ALSO BY GORE VIDAL

*Novels:*
Williwaw
In a Yellow Wood
The City and the Pillar
The Season of Comfort
A Search for the King
Dark Green, Bright Red
The Judgment of Paris
Messiah
Julian
Washington, D.C.
Myra Breckinridge
Two Sisters
Burr
Myron
1876
Kalki
Creation
Duluth
Lincoln
Myra Breckinridge and Myron
Empire
Hollywood
Live from Golgotha

*Short Stories:*
A Thirsty Evil

*Plays:*
An Evening with Richard Nixon
Weekend
Romulus
The Best Man
Visit to a Small Planet

*Essays:*
Rocking the Boat
Reflections Upon a Sinking Ship
Homage to Daniel Shays
Matters of Fact and Fiction
The Second American Revolution
At Home
Screening History

# GORE VIDAL

·

# UNITED STATES

# GORE VIDAL

## UNITED

·

## STATES

ESSAYS

·

1952 – 1992

RANDOM HOUSE
NEW YORK

This work was originally published in hardcover in the United States by Random House, Inc.,
New York, and in Great Britain by Andre Deutsch Limited, London, in 1993.

The essays that appear in this work were originally published in *Architectural Digest, Book
Week, Commentary, Encounter, Esquire, London Sunday Telegraph, Los Angeles Times, The
Nation, The New Statesman, The New York Review of Books, The New York Times Book
Review, New World Writing, The Observer, Partisan Review, Playboy, The Reporter, The
Threepenny Review, The Times, Times Literary Supplement, Vanity Fair,* and *Zero.*

"Paul Bowles's Stories" was originally published as the Introduction to *Collected Stories of
Paul Bowles* (Black Sparrow Press, 1983).

"H. L. Mencken the Journalist" was originally published as the Foreword to *The Impossible
H. L. Mencken: A Selection of His Best Newspaper Stories* edited by Elizabeth Rodgers
(Doubleday/Anchor Books).

Library of Congress Cataloging-in-Publication Data
Vidal, Gore
United States—essays, 1952–1992 / by Gore Vidal
p.      cm.
ISBN 0-679-75572-1
I. Title.
PS3543.I26U55 1992
814'.54—dc20      91-39743

Manufactured in the United States of America
24689753
First Paperback Edition

# AUTHOR'S NOTE

I wrote the first of these pieces in 1952, the year that Eisenhower was elected president, and the last in 1992, the year of Clinton's election. The first piece, "The Twelve Caesars," was written after rereading Suetonius and realizing that I had never before got the point of what he is telling us, not so much about the Caesars as about our common humanity and the nature of power. Apparently, people still miss the point: it took a long time before anyone would publish so "outrageous" a commentary.

This collection represents about two thirds of the essays or pieces that I have published over forty years. They seem to fall naturally into three categories: literature, or the state of the art; politics, or the state of the union; personal responses to people and events, not to mention old movies and children's books, or the state of being. So, herewith, my three states—united.

G.V.
December 1992

# CONTENTS

---·---

# · STATE OF THE ART ·

# 1

## *EVERY ECKERMANN*
## *HIS OWN MAN*

ECKERMANN: I'm delighted that *The New York Review of Books* is still going strong after—what is it now? Fifty years?

VISITOR: Twenty-five, actually.

ECKERMANN: It seems a lot longer.

VISITOR: You appeared in one of the first issues, didn't you, Mr. Eckermann?

ECKERMANN: *Ja,* as Goethe would say. *Zwei Seelen wohnen, ach! in meiner Brust.* But I am my own man now. I am free of Goethe; Wilson, too. *E pluribus meum.*

VISITOR: Only there is no piece in *The New York Review of Books* of twenty-five years ago by anyone called Eckermann. There *is* a curiosity called "Every Man His Own Eckermann," now reprinted in their *Selections* from the first two issues, a self-interview by Edmund Wilson, discussing music and painting, two subjects that he confessed he knew very little about.

ECKERMANN: That was me, if memory serves. As I recall, he—we—knew what we didn't like. On Picasso we anticipated Stassinopoulos

Huffington. Always avant-garde we were in the arts we knew nothing of. Back in Weimar, Wilson is our touchstone.

VISITOR: But surely you . . . I mean Mr. Wilson can no longer contribute.

ECKERMANN: True. That is why, today, whenever I write art criticism, I often sign myself Susan Sontag.

VISITOR: You, Mr. Eckermann, or your own man, wrote "Malthus to Balthus, or the Geometric Art of Silkscreen Reproduction"?

ECKERMANN: In a thousand years no one will know who wrote what or why or if at all. So let's keep those questions moving right along. You would like to know my impression of a small volume called *Selections,* containing a number of pieces from the first two issues of *The New York Review,* which first appeared in 1963. At the time I said, or Wilson said—you see? it hardly matters—"The disappearance of the *Times* Sunday book section at the time of the printers' strike only made us realize it had never existed." Naturally, it sounds even better in the original German!

VISITOR (*quickly*): In *Selections* there are eighteen critical pieces culled from the first two issues. They are written by F. W. Dupee, Dwight Macdonald, Robert Lowell, Mary McCarthy, Elizabeth Hardwick 1, W. H. Auden, Norman Mailer, John Berryman, Irving Howe, Gore Vidal, Alfred Kazin, Elizabeth Hardwick 2, William Styron, Jason Epstein, Allen Tate, Alfred Chester, Richard Wilbur, and Edmund Wilson, and there is a poem by Robert Lowell. What is your immediate impression . . .

ECKERMANN: Of seventeen contributors, eight have fled. Fallen from the perch. Crossed the shining river. Ridden on ahead. Granted, Auden and Berryman and Lowell took early trains, but American poets are obliged to. It's in the by-laws of their union, unlike European poets. Goethe was eighty-three when he cooled it, chatty to the last. But let us look on the bright side: the nine who are still with us are still robust and able to supply bookchat by the yard. Yet *autres temps autres moeurs.* I sometimes think that the long *essai*-attempt (I lapse now into English) may be too much for today's reader, eager for large side-bars and small boxes and lots of coloured ink and numerous Opinions. Oh, how Americans—Brits too, alas—dote on Opinion. But Opinion without Demonstration is worthless. It is the discursive form which the demonstration takes that distinguished *The New York Review* from . . .

VISITOR: *The Times Literary Supplement*?

ECKERMANN: Don't interrupt. The *NYR* made it possible for those writers who don't necessarily have to knock out instant Opinion pieces for money to develop themes that interested them or—the task of criticism—allowed them the space in which to illuminate the work of a forgotten or misunderstood writer. In *Selections,* Allen Tate is splendid on the work of Ford Madox Ford. Since I regard Ford as the finest novelist in English since World War I, I am prejudiced, as well as opinionated. Here's Tate on how the critical biographer should approach Ford:

Ford's best biographer will understand at the outset that Ford himself must be approached as a character in a novel, and that novel by Ford. The complaint, often heard today, that James, Conrad, and Ford were each in his own degree obsessed by "form" or "method" is of course nonsense; but if it were true, would it be less damaging to the vitality of the novel in our day than the obsession with the expressionistic egotism and disorder of American novelists since the War? Ford was not, in the pejorative sense, a formalist. Ford's technique *is* Ford, and he could have had no other.

This echo of Flaubert's "One might almost establish the axiom that there is no such thing as subject. Style in itself being an absolute manner of seeing things." This says a lot about Ford the novelist, Tate the critic, and, perhaps, the *NYR* at the start.

VISITOR: Is there a sort of house style at the *NYR* as there is—or was—at *The New Yorker*?

ECKERMANN: Thank God, no. In *Selections* I was struck by how different the writers are from each other, unlike, say, those at the old *New Yorker,* doomed to conform to a wondrously dull style, chockablock with lots of well-checked little facts, as Gore Vidal pointed out in his review of John Hersey's collection of pieces. In retrospect, Vidal was perhaps too hard on the hapless Hersey and not sufficiently hard on *The New Yorker,* where his work had been, presumably, processed to the consistency of a Kraft cheese. Of course, if Hersey actually writes like that, well . . .

VISITOR: The *NYR* reviewers have been accused of reviewing one another and behaving like any other literary clique.

ECKERMANN: How can there be a clique when hardly anyone knows anyone else? Also, at the beginning, there were far fewer schoolteacher contributors than now. Of course, from time to time, poets often holed up in universities in order not to die but, even so, of the sixteen critics in *Selections,* only three were full-time academics, and academics, then and now, tend to sectarianism—hence, cliquishness. Today the wars of the Literary Theoreticians are bound to leak into the *NYR* and make one, suddenly, nostalgic for a time when Literature not Theory mattered, and Johns Hopkins was known only for its healing arts.

VISITOR: How would you classify the *NYR* politically?

ECKERMANN: Personally, I prefer the *Radical History Review* or *Mother Jones* to *NYR.* But I do think a quarter-century ago we were all a bit more to the true political point than now. Here's Dwight Macdonald on Arthur Schlesinger, Jr., the Kennedy White House apologist:

When he is not confronted with a polemical subject that makes his style taut and forces him to think (which he can do when he has to), Schlesinger likes to slip into something more comfortable. His judgments tend to become official and reverential and to be expressed in the orotundities of the hardened public speaker.

I like that adjective, "hardened." Now if Macdonald were a mere hack of the sort that today fills New York's current papers and magazines, this would have been an *ad hominem* attack on Schlesinger. But Macdonald likes and respects Schlesinger even when, in absolute good faith, he wants to wring his political neck. How to explain personal disinterestedness to a generation that dotes on money, publicity, and personal feuds? How to explain that there are powerful forces—even ideas— abroad that must be analyzed?—and reversed?

Macdonald, in the first issue of the *NYR,* had figured out that we had all been had by the Kennedys (the President was killed a few months later—a *non sequitur,* let me quickly add) and he also detected in Schlesinger's *The Politics of Hope* a shift from the Jefferson-Madison Bill of Rights attitude toward the citizen to the autocratic Jackson and his terrible successors, the Caesars of the National Security State, only now unravelling. Macdonald blows the whistle on Schlesinger's contention, "While the Executive should wield all his powers under the constitution with energy, he should not be able to abrogate the constitution except in face of war, revolution or economic chaos." Macdonald finds this a nice prescription for fascism (what is economic chaos? Black

Monday of October 1987?) . . . I see your eyes are beginning to glaze. I give up. Let me put this in terms that *New York* magazine can grasp. Dwight was jealous of Arthur's success at Camelot and longed, in his heart of hearts, to be flung fully clothed into the pool at Hickory Hill by the dread Ethel Kennedy. Envy is the only credible emotion, isn't it? Never say Eckermann isn't "with it."

VISITOR: But is the *NYR* with it? How have they dealt with black power, gay rights, women . . .

ECKERMANN: F. W. Dupee is superb on James Baldwin's *The Fire Next Time.* Dupee is also a corrective to Flannery O'Connor's contemporary view that if Baldwin hadn't been black, no one would have put up with him*. This is wondrously stupid. If Baldwin had not been black, and gay, he would not have had to behave as he did. Dupee is wondrously subtle on this. As he describes Baldwin's mind and pain, he usefully demonstrates how Baldwin is so much more poignant and effective in his memoir than in those booming sermons of last things.

VISITOR: So much then for politics, Mr. Eckermann. Essentially, the *NYR* is a literary paper . . .

ECKERMANN: Which came along just as literature ceased to be of any general interest. Does anyone—voluntarily—read a book nowadays? Movies are the preferred diversion.

VISITOR: The *Review* has been criticised for not . . . well, doing enough about fiction, about new writers, experimental fiction . . .

ECKERMANN: Except for the genre books, packaged like boxes of cheap Depression candy, there is no longer a novel-reading public. Of course there are the books written to be taught on campus, but they are mere Demonstrations of Theory. For the "educated" public it is filmmaker Woody Allen, not bookmaker Philip Roth, that excites interest.

VISITOR: But if the *NYR* gave more space to "experimental" writing . . .

ECKERMANN: The record's not too bad. In the second issue Richard Poirier was down at the wharf, greeting Pynchon's *V,* while I was startled to reread, in *Selections,* Mary McCarthy's inspired praise of

*See page 1,208 in *The Collected Works of Flannery O'Connor* (Library of America, 1988).

Burroughs's *The Naked Lunch,* a book not much praised at that time, at least not by so celebrated a critic. I say "inspired" because I read the book then and didn't much like it, but now I begin to see things that I had missed first time around. Well, that is what criticism is meant to do—show us what we missed or just plain didn't get.

She is particularly good on Burroughs's humour, "peculiarly American, at once broad and sly. It is the humour of a comedian, a vaudeville performer playing in *One . . .*" Surprisingly for those days, she makes no heavy weather of the fag side of Burroughs, something that the other critics then and now, a quarter-century later, still go on howling about, like the Hilton Kramer on Robert Mapplethorpe in a recent New York paper—truly crazed bigotry of the sort that, outside certain yob papers in England, no paper in the civilized Western world would print.

On that subject, Alfred Chester. He was a glorious writer, tough as nails, with an exquisite ear for the false note; his review of Rechy's *City of Night* is murderously funny, absolutely unfair, and totally true, a trick that only a high critic knows how to pull off. No, I won't show you how it's done. You look tired.

VISITOR: No. No. I'm awake. What did you think of Auden's review of *Anathemata* by David Jones?

ECKERMANN: *Echt* lousy, as Goethe would say. For reasons that Berryman gave in his review of Auden's *The Dyer's Hand.* Auden did

one of two things with books entrusted to him for comment: either he wrote about what interested him at the moment, making some spidery connection with the book in hand, or, with books he felt keen about . . . he quoted from them at agreeable length. Surely the pro sits on and breaks his brains.

It is the ability to break (one's own) brains that makes all the difference. We thought that our job then. Now . . .

VISITOR: Between then and now . . .

ECKERMANN: Then, Baldwin and the black condition, the imperial search for enemies, invasion of Cuba, the turning of "creative" writers from the novel to actual events taken from newspapers (Elizabeth Hardwick's "Grub Street: New York"). Now—or, rather, since—political murders, Vietnam, drugs and the mafia-ization of the society, the federal deficits, the decline of education, of quality of Life, of life of Quality . . . Twenty-five years ago the United States was the world's central economic, military, and intellectual fact. Today, we are, literally, eccentric. I think the *NYR* can take some pride in the way it has handled with a degree of comprehensive dignity a quarter-century of national decline and, law-abiding as we all are (the so-called Molotov cocktail on the cover was actually a Leonardo sketch for a space shuttle—a little leg-pull), we are now simply obeying the second law of thermodynamics, as we run down.

VISITOR: Will *you* be here in 2015?

ECKERMANN: No—Eckermann as his own man will be a thing of the past—rather like books. After all, our Japanese masters currently prefer comic books to book books. As they are now our role models, *The New York Review of Comic Books* will doubtless replace the old *NYR*. But there will be lots more pictures, which will be nice. In any case, the two epochs will be linked here, I hope, by comprehensiveness.

VISITOR: If I comprehend you . . .

ECKERMANN: "Comprehension is only a knowledge adequate to our intention."

VISITOR: Goethe?

ECKERMANN: Kant. *Ich wunsche Ihren noch einen schönen Tag. Have a nice day now.*

VISITOR: Kant?

ECKERMANN: Eckermann. On your way out, open the second shutter so that more light can come in.

*The New York Review of Books*
October 27, 1988

# 2

♦

# NOVELISTS AND CRITICS
# OF THE 1940S

It is a rare and lucky physician who can predict accurately at birth whether a child is to become a dwarf or a giant or an ordinary adult, since most babies look alike and the curious arrangements of chromosomes which govern stature are inscrutable and do not yield their secret order even to the shrewdest eye. Time alone gives definition. Nevertheless, interested readers and writers, like anxious parents and midwives, forever speculate upon the direction and meaning of current literary trends, and professional commentators with grave authority make analyses which the briefest interval often declares invalid. But despite their long historic record of bad guesses, bookish men continue to make judgments, and the recorded derelictions of taste and the erratic judgments of earlier times tend only to confirm in them a sense of complacency: *they* are not we, and did not know; *we* know. To disturb this complacency is occasionally worthwhile, and one way of doing it is to exhume significant critical texts from the recent past. Those of the last century, in particular, provide us with fine warnings.

For instance: "We do not believe any good end is to be effected by fictions which fill the mind with details of imaginary vice and distress and crime, or which teach it instead of endeavoring after the fulfillment of simple and ordinary duty to aim at the assurance of superiority by creating for itself fanciful and incomprehensible perplexities. Rather we believe that the effect of such fictions tends to render those who fall under their influence unfit for practical exertion by intruding on minds which ought to be guarded from impurity the unnecessary knowledge of evil." This was the *Quarterly Review* on George Eliot's *The Mill on the Floss,* and it is really quite well said: the perennial complaint of the professional reviewers and the governors of lending libraries ("enough unpleasant things in the world without reading about them in books").

Or the following attack on preciosity and obscurantism (*Blackwood's Magazine,* 1817): "Mr. Coleridge conceives himself to be a far greater man than the public is likely to admit; and we wish to waken him from what seems to us a most ludicrous delusion. He seems to believe that every tongue is wagging in his praise. . . . The truth is that Mr. Coleridge is but an obscure name in English literature." [Coleridge was forty-five years old at this time and his major work was long since done.] "In London he is well known in literary society for his extraordinary loquacity . . . " And there follows a prolix attack upon the *Biographia Literaria.*

Or this excerpt from an 1848 *Quarterly Review,* deploring the pagan, the sexual, and the vicious:

At all events there can be no interest attached to the writer of *Wuthering Heights*—a novel succeeding *Jane Eyre* and purporting to be written by Ellis Bell—unless it were for the sake of more individual reprobation. For though there is a decided resemblance between the two, yet the aspect of the Jane and Rochester animals in their native state, as Catherine and Heatfield [*sic*], is too odiously and abominably pagan to be palatable even to the most vitiated class of English readers. With all the unscrupulousness of the French school of novels it combines that repulsive vulgarity in the choice of its vice which supplies its own antidote.

Differently worded, these complaints still sound in our press. The Luce editors who cry for an "affirmative" literature echo voices once raised against George Eliot. When middlebrow reviewers deplore "morbidity" in our best writers, they only paraphrase the outrage of those who found the Brontës repellent. And the twitterings of an Orville Prescott when he has discovered a nice and busy book echo the same homely song of those long-dead reviewers who found in the three-volume novels of forgotten lady writers so much warm comfort.

As the essential problems of life remain the same from generation to generation, despite altered conditions, so the problems of literary recognition remain, for contemporaries, peculiarly difficult. Despite the warnings of other times, the impetuous and the confident continue their indiscriminate cultivation of weeds at the expense of occasional flowers.

To consider the writing of any period, including the present, it is perhaps of some importance to examine the climate in which the work is done, to chart if possible the prevailing winds, the weather of the day.

Today there is a significant distinction between the reviewers for popular newspapers and magazines, whom no one interested in literature reads, and the serious critics of the Academy, who write for one another in the quarterlies and, occasionally, for the public in the Sunday supplements. The reviewers are not sufficiently relevant or important to be considered in any but a social sense: they reflect the commonest prejudices and aspirations of the middle class for whom they write, and they need not concern us here.

The critics, however, are significant. They are dedicated men; they are serious; their learning is often respectable. They have turned to the analysis of literature with the same intensity that, born in an earlier time, they might have brought to formal philosophy, to the law, to the ministry. They tend, generically and inevitably, to be absolutists. They believe that by a close examination of "the text," the laws and the crafty "strategies" of its composition will be made clear and the findings will provide "touchstones" for a comparative criticism of other works. So far so good. They have constructed some ingenious and perhaps valuable analyses of metaphysical verse whose order is often precise and whose most disparate images proceed with a calculable wit and logic.

Unfortunately, the novel is not so easily explicated. It is a loose form, and although there is an inherent logic in those books we are accustomed to call great, the deducible "laws" which governed the execution of *Emma* are not going to be of much use in defining *The Idiot*. The best that a serious analyst can hope to do is comment intelligently from his vantage point in time on the way a work appears to him in a contemporary, a comparative, or a historic light; in which case, his opinion is no more valuable than his own subtlety and knowledge. He must be, as T. S. Eliot put it so demurely, "very intelligent." The point, finally, is that he is not an empiricist dealing with measurable quantities and calculable powers. Rather, he is a man dealing with the private vision of another, with a substance as elusive and amorphous as life itself. To *pretend* that there are absolutes is necessary in making relative judgments (Faulkner writes better than Taylor Caldwell), but to *believe* that there are absolutes and to order one's judgments accordingly is folly and disastrous. One is reminded of Matthew Arnold and his touch-stones; it was his conviction that certain lines from a poet by all conceded great might be compared to those of lesser poets to determine their value. Arnold selected Dante as his great poet, an irreproachable choice, but then he misread the Italian, which naturally caused some confusion. Arnold's heirs also demand order, tidiness, labels, ultimate assurance that this work is "good" and that work is "bad," but sooner or later someone misreads the Italian and the system breaks down. In our time there are nearly as many critical systems as there are major critics, which is a pleasing anarchy. The "new critics," as they have been termed (*they* at least dislike being labeled and few will now answer when called), are fundamentally mechanics. They go about dismantling the text with the same rapture that their simpler brothers experience while taking apart combustion engines: inveterate tinkerers both, solemnly playing with what has been invented by others for use, not analysis.

Today's quarterlies are largely house organs for the academic world. They seldom publish imaginative work and one of their most distin-guished editors has declared himself more interested in commentaries on writing than in the writing itself. Their quarrels and schisms and heresies do not in the least resemble the Alexandrians whom they occa-sionally mention, with involuted pride, as spiritual ancestors. Rather, one is reminded of the semantic and doctrinal quarrels of the church fathers in the fourth century, when a diphthong was able to break the civilized world in half and spin civilization into nearly a millennium of darkness. One could invent a most agreeable game of drawing analogies between the fourth century and today. F. R. Leavis and Saint Jerome are perfectly matched, while John Chrysostom and John Crowe Ran-som suggest a possibility. The analogy works amusingly on all levels save one: the church fathers had a Christ to provide them with a primary source of revelation, while our own dogmatists must depend either upon private systems or else upon those proposed by such slender reeds as Matthew Arnold and T. S. Eliot, each, despite his genius, a ritual victim as well as a hero of literary fashion.

But the critics are indefatigable and their game is in earnest, for it is deeply involved not only with literature but with such concrete things as careers in the Academy, where frequent and prestigious publication is important. Yet for all their busyness they are by no means eclectic. In a Henry James year not one will write an analysis of George Meredith. They tend to ignore the contemporary writers, not advancing much later than F. Scott Fitzgerald, whose chief attraction is that he exploded before he could be great, providing a grim lesson in failure that, in its completeness, must be awfully heartening when contemplated on the safe green campus of some secluded school.

Of the critics today, Edmund Wilson, the most interesting and the most important, has shown virtually no interest in the writing of the last fifteen years, his talents engaged elsewhere in the construction of heroic sepulchers for old friends like Fitzgerald and Millay, a likable loyalty but a not entirely useful one. He can of course still make a fine point during a Peacock flurry and he has been startling brilliant in recent essays on Grant and Lincoln, but one can search the pages of that book of his which he calls a "Literary Chronicle of the Forties" without coming upon any but the most cursory mention of the decade's chief talents.

Malcolm Cowley, a good professional literary man, had some sharp things to say recently about the young writers. Although he made almost no reference to the better writing of the day, he did say some accurate things about the university-trained writers, whose work, he feels, is done with too reverent an eye upon their old teachers, the new critics. Cowley speaks out for a hearty freedom from university influence, citing his own generation (the men of the 1920s are loyal to their time if not to one another: *everyone* was a genius then, and liquor was cheap abroad) as being singularly independent of formal instruction. Yet McCullers, Bowles, Capote, etc. (like Hemingway, Faulkner, O'Neill, etc.) are not graduates of universities, and many of the other young lions have had enough war to wash them clean of academicism. Mr. Cowley, like most commentators, tends to bend whatever he finds to his premise. To him there is no single genius who can set the tone for a generation but one wonders if he would recognize that great writer any more than Lord Jeffrey, a century ago, was able to recognize *his* time's greatness? For the Cowleys, the novel stopped at *Gatsby*. That Carson McCullers (whom he does not mention) has influenced many works, that Tennessee Williams has influenced the theater of the world, that Paul Bowles, among others, has reshaped the short story—none of these things impinges on him.

Mr. Cowley's gloom is supported by the young John W. Aldridge, Jr. In his amusing novel *After the Lost Generation* he got onto the subject of "values" (by way of Lionel Trilling and perhaps V. S. Pritchett). After discussing a number of fictitious characters who were writing books (using real, if unlikely, names like Truman Capote and Gore Vidal), he "proved," by the evidence of their works, that they had all failed of greatness because, except for "a pocket or two of manners" (the Army; the South; here and there in New England), there was really nothing left to write about, none of that social conflict out of which comes art, like sparks from a stone grinding metal. His coda indicated that a young writer of singular genius is at this moment hovering in the wings awaiting his cue. It will be interesting to read Mr. Aldridge's next novel.

Yet Mr. Aldridge does have a case: the old authority of church, of settled Puritan morality, *has* broken down, and if one's vision is historically limited to only a few generations in time it might seem that today's novelists are not having the fun their predecessors in the 1920s had, breaking cultural furniture. But to take a longer view, one must recall that the great times for literature and life were those of transition: from the Middle Ages to modern times by way of the Renaissance, from dying paganism to militant Christianity by way of the Antonines, and so on back to Aristophanes. The opportunity for the novelist when Mr. Aldridge's "values" are in the discard is fabulous: to create without wasting one's substance in political or social opposition. What could be more marvelous! Neither Virgil nor Shakespeare had to attack their day's morality or those in authority. They were morally free to write of life, of Henry James's "the main thing." There were certainly inequities and barbarities in sixteenth-century England and first-century Rome, but the writers, affected partly by convention (not to mention the Star Chamber), did not address themselves to attacks upon the government or the time's morality, which, apparently, did not obsess them. Writers, after all, are valuable in spite of their neuroses, obsessions, and rebellions, not because of them. It is a poor period indeed which must assess its men of letters in terms of their opposition to their society. Opposition to life's essential conditions perhaps, or to death's implacable tyranny, is something else again, and universal; but novels, no matter how clever, which attempt to change statutes or moral attitudes are, though useful at the moment, not literature at all. In fact, if Mr. Aldridge were right in his proposition we would have *not* a barren, "subjectless" world for literature but the exact opposite: a time of flowering, of creation without waste and irrelevancy. Unhappily, American society has not changed that much in the last thirty years. There is as much to satirize, as much to protest as ever before, and it will always be the task of the secondary figures to create those useful public books whose momentary effect is as stunning as their literary value is not.

There is no doubt but that the West has come to Malraux's "twilight of the absolute." One awaits with hope the period between when, unencumbered by the junk of dogma, writers can turn to the great things with confidence and delight. Loss of authority by removing targets does not destroy the true novelist, though it eliminates the doctrinaire and those busy critics who use the peculiar yardstick of social usefulness to determine merit. (It is no accident that the few works admired by Mr. Aldridge are those compositions which sturdily and loudly discuss the social scene, or some "pocket" of it—interesting books, certainly, whose public effect is often admirable; though the noise they create seldom persists long enough to enjoy even a first echo.) Actually, one might say that it is only the critic who suffers unduly from the lack of authority. A critic, to criticize, must, very simply, have standards. To have standards he must pretend there is some optimum against which like creations can be measured. By the nature of his own process he is eventually forced, often inadvertently, to accept as absolute those conditions for analysis which he has only tentatively proposed. To be himself significant he needs law and revealed order; without them he is only a civilized man commenting for others upon given works which, temperamentally, he may or may not like without altering the value, if any, of the work examined. With a law, with authority, with faith he becomes something more grand and meaningful; the pytheness through whom passes Apollo's word.

Much of the despondency and apparent confusion in the world of peripheral letters today derives partly from the nervous, bloody age in which we live and partly from that hunger for the absolute which, in our own immediate experience, delivered two great nations into the hands of tyrants, while in our own country the terror of being man alone, unsupported by a general religious belief and undirected by central authority, has reduced many intellectuals either to a bleak nihilism or, worse, to the acceptance of some external authority (Rome, Marx, Freud). One is reminded of Flaubert's comment nearly a century ago: "The melancholy of the ancients seems to me deeper than that of the moderns, who all more or less assume an immortality on the far side of the black pit. For the ancients the black pit was infinity itself; their dreams take shape and pass against a background of unchanging ebony. No cries, no struggles, only the fixity of the pensive gaze. The gods being dead and Christ not yet born [*sic*], there was between Cicero and Marcus Aurelius one unique moment in which there was man."

Our own age is one of man alone, but there are still cries, still struggles against our condition, against the knowledge that our works and days have value only on the human scale; and those who most clearly remember the secure authority of other times, the ordered universe, the immutable moral hierarchies, are the ones who most protest the black pit. While it is perfectly true that any instant in human history is one of transition, ours more than most seems to be marked by a startling variety of conflicting absolutes, none sufficiently great at this moment to impose itself upon the majority whose lives are acted out within an unhuman universe which some still prefer to fill with a vast manlike shadow containing stars, while others behold only a luminous dust which *is* stars, and us as well. This division between those who recognize the unhumanity of creation and those who protest the unchanging ebony sets the tone of our literature, with the imaginative writers inclining (each in his own way) to the first view and their critics to the second. The sense of man not being king of creation (nor even the work of a king of creation) is the burden, directly and indirectly, of modern literature. For the writers there is no reality for man except in his relations with his own kind. Much of the stuff of earlier centuries—like fate, high tragedy, the interventions of *dei ex machina*—have been discarded as brave but outworn devices, not applicable in a world where kings and commoners occupy the same sinking boat.

Those of our writers who might yet enjoy the adjective "affirmative" are the ones who tend to devote themselves to the dramas within the boat, the encompassing cold sea ignored in the passions of the human moment. Most of the worst and a number of the best writers belong to this category. The key words here are "love" and "compassion." And though, like most such devices, they have grown indistinct with use, one can still see them at work, and marvelously so, in the novels of Carson McCullers and certain (though not all) of the plays of Tennessee Williams. Christopher Isherwood once said that to his mind the finest single line in modern letters was: "I have always depended upon the kindness of strangers," from *A Streetcar Named Desire.* At such moments, in such works, the human drama becomes so unbearably intense that time and the sea are blotted out and only the human beings are illuminated as they cease, through the high magic of art, to be mere residents in a time which stops and become, instead, archetypes—elemental figures like those wild gods our ancestors peopled heaven with.

Then there are the writers to whom neither sea nor boat exists. They have accepted some huge fantasy wherein they need never drown, where death is life, and the doings of human beings on a social and ethical level are of much consequence to some brooding source of creation who dispenses his justice along strictly party lines at the end of a gloomy day. To this category belong such talented writers as Graham Greene and Evelyn Waugh. In theory at least, speculation has ended for them; dogma supports them in all things. Yet it is odd to find that the tone of their works differs very little from that of the other mariners adrift. They are, if anything, perhaps a bit more lugubrious, since for them is not the principality of this world.

Finally, there are those who see human lives as the lunatic workings of compulsive animals no sooner born than dead, no sooner dead than replaced by similar creatures born of that proliferating seed which too will die. Paul Bowles is a striking example of this sort of writer as he coolly creates nightmare visions in which his specimens struggle and drown in fantasy, in madness, in death. His short stories with their plain lines of monochromatic prose exploit extreme situations with a chilling resourcefulness; he says, in short, "Let it sink; let us drown."

Carson McCullers, Paul Bowles, Tennessee Williams are, at this moment at least, the three most interesting writers in the United States. Each is engaged in the task of truth-saying (as opposed to saying the truth, which is not possible this side of revelation). Each has gone further into the rich interior of the human drama than any of our immediate predecessors with the possible exception of William Faulkner, whose recent work has unfortunately resembled bad translations from Pindar. On a social level, the hostility shown these essential artists is more significant than their occasional worldly successes, for it is traditional that he who attempts to define man's condition demoralizes the majority, whether relativist or absolutist. We do not want ever to hear that we will die but that first we must live; and those ways of living which are the fullest, the most intense, are the very ones which social man traditionally dreads, summoning all his superstition and malice to combat strangers and lovers, the eternal victims.

The obsessive concern with sexuality which informs most contemporary writing is not entirely the result of a wish *épater le bourgeois* but, more, the reflection of a serious battle between the society man has constructed so illogically and confusedly and the nature of the human being, which needs a considerably fuller expression sexually and emotionally than either the economics or morality of this time will permit. The sea is close. Two may find the interval between awareness and death more meaningful than one alone. Yet while ours is a society where mass murder and violence are perfectly ordinary and their expression in the most popular novels and comic books is accepted with aplomb, any love between two people which does not conform is attacked.

Malcolm Cowley has complained that writers no longer handle some of the more interesting social relationships of man, that there is no good stock-market novel, no Balzacian concern among the better writers with economic motive. His point is valid. The public range of the novel has been narrowed. It would be good to have well-written accounts of the way we live now, yet our important writers eschew, almost deliberately it would seem, the kind of book which provided not only Trollope but Tolstoi with so much power. Mr. Cowley catches quite well the tone of the second-rate good writers (a phenomenon peculiar to this moment; it seems as if a whole generation writes well, though not often to any point); they are concerned with the small scale, and goodness as exemplified by characters resembling the actress Shirley Booth holding out valiantly against villainous forces, usually represented by someone in business. But Mr. Cowley does not mention the novelist from whom these apotheosis-in-the-kitchen writers derive. Carson McCullers, using the small scale, the relations of human beings at their most ordinary, transcends her milieu and shows, in bright glimpses, the potentiality which exists in even the most banal of human relationships, the "we" as opposed to the meager "I."

Or again, in Tennessee Williams's remarkable play *Camino Real,* though the world is shown in a nightmare glass, a vision of those already drowned, there are still moments of private triumphs . . . in Kilroy's love with (not for) the gypsy's daughter and in Lord Byron's proud departure through the gate to *terra incognita,* his last words a reproach and an exhortation: "Make voyages! Make voyages!"

And, finally, most starkly, we have a deliberate act of murder, Gide's *l'acte gratuite,* which occurs at the end of Paul Bowles's *Let It Come Down.* Here the faceless, directionless protagonist, in a sudden storm of rage against his life, all life, commits a murder without reason or passion, and in this one terrible moment (similar perhaps to that of a nation gone to war) he at last finds "a place in the world, a definite status, a precise relationship with the rest of men. Even if it had to be one of open hostility, it was his, created by him." In each of these three writers man acts, through love, through hate, through despair. Though the act in each is different, the common emotion is sufficiently intense to dispel, for a time at least, the knowledge of that cold drowning which awaits us all.

The malady of civilized man is his knowledge of death. The good artist, like the wise man, addresses himself to life and invests with his private vision the deeds and thoughts of men. The creation of a work of art, like an act of love, is our one small "yes" at the center of a vast "no."

The lesser writers whose works do not impress Mr. Cowley despite their correctness possess the same vision as those of the major writers, but their power of illusion is not so great and their magic is only fitful: too often their creatures are only automatons acted upon. Though they may shed light on interesting aspects of ordinary life they do not, in the best sense, illuminate, flood with brilliance, our strange estate.

Among the distinguished second rank of younger writers there is much virtuosity and potentiality. The coolly observant short stories of Louis Auchincloss provide wise social comment of the sort which the Cowleys would probably admire but never seem to read in their haste to generalize. Eudora Welty fashions a subtle line and Jean Stafford, though currently obsessed with literary interior decoration, has in such stories as "The Echo and the Nemesis" displayed a talent which makes all the more irritating her recent catalogues of bric-a-brac, actual and symbolic. John Kelly, whose two novels have been neglected, has created a perverse, operatic world like nothing else in our literature, while the late John Horne Burns, out of fashion for some years, was a brilliant satirist in a time when satire is necessary but difficult to write since to attack successfully one must have a complacent, massive enemy—and though there are numerous villains today, none is entirely complacent.

The serious writers have been attacked by the reviewers for their contempt of narrative and their neglect to fashion "real live characters" (which means familiar stereotypes from Victorian fiction masquerading in contemporary clothes). The reviewers have recognized that a good deal of writing now being done doesn't resemble anything they are used to (although in almost a century there has been a royal line of which they are ignorant . . . from *The Temptation of Saint Anthony* to *The Golden Bowl* to *Mrs. Dalloway*); they still feel most at home with *The Newcomes*, or, if they came to maturity in the 1920s, with *The Sun Also Rises.* When the technique of a play like *Camino Real* seems bizarre and difficult to follow for those accustomed to the imitators of Ibsen, there must be a genuine reason for the change in technique, other than the author's presumed perversity. The change from the exterior to the interior world which has been taking place in literature for at least a century is due not only to a general dissatisfaction with the limitations of naturalism but also to the rise of a new medium, the movies, which, properly used, are infinitely superior to the old novel and to the naturalistic play, especially in the rendering of plain narrative.

*The Quiet One,* a movie, was far superior as a social document (as "art," too, for that matter) to any book published so far in this country dealing with Negro problems. Instinctively, the writers have reacted to the camera. If another medium can handle narrative and social comment so skillfully, even on their lowest aesthetic levels, then the novelist must go deeper, must turn into the maze of consciousness where the camera cannot follow. He must also become wise, and wisdom even in its relative sense was never a notable characteristic of novelists in our language. One can anticipate the direction of the novel by studying that of the painters who, about the time of the still camera's invention, began instinctively to withdraw into a less literal world where they might do work which a machine could not imitate. It is a possibility, perhaps even a probability, that as the novel moves toward a purer, more private expression it will cease altogether to be a popular medium, becoming, like poetry, a cloistered avocation—in which case those who in earlier times might have written great public novels will be engaged to write good public movies, redressing the balance. In our language the novel is but three centuries old and its absorption by the movies, at least the vulgar line of it, is not necessarily a bad thing. In any event, it is already happening.

For the present, however, the tone of the contemporary novel, though not cheerful, is precise. Man is on his own. In certain human actions, in love, in violence, he can communicate with others, touch and be touched, act and in the act forget his fate. The scale is often small. Kings are neglected because, to relativists, all men are the same within eternity. Or rather their crisis is the same. The concern in modern letters is with that crisis which defines the prospect.

In general, the novelists have rejected authority, parting company with their cousins-german the serious critics. To the creative man, religious dogma and political doctrine, when stated in ultimate terms, represent the last enemy, the protean Lucifer in our race's bloody progress. The artist speaks from that awareness of life, that secret knowledge of life in death the absolutists are driven to obscure and to distort, to shape, if possible, to tidy ends.

The interior drama at its most bitterly human comes into sharp focus in the writings of Williams and McCullers, and there are signs that other writers, undismayed by the hostility of the absolutists, may soon provide us with some strength in these last days before the sure if temporary victory of that authoritarian society which, thanks to science, now has every weapon with which to make even the most inspired lover of freedom conform to the official madness.

The thought of heaven, a perennial state of mind, a cheerful conception of what might be in life, in art (if not in death), may yet save our suicidally inclined race—if only because heaven is as various as there are men in the world who dream of it, and writers to evoke that dream. One recalls Constantine (to refer again to the image of the early church) when he teased a dissenting bishop at one of the synods: "Acesius, take a ladder and get up to heaven by yourself." We are fortunate in our time to have so many ladders going up. Each ladder is raised in hope, which is heaven enough.

*New World Writing #4*
1953

# 3

---◆---

# A NOTE ON THE NOVEL

Any discussion of the novel nowadays soon strikes the pessimistic note. It is agreed, for instance, that there are among us no novelists of sufficient importance to act as touchstones for useful judgment. There is Faulkner, but . . . and there is Hemingway, but . . . And that completes the list of near-misses, the others, poor lost legions, all drowned in the culture's soft buzz and murmur. We have embarked upon empire (Rome born again our heavy fate) without a Virgil in the crew, only tarnished silver writers in a bright uranium age, perfunctorily divided by editorialists between the "affirmative" (and good) and the "negative" (and bad). Only cultural researchers (wandering lonely as a crowd) and high critics merit serious attention. From the little red schoolhouse to the library at Alexandria in one generation is the heartening success story of American letters.

Apologists (secret lovers of the novel, few but tender) surveying the seasonal flood of first novels of promise, the smaller wave of second novels of no promise, and, finally, most poignant of all, those minuscule ripples which continue so perversely to assault an indifferent shore— these apologists have noted a spiritual ergot in our country's air which causes good writers to abort young while, tributary to this new myth, lingers the old conviction that American life, even now, lacks the class tensions, the subtle play of manners (Hialeah but no Ascot), the requisite amount of history to make even a small literature. That from Levittown no art may come is still an important critical thesis.

One senses, too, in academic dialogues and explications the unstated burden of the discussion that, at last, all the novels are in. The term is over, the canon assembled if not ordered, the door to the library firmly shut to the irrelevance of new attempts. More ominous, however, than the loss of the higher criticism has been the gradual defection of the public itself. After some three hundred years the novel in English has lost the general reader (or rather the general reader has lost the novel), and I propose that he will not again recover his old enthusiasm.

The fault, if it be a fault, is not the novelist's (I doubt if there ever have been so many interesting and excellent writers as there are now working) but of the audience, an unpleasant accusation to make in a democracy where, ultimately, the taste of the majority is the measure of all things. Nevertheless, appalling education combined with clever new toys has distracted that large public which found pleasure in prose fictions. In an odd way, our civilization has now come full circle: from the Greek mysteries and plays to the printing press and the novel to television and plays again, the audience has returned to the play, and it is now clear that the novel, despite its glories, was only surrogate for the drama, which, confined till this era to theaters, was not generally accessible.

With television (ten new "live" plays a week; from such an awful abundance, a dramatic renaissance *must* come) the great audience now has the immediacy it has always craved, the picture which moves and talks, the story experienced, not reported. In refutation, it may indeed be argued that the large sales of paperback books, both good and bad, are proof that there are millions out there in the dark, hungering for literature. But though it is true that all those books must go *somewhere,* I suggest that their public is not a serious one, that it is simply pursuing secret vices from one bright cover picture to another—consuming, not reading.

Yet all in all, this state of affairs, though disheartening, is by no means tragic. For one thing, those novelists whose interests are in polemic or mere narrative will doubtless join the new Establishment and write plays. Adventure stories, exotic voyages, superficial histories, all the familiar accouterments of the popular novel are now the scenarists' by right of conquest. The novel is left only the best things: that exploration of the inner world's divisions and distinctions where no camera may follow, the private, the necessary pursuit of the whole which makes the novel, at its highest, the humane art that Lawrence called "The one bright book of life."

To strike an optimistic note, if faintly, it may well be that, with unpopularity, the meretricious and the ordinary will desert entirely, leaving only the devoted lashed to the mast. But now the tide is in. The course is set. The charts are explicit, for we are not the first to make the voyage out: the poets long ago preceded us into exile, and one can observe them up ahead, arms outstretched to greet the old enemy, their new companions at the edge of the known world.

*The New York Times Book Review*
August 5, 1956

# 4

◆

## *SATIRE IN THE 1950S*

Malcolm Muggeridge has recently proposed that satire tends to flourish at those times when the Establishment is confident that its eternal truths and verities (to borrow Mr. Faulkner's most famous redundancy) are indeed eternal and therefore impervious to ill-natured wit. Mr. Muggeridge concludes that in an age like ours (other-directed, hydrogen-haunted, artificially tranquilized and doggedly together) satire is more apt to take than administer a beating. He is right in one thing: satire has taken a beating. It hardly exists in the more public art forms, and except for an occasional timid appearance in the novel or on a night-club floor, satire has seldom thrived in our comfortable land. But I suggest that the reasons for this are precisely opposite to those Mr. Muggeridge gives. In the first place, he underestimates the very real complacency of our culture, which despite lowering political weather (those atom bombs again) traditionally holds that boats in any weather are best left un-rocked. Secondly, it would appear to me that satire, historically, has been most useful—and most used—when the moral and religious assumptions of a people about itself are in a state of serious confusion because of some dramatic change for good or ill in that people's fortunes.

As his world and city fell, Aristophanes attacked a demoralized war-minded Administration which did not long survive him. As the Roman Republic disintegrated, Cicero satirized radicals, Catullus satirized the mysteriously amiable Caesar, and Horace ticked off a number of highly placed bores; all this in a time of proscription and violent change. Later, under the Empire, Petronius and Lucan, though good courtiers, had the bad luck to find the Divine Nero irresistibly funny; and their satiric thrusts were rewarded with the optimum Roman prize, that ineluctable warm bath with open veins. Those were not, to say the least, complacent days. Nor can one argue that, fierce palace politics aside, the Roman imperium ever rested on certain common assumptions confidently held. Beyond a glum acceptance of law as necessary to commercial endeavor and the accidental discovery that government is largely a matter of filing and cross-indexing, the Roman state from Sulla to Constantine was gloriously confused in its morality, politics and religion. Confronted by so many rich absurdities and contradictions, satire became a high and useful art in the hands of such various men as Persius, Juvenal, Martial, even St. Paul; though between fatal baths and confinement upon disagreeable islands, the satirists themselves did not always have too good a time of it.

The Christian victory, though it did not bring peace on earth, did at least manage to put a severe leash on the satiric impulse. There are not many recorded attacks on the Church between the Emperor Julian's death and the Reformation, a millennium which—though marked by the usual wars of aggression as well as a number of religious wars (something new under the sun)—qualified supremely, in the West at least, as a period of firmly entrenched spiritual values and therefore a seedbed, one would think, for satire. Yet it was not. And the truth of the matter, of course, is that no well-organized central administration, temporal or spiritual, is apt to allow its beneficiaries the license of laughter at its own expense. Cardinals are no laughing matter in Ireland or in Spain today. Even in America, they must write particularly bad verse to occasion a wary joke or two. Yet in France and Italy, two nations which have been for some time in a state of moral and political confusion, cardinals are stock figures of comedy, cropping up in numerous jokes, good and bad, malicious and amiable. I worry the Roman Church only because it is an elderly institution of great significance morally and therefore an obvious target for useful satire. At present, in America, it is not.

Now I would propose that the United States in its short history has been much too preoccupied uniting and exploring, pioneering and building, inventing and consuming, to give much thought to anything not relevant to the practical and immediate. Not that we have lacked for harsh critics. In fact, most of our country's good writers have been nay-sayers, deploring the day and resolutely pessimistic about tomorrow. On the other hand, our humorists have been jolly and ubiquitous. We all know, rather wearily, about frontier humor. Mark Twain's jokes go on and on and some are funny but none is truly satiric because he was not one to rock the boat. It was his ordeal to be tamed, and the petulance and bitterness of his final book, *What is Man?,* answers as nothing else could why he did not dare question any of his society's basic assumptions.

Henry James observed that it took a great deal of history to make a little bit of literature. I suspect it takes a far more homogeneous, more settled, yet more uneasy society to produce satirists. And if one is to be met by the argument that God forbid things should be any worse simply to make matters easier for one small department of literature, I would be the first to agree that the benign incompetence of the Great Golfer and his Team is certainly preferable to a touchy Nero or to an inscrutable Caesar.

Yet there is a real need for the satirist in our affairs, especially now. Since the Second World War and its horrors there has been a remarkable change in our society. Anti-Semitism seems happily to have vanished, except among the more irritable Jews, while anti-Catholics no longer smile, at least in mixed religious company, when the Vatican certifies that the sun did a dance over Portugal. Even my Southern relatives employ a certain tact in discussing the Problem. A profound tolerance is in the land, a tolerance so profound that it is not unlike terror. One dare not raise one's voice against any religion, idea or even delinquency if it is explicable by a therapist. I suspect that much of the American's hatred of Russia and Communism is simply a siphoning off of other irrational dislikes which, blocked by the stern tolerance of the day, can find expression only in Communist-baiting. I do not propose that we return to the bad old days of holding people responsible for inherited characteristics. Yet I should like to have tolerance learned from within and not have it imposed from without. To put forward a recklessly unsympathetic proposition: As long as any group within the society deliberately maintains its identity, it is, or should be, a fair target for satire, both for its own good and for the society's. Laughing at someone else is an excellent way of learning how to laugh at oneself; and questioning what seem to be the absurd beliefs of another group is a good way of recognizing the potential absurdity of many of one's own cherished beliefs; witness the travels of Gulliver.

It is generally agreed and officially lamented that we are in a new age of conformity. Youth wants security, not adventure. The great questions are not asked because the realization that there are no absolute answers has at last penetrated to the bottom layer of society—and why be curious if the answers are only tentative? Now, if this time is indeed so bland, then according to Muggeridge's law, satire must flourish. Yet satire hardly exists. In perfect comfort the squares grow ever more rectilinear. And to strike the minatory note, if ever there was a people ripe for dictatorship it is the American people today. Should a home-grown Hitler appear, whose voice, amongst the public orders, would be raised against him in derision? Certainly no voice on television: "Sorry, the guy has a lot of fans. Sure, we know he's bad news, but you can't hurt people's feelings. They buy soap, too." And elsewhere there would be the tolerant reflex: "Well, he *could* be right. After all, a lot of people seem to agree with him . . ." And then the iron fist closes, and we start *our* Empire.

I have often chided my Soviet friends on the naïveté of their country's censorship. Newly literate and still awed by the printed word, the Russian governors are terrified of ideas. If only they knew what our governors know: that in a huge egalitarian society no idea which runs counter to the prevailing superstitions can successfully penetrate the national carapace. We give our solemn critics every freedom, including the one to fail to be heard. And fail they do: silence and indifference neutralize the irritant more effectively than brainwashing. Yet this age could be a marvelous one for satirists. Look at the targets: Christianity, Psychiatry, Marxism, Romantic Love, Xenophobia, Science (all capitalized and all regarded with reverence if not admiration). You need only take your pick, and not worry about bad taste. If one can make the cautious laugh by clowning, half the work is done, for laughter is the satirist's anaesthetic: he can then make his incision, darting on before the audience knows what has been done to it. But he must be swift and engaging, or the laughter will turn to indifferent silence, the ultimate censorship.

Where can the American satirist operate today? Not on television, seldom if ever in the movies, and on the stage only if he is willing to play the buffoon. But the novel remains; and it would be good to see those writers with a talent for satire (Randall Jarrell for one) strike boldly at the large targets, without that vitiating diffidence peculiar to the contemporary American novelist. We don't know very much, they seem to say; we are deep of course, often mystic, and we do know that love and compassion are the most beautiful things in the world and in our studies of loneliness we like to show the full potentiality of love (how Flaubert would have satirized these latter-day Bovarists!), but we don't know or want to know any senators, bishops, atomic scientists; as for psychiatrists—well, we like ours: he is a Jungian. Shrinking each into his own skin, our novelists grow more private, and for those who lack genius (the majority), more dull. I do not suggest that everyone turn his hand to satire. It is, after all, only one of a number of ways to get the thing said. Nor do I echo those solid *Forsyte Saga* newspaper reviewers who maintain that what we need is a good novel about the wool trade or building a dam, but what I feel we do need is more engagement in the outer world. And daring. And wit. And, finally, satirists, who are needed as truth is needed—for is not satire, simply, truth grinning in a solemn canting world?

*The Nation*
April 26, 1958

# 5

# NORMAN MAILER'S
# SELF-ADVERTISEMENTS

I first heard of Norman Mailer in the spring of 1948, just before *The Naked and the Dead* was published. I remember thinking meanly: So somebody did it. Each previous war had had its big novel, yet so far there had been none for our war, though I knew that a dozen busy friends and acquaintances were grimly taking out tickets in the Grand War Novel Lottery. I had debated doing one myself and had (I still think) done something better: a small cool hard novel about men on the periphery of the action. *Williwaw* was written when I was nineteen and easily the cleverest young fox ever to know how to disguise his ignorance and make a virtue of his limitations. (What an attractive form the self-advertisement is: one could go on forever relighting one's image!) Not till I began *The City and the Pillar* did I begin to get bored with playing it safe.

I took to the field and have often wondered since, in the course of many excursions, defeats, alarms and ambushes, what it might have been like to have been a safe shrewd custodian of one's talent, playing from strength. I did not suspect then that the ambitious, rather cold-blooded young contemporary who had set out to write the big war novel would one day be in the same fix I was. Not safe. Not wise. Not admired. A fellow victim of the Great Golfer's Age, then no more than a murmur of things to come in the Golfer's murmurous heart.

My first reaction to *The Naked and the Dead* was: it's a fake. A clever, talented, admirably executed fake. I have not changed my opinion of the book since, though I have considerably changed my opinion of Mailer, as he himself has changed. Now I confess I have never read all of *The Naked and the Dead.* I do recall a fine description of soldiers carrying a dying man down a mountain (done almost as well as the same scene in Malraux's earlier work). Yet every time I got going in the narrative I would find myself stopped cold by a set of made-up, predictable characters taken not from life, but from the same novels all of us had read, and informed by a naïveté which was at its worst when Mailer went into his Time-Machine and wrote those passages which resemble nothing so much as smudged carbons of a Dos Passos work.

Sourly, from a distance, that year I watched the fame of Mailer quite surpass that of John Horne Burns and myself, the heroes of the previous year. I should explain for those who have come in late or were around then but inattentive that the O.K. List of writers in 1947 and 1948 was John Horne Burns, Calder Willingham and myself. Capote and Mailer were added in 1948. Willingham was soon dropped; then Burns (my own favorite) sank, and by 1949, in the aftermath of *The City and the Pillar,* I too departed the O.K. List.

"I had the freak of luck to start high on the mountain, and go down sharp while others were passing me"—so Mailer wrote, describing the time after *Barbary Shore* when he unexpectedly joined the rest of us down on the plain. Now the descent, swift or slow, is not agreeable; but on the other hand it is not as tragic as Mailer seems to find it. To be demoralized by the withdrawal of public success (a process as painful in America as the withdrawal of a drug from an addict) is to grant too easily a victory to the society one has attempted to criticize, affect, change, reform. It is clearly unreasonable to expect to be cherished by those one assaults. It is also childish, in the deepest sense of being a child, ever to expect justice. There is none beneath our moon. One can only hope not to be destroyed entirely by injustice and, to put it cynically, one can very often flourish through an injustice obtaining in one's favor. What matters finally is not the world's judgment of oneself but one's own judgment of the world. Any writer who lacks this final arrogance will not survive very long in America.

That wide graveyard of stillborn talents which contains so much of the brief ignoble history of American letters is a tribute to the power of a democracy to destroy its critics, brave fools and passionate men. If there is anything in Mailer's new book which alarms me, it is his obsession with public success. He is running for President, as he puts it. Yet though his best and most interesting works have been unjustly attacked, he should realize that in this most inequitable of worlds his one worldly success was not a very good book, that *The Naked and the Dead* is redolent of "ambition" (in the Mary McCarthy sense of the word—pejorative, needless to say) and a young man's will to be noticed. Mailer himself nearly takes this view: "I may as well confess that by December 8th or 9th of 1941 . . . I was worrying darkly whether it would be more likely that a great war novel would be written about Europe or the Pacific." Ambition and the day coincided and a success was made. Yet it is much less real a book than Burns's *The Gallery,* or even some of the stories of Robert Lowry, works which had the virtue of being felt, possessed entirely by the men who made them, not created out of stern ambition and dogged competence. But, parenthetically, most war books are inadequate. War tends to be too much for any writer, especially one whose personality is already half obliterated by life in a democracy. Even the aristocrat Tolstoi, at a long remove in time, stretched his genius to the breaking point to encompass men and war and the thrust of history in a single vision. Ernest Hemingway in *A Farewell to Arms* did a few good descriptions, but his book, too, is a work of ambition, in which can be seen the beginning of the careful, artful, immaculate idiocy of tone that since has marked both his prose and his legend as he has declined into the sort of fame which, at moments I hope are weak, Mailer seems to crave.

But it is hard for American writers not to measure themselves according to the standards of their time and place. I recall a conversation with Stephen Spender when I lapsed, unconsciously, into the national preoccupation. Some writer had unexpectedly failed, not gone on, blown up. Spender said rather pointedly, "The difference in England is that they want us to be distinguished, to be good." We order things differently; although our example is contagious, for in recent years the popular British press has discovered writers in a way ours never has. Outside the gossip column and the book page no writer except Hemingway is ever mentioned as news in the American press, but let the most obscure young English novelist attack the Establishment and there are headlines in London. Mailer can denounce Eisenhower as much as he likes in *Dissent* but the readers of the *Daily News* will never know Mailer's name, much less the quality of his anger. Publicity for the American writer is of the "personality" kind: a photograph in *Harper's Bazaar,* bland television appearances . . . the writer as minor movie star, and as unheeded.

Mailer and I finally met in 1954. I had just published my last, or perhaps I should say latest, novel, *Messiah,* which was ignored in America. (If it were not for the continuing interest of Europe, especially England, a great many of our writers would not survive as well as they do their various seasons of neglect.) I liked Mailer, though I am afraid my first impression of him was somewhat guarded. I am suspicious of people who make speeches at me, and he is a born cocktail-party orator. I have not the slightest recollection of what we talked about. I do recall telling him that I admired *Barbary Shore,* and he was shrewd enough to observe that probably I had been driven to read it to see if it was really as bad as everyone thought. Of his three novels I find it the most interesting and the least diffuse. It is hallucinatory writing of a kind Mailer attempted, as far as I know, only that one time; and though I think his talents are essentially naturalistic, he does seem again in his new novel (judging from the advance samples he displays in *Advertisements for Myself*) to be trying for that revelation through willful distortion which he achieved in *Barbary Shore.* One is curious to see the result.

I have gone into the chronology of Mailer's days and mine because they run parallel, occasionally crossing, and because the book he has just published is, in effect, an autobiography covering more or less his entire career with particular attention to the days of the Golfer's dull terror. Mailer gives us his life and his work together, and therefore it is impossible to review the book without attempting to make some estimate of both his character and the corpus of his work, the tension of his present and the shape of his future. Mailer is sly to get himself all this attention, but I must point out that it is a very dangerous move for an artist to expose himself so completely. Indeed, in other times it would have been fatal for an artist not yet full grown to show us his sores and wounds, real and illusory strengths. Until very recently the artist was a magician who did his magic in public view but kept himself and his effects a matter of mystery. We know *now* of Flaubert's suffering, both emotional and aesthetic, during the days of his work, but it is hard to imagine what would have happened if the court which prosecuted *Madame Bovary* could have presented as evidence a volume of his letters. In effect, Mailer has anticipated his own posterity. He is giving us now the storms and the uncertainties, private and public, which he has undergone. He has armed the enemy and not entirely pleased his allies.

However, it may be possible to get away with this sort of thing today, for we live in the age of the confession. What Mailer has done is no different in kind from what those deranged and fallen actresses have accomplished in ghost-written memoirs where, with a shrewd eye on the comeback trail, they pathetically confess their sins to Demos, receiving for their tears the absolution of a culture obscenely interested in gossip. I suspect Mailer may create more interest in himself by having made this "clean breast of it" than he would have got by publishing a distinguished novel. The audience no longer consumes novels, but it does devour personalities. Yet what happens after one is eaten? Is one regurgitated? Or does the audience move on to its next dinner of scandal and tears, its previous meal absorbed and forgotten?

But despite a nice but small gift for self-destruction, Mailer is uncommonly adroit, with an eye to the main chance (the writer who lacks this instinct is done for in America; excellence is not nearly enough). I noted with some amusement that, despite his air of candor, he makes no new enemies in this book. He scores off who are lost to him anyway, thus proving that essentially the work is politic. His confessions, when not too disingenuous, are often engaging and always interesting, as he tries to record his confusions. For Mailer does not begin to know what he believes or is or wants. His drive seems to be toward power of a religio-political kind. He is a messiah without real hope of paradise on earth or in heaven, and with no precise mission except that dictated by his ever-changing temperament. I am not sure, finally, that he should be a novelist at all, or even a writer, despite formidable gifts. He is too much a demagogue; he swings from one position of cant to another with an intensity that is visceral rather than intellectual. He is all fragments and pieces. He appears to be looking for an identity, and often it seems that he believes crude celebrity will give it to him again. The author of *The Naked and the Dead,* though not the real Mailer, was at least an identifiable surrogate, and duly celebrated. But Mailer was quickly bored with the war-novelist role, and as soon as possible he moved honorably to a new position: radical politics, in the hope that through Marxist action he might better identify himself to us and to himself. But politics failed him, too. Nor is the new Mailer, prophet of Hip and celebrator of sex and its connection with time, apt to interest him or us for very long.

I also noted at moments toward the end of this book that a reaction was setting in: Mailer started using military allusions. "Back in the Philippines, we . . . "—that sort of thing. And there were references to patrols, ambushes. It was startling. Most of our generation was in the war, usually ingloriously, yet I have never heard a contemporary make any reference to it in a personal way. The war to most of us was a profound irrelevance; traumatic for some, perhaps, but for most no more than an interruption. When the 1959 Mailer reminds us that he was a rifleman on Luzon, I get embarrassed for him and hope he is not going back to his first rôle to get the attention he wants.

Now for the book itself. It is a collection of stories, essays, notes, newspaper columns and part of a play. It begins with his first story at Harvard and ends with part of his new novel. I particularly liked two short stories. "The Language of Men" tells of the problems of an army cook who has an abstract passion for excellence as well as a need for the approbation of the indifferent men who eat what he cooks. His war with them and himself and his will to excel are beautifully shown and in many ways make one of the best stories of its kind I have read, certainly preferable to Hemingway's *The Old Man and the Sea,* which it resembles in theme. But where Hemingway was pretentious and external, Mailer is particular and works with gentle grace from within his characters. The other story, "The Patron Saint of Macdougal Alley," is an amusing portrait of an archetypal drifter, and I think it is of permanent value: we have had this sort of fool in every age, but I have not seen him done quite so well in our day.

By and large, excepting "The White Negro," I did not like the essays and the newspaper columns. Mailer is forever shouting at us that he is about to tell us something we must know or has just told us something revelatory and we failed to hear him or that he will, God grant his poor abused brain and body just one more chance, get through to us so that we will *know.* Actually, when he does approach a point he shifts into a swelling, throbbing rhetoric which is not easy to read but usually has something to do with love and sex and the horror of our age and the connection which must be made between time and sex (the image this bit of rhetoric suggests to me is a limitless gray sea of time with a human phallus desperately poking at a corner of it). He is at his best (who is not?) when discussing himself. He is a born defendant. The piece about getting *The Deer Park* published is especially good, and depressing for what it reveals about our society. But, finally, in every line he writes, despite the bombast, there is uncertainty: Who am I? What do I want? What am I saying? He is Thomas Wolfe but with a conscience. Wolfe's motive for writing was perfectly clear: he wanted fame; he wanted to taste the whole earth, to name all the rivers. Mailer has the same passion for fame but he has a good deal more sense of responsibility and he sees that the thing is always in danger of spinning down into meaninglessness. Nothing is quite enough: art, sex, politics, drugs, God, mind. He is sure to get tired of Hip very soon. Sex will be a dead end for him, because sex is the one purely existential act (to misuse, as he always does, a fashionable adjective of the forties). Sex is. There is nothing more to be done about it. Sex builds no roads, writes no novels, and sex certainly gives no meaning to anything in life but itself. I have often thought that much of D. H. Lawrence's self-lacerating hysteria toward the end of his life must have come out of some "blood knowledge" that the cruel priapic god was mad, bad and dangerous to know, and, finally, not even a palliative to the universal strangeness.

Perhaps what has gone wrong in Mailer, and in many of our fellow clerks, is the sense that human beings to flourish must be possessed by one idea, a central meaning to which all experience can be related. To be, in Isaiah Berlin's bright metaphor, hedgehog rather than fox. Yet the human mind is not capable of this kind of exclusivity. We are none of us hedgehogs or foxes, but both simultaneously. The human mind is in continual flux, and personality is simply a sum of those attitudes which most often repeat themselves in recognizable actions. It is naïve and dangerous to try to impose on the human mind any system of thought which lays claim to finality. Very few first-rate writers have ever subordinated their own apprehension of a most protean reality to a man-made system of thought. Tolstoi's famous attempt in *War and Peace* nearly wrecked that beautiful work. Ultimately, not Christ, not Marx, not Freud, despite their pretensions, has the final word to say about the fact of being human. And those who take solemnly the words of other men as absolute are, in the deepest sense, maiming their own sensibilities and controverting the evidence of their own senses in a fashion which may be comforting to a terrified man but disastrous for an artist.

One of the few sad results of the collapse of the Judeo-Christian ethical and religious systems has been the displacement of those who are absolutists by temperament and would in earlier times have been rabbis, priests, systematic philosophers. As the old Establishment of the West crumbles, the absolutists have turned to literature and the arts, and one by one the arts in the twentieth century have become hieratic. Serious literature has become religion, as Matthew Arnold foresaw. Those who once would have been fulfilled in Talmudic debate or suffered finely between the pull of Rome and the Church of England have turned to the writing of novels and, worse, to the criticism of novels. Now I am not sure that the novel, though it is many things, is particularly suited to didacticism. It is certainly putting an undesirable weight upon it to use it as a pretext for sermons or the resuscitation of antique religious myths. Works of fiction, at best, create not arguments but worlds, and a world by definition is an attitude toward a complex of experience, not a single argument or theme, syllogistically proposed. In the nineteenth century most of our critics (and many of our novelists) would have been writing books of sermons and quarreling over points of doctrine. With religion gone out of the intellectual world they now write solemnly and uneasily about novels; they are clearly impatient with the vulgar vitality of the art, and were it not that they had one another's books about books to analyze, I suspect many of them would despair and falter. The novelists don't seem very bright to the critics, while their commentaries seem irrelevant to the novelists. Yet each affects the other; and those writers who are unduly eager for fame and acceptance will write novels which they hope might interest "religious"-minded critics. The results range from the subliterary bleating of the Beats to Mailer's portentous cry which takes the form of (these words are my paraphrase of Mailer): I am the way and the life ever after, crucify me, you hackers, for mine is a ritual death! Take my flesh and my blood, partake of me and *know* mysteries . . . ! And the curious thing is that they *will* crucify him; they will partake of his flesh; yet no mystery will be revealed. For the priests have created the gods, and they are all of them ritual harvest gods.

I was most struck by a comment of André Gide in the posthumous *Ainsi Soit-il*: "It is affectation that makes so many of today's writings, often even the best among them, unbearable to me. The author takes on a tone that is not natural to him." Of course it is sometimes the work of a lifetime for an artist to discover who he is and it is true that a great deal of good art results from the trying on of masks, the affectation of a persona not one's own. But it seems to me that most of my contemporaries, including Mailer, are—as Gide suggests—desperately trying to convince themselves and the audience that they are something they are not. There is even a certain embarrassment about writing novels at all. Telling stories does seem a silly occupation for one fully grown; yet to be a philosopher or a religious is not easy when one is making a novel. Also, in a society such as ours, where there is no moral, political or religious center, the temptation to fill the void is irresistible. There is the empty throne, so . . . *seize* the crown! Who would not be a king or high priest in such an age? And the writers, each in his own way, are preoccupied with power. Some hope to achieve place through good deportment. Universities are filled with poets and novelists conducting demure and careful lives in imitation of Eliot and Forster and those others who (through what *seems* to have been discretion) made it. Outside the universities one finds the buccaneers who mean to seize the crown by force, blunt Bolingbrokes to the Academy's gentle Richards.

Mailer is a Bolingbroke, a born usurper. He will raise an army anywhere, live off the country as best he can, helped by a devoted underground, even assisted at brief moments by rival claimants like myself. Yet when all is said, none of this is the way to live. And it is not a way (at least it makes the way harder) to create a literature. If it helps Hemingway to think of literature as a Golden Gloves Tournament with himself pounding Maupassant to the mat or fighting Stendhal to a draw, then no doubt the fantasy has been of some use. But there is also evidence that the preoccupation with actual political power is a great waste of time. Mailer has had the honesty to confess that his own competitiveness has wasted him as he worries about reviewers and bad publicity and the seemingly spiteful successes of other novelists. Yet all the time he knows perfectly well that writers are not in competition with one another. The real enemy is the audience, which grows more and more indifferent to literature, an audience which can be reached only by phenomena, by superior pornographies or willfully meretricious accounts of the way we live now. No serious American novelist has ever had any real sense of audience. C. P. Snow made the point that he would, given a choice, prefer to be a writer in England to a writer in America because, for better or worse, the Establishment of his country would read him and know him as he knew them, as the Greek dramatists knew and were known by their city's audience. One cannot imagine the American president, any American president, reading a work by a serious contemporary American writer. This lack of response is to me at the center of Mailer's desperation. He is a public writer, not a private artist; he wants to influence those who are alive at this time, but they will not notice him even when he is good. So each time he speaks he must become more bold, more loud, put on brighter motley and shake more foolish bells. *Anything* to get their attention, and finally (and this could be his tragedy) so much energy is spent in getting the indifferent ear to listen that when the time comes for him to speak there may be not enough strength of creative imagination left him to say what he *knows*. Exhausted, he becomes like Louis Lambert in Balzac's curious novel of the visionary-artist who, having seen straight through to the heart of the mystery, dies mad, murmuring: "The angels are white."

Yet of all my contemporaries I retain the greatest affection for Mailer as a force and as an artist. He is a man whose faults, though many, add to rather than subtract from the sum of his natural achievement. There is more virtue in his failures than in most small, premeditated successes which, in Cynic's phrase, "debase currency." Mailer, in all that he does, whether he does it well or ill, is honorable, and that is the highest praise I can give any writer in this piping time.

*The Nation*
January 2, 1960

# 6

# WRITERS AND THE WORLD

Recently *Variety,* an American paper devoted to the performing arts, reviewed a television program about life inside the Harlem ghetto. The discussion was conducted "by literary oriented . . . Norman Podhoretz, editor of *Commentary* magazine, who initially tried to guide the colloquy along bookish lines. . . ." And apparently failed. "Podhoretz, who described himself as a 'cold, detached intellectual,' is given to verbosity and for about half the program was annoyingly the obtrusive interviewer, more eager to talk than to probe his subject. He receded in the second half, however, and overall was a good foil. . . ."

For several years, *Variety* has been reviewing television's talking writers in precisely the same terms that they review comedians and singers. Mary McCarthy, James Baldwin, Dwight Macdonald are now familiar actors in the world of *Variety.* Yet until this decade, no more than half a dozen writers were known to the mass audience at any given moment. It took a generation of constant performing for someone like Carl Sandburg to become a national figure. Today fame is the work of a night. As a result, any number of contemporary novelists, poets, and critics are known to the innocent millions, who value them not only as entertainers but seem to take them seriously as public moralists. As resonant chorus to the Republic's drama, the writers have replaced the

clergy. It is to Norman Mailer, not to Norman Vincent Peale, that the
television producer turns when he wants a discussion of "America's
Moral Decline" or "The Meaning of Violence."

This dramatic change in literature's estate is not due to any sudden
passion for books among the people. Americans have never liked reading. According to the ubiquitous Dr. Gallup, fifty percent of the adult
population never reads a book once school is done. Nor was the writers'
condition altered by the brief re-creation of Camelot beside the Potomac. It was reassuring to the intellectual community to know that the
thirty-fifth President knew the difference between Saul Bellow and Irwin
Shaw, but it was also true that he preferred Shaw to Bellow and Ian
Fleming to either. What he did respect was success in the arts, which
is not quite the same thing as excellence, though more easily identified.
Finally, it was neither the public nor the New Frontier which glorified
the writers. It was around-the-clock television and its horror of "dead
air."

Producers discovered that one way of inexpensively enlivening the air
is to invite people to talk to one another while the camera records. There
are now literally thousands of talk shows, national and local, ranging
from the *Today* show, which commands the attention of most of the
country's "opinion makers," to late-night educational symposia where
literary men deal with such knotty questions as "Has There Been a
*Really* Important American Novel Since *A Passage to India?*" The
thought of people sitting at home watching other people talk is profoundly sad. But that is the way we live now, electronic villagers tuned
in to the machine if not to the pundits.

In the search for talkers, it was soon discovered that movie stars need
a script and that politicians are not only evasive but apt to run afoul of
the "equal time for the opposition" statute. Of the well known, only the
writers were entirely suitable and perfectly available. From poets
(Auden haggling with Professor Trilling over who was older) to journalists (Walter Lippmann benignly instructing his countrymen in the ways
of history), the writers responded to the Zeitgeist's call with suspicious
alacrity. From the commercialite peddling his latest book-club choice
to the serious critic getting in a good word for *Partisan Review,* the
writers are now public in a way that they have never been before, and
this has created all sorts of problems for them and their admirers, many
of whom believe that it is degrading for a distinguished man of letters
to allow himself to be questioned by an entertainer in front of an audience of forty million people who have not a clue as to who he is other
than the vague knowledge that he has written a book.

To this charge, the highbrow writer usually replies that any sort of exhibitionism is good for selling books. After all, no one would criticize him for giving a paid reading at a university. The middlebrow murmurs something about educating the masses. The lowbrow echoes the highbrow: "exposure" is good for trade. Yet in actual fact, there is no evidence that television appearances sell novels as opposed to volumes of gossip or sex hygiene. Most people who watch television regularly do not read books or much of anything else. Yet this does not deter the talking writers. There are other pleasures and duties than trade. For one thing, those who have strong views of a political or moral nature are free to express them (aesthetic judgments are not encouraged by compères for obvious reasons). Finally if the writer talks often enough, he will acquire a movie-star persona which *ought* eventually to increase the audience for his books if, meanwhile, he has found the time to write them.

But even if the writer who talks well continues to write well, there are those who believe that publicness of any kind must somehow be corrupting, like Hollywood. Americans prefer their serious writers obscure, poor, and, if possible, doomed by drink or gaudy vice. It is no accident that those contemporary writers most admired within the Academy are the ones whose lives were disorderly and disastrous, in vivid contrast to their explicators, quietly desperate upon dull campuses.

From the beginning, the American civilization has been simultaneously romantic and puritan. The World is corrupt. If the virtuous artist does not avoid its pomps and pleasures, he will crack up like Scott Fitzgerald or shoot his brains out like Ernest Hemingway, whose sad last days have assured him a place in the national pantheon which his novels alone would not have done. Of living writers, only Norman Mailer seems willing to live a life that is bound to attract lengthy comment of a cautionary sort. America's literary critics and custodians are essentially moralists who find literature interesting only to the extent that it reveals the moral consciousness of the middle class. The limitations of this kind of criticism were remarked upon more than twenty years ago by John Crowe Ransom, who thought there was a place for at least one ontological critic in the American literary hierarchy. The place of course is still there; still vacant.

"I stayed home and wrote," Flaubert used to say, quoting Horace, and to the serious-minded this priestlike dedication is still the correct way for the good writer to live, even though it means that his biography will be disappointingly slim. Remote from public affairs, the unworldly American artist ought not to be concerned with aesthetic matters either.

Whenever literary questions were put to William Faulkner, he would say, "I'm just a farmer," neglecting to add that for thirty years most of his farming was of a seasonal nature in Hollywood, writing films. Yet he was always given credit for having turned his back upon the World, like J. D. Salinger, who is regarded with a certain awe because he lives entirely withdrawn from everyone. Never photographed, never interviewed, perfectly silent (except when *The New Yorker* is attacked), Mr. Salinger turns out fictions which, for a time, were taken to be more serious than they are because of the entirely admirable way their author lives.

Except for a brief time during the 30s, the notion of the writer as citizen has not been popular. In fact, during the 40s, the intellectual catchword was "alienation." The writers simply ignored the Republic, their full attention reserved for those dramas of the interior where Greek myths are eternally re-enacted in vague places beyond time, and Alcestis wears seersucker and majors in Comp. Lit. at Princeton. The 50s were the time of the Great Golfer, and there was a death in the land to which the only response was the Beats. They were not even alienated. They just went. And felt. Then as swiftly as they appeared, they vanished; nothing but a whiff of marijuana upon the air to mark their exuberant passage. The 60s began with a flourish. The young President detested all rhetoric except his own, in which he resembled most of the writers. A quasi-intellectual, he knew how to flatter even the most irritable man of letters. A master of publicity, he realized the value of having well-known people support him. If James Baldwin was an effective and admired television performer, then it was only common sense to try to win his support.

In 1960 politics and literature officially joined forces. The politician had literary longings; the writer saw himself as president, leading the polity to the good life by means of lysergic acid or the more copious orgasm or whatever bee buzzed loudest in his bonnet. More to the point, through television, the talking writer was able to command an audience in a way few politicians can. Not only is the writer a celebrity, he is also a free agent who does not have to be re-elected or even to be responsible. And so, not unnaturally, writers have been drawn more and more to actual as opposed to symbolic politics. Many worked for the elections of both Kennedy and Johnson. Saul Bellow contemplated writing a biography of Hubert Humphrey. Norman Mailer took credit for Kennedy's election because at a crucial moment in the campaign he gave the candidate the moment's accolade; called him "hipster." After Kennedy's election, writers were regularly invited to the White House. It was a heady thousand days.

But since Johnson's accession, the links between poetry and power have snapped. Literary people annoy and confuse the President. The precise nature of Saul Bellow's achievement does not seem to weigh heavily with him. Nevertheless, like his predecessor, he knows the propaganda value of artists and he has somewhat wistfully tried to win them over. It has not been easy. Despite the good things he has done at home, the President's Asian adventures alarm the talking writers and they talk against him. In retaliation, he has refused to bestow Freedom Medals, Kennedy's order of merit for excellence in science and art. But this state of siege is hardly permanent. For better or worse, the writers are very much in the real world, and the politicians know it.

Simultaneously with their new-found celebrity, the writers have become the beneficiaries of a peculiar crisis in American publishing. Fifteen years ago the mass magazines lost much of their advertising revenue to television. To survive, they were forced to make radical changes. At the prodding of young editors, they began to raid the literary quarterlies. Overnight the work of writers like Bellow, Baldwin, and Paul Goodman replaced those cheerful fictions and bland commentaries that had made the popular magazines the despair of the intellectuals for half a century. All sorts of miracles began to occur: James Baldwin was allowed to deliver a sermon in *The New Yorker,* while Dr. Leslie Fiedler, having deserted raft, Huck, and Jim, became *Playboy*'s "writer of the year." Curiously enough, the readers who had for so long been soothed by Clarence Budington Kelland seemed not to mind the abrasiveness of the new writers. More to the point, young people found them interesting, a matter of some importance to publishers, since the age of the average American is now twenty-seven and growing younger. In fact, those in college form the largest single subculture in the United States, far more numerous, say, than the organized-labor movement or nature's noblemen, the farmers. As a result, courses in contemporary literature have made a generation of young people aware of writers who ordinarily might have gone on to the end in honorable obscurity. This new audience has at last been reflected in the publishing of books, both hard- and soft-cover.

For the first time since New England's brief Indian summer, good writers with some regularity outsell commercial ones in hard cover. In recent years Mary McCarthy has outsold Daphne du Maurier; Bellow has outsold Uris; Auchincloss has outsold O'Hara. Financially, inflation has set in. The paperback publishers are pursuing the new best sellers with advances that go as high as a million dollars. No one knows whether or not the publishers will ever earn back these huge advances, but meanwhile they gain valuable newsstand space, and in the wake of a famous book they can display their less showy wares, which include, often as not, the best books. As a result, a serious and well-reviewed novel which has sold twenty-five hundred copies in hard cover can, in paperback, reach an audience of many thousands of readers, mostly young. This is the first sign that the novel, which has steadily declined as a popular art form in this century, may be able at last to hold its own not only with films and television but also with that high journalism which has so distracted the intellectuals since the Second War.

Affluence, publicity, power, can these things be said to "corrupt" the artist? In themselves, no. Or as Ernest Hemingway nicely put it: "Every whore finds his vocation." Certainly it is romantic melodrama to believe that publicity in itself destroys the artist. Too many writers of the first rank have been devoted self-publicists (Frost, Pound, Yeats), perfectly able to do their work quite unaffected by a machine they know how to run. Toughness is all. Neither Hollywood nor the World destroyed Scott Fitzgerald. He would have made the same mess had he taught at a university, published unnoticed novels, and lived in decorous obscurity. The spoiling of a man occurs long before his first encounter with the World. But the romantic-puritan stereotype dies hard. The misbehavior of the artist thrills the romantic; his subsequent suffering and punishment satisfy the puritan.

Yet today new situations exist, and the old archetypes, never true, seem less relevant than ever. To be outside the World is not necessarily a virtue. To be in the World does not necessarily mean a loss of craft, a fall from grace, a fatness of soul. William Faulkner's thirty years as a movie writer affected his novels not at all. He could do both. Finally, it is truly impertinent to speculate as to whether or not the effect of this or of that on a writer's character is good or bad. What is pertinent is the work he does. Mary McCarthy is no less intelligent a literary critic because she plays games on television. But even if her work should show a sudden falling off, only the simplest moralist would be able to link her appearances as a talking writer to her work as a writing writer.

It has been observed that American men do not read novels because they feel guilty when they read books which do not have facts in them. Made-up stories are for women and children; facts are for men. There is something in this. It is certainly true that this century's romantic estrangement of writer from the World has considerably reduced the number of facts in the American novel. And facts, both literal and symbolic, are the stuff of art as well as of life. In *Moby Dick* Melville saw to it that the reader would end by knowing as much about whaling as he did. But today there are few facts in the American novel, if only because the writers do not know much about anything except their own immediate experience, which is apt to be narrow. It is no accident that the best of American writing since the war has been small, private, interior. But now that the writers have begun to dabble in the World, even the most solipsistic of them has begun to suspect that there are a good many things that other people know that he does not. Though senators tend to be banal in public statements, none is ever quite so wide of the mark as an impassioned novelist giving his views on public affairs, particularly if he accepts the traditional romantic view that passion is all, facts tedious, reflection a sign of coldness (even impotence) and the howl more eloquent than words. Fortunately, as writers come up against the actual World they are bound to absorb new facts, and this ought to be useful to them in their work. As for the World, only good can come of the writers' engagement in public affairs. Particularly in the United States, a nation governed entirely by lawyers, those professional "maintainers of quarrels" whom Henry IV Plantagenet sensibly barred from sitting in Parliament. At last other voices are being heard, if only late at night on television.

The obvious danger for the writer is the matter of time. "A talent is formed in stillness," wrote Goethe, "a character in the stream of the world." Goethe, as usual, managed to achieve both. But it is not easy, and many writers who choose to be active in the World lose not virtue but time, and that stillness without which literature cannot be made. This is sad. Until one recalls how many bad books the World may yet be spared because of the busyness of writers turned Worldly. The romantic-puritans can find consolation in that, and take pleasure in realizing that there is a rude justice, finally, even in the best of worlds.

*Times Literary Supplement* (London)
November 25, 1965

# 7

## LITERARY GANGSTERS

On a rare visit to the theater in the early sixties (visits have been equally rare in other decades), I opened *Playbill,* a throwaway magazine given me by an usher, and saw my own name; then "Golden Age of Television"; then "Chayefsky." I was startled. A half-dozen years had passed since live television drama ended. Why bring up the subject now? And in *Playbill*? I read on. The tone of the piece was shrill, and the substance altogether too familiar. Apparently the television playwrights had not—oh, God, it's that piece again!—been *good.* The writer did not offer much evidence one way or the other, but then did anyone ever see the three thousand or so plays that were done in those years? Better to dismiss the whole lot as *kitsch,* and refer to me, in particular, as "a culture hero of the 50's." Moss creeping up once-heroic limbs, I looked to see who cared so little for television's twenty-one-inch dramatic Renaissance. Richard Gilman. The name—if not the style—was new to me.

Recently, I spent an evening with several other culture heroes, current and past (wherever we meet, there is the Pantheon), and we got onto the subject of literary gangsters. Since the invention of printing, there has been a need for people to write more or less to order for the press. Some of these professionals have been good, some have been bad, and a sizable minority have been gangsters: hit-and-run journalists, without conscience, forced to live precariously by their wits, and those wits are increasingly strained nowadays because there are fewer places to publish in than there used to be, which means a lot more edgy hoods hanging about the playgrounds of the West Side.

The literary gangster's initial problem is a poignant one: how to be noticed? How to occupy a turf of one's own? Having been for a quarter-century an observer of the scene, with a particular interest in literary crime—to use that well-loved *New York Times Book Review* phrase—I would suggest, right off, that the apprentice criminal write the following on the lid of his typewriter: Today's reader is not interested in analysis but opinion, preferably harsh and unexpected. Some years ago a classic caper began with the statement that although Bernard Shaw was a bad playwright, a few pages of his music criticism were not without value. This caused interest. It was also a splendid heist because no attempt was made to prove a case. An opinion was stated loudly, and contrary evidence was ignored. The young apprentice should also feel free to invent sources and quotations, on the ground that readers of even the most high-minded journals know very little about anything, particularly the past. Needless to say, the more violent and *ad hominem* the style, the more grateful his readers will be. Americans like to be told whom to hate. Finally, the gangster can never go wrong if, while appearing to uphold the highest standards (but never define those standards or say just when it was that the theater, for instance, was "relevant"), he attacks indiscriminately the artists of the day, the popular on the ground that to give pleasure to the many is a sign of corruption and the much-admired on the ground that since all values now held by the society are false (for obvious reasons don't present alternative values), any culture hero must reflect perfectly the folly of those who worship him. It is not wise to praise anyone living; unhappily, every now and then, it may be necessary to *appear* to like something done by a contemporary, in which case select a foreign writer like Borges; he is old, admired abroad, and his works are short enough actually to read. In a few years, he can always be dismissed as a culture hero of the "Silly Sixties." Remember that turnover is now as rapid in literary reputations as it is in women's dresses. So keep moving, and if occasionally you contradict yourself, no one will notice, since no one is keeping score.

Was it ever thus? Yes, since antiquity or at least since newspapers. On February 20, 1767, Voltaire wrote a friend, "The infamous trade of vilifying one's colleagues to earn a little money should be left to cheap journalists. . . . It is those wretches who have made of literature an arena for gladiators."

Gladiators, cheap journalists, gangsters, they are always with us. To

the heroes of the forties, John W. Aldridge, Jr., was the first gangster
to appear on the scene, and a source of wonder to us all. In 1947 he set
himself up as—we thought—a legitimate literary businessman, opening
shop with a piece describing the writers of the postwar generation in
which he warmly praised John Horne Burns and myself. The praise
made us think he was not a hood, his shop a legitimate business not a
front. Little did we suspect that Mr. Aldridge was a master literary
criminal who wanted to contribute not simply a modest footnote to each
of our sagas but a terrible full chapter. To achieve this, he even moved
to Connecticut in order to be close to certain of his victims. For several
years he covered them with unctuous praise in print as well as in private.
Meanwhile, he was thoroughly casing the territory. Then he struck. In
a blaze of publicity, Mr. Aldridge bit one by one those very asses he had
with such cunning kissed, earning himself an editorial in *Life* magazine
congratulating him for having shown up the decadence and immorality
of the postwar writers. He has long since faded from the literary scene
as have, fortunately, those scars on which we sit.

Other gangsters today? John Simon was lovingly noted. A Yugoslav
with a proud if somewhat incoherent Serbian style (or is it Croatian?—in
any case, English in his third language), Mr. Simon has for twenty years
slashed his way through literature, theater, cinema. Clanking chains and
snapping whips, giggling and hissing, he has ricocheted from one journal
to another, and though no place holds him for long, the flow of venom
has proved inexhaustible. There is nothing he cannot find to hate. Yet
in his way, Mr. Simon is pure; a compulsive rogue criminal, more
sadistic Gilles de Rais than neighborhood thug.

Robert Brustein, on the other hand, is not pure; he has ambitions
about his station. Mr. Simon knows that he is only an Illyrian gangster
and is blessedly free of side; he simply wants to torture and kill in order
to be as good an American as Mr. Charles Manson, say, or Lyndon
Johnson. But Mr. Brustein wants to matter, to go straight. A failed
theater person, he had/has ambitions not only as director but as an
actor. The actor side of him explains why one always felt he was playing,
in a somewhat hollow way, the part of a stern highbrow critic, and
having the field pretty much to himself because true highbrow critics
don't deal with theater. His specialty was lamentation, a sort of Broadway Old Testament prophet, wailing for a Jerusalem that never was. Mr.
Brustein's ambition has now translated him from literary gangster to
academic bureaucrat at Yale but I'm sure he'll be back one of these days.
Recidivism is a hundred percent in such cases.

My fellow heroes then mentioned Richard Gilman. A notorious hood, they assured me. But except for my brief glimpse of him in the pages of *Playbill* (like Cosa Nostra, they will infiltrate anything), he was just another face, as it were, on the post-office wall. Now I have read him.

It is difficult to know what to say about *The Confusion of Realms.* Mr. Gilman has collected a number of pieces dealing with the novel and the theater, and he presents them to us for . . . what? Our illumination? Admiration? I have read each piece carefully (something no self-respecting gangster would do) and I took many notes. In some ways I found him worse than I expected—gangsters seldom write so dully; he sounds at times as if he were addressing a not-very-bright class in remedial reading. In other ways, he is better than anticipated: he is not above betraying enthusiasm for a living American writer. Yet at the end of 272 pages I could not make out what he was up to—or, more precisely, just what audience he had in mind. His work is too simple for those who know literature and much too long-winded for those who do not but are sufficiently interested to want to know more.

Mr. Gilman's examination of Norman Mailer (last year's obligatory piece) is typical. He writes thousands of words about Mailer; yet says nothing that the Master has not said better about himself (admittedly it is not easy to deal with Mailer since that sly operative is always there first with the most words), concluding with the emotional argument that although Mailer's novels are not much good, it doesn't really matter because he's *ours.* To which the rude answer is he may be yours, but he's certainly not mine. Mr. Gilman goes even farther off the rails when he finds Mailer's passion for being in history (not to mention the press) harmful to him as an artist. I would say it was the making of him. The idea of the artist as priest is much loved in gangsterland. They believe that worldly commitment is corrupting. Yet what about Goethe, Voltaire, Byron or, to come up to date, Günter Grass (admired by John Simon . . . oh, the dread kiss of the Mafioso!)? But bookchat writers have never been able to understand that there is no correct deportment for the good artist. Some are exhibitionists, some are shy; some are political, some are apolitical. What matters is not a writer's personality or politics or private behavior but his books. This should be obvious, but in an age of slick journalism and swift reputation, it is quite forgotten. More to the point, books are no longer much read, while pieces about writers are. Personality is all that matters—as Mailer has neatly grasped—and the chorus does not yet comprehend.

Mr. Gilman's prose style is . . . well, let him speak for himself: "American critics have rarely possessed any substantial philosophical power or interest (Edmund Wilson accomplished important things without having had any such power or interest at all, but would have been more important, I think, if he had had some) and have shied away from metaphysical areas as from a contagion." This is as bad a sentence as I have ever read and though, admittedly, Mr. Gilman is writing about Miss Susan Sontag, whose style is often not much better, some editor ought to have come to his aid.

Stylistically he—but who cares about language? With each generation American prose grows worse, reflecting confused thinking, poor education, and the incomplete assimilation of immigrant English into the old language (see Henry James's remarks on the subject at Bryn Mawr, 1904). Nevertheless, even in a bad time, a writer's prose does give some idea of the way his mind works. From his prose, I should say that Mr. Gilman's mind is slow and uncertain, more at home with moral exhortation than with analysis. The uncertainty is betrayed by the use of adjectives. He likes them in threes, and even fours, resembling in this many popular lady writers (and at least one good one, Nathalie Sarraute): ". . . documents of the white normative Western consciousness and spirit, which blacks in America today have begun to repudiate in ways that are as yet clumsy, painful and confused." Then, on the same page: ". . . hard, local, intransigent, alien [*The Autobiography of Malcolm X*] remains in some sense unassimilable for those of us who aren't black." He is also unnaturally fond of the word "increment," which he occasionally misuses—or at least I think he does: it is often hard to guess his meaning.

For the most part, Mr. Gilman's subjects are as fashionable as his opinions. He believes that black writing cannot be judged by white standards. Good politics but an intellectual cop-out. This is followed by the usual piece on McLuhan, a solemn meditation on Susan Sontag's theory of the new, which we shall get to in a moment, hesitant praise for William Gass and Donald Barthelme, attacks on Rechy's *City of Night* (why bother?) and Updike, whose mastery of English prose makes Mr. Gilman, predictably, uneasy; and then a good deal about the theater, most of it dated ("the extraordinary public awareness of *Macbird!* as a solid fact, a potent presence"). Excepting Barthelme and Gass, the subjects are familiar, the judgments unsurprising, the uneasy self-importance irritating ("I myself, a 'judge' who passes on writing"—the quotes around the word "judge" are the giveaway). But though Mr. Gilman's theories of art are resolutely secondhand, they are still worth examining for what they have to tell us about—how would he put it?—our life today.

Mr. Gilman has his idols—somewhat. He thinks Miss Sontag "one of the most interesting and valuable critics we possess, a writer from whom it's continually possible to learn, even when you're most dissatisfied with what she's saying, or perhaps especially at those times." Mr. Gilman relies heavily on the "or perhapses" that let him off those critical hooks he has a tendency to get himself hung on as his slow, bumbling sentences unfold like bolts of wet wool. Here are two hooks in one sentence: "We might call her a critic of ideas, except that she has always wished to treat ideas sensuously, aesthetically; or decide that she is a philosopher of cultural forms, except that philosophy for her has always been a drama rather than a method." Reading this, one realizes that Mr. Gilman is a serious literary critic even though he does not actually write criticism; a profound thinker were his mind not shallow.

Throughout *The Confusion of Realms,* Mr. Gilman reminds us that the writers he admires (Gass and Barthelme) are making new things, and the ones he cannot endorse, like Mailer, are simply repeating old forms. But again let us listen to his very own voice: *"The Naked and the Dead* remains at bottom a conventional work of literature. As it shapes itself into a tale, it proceeds along predictable lines, creates no convincingly new style, and offers no new purchase on imaginative reality, nothing that can be used by other writers as a model of a way of seeing, or as incontrovertible vision by anyone else." Let us pause (Gilman's "we-ness" is contagious) and try to figure out what he is saying. First, *The Naked and the Dead* is a conventional novel, predictable, no new style, etc. Placed beside Joyce's *Finnegans Wake,* yes, it is an ordinary sort of book, and though one could excuse some of its ordinariness on the ground that most first novels are derivative, let's allow Mr. Gilman the point. Next he tells us that Mailer's novel offers "nothing that can be used by other writers . . . " This is a startling approach to literature. Apparently books are valuable only to the extent that they will help other writers to make newer and better books to be added as links to some sort of Hegelian chain. Could it be, terrible thought, that Mr. Gilman believes in Progress? If I did not know the reading habits of gangsterdom better, I'd suspect him of having read Comte.

Repeatedly, Mr. Gilman rejects what he thinks of as old forms of theater and the novel on the ground "that the distinction between form and content in art was never valid and that we have not simply come into a new use for content as form but into a condition in which seeming content, 'subject matter,' no longer is needed to serve as pretext and instigation for aesthetic action." "Fiction . . . can no longer be (if ever it wholly was) the expression or [sic?] interruption or simulacrum of life and its values . . . " And finally, ". . . fiction ought not to be an employment of language for ends beyond itself, but language in its own right, mysteriously saturated with reality, perpetually establishing a new synthesis of reality and the imagination, and doing this partly by driving out all language which has accomplished an earlier synthesis." As those interested in theories of the novel will recognize, Mr. Gilman has been reading Robbe-Grillet, or at least he has learned about him through Miss Sontag's high Hollywood or Hollywood High prose. They are great drivers-out of language. But to what end? Everyone agrees that three-act plays imitating real people in a real room are as tedious as realistic novels that deal with quotidian affairs. There is no point in reading a novel which could have been written by Galsworthy or—to be just— a novel which might have been written by Joyce. Nevertheless, as Mr. Gilman himself points out—positively insists—writers do use one an- other. Literature cannot be born "new" the instant a writer, even a master, starts to write. Writing is a more complicated matter than that and no critic—much less gangster—has yet cracked the code.

Traditionally, what a critic admires defines him, and makes him a critic rather than a gangster. To Mr. Gilman's credit, he does his best to appreciate certain new-seeming writers. Unfortunately, in controlling the Mafioso side to himself he often sounds like an old hood who now serves, somewhat uncomprehendingly, on the board of a bank whose safe he would rather be cracking. Mr. Gilman likes William Gass, and he writes interestingly about Mr. Gass's novel *Omensetter's Luck*—at least his remarks are interesting to one who has not read the novel. He even communicates enthusiasm, up to a point; then the banker feels compelled to give his report to the board. "The novel *is* Gass's prose, his style, which is not committed to something beyond itself" (a paraphrase of Robbe- Grillet, by the way), "not an instrument of the idea . . . he fashions his tale of the mind, which is the tale of his writing a novel." But then, realizing the extent of his endorsement, Mr. Gilman begins to take it back. He confesses to finding the novel faulty because of "its partial organization along narrative lines, its compulsion to tell a 'story' " (those quotes again: doesn't he know what a story is?) "while its whole internal action struggles against the reductions and untruthfulness of story-telling, while its verbal action is struggling to *be* the story." (Note the assumption that storytelling is false, but putting down words—at random?—is the novel's proper "struggle.") "For narrative, which Bernard Shaw long ago called 'the curse of all serious literature' and which every major novelist since Flaubert has either abandoned or used ironically, is precisely that element of fiction which coerces it and degrades it into being a mere alternative to life, *like* life . . . "

None of this is true. Every major novelist since Flaubert has been as much involved with narrative as those who went before; not to mention Flaubert himself as he meticulously maneuvered his Emmas and Homaises logically from place to place. Specialists even assure us that there is a preordained structure to *Finnegans Wake.* As for Lawrence, Conrad, Hardy, Mann, Musil, Proust, none eschewed or treated with irony narrative. One has only to study those extraordinary scenarios Henry James wrote for each of his works to realize just how important narrative is to a master novelist.

Now, if Mr. Gilman were simply to say that we ought not to read bad novels with familiar plots, who would disagree with him? But wanting to be resonant, and radical, and full of certain French critics (at second-hand, I suspect; curiously enough, he seems not to have read Barthes, nor grasped semiology), he writes such inflated nonsense as "What Gass has written is a work of the imagination and the mind whose study is the mind and imagination themselves as they grant us the instruments of knowing, which are at the same time the sources of all our inability to know." It makes one long for the good old days of Bonnie and Clyde, of Simon and Brustein.

"We are bored," Mr. Gilman suddenly announces, "by most plays today . . . bored by Shakespeare, too, and Molière and Greek tragedy (young people have never been so bored by classics), by Shaw and Pirandello and Brecht. Even by Ionesco and Genet." He is probably right (and writers and teachers like Mr. Gilman have certainly helped make art dull for the many) but he never questions the why of this boredom. Instead he gives us his neo-Robbe-Grillet analysis: "As long as we regard [theater] as illusion instead of a form of reality, we will go on being bored with it as we are bored, ultimately, with all illusions." This is fatuous. People live by illusions. Whether it is that college boy who rises at the end of the lecture and declares, not asks, "Don't you think Bob Dylan is the greatest living poet?" or Richard Nixon not wanting to be the first American President to lose a war or the audience of *Easy Rider,* which knows it is not on the road itself but watching actors on a screen create a naturalistic illusion of freedom that corresponds with their own daydreams, we live by illusion in life as in art. Theater is plays. Plays are simulacra of life just as print (to the astonishment of Robbe-Grillet) stands not for its own black inky self but for words which in turn stand for objects and actions. That words and phrases become corrupt with use and misuse is a perennial problem which only high excellence among writers can solve.

Reading *The Confusion of Realms* (with some continence I have refrained from making any play on the title: a gangster would have gone on and on about it), I find myself wondering who reads this sort of writing and what pleasure and revelation they get from it. Is there a public I know nothing of? Quite possibly. After all, I am often away from the United States. For all I know there are students of education who carefully read (with lips moving?) these long confusions. But I doubt it. With the exception of one piece, there is no ease, no joy, no light in Mr. Gilman's writing. Every sentence seems to have been an effort for him to make, as though he knew he had nothing to say but was impelled for career reasons to set down something. Certainly he has no talent at all for our difficult and various language—by no means a deterrent, let me quickly say, to a literary career in America. Yet it must be a terrible strain to have to keep on doing something one does not do easily or well.

As I write, I have been thinking about other careers for Mr. Gilman. English teaching? No. He would be redundant. Political commentary or action seems out; he shows no great interest in such things. Should he be an actor like Mr. Brustein? Manage a team of lady wrestlers? Work with his hands? But I have no way of knowing his true talents. So accepting him for what he would like to be, a writer, I can hold out some hope. I enjoyed his straightforward description of what happened at the Village Gate when two sets of gangsters (the anarchist hoods led by Mr. and Mrs. Beck and the old guard led by Mr. Brustein) had their showdown. Not having to worry about Culture and Meaning, Mr. Gilman has written a genuinely interesting—even witty—report of the evening (all right, he does bring in Artaud and he refers to that profoundly boring play *The Brig* as "remarkable and revivifying" but for him these are small *bêtises*). He has a surprising gift for psychological description, particularly when he records the Livers' doctrine of love (which is really hate). I particularly liked his reference to the Becks as "pushy martyrs."

Quite seriously, I would advise Mr. Gilman to leave respectable gangsterdom to Mr. Brustein. But not go back to his old ways. Leave them to Mr. Simon, who still prowls the criminal night, switch knife at the ready. Instead, I would very much like to see Mr. Gilman write popular journalism; he has a real talent for it. But I fear he will be deceived by the good reviews he has no doubt already arranged for his book, and so persist in error. But should he go straight, we heroes will gladly allow him to attend us, if not at the Pantheon, as a faithful spear-carrier at high Valhalla.

*Commentary*
March 1970

# 8

*LOVE, LOVE, LOVE*

"Love love love love love love love love love"—give or take a few "loves"—was the entire lyric of a song by Charlie Chaplin and I herewith propose that it be adopted as the American theater's official anthem. Just name your problem, sit back and let love solve it: race prejudice, foreign relations—even Job reeling beneath the unkind attentions of a dubious Yale God gets off the hook at the end through Love, which has now replaced the third-act Marines of a simpler time. On those rare occasions when some other solution tries to creep into the popular theater it either fails or else survives only after whatever alien gold was in it has been transmuted to base Love by the alchemy of production. Granted, Arthur Miller worries his head about problems of the day; but as for his heart—well, scratched he bleeds Love. Even that attention we must pay his salesman is but a command to love him.

Our popular theater ponders, to the exclusion of all else, the pathos of Love withheld, of Love lost, of Love found after three acts of jittery footling while the man learns Tenderness (never the woman, since according to commercial lore, Woman *knows*). Moon-guided, triple-crowned, inscrutable, the American Woman in our theater is never so wise as when she's not thinking at all, just being, and listening with a tiny smile to the third-act speech of the man, who has had to learn

Tenderness the hard way. "Gosh, Marge, I know how it was, but it won't be like that no more, honest, baby, it won't. No, sir, when I got knocked down in that fight with that two-hundred-pound woman in Salt Lake, I knew what we had was all there is and I'm gonna change, Marge, I swear, because that's all there is, what we got . . . love." And Marge, played by an actress weighing-in at ninety-seven tensely muscular pounds, opens her arms slowly as though semaphoring bad news to a foundering ship; she takes his great, empty buffalo head in her arms. "It's all right, Walter," she says in a voice meant to be tender, though aficionados will detect the approaching kill in this last veronica. "I'm *here,* Walter." And the curtain falls.

Yet in all fairness to our commercial theater, the preoccupation with Love was thrust upon it by the society it reflects or tries to reflect. By Love the theater does not mean love in Rousseau's sense (to employ him as a Romantic touchstone, pre-Agony). Nor is Love anything quite so simple as successful copulation, though that of course is of coeval (as Mr. Faulkner would say) importance. After all, one of the few goals our friendly society has set us is a more perfect union; the general failure to achieve it, of course, ensures full employment to mental therapists, causes dramatic religious conversions and, in the case of one talented theater director, has driven him to pad obsessively the crotches of the less flamboyantly hung actors (Aristophanes would have found a joke in that; we can't). No, Love in our theater is not really sex though sex is part of it. Love is a warm druggedness, a surrender of the will and the mind to inchoate feelings of Togetherness. Thought is the enemy; any exercise of mind betrays Love, and Love's vengeance in the theater is terrible, for mind must be broken and made to recant, and then to love Love. But before we score the silliness of our popular theater, we ought to recognize that it reflects, always more baldly than the novel, say, the superstitions and prejudices of the age. The flabbiness of tone in the theater differs only in its oversimplified effects from the same flabbiness in the popular (and sometimes "serious") novel, and, to get to the root, it does no more than reflect the ubiquitous flab of the Great Golfer's reign. Whether Tocqueville's worst fears have come true or not, democracy is too much with us. It has been duly noted how often people now say "I feel" such-and-such to be true rather than "I think" such-and-such to be true. To make that shift of verb unconsciously is to eschew mind and take cover in the cozier, more democratic world of feeling. I suppose there are some who say of others pejoratively, "His feelings are not deep." But if pressed, they would admit that no one really knows what another's feelings are, though it is of course agreed that we are all pretty much alike at heart: sensitive, warm, tender, our moments of bad behavior the result of the green twig's early bending, sure to straighten and flower beneath Love's therapeutic sun. In any case, in our theater feeling is all, and the deliberate exercise of mind is thought an admission of emotional poverty. Particularly mistrusted is Bernard Shaw, whose works are dismissed as displays of debater's tricks, the plots suitable only for adaptation to musical comedy. He did not love Love; worse, he made the devil a Love-lover, and chose as hero Don Juan, a mere life-lover.

Now it is almost too easy to put down Broadway. So much of what's wrong is so obvious that most attacks on our theater lose force because of the target's size. It is impossible with a shotgun at three paces not to hit the Shubert Theater. Yet it is curious how often the serious-minded do miss the essential target. For instance, not long ago a lively young critic fired a familiar blast: no ideas in our theater, too many sensational productions *épater le box office,* too many writers revealing sexual obsessions of depressing singularity. All the usual changes were rung, but then the critic entitled his piece "The Theater Is Losing Its Minds," and confused everything. I don't know how far back his memory, both actual and learned, goes, but if there were ever any minds operative in the American theater it is news to me. Before Eugene O'Neill (whose mastery of ideas was second to none, unless it be his fellow Nobelist Pearl Buck), there was a wasteland of Owen Davises, Avery Hopwoods and Eugene Walters, stretching back to the egregious Royall Tyler, who started the American theater on its mindless way. Two centuries of junk. If anything, there are rather more signs of intelligence stirring now than in the bad old days.

A few months later, our critic was back again. This time he wondered why the better novelists did not bring "mind" to the theater. Or at least why hadn't the theater produced playwrights as good as the novelists on today's List, and he gave the List, betraying himself, I'm afraid, as an incipient Love-lover. Parenthetically, each year there is a short List of the O.K. Writers. Today's List consists of two Jews, two Negroes and a safe floating *goy* of the old American Establishment, just to show there is no prejudice in our Loving world; only the poor old homosexualists are out. It is a list dictated not by any aesthetic but by Good Citizenship. That the writers on it happen to be admirable is irrelevant: Togetherness put them there and we all feel better seeing them belaureled. My young critic is not responsible for today's List, but he showed a certain absence of mind in trying to beat the playwrights with it, because not one of the writers named could be thought of as an intellectual in the sense I assumed he meant (Gide, Camus, even the dervish Genet). They are all good, if fairly standard, writers, more or less in the naturalistic tradition, and, at least in their novels, betray no more mind than do the plays of Arthur Miller.

I find this sort of mistake (taking good writers of one sort and saying they are good writers of quite another sort on the grounds that to be good is good enough) yet another sign of the general corruption of aesthetic and intellectual values in this soft age. The language of criticism now tends to be as inexact as the prose of the works criticized. No one seems to know who or what anyone or anything is. Prevalent is a lazy permissiveness. Our literature as well as our theater seems at times like a terrible kindergarten. Jack is a great novelist because he *feels* he's a great novelist. Anything goes. On every side counterfeit talents flood the exchange. This was always so, but in other times and places there were certain critics whose bite authenticated coinage. They are still with us—but outside the battle, in the Academy.

I have often thought it would be a service to the audience if each writer was forced to refer to himself in a certain style and manner which would make clear what he is. Implicitly, each does, but it is confusing to all but a student of rhetoric. Arthur Miller (he is on my mind because I have just read the Preface to his collected plays) writes of himself not seriously but solemnly. With paralyzing pomp, splitting his infinitives and confusing number, he climbs the steps to the throne, with the enemy syntax crushed beneath his heavy boot: he is our prophet, our king, our guide in the dark. The only thing wrong is that he does not write awfully well. In other times, if one had made such a criticism it would have been quite enough. But Mr. Miller is ready for this stricture (and so are all the other hackers in the kindergarten). "We have had," he reminds those of us who were nodding, "more than one extraordinary dramatist who was a cripple as a writer, and this is lamentable but not ruinous." I suppose he could get out of that one by saying he meant extraordinary to mean just that: extra-ordinary, though of course there is nothing more ordinary than writer-cripples in our theater.

Now by needling the pretensions of Mr. Miller (whom I often admire as a writer-cripple), I don't mean to scout his rightful position in the commercial theater—he is more good than bad as an influence and as a fact—but to draw attention again to the lack of any sense in our aesthetic judgments. Mr. Miller—and all the rest—can get away with just about any evaluation he wants to make of himself, and those who know differently won't bother to straighten out the matter for an audience which seems perfectly content to receive counterfeit bills for checks drawn in good faith. As a result, our commentators are so many Madame Verdurins, hopelessly confused as to true precedence. And the noncounterfeit artist must either go in to table last or make a fool of himself, much as the Baron de Charlus did that curious afternoon.

I happen to like a number of playwrights as people. For some reason they bring out my protective and pedagogic instincts. I like to reassure them, to help them, to give them reading lists. In many ways they are to be admired for stamina, since to be produced on Broadway resembles nothing so much as being shot from a cannon at a fragile net. One should not be surprised if the more sensitive dramatists tend to get a bit punchy. Most of them (I am generalizing hugely, but life is short) experience serious difficulty in reading books, which necessarily limits their fund of general information on any subject not connected with the theater or their own psychoanalysis. The literary world, to the extent they are aware of it at all, seems to them an invidious establishment where writers dislike them because they are better known and make more money than any other sort of writer. They do not realize that, having no interest in language and even less in what we like to think of as mind, they necessarily must earn the indifference of those who do bother with such things. Although in its essential preoccupations our theater cannot help but reflect the day, it has always been estranged not only from its own country's culture but, to strike that tinny gong, from Western civilization. The result has been a curiously artificial development, resembling nothing but itself, like those amoebae which when boxed upon a slide stop their anarchic zooming about and make perfect right angles, as tribute to an imposed environment.

"Weariness of the theatre is the prevailing note of London criticism. Only the ablest critics believe that the theatre is really important; in my time, none of them would claim for it, as I claimed for it, that it is as important as the Church was in the Middle Ages. . . ." Ah, that crisp hopeful voice! Shaw in 1906. "A theatre to me is a place where two or three are 'gathered together.' The apostolic succession from Eschylus to myself is as serious and as continuously inspired as that younger institution, the apostolic succession of the Christian Church." Brave words and perhaps true, though there have not been very many American gatherings-together one would like William Morris to attend. With some justice, intellectuals hold our popular theater in contempt, and one of the reasons seldom explicitly stated is not so much the meretricious-ness of the exhibits—popular art is opportunist at best—as its moments of would-be seriousness. Milton Berle telling low-comedy jokes onstage can be very beguiling; but to be lectured to in a stern tone by a writer considerably more stupid than much of his audience is a somber experi-ence, and were our collective manners not better, theater seats would be torn up and hurled at the stage. Earnest Neanderthals implore us not to persecute minority groups; they exhort us to tenderness; they inform us that war is destructive; they remind us that love is the only connec-tion. There is nothing wrong with these themes except the blunt obvi-ousness with which they are handled and the self-righteous tone of writers whose aesthetic derives partly from mental therapists and partly from those urgent dramas that once made radio wonderful. It is not that one does not admire Arthur Miller's real gifts for theater-writing or his good heart. It is his stunning solemnity which annoys. Stop telling us what we already know! And don't write sentences like: "That he had not the intellectual fluency to verbalize his situation is not the same thing as saying that he lacked awareness, even an overly intensified conscious-ness that the life he had made was without form and inner meaning." That is not a writer writing or a man trying to get through to others; it is the voice of the holder of a degree in Education. One sympathizes with Mr. Miller's passion to be admired, to be thought significant. All of us tend more or less consciously to arrange our personas in an attractive way. But his attempt is saddening because, though he is not taken seriously outside the popular theater and press, he is *almost* good enough to be respected in the way he wants. More to the point, he *should* be good enough: I attribute his failure to the popular theater's estrange-ment from the country's culture.

In the last fifteen years the French theater has been used by Gide, Sartre, Camus, De Montherlant, Genet, Anouilh, Julian Green, Girau-doux—an eclectic list which goes on and on, comprising most of the interesting French writers. And what have we had? Tennessee Williams (whom I happen to admire), Mr. Miller, one small mood play by Carson McCullers, Thornton Wilder in his later, three-cheers-for-Love manner, and, of course, the heady splendors of *J.B.* It is not a heartening record.

The cult of feeling has not only undone much of our theater writing, it has also peculiarly victimized those gentle souls, the actors. They have been taught that "truth" is everything. And what is "truth"? Feeling. And what is feeling? Their own secret core, to which the character they are to interpret must be related. To listen to actors talk about "truth" is a chilling experience. They employ a kind of baby talk compounded of analysts' jargon and the arcane prose of the late Stanislavsky. As one of them said severely of another's performance: "He's not thinking; he's only thinking he's thinking." Our actors have also been taught to condemn the better English or French actors as "technical." "Technical" here *seems* to mean—in these circles words are employed for transient emotive effects, never meaning—that a separation has been made between the actor's own feelings and those the part he is playing calls for. To understand just who Iago is, the "technical" actor will deliberately make the separation. Then, having got the proper range, he will, by an effort of will, inhabit the character, using himself as much or as little as he pleases, his goal being the interpretation of Shakespeare's Iago, *not* the revelation of his own inner state as he grapples with Iago. Our actors may not be able to say a line of verse intelligibly or begin to understand what Iago is all about, but you can bet they will bring floods of irrelevant feelings to the part. It is not acting but group therapy. And the sad thing is that though this kind of acting is usually disagreeable to watch, it is delightful to do. They won't change without a struggle; and since they feel rather than think, they tend to be fanatics about a method whose queen, of course, is the genuinely gifted Kim Stanley. Yet the whole sad mistaken thing is all there in her large bland face, the small eyes turned inward though they seem to be looking out, the whiny voice rising and falling according to the beat of some inner metronome of "truth," her whole being suffused in a nimbus of self-love. The final effect is onanistic.

For some years I would not read Mary McCarthy's theater criticism, after her majestically wrongheaded estimate of *A Streetcar Named Desire.* She not only missed the point to the play but, worse, got carried away by irrelevancies: Williams was really a slob, devoted to success, pretending to be a serious artist while swinging with the Broadway set; worst of all, he was guilty of "ambition." She uses this word several times in her collected pieces to tick off those writers who try, sneakily, to get above their talents. Art climbers are very like social climbers, and Miss McCarthy is a good one to put each in his place. Now I grant that there is something odd in Tennessee Williams's work which not only enrages otherwise reasonable critics but drives them to impute motives to him which are more the business of post-mortem biography than of criticism. I think again of the young critic who wrote recently in *Encounter* that Williams's real theme was incest. Well, his real theme is *not* incest no matter how one chooses to read the plays. One does not dare speculate on what sort of grapevine gossip led to this conclusion; thought certainly had nothing to do with it, though feeling might. But aside from Miss McCarthy's forty whacks at Williams, when I finally came to read her collected criticism I was struck by her remarkable good sense. Uncorrupted by compassion, her rather governessy severity, even cruelty, derives from the useful knowledge that the road to kitsch is paved with good ambitions, and that one must not give the "A" for ambition without also giving simultaneously the "E" for the poor thing effected. The theater needs continual reminders that there is nothing more debasing than the work of those who do well what is not worth doing at all.

A minor phenomenon of the theater today is the milieu: kitchens in Kansas, cold-water flats, Bronx apartments, the lower-middle-class venue depicted in naturalistic terms by "truthful" actors before an audience of overdressed, overfed burghers. How does that audience stand it, even when it's good? Is it that they enjoy a nostalgic *frisson* at looking back to their own origins? Or is there a desire to know about things today, to be instructed by the narcissism of a John Osborne, who tells them: "This is the way we are, young, angry, unique"? The burghers nod and belch softly, and some doze: it is the theater of the editorial and the survey. Even those who dislike Tennessee Williams must give him credit for castrating a hero here, eating one there; and with Elia Kazan racketing the actors about the stage, it is not easy to sleep. I save any further defense of Williams for another occasion, since my intention in these notes is entirely destructive.

And where do we go from here? I confess I have no very clear notion of what I should like to see the theater become. As a playwright I am a sport, whose only serious interest is the subversion of a society that bores and appalls me (no world elsewhere, alas; this is the one to fix). Yet I don't see much change for the good. Plays cost too much to put on. That means investors will be wary of new things. I also suspect that despite the enviable example of the French, our comparable good writers are not apt to be much of an improvement on the ones already in the theater. In England, the Royal Court Theatre has offered hospitality to some of the good writers, but the plays so far produced have been disappointing. In fact, it may very well be that the simplemindedness we score in our playwrights is a necessary characteristic of play-making.

In any case, there is no use in worrying about Broadway. Expect less rather than more intelligence on the stage, especially as costs increase. Revel in the graver efforts, which will more and more resemble *J.B.*—

that portentous magnum of chloroform Elia Kazan so accurately broke across our collective brows, launching us upon a glum sea anodyne. In fact, the former Assistant Secretary of State may well have got our Age's number back in the 1930s, when he decided that a poem should not mean but be. Our theater certainly does not mean; it is. Yet to the extent that it is, it mirrors us. Look in it and you will see quite plain the un-Loved face of Caliban.

*Partisan Review*
Spring 1959

# 9

# THE TOP TEN BEST SELLERS
# ACCORDING TO THE
# SUNDAY NEW YORK TIMES
# AS OF JANUARY 7, 1973

"Shit has its own integrity." The Wise Hack at the Writers' Table in the MGM commissary used regularly to affirm this axiom for the benefit of us alien integers from the world of Quality Lit. It was plain to him (if not to the front office) that since we had come to Hollywood only to make money, our pictures would entirely lack the one basic homely ingredient that spells boffo world-wide grosses. The Wise Hack was not far wrong. He knew that the sort of exuberant badness which so often achieves perfect popularity cannot be faked even though, as he was quick to admit, no one ever lost a penny underestimating the intelligence of the American public. He was cynical (so were we); yet he also truly believed that children in jeopardy *always* hooked an audience, that Lana Turner was convincing when she rejected the advances of Edmund Purdom in *The Prodigal* "because I'm a priestess of Baal," and he thought that Irving Thalberg was a genius of Leonardo proportion because he had made such tasteful "products" as *The Barretts of Wimpole Street* and *Marie Antoinette*.

In my day at the Writers' Table (mid-fifties) television had shaken the industry and the shit-dispensers could now . . . well, flush their products into every home without having to worry about booking a theater. In desperation, the front office started hiring alien integers whose lack of reverence for the industry distressed the Wise Hack who daily lectured us as we sat at our long table eating the specialty of the studio, top-billed as the *Louis B. Mayer Chicken Soup with Matzoh Balls* (yes, invariably, the dumb starlet would ask, What do they do with the rest of the matzoh?). Christopher Isherwood and I sat on one side of the table; John O'Hara on the other. Aldous Huxley worked at home. Dorothy Parker drank at home.

The last time I saw Dorothy Parker, Los Angeles had been on fire for three days. As I took a taxi from the studio I asked the driver, "How's the fire doing?" "You mean," said the Hollywoodian, "the holocaust." The style, you see, must come as easily and naturally as that. I found Dorothy standing in front of her house, gazing at the smoky sky; in one hand she held a drink, in the other a comb which absently she was passing through her short straight hair. As I came toward her, she gave me a secret smile. "I am combing," she whispered, "Los Angeles out of my hair." But of course that was not possible. The ashes of Hollywood are still very much in our hair, as the ten best sellers I have just read demonstrate.

The bad movies we made twenty years ago are now regarded in altogether too many circles as important aspects of what the new illiterates want to believe is the only significant art form of the twentieth century. An entire generation has been brought up to admire the product of that era. Like so many dinosaur droppings, the old Hollywood films have petrified into something rich, strange, numinous—golden. For any survivor of the Writers' Table (alien or indigenous integer), it is astonishing to find young directors like Bertolucci, Bogdanovich, Truffaut reverently repeating or echoing or paying homage to the sort of kitsch we created first time around with a good deal of "help" from our producers and practically none at all from the directors—if one may quickly set aside the myth of the director as *auteur*. Golden-age movies were the work of producer(s) and writer(s). The director was given a finished shooting script with each shot clearly marked, and woe to him if he changed MED CLOSE SHOT to MED SHOT without permission from the front office, which each evening, in serried ranks, watched the day's rushes with script in hand ("We've got some good pages today," they would say; never good film). The director, as the Wise Hack liked to observe, is the brother-in-law.

I think it is necessary to make these remarks about the movies of the thirties, forties, and fifties as a preface to the ten best-selling novels under review since most of these books reflect to some degree the films each author saw in his formative years, while at least seven of the novels appear to me to be deliberate attempts not so much to re-create new film product as to suggest old movies that will make the reader (and publisher and reprinter and, to come full circle, film-maker) recall past success and respond accordingly. Certainly none of the ten writers (save the noble engineer Solzhenitsyn and the classicist Mary Renault) is in any way rooted in literature. For the eight, storytelling began with *The Birth of a Nation.* Came to high noon with, well, *High Noon* and *Mrs. Miniver* and *Rebecca* and *A Farewell to Arms.* Except for the influence of the dead Ian Fleming (whose own work was a curious amalgam of old movies in the Eric Ambler–Hitchcock style with some sado-masochist games added), these books connect not at all with other books. But with the movies . . . ah, the movies!

Let us begin with number ten on your Hit Parade of Fiction, *Two from Galilee,* by Marjorie Holmes. Marjorie is also the author of *I've Got to Talk to Somebody, God* and *Who Am I, God? Two from Galilee* is subtitled significantly, *"A Love Story of Mary and Joseph."* Since the film *Love Story* really took off, what about a love story starring the Mother and the Stepfather of Our Lord? A super idea. And Marjorie has written it. We open with the thirteen-year-old Mary menstruating ("a bloody hand had smitten her in the night"). " 'I am almost fourteen, Father,' she said, 'and I have become nubile this day.' " She is "mad for" Joseph, a carpenter's son; he is mad for her.

Shrewdly Marjorie has taken two young Americans of the lower middle class and placed them in old Galilee. I recognize some of the descriptions as being from the last version of *Ben-Hur* to which I made a considerable contribution. "The couches covered with a silken stuff threaded with gold. The glow from a hanging alabaster lamp. . . ." Luckily, I was on the set at the beginning of the shooting and so was able to persuade the art director to remove tomatoes from Mrs. Ben-Hur Senior's kitchen. Otherwise, Marjorie might have had Hannah prepare a tomato and bacon sandwich for her daughter Mary.

Since Miss Holmes is not an experienced writer, it is difficult to know what, if anything, she had in mind when she decided to tell the Age-Old Story with nothing new to add. True, there are some domestic crises and folksy wrinkles like Joseph's father being a drunk. Incidentally, Joseph and Mary are known by their English names while the other characters keep their Hebrew names. Mary's mother Hannah is fun: a Jewish mother as observed by a gentile housewife in McLean, Virginia, who has seen some recent movies on the subject and heard all the jokes on television.

Hannah worries for her daughter. Will Joseph get into Mary *before* the wedding? "Hannah had no idea what it was like to be a man—this waiting. No woman could comprehend physical passion." Helen Gurley Brown and Germaine Greer will no doubt set Miss Holmes straight on that sexist point. But perhaps the author is reflecting her audience (Who are they, by the way? *Where* are they? Baptists in Oklahoma City? Catholics in Duluth suburbs?) when she writes that Hannah "did not have the faintest concept of the demon-god that entered a youth's loins at puberty and gave him no peace thereafter." Yes, I checked the last noun for spelling. Joseph, incidentally, is such a stud that when Mary is with him "the thing that was between them chimed and quivered and lent discomfort to all."

Suddenly between that chiming, quivering thing and Mary falls the shadow of the Holy Ghost. "Mary's flesh sang," as she experienced "the singing silence of God." Miss Holmes rises to lyricism. "The Holy Spirit came upon her, invaded her body, and her bowels stirred and her loins melted." Obviously entry was not made through the ear as those Renaissance painters who lacked Miss Holmes's powerful realism believed. Mary soon starts wondering why "the blood pumps so painfully in my breast and my bowels run so thin?" She finds out in due course. Joseph has a hard time believing her story until the Holy Spirit tells him to get it together and accept his peculiar role as the antlered saint of a new cult.

At census time the young marrieds set out for Bethlehem, where the local Holiday Inn is full up or, as a passer-by says, " 'The Inn? You'll be lucky to find a corner for the ass at the inn.' " As these quotations demonstrate, Miss Holmes's style is beyond cliché. But when it comes to scene-making, she is sometimes betrayed by the familiarity of her subject matter. If the Story is to be told truly there must be a birth scene, and so she is obliged to write, " 'Some hot water if you can get it,' " adding, " 'Go no further even to fetch a midwife.' " To which a helpful stranger replies, " 'I'll send one of them for one,' " reminding us of the Joan Crawford interview some decades ago when the living legend asked with quiet majesty, "Whom is fooling whom?" Finally, "Each night the great star stood over the stable's entrance. Joseph had never seen such a star, flaming now purple, now white. . . . "

I am told that religioso fiction has a wide audience around the country, and though these books rarely appear on best-seller lists in sinks of corruption like New York City, their overall sales in the country remind us that the enormous audience which flocked to see *Ben-Hur, The Robe, The Ten Commandments* is still waiting to have its simple faith renewed and stimulated with, as the sage at the Writers' Table would say, teats and sand.

Number nine, *The Eiger Sanction,* by Trevanian (just one name) is light years distant from *Two from Galilee.* For one thing, it is sometimes well-written, though hardly, as the blurb tells us, "vintage Huxley." Actually *The Eiger Sanction* is an Ian Fleming byblow and of its too numerous kind pretty good. Fleming once remarked that he wrote his books for warm-blooded heterosexuals. I suspect that Mr. Trevanian (Ms. Trevanian?) is writing for tepid-blooded bisexuals—that is to say, a majority of those who prefer reading kinky thrillers to watching that television set before whose busy screen 90 percent of all Americans spend a third of their waking hours.

Mr. Trevanian's James Bond is called Dr. Jonathan Hemlock. A professor of art, he "moonlights" as a paid assassin for the Search and Sanction Division of CII, an aspect (presumably invented) of the CIA. Dr. Hemlock is engaged to kill those who kill CII agents. With the proceeds from these murders, he buys paintings to hang in the renovated church where he lives on Long Island. He drinks Pichon-Longueville-Baron, worships his "beloved Impressionists" (his taste in pictures is duller than the author suspects), and as for sex, well, he's a tough cookie and finds it temporarily satisfying, "like urination" or "a termination of discomfort, not an achievement of pleasure." This drives women mad.

Mr. Trevanian has a nice gift for bizarre characters. The chief of Search and Sanction is an albino who lives in darkness; he must also undergo periodic changes of blood because he is "one of nature's rarest genealogical phenomena," presumably related to a cadet branch of the Plantagenet family. It seems only yesterday that Sidney Greenstreet was growing orchids in a most sinister greenhouse and chuckling mirthlessly. Actually, that was thirty years ago and writers are now having a difficult time thinking up unlikely traits . . . not to mention names. Unhappily the mind that created Pussy Galore cloned before it went to ashes, and Mr. Trevanian brightly offers us Felicity Arce, Jean-Paul Bidet, Randie Nickers, and a host of other cute names.

But he is also capable of writing most engagingly. "His line of thought was severed by the paternal and the plebeian voice of the pilot assuring him that he knew where they were going." Or, "He intended to give [the book] a handsome review in obedience to his theory that the surest way to maintain position at the top of the field was to advance and support of clearly inferior capacities." More of this and Mr. Trevanian will write himself out of the genre and into Quality Lit, Satire Division. But he must refrain from writing beautifully: "mountain stars still crisp and cold despite the threat of dawn to mute their brilliance," not to mention "organic viscosity of the dark around him"—an inapplicable descrip-

tion of a night in the high Alps worthy of Nathalie Sarraute, as is "Time
had been viscous for Ben, too."

It is sad to report that Mr. Trevanian cannot resist presenting in thin
disguise Mr. and Mrs. Burton and Mr. and Mrs. Onassis. There is
nothing wrong with this if you have a point to make about them. But
he has nothing to say; he simply mentions them in order to express
disdain. No doubt they deserve his Olympian disgust, but he should
leave to Suzy the record of their doings and to the really bad writers the
exploitation of their famous legends. It is interesting, incidentally, to
observe the curiously incestuous feedback of the so-called media. About
a dozen people are known to nearly everyone capable of reading a simply
written book. Therefore the golden dozen keep cropping up in popular
books with the same insistence that their doings dominate the press, and
the most successful exploiters of these legends are the very primitive
writers like Harold Robbins who not only do not know the golden dozen
at first or even second hand but, inexcusably, lack the imagination to
think up anything exciting to add to what the reader has already learned
from gossip columns and magazine interviews. At times while reading
these best sellers I had the odd sensation that I was actually reading a
batch of old Leonard Lyons gossip columns or a copy of *Photoplay* or
anything except a book. But then it is a characteristic of today's writers
(serious as well as commercial) to want their books to resemble "facts"
rather than fiction. *The Odessa File, August 1914, The Eiger Sanction* are
nonfiction titles.

Mr. Trevanian has recourse to that staple of recent fiction the Fag
Villain. Since kikes and niggers can no longer be shown as bad people,
only commies (pre-Nixon) and fags are certain to arouse the loathing
of all decent fiction addicts. I will say for Mr. Trevanian that his Fag
Villain is pretty funny—an exquisite killer named Miles Mellough with
a poodle named Faggot. In fact, Mr. Trevanian in his comic mood is
almost always beguiling, and this bright scenario ought to put new life
into the Bond product. I think even the Wise Hack would have applauded the screenplay I automatically started preparing in my head.
LONG SHOT the Eiger mountain. DAY. As titles begin, CUT TO . . .

*On the Night of the Seventh Moon* belongs to a genre I know very little
about: the Gothic novel for ladies. But I do recall the films made from
the novels of Daphne du Maurier, the queen of this sort of writing. In
fact, I once wrote the screenplay for one of her most powerful works,
*The Scapegoat,* in which the dogged (and in this case hounded) Alec
Guinness played two people. Although Miss du Maurier had written an

up-to-date variation on *The Prisoner of Zenda,* she had somehow got the notion that she had written the passion of St. Theresa. She used to send me helpful memos; and though she could not spell the simplest words or adhere to any agreed-upon grammar, her prose surged with vulgar invention and powerful feeling of the sort that cannot be faked.

I suspect Victoria Holt is also serious about her work. The publishers tell us that she is very popular; certainly she has written many books with magical titles. This one starts rather like *Rebecca:* "Now that I have reached the mature age of twenty-seven I look back on the fantastic adventure of my youth and can almost convince myself that it did not happen. . . ." A sense of warm security begins to engulf the reader at this point. Even the heroine's name inspires confidence: Helena Trant . . . so reminiscent of Helen Trent, whose vicissitudes on radio kept my generation enthralled, not to mention the ever so slight similarity to the name Trapp and all that that truly box-office name suggests; we are almost in the same neck of the woods, too, the Black Forest, 1860. And here is Helen, I mean Helena, asking herself a series of fascinating questions. "Did I suffer some mental aberration? Was it really true—as they tried to convince me—that I, a romantic and rather feckless girl, had been betrayed as so many had before? . . . "

Helena's mother was German (noble); her father English (donnish). Mother dies; girl goes to school in Germany. On a misty day she gets lost in the Black Forest. She is nubile, as Marjorie Holmes would say. Suddenly, riding toward her, "like a hero of the forest on his big white horse," was a godlike young man. He was "tall, broad, and immediately I was aware of what I could only describe then as authority." (How right she was! Though Maximilian is incognito he is really the heir to the local Grand Duchy and—but we are ahead of our story.)

He offers to take her to his hunting lodge. She sits in front of him on his horse ("He held me tightly against him which aroused in me a strange emotion which I had never felt before and which should, of course, have been a warning"). A nice old woman retainer gets her into dry things ("my hair fell about my shoulders; it was thick, dark and straight"). She wants to go back to school but "the mist is too thick." Supper. " 'Allow me to serve you some of this meat,' " says the randy prince. "He did so and I took a piece of rye bread which was hot and crusty and delicious. There was a mixture of spicy pickle and a kind of sauerkraut such as I had never tasted before." Miss Holt knows her readers like a good din from time to time along with romance, and terror. As it turns out, Max doesn't lay Helena despite the demon-god in his loins. A virgin, Helena departs not knowing whom it was she met.

Back to England. Father dead, Helena lives with two aunts. A couple arrive from Germany; they say that they are cousins of her late mother. She goes back to Germany with them. Festival in a small town known as The Night of the Seventh Moon. *He* appears; takes her away with him into the forest. He sends for the couple. They witness his marriage to Helena. She is in a state of ecstasy. For one thing, she is well-groomed. "My best dress; it was of a green silky material with a monk's collar of velvet of a slightly darker shade of green." Remember Joan Fontaine at Manderley? The new clothes? And, ah, the mystery? But Helena has done better than Joan's Max de Winter. She is now Countess Lokenburg. She gloats: "I wondered what the aunts would say when they heard that I had become the wife of a count."

But almost as good as social climbing, there is lust. Max's kiss "made me feel exalted and expectant all at once. It was cruel and yet tender; it was passionate and caressing." Can such happiness last? Certainly not. A mysterious illness; she is out of her head. When she recovers, she is told that on the night of the seventh moon she was taken into the forest and . . . "there criminally assaulted." Those blissful days with Max were all a dream, brought on by a doctor's drug. Meanwhile, she is knocked up. She has the baby; goes back to England. A clergyman falls in love with her and wants to marry her but Helena feels that her past will ruin his career. He is noble: " 'I'd rather have a wife than a bishopric.' "

The plot becomes very complex. Hired to be governess to children of what turns out to be a princely cousin of Max who is married to Wilhelmina because he thinks Helena dead because Wilhelmina's colleagues the supposed cousins of Helena were in a plot to . . . Enough! All turns out well, though it is touch-and-go for a while when her child, the heir to the principality, is kidnapped by the wicked cousin (Raymond Massey in *The Prisoner of Zenda*) who then attacks her. " 'You *are* mad,' I said." He cackles: " 'You will not live to see me rule Rochenstein, but before you die I am going to show you what kind of lover you turned your back on.' " (Mailer's *American Dream*?)

Finally, Helena takes her place at Maximilian's side as consort. Each year they celebrate the night of the seventh moon, and in the year Cousin Victoria Regina dies, "What a beautiful night! With the full moon high in the sky paling the stars to insignificance . . . " Those stars keep cropping up in these books, but then as Bette Davis said to Paul Henreid in the last but one frame of *Now Voyager,* "Don't ask for the moon when we have" (a beat) "the stars!" FADE OUT on night sky filled with stars.

I have never before read a book by Herman Wouk on the sensible ground that I could imagine what it must be like: solid, uninspired, and filled with rabbinical lore. After all, one knows of his deep and abiding religious sense, his hatred of sex outside marriage, his love for the American ruling class. I did see the film of *The Caine Mutiny* (from Queequeg to Queeg, or the decline of American narrative); and I found the morality disturbing. Mr. Wouk has an embarrassing passion for the American goyim, particularly the West Point–Annapolis crowd who stand, he would seem to believe, between him and the Cossacks. In his lowbrow way he reflects what one has come to think of as the *Commentary* syndrome or: all's right with America if you're not in a gas chamber, and making money.

I did see the film *Youngblood Hawke* four times, finding something new to delight in at each visit. When James Franciscus, playing a raw provincial genius like Thomas Wolfe, meets Suzanne Pleshette in a publisher's office, he is told, "She will be your editor and stylist." Well, she pushes these heavy glasses up on her forehead and, my God, she's pretty as well as brilliant and witty, which she proves by saying, "Shall I call you Youngy or Bloody?" The Wise Hack at the Writers' Table always maintained that when boy meets girl they've *got* to meet cute.

*The Winds of War*: 885 pages of small type in which Herman Wouk describes the family of a naval captain just before America enters the Second World War (there is to be a sequel). As I picked up the heavy book, I knew terror, for I am that rarest of reviewers who actually reads every word, and rather slowly. What I saw on the first page was disquieting. The protagonist's name, Victor Henry, put me off. It sounded as if he had changed it from something longer, more exotic, more, shall we say, *Eastern.* But then Henry was the family name of the hero of *A Farewell to Arms* so perhaps Mr. Wouk is just having a little fun with us. Mrs. Henry is called Rhoda; the sort of name someone in New York would think one of *them* would be called out there west of the Hudson. "At forty-five, Rhoda Henry remained a singularly attractive woman, but she was rather a crab." This means that she is destined for extramarital high jinks. "In casual talk [Rhoda] used the swooping high notes of smart Washington women." I grew up in Washington at exactly the same period Mr. Wouk is writing about and I must demur: smart Washington ladies sounded no different from smart New York ladies (no swooping in either city).

Captain Henry is stationed at the War Department. He is "a squat Navy fullback from California, of no means or family." Mr. Wouk quotes from the letter he wrote his congressman asking for an appointment to the Naval Academy. "My life aim is to serve as an officer in the US Navy." We are told he speaks Russian learned from "Czarist settlers in Fort Ross, California." Anyway he got appointed; has risen; is gung ho and wants to command a battleship. The marriage? "Rhoda returned an arch glance redolent of married sex." Elsewhere—the Nazis are on the march.

There are three children. Son Warren was involved in "an escapade involving an older woman and a midnight car crash. The parents had never raised the topic of women, partly from bashfulness—they were both prudish churchgoers, ill at ease with such a topic. . . . " Son Byron is in Siena carrying on with one Nathalie, niece of a famed American Jewish writer, author of *A Jew's Jesus*. Byron has recently turned against his Renaissance studies because " 'I don't believe David looked like Apollo, or Moses like Jupiter.' " Further, " 'The poor idealistic Jewish preacher from the back hills. That's the Lord I grew up with. My father's a religious man; we had to read a chapter of the Bible every morning at home.' "

At this point my worst fears about Mr. Wouk seemed justified. The Russian-speaking Victor Henry who reads a chapter of the Bible every morning to his family and is prudish about sexual matters is, Mr. Wouk wants us to believe, a typical gallant prewar goyisher American naval officer. If I may speak from a certain small knowledge (I was born at West Point, son of an instructor and graduate), I find Mr. Wouk's naval officer incredible—or "incredulous," as they say in best-seller land. There may have been a few religious nuts here and there in the fleet but certainly a naval officer who is about to be posted as an attaché to the American embassy in Berlin would not be one of them. In those days Annapolis was notoriously snobbish and no matter how simple and fundamentalist the background of its graduates, they tended toward worldliness; in fact, a surprising number married rich women. West Pointers were more square but also rowdier. Mr. Wouk's failure to come to terms with the American gentile is not unusual. Few American Jewish writers have been able to put themselves into gentile skins— much less foreskins. With ecumenical relish, Mr. Wouk tells us that son Byron (who marries a Jewish girl) is circumcised.

With an obviously bogus protagonist, Mr. Wouk must now depend upon the cunning of his narrative gift to propel these characters through great events: Berlin under Hitler, Poland during the Nazi invasion, London in the Blitz, Pearl Harbor on December 7, 1941; and not only must he describe the sweep of military and political action but also give us close-ups of Roosevelt, Churchill, Stalin, Hitler, Mussolini. It is Upton Sinclair all over again and, to my astonishment, it is splendid stuff. The detail is painstaking and generally authentic. The naïve portraits of the great men convince rather more than subtler work might have done.

Henry's reports from Berlin attract Roosevelt's attention. Mr. Wouk's portrait of FDR is by no means as sycophantish as one might expect. No doubt the recent revelations of the late President's sexual irregularities have forced the puritan Mr. Wouk to revise his estimate of a man I am sure he regarded at the time as a god, not to mention shield against the Cossacks. With hindsight he now writes, "Behind the jolly aristocratic surface, there loomed a grim ill-defined personality of distant visions and hard purpose, a tough son of a bitch to whom nobody meant very much, except perhaps his family; and maybe not they either." This is not at all bad, except as prose. Unfortunately, Mr. Wouk has no ear for "jolly aristocratic" speech patterns. I doubt if FDR would have called Pug "old top" (though when my father was in the administration the President used to address him, for some obscure reason, as "Brother Vidal").

Also, Mr. Wouk makes strange assumptions. For instance, FDR "wore pince-nez glasses in imitation of his great relative, President Teddy Roosevelt, and he also imitated his booming manly manner; but a prissy Harvard accent made this heartiness somewhat ridiculous." The pince-nez was worn by a good many people in those days, but if FDR was consciously imitating anyone it would have been his mentor, the pince-nezed Woodrow Wilson. T. Roosevelt's voice was not booming but thin and shrill. FDR's accent was neither prissy nor Harvard but Dutchess County and can still be heard among the American nobles now, thank God, out of higher politics.

With extraordinary ease, Mr. Wouk moves from husband to wife to sons to daughter, and the narrative never falters. His reconstruction of history is painless and, I should think, most useful to simple readers curious about the Second War. Yet there is a good deal of pop-writing silliness. We get the Mirror Scene (used by all pop-writers to tell us what the characters look like): "the mirror told her a different story, but even it seemed friendly to her that night: it showed . . . " We get the Fag Villain. In this case an American consul at Florence who will not give the good Jew Jastrow a passport because "people don't see departmental circulars about consuls who've been recalled and whose careers have gone *poof*!" Sumner Welles is briefly glimpsed as a villain (and those who recall the gossip of the period will know why).

Then, of course, there is the problem of Mr. Wouk and sex. Daughter Madeline rooms with two girls and "both were having affairs—one with a joke writer, the other with an actor working as a bellhop. Madeline had found herself being asked to skulk around, stay out late, or remain in her room while one or another pair copulated. . . . She was disgusted. Both girls had good jobs, both dressed with taste, both were college graduates. Yet they behaved like sluts. . . . " But then to Madeline, "sex was a delightful matter of playing with fire, but enjoying the blaze from a safe distance, until she could leap into the hallowed white conflagration of a bridal night. She was a middle class good girl, and not in the least ashamed of it."

Incidentally, Mr. Wouk perpetuates the myth that the SS were all fags. This is now an article of faith with many uneducated Americans on the ground that to be a fag is the worst thing that could befall anyone next to falling into the hands of a fag sadist, particularly the SS guards who were as "alike as chorus boys . . . with blond waved hair, white teeth, bronzed skin, and blue eyes." Actually the SS guards in 1939 were not particularly pretty; they were also not fags. Hitler had eliminated that element.

Mr. Wouk's prose is generally correct if uninspired. The use of the ugly verb "shrill" crops up in at least half the best sellers under review and is plainly here to stay. Also, I suppose we must stop making any distinction between "nauseous" and "nauseated." The book ends with Pearl Harbor in flames and . . . yes, you've guessed it. The stars! "Overhead a clear starry black sky arched" (at least the sky was overhead and not underfoot), "with Orion setting in the west, and Venus sparkling in the east. . . . The familiar religious awe came over him, the sense of a Presence above this pitiful little earth. He could almost picture God the Father looking down with sad wonder at this mischief."

The films *Since You Went Away* and *The Best Years of Our Life* come to mind; not to mention all those *March of Time*s in the Trans-Lux theaters of the old republic as it girded itself for war. But for all Mr. Wouk's idiocies and idiosyncrasies, his competence is most impressive and his professionalism awe-inspiring in a world of lazy writers and TV-stunned readers. I did not in the least regret reading every word of his book, though I suspect he is a writer best read swiftly by the page

in order to get the sweep of his narrative while overlooking the infelici-
ties of style and the shallowness of mind. I realize my sort of slow
reading does a disservice to this kind of a book. But then I hope the
author will be pleased to know that at least one person has actually read
his very long best seller. Few people will. There is evidence that a recent
best seller by a well-known writer was never read by its publisher or by
the book club that took it or by the film company that optioned it.
Certainly writers of book-chat for newspapers *never* read long books
and seldom do more than glance at short ones.

Number six on the best-seller list, *The Camerons,* by Robert Crichton, is a mystifying work. One understands the sincerity of Herman
Wouk, number seven, as he tries to impose his stern morality on an alien
culture, or even that of the dread Marjorie Holmes, number ten, exploiting Bible Belt religiosity with what I trust is some degree of seriousness
(all those chats with God must have made her a fan). But Mr. Crichton
has elected to address himself to characters that seem to be infinitely
remote from him, not to mention his readers. A UK mining town in
what I take to be the 1870s (there is a reference to Keir Hardie, the trade
unionist). With considerable fluency Mr. Crichton tells the story of a
miner's sixteen-year-old daughter who goes to the Highlands to find
herself a golden youth to give her children. She captures a Highland
fisherman, locks him up in the mines for twenty years, and has a number
of children by him who more or less fulfill her "genealogical" (as
Trevanian would say) dream.

Of all these books this one is closest to the movies. The characters all
speak with the singing cadences of Burbank's *How Green Was My
Valley.* Another inspiration is *None But the Lonely Heart,* in which
Ethel Barrymore said to Cary Grant, "Love's not for the poor, son."
Mr. Cameron plays a number of variations on that theme, among them
"Love, in everyday life, is a luxury."

One reads page after page, recalling movies. As always the Mirror
Scene. The Food Scene (a good recipe for finnan haddie). There is the
Fever Breaks Scene (during this episode I *knew* that there would have
to be a tracheotomy and sure enough the doctor said that it was sometimes necessary but that in this case . . .). The Confrontation between
Mr. Big and the Hero. Cameron has been injured while at work; the
mine owner will give him no compensation. Cameron sues; the miners
strike. He wins but not before the Confrontation with the Mob Scene
when the miners turn on him for being the cause of their hunger. There
is even the Illiterate Learning about Literature Scene, inspired by *The*

*Corn Is Green,* in which Bette Davis taught the young Welsh miner John
Dall to read Quality Lit so that he could grow up to be Emlyn Williams.
Well, Cameron goes to the library and asks for *Macbeth* and reads it
to the amazement of the bitter drunken librarian (Thomas Mitchell).

There is the Nubile Scene ("For a small girl she had large breasts and
the shirt was tight and made her breasts stand out, and she kept the
jacket near at hand because she didn't want to embarrass her father if
he came into the room. She had only recently become that way and both
she and her father weren't quite sure how to act about it"). Young Love
Scene (the son's girl friend is named Allison—from *Peyton Place*). At
the end, the Camerons sail for the New World. The first night out
Cameron "wouldn't go down to her then and so he stayed at the rail
and watched the phosphorescent waves wash up against the sides of the
ship and explode in stars."

There is something drastically wrong with this smoothly executed
novel and I cannot figure out what it is other than to suspect that the
author lacks the integrity the Wise Hack insists upon. Mr. Crichton has
decided to tell a story that does not seem to interest him very much. At
those moments when the book almost comes alive (the conflict between
labor and management), the author backs away from his true subject
because socialism cannot be mentioned in best-seller land except as
something innately wicked. Yet technically Mr. Crichton is a good
writer and he ought to do a lot better than this since plainly he lacks
the "integrity" to do worse.

Can your average beautiful teen-age Persian eunuch find happiness
with your average Greek world conqueror who is also a dish and aged
only twenty-six? The answer Mary Renault triumphantly gives us in
*The Persian Boy* is *ne!* Twenty-five years ago *The City and the Pillar*
was considered shocking because it showed what two nubile boys did
together on a hot summer afternoon in McLean, Virginia. Worse, one
of them went right on doing that sort of thing for the rest of his life. The
scandal! The shame! In 1973 the only true love story on the best-seller
list is about two homosexualists, and their monstrous aberration (so
upsetting to moralists like Mr. Wouk) is apparently taken for granted
by those ladies who buy hardcover novels.

At this point I find myself wishing that one had some way of knowing
just who buys and who reads what sort of books. I am particularly
puzzled (and pleased) by the success of Mary Renault. Americans have
always disliked history (of some fifty subjects offered in high school the
students recently listed history fiftieth and least popular) and know

nothing at all of the classical world. Yet in a dozen popular books Mary Renault has made the classical era alive, forcing even the dullest of book-chat writers to recognize that bisexuality was once our culture's norm and that Christianity's perversion of this human fact is the aberration and not the other way around. I cannot think how Miss Renault has managed to do what she has done, but the culture is the better for her work.

I am predisposed to like the novel dealing with history and find it hard to understand why this valuable genre should be so much disdained. After all, every realistic novel is historical. But somehow, describing what happened last summer at Rutgers is for our solemn writers a serious subject, while to re-create Alexander the Great is simply frivolous. Incidentally, I am here concerned only with the traditional novel as practiced by Updike, Tolstoi, George Eliot, Nabokov, the Caldwells (Taylor and Erskine) as well as by the ten writers under review. I leave for another and graver occasion the matter of experimental high literature and its signs.

In *The Persian Boy* Miss Renault presents us with Alexander at the height of his glory as seen through the eyes of the boy eunuch Bagoas. Miss Renault is good at projecting herself and us into strange cultures. With ease she becomes her narrator Bagoas; the book is told in the first person (a device *not* invented by Robert Graves as innocent commentators like to tell us but a classroom exercise going back more than two millennia: write as if you were Alexander the Great addressing your troops before Tyre). Bagoas's father is murdered by political enemies; the boy is enslaved; castrated; rented out as a whore by his first master. Because of his beauty he ends up in the bed of the Great King of Persia, Darius. Alexander conquers Persia; sets fire to Persepolis. The Great King is killed by his own people and Bagoas is presented by one of the murderers to Alexander, who, according to historical account, never took advantage sexually of those he captured. Bagoas falls in love with the conqueror and, finally, seduces him. The love affair continues happily to the end, although there is constant jealousy on Bagoas's side because of Alexander's permanent attachment to his boyhood friend Hephaestion, not to mention the wives he picks up en route.

The effect of the book is phantasmagoric. Marvelous cities, strange landscapes, colliding cultures, and at the center the golden conqueror of the earth as he drives on and on past the endurance of his men, past his own strength. Today when a revulsion against war is normal, the usual commercialite would be inclined to depict Alexander as a Fag

Villain-Killer, but in a note Miss Renault makes the point: "It needs to be borne in mind today that not till more than a century later did a handful of philosophers even start to question the morality of war." Alexander was doing what he thought a man in his place ought to do. The world was there to be conquered.

The device of observing the conqueror entirely through the eyes of an Oriental is excellent and rather novel. We are able to see the Macedonian troops as they appeared to the Persians: crude gangsters smashing to bits an old and subtle culture they cannot understand, like today's Americans in Asia. But, finally, *hubris* is the theme; and the fire returns to heaven. I am not at all certain that what we have here is the "right" Alexander, but right or not, Miss Renault has drawn the portrait of someone who *seems* real yet unlike anyone else, and that divinity the commercialites are forever trying for in their leaden works really does gleam from time to time in the pages of this nice invention.

As a fiction, *August 1914* is not as well managed as Mr. Wouk's *Winds of War*. I daresay as an expression of one man's indomitable spirit in a tyrannous society we must honor if not the art the author. Fortunately the Nobel Prize is designed for just such a purpose. Certainly it is seldom bestowed for literary merit; if it were, Nabokov and not the noble engineer Solzhenitsyn would have received it when the Swedes decided it was Holy Russia's turn to be honored.

Solzhenitsyn is rooted most ambitiously in literature as well as in films. Tolstoi appears on page 3 and Tolstoi hangs over the work like a mushroom cloud. In a sense the novel is to be taken as a dialogue between the creator of *War and Peace* and Solzhenitsyn; with the engineer opposing Tolstoi's view of history as a series of great tides in which the actions of individuals matter not at all. I'm on Solzhenitsyn's side in this debate but cannot get much worked up over his long and wearisome account of Russian military bungling at the beginning of the First World War. The characters are impossible to keep straight, though perhaps future volumes will clarify things. Like *Winds of War*, this is the first of a series.

The book begins with dawn on the Caucasus, towering "so vast above petty human creation, so elemental . . . " The word "vast" is repeated in the next paragraph to get us in the mood for a superspectacle. Then we learn that one of the characters has actually met Tolstoi, and their meeting is recalled on page 17. " 'What is the aim of man's life on earth?' " asks the young man. Tolstoi's reply is prompt: " 'To serve good and thereby to build the Kingdom of Heaven on earth.' " How? " 'Only through love! Nothing else. No one will discover anything better.' " This is best-seller writing with a vengeance.

In due course we arrive at the Mirror Scene: "She was not even comforted by the sight of her naturally rosy skin, her round shoulders, the hair which fell down to her hips and took four buckets of rain water to wash." The Nubile Scene: "She had always avoided undressing even in front of other women, because she was ashamed of her breasts, which were large, big and generous even for a woman of her build." Wisdom Phrases: "The dangers of beauty are well known: narcissism, irresponsibility, selfishness." Or "Evil people always support each other; that is their chief strength." Like Hitler and Stalin? Also, *Christian* Wisdom Phrases: "There is a justice which existed before us, without us and for its own sake. And our task is to *divine* what it is." Not since Charles Morgan's last novel has there been so much profundity in a best-seller.

As for the movies, the best Russian product is recalled, particularly *Battleship Potemkin.* Also, boldly acknowledging the cinema's primacy, Solzhenitsyn has rendered his battle scenes in screenplay form with "=" meaning CUT TO. These passages are particularly inept. *"Mad tearing sound of rifle fire, machine-gun fire, artillery fire!/ Reddened by fire, THE WHEEL still rolls./ = The firelight glitters with savage joy/"* and so on. The Wise Hack would have been deeply disturbed by the presumption of this member of the audience who ought to be eating popcorn in the second balcony and not parodying the century's one true art form that also makes money. From time to time Solzhenitsyn employs the Dos Passos device of random newspaper cuttings to give us a sense of what is going on in August 1914. This works a bit better than the mock screenplay.

At the book's core there is nothing beyond the author's crypto-Christianity, which is obviously not going to please his masters; they will also dislike his astonishing discovery that "the best social order is not susceptible to being arbitrarily constructed, or even to being scientifically constructed." To give the noble engineer his due he is good at describing how things work, and it is plain that nature destined him to write manuals of artillery or instructions on how to take apart a threshing machine. Many people who do not ordinarily read books have bought this book and mention rather proudly that they are reading it, but so far I have yet to meet anyone who has finished it. I fear that the best one can say of Solzhenitsyn is *goré vidal* (a Russian phrase meaning "he has seen grief").

A peculiarity of American sexual mores is that those men who like to think of themselves as exclusively and triumphantly heterosexual are convinced that the most masculine of all activities is not tending to the sexual needs of women but watching other men play games. I have never understood this aspect of my countrymen but I suppose there is a need for it (bonding?), just as the Romans had a need to see people being murdered. Perhaps there is a connection between the American male's need to watch athletes and his fatness: according to a W.H.O. report the American male is the world's fattest and softest; this might explain why he also loves guns—you can always get your revolver up.

I fear that I am not the audience Mr. Dan Jenkins had in mind when he wrote his amiable book *Semi-Tough,* but I found it pleasant enough, and particularly interesting for what it does *not* go into. The narrator is a pro football player who has been persuaded "that it might be good for a pro football stud to have a book which might have a healthy influence on kids." Question: Do young people watch football games nowadays? It seems to me that "jock-sniffers" (as Mr. Jenkins calls them) are of Nixonian age and type—though few have the thirty-seventh president's nose for such pleasures. The unfat and the unsoft young must have other diversions. One wonders, too, if they believe that "a man makes himself a man by whatever he does with himself, and in pro football that means busting his ass for his team."

*Semi-Tough* tells of the preparation for the big game. Apparently, training involves an astonishing amount of drink, pot, and what the narrator refers to as "wool," meaning cunt. There is one black player who may or may not like boys and the narrator clams up on what is a very delicate subject in jock circles. I am not sure Mr. Jenkins is aware of all the reverberations set off by the jokes of one of his white players. Asked why he is an athlete, the stud says, " 'Mainly, we just like to take showers with niggers.' " It is a pity Mary Renault did not write this book. And a pity, come to think of it, that Mr. Jenkins did not write *August 1914,* a subject suitable for his kind of farce. No movie in *Semi-Tough.* As the Wise Hack knows all too well, sports movies bomb at the box office. Perhaps the Warhol factory will succeed where the majors have failed. SHOWER ROOM—LONG SHOT. CUT TO: CLOSE SHOT—SOAP.

At first glance *The Odessa File,* by Frederick Forsyth, looks to be just another bold hard-hitting attack on the Nazis in the form of a thriller masked as a pseudo-documentary. But the proportions of this particular bit of nonsense are very peculiarly balanced. First, the book is dedicated "to all press reporters." The dust jacket tells us that the author worked for Reuters in the early 1960s; it does not give us his nationality but from the odd prose that he writes I suspect his first language is not English. Also the book's copyright is in the name of a company: a tax dodge not possible for American citizens. Next there is an Author's Note. Mr. Forsyth tells us that although he gives "heartfelt thanks" to all those who helped him in his task he cannot name any of them for three reasons. Apparently some were former members of the SS and "were not aware at the time either whom they were talking to, or that what they said would end up in a book." Others asked not to be mentioned; still others are omitted "for their sakes rather than for mine." This takes care of the sources for what he would like us to believe is a true account of the way Odessa (an organization of former SS officers) continues to help its members in South America and the Federal Republic.

After the Author's Note there is a Foreword (by the author). We are told who Adolf Hitler was and how he and the Nazis ruled Germany from 1933 to 1945 and how they organized the SS in order to kill fourteen million "so-called enemies of the Reich," of which six million were Jews. When Germany began to lose the war, "vast sums of gold were smuggled out and deposited in numbered bank accounts, false identity papers were prepared, escape channels opened up. When the Allies finally conquered Germany, the bulk of the mass-murderers had gone."

Well, one knows about Eichmann, and of course Martin Bormann is a minor industry among bad journalists; so presumably there are other "important" SS officers growing old in Paraguay. But do they, as Mr. Forsyth assures us, have an organization called Odessa whose aim is "fivefold"? Firstfold is "to rehabilitate former SS men *into the professions* of the Federal Republic"; second, "to infiltrate at least the lower echelons of political party activity"; third, to provide "legal defense" for any SS killer hauled before a court and in every way possible to stultify the course of justice in West Germany; fourth, to promote the fortunes of former SS members (this seems to be a repeat of the first of the fivefolds); and, five, "to propagandize the German people to the viewpoint that the SS killers were in fact none other than ordinary patriotic soldiers."

This is food for thought. Yet why has one never heard of Odessa? Mr. Forsyth anticipates that question: "changing its name several times" (highly important for a completely secret society), "the Odessa has sought to deny its own existence as an organization, with the result that many Germans are inclined to say that Odessa does not exist. The short answer is: it exists. . . . " We are then assured that the tale he is about to tell represents one of their failures. Obviously fun and games; presumably, there is no such thing as the Odessa but in the interest of making a thriller look like a document (today's fashion in novels) the author is mingling true with "false facts," as Thomas Jefferson would say.

Now for the story. But, no, after the Dedication and the Author's Note and the Foreword there comes a Publisher's Note. Apparently many of the characters in the book are "real people" but "the publishers do not wish to elucidate further because it is in this ability to perplex the reader as to how much is true and how much false that much of the grip of the story lies." The publishers, Viking, write suspiciously like Mr. Forsyth. "Nevertheless, the publishers feel the reader may be interested or assisted to know that the story of former SS Captain Eduard Roschmann, the commandant of the concentration camp at Riga from 1941 to 1944, from his birth in Graz, Austria, in 1908, to his present exile in South America, is completely factual and drawn from SS and West German records." So let us bear this Publisher's Note in mind as we contemplate the story Mr. Forsyth tells.

After the fall of Hitler, Roschmann was harbored at "the enormous Franciscan Monastery in Rome in Via Sicilia." There is no such establishment according to my spies in the order. "Bishop Alois Hudal, the German Bishop in Rome" (Mr. Forsyth seems to think that this is some sort of post) "spirited thousands [of SS] to safety." "The SS men traveled on Red Cross travel documents, issued through the intervention of the Vatican." After a period in Egypt, Roschmann returns to Germany in 1955 under a pseudonym. Thanks to Odessa, he becomes the head of an important firm. He conducts secret research "aimed at devising a tele-guidance system for those rockets [he] is now working on in West Germany. His code name is Vulkan."

Why is Roschmann at work on the rockets? Because Odessa and its evil scientists "have proposed to President Nasser" (whose predecessor Mr. Forsyth thinks was named Naguil), and he "accepted with alacrity, that these warheads on the Kahiras and Zafiras be of a different type. Some will contain concentrated cultures of bubonic plague, and the others will explode high above the ground, showering the entire territory of Israel with irradiated cobalt-sixty. Within hours they will all be dying of the pest or of gamma-ray sickness."

This is splendid Fu Manchu nonsense (infecting the Israelis with bubonic plague would of course start a world epidemic killing the Egyptians, too, while spreading radioactive cobalt in the air would probably kill off a large percentage of the world's population, as any story conference at Universal would quickly conclude). Next Mr. Forsyth presents us with the classic thriller cliché: only one man holds this operation together. Roschmann. Destroy him and Israel is saved.

The plot of course is foiled by a West German newspaperman and its details need not concern us: it is the sort of storytelling that propels the hero from one person to the next person, asking questions. As a stylist, Mr. Forsyth is addicted to the freight-car sentence: "This time his destination was Bonn, the small and boring town on the river's edge that Konrad Adenauer had chosen as the capital of the Federal Republic, because he came from it." (Adenauer came from Cologne but Mr. Forsyth is not one to be deterred by small details: after all, he is under the impression that it was Martin Bormann "on whom the mantle of the Führer had fallen after 1945.") What is important is that Mr. Forsyth and Viking Press want us to believe that the Vatican knowingly saved thousands of SS men after 1945, that six of the ten high-ranking Hamburg police officers in 1964 were former SS men, that President Nasser authorized a clandestine SS organization to provide him with the means to attack Israel with bubonic plague, and that when this plot failed, the Argentine government presumably offered asylum to Captain Roschmann. *Caveat emptor.*

The boldness of author and publisher commands . . . well, awe and alarm. Is it possible now to write a novel in which Franklin Roosevelt secretly finances the German American Bund because he had been made mad by infantile paralysis? Can one write a novel in which Brezhnev is arranging with the American army defectors in Canada to poison Lake Michigan (assuming this is not a redundancy)? Viking would probably say, yes, why not? And for good measure, to ensure success, exploit the prejudices, if possible, of American Jewish readers, never letting them forget that the guilt of the Germans ("dreaming only in the dark hours of the ancient gods of strength and lust and power") for having produced Hitler is now as eternal in the works of bad writers and greedy publishers as is the guilt of the Jews for the death of Jesus in the minds of altogether too many simple Christians. Exploitation of either of these myths strikes me as an absolute evil and not permissible even in the cheapest of fiction brought out by the most opportunist of publishers.

The number one best seller is called *Jonathan Livingston Seagull.* It is a greeting card bound like a book with a number of photographs of seagulls in flight. The brief text celebrates the desire for excellence of a seagull who does not want simply to fly in order to eat but to fly beautifully for its own sake. He is much disliked for this by his peers; in fact, he is ostracized. Later he is translated to higher and higher

spheres where he can spend eternity practicing new flight techniques. It
is touching that this little story should be so very popular because it is
actually celebrating art for art's sake as well as the virtues of noncon-
formity; and so, paradoxically, it gives pleasure to the artless and to the
conforming, to the drones who dream of honey-making in their unchanging hive.

Unlike the other best sellers this work is not so much a reflection of
the age of movies as it is a tribute to Charles Darwin and his high
priestess, the incomparable creatrix of *The Fountainhead* (starring Gary
Cooper and Patricia Neal), Ayn Rand.

There is not much point in generalizing further about these best
sellers. The authors prefer fact or its appearance to actual invention.
This suggests that contemporary historians are not doing their job if to
Wouk and Solzhenitsyn falls the task of telling today's reader about two
world wars and to Forsyth and Trevanian current tales of the cold war.
As Christianity and Judaism sink into decadence, religioso fictions still
exert a certain appeal. It will surprise certain politicians to learn that
sex is of no great interest to best-selling authors. Only *Semi-Tough* tries
to be sexy, and fails. Too much deodorant.

Reading these ten books one after the other was like being trapped
in the "Late Late Show," staggering from one half-remembered movie
scene to another, all the while beginning to suspect with a certain horror
that the Wise Hack at the Writers' Table will be honored and remembered for his many credits on numerous profitable pix long after Isherwood (adapted "The Gambler," with Gregory Peck), Faulkner (adapted
*The Big Sleep,* with Humphrey Bogart), Huxley (adapted *Pride and
Prejudice,* with Greer Garson), Vidal (adapted *Suddenly Last Summer,*
with Elizabeth Taylor) take their humble places below the salt, as it
were, for none of us regarded with sufficient seriousness the greatest art
form of all time. By preferring perversely to write books that reflected
not the movies we had seen but life itself, not as observed by that sterile
machine the camera but as it is netted by a beautiful if diminishing and
polluted language, we were, all in all, kind of dumb. Like Sam, one
should've played it again.

*The New York Review of Books*
May 17 and May 31, 1973

# 10

## FRENCH LETTERS: THEORIES OF THE NEW NOVEL

To say that no one now much likes novels is to exaggerate very little. The large public which used to find pleasure in prose fictions prefers movies, television, journalism, and books of "fact." But then, Americans have never been enthusiastic readers. According to Dr. Gallup, only five percent of our population can be regarded as habitual readers. This five percent is probably a constant minority from generation to generation, despite the fact that at the end of the nineteenth century there were as many bookstores in the United States as there are today. It is true that novels in paperback often reach a very large audience. But that public is hardly serious, if one is to believe a recent *New York Times* symposium on paperback publishing. Apparently novels sell not according to who wrote them but according to how they are presented, which means that *Boys and Girls Together* will outsell *Pale Fire,* something it did not do in hard cover. Except for a handful of entertainers like the late Ian Fleming, the mass audience knows nothing of authors. They buy titles, and most of those titles are not of novels but of nonfiction: books about the Kennedys, doctors, and vivid murders are preferred to the work of anyone's imagination no matter how agreeably debased.

In this, if nothing else, the large public resembles the clerks, one of whom, Norman Podhoretz, observed nine years ago that "A feeling of dissatisfaction and impatience, irritation and boredom with contemporary serious fiction is very widespread," and he made the point that the magazine article is preferred to the novel because the article is useful, specific, relevant—something that most novels are not. This liking for fact may explain why some of our best-known novelists are read with attention only when they comment on literary or social matters. In the highest intellectual circles, a new novel by James Baldwin or William Gass or Norman Mailer—to name at random three celebrated novelists—is apt to be regarded with a certain embarrassment, hostage to a fortune often too crudely gained, and bearing little relation to its author's distinguished commentaries.

An even odder situation exists in the academy. At a time when the works of living writers are used promiscuously as classroom texts, the students themselves do little voluntary reading. "I hate to read," said a Harvard senior to a *New York Times* reporter, "and I never buy any paperbacks." The undergraduates' dislike of reading novels is partly due to the laborious way in which novels are taught: the slow killing of the work through a close textual analysis. Between the work and the reader comes the explication, and the explicator is prone to regard the object of analysis as being somehow inferior to the analysis itself.

In fact, according to Saul Bellow, "Critics and professors have declared themselves the true heirs and successors of the modern classic authors." And so, in order to maintain their usurped dignity, they are given "to redescribing everything downward, blackening the present age and denying creative scope to their contemporaries." Although Mr. Bellow overstates the case, the fact remains that the novel as currently practiced does not appeal to the intellectuals any more than it does to the large public, and it may well be that the form will become extinct now that we have entered the age which Professor Marshall McLuhan has termed post-Gutenberg. Whether or not the Professor's engaging generalities are true (that linear type, for centuries a shaper of our thought, has been superseded by electronic devices), it is a fact that the generation now in college is the first to be brought up entirely within the tradition of television and differs significantly from its predecessors. Quick to learn through sight and sound, today's student often experiences difficulty in reading and writing. Linear type's warm glow, so comforting to Gutenberg man, makes his successors uncomfortably hot. Needless to say, that bright minority which continues the literary culture exists as always, but it is no secret that even they prefer watching movies to reading novels. John Barth ought to interest them more than Antonioni, but he doesn't.

For the serious novelist, however, the loss of the audience should not be disturbing. "I write," declared one of them serenely. "Let the reader learn to read." And contrary to Whitman, great audiences are not necessary for the creation of a high literature. The last fifty years have been a particularly good time for poetry in English, but even that public which can read intelligently knows very little of what has been done. Ideally, the writer needs no audience other than the few who understand. It is immodest and greedy to want more. Unhappily, the novelist, by the very nature of his coarse art, is greedy and immodest; unless he is read by everyone, he cannot delight, instruct, reform, destroy a world he wants, at the least, to be different for his having lived in it. Writers as various as Dickens and Joyce, as George Eliot and Proust, have suffered from this madness. It is the nature of the beast. But now the beast is caged, confined by old forms that have ceased to attract. And so the question is: can those forms be changed, and the beast set free?

Since the Second World War, Alain Robbe-Grillet, Nathalie Sarraute, Michel Butor, Claude Simon, and Robert Pinget, among others, have attempted to change not only the form of the novel but the relationship between book and reader, and though their experiments are taken most seriously on the Continent, they are still too little known and thought about in those countries the late General de Gaulle believed to be largely populated by Anglo-Saxons. Among American commentators, only Susan Sontag in *Against Interpretation, and Other Essays,* published in 1966, has made a sustained effort to understand what the French are doing, and her occasional essays on their work are well worth reading, not only as reflections of an interesting and interested mind but also because she shares with the New Novelists (as they loosely describe themselves) a desire for the novel to become "what it is not in England and America, with rare and unrelated exceptions: a form of art which people with serious and sophisticated [*sic*] taste in the other arts can take seriously." Certainly Miss Sontag finds nothing adventurous or serious in "the work of the American writers most admired today: for example, Saul Bellow, Norman Mailer, James Baldwin, William Styron, Philip Roth, Bernard Malamud." They are "essentially unconcerned with the problems of the novel as an art form. Their main concern is with their 'subjects.' " And because of this, she finds them "essentially unserious and unambitious." By this criterion, to be serious and ambitious in the novel, the writer must create works of prose comparable to those experiments in painting which have brought us to Pop and Op art and in music to the strategic silences of John Cage. Whether or not these experiments succeed or fail is irrelevant. It is enough, if the artist is serious, to attempt new forms; certainly he must not repeat old ones.

The two chief theorists of the New Novel are Alain Robbe-Grillet and Nathalie Sarraute. As novelists, their works do not much resemble one another or, for that matter, conform to each other's strictures. But it is as theorists not as novelists that they shall concern us here. Of the two, Alain Robbe-Grillet has done the most to explain what he thinks the New Novel is and is not, in *Snapshots* and *For a New Novel,* translated by Richard Howard (1965). To begin with, he believes that any attempt at controlling the world by assigning it a meaning (the accepted task of the traditional novelist) is no longer possible. At best, meaning was

an illusory simplification; and far from becoming clearer and clearer because of it, the world has only, little by little, lost all its life. Since it is chiefly in its presence that the world's reality resides, our task is now to create a literature which takes that presence into account.

He then attacks the idea of psychological "depth" as a myth. From the Comtesse de La Fayette to Gide, the novelist's role was to burrow "deeper and deeper to reach some ever more intimate strata." Since then, however, "something" has been "changing totally, definitively in our relations with the universe." Though he does not define that ominous "something," its principal effect is that "we no longer consider the world as our own, our private property, designed according to our needs and readily domesticated." Consequently:

the novel of characters belongs entirely to the past; it describes a period: and that which marked the apogee of the individual. Perhaps this is not an advance, but it is evident that the present period is rather one of administrative numbers. The world's destiny has ceased, for us, to be identified with the rise or fall of certain men, of certain families.

Nathalie Sarraute is also concerned with the idea of man the administrative number in *Tropisms* and in *The Age of Suspicion,* translated by Maria Jolas (1964). She quotes Claude-Edmonde Magny: "Modern man, overwhelmed by mechanical civilization, is reduced to the triple determinism of hunger, sexuality and social status: Freud, Marx and Pavlov." (Surely in the wrong order.) She, too, rejects the idea of human depth: "The deep uncovered by Proust's analyses had already proved to be nothing but a surface."

Like Robbe-Grillet, she sees the modern novel as an evolution from Dostoevsky-Flaubert to Proust-Kafka; and each agrees (in essays written by her in 1947 and by him in 1958) that one of its principal touchstones is Camus's *The Stranger,* a work which she feels "came at the appointed time," when the old psychological novel was bankrupt because, paradoxically, psychology itself, having gone deeper than ever before, "inspired doubts as to the ultimate value of all methods of research." *Homo absurdus,* therefore, was Noah's dove, the messenger of deliverance. Camus's stranger is shown entirely from the inside, "all sentiment or thought whatsoever appears to have been completely abolished." He has been created without psychology or memory; he exists in a perpetual present. Robbe-Grillet goes even further in his analysis:

It is no exaggeration to claim that it is things quite specifically which ultimately lead this man to crime: the sun, the sea, the brilliant sand, the gleaming knife, the spring among the rocks, the revolver . . . as, of course, among these things, the leading role is taken by Nature.

Only the absolute presence of things can be recorded; certainly the depiction of human character is no longer possible. In fact, Miss Sarraute believes that for both author and reader, character is "the converging point of their mutual distrust," and she makes of Stendhal's "The genius of suspicion has appeared on the scene" a leitmotiv for an age in which "the reader has grown wary of practically everything. The reason being that for some time now he has been learning too many things and he is unable to forget entirely all he had learned." Perhaps the most vivid thing he has learned (or at least it was vivid when she was writing in 1947) is the fact of genocide in the concentration camps:

Beyond these furthermost limits to which Kafka did not follow them but to where he had the superhuman courage to precede them, all feeling disappears, even contempt and hatred; there remains only vast, empty stupefaction, definitive total, don't understand.

To remain at the point where he left off or to attempt to go on from there are equally impossible. Those who live in a world of human beings can only retrace their steps.

The proof that human life can be as perfectly meaningless in the scale of a human society as it is in eternity stunned a generation, and the shock of this knowledge, more than anything else (certainly more than

the discoveries of the mental therapists or the new techniques of industrial automation), caused a dislocation of human values which in turn
made something like the New Novel inevitable.

Although Nathalie Sarraute and Alain Robbe-Grillet are formidable
theorists, neither is entirely free of those rhetorical plangencies the
French so often revert to when their best aperçus are about to slip the
net of logic. Each is very much a part of that French intellectual tradition so wickedly described in *Tristes Tropiques* by Lévi-Strauss (1964,
translated by John Russell):

First you establish the traditional "two views" of the question. You then
put forward a common-sensical justification of the one, only to refute it by
the other. Finally, you send them both packing by the use of a third
interpretation, in which both the others are shown to be equally unsatisfactory. Certain verbal maneuvers enable you, that is, to line up the traditional
"antitheses" as complementary aspects of a single reality: form and substance, content and container, appearance and reality, essence and existence, continuity and discontinuity, and so on. Before long the exercise
becomes the merest verbalizing, reflection gives place to a kind of superior
punning, and the "accomplished philosopher" may be recognized by the
ingenuity with which he makes ever-bolder play with assonance, ambiguity,
and the use of those words which sound alike and yet bear quite different
meanings.

Miss Sarraute is not above this sort of juggling, particularly when she
redefines literary categories, maintaining that the traditional novelists
are formalists, while the New Novelists, by eschewing old forms, are the
true realists because

their works, which seek to break away from all that is prescribed, conventional and dead, to turn towards what is free, sincere and alive, will necessarily, sooner or later, become ferments of emancipation and progress.

This fine demagoguery does not obscure the fact that she is obsessed
with form in a way that the traditional writer seldom is. It is she, not
he, who dreams

of a technique that might succeed in plunging the reader into the stream
of those subterranean dreams of which Proust only had time to obtain a
rapid aerial view, and concerning which he observed and reproduced nothing but the broad motionless lines. This technique would give the reader the

illusion of repeating these actions himself, in a more clearly aware, more orderly, distinct and forceful manner than he can do in life, without their losing that element of indetermination, of opacity and mystery, that one's own actions always have for the one who lives them.

This is perilously close to fine lady-writing (Miss Sarraute is addicted to the triad, particularly of adjectives), but despite all protestations, she is totally absorbed with form; and though she dislikes being called a formalist, she can hardly hope to avoid the label, since she has set herself the superb task of continuing consciously those prose experiments that made the early part of the twentieth century one of the great ages of the novel.

In regard to the modern masters, both Robbe-Grillet and Miss Sarraute remark with a certain wonder that there have been no true heirs to Proust, Joyce, and Kafka; the main line of the realistic novel simply resumed as though they had never existed. Yet, as Robbe-Grillet remarks:

Flaubert wrote the new novel of 1860, Proust the new novel of 1910. The writer must proudly consent to bear his own date, knowing that there are no masterpieces in eternity, but only works in history, and that they have survived only to the degree that they have left the past behind them and heralded the future.

Here, as so often in Robbe-Grillet's theorizing, one is offered a sensible statement, followed by a dubious observation about survival (many conventional, even reactionary works have survived nicely), ending with a look-to-the-dawn-of-a-new-age chord, played fortissimo. Yet the desire to continue the modern tradition is perfectly valid. And even if the New Novelists do not succeed (in science most experiments fail), they are at least "really serious," as Miss Sontag would say.

There is, however, something very odd about a literary movement so radical in its pronouncements yet so traditional in its references. Both Miss Sarraute and Robbe-Grillet continually relate themselves to great predecessors, giving rise to the suspicion that, like Saul Bellow's literary usurpers, they are assuming for themselves the accomplishments of Dostoevsky, Flaubert, Proust, Joyce, and Beckett. In this, at least, they are significantly more modest than their heroes. One cannot imagine the Joyce of *Finnegans Wake* acknowledging a literary debt to anyone or Flaubert admitting—as Robbe-Grillet does—that his work is "merely pursuing a constant evolution of a genre." Curiously enough, the writers whom Robbe-Grillet and Miss Sarraute most resemble wrote books which were described by Arthur Symons for the *Encyclopaedia Britannica* as being

made up of an infinite number of details, set side by side, every detail equally prominent. . . . [the authors] do not search further than "the physical basis of life," and they find everything that can be known of that unknown force written visibly upon the sudden faces of little incidents, little expressive movements. . . . It is their distinction—the finest of their inventions—that, in order to render new sensations, a new vision of things, they invented a new language.

*They,* of course, are the presently unfashionable brothers Edmond and Jules de Goncourt, whose collaboration ended in 1870.

In attacking the traditional novel, both Robbe-Grillet and Miss Sarraute are on safe ground. Miss Sarraute is particularly effective when she observes that even the least aware of the traditionalists seems "unable to escape a certain feeling of uneasiness as regards dialogue." She remarks upon the self-conscious way in which contemporary writers sprinkle their pages with "he saids" and "she replied," and she makes gentle fun of Henry Green's hopeful comment that perhaps the novel of the future will be largely composed in dialogue since, as she quotes him, people don't write letters any more: they use the telephone.

But the dialogue novel does not appeal to her, for it brings "the novel dangerously near the domain of the theater, where it is bound to be in a position of inferiority"—on the ground that the nuances of dialogue in the theater are supplied by actors while in the novel the writer himself must provide, somehow, the sub-conversation which is the true meaning. Opposed to the dialogue novel is the one of Proustian analysis. Miss Sarraute finds much fault with this method (no meaningful depths left to plumb in the wake of Freud), but concedes that "In spite of the rather serious charges that may be brought against analysis, it is difficult to turn from it today without turning one's back on progress."

"Progress," "*New* Novel," "permanent creation of tomorrow's world," "the discovery of reality will continue only if we abandon outward forms," "general evolution of the genre" . . . again and again one is reminded in reading the manifestos of these two explorers that we are living (one might even say that we are trapped) in the age of science. Miss Sarraute particularly delights in using quasi-scientific references. She refers to her first collection of pieces as "Tropisms." (According to authority, a tropism is "the turning of an organism, or part of one, in a particular direction in response to some special external stimulus.") She is also addicted to words like "larval" and "magma," and her analogies are often clinical: "Suspicion, which is by way of destroying the character and the entire outmoded mechanism that guaranteed its force, is one of the morbid reactions by which an organism defends itself and seeks another equilibrium. . . ."

Yet she does not like to be called a "laboratory novelist" any more than she likes to be called a formalist. One wonders why. For it is obvious that both she and Robbe-Grillet see themselves in white smocks working out new formulas for a new fiction. Underlying all their theories is the assumption that if scientists can break the atom with an equation, a dedicated writer ought to be able to find a new form in which to redefine the "unchanging human heart," as Bouvard might have said to Pécuchet. Since the old formulas have lost their efficacy, the novel, if it is to survive, must become something new; and so, to create that something new, they believe that writers must resort to calculated invention and bold experiment.

It is an interesting comment on the age that both Miss Sarraute and Robbe-Grillet take for granted that the highest literature has always been made by self-conscious avant-gardists. Although this was certainly true of Flaubert, whose letters show him in the laboratory, agonizing over that double genitive which nearly soured the recipe for *Madame Bovary,* and of Joyce, who spent a third of his life making a language for the night, Dostoevsky, Conrad, and Tolstoi—to name three novelists quite as great—were not much concerned with laboratory experiments. Their interest was in what Miss Sontag calls "the subject"; and though it is true they did not leave the form of the novel as they found it, their art was not the product of calculated experiments with form so much as it was the result of their ability, by virtue of what they were, to transmute the familiar and make it rare. They were men of genius unobsessed by what Goethe once referred to as "an eccentric desire for originality." Or as Saul Bellow puts it: "Genius is always, without strain, avant-garde. Its departure from tradition is not the result of caprice or of policy but of an inner necessity."

Absorbed by his subject, the genius is a natural innovator—a fact which must be maddening to the ordinary writer, who, because he is merely ambitious, is forced to approach literature from the outside, hoping by the study of a masterpiece's form and by an analysis of its content to reconstruct the principle of its composition in order that he may create either simulacra or, if he is furiously ambitious, by rearranging the component parts, something "new." This approach from the outside is of course the natural way of the critic, and it is significant that the New Novelists tend to blur the boundary between critic and novelist. "Critical preoccupation," writes Robbe-Grillet, "far from sterilizing creation, can on the contrary serve it as a driving force."

In the present age the methods of the scientist, who deals only in what can be measured, demonstrated and proved, are central. Consequently, anything as unverifiable as a novel is suspect. Or, as Miss Sarraute quotes Paul Tournier:

There is nobody left who is willing to admit that he invents. The only thing that matters is the document, which must be precise, dated, proven, authentic. Works of the imagination are banned, because they are invented. . . . The public, in order to believe what it is told, must be convinced that it is not being "taken in." All that counts now is the "true fact."

This may explain why so many contemporary novelists feel they must apologize for effects which seem unduly extravagant or made up ("but that's the way it really happened!"). Nor is it to make a scandal to observe that most "serious" American novels are autobiographies, usually composed to pay off grudges. But then the novelist can hardly be held responsible for the society he reflects. After all, much of the world's reading consists of those weekly news magazines in which actual people are dealt with in fictional terms. It is the spirit of the age to believe that any fact, no matter how suspect, is superior to any imaginative exercise, no matter how true. The result of this attitude has been particularly harrowing in the universities, where English departments now do their best to pretend that they are every bit as fact-minded as the physical scientists (to whom the largest appropriations go). Doggedly, English teachers do research, publish learned findings, make breakthroughs in F. Scott Fitzgerald and, in their search for facts, behave as if no work of literature can be called complete until each character has been satisfactorily identified as someone who actually lived and had a history known to the author. It is no wonder that the ambitious writer is tempted to re-create the novel along what he believes to be scientific lines. With admiration, Miss Sontag quotes William Burroughs:

I think there's going to be more and more merging of art and science. Scientists are already studying the creative process, and I think that the whole line between art and science will break down and that scientists, I hope, will become more creative and writers more scientific.

Recently in France the matter of science and the novel was much debated. In an essay called *Nouvelle Critique ou Nouvelle Imposture,* Raymond Picard attacked the new critic Roland Barthes, who promptly defended himself on the ground that a concern with form is only natural since structure precedes creation (an insight appropriated from anthropology, a discipline recently become fashionable). Picard then returned to the attack, mocking those writers who pretend to be scientists, pointing out that they

improperly apply to the literary domain methods which have proved fruitful elsewhere but which here lose their efficiency and rigor. . . . These critical approaches have a scientific air to them, but the resemblance is pure caricature. The new critics use science roughly as someone ignorant of electricity might use electronics. What they're after is its prestige: in other respects they are at opposite poles to the scientific spirit. Their statements generally sound more like oracles than useful hypotheses: categorical, unverifiable, unilluminating.

Picard is perhaps too harsh, but no one can deny that Robbe-Grillet and Nathalie Sarraute often appropriate the language of science without understanding its spirit—for instance, one can verify the law of physics which states that there is no action without reaction, but how to prove the critical assertion that things in themselves are what caused Camus's creature to kill? Yet if to revive a moribund art form writers find it helpful to pretend to be physicists, then one ought not to tease them unduly for donning so solemnly mask and rubber gloves. After all, Count Tolstoi thought he was a philosopher. But whether pseudo-scientists or original thinkers, neither Robbe-Grillet nor Miss Sarraute finds it easy to put theory into practice. As Robbe-Grillet says disarmingly: "It is easier to indicate a new form than to follow it without failure." And he must be said to fail a good deal of the time: is there anything more incantatory than the repetition of the word "*lugubre*" in *Last Year at Marienbad*? Or more visceral than the repetition of the killing of the centipede in *Jealousy*? While Miss Sarraute finds that her later essays are "far removed from the conception and composition of my first book"—which, nevertheless, she includes in the same volume as the essays, with the somewhat puzzling comment that "this first book contains *in nuce* all the raw material that I have continued to develop in my later works."

For Robbe-Grillet, the problem of the novel is—obviously—the problem of man in relation to his environment, a relationship which he believes has changed radically in the last fifty years. In the past, man attempted to personalize the universe. In prose, this is revealed by metaphor: "majestic peaks," "huddled villages," "pitiless sun." "These anthropomorphic analogies are repeated too insistently, too coherently, not to reveal an entire metaphysical system." And he attacks what he holds to be the humanistic view: "On the pretext that man can achieve only a subjective knowledge of the world, humanism decides to elect man the justification of everything." In fact, he believes that humanists will go so far as to maintain that "it is not enough to show man where he is: it must further be proclaimed that man is everywhere." Quite shrewdly he observes: "If I say 'the world is man,' I shall always gain absolution; while if I say things are things, and man is only man, I am immediately charged with a crime against humanity."

It is this desire to remove the falsely human from the nature of things that is at the basis of Robbe-Grillet's theory. He is arguing not so much against what Ruskin called "the pathetic fallacy," as against our race's tendency to console itself by making human what is plainly nonhuman. To those who accuse him of trying to dehumanize the novel, he replies that since any book is written by a man "animated by torments and passion," it cannot help but be human. Nevertheless, "suppose the eyes of this man rest on things without indulgence, insistently: he sees them but he refuses to appropriate them." Finally, "man looks at the world but the world does not look back at him, and so, if he rejects communion, he also rejects tragedy." Inconsistently, he later quotes with admiration Joé Bousquet's "We watch things pass by in order to forget that they are watching us die."

Do those things watch or not? At times Miss Sarraute writes as if she thought they did. Her *Tropisms* are full of things invested with human response ("The crouched houses standing watch all along the gray streets"), but then she is not so strict as Robbe-Grillet in her apprehension of reality. She will accept "those analogies which are limited to the instinctive irresistible nature of the movements . . . produced in us by the presence of others, or by objects from the outside world." For Robbe-Grillet, however, "All analogies are dangerous."

Man's consciousness has now been separated from his environment. He lives in a perpetual present. He possesses memory but it is not chronological. Therefore the best that the writer can hope to do is to impart a precise sense of man's being in the present. To achieve this immediacy, Miss Sarraute favors "some precise dramatic action shown in slow motion"; a world in which "time was no longer the time of real life but of a hugely amplified present." While Robbe-Grillet, in commenting upon his film *Last Year at Marienbad,* declares:

> The Universe in which the entire film occurs is, characteristically, in a perpetual present which makes all recourse to memory impossible. This is a world without a past, a world which is self-sufficient at every moment and which obliterates itself as it proceeds.

To him, the film is a ninety-minute fact without antecedents. "The only important 'character' is the spectator. In his mind unfolds the whole story which is precisely imagined by him." The verb "imagine" is of course incorrect, while the adverb means nothing. The spectator is *not* imagining the film; he is watching a creation which was made in a precise historic past by a writer, a director, actors, cameramen, etc. Yet to have the spectator or reader involve himself directly and temporally in the act of creation continues to be Robbe-Grillet's goal. He wants "a present which constantly invents itself" with "the reader's creative assistance," participating "in a creation, to invent in his turn the work—and the world—and thus to learn to invent his own life." This is most ambitious. But the ingredients of the formula keep varying. For instance, in praising Raymond Roussel, Robbe-Grillet admires the author's "*investigation* which destroys, in the writing itself, its own object." Elsewhere: "The work must seem necessary but necessary for nothing; its architecture is without use; its strength is untried." And again: "The genuine writer has nothing to say. He has only a way of speaking. He must create a world but starting from nothing, from the dust. . . . " It would not seem to be possible, on the one hand, to invent a world that would cause the reader to "invent his own life" while, on the other hand, the world in question is being destroyed as it is being created. Perhaps he means for the reader to turn to dust, gradually, page by page: not the worst of solutions.

No doubt there are those who regard the contradictions in Robbe-Grillet's critical writing as the point to them—rather in the way that the boredom of certain plays or the incompetence of certain pictures are, we are assured, their achievement. Yet it is worrisome to be told that a man can create a world from nothing when that is the one thing he cannot begin to do, simply because, no matter how hard he tries, he cannot dispose of himself. Even if what he writes is no more than nouns and adjectives, who and what he is will subconsciously dictate order. Nothing human is random and it is nonsense to say:

Art is based on no truth that exists before it; and one may say that it expresses nothing but itself. It creates its own equilibrium and its own meaning. It stands all by itself . . . or else it falls.

Which reminds us of Professor Herzog's plaintive response to the philosophic proposition that modern man at a given moment fell into the quotidian: so where was he standing before the fall? In any case, how can something unique, in Robbe-Grillet's sense, rise or fall or be anything except itself? As for reflecting "no truth that existed before it," this is not possible. The fact that the author is a man "filled with torments and passion" means that all sorts of "truths" are going to occur in the course of the writing. The act of composing prose is a demonstration not only of human will but of the desire to reflect truth—particularly if one's instinct is messianic, and Robbe-Grillet is very much in that tradition. Not only does he want man "to invent his own life" (by reading Robbe-Grillet), but he proposes that today's art is "a way of living in the present world, and of participating in the permanent creation of tomorrow's world." It also seems odd that a theory of the novel which demands total existence in a self-devouring present should be concerned at all with the idea of future time since man exists, demonstrably, only in the present— the future tense is a human conceit, on the order of "majestic peaks." As for the use of the adjective "permanent," one suspects that rhetoric, not thought, forced this unfortunate word from the author's unconscious mind.

The ideal work, according to Robbe-Grillet, is

A text both "dense and irreducible"; so perfect that it does not seem "to have touched," an object so perfect that it would obliterate our tracks. . . . Do we not recognize here the highest ambition of every writer?

Further, the only meaning for the novel is the invention of the world. "In dreams, in memory, as in the sense of sight, our imagination is the organizing force of our life, of *our* world. Each man, in his turn, must reinvent the things around him." Yet, referring to things, he writes a few pages later,

They refer to no other world. They are the sign of nothing but themselves. And the only contact man can make with them is to imagine them.

But how is one to be loyal to the actual fact of things if they must be reinvented? Either they are *there* or they are not. In any case, by filtering them through the imagination (reinvention), true objectivity is lost, as he himself admits in a further snarling of his argument: "Objectivity in the ordinary sense of the word—total impersonality of observation—is all too obviously an illusion. But freedom of observation should be possible and yet it is not"—because a "continuous fringe of culture (psychology, ethics, metaphysics, etc.) is added to things, giving them a less alien aspect." But he believes that "humanizing" can be kept to a minimum, if we try "to construct a world both more solid and more immediate. Let it be first of all by their presence that objects and gestures establish themselves and let this presence continue to prevail over the subjective." Consequently, the task of the New Novel is nothing less than to seek

new forms for the novel . . . forms capable of expressing (or of creating) new relations between man and the world, to all those who have determined to invent the novel, in other words, to invent man. Such writers know that the systematic repetition of the forms of the past is not only absurd and futile, but that it can even become harmful: blinding us to our real situation in the world today, it keeps us, ultimately, from constructing the world and man of tomorrow.

With the change of a noun or two, this could easily be the coda of an address on American foreign policy, delivered by Professor Arthur Schlesinger, Jr., to the ADA.

Like Robbe-Grillet, Nathalie Sarraute regards Camus's *The Stranger* as a point of departure. She sees the book's immediate predecessors as "The promising art of the cinema" and "the wholesome simplicity of the new American novel." Incidentally, she is quite amusing when she describes just what the effect of these "wholesome" novels was upon the French during the years immediately after the war:

By transporting the French reader into a foreign universe in which he had no foothold, [they] lulled his wariness, aroused in him the kind of credulous curiosity that travel books inspire, and gave him a delightful impression of escape into an unknown world.

It is reassuring to learn that these works were not regarded with any great seriousness by the French and that Horace McCoy was not finally the master they once hailed him. Apparently the American novel was simply a vigorous tonic for an old literature gone stale. Miss Sarraute is, however, sincerely admiring of Faulkner's ability to involve the reader in his own world. To her the most necessary thing of all is "to dispossess the reader and entice him, at all costs, into the author's territory. To achieve this the device that consists in referring to the leading characters as 'I' constitutes a means." The use of the first person seems to her to be the emblem of modern art. ("Since Impressionism all pictures have been painted in the first person.") And so, just as photography drove painters away from representing nature (ending such ancient arts as that of the miniaturist and the maker of portrait busts), the cinema "garners and perfects what is left of it by the novel." The novel must now go where the camera may not follow. In this new country the reader has been aided by such modern writers as Proust and Joyce; they have so awakened his sensibilities that he is now able to respond to what is beneath the interior monologue, that "immense profusion of sensations, images, sentiments, memories, impulses, little larval actions that no inner language can convey." For her, emphasis falls upon what she calls the sub-conversation, that which is sensed and not said, the hidden counterpoint to the stated theme (obviously a very difficult thing to suggest, much less write, since "no inner language can convey it").

"Bosquet's universe—ours—is a universe of signs," writes Robbe-Grillet. "Everything in it is a sign; and not the sign of something else, something more perfect, situated out of reach, but a sign of itself, of that reality which asks only to be revealed." This answer to Baudelaire's *The Salon of 1859* is reasonable (although it is anthropomorphic to suggest that reality *asks* to be revealed). Robbe-Grillet is equally reasonable in his desire for things to be shown, as much as possible, as they are.

In the future universe of the novel, gestures and objects will be there before being *something;* and they will still be there afterwards, hard, unalterably, eternally present, mocking their own "meaning," that meaning which vainly tries to reduce them to the role of precarious tools, etc.

One agrees with him that the integrity of the nonhuman world should be honored. But what does he mean (that proscribed verb!) when he says that the objects will be *there,* after meaning has attempted to rape them? Does he mean that they will still exist on the page, in some way inviolate in their thing-ness? If he does, surely he is mistaken. What exists on the page is ink; or, if one wishes to give the ink designs their agreed-upon human meaning, letters have been formed to make words in order to suggest things not present. What is on the page are not real things but their word-shadows. Yet even if the things were there, it is most unlikely that they would be so human as to "mock their own meaning." In an eerie way, Robbe-Grillet's highly rhetorical style has a tendency to destroy his arguments even as he makes them; critically, this technique complements ideally the self-obliterating anecdote.

On the question of how to establish the separateness, the autonomy of things, Robbe-Grillet and Miss Sarraute part company. In contemplating her method, she ceases altogether to be "scientific." Instead she alarmingly intones a hymn to words—all words—for they "possess the qualities needed to seize upon, protect and bring out into the open those subterranean movements that are at once impatient and afraid." (Are those subterranean movements really "impatient and afraid"?) For her, words possess suppleness, freedom, iridescent richness of shading, and by their nature they are protected "from suspicion and from minute examination." (In an age of suspicion, to let words off scot-free is an act of singular trust.) Consequently, once words have entered the other person, they swell, explode, and "by virtue of this game of actions and reactions . . . they constitute a most valuable tool for the novelist." Which, as the French say, goes without saying.

But of course words are not at all what she believes they are. All words lie. Or as Professor Frank Kermode put it in *Literary Fiction and Reality*: "Words, thoughts, patterns of word and thought, are enemies of truth, if you identify that with what may be had by phenomenological reductions." Nevertheless, Miss Sarraute likes to think that subterranean movements (tropisms) can be captured by words, which might explain why her attitude toward things is so much more conventional than that of Robbe-Grillet, who writes:

Perhaps Kafka's staircases lead *elsewhere,* but they are *there,* and we look at them step by step following the details of the banisters and the risers.

This is untrue. First, we do not look at the staircases; we look at a number of words arranged upon a page by a conscious human intelligence which would like us to consider, among a thousand other things, the fact of those staircases. Since a primary concern of the human mind is cause and effect, the reader is bound to speculate upon why those staircases have been shown him; also, since staircases are usually built to connect one man-made level with another, the mind will naturally speculate as to what those two levels are like. Only a far-gone schizophrenic (or an LSD tripper) would find entirely absorbing the description of a banister.

Perhaps the most naïve aspect of Robbe-Grillet's theory of fiction is his assumption that words can ever describe with absolute precision anything. At no point does he acknowledge that words are simply fiat for real things; by their nature, words are imprecise and layered with meanings—the signs of things, not the things themselves. Therefore, even if Robbe-Grillet's goal of achieving a total reality for the world of things was desirable, it would not be possible to do it with language, since the author (that man full of torments and passions) is bound to betray his attitude to the sequence of signs he offered us; he has an "interest" in the matter, or else he would not write. Certainly if he means to reinvent man, then he will want to find a way of defining man through human (yes, psychological) relations as well as through a catalogue of things observed and gestures coolly noted. Wanting to play God, ambition is bound to dictate the order of words, and so the subjective will prevail just as it does in the traditional novel. To follow Robbe-Grillet's theory to its logical terminus, the only sort of book which might be said to be *not* a collection of signs of absent things but the actual things themselves would be a collection of ink, paper, cardboard, glue, and typeface, to be assembled or not by the reader-spectator. If this be too heavy a joke, then the ambitious writer must devise a new language which might give the appearance of maintaining the autonomy of things, since the words, new-minted, will possess a minimum of associations of a subjective or anthropomorphic sort. No existing language will be of any use to him, unless it be that of the Trobriand Islanders: those happy people have no words for "why" or "because"; for them, things just happen. Needless to say, they do not write novels or speculate on the nature of things.

The philosophic origins of the New Novel can be found (like most things French) in Descartes, whose dualism was the reflection of a split between the subjective and the objective, between the irrational and the rational, between the physical and the metaphysical. In the last century Auguste Comte, accepting this dualism, conceived of a logical empiricism which would emphasize the "purely" objective at the expense of the subjective or metaphysical. An optimist who believed in human progress, Comte saw history as an evolution toward a better society. For

him the age of religion and metaphysics ended with the French Revolution. Since that time the human race was living in what he termed "the
age of science," and he was confident that the methods of the positive
sciences would enrich and transform human life. At last things were
coming into their own. But not until the twentieth century did the
methods of science entirely overwhelm the arts of the traditional humanists. To the scientific-minded, all things, including human personality, must in time yield their secrets to orderly experiment. Meanwhile,
only that which is verifiable is to be taken seriously; emotive meaning
must yield to cognitive meaning. Since the opacity of human character
has so far defeated all objective attempts at illumination, the New Novelists prefer, as much as possible, to replace the human with objects
closely observed and simple gestures noted but not explained.

In many ways, the New Novel appears to be approaching the "pure"
state of music. In fact, there are many like Miss Sontag who look
forward to "a kind of total structuring" of the novel, analogous to
music. This is an old dream of the novelist. Nearly half a century ago,
Joyce wrote (in a letter to his brother), "Why should not a modern
literature be as unsparing and as direct as song?" Why not indeed? And
again, why? The answer to the second "why" is easy enough. In the age
of science, the objective is preferred to the subjective. Since human
behavior is notoriously irrational and mysterious, it can be demonstrated only in the most impressionistic and unscientific way; it yields
few secrets to objective analysis. Mathematics, on the other hand, is
rational and verifiable, and music is a form of mathematics. Therefore,
if one were to eliminate as much as possible the human from the novel,
one might, through "a kind of total structuring," come close to the state
of mathematics or music—in short, achieve that perfect irreducible
artifact Robbe-Grillet dreams of.

The dates of Miss Sarraute's essays range from 1947 to 1956, those of
Robbe-Grillet from 1955 to 1963. To categorize in the French manner,
it might be said that their views are particularly representative of the
50s, a period in which the traditional-minded (among whom they must
be counted) still believed it possible to salvage the novel—or anything—
by new techniques. With a certain grimness, they experimented. But
though some of their books are good (even very good) and some are bad,
they did not make a "new" novel, if only because art forms do not
evolve—in literature at least—from the top down. Despite Robbe-Grillet's tendency to self-congratulation ("Although these descriptions—
motionless arguments or fragments of scene—have acted on the readers

in a satisfactory fashion, the judgment many specialists make of them remains pejorative"), there is not much in what he has so far written that will interest anyone except the specialist. It is, however, a convention of the avant-garde that to be in advance of the majority is to be "right." But the New Novelists are not in advance of anyone. Their works derive from what they believe to be a need for experiment and the imposition of certain of the methods of science upon the making of novels. Fair enough. Yet in this they resemble everyone, since to have a liking for the new is to be with the dull majority. In the arts, the obviously experimental is almost never denounced *because* it is new: if anything, our taste-makers tend to be altogether too permissive in the presence of what looks to be an experiment, as anyone who reads New York art criticism knows. There is not much likelihood that Robbe-Grillet will be able to reinvent man as a result of his exercises in prose. Rather he himself is in the process of being reinvented (along with the rest of us) by the new world in which we are living.

At the moment, advance culture scouts are reporting with a certain awe that those men and women who were brought up as television-watchers respond, predictably, to pictures that move and talk but not at all to prose fictions; and though fashion might dictate the presence of an occasional irreducible artifact in a room, no one is about to be reinvented by it. Yet the old avant-garde continues worriedly to putter with form.

Surveying the literary output for 1965, Miss Sontag found it "hard to think of any one book [in English] that exemplifies in a *central* way the possibilities for enlarging and complicating the forms of prose litera-ture." This desire to "enlarge" and "complicate" the novel has an air of madness to it. Why not minimize and simplify? One suspects that out of desperation she is picking verbs at random. But then, like so many at present, she has a taste for the random. Referring to William Bur-roughs's resolutely random work *The Soft Machine,* she writes: "In the end, the voices come together and sound what is to my mind the most serious, urgent and original voice in American letters to be heard for many years." It is, however, the point to Mr. Burroughs's method that the voices *don't* come together: he is essentially a sport who is (blessedly) not serious, not urgent, and original only in the sense that no other American writer has been so relentlessly ill-humored in his send-up of the serious. He is the Grand Guy Grand of American letters. But whether or not Miss Sontag is right or wrong in her analyses of specific works and general trends, there is something old-fashioned and touching in her assumption (shared with the New Novelists) that if only we all try hard enough in a "really serious" way, we can come up with the better novel. This attitude reflects not so much the spirit of art as it does that of Detroit.

No one today can predict what games post-Gutenberg man will want to play. The only certainty is that his mind will work differently from ours; just as ours works differently from that of pre-Gutenberg man, as Miss Frances Yates demonstrated so dramatically in *The Art of Memory*. Perhaps there will be more Happenings in the future. Perhaps the random will take the place of the calculated. Perhaps the ephemeral will be preferred to the permanent: we stop in time, so why should works of art endure? Also, as the shadow of atomic catastrophe continues to fall across our merry games, the ephemeral will necessarily be valued to the extent it gives pleasure in the present and makes no pretense of having a future life. Since nothing will survive the firewind, the ashes of one thing will be very like those of another, and so what matters excellence?

One interesting result of today's passion for the immediate and the casual has been the decline, in all the arts, of the idea of technical virtuosity as being in any way desirable. The culture (*kitsch* as well as camp) enjoys singers who sing no better than the average listener, actors who do not act yet are, in Andy Warhol's happy phrase, "super-stars," painters whose effects are too easily achieved, writers whose swift flow of words across the page is not submitted to the rigors of grammar or shaped by conscious thought. There is a general Zen-ish sense of why bother? If a natural fall of pebbles can "say" as much as any shaping of paint on canvas or cutting of stone, why go to the trouble of recording what is there for all to see? In any case, if the world should become, as predicted, a village united by an electronic buzzing, our ideas of what is art will seem as curious to those gregarious villagers as the works of what we used to call the Dark Ages appear to us.

Regardless of what games men in the future will want to play, the matter of fiction seems to be closed. Reading skills—as the educationalists say—continue to decline with each new generation. Novel reading is not a pastime of the young now being educated, nor, for that matter, is it a preoccupation of any but a very few of those who came of age in the last warm years of linear type's hegemony. It is possible that fashion may from time to time bring back a book or produce a book which arouses something like general interest (Miss Sontag darkly suspects that "the nineteenth-century novel has a much better chance for a comeback than verse drama, the sonnet, or landscape painting"). Yet it is literature itself which seems on the verge of obsolescence, and not so much because the new people will prefer watching to reading as because the language in which books are written has become corrupt from misuse.

In fact, George Steiner believes that there is a definite possibility that "The political inhumanity of the twentieth century and certain elements in the technological mass-society which has followed on the erosion of European bourgeois values have done injury to language. . . . " He even goes so far as to suggest that for now at least silence may be a virtue for the writer—when

language simply ceases, and the motion of spirit gives no further outward manifestation of its being. The poet enters into silence. Here the word borders not on radiance or music, but on night.

Although Mr. Steiner does not himself take this romantic position ("I am not saying that writers should stop writing. This would be fatuous"), he does propose silence as a proud alternative for those who have lived at the time of Belsen and of Vietnam, and have witnessed the perversion of so many words by publicists and political clowns. The credibility gap is now an abyss, separating even the most honorable words from their ancient meanings. Fortunately, ways of communication are now changing, and though none of us understands exactly what is happening, language is bound to be affected.

But no matter what happens to language, the novel is not apt to be revived by electronics. The portentous theorizings of the New Novelists are of no more use to us than the self-conscious avant-gardism of those who are forever trying to figure out what the next "really serious" thing will be when it is plain that there is not going to be a next serious thing in the novel. Our lovely vulgar and most human art is at an end, if not the end. Yet that is no reason not to want to practice it, or even to read it. In any case, rather like priests who have forgotten the meaning of the prayers they chant, we shall go on for quite a long time talking of books and writing books, pretending all the while not to notice that the church is empty and the parishioners have gone elsewhere to attend other gods, perhaps in silence or with new words.

*Encounter*
December 1967

# 11

# THE HACKS OF
# ACADEME

*The Theory of the Novel: New Essays,* edited by John Halperin. The two articles arouse suspicion. *The* theory? *The* novel? Since there is no such thing as the novel, how can there be a single theory? Or is the editor some sort of monist? Blinkered hedgehog in wild fox country? The jacket identifies Mr. Halperin as "Associate Professor and Director of Graduate Studies in the Department of English at the University of Southern California." This is true academic weight. "He is also the author of *The Language of Meditation: Four Studies in Nineteenth-Century Fiction* and *Egoism and Self-Discovery in the Victorian Novel.*" Well, meditation if not language is big in Southern California, where many an avocado tree shades its smogbound Zen master, while the Victorian novel continues to be a growth industry in academe. Eagerly, one turns to Professor Halperin's "A Critical Introduction" to nineteen essays by as many professors of English. Most are American; most teach school in the land of the creative writing course.

"Christ left home at twelve." Professor Halperin's first sentence is startlingly resonant, to use an adjective much favored by the contributors, who also like "mythopoeic," "parameter" (almost always misused), "existential" (often misused), "linear," "schematic" and "spatial." Professor Halperin tells us that during the lifetime of Nazareth's gift to the joy of nations, poetry's age . . . was in the thousands of years and drama's in the hundreds. It was not until a millennium and a half later that the gestation period of the novel began. Thus it is not surprising, three quarters of the way through the twentieth century, that we find ourselves with a growing but still relatively small body of critical *theory* pertaining to the novel . . .

This is sweet innocence; also, ignorance. Two very good novels (*Satyricon, Golden Ass*) were written by near-contemporaries of the gentle Nazarene. Later, during the so-called long "gestation," other cultures were lightened (as William Faulkner would put it) of novels as distinguished as the Lady Murasaki's *Tale of Genji* (c. A.D. 1005).

But Professor Halperin is not very interested in novels. Rather:

It is the purpose of the present volume to reflect and hopefully to deal with some of the more radical issues of contemporary novel-theory. . . . This collection, containing original essays of theoretical cast written especially for this volume by some of the most distinguished critics of our time, hopefully will be a major addition to the growing corpus of theoretical approaches to fiction.

Professor Halperin has not an easy way with our rich language. Nevertheless, one opens his book in the hope that the prose of "some of the most distinguished critics of our time" will be better than his own. Certainly the great names are all here: Meir Sternberg, Robert Bernard Martin, Irving H. Buchen, Alan Warren Friedman, Max F. Schulz, Alice R. Kaminsky, George Levine, John W. Loofourow, Marvin Mudrick, Walter F. Wright, Robert B. Heilman, Richard Harter Fogle, Dorothea Krook. Also Leon Edel, Leslie A. Fiedler, Walter Allen and Frank Kermode. *Un sac mixte,* as Bouvard might have said to Pécuchet.

Professor Halperin quotes approvingly Barthes's

Flaubert . . . finally established Literature as an object, through promoting literary labour to the status of a value; form became the end-product of craftsmanship, like a piece of pottery or a jewel . . . [The] whole of Literature, from Flaubert to the present day, became the problematics of language.

Professor Halperin adds his own gloss.

Modern theoretical novel-criticism . . . is occupied less with the novel as a mimetic and moral performance than with the novel as an autonomous creation independent of or at least not wholly dependent on the real world. The world of the autonomous novel may inevitably resemble our own, but it is not created as a conscious representation of anything outside itself.

American professors of English have never had an easy time with French theoreticians of the novel (close scrutiny of the quotation from Barthes reveals that it was taken from an English not an American translation). Nevertheless, despite various hedges like "may inevitably," Professor Halperin has recklessly enrolled himself in the school of Paris (class of '56). As a result, he believes that the autonomous novel "is not created as a conscious representation of anything outside itself." Aside from the presumption of pretending to know what any writer has in mind (is he inevitably but not consciously describing or mimicking the real world?), it is naïve to assume that a man-made novel can ever resemble a meteor fallen from outer space, a perfectly autonomous artifact whose *raison d'être* is "with the relationships among the various structural elements within the work of fiction itself" rather than "between reader and text." Apparently the novel is no longer what James conceived it, a story told, in Professor Halperin's happy phrase, from "the limited perspective of a single sentient consciousness." And so, in dubious battle, unconscious sentiencies clash in the English departments of the West with insentient consciousnesses.

The first essay is called "What is Exposition?" This subject plainly troubles Professor Meir Sternberg. At a loss for the right words, he resorts to graphics. An inverted "V" occupies the top of one page. At the foot of the left leg is the word "introduction"; then "exciting force"; then "rise." The apex of the inverted "V" is labeled "climax." Partway down the right leg is the word "fall," while at the base occurs the somber word "catastrophe." This treasure-seeker's map to tragedy is something called "Freytag's pyramid," which the eponymous architect set up in the desert of novel-theory to show how "time-honored" exposition works in tragedy.

Professor Sternberg then adds his own markings to the sand. "Suppose an author wishes to compose a narrative which is to consist of three motifs: a1, a2, a3. These motifs, arranged in an order in which a2 follows a1 in a time and a3 follows a2, will form the *fabula* of his story." The sequence of numbered a's is then arranged vertically on the page, and casts almost as minatory a shadow as Freytag's pyramid. Later Professor Sternberg assembles a positively Cheopsean structure with such parallel headings as "story," "*fabula,*" "plot," "*sujet,*" a monster

Rosetta stone with which to confound strawman Freytag. The resulting *agon* (or duel or *lutte*) in the desert is very elaborate and not easy to follow. Occasionally there is a simple sentence like: "A work of fiction presents characters in action during a certain period of time." But, by and large, sentences are as elaborate as the ideas that they wish to express are simple. And so, as the sun sinks behind the last tautology, our guide sums up: "As my definition of it clearly implies, exposition is a time problem *par excellence.*" (Instructor's note: Transpose "it" and "exposition.")

Further on in the Sahelian wilderness we meet Professor Irving H. Buchen. At first, one is charmed: "Critics may need novels to be critics but novels do not need critics to be novels." This is fine stuff. The pathetic fallacy is at last able to define for us that mysterious entity "the living novel." Professor Buchen likes his literature lean.

Almost all novelistic failures, especially significant ones, are the result of crushing richness. Plenitude swelled to bursting Fielding's *Tom Jones,* deluged Conrad's *Nostromo,* over-refined Proust's sensibility, and transformed Joyce in *Finnegans Wake* into a self parodist.

Solution? "The key to the artistry of the novel is managing fecundity." The late Margaret Sanger could not have put it better.

Although Professor Buchen's "The Aesthetics of the Supra-Novel" deals only in the obvious, his footnotes are often interesting. Occasionally a shy aphorism gleams like a scarab in the sand. "The novel is not a given form; it is given to be formed." Pondering the vast amount of "novel-theory" written for classrooms, he notes that this process of over-explicating texts produces

new novelists who, like the re-issue of older novelists, seemed to be buttressed both in front and in back. Finally, virtually every facet of the novel has been subjected to structural, stylistic, formalistic, epistemological processing. Aside from some outstanding seminal pieces, what is instructive about the entire theoretical enterprise is that it has created a Frankenstein.

I assume that he means the monster and not the baron. In any case, relieved of those confining "parameters" of "novel-theory" (also known as "book-chat"), Professor Buchen's footnotes betray glimmers of true intelligence.

In general, Professor Halperin's novel-theorists have nothing very urgent or interesting to say about literature. Why then do they write when they have nothing to say? Because the ambitious teacher can only rise in the academic bureaucracy by writing at complicated length about writing that has already been much written about. The result of all this book-chat cannot interest anyone who knows literature while those who would like to learn something about books can only be mystified and discouraged by these commentaries. Certainly it is no accident that the number of students taking English courses has been in decline for some years. But that is beside the point. What matters is that the efforts of the teachers now under review add up to at least a half millennium of academic tenure.

Although The Novel is not defined by Professor Halperin's colleagues, some interesting things are said about novels. Professor Frank Kermode's "Novel and Narrative" is characteristically elegant. In fact, so fine-meshed is his prose that one often has to reread whole pages but then, as Kant instructs us, "comprehension is only a knowledge adequate to our intention." Kermode is particularly good on the virtues and demerits of Roland Barthes, no doubt because he has actually read Barthes and not relied upon the odd quotation picked up here and there in translation. Kermode tends to pluralism and he is unimpressed by the so-called great divide between the mimetic fiction of the past and the autonomous fiction of the present. "It seems doubtful, then, whether we need to speak of some great divide—a strict historical *coupure*—between the old and new." Minor complaint: I do wish Kermode would not feel obliged always to drag in the foreign word whose meaning is no different from the English equivalent. Also, my heart sinks every time he fashions a critical category and then announces firmly: "I shall call it, hermeneutic activity." As for the great divide:

There are differences of emphasis, certainly, as to what it is to read; and there are, within the narratives themselves, rearrangement of emphasis and interest. Perhaps, as metacritics often allege, these are to be attributed to a major shift in our structures of thought; but although this may be an efficient cause of the mutation of interests it does not appear that the object of those interests—narrative—imitates the shift.

Phrased like a lawyer and, to my mind, demonstrably true. Nevertheless, the other "most distinguished critics" seem to believe that there has indeed been at least a gap or split or *coupure* between old and new writing, requiring, if not a critical bridge, an academic's bandage.

Professor Leon Edel chats amiably about "Novel and Camera," reminding us that Robbe-Grillet's reliance on the close-shot in his novels might have something to do with his early training as an agronomist where the use of a microscope is essential. Professor Edel notes that the audience for the novel is dwindling while the audience for films, television, comic books continues to grow; he echoes Saul Bellow:

Perhaps we have had too many novels. People no longer seem to need them. On the other hand, pictorial biographies—real pictures of real lives—exist in abundance, and there will be more of these in the coming year. The camera is ubiquitous.

In "Realism Reconsidered," Professor George Levine has a number of intelligent things to say about writing. Although limited by a certain conceit about his own place in time ("Reality has become problematic in ways the Victorians could only barely imagine"), he is aware that the word "reality" is protean: even the French ex-agronomist wants to be absolutely realistic. Buttressed by Auerbach, Gombrich and Frye, Professor Levine's meditation on realism in the novel is not only sensible but his sentences are rather better than those of his fellow most-distinguished critics. There is a plainness reminiscent of Edmund Wilson. Possibly because:

My bias, then, is historical. . . . What is interesting here is that at one point in European history writers should have become so self-conscious about truth-telling in art [which I take to imply the growth of doubt about art in society] that they were led to raise truth-telling to the level of doctrine and to imply that previous literatures had not been telling it.

Then Levine states the profound truth that "fiction is fiction," ruling out Truth if not truth. Or as Calvin Coolidge said in a not too dissimilar context: "In public life it is sometimes necessary in order to appear really natural to be actually artificial."

"The Death and Rebirth of the Novel." The confident ring of the title could only have been sounded by America's liveliest full-time professor and seducer of the *Zeitgeist* (no proper English equivalent), Leslie A. Fiedler. A redskin most at home in white clown makeup, Fiedler has given many splendid performances over the years. From a secure heterosexual base, he has turned a bright amused eye on the classic American *goyim* and finds them not only homoerotic to a man (or person as they say nowadays) but given to guilty pleasures with injuns like Queequeg, with niggers like Jim. As far as I know, Fiedler has yet to finger an American-Jewish author as a would-be reveler in the savage Arcadia of Sodom-America, but then that hedge of burning bushes no doubt keeps pure the American Jewish writer/person.

Fiedler reminds us that for a "century or more" the leading novelists and a good many critics have forgotten "that at its most authentic the novel is a form of popular art." But he shares the academic delusion that the novel was invented in the middle of the eighteenth century by "that extraordinary anti-elitist genius" Samuel Richardson, who launched "the first successful form of Pop Art." For Fiedler, Richardson reflects little of what preceded him (the epic, the ballad) but he made possible a great deal that has come since: "the comic strip, the comic book, cinema, TV." After the Second World War, the appearance of mass-production paperback books in the supermarkets of the West was insurance against the main line of the novel becoming elitist, for "the machine-produced commodity novel is, therefore, dream literature, mythic literature, as surely as any tale told over the tribal fire." Consequently, "form and content, in the traditional sense, are secondary, optional if not irrelevant—since it is, in the first instance, primordial images and archetypal narrative structures that the novel is called on to provide." Fiedler believes that dream-literature (*Pickwick Papers, Valley of the Dolls*) is peculiarly "immune to formalist criticism." Further, "it sometimes seems as if all such novels want to metamorphose into movies . . . a kind of chrysalis yearning to be a butterfly."

Certainly Pop narratives reveal the society's literally vulgar day-dreams. Over and over again occur and recur the sex lives and the murders of various Kennedys, the sphinx-like loneliness of Greta Garbo, the disintegration of Judy Garland or, closer to the heart of academe, the crack-up of Scott Fitzgerald in Hollywood, the principal factory of this century's proto-myths. Until recently no Art Novelist (Fiedler's phrase) would go near a subject as melodramatic as the collapse of a film star or the murder of a president. Contemporary practitioners of the Art Novel ("beginning with, perhaps, Flaubert, and reaching a climax in the work of Proust, Mann and Joyce") are doggedly at work creating "fiction intended not for the market-place but the library and classroom; or its sub-variety, the Avant-Garde Novel, which foresees immediate contempt followed eventually by an even securer status in future Museums of Literary Culture."

To put it as bluntly as possible, it is incumbent on all who write fiction or criticism in the disappearing twentieth century to realize that the Art Novel or Avant-Garde Novel is in the process of being abandoned wherever fiction remains most alive, which means that that sub-genre of the novel is dying if not dead.

Although Fiedler's funeral oration ought to alarm those teachers who require a certain quantity of serious "novel writing" so that they can practice "novel criticism," I suspect that they will, secretly, agree with him. If all the Art Novels have been written, then no one need ever run the risk of missing the point to something new. After all, a lot can still be written about the old Modern masterpieces.

As always, Fiedler makes some good sense. He can actually see what is in front of him and this is what makes him such a useful figure. Briskly, he names four present-day practitioners of the Art Novel of yesteryear: Bellow, Updike, Moravia, Robbe-Grillet. This is an odd grouping, but one sees what he means. Then he gives two examples of what he calls, approvingly, "the Anti-art Art Novel." One is Nabokov's *Pale Fire.* The other is John Barth's *Giles Goat-Boy*: "a strange pair of books really"—note the first sign of unease—

the former not quite American and the latter absolutely provincial American. Yet they have in common a way of using typical devices of the Modernist Art Novel, like irony, parody, travesty, exhibitionistic allusion, redundant erudition, and dogged experimentalism, not to extend the possibilities of the form but to destroy it.

This is nonsense. Professor (Emeritus) Nabokov's bright clever works are very much in the elitist Art-Novel tradition. It is true that the Black Swan of Lac Léman makes fun of American academics and their ghastly explications, but his own pretty constructions are meant to last forever. They are not autonomous artifacts designed to "self-destruct."

*Giles Goat-Boy* is a very bad prose-work by Professor John Barth. Certainly the book is not, as Fiedler claims,

a comic novel, a satire intended to mock everything which comes before it . . . it is itself it mocks, along with the writer capable of producing one more example of so obsolescent a form, and especially us who are foolish enough to be reading it. It is as if the Art Novel, aware that it must die, has determined to die laughing.

With that, Professor Fiedler goes over the side of Huck's raft. Whatever Professor Barth's gifts, humor, irony, wit are entirely lacking from his ambitious, garrulous, jocose productions. If this is the Anti-art Art Novel, then I predict that it will soon be superseded by the Anti-Anti-art Art Novel, which will doubtless prove to be our moribund friend the Art Novel. I suspect that the works of Professor Barth are written not so much to be read as to be taught. If this is the case then, according to Fiedler's own definition, they are Art Novels. Certainly they are not destined for the mass marketplace where daydreams of sex and of money, of movie stars and of murdered presidents are not apt to be displaced by a leaden narrative whose burden is (oh, wit, oh, irony) the universe is the university is the universe.

Happily, Fiedler soon abandons the highlands of culture for those lowlands where thrive science fiction and the Western, two genres that appear to reflect the night mind of the race. Fiedler mentions with approval some recent "neo-Pop Novels." *Little Big Man* excites him and he is soon back on his familiar warpath as white skin confronts redskin. Yet why the "neo" in front of Pop? Surely what used to be called "commercial fiction" has never ceased to reflect the dreams and prejudices of those still able to read. Fiedler does not quite deal with this. He goes off at a tangent. "At the moment of the rebirth of the novel, all order and distinction seem lost, as High Art and Low merge into each other, as books become films. . . . " Fiedler ends with an analysis of a novel turned into film called *Drive, He Said,* and he suggests that "therapeutic" madness may be the next chapter in our collective dreaming: injuns, niggers, subversives . . . or something.

Rebirth of the novel? That seems unlikely. The University-novel tends to be stillborn, suitable only for classroom biopsy. The Public-novel continues to be written but the audience for it is drifting away. Those brought up on the passive pleasures of films and television find the act of reading anything at all difficult and unrewarding. Ambitious novelists are poignantly aware of the general decline in what Professor Halperin would call "reading skills." Much of Mr. Donald Barthelme's latest novel, *The Dead Father,* is written in a kind of numbing baby talk reminiscent of the "see Jane run" primary school textbooks. Of course Mr. Barthelme means to be ironic. Of course he knows his book is not very interesting to read, but then life is not very interesting to live either. Hopefully, as Professor Halperin would say, the book will self-destruct once it has been ritually praised wherever English is taught but not learned.

Obviously what Fiedler calls the Art Novel is in more trouble than the Pop novel. Movies still need larvae to metamorphose into moths.

The Anti-art Art Novel does not exist despite the nervous attempts of teachers to find a way of making the novel if not news, really and truly new. I think it unlikely that Barthes, Barth and Barthelme will ever produce that unified field theory of Art-Novel writing and theory so long dreamed of by students of Freytag's pyramid.

Meanwhile, the caravans bark, and the dogs move on. Last December the Modern Language Association met in San Francisco. According to a reliable authority, the most advanced of the young bureaucrats of literature were all reading and praising the works of Burroughs. Not William, Edgar Rice.

*Times Literary Supplement*
February 20, 1976

# 12

·

# *AMERICAN PLASTIC: THE MATTER OF FICTION*

The New Novel is close to forty years old. Although forty is young for an American presidential candidate or a Chinese buried egg, it is very old indeed for a literary movement, particularly a French literary movement. But then what, recently, *has* one heard of the New Novel, whose official *vernissage* occurred in 1938 with Nathalie Sarraute's publication of *Tropismes*? The answer is not much directly from the founders but a good deal indirectly, for, with characteristic torpor, America's Departments of English have begun slowly, slowly to absorb the stern aesthetics of Sarraute and Robbe-Grillet, not so much through the actual writing of these masters as through their most brilliant interpreter, the witty, meta-camp sign-master and analyst of *le degré zéro de l'écriture* Roland Barthes, whose amused and amusing saurian face peers like some near-sighted chameleon from the back of a half-dozen slim volumes now being laboriously read in Academe.

Barthes has also had a significant (or signifying) effect on a number of American writers, among them Mr. Donald Barthelme. Two years ago Mr. Barthelme was quoted as saying that the only American writers worth reading are John Barth, Grace Paley, William Gass, and Thomas Pynchon. Dutifully, I have read all the writers on Mr. Barthelme's list, and presently I will make my report on them. But first, a look at M. Barthes.

For over twenty years Barthes has been a fascinating high critic who writes with equal verve about Charlie Chaplin, detergents, Marx, toys, Balzac, structuralism, and semiology. He has also put the theory of the New Novelists rather better than they have themselves, a considerable achievement since it is as theoreticians and not as practitioners that these writers excel. Unlike Sarraute, Robbe-Grillet, and Butor, Professor Barthes is much too clever actually to write novels himself, assuming that such things exist, new or old, full of signs or not, with or without sequential narratives. Rather, Barthes has remained a commentator and a theoretician, and he is often pleasurable to read though never blissful, to appropriate his own terminology.

Unlike the weather, theories of the novel tend to travel from east to west. But then, as we have always heard (sometimes from the French themselves), the French mind is addicted to the postulating of elaborate systems in order to explain everything, while the Anglo-American mind tends to shy away from unified-field theories. We chart our courses point to point; they sight from the stars. The fact that neither really gets much of anywhere doesn't mean that we haven't all had some nice outings over the years.

Nine years ago I wrote an exhaustive and, no doubt, exhausting account of the theory or theories of the French New Novel. Rejected by the American literary paper for which I had written it (subject not all that interesting), I was obliged to publish in England at the CIA's expense. Things have changed since 1967. Today one can hardly pick up a Serious literary review without noting at least one obligatory reference to Barthes, or look at any list of those novelists currently admired by American English departments without realizing that although none of these writers approaches zero degree, quite a few are on the chilly side. This is not such a bad thing. Twice, by the way, I have used the word "thing" in this paragraph. I grow suspicious, as one ought to be in zero-land, of all *things* and their shadows, words.

Barthes's American admirers are particularly fascinated by semiology, a quasi-science of signs first postulated by Ferdinand de Saussure in his *Course in General Linguistics* (1916). For some years the school of Paris and its American annex have made much of signs and signification, linguistic and otherwise. Barthes's *Elements of Semiology* (1964) is a key work and not easy to understand. It is full of graphs and theorems as well as definitions and puzzles. Fortunately, Susan Sontag provides a useful preface to the American edition of *Writing Degree Zero,* reminding us that Barthes "simply takes for granted a great deal that we do not." Zero degree writing is that colorless "white" writing (first defined and named by Sartre in his description of Camus's *L'Étranger*). It is a language in which, among other things and nothings, metaphor and anthropomorphizing are eliminated. According to Sontag, Barthes is reasonable enough to admit that this kind of writing is but *"one* solution to the disintegration of literary language."

As for semiology or the "science" of signs, Barthes concedes that "this term, *sign,* which is found in very different vocabularies . . . is for these very reasons very ambiguous." He categorizes various uses of the word "from the Gospels to Cybernetics." I should like to give him a use of the word he seems not to know. The word for "sign" in Sanskrit is "lingam," which also means "phallus," the holy emblem of our Lord Shiva.

In *S/Z* (1970) Barthes took "Sarrasine," a Balzac short story, and subjected it to a line-by-line, even a word-by-word analysis. In the course of this assault, Barthes makes a distinction between what he calls the "readerly text" and the "writerly text" (I am using Mr. Richard Miller's translation of these phrases). Barthes believes that "the goal of literary work (of literature as work) is to make the reader no longer a consumer, but a producer of the text. Our literature is characterized by the pitiless divorce . . . between the producer of the text and its user, between its owner and its customer, between its author and its reader. This reader is thereby plunged into a kind of idleness—he is intransitive; he is, in short, *serious.* Opposite the writerly text, then, is its counter-value, its negative, reactive value: what can be read but not written: the *readerly.* We call any readerly text a classic text." Then "the writerly is the novelistic without the novel, poetry without the poem. . . . But the readerly texts? They are products (and not productions), they make up the mass of our literature. How [to] differentiate this mass once again?"

Barthes believes that this can be done through *"interpretation* (in the Nietzschean sense of the word)." He has a passion, incidentally, for lizardlike dodges from the direct statement by invoking some great reverberating name as an adjective, causing the reader's brow to contract. But then the lunges and dodges are pretty much the matter as well as the manner of Barthes's technique as he goes to work on Balzac's short story of a man who falls in love with a famous Italian singer who turns out to be not the beautiful woman of his dreams but a castrated Neapolitan boy.

I do not intend to deal with Barthes's "interpretation" of the text. It is a very elaborate and close reading in a style that seems willfully complicated. I say willfully because the text of itself is a plain and readerly one in no need of this sort of assistance, not that Barthes wants to assist either text or reader. Rather he means to make for his own delectation or bliss a writerly text of his own. I hope that he has succeeded.

Like so many of today's academic critics, Barthes resorts to formulas, diagrams; the result, no doubt, of teaching in classrooms equipped with blackboards and chalk. Envious of the half-erased theorems—the prestigious *signs*—of the physicists, English teachers now compete by chalking up theorems and theories of their own, words having failed them yet again.

Fair stood the wind for America. For twenty years from the east have come these thoughts, words, signs. Let us now look and see what our own writers have made of so much exciting heavy weather, particularly the writers Mr. Donald Barthelme has named. Do they show signs of the French Pox?

Two years ago, I had read some of Gass, tried and failed to read Barth and Pynchon. I had never read Mr. Barthelme and I had never heard of Grace Paley. I have now made my way through the collected published works of the listed writers as well as through Mr. Barthelme's own enormous output. I was greatly helped in my journey through these texts by Mr. Joe David Bellamy's *The New Fiction,* a volume containing interviews with most of the principals and their peers.

Over the years I have seen but not read Donald Barthelme's short stories in *The New Yorker.* I suppose I was put off by the pictures. Barthelme's texts are usually decorated with perspective drawings, ominous faces, funny-looking odds and ends. Let the prose do it, I would think severely, and turn the page, looking for S. J. Perelman. I was not aware that I was *not* reading one who is described in *The New Fiction* as, "according to Philip Stevick . . . 'the most imitated fictionist in the United States today.' " Mr. Stevick is plainly authority to the interviewer, who then gets Barthelme to say a number of intelligent things about the life of a "fictionist" today. Mr. Barthelme tells us that his father was "a 'modern' architect." Incidentally, it is now the fashion to put quotes around any statement or word that might be challenged. This means that the questionable word or statement was not meant literally but ironically or "ironically." Another way of saying, "Don't hit me. I didn't really 'mean' it." As son of a School of Barnstone architect, Barthelme came naturally by those perspective drawings that so annoyed (and still annoy) me. He has worked as an editor and "I enjoy editing and enjoy doing layout-problems of design. I could very cheerfully be a typographer."

Barthelme's first book, *Come Back, Dr. Caligari,* contains short stories written between 1961 and 1964. This was the period during which Sarraute and Robbe-Grillet and Barthes were being translated into English. Although Robbe-Grillet's *For a New Novel* was not translated until 1965, Nathalie Sarraute's *Tropismes* was translated in 1963 as were such essential novels as *Le Planétarium, Fruits d'or, Jalousie,* and *Le Voyeur.* I note the fact of translation only because Barthelme admits to our common "American lack-of-language." Most American and English writers know foreign literature only through translation. This is bad enough when it comes to literature but peculiarly dangerous when it comes to theory. One might put the case that without a French education there is no way of comprehending, say, Roland Barthes (Sontag suggests as much). One can only take a piece here, a piece there, relate it to the tradition that one knows, and hope for the best. There is comfort, however, in knowing that the French do not get the point to us either.

The stories in *Come Back, Dr. Caligari* are fairly random affairs. Barthelme often indulges in a chilling heterosexual camp that is, nevertheless, quite a bit warmer than zero degree centigrade. There are funny names and cute names. Miss Mandible. Numerous non sequiturs. Dialogue in the manner not only of Ionesco but of Terry Southern (another Texas master). One can read any number of Barthelme's lines with a certain low-keyed pleasure. But then silliness stops the eye cold. " 'You're supposed to be curing a ham.' 'The ham died,' she said." The Marx Brothers could get a big laugh on this exchange because they would already have given us a dozen other gags in as many minutes. Unhappily one small gag on its own shrivels and dies. " '*You* may not be interested in absurdity,' she said firmly, 'but absurdity is interested in *you.*' "

Three years later came *Snow White.* This fiction was billed by the publisher as "a perverse fairy tale." The book is composed of fairly short passages. Quotation marks are used to enclose dialogue and there are the usual number of "he saids," and "she replied." This is an important point. *Truly* new writing eliminates quotation marks and "he saids." Barthelme is still cooking on a warm stove. The seven dwarfs are indistinguishable from one another and from the heroine. But the somewhat plodding tone of this work holds the attention rather better than did any of those fragments in the first volume. Yet Barthelme is compelled always to go for the easy twist. "Those cruel words remain locked in his lack of heart." Also, he writes about the writing he is writing:

We like books that have a lot of *dreck* in them, matter which presents itself as not wholly relevant (or indeed at all relevant) but which, carefully attended to, can supply a kind of "sense" of what is going on. This kind of "sense" is not to be obtained by reading between the lines (for there is nothing there, in those white spaces) but by reading the lines themselves. . . .

Roland Barthes, his mark.

*Unspeakable Practices, Unnatural Acts* (1968) contains fifteen pieces mostly published in *The New Yorker.* Occasionally the text is broken with headlines in the Brechtian manner. With film subtitles. With lists. One list called *Italian Novel* names sixteen Italian writers "she" was reading. Most are fashionable; some are good; but the premier Sciascia has been omitted. *What can this mean?*

Many proper names from *real* life appear in these texts. Paul Goodman, J. B. Priestley, Julia Ward Howe, Anthony Powell, Godard. Also *Time, Newsweek,* the Museum of Modern Art. Curiously enough those names that are already invested with an *a priori* reality help the texts which, as usual, maunder, talking to themselves, keeping a dull eye out for the odd joke as the author tries not to be himself a maker of dreck but an arranger of dreck.

The most successful of the lot is "Robert Kennedy Saved from Drowning." The reader brings to the story an altogether too vivid memory of the subject. We learn from the interview in Bellamy's book that, though the story "is, like, made up," Barthelme did use a remark that he heard Kennedy make about a geometric painter (" 'Well, at least we know he has a ruler' " . . . high wit from Camelot). Yet the parts that are not, like, made up are shrewd and amusing and truthful (relatively, of course). Also, the see-Jane-run style is highly suited to a parody of a contemporary politician on the make as he calculates his inanities and holds back his truths (relative—and relatives, too) and rage. Mr. William Gass takes an opposite view of this story. "Here Barthelme's method fails; for the idea is to *use* dreck, not write about it." But surely one can do both. Or neither. Or one. Or the other. But then Mr. Gass thinks that Barthelme at his best "has the art to make a treasure out of trash. . . . "

Throughout Barthelme's work one notes various *hommages* to this writer or that (who lives at Montreux? and where will one hear the ultimate message *Trink*?); some are a bit too close. For instance, the famous opening scene of Beckett's *Molloy* in which a father is carrying his son becomes in "A Picture History of the War": "Kellerman, gigantic with gin, runs through the park at noon with his naked father slung under one arm."

*City Life* (1970). Fourteen short stories, much as before except that now Barthelme is very deep into fiction's R and D (Research and Development) as opposed to the old-fashioned R and R (Rest and Recuperation). There are, galore, graphics. Big black squares occupy the center of white pages. Elaborate studies in perspective. Lots of funny old pictures. There are wide white margins, nice margins, too. There are pages of questions and answers (Q and A). Father returns. In fact, the first paragraph of the first story is: "An aristocrat was riding down the street in his carriage. He ran over my father."

It must be said that America's most imitated young writer is also not only the most imitable but one of the most imitative. *Hommage* to Robbe-Grillet:

Or a long sentence moving at a certain pace down the page aiming for the bottom—if not the bottom of this page then of some other page—where it can rest, or stop for a moment to think about the questions raised by its own (temporary) existence, which ends when the page is turned, or the sentence falls out of the mind that holds it (temporarily) in some kind of an embrace

and so on for eight whole pages with *not one full stop,* only a breaking off of the text, which is called "Sentence." The only development in "Sentence" is that what looks to be Robbe-Grillet at work in the first lines turns gradually (temporarily) into something like Raymond Roussel. Not quite zero degree: at the frozen pole no sentence ever thinks or even "thinks."

*Sadness* (1972). More stories. More graphics. The pictures are getting better all the time. There is a good one of a volcano in eruption. The prose . . . as before. Simple sentences. "Any writer in the country can write a beautiful sentence," Barthelme has declared. But he does not want to be like any writer in the country: "I'm very interested in awkwardness: sentences that are awkward in a particular way." What is "beauty," one wonders, suspicious of words. What, for that matter, is "awkward" or "particular"? But we do know all about sentences and occasionally among the various tributes to European modern masters (in translation), certain themes (or words) reoccur. One is the father. Of that more later. Also, drunkenness. In fact, alcohol runs like a torrent through most of the writers I have been reading. From Barthelme to Pynchon there is a sense of booziness, nausea, hangover.

I say: "I'm forty. I have bad eyes. An enlarged liver."
"That's the alcohol," he says.
"Yes," I say.
"You're very much like your father, there."

The only pages to hold me were autobiographical. Early dust-jacket pictures of Barthelme show an amiable-looking young man upon whose full upper lip there is a slight shadow at the beginning of the lip's bow. The dust jacket of *Sadness* shows a bearded man with what appears to be a harelip. Barthelme explains that he has had an operation for a "basal-cell malignancy" on his upper lip. True graphics, ultimately, are not old drawings of volcanoes or of perspective but of the author's actual face on the various dust jackets, aging in a definitely serial way with, in Barthelme's case, the drama of an operation thrown in, very much in the R and R tradition, and interesting for the reader though no doubt traumatizing for the author.

*Guilty Pleasures* (1974). This writer cannot stop making sentences. I have stopped reading a lot of them. I feel guilty. It is not pleasurable to feel guilty about not reading every one of those sentences. I do like the pictures more and more. In this volume there are more than thirty pictures. In the prose I spotted *hommages* to Calvino, Borges, early Ionesco. I am now saving myself for *The Dead Father,* the big one, as they say on Publisher's Row, the first big novel, long awaited, even heralded.

In *The Pleasure of the Text,* published just before *The Dead Father* (and by the same American publisher), Roland Barthes observes: "Death of the Father would deprive literature of many of its pleasures. If there is no longer a Father, why tell stories? Doesn't every narrative lead back to Oedipus? Isn't storytelling always a way of searching for one's origin. . . . As fiction, Oedipus was at least good for something: to make good novels. . . ." Apparently Barthelme took the hint. In *The Dead Father* a number of people are lugging about the huge remains of something called The Dead Father. Only this monster is not very dead because he talks quite a bit. The people want to bury him but he is not all that eager to be buried. Barthelme ends his book by deliberately burying the eponymous hero and, perhaps, fiction too. All of this is very ambitious.

Barthelme's narrative is reasonably sequential if lacking in urgency. There is, as always, Beckett: "said Julie, let us proceed. / They proceeded." Within the book is A Manual for Sons, written in a splendid run-on style quite at odds with the most imitated imitable writing that surrounds this unexpectedly fine burst of good writing on the nature of fathers, sons. For the record: there are no quotation marks. And no pictures. There is one diagram of a *placement;* but it is not much fun.

I am not sure that my progress through all these dull little sentences has been entirely justified by A Manual for Sons, but there is no doubt that beneath the mannerisms, the infantile chic, the ill-digested culture of an alien world, Barthelme does have a talent for, of all things in this era, writing. Shall I quote an example? I think not. Meanwhile, Barthelme himself says, "I have trouble reading, in these days. I would rather drink, talk or listen to music. . . . I now listen to rock constantly." Yes.

I can only assume that Grace Paley is a friend of Mr. Barthelme because she does not belong to what a certain Hack of Academe named Harry T. Moore likes, mistakenly, to call a *galère.* Paley is a plain short-story writer of the R and R school, and I got a good deal of pleasure from reading her two collections of short stories, *The Little Disturbances of Man* (with the nice subtitle: "Stories of Men and Women at Love") and *Enormous Changes at the Last Minute.* She works from something very like life . . . I mean "life"; she has an extraordinary ear for the way people sound. She do the ethnics in different voices. Although she tends, at times, to the plain-Jane or see-Jane-run kind of writing, her prose has such a natural energy that one is not distracted, a sign of good writing if not of a blissful text (she is close to boiling, in any case, and will never freeze).

With William Gass we are back in R and D country. I read Gass's first novel *Omensetter's Luck* in 1966 and found much to admire in it. Gass's essays are often eerily good. At his best, he can inhabit a subject in a way that no other critic now writing can do (see, in particular, his commentaries on Gertrude Stein). He seems not to have enjoyed being interviewed in Bellamy's collection, and his tone is unusually truculent (of New York quality lit. types: "I snub them"). It should be noted that of the writers admired by Barthelme only William Gass is an intellectual in the usual sense (I put no quotes around the words "intellectual," "usual," or "sense"). Gass's mind is not only first-rate but far too complex to settle for the easy effects of, say, Mr. Barthelme. But then: "As a student of philosophy, I've put in a great deal of time on the nature of language and belong, rather vaguely, to a school of linguistic philosophy which is extremely skeptical about the nature of language itself."

Gass has a complaint about Barth, Borges, and Beckett: "occasionally their fictions, conceived as establishing a metaphorical relationship between the reader and the world they are creating, leave the reader too passive." This is fair comment, though open to the question: just what is passive in this context? Ought the reader to be dancing about the room? blood pressure elevated? adrenaline flowing as he and the text battle one another? But then Gass shifts ground in his next sentence but one: "I have little patience with the 'creative reader.' " In other words the ideal reader is active but not creative. Quotation marks are now in order to protect these adjectives from becoming meaningless.

"I rarely read fiction and generally don't enjoy it." Gass is as one with the other R and D writers of fiction today. Although they do not read with any pleasure what anyone else is doing, they would like, naturally, to be themselves read with pleasure . . . by whom? Perhaps a college of writerly texts, grave as cardinals.

Gass himself is a curious case. Essentially, he is a traditional prose writer, capable of all sorts of virtuoso effects on the inner ear as well as on the reading eye. Yet he appears to have fallen victim to the R and D mentality. Speaking of a work in progress, "I hope that it will be really original in form and in effect, although mere originality is not what I'm after." This is worthy of Jimmy Carter.

Fiction has traditionally and characteristically borrowed its form from letters, journals, diaries, autobiographies, histories, travelogues, news stories, backyard gossip, etc. It has simply *pretended* to be one or other of them. The history of fiction is in part a record of the efforts of its authors to create for fiction in its own forms. Poetry has its own. It didn't borrow the ode from somebody. Now the novel is imagined news, imagined psychological or sociological case studies, imagined history . . . feigned, I should say, not imagined. As Rilke shattered the journal form with *Malte,* and Joyce created his own for *Ulysses* and *Finnegan,* I should like to create mine.

There seems to me to be a good deal wrong not only logically but aesthetically and historically with this analysis. First, poetry has never *had* its form. The origins of the ode are ancient but it was once created if not by a single ambitious schoolteacher, then by a number of poets roving like Terence's rose down the centuries. Certainly in this century poetry has gone off in as many directions as the novel, an art form whose tutelary deity is Proteus. The more like something else the novel is, the more like its true self it is. And since we do not *have* it, we can go on making it. Finally, whether or not a work of art is feigned or imagined is irrelevant if the art is good.

Like many good books, *Omensetter's Luck* is not easy to describe. What one comes away with is the agreeable memory of a flow of language that ranges from demotic Midwest ("I just up and screams at him—thump thump thump, he'd been going, die die die—I yell . . . ") to incantatory ("For knowledge, for good and evil, would Eve have set her will against her Father's? Ah, Horatio . . . "). In his interview the author tells us that he knows nothing of the setting (an Ohio river town); that everything is made up. He also confesses, "I haven't the dramatic imagination at all. Even my characters tend to turn away from one another and talk to the void. This, along with my inability to narrate, is my most serious defect (I think) as a writer and incidentally as a person."

The stories in *In the Heart of the Heart of the Country* seem to me to be more adventurous and often more successful than the novel. "The Pedersen Kid" is beautiful work. In a curious way the look of those short sentences on pages uncluttered with quotation marks gives the text a visual purity and coldness that perfectly complements the subject of the story, and compels the reader to know the icy winter at the country's heart. In most of these stories the prevailing image is winter.

Billy closes his door and carries coal or wood to his fire and closes his eyes, and there's simply no way of knowing how lonely and empty he is or whether he's as vacant and barren and loveless as the rest of us are—here in the heart of the country.

At actual zero degree, Gass, perversely, blazes with energy.

The title story is the most interesting of the collection. Despite a sign or two that the French virus may have struck: "as I write this page, it is eleven days since I have seen the sun," the whole of the story (told in fragments) is a satisfying description of the world the narrator finds himself in, and he makes art of the quotidian:

My window is a grave, and all that lies within it's dead. No snow is falling. There's no haze. It's not still, not silent. Its images are not an animal that waits, for movement is no demonstration.

What is art?

Art is energy shaped by intelligence. The energy that the text of *Madame Bovary* generates for the right reader is equal to that which sustains the consumer of *Rebecca*. The ordering intelligence of each writer is, of course, different in kind and intention. Gass's problem as an artist is not so much his inability to come up with some brand-new Henry Ford–type invention that will prove to be a breakthrough in world fiction (this is never going to happen) as what he calls his weak point—a lack of dramatic gift—which is nothing more than low or rather intermittent energy. He can write a dozen passages in which the words pile up without effect. Then, suddenly, the current, as it were, turns on again and the text comes to beautiful life (in a manner of speaking of course . . . who does not like a living novel? particularly one that is literate).

I have seen the sea slack, life bubble through a body without a trace, its spheres impervious as soda's.

For a dozen years I have been trying to read *The Sot-Weed Factor*. I have never entirely completed this astonishingly dull book but I have read most of John Barth's published work and I feel that I have done him, I hope, justice. There is a black cloth on my head as I write.

First, it should be noted that Barth, like Gass, is a professional schoolteacher. He is a professor of English *and* Creative Writing. He is extremely knowledgeable about what is going on in R and D land and he is certainly eager to make his contribution. Interviewed, Barth notes "the inescapable fact that literature—because it's made of the common stuff of language—seems more refractory to change in general than the other arts." He makes the obligatory reference to the music of John Cage. Then he adds, sensibly, that "the permanent changes in fiction from generation to generation more often have been, and are more likely to be, modifications of sensibility and attitude rather than dramatic innovations in form and technique."

Barth mentions his own favorite writers. Apparently "Borges, Beckett and Nabokov, among the living grand masters (and writers like Italo Calvino, Robbe-Grillet, John Hawkes, William Gass, Donald Bar-

thelme)—*have* experimented with form and technique and even with
the *means* of fiction, working with graphics and tapes and things. . . . "
What these writers have in common (excepting Robbe-Grillet) "is
a more or less fantastical, or as Borges would say, 'irrealist,' view of
reality. . . . " Barth thinks—hopes—that this sort of writing will characterize the seventies.

What is "irrealism"? Something that cannot be realized. This is a
curious goal for a writer though it is by no means an unfamiliar terminus
for many an ambitious work. Further, Barth believes that realism is "a
kind of aberration in the history of literature." I am not exactly sure
what he means by realism. After all, the Greek myths that he likes to
play around with were once a "reality" to those who used them as stuff
for narrative. But then Barth broods. "Perhaps we should *accept* the fact
that writing and reading are essentially linear activities and devote our
attention as writers to those aspects of experience that can best be
rendered linearly—with words that go left to right across the page;
subjects, verbs and objects; punctuation!" He ends with the rather plaintive, "The trick, I guess, in any of the arts at this hour of the world, is
to have it both ways." How true!

*The Floating Opera* (1956) and *The End of the Road* (1958) are two
novels of a kind and that kind is strictly R and R, and fairly superior R
and R at that. The author tells us that they were written in his twenty-
fourth year, and a good year it was for him. Publishers meddled with the
ending of the first novel. He has since revised the book and that is the
version I read. It is written in first person demotic (Eastern Shore of
Maryland, Barth's place of origin). The style is garrulous but not unattractive. "I was just thirty-seven then, and as was my practice, I greeted
the new day with a slug of Sherbrook from the quart on my window sill.
I've a quart sitting there now, but it's not the same one. . . . "

There is a tendency to put too much in, recalling Barthes's "The
Prattle of Meaning" (*S/Z*): certain storytellers

impose a dense plenitude of meaning or, if one prefers, a certain redundancy, a kind of semantic prattle typical of the archaic—or infantile—era
of modern discourse, marked by the excessive fear of failing to communicate
meaning (its basis); while, in reaction, in our latest—or "new" novels,

the action or event is set forth "without accompanying it with its signification."

Certainly Barth began as an old-fashioned writer who wanted us to know all about the adulteries, money-hassling, and boozing on what sounded like a very real Eastern Shore of a very real Maryland, as lacking in bears as the seacoast of Illyria: "Charley was Charley Parks, an attorney whose office was next door to ours. He was an old friend and poker partner of mine, and currently we were on opposite sides in a complicated litigation. . . . "

In 1960 Barth published *The Sot-Weed Factor.* The paperback edition is adorned with the following quotation from *The New York Times Book Review*: "Outrageously funny, villainously slanderous. . . . The book is a brass-knuckled satire of humanity at large. . . . " I am usually quick, even eager, to respond to the outrageously funny, the villainously slanderous . . . in short, to *The New York Times* itself. But as I read on and on, I could not so much as summon up a smile at the lazy jokes and the horrendous pastiche of what Barth takes to be eighteenth-century English (" ' 'Tis not that which distresses me; 'tis Andrew's notion that I had vicious designs on the girl. 'Sheart, if anything be improbable, 'tis . . . ' "). I stopped at page 412 with 407 pages yet to go. The sentences would not stop unfurling; as Peter Handke puts it in *Kaspar*: "Every sentence helps you along: you get over every object with a sentence: a sentence helps you get over an object when you can't really get over it, so that you really get over it," etc.

To read Barth on the subject of his own work and then to read the work itself is a puzzling business. He talks a good deal of sense. He is obviously intelligent. Yet he tells us that when he turned from the R and R of his first two novels to the megalo-R and R of *The Sot-Weed Factor,* he moved from "a merely comic mode to a variety of farce, which frees your hands even more than comedy does." Certainly there are comic aspects to the first two books. But the ponderous jocosity of the third book is neither farce nor satire nor much of anything except English-teacher-writing at a pretty low level. I can only assume that the book's admirers are as ignorant of the eighteenth century as the author (or, to be fair, the author's imagination) and that neither author nor admiring reader has a sense of humor, a fact duly noted about Americans in general—and their serious ponderous novelists in particular—by many peoples in other lands. It still takes a lot of civilization gone slightly high to make a wit.

*Giles Goat-Boy* arrived on the scene in 1966. Another 800 pages of ambitious schoolteacher-writing: a book to be taught rather than read. I shall not try to encapsulate it here, other than to say that the central metaphor is the universe is the university is the universe. I suspect that this will prove to be one of the essential American university novels and to dismiss it is to dismiss those departments of English that have made such a book possible. The writing is more than usually clumsy. A verse play has been included. *"Agnora:* for Pete's sake, simmer down, boys. Don't you think / I've been a dean's wife long enough to stink / my public image up?"

Barth thinks that the word "human" is a noun; he also thinks that Giles is pronounced with a hard "g" as in "guile" instead of a soft "g" as in "giant." But then the unlearned learned teachers of English are the new barbarians, serenely restoring the Dark Ages.

By 1968 Barth was responding to the French New Novel. *Lost in the Funhouse* is the result. A collection (or, as he calls it, a "series") of "Fiction for Print, Tape, Live Voice." Barth is not about to miss a trick now that he has moved into R and D country. The first of the series, "Night-Sea Journey," should—or could—be on tape. This is the first-person narrative of a sperm heading, it would appear, toward an ovum, though some of its eschatological musings suggest that a blow-job may be in progress. Woody Allen has dealt more rigorously with this theme.

The "story" "Lost in the Funhouse" is most writerly and self-conscious; it chats with the author who chats with it and with us. "Description of physical appearance and mannerisms is one of several standard methods of characterization used by writers of fiction." Thus Barth distances the reader from the text. A boy goes to the funhouse and. . . . "The more closely an author identifies with the narrator, literally or metaphorically, the less advisable it is, as a rule, to use the first-person narrative viewpoint." Some of this schoolteacherly commentary is amusing. But the ultimate effect is one of an ambitious but somewhat uneasy writer out to do something brand-new in a territory already inhabited by, among other texts that can read and write, the sinister *Locus Solus,* the immor(t)al *Tlooth* and the dexterous *A Nest of Ninnies.*

It is seldom wise for a born R and R writer to make himself over into an R and D writer unless he has something truly formidable and new to show us. Barth just has books. And sentences. And a fairly clear idea of just how far up the creek he is without a paddle. "I believe literature's not likely ever to manage abstraction successfully, like sculpture for example, is that a fact, what a time to bring up that subject. . . ." What a time! And what is the subject, Alice? Incidentally, Barth always uses quotation marks and "he saids."

In 1972 Barth published three long stories in a volume called *Chimera.* Two of the stories are based on Greek myths, for are they not, as admirers of Jung declare, part of the racial memory, the common stock of all our dreams and narratives? Well, no, they are not. The Greek myths are just barely relevant to those Mediterranean people who still live in a landscape where the *anima* of a lost world has not yet been entirely covered with cement. The myths are useful but not essential to those brought up on the classics, the generation to which Dr. Jung (and T. S. Eliot) belonged; and of course they are necessary to anyone who would like to understand those works of literature in which myth plays a part. Otherwise they are of no real use to Americans born in this century. For us Oedipus is not the doomed king of Thebes but Dr. Freud's depressing protagonist, who bears no relation at all to the numinous figure that Sophocles and Euripides portrayed. Thebes is another country, where we may not dwell.

Joyce's *Ulysses* is often regarded as a successful attempt to use Greek myth to shore up a contemporary narrative. But it is plain to most noncreative readers that the myth does not work at all in Joyce's creation and were it not for his glorious blarney and fine naturalistic gifts, the book's classical structure alone could not have supported the novel. Since Joyce, alas, the incorporation of Greek myth into modern narrative has been irresistible to those who have difficulty composing narrative, and no Greek. These ambitious writers simply want to give unearned resonance to their tales of adultery on the Eastern Shore of Maryland, of misbehavior in faculty rooms, of massive occlusions in the heart of the country. But the results are deeply irritating to those who have some sense of the classical world and puzzling, I would think, to those taking English courses where the novel is supposed to have started with Richardson.

Barth has browsed through Robert Graves's *The Greek Myths* (and gives due acknowledgment to that brilliantly eccentric custodian of the old world). At random, I would guess, Barth selected the story of Bellerophon (tamer of Pegasus) for modernizing; also, more to his point, Perseus, the slayer of Medusa. The first story is taken from Arabian mythology, a narrative called "Dunyazadiad," as told by the "kid sister of Scheherazade." It should also be noted that two of the stories in *Lost in the Funhouse* were wacky versions of certain well-known highjinks in old Mycenae.

The kid sister of Scheherazade is a gabby co-ed who mentions with awe the academic gifts of her sister "Sherry," "an undergraduate arts-and-sciences major at Banu Sasan University. Besides being Homecoming

Queen, valedictorian-elect, and a four-letter varsity athlete. . . . Every graduate department in the East was after her with fellowships." This unbearable cuteness has a sinister side. Since Barth's experience of literature and the world is entirely that of a schoolteacher, he appears to take it for granted that the prevailing metaphor for his own life (and why not all life itself?) is the university. There is also an underlying acceptance of the fact that since no one is ever going to read him except undergraduates in American universities, he had better take into account that their reading skills are somewhat underdeveloped, their knowledge of the way society works vague, and their culture thin.

Barth's *Hamlet* would no doubt begin, "Well, I guess flunking out of Rutgers is no big deal when I got this family up in Wilmington where we make these plastics that, like, kill people but I'm changing all that or I was going to up until my mother went and married this asshole uncle of mine. . . . " Perhaps this is the only way to get the classics into young television-shrunk minds. But the exercise debases both classics and young minds. Of course Barth is no fool. He is often quick to jump in and forestall criticism. Sherry's kid sister remarks: "currently, however, the only readers of artful fiction were critics, other writers, and unwilling students who, left to themselves, preferred music and pictures to words."

Sherry is helped in her literary efforts to think up 1001 stories by a genie who is, like so many of Barth's male protagonists, a *thoroughly good person*: his policy "was to share beds with no woman who did not reciprocate his feelings." For a United Statesman (posing as an Arabian genie), this is true heterosexual maturity. In case we missed Barth's first testimonial to the genie's niceness, we are later told that "he was no more tempted to infidelity than to incest or pederasty." I guess this makes him about the best genie on campus. Between Genie and Sherry there is a lot of talk about the nature of fiction, which is of course the only reason for writing university fiction. There is not a glimmer of intelligence in this jaunty tale.

Barth was born and grew up a traditional cracker-barrelly sort of American writer, very much in the mainstream—a stream by no means polluted or at an end. But he chose not to continue in the vein that was most natural to him. Obviously he has read a good deal about Novel Theory. He has the standard American passion not only to be original but to be great, and this means creating one of Richard Poirier's "worlds elsewhere": an alternative imaginative structure to the mess that we have made of our portion of the Western hemisphere. Aware of French theories about literature (but ignorant of the culture that has produced those theories), superficially acquainted with Greek myth, deeply involved in the academic life of the American university, Barth is exactly the sort of writer our departments of English were bound, sooner or later, to produce. Since he is a writer with no great gift for language either demotic or mandarin, Barth's narratives tend to lack energy; and the currently fashionable technique of stopping to take a look at the story as it is being told simply draws attention to the meagerness of what is there.

I am obliged to remark upon the sense of suffocation one experiences reading so much bad writing. As the weary eyes flick from sentence to sentence, one starts *willing* the author to be good. Either I have become shell-shocked by overexposure to the rockets' red glare and bombs bursting in air or Barth has managed a decent narrative in "Perseid." As usual, the language is jangling everyday speech: "Just then I'd've swapped Mycenae for a cold draught and a spot of shade to dip it in. . . . " The gods and demigods are straight from Thorne Smith, who ought to be regarded, in Harry T. Moore's *galère,* as the American Dante. But the story of the middle-aged Perseus and his problems of erection (and love) with a young girl seems at times authentic, even true . . . despite Barth's unremitting jocosity: " 'Were you always psychosexually weak, or is that Andromeda's doing?' "

In some ways, the writers' interviews are more revealing about the state of fiction than the books they write. The twelve writers interviewed for Joe David Bellamy's book often sound truculent; also, uneasy. For instance, John Gardner (whose *Grendel* I much admired) is very truculent, but then Mr. Barthelme is on record as not admiring him; this cannot help but hurt. Gardner is as much his own man as anyone can be who teaches school and wants to get good reviews from his fellow teachers in *The New York Times Book Review.* Yet he dares to say of *The Sot-Weed Factor*: "nothing but a big joke. It's a philosophical joke; it might even be argued that it's a philosophical advance. But it ain't like Victor Hugo." It also ain't an advance of any kind. Although Gardner is myth-minded, he is much more intuitive and authentic than the usual academic browser in Robert Graves's compendium. Gardner also knows where proto-myths are to be found: Walt Disney's work, for one.

Gardner tells us that "most writers today are academicians: they have writing or teaching jobs with universities. In the last ten years the tone of university life and of intellectuals' responses to the world have changed. During the Cold War there was a great deal of fear and cynicism on account of the Bomb." Gardner then makes the astonishing suggestion that when the other Americans (those somewhat unreal millions condemned to live off-campus) turned against the Vietnam war (after eight years of defeat), the mood changed in the universities as the academicians realized that "the people around you are all working hard to make the world better." A startling observation. In any case, the writers of University or U-novels will now become more life-affirming than they were in the sad sixties; "notable exceptions are writers who very carefully stay out of the mainstream and therefore can't be influenced by the general feeling of people around them."

At first I thought Gardner was joking. But I was wrong. He really believes that the mainstream of the world is the American university and that a writer outside this warm and social-meliorizing ambience will fall prey to old-fashioned cynicism and hardness of heart. For instance, "Pynchon stays out of universities. He doesn't know what chemists and physicists are doing; he knows only the pedantry of chemistry and physics. When good chemists and physicists talk about, say, the possibility of extraterrestrial life, they agree that for life to be evolved beyond our stage, creators on other planets must have reached decisions we now face." Removed from the academic mainstream and its extraterrestrial connections, Pynchon's *Gravity's Rainbow* is just an apocalyptic "whine."

Fortunately, Gardner's imagination is fabulous; otherwise, he would be fully exposed in his work as being not only *not* in the mainstream of American society but perfectly irrelevant in his academic *cul de sac.* Yet if he is right that most contemporary writers are also teaching school and listening in on warm-hearted life-enhancing physicists and chemists as they talk of their peers on other planets, then literature has indeed had its day and there will be no more books except those that teachers write to teach.

Although Barthelme has mentioned Pynchon as one of the writers he admires, neither Gass nor Barth refers to him and Gardner thinks him a "whiner" because he no longer spawns in the mainstream of Academe. I daresay that it will come as news to these relatively young writers that American literature, such as it is, has never been the work of schoolteachers. Admittedly, each year it is harder and harder for a writer to make a living from writing, and many writers must find the temptation to teach overwhelming. Nevertheless, those of us who emerged in the forties (Roosevelt's children) regarded the university (as did our predecessors) as a kind of skid row far worse than a seven-year writer's contract at Columbia (the studio, not the university). Except for Saul Bellow, I can think of no important novelist who has taught on a regular basis throughout a career.

I find it admirable that of the nonacademics Pynchon did not follow the usual lazy course of going for tenure as did so many writers—no, "writers"—of his generation. He is thirty-nine years old and attended Cornell (took a class from former Professor V. Nabokov); he is eminently *academebile.* The fact that he has got out into the world (somewhere) is to his credit. Certainly he has not, it would seem, missed a trick; and he never whines.

Pynchon's first novel, *V.,* was published in 1963. There is some similarity to other R and D works. Cute names abound. Benny Profane, Dewey Gland, Rachel Owlglass. Booze flows through scene after scene involving members of a gang known as The Whole Sick Crew. The writing is standard American. "Kilroy was possibly the only objective onlooker in Valletta that night. Common legend had it he'd been born in the U.S. right before the war, on a fence or latrine wall." Above this passage is a reproduction of the classic Kilroy sketch; below this passage there is a broken-line Kilroy. These are the only graphics in a long book that also contains the usual quotation marks and "he says." All in all, a naturalistic rendering of an essentially surrealist or perhaps irrealist subject, depending on one's apprehension of the work.

Benny Profane is described as "a schlemihl and human yo-yo." He is a former sailor. On Christmas Eve 1955 he is in Norfolk, Virginia. He goes into a bar, "his old tin can's tavern on East Main Street." People with funny names sing songs at each other (lyrics provided in full by the author) and everyone drinks a lot. There is vomiting. Scene with a girl: "What sort of Catholic was she? Profane, who was only half Catholic (mother Jewish), whose morality was fragmentary (being derived from experience and not much of it). . . . " Profane is "girl-shy" and fat. " 'If I was God . . . ' " begins a fantasy. Definitely a clue to the state of mind of the creator of the three books I have been reading.

A shift from Profane to "Young Stencil, the world adventurer" and the mystery woman V. Elliptical conversation (1946) between a margravine and Stencil (whose father Sidney was in the British foreign office; he died in Malta "while investigating the June Disturbances"). They sit on a terrace overlooking the Mediterranean. "Perhaps they may have felt like the last two gods." Reference to an entry in father's journal, " 'There is more behind and inside V. than any of us had suspected. Not who, but what: what is she.' " Stencil pursues the idea of V. A quest: "in the tradition of *The Golden Bough* or *The White Goddess.* "

From various references to Henry Adams and to physics in Pynchon's work, I take it that he has been influenced by Henry Adams's theory of history as set forth in *The Education of Henry Adams* and in the posthumously published "The Rule of Phase Applied to History." For Adams, a given human society in time was an organism like any other in the universe and he favored Clausius's speculation that "the entropy of the universe tends to a maximum" (an early Pynchon short story is called "Entropy").

Maximum entropy is that state at which no heat/energy enters or leaves a given system. But nothing known is constant. The Second Law of Thermodynamics appears to be absolute: everything in time loses energy to something else and, finally, drops to zero (centigrade) and dies or, perhaps, ceases to be matter as it was and becomes anti-matter. Question: to anti-matter are we anti-anti-matter or no matter at all?

I have little competence in the other of Lord Snow's celebrated two cultures. Like so many other writers I flunked physics. But I know my Adams and I can grasp general principles (without understanding how they have been arrived at); in any case, to make literature, a small amount of theory is enough to provide commanding metaphors. Pynchon's use of physics is exhilarating and as an artist he appears to be gaining more energy than he is losing. Unlike the zero writers, he is usually at the boil. From Adams he has not only appropriated the image of history as Dynamo but the attractive image of the Virgin. Now armed with these concepts he embarks in *V.* on a quest, a classic form of narrative, and the result is mixed, to say the least.

To my ear, the prose is pretty bad, full of all the rattle and buzz that were in the air when the author was growing up, an era in which only the television commercial was demonically acquiring energy, leaked to it by a declining Western civilization. Happily, Pynchon is unaffected by the French disease, except for one passage: "Let me describe the room. The room measures 17 by 11 ½ feet by 7 feet. The walls are lathe and plaster. . . . The room is oriented so that its diagonals fall NNE/SSW, and NW/SE." As another ex-seaman, I appreciate Pynchon's ability to box the compass, something no French ice-cream vendor could ever do. With this satisfying send-up, Pynchon abandons the New Novel for his own worlds and anti-worlds.

The quest for V. (the Virgin? or nothing much?) takes Stencil to Valletta, capital of Malta, a matriarchal island, we are told, where manhood must identify itself with the massive rock. There are clues. False scents. Faust is on the scene. And Profane is also in Malta. The prose is very close to that of the comic books of the fifties:

"Thirteen of us rule the world in secret."

"Yes, yes. Stencil went out of his way to bring Profane here. He should have been more careful; he wasn't. Is it really his own extermination he's after?"

Maijstral turned smiling to him. Gestured behind his back at the ramparts of Valletta. "Ask her," he whispered. "Ask the rock."

Energy nicely maintained; controlling intelligence uneven.

With *The Crying of Lot 49* (1966) Pynchon returns to the quest, to conspiracy. Cute names like Genghis Cohen, an ancient Hollywood joke. Bad grammar: "San Narciso lay further south," "some whirlwind rotating too slow for her heated skin." A lot of booze. Homophobia. Mysteries. It would appear that most of the courses Pynchon took at Cornell are being used: first-year physics, psychology, Jacobean tragedy—but then his art is no doubt derived "from experience and not much of that."

This time the grail is an alternative postal service. Haunting the narrative is the noble house of Thurn and Taxis (the wife of a descendant was a literary agent in the United States: known to Pynchon? Also, Rilke's patroness was a princess of that house). Jokes: " 'I was in the little boys' room,' he said. 'The men's room was full.' " There are numerous images of paranoia, the lurking "they" who dominate the phantom postal service of the Tristero (sometimes spelled Trystero), a mirror-alternative in earlier times to the Thurn and Taxis postal monopoly. "While the Pony Express is defying deserts, savages and sidewinders, Tristero's giving its employees crash courses in Siouan and Athapascan dialects. Disguised as Indians their messengers mosey westward. Reach the coast every time, zero attrition rate, not a scratch on them. The entire emphasis now toward silence, impersonation, opposition masquerading as allegiance.' " Well, Joyce also chose exile, cunning, silence, but eschewed allegiance's mask. Lot 49 has been cried. Who will bid?

*Gravity's Rainbow* (1973) contains close to 900 densely printed pages. For a year I have been reading in and at the text. Naturally, I am impressed that a clear-cut majority of the departments of English throughout North America believe this to be the perfect teachers' novel. I am sure that they are right. Certainly no young writer's book has been so praised since Colin Wilson's *The Outsider.*

The first section of *Gravity's Rainbow* is called "Beyond the Zero." Plainly a challenge not only to *l'écriture blanche* but to proud entropy itself. Pynchon has now aimed himself at anti-matter, at what takes place beyond, beneath the zero of freezing, and death. This is superbly ambitious and throughout the text energy hums like a . . . well, dynamo.

The narrative begins during the Second War, in London. Although Pynchon works hard for verisimilitude and fills his pages with period jabber, anachronisms occasionally jar (there were no "Skinnerites" in that happy time of mass death). The controlling image is that of the V-2, a guided missile developed by the Germans and used toward the end of the war (has Pynchon finally found V.? and is she a bomb?). There is an interesting epigraph from Werner von Braun: "Nature does not know extinction; all it knows is transformation." Braun believes "in the continuity of our spiritual existence after death." So much then for zero degree. This quasi-Hindu sentiment is beguiling and comforting and, no doubt, as concerns matter, true: in time or phases, energy is always lost but matter continues in new arrangements. Personally, I find it somber indeed to think that individual personality goes on and on beyond zero, time. But I am in a minority: this generation of Americans is god-hungry and craves reassurance of personal immortality. If Pynchon can provide it, he will be as a god—rather his intention, I would guess.

It is curious to read a work that excites the imagination but disturbs the aesthetic sense. A British critic no longer in fashion recently made the entirely unfashionable observation that prose has everywhere declined in quality as a result of mass education. To compare Pynchon with Joyce, say, is to compare a kindergartener to a graduate student (the permanent majority of the culturally inadequate will promptly respond that the kindergartener *sees* more clearly than the graduate student and that his incompetence with language is a sign of innocence not ignorance and hence grace). Pynchon's prose rattles on and on, broken by occasional lengthy songs every bit as bad, lyrically, as those of Bob Dylan.

> *Light-up, and-shine, you—in-candescent Bulb Ba-bies!*
> *Looks-like ya got ra-bies*
> *Just lay there foamin' and a-screamin' like a buncha little demons,*
> *I'm deliv'rin' unto you a king-dom of roa-ches. . . .*

England. Germany. Past. Present. War. Science. Telltale images of approaching . . . deity? Two characters with hangovers "are wasted gods urging on a tardy glacier." Of sandbags at a door, "provisional pyramids erected to gratify curious gods' offspring." And "slicks of nighttime

vomit, pale yellow, clear as the fluids of gods." Under deity, sex is
central to this work of transformation. A character's erections achieve
a mysterious symbiosis with the V-2s. A sadist abuses a young man and
woman. "Every true god must be both organizer and destroyer." A
character declaims: " 'If only S and M could be established universally,
at the family level, the state would wither away.' " This is a nice joke
(although I thought S and M was already universal at the family level).
" 'Submit, Gottfried. Give it all up. See where she takes you. Think of
the first time I fucked you. . . . Your little rosebud bloomed.' " Hard
to believe that it is close to a decade since that pretty moss tea-rose was
first forced, as it were, in my greenhouse.

Eventually, the text exhausts patience and energy. In fact, I suspect
that the energy expended in reading *Gravity's Rainbow* is, for anyone,
rather greater than that expended by Pynchon in the actual writing. This
is entropy with a vengeance. The writer's text is ablaze with the heat/
energy that his readers have lost to him. Yet the result of this exchange
is neither a readerly nor a writerly text but an uneasy combination of
both. Energy and intelligence are not in balance, and the writer fails in
his ambition to be a god of creation. Yet his ambition and his failure
are very much in the cranky, solipsistic American vein, and though I
doubt if anyone will ever want to read all of this book, it will certainly
be taught for a very long (delta) time: "approaching zero, eternally
approaching, the slices of time growing thinner and thinner, a succession of rooms each with walls more silver, transparent, as the pure light
of the zero comes nearer. . . ." Everything is running down. We shall
freeze. Then what? A film by Stanley Kubrick?

Richard Poirier is more satisfied than I with Pynchon's latest work.
For one thing, he is awed by the use of science. Approvingly, he quotes
Wordsworth's hope that the poet would one day "be ready to follow the
steps of the Man of science, not only in those general indirect effects,
but he will be at his side, carrying sensation into the midst of science
itself." Pynchon would appear to fulfill Wordsworth's reverie. He is as
immersed in contemporary physics and cybernetics as Henry Adams
was in the scientific theories of *his* day. But the scientific aspects of
Pynchon's work will eventually become as out-of-date as those of Henry
Adams. Science changes: one day we are monists, the next day plural-
ists. Proofs are always being disproven by other proofs. At the end, there
are only words and their arrangement.

Poirier compares Pynchon to the Faulkner of *Absalom, Absalom* and
finds both likeness and a significant difference, for "this genius of our

day is shaped by thermodynamics and the media, by Captain Marvel rather than by Colonel Sartoris." This is no doubt a true description, but is the result as good? or good? What I find to be tedious and random in Pynchon's list-making, Poirier sees as so many

Dreiserian catalogues of the waste materials of our world that only by remaining resolutely on the periphery, without ever intruding himself into the plotting that emanates from his material, only then can he see what most humanly matters.

"Matter," a verb. "Matter," a noun. The matter of fiction has been expanded by Pynchon's ascent from zero degree (writing as well as centigrade); nevertheless, entropy is sovereign. That which gains energy/heat does so at the expense of that which is losing energy/heat to it. At the end there is only the cold and no sublunary creatures will ever know what songs the quasars sing in their dark pits of anti-matter.

I cannot help but feel a certain depression after reading Mr. Barthelme's chosen writers. I realize that language changes from generation to generation. But it does not, necessarily, improve. The meager rattling prose of all these writers, excepting Gass, depresses me. Beautiful sentences are not easy to write, despite Mr. Barthelme's demur. Since beauty is relative only to intention, there are doubtless those who find beauty in the pages of books where I find "a flocculent appearance, something opaque, creamy and curdled, something powerless ever to achieve the triumphant smoothness of Nature. But what best reveals it for what it is is the sound it gives, at once hollow and flat; its noise is its undoing, as are its colors, for it seems capable of retaining only the most chemical-looking ones. Of yellow, red and green, it keeps only the aggressive quality. . . ." What is "it"? The work of the new American formalists? No, "it" is plastic, as described by Barthes in *Mythologies*.

The division between what I have elsewhere called the Public-novel and the University-novel is now too great to be bridged by any but the occasional writer who is able to appeal, first to one side, then to the other, fulfilling the expectations (more or less) of each. I find it hard to take seriously the novel that is written to be taught, nor can I see how the American university can provide a base for the making of "new" writing when the American university is, at best, culturally and intellectually conservative and, at worst, reactionary.

Academics tell me that I am wrong. They assure me that if it were not for them, the young would never read the Public-novels of even the

recent past (Faulkner, Fitzgerald). If this is true, then I would prefer
for these works decently to die rather than to become teaching-tools,
artifacts stinking of formaldehyde in a classroom (original annotated
text with six essays by the author and eight critical articles examining
the parameters of the author's vision). But the academic bureaucracy,
unlike the novel, will not wither away, and the future is dark for literature. Certainly the young in general are not going to take up reading
when they have such easy alternatives as television, movies, rock. The
occasional student who might have an interest in reading will not survive a course in English, unless of course he himself intends to become
an academic bureaucrat.

As for Thomas Pynchon, one can applaud his deliberate ascent from
Academe into that dangerous rainbow sky in which he will make his
parabola and fall as gravity pulls him back to where he started, to
Academe, to zero, or to (my first graphic, ever) ○.

*The New York Review of Books*
July 15, 1974

◆

# THOMAS LOVE PEACOCK: THE NOVEL OF IDEAS

What is a novel for? To be read is the simple answer. But since fewer and fewer people want to read novels (as opposed to what the conglomerate-publishers call "category fiction"), it might be a good idea to take a look at what is being written, and why; at what is being read, and why.

In *Ideas and the Novel* Mary McCarthy notes that since the time of Henry James, the serious novel has dealt in a more and more concentrated—if not refined—way with the moral relations of characters who resemble rather closely the writer and his putative reader. It is not, she says, that people actually write Jamesian novels; rather, "The Jamesian model remains a standard, an archetype, against which contemporary impurities and laxities are measured." In addition, for Americans, sincerity if not authenticity is all-important; and requires a minimum of invention.

During the last fifty years, the main line of the Serious American Novel has been almost exclusively concerned with the doings and feelings, often erotic, of white middle-class Americans, often schoolteachers, as they confront what they take to be life. It should be noted that these problems seldom have much or anything to do with politics, with theories of education, with the nature of the good. It should also be noted that the tone of the Serious Novel is always solemn and often vatic. Irony and wit are unknown while the preferred view of the human estate is standard American, which is to say positive. For some reason, dialogue tends to be minimal and flat.

Virginia Woolf thought that the Victorian novelists "created their characters mainly through dialogue." Then, somehow, "the sense of an audience" was lost. "*Middlemarch* I should say is the transition novel: Mr. Brooke done directly by dialogue: Dorothea indirectly. Hence its great interest—the first modern novel. Henry James of course receded further and further from the spoken word, and finally I think only used dialogue when he wanted a very high light."

Today's Serious Novel is not well lit. The characters do, say, and think ordinary things, as they confront those problems that the serious writer must face in his everyday life. Since the serious novel is written by middle-class, middlebrow whites, political activists, intellectuals, members of the ruling classes, blacks seldom make appearances in these books, except as the odd flasher.

Predictably, despite the reflexive support of old-fashioned editors and book-reviewers, the Serious Novel is of no actual interest to anyone, including the sort of people who write them: they are apt to read Agatha Christie, if they read at all. But then, this is an old story. In 1859, Nathaniel Hawthorne, having just perpetrated that "moonshiny Romance" (his own phrase) *The Marble Faun,* wrote to his publishers: "It is odd enough, moreover, that my own individual taste is for quite another class of works than those which I myself am able to write." Sensible man, he preferred Trollope to himself. Nevertheless, in a sort of void, Serious Novels continue to be published and praised, but they are not much read.

What is a novel for, if it is *not* to be read? Since the rise of modernism a century ago—is there anything quite as old or as little changed as modern literature?—the notion of the artist as saint and martyr, reviled and ignored in his own time, has had a powerful appeal to many writers and teachers. Echoing Stendhal, the ambitious artist will write not for the people of his own day but for the residents of the next century—on the peculiar ground that the sort of reader who preferred Paul de Kock to Stendhal in the nineteenth century and Barbara Cartland to Iris Murdoch in our own will have developed an exquisite sensibility by the year 2080. These innocents seem not to understand that posterity is a permanent darkness where no whistle sounds. It is reasonable to assume that, by and large, what is not read now will not be read, ever. It is also reasonable to assume that practically nothing that is read now will be read later. Finally, it is not too farfetched to imagine a future in which novels are not read at all. But, for the present, if a Serious Novel is not going to be read, it can always be taught—if it is so made as to be more teacherly than readerly. Further, if the serious student keeps on going to school and acquiring degrees, he will find that not only is his life enhanced by the possession of tools with which to crack the code of rich arcane texts but he will also be able to earn a living by teaching others to teach books written to be taught. Admittedly, none of this has much to do with literature but, as a way of life, it is a lot easier than many other—phrase? Service-oriented Fields.

Although there is no reason why the universities should not take over the Serious Novel and manufacture it right on campus, there are signs that the magistri ludi of Academe are now after more glorious game. Suddenly, simultaneously, on many campuses and in many states, a terrible truth has become self-evident. *The true study of English studies is English studies.* If this truth is true, then the novel can be dispensed with. As our teachers begin to compose their so-called "charters," setting forth powerful new theories of English studies, complete with graphs and startling neologisms, the dream of the truly ambitious schoolteacher will be fulfilled and the interpreter-theorist will replace the creator as culture hero.

Meanwhile, in the real world—take the elevator to the mezzanine, and turn left; you can't miss it—what sort of novels are still read, *voluntarily,* by people who will not be graded on what they have read?

Conglomerate-publishers are a good consumer guide, catering, as they do, to a number of different, not always contiguous publics: Gothic stories, spy thrillers, Harlequin romances . . . each genre has its measurable public. Occasionally, books are written which appear to fit a genre but transcend it because they are works of the imagination, dealing with the past or the future; with alternative worlds. Although these books cannot be truly serious because they are not, literally, *true,* there is no serious American novelist who can write as well or as originally (not a recommendation, perhaps) as John Fowles or William Golding, two English writers whose works are often read outside institutions. Yet neither Fowles nor Golding is taken with any great seriousness by American schoolteachers. Fowles is regarded as a sort of Daphne du Maurier with grammar while Golding is known as the author of a book that the young once fancied—and so was taught in the lower grades. For reasons that have to do with the origins of the United States, Americans will never accept any literature that does not plainly support the prejudices and aspirations of a powerful and bigoted middle class which is now supplementing its powerful churches with equally powerful universities where what is said and thought and imagined is homogenized to a degree that teachers and students do not begin to suspect because they have never set foot outside the cage that they were born in. Like the gorilla who was taught to draw, they keep drawing the bars of their cage; and think it the world.

Historical novels and political novels can never be taken seriously because true history and disturbing politics are not acceptable subjects. Works of high imagination cause unease: if it didn't really happen, how can your story be really *sincere* . . . ? The imaginative writer can never be serious unless, like Mr. Thomas Pynchon, he makes it clear that he is writing about Entropy and the Second Law of Thermodynamics and a number of other subjects that he picked up in his freshman year at Cornell. English teachers without science like this sort of thing while physicists are tempted to write excited letters to literary journals. Thus, the Snow-called gap between the two cultures looks to be bridged, while nothing at all has been disturbed in the way that the society obliges us to see ourselves.

One of the great losses to world literature has been the novel of ideas. Or the symposium-novel. Or the dialogue-novel. Or the. . . . One has to search for some sort of hyphenate even to describe what one has in mind. Mary McCarthy calls it the "conversation novel."

From Aristophanes to Petronius to Lucian to Rabelais to Swift to Voltaire to Thomas Love Peacock, there has been a brilliant line of satirical narratives and had it not been for certain events at the beginning of the nineteenth century in England, this useful form might still be with us, assuming that those who have been brought up on sincere simple Serious Novels would appreciate—or even recognize—any play of wit at the expense of dearly held serious superstitions. Where the True is worshiped, truth is alien. But then to be middle class is to be, by definition, frightened of losing one's place. Traditionally, the virtuous member of the middle class is encouraged to cultivate sincerity and its twin, hypocrisy. The sort of harsh truth-telling that one gets in Aristophanes, say, is not possible in a highly organized zoo like the United States where the best cuts are flung to those who never question the zoo's management. The satirist breaks with his origins; looks at things with a cold eye; says what he means, and mocks those who do not know what *they* mean.

It is significant that the only American writer who might have taken his place in the glittering line was, finally, scared off. Since Mark Twain was not about to lose his audience, he told dumb jokes in public while writing, in private, all sorts of earth-shattering notions. Twain thought that if there was a God, He was evil. Twain's poignant invention, Huck, is a boy who wants to get his ass out of the serious, simple, sincere, bigoted world on whose fringe he was born. He is a lovely, true evocation. But he is in flight; can't cope; knows something is wrong. There is a world elsewhere, he suspects; but there are practically no people in it—it is the territory.

Every quarter century, like clockwork, there is a Peacock revival. The great tail feathers unfurl in all their Pavonian splendor, and like-minded folk delight in the display; and that's the end of that for the next twenty-five years. Although it is now too late in history to revive either Peacock or the conversation novel, Marilyn Butler in *Peacock Displayed* has written an admirable book about a valuable writer.

Thomas Love Peacock was born in 1785; he died in 1866. He was well read in Greek, Latin, French, and Italian literature; he was an early and knowledgeable devotee of opera, particularly Mozart, Rossini, Bellini. Since he did not go to school after the age of twelve, he was able to teach himself what he wanted to know, which was a lot. In 1819, he was taken on by the East India Company where he worked until his retirement in 1856. He associated at India House with James and John Stuart Mill; he was a lifelong friend of Jeremy Bentham and of Byron's friend John Cam Hobhouse. For three years, he was close to Shelley; and got him to read the classics. Peacock's wife went mad while his daughter Mary Ellen married a bearded, dyspeptic, cigarette-smoker—three demerits in Peacock's eyes. George Meredith was less than an ideal son-in-law, particularly at table. Some of Mary Ellen's recipes survive. Ingredients for Athenian Eel and Sauce: "Half a pint of good Stock. One tablespoon of Mushroom Ketchup. One mustard-spoonful of Mustard. One dessert spoonful of Shalot Vinegar. One dessert spoonful of Anchovy Sauce. One dessert spoonful of Worcester Sauce. Marjoram and Parsley." That was just the sauce. Meanwhile, cut the eels in pieces. . . . When Mary Ellen deserted Meredith for the painter Henry Wallis, Meredith's digestive tract must have known a certain relief. Later he memorialized his father-in-law as Dr. Middleton in *The Egoist*. Mary Ellen died young. Despite the deaths of children and a wife's madness, one has the sense that Peacock's long life was happy; but then he was a true Epicurean.

Peacock began as a poet in the didactic Augustan style. He was much interested in politics, as were most of the English writers of the late eighteenth and early nineteenth centuries. Butler is particularly good in setting Peacock firmly in a world of political faction and theorizing. By the time Peacock was of age, the American and French revolutions had happened. The ideas of Rousseau and Paine were everywhere talked of, and writers wrote in order to change society. As a result, what was written was considered more important than who wrote it—or even read it. The writer as his own text was unknown because it was unthinkable, while the writer as sacred monster was not to emerge until mid-century. Ironically, Peacock's idealistic friend Shelley was to be Sacred Monster Number Two. Number One was Byron (who figures as Mr. Cypress in Peacock's *Nightmare Abbey*).

In the first quarter of the century, British intellectual life was mostly Scottish. The *Edinburgh Review*'s chief critic was Francis Jeffrey, a liberal Whig who tended to utilitarianism: to what social end does the work in question contribute? Will it or won't it *do*? This was Jeffrey's narrow but, obviously, useful approach to literature. Peacock was also a utilitarian; and subscribed to his friend Bentham's dictum: "the greatest good of the greatest number." But Peacock regarded the *Edinburgh Review* ("that shallow and dishonest publication") as much too Whiggish and class-bound. Peacock seems always to have known that in England the Whig-versus-Tory debate was essentially hollow because "though there is no censorship of the press, there is an influence widely diffused and mighty in its operation that is almost equivalent to it. The whole scheme of our government is based on influence, and the immense number of genteel persons, who are maintained by the taxes, gives this influence an extent and complication from which few persons are free. They shrink from truth, for it shews those dangers which they dare not face." Thus, in our own day, *The New York Times* reflects the will of the administration at Washington which in turn reflects the will of the moneyed interests. Should a contemporary American writer point out this connection, he will either be ignored or, worse, found guilty of Bad Taste, something that middle-class people are taught at birth forever to eschew.

The debate that helped to shape Peacock (and the century) was between Shelley's father-in-law William Godwin and the Reverend Thomas Malthus. The anarchist Godwin believed in progress; thought human nature perfectible. He believed society could be so ordered that the need for any man to work might be reduced to an hour or two a day. Godwin's *Political Justice* and *The Enquirer* inspired Malthus to write

*An Essay on the Principle of Population,* published in 1798. Everyone knows Malthus's great proposition: "Population, when unchecked, increases in a geometrical ratio. Subsistence increases only in an arithmetical ratio. A slight acquaintance with numbers will show the immensity of the first power in comparison with the second." This proposition is still being argued, as it was for at least two millennia before Malthus. At the time of Confucius, China was underpopulated; yet all ills were ascribed to overpopulation: "When men were few and things were many," went an already ancient saying, "there was a golden age; but now men are many and things are few and misery is man's lot."

In a series of dialogue-novels, Peacock enlarged upon the debate. *Headlong Hall* appeared in 1816. As Butler notes: "Peacock's satires are all centered on a recent controversy large in its ideological implications but also amusingly rich in personality and detail. For its full effect, the satire requires the reader to be in the know." This explains why the form is not apt to be very popular. At any given moment too few people are in the know about much of anything. As time passes, the urgencies of how best to landscape a park—a debate in *Headlong Hall*—quite fades even though the various points of view from romantic to utilitarian are eternal.

Aristophanes made jokes about people who were sitting in the audience at the theatre of Dionysos. When we do know what's being sent up—Socrates' style, say—the bright savagery is exciting. But who is Glaucon? And what did he steal? Happily, most of Peacock's characters (based on Shelley, Byron, Coleridge, Malthus, et al.) are still well enough known to some readers for the jokes to work. More important, the tone of Peacock's sentences is highly pleasing. He writes a stately, balanced prose that moves, always, toward unexpected judgment or revelation.

Peacock begins a review of Thomas Moore's novel *The Epicurean* with: "This volume will, no doubt, be infinitely acceptable to the ladies 'who make the fortune of new books.' Love, very intense; mystery, somewhat recondite; piety, very profound; and philosophy, sufficiently shallow. . . . In the reign of the emperor Valerian, a young Epicurean philosopher is elected chief of that school in the beginning of his twenty-fourth year, a circumstance, the author says, without precedent, and we conceive without probability."

*Melincourt* was published in 1817, starring a truly noble savage, a monkey called Sir Oran Haut-ton. Malthus makes an appearance as Mr. Fax. Sir Oran, though he cannot speak, is elected to Parliament. *Night-*

*mare Abbey* (1818) is a take-off on the cult of melancholy affected, in one way, by Byron (Mr. Cypress) and, in another, by Coleridge (Mr. Flosky). Shelley appears as Scythrop, though Butler makes the point that neither Shelley nor Peacock ever admitted to the likeness. Mr. Cypress has quarreled with his wife; he sees only darkness and misery as man's estate. Peacock works in actual lines from *Childe Harold* to mock if not Byron Byronism, while Mr. Flosky's dialogue is filled with metaphysical conceits that even he cannot unravel. Scythrop is not practical.

Peacock's next two works, *Maid Marian* (1818) and *The Misfortunes of Elphin* (1829), are set, respectively, in the late twelfth century and the sixth century. But Robin Hood's England is used to illuminate Peacock's dim view of the Holy Alliance of his own day while sixth-century Wales is used to savage Wellington's current Tory administration. *Crotchet Castle* (1831) is like the early books in form: culture is the theme. One of the characters is Dr. Folliott, a philistine Tory who mocks those who would improve man's lot. Since Dr. Folliott has been thought to be a voice for his creator, serious critics have tended to dismiss Peacock as a crotchety, unserious hedonist whose tastes are antiquarian and whose political views are irrelevant. Butler takes exception to this; she thinks that Folliott's likeness to his creator "cannot in fact survive a close reading." On education, Folliott advances opinions that were not Peacock's:

I hold that there is every variety of natural capacity from the idiot to Newton and Shakespeare; the mass of mankind, midway between these extremes, being blockheads of different degrees; education leaving them pretty nearly as it found them, with this single difference, that it gives a fixed direction to their stupidity, a sort of incurable wry neck to the thing they call their understanding.

I rather suspect that Peacock, in a certain mood, felt exactly as Dr. Folliott did. He also possessed negative capability to a high degree. In this instance, he may well be saying what he thinks at the moment, perfectly aware that he will think its opposite in relation to a different formulation on the order, say, of certain observations in Jefferson's memoirs which he reviewed in 1830. Peacock was absolutely bowled over by the mellifluous old faker's announcement that between "a government without newspapers, or newspapers without a government" he would choose the latter. This is, surely, one of the silliest statements ever made by a politician; yet it is perennially attractive to—yes, journalists. In any case, Jefferson was sufficiently sly to add, immediately, a line that is seldom quoted by those who love the sentiment: "But I should mean that every man should receive those papers, and be capable of reading them." The last phrase nicely cancels all that has gone before. Jefferson was no leveler.

In any case, the endlessly interesting controversy of who should be taught what and how and why is joined in this bright set of dialogues and every position is advanced. We get the Tory view, as published by the Rev. E. W. Grinfield; he thought that the masses need nothing more than to have religion and morals instilled in them: "We inculcate a strong attachment to the constitution, *such as it now is;* we teach them to love and revere our establishments in Church and State, even *with all their real or supposed imperfections;* and we are far more anxious to make them good and contented citizens, than to fit them for noisy patriots, who would perhaps destroy the constitution whilst pretending to correct it." There, in one sentence, is the principle on which American public education is based (*vide* Frances FitzGerald's *America Revised*).

In opposition to Grinfield is John Stuart Mill:

I thought, that while the higher and richer classes held the power of government, the instruction and improvement of the mass of the people were contrary to the self-interest of those classes, because tending to render the people more powerful for throwing off the yoke; but if the democracy obtained a large, and perhaps the principal share, in the governing power, it would become the interest of the opulent classes to promote their education, in order to ward off really mischievous errors, and especially those which would lead to unjust violations of property.

This has proven to be idealistic. Neither Washington nor Moscow thinks it worthwhile to teach their citizens to address themselves to "real or supposed imperfections" in the system. Rather, to keep the citizens "good and contented" is the perennial aim of powerful governing classes or, as one of Peacock's Tory characters puts it: "Discontent increases with the increase of information."

Five years before Peacock's death at eighty-one, he published the most satisfying of his works (I still don't know what to call them: they are not novels as novels were written then or now, and they are not theatre pieces even though many pages are set up like a playscript), *Gryll*

*Grange.* The subject is everything in general, the uses of the classics in particular. The form is resolutely Pavonian. Each character represents a viewpoint; each makes his argument.

Here is an example of Peacock when he slips into dialogue.

LORD CURRYFIN: Well, then, what say you to the electric telegraph, by which you converse at the distance of thousands of miles? Even across the Atlantic, as no doubt we shall do yet.

MR. GRYLL: Some of us have already heard the Doctor's opinion on the subject.

THE REVEREND DOCTOR OPIMIAN: I have no wish to expedite communication with the Americans. If we could apply the power of electrical repulsion to preserve us from ever hearing anything more of them, I should think that we had for once derived a benefit from science.

MR. GRYLL: Your love for the Americans, Doctor, seems something like that of Cicero's friend Marius for the Greeks. He would not take the nearest road to his villa, because it was called the Greek-road. Perhaps if your nearest way home were called the American-road, you would make a circuit to avoid it.

THE REVEREND DOCTOR OPIMIAN: I am happy to say that I am not put to the test. Magnetism, galvanism, electricity, are "one form of many names." Without magnetism, we should never have discovered America; to which we are indebted for nothing but evil; diseases in the worst form that can afflict humanity, and slavery in the worst form in which slavery can exist. The Old World had the sugarcane and the cotton-plant, though it did not so misuse them. Then, what good have we got from America? What good of any kind, from the whole continent and its islands, from the Esquimaux to Patagonia?

MR. GRYLL: Newfoundland salt fish, Doctor.

THE REVEREND DOCTOR OPIMIAN: That is something, but it does not turn the scale.

MR. GRYLL: If they have given us no good, we have given them none.

THE REVEREND DOCTOR OPIMIAN: We have given them wine and classical literature; but I am afraid Bacchus and Minerva have equally "Scattered their bounty upon barren ground." On the other hand, we have given the red men rum, which has been the chief instrument of their perdition. On the whole, our intercourse with America has been little else than interchange of vices and diseases.

LORD CURRYFIN: Do you count it nothing to have substituted civilized for savage men?

THE REVEREND DOCTOR OPIMIAN: Civilized. The word requires definition. But looking into futurity, it seems to me that the ultimate tendency of the change is to substitute the worse for the better race; the Negro for the Red Indian. The Red Indian will not work for a master. No ill-usage will make him. Herein, he is the noblest specimen of humanity that ever walked the earth. Therefore, the white men exterminate his race. But the time will come, when, by mere force of numbers, the black race will predominate, and exterminate the white.

Mr. Falconer remonstrates that "the white slavery of our [English] factories is not worse than the black slavery of America. We have done so much to amend it, and shall do more. Still much remains to be done." Opimian responds: "And will be done, I hope and believe. The Americans do nothing to amend their system." When Lord Curryfin remarks that he has met many good Americans who think as Doctor Opimian does, the response is serene: "Of that I have no doubt. But I look to public acts and public men."

In the half century between Peacock's first work and his last, the novel was transformed by Dickens and the comedy of character replaced the comedy of ideas. In fact, character—the more prodigious the better—was the novel. In the year of *Gryll Grange* (1860), the novel was about to undergo yet another change with the publication of *The Mill on the Floss.* In the everyday world of George Eliot's characters the play of intelligence is quite unlike that of Peacock, since the only vivid intelligence in an Eliot novel is that of the author or, as Mary McCarthy writes: ". . . the kind of questions her characters put to themselves and to each other, though sometimes lofty, never question basic principles such as the notion of betterment or the inviolability of the moral law."

Elsewhere in *Ideas and the Novel,* McCarthy contrasts Peacock with James. Where James managed to exclude almost everything in the way of ideas from the novel in order to concentrate on getting all the way 'round, as it were (oh, *as it were!*), his made-up characters, "consider Thomas Love Peacock," she writes. "There the ordinary stuff of life is swept away to make room for abstract speculation. That, and just that, is the joke. . . . In hearty, plain-man style (which is partly a simulation),

Peacock treats the brain's sickly products as the end-result of the general disease of modishness for which the remedy would be prolonged exposure to common, garden reality." But that was written of *Nightmare Abbey*: common, garden reality flourishes during the debates in *Gryll Grange,* a book which Butler believes "occupies the same position in Peacock's oeuvre as *The Clouds* in that of Aristophanes: both seem less directly political than usual because the author's approach is oblique and fantastic, almost surreal."

It is fitting that in *Gryll Grange* the characters are composing a comedy in the Aristophanic manner while the book itself is a variation on Old Comedy. Although the tone of this old man's work is highly genial, he still strikes with youthful vigor the negative. He still says no to Romanticism which had, by then, entirely triumphed, and which, not much changed, continues to dominate our own culture.

In a review of C. O. Müller's *A History of the Literature of Ancient Greece,* Peacock explains the value of the negative: "there is much justice in the comparison of Lucian and Voltaire. The view is not only just, it is also eminently liberal. That 'the results of the efforts of both against false religion and false philosophy were merely negative'; that they had 'nothing tangible to substitute for what they destroyed,' is open to observation." Indeed it is. After all, this is the constant complaint of those who support the crimes and injustices of the status quo. Peacock proceeds to observe, "To clear the ground of falsehood is to leave room for the introduction of truth. Lucian decidedly held that moral certainty, a complete code of duty founded on reason, existed in the writings of Epicurus; and Voltaire's theism, the belief in a pervading spirit of good, was clear and consistent throughout. The main object of both was, by sweeping away false dogmas, to teach toleration. Voltaire warred against opinions which sustained themselves by persecution."

Needless to say, there is no more certain way of achieving perfect unpopularity in any society than to speak against the reigning pieties and agreed-upon mendacities. The official line never varies: To be negative is to be bad; to be positive is to be good. In fact, that is even more the rule in our society than it was in Peacock's smaller world where the means to destroy dissent through censorship or ridicule or silence were not as institutionalized as they are now.

Even so, Peacock himself was forced to play a very sly game when he dealt with the Christian dictatorship of England. After giving an admiring account of Epicurus' "favorite dogma of the mortality of the soul," he remarks, "In England, we all believe in the immortality of the

soul" because "the truth of the Christian Religion is too clearly established amongst us to admit of dispute." In his novels, he treated Christianity with great caution. What he really thought of a religion that was
the negation of all that *he* held positive only came to light posthumously.

In 1862, a year after Mary Ellen's death, he sent to the printers a poem
he had written in Greek on Jesus' exuberantly vicious tirade (Matthew
10:34): "Think not that I am come to send peace on earth: I came not
to send peace, but a sword." The executors of Peacock's estate suppressed the poem; and only the last lines survive in translation. A pagan
appears to be exhorting a crowd to "come now in a body and dash in
pieces" this armed enemy, Jesus. "Break in pieces, hurl down him who
is a seller of marvels, him who is hostile to the Graces, and him who
is abominable to Aphrodite, the hater of the marriage bed, this mischievous wonder-worker, this destroyer of the world, CHRIST." There are
times when positive capability must masquerade as negative.

Butler is at her most interesting when she relates Peacock to our own
time where "students of literature are taught to think more highly of
introspection than of objectivity, to isolate works of art from their social
context, and to give them a high and special kind of value." She ascribes
this to "the early nineteenth century irrationalist reaction—Romanticism—[which] is a current movement still. . . . In England at the close
of the Napoleonic Wars, Romanticism was perceived to encourage indifference to contemporary politics, or to offer outright aid to illiberal
governments. A literature that is concerned with style, and with feeling,
rather than with intellect and reason, may be merely decorative; in
relation to practical affairs, it will almost certainly be passive."

One can understand the emphasis that our universities continue to
place on the necessary separation of literature from ideas. "We are
stunned," writes Butler, "by reiteration into believing that what the
world wants is positive thinking. Peacock makes out a case, illustrated
by Voltaire, for negative thinking, and its attendant virtues of challenge,
self-doubt, mutual acceptance, and toleration." Finally, "Since Coleridge we have been fond of the artist-prophet, and the art-work which
is monologue, or confession, or even opium dream. Peacock, whose art
is based on the dialogue, has waited a long time for his turn to be heard."

I don't know how these things are being arranged in Butler's England
but the passive yea-sayer who has no ideas at all about politics, religion,
ethics, history is absolutely central to our syllabus and his only competition is the artist as advertiser of sweet self alone. The culture would not

have it otherwise and so, as McCarthy puts it, "in the place of ideas, images still rule the roost, and Balzac's distinction between the *roman idée* and the *roman imagé* appears to have been prophetic, though his order of preference is reversed."

In *Ideas and the Novel,* McCarthy joins in the battle (assuming that this is not just a skirmish in a byway where the mirror lies shattered). Although McCarthy takes the Pavonian side, she moves beyond Peacock's satiric dialogue-novels to those formidable nineteenth-century novelists to whom ideas are essential and, for her, it is James not Coleridge who is terminus to this line. "When you think of James in the light of his predecessors," she writes, "you are suddenly conscious of what is not there: battles, riots, tempests, sunrises, the sewers of Paris, crime, hunger, the plague, the scaffold, the clergy, but also minute particulars such as you find in Jane Austen—poor Miss Bates's twice-baked apples."

McCarthy is particularly interesting when she examines Victor Hugo, a great novelist doomed to be forever unknown to Americans. She examines Hugo's curious way of staying outside his characters whose "emotions are inferred for us by Victor Hugo and reported in summary form." Hugo deals with ideas on every subject from capital punishment to argot. He is also possessed by an Idea: "The manifest destiny of France to lead and inspire was identified by Hugo with his own mission to the nation as seer and epic novelist." McCarthy's survey of this sort of, admittedly, rare master (Tolstoi, Dostoevsky, Manzoni, Balzac, Stendhal, George Eliot) is illuminating, particularly when she discusses "the ambition to get everything in, to make this book *the* Book," a passion still to be found post-James in Proust and Joyce "Though public spirit as an animating force was no longer evident (in fact the reverse) . . . the ambition to produce a single compendious sacred writing survived, and we may even find it today in an author like Pynchon (*Gravity's Rainbow*)."

It is usual in discussion of the novel (what is it for? what is it?) to point to the displacement that occurred when the film took the novel's place at the center of our culture. What James had removed from the novel in the way of vulgar life, film seized upon: "It was not until the invention of the moving-picture," writes McCarthy, "that the novel lost its supremacy as purveyor of irreality to a multitude composed of solitary units." McCarthy goes on to make the point that "unlike the novel, the moving-picture, at least in my belief, cannot be an idea-spreader; its images are too enigmatic, e.g., Eisenstein's baby carriage bouncing down those stairs in *Potemkin.* A film cannot have a spokesman or chorus character to point the moral as in a stage play; that function is assumed by the camera, which is inarticulate. And the absence of spokesmen in the films we remember shows rather eerily that with the cinema, for the first time, humanity has found a narrative medium that is incapable of thought."

If McCarthy's startling insight is true (I *think* it is), the curious invention by the French of the auteur-theory begins to make a degree of sense. Aware that something was missing in films (a unifying intelligence), M. Bazin and his friends decided that the camera's lens was nothing but a surrogate for the director who held it or guided it or aimed it, just as the painter deploys his brush. For M. Bazin *et cie.,* the director is the unifying intelligence who controls the image and makes sense of the piece: he is The Creator. Needless to say, this perfect misapprehension of the way movies were made in Hollywood's Golden Age has been a source of mirth to those who were there.

The movie-goer is passive, unlike the reader; and one does not hear a creator's voice while watching a movie. Yet, curiously enough, the kind of satire that was practiced by Aristophanes might just find its way onto the screen. As I watched *Airplane!,* I kept hoping that its three auteurs (bright show-biz kids) would open up the farce. Include President Carter and his dread family; show how each would respond to the near-disaster. Add Reagan, Cronkite, the Polish Pope. But the auteurs stuck to the only thing that show-biz people ever know about—other movies and television commercials. Although the result is highly enjoyable, a chance was missed to send up a whole society in a satire of the Old Comedy sort.

At the end of McCarthy's notes on the novel, she looks about for new ways of salvaging a form that has lost its traditional content. She thinks that it might be possible, simply, to go back in time: "If because of ideas and other unfashionable components your novel is going to seem dated, don't be alarmed—date it." She mentions several recent examples of quasi-historical novels; she also notes that "in the U.S.A., a special license has always been granted to the Jewish novel, which is free to juggle ideas in full public; Bellow, Malamud, Philip Roth still avail themselves of the right, which is never conceded to us goys." With all due respect to three interesting writers, they don't use their "concession" with any more skill than we mindless goys. The reason that they sometimes appear to be dealing in ideas is that they arrived post-James. Jewish writers over forty do—or did—comprise a new, not quite American class, more closely connected with ideological, argumentative Europe (and Talmudic studies) than with those of us whose ancestors killed Indians, pursued the white whale, suffered, in varying degrees, etiolation as a result of overexposure to the Master's lesson. In any case, today's young Jewish writers are every bit as lacking in ideas as the goyim.

McCarthy admires Robert Pirsig's *Zen and the Art of Motorcycle Maintenance,* "an American story of a cross-country trip with philosophical interludes." She believes that "if the novel is to be revitalized, maybe more such emergency strategies will have to be employed to disarm and disorient reviewers and teachers of literature, who, as always, are the reader's main foe." They are not the writer's ally either—unless he conforms to their kitsch romantic notions of what writing ought to be or, more to the point, what it must never be.

Although I suspect that it is far too late for emergency strategies, one final tactic that *might* work is to infiltrate the genre forms. To fill them up, stealthily, with ideas, wit, subversive notions: an Agatha Christie plot with well-cut cardboard characters that demonstrated, among other bright subjects, the rise and fall of monetarism in England would be attractive to all sorts of readers and highly useful.

In any case, write what you know will always be excellent advice for those who ought not to write at all. Write what you think, what you imagine, what you suspect: that is the only way out of the dead end of the Serious Novel which so many ambitious people want to write and no one on earth—or even on campus—wants to read.

*The New York Review of Books*
December 4, 1980

# 14

## MEREDITH

"He did the best things best." Henry James's famous epitaph for George Meredith strikes an ominous note. "He was the finest contriver," wrote E. M. Forster, noun carefully chosen to deflate reluctant superlative. Literary critics tend to regard Meredith's novels much the way music critics responded a few years ago to a singer with a three-octave range; absolutely secure in her highest and lowest notes, she lacked nothing save that middle register in which most music is written. Nevertheless, virtuosity of any kind is so rare in the arts that other artists tend to be fascinated by it. In a letter to Stevenson, James refers to Meredith's "charming *accueil,* his impenetrable shining scales, and the (to me) general mystery of his perversity." Charm and glitter; mystery and perversity.

In the Clark Lectures for 1969 V. S. Pritchett (a critic who can usually be counted on to do the good things well) does his best to come to terms with the Meredithean mystery, and in the process says a number of things about the English novel in general, and its comic tradition in particular.

Mr. Pritchett proposes three literary categories: the masculine, the feminine, and the mythic or fantastic. The masculine line is concerned with the life of the town—that is, "the world" in the eighteenth-century sense. Fielding, Scott, Austen, George Eliot "are robust and hard-headed. They know that in the long run feeling must submit to intelligence." The feminine tradition reverses the field. "The disorderly, talkative, fantasticating tradition" of Sterne in which "the 'I' is not a fixture; it dissolves every minute. . . . Not action but inaction, being washed along by the tide is the principle, astonished that we are a form of life." Among the feminine, Peacock, some of Meredith and Dickens, Firbank, Virginia Woolf, Joyce, with Beckett now busily—no, not busily—contriving game's end.

The fantastic or mythic line reflects a shift in emphasis. Town has been replaced by impersonal city. The Great Crowding has begun. Obsession flourishes, and worldly conversation is replaced by solipsistic monologue. Dickens's characters now "speak as if they were the only persons in the world." People "whose inner life was hanging out, so to speak, on their tongues, outside their persons." Mr. Pritchett's categories are nicely drawn and useful if not strictly applied—as Mrs. Woolf once noted, the best writers are androgynes.

Mr. Pritchett examines in some detail *Harry Richmond, The Ordeal of Richard Feverel* (of all English novelists, Meredith wrote morning best), *The Egoist,* and *Beauchamp's Career* ("His by-elections are very real"). Education and ordeal are the recurring themes. "Meredith is above all a novelist of youth and growth; for he accepts with pleasure the conceit, the severity, the aggressiveness and self-encumberedness of young men and women, the uncritical impulses and solemn ambitions."

The technique of the novels is theatrical. A series of carefully staged conflicts provide the ordeal through which the hero must pass if he is to arrive at that clarification and sad wisdom which can only be achieved when all pride and self-delusion are burnt away. But it is not the inventions which give the novels their force, it is Meredith himself. He is constantly at stage center, commenting in a first person altogether too singular upon the narrative, upstaging at will his own bright creations. Yet for those of us who are devotees (interest is now declared), Meredith's energy, wit, comedic invention are not only satisfying but like no one else's.

Also, for those who care about such things, Meredith was an innovator whose "originality lies in rejecting realism and parcelling out events among people's minds." While his "dialogue brings in the modern wave. It is brisk, abrupt, allusive and born to its moment. . . ." Finally, he concerns himself with that ever-valid theme, the crippling aspects of egoism and "the death of heart and sense, in those who feed back a false public image into private life." In this, the Tory-Radical Meredith was responding fiercely to those incorrigible self-lovers, the ruling class of his place and time. Only connect? No, only erupt, he seems to say, and in the bright lava flow, if not a cleansing an illumination.

The legend of Meredith's difficult style has been a formidable and now, one suspects, permanent barrier to that dwindling crew of eccentrics who enjoy reading novels. Yet the famous style is no more demanding than Proust's, simpler than Joyce's, less enervating than Beckett's, and if one makes the effort to submit to its strange rhythm, quite addictive in the end. But despite Mr. Pritchett's efforts it is unlikely that Meredith will ever again be much read except by those solemn embalmers, the Specialists in English Lit., for we live at a chiliastic time when even Cyril Connolly has been forced, he tells us, to give up reading Henry James on the grounds that nowadays one can only cope with a single slow exigent master and his is Proust.

Meredith was always odd bird out in Britain's literary aviary. All plumes and hectic color, he is total Cavalier, and so anathema to those Roundheads who form a permanent majority in the literary worlds of both Atlantic East and Atlantic West. The puritan dislike of show, of wit, of uncommon skill continues as relentlessly today as it did in his own time. But (these "buts" are a feeble attempt at selling Meredith) he had a "young pre-adult heart like Dickens"; also unusual among English writers, he not only liked women, he liked them as equals. His comic creations were of such a high order that Mark Twain stole a pair (The Duke and the Dauphin) from *Harry Richmond* in order to enliven *Huckleberry Finn.* As for Meredith's beautifully concentrated elliptical dialogue, it continues to sound in the work of Ivy Compton-Burnett and her imitators while, according to Mr. Pritchett, ". . . the sardonic and reiterated stress on a single essence in his characters" was an influence on D. H. Lawrence. If nothing else, Meredith is a permanent footnote to the great puritan tradition.

"A very honorable disinterested figure in his old age," wrote Henry James, "and very superior to any other here, in his scorn of the beefy British public and all its vulgarities and brutalities." A century later that beefy public is busy writing most of the novels (though still not reading them) and the great good (yes, often silly) places that those two mandarins so powerfully imagined are casualties of lost empire, class shiftings and, above all, that electronic revolution that has found a new way of peopling the popular imagination with alternative worlds. Mr. Pritchett acknowledges as much and notes that Meredith's highly subjective tone is "not so far from the agitated prose of those modern writers who seem to have sensed that the prose of the future will be heard and seen, and perhaps never read."

As prose fiction stutters into silence, it is possible to look back without sadness (three centuries is quite long enough for any literary form) and note that the imperium James and Meredith dreamed of was just that, a territory translated from the quotidian by a rare combination of will and genius. They knew that literature was (let us use the past tense) never a democracy or even a republic. It was a kingdom, and there for a time ruled George Meredith, the tailor's son whose unique art made him what all of Richmond Roy's con-man's cleverness could not, a king.

*The Times* (London)
May 2, 1970

# 15

## THE BOOKCHAT
## OF HENRY JAMES

On the evening of January 12, 1905, President and Mrs. Theodore Roosevelt held a reception for the diplomatic corps. After the reception, a limited number of grandees were given a dinner; among those so distinguished was Henry James, who was staying across the street at the house of Henry Adams. The reception had been boycotted by Adams himself, who found it impossible to finish a sentence once the voluble president was wound up. But Adams sent over his houseguests, James, John La Farge, and Augustus Saint-Gaudens.

The confrontation between Master and Sovereign contained all the elements of high comedy. Each detested the other. James regarded Roosevelt as "a dangerous and ominous jingo" as well as "the mere monstrous embodiment of unprecedented and resounding noise" while Theodore Rex, as the Adams circle dubbed him, regarded the novelist as "a miserable little snob" and, worse, "effete." As it turned out, snob and jingo were each on his best behavior that night, and James, in a letter to Mary Cadwalader Jones, noted that the president was "a really extraordinary creature for native intensity, veracity and *bonhomie.*" What TR thought of his guest on that occasion is not recorded, but he could never have been approving of James, who had settled in England, had never roughed it, had never ridden, roughly, up Kettle Hill (to be renamed San Juan, since no one could be the hero of anything so homely as a kettle).

But the true high comedy of that January evening was that the two great men were meeting not as literary lion and president but as book reviewer and author reviewed. Seven years earlier, James had given Roosevelt (an indefatigable writer of echoing banality) a very bad review in the English paper *Literature.* Although reviews were not signed in those days, concerned authors could almost always find out who had done them in, and if the wielder of the axe were a writer of James's fame, the secret could never have been kept for long.

James begins, blandly,

Mr. Theodore Roosevelt appears to propose [the first verb is a hint of fun to come]—in *American Ideals and Other Essays Social and Political*—to tighten the screws of the national consciousness as they have never been tightened before. The national consciousness for Mr. Theodore Roosevelt is, moreover, at the best a very fierce affair.

James then suggests that this approach is not only overwrought but vague.

It is "purely as an American," he constantly reminds us, that each of us must live and breathe. Breathing, indeed, is a trifle; it is purely as Americans that we must think, and all that is wanting to the author's demonstration is that he shall give us a receipt for the process. He labours, however . . . under the drollest confusion of mind.

All in all, TR was saintly to put such an un-American reviewer at his dinner table, separated from his own intensely American self by a single (American) lady. Of course, in April 1898, James could not have known that the author, a mere assistant secretary of the Navy, was glory-bound. Yet if he had, the Jamesian irony (so like that of his friends John Hay and Henry Adams, and so deeply deplored, in retrospect, by the president) could not resist serving up such quotes as,

"The politician who cheats or swindles, or the newspaperman who lies in any form, should be made to feel that he is an object of scorn for all honest men." That is luminous; but, none the less, "an educated man must not go into politics as such; he must go in simply as an American . . . or he will be upset by some other American with no education at all . . ." A better way perhaps than to barbarize the upset—already, surely, sufficiently unfortunate—would be to civilize the upsetter.

For James, whatever useful insights that politician Roosevelt might have are undone "by the puerility of his simplifications."

The Library of America has seen fit to publish in one volume all of James's book reviews on American and English writers, as well as a number of other meditations on literature. To read the book straight through (1413 pages of highly uneven bookchat) is to get to know Henry James in a way that no biographer, not even the estimable Leon Edel, the present editor, can ever capture. Here one can study the evolution of James's taste and mind.

As a critic, James began far too young. From age twenty-three to twenty-five, he was reviewing everything that came to hand for the *North American Review* and *The Nation.* He was still an American resident: He did not set out from the territory for old Europe until John Hay, then at the *New York Tribune,* sent him to Paris as a general correspondent (1875–1876). By 1878 he was settled in England, his domicile to the end.

In London, he wrote *French Poets and Novelists,* and a long study of Hawthorne. In 1878, "I had ceased to 'notice' books—that faculty seemed to diminish for me, perversely, as my acquaintance with books grew." Fortunately for the readers of this volume, in 1898 James became a householder. In need of money, he went back to book reviewing for a year or two and produced some of his most interesting pieces. Finally, in 1914, he wrote *The New Novel,* in which he threaded his way, as best he could, among the young Turks—H. G. Wells and Arnold Bennett and (they meet at last! the great tradition) D. H. Lawrence, whose *Sons and Lovers* James remarks "hang(s) in the dusty rear of Wells and Bennett."

There is a lifelong prejudice in James against the slice-of-life novel as opposed to the consciously shaped work of art. (Yet, paradoxically, he is enthralled by Balzac, on whom he was lecturing in 1905.) In that sense, he is the snob that Theodore Rex called him. Although he is most comfortably at home in fairly high society, his true subject is displaced, classless, innocent Americans with money, at sea in old Europe which, at the beginning of his career, he saw as beguiling and dangerous and, at the end, quite the reverse: Old Europe was no match for young America's furious energy and ruthless, mindless exertion of force. But the milieu of *Sons and Lovers* depressed him, as did that of Thomas Hardy, whose village oafs he quotes at length in a review of *Far from the Madding Crowd.*

James, justifiably, hated dialect novels, American or English. Hardy's "inexhaustible faculty for spinning smart dialogue makes him forget that dialogue in a story is after all but episode. . . ." The book "is inordinately diffuse, and, as a piece of narrative, singularly inartistic. The author has little sense of proportion, and almost none of composition." Worse, the book is much too long (this from James the First not yet Old Pretender), thanks to the tradition of the three-volume novel. "Mr. Hardy has gone astray very cleverly, and his superficial novel is a really curious imitation of something better."

Yet with George Eliot, whom he admires, he notes of *Silas Marner,* "Here, as in all George Eliot's books, there is a middle life and a low life; and here, as usual, I prefer the low life." This is James, aged twenty-three, indicating that Eliot does not feel quite at home in middle life much less high life. But twenty years later, a wiser James sums up the great novelist:

What *is* remarkable, extraordinary—and the process remains inscrutable and mysterious—is that this quiet, anxious, sedentary, serious, invalidical English lady, without animal spirits, without adventures or sensations, should have made us believe that nothing in the world was alien to her; should have produced such rich, deep, masterly pictures of the multiform life of man.

In the notorious case of Walt Whitman one can observe James's evolution from disdainful, supercilious, but observant youth to mystified, awed admirer. Of *Drum-Taps* he writes (1865),

It has been a melancholy task to read this book; and it is a still more melancholy one to write about it. . . . It exhibits the effort of an essentially prosaic mind [and] frequent capitals are the only marks of verse in Mr. Whitman's writing . . . As a general principle, we know of no circumstance more likely to impugn a writer's earnestness than the adoption of an anomalous style. He must have something very original to say if none of the old vehicles will carry his thoughts. Of course, he *may* be surprisingly original. Still, presumption is against him. . . . This volume is an offense against art.

He scolds Whitman for crowning himself the national poet: "You cannot entertain and exhibit ideas; but, as we have seen, you are prepared to incarnate them." This was the point, of course, to Whitman; but young James can only groan, "What would be bald nonsense, and dreary platitudes in anyone else becomes sublimity in you." A quarter century later, Whitman has become "the good Walt." Of *Calamus* (Whitman's highly adhesive letters to the working-class lad Pete Doyle): "There is not even by accident a line with a hint of style—it is all flat, familiar, affectionate, illiterate colloquy" yet "the record remains, by a mysterious marvel, a thing positively delightful. If we can ever find out why, it must be another time. The riddle meanwhile is a neat one for the sphinx of democracy to offer." When the riddle was "solved" by Dr. Kinsey in 1948, the Republic had a nervous breakdown, which continues to this day.

One is constantly surprised by the spaciousness of James's sympathies as he got older. In time, the vulgarity of Whitman was seen for what it is, the nation itself made flesh. Edith Wharton in *A Backward Glance* writes,

It was a joy to me to discover that James thought [Whitman] the greatest of American poets. *Leaves of Grass* was put into his hands, and all that evening we sat rapt while he wandered from "The Song of Myself" to "When Lilacs Last in the Dooryard Bloom'd."

On the other hand, no sentiment was ever exempt from his critical irony, and James could not resist exclaiming, at the reading's end, "Oh, yes, a great genius; undoubtedly a very great genius! Only one cannot help deploring his too-extensive acquaintance with foreign languages." Like the late Tennessee Williams, Whitman loved foreign phrases and usually got them wrong.

The fact that one is never told just how James's heroes make their money was neither coyness nor disdain: It was simply a blank, as he confessed in 1898: "Those who know [business] are not the men to paint it; those who might attempt it are not the men who know it." One wonders what his friend the author of *The Rise of Silas Lapham* thought of the alleged absence in our literature of the businessman—of "the magnificent theme *en disponibilité.*"

James was very much interested in "the real world"; and not without a certain shrewdness in political matters. Surprisingly, he reviews in *The*

*Nation* (1875) Charles Nordhoff's *The Communistic Societies of the United States, from Personal Visit and Observation, Etc.,* a book once again in print. Nordhoff was a Prussian-born American journalist who covered the Civil War for the *New York Herald.* In the 1870s, he decided to investigate applied communism in the United States, as demonstrated by the Oneida, Amana, Mount Lebanon, and Shaker groups. "Hitherto," Nordhoff writes, "very little, indeed almost nothing definite and precise, has been made known concerning these societies; and Communism remains loudly but very vaguely spoken of, by friends as well as enemies, and is commonly either a word of terror or contempt in the public prints." *Tout ça change,* as the good Walt might have said.

For over a century, communism has been the necessary enemy of our republic's ruling oligarchy. Yet before 1917, communism was not associated with totalitarianism or Russian imperialism or the iron rule of a *nomenklatura.* Communism was simply an economic theory, having to do with greater efficiency in production as a result of making those who did the work the owners. James grasps this principle rather better than most of his contemporaries, and he commends Nordhoff for his ability to show us

communistic life from the point of view of an adversary to trades-unions, and to see whether in the United States, with their vast area for free experiments in this line, it might not offer a better promise to workingmen than mere coalitions to increase wages and shorten the hours of labor.

Although he thinks Nordhoff (probably a closet German socialist) tends to "dip his pen into rose-color," James is intrigued by the material efficiency of the societies. He is also appalled by their social customs: Some are celibate, some swap mates. "One is struck, throughout Mr. Nordhoff's book, with the existence in human nature of lurking and unsuspected strata, as it were, of asceticism, of the capacity for taking a grim satisfaction in dreariness." Then James adds with characteristic sly irony: "Remember that there are in America many domestic circles in which, as compared with the dreariness of private life, the dreariness of Shakerism seems like boisterous gaiety."

Predictably, James deplores the "attempt to organize and glorify the detestable tendency toward the complete effacement of privacy in life and thought everywhere so rampant with us nowadays." Would that he could move among us today and revel in our government's call for obligatory blood and urine tests. "But [lack of privacy] is the worst fact chronicled in Mr. Nordhoff's volume, which, for the rest, seems to establish fairly that, under certain conditions and with strictly rational hopes, communism in America may be a paying experiment." Now that I have revived these lines, James, already banned in certain public libraries for pornography (*The Turn of the Screw,* what else?), can now be banned as a communist. A small price, all in all, to pay for freedom.

As the complete Henry James is to be republished in the Library of America, it is amusing to read what he has to say of the other novelists in the series, also, more to the point, what he does *not* have to say. For instance, there is no mention of Jack London, whose best work was done before James died in 1916. Although the inner life of a dog in the Arctic Circle might not have appealed to the Master, James might have found a good deal to ponder in *The Sea Wolf* and *The Iron Heel.* Stephen Crane appears in his letters (and his life; he liked him, not her) but there is no reference to Crane anywhere in the flow, the torrent, of names like Alger, Bazley, Channing, Fletcher, Gannett, Sedley, Spofford, Whitney . . .

James's study of Hawthorne is famous; it is also full of evasive high praise: James did not care for romance; yet Hawthorne's one "real" novel, *The Blithedale Romance,* which is not, to me, a romance at all, is to James notable for its "absence of satire . . . of its not aiming in the least at satire." I thought the whole thing a splendid send-up of Brook Farm, and Zenobia a truly comic character. In any case, Hawthorne is the only American novelist to whom James pays full homage.

He does do justice to his friend Howells. He certainly applauds Howells's ability for "definite notation"; yet he doesn't much care for Howells's ladies. But Howells is not writing about the drawing room; he writes about men, work, business. Bartley Hubbard is a splendid invention—the newspaperman as inventor—while the story of Silas Lapham does for the paint business what Balzac so magically did for paper. James (writing for lady readers?) looks elsewhere.

Fenimore Cooper is mentioned, blandly, twice, while Melville is dismissed in the following line: "the charming *Putnam* [magazine] of faraway years—the early fifties . . . the prose, as mild and easy as an Indian summer in the woods, of Herman Melville, of George William Curtis and 'Ik Marvel.' "

Mark Twain, with whom Henry James was forced so titanically to contest in the pages of Van Wyck Brooks (James lost), is mentioned only once: "In the day of Mark Twain there is no harm in being reminded that the absence of drollery may, at a stretch, be compensated by the presence of sublimity." So much for the Redskin Chief from the Paleface Prince. Finally, James praises his friend Mrs. Wharton, with the no longer acceptable but perfectly apt characterization: "of the masculine conclusion tending to crown the feminine observation."

James is on happier ground when dealing with English and French writers. As for the Russians, except for Turgenev, whom he knew, they seem to have made no impression. There is a perfunctory nod to Tolstoi (1914) in a survey of the new novel. Tolstoi is "the great Russian" whose influence can be detected in the world of Wells and Bennett. The name Dostoevsky is added to a list of deliberately disparate writers. Admittedly, by then (1897) James had ceased to be a working reviewer as opposed to being an occasional writer of "London Notes" for *Harper's,* with a tendency "to pass judgment in parenthesis," something he maintained that the critic by him admired, Matthew Arnold, never did.

  Henry James's admiration of the never entirely fashionable and often despised Balzac is to his eternal credit as a critic. On the other hand, his attitude to Flaubert, whom he knew, is very odd indeed. He thought that Flaubert (whom he could see all 'round, he once declared) had produced a single masterpiece; and that was that. He seems not to have got the point to *Sentimental Education,* the first truly "modern novel," which demonstrated for the first time in literature the fact that life is simply drift and though *Bouvard and Pécuchet* is unfinished, the notion is still splendid if droll (James, who was, in life, the essence of drollery, did not much care for levity in the novel, *tant pis*).

  It is always easy to make fun of book reviewers, and what we take now to be, in our superior future time, their mistakes. But he *is* wrong-headed when he writes (1876): "Putting aside Mme. Sand, it is hard to see who among the French purveyors of more or less ingenious fiction, is more accomplished than [M. Octave Feuillet]. There are writers who began with better things—Flaubert, Gustave Droz, and Victor Cherbuliez—but they have lately done worse, whereas Mr. Feuillet never falls below himself." Flaubert had been lately doing such "worse" things as publishing *Sentimental Education* (1869) and *The Temptation of Saint Anthony* (1874), while *Three Tales* would be published the next year. James had read one of them:

Gustave Flaubert has written a story about the devotion of a servant-girl to a parrot, and the production, highly finished as it is, cannot, on the whole, be called a success. We are perfectly free to call it flat, but I think it might have been interesting; and I, for my part, am extremely glad he should have written it; it is a contribution to our knowledge of what can be done—or what cannot. Ivan Turgenev has written a tale about a deaf and dumb serf and a lap-dog, and the thing is touching, loving, a little masterpiece. He struck the note of life where Flaubert missed it—he flew in the face of a presumption and achieved a victory.

James is never on thinner ice than when he goes on about "presumptions," as if the lovely art was nothing but constant presuming. In *The Art of Fiction* (1884), he is more open: "There is no impression of life, no manner of seeing it and feeling it, to which the plan of the novel may not offer a place; you have only to remember that talents so dissimilar as those of Alexander Dumas and Jane Austen, Charles Dickens and Gustave Flaubert have worked in this field with equal glory." *Equal* is not the right word; but *glory* is.

The usually generous James cannot entirely accept Flaubert, the one contemporary writer whose dedication to his art was comparable to his own. Although James goes on and on about the greatness of *Madame Bovary,* he cannot, simultaneously, resist undermining it.

Nothing will ever prevent Flaubert's heroine from having been an extremely minor specimen, even of the possibilities of her own type, a twopenny lady, in truth, of an experience so limited that some of her chords, it is clear, can never be sounded at all. It is a mistake, in other words, to speak of any feminine nature as consummately exhibited, that is exhibited in so small a number of its possible relations. Give it three or four others, we feel moved to say—"then we can talk."

Plainly, Flaubert's version of a "twopenny lady" is not the portrait of a lady of the sort that James could happily "talk" about. I suspect, finally, that James not only did not like Flaubert's writing but that he had serious moral reservations about French literature in general: "There are other subjects," he wrote plaintively, "than those of the eternal triangle of the husband, the wife and the lover." Among critics, James is hardly a master; rather, he is a master of the novel who makes asides that are, often, luminous; as often, not.

In the spring of 1948, I was received in Paris by André Gide at 1 *bis* rue Vaneau. I spent a pleasant hour with the Master and John Lehmann, my English publisher. We talked of literature, of national differences, of changing fashions, of James. Then Gide (the proud translator of Conrad) asked, "What is it that you Americans—and English—see in Henry James?" I could only stammer idiocies in my schoolboy French. Ironically, now, nearly forty years later, I find myself explaining to the young that there was once a famous French writer named André Gide. Fashions change but, as George Santayana remarked, "it would be insufferable if they did not." Each generation has its own likes and dislikes and ignorances.

In our postliterary time, it is hard to believe that once upon a time a life could be devoted to the perfecting of an art form, and that of all the art forms the novel was the most—exigent, to use a modest word. Today the novel is either a commodity that anyone can put together, or it is an artifact, which means nothing or anything or everything, depending on one's literary theory. No longer can it be said of a writer, as James said of Hawthorne in 1905: "The grand sign of being a classic is that when you have 'passed,' as they say at examinations, you have passed; you have become one once for all; you have taken your degree and may be left to the light and the ages." In our exciting world the only light cast is cast by the cathode-ray tube; and the idea of "the ages" is, at best, moot—mute?

*The New York Review of Books*
November 6, 1986

# 16

·

## THE GOLDEN BOWL
## OF HENRY JAMES

**I**

A century ago, Mrs. Henry Adams confided to her diary: "It is high time Harry James was ordered home by his family. He is too good a fellow to be spoiled by injudicious old ladies in London—and in the long run they would like him all the better for knowing and living in his own country. He had better go to Cheyenne and run a hog ranch. The savage notices of his Hawthorne in American papers, all of which he brings me to read, are silly and overshoot the mark in their bitterness, but for all that he had better not hang around Europe much longer if he wants to make a lasting literary reputation." That same year the egregious Bret Harte observed, sadly, that Henry James "looks, acts, thinks like an Englishman and writes like an Englishman."

But the thirty-seven-year-old James was undeterred by public or private charges of un-Americanism; he had every intention of living the rest of a long and productive life in England. Since he was, in the phrase of his older brother William, like all the Jameses a native only of the James family, the Wyoming pig farmer who might have been preferred rooting, as it were (Oh, as it were!—one of his favorite phrases: a challenge to the reader to say, As it were *not*?), for those truffles that are to be found not beneath ancient oak trees in an old country but in his own marvelous and original consciousness, James did nothing like an Englishman—or an American. He was a great fact in himself, a new world, a *terra incognita* that he would devote all his days to mapping for the rest of us. In 1880 James's American critics saw only the fussy bachelor expatriate, growing fat from too much dining out; none detected the sea change that was being undergone by what had been, until then, an essentially realistic American novelist whose subject had been Americans in Europe, of whom the most notorious was one Daisy Miller, eponymous heroine of his first celebrated novel (1878).

But by 1880, James was no longer able—or willing?—to render American characters with the same sureness of touch. For him, the novel must now be something other than the faithful detailing of familiar types engaged in mating rituals against carefully noted backgrounds. Let the Goncourts and the Zolas do that sort of thing. James would go further, much as Flaubert had tried to do; he would take the usual matter of realism and heighten it; and he would try to create something that no writer in English had ever thought it possible to do with a form as inherently loose and malleable as the novel: He would aim at perfection. While James's critics were complaining that he was no longer American and could never be English, James was writing *The Portrait of a Lady,* as nearly perfect a work as a novel can be. From 1881, James was the master of the novel in English in a way that no one had ever been before; or has ever been since. Even that Puritan divine, F. R. Leavis, thought *The Portrait* "one of the great novels of the English language."

Over the next twenty years, as James's novels got longer and longer, they became, simultaneously and oddly, more concentrated. There are fewer and fewer characters (usually Americans in a European setting but Americans at some psychic distance from the great republic) while the backgrounds are barely sketched in. What indeed *are* the spoils of the house Poynton? James never tells us what the "old things" are that mother and son fight for to the death. Balzac would have given us a catalogue, and most novelists would have indicated something other than an impression of a vague interior perfection. As James more and more mastered his curious art, he relied more and more on the thing *not* said for his essential dramas; in the process, the books become somewhat closer to theater than to the novel-tradition that had gone before him. Famously, James made a law of the single viewpoint; and then constantly broke it. In theory, the auctorial "I" of the traditional novel was to be banished so that the story might unfold much like a play except that the interpretation of scenes (in other words, who is thinking what) would be confined to a single observer if not for an entire book, at least for the scene at hand. Although James had sworn to uphold forever his own Draconian law, on the first page of *The Ambassadors*, where we meet Strether, the principal consciousness of the story and the point of view from which events are to be seen and judged, there is a startling interference by the author, Mr. James himself, who states, firmly: "The principle I have just mentioned . . ." Fortunately, no more principles are mentioned by the atavistic "I."

There is the familiar joke about the three styles of Henry James: James the First, James the Second, and the Old Pretender. Yet there are indeed three reigns in the Master's imagined kingdom. James I is the traditional nineteenth-century novelist, busy with the usual comings and goings of the ordinary fiction writer; James II is the disciplined precise realist whose apotheosis is *The Portrait of a Lady*. From 1890 to 1895 there is a break in the royal line: James turns to the theater; and most beautifully fails. Next comes the restoration. James returns in triumph to the novel—still James II (for purposes of simile, Charles II as well); and then, at the end, the third James, the Old Pretender, the magician who, unlike Prospero, breaks not his staff but a golden bowl.

After 1895, there is a new heightening of effect in James's narratives; he has learned from the theater to eliminate the nonessential but, paradoxically, the style becomes more complex. The Old Pretender's elaborateness is due, I should think, to the fact that he had now taken to dictating his novels to a series of typewriter operators. Since James's conversational style was endlessly complex, humorous, unexpected—euphemistic where most people are direct and suddenly precise where avoidance or ellipsis is usual—the last three novels that he produced (*The Ambassadors*, 1903; *The Wings of the Dove*, 1902; and *The Golden Bowl*, 1904) can be said to belong as much to the oral tradition of narrative as to the written.

James was fifty-seven when he started *The Ambassadors* and sixty-one when he completed *The Golden Bowl*. In those five years he experienced a late flowering without precedent among novelists. But then he was more than usually content in his private life. He had moved out of London; and he had established himself at the mayoral Lamb House in Rye. If there is an eternal law of literature, a *pleasant* change of house for a writer will produce an efflorescence. Also, at sixty, James fell in love with a young man named Jocelyn Persse. A charming Anglo-Irish man-about-town, Persse was not at all literary; and somewhat bewildered that James should be in his thrall. But, for James, this attractive young extrovert must have been a great improvement over his predecessor in James's affection, Hendrik Andersen, the handsome sculptor of megalomaniac forms. Andersen had been trouble. Persse was good company: "I rejoice greatly in your breezy, heathery, grousy—and housey, I suppose—adventures and envy you, as always, your exquisite possession of the Art of Life which beats any Art of mine hollow." This "love affair" (with the Master, quotes are always necessary because we lack what Edith Wharton would call the significant data) had a most rejuvenating effect on James, and the first rapturous days with Persse coincided with the period in which he was writing *The Golden Bowl.*

A decade earlier (November 28, 1892) Henry James sketched in his notebook the first design for *The Golden Bowl*: ". . . a father and daughter—an only daughter. The daughter—American of course—is engaged to a young Englishman, and the father, a widower and still youngish, has sought in marriage at exactly the same time an American girl of very much the same age as his daughter. Say he has done it to console himself in his abandonment—to make up for the loss of the daughter, to whom he has been devoted. I see a little tale, *n'est-ce pas?*—in the idea that they all shall have married, as arranged, with this characteristic consequence—that the daughter fails to hold the affections of the young English husband, whose approximate mother-in-law the pretty young second wife of the father will now have become." James then touches upon the commercial aspect of the two marriages: "young Englishman" and "American girl" have each been bought. They had also known each other before but could not marry because each lacked money. Now "they spend as much of their time together as the others do, and for the very reason that the others spend it. The whole situation works in a kind of inevitable rotary way—in what would be called a vicious circle. The *subject* is really the pathetic simplicity and good faith of the father and daughter in their abandonment . . . he peculiarly paternal, she passionately filial." On Saint Valentine's Day 1895, James again adverts to the story which now demands to be written, though he fears "the adulterine element" might be too much for his friend William Dean Howells's *Harper's Magazine.* "But may it not be simply a question of handling that?"

Seven years later, James was shown a present given the Lamb family by King George I: It is a golden bowl. The pieces have now begun to come together. James has just completed, in succession, *The Ambassadors* and *The Wings of the Dove.* Comfortably settled in the garden room at Lamb House (later to be inhabited by E. F. Benson's dread Miss Mapp and then the indomitable Lucia; later still, to be blown up in World War II), James wrote, in slightly more than a year, what he himself described to his American publisher as "distinctly the most done of my productions—the most composed and constructed and completed. . . . I hold the thing the solidest, as yet, of all my fictions." The "as yet" is splendid from a sixty-one-year-old writer. Actually, *The Golden Bowl* was to be the last novel that he lived to complete, and it has about it a kind of spaciousness—and even joy—that the other novels do not possess. In fact, *pace* F. R. Leavis, I do not think James has in any way lost his sense of life or let slip "his moral taste" (what a phrase!).

2

When I first read *The Golden Bowl,* I found Amerigo, the Prince, most sympathetic. I still do. I also found—and find—Charlotte the most sympathetic of the other characters; as a result, I don't think that her creator does her justice or, perhaps, he does her too much conventional justice, as he sentences her to a living death. But then James *appears* to accept entirely the code of the class into which he has placed both himself in life and the characters in his book. This means that the woman must always be made to suffer for sexual transgression while the man suffers not at all or, in the case of the Prince, very little—although the renewed and intensified closeness to Maggie may well be a rarefied punishment that James only hints at when, for the last time, he shuts the door to the golden cage on Husband and Wife Victrix. For once, in James, the heiress has indisputably won; and the other woman, the enchantress, is routed.

I barely noticed Adam Verver the first time I read the book. I saw him as an aged (at forty-seven!) proto–J. Paul Getty, out "to rifle the Golden Isles" in order to memorialize himself with a museum back home—typical tycoon behavior, I thought; and thought no more. But now that he could be my younger brother (and Maggie an exemplary niece), I regard him with new interest—not to mention suspicion. What is he up to? He is plainly sly; and greedy; and although the simultaneous possession and ingestion of confectionary is a recurrent James theme, my God, how this father and daughter manage to both keep and devour the whole great world itself! They buy the handsome Prince, a great name, *palazzi,* the works. They buy the brilliant Charlotte. But they do not know that the two beauties so triumphantly acquired are actually a magnificent pair, destined to be broken up by Maggie when she discovers the truth, and, much as Fanny Assingham smashes the golden bowl into three parts and pedestal, Maggie breaks the adulterine situation into three parts: Amerigo, Charlotte, and Adam (she is, plainly, pedestal). Then, adulterine world destroyed, Maggie sends Adam and Charlotte home to American City at the heart of the great republic.

Best of all, from Maggie's viewpoint, Charlotte does not know for certain even then that Maggie knows all—a real twist to the knife for in a James drama *not* to know is to be the sacrificial lamb. Once Mr. and Mrs. Adam Verver have gone forever, the Prince belongs absolutely to Maggie. One may or may not like Maggie (I don't like what she does or, indeed, what she is) but the resources that she brings to bear, first *to know* and then *to act,* are formidable. Yet there is a mystery in my second experience of the novel which was not present thirty years ago. What, finally, does Adam Verver know? And what, finally, does he do? Certainly father and daughter are so perfectly attuned that neither has to *tell* the other anything at all about the unexpected pair that they have acquired for their museum. But does Maggie lead him? Or does he manage her? Can it be that it is Adam who pulls all the strings, as befits the rich man who has produced a daughter and then bought her—and himself—a life that even he is obliged to admit is somewhat selfish in its perfection?

As one rereads James's lines in his notebook, the essentially rather banal short story that he had in mind has changed into a wonderfully luminous drama in which nothing is quite what it seems while James's pious allusion to the subject as "really the pathetic simplicity and good faith of the father and daughter in their abandonment" is plain nonsense. James is now giving us monsters on a divine scale.

I think the clue to the book is the somewhat, at first glance, over-obvious symbol of the golden bowl. Whatever the king's christening gift was made of, James's golden bowl proves to be made not of gold but of gilded crystal, not at all the same thing; yet the bowl is massy and looks to be gold. The bowl is first seen in a Bloomsbury shop by Charlotte, who wants to buy a wedding present for her friend Maggie. Charlotte cannot afford anything expensive, but then, as she remarks to her lover, Maggie's groom-to-be, " 'She's so modest,' she developed—'she doesn't miss things. I mean if you love her—or, rather, I should say, if she loves you. She lets it go.' " The Prince is puzzled by this use of *let,* one of James's two most potent verbs (the other is *know*): "She lets what—?" Charlotte expatiates on Maggie's loving character. She wants nothing but to be kind to those she believes in: "It's of herself that she asks efforts."

At first the bowl enchants Charlotte. But the shop owner overdoes it when he says that he has been saving it for a special customer. Charlotte knows then that there must be a flaw and says as much. The dealer rises to the challenge: "But if it's something you can't find out, isn't it as good as if it were nothing?" Charlotte wonders how—or if—one can give a present that one knows to be flawed. The dealer suggests that the flaw be noted to the recipient, as a sign of good faith. In any case, the bowl is a piece of solid crystal and crystal, unlike glass, does not break; but it can shatter "on lines and by laws of its own." Charlotte decides that she cannot afford the bowl; she joins Amerigo, who has been waiting for her in the street. He had seen the flaw at once. *"Per Dio,* I'm superstitious! A crack is a crack—and an omen's an omen."

For the moment, that is the end of the bowl itself. But James has now made the golden bowl emblematic, to use a Dickens word, of the relations between the lovers and their legal mates. To all appearances, the world of the two couples is a flawless rare crystal, all of a piece, beautifully gilded with American money. Of the four, the Prince is the first to detect the flaw; and though he wanted no part of the actual bowl, he himself slips easily into that adulterine situation which is the flaw in their lives. Charlotte refused to buy the bowl because she could not, simply, pay the price; yet she accepts the adultery—and pays the ultimate price.

In due course, Maggie acquires the bowl as a present for her father. Although she does not detect the flaw, the dealer believes himself mysteriously honor-bound to come to her house and tell her that the flaw is there. During his confession, he notices photographs of the Prince and Charlotte; tells Maggie that they were in his shop together. Thus, she learns that they knew each other before her marriage and, as she tells Fanny, "They went about together—they're known to have done it. And I don't mean only before—I mean after."

As James's other triumph of knowledge gained through innocence was called *What Maisie Knew,* so this story might easily have been called

*When Maggie Knew.* As the bowl is the symbol of the flawed marriages, so the line: "knowledge, knowledge was a fascination as well as a fear," stands as a sort of motto to this variation on one of our race's earliest stories, Adam and Eve and the forbidden fruit of knowledge which, once plucked, let the first human couple know both the joys of sex and the pain of its shadow, death. But if James was echoing in his last novel one of the first of all our stories, something is missing: the serpent-tempter. Is it Adam Verver? Or is he too passive to be so deliberate an agent? Actually, the shop owner is the agent of knowledge; but he is peripheral to the legend. Fanny Assingham has something slightly serpentine about her. Certainly, she is always in the know, but she is without malice. In fact, she prefers people *not* to know, and so she makes the splendid gesture of smashing the bowl and, presumably, the knowledge that the bowl has brought Maggie. But it is too late for that. Maggie moves into action. She sets out to rid herself of Charlotte because "I want a happiness without a hole in it. . . . The golden bowl—as it *was* to have been."

In the first of a series of splendid confrontations, Maggie tells the Prince that she knows. He, in turn, asks if Adam knows. "Find out for yourself!" she answers. Maggie is now having, as James colloquially puts it, "the time of her life—she knew it by the perpetual throb of this sense of possession, which was almost too violent either to recognize or to hide." Again, "possession." When the suspicious Charlotte confronts her in the garden (of Eden?) at Fawns, Maggie lies superbly; and keeps her enemy in ignorance, a worse state—for her—than even the United States. Finally, Maggie's great scene with her father is significant for what is not said. No word is spoken by either against Charlotte; nor is there any hint that all is not well with Amerigo and Maggie. But James's images of Maggie and Adam together in the garden—again the garden at Fawns (from the Latin *fons*: spring or source?)—are those of a husband and wife at the end or the beginning of some momentous change in their estate. The images are deliberately and precisely marital: "They were husband and wife—oh, so immensely!—as regards other persons." The reference here is to house party guests but the implication is that "other persons" include her husband and his wife. They speak of their social position and its ambiguities, of the changes that their marriages have made. She is a princess. He is the husband of a great lady of fashion. They speak of the beauty and selfishness of their old life.

Maggie remarks of her husband that "I'm selfish, so to speak, *for* him." Maggie's aria on the nature of jealousy (dependent in direct ratio on the degree of love expended) is somewhat mystifying because she may "seem often not to know quite *where* I am." But Adam appears to know exactly where he is: "I guess I've never been jealous." Maggie affirms that that is because he is "beyond everything. Nothing can pull *you* down." To which Adam responds, "Well, then, we make a pair. We're all right." Maggie reflects on the notion of sacrifice in love. The ambiguities are thick in the prose: Does she mean, at one point, the Prince or Charlotte or Adam himself? But when she says, "I sacrifice you," all the lines of the drama cross and, as they do, so great is the tension that James switches the point of view in mid-scene from daughter to father as James must, for an instant, glimpse Adam's response to this declaration: "He had said to himself, 'She'll break down and name Amerigo; she'll say it's to him she's sacrificing me; and it's by what that will give me—with so many other things too—that my suspicion will be clinched.' " Actually, this is supposed to be Maggie's view of what her father senses, but James has simply abandoned her in mid-consciousness for the source of her power, the father-consort. How Adam now acts will determine her future. He does not let her down. In fact, he is "practically *offering* himself, pressing himself upon her, as a sacrifice . . ." The deed is done. He will take Charlotte back to American City. He will leave the field to Maggie.

Adam has been sacrificed. But has he? This is the question that reverberates. Maggie finds herself adoring him for his stillness and his power; and for the fact "that he was always, marvellously, young—which couldn't but crown, at this juncture, his whole appeal to her imagination." She gives him the ultimate accolade: "I believe in you more than anyone." They are again as one, this superbly monstrous couple. "His hands came out, and while her own took them he drew her to his breast and held her. He held her hard and kept her long, and she let herself go; but it was an embrace that august and almost stern, produced, for its intimacy, no revulsion and broke into no inconsequence of tears."

Where Maggie leaves off and Adam begins is not answered. Certainly, incest—a true Jamesian "horror"—hovers about the two of them, though in a work as delicately balanced as this the sweaty deed itself seems irrelevant and unlikely. It is enough that two splendid monsters have triumphed yet again over everyone else and, best of all, over mere human nature. But then Maggie contains, literally, the old Adam. He is progenitor; and the first cause; *fons.*

It is Adam who places Charlotte in her cage—a favorite Jamesian image; now James adds the image of a noose and silken cord by which Adam leads her wherever he chooses—in this case to the great republic of which Fanny observes to Maggie: "I see the long miles of ocean and the dreadful great country, State after State—which have never seemed to me so big or so terrible. I see *them* at last, day by day and step by step, at the far end—and I see them never come back." It is as if a beautiful, wealthy, American young woman of today were doomed to spend her life entirely in London. But the victorious Maggie believes that Charlotte will probably find life back home "interesting" while she and her father are the real losers because they are now forever parted. But Fanny is on to her. Fanny gets Maggie to confess that what was done not only suits her ("I let him go") but was indeed no more than the successful execution of Adam's master plan: "Mrs. Assingham hesitated, but at last her bravery flared. 'Why not call it then frankly his complete success?' " Maggie agrees that that is all that is left for her to do.

At the end, Adam has brought together Maggie and Amerigo. James now throws all the switches in the last paragraph:

[Amerigo] tried, too clearly, to please her—to meet her in her own way; but with the result only that, close to her, her face kept before him, his hands holding her shoulders, his whole act enclosing her, he presently echoed: " 'See'? I see nothing *but* you." And the truth of it had, with this force, after a moment, so strangely lighted his eyes that, as for pity and dread of them, she buried her own in his breast.

The golden cage has shut on them both. She is both jailer and prisoner. She is both august and stern. In the book's last line the change of the word *dread* to *awe* would have made the story a tragedy. But James has aimed at something else—another and higher state for the novel (for life, too, that poor imitation of art with its inevitable human flaw): He has made gods of his characters; and turned them all to gold.

Years earlier, when James first saw the gilded Galerie d'Apollon in the palace of the Louvre, he had "an immense hallucination," a sense of cosmic consciousness; and over the years he often said that he could, all in all, take quite a lot of gold. At the end of Henry James's life, in a final delirium, he thought that he was the Emperor Napoleon; and as the Emperor, he gave detailed instructions for the redoing of the Tuileries and the Louvre: and died, head aswarm with golden and imperial visions. Fortunately, he had lived long enough to make for us *The Golden Bowl*, a work whose spirit is not imperial so much as it is ambitiously divine.

# 17
·

# *LOGAN PEARSALL SMITH*
# *LOVES THE ADVERB*

Should the human race survive the twentieth of those wondrous centuries since shepherds quaked at the sight of God's birth in a Middle Eastern stable (all in all, a bad career move), our century will be noted more for what we managed to lose along the way than for what we acquired. Although the physical sciences took off, literally, and some rightly stuffed American men with nothing much to say lurched about the moon, sublunary population was allowed to get out of control to such an extent that much of the earth's good land was covered with cement in order to house the new arrivals while the waters of the globe are now so poisoned that on the just and the unjust alike pale acid rain everywhere softly falls. As we get more people, we lose "amenities" of every sort.

The century that began with a golden age in all the arts (or at least the golden twilight of one) is ending not so much without art as without the idea of art, while the written culture that was the core of every educational system since the fifth century B.C. is now being replaced by sounds and images electronically transmitted. As human society abandoned the oral tradition for the written text, the written culture is giving way to an audiovisual one. This is a radical change, to say the least, and none of us knows quite how to respond. Obviously the change cannot be all bad. On the other hand, what is to become of that written language which was for two millennia wisdom's only mold? What is to become of the priests of literature, as their temples are abandoned? What happens to the work of (now one strikes plangently the diminuendo!) Logan Pearsall Smith?

It is startling to think that someone like Pearsall Smith actually lived most of his life in our century. Entirely possessed by the idea of literature, Logan was besotted with language and "the lovely art of writing." As a result, he spent almost as much time searching for the right unhackneyed adjective to describe the moon (one of whose Latin names is Trivia) as any of that body's recent callers spent in getting there. He even belonged to something called the Society for Pure English, surely long since dispersed, along with its objective. Yet he was not a pedant; he believed in "Idiom before Grammar." Finally, like so many of us, in old age, Logan fell in love—with the adverb.

There is something heroic in all this. There is also something beautifully irrelevant to a culture where the idea of literature is being erased by the word processor while even its memory is less than green in the minds of those proud schoolteachers who are currently charting for themselves vast cosmogonies of words and signs in the vacuum of Academe. Logan actually thought that there was such a thing as good—even fine—writing. Today hardly anyone knows the difference between good and bad prose while those who do know had better keep quiet about it: Literary excellence is not only undemocratic but tends to subvert teacherly texts.

Logan Pearsall Smith was born October 18, 1865, the son of a wealthy Philadelphia Quaker who, rather abruptly, left the family glass business and became an evangelist, preaching the Higher Life. Then, as abruptly, inspired by venery, he quit preaching. Logan's mother became—and remained—a writer of best-selling uplifting books. Logan lost his own faith at eleven—vanished while up a cherry tree, he said. But he remained to the end of his days a Quaker at heart, modest, self-aware, self-mocking. Happily, he was as hard on others as on himself.

England delighted in the Smiths; and they in England. The family settled there. In due course, one daughter married Bertrand Russell; another married Bernard Berenson. One niece married Virginia Woolf's brother; another niece married Lytton Strachey's brother. After Harvard and Oxford, Logan married literature and lived happily ever after, with occasional lapses into a kind of madness, the inevitable fate of one who has been denied not only the word processor but the Apple home computer in which to encode Thoughts.

As a young man, Logan had known and delighted in Walt Whitman of nearby Camden, New Jersey (described in Logan's memoir *Unforgotten Years,* 1939); but most of his life was spent in England, where he worshipped Henry James; knew Bernard Shaw and the Webbs; was related to Bloomsbury. Since Logan had an income, he could follow his own literary pursuits: making anthologies of Milton and Shakespeare and Jeremy Taylor; collecting aphorisms by others; making up his own. He was a favorite of those, like James, whom he regarded as masters. He was less favorably regarded by others. Mrs. Woolf was actually unkind about Uncle Logan. But Logan held his own. He confessed, in a letter to her (November 2, 1932): "I may have mocked at Bloomsbury because mockery is my favorite pastime, and also perhaps (to take a darker view into that dark cabinet, the human heart) because I was not admitted to its conclaves." But then, he sweetly added, "I know from my own feeling how justly critics resent criticism, and mockers being mocked."

In 1913 Logan became a British subject. On March 2, 1946, he died and his former secretary, Cyril Connolly, wrote in *The New Statesman*: "Two weeks before his death a friend asked him half jokingly if he had discovered any meaning in life. 'Yes,' he replied, 'there is a meaning; at least for me, there is one thing that matters—to set a chime of words tinkling in the minds of a few fastidious people.' "

Logan devoted his life to getting his own sentences right. Edmund Wilson did not think he always succeeded; "in spite of his cult of writing . . . he [never] became a real master. His prose is rather pale and dead." But the Anglophobe Wilson was not well disposed toward the Anglophilic Logan. Later, Wilson came to see the virtue of Logan the miniaturist, the creator of *Trivia.*

A lover of language, Logan was always on the lookout for sentences, phrases, *aperçus, pensées* (he found fascinating the fact that the last two words have no English equivalents); he delighted in the splendors of seventeenth-century English prose, particularly that of Jeremy Taylor. He wrote appreciatively of Montaigne, De Sévigné, and Sainte-Beuve. But he was at his best when he wrote of "fine writing" and the works of the English aphorists.

As a writer, Logan himself was very much school of America's own (now seldom read) Emerson who was at *his* best in "the detached—and the detachable—sentence." Logan quotes Emerson on literature (in *English Aphorists*): "People do not deserve to have good writing, they

are so pleased with the bad." And, "In every work of genius we recognize our own rejected thoughts; they come back to us with a certain
alienated majesty." And, of course, "Poets are not to be seen."

During the years that Logan was writing about other people's writing
and collecting other writers' phrases, he was himself working on his own
library of miniature portraits, narratives, descriptions, and other
"trivia." (In 1755 Samuel Johnson nicely defined the word *trivial* as
"vile, worthless, vulgar, such as may be picked up in the highway.")
Logan saw himself as the latest in a line that extends in French from
La Rochefoucauld's *Maximes* and Pascal's *Pensées* to Jules Renard's
notebooks ("I find that when I do not think of myself I do not think at
all"). In English the line begins with Bacon and includes Chesterfield,
Blake, Hazlitt, Emerson. Just what it is these writers do is hard to
explain in English because we lack the words—in itself something of a
giveaway. These sharp thrusts are not really maxims or wisecracks or
thoughts; yet they are often indistinguishable from them. At one point,
Logan uses the word "illuminations"; and he notes that for those
"whom the spectacle of life as it is, stripped of its illusions, possesses an
inexhaustible fascination, for such students of human nature there will
always be a great attraction in these profound X-rays of observation,
which reveal the bones beneath the flesh; these acute and penetrating
phrases which puncture man's pretensions and bring him disenflated to
the earth."

Logan Pearsall Smith joined the glittering line in 1902 when he published, privately, a truly slender volume, *Trivia,* "from the papers of one
Anthony Woodhouse." He thought a pseudonym necessary. So did
Mother. "It is certainly very quaint and interesting," wrote Hannah
Smith, "but it is what I would suppose would be called very 'precious,'
as it begins nowhere and ends nowhere and leads to nothing." The
terminus that Hannah Smith could not see in her son's work was, of
course, perfection—a matter of no consequence to a believer in the
Higher Life. Fifteen years later, Constable republished *Trivia,* and its
author became agreeably if not enormously famous on both sides of the
Atlantic. In 1921 he published *More Trivia;* then came *Afterthoughts*
and, in 1933, all of his illuminations were gathered into one volume, *All
Trivia* (containing the never-before-published *Last Words*).

When *Unforgotten Years* was distributed by the Book-of-the-Month
Club in 1939, Logan became popular. Although he liked to quote Aristippus of Cyrene ("I am taken by these things, but they do not take me
in"), he was delighted. In 1895, Henry James had warned him that

loneliness was the dedicated artist's lot. Now Logan was taken up by a new generation of writers and remembered anew by an old generation of hostesses or, as he wrote one of the former, Hugh Trevor-Roper (June 26, 1941): "I will admit a weakness for one cup of poison, that of social success, whose flavor, as far as I have tasted it, is delicious and which I have never known anyone resist to whom it has been proffered. *Power* is, I believe, even more poisonous and more delicious, but that I have never tasted."

But despite sprigs of laurel and windfall checks, he kept on writing and reading, "miscellaneously," more or less well served by a series of secretaries, of whom the most celebrated was Cyril Connolly and the most aggrieved Robert Gathorne-Hardy, later his biographer. Logan himself never ceased to serve the English language and its literature. In 1924, when the seventeen-year-old Dwight Macdonald wrote him an admiring letter about *Trivia,* Logan responded: ". . . I don't think I had any natural gift for writing. But the art of prose, unlike that of poetry, is one that can be learnt." Also, "the amused observation of one's own self is a veritable gold mine whose surface has hardly yet been scratched." In 1945, he wrote Trevor-Roper, "My life has been spent in mooning over that little book [*All Trivia*], as it was my fantastic daydream to write a little book which should live on after my own unregretted departure."

Edmund Wilson came around in 1950: "I always used to think *Trivia* overrated. A certain amount of it, to be sure; and yet there *is* something in it, something dry, independent, even tough. There are things which one took in at a glance when one first picked up the book and looked through it, and yet which ever since have stuck in one's mind . . . in dealing with incidents frankly infinitesimal [four *in*'s in six lines is a record, Mr. Wilson], somehow succeeds in [a fifth!] being impressively truthful . . ."

The French have a phrase, *l'esprit de l'escalier,* which means, literally, "the wit of the staircase," referring to all those marvelous things that you did *not* say at the party which now occur to you as you descend the staircase en route to the exit. Fortunately, Logan saw to it that his own staircase-musings were not only polished highly but memorialized for all time. Whatever he may or may not have said at the party, he certainly had ample time to get it right on the stairs.

For what is now close to forty years a number of Logan's lines or anecdotes or volumes-in-miniature have stuck in my mind. "The Ear-Trumpet," for instance. At table, a deaf lady asks Logan to repeat a phrase he has too proudly let drop, which is, to his horror, as he booms it over and over again, "the interstices of their lives." This story later reverberated for me in a Washington, D.C., drawing room when a deaf lady asked a solemn man his name and he replied, solemnly, "I am Senator Bourke C. Hickenlooper of Iowa." She then asked him to repeat his name, which he did. "Now I have it!" she said at last. "How deaf I've become!" She gave a contented laugh. "And to think that I thought that you said your name was Senator Bourke C. Hickenlooper of Iowa." Thus, Logan chimes for me down the radioactive dusted corridors of the twentieth century.

To the extent that there will always be a few voluntary readers, Logan ought always to have some of them. *All Trivia* is a whole library in miniature. He retells legends and composes entire novels and biographies in a page while producing eternal wisdom as well as life-enhancing malice in a series of phrases: "Those who set out to serve both God and Mammon soon discover that there is no God," or "If you want to be thought a liar, always tell the truth." Logan has also written if not his urn burial his demitasse burial when he contemplates his world as posterity is apt to see it: "a dusty set of old waxworks simpering inanely in the lumber-room of Time." But then, as he comments in *English Aphorists,* "On the whole [the aphorists] are a malicious lot; their object is not to extricate man from the mire of his condition, but rather to roll him more deeply in it. So much do they enjoy fishing in muddy waters, that they are not unwilling to pursue their sport even in their own bosoms." He made fun of himself; he also made fun of those critics who disliked fine writing, pointing out that they have nothing to fear from it, since "the fever of perfection is not catching. . . ." In any case, "If you write badly about good writing, however profound may be your convictions or emphatic your expressions of them, your style has a tiresome trick (as a wit once pointed out) of whispering 'Don't listen!' in your reader's ear."

Presciently, Logan feared the insect world and its possible analogy to ours. "I hate . . . their cold intelligence; their stereotyped, unremitting industry repels me." Long before the DNA code was discovered, Logan feared a predetermined universe where "we are forced like the insects and can't help it, to undergo all the metamorphoses preordained for our species." But this laconic master is making me garrulous. Read him and hear the chimes at two minutes, or whatever it is, to midnight. Listen.

*The New York Review of Books*
March 29, 1984

# 18

◆

# WILLIAM DEAN HOWELLS

I

On May 1, 1886, American workers in general and Chicago's workers in particular decided that the eight-hour workday was an idea whose time had come. Workers demonstrated, and a number of factories were struck. Management responded in kind. At McCormick Reaper strikers were replaced by "scabs." On May 3, when the scabs left the factory at the end of a long traditional workday, they were mobbed by the strikers. Chicago's police promptly opened fire and America's gilded age looked to be cracking open.

The next night, in Haymarket Square, the anarchists held a meeting presided over by the mayor of Chicago. A thousand workers listened to many thousands of highly incendiary words. But all was orderly until His Honor went home; then the police "dispersed" the meeting with that tact which has ever marked Hog City's law-enforcement officers. At one point, someone (never identified) threw a bomb; a number of policemen and workers were killed or wounded. Subsequently, there were numerous arrests and in-depth grillings.

Finally, more or less at random, eight men were indicted for "conspiracy to murder." There was no hard evidence of any kind. One man was

not even in town that day while another was home playing cards. By
and large, the great conservative Republic felt no compassion for anarchists, even the ones who had taken up the revolutionary game of bridge;
worse, an eight-hour workday would drive a stake through the economy's heart.

On August 20, a prejudiced judge and jury found seven of the eight
men guilty of murder in the first degree; the eighth man (who had not
been in town that night) got fifteen years in the slammer because he had
a big mouth. The anarchists' counsel, Judge Roger A. Pryor, then
appealed the verdict to the Supreme Court.

During the short hot summer of 1886, the case was much discussed. The
peculiar arbitrariness of condemning to death men whom no one had
seen commit a crime but who had been heard, at one time or another,
to use "incendiary and seditious language" was duly noted in bookish
circles. Yet no intellectual of the slightest national importance spoke up.
Of America's famous men of letters, Mark Twain maintained his habitual silence on any issue where he might, even for an instant, lose the love
of the folks. Henry James was in London, somewhat shaken by the
recent failure of not only *The Bostonians* but *The Princess Casamassima*.
The sad young man of *The Princess Casamassima* is an anarchist, who
has had, like James himself that year, "more news of life than he knew
what to do with." Although Henry Adams's education was being conducted that summer in Japan, he had made, the previous year, an
interesting comment on the American political system—or lack of one:

Where no real principle divides us . . . some queer mechanical balance holds
the two parties even, so that changes of great numbers of voters leave no
trace in the sum total. I suspect the law will someday be formulated that
in democratic societies, parties tend to an equilibrium.

As the original entropy man, Adams had to explain, somehow, the
election of the Democrat Grover Cleveland in 1884, after a quarter-
century of Republican abolitionist virtue and exuberant greed.

Of the Republic's major literary and intellectual figures (the division
was not so clearly drawn then between town, as it were, and gown), only
one took a public stand. At forty-nine, William Dean Howells was the
author of that year's charming "realistic" novel, *Indian Summer;* he
was also easily the busiest and smoothest of America's men of letters.
Years before, he had come out of Ohio to conquer the world of litera-

ture; and had succeeded. He had been the first outlander to be editor
of the *Atlantic Monthly.* In the year of the Haymarket Square riot, he
had shifted the literary capital of the country from Boston to New York
when he took over *Harper's Monthly,* for which he wrote a column
called "The Editor's Study"; and a thousand other things as well. That
summer Howells had been reading Tolstoi. In fact, Tolstoi was making
a socialist out of him; and Howells was appalled by Chicago's judge,
jury, and press. He was also turning out his column, a hasty affair by
his own best standards but positively lapidary by ours.

In the September 1886 issue of *Harper's,* Howells, who had done so
much to bring Turgenev and Tolstoi to the attention of American
readers, decided to do the same for Dostoevsky, whose *Crime and
Punishment* was then available only in a French translation. Since Howells had left school at fifteen, he had been able to become very learned
indeed. He had taught himself Latin and Greek; learned Spanish, German, Italian, and French. He read many books in many languages, and
he knew many things. He also wrote many books; and many of those
books are of the first rank. He was different from us. Look at Dean run!
Look at Dean read! Look-say what Dean writes!
  While the Haymarket Square riots were causing Howells to question
the basis of the American "democracy," he was describing a Russian
writer who had been arrested for what he had written and sent off to
Siberia where he was taken out to be shot but not shot—the kind of fun
still to be found to this very day south of our borders where the dominoes roam. As Howells proceeded most shrewdly to explain Dostoevsky
to American readers, he rather absently dynamited his own reputation
for the next century. Although he admired Dostoevsky's art, he could
find little similarity between the officially happy, shadowless United
States and the dark Byzantine cruelties of czarist Russia:

It is one of the reflections suggested by Dostoevsky's book that whoever
struck a note so profoundly tragic in American fiction would do a false and
mistaken thing. . . . Whatever their deserts, very few American novelists
have been led out to be shot, or finally expelled to the rigors of a winter at
Duluth. . . . We invite our novelists, therefore, to concern themselves with
the more smiling aspects of life, which are the more American, and to seek
the universal in the individual rather than the social interests. It is worth
while even at the risk of being called commonplace, to be true to our
well-to-do actualities.

This was meant to be a plea for realism. But it sounded like an invitation to ignore the sort of thing that was happening in Chicago. Ironists are often inadvertent victims of their own irony.

On November 2, 1887, the Supreme Court denied the anarchists' appeal. On November 4, Howells canvased his literary peers. What to do? The dedicated abolitionist of thirty years earlier, George William Curtis, whose lecture *Political Infidelity* was a touchstone of political virtue, and the noble John Greenleaf Whittier agreed that something must be done; but they were damned if they were going to do it. So the belletrist who had just enjoined the nation's scribblers to address themselves to the smiling aspects of a near-perfect land hurled his own grenade at the courts.

In an open letter to the *New York Tribune* (published with deep reluctance by the ineffable Whitelaw Reid) Howells addressed all right-thinking persons to join with him in petitioning the governor of Illinois to commute the sentences. No respectable American man of letters had taken on the American system since Thomas Paine, who was neither American nor respectable. Of the Supreme Court, Howells wrote, it "simply affirmed the legality of the forms under which the Chicago court proceeded; it did not affirm the propriety of trying for murder men fairly indictable for conspiracy alone . . ." The men had been originally convicted of "constructive conspiracy to commit murder," a star-chamberish offense, based on their fiery language, and never proved to be relevant to the actual events in Haymarket Square. In any case, he made the point that the Supreme Court

by no means approved the principle of punishing them because of their frantic opinions, for a crime which they were not shown to have committed. The justice or injustice of their sentence was not before the highest tribunal of our law, and unhappily could not be got there. That question must remain for history, which judges the judgment of courts, to deal with; and I, for one, cannot doubt what the decision of history will be.

Howells said that the remaining few days before the men were executed should be used to persuade the governor to show mercy. In the course of the next week the national press attacked Howells, which is what the American system has a national press for.

On November 11, four of the men, wearing what looked like surgical gowns, were hanged. Of the others, one had committed suicide and two had had their sentences commuted. On November 12, Howells, undaunted by the national hysteria now directed as much against him as against the enemies of property, wrote another public letter:

It seems of course almost a pity to mix a note of regret with the hymn of thanksgiving for blood growing up from thousands of newspapers all over the land this morning; but I reflect that though I write amidst this joyful noise, my letter cannot reach the public before Monday at the earliest, and cannot therefore be regarded as an indecent interruption of the Te Deum.

By that time journalism will not have ceased, but history will have at least begun. All over the world where civilized men can think and feel, they are even now asking themselves, For what, really, did those four men die so bravely? Why did one other die so miserably? Next week the journalistic theory that they died so because they were desperate murderers will have grown even more insufficient than it is now for the minds and hearts of dispassionate inquirers, and history will make the answer to which she must adhere for all time, *They died in the prime of the first Republic the world has ever known, for their opinions' sake* [original emphasis].

Howells then proceeds to make the case against the state's attorney general and the judge and the shrieking press. It is a devastating attack: "I have wished to deal with facts. One of these is that we had a political execution in Chicago yesterday. The sooner we realize this, the better for us." As polemic, Howells's letter is more devastating and eloquent than Emile Zola's *J'accuse;* as a defense of the right to express unpopular opinions, it is the equal of what we mistakenly take to be the thrust of Milton's *Areopagitica.*

Unfortunately, the letter was not published in the year 1887. Eventually, the manuscript was found in an envelope addressed to Whitelaw Reid. The piece had been revised three times. It is possible that a copy had been sent to Reid who had not published it; it is possible that Howells had had second thoughts about the possibilities of libel actions from judge and state's attorney general; it is possible that he was scared off by the general outcry against him. After all, he had not only a great career to worry about but an ill wife and a dying daughter. Whatever the reason, Howells let his great moment slip by. Even so, the letter-not-sent reveals a powerful mind affronted by "one of those spasms of paroxysmal righteousness to which our Anglo-Saxon race is peculiarly subject . . ." He also grimly notes that this "trial by passion, by terror, by prejudice, by hate, by newspaper" had ended with a result that has won "the approval of the entire nation."

I suspect that the cautious lifetime careerist advised the Tolstoian socialist to cool it. Howells was in enough trouble already. After all, he was the most successful magazine editor in the country; he was a best-selling novelist. He could not afford to lose a public made up mostly of ladies. So he was heard no more on the subject. But at least he, alone of the country's writers, had asked, publicly, on November 4, 1887, that justice be done.

Howells, a master of irony, would no doubt have found ironic in the extreme his subsequent reputation as a synonym for middle-brow pusil-lanimity. After all, it was he who was the spiritual father of Dreiser (whom he did nothing for, curiously enough) and of Stephen Crane and Harold Frederic and Frank Norris, for whom he did a very great deal. He managed to be the friend and confidant of both Henry James and Mark Twain, quite a trick. He himself wrote a half-dozen of the Republic's best novels. He was learned, witty, and generous.

Howells lived far too long. Shortly before his death at the age of eighty-four, he wrote his old friend Henry James: "I am comparatively a dead cult with my statues cut down and the grass growing over me in the pale moonlight." By then he had been dismissed by the likes of Sinclair Lewis as a dully beaming happy writer. But then Lewis knew as little of the American literary near-past as today's writers know, say, of Lewis. If Lewis had read Howells at all, he would have detected in the work of this American realist a darkness sufficiently sable for even the most lost-and-found of literary generations or, as Howells wrote James two years after the Haymarket Square riots: "After fifty years of optimistic content with 'civilization' and its ability to come out all right in the end, I now abhor it, and feel that it is coming out all wrong in the end unless it bases itself on a real equality." What that last phrase means is any-one's guess. He is a spiritual rather than a practical socialist. It is interesting that the letter was written in the same year that Edward Bellamy's *Looking Backward: 2000–1887* was published. The ideas of Robert Owen that Howells had absorbed from his father (later a Swe-denborgian like Henry James, Sr.) were now commingled with the theories of Henry George, the tracts of William Morris, and, always, Tolstoi. Howells thought that there must be a path through the political jungle of a republic that had just hanged four men for their opinions; he never found it. But as a novelist he was making a path for himself and for others, and he called it realism.

2

On Thanksgiving Day 1858, the twenty-one-year-old Howells was received at the court of the nineteen-year-old first lady of Ohio, Kate Chase, a handsome ambitious motherless girl who acted as hostess to her father the governor, Salmon P. Chase, a handsome ambitious wifeless man who was, in Abraham Lincoln's thoughtful phrase, "on the subject of the Presidency, a little insane."

Howells had grown up in Ohio; his father was an itinerant newspaper editor and publisher. He himself was a trained printer as well as an ambitious but not insane poet. Under the influence of Heine, he wrote a number of poems; one was published in the *Atlantic Monthly*. He was big in Cleveland. Howells and Kate got on well; she teased him for his social awkwardness; he charmed her as he charmed almost everyone. Although he wrote about the doings of the Ohio legislature for the Cincinnati *Gazette,* he preferred the company of cultivated ladies to that of politicians. A passionate autodidact, he tended to prefer the company of books to people. But through Kate he met future presidents and was served at table by his first butler.

In a sense the Chase connection was the making of Howells. When Lincoln won the Republican presidential nomination in 1860, Howells was chosen, somewhat improbably, to write a campaign biography of the candidate. Characteristically, Howells sent a friend to Springfield to chat with the subject of his book; he himself never met Lincoln. He then cobbled together a book that Lincoln did not think too bad. One suspects that he did not think it too good, either. Shortly before the president was shot, he withdrew the book for the second time from the Library of Congress: nice that he did not have a copy of it on the coffee table in the Blue Room, but then Lincoln was so unlike, in so many ways, our own recent sovereigns.

Once Lincoln was president, Chase became secretary of the treasury. Chase proposed that the campaign biographer be rewarded with a consulate. But nothing happened until Howells himself went to Washington where he found an ally in Lincoln's very young and highly literary second secretary, John Hay, who, with the first secretary, John Nicolay, finally got Howells the consulate at Venice.

It is odd to think that a writer as curiously American as Howells should have been shaped by the Most Serene Republic at a bad moment in that ancient polity's history—the Austrian occupation—rather than by the United States at the most dramatic moment in that polity's history: the Civil War. Odd, also, that Howells managed, like the other two major writers of his generation, to stay out of the war. Neither Mark Twain nor Henry James rushed to the colors.

Since Howells had practically no official work to do, he learned Italian and perfected his German and French. He turned out poems that did not get printed in the *Atlantic*. "Not one of the MSS you have sent us," wrote the editor, "swims our seas." So Howells went off the deep end, into prose. He wrote Venetian sketches of great charm; he was always to be a good—even original—travel writer. Where the previous generation of Irving and Hawthorne had tended to love far too dearly a ruined castle wall, Howells gave the reader not only the accustomed romantic wall but the laundry drying on it, too. The Boston *Advertiser* published him.

Then came the turning point, as Howells termed it, in his life. He had acquired a charming if garrulous wife, who talked even more than Mark Twain's wife, or as Twain put it, when Elinor Howells entered a room "dialogue ceased and monologue inherited its assets and continued the business at the old stand." Howells wrote a serious study of the Italian theater called "Recent Italian Comedy," which he sent to the *North American Review*, the most prestigious of American papers, coedited by his friend James Russell Lowell and Charles Eliot Norton. At the time, Boston and Cambridge were in the throes of advanced Italophilia. Longfellow was translating Dante; and all the ladies spoke of Michelangelo. Lowell accepted the essay. Howells was now on his way, as a *serious* writer.

After nearly four years in Venice, which he did not much care for, Howells returned to New York. With a book of sketches called *Venetian Life* at the printers, he went job hunting. He was promptly hired by E. L. Godkin to help edit *The Nation*. Not long after, he was hired by the *Atlantic Monthly* as assistant to the editor; then from 1871 to 1881 he was editor in chief. In Boston, Howells was now at the heart of an American literary establishment which had no way of knowing that what looked to be eternal noon was actually Indian summer—for New England.

Just before Howells had gone to Venice, he had made the rounds of New England's literary personages. He had met Holmes and Hawthorne whom he had liked; and Emerson whom he had not. Now, at the *Atlantic*, every distinguished writer came his editorial way; and soon he himself would be one of them. But what sort of writer was he to be? Poetry was plainly not his métier. Journalism was always easy for him, but he was ambitious. That left the novel, an art form which was not yet entirely "right." The American product of the 1860s was even less "aesthetic" than the English and neither was up to the French, who were, alas, sexually vicious, or to the Russians, who were still largely untranslated except for the Paris-based Turgenev. At this interesting moment, Howells had one advantage denied his contemporaries, always excepting Henry James. He could read—and he had read—the new Europeans in the original. He went to school to Zola and Flaubert. Realism was in the European air, but how much reality could Americans endure? Out of the tension between the adventurousness of Flaubert and the edgy reticence of Hawthorne came the novels of William Dean Howells.

From Heine, Howells had learned the power of the plain style. Mark Twain had also learned the same lesson—from life. Whereas the previous generation of Melville and Hawthorne had inclined to elevated, even "poetic" prose, Twain and Howells and James the First were relatively straightforward in their prose and quotidian in their effects—no fauns with pointed ears need apply. In fact, when Howells first met Hawthorne, he shyly pointed to a copy of *The Blithedale Romance* and told the great man that that was his own favorite of the master's works. Hawthorne appeared pleased; and said, "The Germans like it, too."

But realism, for Howells, had its limits. He had grown up in a happy if somewhat uncertain environment: His father was constantly changing jobs, houses, religions. For a writer, Howells himself was more than usually a dedicated hypochondriac whose adolescence was shadowed by the certainty that he had contracted rabies which would surface in time to kill him at sixteen. Like most serious hypochondriacs, he enjoyed full rude health until he was eighty. But there were nervous collapses. Also, early in life, Howells had developed a deep aversion to sexual irregularity, which meant any form of sexuality outside marriage. When his mother befriended a knocked-up seamstress, the twelve-year-old Howells refused to pass her so much as the salt at table.

In Venice he could not get over the fact that there could be no social intercourse of any kind with unmarried girls (unlike the fun to be had with The American Girl, soon to be celebrated not only by Henry James but by Howells himself), while every married woman seemed bent on flinging even the purest of young bachelors into the sack. Doubtless, he kept himself chaste until marriage. But he railed a good deal against European decadence, to the amusement of the instinctively more worldly, if perhaps less operative Henry ("Oh, my aching back!") James, who used to tease him about the latest descriptions of whorehouses to be found in French fiction. Nevertheless, for a writer who was to remain an influence well into the twentieth century, an aversion to irregular sexuality was not apt to endear him to a later generation which, once it could put sex into the novel, proceeded to leave out almost everything else. Where the late-nineteenth-century realistic novel might be said to deal with social climbing, the twentieth-century novel has dealt with sexual climbing, an activity rather easier to do than to write about.

The Library of America now brings us four of Howells's novels written between 1875 and 1886. Before the publications of these four novels, Howells had already published his first novel *Their Wedding Journey* (1871); his second novel *A Chance Acquaintance* (1873); as well as sketches of Italy, people, and yet another personage. Elinor Mead Howells was a cousin of President Rutherford (known to all good Democrats as Rather-fraud) B. Hayes. So the campaign biographer of Lincoln, duly and dutifully and dully, wrote a book called *Sketch of the Life and Character of Rutherford B. Hayes* (1876). Thanks to Cousin Hayes, Howells was now able to reward those who had helped him. James Russell Lowell was sent to London as American ambassador.

Of the books written before *A Foregone Conclusion* (the first of the four now reissued), the ever-polite but never fraudulent Turgenev wrote Howells in 1874:

Accept my best thanks for the gracious gift of your delightful book *Their Wedding Journey,* which I have read with the same pleasure experienced before in reading *A Chance Acquaintance* and *Venetian Life.* Your literary physiognomy is a most sympathetic one; it is natural, simple and clear— and in the same time—it is full of unobtrusive poetry and fine humor. Then—I feel the peculiar American stamp on it—and that is not one of the least causes of my relishing so much your works.

This was written in English. In a sense, Turgenev is responding to Howells's championing of his own work (Howells had reviewed *Lisa* and *Rudin*) but he is also responding to a sympathetic confrere, a young writer whom he has influenced though not so much as has "the peculiar American stamp." Unfortunately, Turgenev never lived to read the later books. It would be interesting to see what he might have made of *A Modern Instance,* a book as dark and, at times, as melodramatic as a novel by Zola whose *L'Assommoir* Turgenev disliked.

. . .

*A Foregone Conclusion* (1875) has, as protagonist, the—what else?—
American consul at Venice. The consul is a painter (young writers
almost always make their protagonists artists who practice the one art
that they themselves know nothing about: It's the light, you see, in
Cimabue). The consul attracts a young priest, Don Ippolito, who wants
to emigrate to America and become an inventor. It is no accident that
practically the first building in Washington to be completed in imperial
marble splendor was the Patent Office. Don Ippolito is a sort of Italian
Major Hoople. The inventions don't really work but he keeps on because
"Heaven only knows what kind of inventor's Utopia our poor, patent-
ridden country appeared to him in those dreams of his, and I can but
dimly figure it to myself." Here the auctorial "I" masquerades as the
"I" of the consul, Ferris, who is otherwise presented in the objective
third person. Howells has not entirely learned Turgenev's lesson: stay
out of the narrative. Let the characters move the narration and the
reader. Howells's native American garrulousness—and tendentious-
ness—occasionally breaks in.

Enter, inexorably, middle-aged American lady and daughter—Mrs.
Vervain and Florida. This was four years before Howells's friend sicked
*Daisy Miller* on to a ravished world. But then The American Girl was
to be a Howells theme, just as it was to be James's and, later, and in a
much tougher way, Mrs. Wharton's. As every writer then knew, the
readers of novels were mostly women, and they liked to read about the
vicissitudes of young women, preferably ladies. But while James would
eventually transmute his American girls into something that Euripides
himself might find homely (e.g., Maggie Verver), Howells tends, gently,
to mock. Incidentally, I do not believe that it has ever before been noted
that the portrait of Florida is uncannily like Kate Chase.

It is a foregone conclusion that American girl and American mother
("the most extraordinary combination of perfect fool and perfect lady
I ever saw") will miss the point to Don Ippolito and Venice and Europe,
and that he will miss the point to them. Don Ippolito falls in love with
Florida. The Americans are horrified. How can a priest sworn to celibacy . . . ? Since they are Protestants, the enormity of his fall from
Roman Catholic grace is all the greater. Although Don Ippolito is
perfectly happy to give up the Church, they will not let him. Mother
and daughter flee. As for Ferris, he has misunderstood not only Don
Ippolito but Florida's response to him. Don Ippolito dies—with the
comment to Ferris, "You would never see me as I was."

The consul goes home to the States and joins the army. Like so many
other characters in the works of those writers who managed to stay out
of the Civil War, Ferris has a splendid war: "Ferris's regiment was sent
to a part of the southwest where he saw a good deal of fighting and fever
and ague" (probably a lot easier than trying to get a job at the *Atlantic*).
"At the end of two years, spent alternately in the field and the hospital,
he was riding out near the camp one morning in unusual spirits, when
two men in butternut fired at him: one had the mortification to miss him;
the bullet of the other struck him in the arm. There was talk of amputa-
tion at first . . ." Pre-dictaphone and word processor, it was every
writer's nightmare that he lose his writing arm. But, worse, Ferris is a
painter: *he can never crosshatch again.* Broke, at a loose end, he shows
an old picture at an exhibition. Florida sees the picture. They are reunited. Mrs. Vervain is dead. Florida is rich. Ferris is poor. What is to
be done?

It is here that the avant-garde realism of Howells shoves forward the
whole art of the popular American novel: "It was fortunate for Ferris,
since he could not work, that she had money; in exalted moments he
had thought this a barrier to their marriage; yet he could not recall
anyone who had refused the hand of a beautiful girl because of the
accident of her wealth, and in the end, he silenced his scruples." This
is highly satisfying.

Then Howells, perhaps a bit nervous at just how far he has gone in
the direction of realism, tosses a bone of marzipan to the lady-reader:
"It might be said that in many other ways he was not her equal; but one
ought to reflect how very few men are worthy of their wives in any
sense." Sighs of relief from many a hammock and boudoir! How well
he knows the human heart.

Howells smiles at the end; but the smile is aslant, while the point to
the tragedy (not Ferris's for he had none, but that of Don Ippolito) is
that, during the subsequent years of Ferris's marriage, Don Ippolito
"has at last ceased to be even the memory of a man with a passionate
love and a mortal sorrow. Perhaps this final effect in the mind of him
who has realized the happiness of which the poor priest vainly dreamed
is not the least tragic phase of the tragedy of Don Ippolito."

This coda is unexpectedly harsh—and not at all smiling. A priest
ought not to fall in love. It is a foregone conclusion that if you violate
the rules governing sexuality, society will get you, as Mrs. Wharton
would demonstrate so much more subtly in *The Age of Innocence;* and

Henry James would subtly deny since he knew, in a way that Howells did not, that the forbidden cake could be both safely eaten and kept. It is an odd irony that the donnée on which James based *The Ambassadors* was a remark that the fifty-seven-year-old Howells made to a friend in Paris: No matter what, one ought to have one's life; that it was too late for him, personally, but for someone young . . . "Don't, at any rate, make *my* mistake," Howells said. "Live!"

Kenneth S. Lynn has put the case, persuasively to my mind, that the "happy endings" of so many of Howells's novels are deliberately "hollow or ironic. After all, it was Howells who had fashioned the, to Edith Wharton, "lapidary phrase": Americans want tragedies with happy endings. There are times when Howells's conclusion—let's end with a marriage and live happily ever after—carry more formidable weight than the sometimes too-lacquered tragic codas of James: "We shall never be again as we were." The fact is that people are almost always exactly as they were and they will be so again and again, given half a chance.

At forty-four, the highly experienced man of letters began his most ambitious novel, *A Modern Instance.* Although the story starts in a New England village, the drama is acted out in the Boston of Howells's professional life, and the very unusual protagonist is a newspaperman on the make who charms everyone and hoodwinks a few; he also puts on too much weight, steals another man's story, and makes suffer the innocent young village heiress whom he marries. In a sense, Howells is sending himself up; or some dark side of himself. Although Bartley Hubbard is nowhere in Howells's class as a writer, much less standard-bearer for Western civilization, he is a man who gets what he wants through personal charm, hard work, and the ability to write recklessly and scandalously for newspapers in a way that the young William Randolph Hearst would capitalize on at century's end, thus making possible today's antipodean "popular" press, currently best exemplified by London's giggly newspapers.

Unlike Howells, or the Howells that we think we know, Bartley is sexually active; he is not about to make the Howells-Strether mistake. He *lives* until he is murdered by a man whom he may have libeled in a western newspaper. It would have been more convincing if an angry husband had been responsible for doing him in, but there were conventions that Howells felt obliged to observe, as his detractors, among them

Leslie Fielder, like to remind us. Mr. Fiedler writes in *Love and Death in the American Novel* (1975):

Only in *A Modern Instance,* written in 1882 [*sic*: 1881], does Howells deal for once with a radically unhappy marriage; and here he adapts the genteel-sentimental pattern which had substituted the bad husband (his Bartley Hubbard has "no more moral nature than a baseball") for the Seducer, the long-suffering wife for the Persecuted Maiden or fallen woman.

Mr. Fiedler, of course, is—or was in 1960—deeply into "the reality of dream and nightmare, fantasy and fear," and for him Howells is "the author of flawlessly polite, high-minded, well-written studies of un-tragic, essentially eventless life in New England—the antiseptic upper-middlebrow romance. Yet his forty books [*sic*: he means novels, of which Howells wrote thirty-five; there are close to one hundred books], in which there are no seductions and only rare moments of violence, are too restrictedly 'realistic', too . . . ," *et cetera.*

Mr. Fiedler gets himself a bit off the hook by putting those quotes around the word realistic. After all, Howells had developed an aesthetic of the novel: and if he preferred to shoot Bartley offstage, why not? The classic tragedians did the same. He also inclined to Turgenev's view that the real drama is in the usual. Obviously, this is not the way of the romantic writer but it is a no less valid way of apprehending reality than that of Melville or Faulkner, two writers Howells would have called "romancers," about as much a term of compliment with him as "too unrestrictedly 'realistic' " is to Mr. Fiedler. Without rehashing the tired Redskin versus Paleface debate of the 1940s, it should be noted that there is something wrong with a critical bias that insists upon, above all else, "dream and nightmare, fantasy and fear" but then when faced with the genuine article in, say, the books of William Burroughs or James Purdy or Paul Bowles starts to back off, nervously, lighting candles to The Family and all the other life-enhancing if unsmiling aspects of American life that do *not* cause AIDS or social unrest.

Whatever our romantic critics may say, Bartley Hubbard is an arche-typal American figure, caught for the first time by Howells: the amiable, easygoing bastard, who thinks nothing of taking what belongs to an-other. Certainly Mark Twain experienced the shock of recognition when he read the book: "You didn't intend Bartley for me but he *is* me just the same . . ." James, more literary, thought the character derived from

Tito, in the one (to me) close-to-bad novel of George Eliot, *Romola.* In later years Howells said that he himself was the model. Who was what makes no difference. There is only one Bartley Hubbard, and he appears for the first time in the pages of a remarkable novel that opened the way to Dreiser and to all those other realists who were to see the United States plain. The fact that there are no overt sexual scenes in Howells ("no palpitating divans," as he put it) does not mean that sexual passion is not a powerful motor to many of the situations, as in life. On the other hand, the fact that there are other motors—ambition, greed, love of power—simply extends the author's range and makes him more interesting to read than most writers.

In this novel, Howells is interesting on the rise of journalism as a "serious" occupation. "There had not yet begun to be that talk of journalism as a profession which has since prevailed with our collegians . . ." There is also a crucial drunk scene in which Bartley blots his copybook with Boston; not to mention with his wife. It is curious how often Howells shows a protagonist who gets disastrously drunk and starts then to fall. Mark Twain had a dark suspicion that Howells always had *him* in mind when he wrote these scenes. But for Mr. Fiedler, "drunkenness is used as a chief symbol for the husband's betrayal of the wife." Arguably, it would have been better (and certainly more manly) if Bartley had cornholed the Irish maid in full view of wife and child, but would a scene so powerful, even *existential,* add in any way to the delicate moral balances that Howells is trying to make?

After all, Howells is illuminating a new character in American fiction, if not life, who, as "he wrote more than ever in the paper . . . discovered in himself that dual life, of which every one who sins or sorrows is sooner or later aware: that strange separation of the intellectual activity from the suffering of the soul, by which the mind toils on in a sort of ironical indifference to the pangs that wring the heart; the realization that in some ways his brain can get on perfectly well without his conscience." This is worthy of the author of *Sentimental Education;* it is also the kind of insight about post-Christian man that Flaubert so often adverted to, indirectly, in his own novels and head-on in his letters.

*The Rise of Silas Lapham* (1885) begins with Bartley Hubbard brought back to life. It is, obviously, some years earlier than the end of *A Modern Instance.* Bartley is interviewing a self-made man called Silas Lapham who has made a fortune out of paint. Lapham is the familiar diamond in the rough, New England Jonathan style. He has two pretty daughters, a sensible wife, a comfortable house; and a growing fortune, faced with all the usual hazards. Howells makes the paint business quite as interesting as Balzac made paper making. This is not entirely a full-hearted compliment to either; nevertheless, each is a novelist fascinated by the way the real world works; and each makes it interesting to read about.

In a sense, Silas Lapham's rise is not unlike that of William Dean Howells: from a small town to Boston back street to Beacon Street on the Back Bay. But en route to the great address there are many lesser houses and Howells is at his best when he goes house hunting—and building. In fact, one suspects that, like Edith Wharton later, he would have made a splendid architect and interior decorator. In a fine comic scene, a tactful architect (plainly the author himself) guides Lapham to Good Taste. " 'Of course,' resumed the architect, 'I know there has been a great craze for black walnut. But it's an ugly wood . . .' " All over the United States there must have been feminine gasps as stricken eyes were raised from the page to focus on the middle distance where quantities of once-beauteous black shone dully by gaslight; but worse was to come: " '. . . and for a drawing room there is really nothing like white paint. We should want to introduce a little gold here and there. Perhaps we might run a painted frieze round under the cornice—garlands of roses on a gold ground; it would tell wonderfully in a white room.' " From that moment on, no more was black walnut seen again in the parlors of the Republic, while the sale of white paint soared; gold, too.

The rise of Lapham's house on Beacon Hill is, in a sense, the plot of the book, as well as the obvious symbol of worldly success. Howells makes us see and feel and smell the house as it slowly takes shape. Simultaneously, a young man called Tom Corey wants to work for Lapham. Since Corey belongs to the old patriciate, Lapham finds it hard to believe Corey is serious. But the young man is sincere; he really likes the old man. He must also work to live. There are romantic exchanges between him and the two daughters; there is an amiable mix-up. Finally, Tom says that it is Penelope not her sister whom he wants to marry. Mr. and Mrs. Lapham are bemused. In the world of the Coreys they are a proto–Maggie and Jiggs couple.

Corey takes Lapham to a grand dinner party where the old man gets drunk and chats rather too much. It is the same scene, in a sense, as Bartley's fall in the earlier novel, but where Bartley could not have minded less the impression he made, Lapham is deeply humiliated; and the fall begins. He loses his money; the new house burns down; by then, the house is an even more poignant character than Lapham, and the reader mourns the white-and-gold drawing room gone to ash. But there is a happy enough ending. Maggie and Jiggs return to the Vermont village of their origin (which they should never have left?) while Corey marries Penelope.

It would be easy to point out traits in Penelope's character which finally reconciled all her husband's family and endeared her to them. These things continually happen in novels; and the Coreys, as they had always promised themselves to do, made the best, and not the worst, of Tom's marriage. . . . But the differences remained uneffaced, if not uneffaceable, between the Coreys and Tom Corey's wife.

The young couple move from Boston. Then Howells shifts from the specific to the general:

It is certain that our manners and customs go for more in life than our qualities. The price that we pay for civilization is the fine yet impassable differentiation of these. Perhaps we pay too much; but it will not be possible to persuade those who have the difference in their favor that this is so. They may be right; and at any rate the blank misgiving, the recurring sense of disappointment to which the young people's departure left the Coreys is to be considered. That was the end of their son and brother for them; they felt that; and they were not mean or unamiable people.

This strikes me as a subtle and wise reading of the world—no, not *a* world but *the* world; and quite the equal of James or Hardy.

Whether or not this sort of careful social reading is still of interest to the few people who read novels voluntarily is not really relevant. But then today's "serious" novel, when it is not reinventing itself as an artifact of words and signs, seldom deals with the world at all. One is no longer shown a businessman making money or his wife climbing up or down the social ladder. As most of our novelists now teach school, they tend to tell us what it is like to be a schoolteacher, and since schoolteachers have been taught to teach others to write only about what they know, they tell us what they know about, too, which is next to nothing about the way the rest of the population of the Republic lives.

In a sense, if they are realists, they are acting in good faith. If you don't know something about the paint business you had better not choose a protagonist who manufactures paint. Today, if the son of an Ohio newspaper editor would like to be a novelist, he would not quit school at fifteen to become a printer, and then learn six languages and do his best to read all the great literary figures of the present as well as of the past so that he could introduce, say, Barthes or Gadda to the American public while writing his own novels based on a close scrutiny of as many classes of society as he can get to know. Rather, he would graduate from high school; go on to a university and take a creative writing course; get an M.A. for having submitted a novel (about the son of an Ohio editor who grew up in a small town *and found out about sex* and wants to be a writer and so goes to a university where he submits, etc.).

Then, if he is truly serious about a truly serious literary career, he will become a teacher. With luck, he will obtain tenure. In the summers and on sabbatical, he will write novels that others like himself will want to teach just as he, obligingly, teaches their novels. He will visit other campuses as a lecturer and he will talk about his books and about those books written by other teachers to an audience made up of ambitious young people who intend to write novels to be taught by one another to the rising generation and so on and on. What tends to be left out of these works is the world. World gone, no voluntary readers. No voluntary readers, no literature—only creative writing courses and English studies, activities marginal (to put it tactfully) to civilization.

3

Civilization was very much on Howells's mind when he came to write *Indian Summer* (1886). He deals, once more, with Americans in Italy. But this time there are no Don Ippolitos. The principals are all Americans in Florence. A middle-aged man, Theodore Colville, meets, again, Mrs. Bowen, a lady who once did not marry him when he wanted to marry her. She married a congressman. She has a young daughter, Effie. She is a widow.

Colville started life as an architect, a suitable occupation for a Howells character; then he shifted to newspaper publishing, an equally suitable profession. In Des Vaches, Indiana, he published, successfully, the *Democrat-Republican* newspaper. Although he lost a race for Congress, he has received from former political opponents "fulsome" praise. Like most American writers Howells never learned the meaning of the word *fulsome.* Colville then sold his newspaper and went to Europe because "he wanted to get away, to get far away, and with the abrupt and total change in his humor he reverted to a period in his life when journalism and politics and the ambition of Congress were things undreamed of." He had been young in Italy, with a Ruskinian interest in architecture; he had loved and been rejected by Evelina—now the widow Bowen. He looks at Florence: "It is a city superficially so well known that it affects one somewhat like a collection of views of itself: they are from the most striking points, of course, but one has examined them before, and is disposed to be critical of them." The same goes for people one has known when young.

Mrs. Bowen has a beautiful young friend named Imogene. Colville decides that he is in love with Imogene, and they drift toward marriage. There are numerous misunderstandings. Finally, it is Mrs. Bowen not Imogene who is in love with Colville. The drama of the three of them (a shadowy young clergyman named Morton is an undelineated fourth) is rendered beautifully. There are many unanticipated turns to what could easily have been a simpleminded romantic novella.

When Colville is confronted with the thought of his own great age (forty-one), he is told by a very old American expatriate:

At forty, one has still a great part of youth before him—perhaps the richest and sweetest part. By that time the turmoil of ideas and sensations is over; we see clearly and feel consciously. We are in a sort of quiet in which we peacefully enjoy. We have enlarged our perspective sufficiently to perceive things in their true proportion and relation; we are no longer tormented with the lurking fear of death, which darkens and imbitters our earlier years; we have got into the habit of life; we have often been ailing and we have not died . . .

Finally, "we are put into the world to be of it." Thus, Howells strikes the Tolstoian note. Yes, he is also smiling. But even as *Indian Summer* was being published, its author was attacking the state of Illinois for the murder of four workmen. He also sends himself up in the pages of his own novel. A Mrs. Amsden finds Colville and Imogene and Effie together after an emotional storm. Mrs. Amsden remarks that they form an interesting, even dramatic group:

"Oh, call us a passage from a modern novel," suggested Colville, "if you're in a romantic mood. One of Mr. James's."

"Don't you think we ought to be rather more of the great world for that? I hardly feel up to Mr. James. I should have said Howells. Only nothing happens in that case."

For this beguiling modesty Howells no doubt dug even deeper the
grave for his reputation. How can an American novelist who is ironic
about himself ever be great? In a nation that has developed to a high
art advertising, the creator who refuses to advertise himself is immediately suspected of having no product worth selling. Actually, Howells
is fascinated with the interior drama of his characters, and quite a lot
happens—to the reader as well as to the characters who are, finally,
suitably paired: Imogene and Mr. Morton, Colville and Mrs. Bowen.

The Library of America has served William Dean Howells well.
Although the spiritual father of the library, Edmund Wilson, did not
want this project ever to fall into the hands of the Modern Language
Association, all four of the novels in the present volume bear the proud
emblem of that association. One can only assume that there are now
fewer scholars outside academe's groves than within. I found no misprints; but there are eccentricities.

In *A Modern Instance* (p. 474) we read of "the presidential canvas of
the summer"; then (p. 485) we read "But the political canvass . . ." Now
a tent is made of canvas and an election is a canvass of votes. It is true
that the secondary spelling of "canvass" is "canvas" and so allowable;
nevertheless, it is disturbing to find the same word spelled two ways
within eleven pages. On page 3 the variant spelling "ancles" is used for
"ankles." On page 747 Howells writes "party-colored statues" when,
surely, "parti-colored" was nineteenth-century common usage as opposed to the Chaucerian English "party." Of course, as the editors tell
us, "In nineteenth-century writings, for example, a word might be
spelled in more than one way, even in the same work, and such variations might be carried into print."

Anyway, none of this is serious. There are no disfiguring footnotes.
The notes at the back are for the most part helpful translations of foreign
phrases in the text. The chronology of Howells's life is faultless but
perhaps, skimpy. For those who are obliged for career reasons to read
Howells, this is a useful book. For those who are still able to read novels
for pleasure, this is a marvelous book.

For some years I have been haunted by a story of Howells and that most
civilized of all our presidents, James A. Garfield. In the early 1870s
Howells and his father paid a call on Garfield. As they sat on Garfield's
veranda, young Howells began to talk about poetry and about the poets
that he had met in Boston and New York. Suddenly, Garfield told him
to stop. Then Garfield went to the edge of the veranda and shouted to

his Ohio neighbors. "Come over here! He's telling about Holmes, and Longfellow, and Lowell, and Whittier!" So the neighbors gathered around in the dusk; then Garfield said to Howells, "Now go on."

Today we take it for granted that no living president will ever have heard the name of any living poet. This is not, necessarily, an unbearable loss. But it is unbearable to have lost those Ohio neighbors who actually read books of poetry and wanted to know about the poets.

For thirty years bookchat writers have accused me of having written that the novel is dead. I wrote no such thing but bookchat writers have the same difficulty extracting meaning from writing as presidents do. What I wrote was, "After some three hundred years the novel in English has lost the general reader (or rather the general reader has lost the novel), and I propose that he will not again recover his old enthusiasm." Since 1956, the audience for the serious (or whatever this year's adjective is) novel has continued to shrink. Arguably, the readers that are left are for the most part involuntary ones, obliged by the schools to read novels that they often have little taste for. The fact that a novelist like Howells—or even Bellow—is probably no longer accessible to much of anyone would be bearable if one felt that the sense of alternative worlds or visions or—all right, Leslie—nightmares, fantasies, fears could be obtained in some other way. But movies are no substitute while television is, literally, narcotizing: The human eye was not designed to stare at a light for any length of time. Popular prose fictions are still marketed with TV and movie tie-ins, but even the writers or word-processors of these books find it harder and harder to write simply enough for people who don't really know how to read.

Obviously, there is a great deal wrong with our educational system, as President Reagan recently, and rather gratuitously, noted. After all, an educated electorate would not have elected him president. It is generally agreed that things started to go wrong with the schools after the First World War. The past was taught less and less, and Latin and Greek ceased to be compulsory. Languages were either not taught or taught so badly that they might just as well not have been taught at all, while American history books grew more and more mendacious, as Frances FitzGerald so nicely described (*America Revised*, 1979), and even basic geography is now a nonsubject. Yet the average "educated" American has been made to believe that, somehow, the United States must lead the world even though hardly anyone has any information at all about those countries we are meant to lead. Worse, we have very little information about our own country and its past. That is why it is not really possible to compare a writer like Howells with any living American writer because Howells thought that it was a good thing to know as much as possible about his own country as well as other countries while our writers today, in common with the presidents and paint manufacturers, live in a present without past among signs whose meanings are uninterpretable.

Edmund Wilson's practical response was to come up with the idea of making readily available the better part of American literature; hence, the Library of America. It is a step in the right direction. But will this library attract voluntary readers? Ultimately—and paradoxically—that will depend on the schools.

Since no one quite knows what a university ought to do, perhaps *that* should be the subject of our educational system. What variety of things should *all* educated people know? What is it that we don't know that we need to know? Naturally, there is a certain risk in holding up a mirror to the system itself (something the realistic novelist always used to do) because one is apt to see, glaring back, the face of Caliban or, worse, plain glass reflecting glass. But something must now be done because Herzen's terrible truth is absolutely true: "The end of each generation is itself."

*The New York Review of Books*
October 27, 1983

# OSCAR WILDE:
# ON THE SKIDS AGAIN

Must one have a heart of stone to read *The Ballad of Reading Gaol* without laughing? (In life, practically no one ever gets to kill the thing he hates, much less loves.) And did not *De Profundis* plumb for all time the shallows of the most-reported love affair of the past hundred years, rivaling even that of Wallis and David, its every nuance (O Bosie!) known to all, while trembling rosy lips yet form, over and over again, those doom-laden syllables *The Cadogan Hotel*? Oscar Wilde. Yet again. Why?

In *Four Dubliners* (1987), Richard Ellmann published essays on Yeats, Joyce, Wilde, and Beckett. "These four," he admits, "make a strange consortium. Yet resemblances of which they were unaware begin to appear." Certainly no one could detect these resemblances better than the late Professor Ellmann, who devoted much of a distinguished career to Joyce and Yeats. He tells us that at eighteen Yeats heard Wilde lecture, while Joyce, at twenty, met Yeats and called him too old. In 1928 young Beckett met Joyce and they became friends. . . . So much for the traffic, somewhat more to the point, "Wilde and Yeats reviewed each other's work with mutual regard, and sometimes exploited the same themes. Joyce memorialized Wilde as a heroic victim, and repeatedly quoted or referred to him in his writings later. Beckett was saturated in all their works. . . . Displaced, witty, complex, savage they companion each other." I wonder.

Since Ellmann had already written magisterial works on two of the four, symmetry and sympathy plainly drew him to a third; hence, this latest biography of Wilde, this last biography of Ellmann, our time's best academic biographer. Although Ellmann was unusually intelligent, a quality seldom found in academe or, indeed, on Parnassus itself, Wilde does not quite suit his schema or his talent. Aside from the fact that the four Dubliners, as he acknowledges, "were chary of acknowledging their connection," I suspect that the controlling adjective here is "academic." To an academic of Ellmann's generation, explication is all.

The problem with Wilde is that he does not need explication or interpretation. He needs only to be read, or listened to. He plays no word games other than that most mechanical of verbal tricks: the paradox. When he rises to the sublime in poetry or prose there is so much purple all over the place that one longs for the clean astringencies of Swinburne.

On those occasions when Wilde is true master, the inventor of a perfect play about nothing and everything, we don't need to have the jokes explained. One simply laughs and wonders why no one else has ever been able to sustain for so long so flawlessly elegant a verbal riff. I would not like to rise in the academic world with a dissertation on Wilde's masterpiece and I suspect (but do not know) that hardly anyone has tried, particularly now that ever-easy Beckett's clamorous silences await, so temptingly, tenure seekers.

All in all, Wilde provides little occasion for Ellmann's formidable critical apparatus. Where Ellmann showed us new ways of looking at Yeats and, above all, at Joyce, he can do nothing more with Wilde than fit him into a historical context and tell, yet again, the profane story so well known to those who read. Is this worthwhile? I am not so sure. Ellmann does straighten out earlier versions of the gospel—or bad news, I suppose one should say. He rises to the essential prurience; and it is interesting to know that at thirty-one, after a lifetime of vigorous heterosexuality which had given him not only two children but syphilis, Wilde was seduced by Robert Ross, then aged seventeen, at Oxford. It is also interesting to know that Wilde, unlike Byron, Charlemagne, and Lassie, was not into buggery, preferring either oral sex or the Dover-sole kiss *cum* intercrural friction. What a one-time warden of All Souls did for Lawrence, Ellmann now does for Wilde. Future generations will be in his—their—debt.

Future generations. Now let us be relevant, the essential task of the irrelevant (O Oscar!): *Will there be future generations?* The British press of the AIDSy eighties thinks not. According to the *Daily Mail,* the last man on earth died in 1986, clutching to his dehydrated bosom a portrait of Margaret Thatcher. According to the *New York Post* (an Australian newspaper whose editors are able to do simple sums), the human race will be dead by century's end due to rabid homos and drug takers (mostly black and Hispanic and viciously opposed to prayer in America's chaste bookless schools). Therefore, it is now necessary to trot out an Oscar Wilde suitable for our anxious plague-ridden times. In the four decades since the Second World War, Wilde has gradually become more and more a victim-hero of a hypocritical society whose most deeply cherished superstitions about sex were to be violently shaken, first, by the war, where the principal secret of the warrior male lodge was experienced by millions on a global scale and, second, by Dr. Alfred C. Kinsey, who reported that more than one third of the triumphant Butch Republic's male population had participated in the tribal mysteries. The revolution in consciousness attributed to the Beatles and other confusions of the 1960s actually took place in the 1940s: war and Kinsey, penicillin and the Pill. As a result, Oscar Wilde ceased to be regarded as a criminal; he had been nothing worse than maladjusted to a society that was not worth adjusting to. Wilde himself became a symbol of mental if not of physical health: Ellmann pinpoints the when and how of the syphilis that killed him when every orifice, suddenly, hugely, voided in a Paris hotel room. The cumulative effect of Ellmann's Wilde may suit altogether too well the AIDSy Eighties.

Currently, our rulers are tightening the screws; too much sexual freedom is bad for production and, even worse, for consumption. Sex is now worse than mere sin; it is murderous. In the selfish pursuit of happiness another may die. One understands those paranoids who think that AIDS was deliberately cooked up in a laboratory, for the idea of plague is endlessly useful, transforming society-persecutor into society-protector: urine samples here, blood tests there.

Although Ellmann certainly did not set out to recast Wilde for our dismal age, he was, like the rest of us, a part of the way we live now, and his Wilde is more cautionary tale than martyr-story. There is the obligatory Freudianism. *Cherchez la mère* is indulged in, legitimately, I suppose. Jane Wilde, self-dubbed Speranza Francesca, was, if not larger than life, a good deal larger than average. A Protestant, Lady Wilde kept a literary salon rather than saloon in Dublin, favored an independent Ireland, wrote thundering verse worthy of her son (anent child-nurture: "Alas! The Fates are cruel. / Behold Speranza making gruel!"). She loved sensation-making and came into her own at a treason trial in Dublin, where she was gaveled down by the judge as she tried to make herself, rather than the defendant, the fount of sedition. Later, she endured the trial for seduction, of her husband, Sir William, an oculist. Trials were, rather ominously, her ice cream. Son deeply admired mother and vice versa. But Ellmann controls himself: "However accommodating it is to see a maternal smothering of masculinity as having contributed to [Oscar's] homosexuality there is reason to be skeptical."

Although Ellmann has not worked out that homosexual is an adjective describing an act not a noun descriptive of a human being, he has been able to assemble data which he then tests against fashionable theory; in this case he finds theory wanting. Oscar was a brilliant creature neither more nor less "masculine" than any other man. What he learned from his mother was not how to be a woman but the importance of being a Show-off and a Poet and a questioner of whatever quo was currently status. He also inherited her talent for bad poetry. In due course, he re-created himself as a celebrity (a terrible word that has been used in our sense since the mid-1800s), and he was well known long before he had actually done anything at all of note. The Anglo-Irish gift of the gab, combined with an actor's timing, made him noticeable at Oxford and unescapable in London's drawing rooms during the 1880s. He invented a brand-new voice for himself (the Irish brogue, no matter how Merrion Squared, was dispensed with), and Beerbohm reports on his "mezzo voice, uttering itself in leisurely fashion, with every variety of tone." He also took to gorgeous costumes that set off his large ungainly figure to splendid disadvantage. With the death of Sir William, he possessed a small inheritance, expensive tastes and no focused ambition other than poetry, a common disease of that day; also, as Yeats put it, "the enjoyment of his own spontaneity."

What is most interesting in Ellmann's account is the intellectual progress of Wilde. He is particularly good on Wilde's French connection, much of it unknown to me, though I once asked André Gide several searching questions about his friend, and Gide answered me at length. That was in 1948. I have now forgotten both questions and answers. But until I read Ellmann I did not know how well and for how long the two had known each other and what an impression Wilde ("Creation began when you were born. It will end on the day you die") had made on Gide's tormented passage through that strait gate that leads the few to life.

As a result of a collection of fairy tales, *The Happy Prince* (a revelation to at least one American child forty years later), Wilde became famous for writing as well as for showing off, and Paris stirred, as it sometimes will, for an Anglo (the Celtic distinction is unknown there). With the publication of the dialogue "The Decay of Lying," Wilde took note of a change of direction in literature, and the French were both startled and delighted that the cultural wind was coming from the wrong side of the channel. Ellmann writes,

In England decadence had always been tinged with self-mockery. By 1890, symbolism, not decadence, had the cry, as Wilde acknowledged in the preface to *Dorian Gray.* "All art is at once surface and symbol. Those who go beneath the surface do so at their peril. Those who read the symbol do so at their peril." These aphorisms were a bow to Stéphane Mallarmé, whom he had visited in February 1891, when he was writing the preface.

Wilde then proceeded to conquer Parisian literary life in much the same way that he had the drawing rooms of London and the lecture halls of the United States. Incidentally, Ellmann's list of the number of places where Wilde spoke is positively presidential. In hundreds of cities and towns he lectured on the Beautiful, with numerous household hints. In his two chats "The House Beautiful" and "The Decorative Arts," he foreshadowed today's how-to-do-it books. He was a sensation. My twelve-year-old grandfather (during Reconstruction, southern boys were bred early and often) recalled Wilde's performance (July 15, 1882) at the Opera House in Vicksburg, Mississippi: "He wore," and the old man's voice trembled, "a *girdle,* and he held a flower in his hand." Happily, my grandfather never knew that two weeks later Wilde was received by General Grant. (As I write these lines, I wonder *how* did he know that Wilde was wearing a girdle?)

The siege of Paris was swift, the victory total. Symbolism did not need to lay siege to Wilde; he surrendered to the modernist movement, now the world's oldest *vague,* whose long roar shows no sign of withdrawing. Wilde also appropriated Mallarmé's unfinished *Hérodiade* for his own *Salomé,* written in French for Bernhardt; but the play was admired. It is interesting just how learned the writers of the last century were: The educational system Greeked and Latined them; other languages came easily to them, cultures, too. Today's writers know very little about anything. But then those who teach cannot be taught.

During the enchantment of Paris, Wilde himself was, significantly, overwhelmed by Huysmans's *À Rebours,* still a touchstone as late as the

1940s. The young Proust was impressive to Wilde because of his "enthu-siasm for English literature, especially for Ruskin (whom he translated) and George Eliot . . ." But when Proust invited him to dinner, Wilde arrived before Proust: "I looked at the drawing room and at the end of it were your parents, my courage failed me." Wilde departed, after the thoughtful observation to M. and Mme. Proust: "How ugly your house is."

With the local cat-king, Edmond de Goncourt, Wilde was no less magisterial. In a newspaper piece, Goncourt had got all wrong Wilde's remarks about Swinburne, while Wilde himself was sneered at as "this individual of doubtful sex, with a ham actor's language, and tall stories." Wilde chose to ignore the personal attack in a letter that set straight the gossip: "In Swinburne's work we meet for the first time the cry of flesh tormented by desire and memory, joy and remorse, fecundity and steril-ity. The English public, as usual hypocritical, prudish, and philistine, has not known how to find the art in the work of art: it has searched for the man in it." *Tiens!* as Henry James liked to write in his notebook. The biographer has license to go a-hunting for the man; the critic not; the reader—why not just read what's written?

Wilde, the playwright, is duly recorded, duly celebrated. Ellmann has some nice greenroom gossip for those who like that sort of thing. It is interesting to know that when Beerbohm Tree addressed a "brilliant lady" on stage he did so with his back to the audience (a Bernhardt trick, too). But then when he had an epigram to launch, he would turn to face the audience, to their ravishment. For those who like such things, there is also a very great deal about Wilde's love affair with a boring boy-beauty called Bosie. At this late date it is no longer a story worth retelling, and if Ellmann has added anything new to it I did not notice. The trial. Prison. Exile. The usual. I suspect that one of the reasons we create fiction is to make sex exciting; the fictional meeting between Vautrin and Lucien de Rubempré at the coach house in Balzac's *Illu-sions Perdues* is one of the most erotic ever recorded. But details of the real Oscar and Bosie in bed together or in combination with bits and pieces of England's adenoidal trade, more gifted at blackmail than ganymedery, create for the reader neither tumescence nor moistness; rather, one's thoughts turn somberly to laundry and to the brutal horror of life in a world without dry cleaning.

Ellmann's literary criticism is better than his telling of the oft-told tale. He is particularly good on *Dorian Gray,* a book truly subversive of the society that produced it—and its author. He is interesting on

Wilde's conversion to a kind of socialism. Of Wilde's essay "The Soul of Man Under Socialism," Ellmann tells us that it "is based on the paradox that we must not waste energy in sympathizing with those who suffer needlessly, and that only socialism can free us to cultivate our personalities. Charity is no use—the poor are . . . right to steal rather than to take alms." On the other hand, Wilde was wary of authoritarianism, so often socialism's common-law helpmeet. In the end, Wilde veered off into a kind of anarchy; and defined the enemy thus:

There are three sorts of despots. There is the despot who tyrannizes over the body. There is the despot who tyrannizes over the soul. There is the despot who tyrannizes over the soul *and* body alike. The first is called the Prince. The second is called the Pope. The third is called the People.

Joyce was impressed by this and borrowed it for *Ulysses.* Inadvertently (I suspect), Richard Ellmann does make it clear that for all the disorder of Wilde's life he was never, in the Wordsworthian sense, "neglectful of the universal heart."

Yeats thought Wilde a man of action, like Byron, who had got waylaid by literature. When this was repeated to Wilde, he made an offhand remark about the boredom of Parliament. But Yeats did sense in Wilde the energy of the actor: of one who acts, rather than of one who simply, bemusedly *is*—the artist. But whatever Wilde might or might not have done and been, he was an extremely good man and his desire to subvert a supremely bad society was virtuous. Cardinal Newman, writing of their common day, said, "The age is so very sluggish that it will not hear you unless you bawl—you must first tread on its toes, and then apologise." But behavior suitable for an ecclesiastical busybody is all wrong for Oscar Wilde, whose only mistake was to apologize for his good work and life.

*The Times Literary Supplement* (London)
October 2–8, 1987

# 20

# BERNARD SHAW'S
# HEARTBREAK HOUSE

"Heartbreak House . . . rhapsodized about love; but it believed in cruelty. It was afraid of the cruel people; and it saw that cruelty was at least effective. Cruelty did things that made money, whereas Love did nothing but prove the soundness of LaRochefoucauld's saying that very few people would fall in love if they had never read about it. Heartbreak House in short did not know how to live at which point all that was left to it was the boast that at least it knew how to die: a melancholy accomplishment which the outbreak of war presently gave it practically unlimited opportunities of displaying. Thus were the first-born of Heartbreak House smitten; and the young, the innocent, the hopeful expiated the folly and worthlessness of their elders."

That is from Bernard Shaw's odd preface to his even odder play, now revived on Broadway. The preface is odd, among other things, because it is written with the wrong sort of hindsight. Shaw did not know when he began the play in 1913 that the first-born were going to be struck down. Nor is there any reference to war, actual or impending, in the first two acts. The third act, however, was completed after the first aerial bombardments in history, and Shaw, rather casually, uses this serendipitous, for him, horror to drop a bomb and end the play. Yet it is not the residents of Heartbreak House or their first-born who get blown up; only a businessman and a burglar expiate the folly and worthlessness of . . . what? Not Heartbreak House certainly; capitalism, perhaps.

Everything about the play is queer, even its production history. Plans to put it on during the war went awry. Shaw finally published it, with preface, in 1919. Not until 1920 was the play produced, in New York. The next year it got to the West End. The preface is unique in Shaw for its bitterness and the play . . . well, there are those who put it first among his work and there are those who don't know what to think of it. I'm afraid after seeing it performed for the first time the other day that I liked it a good deal less than I thought I did from having read it; parenthetically, I should put quite plainly here at the beginning that I regard Bernard Shaw as the best and most useful dramatist in English since the author of *Much Ado About Nothing* turned gentleman and let fall the feather.

What is Heartbreak House? In the context of the play it stands for the ruling class of England pre-1914: the "nice people," somewhat educated, somewhat sensitive, somewhat independent financially (their cousins the hearties lived over at Horseback Hall). They were devotees of laissez-faire; they rhapsodized about love—but I have already quoted Shaw's indictment. Heartbreak House, of course, is only another name for our new friend the Establishment, a protective association made up of public-school boys who come down from Oxbridge to take over Whitehall, the Church of England, the BBC, Fleet Street, the better-looking girls, and everything else that's fun, while (so young writers tell us) sneering at the newly articulate *Lumpenproletariat* who have gone to red-brick colleges where, if one reads the new novels accurately, the main course given is Opportunism: Don't reform, adapt. The jocose nihilism of many of the anti-Establishment novels and plays is no more than a love-hate acceptance of the Establishment; the Kingsley Amises approach it on its own terms in a way Shaw would have detested. Where he would have leveled Heartbreak House to make way for a carefully planned housing project, the new attackers of the Establishment merely want to move into some of those nice rooms at the top, an attitude ignoble to a socialist and hopelessly petty to an outsider who is aware that the rooms at the top of a diminished England are not much better than those directly under. The Establishment has only an island to tend, while Heartbreak House, with Asquith and Bonar Law and Ramsay Mac for weekend guests, governed much of the world. To put it plain, Shaw's target was important; and he knew what he wanted, which was not to adapt, or to make his own way, but to reform.

I think we know pretty much what Shaw intended to do in *Heartbreak House,* yet what actually did he do in the play itself? For one thing, it is improvised work. Shaw admitted he made it up as he went along, not knowing from day to day what his characters would do or say or become. He always tended to work this way, regarding a play essentially as an organism with a life of its own; one need only nurture it and let it assume its own shape. He even used to keep a checkerboard at hand to remind him who was onstage and who was off at any given moment in the writing. There is no doubt this method served him as well as any other; his night mind was not, to say the least, fantastic. I am sure deep in his unconscious there lurked not the usual nightmare monsters of the rest of us but yards of thesis, antithesis, and synthesis, all neatly labeled and filed. Yet in *Heartbreak House* Shaw's improvisatory genius breaks down; he keeps marching into conversational culs-de-sac.

For example, in the second act the play comes to a grinding halt after Boss Mangan, recovered from hypnotic trance, denounces and is denounced by those who happen to be onstage at the moment, and exits. Then Captain Shotover tosses a Delphic phrase or two upon the night and paddles off. (Later the Captain, while again trying for an exit, says, almost apologetically: "I must go in and out," a compulsion he shares with everyone else in this play; they all go in and out at whim.) This ill-madeness is often beguiling except on those occasions when it defeats the author, who finds himself with nobody left onstage except a couple who don't have much of anything to say to one another at the moment. It is then that Shaw invariably, shamelessly, brings on the New Character, who is very often a member of the lower classes with a colorful speech pattern usually written out phonetically in the text. This time he is the Burglar, a comic character right out of Dickens, where Shaw claimed, not entirely facetiously, to have got most of his characters, at least those who are not himself. The Burglar is one of Shaw's standbys, used in play after play; he is awful, but at least he starts the second act moving again and gives it a certain vivacity. As usual, Shaw, delighted with his own cunning, starts tying up ends; the Burglar is really the Captain's old bos'n, the nurse's husband, etc., etc. And now let's have a long chat about the poor and the exploited, the exploiters and the *rentiers,* and then end the act.

As a rule, Shaw's arbitrariness does not disturb. After all, he is conducting a seminar with enormous wit and style and we don't much mind his more casual contrivances. But in this play they don't come off.

I think it has to do with a fundamental conflict between characters and settings. The characters, of course, are our old friends the Bernard Shaw Team of Fabian Debaters; we know each one of them already. But what are they doing in this peculiar Midsummer's Eve *ambiance*? They seem a bit puzzled, too. As they debate with their usual ease they tend nervously to eye the shrubbery: Are there elves at the bottom of that garden? Have we been booked into an allegory? Are we going to find out we're all dead or something? Steady, chaps, the old boy's got us into one of *those* plays. They rattle on bravely but they are clearly ill at ease, and so is the audience. I think it was one of the New York daily reviewers who observed that the mood is not Chekhov but J. M. Barrie. Which is exactly right. We are led to expect magic, fey girls upon the heath, and revelation through fantasy. But we get none of it. Instead we are offered the old Debating Team in top form but in the wrong place and mood (oh, for that dentist's office!). As a result the debaters recede as characters; we grow indifferent to them; they are too humorous in the original sense of the word. Especially Ellie, Shaw's super-girl. In this version she is more than ever iron, ready to mother not heroes but heroines. Shaw dotes on Ellie; I found her purest drip-torture. Halfway through the play I had a startling *aperçu*: Shaw regarded himself not as a man or an artist or a social meliorist but as a kind of superwoman, a chaste spinster fiercely armed with the umbrella of dialectic, asexual limbs blue-stockinged, and tongue wagging. Of all the debaters assembled, I liked only Captain Shotover, because his dottiness contrasted agreeably with the uneasy predictability of his teammates.

Finally, at the play's end, I found myself entirely confused as to what Shaw intended. Shaw is not, even when he would like to be, an impressionist, a Chekhov turning life before our eyes to no end but that life observed is sufficient. Look, we live, we are, says Chekhov. While Shaw declares briskly: Pull up your socks! Fall in line there. Come along now. Double-quick march and we'll overtake the future by morning! One loves Shaw for his optimism, but moonlight is not a time for marching, and *Heartbreak House* is a moonlight play, suitable for recapturing the past. Elegy and debate cancel one another out. Nor is the work really satiric, an attack on "folly and worthlessness." These people are splendid and unique, and Shaw knows it. He cannot blow them up at the end.

Shaw's prefaces—no matter how proudly irrelevant their content may, at first, seem to the play that follows (sometimes a bit forlornly)— usually turn out to be apposite or at least complementary. But not this preface. In fact, it is misleading. Shaw talks about Chekhov. He finds the country-house mentality Chekhov *seems* to be writing about endemic to Europe, part of the sweet sickness of the bourgeoisie. Therefore Shaw will examine the same house in the same way, only in English terms. Ever since that preface, we have all dutifully considered this play in terms of Chekhov. Does it compare? Is it as good? Why is it *un*like? It is true that both are dealing with the same dying society of "nice people," but where Chekhov's interest was the "nice people," Shaw's interest was the dying society and the birth pains of the new.

Shaw once told Sir Cedric Hardwicke that he had no idea how to end the play until the first bombs fell. I suspect he had originally planned to allow Captain Shotover to attain "the Seventh Degree of concentration," thereby detonating the dynamite he had stored in the gravel pit and blowing up the enemy Mangan. As it was, at the last minute, the bomb from the Zeppelin did the trick even better, providing Shaw quite literally with a god from the machine. Then, almost as an afterthought, Shaw comes to the point:

HECTOR: Well, I don't mean to be drowned like a rat in a trap. I still have the will to live. What am I to do?

CAPTAIN SHOTOVER: Do? Nothing simpler. Learn your business as an Englishman.

HECTOR: And what may my business as an Englishman be, pray?

CAPTAIN SHOTOVER: Navigation. Learn it and live; or leave it and be damned.

And that's it. Captain Shotover, supposed to have sold his soul to the devil, to have meddled with mysticism, to have mastered the *non sequitur,* turns out to be a good Fabian socialist after all. Obviously, Shotover was a humbug mystic, excusably deranged by the setting Shaw put him in; not until faced with his world's extinction does he throw off the mask of dottiness to reveal the bright, hard, intelligent face of Bernard Shaw, who to this day has a good deal to tell us about the danger of a society drifting as opposed to one which has learned the virtue of setting a deliberate course by fixed stars. To navigate is to plan. Laissez-faire, though always delightful for a few, in crisis is disastrous for all. There is no alternative to a planned society; that is the burden of the Shaw debate. Almost as an afterthought he makes this familiar point as the bomb drops near Heartbreak House.

The production now on view is ambitious, and at many points successful. As usual, I found myself more attentive to the audience than to the play. As they say in physics, there is no action without reaction. I can think of no urgent reason for writing about productions in the theater unless one also writes about the audience, too. The play acts upon the audience, which is society today; the audience reacts and in its reaction one can get a sense of the superstitions and prejudices which obtain. Theater can be revelatory. In fact, I wish sociologists would spend more time in the theater and less in conducting polls and drawing graphs. Any audience at *Tea and Sympathy* or *Auntie Mame* will tell them more about the way we live now than a house-to-house canvass from Morristown to White Plains with pad and pencil.

In the case of an old play like *Heartbreak House* one may also use it as a touchstone. In the 1920s it seemed one thing, in the 1930s another, and so on. To those watching, the day I saw it, *Heartbreak House* was a delightful place, menaced by burglars, self-made men, and Zeppelins. The clothes were chic yet quaint and every woman saw herself up there pouring tea for weak enamored men who tended to burst into tears while the ladies talked a bright blue streak. Whenever the debate really got going, 1959's attention flagged: Is that a rubber plant? Can they still get egret feathers or is that an imitation? Did you leave the keys in the car? . . . Bernard Shaw, I'm afraid, was being taken for Oscar Wilde, and afflicted with un-Wildean *longueurs*. But then we are not used to debate at any level. If Bernard Shaw, who made the act of argument as pleasurable as any writer who ever lived, cannot hold his audience except by predictable paradoxes and references to adultery and all the familiar junk of the Commercialites, we the audience are in a bad way. Although in fairness it must be admitted that talking about society and the better life and planning of any sort has never been a characteristic of the Anglo-American mind.

All in all, reservations about this particular play aside, I hope it runs forever and gives heart to those who expect the theater to be something more than a business for those who, in their calculated desire to please us, only make us more than ever absent of mind.

*The Reporter*
November 26, 1959

# 21

---◆---

# MAUGHAM'S
# HALF & HALF

## I

Mr. Robert Calder has written a biography of W. Somerset Maugham in order to redress, nicely, I think, some recent studies of the man who was probably our century's most popular novelist as well as the most successful of Edwardian playwrights. Maugham's last biographer, Mr. Ted Morgan, concentrated morbidly on the incontinences and confusions of a mad old age while scanting works and bright days. Doubtless, he was influenced by the young Maugham's remark:

I cannot understand why a biographer, having undertaken to give the world details of a famous man's life, should hesitate, as so often happens, to give details of his death . . . Our lives are conditioned by outer circumstances but our death is our own.

Not, as it proves, with Mr. Morgan on the case. But then, as demonstrated by Mr. Morgan and other biographers of known sexual degenerates (or merely suspected—Lennon, Presley, by one A. Goldman, the master of that expanding cottage industry, Bioporn), a contemptuous adversarial style seems to be the current . . . norm. Despite the degenerate's gifts, he is a Bad Person; worse, he is Immature; even worse, he is Promiscuous. Finally, he is demonstrably more Successful than his biographer, who is Married, Mature, Monogamous, and Good.

Although Mr. Calder is MMM&G, he does believe that

Morgan's antipathy to the man is most damaging. Though his treatment of Maugham's homosexuality is more explicit than anything previously published, it always emphasizes the nasty procuring side of his homosexual life.

Yet even a gentle schoolteacher in Saskatchewan like Mr. Calder must know that the men of Maugham's generation paid for sex with men or women or both (the last century was prostitution's Golden Age—for the buyer, of course). Would Mr. Calder think it relevant to note and deplore as immature if Joseph Conrad, say, had visited women prostitutes? I doubt it. Obviously a double standard is at work here. What is sheer high animal spirits in the roaring boy who buys a pre-feminist girl is vileness in the roaring boy who buys another boy.

To Mr. Calder's credit, he does his best to show the amiable side to the formidable Mr. Maugham—the side that Mr. Calder terms "Willie," as he was known to friends. But our schoolteacher also distances himself from "nastiness" in his acknowledgments where he notes "the unqualified encouragement of my parents, and my children—Alison, Kevin, Lorin, and Dani." (Did they pipe "What's rough trade, Daddy?" with *unqualified* encouragement?) No matter. By and large, children, your Daddy has done the old fruitcake proud.

Maugham spent his first twenty-six years in the nineteenth century and for the subsequent sixty-five years he was very much a nineteenth-century novelist and playwright. In many ways he was fortunately placed, though he himself would not have thought so. He was born in Paris where his lawyer father did legal work for the British Embassy, and his mother was a popular figure in Paris society. Maugham's first language was French and although he made himself into the premier English storyteller, his prose has always had a curious flatness to it, as if it wanted to become either Basic English or Esperanto or perhaps go back into French.

Maugham's self-pity, which was to come to a full rather ghastly flowering in *Of Human Bondage,* is mysterious in origin. On the demerit side, he lost a beloved mother at eight; lost three older brothers to boarding school (all became lawyers and one Lord Chancellor); lost, at eleven, a not-so-well-loved father. He was then sent off to a clergyman uncle in Whitstable—home of the oyster—and then to the standard dire school of the day. On the credit side, under his father's will, he got £150 a year for life, enough to live on. He was well-connected in the professional upper middle class. He had the run of his uncle's considerable library—the writer's best education. When he proved to be sickly, he was sent to the south of France; when, at seventeen, he could endure his school no more, he was sent to Heidelberg and a merry time.

On balance, the tragic wound to which he was to advert throughout a long life strikes me as no more than a scratch or two. Yes, he wanted to be taller than five foot seven; yes, he had an underslung jaw that might have been corrected; yes, he stammered. But . . . *tant pis,* as he might have observed coldly of another (used in a novel, the phrase would be helpfully translated).

Yet something *was* gnawing at him. As he once observed, sardonically, to his nephew Robin Maugham, "Jesus Christ could cope with all the miseries I have had to contend with in life. But then, Jesus Christ had advantages I don't possess." Presumably, Jesus was a six-foot-tall blond blue-eyed body-builder whereas Maugham was slight and dark with eyes like "brown velvet," and, of course, Jesus' father owned the shop. On the other hand, Maugham was not obliged to contend with the sadomasochistic excitement of the Crucifixion, much less the head-turning rapture of the Resurrection. It is the common view of Maugham biographers that the true tragic flaw was homosexuality, disguised as a club foot in *Of Human Bondage*—or was that the stammer? Whatever it was, Maugham was very sorry for himself. Admittedly, a liking for boys at the time of Oscar Wilde's misadventures was dangerous but Maugham was adept at passing for MMM&G: he *appeared* to have affairs with women, not men, and he married and fathered a daughter. There need not have been an either/or for him.

Maugham's career as a writer was singularly long and singularly successful. The cover of each book was adorned with a Moorish device to ward off the evil eye: the author knew that too much success over-excites one's contemporaries, not to mention the gods. Also much of his complaining may have been prophylactic: to avert the Furies if not the book-chatterers, and so he was able to live just as he wanted for two thirds of his life, something not many writers—or indeed anyone else—ever manage to do.

At eighteen, Maugham became a medical student at St Thomas's Hospital, London. This London was still Dickens's great monstrous invention where "The messenger led you through the dark and silent streets of Lambeth, up stinking alleys and into sinister courts where the police hesitated to penetrate, but where your black bag protected you from harm." For five years Maugham was immersed in the real world, while, simultaneously, he was trying to become a writer. "Few authors," Mr Calder tells us, "read as widely as Maugham and his works are peppered with references to other literature." So they are—peppered indeed—but not always seasoned. The bilingual Maugham knew best the French writers of the day. He tells us that he modelled his short stories on Maupassant. He also tells us that he was much influenced by Ibsen, but there is no sign of that master in his own school of Wilde comedies. Later, he was awed by Chekhov's stories but, again, he could never "use" that master because something gelled very early in Maugham the writer, and once his own famous tone was set it would remain perfectly pitched to the end.

In his first published novel, *Liza of Lambeth* (1897), Maugham raised the banner of Maupassant and the French realists but the true influence on the book and its method was one Arthur Morrison, who had made a success three years earlier with *Tales of Mean Streets.* Mr. Calder notes that Morrison,

writing with austerity and frankness . . . refused to express sympathy on behalf of his readers so that they could then avoid coming to terms with the implications of social and economic inequality. Maugham adopted this point of view in his first novel, and was therefore, like Morrison, accused of a lack of conviction.

In general, realists have always been open to the charge of coldness, particularly by romantics who believe that a novel is essentially a sermon, emotional and compassionate and so inspiring that after the peroration, the reader, wiser, kinder, *bushier* indeed, will dry his eyes and go forth to right wrong. This critical mindset has encouraged a great deal of bad writing. The unemotional telling of a terrible story is usually more effective than the oh, by the wind-grieved school of romantic (that is, self-loving) prose. On the other hand, the plain style can help the dishonest, pusillanimous writer get himself off every kind of ideological or ethical hook. Just the facts, ma'am. In this regard, Hemingway, a literary shadow-self to Maugham, was our time's most artful dodger, all busy advancing verbs and stony nouns. Surfaces coldly rendered. Interiors unexplored. Manner all.

For someone of Maugham's shy, highly self-conscious nature (with a secret, too) the adoption of classic realism, Flaubert with bitters, was inevitable. Certainly, he was lucky to have got the tone absolutely right in his first book, and he was never to stray far from the appearance of plain story-telling. Although he was not much of one for making up things, he could always worry an anecdote or bit of gossip into an agreeable narrative. Later, as the years passed, he put more and more effort—even genius—into his one triumphant creation, W. Somerset Maugham, world-weary world-traveller, whose narrative first person became the best-known and least wearisome in the world. At first he called the narrator "Ashenden" (a name carefully chosen so that the writer would not stammer when saying it, unlike that obstacle course for stammerers, "Maugham"); then he dropped Ashenden for Mr. Maugham himself in *The Razor's Edge* (1944). Then he began to appear, as narrator, in film and television dramatisations of his work. Thus, one of the most-read novelists of our time became widely known to those who do not read.

Shaw and Wells invented public selves for polemical reasons, while Mark Twain and Dickens did so to satisfy a theatrical need, but Maugham contrived a voice and a manner that not only charm and surprise in a way that the others did not, but where they were menacingly larger than life, he is just a bit smaller (5′ 7″), for which he compensates by sharing with us something that the four histrionic masters would not have dreamed of doing: inside gossip. It is these confidences that made Maugham so agreeable to read: *nothing,* he tells us with a smile, *is what it seems.* That was his one trick, and it seldom failed. Also, before D. H. Lawrence, Dr. Maugham (obstetrician) knew that women, given a fraction of a chance, liked sex as much as men did. When he said so, he was called a misogynist.

In October 1907, at thirty-three, Maugham became famous with the triumphant production of *Lady Frederick* (one of six unproduced plays that he had written). Maugham ravished his audience with the daring trick of having the star—middle-aged with ardent unsuitable youthful admirer—save the boy from his infatuation by allowing him to see her un-made-up at her dressing-table. So stunned is the lad by the difference between the beauty of the *maquillage* and the crone in the mirror that he is saved by her nobleness, and right before our eyes we see "nothing is what it seems" in spades, raw stuff for the theatre of those days.

By 1908 Maugham had achieved the dream of so many novelists: he had four plays running in the West End and he was financially set for life. In that same year, the sixty-five-year-old impecunious Henry James was having one last desperate go at the theatre. To Edith Wharton he wrote that he was

working under a sudden sharp solicitation (heaven forgive me!) for the Theatre that I had, as a matter of life or death, to push through with my play, or rather with my 2 plays (for I'm doing two), the more important of which (though an abject little cochonnerie even *it,* no doubt!) is to be produced . . . I have been governed by the one sordid & urgent consideration of the possibility of making some money . . . Forgive so vulgar a tale—but I am utterly brazen about it; for my base motive is all of that brassy complexion—till sicklied o'er with the reflection of another metal.

But it was to Maugham, not the Master, that the other metal came.

Maugham enjoyed his celebrity; he was a popular diner-out; he was, when he could get the words out, something of a wit. He was eminently marriageable in Edwardian eyes. So which will it be—the lady or the tiger/man? Mr. Calder cannot get enough of Maugham the faggot in conflict with Maugham the potential MMM&G. Will good drive out evil? Maturity immaturity?

Unhappily, the witch-doctor approach to human behaviour still enjoys a vogue in academe and Mr. Calder likes to put his subject on the couch, while murmuring such Freudian incantations as "loss of a beloved mother, the lack of a father with whom to identify . . . followed a common pattern in the development of homosexuality." That none of this makes any sense does not alter belief: in matters of faith, inconvenient evidence is always suppressed while contradictions go unnoticed. Nevertheless, witch-doctors to one side, witches did—and do—get burned, as Oscar Wilde discovered in 1895, and an entire generation of same-sexers were obliged to go underground or marry or settle in the south of France. I suspect that Maugham's experiences with women were not only few but essentially hydraulic. Writers, whether same-sexers or other-sexers, tend to have obsessive natures; in consequence, they cross the sexual borders rather less often than the less imaginative who want, simply, to get laid or even loved. But whereas a same-sexer like Noël Coward never in his life committed an other-sexual act ("Not even with Gertrude Lawrence?" I asked. "Particularly not with Miss Lawrence" was the staccato response), Dr. Maugham had no fear of vaginal teeth—he simply shut his eyes and thought of Capri.

At twenty-one Maugham was well and truly launched by one John Ellingham Brooks, a littérateur who lived on Capri, then known for the easy charm of its boys. "The nasty procuring side" of Maugham started in Capri and he kept coming back year after year. At ninety, he told a reporter, "I want to go to Capri because I started life there." In old age, he told Glenway Wescott that Brooks was his first lover. This is doubtful. Maugham told different people different things about his private life, wanting always to confuse. Certainly, for sheer energetic promiscuity he was as athletic as Byron; with a club foot, what might he not have done! Even so, "He was the most sexually voracious man I've ever known," said Beverley Nichols, the journalist and one-time Maugham secretary, who knew at first hand. Robin Maugham and the last companion, Alan Searle, agreed.

Ironically, within a dozen years of Wilde's imprisonment, Maugham was the most popular English playwright. Unlike the reckless Oscar, Maugham showed no sign of ever wanting to book so much as a room at the Cadogan Hotel. Marriage it would be. With Syrie Barnardo Wellcome, an interior decorator much liked in London's high bohemia. Fashionable wife for fashionable playwright. A daring woman of the world—an Iris March with a green hat *pour le sport*—Syrie wanted a child by Maugham without wedlock. Got it. As luck—hers and his—would have it, Maugham then went to war and promptly met the great love of his life, Gerald Haxton.

For a time Maugham was a wound dresser. Gerald was in the Ambulance Corps. They were to be together until Gerald's death twenty-nine years later, "longer than many marriages," observes the awed Mr. Calder. But there was a good deal of mess to be cleaned up along the way. Haxton could not go to England: he had been caught by the police in bed with another man. Maugham himself did not want, finally, to be even remotely MMM&G. Syrie suffered. They separated. Toward the end of his life, Maugham tried to disinherit his daughter on the ground that she was not his but, ironically, he had got a door prize for at least one dutiful attendance and she was very much his as anyone who has ever seen her or her descendants can attest: the saturnine Maugham face still gazes by proxy upon a world where nothing else is ever what it seems.

During the war, Maugham was hired by the British secret service to go to Moscow and shore up the Kerensky government. He has written of all this in both fiction (*Ashenden*—literary ancestor to Eric Ambler, Ian Fleming, John le Carré) and two books of memoirs. Unfortunately, the mission to Moscow was aborted by the overthrow of Kerensky.

Maugham developed tuberculosis. During twenty months in a Scottish sanatorium he wrote four of his most popular plays, including *The Circle* and the highly successful novel *The Moon and Sixpence,* where a Gauguin-like English painter is observed by the world-weary Ashenden amongst Pacific palms. Maugham wrote his plays rather the way television writers (or Shakespeare) write their serials—at great speed. One week for each act and a final week to put it all together. Since Mr. Calder is over-excited by poor Willie's rather unremarkable (stamina to one side) sex life, we get far too little analysis of Maugham's writing and of the way that he worked, particularly in the theatre. From what little Mr. Calder tells us, Maugham stayed away from rehearsals but, when needed, would cut almost anything an actor wanted. This doesn't sound right to me but then when one has had twenty play productions in England alone, there is probably not that much time or inclination to perfect the product. In any case, Mr. Calder is, as he would put it, "disinterested" in the subject.

In 1915, while Maugham was spying for England, *Of Human Bondage* was published. Maugham now was seen to be not only a serious but a solemn novelist—in the ponderous American manner. The best that can be said of this masterpiece is that it made a good movie and launched Bette Davis's career. I remember that on all the pre-Second War editions, there was a quotation from Theodore Dreiser to the effect that the book "has rapture, it sings." Mr. Calder does not mention Dreiser but Mr. Frederic Raphael does, in his agreeable picture book with twee twinkly text, *Somerset Maugham and His World* (1977). Mr. Raphael quotes from Dreiser, whom he characterises as "an earnest thunderer in the cause of naturalism and himself a Zolaesque writer of constipated power." Admittedly, Dreiser was not in a class with Margaret Drabble but—constipated?*

The Maugham persona was now perfected in life and work. Maugham's wit was taken for true evil as he himself was well known, despite all subterfuge, to be non-MMM&G. Mr. Calder is disturbed by Maugham's attempts at epigrams in conversation. Sternly, Mr. Calder notes: "Calculated flippancy was nonetheless a poor substitute for natural and easy insouciance." But despite a near-total absence of easy insouciance, Maugham fascinated everyone. By 1929 he had settled into his villa at Cap Ferrat; he was much sought after socially even though

---

*Mr. Raphael has many opinions about books that he has not actually read. You will see him at his glittering best in the *Times,* in his obituary of Gore Vidal (date to come).

the Windsors, the Churchills, the Beaverbrooks all knew that Haxton was more than a secretary. But the very rich and the very famous are indeed different from really real folks. For one thing, they often find funny the MMM&Gs. For another, they can create their own world and never leave it if they choose.

It is a sign of Maugham's great curiosity and continuing sense of life (even maturity) that he never stopped travelling, ostensibly to gather gossip and landscape for stories, but actually to come alive and indulge his twin passions, boys and bridge, two activities far less damaging to the environment than marriages, children, and big-game hunting. Haxton was a splendid organiser with similar tastes. Mr. Calder doesn't quite get all this but then his informants, chiefly nephew Robin Maugham and the last companion, Alan Searle, would have been discreet.

During the Second War, Maugham was obliged to flee France for America. In Hollywood he distinguished himself on the set of *Dr. Jekyll and Mr. Hyde.* George Cukor had explained to Willie how, in this version of the Stevenson story, there would be no horrendous make-up change for the star, Spencer Tracy, when he turned from good Dr. Jekyll into evil Mr. Hyde. Instead, a great actor, Tracy, would bring forth both evil and good from within. Action! Tracy menaces the heroine. Ingrid Bergman cowers on a bed. Tracy simpers, drools, leers. Then Maugham's souciant voice is heard, loud and clear and stammerless. "And which one is he supposed to be now?"

During this time, the movie of *The Moon and Sixpence* was released—the twenty-third Maugham story to be filmed. Maugham himself travelled restlessly about the East coast, playing bridge. He also had a refuge in North Carolina where, while Maugham was writing *The Razor's Edge,* Haxton died. For a time Maugham was inconsolable. Then he took on an amiable young Englishman, Alan Searle, as secretary-companion, and together they returned to the Riviera where Maugham restored the war-wrecked villa and resumed his life.

One reason, prurience aside, why Mr. Calder tells us so much about Maugham's private life (many kindnesses and charities are duly noted) is that Maugham has no reputation at all in North American academe where Mr. Calder is a spear-carrier. The result is a lot of less than half-praise: "His career had been largely a triumph of determination and will, the success in three genres of a man not naturally gifted as a writer." Only a schoolteacher innocent of how literature is made could have written such a line. Demonstrably, Maugham was very talented at doing what he did. Now, this is for your final grade, *what* did he do? Describe, please. Unfortunately, there aren't many good describers (critics) in any generation. But I shall give it a try, presently.

At seventy-two, Maugham went to Vevey, in Switzerland, where a Dr. Niehans injected ageing human organisms with the cells of unborn sheep, and restored youth. All the great came to Niehans, including Pius XII—in a business suit and dark glasses, it was said—an old man in no hurry to meet his Jewish employer. Thanks perhaps to Niehans, Maugham survived for nearly fifteen years in rude bodily health. But body outlived mind and so it was that the senile Maugham proceeded to destroy his own great invention, W. Somerset Maugham, the teller of tales, the man inclined to the good and to right action and, above all, to common sense. By the time that old Maugham had finished with himself, absolutely nothing was what it seemed and the double self-portrait that he had given the world in *The Summing Up* and *A Writer's Notebook* was totally undone by this raging Lear upon the Riviera, who tried to disinherit his daughter while adopting Searle as well as producing *Looking Back,* a final set of memoirs not quite as mad as Hemingway's but every bit as malicious. With astonishing ingenuity, the ancient Maugham mined his own monument; and blew it up.

For seven decades Maugham had rigorously controlled his personal and his artistic life. He would write so many plays, and stop; and did. So many short stories . . . He rounded off everything neatly, and lay back to die, with a quiet world-weary smile on those ancient lizard lips. But then, to his horror, he kept on living, and having sex, and lunching with Churchill and Beaverbrook. Friends thought that Beaverbrook put him up to the final memoir, but I suspect that Maugham had grown very bored with a lifetime of playing it so superbly safe.

2

It is very difficult for a writer of my generation, if he is honest, to pretend indifference to the work of Somerset Maugham. He was always so entirely *there.* By seventeen I had read all of Shakespeare; all of Maugham. Perhaps more to the point, he dominated the movies at a time when movies were the lingua franca of the world. Although the French have told us that the movie is the creation of the director, no one in the Twenties, Thirties, Forties paid the slightest attention to who had directed *Of Human Bondage, Rain, The Moon and Sixpence, The Razor's Edge, The Painted Veil, The Letter.* Their true creator was W. Somerset Maugham, and a generation was in thrall to his sensuous, exotic imaginings of a duplicitous world.

Although Maugham received a good deal of dutiful praise in his lifetime, he was never to be taken very seriously in his own country or the United States, as opposed to Japan where he has been for two thirds of a century the most read and admired Western writer. Christopher Isherwood tells us that he met Maugham at a Bloomsbury party where Maugham looked most ill-at-ease with the likes of Virginia Woolf. Later Isherwood learned from a friend of Maugham's that before the party, in an agony of indecision, as the old cliché master might have put it, he had paced his hotel sitting room, saying, "I'm just as good as they are."

I suspect that he thought he was probably rather better *for what he was,* which was not at all what they were. Bloomsbury disdained action and commitment other than to Art and to Friendship (which meant going to bed with one another's husbands and wives). Maugham liked action. He risked his life in floods, monsoons, the collapse of holy Russia. He was worldly like Hemingway, who also stalked the big game of wild places, looking for stories, self. As for what he thought of himself, Mr. Calder quotes Maugham to the headmaster of his old school: "I think I ought to have the OM [Order of Merit] . . . They gave Hardy the OM and I think I am the greatest living writer of English, and they ought to give it to me." When he did get a lesser order, Companion of Honour, he was sardonic: "It means very well done . . . but."

But. There is a definite but. I have just reread for the first time in forty years *The Narrow Corner,* a book I much admired; *The Razor's Edge,* the novel on which the film that I found the ultimate in worldly glamour was based; *A Writer's Notebook,* which I recalled as being very wise; and, yet again, *Cakes and Ale.* Edmund Wilson's famous explosion at the success of Maugham in general and *The Razor's Edge* in particular is not so far off the mark.

The language is such a tissue of clichés that one's wonder is finally aroused at the writer's ability to assemble so many and at his unfailing inability to put anything in an individual way.

Maugham's reliance on the banal, particularly in dialogue, derived from his long experience in the theatre, a popular art form in those days. One could no more represent the people on stage without clichés than one could produce an episode of *Dynasty*: Maugham's dialogue is a slightly sharpened version of that of his audience.

Both Wilde and Shaw dealt in this same sort of realistic speech but Shaw was a master of the higher polemic (as well as of the baleful clichés of the quaint working-man, rendered phonetically to no one's great delight) while Wilde made high verbal art of clichés so slyly crossed as to yield incongruent wit. But for any playwright of that era (now, too), the *mot juste* was apt to be the correctly deployed *mot banal*. Maugham's plays worked very well. But when Maugham transferred the tricks of the theatre to novel writing, he was inclined not only to write the same sort of dialogue that the stage required but in his dramatic effects he often set his scene with stage directions, ignoring the possibilities that prose *with* dialogue can yield. The economy won him many readers, but there is no rapture, song. Wilson, finally, puts him in the relation of Bulwer-Lytton to Dickens: "a half-trashy novelist who writes badly, but is patronized by half-serious readers who do not care much about writing." What ever happened to those readers? How can we get them back?

Wilson took the proud modernist view that, with sufficient education, everyone would want to move into Axel's Castle. Alas, the half-serious readers stopped reading novels long ago, while the "serious" read literary theory, and the castle's ruins are the domain of literary archaeologists. But Wilson makes a point, inadvertently: if Maugham is half-trashy (and at times his most devoted admirers would probably grant that) what, then, is the other half, that is not trash? Also, why is it that just as one places, with the right hand, the laurel wreath upon his brow, one's left hand starts to defoliate the victor's crown?

*A Writer's Notebook* (kept over fifty years) is filled with descriptions of sunsets and people glimpsed on the run. These descriptions are every bit as bad as Wilson's (in *The Twenties*) and I don't see why either thought that writing down a fancy description of a landscape could—or should—be later glued to the page of a novel in progress. Maugham's descriptions, like Wilson's, are disagreeably purple while the physical descriptions of people are more elaborate than what we now put up with. But Maugham was simply following the custom of nineteenth-century novelists in telling us whether or not eyebrows grow together while noting the exact placement of a wen. Also, Dr. Maugham's checklist is necessary for diagnosis. Yet he does brood on style; attempts to make epigrams. "Anyone can tell the truth, but only very few of us can make epigrams." Thus, young Maugham, to which the old Maugham retorts, "In the nineties, however, we all tried to."

In the preface, Maugham expatiates on Jules Renard's notebooks, one of the great delights of world literature and, as far as I can tell, unknown to Anglo-Americans, like so much else. Renard wrote one small master-piece, *Poil de Carotte,* about his unhappy childhood—inhuman bondage to an evil mother rather than waitress.

Renard appeals to Maugham, though "I am always suspicious of a novelist's theories, I have never known them to be anything other than a justification of his own shortcomings." Well, that is commonsensical. In any case, Maugham, heartened by Renard's marvelous notebook, decided to publish his own. The tone is world-weary, modest. "I have retired from the hurly-burly and ensconced myself not uncomfortably on the shelf." Thus, he will share his final musings.

There is a good deal about writing. High praise for Jeremy Taylor:

He seems to use the words that come most naturally to the mouth, and his phrases, however nicely turned, have a colloquial air . . . The long clauses, tacked on to one another in a string that appears interminable, make you feel that the thing has been written without effort.

Here, at twenty-eight, he is making the case for the plain and the flat and the natural sounding:

There are a thousand epithets with which you may describe the sea. The only one which, if you fancy yourself a stylist, you will scrupulously avoid is *blue;* yet it is that which most satisfies Jeremy Taylor . . . He never surprises. His imagination is without violence or daring.

Of Matthew Arnold's style, "so well suited to irony and wit, to exposi-tion . . . It is a method rather than an art, no one more than I can realize what enormous labour it must have needed to acquire that mellifluous cold brilliance. It is a platitude that simplicity is the latest acquired of all qualities . . ." The interesting giveaway here is Maugham's assump-tion that Arnold's style must have been the work of great labour. But suppose, like most good writers, the style was absolutely natural to Arnold and without strain? Here one sees the hard worker sternly shaping himself rather than the natural writer easily expressing himself as temperament requires:

My native gifts are not remarkable, but I have a certain force of character which has enabled me in a measure to supplement my deficiencies. I have common sense . . . For many years I have been described as a cynic; I told the truth. I wish no one to take me for other than I am, and on the other hand I see no need to accept others' pretences.

One often encounters the ultimate accolade "common sense" in these musings. Also, the conceit that he is what you see, when, in fact, he is not. For instance, his native gifts for narrative were of a very high order. While, up to a point, he could tell the truth and so be thought cynical, it was always "common sense," a.k.a. careerism, that kept him from ever saying all that he knew. Like most people, he wanted to be taken for what he was not; hence, the great invention W. Somerset Maugham.

Maugham uses his Moscow experience to good literary advantage. He reads the Russians. Marvels at their small cast of characters. Notes that no one in a Russian book ever goes to an art gallery. Later, he travels through America, wondering what the people on the trains are really like. Then he reads, with admiration, *Main Street,* where he detects the emergence of a complex caste system: "The lip service which is given to equality occasions a sort of outward familiarity, but this only makes those below more conscious of the lack of inward familiarity; and so nowhere is class-hatred likely to give rise in the long run to more bitter enmity."

Maugham was alert to the persisting problem of how to be a writer at all: certainly the writer "must never entirely grow up . . . It needs a peculiar turn of mind in a man of fifty to treat with great seriousness the passion of Edwin for Angelina." Or Edmund for Daisy. "The novelist is dead in the man who has become aware of the triviality of human affairs. You can often discern in writers the dismay with which they have recognized this situation in themselves." He notes how Flaubert turned from *Madame Bovary* to *Bouvard et Pécuchet,* George Eliot and H. G. Wells to "sociology," Hardy to *The Dynasts*—a step farther up Parnassus but no one thought so then.

Maugham's great enthusiasm is for Chekhov, a fellow doctor, playwright, and short-story writer:

He has been compared with Guy de Maupassant, but one would presume only by persons who have read neither. Guy de Maupassant is a clever story-teller, effective at his best—by which, of course, every writer has the right to be judged—but without much real relation to life . . . But with

Chekhov you do not seem to be reading stories at all. There is no obvious cleverness in them and you might think that anyone could write them, but for the fact that nobody does. The author has had an emotion and he is able so to put it in words that you receive it in your turn. You become his collaborator. You cannot use of Chekhov's stories the hackneyed expression of the slice of life, for a slice is a piece cut off and that is exactly the impression you do not get when you read them; it is a scene seen through the fingers which you know continues this way and that though you only see a part of it.

Mr. Maugham knows very well what literature is, and how great effects are, if not made, received.

Finally, he makes a bit of literature in one of the notebook entries. A popular writer of the day, Haddon Chambers, is dead. He is known for one phrase, "the long arm of coincidence." Maugham does a short amusing sketch of Chambers, the man and the writer; then he concludes: "I seek for a characteristic impression with which to leave him. I see him lounging at a bar, a dapper little man, chatting good-humouredly with a casual acquaintance of women, horses and Covent Garden opera, but with an air as though he were looking for someone who might at any moment come in at the door." That is very fine indeed, and Mr. Chambers still has a small corner of life in that bar, in that paragraph.

My only memory of *The Razor's Edge* (1944) was that of an American lady who threw a plate at the narrator, our own Mr. Maugham, with the cry, "And you can call yourself an English gentleman," to which Mr. Maugham, played urbanely in the movie by Herbert Marshall, responded niftily, "No, that's a thing I've never done in all my life." The scene has remained in my memory all these years because it is almost the only one in the book that has been dramatised. Everything else is relentlessly told. The first-person narrator, so entirely seductive in the short stories, is now heavy, garrulous, and awkward, while the clichés are not only "tissued" but Maugham even cocks, yes, a snook at his critics by recording every one of an American businessman's relentless banalities. Of course, the author is sixty-nine. Maugham's view of the world was consistent throughout his life. Intrigued by religion, he remained an atheist. Vedanta was attractive, but reincarnation was simply not common sense. If you had no recollection of any previous incarnations, what was the point? For all practical purposes the first carnation was extinct when it died, and all the others random. But during the

Second War there was a lot of musing about the meaning of it all, and out of that age's anxiety did come Thomas Mann's masterpiece, *Dr. Faustus.*

Maugham stalks similar game. Again, the narrator is our Mr. Maugham, the all-wise, all-tolerant Old Party who knows a thing or two. Nearby, on the Riviera, lives Elliot Templeton, an elegant snobbish old queen whose identity was revealed for the first time in the pages of *The New York Review of Books* (September 29, 1983) as Henry de Courcey May. (Mr. Calder thinks that the character is, in part, Chips Channon, but Chips is separately present as Paul Barton, another American social climber.) Elliott is an amusing character (Mr. Calder finds him "brilliant") but Maugham can't do very much with him other than give him a Chicago niece. And money, Paris. Love. The niece is in love with Larry Darrell—why a name so close to real life Larry Durrell? Maugham's names for characters (like Hemingway's) are standard for the time—highly forgettable Anglo-Saxon names. Why? Because novels were read by a very large public in those days and any but the most common names could bring on a suit for libel.

Larry does not want to go to work, he wants to "loaf." This means that he has spiritual longings: what does it all mean? He wants to know. He loses the girl to a wealthy young man who doesn't care what it may or may not mean. In pursuit of *it,* Larry becomes very learned in Germany; he works in a coal mine; he goes to India and discovers Vedanta. He returns to the world perhaps with *it* or perhaps not since *it* is an illusion like all else.

Maugham and Larry sit up all night in a bistro while Larry tells him the entire story of his life, much of which Maugham has already told us: it is very dangerous to be your own narrator in a book. Finally, as the dawn like a frightened Scottish scone peeps through the bistro window, Larry tells and tells about India. And Vedanta.

Larry wants nothing less than Enlightenment. Does he achieve it? Maugham teases us. Yes, no, it's all the same, isn't it? There are several short stories intercut with Larry's passion play: a brilliant poetic girl becomes a drunken drug-ridden hag and ends up on the Riviera and in the Mediterranean, murdered by a piece of trade. Proof to Mr. Calder and his Freudian friends that because Maugham liked males he (what else?) hated females. This is one of the rocks on which the whole Freudian structure has been, well . . . erected. For the witch-doctors, Maugham's invention of such a woman is *prima facie* evidence of his hatred of the opposite sex, which vitiated his work and made it impossible for him to be truly great and married. Yet in real life it is the other-sexers (Hemingway) who hate women, and the same-sexers (Maugham) who see them not as women but, as someone observed of Henry James's response to the ladies, as people. Finally, even the most confused witch-doctor must have stumbled upon that essential law of human behaviour: one cannot hate what one cannot love. Nevertheless, as members of chemistry departments still search for cold fusion, so dedicated English teachers still seek to crack the fairy code.

Depressed, I move on to *The Narrow Corner*. On the first page, the energy is switched on. First chapter: "All this happened a good many years ago." That's it. One settles in. Second chapter begins. "Dr Saunders yawned. It was nine o'clock in the morning." An English doctor (under a cloud in England—abortion? We are not told). He practices medicine in the Chinese port of Fu-chou. There is no Mrs. Saunders. There is a beautiful Chinese boy who prepares his opium pipes. Sentences are short. Descriptions of people are never tedious. We inhabit Dr. Saunders's mind for most of the book though, as always, Maugham will shift the point of view to someone else if for some reason Dr. Saunders is not witness to a necessary scene. This is lazy but a lot better than having someone sit down and tell you the story of his life, in quotation marks, page after page.

Dr. Saunders is offered a great deal of money to operate on a rich Chinese opium trafficker, domiciled on the island of Takana in the distant Malay archipelago (a trip as momentous and hazardous in those days as one from Ann Arbor to East Anglia today). By page seven the trip has been made and a successful operation for cataract has been performed. Now Dr. Saunders and beautiful Chinese boy are looking for a ship to get them home again. Enter Captain Nichols, a man under numerous clouds, but a first-class English skipper. Dr. Saunders is amused by the rogue who has arrived aboard a lugger out of Sydney, destination vague. They spar. Each notes the other's cloud. Will Dr. Saunders leave the island aboard Nichols's boat?

Dr Saunders was not a great reader. He seldom opened a novel. Interested in character, he liked books that displayed the oddities of human nature, and he had read over and over again Pepys and Boswell's Johnson, Florio's Montaigne and Hazlitt's essays . . . He read neither for information nor to improve his mind, but sought in books occasion for reverie.

In 1938, George Santayana dismissed Maugham's stories; "They are not pleasing, they are not pertinent to one's real interests, they are not true; they are simply plausible, like a bit of a dream that one might drop into in an afternoon nap." Yet, perhaps, that is a necessary condition of narrative fiction, a plausible daydreaming. Although Maugham could never have read Santayana's letter to a friend, he returns the compliment in *A Writer's Notebook:*

I think Santayana has acquired his reputation in America owing to the pathetically diffident persuasion of Americans that what is foreign must have greater value than what is native . . . To my mind Santayana is a man who took the wrong turning. With his irony, his sharp tongue, common-sense and worldly wisdom, his sensitive understanding, I have a notion that he could have written semi-philosophical romances after the manner of Anatole France which it would have been an enduring delight to read . . . It was a loss to American literature when Santayana decided to become a philosopher rather than a novelist.

Kindly vocational guidance from Uncle Willie; or it takes one to . . .

The plot: aboard the lugger is an edgy young Australian beauty (this was Maugham's one and only crypto-fag novel). Fred Blake is also under a cloud but where Doctor and Skipper each wears his cloud *pour le sport,* Fred seems ready to jump, as they say, out of his skin. It is finally agreed that the Doctor accompany them to one of the Dutch islands where he can find a ship for home. They embark. There is a storm at sea, not quite as well rendered as that in *Williwaw,* but Maugham's influence permeates those chaste pages, even down to the annoying use of *i* and *ii* as chapter heads. Plainly, the book had a large effect on the youthful war writer.

Finally, they arrive at the Dutch island of Banda Neira. There are substantial Dutch houses with marble floors, relics of a former prosperity, as well as nutmeg trees, all the props. They encounter a noble Danish youth, Eric Christessen, who in turn introduces them to a one-time English school teacher, Frith, and his daughter, Louise. The saintly Eric is in love with beautiful Louise, who is enigmatic. Dr. Saunders sees the coming tragedy but the others are unaware, particularly the trusting Eric, who says, early on, how much he likes the East. "Everyone is so nice. Nothing is too much trouble. You cannot imagine the kindness I've received at the hands of perfect strangers." I was not the only American writer to be influenced by this book.

In 1948, after Tennessee Williams had read my "bold" novel, *The City and the Pillar,* we tried to remember what books we had read that dealt, overtly or covertly, with same-sexuality. Each had a vivid memory of *The Narrow Corner.* According to Mr. Calder, Maugham himself was somewhat nervous of his romantic indiscretion. "Thank heavens nobody's seen it," he said to his nephew Robin at about the same time that Tennessee and I were recalling a novel each had intensely "seen." Another novel that each had read was James M. Cain's *Serenade* (1937), where bisexual singer loses voice whenever he indulges in same-sex but gets it back when he commits other-sex, which he does, triumphantly, in Mexico one magical night in the presence of—get cracking, Williams scholars—an iguana.

Fred and Louise couple for a night. Eric finds out and kills himself. Louise is sad but confesses to the doctor that she really did not love Eric, who had been enamoured not so much of her as of her late mother. She is, in her quiet way, a startling character. The lugger sails away. Then Fred's cloud is revealed: by accident, he murdered the husband of an older woman who had been hounding him. Fred's lawyer father is a great power in the corrupt government of New South Wales (*tout ça change,* as we say in Egypt), Fred is whisked away by Captain Nichols. In due course, it is learned that Fred is supposed to have died in a flu epidemic. So he is now a nonperson under two clouds. Dr. Saunders leaves them. Some time later, Dr. Saunders is daydreaming in Singapore when Nichols reappears. Fred fell overboard and drowned. Apparently all his money was in his belt which so weighed him down . . . Worse, he had won all of Nichols's money at cribbage. Plainly, the doomed boy had been killed for his money which, unknown to Nichols, he took with him to Davy Jones's locker. Nothing is . . .

The novel still has all of its old magic. There is not a flaw in the manner except toward the end where Maugham succumbs to sentiment. Fred:

'Eric was worth ten of her. He meant all the world to me. I loathe the thought of her. I only want to get away. I want to forget. How could she trample on that lone noble heart!' Dr Saunders raised his eyebrows. Language of that sort chilled his sympathy. 'Perhaps she's very unhappy,' he suggested mildly.

'I thought you were a cynic. You're a sentimentalist.'

'Have you only just discovered it?'

Sincerity in a work of art is always dangerous and Maugham, uncharacteristically, lets it mar a key scene because, by showing that boy cared more for boy than girl, he almost gives away at least one game. But recovery was swift and he was never to make that mistake again. As he observed in *Cakes and Ale*:

I have noticed that when I am most serious people are apt to laugh at me, and indeed when after a lapse of time I have read passages that I wrote from the fullness of my heart I have been tempted to laugh at myself. It must be that there is something naturally absurd in a sincere emotion, though why there should be I cannot imagine, unless it is that man, the ephemeral inhabitant of an insignificant planet, with all his pain and all his striving is a jest in an eternal mind.

What then of *Cakes and Ale*? The story is told in the first person by the sardonic Ashenden, a middle-aged novelist (Maugham was fifty-six when the book was published in 1930). The manner fits the story, which is not told but acted out. What telling we are told is simply Maugham the master essayist, heir of Hazlitt, commenting on the literary world of his day—life, too. In this short novel he combines his strengths—the discursive essay "peppered" this time with apposite literary allusions to which is added the high craftsmanship of the plays. The dialogue scenes are better than those of any of his contemporaries while the amused comments on literary ambition and reputation make altogether enjoyable that small, now exotic, world.

Plot: a great man of letters, Edward Driffield (modelled on Thomas Hardy), is dead and the second wife wants someone to write a hagiography of this enigmatic rustic figure whose first wife had been a barmaid; she had also been a "nymphomaniac" and she had left the great man for an old lover. The literary operator of the day, Alroy Kear (Maugham's portrait spoiled the rest of poor Hugh Walpole's life), takes on the job. Then Kear realises that Ashenden knew Driffield and his first wife, Rosie. When Ashenden was a boy, they had all lived at the Kentish port, Blackstable. The first line of the book:

I have noticed that when someone asks for you on the telephone and, finding you out, leaves a message . . . as it's important, the matter is more often important to him than to you. When it comes to making you a present or doing you a favour most people are able to hold their impatience within reasonable bounds.

Maugham is on a roll, and the roll continues with great wit and energy to the last page. He has fun with Kear, with Driffield, with himself, with Literature. Ashenden purrs his admiration for Kear: "I could think of no one of my contemporaries who had achieved so considerable a position on so little talent." He commends Kear's largeness of character. On the difficult business of how to treat those who were once equals but are now failed and of no further use at all, Kear "when he had got all he could from people . . . dropped them." But Maugham is not finished:

Most of us when we do a caddish thing harbour resentment against the person we have done it to, but Roy's heart, always in the right place, never permitted him such pettiness. He could use a man very shabbily without afterward bearing him the slightest ill-will.

This is as good as Jane Austen.

Will Ashenden help out even though it is clear that second wife and Kear are out to demonise the first wife, Rosie, and that nothing that Ashenden can tell them about her will change the game plan? Amused, Ashenden agrees to help out. He records his memories of growing up in Blackstable, of the Driffields who are considered very low class indeed: Ashenden's clergyman uncle forbids the boy to see them, but he does. Rosie is a creature of air and fire. She is easy, and loving, and unquestioning. Does she or does she not go to bed with her numerous admirers in the village and later in London where Ashenden, a medical student, sees them again (they had fled Blackstable without paying their bills)?

In London Driffield's fame slowly grows until he becomes the Grand Old Man of Literature. Ashenden's secret—for the purposes of the narrative—is that he, too, had an affair in London with Rosie and when he taxed her with all the others, she was serene and said that that was the way she was and that was that. As writer and moralist Maugham has now travelled from the youthful blurter-out of the truth about woman's potential passion for sex to an acceptance that it is a very good thing indeed and what is wrong with promiscuity if, as they say, no one is hurt? In the end Rosie leaves Driffield for an old love; goes to New York, where, presumably, she and old love are long since dead.

As the narrative proceeds, Maugham has a good deal of fun with the literary world of the day, where, let us note, not one academic can be found (hence its irrelevance?). On the subject of "longevity is genius," he thinks old extinct volcanoes are apt to be praised as reviewers need fear their competition no longer:

But this is to take a low view of human nature and I would not for the world lay myself open to a charge of cheap cynicism. After mature consideration I have come to the conclusion that the real reason for the applause that comforts the declining years of the author who exceeds the common span is that intelligent people after thirty read nothing at all.

This auctorial self-consciousness now hurls old Maugham into the mainstream of our *fin-de-siècle* writing where texts gaze upon themselves with dark rapture. "As they grow older the books they read in their youth are lit with its glamour and with every year that passes they ascribe greater merit to the author that wrote them." Well, that was then; now most intelligent readers under thirty read nothing at all that's not assigned.

"I read in the *Evening Standard* an article by Mr. Evelyn Waugh in the course of which he remarked that to write novels in the first person was a contemptible practice . . . I wish he had explained why . . ." Maugham makes the modest point that with "advancing years the novelist grows less and less inclined to describe more than what his own experience has given him. The first-person singular is a very useful device for this limited purpose."

In *Looking Back,* Maugham "explains" his uncharacteristic portrait of a good and loving woman who gave of herself (sympathy, please, no tea) as being based on an actual woman/affair. Plainly, it is not. But this charade is harmless. What he has done is far better: he makes a brand-new character, Rosie, who appears to be a bad woman, but her "badness" is really goodness. Once again, nothing is what it seems. To the end this half-English, half-French writer was a dutiful and often worthy heir to his great forebears Hazlitt and Montaigne.

Posterity? That oubliette from which no reputation returns. Maugham:

I think that one or two of my comedies may retain for some time a kind of pale life, for they are written in the tradition of English comedy . . . that began with the Restoration dramatists . . . I think a few of my best short stories will find their way into anthologies for a good many years to come if only because some of them deal with circumstances and places to which the passage of time and the growth of civilization will give a romantic glamour. This is slender baggage, two or three plays and a dozen short stories . . .

But then it is no more than Hemingway, say, will be able to place in the overhead rack of the economy section of that chartered flight to nowhere, Twentieth Century Fiction.

I would salvage the short stories and some of the travel pieces, but I'd throw out the now-too-etiolated plays and add to Maugham's luggage *Cakes and Ale,* a small perfect novel, and, sentimentally, *The Narrow Corner.* Finally, Maugham will be remembered not so much for his own work as for his influence on movies and television. There are now hundreds of versions of Maugham's plays, movies, short stories available on cassettes, presumably forever. If he is indeed half-trashy, then one must acknowledge that the other half is of value; that is, *classicus,* "belonging to the highest class of citizens," or indeed of any category; hence, our word "classic"—as in Classics *and* Commercials. Emphasis added.

*The New York Review of Books*
February 1, 1990

# 2 2

·

## *FORD'S WAY*

When the old New Criticism separated Author from Text, the person and place of Author became irrelevant to any rigorous scrutiny of parthenogenetic Text. Since that split occurred more than a half century ago, Text has given way to Theory. Today, with neither significant Text nor lively Author, powerful schoolteachers issue charters to be studied by adepts within the plywood of Academe, where involuntary readers search for validating signs and significations among the entrails of the latest Theory, etherised, as it were, upon a *tabula rasa*. Lately those American schoolteachers who practise Literary Theory have taken to referring to themselves as avant-garde. (At least that was the phrase that I think I heard. The telephone connection was faulty. When I asked what was the garde they were avant to, there was only transatlantic stammering.) In any case, like early Christians we live now in the Piscine Age, with Scorpio rising.

Back in the days of the Scales, there were critics who used to describe what they had read in order to attract and illuminate those common readers who had volunteered to join what was agreed by all to be civilization as written down. The lord of the Scales at mid-century was Edmund Wilson: a true American, he believed in progress. In time, with effort and sufficient goodwill, he believed that the "half-serious reader"

would become serious, and after first disembarking at the Finland station he would book a room at Axel's Castle, and there know the sublime.
But none of this happened. Railroads were superseded by airlines (significantly, in Europe, the train is coming back) and Axel's Castle is now
a part of the B. Dalton chain of motels. As a source of interest for the
serious, film has replaced the novel as the novel replaced the poem in
the last century, soon to be, for us, but one.

The half-serious reader of yesteryear is now the film-buff. The "educated"—that is, functionally literate public—looks at television a great
deal and reads many magazines and newspapers. They read few novels
and though a few of these few are read by hundreds of thousands of
passionately non-serious readers, that is still a small number in a country where something like three hundred million people buzz in and out.
If a new novel is highly praised it might be consumed by five thousand
readers. Edna St. Vincent Millay's verse used to be read in greater
quantities.

Exactly forty years ago I wrote that the novel had lost the general
public for good. Since this was unacceptable news to the ambitious
pen-person, my simple rather obvious statement became: he says the
novel is dead. My words were then made an occasion for the celebrating
of astonishing new talent, testifying to the rare rude health of Lawrence's bright book of life. Well, the truth has never helped anyone who
wanted to write fiction, and perhaps it is just as well that once Author
was driven from the Grove, the Text in its turn should be deconstructed
and abandoned as well in favour of Theory.

Such is the overview from Parnassus. Up close, here on the ground,
pen-persons still charge about hawking their wares, and American
schoolteachers still delight in appropriating for themselves the dignity
and authority of the great makers of literature. But even as they prance
about, English departments are losing would-be adepts even faster than
Christian churches are losing priests, and the celebration of Pulitzer Eve
and Booker Day are as nothing compared to the evangelical hordes that
celebrate the celluloid Host at Cannes. Nevertheless, here, on the
ground where we all must live until we, too, are simply history—that
ultimate act of imagination—novels are still being written for the many
by the—no, not few, the many. In England there are more novelists than
novel-readers. But even in deliciously perverse backward little England
the separation of Text from Author has had a most unexpected effect.
The Text as object of interest has little or no interest for readers,
while the Author as subject has come into his terrible own. Faced with

reading *Across the River and into the Trees,* even the idlest of half-serious readers will turn to a biography of Hemingway. The phenomenon of the past twenty years has been the replacement of Text by Author's life, usually the work of a word-processor, manipulated by a journalist or beautiful-letters writer.

In England, after the Guelph-Pooters and that con-man for all seasons, Churchill, Bloomsbury is the most popular continuing saga for half-serious readers. Who will breast *The Waves* when Mrs. Woolf's diaries and letters are all now at hand like a life-preserver? What real reader does not know every detail of the private lives of the Bloomsbury writers and painters even better than those of his own acquaintance? I once knew, alas, not well, a sensitive high-strung English woman— nerves, indeed, stretched perilously taut—who said that if ever again, even by accident, she were to come across the name Carrington in print, she would kill herself. She . . . Mine eyes dazzle.

In freedom's land the lives of our midcentury poets are studied with all the pity and awe that each sought as he proceeded along his dolorous way to a supremely calculated death through falling from a high place— metaphor!—into a berry patch, or through placing—even more triumphant *closing* metaphor!—a plastic bag over the head in order to suffocate. Who needs *anyone's* poems when we have before us, with footnotes, so many lives gallantly given for the graduate schools?

Today's bookstores are crowded with the lives of writers whose books one would not dream of reading. Where the latest serious novel may sell a few thousand copies, a life of any truly messy author will sell the way novels once did. Look through the pages of any serious journal and you will find that books about writers will outnumber books by writers. Fortunately, every now and then, one of these books may have a missionary function. Such is the case of Alan Judd, who has nicely produced for us *Ford Madox Ford,* whose previous compendious biographer liked neither man nor work, if one has read correctly Arthur Mizener's *The Saddest Story.*

Mr. Judd is himself a lively writer with an attractive conversational style. He never bores. He likes Ford the man as perceived through that perfect confusion known as history (a.k.a. the survivors' revenge). He is shrewd about the novel in general and those novels by Ford in particular, which is pleasing to one who would place Ford among this century's half-dozen major novelists in English. In order to avoid disorder, the names of the other five will not—repeat *not*—be released until January 1, 2000 A.D. at noon. Yet even as one writes the word "major" the whole

game seems hardly worth playing. If Ford is no longer interesting to the
few who read voluntarily, no critic's praise is going to be of much use
beyond providing a small signpost at a largely abandoned crossroads,
whose only travelled lane leads to Academe, which is nowhere in the
yellow wood.

Anyway, over there, through the woods, you may find the best of
historical novels, which is to say a novel that takes place in history (a
category almost as valid if not as dignified as the one that takes place
each summer at Bread Loaf), *The Fifth Queen,* whose subject is not so
much the story of the eighth Henry's fifth wife as of Tudor England, and
the beginning of the modern world that Ford still lived in. We occupy
far different quarters in time, and no one has yet fixed the date when
we ceased to be modern and became merely contemporary; yet somewhere close to the dateline is Ford's *The Good Soldier,* a book he called
his Great Auk's egg; into this he put everything that he knew about the
novel, whose art is entirely dependent on what is left out. Finally, he
wrote the three—or four?—volumes known as *Parade's End,* and for
those who continue to find satisfaction in, say, Flaubert's *Sentimental
Education* or Proust's even longer deeper river, Ford has provided easily
the best set of English variations on the theme of time and what it does
to love and appetite and all the rest, including that now quaint concept,
honour. Along with those three masterpieces, Ford wrote some seventy
other books. "I never knew him when he was not writing a book," said
Katherine Anne Porter. But in a world where books were read voluntarily, this was the normal condition of the born writer; today, however,
when one looks on all those books that bear Ford's name, even the most
eccentric fan becomes intimidated and cannot finish, say, *The Rash Act,*
which Judd admires.

So why isn't Ford on every syllabus? Why is Judd as defensive in tone
as his predecessor Arthur Mizener was offensive? Why do the remaining
"voluntaries" not seem to know Ford's best work? Judd provides some
reasons. As he is English and so, administratively at least, is his subject,
there is a bit of confusion here about class and category, always big
trouble in those now sunny northern isles. Class, category—even nationality. Ford's father, Franz Hueffer, was born in Münster—musical
Hun with money, who had married into the Rossetti circle, oily lot; was
connected with the Garnetts—a small anchor there. Even so, an English
writer who was born Huffer or Hueffer, December 17, 1873? Difficult.
Ford went to top-drawer-but-three schools in England; was blond, Germanic, blue-eyed; fortunately, as Judd nicely notes, "He was always

tall," which may have been some slight compensation for a Hunnish name during the Thirty Years German War now ending, as I write, in a shower of ecus. In due course, the name was changed from Hueffer to Ford. But nothing helped class its owner. As all good writers are, by their work, socially de-classed, he was not unique. But something about him *was* off-putting. Hemingway didn't like his smell. David Garnett confessed to a physical distaste for Ford . . . "too mobile lips." Ford was also pretty fat from maturity on; he smoked and drank far too much and he was besotted by women. This last would do him no good at all in a certain set of very peculiar islands where women are only appreciated by novelists like Henry James, who lusted for men, while in the great republic to the west women figure only as interlocutors of some agonized Man, awash with testosterone, as he tries to do and be what a man must do and be in spite of women, all of them ball-cutters except for, maybe, the rare bore-proof Italian Contessa who can be relied on to ask, at intervals, like a metronome, "Tell me again, Papa, what it was you did that was so manly and so brave and so true in *La Guerra Grande.*"

Until recently, when writing in England became a respectable hereditary occupation, to be a writer at all in a bourgeois society was to banish oneself to the margin. But Ford was born to be, proudly, an artist. The young Hueffers "grew up conscious of themselves as heirs to a culture that transcended national boundaries." Hence, Ford could easily and naturally befriend an icy Pole with a Berlitz problem, responding to the dictum of his beloved grandfather, the painter Ford Madox Brown, who maintained that to work hard for a genius greater than one's own is the highest virtue. Yet good as Ford was to others, he seemed to set everyone's teeth on edge. From youth "he had been an exponent of the Grand Manner"; he spoke of Art not cricket. He was "oracular without repartee or cruelty"; finally, "he never signposted his irony . . . and so it was often missed." That is one clue to his unpopularity. The British can recognise irony only when it is dispensed with an old auntie-ish twinkle, like that of E. M. Forster, while Americans have yet to discover there is such a thing. Once we do, the national motto will produce gargantuan laughter from sea to shining sea. *E pluribus unum* indeed!

Judd is very funny about one of Ford's rambles. Apparently Shakespeare had an ancestor called Hill; so did Ford. So, he mused, perhaps he was a descendant of Shakespeare, the sort of remark that could demoralise an American faculty room, impervious to his freighted tagline: "*Someone* has to be."

Ford's unnatural liking for women and their company did him no good with the English. The fact that he was hopeless in his relations with women did him no harm with women in those days before Eve's shovel reclaimed the Garden. Stella Bowen: "He had a genius for creating confusion." As a conscientious biographer Judd is obliged to tell us about Ford's wives and mistresses, the sort of thing one tends to skip in biographies unless, as in the case of an American modernist poet, there is nothing else to write about save prescription drugs and prizes and tenure. Judd makes Ford's private life sound as interesting as it is possible to make that sort of thing. Early marriage to Elsie; affair with her sister Mary; then on to dashing syphilitic Violet Hunt, the Morgan Le Fay of Edwardian biographies, who once ravished the youthful lizard-lovely body of W. Somerset Maugham, thus ensuring his life-long allegiance to Sodom. Then there comes the Australian Miss Stella Bowen, who kept a written record, usually a fatal business for a loved one, but Ford comes out well in her accounts: then on to Jean Rhys followed by a twilight love with what sounds like a nice American, who survived (survives?). By Elsie, there were two daughters: one became a nun and never saw Ford again; the other did not become a nun and never saw him again. What to make of this? Nothing at all. Just a life.

I must confess to lifelong boredom with the main purpose of literary biography: the Life as opposed to the Work, which is, after all, all. I have also never had the slightest interest in knowing on whom a writer has based the character of Jeff, say, and should Jeff's affair with Jane be just like a real-life one with Gladys, I feel gravity tugging at the volume in my hand. It makes not the slightest difference whether or not one knows a writer's raw material because it is *what* he does with the stuff of his life that matters, and *how* he does it is to be found in the surviving words not in long since made beds. George Painter's enjoyable re-creation of Proust's world is a distinguished work in its own right, but it sheds not a gleam of light on Proust's great fiction. Was Madame Verdurin the Duchesse de Montmorency *ci-devant* Blumenthal? Yes, no, maybe, in part—so what? Although the game is fun to play for its own sake, it is not the sort of game that an English teacher ought to encourage his students to play. It is enough that they learn how to read and understand the fiction *tout court;* to perceive what it is on the page that makes, as the Master said with unusual hard preciseness, *Interest.*

One does not want to discourage the great mills that now churn out literary biography along with bio- and necro-porn. I think that a certain amount of an author's private life is useful in establishing who he was;

and if certain figures influenced him greatly, then one might just as well describe them, as Judd does Marwood, Ford's "model" for the doomed gentleman character of his best work. Beyond that, there is only pointless strain if one seeks to find the originals for characters that are themselves autonomous upon the page and should need no historical antecedent to give them life. This is also applicable, most poignantly, to history itself. But that lesson is for another day.

What interests one in Ford's case? Bloomsbury has turned out to be the epic novel of the twentieth century (will Cousin Maynard take Lytton's Duncan away from him while in the wings a ballerina warms up at the barre?) But contra Bloomsbury there is another epic narrative, lightly described in Miranda Seymour's *A Ring of Conspirators*. This subversive ring was centred in and around Romney Marsh. Personally, I find the ring more congenial and interesting than overblown Bloomsbury and it is within the ring that Ford came into his own as a young writer, established at Pent Farm. Nearby, Henry James, Joseph Conrad and Stephen Crane, who did so much better in prose what Hemingway was later to be credited for. Also the popular enchanter, H. G. Wells.

Judd's story gets very interesting indeed when he describes the unlikely collaboration of Ford and Conrad, which did the former permanent harm in the eyes of bookchatland while benefiting, if nothing else, the Pole's English. Mindful of grandfather's injunction to help genius, Ford at twenty-four made himself available to the forty-one-year-old Conrad. The results of their joint efforts (*The Inheritors, Romance, The Nature of a Crime*) are not memorable, but the fact that a young man with his own work to do should help a down-at-heels foreigner suggests altruism, a quality as hated by the generality as it is rare. Practically, Conrad was the gainer, though gratitude was not in his nature—but then Conrad was a rare sort of coincidence and had he not invented himself, no one else would have wanted to except, perhaps, Ford. But then Ford had a dowsing-rod for genius and hardly ever made a mistake from the pre-war (No. 1) Ezra Pound to the pre-war (No. 2) Robert Lowell. Later as an entrepreneur ("There entered then into me the itch of trying to meddle in English literary affairs"), he edited the *English Review* (1908–09) and, later still, the *Transatlantic Review* (1924–5). Most of the great figures of the Old Modernism owed him a good deal, and repaid him predictably with malice.

If nothing else, Ford gained an audience in Conrad. Each thought the novel could be high art, whose author's non-presence was an irradiating holy ghost: "What is to be aimed at in a style is something so unobtrusive and so quiet—and so beautiful if possible—that the reader should not know he is reading, and be conscious only that he is living in the life of the book . . . a book so quiet in tone, so clearly and so unobtrusively worded, that it should give the effect of a long monologue spoken by a lover at a little distance from his mistress's ear—a book about the invisible relationships between man and man," and so on. There is hardly any novelist who would not more or less subscribe to this prescription.

Ford is stern if not rigid about the intrusion of self. Of *Tess of the D'Urbervilles,* "Hardy was not content mercilessly to render but intervened and pleaded." Better, simply, to show. In this Ford was like the other conspirators. Crane's power was in his apparent absence from his seen-heard narrative. Writer Crane is everything and nothing, like the weather, while James's theory of point of view has now a Sinai-esque power to it. To Ford, "it is, for instance, an obvious and unchanging fact that if an author intrudes his comments into the middle of a story he will endanger the illusion conveyed by that story—but a generation of readers may come along who would prefer witnessing the capers of the author [Richard Poirier's "performing self"] to being carried away by stories and that generation of readers may coincide with a generation of writers tired of self-obliteration . . . then you will have a movement toward diffuseness, backboneless sentences, digressions and inchoateness." He had seen ahead to our own time while officiating at the birth in English of Modernism, giving Joyce, during the accouchement, the inspired interim title for *Finnegans Wake, Work in Progress,* parts of which Ford published. In the 1920s and 30s, Ford saw himself as a link between the garde of the past, Meredith, Hardy, James, and the avant-garde, Joyce, Pound, Lawrence, whose hangers-on, like Hemingway, wanted to abolish the past and be themselves the only morning of the only world to matter. Ford's insistence on the power of the predecessors made him look old-fashioned and pompous to those who painted their workrooms red in order to remind themselves to be modern. But whatever theory Ford as practitioner might hold, he never lost his passion for the making and delivery of literature to voluntary readers: "If a boy tells me he does not like Virgil, I tell him to find something he does like and to read it with attention."

Judd thinks Ford's poems much underrated. He wrote them, according to Robert Lowell, "with his left hand—casually and even contemptuously." Judd has included several very long swatches not only to show us what Ford could do in that line but to fill in the narrative gaps. There are nice lines here and there but the effect, finally, is that of Frost on a bad day; yet as Pound reminds us, "that style of poetry we have come to take for granted but when (Ford) started it he was virtually alone." Pound acknowledged his own debt to Ford, as did Lowell, Tate, William Carlos Williams . . . The poetry, like the prose, unfurls rather like monologue with many dashes and ellipses. In life, we are told, Ford's voice was superbly pitched for intimate narrative, and so it is in the best of his work. The only flaw is the awful copiousness, and the unblottedness: ". . . he would often sit and play patience, working it out, word for word, and then simply do it. He revised very little and disliked even proofreading." Plainly, a swift-drying egg-tempera master ill-suited for slow oils. Since the best writers have nothing to say, only to add, Ford said it all at once and so was not left with those second thoughts—inspired blots—that ultimately add the highest interest.

As is so often the case, Ford's life went on until it stopped. Judd is a pleasant tour guide, with an easy colloquial style that occasionally goes beyond mere prose to something menacing and new: "Quite what passed between she and Mary, like what passed between Mary and Ford, we do not know." This is superb, and reminiscent, if I may drop for an instant the reviewer's anonymous mask, of the butler's line from *Duluth,* "Whom shall I say is calling she?" There are mistakes—it is George Davis, not Davies, who, at *Harper's Bazaar,* published so many good writers. There are delights: Judd's description of Henry James, from Ford's point of view, captures with rare distinction the Master's cosy cruelty. But then Ford's simpleness excited the malice of the intricate. Witness Conrad's tribute to *The Fifth Queen*: "The swansong of historical romance and, frankly, I am glad to have heard it."

Judd accompanies the good soldier to America, to teaching (at Olivet); then back to France and death at sixty-one. He notes again and again Ford's faculty for irritating people, and much is made of his lying, which seems to have been nothing more than a dressing-up and rearrangement of data which in their original form lacked—what shall I say? colour? interest? Most people, writers or not, do this. Certainly, Ford never lied deliberately in order to harm others, as did Truman Capote, or to make himself appear brave and strong and true as did Hemingway, whose own lying finally became a sort of art-form by the time he got round to settling his betters' hash in *A Moveable Feast.* Ford's essential difference from the others was the fact that he was all along what he had imagined himself to be, that latterday unicorn, a gentleman. He enlisted in the Army when he was overage. He saw action, and stayed overseas when he could have gone home. For some reason the voluntariness of his enlistment—like so much else—upsets American book-chatters, particularly Arthur Mizener, who only finds fault with the (by military standards) elderly Ford's clumsiness as a soldier. After all, he was there, and he did not need to be there, unlike the ambulance drivers, say, who were under no military orders to die when told to.

In the wars of Venus, Ford did not traduce publicly his various mates; he kept a Tietjens silence no matter how goaded. In literary matters he lacked "envy to an almost dangerous degree . . ." He believed above all in the importance of art—specifically the art of the novel, which puts him well outside contemporary taste, not to mention Theory. Finally, Ford thought there was such a thing as honour, a set of values by which a life and a work could be measured. In the Piscine age the word honour has no meaning at all for Americans, and who would be so cruel as to ask a Brit of today what honour is as opposed to was?

*The Times Literary Supplement* (London)
June 22–28, 1990

# 23

---◆---

# *THE SEXUS*
# *OF HENRY MILLER*

In 1949 Henry Miller sent his friend Lawrence Durrell the two volumes of *Sexus* that together comprise one of the seven sections of his long-awaited masterwork, *The Rosy Crucifixion* (Rosicrucian?). The other parts are titled *Nexus, Plexus,* and presumably anything else that ends in "exus." Durrell's reaction to *Sexus* has been published in that nice book, *Lawrence Durrell and Henry Miller: A Private Correspondence*: "I must confess I'm bitterly disappointed in [*Sexus*], despite the fact that it contains some of your very best writing to date. But, my dear Henry, the moral vulgarity of so much of it is artistically painful. These silly meaningless scenes which have no *raison d'être,* no humor, just childish explosions of obscenity—what a pity, what a terrible pity for a major artist not to have a critical sense enough to husband his force, to keep his talent aimed at the target. What on earth possessed you to leave so much twaddle in?"

Miller's response was serene and characteristic. "I said it before and I repeat it solemnly: I am writing exactly what I want to write and the way I want to do it. Perhaps it's twaddle, perhaps not. . . . I am trying to reproduce in words a block of my life which to me has the utmost significance—every bit of it. Not because I am infatuated with my own ego. You should be able to perceive that only a man without ego could write thus about himself. (Or else I am really crazy. In which case, pray for me.)"

*Sexus* is a very long book about a character named Henry Miller (though at times his first name mysteriously changes to Val) who lives in Brooklyn (circa 1925) with a wife and daughter; he works for the Cosmodemonic Telegraph Company of North America (Western Union) and conducts an affair with a dance-hall girl named Mara (whose first name changes to Mona halfway through and stays Mona). In the course of six hundred and thirty-four pages, the character Henry Miller performs the sexual act many times with many different women, including, perversely, his wife, whom he does not much like. By the end of the book he has obtained a divorce and Mara-Mona becomes his second or perhaps third wife, and he dreams of freedom in another land.

Because of Miller's hydraulic approach to sex and his dogged use of four-letter words, *Sexus* could not be published in the United States for twenty-four years. Happily, the governors of the new American Empire are not so frightened of words as were the custodians of the old Republic. *Sexus* can now be dispensed in our drugstores, and it will do no harm, even without prescription.

Right off, it must be noted that only a total egotist could have written a book which has no subject other than Henry Miller in all his sweet monotony. Like shadows in a solipsist's daydream, the other characters flit through the narrative, playing straight to the relentless old exhibitionist whose routine has not changed in nearly half a century. Pose one: Henry Miller, sexual athlete. Pose two: Henry Miller, literary genius and life force. Pose three: Henry Miller and the cosmos (they have an understanding). The narrative is haphazard. Things usually get going when Miller meets a New Person at a party. New Person immediately realizes that this is no ordinary man. In fact, New Person's whole life is often changed after exposure to the hot radiance of Henry Miller. For opening the door to Feeling, Miller is then praised by New Person in terms which might turn the head of God—but not the head of Henry Miller, who notes each compliment with the gravity of the recording angel. If New Person is a woman, then she is due for a double thrill. As a lover, Henry Miller is a national resource, on the order of Yosemite National Park. Later, exhausted by his unearthly potency, she realizes that for the first time she has met Man . . . one for whom *post coitum* is not *triste* but rhetorical. When lesser men sleep, Miller talks about the cosmos, the artist, the sterility of modern life. Or in his own words: ". . . our conversations were like passages out of *The Magic Mountain*, only more virulent, more exalted, more sustained, more provocative, more inflammable, more dangerous, more menacing, and much more, ever so much more, exhausting."

Now there is nothing inherently wrong with this sort of bookmaking. The literature of self-confession has always had an enormous appeal, witness the not entirely dissimilar successes of Saints Augustine and Genet. But to make art of self-confession it is necessary to tell the truth. And unless Henry Miller is indeed God (not to be ruled out for lack of evidence to the contrary), he does not tell the truth. Everyone he meets either likes or admires him, while not once in the course of *Sexus* does he fail in bed. Hour after hour, orgasm after orgasm, the great man goes about his priapic task. Yet from Rousseau to Gide the true confessors have been aware that not only is life mostly failure, but that in one's failure or pettiness or wrongness exists the living drama of the self. Henry Miller, by his own account, is never less than superb, in life, in art, in bed. Not since the memoirs of Frank Harris has there been such a record of success in the sack. Nor does Miller provide us with any sort of relief. One could always skip Frank Harris's erotic scenes in favor of literary and political gossip. But Miller is much too important for gossip. People do not interest him. Why should they? They are mere wedding guests: he is the Ancient Mariner.

At least half of *Sexus* consists of tributes to the wonder of Henry Miller. At a glance men realize that he *knows.* Women realize that he *is.* Mara-Mona: "I'm falling in love with the strangest man on earth. You frighten me, you're so gentle . . . I feel almost as if I were with a god." Even a complete stranger ("possibly the countess he had spoken of earlier") is his for the asking the moment she sees him. But, uniquely, they both prefer to chat. The subject? Let the countess speak for herself: "Whoever the woman is you love, I pity her . . . Nobody can hold you for long . . . You make friends easily, I'm sure. And yet there is no one whom you can really call your friend. You are alone. You will always be alone." She asks him to embrace her. He does, chastely. Her life is now changed. "You have helped, in a way . . . You always help, indirectly. You can't help radiating energy, and that is something. People lean on you, but you don't know why." After two more pages of this keen analysis, she tells him, "Your sexual virility is only the sign of a greater power, which you haven't begun to use." She never quite tells him what this power is, but it must be something pretty super because everyone else can also sense it humming away. As a painter friend (male) says, "I don't know any writer in America who has greater gifts than you. I've always believed in you—and I will even if you prove to be a failure." This is heady praise indeed, considering that the painter has yet to read anything Miller has written.

Miller is particularly irresistible to Jews: "You're no Goy. You're a black Jew. You're one of those fascinating Gentiles that every Jew wants to shine up to." Or during another first encounter with a Jew (Miller seems to do very well at first meetings, less well subsequently): "I see you are not an ordinary Gentile. You are one of those lost Gentiles—you are searching for something . . . With your kind we are never sure where we stand. You are like water—and we are rocks. You eat us away little by little—not with malice, but with kindness . . ." Even when Miller has been less than loyal in his relations with others, he is forgiven. Says a friend: "You don't seem to understand what it means to give and take. You're an intellectual hobo . . . You're a gangster, do you know that?" He chuckled. "Yes, Henry, that's what you are—you're a spiritual gangster." The chuckle saves the day for lovable Henry.

Yet Henry never seems to do anything for anyone, other than to provide moments of sexual glory which we must take on faith. He does, however, talk a lot and the people he knows are addicted to his conversation. "Don't stop talking now . . . please," begs a woman whose life is being changed, as Henry in a manic mood tells her all sorts of liberating things like "Nothing would be bad or ugly or evil—if we really let ourselves go. But it's hard to make people understand that." To which the only answer is that of another straight man in the text who says, "You said it, Henry. Jesus, having you around is like getting a shot in the arm." For a man who boasts of writing nothing but the truth, I find it more than odd that not once in the course of a long narrative does anyone say, "Henry, you're full of shit." It is possible, of course, that no one ever did, but I doubt it.

Interlarded with sexual bouts and testimonials are a series of prose poems in which the author works the cosmos for all it's worth. The style changes noticeably during these arias. Usually Miller's writing is old-fashioned American demotic, rather like the prose of one of those magazines Theodore Dreiser used to edit. But when Miller climbs onto the old cracker barrel, he gets very fancy indeed. Sentences swell and billow, engulfing syntax. Arcane words are put to use, often accurately: ecto-plasmic, mandibular, anthropophagous, terrene, volupt, occipital, fatidical. Not since H. P. Lovecraft has there been such a lover of language. Then, lurking pale and wan in this jungle of rich prose, are the Thoughts: "Joy is founded on something too profound to be understood and communicated: To be joyous is to be a madman in a world of sad ghosts." Or: "Only the great, the truly distinctive individuals resemble one another. Brotherhood doesn't start at the bottom, but at the top." Or: "Sex and poverty go hand in hand." The interesting thing about the Thoughts is that they can be turned inside out and the effect is precisely the same: "Sex and affluence go hand in hand," and so on.

In nearly every scene of *Sexus* people beg Miller to give them The Answer, whisper The Secret, reveal The Cosmos; but though he does his best, when the rosy crucial moment comes he invariably veers off into platitude or invokes high mysteries that can be perceived only through Feeling, never through thought or words. In this respect he is very much in the American grain. From the beginning of the United States, writers of a certain kind, and not all bad, have been bursting with some terrible truth that they can never quite articulate. Most often it has to do with the virtue of feeling as opposed to the vice of thinking. Those who try to think out matters are arid, sterile, anti-life, while those who float about in a daffy daze enjoy copious orgasms and the happy knowledge that they are the salt of the earth. This may well be true but Miller is hard put to prove it, if only because to make a case of any kind, cerebration is necessary, thereby betraying the essential position. On the one hand, he preaches the freedom of the bird, without attachments or the need to justify anything in words, while on the other hand, he feels obligated to write long books in order to explain the cosmos to us. The paradox is that if he really meant what he writes, he would not write at all. But then he is not the first messiah to be crucified upon a contradiction.

It is significant that Miller has had a considerable effect on a number of writers better than himself—George Orwell, Anaïs Nin, Lawrence Durrell, to name three at random—and one wonders why. Obviously his personality must play a part. In the letters to Durrell he is a most engaging figure. Also, it is difficult not to admire a writer who has so resolutely gone about his own business in his own way without the slightest concession to any fashion. And though time may have turned the Katzenjammer Kid into Foxy Grandpa, the old cheerful anarchy remains to charm.

Finally, Miller helped make a social revolution. Forty years ago it was not possible to write candidly of sexual matters. The door was shut. Then the hinges were sprung by D. H. Lawrence, and Miller helped kick it in. Now other doors need opening (death is the new obscenity). Nevertheless, at a certain time and in a certain way, Henry Miller fought the good fight, for which he deserves not only our gratitude but a permanent place of honor in that not inconsiderable company which includes such devoted figures as Havelock Ellis, Alfred C. Kinsey, and Marie C. Stopes.

*Book Week*
August 1, 1965

# 24

·

# PEN PALS:
# HENRY MILLER AND
# LAWRENCE DURRELL

The dust-jacket of *The Durrell-Miller Letters 1935–80,* edited by Ian S. MacNiven, shows three protagonists sprawled in a shallow wine-dark sea—Lawrence Durrell, Henry Miller, and Henry Miller's numinous cock. Needless to say, it is the third that not only rivets attention but commands nostalgia and, well, let us be honest, pity and awe. Like so many celebrities caught off-guard, the protagonist of a million words looks slightly exhausted and rather smaller than one recalls it from Literature; and yet even in its fragile state one senses that humming hydraulic energy which made it the stuff of legend in the first place. Durrell, beautiful leprechaun in his twenties, cradles modestly—nervously?—raised knees while on his lips there is a virginal archaic smile. The rest of Henry Miller looks rather like a frustrated stage-mother about to burst into a chorus of "Everything's Coming Up Roses" from *Gypsy.*

In the preface by Alfred Perlès, a friend of the two if not the three, all sorts of high claims are made for their correspondence now that "There are more letters being written . . . than ever before in the history of man." This is inaccurate. For half a century, the telephone conversation has largely replaced letter-writing; and since only mad American presidents tape their conversations, the unique telephone artistry of a

Truman Capote, say, is forever lost to us except as a nasal whine in the
aural memory of ageing listeners.

Perlès does describe how he was present when Durrell came to Paris
to meet Miller in 1937. Durrell was twenty-five; Miller was forty-six.
Two years earlier, Durrell had read Miller's underground success,
*Tropic of Cancer,* and thus began a correspondence that was to continue
to the end of Miller's life. Unalike in background, they also proved to
be far more unalike as writers than either suspected. But at the beginning there is only joy as the two Outsiders plot the storming of Parnassus and the setting up of a new god that will look suspiciously like the
holy ghost of their trinity.

Miller was that rarest of literary types: a true American proletarian
who had somehow discovered literature and then, in a wacky autodidac-
tic way, made himself a master of a kind. If he often sounded like the
village idiot, that was because, like Whitman, he was the rest of the
village as well. Durrell's background was conventional; a product of
the civil service mandarin class, he was born in India and sent home to
school in England. School didn't take; so he absconded with his wid-
owed mother to Corfu and took up writing. Durrell's first letter:

*Tropic* turns the corner into a new life which has regained its bowels
. . . I love its guts. I love to see the canons of oblique and pretty emotions
mopped up; to see every whim-wham and bagatelle of our contemporaries
from Eliot to Joyce dunged under. God give us young men the guts to plant
daisies on top and finish the job.

As a Britisher, Durrell's images here are—and continued for some time
to be—related more to the water-closet and the bowels (*The Black Book*
is at its most daring with the fart) than to the priapic and its conventional fodder, Miller's territory. Miller responds: "I particularly prize
your letter because it's the kind of letter I would have written myself
had I not been the author of the book." In due course, they meet. Miller
is certain of his own genius. Durrell fears that he himself can never be
much more than another Somerset Maugham. But priapic Miller has
seriously stirred him and, as Durrell will prove to be the better writer
of the two (if one can compare a lemon to a banana), the *blague* that
they bat across numerous great seas and oceans for forty-five years is
endearing, hilarious and sometimes wise.

The early letters are mostly about literary self-promotion, a sombre
subject. They may be Outsiders but they want to be published and well

reviewed by the likes of Cyril Connolly. On the other hand, George Orwell's meditations on Miller are not appreciated. Durrell: "Orwell is a nice man, but ignorant." Miller: "Orwell-pfui! That man lacks nearly everything in my opinion. He hasn't even a good horizontal view." Eliot is a problem because Durrell is a poet and Eliot is . . . Eliot. Eventually Durrell earns Eliot's praise ("Lawrence Durrell's *Black Book* is the first piece of work by a new English writer to give me any hope for the future of prose fiction"). Later Durrell arranges a meeting between Eliot and Miller; the papal benediction is somewhat coolly bestowed on the village.

The private lives of the two correspondents do not take up much space in their letters. Over the decades, a great many wives and women come and go; a number of children get born. Houses are moved into and out of. Durrell, who is very much a house-person, is forever obliged to move away from that perfect Ionian retreat (for years he was with the British diplomatic service—Argentina, Yugoslavia), while the Bohemian Miller settles down, for most of their correspondence, in California; first, at Big Sur; then on the prosperous Pacific Palisades. Their one continuing link is Anaïs Nin, with whom Miller was conducting an affair when they first met. By profession a muse to greatness, Anaïs had powerful literary longings of her own (she kept a diary, wrote poetic prose); but she would have settled for movie stardom—Luise Rainer, Carmen Miranda, it made no difference—or indeed *anything* that would have made her "a legend," as she referred to herself in later life with no trace, ever, of humour. Fortunately, to the end of her life, Anaïs was married to a wealthy and highly complaisant banker who made it possible for her to publish Miller and herself in pre-war Paris, and bemuse genius.

Durrell mailed Miller the only copy of *The Black Book,* with the airy advice to throw it away if he didn't like it. Miller replied with true feeling: "Why not put in a carbon when you write? What's to prevent it? You will find that you save time and energy." As it was, Henry and Anaïs typed out copies of the book. In the old pre-Xerox world, that was love, dedication. Then they got Kahane's Obelisk Press to publish Durrell in 1938. Miller himself proof-read the book: "I would suggest now, when you receive your copy, that you re-read with an eye to reducing the verbiage . . . You will lose nothing by cutting." In later years Durrell will *tu quoque* this with a vengeance.

Finally, in the summer of 1937, the Durrells meet Miller and Anaïs in Paris. Harmony reigns. Miller is then persuaded to come to Greece,

out of which comes perhaps his best book, *The Colossus of Maroussi,*
based on an outsized, in every sense, fixture in Athens, George Katsim-
balis. Although no politics other than literary is touched on in the letters
of this period, Miller is suddenly terrified by the international situation.
September 1938:

. . . maybe I might find a way to get to Corfu—*if it's safe there?* . . .
Everything would be OK if Anaïs could depend on receiving money from
London regularly . . . Five minutes alone with Hitler and I could have
solved the whole damned problem. They don't know how to deal with the
guy. He's temperamental—and terribly earnest. Somebody has to make him
laugh, or we're all lost.

Plainly the funereal Chamberlain had insufficiently tickled the Führer's
funny-bone. In any case, Miller was all for saving one's own skin:
"Don't let your countrymen play on your emotions. England hasn't a
bloody chance, nor France . . ." But Miller was consistent: *sauve qui peut*
was all that one could do in a world that he had rejected at every level.

Durrell was more conventional; he went to work for the British
Council in Greece. Miller went back to America where, except for an
occasional trip, he would end his days, a cult figure, and content because
he knew "A hundred years from now the phrases I let drop here and
there, in the books and in the letters, will be studied to prove this and
that about me, I know it. But now, even now, I am struck by the
prophetic element which is an essential part of me." Well, we all have
those days but Miller seems to have had them every day.

Over the years Durrell's letters begin to sound more like himself and
less like Miller. Miller never varies; he pounds his big drum, but he is
capable of the shrewd aside, especially his curious love-hate for his
native land upon whose west coast, so close to the Asia of his imagination, he is perched, surrounded by fellow enthusiasts for Zen, astrology,
Lao Tse. Happily, too, his psychic powers never desert him: (1941)
". . . whether the US enters the war or not, there will be a world-wide
revolution to finish this off. *You* will yet see a wonderful period. Neither
England nor Germany will win. We're in for the greatest change the
earth has known."

Fame comes at last to Durrell with *Justine* and the rest of the Alexandria Quartet, much underestimated, in my view, particularly in an age
when explication and literary theory are sovereign and so much teacherly sense as well as nonsense could be made of his works. Each master

affects to find fame a drag: too many intrusions, etc. They are not much interested in other writers except for the ones who admire them. Miller does send Durrell Kerouac's *Dharma Bums.* Durrell's response is sharp:

. . . found it unreadable; no, I admire it in a way, as I admire *Catcher in the Rye.* It is social realism as the Russians understand it. But out of the emptiness really of this generation of self-pitying cry-babies . . . It is only here that I think America is really harming you, making you critically soft; beware of cowboy evangelism and Loving Everything and Everybody Everywhere.

Finally, of the Beats, "They are turning the novel into a skating rink; I am trying to make it a spiral staircase."

Miller strikes back—*re* America: "I loathe everything about it more and more. It's the land of doom." He reiterates his praise for Kerouac's prose; denies he himself is critically soft because he won't read "the celebrities." Durrell comes back even harder: "I found [*Dharma Bums*] really corny and deeply embarrassing (Read pages 30–33 aloud in a strong American voice); and worst of all pretentious . . . As for the writing, yes it's fluent . . . but it has that breathless wondering lisp, the prattling tone which seems to have been handed down to American writers by Anita Loos." Durrell the critic is now zeroing in on his one-time master. But then Miller is having problems with the Quartet. "You know with whom, in some ways, you have a kinship? Malaparte." The *farceur* to end all *farceurs*!

In 1949 Durrell sends Miller a wire: "*Sexus* deliberately bad will completely ruin reputation unless withdrawn revised Larry." Miller bides his time; then he writes of *Monsieur* (1974):

Somewhere after the marvellous episode in the tent . . . the book seemed to fall apart, forgive me for saying so . . . I kept wondering as I read if you had an American publisher for it. (I can't see more than a few hundred Americans capable of reading a book like this.)

In the end the great friendship holds up even though each doesn't really much care for what the other does, a sign not of invidiousness but of mastery. If one thought that someone else could do what one did, one would not do it, for the work of any artist is, to him, by its nature and its intention incomparable; otherwise, he would not bother to write at all.

The 1960s were not as much to Miller's liking as one might have suspected. After watching the Democratic convention on television, he remarks, "How clean a dictatorship like de Gaulle's seems." (This is wiser than he knows. I was a delegate to that convention, chosen not by the people of New York State but by the boss of Tammany, Carmine di Sapio, with orders to vote for Kennedy.) "If Kennedy is our next president . . . something will happen . . . and if Kennedy dies in office we'll have Johnson from Texas, about the narrowest-minded group of people in America, Texans." For once Miller's crystal ball was functioning. He also detested the mindless violence of *Bonnie and Clyde,* an emblematic film of the day. Durrell sees the film as

. . . a US version of the Babes in the Wood. They knew not what the hell they were doing, this is what was frightening on the moral *plane;* its application to young America (or England for that matter—for England has become a sub-culture of the US now) was not only accurate but terrifying. To do ill without having any value in mind which the act represents— that is what flatters the young . . . they feel they are like that—not bad but just lost.

Whatever the ageing duo's faults, easy riding was never one of them.

In the 1970s each is more or less preoccupied by the Nobel Prize, a sort of rigged good citizenship medal, awarded by a largely monolingual club of a small nation noted for its literary taste, cuisine and criminal detection (clue: *not* Belgium). It is fascinating to learn, from Durrell, that an interesting but not exactly Great Citizen, Denis de Rougemont, "missed the Nobel this year by very little" (1971). In 1978 Durrell writes, "I fear your indiscretions will result in Miss De Johngh [sic] and Normal [sic] Mailer being the next. I think to get that sort of prize one must be a sort of UNESCO wire-puller and president of PEN—like Mario Praz (Premier Prix Zagreb, Prix d'Honneur Kiev, etc. etc.)." But Miller is optimistic: "No, I wasn't robbed of Prize by Singer—my applications are for 1979." Obviously they have come a long way from literary outlaws to literary intriguers. Miller: "I must tell you some other time how I offended Artur Lundkvist, Swedish poet and translator (Head of Lit. Committee there!) . . . Let me only say this—there are no greater, no more colossal bores than most Scandinavians, with Sweden in the lead." Durrell responds:

"I didn't know that Lundkvist was on the Committee—he is a Com and received the Prix Lenin; it explains why I lost that year to Steinbeck . . . What the hell."

Towards the close each is truly bemused by the rise of their common muse, Anaïs Nin, who has begun to publish her diaries; she is also rewriting them as she goes along, paying off new as well as old scores. She is Kali incarnate, whom John Dowson describes in *A Classical Dictionary of Hindu Mythology* as "a hideous and terrible countenance, dripping with blood, encircled with snakes, hung round with skulls and human heads, and in all respects resembling a fury rather than a goddess." Over the years Anaïs had managed to quarrel with all her Dauphins (she was Joan of Arc), including me. As Miller grew more famous, she grew bitter. When Durrell, now celebrated too, mentioned in an article that Hugo was her husband, he "had to do a public repentance with sackcloth and ashes." It was Anaïs's special joy to be married to two men at the same time, and no interviewer was too humble not to be taken promptly into her confidence, and then sworn to secrecy. Miller was, until the end, more tolerant of her than Durrell or my estranged self. Miller does wonder (1975), "Why she 'denies' Hugo, who treated her so wonderfully, I can't make out. But talk of 'deceivers'! She takes the cake. We are lucky to be spared, eh?" After Anaïs's death, Durrell writes (1977): "As for Anaïs I suppose the fur will start flying now as they search for the real girl among the four or five masks she left lying about with false clues attached to them." Of course each mask was just like the others and—*honi soit qui mal y pense* . . . Later (1979) Miller has read what purports to be an interview with his ex-wife June: "Scurrilous and full of lies. (She even beats Anaïs at it.)" He then makes a comparison that I thought I was the only one of Anaïs's Dauphins to have noted: "Am now reading a biography of Marie Corelli, my female favorite. Resemblance to Anaïs again. But Corelli more pure, more strong. . . ." There is a lot to this, and though Anaïs will never be more than a series of busy footnotes clacking like castanets through the biographies of others, Marie Corelli might be usefully revived. Certainly, *Sorrows of Satan* is—dare I confess it?—Bookeresque in its moral propriety.

On June 1, 1980, Henry Miller died beside the Pacific Ocean. Durrell continued. Different as the two writers are, each understood Flaubert's axiom "that there is no such thing as subject. Style in itself being an absolute manner of seeing things. All possible prosodic variations have been discovered; but that is far from being the case with prose." Each deployed his own prose over a lifetime, and though I would rather read Durrell than Miller, our literary landscape would be even more lunar than it is had the two of them not passed, so goonily, so cheerfully, so originally through this sad century.

*The Times Literary Supplement* (London)
September 9–15, 1988

# 25

---  ·  ---

# EDMUND WILSON:
# THIS CRITIC AND
# THIS GIN AND
# THESE SHOES

On February 2, 1821, gin-drinker Lord Byron wrote in his Ravenna Journal: "I have been considering what can be the reason why I always wake at a certain hour in the morning, and always in very bad spirits—I may say, in actual despair and despondency, in all respects—even of that which pleased me overnight. . . . In England, five years ago, I had the same kind of hypochondria, but accompanied with so violent a thirst that I have drank as many as fifteen bottles of soda-water in one night, after going to bed, and been still thirsty. . . . What is it?—liver?"

In Edmund Wilson's journal, published as *Upstate,* he wrote, in 1955: "One evening (August 13, Saturday) I drank a whole bottle of champagne and what was left of a bottle of old Grand-Dad and started on a bottle of red wine—I was eating Limburger cheese and gingersnaps. This began about five in the afternoon—I fell asleep in my chair, but woke up when Beverly came, thinking it was the next morning. I decided to skip supper; and felt queasy for the next twenty-four hours." The sixty-year-old Wilson does not ask, what is it? as Byron did. Wilson knows. "This kind of life," he writes, rather demurely, "in the long run, does, however, get rather unhealthy."

About the time that Wilson was munching on those gingersnaps and Limburger cheese, washed down with fiery waters, I received a letter from Upton Sinclair (whom I had never met), asking me about something. Then, obsessively, from left field, as it were, Sinclair denounced John Barleycorn. In the course of a long life, practically every writer Sinclair had known had died of drink, starting with his friend Jack London. Needless to say, this was not the sort of unsolicited letter that one likes to read while starting on one's fifteenth bottle of soda water, or to be precise and up-to-date, Coca-Cola, Georgia's sole gift to a nation whose first century was recently described in a book titled *The Alcoholic Republic* . . . of letters, I remember adding to myself when I first saw the book.

In this century, it would be safe to say that a significant percent of American writers are to a greater or lesser degree alcoholics and why this should be the case I leave to the medicine men. Alcoholism ended the careers of Hemingway, Fitzgerald, and Faulkner, to name three fashionable novelists of our mid-century. Out of charity toward the descendants and keepers of the still flickering flames of once glorious literary figures, I shall name no other names. Heavy drinking stopped Hemingway from writing anything of value in his later years; killed Fitzgerald at forty-four; turned the William Faulkner of *As I Lay Dying* into a fable.

Meanwhile, the contemporary of these three blasted stars, Edmund Wilson, outlived and outworked them all; he also outdrank them. Well into his seventies, Wilson would totter into the Princeton Club and order a half dozen martinis, to be prepared not sequentially but simultaneously—six shining glasses in a bright row, down which Wilson would work, all the while talking and thinking at a rapid pace. To the end of a long life, he kept on making the only thing he thought worth making: sense, a quality almost entirely lacking in American literature where stupidity—if sufficiently sincere and authentic—is deeply revered, and easily achieved. Although this *was* a rather unhealthy life in the long run, Wilson had a very long run indeed. But then, he was perfect proof of the proposition that the more the mind is used and fed the less apt it is to devour itself. When he died, at seventy-seven, he was busy stuffing his head with irregular Hungarian verbs. Plainly, he had a brain to match his liver.

Edmund Wilson was the last of a leisurely educated generation who were not obliged, if they were intellectually minded, to join the hicks and hacks of Academe. Wilson supported himself almost entirely by literary journalism, something not possible today if only because, for all practical purposes, literary journalism of the sort that he practiced no longer exists. Instead, book-chat is now dominated either by academic bureau-crats, crudely pursuing bureaucratic careers, or by journalists whose "leprous jealousy" (Flaubert's pretty phrase) has made mephitic the air of our alcoholic literary republic. But then, Flaubert thought that "crit-ics write criticism because they are unable to be artists, just as a man unfit to bear arms becomes a police spy." Wilson would have challenged this romantic notion. Certainly, he would have made the point that to write essays is as much an aspect of the literary artist's temperament as the ability to evoke an alien sensibility on a page while sweating to avoid a double genitive. In any case, Wilson himself wrote stories, plays, novels. He knew how such things were made even if he was not entirely a master of any of these forms.

Of what, then, was Edmund Wilson a master? That is a question in need of an answer, or answers; and there are clues in the book at hand, *The Thirties: From Notebooks and Diaries of the Period.* At the time of Wilson's death, eight years ago, he was editing the notebooks that dealt with the Twenties. He had already finished *Upstate,* a chronicle of his works and days from the early Fifties to 1970. *Upstate* is a highly satisfactory Wilsonian book, filled with sharp personal details, long scholarly asides on those things or people or notions (like New York religions) that had caught his fancy. Although he had planned to rework his earlier records, he soon realized that he might not live long enough to complete them. He then designated, in his will, that Professor Leon Edel edit the remains, with the injunction that the text be published the way he wrote it, except for straightening out "misspellings and faulty punctuations" (but not, apparently, faulty grammar: Wilson often "feels badly"—it *is* liver). With *The Thirties,* Professor Edel had his work cut out for him because, he writes, "It is clear from the condition of the typescript that [Wilson] intended to do much more work on this book." That is understatement.

At the beginning of the Thirties, Wilson completed *Axel's Castle;* at the end, he had finished *To the Finland Station.* He wrote for *The New Republic,* supported, briefly, the American Communist party, visited the Soviet Union, Detroit, Appalachia, Scotsboro, and tried a season of teaching at the University of Chicago. The decade, in a sense, was the making of him as critic and triple thinker. Emotionally, it was shatter-ing: in 1930 he married Margaret Canby; in 1932 she died. He also conducted a wide range of affairs, many on the raunchy side.

Professor Edel rather flinches at Wilson's "record of his own copula-tions" in general and the notes about his marriage in particular (so unlike the home life of our own dear Master): "some readers may be startled by this intimate candid record of a marriage." But Professor Edel is quick to remind us that this is all part of "the notebooks of a chronicler, a way of tidying the mind for his craft of criticism. . . . He tries, rather, to be a camera, for this is what he finds most comfortable." Well, yes and no.

In 1930 Edmund Wilson was thirty-five. He was a member of the minor Eastern gentry, a Princeton graduate, a World War I overseas noncombatant. In the Twenties, he had lived the life of the roaring boy but unlike the other lads that light-footed it over the greensward, he never stopped reading and writing and thinking. Thanks, in large part, to the Christers who had managed to prohibit the legal sale of spirits, alcohol was as much a curse to that generation as Gin Lane had been to the poor of eighteenth-century London. I suspect that a great deal of the grimness of this volume is a result of hangover and its concomitant despairs. At the same time, it is the record of an astonishing constitution: Wilson would write while he was drinking—something I should not have thought possible for anyone, even his doomed friend Scott Fitzgerald.

From thirty-five to forty-five men go from relative youth to middle age. The transit is often rocky. As a man's life settles into a rut, in mindless rut the man is apt to go. Certainly, this was true of Wilson, as readers of *Memoirs of Hecate County* might have suspected and as readers of *The Thirties* will now know for certain. During the so-called "ignoble" decade, despite constant drinking, Wilson was sexually very active. He enjoyed trade in the form of the Slavic Anna, a working-class woman whose proletarian ways fascinated him. He had sex with a number of those women who used to hang about writers, as well as with ladies at the edge of the great world. He bedded no Oriane but he knew at least one Guermantes *before* her translation to the aristocracy.

Although Wilson's bedmates are sometimes masked by initials, he enjoys writing detailed descriptions of what Professor Edel calls his "copulations." These descriptions are mechanistic, to say the least. Since they are not connected with character, they are about as erotic as a *Popular Mechanics* blueprint of the sort that is said to appeal to the growing boy. I am not sure just why Wilson felt that he should write so much about cock and cunt except that in those days it was a very daring thing to do, as Henry Miller had discovered when his books were burned and as Wilson was to discover when his own novel, *Memoirs of Hecate County,* was banned.

In literature, sexual revelation is a matter of tact and occasion. Whether or not such candor is of interest to a reader depends a good deal on the revealer's attitude. James Boswell is enchanting to read on sex because he is by self, as well as by sex, enchanted and possessed. The author of *My Secret Life* (if for real) is engaging because he is only interested in getting laid as often as possible in as many different ways and combinations. We also don't know what he looks like—an important aid to masturbation. Frank Harris (not for real) has the exuberance of a natural liar and so moves the reader toward fiction.

The list now starts to get short. The recently published (in English) letters of Flaubert are interesting because he has interesting things to say about what he sees and does in the brothels and baths of North Africa. Also, tactfully, mercifully, he never tells us what he feels or Feels. The sex that Flaubert has with women and men, with boys and girls, is fascinating to read about (even though we know exactly how *he* looks). This is due, partly, to the fact that his experiences are, literally, exotic as well as erotic and, partly, to that famous tone of voice. Today one is never quite certain why memoirists are so eager to tell us what they do in bed. Unless the autobiographer has a case to be argued, I suspect that future readers will skip those sexual details that our writers have so generously shared with us in order to get to the gossip and the jokes.

In Wilson's notebooks, he liked to describe sex in the same way that he liked "doing" landscapes. "It is certainly very hard," he concedes, "to write about sex in English without making it unattractive. *Come* is a horrible word to apply to something ecstatic." Finally, he did neither sex scenes nor landscapes very well. But in sexual matters, he has no real case to make, unlike, let us say, the committed homosexualist who thinks, incorrectly, that candor will so rend the veil that light will be shed upon what the society considers an abominable act and in a blaze of clarity and charity all will be forgiven. This is naïve, as Wilson himself demonstrates in these pages. He was very much an American of his time and class and the notebooks are filled with innumerable references to "fairies" that range from derisive to nervous; yet Wilson also admits to occasional homosexual reveries which he thought "were a way of living in the grip of the vise, getting away into a different world where those values that pressed me did not function."

Nevertheless, it is disquieting to find Wilson, in the Thirties (having admired Proust and Gide), quite unable to accept the fact that a fairy could be a major artist. In *Axel's Castle,* he has great trouble admitting, or not admitting, the sexual source of Proust's jealousy.

On the other hand, he made a curious and admirable exception in the case of Thornton Wilder.

During the Twenties and Thirties, Wilder was one of the most celebrated and successful American novelists. He was also one of the few first-rate writers the United States has produced. Fortunately for Wilder's early reputation, he was able to keep his private life relatively secret. As a result, he was very much a hero in book-chat land. In *The Twenties* Wilson describes a meeting with Wilder. He was startled to find Wilder "a person of such positive and even peppery opinions." Wilson had not read any of Wilder's novels because he thought that "they must be rather on the fragile and precious side" (what else can a fairy write?). As it turned out, each had been reading the new installment of Proust's novel and Wilson was delighted to find that Wilder thought Saint Loup's homosexuality unjustified. Over the years, Wilson was to review Wilder seriously and well. When Wilder was the victim of a celebrated Marxist attack, Wilson came to Wilder's defense—not to mention literature's. But the word was out and Thornton Wilder's reputation never recovered; to this day, he is a literary nonperson. Nevertheless, it is to Wilson's credit that he was able to overcome his horror of fairydom in order to do justice to a remarkable contemporary.

Of a certain Victorian Englishman it was said that no lady's shoe, unescorted, was safe in his company. It could be said of Edmund Wilson that, like Cecil B. DeMille, "he never met a woman's foot he didn't like." Is there any reader of Wilson's novel *I Thought of Daisy* who does not recall Wilson's description of a girl's feet as being like "moist cream cheeses"? But Wilson's podophilia did not stop there: he could have made a fortune in women's footwear. From *The Thirties*: ". . . shoes, blue with silver straps, that arched her insteps very high . . . ," "Katy's little green socks and untied gray moccasins . . . ," "young Scotch girl M.P. [with] large feet bulging out of black shoes . . . ," ". . . silver open-work shoes that disclosed her reddened toenails, such a combination as only she could wear. . . ." In *The Thirties,* I counted twenty-four references to shoes and feet; each, let me quickly say, belonging to a woman. When it came to shoes, Wilson was sternly heterosexual—not for him the stud's boot or the little lad's Ked. But, to be absolutely precise, there is one very odd reference. Wilson is struck by the number of Chicago men who wear spats. Reverie: "Excuse me, sir. But a hook is loose on your left spat. As chance would have it, I have with me a spats-hook. If you'll allow me, sir. . . ." Whenever Wilson strikes the Florsheim note, he is in rut.

As a lover, Wilson is proud of his "large pink prong." (Surely, Anaïs Nin said it was "short and puce"—or was that Henry Miller's thumb?) In action, "My penis went in and out so beautifully sensitively, caressing (me) each time so sweet-smoothly (silkily). . . ." Yet he refers, clinically, to his "all too fat and debauched face" not to mention belly. He was a stubby little man who drank a lot. But his sexual energy matched his intellectual energy; so much for Freud's theory of sublimation.

The section called "The Death of Margaret" is fascinating, and quite unlike anything else he was ever to write. He started scribbling in a notebook aboard an airliner in 1932, en route to California where his wife of two years had just died of a fall. A compulsive writer, Wilson felt, instinctively, that by a close running description of what he saw from the plane window and in the air terminals he could get control of the fact of death and loss, or at least neutralize the shock in the act of re-creation. He writes a good many impressionistic pages of the trip before he gets to Margaret. Some very odd items: "—touching fellow passenger's thigh, moving over to keep away from it, did he move, too?—shutting eyes and homosexual fantasies, losing in vivid reality from Provincetown, gray, abstract, unreal sexual stimulus—also thought about coming back with Jean Gorman on train as situation that promises possibilities; but couldn't stomach it—young man too big, not my type—" Then impressions of his time together with Margaret: "I felt for the first time how she'd given me all my self-confidence, the courage that I hadn't had before to say what I thought. . . ."

In Santa Barbara, he stays with her family. "At Mrs. Waterman's house [Margaret's mother], when I began to cry, she said, I've never broken down. . . ." "Second night: homosexual wet dream, figures still rather dim, a boy. Third night: nightmare—the trolls were in the dark part of the cellar. . . ." Finally, the inevitable epitaph; "After she was dead, I loved her." That is the story of every life—and death. For the next decade, Wilson dreams of Margaret and writes down the dreams. In these dreams he usually knows that she is dead but, somehow, they can overcome this obstacle. They don't; even in dreams. Eurydice always stays put: It is the blight man was born for.

During the Thirties, Wilson's interests were more political than literary. The Depression, the New Deal, the Soviet experiment absorbed him. Wilson is at his most attractive and, I should think, characteristic when he describes going to Russia. He wanted to think well of communism, and, to a point, he was enthralled by the "classless" society and by the way that one man, Lenin, "has stamped his thought and his language on a whole people." This is not the treason but the very nature of the true clerk: the word as absolute can be motor to behavior and to governance. Gradually, Wilson is disillusioned about Stalin and the state he was making.

But what is fascinating to read today is not Wilson's account of what he saw and did but the way that he goes about taking on a subject, a language, a world. This is what sets him apart from all other American critics. He has to get to the root of things. He will learn Hebrew to unravel the Dead Sea scrolls. Read a thousand windy texts to figure out the Civil War. Learn Russian to get past the barrier of Constance Garnett's prose. He was the perfect autodidact. He wanted to know it all. Or, as he wrote, after he had a nervous breakdown in the Thirties, "I usually know exactly what I want to do, and it has only been when I could not make up my mind that I have really gone to pieces."

Early in *The Thirties,* Wilson is a fellow traveler of the American communists' *faute de mieux.* He can see no other way out of the Depression than an overthrow of the form of capitalism that had caused it. Before the election of 1932, he wrote: "Hoover stands frankly for the interests of the class who live on profits as against the wage-earning classes. Franklin Roosevelt, though he speaks as a Democrat in the name of the small businessmen and farmers and is likely to be elected by them in the expectation that he can do something for them, can hardly be imagined effecting any very drastic changes in the system which has allowed him to get into office. Whatever amiable gestures he may make, he will be largely controlled by the profit-squeezing class just as Hoover is." This is prescient. Apropos the fireside chats: "Roosevelt's unsatisfactory way of emphasizing his sentences, fairyish, or as if there weren't real conviction behind him—in spite of his clearness and neatness—but regular radio announcers, I noticed later, did the same thing. (The remoteness of the speaker from his audience.)" It is a pity that Wilson, who was on the fringes of the New Deal, never got to know the president. "Roosevelt is reported to have answered when someone had said to him that he would either be the best president the country had ever had or the most hated: No—that he would either be the most popular or the last."

Wilson often traveled to Washington in the Thirties and he had a sense of the place (derived from Henry Adams?) that makes him sound like one of us cliff-dwellers: "Washington is really a hollow shell which holds the liberalism of the New Deal as easily as the crooks and thugs of the Harding Administration—no trouble to clean it out every night and put something else in the past Administration's place."

Wilson goes to see one Martha Blair—"a rather appealing mouth and slim arms, though pale thyroid eyes: pink flowered print dress, with sleeves that gave a glimpse of her upper arms . . . she complained of the small town character of Washington—if you said you had another engagement, people asked you what it was—when she had said she was going to Virginia for the weekend they had asked her where in Virginia." It is odd to see this old formidable "socialite" of my childhood (she was then in her early thirties) as viewed from a totally different angle. Martha Blair kept company in those days with Arthur Krock of *The New York Times.* They were known as Martha'n'Artha. Wilson thinks they were married in 1934. I don't. At about that time, I remember there was a great row between my mother and her husband over whether or not the unmarried couple Martha and Arthur could stay overnight at our house in Virginia—where she was so often headed. My mother won that round. They were often at Merrywood, and Arthur Krock was the first Jew that I ever met. Anti-Semitism was in full boisterous American flower in the Thirties, and Wilson's record of conversations and attitudes haunt a survivor in much the same way that the background of a Thirties movie will reverse time, making it possible to see again a *People's Drug* store (golden lettering), straw hats, squared-off cars, and the actual light that encompassed one as a child, the very same light that all those who are now dead saw then.

Wilson notes, rather perfunctorily, friends and contemporaries. Scott Fitzgerald makes his usual appearances, and in his usual state. Once again we get the Hemingway-Wilson-Fitzgerald evening. "When Scott was lying in the corner on the floor, Hemingway said, Scott thinks that his penis is too small. (John Bishop had told me this and said that Scott was in the habit of making this assertion to anybody he met—to the lady who sat next to him at dinner and who might be meeting him for the first time.) I explained to him, Hemingway continued, that it only seemed to him small because he looked at it from above. You have to look at it in the mirror. (I did not understand this.)" I have never understood what Hemingway meant either. For one thing, Fitzgerald had obviously studied his diminutive part in a mirror. Even so, he would still be looking down at it unless, like a boy that I went to school with, he could so bend himself as to have an eye to eye, as it were, exchange with the Great American (Male) Obsession.

"Scott Fitzgerald at this time [1934] had the habit of insulting people, and then saying, if the victim came back at him: 'Can't take it, huh?' (I learned years later from Morley Callaghan that this was a habit of Hemingway's, from whom Scott had undoubtedly acquired it.)" There is altogether too little about Wilson's friend Dawn Powell, one of the wittiest of our novelists, and the most resolutely overlooked. But then American society, literary or lay, tends to be humorless. What other culture could have produced someone like Hemingway and *not* seen the joke?

Wilson's glimpses of people are always to the point. But they are brief. He is far more interested in writing descriptions of landscapes. I cannot think where the terrible habit began. Since Fitzgerald did the same thing in his notebooks, I suppose someone at Princeton (Professor Gauss? Project for a scholar-squirrel) must have told them that a writer must constantly describe things as a form of finger-exercise. The result is not unlike those watercolors Victorian girls were encouraged to turn out. Just as Wilson is about to tell us something quite interesting about e. e. cummings, he feels that he must devote a page or two to the deeply boring waterfront at Provincetown. A backdrop with no action in front of it is to no point at all.

There were trolls in the cellar of Wilson's psyche, and they tended to come upstairs "When I was suffering from the bad nerves of a hang-over. . . ." There is also an echo of Mrs. Dalloway's vastation in the following passage: "Getting out of an elevator in some office building—I must have been nervously exhausted—I saw a man in a darkened hall—he was in his shirt sleeves with open neck, had evidently been working around the building—his eyes were wide open, and there seemed to be no expression on his face: he looked, not like an ape, but like some kind of primitive man—and his staring face, as I stared at him, appalled me: humanity was still an animal, still glaring out of its dark caves, not yet having mastered the world, not even comprehending what he saw. I was frightened—at him, at us all. *The horrible look of the human race.*"

As a critic, Wilson was not always at his best when it came to the design or pattern of a text—what used to be called aesthetics. He liked data, language. He did not have much sympathy for the New Critics with their emphasis on text *qua* text. After all, nothing human exists in limbo; nothing human is without connection. Wilson's particular genius lay in his ability to make rather more connections than any other critic of his time. As Diderot said of Voltaire: "He knows a great deal and our young poets are ignorant. The work of Voltaire is full of things; their works are empty."

But Wilson was quite aware that "things" in themselves are not enough. Professor Edel quotes from Wilson's Princeton lecture: "no matter how thoroughly and searchingly we may have scrutinized works of literature from the historical and biographical point of view . . . we must be able to tell the good from the bad, the first-rate from the second-rate. We shall not otherwise write literary criticism at all."

We do not, of course, write literary criticism at all now. Academe has won the battle in which Wilson fought so fiercely on the other side. Ambitious English teachers now invent systems that have nothing to do with literature or life but everything to do with those games that must be played in order for them to rise in the academic bureaucracy. Their works are empty indeed. But then, their works are not meant to be full. They are to be taught, not read. The long dialogue has broken down. Fortunately, as Flaubert pointed out, the worst thing about the present is the future. One day there will be no. . . . But I have been asked not to give the game away. Meanwhile, I shall drop a single hint: Only construct!

*The New York Review of Books*
September 25, 1980

# 26

# F. SCOTT FITZGERALD'S
# CASE

Francis Scott Fitzgerald was born 1896 in St. Paul, Minnesota; he died 1940 in Hollywood, California, at 1443 North Hayworth Avenue, within walking distance of Schwab's drugstore, then as now a meeting place for those on their way up or down in what is still known in that part of the world as The Industry, elsewhere as the movies.

Between 1920 and 1940, Fitzgerald published four novels, 160 short stories, some fragments of autobiography. He worked on a dozen film scripts. He also wrote several thousand letters, keeping carbon copies of the ones most apt to present posterity with his side of a number of matters that he thought important. Although very little of what Fitzgerald wrote has any great value as literature, his sad life continues to provide not only English Departments but the movies with a Cautionary Tale of the first magnitude. Needless to say, Scott Fitzgerald is now a major academic industry. Currently, there are two new models in the bookstores, each edited by Professor Matthew J. Bruccoli. *The Notebooks of F. Scott Fitzgerald* contains all 2,078 notebook entries while *Correspondence of F. Scott Fitzgerald* includes letters to as well as from Fitzgerald.

A quick re-cap of the Fitzgerald career: in 1920, he published *This Side of Paradise* and married the handsome Zelda Sayre. In 1921, they set out for the territory—in those days, Europe. But the Fitzgeralds' Europe was hardly the Europe of James's "The Passionate Pilgrim." The Fitzgeralds never got around to seeing the sights because, as Jazz Age celebrities, they were the sights. They wanted to have a good time and a good time was had by all for a short time. Then things fell apart. Crash of '29. Zelda's madness. Scott's alcoholism. As Zelda went from one expensive *clinique* to another, money was in short supply. Scott's third and best novel, *The Great Gatsby* (1925), did not make money. Novel number four did not come easily. Back to America in 1931: Baltimore, Wilmington. Fitzgerald made two trips to Hollywood where he wrote movie scripts for money; he made the money but no movies.

The relative failure of *Tender Is the Night* (1934) came at a time when Fitzgerald's short stories no longer commanded the sort of magazine prices that had made the living easy in the Twenties. After a good deal of maneuvering, Fitzgerald wangled a six-month contract as a staff writer for MGM. At $1,000 a week, he was one of the highest paid movie writers. From 1937 to 1940, Fitzgerald wrote movies in order to pay his debts; to pay for Zelda's sanitarium and for his daughter's school; to buy time in which to write a novel. Despite a dying heart, he did pretty much what he set out to do.

In a sense, Fitzgerald's final days are quite as heroic as those of General Grant, as described in *General Grant's Last Stand,* a book that the Scribner's editor, Maxwell Perkins, rather tactlessly sent Fitzgerald after reading the three sad autobiographical sketches in *Esquire* (reprinted, posthumously, by Edmund Wilson in *The Crack-Up*).

"I enjoyed reading *General Grant's Last Stand,*" Fitzgerald replied with considerable dignity under the circumstances, "and was conscious of your particular reasons for sending it to me. It is needless to compare the difference in force of character between myself and General Grant, the number of words he could write in a year" (while dying of cancer, dead broke), "and the absolutely virgin field which he exploited with the experiences of a four-year life under the most dramatic of circumstances." It was also needless to mention that despite a failed presidency, a personal bankruptcy, a history of alcoholism, Grant had had such supreme victories as Shiloh, Vicksburg, Appomattox, while Fitzgerald had had only one—*The Great Gatsby,* a small but perfect operation comparable, say, to Grant's investiture of Fort Donelson.

At the time of Fitzgerald's death in 1940, he was already something of a period-piece, a relic of the Jazz Age, of flappers and bathtub gin. The last decade of Fitzgerald's life began with the Depression and ended with World War II; midway through the Thirties, the Spanish Civil War politicized most of the new writers, and many of the old. Predictably, Ernest Hemingway rode out the storm, going triumphantly from the bad play *The Fifth Column* to the bad novel *For Whom the Bell Tolls* (Fitzgerald's comment: "a thoroughly superficial book with all the profundity of *Rebecca*"). Nevertheless, with characteristic panache, the great careerist managed to keep himself atop the heap at whose roomy bottom Fitzgerald had now taken up permanent residence.

But, sufficiently dramatized, failure has its delights, as Fitzgerald demonstrated in those autobiographical pieces which so outraged his old friend, John Dos Passos, who wrote: "Christ, man, how do you find time in the middle of the general conflagration to worry about all that stuff?" But all that stuff was all that Fitzgerald ever had to deal with and he continued to confront his own private conflagration until it consumed him, while eating chocolate on a winter's day just off Sunset Boulevard.

At Princeton, Fitzgerald and Edmund Wilson were friends; they continued to be friends to the end even though Wilson was an intellectual of the most rigorous sort while Fitzgerald was barely literate. Yet they must have had something in common beyond shared youth, time, place, and I suspect that that something was the sort of high romanticism which Fitzgerald personified and Wilson only dreamed of, as he pined for Daisy.

When Wilson put together a volume of Fitzgeraldiana and called it *The Crack-Up*, the dead failed writer was totally, if not permanently, resurrected. Since 1945, there have been hundreds, perhaps thousands of biographies, critical studies, Ph.D. theses written about Fitzgerald. Ironically, the movies which so fascinated and frustrated Fitzgerald have now turned him and Zelda into huge mythic monsters, forever sweeping 'round to *Wiener* waltzes en route to the last reel where they sputter out like a pair of Roman candles on a rainy Fourth of July— disenchanted, beloved infidels.

For Americans, a writer's work is almost always secondary to his life—or life-style, as they say nowadays. This means that the novelist's biographer is very apt to make more, in every sense, out of the life than the writer who lived it. Certainly, Fitzgerald's personal story is a perennially fascinating Cautionary Tale. As for his novels, the two that were popular in his lifetime were minor books whose themes—not to mention titles—appealed enormously to the superstitions and the prejudices of the middle class: *This Side of Paradise* and *The Beautiful and Damned*—if that last title isn't still a lu-lu out on the twice-born circuit where Cleaver and Colson flourish, I will reread the book. But when Fitzgerald finally wrote a distinguished novel, the audience was not interested. What, after all, is the *moral* to Gatsby? Since there seemed to be none, *The Great Gatsby* failed and that was the end of F. Scott Fitzgerald, glamorous best seller of yesteryear, bold chronicler of girls who kissed. It was also to be the beginning of what is now a formidable legend: the "archetypal" writer of whom Cyril Connolly keened (in *The New Yorker,* April 10, 1948) "the young man slain in his glory." Actually, the forty-four-year-old wreck at the bottom of Laurel Canyon was neither young nor in his glory when he dropped dead. But five years later, when Wilson itemized the wreckage, he re-created for a new generation the bright, blond youth, forever glorious, doomed.

Professor Bruccoli's edition of *The Notebooks* comes highly recommended. Mr. James Dickey, the poet and novelist, thinks that "they should be a bible for all writers. But one does not have to be a writer to respond to them—these *Notebooks* make writers of us all." If true, this is indeed a breakthrough. Why go to Bread Loaf when you, too, can earn good money and get tenure by reading a single book? Mr. Budd Schulberg, the novelist, says, "Of all the Notebook masters, beyond Butler, Bennett, even Jules Renaud [*sic*], Fitzgerald emerges—in our judgment—as not only the most thorough and professional but the most entertaining and evocative." This is a stunning assessment. Better than Butler? Better than Jules Renard? Rush to your bookstore! At last, an aphorist superior to the man who wrote in his *cahier,* "I find that when I do not think of myself, I do not think at all."

Professor Bruccoli is understandably thrilled by *The Notebooks* which "were [Fitzgerald's] workshop and chronicle. They were his literary bankroll. They were also his confessional." Edmund Wilson disagrees. In the introduction to *The Crack-Up,* Wilson notes that, even at Princeton, Fitzgerald had been so much an admirer of Butler's *Notebooks* that when he came to fill up his own notebooks it was "as if he were preparing a book to be read as well as a storehouse for his own convenience. . . . Actually, he seems rarely to have used them."

The entries range from idle jottings, proper names, and jokes to extended descriptions and complaints. I fear that I must part company with Wilson, who finds these snippets "extremely good reading." For one thing, many entries are simply cryptic. "Hobey Baker." That's all. Yes, one knows—or some of us know—that Baker was a golden football player at Princeton in Fitzgerald's day. So what? The name itself is just

a name and nothing more. As for the longer bits and pieces, they serve
only to remind us that even in his best work, Fitzgerald had little wit
and less humor. Although in youth he had high spirits (often mistaken
in freedom's home for humor) these entries tend toward sadness; certainly, he is filled with self-pity, self-justification, self . . . not love so
much as a deep and abiding regard.

In general, Fitzgerald's notes are just notes or reminders. Here are
some, presumably numbered by Professor Bruccoli:

|      |                                                         |
|------|---------------------------------------------------------|
| 12   | Sgt. Este                                               |
| 137  | Ogden and Jesus                                         |
| 375  | Let's all live together.                                |
| 975  | Paul Nelson from School Play Onward                     |
| 1058 | Tie up with Faulkner—Lord Fauntleroy. [If only he had!] |
| 1128 | De Sano tearing the chair                               |
| 1270 | Actors the clue to much                                 |
| 1411 | Bunny Burgess episode of glass and wife.                |
| 1443 | The rejection slips                                     |
| 1463 | Memory of taking a pee commencement night               |
| 1514 | Coat off in theatre                                     |

I'm not at all sure how these little notes can make writers of us all or
even of Fitzgerald. Certainly, they do not entertain or evoke in their
present state. One can only hope that Professor Bruccoli will one day
make for us a skeleton key to these notes so that we can learn just what
it was that Bunny B. did with his wife and the glass. In the meantime,
I shall personally develop item 1069: "The scandal of 'English Teaching.' "

There is a section devoted to descriptions of places, something Fitzgerald was very good at in his novels. Number 142 is a nice description
of Los Angeles, "a city that had tripled its population in fifteen years,"
where children play "on the green flanks of the modern boulevard
. . . with their knees marked by the red stains of the mercurochrome era,
played with toys with a purpose—beams that taught engineering, soldiers that taught manliness, and dolls that taught motherhood. When
the dolls were so banged up that they stopped looking like real babies
and began to look like dolls, the children developed affection for them."
That is sweetly observed. But too many of these descriptions are simply
half-baked or strained. The description of a place or mood that is not
in some way connected to action is to no point at all.

Those journals and notebooks that are intended to be read must, somehow, deal with real things that are complete in themselves. Montaigne does not write: "Cardinal's house at Lucca," and leave it at that. But then Montaigne was a man constantly thinking about what he had read and observed in the course of a life in the world. Fitzgerald seems not to have read very much outside the Romantic tradition, and though his powers of observation were often keen and precise when it came to the sort of detail that interested him (class differences, remembered light), he had no real life in the world. Early on, he chose to live out a romantic legend that had no reference to anything but himself and Zelda and the child.

As I read *The Notebooks,* I was struck by the lack of literary references (other than a number of quite shrewd comments about Fitzgerald's contemporaries). Although most writers who keep notebooks make random jottings, they also tend to comment on their reading. Fitzgerald keeps an eye out for the competition and that's about it. By the time I got to the section labeled "Epigrams, Wise Cracks and Jokes," I wondered if he had ever read Gide. Whether or not he had read Gide is forever moot. But he had certainly heard of him. "Andre Gide lifted himself by his own jockstrap so to speak—and one would like to see him hoisted on his own pedarasty [*sic*]." Epigram? Wisecrack? Joke?

In these *Notebooks* Fitzgerald makes rather too many nervous references to fairies and pansies. But then his attitudes toward the lesser breeds were very much those of everyone else in those days: "1719 the gibbering dinges on the sidewalks; 1921 Arthur Kober type of Jew without softness . . . trying to realize himself outside of Jewry; 1974 *Native Son*—A well written penny dreadful with the apparent moral that it is good thing for the cause when a feeble minded negro runs amuck."

There are lines from *The Notebooks* which have been much used in biographies of Fitzgerald; even so, they still retain their pathos: "1362 I left my capacity for hoping on the little roads that led to Zelda's sanitarium." But most of the personal entries are simply sad and not very interesting. To hear him tell it, again and again: once upon a time, he was a success and now he's a failure; he was young and now he's middle-aged.

Out of 2,078 entries, I can find only one line worthy of Jules Renard: "In order to bring on the revolution it may be necessary to work inside the communist party." That's funny. Otherwise, Fitzgerald's observations resemble not Jules Renard but, as Mr. Schulberg has noted, Jules Renaud.

One would have thought that Andrew Turnbull's collection of Fitzgerald's letters was all that any reasonable admirer of Fitzgerald would ever need. Fitzgerald was not exactly the sort of letter-writer for whose *pensées* one sprints, as it were, to the mailbox to see if he's remembered to write. When Fitzgerald is not asking for money, he is explaining and complaining. But Professor Matthew J. "research begets research" Bruccoli thinks otherwise. In *Correspondence* he now gives us an altogether too rich display of Fitzgerald's letters complete with the master's astonishing misspellings; fortunately, he has had the good sense, even compassion for the reader, to include a number of interesting letters *to* Fitzgerald. If the marvelous letters of Zelda do not make this project absolutely worthwhile, they at least provide some literary pleasure in the course of a correspondence which, on Fitzgerald's side, is pretty depressing.

Certainly, Fitzgerald had a good deal to gripe about and, to a point, these cries at midnight are poignant. But they are also monotonous. Since Fitzgerald's correspondence is of current interest to a number of American graduate students, the letters deserve preservation but not publication. One can enjoy the letters of Lord Byron and Virginia Woolf without any particular knowledge of their works or even days. But Fitzgerald has not their charm or brutal force. On those rare occasions when he is not staring into the mirror, he can be interesting. "I'd like to put you on to something about Steinbeck," he wrote Wilson a month before he died. "He is a rather cagey cribber. Most of us begin as imitators but it is something else for a man of his years and reputation to steal a whole scene as he did in 'Mice and Men.' I'm sending you a marked copy of Norris' 'McTeague' to show you what I mean. His debt to 'The Octupus' is also enormous and his balls, when he uses them, are usually clipped from Lawrence's 'Kangeroo.' "

Precocious talents mature slowly if at all. Despite youthful success, there is something "hurried," as Fitzgerald put it, about his beginnings. Hurried and oddly inauspicious: the soldier who never fought (at one point he served under Captain Dwight D. Eisenhower—what did they talk about?) and the athlete who never competed. Yet, at twenty-one, Fitzgerald wrote Wilson: "God! How I miss my youth—that's only relative of course but already lines are beginning to coarsen *in other people* and that's the sure sign. I don't think you ever realized at Princeton the childlike simplicity that lay behind all my petty sophistication and my lack of a real sense of honor." Even before Fitzgerald had a past to search for, he was on the prowl for lost time, "borne back ceaselessly into the past."

The most curious aspect of Fitzgerald's early days was his relationship with Monsignor Sigourney Webster Fay at the Newman School. Fitzgerald was an uncommonly bright and pretty boy and, from the tone of the letters that Fay wrote him, pederasty was very much in the air. At one point, in 1917, Fitzgerald was to accompany Fay on a mission to Russia in order to bring the Greek Orthodox Church back to Rome. But the Bolsheviks intervened. Even so, the whole project has a Corvoesque dottiness that is appealing, and one wonders to what extent Fitzgerald understood the nature of his loving friend whose assistant at the Newman School, Father William Hemmick ("with his silver-buckled pumps and cassocks tailored in Paris"), was to end his days in Rome, surrounded by golden ephebes, a practicing fairy, whose apotheosis was to come that marvelous day when, with all the gravity and splendor that robes by Lanvin can bestow, Monsignor Hemmick, in the very teeth, as it were, of the Vicar of Christ on earth, united in marriage, before the cameras of all the world, Tyrone Power and Linda Christian. One thing about Scott, he was show-biz from the start. Fay appears as Father Darcy in *This Side of Paradise.* Fitzgerald's letters to Fay have vanished. Professor Bruccoli tells us that "they are believed to have been destroyed by Fay's mother after his death."

Since many of these letters deal with the personality of Fitzgerald (his drinking, marriage, friendships), it is not entirely idle to speculate—but pretty idle, even so—on Fitzgerald's sex life. There are very few youths as handsome as Fitzgerald who go unseduced by men or boys in the sort of schools that he attended. Zelda's occasional accusations that Fitzgerald was homosexual have usually been put down to the fact that she was either off her rocker or, mounted on that rocker, she was eager to wound Fitzgerald, to draw psychic blood. In a position paper which Fitzgerald may or may not have sent Zelda when she was hospitalized, he wrote: "The nearest I ever came to leaving you was when you told me you [thought] that I was a fairy in the Rue Palatine. . . ." The answer to that one is, stay away from the Rue Palatine.

Unfortunately, the street had its fascination for both of them. Zelda was drawn to Madame, her ballet teacher, while Fitzgerald made the acquaintance of a Paris tough (in the Rue Palatine?) and brought him back to America as a butler and "sparring partner." In any case, Zelda managed to so bug her husband on the subject that one day in Paris when he came to take Morley Callaghan's arm, he suddenly let go. "It was like holding on to a cold fish. You thought I was a fairy, didn't you?" In *That Summer in Paris* Callaghan says that he wished that he had been "more consoling, more demonstrative with him that night."

Whatever Fitzgerald's sexual balance, there is no doubt that he was totally absorbed in Zelda. There is little doubt that he was impotent a good deal of the time because anyone who drinks as much as Fitzgerald drank will lose, temporarily at least, the power of erection. In *Papa: A Personal Memoir,* Hemingway's son, an M.D., has made this point about his own hard-drinking father.

"One of the many ironies that inform the career of F. Scott Fitzgerald is that the writer who died 'forgotten' in 1940 is the most fully documented American author of this century." Professor Bruccoli rather smacks his lips in the introduction to the *Correspondence.* "We know more about Fitzgerald than about any of his contemporaries because he preserved the material. . . . The best Fitzgerald scholar of us was F. Scott Fitzgerald." Typing out these words I have a sense of perfect madness. *Scholar* of Fitzgerald? One sees the need for scholars of Dante, Rabelais, Shakespeare. But scholar of a contemporary popular writer who needs no introduction? Isn't this all a bit out of proportion? Are the academic mills now so huge and mindless that any writer of moderate talent and notoriety is grist? All the time wasted in collecting every scrap of paper that Fitzgerald scribbled on might be better spent in trying to understand, say, the nature of that society which produced the Fitzgerald who wrote those letters. But today's literary scholars are essentially fact-collectors, scholar-squirrels for whom every season's May.

That said, one must be grateful to this particular scholar-squirrel for publishing sixty-two of Zelda's letters to Fitzgerald. Like all her other writings, the letters are both beautiful and evocative. After a frantic attempt to become a ballerina, Zelda went clinically mad. From various sanitariums she did her best to tell Fitzgerald what going mad is like: "Every day it seems to me that things are more barren and sterile and hopeless—In Paris, before I realized that I was sick, there was a new significance to everything: stations and streets and façades of buildings—colors were infinite; part of the air, and not restricted by the lines that encompassed them and lines were free of the masses they held. . . . Then the world became embryonic in Africa—and there was no need for communication. The Arabs fermenting in the vastness; the curious quality of their eyes and the smell of ants; a detachment as if I was on the other side of a black gauze—a fearless small feeling, and then the end at Easter. . . ." (This quotation is from Nancy Milford's *Zelda.*) "I would have liked to dance in New York this fall, but where am I going to find again these months that dribble into the beets of the clinic garden?" And "I have been living in vaporous places peopled with one-dimensional figures and tremulous buildings until I can no longer tell an optical illusion from a reality . . . that head and ears incessantly throb and roads disappear. . . . Was it fun in Paris? Who did you see there and was the Madeleine pink at five o'clock and did the fountains fall with hollow delicacy into the framing of space in the Place de la Concorde and did the blue creep out from behind the Colonades of the rue de Rivoli through the grill of the Tuileries and was the Louvre gray and metallic in the sun and did the trees hang brooding over the cafés and were there lights at night and the click of saucers and the auto horns that play de Bussey. . . ."

A master of weather and landscape, Zelda was almost as good with people. She was one of the first to realize that Hemingway was "phony as a rubber check." When she read *A Farewell to Arms* in manuscript, she said that the prose sounded "pretty damned Biblical" while *The Sun Also Rises* was "bullfighting, bull-slinging and bullshit." Of Edmund Wilson, she wrote: "Bunny's mind is too speculative. Nothing but futures, of the race, of an idea, of politics, of birth control. Just constant planning and querulous projecting and no execution. And he drinks so much that he cares more than he would." No doubt, Fitzgerald was as charmed by the letters as we are. But he also understood her almost as well as he did his lifelong subject, himself. "Her letters," he wrote, "are tragically brilliant on all matters except those of actual importance. How strange to have failed as a social creature—even criminals do not fail that way—they are the law's 'Loyal Opposition' so to speak. But the insane are always mere guests on earth, eternal strangers, carrying around broken dialogues that they cannot read."

Zelda and Scott. In a curious way Zelda and Scott were meant to be perfectly combined in Plato's sense. Since this is not possible for us, each became shadow to the other and despite mutual desire and pursuit, no whole was ever achieved.

In July of 1922, Mr. and Mrs. Fitzgerald were offered the leads in a movie version of *This Side of Paradise.* Andrew Turnbull says that they turned down the offer. In 1927, Mr. and Mrs. Fitzgerald spent two months in Hollywood where he was contracted to write an original screenplay for Constance Talmadge. Although the screenplay was not used, Fitzgerald got his first look at the place where he was to live and die. In 1931, he came back to Hollywood for five weeks' work on *Red-Headed Woman* at MGM. Although Fitzgerald's script was not used, he got to know the boy genius Irving Thalberg, whose "tasteful" films

*(The Barretts of Wimpole Street)* were much admired in those days. On one occasion (recorded in the story "Crazy Sunday") Fitzgerald held riveted a party at the Thalbergs with a drunken comedy number. Movie stars do not like to be upstaged by mere writers, especially drunk writers. But next day, the hostess, the ever-gracious Norma Shearer, wired Fitzgerald (no doubt after an apologetic *mea culpa* that has not survived), "I thought you were one of the most agreeable persons at our tea." In Hollywood that means you're fired; he was fired.

All Americans born between 1890 and 1945 wanted to be movie stars. On Scott Fitzgerald's first trip to Hollywood, he was given a screen test (where is it?). As early as 1920, Fitzgerald tells how "summoned out to Griffith's studio on Long Island, we trembled in the presence of the familiar faces of the *Birth of a Nation*. . . . The world of the picture actors was like our own in that it was in New York, but not of it." Later, Zelda's passion to become a ballerina was, at its core, nothing except a desire to be A Star. But like so many romantics, then and now, the Fitzgeralds did not want to go through the grim boring business of becoming movie stars. Rather they wanted to live as if they were *inside* a movie. Cut to Antibes. Dissolve to the Ritz in Paris. Fade to black in Hollywood. Each lived long enough and suffered enough to realize that movies of that sort are to be made or seen, not lived. But by then she was in a sanitarium full-time and he was a movie hack.

In "Pasting It Together" (March 1936) Fitzgerald, aged forty, made note of a cultural change that no one else seemed to have noticed.

I saw that the novel, which at my maturity was the strongest and supplest medium for conveying thought and emotion from one human being to another, was becoming subordinated to a mechanical and communal art that, whether in the hands of Hollywood merchants or Russian idealists, was capable of reflecting only the tritest thought, the most obvious emotion. It was an art in which words were subordinate to images, where personality was worn down to the inevitable low gear of collaboration. As long past as 1930, I had a hunch that the talkies would make even the best-selling novelist as archaic as silent pictures.

Fitzgerald was right. Forty-four years later, it is the film school that attracts the bright young people while the writers' workshop caters to those whose futures will not be literary but academic. Today, certainly, no new novel by anyone commands the sort of world attention that a new film automatically gets. Yet, for reasons obscure to me, novelists still continue to echo Glenway Wescott, who wrote that Fitzgerald's hunch was "a wrong thought indeed for a novelist." I should have thought it was not wrong but inevitable.

A decade later, when I wrote that the film had replaced the novel as the central art form of our civilization, I was attacked for having said that the novel was dead and I was sent reading lists of grand new novels. Obviously, the serious novel or art-novel or whatever one wants to call the novel-as-literature will continue to be written; after all, poetry is flourishing without the patronage of the common reader. But it is also a fact that hardly anyone outside of an institution is ever apt to look at any of these literary artifacts. Worse, if the scholar-squirrel prevails, writers will not be remembered for what they wrote but for the Cautionary Tales that their lives provide. Meanwhile the sharp and the dull watch movies; discuss movies; dream movies. Films are now shown in the classroom because it is easier to watch Pabst than to read Dreiser. At least, it *was* easier. There is now some evidence that the current television-commercial generation is no longer able to watch with any degree of concentration a two-hour film without breaks. Thus, Pabst gives way to the thirty-second Oil of Olay spot.

In our epoch, only a few good writers have been so multitalented or so well situated in time and place that they could use film as well as prose. Jean Cocteau, Graham Greene. . . . who else? Certainly not Faulkner, Sartre, Isherwood, Huxley. In the heyday of the Hollywood studios no serious writer ever got a proper grip on the system. But then few wanted to. They came to town to make money in order to buy time to write books. But Fitzgerald was more prescient than many of his contemporaries. He realized that the novel was being superseded by the film; he also realized that the film is, in every way, inferior as an art form to the novel—if indeed such a collective activity as a movie can be regarded as an art at all. Even so, Fitzgerald was still enough of an artist or romantic egotist to want to create movies. How to go about it?

In those days, the producer was all-powerful and everyone else was simply a technician to be used by the producer. Naturally, there were "stars" in each technical category. A super-hack writer like Ben Hecht could influence the making of a film in a way that, often, the director-technician could not or, as Fitzgerald put it in a letter to Matthew Josephson (March 11, 1938),

In the old days, when movies were a stringing together of the high points in the imagination of half a dozen drunken ex-newspapermen, it was true that the whole thing was the director. He coordinated and gave life to the material—he carried the story in his head. There is a great deal of carry-over from those days, but the situation of *Three Comrades,* where Frank Borzage had little more to do than be a sort of glorified cameraman, is more typical of today. A Bob Sherwood picture, for instance, or a Johnny Mahin script, could be shot by an assistant director or a script girl, and where in the old days an author would have jumped at the chance of becoming a director, there are now many, like Ben Hecht and the aforesaid Mahin, who hate the eternal waiting and monotony of the modern job.

Although Fitzgerald underplays the power of the producer (in the case of *Three Comrades* the witty and prodigious writer-director Joe Mankiewicz), he is right about the low opinion everyone had of the director and the importance, relatively speaking, of the super-hack writers who pre-directed, as it were, each film by incorporating in their scripts the exact way that the film was to be shot. This was still pretty much the case when I was a writer under contract to MGM a dozen years after Fitzgerald's death. Scott was still remembered, more or less fondly.

"But," as the Wise Hack at the Writers' Table said, "there wouldn't've been all this revival stuff, if he'd looked like Wallace Beery." The Wise Hack had only contempt for Edmund Wilson's labors to restore Fitzgerald's reputation. "The Emperor's tailor," he snapped. At the Writers' Table we all snapped or riposted or even, sometimes, like Fitzgerald, shrilled.

When I said that I'd never much liked Fitzgerald's face in the early photographs but found the later ones touching because he always looked as if he was trying very hard not to scream, the Wise Hack said, "No. Not scream, whimper. There was never such a whiner. God knows why. He had a good time around here. Joe admired him. Got him a credit. Got his contract renewed. Whole thing started with Eddie Knopf who was queer for writers. It was him who talked the studio into taking Fitzgerald, the trick of the week after all that shit he shoveled in *Esquire* about what a drunk he was. Then Joe puts him on *Three Comrades* because he thought he could get some good period stuff out of him. Then when that didn't work, Joe got old Ted Paramore to help out on the script. But that didn't work either. First day on the set, Maggie Sullavan says, 'I can't say these lines,' and so Joe has to rewrite the whole damned thing. So why should Scott be pissed off? He knew enough to know that in this business the writer is the woman."

But Scott was pissed off at what Mankiewicz had done to the script of the only film on which Fitzgerald's name was ever to appear and for him to get what is known in the trade as a credit (debit is usually the better word) was a giant step toward big money, autonomy, freedom or, as Fitzgerald wrote Zelda (Fall 1937), "If I can finish one *excellent* picture to top *Three Comrades* I think I can bargain for better terms— more rest *and* more money." To Beatrice Dance he wrote (November 27, 1937), "I've been working on a script of *Three Comrades*, a book that falls just short of the 1st rate (by Remarque)—it leans a little on Hemingway and others but tells a lovely tragic story." To the same woman, a sadder if no wiser Fitzgerald wrote four months later, "*Three Comrades*, the picture I have just finished, is in production and though it bears my name, my producer could not resist the fascination of a pencil and managed to obliterate most signs of my personality." To his mother-in-law, Fitzgerald wrote in the next month (April 23, 1938): "*Three Comrades* should be released within ten days, and a good third of that is absolutely mine." But a few weeks later he wrote his sister-in-law: "*Three Comrades* is awful. It was *entirely* rewritten by the producer. I'd rather Zelda didn't see it."

But Zelda saw it and thought that a lot of it was very good even though

there isn't any dramatic continuity—which robs the whole of suspense. I know it's hard to get across a philosophic treatise on the screen, but it would have been better had there been the sense of some inevitable thesis making itself known in spite of the characters—or had there been the sense of characters dominated by some irresistible dynamic purpose. It drifts; and the dynamics are scattered and sporadic rather than cumulative or sustained.

Even in the loony bin, Zelda was a better critic than the ineffable Frank Nugent of *The New York Times* (who loved the picture) or Fitzgerald, who had written a so-so first draft of a film that was to be altered not only during a collaboration with one Ted *(The Bitter Tea of General Yen)* Paramore but, finally, redone by the producer Joe Mankiewicz.

Fitzgerald's first-draft screenplay was completed September 1, 1937. Edited by the ubiquitous Professor Bruccoli, Fitzgerald's screenplay was published in 1978, along with the various letters that Fitzgerald wrote but did not always send to Mankiewicz and the heads of the studio as well as the position paper that he did give to his collaborator Paramore. In an afterword, Professor Bruccoli gives a short history of the film's production; he also compares the penultimate screenplay with Fitzgerald's first draft.

Now I have always been suspicious of the traditional Cautionary Tale of Fitzgerald's fragile genius, broken on the rack of commerce by "an ignorant and vulgar gent" (Fitzgerald in a letter to Beatrice Dance, four months after the picture's release). Inspired and excited by Professor Bruccoli's researches, I have now turned scholar-squirrel myself. I have penetrated the so-called "vault" at MGM where I was allowed to read not only a copy of the actual shooting script of *Three Comrades* (dated February 2, 1938) but also the revisions that Mankiewicz made during the course of the filming. I also know the answer to the question that has so puzzled my fellow squirrels: did Mankiewicz ever receive Fitzgerald's letter of protest, dated January 20, 1938? He. . . . But let us not get ahead of our story.

On November 5, 1937, the first Fitzgerald-Paramore script was handed in. There was a story conference: one can imagine what it was like. Mankiewicz talking rapidly, eyes opening wide for emphasis while the faded Fitzgerald thought about the last drink—and the next drink; and Paramore did whatever it is that Paramores did or do. Subsequently, two more revised scripts were handed in by Fitzgerald-Paramore. Then between their last script, dated December 21, and the script of January 21, *something happened.*

On January 20, the day before the penultimate script was mimeographed, Fitzgerald wrote Mankiewicz a furious letter in which he attacked the radical changes that Mankiewicz had made in the script. Although Mankiewicz is on record as saying that "Scott Fitzgerald really wrote very bad spoken dialogue," I don't think that this is true. But we shall never know for certain because little of his dialogue ever made it to the screen. In the case of *Three Comrades,* Fitzgerald thought that "37 pages mine about ⅓." I'd say it was rather less.

In Fitzgerald's original script the boy-girl dialogues are charming and, curiously enough, far less wordy than the final version's. Fitzgerald's lack of humor might not have been so noticeable in an anti-Nazi tear-jerker were it not for the fact that Mankiewicz is one of the few genuine wits ever to come out of Hollywood. Where Fitzgerald's dialogue tended to be too sweet, Mankiewicz's dialogue was often pretty sour; the combination was not entirely happy. In any case, Fitzgerald never did get the point to Mankiewicz's jokes.

Fitzgerald's original script was overlong and somewhat confusing. In an excess of conscientiousness, he had studied so many old movies that there was hardly a cliché that he overlooked. When the hero telephones the heroine's sanitarium "CUT TO: QUICK TRAVELING SHOT OF A LINE OF TELEPHONE POLES IN WINTER—The line goes up a snowy mountain. CUT TO:" . . . Mel Brooks cutting the line.

Remarque's story of three German World War I buddies who go into the car-repair business during the rise of the Nazis was plainly not congenial to Fitzgerald's talents but since he needed the money, he did what all good writers who write for hire instinctively do: he pulled the narrative in his own direction. He made the German girl Pat (a rich girl now poor) into a Fitzgerald heroine and he made the boy Bobby (Erich in the final script) into a Fitzgerald hero. Once again, Scott and Zelda light up if not the sky the first-draft screenplay. Erich now has an unacknowledged drinking problem—hardly a page goes by that he doesn't think of bottles of rum or ask for a double whisky (not the usual tipple of your average Weimar Republic worker-lad). Erich's two comrades and the cleaning woman also, as they say in the script, "prosit" quite a lot.

When Pat is dying of tuberculosis in a sanitarium, Fitzgerald has a field day and much of the dialogue is charming. But even in Culver City, Fitzgerald could not escape the shadow of his monstrous friend Hemingway. "*Pat (as if to herself):* It's raining. It's been raining too long. At night sometimes when I wake, I imagine we're quite buried under all the rain." Fans of *A Farewell to Arms* will recall the soon-to-be-dying Catherine's speech as "All right. I'm afraid of the rain because sometimes I see me dead in it." Told that this is all nonsense, Catherine agrees: "It's all nonsense. It's only nonsense. I'm not afraid of the rain. I'm not afraid of the rain. Oh, oh, God, I wish I wasn't.' She was crying. I comforted her and she stopped crying. But outside it kept on raining." There was a lot of rain in those days. Luckily most of it was outside.

Fitzgerald was not entirely at ease with the talk of young men in the car-repair business. He was also hampered by Hollywood's insistence that an English-speaking film about Germans in Germany should be loaded with *achs* and *auf Wiedersehens* and *Herrs.* Mankiewicz also maintains the silliness: the one *auf Wiedersehen* in the script is his. Since profanity was not allowed in those chaste days, Fitzgerald has the lower orders accuse one another of being "twerps," "squirts," "greasepots," when today he would doubtless have used the more succinct if somewhat bleak epithet for all seasons and occasions "ass-hole." Fitzgerald also loaded the script with such epithets as "Holy Cats!" and "Great Snakes!" Wisely, Mankiewicz replaced Scott's cats and snakes with emotion-charged ellipses.

Now for Fitzgerald's January 20 letter. According to Professor Bruccoli, "Mankiewicz has stated that he never received this letter, which survives in a carbon copy in Fitzgerald's papers. Since there is no closing on the letter, it is possible that Fitzgerald did not send it." But Fitzgerald sent the letter; *and Mankiewicz read the letter.* Proof?

In Fitzgerald's script the boy and the dying girl are on a balcony, gazing out over what is supposed to be Thomas Mann's magic mountain but is actually Sonja Henie's winter wonderland. "*Pat:* Is that the road home? *Erich:* Yes. *Pat:* How far is it? *Erich:* About five hundred miles. In May you'll be starting back along that road. *Pat:* In May. My God, in May!" Fitzgerald left it at that—and why not? The dialogue comes straight from Remarque's novel.

Mankiewicz kept the dialogue. But then he moved the couple off the balcony and into Pat's bedroom at the sanitarium. Daringly, they sit on the bed for a really serious chat. After Pat's "*(unbelievingly):* In May. My God, in May!" Mankiewicz adds: "*(a pause then she turns to him):* But we're not saying what we should be saying this first time together. *(he looks at her puzzled)* All these months I'd figured out what you would say and I would say—word for word. Do you want to hear? *(he nods, smiling)* We'd be sitting here on the foot of this bed like this, hand in hand, and you'd ask, what time is it and I'd say that doesn't matter now. We love each other beyond time and place now. And you'd say, that's right. God's in this room with us, lightning's in this room, and the sea and the sky and the mountains are in this room with us. And you'd kiss me on the forehead and I'd say, how cool your lips are, don't move away—*(he kisses her on the forehead).* And you'd say, ought I to be in this room now? Aren't we breaking the rules? And I'd say must I start now—not breaking them—*(he looks into her eyes, unsmiling)* because I can't let you go and then you'd say hello, Pat, and I'd say, Erich, hello, and suddenly it would all be so real it would stab my heart and—*Erich:* But—darling—" They embrace "fiercely" and the camera sails out the window en route to the magic mountain and Settembrini and Naphta in the distance.

After Fitzgerald read this scene, he wrote Mankiewicz that Pat's big speech is "utter drool out of *True Romances* . . . God and 'cool lips,' whatever they are, and lightning and elephantine play on words. The audience's feeling will be 'Oh, go on and die.' "

Now if there is ever any way of making nervous the sardonic Mankiewicz it is to call him corny. Like Billy Wilder, he does not go in for scenes out of *True Romances.* Between January 20 and February 2 Mankiewicz rewrote the scene. He cut out "God" and "cool lips" and "lightning." Here is Pat's aria revised: "Well, we'd be laying here on the foot of this bed just like this, and I'd ask, is that the road home? And you'd say yes, it's six hundred kilometers. And I'd say, that doesn't matter now. We love each other beyond time and place now. You'd say, that's right—and you'd kiss me."\* And five months later there was not, as they used to say, a dry seat in any cinema of the republic when Margaret Sullavan husked those words to Robert Taylor.

What Fitzgerald had not realized was that dialogue must be precisely cut in quality to the player's talents and in length to the player's salary. Margaret Sullavan was a star whose deathbed scenes were one of the great joys of the Golden Age of the movies. Sullavan never simply kicked the bucket. She made speeches, as she lay dying; and she was so incredibly noble that she made you feel like an absolute twerp for continuing to live out your petty life after she'd ridden on ahead, to the accompaniment of the third movement of Brahms's First Symphony.

Fitzgerald's death scene went like this: Pat is all in a heap beside her bed, as Erich enters. "*Erich:* Pat—oh, Pat. *(He raises her, supports her. Pat's head wobbles on her shoulders)* Help—somebody! *Pat: (very low)* It's all right—it's hard to die—but I'm quite full of love—like a bee is full of honey when it comes back to the hive in the evening." On this grammatical error, "her eyes close in death." Joe will fix that line, I thought, as I put to one side Scott's version and picked up the shooting script. But, no, Mankiewicz's final words for Pat are: "It's all right for me to die, darling—and it's not hard—when I'm so full of love." Joe, I say to myself, tensing, make her say "as." But, alas, Miss Sullavan dies "like a bee is full of honey when it comes home in the evening." At least Mankiewicz got rid of Fitzgerald's hive.

In the novel, Remarque killed Pat more realistically—she doesn't talk all that much. But then she had already made her great speech a few pages earlier on why it's OK to be dying because she has Erich's love: "Now it's hard; but to make up, I'm quite full of love, *as* a bee is full of honey when it comes back to the hive in the evening." (Emphasis added by me.) Curiously enough, *there is no rain in the book.* But then the *Föhn* is blowing.

Mankiewicz's main contribution to this tear-jerker was an anti-Nazi subplot which the Breen office objected to. They wanted the German thugs to be communists. When Mankiewicz threatened to quit, the

---

\*From the MGM release *Three Comrades* © 1938 Loew's Incorporated. Copyright renewed 1965 by Metro-Goldwyn-Mayer Inc.

Breen office backed down; and the film was politically daring for its time. Mankiewicz also added a certain wit to the girl's part, annoying Fitzgerald. He thought that Mankiewicz had made Pat "a sentimental girl from Brooklyn"—a mildly anti-Semitic swipe which was off the mark: Mankiewicz's jokes were usually rather good and as much in character as anything else in the film. Incidentally, for those who subscribe to the *auteur* theory, Frank Borzage was in no way involved with the actual creation of the film that he humbly directed.

Professor Bruccoli tells us that "after MGM dropped his option in 1939, Fitzgerald freelanced at other studios before starting *The Last Tycoon*—which, in its unfinished state, is the best Hollywood novel ever written. In 1977 Hollywood turned *The Last Tycoon* into the worst movie ever made." Well, I am sure that Professor Bruccoli does not regard himself as a literary or film critic. He is a scholar-squirrel and the nuts that he gathers from past Mays are great fun to crack. To say that *The Last Tycoon* is the best Hollywood novel is like saying *Edwin Drood* is the best mystery novel ever written. Since *The Last Tycoon* is a fragment and nothing more, it's not the best anything. *The Day of the Locust, The Slide Area,* the crudely written but well-observed *What Makes Sammy Run?* are far more interesting "Hollywood novels" than the fragment Fitzgerald left behind, while to say that *The Last Tycoon* is the worst film Hollywood ever made is silly squirrel-talk. At the risk of betraying an interest, I would propose not the worst film *ever* made (critics are not allowed to use the sort of hyperbole that scholar-squirrels may indulge in) but a film that was certainly much worse than *The Last Tycoon* (and based on, dare I say? a rather better work), *Myra Breckinridge.*

Recently, I ran into the Wise Hack. He was buying the trade papers at the newsstand in the Beverly Hills Hotel. He is very old but still well turned out (blue cashmere blazer, highly polished ox-blood loafers with tassels); he owns a shopping center in downtown Encino; he has emphysema. Although he still keeps up with the latest movie deals, he seldom goes to the movies. "Too many cars," he says vaguely.

When I mentioned Fitzgerald, he sighed. "At least Ketti made some money out of him." It took me a moment to realize that he was referring to Ketti Frings who had written, in 1958, a successful stage version of *Look Homeward, Angel.*

"Did you hear the latest Polish joke?" The Wise Hack's little eyes gleamed behind thick glasses. "This Polish star, she comes to Hollywood to make a picture and she," the Wise Hack wheezed with delight, "*she fucks the writer!*"

Poor Scott: "He had come a long way to this blue lawn, and his dream must have seemed so close that he could hardly fail to grasp it. He did not know that it was already behind him, somewhere back in that vast obscurity beyond the city, where the dark fields of the republic rolled on under the night." *Habent sua fata libelli.* Writers have their scholar-squirrels.

*The New York Review of Books*
May 1, 1980

# 27

### DAWN POWELL:
### THE AMERICAN WRITER

I

Once upon a time, New York City was as delightful a place to live in as to visit. There were many amenities, as they say in brochures. One was something called Broadway, where dozens of plays opened each season, and thousands of people came to see them in an area which today resembles downtown Calcutta without, alas, that subcontinental city's deltine charm and intellectual rigor.

One evening back there in once upon a time (February 7, 1957, to be exact) my first play opened at the Booth Theatre. Traditionally, the playwright was invisible to the audience: One hid out in a nearby bar, listening to the sweet nasalities of Pat Boone's rendering of "Love Letters in the Sand" from a glowing jukebox. But when the curtain fell on this particular night, I went into the crowded lobby to collect some-one. Overcoat collar high about my face, I moved invisibly through the crowd, or so I thought. Suddenly a voice boomed-tolled across the lobby. *"Gore!"* I stopped; everyone stopped. From the cloakroom a small round figure, rather like a Civil War cannon ball, hurtled toward me and collided. As I looked down into that familiar round face with its snub nose and shining bloodshot eyes, I heard, the entire crowded lobby heard: *"How could you do this?* How could you *sell out* like this?

To *Broadway*! To *Commercialism*! How could you give up *The Novel*? Give up the *security*? The security of knowing that every two years there will be—like clockwork—*that five-hundred-dollar advance*!" Thirty years later, the voice still echoes in my mind, and I think fondly of its owner, our best comic novelist. "The field," I can hear Dawn Powell snarl, "is not exactly overcrowded."

On the night that *Visit to a Small Planet* opened, Dawn Powell was fifty-nine years old. She had published fourteen novels, evenly divided between accounts of her native Midwest (and how the hell to get out of there and make it to New York) and the highly comic New York novels, centered on Greenwich Village, where she lived most of her adult life. Some twenty-three years earlier, the Theatre Guild had produced Powell's comedy *Jig Saw* (one of *her* many unsuccessful attempts to sell out to commercialism), but there was third-act trouble and, despite Spring Byington and Ernest Truex, the play closed after forty-nine performances.

For decades Dawn Powell was always just on the verge of ceasing to be a cult and becoming a major religion. But despite the work of such dedicated cultists as Edmund Wilson and Matthew Josephson, John Dos Passos and Ernest Hemingway, Dawn Powell never became the popular writer that she ought to have been. In those days, with a bit of luck, a good writer eventually attracted voluntary readers and became popular. Today, of course, "popular" means bad writing that is widely read while good writing is that which is taught to involuntary readers. Powell failed on both counts. She needs no interpretation and in her lifetime she should have been as widely read as, say, Hemingway or the early Fitzgerald or the mid O'Hara or even the late, far too late, Katherine Anne Porter. But Powell was that unthinkable monster, a witty woman who felt no obligation to make a single, much less a final, down payment on Love or The Family; she saw life with a bright Petronian neutrality, and every host at life's feast was a potential Trimalchio to be sent up.

In the few interviews that Powell gave, she often mentions as her favorite novel, surprisingly for an American, much less for a woman of her time and place, the *Satyricon*. This sort of thing was not acceptable then any more than it is now. Descriptions of warm, mature, heterosexual love were—and are—woman's writerly task, and the truly serious writers really, heartbreakingly, flunk the course while the pop ones pass with bright honors.

Although Powell received very little serious critical attention (to the extent that there has ever been much in our heavily moralizing culture), when she did get reviewed by a really serious person like Diana Trilling (*The Nation,* May 29, 1948), *la* Trilling warns us that the book at hand is no good because of "the discrepancy between the power of mind revealed on every page of her novel [*The Locusts Have No King*] and the insignificance of the human beings upon which she directs her excellent intelligence." Trilling does acknowledge the formidable intelligence but because Powell does not deal with morally complex people (full professors at Columbia in mid journey?), "the novel as a whole . . . fails to sustain the excitement promised by its best moments."

Apparently, a novel to be serious must be about very serious—even solemn—people rendered in a very solemn—even serious—manner. Wit? What is that? But then we all know that power of mind and intelligence count for as little in the American novel as they do in American life. Fortunately neither appears with sufficient regularity to distress our solemn middle-class middlebrows as they trudge ever onward to some Scarsdale of the mind, where the red light blinks and blinks at pier's end and the fields of the republic rush forward ever faster like a rug rolling up.

Powell herself occasionally betrays bewilderment at the misreading of her work. She is aware, of course, that the American novel is a middle-brow middle-class affair and that the reader/writer must be as one in pompous self-regard. "There is so great a premium on dullness," she wrote sadly (Robert Van Gelder, *Writers and Writing,* New York: Scribner's, 1946), "that it seems stupid to pass it up." She also remarks that

it is considered jolly and good-humored to point out the oddities of the poor or of the rich. The frailties of millionaires or garbage collectors can be made to seem amusing to persons who are not millionaires or garbage collectors. Their ways of speech, their personal habits, the peculiarities of their thinking are considered fair game. I go outside the rules with my stuff because I can't help believing that the middle class is funny, too.

Well, she was warned by four decades of bookchatterers.

My favorite was the considered judgment of one Frederic Morton (*The New York Times,* September 12, 1954):

But what appears most fundamentally lacking is the sense of outrage which serves as an engine to even the most sophisticated [*sic*] satirist. Miss Powell does not possess the pure indignation that moves Evelyn Waugh to his absurdities and forced Orwell into his haunting contortions. Her verbal equipment is probably unsurpassed among writers of her genre—but she views the antics of humanity with too surgical a calm.

It should be noted that Mr. Morton was the author of the powerful, purely indignant, and phenomenally compassionate novel, *Asphalt and Desire.* In general, Powell's books usually excited this sort of commentary. (Waugh *indignant*? Orwell hauntingly *contorted*?) The fact is that Americans have never been able to deal with wit. Wit gives away the scam. Wit blows the cool of those who are forever expressing a sense of hoked-up outrage. Wit, deployed by a woman with surgical calm, is a brutal assault upon nature—that is, Man. Attis, take arms!

Finally, as the shadows lengthened across the greensward, Edmund Wilson got around to his old friend in *The New Yorker* (November 17, 1962). One reason, he tells us, why Powell has so little appeal to those Americans who read novels is that "she does nothing to stimulate feminine day-dreams [sexist times!]. The woman reader can find no comfort in identifying herself with Miss Powell's heroines. The women who appear in her stories are likely to be as sordid and absurd as the men." This sexual parity was—is—unusual. But now, closer to century's end than 1962, Powell's sordid, absurd ladies seem like so many Mmes. de Staël compared to our latter-day viragos.

Wilson also noted Powell's originality: "Love is not Miss Powell's theme. Her real theme is the provincial in New York who has come on from the Middle West and acclimatized himself (or herself) to the city and made himself a permanent place there, without ever, however, losing his fascinated sense of an alien and anarchic society." This is very much to the (very badly written) point. Wilson finds her novels "among the most amusing being written, and in this respect quite on a level with those of Anthony Powell, Evelyn Waugh, and Muriel Spark." Wilson's review was of her last book, *The Golden Spur;* three years later she was dead of breast cancer. "Thanks a lot, Bunny," one can hear her mutter as this belated floral wreath came flying through her transom.

Summer. Sunday afternoon. Circa 1950. Dawn Powell's duplex living room at 35 East Ninth Street. The hostess presides over an elliptical aquarium filled with gin: a popular drink of the period known as the martini. In attendance, Coby—just Coby to me for years, her *cavaliere servente;* he is neatly turned out in a blue blazer, rosy faced, sleek silver hair combed straight back. Coby can talk with charm on any subject. The fact that he might be Dawn's lover has never crossed my mind. They are so old. A handsome, young poet lies on the floor, literally at the feet of e. e. cummings and his wife, Marion, who ignore him. Dawn casts an occasional maternal eye in the boy's direction; but the eye is more that of the mother of a cat or a dog, apt to make a nuisance. Conversation flows. Gin flows. Marion Cummings is beautiful; so indeed is her husband, his eyes a faded denim blue. Coby is in great form. Though often his own subject, he records not boring triumphs but improbable disasters. He is always broke, and a once distinguished wardrobe is now in the hands of those gay receivers, his landladies. This afternoon, at home, Dawn is demure; thoughtful. "Why," she suddenly asks, eyes on the long body beside the coffee table, "do they never have floors of their own to sleep on?"

Cummings explains that as the poet lives in Philadelphia he is too far from his own floor to sleep on it. Not long after, the young poet and I paid a call on the Cummingses. We were greeted at the door by an edgy Marion. "I'm afraid you can't come in." Behind her an unearthly high scream sounded. "Dylan Thomas just died," she explained. "Is that Mr. Cummings screaming?" asked the poet politely, as the keening began on an even higher note. "No," said Marion. "That is not Mr. Cummings. That is Mrs. Thomas."

But for the moment, in my memory, the poet is forever asleep on the floor while on a balcony high up in the second story of Dawn's living room, a gray blurred figure appears and stares down at us. "Who," I ask, "is that?"

Dawn gently, lovingly, stirs the martinis, squints her eyes, says, "My husband, I think. It is Joe, isn't it, Coby?" She turns to Coby, who beams and waves at the gray man, who withdraws. "Of course it is," says Coby. "Looking very fit." I realize, at last, that this is a *ménage à trois* in Greenwich Village. My martini runs over.

**2**

To date the only study of Dawn Powell is a doctoral dissertation by Judith Faye Pett (University of Iowa, 1981). Miss Pett has gathered together a great deal of biographical material for which one is grateful. I am happy to know, at last, that the amiable Coby's proper name was Coburn Gilman, and I am sad to learn that he survived Dawn by only two years. The husband on the balcony was Joseph Gousha, or Goushé, whom she married November 20, 1920. He was musical; she literary, with a talent for the theater. A son was born retarded. Over the years, a fortune was spent on schools and nurses. To earn the fortune, Powell did every sort of writing, from interviews in the press to stories for ladies' magazines to plays that tended not to be produced to a cycle of novels about the Midwest, followed by a cycle of New York novels, where she came into her own, dragging our drab literature screaming behind her. As doyenne of the Village, she held court in the grill of the Lafayette Hotel—for elegiasts the Lafayette was off Washington Square, at University Place and Ninth Street.

Powell also runs like a thread of purest brass through Edmund Wilson's *The Thirties:* "It was closing time in the Lafayette Grill, and Coby Gilman was being swept out from under the table. Niles Spencer had been stuttering for five minutes, and Dawn Powell gave him a crack on the jaw and said, '*Nuts* is the word you're groping for.' " Also, "[Peggy Bacon] told me about Joe Gousha's attacking her one night at a party and trying to tear her clothes off. . . . I suggested that Joe had perhaps simply thought that this was the thing to do in Dawn's set. She said, 'Yes: he thought it was a social obligation.' " Powell also "said that Dotsy's husband was very much excited because the Prince of Wales was wearing a zipper fly, a big thing in the advertising business." A footnote to this text says that "Dawn Powell (1897–1965)" and Wilson carried on a correspondence in which she was Mrs. Humphry Ward and he "a seedy literary man named Wigmore." Later, there is a very muddled passage in which, for reasons not quite clear, James Thurber tells Dawn Powell that she does not *deserve* to be in the men's room. That may well be what it was all about.

I have now read all of Powell's novels and one of the plays.* Miss Pett provides bits and pieces from correspondence and diaries, and fragments of bookchat. Like most writers, Powell wrote of what she knew. There-

---

*I have omitted an interesting short novel because it is not part of the New York cycle. Powell made one trip to Europe after the war. Although Paris was no match for the Village, Powell, ever thrifty, uses the city as a background for a young man and woman trapped in *A Cage for Lovers* (published the year that Dawn roared at me in the Booth Theatre). The girl is a secretary-companion to a monster-lady, and the young man her chauffeur. The writing is austere; there are few characters; the old lady, Lesley Patterson, keeper of the cage, is truly dreadful in her loving kindness. In a rather nice if perhaps too neat ending, they cage *her* through her need to dominate. Thus, the weak sometimes prevail.

fore, certain themes recur, while the geography does not vary from that
of her actual life. As a child, she and two sisters were shunted about
from one midwestern farm or small town to another by a father who was
a salesman on the road (her mother died when she was six). The maternal grandmother made a great impression on her and predisposed her
toward boardinghouse life (as a subject not a residence). Indomitable old
women, full of rage and good jokes, occur in both novel cycles. At
twelve, Powell's father remarried, and Dawn and sisters went to live on
the stepmother's farm. "My stepmother, one day, burned up all the
stories I was writing, a form of discipline I could not endure. With thirty
cents earned by picking berries I ran away, ending up in the home of
a kind aunt in Shelby, Ohio." After graduation from the local high
school, she worked her way through Lake Erie College for Women in
Painesville, Ohio. I once gave a commencement address there and was
struck by how red-brick New England Victorian the buildings were. I
also found out all that I could about their famous alumna. I collected
some good stories to tell her. But by the time I got back to New York
she was dead.

Powell set out to be a playwright. One play ended up as a movie while
another, *Big Night,* was done by the Group Theatre in 1933. But it was
the First World War not the theater that got Powell out of Ohio and
to New York in 1918, as a member of the Red Cross: The war ended
before her uniform arrived. Powell wrote publicity. Married. Wrote
advertising copy (at the time Goushé or Gousha was an account executive with an advertising agency). Failure in the theater and need for
money at home led her to novel writing and the total security of that
five-hundred-dollar advance each of us relied on for so many years.
Powell's first novel, *Whither,* was published in 1925. In 1928 Powell
published *She Walks in Beauty,* which she always maintained, mysteriously, was really her first novel. For one thing, the Ohio heroine of
*Whither* is already in New York City, like Powell herself, working as
a syndicated writer who must turn out thirty thousand words a week
in order to live (in Powell's case to pay for her child's treatments). In
a sense, this New York novel was premature; with her second book,
Powell turns back to her origins in the Western Reserve, where New
Englanders had re-created New England in Ohio; and the tone is dour
Yankee, with a most un-Yankeeish wit.

The Ohio cycle begins with *She Walks in Beauty,* which is dedicated
to her husband, Joe. The story is set in Powell's youth before the First
World War. The book was written in 1927. Popular writers of the day:
Thornton Wilder had published *The Bridge of San Luis Rey* in the same

year as Powell's first but really second novel. Louis Bromfield received the Pulitzer Prize for *Early Autumn* (a favorite Bromfield phrase, "candy pink and poison green," occasionally surfaces in Powell) while Cather's *Death Comes for the Archbishop* was also published in 1927. The year 1925, of course, had been the most remarkable in our literary history. After commemorating life in the Midwest, Sinclair Lewis brought his hero Arrowsmith to New York City, a pattern Powell was to appropriate in her Ohio cycle. Also in that miraculous year alongside, as it were, *Whither*: Theodore Dreiser's *An American Tragedy*, Dos Passos's *Manhattan Transfer*, Fitzgerald's *The Great Gatsby*. It is interesting that Dreiser, Lewis, Hemingway, Fitzgerald, Dos Passos, and the popular Bromfield were all, like Powell, midwesterners with a dream of some other great good place, preferably Paris but Long Island Sound and social climbing would do.

Powell briskly shows us the town of Birchfield. Dorrie is the dreamy, plain, bright sister (always two contrasting sisters in these early novels); she stands in for Powell. Linda is the vain, chilly one. Aunt Jule keeps a boardinghouse. The Powell old lady makes her debut: "She pinned her muslin gown at the throat, dropped her teeth with a cheerful little click in the glass of water on the table, and turned out the gas." The "cheerful" launches us on the Powell style. The story is negligible: Who's going to make it out of the sticks first. In the boardinghouse there is an old man who reads Greek; his son has already made it to the big city, where he is writing a trilogy. Powell doesn't quite see the fun of this yet. But Dorrie falls for the young man, Dorrie "with that absurd infantile tilt to her nose" (Dawn to a T). Also Dorrie's tact is very like her creator's. A theatrical couple of a certain age are at the boardinghouse. The actress, Laura, tries on a hat. " 'It will look wonderful on Linda,' Dorrie vouchsafed pleasantly. 'It's too young for you, Aunt Laura.' " The adverb "pleasantly" helps make the joke, a point of contention between no-adverbs Graham Greene and myself. I look to the adverb for surprise. Greene thinks that the verb should do all the work.

Dorrie observes her fellow townspeople—nicely? "He had been such a shy little boy. But the shyness had settled into surliness, and the dreaminess was sheer stupidity. Phil Lancer was growing up to be a good Birchfield citizen." Points of view shift wildly in Powell's early books. We are in Linda's mind, as she is about to allow a yokel to marry her. "Later on, Linda thought, after they were married, she could tell him she didn't like to be kissed." The book ends with Dorrie still dreaming that the trilogist will come and take her off to New York.

. . .

In 1929 came *The Bride's House.* One suspects that Powell's own wit was
the result of being obliged for so long to sing for her supper in so many
strange surroundings: "Lotta's children arrived, . . . three gray, horrid-
looking little creatures and their names were Lois and Vera and Custer
. . . 'We've come to stay!' they shouted. . . . 'We've come to stay on the
farm with Uncle Stephen and Aunt Cecily. Aren't you glad?' " No one
is, alas. But these children are well-armored egotists. " 'She tells lies,'
Lois hissed in George's ear. 'I'm the pretty one and she's the bright one.
She told the conductor we lived in the White House. She's a very bad
girl and mother and I can't do a thing with her. . . . Everything she says
is a lie, Cousin Sophie, except when it hurts your feelings then it's
true.' " A child after absolutely no one's heart.

Unfortunately, Powell loses interest in the children; instead we are
told the story of Sophie's love for two men. The grandmother character
makes a dutiful appearance, and the Powell stock company go rather
mechanically through their paces. Powell wants to say something original about love but cannot get the focus right: "A woman needed two
lovers, she finally decides, one to comfort her for the torment the other
caused her." This is to be a recurring theme throughout Powell's work
and, presumably, life: Coby versus Joe? or was it Coby *and* Joe?

*Dance Night* (1930) is the grittiest, most proletarian of the novels. There
are no artists or would-be artists in Lamptown. Instead there is a railroad junction, a factory, the Bon Ton Hat Shop, where the protagonists,
a mother and son, live close to Bill Delaney's Saloon and Billiard Parlor.
Like the country, the town has undergone the glorious 1920s boom; now
the Depression has begun to hit. Powell charts the fortunes of the
mother-milliner, Elsinore Abbott, and her adolescent son, Morry. Elsinore's husband is a traveling salesman; he affects jealousy of his wife,
who has made a go of her shop but given up on her life.

Morry gets caught up in the local real estate boom. He also gets
involved with a waif, Jen, from an orphanage, who has been adopted by
the saloon-keeper as a sort of indentured slave. Jen dreams of liberating
her younger sister, Lil, from the home where their mother had deposited
them. Jen is not much of an optimist: "People last such a little while
with me. There's no way to keep them, I guess, that's why I've got to
go back for Lil because I know how terrible it is to be left always—never
see people again." It took Powell a long time to work all this out of her
system. Happily, farce intrudes. A young swain in a romantic moment
"slid his hand along her arm biceps and pressed a knuckle in her

arm-pit. 'That's the vein to tap when you embalm people,' he said, for he was going to be an undertaker.''

The highest work for a Lamptown girl is telephone operator, then waitress, then factory hand. Powell has a Balzacian precision about these things; and she remembers to put the price tag on everything. Money is always a character in her novels, as it was in Balzac's. In fact, Powell makes several references to Balzac in her early books as well as to his Eugénie Grandet.

Morry grows up, and his mother hardly notices him: "She had moved over for Morry as you would move over for someone on a street car, certain that the intimacy was only for a few minutes, but now it was eighteen years and she thought, why Morry was hers, hers more than anything else in the world was." This revelation shatters no earth for her or for him; and one can see how distressing such realism must have been—as it still is—for American worshipers of the family. Love, too.

Morry gets involved with a builder who indulges him in his dreams to create handsome houses for a public that only wants small lookalike boxes jammed together. Meanwhile, he loves Jen's sister, Lil, while Jen loves him: a usual state of affairs. The only bit of drama, indeed melo-drama, is the return of Morry's father; there is a drunken fight between father and son, then a row between father and Elsinore, whom he accuses, wrongly, of philandering. Finally, "wearing down her barri-ers," she reaches for a pistol: "This was one way to shut out words. . . . She raised the gun, closed her eyes and fired." Although everyone knows that she killed her husband the town chooses to believe it was suicide, and life goes on. So does Morry who now realizes that he must go away: "There'd be no place that trains went that he wouldn't go."

In 1932, Powell published *The Tenth Moon*. This is a somewhat Cather-esque novel composed with a fuguelike series of short themes (the influence of her ex-music-critic husband?). Connie Benjamin is a village Bovary, married to a cobbler, with two daughters; she once dreamed of being a singer. Connie lives now without friends or indeed a life of any kind in a family that has not the art of communication with one another. Connie daydreams through life while her daughters fret ("They went to bed at ten but whispered until twelve, remembering through all their confidences to tell each other nothing for they were sisters"). The hus-band works in amiable silence. Finally, Connie decides to have a social life. She invites to supper her daughter's English teacher; she also invites the music teacher, Blaine Decker, an exquisite bachelor, as adrift as Connie in dreams of a career in music that might have been.

Powell now introduces one of her major themes: the failed artist who with luck, might have been—what? In dreams, these characters are always on stage; in life, they are always in the audience. But Blaine has actually been to Paris with his friend, a glamorous one-shot novelist, Starr Donnell (Glenway Wescott?). Blaine and Connie complement and compliment each other. Connie realizes that she has been "utterly, completely, hideously unhappy" for fifteen years of marriage. Yet each pretends there are compensations to village life and poverty. " 'Isn't it better, I've often thought,' she said, 'for me to be here keeping up with my interests in music, keeping my ideals, than to have failed as an opera singer and been trapped into cheap musical comedy work?' " To hear them tell it, they are as one in the contentment of failure.

But Blaine still hears his mother's voice from offstage, a Powellesque killer: "I sometimes wonder, Blaine, if I didn't emphasize the artistic too much in your childhood, encouraging you and perhaps forcing you beyond your real capacity in music. It was only because you did so poorly in school, dear. . . ." Powell always knows just how much salt a wound requires.

Although the dreamers "talked of music until the careers they once planned were the careers they actually had but given up for the simple joys of living," knowing "success would have destroyed us," Connie goes too far. First, she tries indeed to sing and, for an instant, captures whatever it was she thought that she had and promptly hemorrhages—tuberculosis. Second, she confides to Blaine that she lost a career, home, virginity to Tony the Daredevil, a circus acrobat, who abandoned her in Atlantic City, where the kindly cobbler met and married her. He needed a wife; she could not go home. Blaine is made furious by the truth.

Then daughter Helen runs off with a boy, and the dying Connie pursues her. She finds that Helen has not only managed to get herself a job with a theatrical stock company but she is about to drop the boy; and Connie "knew almost for a certainty that Helen would climb the heights she herself had only glimpsed." Connie goes home to die, and Powell shifts to the dying woman's point of view:

When Dr. Arnold's face flashed on the mirror she thought, "This must be the way one dies. People collect on a mirror like dust and something rushes through your mind emptying all the drawers and shelves to see if you're leaving anything behind." . . . What a pity, she thought, no one will ever know these are my last thoughts—that Dr. Arnold's mouth was so small.

At the end Connie is spared nothing, including the knowledge that her husband never believed that she came of a good family and studied music and only fell once from grace with an acrobat. Blaine goes off to Paris as a tour guide.

With *The Story of a Country Boy* (1934) she ends the Ohio cycle. This is the most invented of the novels. There is no pretty sister, no would-be artist, no flight from village to city. Instead Powell tells the story of a conventional young man, a country boy, who becomes a great success in business; then he fails and goes home to the country, no wiser than before. Ironically, Powell was doing the exact reverse in her own life, putting down deep lifelong roots in that village called Greenwich, far from her own origins. In a sense, this book is a good-bye to all that.

Again, one gets the boom and bust of the twenties and early thirties. Chris Bennett is the all-American boy who makes good. He is entirely self-confident and sublimely unaware of any limitations. Yet, in due course he fails, largely because he lacks imagination. There is a good deal of Warren Harding, Ohio's favorite son, in his makeup. He is more striking in appearance than reality. Also, Powell was becoming more and more fascinated by the element of chance in life, as demonstrated by Harding's incredible election (those were simple times) to the presidency. "Chris could not remember ever being unsure of himself except in little details of social life where his defects were a source of pride rather than chagrin." He also wonders "if pure luck had brought him his success." He is right to wonder: It has. When he finally looks down from the heights he falls. No fatal flaw—just vertigo.

A splendid new character has joined the stock company, a former U.S. senator who sees in Chris the sort of handsome mediocrity that, properly exploited, could be presidential. John J. Habbiman's drunken soliloquies are glorious:

"Tell them I died for Graustark," said the Senator in a faraway voice. He sombrely cracked peanuts and ate them, casting the shells lightly aside with infinite grace. "What wondrous life is this I lead. Ripe apples drop about my head."

Powell also developed an essayistic technique to frame her scenes. A chapter will begin with a diversion:

In the utter stillness before dawn a rat carpentered the rafters, a nest of field mice seduced by unknown applause into coloratura ambitions, squeaked and squealed with amateur intensity. . . . Here, at daybreak, a host of blackbirds were now meeting to decide upon a sun, and also to blackball from membership in the committee a red-winged blackbird.

Unfortunately, her main character is too schematic to interest her or the reader. In any case, except for one final experiment, she has got Ohio out of her system; she has also begun to write more carefully, and the essays make nice point counterpoint to the theatricality of her scene writing.

The theater is indeed the place for her first New York invention, *Jig Saw* (1934), a comedy. The gags are generally very good but the plotting is a bit frantic. Claire is a charming lady, whose eighteen-year-old daughter, Julie, comes to stay with her in a Manhattan flat. Claire has a lover; and a best woman friend to make the sharper jokes. Julie "is a very well brought up young lady—easy to see she has not been exposed to home life." Again it takes two to make a mate: "It takes two women to make your marriage a success." To which Claire's lover, Del, responds, "Have it your way—then Claire and I have made a success of my marriage to Margaret."

A young man, Nathan, enters the story. Both mother and daughter want him. Julie proves to be more ruthless than Claire. Julie moves in on Nathan and announces their coming marriage to the press. He is appalled; he prefers her mother. But Julie is steel: "I can make something of you, Nate. Something marvelous." When he tries to talk her out of marriage, she declares, "I expect to go through life making sacrifices for you, dear, giving up my career for you." When he points out that she has never had a career, she rises to even greater heights: "I know. That's what makes it all the more of a sacrifice. I've never had a career. I never will have. Because I love you so much." Nate is trapped. Claire wonders if she should now marry Del, but he advises against it: "You're the triangular type. . . ." With a bit of the sort of luck that so fascinated Powell by its absence in most lives, she might have had a successful commercial career in the theater. But that luck never came her way in life, as opposed to imagination. Finally, Powell's bad luck on Broadway was to be our literature's gain.

## 3

The New York cycle begins with *Turn, Magic Wheel* (1936), dedicated to Dwight Fiske, a sub-Coward nightclub performer for whom Powell wrote special material. Powell now writes about a writer, always an edgy business. Dennis Orphen is a male surrogate for Powell herself. He is involved with two women, of course. He is also on the scene for good: He reappears in almost all her books, and it is he who writes finis to *The Golden Spur,* some twenty years later, as the Lafayette Hotel is being torn down and he realizes that his world has gone for good. But in 1936 Dennis is eager, on the make, fascinated by others: "his urgent need to know what they were knowing, see, hear, feel what they were sensing, for a brief moment to *be* them." He is consumed by a curiosity about others which time has a pleasant way of entirely sating.

Corinne is the profane love, a married woman; Effie is the sacred love, the abandoned wife of a famous writer called Andrew Callingham, Hemingway's first appearance in Powell's work. Effie is a keeper of the flame; she pretends that Andrew will come back: "Why must she be noble, frail shoulders squared to defeat, gaily confessing that life was difficult but that was the way things were?" Dennis publishes a *roman à clef,* whose key unlocks the Callingham/Hemingway story, and he worries that Effie may feel herself betrayed because Dennis completely dispels her illusion that the great man will return to her. As Dennis makes his New York rounds, the Brevoort Café, Longchamps, Luchow's, he encounters Okie, the ubiquitous man about town who will reappear in the New York novels, a part of their Balzacian detail. Okie edits an entertainment guide magazine, writes a column, knows everyone, and brings everyone together. A party is going on at all hours in different parts of the town, and Powell's characters are always on the move, and the lines of their extramarital affairs cross and recross. The essays now grow thoughtful and there are inner soliloquies:

Walter missed Bee now but sometimes he thought it was more fun talking to Corinne about how he loved Bee than really being with Bee, for Bee never seemed to want to be alone with him, she was always asking everyone else to join them. In fact the affair from her point of view was just loads of fun and that was all. She never cried or talked about divorce or any of the normal things, she just had a fine time as if it wasn't serious at all.

Powell is much concerned with how people probably ought to behave but somehow never do. The drinking is copious: "Corinne went into the ladies room and made up again. It was always fun making up after a few Pernods because they made your face freeze so it was like painting a statue." Of course, "Walter was as mad as could be, watching the cunning little figure in the leopard coat and green beret patter out of the room." Whenever "cunning" or "gaily" or "tinkling" is used, Powell is stalking dinner, with the precision of a saber-toothed tiger. She also notes those "long patient talks, the patient civilized talks that, if one knew it, are the end of love."

There are amusing incidents rather than a plot of the sort that popular novels required in those days: Effie is hurt by Orphen's portrayal of her marriage in his book; Corinne vacillates between husband and lover; the current Mrs. Callingham goes into the hospital to die of cancer. There are publishers who live in awe of book reviewers with names like Gannett, Hansen, Paterson. One young publisher "was so brilliant that he could tell in advance that in the years 1934–35 and –36 a book would be called exquisitely well-written if it began: 'The boxcar swung out of the yards. Pip rolled over in the straw. He scratched himself where the straw itched him.' " Finally, the book's real protagonist is the city:

In the quiet of three o'clock the Forties looked dingy, deserted, incredibly nineteenth century with the dim lamps in dreary doorways; in these midnight hours the streets were possessed by their ancient parasites, low tumble-down frame rooming houses with cheap little shops, though by day such remnants of another decade retreated obscurely between flamboyant hotels.

*That* city is now well and truly gone.

"Fleetingly, Effie thought of a new system of obituaries in which the lives recorded were criticized, mistaken steps pointed out, structure condemned, better paths suggested." This is the essence of Dawn Powell: The fantastic flight from the mundane that can then lead to a thousand conversational variations, and the best of her prose is like the best conversation where no *escalier* is ever wit's receptacle. As a result, she is at her best with The Party; but then most novels of this epoch were assembled around The Party, where the characters proceed to interact and the unsayable gets said. Powell has a continuing hostess who is a variation on Peggy Guggenheim, collecting artists for gallery and bed. There is also a minor hostess, interested only in celebrities and meaningful conversation. She quizzes Dennis: " 'Now let's talk,' she commanded playfully [Powell's adverbs are often anesthetic preparatory for surgery]. 'We've never really had a nice talk, have we, Dennis? Tell me how you came to write? I suppose you had to make money so you just started writing, didn't you?' " Callingham himself comes to The Party. Powell's affection for the real Hemingway did not entirely obscure his defects, particularly as viewed by an ex-wife, Effie, who discovers to her relief "there was no Andy left, he had been wiped out by Callingham the Success as so many men before him had been wiped out by the thing they represented." Effie frees herself from him and settles back into contented triangularity with Dennis and Corinne. Cake had; ingested, too.

In 1938, with *The Happy Island,* the Powell novel grows more crowded and The Party is bigger and wilder. This time the rustic who arrives in the city is not a young woman but a young man. Powell is often more at home with crude masculine protagonists, suspecting, perhaps, that her kind of tough realism might cause resentment among those who think of women as the fair sex.

A would-be playwright, Jeff Abbott (related to Morry?), arrives on the bus from Silver City; a manager has accepted his play with the ominous telegram, CASTING COMPLETE THIRD ACT NEEDS REWRITING [like that of *Jig Saw*] COME IMMEDIATELY. Jeff has two friends in the city. One is Prudence Bly, a successful nightclub singer; the other is Dol, a gentleman party giver and fancier of young men. At the book's end, Dol gives great offense by dying, seated in a chair, at his own party. How like him! the guests mutter.

Prudence is the most carefully examined of Powell's women. She is successful; she drinks too much; she is seldom involved with fewer than two men. But it is the relationships between women that make Powell's novels so funny and original. Jean Nelson, a beautiful dummy, is Prudence's best friend; each needs the other to dislike. At the novel's beginning, Jean has acquired Prudence's lover Steve. The two girls meet for a serious drunken chat over lunch. "You aren't jealous of me, are you, Prudence?" "*Jealous?* Jealous? Good God, Jean, you must think this is the Middle Ages!" Prudence then broods to herself:

Why do I lunch with women anyway? . . . We always end up sniveling over men and life and we always tell something that makes us afraid of each other for weeks to come. . . . Women take too much out of you, they drink too much and too earnestly. They drink the way they used to do china painting, and crewel work and wood burning.

In the restaurant things grow blurred: " 'You're so good to everyone,' sighed Jean. 'You really are.' Nothing could have enraged Prudence more or been more untrue." Finally, Jean goes: "Prudence looked meditatively after Jean as she wove her way earnestly through tables and knees. The girl did look like a goddess but the trouble was she walked like one, too, as if her legs had been too long wound in a flag."

Prudence's forebears include, yet again, the eccentric grandmother. This one is rich, and "Prudence was always glad her grandmother had been neither kind nor affectionate." The escape from Silver City had been easy. The grandmother was indifferent to everyone, including "her surly young Swedish chauffeur." A great traveler, Mrs. Bly "always wanted to buy one dinner with two plates, as if he were a Pekinese, and, more alarming still, to take one room in the hotels where they stayed. . . . After all, she explained, she always slept with her clothes on so there was nothing indecent in it." In addition, Mrs. Bly is a sincere liar, who believes that she was on the *Titanic* when it was sunk; and was courted by the czar.

Jeff Abbott and Prudence meet. They have an affair. Jeff is sublimely humorless, which intrigues Prudence. He is also a man of destiny, doomed to greatness in the theater. " 'I never yet found anything to laugh at in this world,' said Jeff. 'You never heard of a great man with a sense of humor, did you? Humor's an anesthetic, that's all, laughing gas while your guts are jerked out.' " Since they are not made for each other, marriage is a real possibility. Prudence is growing unsure of herself:

She could not find the place where the little girl from Ohio, the ambitious, industrious little village girl, merged into the *Evening Journal* Prudence Bly, *The Town and Country* Bly. There were queer moments between personalities, moments such as the hermit crab must have scuttling from one stolen shell to the next one. . . . Prudence Bly was not so much a person as a conspiracy.

Then Powell, in a quick scuttle, briefly inhabits her own shell:

Prudence slew with a neat epithet, crippled with a true word, then, seeing the devastation about her and her enemies growing, grew frightened of revenge, backed desperately, and eventually found the white flag of Sentimentality as her salvation. For every ruinous *mot* she had a tear for motherhood.

The failure of Jeff's powerful play does not disturb him, and Prudence is somewhat awed since worldly success is the only thing that makes the island happy. But "he belongs to the baffling group of confident writers who need no applause. For them a success is not a surprise but cause for wonder that it is less than international. . . . A failure proves that a man is too good for his times." When he says he wants to buy a farm in the Midwest and settle down and write, Prudence is astonished. When he does exactly that, she goes with him. Integrity at last. No more glamour. No more happy island. Only fields, a man, a woman. In no time at all, she is climbing the walls and heading back to New York where she belongs. Since Jean has let go of Steve, he receives her amiably (but then hardly anyone has noticed her departure). The book ends with: "Prudence's looks, [Steve] reflected with some surprise, were quite gone. She really looked as hard as nails, but then so did most women eventually." That excellent worldly novelist Thackeray never made it to so high a ground.

*Angels on Toast* (1940); war has begun to darken the skyline. But the turning wheel's magic is undiminished for Ebie, a commercial artist, whose mother is in the great line of Powell eccentrics. Ebie lives with another working woman, Honey, who "was a virgin (at least you couldn't prove she wasn't), and was as proud as punch of it. You would have thought that it was something that had been in the family for generations." But Ebie and Honey need each other to talk at, and in a tavern

where O. Henry used to go . . . they'd sit in the dark smoked-wood booth drinking old-fashioneds and telling each other things they certainly wished later they had never told and bragging about their families, sometimes making them hot-stuff socially back home, the next time making them romantically on the wrong side of the tracks. The family must have been on wheels back in the Middle West, whizzing back and forth across tracks at a mere word from the New York daughters.

Brooding over the novel is the downtown Hotel Ellery. For seventeen dollars a week Ebie's mother, Mrs. Vane, lives in contented genteel squalor.

BAR and GRILL: it was the tavern entrance to a somewhat medieval looking hotel, whose time-and-soot-blackened façade was frittered with fire-escapes, . . . its dark oak-wainscotting rising high to meet grimy black walls, its ship windows covered with heavy pumpkin chintz. . . . Once in you were in for no mere moment. . . . The elderly lady residents of the hotel were without too much obvious haste taking their places in the grill-room, nodding and smiling to the waitresses, carrying their knitting and a slender volume of some English bard, anything to prop against their first Manhattan . . . as they sipped their drinks and dipped into literature. It was sip and dip, sip and dip until cocktail time was proclaimed by the arrival of the little cocktail sausage wagon.

In its remoteness, this world before television could just as easily be that of *St. Ronan's Well.*

It is also satisfying that in these New York novels the city that was plays so pervasive a role. This sort of hotel, meticulously described, evokes lost time in a way that the novel's bumptious contemporary, early talking movies, don't.

Another curious thing about these small, venerable, respectable hotels, there seemed no appeal here to the average newcomer. BAR and GRILL, for instance, appealed to seemingly genteel widows and spinsters of small incomes. . . . Then there were those tired flashes-in-the-pan, the one-shot celebrities, and, on the other hand, there was a gay younger group whose loyalty to the BAR and GRILL was based on the cheapness of its martinis. Over their simple dollar lunches (four martinis and a sandwich) this livelier set snickered at the older residents.

Ebie wants to take her mother away from all this so that they can live together in Connecticut. Mrs. Vane would rather die. She prefers to lecture the bar on poetry. There is also a plot: two men in business, with wives. One has an affair with Ebie. There is a boom in real estate; then a bust. By now, Powell has mastered her own method. The essay-beginnings to chapters work smartly:

In the dead of night wives talked to their husbands, in the dark they talked and talked while the clock on the bureau ticked sleep away, and the last street cars clanged off on distant streets to remoter suburbs, where in new houses bursting with mortgages and the latest conveniences, wives talked in the dark, and talked and talked.

The prose is now less easygoing; and there is a conscious tightening of the language although, to the end, Powell thought one thing was different *than* another while always proving not her mettle but metal.

.    .    .

Powell is generally happiest in the BAR and GRILL or at the Lafayette or Brevoort. But in *A Time to Be Born* (1942) she takes a sudden social leap, and lands atop the town's social Rockies. Class is the most difficult subject for American writers to deal with as it is the most difficult for the English to avoid. There are many reasons. First, since the Depression, the owners of the Great Republic prefer not to be known to the public at large. Celebrities, of the sort that delight Powell, fill the newspapers while the great personages are seldom, if ever, mentioned; they are also rarely to be seen in those places where public and celebrities go to mingle. "Where," I asked the oldest of my waiter-acquaintances at the Plaza (we've known each other forty years), "have the nobles gone?" He looked sad. "I'm told they have their own islands now. Things"—he was vague—"like that."

As I read my way through Powell I noted how few names she actually does drop. There is a single reference to the late Helen Astor, which comes as a mild shock. Otherwise the references are no more arcane than Rockefeller equals money (but then John D. had hired the first press agent). In a sense, midwesterners were the least class-conscious of Americans during the first half of the twentieth century and those who came from the small towns (Hemingway, Dreiser, Powell herself) ignore those drawing rooms where Henry James was at home amongst pure essences, whose source of wealth is never known but whose knowledge of what others know is all that matters. Powell, agreeably, knows exactly how much money everyone makes (not enough) and what everything costs (too much). As for value, she does her best with love, but suspects the times are permanently inflationary for that overhyped commodity. Powell never gets to Newport, Rhode Island, in her books but she manages Cape Cod nicely. She inclines to the boozy meritocracy of theater and publishing and the art world both commercial and whatever it is that Fifty-seventh Street was and is.

But in *A Time to Be Born,* she takes on the highest level of the meritocracy (the almost-nobles) in the form of a powerful publisher and his high-powered wife, based, rather casually, on Mr. and Mrs. Henry Luce. At last Powell will have a fling at those seriously important people Diana Trilling felt that she was not up to writing about. But since one person is pretty much like another, all are as one in art, which alone makes the difference. Humble Ebie is neither more nor less meaningful than famous Amanda. It's what's made of them in art. Powell does have a good deal of fun with Julian and Amanda Evans, and the self-important grandeur of their lives. But Powell has no real interest in power or, more to this particular point, in those whose lives are devoted to power over others. Powell is with the victims. The result is that the marginal characters work rather better than the principals. One never quite believes that Julian owns and operates sixteen newspapers. One does believe Vicki Haven, who comes from the same Ohio town as Amanda, authoress of a *Forever Amber* best seller that has been written for her by the best pen-persons and scholar-squirrels that Julian's money can buy. Ken Saunders, a reasonably failed hack, gets Powell's full attention: he is a friend of Dennis Orphen, who makes an obligatory appearance or two as does the great novelist, Andrew Callingham, still hugely at large.

Powell sets *A Time* (magazine?) *to Be Born* in that time *not* to be born, the rising war in the West:

This was a time when the true signs of war were the lavish plumage of the women; Fifth Avenue dress shops and the finer restaurants were filled with these vanguards of war. Look at the jewels, the rare pelts, the gaudy birds on elaborate hair-dress and know that war was here; already the women had inherited the earth. The ominous smell of gunpowder was matched by a rising cloud of Schiaparelli's *Shocking.* The women were once more armed, and their happy voices sang of destruction to come. . . . This was a time when the artists, the intellectuals, sat in cafés and in country homes and accused each other over their brandies or their California vintages of traitorous tendencies. This was a time for them to band together in mutual antagonism, a time to bury the professional hatchet, if possible in each other. . . . On Fifth Avenue and Fifty-fifth Street hundreds waited for a man on a hotel window ledge to jump; hundreds waited with craning necks and thirsty faces as if this single person's final gesture would solve the riddle of the world. Civilization stood on a ledge, and in the tension of waiting it was a relief to have one little man jump.

I know of no one else who has got so well the essence of that first war-year before we all went away to the best years of no one's life.

Again the lines of love and power cross and recross as they do in novels and often, too, in life. Since Julian publishes newspapers and magazines and now propaganda for England, much of it written in his wife's name, there is a Sarrautesque suspicion of language in Powell's reflections. A publisher remarks, "A fact changes into a lie the instant it hits print." But he does not stop there. "It's not print, it's the word," he declares. "The Spoken Word, too. The lie forms as soon as the breath of thought hits air. You hear your own words and say— 'That's not what I mean. . . .' " Powell is drawing close to the mystery of literature, life's quirky—quarkish—reflection.

Amanda's power world does not convince quite as much as the Village life of Vicki and Ken and Dennis Orphen. Earlier readers will be happy to know that cute Corinne "had considered leaving her husband for Dennis Orphen for two or three years, and during her delay" the husband had divorced her "with Corinne still confused by this turn of events. . . . She wanted a little more time to consider marrying Dennis." When in doubt, do nothing, is the Powellesque strategy for life. Ken goes back and forth between Amanda and Vicki. For a time Amanda is all-conquering:

She knew exactly what she wanted from life, which was, in a word, everything. She had a genuine distaste for sexual intimacy . . . but there were so many things to be gained by trading on sex and she thought so little of the process that she itched to use it as currency once again.

This time with the great writer-hunter Callingham. As it is, ironically, she gets knocked up by Ken and falls out with Julian. But she is never not practical: On the subject of writing, she believes that "the tragedy of the Attic poets, Keats, Shelley, Burns was not that they died young but that they were obliged by poverty to do all their own writing." Amanda's descendants are still very much with us: sweet lassies still saddened at the thought of those too poor to hire someone who will burn with a bright clear flame, as he writes their books for them.

It is plain that Powell was never entirely pleased with the Ohio cycle. She had a tendency to tell the same story over and over again, trying out new angles, new points of view, even—very occasionally—new characters. Finally, in mid-war, she made one last attempt to get Ohio (and herself) right. *My Home Is Far Away* (1944) is lapidary—at least compared to the loose early works. New York has polished her style; the essays glitter convincingly. The rural family is called Willard. A Civil War veteran for a grandfather; missing the odd eye, limb. Two sisters again: Lena the pretty one, Marcia the bright one. Powell again holds up the mirror to her past: "The uncanniness of [Marcia's] memory was not an endearing trait; invariably guests drew respectfully away from the little freak and warmed all the more to the pretty unaffected normalcy of little Lena." The book begins when father, mother, daughters leave a contented home. Suddenly, there is a nightmare vision: A man in a balloon floats across a starry sky. Home is now forever faraway.

Too clever by more than half and too much obliged throughout a peripatetic childhood to sing for a supper prepared by tone-deaf strangers, Powell hammered on the comic mask and wore it to the end. But when the dying mother has a horrendous vision of the man in the balloon, the mask blinks—for the last time.

Aunt Lois has a boardinghouse. The girls work. The old ladies are more than ever devastating. " 'A grandmother doesn't like children any more than a mother does,' she declared. 'Sometimes she's just too old to get out of tending them, that's all, but I'm not.' " Lena goes first. Then Marcia leaves town, as Powell left town, and catches that train "which will go everywhere on earth that is not home." On a foggy pane of glass, she writes, with her finger, *Marcia Willard*. Dawn Powell.

## 4

After the war, Powell returned to the New York cycle for good. She published a book of short stories, *Sunday, Monday and Always* (1952). There are occasional ill-omened visits back home but no longer does she describe the escape; she has escaped for good. There are some nice comic moments. Edna, a successful actress, comes home to find her rustic family absorbed in radio soap operas. Although she is quite willing to describe her exciting life, the family outmaneuvers her. " 'Well, Edna,' cackled Aunt Meg, hugging her. 'I declare I wouldn't have known you. Well, you can't live that life and not have it show, they tell me.' " The "they tell me" is masterful. Powell's ear for the cadences of real-life talk only improved with time.

The final New York novels, *The Locusts Have No King* (1948), *The Wicked Pavilion* (1954), and *The Golden Spur* (1962), demonstrate Powell's ultimate mastery of subject, art, self. Where the last two are near-perfect in execution, *The Locusts Have No King* ("yet they, all of them go forth by bands": Proverbs) shares some of the helter-skelterness of the early books. It is as if before Powell enters her almost-benign Prospero phase, she wants to cut loose once more at The Party.

This time the literary scene of the forties gets it. The protagonist, Frederick Olliver, is a young man of integrity (a five-hundred-dollar-advance man) and literary distinction and not much will. He has been having an affair with Lyle, part of a married team of writers: Lyle is all taste and charm. But Frederick Olliver meets Dodo in a bar. Dodo is deeply, unrepentantly vulgar and self-absorbed. She says, "Pooh on you," and talks baby talk, always a sign for Powell of Lilithian evil. They meet in one of Powell's best bars downtown, off Rubberleg Square, as she calls it. The habitués all know one another in that context and, often, no other: parallel lives that are contiguous only in the confines of a cozy bar.

Frederick takes Dodo to a publisher's party (our friend Dennis is there) and Dodo manages to appall. Lyle is hurt. Everyone is slightly fraudulent. A publisher who respects Frederick's integrity offers him the editorship of *Haw,* a low publication which of course Frederick makes a success of. Lyle writes her husband's plays. There is a literary man who talks constantly of Jane Austen, whom he may not have read, and teaches at the League for Cultural Foundations (a.k.a. The New School), where "classes bulged with middle-aged students anxious to get an idea of what it would be like to have an idea." But under the usual bright mendacities of happy island life, certain relationships work themselves out. The most Powellesque is between two commercial artists, Caroline and Lorna:

Ever since their marriages had exploded Caroline and Lorna had been in each other's confidence, sharing a bottle of an evening in Lorna's studio or Caroline's penthouse. In fact they had been telling each other everything for so many years over their cups that they'd never heard a word each other had said.

In an ecstasy of female bonding, they discuss their lost husbands:

They told each other of their years of fidelity—and each lamented the curse of being a one-man woman. Men always took advantage of their virtue and Caroline agreed with Lorna that, honestly, if it could be done over again, she'd sleep with every man who came along instead of wasting loyalty on one undeserving male. After a few drinks, Caroline finally said she had slept with maybe forty or fifty men but only because she was so desperately unhappy. Lorna said she didn't blame anyone in Caroline's domestic situation for doing just that, and many times wished she had not been such a loyal sap about George, but except for a few vacation trips and sometimes being betrayed by alcohol she had really never—well, anyway, she didn't blame anyone.

Revelations bombard deaf ears. "Frequently they lost interest in dinner once they had descended below the bottle's label and then a remarkable inspiration would come to open a second bottle and repeat the revelations they had been repeating for years to glazed eyes and deaf ears." Finally, "Both ladies talked in confidence of their frustrations in the quest for love, but the truth was they had gotten all they wanted of the commodity and had no intention of making sacrifice of comfort for a few Cupid feathers." Powell was a marvelous sharp antidote for the deep-warm-sincere love novels of that period. Today she is, at the least, a bright counterpoint to our lost-and-found literary ladies.

Powell deals again with the, always to her, mysterious element of luck in people's careers. When one thinks of her own bad luck, the puzzlement has a certain poignancy. But she can be very funny indeed about the admiration that mediocrity evokes on that happy island where it has never been possible to be too phony. Yet when Frederick, free of his bondage to Dodo, returns to Lyle, the note is elegiac: "In a world of destruction one must hold fast to whatever fragments of love are left, for sometimes a mosaic can be more beautiful than an unbroken pattern." We all tended to write this sort of thing immediately after Hiroshima, *mon assassin.*

*The Wicked Pavilion* (1954) is the Café Julien is the Lafayette Hotel of real life. The title is from *The Creevey Papers,* and refers to the Prince Regent's Brighton Pavilion, where the glamorous and louche wait upon a mad royal. Dennis Orphen opens and closes the book in his by now familiarly mysterious way. He takes no real part in the plot. He is simply still there, watching the not-so-magic wheel turn as the happy island grows sad. For him, as for Powell, the café is central to his life. Here he writes; sees friends; observes the vanity fair. Powell has now become masterful in her setting of scenes. The essays—preludes, overtures—are both witty and sadly wise. She has also got the number to Eisenhower's American, as she brings together in this penultimate rout all sorts of earlier figures, now grown old: Okie is still a knowing man about town and author of the definitive works on the painter Marius; Andy Callingham is still a world-famous novelist, serene in his uncontagious self-love; and the Peggy Guggenheim figure is back again as Cynthia, an art gallery owner and party giver. One plot is young love: Rick and Ellenora who met at the Café Julien in wartime and never got enough of it or of each other or of the happy island.

A secondary plot gives considerable pleasure even though Powell lifted it from a movie of the day called *Holy Matrimony* (1943) with Monty Woolley and Gracie Fields, from Arnold Bennett's novel *Buried Alive.* The plot that Powell took is an old one: A painter, bored with life or whatever, decides to play dead. The value of his pictures promptly goes so high that he is tempted to keep on painting after "death." Naturally, sooner or later, he will give himself away: Marius paints a building that had not been built before his "death." But only two old painter friends have noticed this, and they keep his secret for the excellent reason that one of them is busy turning out "Marius" pictures, too. Marius continues happily as a sacred presence, enjoying in death the success that he never had in life: "Being dead has spoiled me," he observes. It should be noted that the painting for this novel's cover was done by Powell's old friend, Reginald Marsh.

A new variation on the Powell young woman is Jerry: clean-cut, straight-forward, and on the make. But her peculiar wholesomeness does not inspire men to give her presents; yet "the simple truth was that with her increasingly expensive tastes she really could not afford to work. . . . As for settling for the safety of marriage, that seemed the final defeat, synonymous in Jerry's mind with asking for the last rites." An aristocratic lady, Elsie, tries unsuccessfully to launch her. Elsie's brother, Wharton, and sister-in-law, Nita, are fine comic emblems of respectable marriage. In fact, Wharton is one of Powell's truly great and original monsters, quite able to hold his own with Pecksniff:

Wharton had such a terrific reputation for efficiency that many friends swore that the reason his nose changed colors before your very eyes was because of an elaborate Rimbaud color code, indicating varied reactions to his surroundings. . . . Ah, what a stroke of genius it had been for him to have found Nita! How happy he had been on his honeymoon and for years afterward basking in the safety of Nita's childish innocence where his intellectual shortcomings, sexual coldness and caprices—indeed his basic ignorance—would not be discovered. . . . He was well aware that many men of his quixotic moods preferred young boys, but he dreaded to expose his inexperience to one of his own sex, and after certain cautious experiments realized that his anemic lusts were canceled by his overpowering fear of gossip. . . . Against the flattering background of Nita's delectable purity, he blossomed forth as the all-round He-man, the Husband who knows everything. . . . He soon taught her that snuggling, hand-holding, and similar affectionate demonstrations were kittenish and vulgar. He had read somewhere, however, that breathing into a woman's ear or scratching her at the nape of the neck drove her into complete ecstasy. . . . In due course Nita bore him four daughters, a sort of door prize for each time he attended.

The Party is given by Cynthia now, and it rather resembles Proust's last roundup: "There are people here who have been dead twenty years," someone observes, including "the bore that walks like a man." There is a sense of closing time; people settle for what they can get. "We get sick of our clinging vines, he thought, but the day comes when we suspect that the vines are all that hold our rotting branches together." Dennis Orphen at the end records in his journal the last moments of the wicked pavilion as it falls to the wrecker's ball:

It must be that the Julien was all that these people really liked about each other for now when they chance across each other in the street they look through each other, unrecognizing, or cross the street quickly with the vague feeling that here was someone identified with unhappy memories—as if the other was responsible for the fall of the Julien.

What had been a stage for more than half a century to a world is gone and "those who had been bound by it fell apart like straws when the baling cord is cut and remembered each other's name and face as part of a dream that would never come back."

In 1962, Powell published her last and, perhaps, most appealing novel, *The Golden Spur*. Again, the protagonist is male. In this case a young man from Silver City, Ohio (again), called Jonathan Jaimison. He has come to the city to find his father. Apparently twenty-six years earlier his mother, Connie, had had a brief fling with a famous man in the Village; pregnant, she came home and married a Mr. Jaimison. The book opens with a vigorous description of Wanamaker's department store being torn down. Powell is now rather exuberant about the physical destruction of her city (she wrote this last book in her mid-sixties, when time was doing the same to her). There is no longer a Dennis Orphen on the scene; presumably, he lies buried beneath whatever glass-and-cement horror replaced the Lafayette. But there are still a few watering holes from the twenties, and one of them is The Golden Spur, where Connie mingled with the bohemians.

Jonathan stays at the Hotel De Long, which sounds like the Vanderbilt, a star of many of Powell's narratives. Jonathan, armed with Connie's cryptic diary, has a number of names that might be helpful. One is that of Claire van Orphen (related to Dennis?), a moderately successful writer, for whom Connie did some typing. Claire now lives embalmed in past time. She vaguely recalls Connie, who had been recommended to her by the one love of her life, Major Wedburn, whose funeral occurs the day Jonathan arrives at the De Long. Claire gives

Jonathan possible leads; meanwhile, his presence has rejuvenated her. She proposes to her twin sister, Bea, that they live together and gets a firm no. The old nostalgia burned down long ago for the worldly Bea. On the other hand, Claire's career is revived, with the help of a professionally failed writer who gets "eight bucks for fifteen hundred words of new criticism in a little magazine or forty for six hundred words of old criticism in the Sunday book section." He studies all of Claire's ladies' magazine short stories of yesteryear; he then reverses the moral angle:

"In the old days the career girl who supported the family was the heroine, and the idle wife was the baddie," Claire said gleefully. "And now it's the other way round. In the soap operas, the career girl is the baddie, the wife is the goodie because she's better for *business*. . . . Well, you were right. CBS has bought the two [stories] you fixed, and Hollywood is interested."

Powell herself was writing television plays in the age of Eisenhower and no doubt had made this astonishing discovery on her own.

Jonathan is promptly picked up by two girls at The Golden Spur; he moves in with them. Since he is more domestic than they, he works around the house. He is occasionally put to work in bed until he decides that he doesn't want to keep on being "a diaphragm-tester." Among his possible fathers is Alvine Harshawe alias Andrew Callingham alias Ernest Hemingway. Alvine is lonely; "You lost one set of friends with each marriage, another when it dissolved, gaining smaller and smaller batches each time you traded in a wife." Alvine has no clear memory of Connie but toys with the idea of having a grown son, as does a famous painter named Hugow. Another candidate is a distinguished lawyer, George Terrence, whose actress daughter, unknown to him, is having an affair with Jonathan. Terrence is very much school of the awful Wharton of *The Wicked Pavilion,* only Terrence has made the mistake of picking up a young actor in the King Cole Bar of the St. Regis Hotel; the actor is now blithely blackmailing him in a series of letters worthy of his contemporary Pal Joey. Terrence welcomes the idea of a son but Jonathan shies away: He does not want his affair with the daughter to be incestuous.

Finally, Cassie, the Peggy Guggenheim character, makes her appearance, and The Party assembles for the last time. There are nice period touches: girls from Bennington are everywhere. While Cassie herself "was forty-three—well, all right, forty-eight, if you're going to count every lost weekend—and Hugow's betrayal had happened at birthday time, when she was frightened enough by the half-century mark reaching out for her before she'd even begun to have her proper quota of love." Cassie takes a fancy to Jonathan and hires him to work at her gallery. He has now figured out not only his paternity but his maternity and, best of all, himself. The father was Major Wedburn, who was, of course, exactly like the bore that his mother, Connie, married. The foster father appears on the scene, and there is recognition of this if not resolution. As for Connie, she had slept with everyone who asked her because "she wanted to be whatever anybody expected her to be, because she never knew what she was herself." Jonathan concludes, "That's the way I am." At an art gallery, he says, "I have a career of other people's talents."

The quest is over. Identity fixed. The Party over, Jonathan joins Hugow in his cab. "He was very glad that Hugow had turned back downtown, perhaps to the Spur, where they could begin all over." On that blithe note Powell's life and lifework end; and the wheel stops; the magic's gone—except for the novels of Dawn Powell, all of them long since out of print just as her name has been erased from that perpetually foggy pane, "American Literature."

*The New York Review of Books*
November 5, 1987

# 28

———————— • ————————

# JOHN O'HARA

In 1938, writing to a friend, George Santayana described his first (and presumably last) encounter with the writing of Somerset Maugham. "I could read these [stories], enticed by the familiarity he shows with Spain, and with Spanish Americans, in whose moral complexion I feel a certain interest; but on the whole I felt . . . wonder at anybody wishing to write such stories. They are not pleasing, they are not pertinent to one's real interests, they are not true; they are simply graphic or plausible, like a bit of a dream that one might drop into in an afternoon nap. Why record it? I suppose it is to make money, because writing stories is a profession . . ." In just such a way, the Greek philosophers condemned the novels of the Milesian school. Unpleasing, impertinent, untruthful—what else can one say about these fictions except to speculate idly on why grown men see fit to write them. Money? There seems nothing more to be said.

Yet there is at least one good reason for a serious consideration of popular writing. "When you are criticizing the Philosophy of an epoch," wrote Alfred Whitehead in *Adventures Of Ideas,* "do not chiefly direct your attention to those intellectual positions which its exponents feel it necessary to defend. There will be some fundamental assumption which adherents of all the various systems within the epoch unconsciously

presuppose." Writers of fiction, even more than systematic philosophers, tend to reveal unconscious presuppositions. One might even say
that those writers who are the most popular are the ones who share the
largest number of common assumptions with their audience, sublimi-
nally reflecting prejudices and aspirations so obvious that they are never
stated and, never stated, never precisely understood or even recognized.
John O'Hara is an excellent example of this kind of writer, and useful
to any examination of what we are.

Over the last three decades, Mr. O'Hara has published close to thirty
volumes of stories, plays, essays and novels. Since 1955 he has had a
remarkable burst of activity: twelve books. His most recent novel, *Elizabeth Appleton,* was written in 1960 but kept off the market until 1963 in
order that five other books might be published. His latest collection of
short stories, *The Hat on the Bed,* is currently a best seller and apparently gives pleasure to the public. In many ways, Mr. O'Hara's writing
is precisely the sort Santayana condemned: graphic and plausible, impertinent and untrue. But one must disagree with Santayana as to *why*
this sort of work is done (an irrelevant speculation, in any case). Money
is hardly the motive. No man who devotes a lifetime to writing can ever
be entirely cynical, if only because no one could sustain for a lifetime
the pose of being other than himself. Either the self changes or the
writing changes. One cannot have it both ways. Mr. O'Hara uses himself
quite as fully and obsessively as William Faulkner. The difference between them lies in capacity, and the specific use each makes of a common obsession to tell what it is like to be alive. But where Faulkner
re-created his society through a gifted imagination, Mr. O'Hara merely
reflects that society, making him, of the two, rather the more interesting
for our immediate purpose, which is to examine through certain popular
works the way we live now.

Mr. O'Hara's work is in the naturalistic tradition. "I want to get it
all down on paper while I can. The U.S. in this century, what I know,
and it is my business to write about it to the best of my ability with the
sometimes special knowledge that I have." He also wants "to record the
way people talked and thought and felt, and to do it with complete
honesty and variety." In this, he echoes Sinclair Lewis, Emile Zola, and
(rather dangerously) the brothers Goncourt.

*The Hat on the Bed* is a collection of twenty-four short stories. They
are much like Mr. O'Hara's other short stories, although admirers seem
to prefer them to earlier collections. Right off, one is aware of a passionate interest in social distinctions. Invariably we are told not only what

university a character attended but also what prep school. Clothes, houses, luggage (by Vuitton), prestigious restaurants are all carefully noted, as well as brand names. With the zest of an Internal Revenue man examining deductions for entertainment, the author investigates the subtle difference between the spending of old middle-class money and that of new middle-class money. Of course social distinctions have always been an important aspect of the traditional novel, but what disturbs one in reading Mr. O'Hara is that he does so little with these details once he has noted them. If a writer chooses to tell us that someone went to St. Paul's and to Yale and played squash, then surely there is something about St. Paul's and Yale and squash which would make him into a certain kind of person so that, given a few more details, the reader is then able to make up his mind as to just what that triad of experience means, and why it is different from Exeter-Harvard-la-crosse. But Mr. O'Hara is content merely to list schools and sports and the makes of cars and the labels on clothes. He fails to do his own job in his own terms, which is to show us *why* a character who went to Andover is not like one who went to Groton, and how the two schools, in some way, contributed to the difference. It would seem that Mr. O'Hara is excited by fashionable schools in much the same way that Balzac was by money, and perhaps for the same reason, a cruel depriva-tion. Ernest Hemingway (whose malice was always profound) once announced that he intended to take up a collection to send John O'Hara through Yale. In his own defense, Mr. O'Hara has said that his genera-tion did care passionately about colleges. Granting him this, one must then note that the children and grandchildren of his contemporaries do not care in the *same* way, a fact he seems unaware of.

The technique of the short stories does not vary much. The prose is plain and rather garrulous; the dialogue tends to run on, and he writes most of his stories and novels in dialogue because that is not only the easiest kind of writing to read but the easiest to do. In a short story like "The Mayor" one sees his technique at its barest. Two characters meet after three pages of setting up the scene (describing a hangout for the town's politicians and setting up the personality of the mayor, who often drops in). Then two characters start to talk about a third character (the mayor) and his relationship with a fourth, and after some four pages of dialogue—and one small uninteresting revelation—the story is over. It has been, in Santayana's image, a daydream. One has learned nothing, felt nothing. Why record it?

Another short story, "How Can I Tell You?" is purest reverie. Once upon a time there was a car salesman who by all worldly standards is a success; he even gets on well with his wife. All things conspire to make him happy. But he suffers from accidie. The story begins *in medias res.* He is making an important sale. The woman buying the car talks to him at great length about this and that. Nothing particularly relevant to the story is said. The dialogue wanders aimlessly in imitation of actual speech as it sounds to Mr. O'Hara's ear, which is good but unselective, with a tendency to use arcane slang ("plenty of glue") and phonetic spellings ("wuddia"). Yet despite this long conversation, the two characters remain vague and undefined. Incidentally, Mr. O'Hara almost never gives a physical description of his characters, a startling continence for a naturalistic writer, and more to be admired than not.

The woman departs. The salesman goes to a bar, where the bartender immediately senses that "You got sumpn eatin' you, boy." The salesman then goes home. He looks at his sleeping wife, who wakes up and wants to know if something is wrong. "How the hell can I tell you when I don't know myself?" he says. She goes back to sleep. He takes down his gun. He seems about to kill himself when his wife joins him and says, "Don't. Please?" and he says, "I won't." And there the story ends. What has gone wrong is that one could not care less about this Richard Cory (at least we were told that the original was full of light and that people envied him), because Mr. O'Hara's creation has neither face nor history. What the author has shown us is not a character but an event, and though a certain kind of writing can be most successful dealing only with events, this particular story required character shown from the inside, not a situation described from the outside and through dialogue.

*Elizabeth Appleton,* O'Hara's latest novel, takes place in a Pennsylvania university town. Will the dean, Elizabeth's husband, be made president of the college? He is a popular choice, and in line for the post. Elizabeth has been a conscientious faculty wife, in spite of being "aristocratic" (her family used to go to Southampton in the summer). Elizabeth also has money, a fact which her patrician good taste insists she hide from her husband's world. But hidden or not, for those who know true quality Elizabeth is the real thing. She even inspires the reverence of a former New York policeman who happens to be sitting next to her during a plane trip. There has been bad weather. Danger. Each is brave. The danger passes. Then they talk of . . . what else do Mr. O'Hara's people talk of in a pinch? Schools. "You're a New York girl, even if you did get on at Pittsburgh." Elizabeth allows that this is so. Then with that uncanny shrewdness the lower orders often demonstrate when they are in the presence of their betters, the flatfoot asks, "Did you ever go to Miss Spence's Finishing School? I used to help them cross the street when I was in that precinct." No Franklin High School for him. "I went to Miss Chapin's," says Elizabeth quietly, as if declaring, very simply, that she is a Plantagenet. Needless to say, the fuzz knows all about Chapin, too. He is even more overcome when he learns her maiden name. He knows exactly who her father was. He even recalls her family house "on the north side of Fifty-Sixth between Madison and Park. Iron grillwork on the ground floor windows. . . . Those were the good days, Mrs. Appleton, no matter what they say," he declares in an ecstasy of social inferiority.

Like so many of O'Hara's novels, the book seems improvised. The situation is a simple one. Appleton is expected to become Spring Valley's next president. He wants the job, or nearly (readers of the late John P. Marquand will recognize with delight that hesitancy and melancholy which inevitably attend success in middle age. Is this all there is to it? Where are my dreams, my hopes, my love?). Elizabeth wants the promotion, partly for her husband's sake, partly because she is guilty because *she has had an affair.* It is over now, of course. Her lover has taken to drink. But with the aid of flashbacks we can savor the quality of their passion, which turns out to have been mostly talk. Sometimes they talked about schools, sometimes about games; occasionally they discussed the guilt each feels toward her husband, and the possibility of their own marriage one day. But aside from talk nothing happens. In fact, there is almost no action in Mr. O'Hara's recent work. Everything of consequence takes place offstage, to be reported later in conversation—perhaps his only resemblance to classical literature.

To be effective, naturalistic detail must be not only accurate but relevant. Each small fact must be fitted to the overall pattern as tightly as mosaic. This is a tiresomely obvious thing to say, but repetition does not seem to spoil the novelty of it as criticism. Unfortunately Mr. O'Hara does not relate things one to the other, he simply puts down the names of schools, resorts, restaurants, hotels for the simple pleasure of recording them (and perhaps, magically, possessing them in the act of naming). If he can come up with the name of an actual entertainer who performed in a real club of a known city in a particular year, he seems to feel that his work as recorder has been justified. This love of minutiae for their own sake can be as fatal to the serious novelist as it is necessary to the success of the popular writer . . . which brings us to the audience and its unconscious presuppositions.

Right off, one is struck by the collective narcissism of those whose tastes create the best-seller lists. Until our day, popular writers wrote of kings and queens, of exotic countries and extreme situations, of worlds totally unlike the common experience. No longer. Today's reader wants to look at himself, to find out who *he* is, with an occasional glimpse of his next-door neighbor. This self-absorption is also reflected in the ubiquitous national polls which fascinate newspaper readers and in those magazine articles that address themselves with such success to the second person singular. Certainly, fiction is, to a point, an extension of actual life, an alternative world in which a reader may find out things he did not know before and live in imagination a life he may not live in fact. But I suggest that never before has the alternative world been so close to the actual one as it is today in the novels of John O'Hara and his fellow commercialites. Journalism and popular fiction have merged, and the graphic and the plausible have become an end in themselves. The contemporary public plainly prefers mirrors to windows.

The second unconscious presupposition Mr. O'Hara reveals is the matter of boredom. Most of the people he describes are bored to death with their lives and one another. Yet they never question this boredom, nor does their author show any great awareness of it. He just puts it all down. Like his peers, he reflects the *taedium vitae* without seeming to notice it. Yet it lurks continually beneath the surface, much the way a fear of syphilis haunted popular writing in the nineteenth century. One can read O'Hara by the yard without encountering a single character capable of taking pleasure in anything. His creatures are joyless. Neither art nor mind ever impinges on their garrulous self-absorption. If they read books, the books are by writers like Mr. O'Hara, locked with them in a terrible self-regard. Strangely enough, they show little true curiosity about other people, which is odd since the convention of each story is almost always someone telling someone else about so-and-so. They want to hear gossip but only in a desultory, time-passing way.

Finally, there is the matter of death. A recent survey among young people showed that since almost none believed in the continuation of personality after death, each felt, quite logically, that if this life is all there is, to lose it is the worst that can happen to anyone. Consequently, none was able to think of a single "idea," political or moral, whose defense might justify no longer existing. To me this is the central underlying assumption of our society and one which makes us different from our predecessors. As a result, much of the popular writers' glumness reflects the unease of a first generation set free from an attitude toward death which was as comforting as it was constraining. Curiously enough, this awareness is responsible for one of Mr. O'Hara's few entirely successful works, the short story "The Trip," from *Assembly*.

An elderly New York clubman is looking forward to a boat trip to England, the scene of many pleasures in his youth (the Kit Kat Club with the Prince of Wales at the drums, etc.). He discusses the trip with his bridge partners, a contented foursome of old men, their pleasant lives shadowed only by the knowledge of death. An original member of the foursome died some years earlier, and there had been some criticism of him because he had collapsed "and died while playing a hand. The criticism was mild enough, but it was voiced, one player to another; it was simply that Charley had been told by his doctor not to play bridge, but he had insisted on playing, with the inevitable, extremely disturbing result." But there were those who said how much better it was that Charley was able to die among friends rather than in public, with "policemen going through his pockets to find some identification. Taxi drivers pointing to him. Look, a dead man." Skillfully O'Hara weaves his nightmare. Shortly before the ship is to sail for England, one of the foursome misses the afternoon game. Then it is learned that he has died in a taxicab. Once again the "inevitable, extremely disturbing" thing has happened. The trip is called off because "I'd be such a damn nuisance if I checked out in a London cab." This particular story is beautifully made, and completely effective. Yet Boccaccio would have found it unfathomable: isn't death everywhere? and shouldn't we crowd all the pleasure that we can into the moment and hope for grace? But in Mr. O'Hara's contemporary mirror, there is neither grace nor God nor— one suspects—much pleasure in living.

Why our proud Affluency is the way it is does not concern us here. Enough to say that Mr. O'Hara, for all his faults, is a reliable witness to our self-regard, boredom, and terror of not being. Nor is he without literary virtues. For one thing, he possesses that rare thing, the narrative gift. For another, he has complete integrity. What he says he sees, he sees. Though his concern with sex used to trouble many of the Good Gray Geese of the press, it is a legitimate concern. Also, his treatment of sexual matters is seldom irrelevant, though touchingly old-fashioned by today's standards, proving once again how dangerous it is for a writer to rely too heavily on contemporary sexual mores for his effects. When those mores change, the moments of high drama become absurd. "Would you marry me if I weren't a virgin?" asks a girl in one of the early books. "I don't know. I honestly don't know," is the man's agonized response, neither suspecting that even as they suffer, in literature's womb Genet and Nabokov, William Burroughs and Mary McCarthy are stirring to be born. But despite Mr. O'Hara's passionate desire to show things as they are, he is necessarily limited by the things he must look at. Lacking a moral imagination and not interested in the exercise of mind or in the exploration of what really goes on beneath that Harris tweed suit from J. Press, he is doomed to go on being a writer of gossip who is read with the same mechanical attention any newspaper column of familiar or near-familiar names and places is apt to evoke. His work, finally, cannot be taken seriously as literature, but as an unconscious record of the superstitions and assumptions of his time, his writing is "pertinent" in Santayana's sense, and even "true."

*The New York Review of Books*
April 16, 1964

# 29

# JOHN HORNE BURNS

In 1947 *The Gallery* by John Horne Burns was published, to great acclaim: the best book of the Second War. That same year Burns and I met several times, each a war novelist and each properly wary of the other. Burns was then thirty-one with a receding hairline above a face striking in its asymmetry, one ear flat against the head, the other stuck out. He was a difficult man who drank too much, loved music, detested all other writers, and wanted to be great (he had written a number of novels before the war, but none was published). He was also certain that to be a good writer it was necessary to be homosexual. When I disagreed, he named a half dozen celebrated contemporaries, "A pleiad," he roared delightedly, "of pederasts!" But what about Faulkner, I asked, and Hemingway. He was disdainful. Who said *they* were any good? And besides, hadn't I heard how Hemingway once . . .

I never saw Burns after 1947. But we exchanged several letters. He was going to write a successful play and become rich. He was also going to give up teaching in a prep school and go live in Europe. He did achieve Europe, but the occasion of the return was not happy. His second novel, *Lucifer with a Book* (1949), was perhaps the most savagely and unjustly attacked book of its day. Outraged, and with good reason, Burns exchanged America for Italy. But things had started to go wrong for him, and Italy did not help. The next novel, *A Cry of Children* (1952), was bad. He seemed to have lost some inner sense of self, gained in the war, lost in peace. He disintegrated. Night after night, he would stand at the Excelsior Hotel bar in Florence, drinking brandy, eating hard candy (he had a theory that eating sugar prevents hangovers . . . it does not), insulting imagined enemies and imagined friends, and all the while complaining of what had been done to him by book reviewers. In those years one tried not to think of Burns: it was too bitter. The best of us all had taken the worst way. In 1958 when I read that he was dead, I felt no shock. It seemed right. One only wondered how he had achieved extinction. Sunstroke was the medical report. But it being Burns, there were rumors of suicide, even of murder; however, those who knew him at the last say that his going was natural and inevitable. He was thirty-seven years old.

Twenty-one years ago the U.S. Army occupied Naples and John Horne Burns, a young soldier from Boston—Irish, puritan, unawakened—was brought to life by the human swarm he encountered in the Galleria Umberto, "a spacious arcade opening off Via Roma. . . . It was like walking into a city within a city." From this confrontation Burns never recovered. As he put it, "I thought I could keep a wall between me and the people. But the monkeys in the cage reach out and grab the spectator who offers them a banana." It was the time when cigarettes, chocolate, and nylons were exchanged for an easy sex that could become, for a man like Burns, unexpected love. He was startled to find that Italians could sell themselves with no sense of personal loss and, unlike their puritan conquerors, they could even take pleasure in giving pleasure; their delight in the fact of life persisted, no matter how deep the wound. Unlike "the Irish who stayed hurt all their lives, the Italians had a bounce-back in them."

*The Gallery* is a collection of "Portraits" and "Promenades"; a study of men and women brought together in one way or another by the fact of the Galleria and war. The characters, some shadowy, some startlingly brilliant, have sex, make love, lose themselves, find themselves. A young soldier retreats into visions of himself as Christ; a major in censorship builds himself a bureaucratic empire; a Catholic chaplain quibbles with a Protestant chaplain; a soldier grimly endures the VD ward and wonders how he could ever have loved the girl who put him there; and Momma, a genial Italian lady, presides over the Galleria's queer bar, finding her charges mysteriously *simpatico,* quite unlike the other conquerors. Finally, it is not so much what these characters do as the effect that Naples has on them. One discovers "the difference between love and Having Sex." To another: "It seemed that in our lethargic and compassionate caresses we were trying to console each other for every hurt the world had ever inflicted." To the demented visionary: "These people are all in search of love. The love of God, or death, or of another human being. They're all lost. That's why they walk so aimlessly. They all feel here that the world isn't big enough to hold them—and look at the design of this place. Like a huge cross laid on the ground, after the corpus is taken off the nails."

In the classic tradition of northern visitors to the South, Burns is overwhelmed by the spontaneity of the Italians. Even their rapacity and cruelty strike him as being closer to some ideal of the human than the moral numbness of the Americans. He contrasts Italian delicacy in human matters with the harshness of our own soldiers and their pathological loathing of the "inferior" races which war forced them to deal with. For the thousandth time in history, gross northern warriors were loose among the ancient civilization at the edge of the middle sea, and for Burns it was a revelation to realize that he belonged not to an army of civilized liberators but to a barbarian horde humanly inferior to the conquered.

Burns's style is energetic, very much that of the 40s, with distracting attempts at phonetic spelling ("furren" for "foreign") and made-up verbs ("he shrilled"). Burns's ear for dialogue was not always true; his dislike of those speaking often came between him and accuracy. He was also sometimes operatic in his effects (penicillin hurled at the Galleria: symbolic revenge). But when he is good, the style has a compelling drive that displays the national manner at its best. "Their faces complemented one another as a spoon shapes what it holds," thinks a character who has "contracted a bad case of irrelevance."

Of the well-known books of the Second War, I have always thought that only Burns's record was authentic and felt. To me the others are redolent of ambition and literature. But for Burns the war was authentic revelation. In Naples he fell in love with the idea of life. And having obtained a sense of his own identity, he saw what life might be. That the vision was a simple one makes no difference. It was his. "There'll be Neapolitans alive in 1960. I say, more power to them. They deserve to live out the end of their days because they caught on sooner than we how simple human life can be, uncomplicated by advertising and Puritanism and those loathsome values of a civilization in which everything is measured in terms of commercial success." His indictment is now a cliché, but it struck a nerve twenty years ago. Also I suspect he never understood his own people very well; nor do I think he would have been so entirely pleased by the Neapolitans of 1960 who, in their relative affluence, have begun to resemble us. But the spirit of his revelation remains true. "For I got lost in the war in Naples in August 1944. Often from what I saw I lost the power of speech. It seemed to me that everything happening there could be happening to me. A kind of madness, I suppose. But in the twenty-eighth year of my life I learned that I too must die. Until that time the only thing evil that could be done to me would be to hurry me out of the world before my time. Or to thwart my natural capacities. If this truth held for me, it must be valid for everybody else in the world."

Burns hurried himself out of the world before his time. But he had had his moment. And now that the war we lived through is history, we are able to recognize that the novel he wrote about it is literature. Burns was a gifted man who wrote a book far in excess of his gift, making a masterpiece that will endure in a way he himself could not. Extreme circumstances made him write a book which was better than his talent, an unbearable fate for an ambitious artist who wants to go on, but cannot—all later work shadowed by the splendid accident of a moment's genius. I suspect that once Burns realized his situation, he chose not to go on, and between Italian brandy and Italian sun contrived to stop.

As for the man, Burns had the luck to know, if only briefly, what it was to be alive with all senses responsive to all things; able to comprehend another person and to share that truth which is "valid for everybody else." Describing a soldier much like himself, even to the first name, Burns shows us a man discovering himself for the first time in the act of love on a hot August night. But then, love made, he is too keyed up to fall asleep, too restless with discovery; and so he is soothed and comforted in the dark, and the whispered Italian of his companion strikes the note of epitaph: "Buona notte e sogni d'oro. . . . Dormi, John."

*The New York Times Book Review*
May 30, 1965

# 30

·

# *JOHN DOS PASSOS*
# *AT MIDCENTURY*

There is a terrible garrulousness in most American writing, a legacy no doubt of the Old Frontier. But where the inspired tall-talesman of simpler days went on and on, never quite certain and never much caring what the next load of breath might contain, at his best he imparted with a new demotic flare the sense of life-living. Unfortunately, since these first originals the main line of the American novel has reverted to incontinent heirs, to the gabblers, maunderers, putters-in of everything. Watch: Now the man goes into the barbershop and sees four chairs with two people in them, one with a beard and the other reading a comic book about Bugs Bunny, then the man sits in the chair, he thinks of baby's first curls shorn and (if he's been analyzed) of castration, as he lists for us the labels on every bottle of hair tonic on the shelf, records every word the barber has to say about the Series—all the time wondering what happened to the stiff white brush smelling of stale powder they used to brush the back of your neck with. . . . To get that haircut the true gabbler will devote a dozen pages of random description and dialogue none of which finally has anything to do with his novel's theme, assuming there is one. It was included at that moment because the gabbler happened to think of a visit to a barber, the way good old Tom Wolfe once named all the rivers of America because he felt like it.

For every Scott Fitzgerald concerned with the precise word and the selection of relevant incident, there are a hundred American writers, many well regarded, who appear to believe that one word is just as good as another, and that anything which pops into the head is worth putting down. It is an attitude unique to us and deriving, I would suspect, from a corrupted idea of democracy: if everything and everyone is of equal value, then any word is as good as any other word to express a meaning, which in turn is no more valuable than any other meaning. Or to put it another way, if everyone is equally valuable, then anything the writer (who is valuable) writes must be of value, so why attempt selection? This sort of writing, which I call demotic, can be observed at its purest in the recent work of Jack Kerouac.

Thackeray said of Smollett, "I fancy he did not invent much." There it all is: the two kinds of writer, underscored by the choice of verb. To fancy. To invent. Most of our writers tend to be recorders. They tell us what happened last summer, why the marriage went wrong, how they lost custody of the children, how much they drank and whom they laid, and if they are demoticists the task of ordering that mass of words and impressions put between covers will be the reader's. Of all the recorders of what happened last summer—or last decade—John Dos Passos is the most dogged. Not since the brothers Goncourt has there been such a dedication to getting down exactly what happened, and were it not for his political passions he might indeed have been a true camera to our time. He invents little; he fancies less. He is often good when he tells you something through which he himself has lived, and noted. He is well equipped to be a good social critic, which is the role he has cast for himself: conscience to the Republic, stern reminder of good ways lost, of useful ways not taken.

With what seems defiance, the first two pages of John Dos Passos's new novel *Midcentury* are taken up with the titles of his published work, proudly spaced, seventeen titles to the first page, sixteen to the second: thirty-three books, the work of some forty years. The list is testament to Dos Passos's gallantry, to his stubbornness, and to his worldly and artistic failure. To paraphrase Hollywood's harsh wisdom, the persistent writer is only as good as his last decade. Admired extravagantly in the 20s and 30s, Dos Passos was largely ignored in the 40s and 50s, his new works passed over either in silence or else noted with that ritual sadness we reserve for those whose promise to art was not kept. He himself is aware of his own dilemma, and in a recent novel called *The Great Days* he recorded with brave if bewildered objectivity a decline similar to his own. I shall not try to ring the more obvious changes suggested by his career. Yet I should note that there is something about Dos Passos which makes a fellow writer unexpectedly protective, partly out of compassion for the man himself, and partly because the fate of Dos Passos is a chilling reminder to those condemned to write for life that this is the way it almost always is in a society which, to put it tactfully, has no great interest in the development of writers, a process too slow for the American temperament. As a result our literature is rich with sprinters but significantly short of milers.

Right off, let me say that unlike most of Dos Passos's more liberal critics, I never cared much for his early work even at its best. On the other hand, I have always enjoyed, even admired, the dottiness of his politics. His political progress from Radical Left to Radical Right seems to me very much in the American grain, and only the most humorless of doctrinaire liberals should be horrified. After all, it is not as if Dos Passos were in any way politically significant. Taken lightly, he gives pleasure. There is a good deal of inadvertent comedy in his admiration for such gorgeous Capitoline geese as Barry Goldwater, while page after page of *Midcentury* is vintage Old Guard demagoguery. For instance there is that old Bourbon comforter "Roosevelt's war" for the Second World War, while, every now and then, a passage seems almost to parody Wisconsin's late wonder:

Hitler's invasion of the Soviet Union cut off support from the Communists. Stalin needed quick help. Warmonger Roosevelt became the Communists' god. . . . War work meant primarily help for the Soviets to many a Washington bureaucrat.

That "many" is superb. "I have here in my hand a list of MANY Washington bureaucrats who . . ." Politically, to make an atrocious pun, Dos Passos is for the Byrds.

*Midcentury* is about the American labor movement from, roughly, the New Deal to the present, with occasional reminiscences of earlier times. The form of the book is chaotic. There are prose poems in italics, short impressionistic biographies of actual public figures, several fictional narratives in which various men and women are victimized by labor unions. And of course his patented device from *USA*: using newspaper headlines and fragments of news stories to act as counterpoint to the narration, to give a sense of time and place.

To deal with this last device first. In *USA* it was effective. In that book, Dos Passos stumbled on an interesting truth: nearly all of us are narcotized by newspapers. There is something about the way a newspaper page is set which, if only from habit, holds the attention no matter how boring the matter. One does read on, waiting for surprise or titillation. The success of the gossip column is no more than a crude exploitation of newspaper addiction. Even if you don't want to know what the Duchess of Windsor said to Elsa Maxwell or learn what stranger in the night was visited by Sir Stork, if your eye is addicted you will read on numbly.

(Parenthetic note to writers on the make and a warning to exploited readers: any column of text, even this one, will hold the eye and the attention of the reader if there are sufficient familiar proper names. Nat King Cole, Lee Remick, Central Park, Marquis de Sade, Senator Bourke Hickenlooper, Marilyn Monroe. See? I trapped a number of you who'd skimmed the denser paragraphs above, deciding it was pretty dull literary stuff. "Marquis de Sade? Must've skipped something. Let's see, there's 'titillation' . . . no, 'Hollywood' . . . no.")

Also, dialogue has almost the same effect on the eye as names and newspaper headlines. In an age of worsening prose and declining concentration, most readers' attention will wander if there is too much unbroken text. On the other hand, even the most reluctant reader enjoys descending the short sprightly steps of dialogue on the page, jumping the descriptions, to shift the metaphor, as a skilled rider takes hedges in a steeplechase.

The newspaper technique is a good one; but to make it work the excerpts ought, minimally, to have some bearing on the narrative. In *Midcentury* one has the impression that Dos Passos simply shredded a few newspapers at random and stuffed them between the chapters as a form of excelsior to keep the biographies from bumping into one another. On the whole these biographies provide the book with its only interest, although the choice of subjects is inscrutable. Walter Reuther, John L. Lewis, James Hoffa are relevant to a novel dealing with organized labor, but then why include Robert Oppenheimer and Eleanor Roosevelt? And what exactly *is* Sam Goldwyn doing in the book? Or James Dean, that well-known statesman of organized labor? But, disregarding the irrelevance of many of the subjects, Dos Passos handles his impressionistic technique with a good deal of cunning. It is a tribute to his method that I was offended by the job he did on Mrs. Roosevelt. He is wonderfully expert at the precise, low blow. Thus, referring to Oppenheimer's belated political awakening (and turn to the Left): "Perhaps he felt the need to expiate the crime of individuality (as much of a crime to the solid citizens of the American Legion posts as to party function- aries Moscow-trained in revolution)." That's good stuff. He may not make the eagle scream, but he can certainly get the geese to honking. Yet despite his very pretty malice, the real reason the biographies work is again newspaper addiction: we know the subjects already. Our memo- ries round the flat portraits; our prejudices do the author's work.

Finally, we come to the fictional characters, buried beneath headlines, feature stories and prose poems. (*Walking the earth under the stars, musing midnight in midcentury, a man treads the road with his dog; the dog, less timebound in her universe of stench and shrill, trots eager ahead. . . .* Not since Studs Lonigan's old buddy Weary Reilley was making the scene has there been such word-music, I mean wordmusic.) Excepting one, the invented characters are cast in solid cement. Dos Passos tells us this and he tells us that, but he never shows us anything. He is unable to let his characters alone to see which will breathe and which will not. The only story which comes alive is a narrative by a dying labor organizer and onetime Wobbly who recalls his life; and in those moments when Dos Passos allows him to hold the stage, one is most moved. If Dos Passos were a novelist instead of a pamphleteer he would have liberated this particular character from the surrounding cement and made a book of him, and in that book, simply told, not only made all his urgent polemical points but art as well. As it is, Dos Passos proves a point well taken by Stendhal: "Politics, amidst the interests of the imagination, are a pistol shot in the middle of a concert. This noise is ear-rending, without being forceful. It clashes with every instrument."

Dos Passos ends his book with a sudden lashing out at the youth of the day. He drops the labor movement. He examines James Dean. Then he does a Salingeresque first-person narrative of an adolescent who stole some credit cards (remember a similar story in *Life*?) and went on a spree of conspicuous consumption. Despite stylistic confusions, Dos Passos is plain in his indictment: doomed is our pleasure-loving, scorn- ful, empty, flabby modern youth, product of that midcentury dream in which, thanks to the do-gooders, we have lost our ancient Catonian virtue. I found the indictment oddly disgusting. I concede that there is some truth in everything Dos Passos says. But his spirit strikes me as sour and mean and, finally, uncomprehending. He has mistaken the decline of his own flesh and talent for the world's decline. This is the old man's folly, which a good artist or a generous man tries to avoid. Few of us can resist celebrating our own great days or finding fault with those who do not see in us now what we were or might have been. Nor is it unnatural when contemplating extinction to want, in sudden raging moments, to take the light with one. But it is a sign of wisdom to recognize one's own pettiness and not only to surrender vanity to death, which means to take it anyway, but to do so with deliberate grace as exemplar to the young upon whom our race's fragile continuity, which is all there is, depends. I should have thought that that was why one wrote—to make something useful for the survivors, to say: I was and now you are, and I leave you as good a map as I could make of my own traveling.

*Esquire*
May 1961

## 31

### BOOK REPORT

Can you hear me? Oh, good. Then I won't have to use this thing. It scares me to death! My husband always tells me, "Marian, you and your mother may not be very good but you're certainly loud enough when you give a book report." That's what he always says. Now then: the book I'm going to talk to you about today is by an American writer named Robert Penn Warren. Robert Penn Warren. He has written some poems, and of course most of us read his book a few years ago called *All the King's Men,* which they later made a movie out of and ruined, the way they always do. Mr. Warren's new book is a historical—*an* historical—novel *with a difference.* It begins with a beautiful quotation from a poem by A. E. Housman, the poet: "When shall I be dead and rid of the wrong my father did?"

And that's just what it's about. About Amantha Starr, a beautiful girl of sixteen, raised in Ohio, where she'd been sent to be educated by her father—sent by her father to be educated—a wealthy Kentucky plantation owner. When suddenly he dies, she comes home for his funeral, where she finds that not only did he die bankrupt, but that she is really a Negress, the daughter of one of his slaves, and she has to be sold to pay off these debts he left. Well, this is how the story starts. A really awful situation for a girl to be in. One day she had everything money and refinement could bring, and the next day she is a slave. The very first sentence of the book is filled with symbolism: "Oh, who am I? For so long that was, you might say, the cry of my heart." And then there follows a description of this wonderful house she lived in in Kentucky, south of Lexington, near Danville: a two-story brick house with a chimney at each end and a portico with pillars. The most beautiful house you could imagine! All of which she lost when she found she was colored and sold to a dealer who took her to New Orleans where she was put up for sale in the slave market as a slave.

Fortunately, she was bought by the most interesting person in the book, a fascinating older man with a lame leg who always walked with a heavy blackthorn stick with a great silver knob. His name was Hamish Bond, and he became her protector. Not until much later does she find out that he's really not named Bond but Hinks, that he was raised in Baltimore where he was a slave trader, going to Africa regularly and bringing back Negroes. He had some awful experiences in Africa. One in particular, a description of a massacre, is really gruesome where these Amazon women go through an entire village, slaughtering all the men, women and children because they're so enormous and bloodthirsty, much stronger than men. When Hamish, whose real name is Hinks, tries to keep one of the Amazons from killing a baby, this is what happens: "I just shoved her a little. It's very peculiar the way you have a habit. I just shoved her gentle because she was, in a way of speaking, a lady, and I had learned manners back in Baltimore. Here she was a crocodile-hided, blood-drinking old frau, who had been in her line of business for twenty years, and I caught myself making allowance for a lady." Well, he wished he hadn't, because right after he pushed her she slashed his leg with a big razor, making a long jagged cut which is what made him lame and why he had to always walk with that blackthorn cane with the silver knob.

Anyway, Hamish was kind in his brooding way to Amantha, and he treated her like she was really a lady which made her feel a bit better about being a slave. As somebody in the book says, the trouble with Hamish is he has "kindness like a disease." Another fascinating character Amantha meets is Hamish's *k'la* (meaning Negro best friend) Rauru, "whose eyes were wide, large and deepest, his nose wide but not flattened, the underlip full if not to the comic fullness favored in the minstrel shows of our day, and the corners of the mouth were drawn back so that the effect of that mouth was one of arrogant reserve and not blubbering docility."

Hamish was a very unusual man, especially after the Civil War started. One night there is a storm at Hamish's house—and Hamish takes Amantha in his arms while the rain blows in the window and she knows for the first time what love is. "With the hand of Hamish Bond laid to my side, and the spreading creep and prickle of sensation across the softness of my belly from the focus of Hamish Bond's sandpaper thumb, and the unplaiting and deliquescence of the deep muscles of thighs were as much History as any death-cry at the trenchlip or in the tangle of the abatis."

Can you still hear me? Well, that's how she feels as she discovers what love is and this maybe is the only serious fault in the book. I mean *would* a young girl like Amantha, even though she was well educated in Oberlin, Ohio, think thoughts quite like *that*? I mean, older more experienced women would, but would she? However, Mr. Warren writes poetic English and we can certainly excuse an occasional symbolic sentence like that. Well, there are many beautiful passages like this in the book, but the story never gets bogged down and the parts about the Civil War are really fascinating. Especially in New Orleans where she meets, completely by accident, Seth Parton, her girlhood sweetheart, who is now an officer in the Union Army, and also Tobias Sears, "the New England idealist to whom the butcheries of war must be justified by 'truth.'" I don't think it will spoil the book any if I tell you that everything ends all right with Tobias and Amantha . . . Miss Manty, as everybody calls her . . . together in quite a beautiful and touching ending.

I'd like to say something, by the way, if I may make a digression, about the much-maligned historical novel . . . the "bosom books" as they are disdainfully called by some critics, who think they know everything and can't keep from tearing apart books like Mr. Warren's. Now, I know and you know that maybe these books aren't *exactly* history, but they're awfully close, some of them, especially this one, and I can't help but think of Mrs. Gregg Henderson's fascinating report some meetings ago about the boys in Korea who were captured and tortured and brainwashed by the Chinese Communists who found that American boys were easy to break down BECAUSE THEY DID NOT KNOW ENOUGH ABOUT AMERICAN HISTORY AND WHY THEY WERE FIGHTING. Most of us here are mothers and we all know the trouble we have getting boys to read about history and all the things which don't seem important to them until they're caught by the enemy, when it's too late. So I don't think it's fair to make fun of novels that may be a little romantic but are still very useful ways of teaching what America is to people who are never going to read history or really deep things. I think Mr. Warren has done a wonderful job of bringing to life the Civil War and certain problems of that time—and frankly, I don't care a penny what the critics say about the book. After all, if people didn't want books like this, writers wouldn't write them and publishers wouldn't publish them. You can't argue with facts!

This book has been high on the best-seller list, and the movies have bought it, though they'll probably ruin it like they always do. A lot of people are going to be hearing about Amantha Starr and the Civil War. And they'll learn something. I firmly believe that these characters will stay with you for many a long day. Rau-ru, Miss Manty, the Amazons who go into that village killing all the men, Hamish Bond with his heavy blackthorn stick with the great silver knob—all these wonderful characters come alive for you in the pages of *Band of Angels* by Robert Penn Warren, published by Random House, three hundred and seventy-five pages long. Long? I wanted it to go on forever, and so will you!

*Zero*
Spring 1956

# V. S. PRITCHETT
## AS "CRITIC"

Thirty-three years ago in a preface to *The Living Novel,* V. S. Pritchett described how it was that he came to be the "critic" that he is. I put quotes around the word critic because that is what he himself does when, with characteristic modesty, he tells us how he stopped writing novels and short stories during World War II and turned to criticism. "Without leisure or freedom to write what I wanted, I could at least read what I wanted, and I turned to those most remarkable men and women: the great novelists of the past, those who are called the standard novelists." As he read, he made notes. These notes or reports or reviews were first published in the *New Statesman* and *The Nation;* then collected in *The Living Novel.* Since 1946 he has continued to report regularly on his reading, and *The Myth Makers* is his latest collection of literary essays.

It is interesting to read what Pritchett had to say in 1946 about the impression made on him by "what are called the Standard Novelists [who] have the set air of an officially appointed committee. We had fallen into the error of believing that they were written for critics, for literary historians, for students or for leisured persons of academic tastes; and people who read only the best authors usually let one know it. We had easily forgotten that the masters, great and small, remembered or neglected, were the freshest, the most original, the most importunate and living novelists of their time; that they stood above their contemporaries and survived them, because they were more readable, more entertaining, more suggestive and incomparably more able than the common run of novelist."

There are certain truths so true that they are practically unbelievable.

"We have only to glance," Pritchett continues, "at the second-rate novelists to see how they differ in this sense [of contemporaneity] from the masters. The second-rate are rarely of their time. They are not on the tip of the wave. They are born out of date and out of touch and are rooted not in life but in literary convention."

One thinks of all those busy teachers of English whose spare time is devoted to re-creating yet another version of dead Finnegan and his long-since celebrated wake; or of the *really* ambitious teacher-writer who wants so much for literature to achieve the pure heights of music (an aside, by the way, not a goal of Joyce); or of the would-be master of the two cultures who wants to encompass within a construct of narrative prose all the known laws, let us say, of thermodynamics. Our universities are positively humming with the sound of fools rushing in. The odd angel bleakly hovers; casts no shadow.

During the last third of a century, V. S. Pritchett has continued to be the best English-language critic of . . . well, the *living* novel. How does he do it? And what is it that he does? To begin with, unlike most critics, Pritchett is himself a maker of literature. He is a marvelous short-story writer; if he is less successful as a novelist, it is because, perhaps, he lacks "the novelist's vegetative temperament," as he remarks of Chekhov.

At work on a text, Pritchett is rather like one of those amorphic sea-creatures who float from bright complicated shell to shell. Once at home within the shell, he is able to describe for us in precise detail the secrets of the shell's interior; and he is able to show us, from the maker's own angle, the world the maker saw.

Of Dostoevsky: "Life stories of endless complexity hang shamelessly out of the mouths of his characters, like dogs' tongues, as they run by; the awful gregariousness of his people appears simultaneously with the claustrophobia and the manias of their solitude." Plainly, Pritchett's negative capability is well developed. He has a remarkable affinity for writers entirely different from that tradition of comic irony which has produced most of the best of English literature—including his own— and quite a lot of the bad. It is eerie to observe with what ease Pritchett occupies the shell of a writer who "is a sculptor of molten figures. . . . If anyone took up alienation as a profession it was [Dostoevsky]."

Finally, "Dostoevsky's style: it is a talking style in which his own voice and the voices of all his characters are heard creating themselves, as if all were narrators without knowing it."

The first job of a critic is to describe what he has read. This is a lot more difficult than one might suspect. I have often thought that one of the reasons why there have been so few good American literary critics is that those Americans who do read books tend to be obsessed with the personality of the author under review. The politics, sex, class of the author are all-important while the book at hand is simply an excuse to discuss, say, the anti-Semitism of Pound, the homosexuality of Whitman, the social climbing of James. Since the American character is essentially tendentious and sectarian, the American critic must decide in advance whether or not the writer he is writing about is a Good Person; that is, one who accepts implicitly all the going superstitions (a.k.a. values [*sic*]) of the middle class of the day. If the writer is a GP, then what he writes is apt to be good. If he is a BP, forget it.

In the Forties, the New Critics faced up to this national tendency and for a time their concentration on the text *qua* text provided a counterweight. But these paladins of the word have long since faded away, and the character of the United Statesman seems immutable. Or as the founder of *The Nation* put it more than a century ago: "The great mischief has always been that whenever our reviewers deviate from the usual and popular course of panegyric, they start from and end in personality, so that the public mind is almost sure to connect unfavorable criticism with personal animosity." Today, our critics either moralize *ad hominem* or, most chillingly (an "advance" since Godkin's time), pretend that the art of literature is one of the physical sciences and so in desperate need of neologisms, diagrams, laws.

The personality of a writer obviously has some relevance to what he writes, particularly if he is dead and the life has been publicly examined. But it takes great tact to know how to use gossip. Pritchett seldom loses sight of the fact that he is writing about writing, and not about writers at home. In a review of a life of Tolstoi, he observes, "Like the Lawrences and the Carlyles, the Tolstois were the professionals of marriage; they knew they were not in it for their good or happiness, that the relationship was an appointed ordeal, an obsession undertaken by dedicated heavyweights." This is personal; this is relevant . . . at least when discussing a book about the life of a major novelist. Pritchett rarely judges a living writer whose character cannot be known for certain, as opposed to his literary persona, which is fair game.

Pritchett's only American lapse occurs in his discussion of Jean

Genet, a writer whose luminous stupidity put Sartre in mind of the saints. Pritchett remarks that the brilliance of Genet's prose is often undone by the "sudden descents into banal reflection and in overall pretentiousness" while "the lack of charity is an appalling defect and one rebels against the claustrophobia." But then he remarks that "there are scarcely any women in Genet's novels and although this is due to his homosexuality, which is passive and feminine, it has an obvious root in his rage at being abandoned by his mother, who was a prostitute."

We don't know what either "passive" or "feminine" means in this context. As for "obvious root," is it so obvious? And why bad-mouth poor old Mrs. Genet? No guesswork about living writers unless they decide to tell all; in which case, *caveat lector.*

In *The Myth Makers,* Pritchett deals with nineteen writers entirely outside the Anglo-American tradition: seven Russians, five French, five writers of Spanish or Portuguese, Strindberg and Kafka. In other words, Pritchett has removed himself from ancestral ground. Although he is as familiar with French literature as he is with English (in this he very much resembles another Tory critic, the splendid, no longer read George Saintsbury), it must have been a considerable stretch for him to deal with the likes of Eça de Queiroz. If it was, he shows no strain.

Pritchett is at his best with the French; and if it does not take much critical acumen to write intelligently about Flaubert, it does take considerable intelligence to say something new about him ("Flaubert presented the hunger for the future, the course of ardent longings and violent desires that rise from the sensual, the horrible, and the sadistic"), or to illuminate a writer like George Sand, whose "people and landscapes are silhouettes seen in streams of sheet lightning. . . . She was half Literature."

Pritchett has new things to say about the differences between French and English, and how translation to English particularly undoes many of George Sand's effects. "If there is a loss it is because English easily droops into a near-evangelical tune; our language is not made for operatic precisions and we have a limited tradition of authorized hyperbole. Abstractions lose the intellectual formality that has an exact ring in French. . . . She had little sense of humor." This is excellent, and valuable. One thinks of other examples. Although Anaïs Nin was never taken seriously in England, the French eventually came to appreciate her solemn hieratic prose while the Americans, predictably, celebrated her personality. She had little sense of humor.

If there can be said to be a unifying argument to these nineteen essays, it has to do with time and the novel. Pritchett approves Bakhtin's notion that Dostoevsky is "the inventor of a new genre, the polyphonic novel. . . . There is a plurality of voices inner and outer, and they retain 'their unmergedness.' " Pritchett continues with Bakhtin's argument that "the traditional European novel is 'monological,' a thing of the past, and if Dostoevsky's novels seem a chaos compared, say, with *Madame Bovary,* so much the worse for the tradition. Man is not an object but another subject."

In Machado de Assis, Pritchett finds another kind of novel, "constructed by a short-story-teller's mind, for he is a vertical, condensing writer who slices through the upholstery of the realist novel into what is essential. He is a collector of the essences of whole lives and does not labor with chronology, jumping back or forward confidently in time as it pleases him." As for *One Hundred Years of Solitude,* "Márquez seems to be sailing down the blood stream of his people as they innocently build their town in the swamp, lose it in civil wars, go mad in the wild days of the American banana company and finally end up abandoned."

Unexpectedly, Pritchett regards the fabulist Borges as "a master of the quotidian, of conveying a whole history in two or three lines that point to an exact past drama and intensify a future one." Pritchett examines *The Circular Ruins* in which a teacher takes refuge in the ruins of a temple in order "to dream a man." Finally, Borges says of his character (*his* character?), "With relief, with humiliation, with terror, he understood that he too was a mere appearance dreamed by another." Pritchett wonders where this solipsistic conceit comes from. I shall be helpful. Borges got it from Chuang-tze, who wrote at the beginning of the third century B.C. Chuang-tze or "Chou dreamed that he was a butterfly. Then he woke up and found to his astonishment that he was Chou. But it was hard to be sure whether he really was Chou and had only dreamed that he was a butterfly, or was really a butterfly, and was only dreaming that he was Chou."

The most interesting piece in this collection deals with Goncharov, whose *Oblomov* is one of those great novels that are all of a piece and, inexplicably, like nothing else. Since Goncharov wrote only three novels in the course of what must have been a singularly discouraging life (he was State Censor), it is all the more extraordinary that this unique creation should have happened to him. Oblomov surely dreamed Goncharov. Who else would have bothered? "From what leak in a mind so small and sealed," writes Pritchett, "did the unconscious drip out and produce the character of Oblomov, the sainted figure of nonproductive sloth and inertia; one of those creatures who become larger and larger as we read?" There is no answering this question. "Genius is a spiritual greed," Pritchett remarks apropos Chekhov. But the Censor seems to have been greedier for food than for things of the spirit. Nevertheless, "From Sterne he learned to follow a half-forgotten tune in his head." Then Pritchett notes a difference between East and West in the ways of perceiving events. "If the Western calendared attitude to plot and precise action escaped [Goncharov], he had on his side the Russian sense of the hours of the day running through his scenes and people like a stream or continuous present." One *saw* Madame Bovary at a distance, plain; one *sees* Oblomov close-up, vivid in his sloth.

When Pritchett is obliged to deal with literary biographers and critics, he is generous and tactful. Only once does he express his horror at what the hacks of Academe have done to our language. Professor Victor Brombert's *The Novels of Flaubert: A Study of Themes and Techniques* provides the occasion. Pritchett quotes Professor Brombert at length; he praises things in the professor's book. But Pritchett finds disturbing the fact that the professor does not write well. Although this mild disability would go unremarked (and unnoticed in the land of the tin ear), for Pritchett

It is depressing to find so good a critic of Flaubert—of all people—scattering academic jargon and archaisms in his prose. The effect is pretentious and may, one hopes, be simply the result of thinking in French and writing in English; but it does match the present academic habit of turning literary criticism into technology. One really cannot write of Flaubert's "direction for monstrous forms" or of "vertiginous proliferation of forms and gestures"; "dizzying dilation," or "volitation"; "lupanar"—when all one means is "pertaining to a brothel." Philosophers, psychologists, and scientists may, I understand, write of "fragmentations" that suggest "a somnambulist and oneiric state." But who uses the pretentious "obnubilate" when they mean "dim" or "darkened by cloud"? Imaginative writers know better than to put on this kind of learned dog. The duty of the critic is to literature, not to its surrogates. And if I were performing a textual criticism of this critic I would be tempted to build a whole theory on his compulsive repetition of the word "velleities." Words and phrases like these come from the ingenuous and fervent pens of *Bouvard and Pécuchet*.

Literary criticism does not add to its status by opening an intellectual hardware store.

Unfortunately, the hardware store is pretty much all that there is to "literary criticism" in the United States. With a few fairly honorable exceptions, our academics write Brombertese, and they do so proudly. After all, no one has ever told them that it is not English. The fact that America's English departments are manned by the second-rate is no great thing. The second-rate must live, too. But in most civilized countries the second-rate are at least challenged by the first-rate. And score is kept in literary journals. But as McDonald's drives out good food, so these hacks of Academe drive out good prose. At every level in our literary life they flourish. In fact, they have now taken to writing the sort of novels that other tenured hacks can review and teach. Entire issues of "literary journals" are written by them. Meanwhile, in the universities, they are increasing at a positively Malthusian rate; and an entire generation of schoolteachers and book chatterers now believes that an inability to master English is a sign of intellectual grace, and that a writer like Pritchett is not to be taken seriously because he eschews literary velleities for literary criticism. Madame Verdurin has won the day.

Even so, it is good to know that our last critic in English is still at work, writing well—that is, writing as if writing well mattered. It would be nice if Sir Victor lived forever.

*The New York Review of Books*
June 28, 1979

# 33

# THE GREAT WORLD
# AND
# LOUIS AUCHINCLOSS

"What a dull and dreary trade is that of critic," wrote Diderot. "It is so difficult to create a thing, even a mediocre thing; it is so easy to detect mediocrity." Either the great philosophe was deliberately exaggerating or Americans have always lived in an entirely different continuum from Europe. For us the making of mediocre things is the rule while the ability to detect mediocrity or anything else is rare.

Don't knock, boost! was the cry of Warren Harding. To which the corollary was plain: anyone who knocks is a bad person with a grudge. As a result, the American has always reacted to the setting of standards rather the way Country Dracula responds to a clove of garlic or a crucifix. Since we are essentially a nation of hustlers rather than makers, any attempt to set limits or goals, rules or standards, is to attack a system of free enterprise where not only does the sucker not deserve that even break but the honest man is simply the one whose cheating goes undetected. Worse, to say that one English sentence might be better made than another is to be a snob, a subverter of the democracy, a Know Nothing enemy of the late arrivals to our shores and its difficult language.

Moralizing is as natural to the American book-chat writer as it is to the rest of our countrymen—a sort of national tic. Naturally, there are fashions in goodness owing to changes in the Climate of Opinion (current forecast: Chomsky occluded, low pressure over the black experience, small Stravinsky-Craft warnings). Also, the American university has come into its terrible own. Departments of English now produce by what appears to be parthenogenesis novels intended only for the classroom; my favorite demonstrated that the universe is—what else?—the university. Occasionally, a university novel (or U-novel) will be read by the general (and dwindling) public for the novel; and sometimes a novel written for that same public (P-novel) will be absorbed into Academe, but more and more the division between the two realms grows and soon what is written to be taught in class will stay there and what is written to be read outside will stay there, too. On that day the kingdom of prose will end, with an exegesis.

Meanwhile, book-chat, both P and U, buzzes on like some deranged bumblebee with a taste for ragweed; its store of bitter honey periodically collected and offered the public (?) in books with titles like *Literary Horizons: A Quarter Century of American Fiction,* by Granville Hicks, one of the most venerable bees in the business, a nice old thing who likes just about everything that's "serious" but tends to worry more about the authors than their books. Will X develop? Get past the hurdle of The Second Novel (everyone has One Novel in him, the First) or will fashion destroy him? Drink? Finally, does he deserve to be memorialized in *Literary Horizons*? Mr. Hicks's list of approved novelists contains one black, one Catholic, one Southern Wasp and six Jews. That is the standard mix for the seventies. The fifties mix would have been six Southern Wasps, one Jew, no black, etc.

For those who find puzzling the high favor enjoyed by the Jewish novelist in today's book-chat land, I recommend Mr. Alfred Kazin's powerful introduction to *The Commentary Reader,* "The Jew as Modern American Writer." Mr. Kazin tells us, with pardonable pride, that not only are Jews "the mental elite of the power age" but "definitely it was now [1966] the thing to be Jewish." As a result, to be a Jew in America is the serious subject for a P- or even U-novel, while to be a Wasp is to be away from the creative center; the born Catholic (as opposed to a convert) is thought at best cute (if Irish), at worst silly (if drunken Irish). In the permissive sixties, Negroes were allowed to pass themselves off as blacks and their books were highly praised for a time, but then there was all that trouble in the schools and what with one thing or another the black writers faded away except for James Baldwin, Mr. Hicks's token nigger. Yet even Mr. Hicks is worried about Mr.

Baldwin. Does he *really* belong on the List? Is it perhaps time for his
"funeral service" as a writer? Or will he make one final titanic effort and
get it all together and write The Novel?

Like Bouvard, like Pécuchet, like every current book-chatterer, Hicks
thinks that there really is something somewhere called The Novel which
undergoes periodic and progressive change (for the better—this is
America!) through Experiments by Great Masters. Consequently the
Task of the Critic is to make up Lists of Contenders and place his bets
accordingly. Not for Mr. Hicks Brigid Brophy's truism: there is no such
thing as The Novel, only novels.

At any given moment the subject or the matter of American fiction
is limited by the prevailing moral prejudices and assumptions of the
residents in book-chat land. U-novels must always be predictably experimental while the respectable P-novel is always naturalistic, usually
urban, often Jewish, always middle-class, and, of course, deeply, sincerely heterosexual.

Conscious of what the matter of fiction *ought* to be, Mr. Hicks somewhat nervously puts Louis Auchincloss on his list. On the one hand,
Auchincloss deals entirely with the American scene, writes in a comfortably conventional manner, and is one of the few intellectuals who write
popular novels. On the other hand, despite these virtues, Auchincloss
is not much thought of in either the P or the U world and Mr. Hicks
is forced to buzz uneasily: "Although I have read and reviewed most
of Louis Auchincloss's work in the past twelve years, I hesitated about
including him in this volume." So the original Debrett must have felt
when first called upon to include the Irish peerage. "Certainly he has
not been one of the movers and shakers of the postwar period." As
opposed, presumably, to Reynolds Price, Wright Morris, Herbert Gold,
Bernard Malamud, and the other powerhouses on Mr. Hicks's list.
Actually, only two or three of Mr. Hicks's writers could be said to have
made any contribution at all to world literature. But that is a matter of
taste. After all, what, Pontius, *is* literature?

Mr. Hicks returns worriedly to the *matter* of fiction. Apparently
Auchincloss "has written for the most part about 'good' society, the
well-to-do and the well-bred. And he has written about them with
authority. What bothers me is not that he writes about this little world
but that he seems to be aware of no other. Although he is conscious of
its faults, he never questions its values in any serious way." This is
fascinating. I have read all of Auchincloss's novels and I cannot recall
one that did not in a most serious way question the values of his "little
world." Little world!

It is a tribute to the cunning of our rulers and to the stupidity of our intellectuals (book-chat division, anyway) that the world Auchincloss writes about, the domain of Wall Street bankers and lawyers and stock-brokers, is thought to be irrelevant, a faded and fading genteel-gentile enclave when, in actual fact, this little world comprises the altogether too vigorous and self-renewing ruling class of the United States—an oligarchy that is in firm control of the Chase Manhattan Bank, American foreign policy, and the decision-making processes of both the Republican and Democratic parties; also, most "relevantly," Auchincloss's characters set up and administer the various foundations that subsidize those universities where academics may serenely and dully dwell like so many frogs who think their pond the ocean—or the universe the university.

Of all our novelists, Auchincloss is the only one who tells us how our rulers behave in their banks and their boardrooms, their law offices and their clubs. Yet such is the vastness of our society and the remoteness of academics and book-chatterers from actual power that those who should be most in this writer's debt have no idea what a useful service he renders us by revealing and, in some ways, by betraying his class. But then how can the doings of a banker who is white and gentile and rich be *relevant* when everyone knows that the only meaningful American experience is to be Jewish, lower-middle-class, and academic? Or (in Mr. Hicks's words), "As I said a while ago and was scolded for saying, the characteristic hero of our time is a misfit." Call me Granville.

Ignorance of the real world is not a new thing in our literary life. After the Second World War, a young critic made a splash with a book that attributed the poverty of American fiction to the lack of a class system—a vulgar variation on Henry James's somewhat similar but usually misunderstood observations about American life. This particular writer came from a small town in the Midwest; from school, he had gone into the service and from there into a university. Since he himself had never seen any sign of a class system, he decided that the United States was a truly egalitarian society. It should be noted that one of the charms of the American arrangement is that a citizen can go through a lifetime and never know his true station in life or who his rulers are.

Of course our writers know that there are rich people hidden away somewhere (in the gossip columns of Suzy, in the novels of Louis Auchincloss), but since the Depression the owners of the country have played it cool, kept out of sight, consumed inconspicuously. Finally, no less a P (now P-U)-writer than that life-long little friend of the rich Ernest Hemingway felt obliged to reassure us that the rich are really just folks. For the P-writer the ruling class does not exist as a subject for fiction if only because the rulers are not to be found in his real world of desperate suburbs. The U-writer knows about the Harkness plan—but then what is a harkness? Something to do with horse racing? While the names that the foundations bear do not suggest to him our actual rulers—only their stewards in the bureaucracy of philanthropy, the last stronghold of the great immutable fortunes.

The serious P-writer knows that he must reflect the world he lives in: the quotidian of the average man. To look outside that world is to be untrue and, very possibly, undemocratic. To write about the actual rulers of the world we live in (assuming that they exist, of course) is to travel in fantasy land. As a result, novels to do with politics, the past, money, manners, power are as irrelevant to the serious P-writer as are the breathy commercial fictions of all the Irvingses—so unlike the higher relevancies of all the Normans.

In a society where matters of importance are invariably euphemized (how can an antipersonnel weapon actually kill?) a writer like Louis Auchincloss who writes about the way money is made and spent is going to have a very hard time being taken seriously. For one thing, it is now generally believed in book-chat land that the old rich families haven't existed since the time of Edith Wharton while the new-rich are better suited for journalistic exposés than for a treatment in the serious P- or U-novel. It is true that an indiscriminate reading public enjoys reading Auchincloss because, unlike the well-educated, they suspect that the rich are always with us and probably up to no good. But since the much-heralded death of the Wasp establishment, the matter of Auchincloss's fiction simply cannot be considered important.

This is too bad. After all, he is a good novelist, and a superb short-story writer. More important, he has made a brave effort to create his own literary tradition—a private oasis in the cactus land of American letters. He has written about Shakespeare's penchant for motiveless malignity (a peculiarly American theme), about Henry James, about our women writers as the custodians and caretakers of the values of that dour European tribe which originally killed the Indians and settled the continent.

Mr. Hicks, with his eerie gift for misunderstanding what a writer is writing about, thinks that Auchincloss is proudly showing off his class while bemoaning its eclipse by later arrivals. Actually, the eye that Auchincloss casts on his own class is a cold one and he is more tortured than complacent when he records in book after book the collapse of the

Puritan ethical system and its replacement by—as far as those of us now living can tell—nothing. As for the ruling class being replaced by later arrivals, he knows (though they, apparently, do not) that regardless of the considerable stir the newcomers have made in the peripheral worlds of the universities, showbiz, and book-chat, they have made almost no impact at all on the actual power structure of the country.

Auchincloss deals with the masters of the American empire partly because they are the people he knows best and partly, I suspect, because he cannot figure them out to his own satisfaction. Were they better or worse in the last century? What is good, what is bad in business? And business (money) is what our ruling class has always been about; this is particularly obvious now that the evangelical Christian style of the last century has been abandoned by all but the most dull of our rulers' employees (read any speech by any recent president to savor what was once the very sound of Carnegie, of Gould, and of Rockefeller).

Finally, most unfashionably, Auchincloss writes best in the third person; his kind of revelation demands a certain obliqueness, a moral complexity which cannot be rendered in the confessional tone that marks so much of current American fiction, good and bad. He plays God with his characters, and despite the old-fashionedness of his literary method he is an unusually compelling narrator, telling us things that we don't know about people we don't often meet in novels—what other novelist went to school with Bill and McGenghis Bundy? Now, abruptly, he ceases to play God. The third person becomes first person as he describes in *A Writer's Capital* the world and the family that produced him, a world and family not supposed either by their own standards or by those of book-chat land to produce an artist of any kind.

I must here confess to an interest. From the time I was ten until I was sixteen years old my stepfather was Hugh D. Auchincloss, recently saluted by a society chronicler as "the first gentleman of the United States"—to the enormous pleasure and true amazement of the family. The Auchinclosses resemble the fictional Primes in *The Embezzler,* a family that over the years has become extraordinarily distinguished for no discernible reason or, as Louis puts it, "There was never an Auchincloss fortune . . . each generation of Auchincloss men either made or married its own money."

Plainly, even sharply, Louis chronicles the family's history from their arrival in America (1803) to the present day. He is realistic about the family's pretensions though he does not seem to be aware of the constant chorus of criticism their innumerable in-laws used to (still do?) indulge in. I can recall various quasi-humorous rebellions on the part of the in-laws (once led by Wilmarth Lewis) at the annual clan gathering in New York. What the in-laws could never understand was the source of the family's self-esteem. After all, what had they ever *done*? And didn't they come to America a bit late by true "aristocratic" standards? And hadn't they been peddlers back in Scotland who had then gone into *dry goods* in New York? And what was so great about making blue jeans? Besides, weren't they all a bit too dark? What about "those grave, watery eyes over huge aquiline noses"? And wasn't there a rumor that they had Italian blood? And when you come right down to it didn't they look (this was only whispered at Bailey's Beach, muttered in the men's room of the Knickerbocker) *Jewish*?

In the various peregrinations of the branch of the family that I was attached to (I almost wrote "assigned to": sooner or later the Auchin-closses pick up one of everything, including the cutest of the presidents), I never came across Louis, who was, in any case, eight years older than I. Right after the war when I was told that a Louis Auchincloss had written a novel, I said: Not possible. No Auchincloss could write a book. Banking and law, power and money—that is their category.

From reading Louis's memoir I gather that that was rather his own view of the matter. He had a good deal to overcome and this is reflected in the curiously tense tone of his narrative. He had the bad luck, for a writer, to come from a happy family, and there is no leveler as great as a family's love. Hatred of one parent or the other can make an Ivan the Terrible or a Hemingway; the protective love, however, of two devoted parents can absolutely destroy an artist. This seems to have been particularly true in the case of Louis's mother. For one thing she knew a good deal about literature (unlike every other American writer's mother) and so hoped that he would not turn out to be second-rate, and wretched.

From the beginning, Louis was a writer: word-minded, gossip-prone, book-devouring. In other words, a sissy by the standards of the continuing heterosexual dictatorship that has so perfectly perverted in one way or another just about every male in the country. The sensitive, plump, small boy like Louis has a particularly grim time of it but, happily, as the memoir shows, he was able eventually to come to grips with himself and society in a way that many of the other sensitive, plump boys never could. A somber constant of just about every American literary gathering is the drunk, soft, aging writer who bobs and weaves and jabs pathetically at real and imagined enemies, happy in his ginny madness that he is demonstrating for all the world to see his so potent manliness.

By loving both parents more or less equally, Auchincloss saw through the manly world of law and finance; saw what it did to his father, who suffered, at one point, a nervous breakdown. Not illogically, "I came to think of women as a privileged happy lot. With the right to sit home all day on sofas and telephone, and of men as poor slaves doomed to go downtown and do dull, soul-breaking things to support their families." As for Wall Street, "never shall I forget the horror inspired in me by those narrow dark streets and those tall sooty towers. . . ." The story of Auchincloss's life is how he reconciled the world of father with that of mother; how he became a lawyer and a novelist; how the practice of law nourished his art and, presumably, the other way around, though I'm not so sure that I would want such a good novelist creating a trust for me.

Groton, Yale, Virginia Law School, the Navy during the Second World War, then a Manhattan law firm, psychoanalysis, marriage, children, two dozen books. Now from the author's middle age, he looks back at himself and our time, holding the mirror this way and that, wondering why, all in all, he lacked the talent early on for being happy, for being himself. With characteristic modesty, he underplays his own struggle to reconcile two worlds, not to mention the duality of his own nature. Yet I suspect that having made himself a writer, he must have found demoralizing the fact that the sort of writing he was interested in doing was, simply, not acceptable to the serious U- or even the serious P-book-chatterers.

The literary line to which Auchincloss belongs was never vigorous in the United States—as demonstrated by its master Henry James's wise removal to England. Edith Wharton moved to France, but remained an American; even so, to this day, she is regarded as no more than pale James. Since Mrs. Wharton, the novel of manners has been pretty much in the hands of commercialites. Neither the insider Marquand nor the outsider O'Hara is taken seriously in U-land while in P-land they were particularly denigrated after the war when book-chat was no longer written by newspapermen who were given books to review because they were not good enough to write about games but by young men and women who had gone to universities where the modern tradition (*sic*) was entirely exotic: Joyce and Lawrence, Proust and Kafka were solemnly presented to them as the models worth honoring or emulating. It is true that right after the war James made a comeback, but only as an elaborate maker of patterns: *what* Maisie knew was not so important as her way of telling what she knew.

The early fifties was not a good time for a writer like Louis Auchincloss. But it could have been worse: at least he did not have to apologize
for his class because, pre-Camelot, no American writer had a clue who
or what an Auchincloss was. Yet even then his novels never much
interested his fellow writers or those who chatted them up because he
did not appear to deal with anything that really mattered, like the recent
war, or being Jewish/academic/middle-class/heterosexual in a world of
ball-cutters. No one was prepared for dry ironic novels about our rulers—not even those social scientists who are forever on the lookout for
the actual bill of sale for the United States.

Auchincloss himself was no help. He refused to advertise himself. If
the book-chatterers had no idea what Sullivan and Cromwell was, he
wasn't going to tell them. He just showed the firm in action. He also
knew, from the beginning, what he was doing: "I can truly say that I
was never 'disillusioned' by society. It was perfectly clear from the
beginning that I was interested in the story of money: how it was made,
inherited, lost, spent." Not since Dreiser has an American writer had
so much to tell us about the role of money in our lives. In fascinating
detail, he shows how generations of lawyers have kept intact the great
fortunes of the last century. With Pharaonic single-mindedness they
have filled the American social landscape with pyramids of tax-exempt
money, to the eternal glory of Rockefeller, Ford, et al. As a result, every
American's life has been affected by the people Auchincloss writes so
well about.

I cannot recall where or when I first met Louis. He lists me among
a dozen writers he met twenty years ago at the Greenwich Village flat
of the amiable novelist Vance Bourjaily and his wife. I do recall the
curiosity I had about him: how on earth was he going to be both a lawyer
and a writer (a question entirely subjective: how could I write what I
did and be an effective politician? Answer: forget it). I can't remember
how he answered the question or if he did. I was amused by the reaction
of other writers to him. They knew—particularly the wives or girl
friends—that there was something "social" about him but that was
neither a plus nor a minus in the Eisenhower era. Earlier it would have
been a considerable handicap. In my first years as a writer, I was often
pleased to be identified with the protagonist of *The City and the
Pillar*—a male prostitute. After all, that was a *real* identity, I thought,
sharing the collective innocence.

Louis moved through these affairs with considerable charm and he
exaggerates when he writes: "The fact that I was a Wall Street lawyer,

a registered Republican, and a social registrite was quite enough for half the people at any one party to cross me off as a kind of duckbill platypus not to be taken seriously." Rather wistfully, he observes: "I am sure I had read more books by more of the guests at any one party than anyone else." I am sure that he had. But then it has always been true that in the United States the people who ought to read books write them. Poor Louis who *knew* French and American literature, who "kept up" with what was going on, now found himself in a literary society of illiterate young play-actors. Overexcited by the publicity surrounding Hemingway and Fitzgerald, they had decided to imitate these "old masters." At least a dozen were playing Hemingway—and several grizzled survivors still are. Certainly no one was himself—but then selves are hard to come by in America. So, in a way, Louis was indeed like a platypus in that farmyard of imitation roosters. After all, he didn't resemble any famous writer we had ever heard of. He was simply himself, and so odd man out to the young counterfeiters.

Since then, Auchincloss has learned (through psychoanalysis, he tells us) that "a man's background is largely of his own creating." Yet pondering the response to this discovery as expressed in his work, he writes,

American critics still place a great emphasis on the fact of background on character, and by background they mean something absolute which is the same for all those in the foreground. Furthermore, they tend to assume that the effect of any class privilege in a background must be deleterious to a character and that the author has introduced such a background only to explain the harm done. Now the truth is that the background to most of my characters has been selected simply because it is a familiar one to me and is hence more available as a model. . . . I cannot but surmise that the stubborn refusal on the part of many critics to see this is evidence of a resentment on their part against the rich, a resentment sometimes carried to the point of denying that a rich man can be a valid subject for fiction. . . . Such a point of view would have been, of course, ridiculous in the eighteenth or nineteenth centuries when the great bulk of the characters of fiction came from the upper or upper middle class. Critics did not resent Anna Karenina or Colonel Newcome.

Louis Auchincloss's latest book, *The Partners,* is a collection of related short stories set in a New York law firm. A merger has been proposed between the demure firm of the partners and a larger, flashier firm. Old values (but are they really values?) combat new forces. Invariably those who do the right self-sacrificing thing end up echoing Mrs. Lee in Henry Adams's *Democracy*: "The bitterest part of all this horrid story is that nine out of ten of your countrymen would say I have made a mistake." By not marrying a blackguard senator.

The author's virtues are well displayed: almost alone among our writers he is able to show in a convincing way men at work—men at work discreetly managing the nation's money, selecting its governors, creating the American empire. Present, too, are his vices. Narrative is sometimes forced too rapidly, causing characters to be etiolated while the profound literariness of the author keeps leaking into the oddest characters. I am sure that not even the most civilized of these Wall Street types is given to quoting *King Lear* and Saint-Simon quite as often as his author has him do. Also, there are the stagy bits of writing that recur from book to book—hands are always "flung up" by Auchincloss characters; something I have never seen done in real life west of Naples.

One small advance: in each of Auchincloss's previous books sooner or later the author's Jamesian fascination with the theater intrudes and, when it does, I know with terrible foreboding that I shall presently see upon the page that somber ugly word "scrim." I am happy to report that in *The Partners* there is no scrim; only the author's elegant proscenium arch framing our proud, savage rulers as they go single-mindedly about their principal task: the preserving of fortunes that ought to be broken up.

*The New York Review of Books*
July 18, 1974

# 34

## MISS SONTAG'S
## NEW NOVEL

The beginning of a novel tends to reveal the author's ambition. The implicit or explicit obeisance he pays to previous works of literature is his way of "classing" himself, thereby showing interest in the matter. But as he proceeds, for better or worse his true voice is bound to be heard, if only because it is not possible to maintain for the length of a novel a voice pitched at a false level. Needless to say, the best and the worst novels are told in much the same tone from beginning to end, but they need not concern us here.

In the early pages of *Death Kit,* Susan Sontag betrays great ambition. Her principal literary sources are Nathalie Sarraute, Robbe-Grillet, Sartre, and Kafka, and she uses these writers in such a way that they must be regarded not so much as influences upon her prose as collaborators in the act of creation. Contemplating Nathalie Sarraute's *Portrait of a Man Unknown,* Sartre made much of Sarraute's "protoplasmic vision" of our interior universe: roll away the stone of the commonplace and we will find running discharges, slobberings, mucus; hesitant, amoeba-like movements. The Sarraute vocabulary is incomparably rich in suggesting the slow centrifugal creeping of these viscous, live solutions. "Like a sort of gluey slaver, their thought filtered into him, sticking to him, lining his insides." This is a fair description of Sarraute's manner, which Miss Sontag has entirely appropriated.

The first few pages of *Death Kit* are rich with Sarrautesque phrases: "inert, fragile, sticky fabric of things," "the soft inter-connected tissue-like days," "surfaces of people deformed and bloated and leaden and crammed with vile juices" (but Miss Sarraute would not have written "leaden" because a bloated person does not suggest metal; more to the point, "leaden" is not a soft, visceral word), "his jellied porous boss" (but isn't the particular horror of the true jelly its consistency of texture? a porous jelly is an anomaly). Fortunately, once past the book's opening, Miss Sontag abandons the viscous vision except for a brief reprise in mid-passage when we encounter, in quick succession, "affable gelatinous Jim Allen," "chicken looks like boiled mucus," "oozing prattling woman," "sticky strip of words." But later we are reminded of Miss Sarraute's addiction to words taken from the physical sciences. In "The Age of Suspicion" (an essay admired by Miss Sontag in her own collection of essays *Against Interpretation*), Miss Sarraute wrote that the reader "is immersed and held under the surface until the end, in a substance as anonymous as blood, a magma without name or contours." Enchanted by the word "magma," Miss Sontag describes *her* characters as being "All part of the same magma of sensation, in which pleasure and pain are one." But Miss Sarraute used the word precisely, while Miss Sontag seems not to have looked it up in the dictionary, trusting to her ear to get the meaning right, and failing.

The plot of *Death Kit* is elaborate. Aboard the Privateer (yes), a train from Manhattan to Buffalo, Diddy (a divorced man in his thirties who inhabits a life he does not possess) observes a blind girl and an older woman. He wonders who they are; he also meditates on the other occupants of the compartment (as in Proust). Then the train stalls in a tunnel. The lights go out. After what seems a long time, Diddy gets off the train. He makes his way in the dark to the front of the train, where he finds a workman removing a barrier. When the man does not respond to his questions, Diddy grows alarmed. Finally the man does speak: he appears to threaten Diddy, who kills him with a crowbar, a murder which is almost gratuitous, almost Gide. Diddy returns to the compartment to find the older woman asleep. He talks to the blind girl, whose name is Hester (*The Scarlet Letter*?). Then the train starts and he takes Hester to the washroom, where, excited by his murder (Mailer's *An American Dream*), he makes love to her. Later Hester tells him that he did not leave the compartment and so could not have killed the workman. But of course she is blind, while the older woman, her aunt, was asleep and so cannot bear witness. In any case, hallucination has begun, and we are embarked upon another of those novels whose contemporary source is Kafka. Do I wake or sleep?

Diddy dreams a very great deal and his dreams are repeated at length. When awake, he attends business meetings of his company, whose trademark is a gilded dome, whose management is conservative, whose business is worldwide, whose prospects are bad . . . too much undercutting from the East (what can Miss Sontag *mean*?). He broods about the "murder" and moons about Hester, who is in a local clinic waiting for an operation to restore her sight. Diddy visits her; he loves her. But he is still obsessed by the murder. In the press he reads that a workman named Angelo Incarnadona (incarnated angel) was killed in the tunnel by the Privateer, which had not, apparently, stalled in the tunnel. Diddy's quest begins. Did he kill the angel? He talks to the widow, who tells him that the body was cremated; he is safe, there can never be an investigation. Meanwhile Hester's operation is a failure. But Diddy has decided to marry her. They return to Manhattan. He quits his job. They withdraw from the world, seldom leaving his apartment. Slowly he begins to fade, grows thinner, vaguer. Finally he (apparently) takes Hester with him to the tunnel in an effort to make her *see* what it was that he did . . . or did he (Diddy)? In the tunnel they find a workman similar to the angel made flesh: again the man is at work removing a barrier. The scene more or less repeats the original, and once again Diddy separates the angel from its fleshly envelope with a crowbar. Then he makes love to Hester on the tunnel floor. But now we cease to see him from the outside. We enter his declining world, we become him as he walks naked through one subterranean room after another, among coffins and corpses heavy with dust, and in this last progress, simply written, Miss Sontag reveals herself as an artist with a most powerful ability to show us what it is she finally, truly sees.

The flash of talent at the book's end makes all the more annoying what precedes it. Miss Sontag is a didactic, naturalistic, Jewish-American writer who wants to be an entirely different sort of writer, not American but high European, not Jewish but ecumenical, not naturalistic in style but allusive, resonant, ambiguous. It is as an heiress to Joyce, Proust, and Kafka that she sees herself; her stand to be taken on foreign rather than on native ground. The tension between what she is and what she would like to be creates odd effects. She presents Diddy as a Gentile. But, to make a small point, middle-class American goyim do not address each other continually by name while, to make a larger point, Diddy's possession of a young brother who is a virtuoso musician seems better suited to a Clifford Odets drama than to one by Sherwood Anderson or William Faulkner. But Miss Sontag is nothing if not contemporary and perhaps she is reflecting the current fashion for Jewish writers to disguise Jewish characters as Gentiles, in much the same way that the homosexualists in our theater are supposed to write elaborate masquerades in which their own pathological relationships are depicted as heterosexual, thus traducing women and marriage. These playwrights have given us all many an anxious moment. Now the Jewish novelists are also indulging in travesty, with equally scandalous results.

As for style, Miss Sontag demonstrates a considerable gift for naturalistic prose, particularly in the later parts of the book when she abandons her sources and strikes out on her own. But she is not helped by the form in which she has cast her work. For no apparent reason, certain passages are indented on the page, while at maddeningly regular but seemingly random intervals she inserts the word "now" in parenthesis. If she intends these (now)s to create a sense of immediacy, of presentness, she fails. Also, though the story is told in the third person, on four occasions she shifts to the first person plural. It is a nice surprise, but one that we don't understand. Also, her well-known difficulties in writing English continue to make things hard for her. She is altogether too free with "sort ofs" and "kind ofs" and "reallys"; she often confuses number, and her ear, oddly enough, is better attuned to the cadences of the lower orders than to those of the educated. In the scenes between Diddy and the dead workman's widow, she writes not unlike Paddy Chayefsky at his best. She is, however, vulgar at moments when she means not to be, and on several occasions she refers to someone as "balding," betraying, if nothing else, her lovely goosey youth: those of us battered by decades of Timestyle refuse to use any word invented by that jocose and malicious publishing enterprise which has done so much to corrupt our Empire's taste, morals, and prose.

In a strange way, Miss Sontag has been undone as a novelist by the very thing that makes her unique and valuable among American writers: her vast reading in what English Departments refer to as comparative literature. As a literary broker, mediating between various contemporary literatures, she is awesome in her will to understand. This acquired culture sets her apart from the majority of American novelists (good and bad) who read almost nothing, if one is to admit as evidence the meager texture of their works and the idleness of their occasional commentaries. When American novelists do read, it is usually within the narrow limits of the American canon, a strange list of minor provincial writers grandiosely inflated into "world classics." Certainly few of our writers know anything of what is now being written in Europe, particularly in France. Yet for all the aridities and pretensions of the French "New Novelists," their work is the most interesting being done anywhere, and not to know what they are up to is not to know what the novel is currently capable of. As an essayist (and of course interpreter!) Miss Sontag has been, more than any other American, a link to European writing today. Not unnaturally, her reading has made her impatient with the unadventurous novels which our country's best-known (and often best) writers produce. She continues to yearn, as she recently wrote, for a novel "which people with serious and sophisticated [*sic*] taste in the other arts can take seriously," and she believes that such a work might be achieved "by a kind of total structuring" that is "analogous to music." This is all very vague, but at least she is radical in the right way; also her moral seriousness is considerably enhanced by a perfect absence of humor, that most devastating of gifts usually thrust at birth upon the writer in English. Unhindered by a sense of humor, she is able to travel fast in the highest country, unafraid of appearing absurd, and of course invulnerable to irony.

Unfortunately, Miss Sontag's intelligence is still greater than her talent. What she would do, she cannot do—or at least she has not done in *Death Kit,* a work not totally structured, not even kind of. Worse, the literary borrowings entirely obscure her own natural talent while the attitudes she strikes confuse and annoy, reminding one of Gide's weary complaint that there is nothing more unbearable than those writers who assume a tone and manner not their own. In the early part of *Death Kit,* Miss Sontag recklessly uses other writers in much the same way that certain tribes eat parts of their enemies in the hope that, magically, they may thus acquire the virtues and powers of the noble dead. No doubt the tribesmen do gain great psychological strength through their cannibalizing, but in literature only writers of the rank of Goethe and Eliot can feed promiscuously and brazenly upon the works of other men and gain strength. Yet the coda of Miss Sontag's novel suggests that once she has freed herself of literature, she will have the power to make it, and there are not many American writers one can say that of.

*Book World*
September 10, 1967

# 35

---
⬦
---

## *LESSING'S SCIENCE FICTION*

Currently, there are two kinds of serious-novel. The first deals with the Human Condition (often confused, in Manhattan, with marriage) while the second is a word-structure that deals only with itself. Although the Human Condition novel can be read—if not fully appreciated—by any moderately competent reader of the late Dame Agatha Christie, the second cannot be read at all. The word-structure novel is intended to be taught, rather like a gnostic text whose secrets may only be revealed by tenured adepts in sunless campus chapels. Last month, a perfect example of the genre was extravagantly praised on the ground that here, at last, was a "book" that could not, very simply, be read at all by anyone, ever.

The only thing that the two kinds of serious-novel have in common is the fact that in each case the creator has taken *extraordinary risks with his talents.* He has driven his art and mind to the fullest limit of prose; and beyond. He has gambled recklessly with his gifts; been deer to his own gun; been brave, brave. On the other hand, the serious-writer's reader's courage has gone entirely unremarked and the slopes of Parnassus are now planted thick with the shallow graves of those gallant readers who risked their all in dubious battle with serious-texts, and failed—their names known only to whatever god makes the syllabus.

Nevertheless, despite the glory of risk-taking and the applause of tens of book-chatterers, today's serious-novelist often betrays a certain edginess whenever he feels obliged to comment publicly on his art. He is apt to admit that the word-structure novel is unsatisfying while the Human Condition novel tends to look more and more like old movies or, worse, like new movies. Needless to say, the fact that hardly anyone outside an institution wants to read a serious-novel has never been a deterrent to our serious-novelists—rather the reverse. They know that silence, cunning, exile all add up to exegesis. But is that enough? I suspect that a crisis is now at hand and that the serious-novel, as we lucky few have known it, may be drawing to a close.

At the risk of poaching on that territory where the buffalo and Leslie Fiedler roam, one might make the case that owing to some sort of perfect misunderstanding about the nature of literature, our ungifted middlebrows have taken over the serious-novel while those highbrows who tend to create an epoch's high literature appear not to be "serious" at all. In any case, the thing is now so muddled that it will be a long time before all this is sorted out. Certainly it will be a long time before anyone can ever again state with George Eliot's serenity and confidence that "Art must be either real and concrete or ideal and eclectic. Both are good and true in their way, but my stories are of the former kind." What, we hear our middlebrows begin to buzz, is real? concrete? ideal? eclectic? *What is art?* Whatever art is, it is not our day's serious-novel, whose texture so closely resembles that gelidity in which great Satan is forever mired at the center of hell's inner ring.

Although Doris Lessing has more in common with George Eliot than she has with any contemporary serious-novelist, she is not always above solemnity, as opposed to mere seriousness. Somewhat solemnly, Lessing tells us in the preface to her new novel *Shikasta* that there may indeed be something wrong with the way that novels are currently being written. She appears not to be drawn to the autonomous word-structure. On the other hand, she is an old-fashioned moralist. This means that she is inclined to take very seriously the quotidian. The deep—as opposed to strip—mining of the truly moral relationship seems to me to be her territory. I say "seems" because I have come to Lessing's work late. I began to read her with *Memoirs of a Survivor,* and now, with *Shikasta,* I have followed her into the realms of science fiction where she is making a continuum all her own somewhere between John Milton and L. Ron Hubbard.

Lessing tells us that, originally, she thought that she might make a single volume out of certain themes from the Old Testament (source of so much of our dreaming and bad behavior) but that she is now launched on a series of fables about interplanetary dominations and powers. "I feel as if I have been set free both to be as experimental as I like, and as traditional." I'm not sure what she means by "experimental" and "traditional." At best, Lessing's prose is solid and slow and a bit flat-footed. She is an entirely "traditional" prose writer. I suspect that she did not want to use the word "imaginative," a taboo word nowadays, and so she wrote "experimental."

In any case, like the splendid *Memoirs of a Survivor*, *Shikasta* is the work of a formidable imagination. Lessing can make up things that appear to be real, which is what storytelling is all about. But she has been sufficiently influenced by serious-writing to feel a need to apologize. "It is by now commonplace to say that novelists everywhere are breaking the bonds of the realistic novel because what we all see around us becomes daily wilder, more fantastic, incredible. . . . The old 'realistic' novel is being changed, too, because of influences from that genre loosely described as space fiction." Actually, I have seen no very vivid sign of this influence and I don't suppose that she has either. But it is not unusual for a writer to regard his own new turning as a highway suddenly perceived by all, and soon to be crowded with other pilgrims en route to the City on the Hill.

If this book has any recent precursor, it is Kurt Vonnegut, Jr. Lessing has praised him elsewhere: "Vonnegut is moral in an old-fashioned way . . . he has made nonsense of the little categories, the unnatural divisions into 'real' literature and the rest, because he is comic and sad at once, because his painful seriousness is never solemn. Vonnegut is unique among us; and these same qualities account for the way a few academics still try to patronize him. . . ."

Lessing is even more influenced by the Old Testament. "It is our habit to dismiss the Old Testament altogether because Jehovah, or Jahve, does not think or behave like a social worker." So much for JC, doer of good and eventual scientist. But Lessing's point is well taken. Because the Old Testament's lurid tales of a furious god form a background to Jesus' "good news," to Mohammed's "recitations," to the Jewish ethical sense, those bloody tales still remain an extraordinary mythic power, last demonstrated in full force by Milton.

In a sense, Lessing's *Shikasta* is a return more to the spirit (not, alas, the language) of Milton than to that of Genesis. But Lessing goes Milton one better, or worse. Milton was a dualist. Lucifer blazes as the son of morning; and the Godhead blazes, too. Their agon is terrific. Although

Lessing deals with opposites, she tends to unitarianism. She is filled with the spirit of the Sufis, and if there is one thing that makes me more nervous than a Jungian it is a Sufi. Lessing believes that it is possible "to 'plug in' to an overmind, or Ur-mind, or unconscious, or what you will, and that this accounts for a great many improbabilities and 'coincidences.' " She does indeed plug in; and *Shikasta* is certainly rich with improbabilities and "coincidences." Elsewhere ("In the World, Not of It"), Lessing has expressed her admiration for one Idries Shah, a busy contemporary purveyor of Sufism (from the Arab word *suf,* meaning wool . . . the costume for ascetics).

Idries Shah has been characterized in the pages of *The New York Review of Books* as the author of works that are replete with "constant errors of fact, slovenly and inaccurate translations, even the misspelling of Oriental names and words. In place of scholarship we are asked to accept a muddle of platitudes, irrelevancies, and plain mumbo-jumbo." Lessing very much admires Idries Shah and the woolly ones, and she quotes with approval from Idries Shah's *The Dermis Probe* in which *he* quotes from M. Gauquelin's *The Cosmic Clocks.* "An astonishing parallel to the Sufi insistence on the relatively greater power of subtle communication to affect man, is found in scientific work which shows that all living things, including man, are 'incredibly sensitive to waves of extraordinarily weak energy—when more robust influences are excluded.' " This last quotation within a quotation is the theme of *Shikasta.*

It is Lessing's conceit that a benign and highly advanced galactic civilization, centered on Canopus, is sending out harmonious waves hither and yon, rather like Milton's god before Lucifer got bored. Canopus lives in harmony with another galactic empire named Sirius. Once upon a time warp, the two fought a Great War but now all is serene between the galaxies. I can't come up with the Old Testament parallel on that one. Is Canopus Heaven versus Sirius' Chaos? Anyway, the evil planet Shammat in the galactic empire of Puttiora turns out be our old friend Lucifer or Satan or Lord of the Flies, and the Planet Shikasta (that's us) is a battleground between the harmonious vibes of Canopus and the wicked vibes of Shammat, which are constantly bombarding our planet. In the end, Lucifer is hurled howling into that place where he prefers to reign and all is harmony with God's chilluns. Lessing rather lacks negative capability. Where Milton's Lucifer is a joy to contemplate, Lessing's Shammat is a drag whose planetary agents sound like a cross between Tolkien's monster and Sir Lew Grade.

Lessing's narrative devices are very elaborate. Apparently, the

Canopian harmonious future resembles nothing so much as an English Department that has somehow made an accommodation to share its "facilities" with the Bureau of Indian Affairs. The book's title page is daunting: "Canopus in Argos: Archives" at the top. Then "Re: Colonised Planet 5" (as I type this, I realize that I've been misreading "Re: Colonised" as recolonised): then "Shikasta"; then "Personal, Psychological, Historical Documents Relating to Visit by JOHOR (George Sherban) Emissary (Grade 9) 87th of the Period of the Last Days." At the bottom of the page, one's eye is suddenly delighted by the homely phrase "Alfred A. Knopf New York 1979." There is not much music in Lessing spheres.

Like the Archangel Michael, Johor travels through Shikasta's time. The planet's first cities were so constructed that transmitters on Canopus could send out benign waves of force; as a result, the local population (trained by kindly giants) were happy and frolicsome. "Canopus was able to feed Shikasta with a rich and vigorous air, which kept everyone safe and healthy, and above all, made them love each other. . . . This supply of finer air had a name. It was called SOWF—the substance-of-we-feeling—I had of course spent time and effort in working out an easily memorable syllable." Of course. But the SOWF is cut off. The cities of the plain are blasted. The Degenerative Disease begins and the race suffers from "grandiosities and pomps," short life spans, bad temper. The Degenerative Disease is Lessing's equivalent for that original sin which befell man when Eve bit on the apple.

There is a certain amount of fun to be had in Johor's tour of human history. He is busy as a bee trying to contain the evil influence of Shammat, and Lessing not only brings us up to date but beyond: the Chinese will occupy Europe fairly soon. Lessing is a master of the eschatological style and *Memoirs of a Survivor* is a masterpiece of that genre. But where the earlier book dealt with a very real London in a most credible terminal state, *Shikasta* is never quite real enough. At times the plodding style does make things believable, but then reality slips away . . . too little SOWF, perhaps. Nevertheless, Lessing is plainly enjoying herself and the reader can share in that enjoyment a good deal of the time. But, finally, she lacks the peculiar ability to create alternative worlds. For instance, she invents for the human dead a limbo she calls Zone 6. This shadowy place is a cross between Homer's Hades and the Zoroastrian concept of that place where eternal souls hover about, waiting to be born. Lessing's descriptions of the undead dead are often very fine, but when one compares her invention with Ursula Le Guin's somewhat similar land of the dead in the *Earthsea* trilogy, one is aware that Le Guin's darkness is darker, her coldness colder, her shadows more dense and strange.

Lessing's affinity for the Old Testament combined with the woolliness of latter-day Sufism has got her into something of a philosophical muddle. Without the idea of free will, the human race is of no interest at all; certainly, without the idea of free will there can be no literature. To watch Milton's Lucifer serenely overthrow the controlling intelligence of his writerly creator is an awesome thing. But nothing like this happens in Lessing's work. From the moment of creation, Lessing's Shikastans are programmed by outside forces—sometimes benign, sometimes malign. They themselves are entirely passive. There is no Prometheus; there is not even an Eve. The fact that in the course of a very long book Lessing has not managed to create a character of the slightest interest is the result not so much of any failure in her considerable art as it is a sign that she has surrendered her mind to SOWF, or to the woollies, or to the Jealous God.

Obviously, there is a case to be made for predetermination or predestination or let-us-now-praise B. F. Skinner. Lessing herself might well argue that the seemingly inexorable DNA code is a form of genetic programming that could well be equated with Canopus' intervention and that, in either case, our puny lives are so many interchangeable tropisms, responding to outside stimuli. But I think that the human case is more interesting than that. The fact that no religion has been able to give a satisfactory reason for the existence of evil has certainly kept human beings on their toes during the brief respites that we are allowed between those ages of faith which can always be counted upon to create that we-state which seems so much to intrigue Lessing and her woollies, a condition best described by the most sinister of all Latin tags, *e pluribus unum*.

Ultimately, *Shikasta* is not so much a fable of the human will in opposition to a god who has wronged the fire-seeker as it is a fairy tale about good and bad extraterrestrial forces who take some obscure pleasure in manipulating a passive ant-like human race. Needless to say, Doris Lessing is not the first to incline to this "religion." In fact, she has considerable competition from a living prophet whose powerful mind has envisaged a race of god-like Thetans who once lived among us; they, too, overflowed with SOWF; then they went away. But all is not lost. The living prophet has told us their story. At first he wrote a science fiction novel, and bad people scoffed. But he was not dismayed.

He knew that he could save us; bring back the wisdom of the Thetans; "clear" us of badness. He created a second holy book, *Dianetics.* Today he is the sole proprietor of the Church of Scientology. Doris Lessing would do well to abandon the woolly Idries Shah in favor of Mr. L. Ron Hubbard, who has already blazed that trail where now she trods— treads?—trods.

*The New York Review of Books*
December 20, 1979

# 36

## CHRISTOPHER ISHERWOOD'S KIND

In 1954 I had lunch with Christopher Isherwood at MGM. He told me that he had just written a film for Lana Turner. The subject? Diane de Poitiers. When I laughed, he shook his head. "Lana can do it," he said grimly. Later, as we walked about the lot and I told him that I hoped to get a job as a writer at the studio since I could no longer live on my royalties as a novelist (and would not teach), Christopher gave me as melancholy a look as those bright—even harsh—blue eyes can affect. "Don't," he said with great intensity, posing against the train beneath whose wheels Greta Garbo as Anna Karenina made her last dive, "become a hack like me." But we both knew that this was play-acting. Like his friend Aldous Huxley (like William Faulkner and many others), he had been able to write to order for movies while never ceasing to do his own work in his own way. Those whom Hollywood destroyed were never worth saving. Not only has Isherwood written successfully for the camera, he has been, notoriously, in his true art, *the* camera.

"I am a camera." With those four words at the beginning of the novel *Goodbye to Berlin* (1939), Christopher Isherwood became famous. Because of those four words he has been written of (and sometimes written off) as a naturalistic writer, a recorder of surfaces, a film director *manqué*. Although it is true that, up to a point, Isherwood often appears to be recording perhaps too impartially the lights, the shadows, the lions that come within the area of his vision, he is never without surprises; in the course of what looks to be an undemanding narrative, the author will suddenly produce a Polaroid shot of the reader reading, an alarming effect achieved by the sly use of the second person pronoun. You never know quite where *you* stand in relation to an Isherwood work.

During the half century that Christopher Isherwood has been more or less at the center of Anglo-American literature, he has been much scrutinized by friends, acquaintances, purveyors of book-chat. As memoirs of the Twenties, Thirties, Forties now accumulate, Isherwood keeps cropping up as a principal figure, and if he does not always seem in character, it is because he is not an easy character to fix upon the page. Also, he has so beautifully invented himself in the Berlin stories, *Lions and Shadows, Down There on a Visit,* and now *Christopher and His Kind,* that anyone who wants to snap yet again this lion's shadow has his work cut out for him. After all, nothing is harder to reflect than a mirror.

To date the best developed portrait of Isherwood occurs in Stephen Spender's autobiography *World Within World* (1951). Like Isherwood, Spender was a part of that upper-middle-class generation which came of age just after World War I. For the lucky few able to go to the right schools and universities, postwar England was still a small and self-contained society where everyone knew everyone else. In fact, English society was simply an extension of school. But something disagreeable had happened at school just before the Isherwoods and Spenders came on stage. World War I had killed off the better part of a generation of graduates, and among the graduated dead was Isherwood's father. There was a long shadow over the young . . . of dead fathers, brothers; also of dead or dying attitudes. Rebellion was in the air. New things were promised.

In every generation there are certain figures who are who they are at an early age: stars *in ovo.* People want to know them; imitate them; destroy them. Isherwood was such a creature and Stephen Spender fell under his spell even before they met.

At nineteen Spender was an undergraduate at Oxford; another undergraduate was the twenty-one-year-old W. H. Auden. Isherwood himself (three years Auden's senior) was already out in the world; he had got himself sent down from Cambridge by sending up a written examination. He had deliberately broken out of the safe, cozy university world, and the brilliant but cautious Auden revered him. Spender writes how, "according to Auden, [Isherwood] held no opinions whatever about anything. He was wholly and simply interested in people. He did not like or dislike them, judge them favorably or unfavorably. He simply regarded them as material for his Work. At the same time, he was the Critic in whom Auden had absolute trust. If Isherwood disliked a poem, Auden destroyed it without demur."

Auden was not above torturing the young Spender: "Auden withheld the privilege of meeting Isherwood from me." Writing twenty years later, Spender cannot resist adding, "Isherwood was not famous at this time. He had published one novel, *All the Conspirators,* for which he had received an advance of £30 from his publishers, and which had been not very favorably reviewed." But Isherwood was already a legend, as Spender concedes, and worldly success has nothing to do with legends. Eventually Auden brought them together. Spender was not disappointed:

He simplified all the problems which entangled me, merely by describing his own life and his own attitudes towards these things. . . . Isherwood had a peculiarity of being attractively disgusted and amiably bitter. . . . But there was a positive as well as negative side to his beliefs. He spoke of being Cured and Saved with as much intensity as any Salvationist.

In Isherwood's earliest memoir, *Lions and Shadows* (1938), we are given Isherwood's first view of Spender, a sort of reverse-angle shot (and known to Spender when he wrote *World Within World*): "[Spender] burst in upon us, blushing, sniggering loudly, contriving to trip over the edge of the carpet—an immensely tall, shambling boy of nineteen, with a great scarlet poppy-face, wild frizzy hair, and eyes the violent color of bluebells." The camera turns, watching it all. "In an instant, without introductions, we were all laughing and talking at the top of our voices. . . . He inhabited a world of self-created and absorbing drama, into which each new acquaintance was immediately conscripted to play a part. [Spender] illuminated you" (the second person now starts to take hold: the film's *voice-over* has begun its aural seduction) "like an expressionist producer, with the crudest and most eccentric of spot-lights: you were transfigured, became grandiose, sinister, brilliantly ridiculous or impossibly beautiful, in accordance with his arbitrary, prearranged conception of your role." *You, spot-light, producer. . . .*

In *The Whispering Gallery,* the publisher and critic John Lehmann describes his first meeting with Spender in 1930 and how he "talked a great deal about Auden, who shared (and indeed had inspired) so many of his views, and also about a certain young novelist Christopher Isherwood, who, he told me, had settled in Berlin in stark poverty and was an even greater rebel against the England we lived in than he was. . . ." When Lehmann went to work for Leonard and Virginia Woolf at the Hogarth Press, he got them to publish Isherwood's second novel, *The Memorial.*

Lehmann noted that the generation's Novelist was

much shorter than myself, he nevertheless had a power of dominating which small people of outstanding intelligence or imaginative equipment often possess. One of my favorite private fancies has always been that the most ruthless war that underlies our civilized existence . . . is the war between the tall and the short.

Even so, "It was impossible not to be drawn to him. . . . And yet for some months after our first meeting . . . our relations remained rather formal: perhaps it was the sense of alarm that seemed to hang in the air when his smile was switched off, a suspicion he seemed to radiate that one might after all be in league with the 'enemy,' a phrase which covered everything he had, with a pure hatred, cut himself off from in English life. . . ."

In 1931 a cold transatlantic eye was turned upon both Isherwood and Spender. The twenty-year-old Paul Bowles presented himself to Isherwood in Berlin. "When I came to Isherwood," Bowles records in *Without Stopping,* "he said he would take me himself to Spender." Bowles did not approve of Spender's looking and acting the part of a poet: "Whether Spender wrote poetry or not seemed relatively unimportant; that at all costs the fact should not be evident was what should have mattered to him." Bowles acknowledges that this primness reflected the attitudes of his Puritan family and background. "I soon found that Isherwood with Spender was a very different person from Isherwood by himself." But then the camera and its director are bound to alter according to light, weather, cast. "Together they were overwhelmingly British, two members of a secret society constantly making references to esoteric data not available to outsiders." This strikes me as an accurate and poignant description of the difference between American and English writers. The English tend to play off (and with) one another; while the Americans are, if not Waldenized solitaries, Darwinized predators constantly preying upon one another. I think it significant that when Paul

Bowles came to write *his* autobiography, he chose a prose style not unlike that of Julius Caesar's report on how he laid waste Gaul.

"At all our meetings I felt that I was being treated with good-humored condescension. They accepted Aaron [Copland], but they did not accept me because they considered me too young and uninteresting; I never learnt the reason, if there was one, for this exclusion by common consent." Bowles describes a British girl he met with Isherwood. She was called Jean Ross "(When Christopher wrote about her later, he called her Sally Bowles)."

In *Christopher and His Kind*, Isherwood sets up the by now obligatory reverse-angle shot: "(Sally Bowles's second name was chosen for her by Christopher because he liked the sound of it and also the looks of its owner, a twenty-year-old American whom he met in Berlin in 1931. The American thought Christopher treated him with 'good-humored condescension'; Christopher thought the American aloof. . . .)" Apparently, there was a near-miss in Berlin.

*Christopher and His Kind* describes Isherwood's life from 1929 to 1939. The narrative (based on diaries and written, generally, in the third person) takes up where *Lions and Shadows* ends with "twenty-four-year-old Christopher's departure from England on March 14, 1929, to visit Berlin for the first time in his life." The book ends a decade later when Isherwood emigrates to the United States. Of *Lions and Shadows*, Isherwood says that it describes his "life between the ages of seventeen and twenty-four. It is not truly autobiographical, however. The author conceals important facts about himself . . . and gives his characters fictitious names." But "The book I am now going to write will be as frank and factual as I can make it, especially as far as I myself am concerned." He means to be sexually candid; and he is. He is also that rarest of creatures, the objective narcissist; he sees himself altogether plain and does not hesitate to record for us the lines that the face in the mirror has accumulated, the odd shadow that flaws character.

I have just read the two memoirs in sequence and it is odd how little Isherwood has changed in a half century. The style is much the same throughout. The shift from first to third person does not much alter the way he has of looking at things and it is, of course, the *precise* way in which Isherwood perceives the concrete world that makes all the difference. He is particularly good at noting a physical appearance that suggests, through his selection of nouns, verbs, a psychic description. This is from *Lions and Shadows*:

[Chalmers] had grown a small moustache and looked exactly my idea of a young Montmartre poet, more French than the French. Now he caught sight of us, and greeted me with a slight wave of the hand, so very typical of him, tentative, diffident, semi-ironical, like a parody of itself. Chalmers expressed himself habitually in fragments of gestures, abortive movements, half-spoken sentences. . . .

Then the same sharp eye is turned upon the narrator:

Descending the staircase to the dining-room, I was Christopher Isherwood no longer, but a satanically proud, icy, impenetrable demon; an all-knowing, all-pardoning savior of mankind; a martyr-evangelist of the tea-table, from which the most atrocious drawing-room tortures could wring no more than a polite proffer of the buttered scones.

This particular *auteur du cinéma* seldom shoots a scene without placing somewhere on the set a mirror that will record the *auteur* in the act of filming.

At the time of the publication of *Lions and Shadows* in 1938, Isherwood was thirty-four years old. He had published three novels: *All the Conspirators, The Memorial, Mr. Norris Changes Trains.* With Auden he had written the plays *The Dog Beneath the Skin* and *The Ascent of F6.* Finally, most important of all, the finest of his creations had made a first appearance in *Mr. Norris Changes Trains;* with no great fuss or apparent strain, Isherwood had invented Isherwood. The Isherwood of the Berlin stories is a somewhat anodyne and enigmatic narrator. He is looking carefully at life. He does not commit himself to much of anything. Yet what might have been a limitation in a narrator, the author, rather mysteriously, made a virtue of.

Spender describes Isherwood in Berlin as occasionally "depressive, silent or petulant. Sometimes he would sit in a room with Sally Bowles or Mr. Norris without saying a word, as though refusing to bring his characters to life." But they were very much *his* characters. He lived "surrounded by the models for his creations, like one of those portraits of a writer by a bad painter, in which the writer is depicted meditating in his chair whilst the characters of his novels radiate round him under a glowing cloud of dirty varnish. . . ." Isherwood had rejected not only the familiar, cozy world of Cambridge and London's literary life but also the world of self-conscious aestheticism. He chose to live as a proletarian in Berlin where, Spender tells us, "He was comparatively poor and almost unrecognized. His novel, *All the Conspirators,* had been remaindered," Spender notes yet again. Nevertheless, Spender realized that Isherwood

was more than a young rebel passing through a phase of revolt against parents, conventional morality, and orthodox religion. . . . He was on the side of the forces which make a work of art, even more than he was interested in art itself. . . . His hatred of institutions of learning and even of the reputation attached to some past work of art, was really hatred of the fact that they came between people and their direct unprejudiced approach to one another.

In *Lions and Shadows* Isherwood writes of school, of friendships, of wanting to be . . . well, Isherwood, a character not yet entirely formed. Auden appears fairly late in the book though early in Isherwood's life: they were together at preparatory school. Younger than Isherwood, Auden wanted "to become a mining engineer. . . . I remember him chiefly for his naughtiness, his insolence, his smirking tantalizing air of knowing disreputable and exciting secrets." Auden was on to sex and the others were not.

Auden and Isherwood did not meet again for seven years. "Just before Christmas, 1925, a mutual acquaintance brought him in to tea. I found him very little changed." Auden "told me that he wrote poetry nowadays: he was deliberately a little over-casual in making this announcement. I was very much surprised, even rather disconcerted." But then, inevitably, the Poet and the Novelist of the age formed an alliance. The Poet had further surprises for the Novelist. Auden's "own attitude to sex, in its simplicity and utter lack of inhibition, fairly took my breath away. He was no Don Juan: he didn't run around hunting for his pleasures. But he took what came to him with a matter-of-factness and an appetite as hearty as that which he showed when sitting down to dinner."

Art and sex: the two themes intertwine in Isherwood's memoirs but in the first volume we do not know what the sex was all about: the reticences of the Thirties forbade candor. Now in *Christopher and His Kind,* Isherwood has filled in the blanks; he is explicit about both sex and love. Not only did the Poet and the Novelist of that era lust for boys, there is some evidence that each might have echoed Marlowe's mighty line: I have found that those who do not like tobacco and boys are fools.

"The book I am now going to write will be as frank and factual as

I can make it, especially as far as I myself am concerned." Then the
writer shifts to the third person: "At school, Christopher had fallen in
love with many boys and been yearningly romantic about them. At
college he had at last managed to get into bed with one. This was due
entirely to the initiative of his partner, who, when Christopher became
scared and started to raise objections, locked the door and sat down
firmly on Christopher's lap." For an American twenty-two years
younger than Christopher, the late development of the English of that
epoch is astonishing. In Washington, D.C., puberty arrived at ten,
eleven, twelve, and sex was riotous and inventive between consenting
paeds. Yet Tennessee Williams (fourteen years my senior) reports in his
*Memoirs* that neither homo- nor heterosexuality began for him until his
late twenties. On the other hand, he did not go to a monosexual school
as I did, as Isherwood and his kind did.

Isherwood tells us that "other experiences followed, all of them enjoyable but none entirely satisfying. This was because Christopher was
suffering from an inhibition, then not unusual among upper-class homosexuals; he couldn't relax sexually with a member of his own class or
nation. He needed a working-class foreigner." Germany was the answer.
"To Christopher, Berlin meant Boys." Auden promptly introduced him
to the Cosy Corner, a hangout for proletarian youths, and Christopher
took up with a blond named Bubi, "the first presentable candidate who
appeared to claim the leading role in Christopher's love myth."

John Lehmann's recently published "novel" *In the Purely Pagan
Sense* overlaps with Isherwood's memoirs not only in time and place but
in a similar sexual preoccupation. "I was obsessed," writes Lehmann's
narrator, "by the desire to make love with boys of an entirely different
class and background. . . ." This desire for differentness is not unusual:
misalliance has almost always been the name of the game hetero or
homo or bi. But I suspect that the upper-middle-class man's desire for
youths of the lower class derives, mainly, from fear of his own class.
Between strongly willed males of the Isherwood-Auden sort, a sexual
commitment could lead to a psychic defeat for one of the partners.

The recently published memoirs of Isherwood's contemporary Peter
Quennell *(The Marble Foot)* describe how an upper-class *heterosexual*
English writer was constantly betrayed by women of his own class.
Apparently, Quennell is much too tender, too romantic, too . . . well,
feminine to avoid victimization by the ladies. A beautiful irony never to
be understood by United States-men given to the joys of the sexual
majority is that a homosexualist like Isherwood cannot with any ease

enjoy a satisfactory sexual relationship with a woman because he himself is so entirely masculine that the woman presents no challenge, no masculine hardness, no exciting *agon.* It is the heterosexual Don Juan (intellectual division) who is the fragile, easily wounded figure, given to tears. Isherwood is a good deal less "feminine" (in the pre-women's lib sense of the word) than Peter Quennell, say, or Cyril Connolly or our own paralyzingly butch Ernest Hemingway.

Isherwood describes his experiments with heterosexuality: "She was five or six years older than [Christopher], easygoing, stylish, humorous. . . . He was surprised and amused to find how easily he could relate his usual holds and movements to his unusual partner. He felt curiosity and the fun of playing a new game. He also felt a lust which was largely narcissistic. . . ." Then: "He asked himself: Do I now want to go to bed with more women and girls? Of course not, as long as I can have boys. Why do I prefer boys? Because of their shape and their voices and their smell and the way they move. And boys can be romantic. I can put them into my myth and fall in love with them. Girls can be absolutely beautiful but never romantic. In fact, their utter lack of romance is what I find most likeable about them." There is a clear-eyed healthiness (if not great accuracy) about all this.

Then Isherwood moves from the personal to the general and notes the lunatic pressure that society exerts on everyone to be heterosexual, to deny at all costs a contrary nature. Since heterosexual relations proved to be easy for Isherwood, he could have joined the majority. But he was stopped by Isherwood the rebel, the Protestant saint who declared with the fury of a Martin Luther: "even if my nature were like theirs, I should still have to fight them, in one way or another. If boys didn't exist, I should have to invent them." Isherwood's war on what he has called, so aptly, "the heterosexual dictatorship" has been unremitting and admirable.

In Berlin Isherwood settled down with a working-class boy named Heinz and most of *Christopher and His Kind* has to do with their life together during the time when Hitler came to power and the free and easy Berlin that had attracted Isherwood turned ugly. With Heinz (whose papers were not in order), Isherwood moved restlessly about Europe: Copenhagen, Amsterdam, the Canary Islands, Brussels. In the end Heinz was trapped in Germany, and forced to serve in World War II. Miraculously, he survived. After the war, Isherwood met Heinz and his wife—as pleasant an end as one can imagine to any idyll of that neo-Wagnerian age.

Meanwhile, Isherwood the writer was developing. It is during this period that the Berlin stories were written; also, *Lions and Shadows.* Also, the collaboration with Auden on the last of the verse plays. Finally, there is the inevitable fall into the movies . . . something that was bound to happen. In *Lions and Shadows* Isherwood describes how "I had always been fascinated by films. . . . I was a born film fan. . . . The reason for this had, I think, very little to do with 'Art' at all; I was, and still am, endlessly interested in the outward appearance of people—their facial expressions, their gestures, their walk, their nervous tricks. . . . The cinema puts people under a microscope: you can stare at them, you can examine them as though they were insects."

Isherwood was invited to write a screenplay for the director "Berthold Viertel [who] appears as Friedrich Bergmann in the novelette called *Prater Violet,* which was published twelve years later." Isherwood and the colorful Viertel hit it off and together worked on a film called *Little Friend.* From that time on the best prose writer in English has supported himself by writing movies. In fact, the first Isherwood work that I encountered was not a novel but a film that he wrote called *Rage in Heaven*: at sixteen I thought it splendid. "The moon!" intoned the nutty Robert Montgomery. "It's staring at me, like a great Eye." Ingrid Bergman shuddered. So did I.

It is hard now for the young who are interested in literature (a tiny minority compared to the young who are interested in that flattest and easiest and laziest of art forms: the movies) to realize that Isherwood was once considered "a hope of English fiction" by Cyril Connolly, and a master by those of us who grew up in World War II. I think the relative neglect of Isherwood's work is, partly, the result of his expatriation. With Auden, he emigrated to the United States just before the war began, and there was a good deal of bitter feeling at the time (they were clumsily parodied by the unspeakable Evelyn Waugh in *Put Out More Flags*). Ultimately, Auden's reputation was hardly affected. But then poets are licensed to be mad, bad, and dangerous to read, while prose writers are expected to be, if not responsible, predictable.

In America Isherwood was drawn first to the Quakers; then to Vedanta. Lately, he has become a militant spokesman of Gay Liberation. If his defense of Christopher's kind is sometimes shrill . . . well, there is a good deal to be shrill about in a society so deeply and so mindlessly homophobic. In any case, none of Isherwood's moral preoccupations is apt to endear him to a literary establishment that is, variously, academic, Jewish/Christian, middle-class, and heterosexual. Yet he has written some of his best books in the United States, including the memoir at hand and the novels *A Single Man* and *A Meeting by the River.* Best of all, he still views the world aslant despite long residence in Santa Monica, a somber place where even fag households resemble those hetero couples photographed in *Better Homes and Gardens,* serving up intricate brunches 'neath the hazel Pacific sky.

What strikes me as most remarkable in Isherwood's career has not been so much the unremitting will to be his own man as the constant clarity of a prose style that shows no sign of slackness even though the author is, astonishingly, in his seventies. There is a good deal to be said about the way that Isherwood writes, particularly at a time when prose is worse than ever in the United States, and showing signs of etiolation in England. There is no excess in an Isherwood sentence. The verbs are strong. Nouns precise. Adjectives few. The third person startles and seduces, while the first person is a good guide and never coy.

Is the Isherwood manner perhaps *too* easy? Cyril Connolly feared that it might be when he wrote in *Enemies of Promise* (1938): "[Isherwood] is persuasive because he is so insinuatingly bland and anonymous, nothing rouses him, nothing shocks him. While secretly despising us he could not at the same time be more tolerant. . . . Now for this a price has to be paid; Herr Issyvoo" (Connolly is contemplating Isherwood's Berlin stories) "is not a dumb ox, for he is not condemned to the solidarity with his characters and with their background to which Hemingway is bound by his conception of art, but he is much less subtle, intelligent and articulate than he might be." Isherwood answered Connolly: "In conversation, Isherwood . . . expressed his belief in construction as the way out of the difficulty. The writer must conform to the language which is understood by the greatest number of people, to the vernacular, but his talent as a novelist will appear in the exactness of his observation, the justice of his situations and in the construction of his book."

Isherwood has maintained this aesthetic throughout a long career. When he turned his back on what Connolly termed Mandarin writing, he showed considerable courage. But the later Isherwood is even better than the early cameraman because he is no longer the anonymous, neutral narrator. He can be shocked; he can be angry.

In *Christopher and His Kind,* Isherwood wonders what attitude to take toward the coming war with Germany. "Suppose, Christopher now said to himself, I have a Nazi Army at my mercy. I can blow it up by pressing a button. The men in the army are notorious for torturing and murdering civilians—all except one of them, Heinz. Will I press the button? No—wait: Suppose I know that Heinz himself, out of cowardice or moral infection, has become as bad as they are and takes part in all their crimes? Will I press that button, even so? Christopher's answer, given without the slightest hesitation, was: Of course not." That is the voice of humanism in a bad time, and one can only hope that thanks to Christopher's life and work, his true kind will increase even as they refuse, so wisely, to multiply.

*The New York Review of Books*
December 9, 1976

# 37

# ON PRETTINESS

In the fifteenth century the adjective "pretty" joined the English language (derived from the Old Teutonic noun *pratti* or *pratta,* meaning trick or wile). At first everyone thought the world of pretty. To be a pretty fellow was to be clever, apt, skillful; a pretty soldier was gallant and brave; a pretty thing was ingenious and artful. It was not until the sixteenth century that something started to go wrong with the idea of prettiness. Although women and children could still take pleasure in being called pretty, a pretty man had degenerated into a fop with a tendency to slyness. Pretty objects continued to be admired until 1875 when the phrase "pretty-pretty" was coined. That did it. For the truly clever, apt, and skillful, the adjective pretty could only be used in the pejorative sense, as I discovered thirty years ago while being shown around King's College by E. M. Forster. As we approached the celebrated chapel (magnificent, superb, a bit much), I said, "Pretty." Forster thought I meant the chapel when, actually, I was referring to a youthful couple in the damp middle distance. A ruthless moralist, Forster publicized my use of the dread word. Told in Fitzrovia and published in the streets of Dacca, the daughters of the Philistines rejoiced; the daughters of the uncircumcised triumphed. For a time, my mighty shield was vilely cast away.

In the last thirty years the adjective pretty has been pretty much abandoned, while the notion of beauty has become so complex that only the dullest of the daughters of the uncircumcised dares use it. Santayana was the last aesthetician to describe beauty without self-consciousness; and that was in 1896. As a result, we now live in a relativist's world where one man's beauty is another man's beast. This means that physical ugliness tends to be highly prized on the ground that it would be not only cruel, but provocative for, let us say, a popular performer to look better than the plainest member of the audience. This is democracy at its most endearing; and only a beauty or a Beaton would have it otherwise.

Sir Cecil Beaton's latest volume of diaries has now been published in the seventy-fourth year of a life devoted to the idea of beauty in people, clothes, décor, landscape, and manners. To the extent that Sir Cecil falls short of beauty in his life and work, he is merely pretty. But that is not such a bad thing. Quite the contrary. Sir Cecil . . . no, I think we had better call him Beaton, in honor of his own creation as opposed to the Queen's. Beaton is the oldest if not the last of a long line of minor artists who have given a good deal of pleasure to a good many people. He is a celebrated photographer. Unfortunately, I cannot judge his pictures because all photographs tend to look alike to me in their busy flatness. For half a century photography has been the "art form" of the untalented. Obviously some pictures are more satisfactory than others, but where is credit due? To the designer of the camera? to the finger on the button? to the law of averages? I was pleased to note in Beaton's pages that Picasso thought the same.

It is as a designer for the theatre that Beaton is at his best. But then clothes and sets are in the round, not flat upon the page. Beaton is absolutely stage-struck, and so wonderfully striking in his stage effects. There is no sense of strain in his theatre work except, perhaps, when he acts. Years ago I saw him in a play by (I think) Wilde. Like an elegant lizard just fed twenty milligrams of Valium, Beaton moved slowly about the stage. The tongue flicked; the lips moved; no word was audible.

Now we have Beaton's written words; and they are most vivid: contents of diaries kept from 1963 to 1974. The mood is often grim. He does not like getting old. He has also not learned that, after fifty, you must never look into a mirror whose little tricks you don't already know in advance. The same goes for eyes. At the Rothschild place in Mouton, he takes a good look at himself in a strange mirror. He is rewarded for his recklessness:

I was really an alarming sight—wild white hair on end, most of the pate quite bald: chins sagging with a scraggly tissued neck: pale weak eyes without their former warmth. But this could not be me!

More somber details are noted. Finally, "How could I make the effort to dress myself up in picturesque clothes and try to be attractive to a group of highly critical people?" I am sure that he managed.

*The Parting Years* is a haphazard collection of pages taken at what seems to be random from a number of diaries. No attempt has been made to link one thing to another. He arrives in New York to design a production of *La Traviata*. Alfred Lunt is the director. It is all very exciting. But, for the reader, the curtain never goes up. How did the production go? Who sang? There are numerous odd lacunae:

Oliver Lyttleton, whose desire to amuse has increased with the years to the extent that he is a real bore, made one funny joke. The evening was a great success.

*But what was the joke?* On second thoughts, perhaps that is Beaton's strategy. In *Orlando,* Virginia Woolf never allowed us to hear the brilliant dialogue of Alexander Pope.

Beaton is a good travel-writer. He has a sharp eye for those horrors of travel that delight the sedentary reader far more than set descriptions of beautiful or even pretty places. South America in general and Poland in particular do not get high marks. The first is too steep; the second too flat. But Beaton is quite as strict with things English. The cathedrals get a thorough going-over. "Exeter Cathedral, more squat than Salisbury, but original and successful, with a frieze of carvings on the façade." Next term if Exeter C. joins *wholeheartedly* in house-games there is no reason why that squatness can't be trimmed down. On the other hand, poor "Wells Cathedral did not look its best. It has a certain character but is not really impressive as a creative expression of devotion." Wells C. might do better at a different school.

Beaton is too much the stoic to strike too often the valetudinarian note. But when he does, the effect is chilling. He looks at himself with the same cold eye that he turns upon slovenly Wells Cathedral.

I don't really feel that I am ever going to come into my own, to justify myself and my existence by some last great gesture. I am likewise certain that nothing I have done is likely to live long after me.

This is no doubt true. Yet one cannot help but admire a man in his seventies who still makes a living by his wits in the world of theatre and fashion where Americans with hearts of stone and egos of brass dominate ("I put up with Americans willingly only when I am on business bent").

Beaton never ceases to be interested in seeing new places, meeting new talent. He checks out The Rolling Stones at the beginning of their fame. He takes up the town's new artist, David Hockney. Meanwhile, he continues to make the rounds of the old from Picasso to Coward. He almost always has something shrewd to say—except of famous hostesses. They get elaborate bread-and-butter-letter eulogies best left unpublished. Beaton is most generous with the young. But then, it is always easier to prefer the young to one's contemporaries. Witness:

*April 11, 1966:* So Evelyn Waugh is in his coffin. Died of snobbery. Did not wish to be considered a man of letters; it did not satisfy him to be thought a master of letters: it did not satisfy him to be thought a master of English prose. He wanted to be a duke . . .

Beaton and Waugh had known each other at school. Each was a social climber; and each was on to the other. Yet Beaton appears to have got a good deal of pleasure out of his nimble run up the ladder, as opposed to Waugh, who huffed and puffed and "would suddenly seem to be possessed by a devil and do thoroughly fiendish things." It is a pity that there is no present-day writer able to do for this pretty couple what Max Beerbohm did for a similar pair in "Hilary Maltby and Stephen Braxton."

As might be expected, the book is full of obituaries. Outliving contemporaries is always a joy, up to a point. Beaton usually gets the point. Of the Duke of Windsor, he "had never shown any affection for or interest in me." Beaton also notes that the Duke "was inclined to be silly." That is putting it mildly. The Duke's stupidity was of a perfection seldom encountered outside institutions. Of James Pope-Hennessy, he "had 'quality,' was intelligent, and intellectual and serious and yet good company." Beaton is a bit wary of intellectuals. He is better at describing figures like Chanel. He is also good on performers, noting the odd but illuminating detail. Alan Bates

has invented an original sense of humor. It takes a while to realize what he is up to. . . . He has grown his hair very shaggily long. This is obviously to compensate for the width of the neck which has now become almost inhumanly large.

Much of *The Parting Years* will be mysterious to those not intimately acquainted with the theatre and High Bohemia. Even those who have some knowledge of the terrain will get lost from time to time. First names appear without last names. And last names without first names. It is often hard to figure out just who is who. There is one most intriguing encounter, set in New York. I quote the scene in its entirety. "Truman came back with me to the hotel. We talked over whiskies and sodas until I realized that by English time it was 7.30 in the morning." That's all. What, one wonders, did Beaton and the former president have to say to one another? News of the Queen? Of course. But that wouldn't go on until 7:30 A.M. Lady Juliet Duff's failing health? Yes. But one illness is much like another. Music? That must be it. The thirty-third president loved to play the piano. They talked of Horowitz. Of young Van Cliburn who played at Potsdam for Truman and ("Uncle Joe") Stalin. But then, surely, Truman must have mentioned President Johnson. *What did he say?* For once, Beaton is too discreet, unlike his earlier diaries.

I was in Switzerland when Beaton's revelations about his "affair" with Greta Garbo were published in a German magazine. The only comment that I heard her make was glum: "And people think that I am pair-annoyed." But it is the nature of the dandy to flaunt brilliant plumes. In this, Beaton resembles the kingfisher, a bird that flies

so quickly that by the time one says "Look!" they have gone. This most brilliant metallic bird is said to have such an unpleasant smell for other birds that it is solitary and safe.

The Greek word for kingfisher is "halcyon"—born of the sea. For two weeks at the winter solstice the kingfisher's nest is supposed to float on a tranquil sea until the eggs are hatched. Twice Beaton uses the word "halcyon" to describe days in summer. But halcyon can refer only to calm and peaceful winter days, of the sort that this bright kingfisher deserves for the pleasure that he has given to all those who for so many years have watched ("Look!") his swift, pretty flight.

*New Statesman*
March 17, 1978

# 38

WHY I AM
EIGHT YEARS YOUNGER
THAN ANTHONY BURGESS

I saw them coming, an army of two with banners. He was tall, pale, eyes narrowed from cigarette smoke of his own making (an eighty-a-day man for years); she was small, round faced, somewhat bloated. In the gracious plywood-paneled room, the hard stuff was flowing, and the flower of British bookchat and publishing was on hand to drink it all up in honor, not quite the noun, of my return, after a decade's absence, to Literature, with a long reflection on the origins of Christianity, novelly disguised as a novel. The year, 1964.

She said in a loud clear voice, "You," and then I ceased to understand her, "chung cheers boog sightee Joyce yearsen roscoe conkling." I am certain that I heard the name of the nineteenth-century New York senator, and I turned to the man—the senator's biographer?—and saw, like infected buttonholes, eyes I dare not meet in dreams. "Tchess." He took up the refrain. "Boog Joyce venially blind, too, bolder." I had been drinking, but not that much, while the tall man appeared sober. Obviously, I was having my chronic problem with English voices: the low rapid mumble, the urgent wheeze, the imploding diphthong, vowels wrongly stressed, and consonants long since gone west with the thirteen colonies.

We were separated. I was told that I had been talking to Anthony

Burgess and his wife, Lynne. Burgess had written some comic novels about life east of Maugham—or Suez; now there was a new book called *A Clockwork Orange.* I knew nothing of him except for one splendid anecdote. Under another name, he had reviewed one of his own books in a British paper. The Brits were horrified. I was delighted: Whitman had done the same. Besides, I was stern, shouldn't there be at least one review in all of England written by someone who had actually read the book?

Again the army approached, banners raised high. We worked out a common language. Lynne was pissed off that my novel *Julian* was a Book Society choice. She was even more annoyed when I wanted to know what the Book Society was. I had a vision of aged flappers reciting Dorothy Richardson over sugary tea. The society was like an American book club, she growled. I apologized. This was not enough. Truth crackled in the air. A novel by Burgess had finally been chosen, in 1961; yet *he was eight years my senior.* I was too young to be so honored. I mounted my high horse, tethered conveniently near. "I have written more books than Mr. Burgess," I said, settling myself into the saddle. "And over a greater length of time." Swift, suspicious adding and subtracting was done as we ate small but heavy sausages, diapered in a fried bread and speared with lethal plastic toothpicks. True, eighteen years had passed since my first book was published (at twenty) and a mere seven years since his first (at thirty-seven) but he was certain that he was well ahead in units of production. I was not. But before I could begin the long count, he said, "Anyway, I'm actually a composer." This was superb, and I ceded the high ground to him. Lynne did not. She rounded on him: You are *not* a composer. Pussy-whipped, he winced and muttered, "roscoe g. conkling." As I rode off into the night, no boyish treble sounded, "Shane!"

Four years later Lynne was dead of the drink (cirrhosis of the liver). In due course, Burgess married an Italian, lived in Rome, and from time to time our paths crossed, cross. Now, twenty-three years after our first meeting, he is suddenly, astonishingly, seventy years old (I remain, throughout eternity, eight years his junior), and the author of twenty-eight novels and dozens of odd volumes on this and that as well as a part-time laborer in television and films and the theater, where he recently distinguished himself with an adaptation of *Cyrano* that changed everyone's view of that familiar but not-so-high war horse.

· · ·

Burgess has now published *Little Wilson and Big God,* "Being the First Part of the Autobiography," which, long as it is, takes him only to the age of forty-two in 1959 when he was told that he had an inoperable brain tumor, and a year to live. In order to provide for Lynne, he started turning out books at a prodigious rate, and now, twenty years after her death, he still, undead, goes on. Incomparable British medicine ("In point of fact, Dr. Butterfingers, that's *my* scalpel you're standing on") is responsible for the existence of easily the most interesting English writer of the last half century. Like Meredith, Burgess does the best things best; he also does the worst things pretty well, too. There is no other writer like him, a cause of some alarm to others—him, too. Now, in the sad—the vain, I fear—hope that once we've known the trouble he's seen we will forgive him his unfashionable originality and prodigiousness, he makes confession not to merciful God but to merciless us.

The subject of the first part of the autobiography bears, I should guess, very little resemblance to the man who wrote it, who, in turn, bears no resemblance at all to the John Wilson that he was born and continued to be until his relatively late blossoming as a novelist. It is not that he bears false witness; it is, simply, the problem of recalling past time as it occurs to someone in a present where "I have trouble with memory, especially of names." Also, this testament is not extravagantly and carefully shaped like one of his novels; rather, it is doggedly improvised (from diaries? There is a single reference to a diary).

Burgess tells us that in 1985, he was in New York's Plaza Hotel, waiting for a car to take him to the airport. Suddenly, like Gibbon on the steps of Santa Maria d'Aracoeli, he decided to tell this story. But when he started to write, I don't think that he had a clue where he was going or how he was going to get there. Fortunately, he has not the gift of boredom. He can make just about anything interesting except on those occasions when he seems to be writing an encoded message to N. Chomsky, in celebration not so much of linguistics as his own glossolalia, so triumphantly realized in his screenplay *Quest for Fire.*

But the narrative itself is in order. Born John Wilson, February 25, 1917, in Manchester, England; father arrives home from the First World War to find wife and daughter dead of the influenza epidemic; in the same room as the corpses, young Wilson lies, giggling, in his crib. I am not sure if every detail is meant to stand up in court, but certainly Burgess, as artist always on oath (as opposed to defendant in the dock), is keeping close to the essential facts of the case. The father is musical; plays piano in silent movie houses; marries a second time to a woman of some means who becomes a tobacconist. Young Wilson is solidly lower-middle-class and might have made it up to mid-middle-class were it not for the fact that Celtic blood flows in his veins and so, as a Roman Catholic, he was literally set apart from the Protestant majority and was sent to church schools where the good brothers, as is their wont, managed to detach him from his faith. When Burgess starts to question Holy Church, a priest remarks that this is plainly a case of Little Wilson and Big God; hence the book's title, the author's problem.

There is a great deal of carefully described sex. Although Burgess had had sex with girls at an early age, and once observed another boy masturbating, he himself did not know how to masturbate until late adolescence; even more traumatic and poignant, he was equally ignorant of lending libraries. For me, Burgess demonstrates, yet again, how uninteresting the sexual lives of others are when told by them. At one point, he remarks that most literature is about sex. If true, then, perhaps, that is why it is necessary for us to have literature. Once the imagination has, kinetically, translated the act from bed to page excitement begins. But nothing happens when a writer, or anyone, tells us what he himself has actually done in bed or on the floor or in the bushes, where Burgess was caught in the army. Nevertheless, from Frank Harris to Henry Miller to Tennessee Williams to Burgess, there is a weird desire to tell us all, and the rest of us (unless we lust for aged auctorial flesh) start to skip, looking for gossip, jokes, wisdom, or just a good sentence.

Of course, Burgess was brought up, as was I, before the Second World War. In those days, in most circles (not mine, happily) sex and guilt were one and the same, and a new religion was even based on the idea of universal sexual repression (the universe, as symbolized by a corner of bourgeois Vienna) which could only be raised through confession. It is not until mid-career that Burgess suspects that there may be other sources of joy if little guilt, like the perfect bowel movement, which his eponymous hero-poet, the costive Enderby, pursues like a mad surfer waiting upon the perfect wave.

In youth, Burgess must have found bewildering the variety of his talents. He was, first, a musician entirely bewitched by that arithmetical muse. He could remember a thousand popular songs. Wistfully, he suggests that even to this day he could earn his living as a cocktail-bar pianist. But he was more ambitious than that. He set poems, wrote symphonies, attempted operas. He still does, he tells us, somewhat defensively because parallel to his successful literary career, he has been a not-so-successful composer. Plainly, he is puzzled. Are they right? Is he any good? Currently he is working on an opera about Freud ("Show Me Your Dream, I'll Show You Mine"?). So, perhaps, there is method to his recollections here of early sexual experiences.

Nevertheless, it is an article of faith (bad) in our dull categorizing time that no one may practice more than a single art; even worse, within the house of literature itself, the writer must keep to only one, preferably humble, room; yet a gift for any art is almost always accompanied by at least the ability to master one or more of the other arts. This is a secret of genius's lodge that is kept from every faculty room lest there be nervous breakdowns and losses of faith and transfers from English studies to physics. But where Goethe, say, was allowed his universality, today's artist is expected to remain cooped up in mediocrity's vast columbarium. The reputation of our best short-story writer, Paul Bowles, has suffered because he is, equally, a fine composer: For musicians, he is a writer, for writers a composer.

Along with music, Burgess had a talent for drawing; fortunately, he is also color-blind; otherwise he might have been pecked to death by angry crows at the Tate. Finally, he could write, but it was a long time before he allowed that old shoe of an art to bemuse him. I suspect that Burgess has been severely shaken by those music critics who have put him in his place, high in the gallery of Albert Hall; as a result, he believes that they are probably right because one person cannot be more than one thing. To a born-again atheist like myself, it is clear that each of us has multiple selves, talents, perceptions. But to the Roman Catholic, unity is all. At birth, each is handed One Immortal Soul, and that's that. One god for each; one muse for each. Then, at the end, we all line up. Good to the right. Bad to the left. All right! Now let's hear those voices raised in praise of HIM. Because—Heee-res De Lawd! Burgess! Less vibrato. This isn't Heaven, you know.

Three themes emerge in the course of the autobiography. The first, religion. What it means to be lower-middle-class Roman Catholic in the English mid-Midlands; what it means to lose—or lapse from—one's faith; what it means to be forever on the alert for another absolute system to provide one with certainty about everything. At one point, in Southeast Asia, Burgess was tempted to convert to Islam. But Islamic bigotry distressed him, and he backed away. Now,

in old age I look back on various attempts to cancel my apostasy and become reconciled to the Church again. This is because I have found no metaphysical substitute for it. Marxism will not do, nor will the kind of sceptical humanism that Montaigne taught. I know of no other organization that can both explain evil and, theoretically at least, brandish arms against it.

This is bewildering to an American of the Enlightenment; but as the twig was bent . . . Also, to the extent that Burgess has any political ideas at all, he's deeply reactionary and capable of such blimpisms as, "In February the Yalta Conference sold half of Europe to the Russians."

The second theme is sex. After the glut of the salacious sexy seventies, and the hysteria of the anxious AIDSy eighties, it is hard for those who grew up after the great divide—the Second World War—to realize that just about the only thing any of us ever thought about was getting laid. Burgess went into the British army at twenty-three in 1940. Three years later, at seventeen, I went into the American army. Each got out of the army in 1946; each with the neither-fish-nor-fowl rank of warrant officer. Although Burgess was for all practical purposes married to Lynne when he was scooped up by the army, he, too—like the rest of us—was introduced to a world of sex where every traditional barrier had fallen with a crash. There was a general availability unknown to previous generations of European—much less American—Christendom. Those of us who joined the orgy in our teens often failed, in later life, to acquire the gift of intimacy. Burgess himself had other problems; innocently— always innocently—he tells us about them, unaware that an autobiography is no place for truth as opposed to the true: Augustine's sententious nonsense about those pears should have taught him that.

Because Burgess had no mother, he writes,

I was not encouraged to express tenderness. I was reared emotionally cold. . . . I regret the emotional coldness that was established then and which, apart from other faults, has marred my works.

At least one dull American bookchat writer thought that this was really insightful stuff and moved Burgess several rungs down the literary ladder. He cannot love; ergo, he cannot write. He is not warm; ergo, he is not good. He is cold; ergo, he is bad. Burgess is very conscious of his reviewers but I do not think that he has ever quite grasped the deep ignorance of the average American bookchat writer, who is in place to celebrate obedience and conformity to that deadly second-rateness which has characterized our garrison state for the last third of a century.

Recently a television documentary on one of our public schools was screened for the local school board. The board was near rapture. But when the public saw the film, the board realized that what they had admired, the successful attempt to destroy individuality in the young, did not play so well with the TV audience, hardly themselves naysayers. Since power not sex is true motor to human life, the powerless often prefer to die. That is why today's young do not eat goldfish. They kill themselves.

Burgess's thirty-year marriage is more harrowing to read about than, perhaps, to have lived. At first, he was obliged to share Lynne with a pair of well-off brothers, one of whom might bring her the money that he could not. Then Burgess attended the party that was the Second World War. Finally, Lynne and the brothers parted and the open marriage of the Burgesses gaped anew. Postwar, Burgess taught in Malaya and Brunei. He and she each drank a bottle of gin a day. She made love to a number of men; he to women. She fought with everyone; demanded a divorce; was reconciled by the publication of his first books. Fortunately, he enjoys being humiliated by women, a theme that runs through the novels, giving them their sexual edge (see the final Enderby volume). Fascinating but mysterious—like Grace. Anyway, he loved her, he tells us, for thirty years.

Religion, sex, art—three themes that, unlike the Trinity, never become one. Finally, despite the distractions of the first two, it is the third that matters because that is all that's ever left. Burgess himself does not seem quite to know what to make of his novels. Wistfully, he goes on about music and the structure of language but, in the end, he is a writer of prose, a novelist, a sometime movie and television writer. There was a time whenever a producer came to me for a script on Jesus or the Borgias, or even Jesus and the Borgias, I'd send them on to Burgess, who would oblige. Today, he is the best literary journalist alive, as V. S. Pritchett is the best literary critic. Pritchett, of course, modestly opts for the word *journalist,* aware that the high ground of criticism is currently occupied by academic literary theoreticians who have presided, during the last two decades, over a 60 percent drop in English studies. Well, if you can't lick 'em, change the game.

This is not the place (nor does space afford, as Henry James would coyly note, having filled his review of some dim novel with a series of glittering false starts) to describe the twenty-eight novels of Anthony Burgess. So I shall stick to what he himself has to say about them in his memoir. One thing becomes clear: Like so many highly serious brilliant men, he has no natural humor or comic sense as opposed to verbal wit. Bewitched by *Finnegans Wake,* he dreamed of the marriage of high literature to high music. When he wrote his first novel, about wartime Gibraltar, he gave it to an editor at Heinemann. "It was, he said, funny. I had not, in fact, intended it to be funny, but I assumed the right posture of modesty on this revelation that I was a coming comic novelist." Dutifully—seriously?—he wrote several more novels set east of Suez and each turned out comic, even though he was writing of sad exotic places, and people; but, of course, he was writing about the painful untidy lives of Anthony and Lynne in far-off places where, as Horace (no, not Greeley) so pithily put it, "People change their skies, not their feelings, when they rush overseas." The *rush* is often funny while *overseas,* for the Brits, always is. Thus tragedy turns out comedy.

Of Burgess's fourth novel (*The Right to an Answer*) he writes, it "was almost entirely invention. That I could invent was the final proof, to me, that I had not mistaken my vocation." For the Burgess reader, the great breakthrough came after his death sentence, when he was furiously writing and inventing. In 1944, the pregnant Lynne had been robbed and beaten up in a London street by four American soldiers. She aborted. Burgess turned this true story into a novel that he has small regard for because the world at large has such a high regard for the film version, done by another, of *A Clockwork Orange.* Burgess hurls the story into a future London where four local louts have been Sovietized and speak a new vulgate, part London prole, part Russian. The result is chilling, and entirely other. When Burgess moves away from his own immediate life, his books come most startlingly alive, if ink markings on mute paper can ever be called a life form or even its surrogate.

In the light of his three obsessions, Burgess wanted to bring God into the novel in a big way, with Berlioz-cum-Joyce symbolism, and resonating like a struck cymbal with atavistic Lorenzian blood myths. Happily, he failed. Of an early novel, he writes, "The realism overcame the symbolism. This usually happens when the novelist possesses, which Joyce did not, a genuine narrative urge." One detects a regret here, an acknowledgment that the Wilsonian passion for *Finnegans Wake* has no place in the Burgessian novel. But then, "I see that the novel, an essentially comic and Protestant art form, is no place for the naked posturing of religious guilt." He means of course the English novel in this century. A twentieth-century novel each of us admires, *Doctor Faustus,* has roots in the human bloodstream (spirochete-ridden as it is) in a way not allowed by our meager culture and overrich language.

If Burgess is obsessed with sex in his memoirs, he uses sex judiciously in his novels and in the best (he will not agree), The Enderby Four, as I call them—*Inside Mr. Enderby, Enderby Outside, The Clockwork Testament, or Enderby's End,* and *Enderby's Dark Lady*—he uses his obsession much as Nabokov did in *Lolita* to make a thousand and one points about literature and life and their last human sanctuary, the motels of America. On the showing of the fugitive poems in the autobiography, Burgess himself is not much of a poet but his invention, the poet Enderby, on the showing of *his* poems is one of the finest of contemporary poets and ought to be anthologized as himself, with symposia devoted to his art, and no reference to Wilson/Burgess as amanuensis. There is no invention quite so extraordinary as that which surpasses, at inventing, the original inventor. Baron Frankenstein's creation just hangs out. But Enderby's poems have the effect that only the best writing can have on a reader who also writes. They make him want to write poems, too; and surpass self.

The Burgess who doubts his cosmic sense or, rather, was slightly appalled that his "serious" works made others laugh must know by now that the highest art, which is comedy, is grounded in obsession. With a bit of luck (a Roman Catholic education?) Melville might have created a masterpiece in *Moby-Dick.* As it is, we laugh—though not enough—at Captain Ahab (*Pierre* is funnier). But Burgess was wise enough to allow *his* obsessions with religion, sex, language, to work themselves out as comedy. Also, he has been able to put to good use his passion, rather than obsession, for language and its forms, and his lively restless inventions have considerably brightened the culturally flat last years of our century. How he managed to do this is implicit, if not always explicit, in the pages of *Little Wilson and Big God,* which might better be called *Little Wilson and Big Burgess,* who did it his, if not His, way.

*The New York Review of Books*
May 7, 1987

# *FREDERIC PROKOSCH:*
# *THE EUROPEAN CONNECTION*

**I**

In August 1939, I crossed the border from France into Italy. At thirteen I was already Henry James's passionate pilgrim; and the principal object of my pilgrimage was those remnants of the Roman empire which I had come to know so well from that glorious film *The Last Days of Pompeii,* not to mention its Plautine counterpart, the sympathetic Eddie Cantor's *Roman Scandals*: a thousand compelling celluloid images complemented by the texts of *Tales from Livy* and Suetonius's mind-boggling gossip.

At the train's first stop in Italy—Ventimiglia?—fascist guards gave the fascist salute just as they had done in all those newsreels where Hitler and Mussolini were perpetual Gog and Magog to our days, grotesque cinematic fictions soon to break out of the honey-odored darkness of the art-deco Trans-Lux theaters and become real-life monsters in spades.

Yet on my first trip down the Italian peninsula, in the company of a group of schoolboys and masters, I seldom looked out the train's windows. I was reading a paperback edition of *The Seven Who Fled* by Frederic Prokosch. For the next week I was in two places at once. I was

in the Rome that I had so long imagined. I was also fleeing across an
Asia that had been entirely imagined by Prokosch. One hot, airless
August morning, as I walked up the Via Tritone and into the Piazza
Barberini, I realized that I was, simultaneously, in the desert southwest
of Urga and in prewar (yes, we knew it was prewar then) Rome, facing
the Bristol Hotel, where lived, unknown to me, another writer that I was
soon to read, George Santayana, whose *The Last Puritan* was to have
much the same revelatory effect on me as the romantic eroticism of *The
Seven Who Fled.*

From the ages of seventeen to twenty I was in the American army.
Wherever I was stationed—at least in the United States—I would go to
the post library and look up Prokosch. In the years since I first discovered him he had published three more novels. He was something of a
cult in the army, and on the outside, too. During the summer of 1945
I was on leave at East Hampton, Long Island. I had finished my first
novel. I had another six months to serve in the army.

I cannot remember how I met Prokosch but one day there he was on
the beach. Somehow it had never occurred to me that the two fascinating words that made up his name might actually belong to a living
person, aged thirty-eight. It is true that I had looked carefully at the
photographs on the dust jackets. But one might just as well have been
looking at pictures of Byron. Certainly the dust-jacket biographies were
brief and uninformative. He seemed to spend a lot of time in Europe;
and that was it. Now there he was on the white beach, a dark-haired,
black-eyed man, who looked more like a pirate than a writer.

In *Voices: A Memoir,* Prokosch writes of that summer: "I took a room
in one of the cottages of the Sea Spray Inn. . . . Every evening I'd go
wandering along the beach and watch the breakers. There were days
when they kept pounding at the sand with their shining fists and there
were days when they slid shoreward with a snakelike malevolence." In
this one offhand description, Prokosch displays his characteristic investiture of nature with the human and the human with the natural—
Ruskin's so-called "pathetic fallacy" which was to be denounced yet
again by the French "new novelists" as the unforgivable (for an entire
literary season) anthropomorphizing of nature's neutral otherness. Nevertheless, central to Prokosch's vision of the material world is a creation
that can only be recorded by the human eye, itself both subject and
object—the sole measurer of light and inevitable victim of darkness. For
Prokosch, a landscape observed is an extension of the human, particu-

larly if the landscape is one that he himself has invented, like the Asia of *The Asiatics* and *The Seven Who Fled.*

Personally, I found Prokosch amiable but distant. Now that I have read *Voices,* I can see that he was not used to being the found writer of a younger writer; rather, he himself was a dedicated finder of older artists and wise men, and the memoir that he has written is curiously selfless. The voice one hears is not so much his as the voices of those whom he has admired or at least listened closely to. By and large, he has chosen not to praise himself, the memoirist's usual task. Instead he has tried to distill the essence of each voice rather than what might have been exactly said. Since he and I often saw the same people at the same time (in the case of Santayana, we must have been alternating our visits to the Convent of the Blue Nuns, neither letting on to the other that he was making pilgrimages to the old man's cell), it is fascinating for me to hear what Santayana said to him as opposed to what he said to me. Particularly when . . .

But, first, who is Frederic Prokosch? He was born in Wisconsin in 1908, the son of a Sudeten-Czech linguist and philologist. Prokosch's childhood was surprisingly Twainesque: Prairie du Sac, Wisconsin; Austin, Texas; and rural Pennsylvania, where his father taught at Bryn Mawr. As a youth, Prokosch's interests were about evenly divided between the arts—literature, painting—and tennis. Eventually, Professor Edouard Prokosch moved on to Yale, where Frederic got a doctorate in Middle English. In 1935 Prokosch was at King's College, Cambridge, when *The Asiatics* was published. Like Byron, he was suddenly famous.

*The Seven Who Fled* (1937) was equally successful. He also published poetry, which was praised by Yeats. During the war he worked for the Office of War Information in Lisbon and Stockholm. To date, he has written sixteen novels, four volumes of poetry, and he has translated into English Louise Labé and Friedrich Hölderlin. For thirty years he has been completely out of fashion in America (a place the late Philip Rahv used to call Amnesia), but the French continue to find his novels fascinating, and he has been praised in that country by critics as various as Gide and Camus and Queneau, while the first translation into French of *The Seven Who Fled* was made by Marguerite Yourcenar. He lives now in the south of France. He continues to write; he makes, by hand, miniature editions of poets whom he admires; he collects butterflies (I wish he had published more of his correspondence with Nabokov, another literary lepidopterist).

For those concerned with Significant Literary Trends in Modern Literature (so different from our own high culture's English Studies' English Studies), Prokosch is a precursor of the currently fashionable Latin American school of writing, which has managed to break more than a hundred years of beautifully resonant silence with the sort of precise rendering of imagined human landscapes that Prokosch had invented and perfected in the thirties. Since Prokosch's novels have always been available in French translations, his inventions have much influenced those Latin Americans who have always looked—and continue to look—to Paris for guidance. García Márquez would not write the way that he does if Prokosch had not written the way that he did. At a time when the American novel was either politically *engagé* or devoted to the homespun quotidian, Prokosch's first two novels were a half-century ahead of their time. This did him no good in the medium-long run.

After forty-four years, I have reread *The Seven Who Fled.* To my surprise, I actually remembered some of it. I also found that much of what had been magical for me still works. But then the picaresque novel has the unique advantage of *being* . . . Also, what is not dated cannot truly date; and if the writer has chosen to render imagined people in an imagined landscape with history firmly kept to the margin of *his* story, the work will always be what it is, in the present tense. On the other hand, the last two pages of the first edition which I have been reading are ominously dated.

First, there is a page with the words: "The Harper Prize Novel Contest *Its History and Terms.*" On the next page, the publisher tells us that the judges of the 1937 contest are Louis Bromfield, Sinclair Lewis, and Thornton Wilder. Recently, I read that Tennessee Williams (circa 1937) said that his favorite writer was Louis Bromfield while I remember writing (circa 1950) that Thornton Wilder was mine. The publisher now hits hard the Ozymandias note: "The first Harper Prize was awarded in 1922 to Margaret Wilson's *The Able McLaughlins,* which also received the Pulitzer Prize. The second winner was Anna Parrish's *The Perennial Bachelor.* The third was *The Grandmothers* by Glenway Wescott, the fourth Julian Green's *The Dark Journey,* the fifth Robert Raynold's *Brothers in the West,* and the sixth Paul Horgan's *The Fault of Angels.* The seventh award went to H. L. Davis's *Honey in the Horn,* which also won the Pulitzer Prize. To this distinguished list is now added *The Seven Who Fled* by Frederic Prokosch."

Happily, we have now got literature sorted out and we all know exactly who's who and why. The absolute permanence of the *oeuvre* (there is no other word, in French at least) of Joyce Carol Oates, say, is, very simply, a fact that no American English teacher—as opposed, perhaps, to an English American teacher—would for an instant challenge. But then the nice thing about being now is being right, and the bad thing about being then is being wrong, not to mention forgotten. Could any of these prize-winning books have been any good? It beats me. Of the lot, I read and somewhat admired *The Grandmothers*. I have read Julian Green but not *The Dark Journey*. The rest are simply dusty titles, swept up by time's winged wastebasket wherein alabaster cities as well as fruited plains are all as one forgot by Amnesia the Beautiful.

*The Seven Who Fled* is filled with energy and color. The somewhat unfocused romanticism of Prokosch's poetry works very well indeed when deployed as prose narrative. From Kashgar, at the center of Asia, seven Europeans flee the armies of the youthful General Ma, who ranges up and down Tashkent while Russia and China begin to press upon the borders of that disintegrating state. In the thirties, much was made of the fact that Prokosch had never set foot in the Asia that he had invented for *The Asiatics* and *The Seven Who Fled*. Since then, other writers have invented jungles in South America not to mention those brilliant invisible cities of Asia that Calvino's Marco Polo saw.

For each of the seven characters, there is at least one reverie of an earlier non-Asiatic time. For the Englishman Layeville there is a glimpse of the world in which Prokosch himself had been living:

And Cambridge. Those ingratiating days of hesitation and unreality! Those platonic hours upon the grass lit by the rays of sunlight slanting through the leaves, or among the scattered dusty books lit by rays that slanted through the high windows. Their very unreality indeed gave them a magical and melancholy innocence, not that of childhood, but that of pure seclusion. The elaborate pleas for a new order; the eloquent disputations of social justice; ardors and ambitions which made every moment seem important and profound.

Yes, Prokosch met Guy Burgess at Cambridge; no, Prokosch was not political. But his character Layeville is fulfilled in youth at school:

So that, little by little, he became familiar with the chilling pangs endured by those who have lost, somewhere amongst the ardors of childhood and youth, all power to love.

There is an astonishing sexual tension in Prokosch's early books that is as hard to define as it is impossible not to sense. The sexual takes unexpected forms. One of the seven kills another man, a gratuitous but altogether necessary act that is, in its dreamlike rendering, highly sexual, presaging Genet and Paul Bowles. As a writer, Prokosch is not so much a conscious mind as a temperament through which the human condition, as imagined by him, flows—and merges with the nonhuman. For Prokosch, each of the seven who flees is both generalized essence and specified ape, while the dark gravel-strewn Gobi beneath the sheltering sky that does not shelter is simply an extension of a shifting, living cosmos where man is in all things that man observes; and the only constant is change—hence, the romantic's agony. Or:

He could see that the snow was leading a life of its own, precisely like the earth or the sea: but sterile, secret, silvery, its love so to speak turned forever upon fragments of its own self and destined to fruitlessness and silence. A million crystals of infinite complexity, living for nothing else but the gradual destruction of their own perfect selves, growing slowly into each other, moving silkily downward during each moment of sunlight, motionless again at night, and then in the warm sun again becoming amorous and weak, like vast degenerate tribes drifting together, flowing away; demonstrating how close to one another were purity and decay, perfection and death.

Thus he makes the snow a metaphor for the human; and makes the snow snow; and makes sentences: "Sentences must stir in a book like leaves in a forest," wrote Flaubert, "each distinct from each, despite their resemblance."

2

The title of Prokosch's current memoir is significant: *Voices.* In a sense, it is an ironic commentary on the ancient complaint that he was always, as a novelist, too much concerned with place and not enough with people. Actually, it was his special genius to realize that place approached as if it were character *is* human since only a human mind can evoke a landscape never before seen on earth except in the author's mind. But now Prokosch has turned from those dreams of imaginary places (and recollections of the past, as in his reconstruction of Byron in *The Missolonghi Manuscript*) to the voices that he has heard in life and now recollects in memory.

Most young writers are eager, for a time at least, to meet the great figures of the day. At nineteen I was fascinated to meet Prokosch because his books had had a profound effect on my early adolescent self. He found this amusing: "How *sensitive* you must have been!" And the pirate's laugh would roar. Later he found it amusing that in the summer of 1948—when I was not enjoying the success of my third novel, *The City and the Pillar*—I should want to meet Gide and Santayana and Sartre. . . . He gave me the impression that this sort of busy-ness was somehow vulgar. I wish now that I had known then that he himself had been a resolute collector of all sorts of rare artist-butterflies and that he had continued to add to his collection until he withdrew himself entirely from the literary world, as most writers who write eventually do.

But, plainly, the voices he once heard persist in memory, and now he has put them down. From youth, he tells us, he had got into the habit of taking down conversations. He had begun with his father's friend Thomas Mann, who came to call on the family at Bryn Mawr. "I kept staring with fascination at the back of Thomas Mann. The stars were beginning to shine and a mist hung over the hockey field. His head rose from his shoulders like a moss-grown rock and the words he was uttering spread from his skull like antlers." Among those words: " 'The fatal thing,' he said, 'is that Tolstoi had no irony. It is a miracle that he managed to write as well as he did. Irony in a novel is like the salt in a pea soup. It gives the flavor, the nuance. Without the salt it is insipid.' " This is *echt* Mann, for whom food was always a metaphor, and the heavier the food the heavier the metaphor. "After he left I went to my bedroom and wrote it all down, and this was the first of the dialogues that I scribbled faithfully in my notebooks."

Prokosch glimpsed "an abyss at the core of greatness" in Mann. The abyss or vastation or, simply, *Weltschmerz* was to be a recurring theme in Prokosch's own travels among Heine's foreign cities: "It was a journey in search of the artist as a hero, as an enigma, as a martyr, as a revelation, and finally as a fragment of humanity."

While an undergraduate at Haverford, Prokosch and a culture-vulture classmate spent a summer in Paris, where they called on Gertrude Stein and Alice B. Toklas. The ladies were just back from Spain. Gertrude relates: "The Goyas were very nice and the El Grecos were more than adequate but I felt no rapport with the Murillos or the Zurbaráns. Alice said that she profoundly distrusted the Zurbaráns but we trusted Mallorca when we came to Mallorca." As for Paris, Gertrude confessed that in the early days, "there were moments when I was homesick but they gradually grew less frequent. I still had friends in America and I wrote them some letters and we ate cornbread with molasses and apple pie on Sundays and on certain occasions a bit of cheese with the pie. One has these native habits and it is foolish to defy them. . . . Even Alice who is a gypsy has her own deep Americanism."

Prokosch has always had a habit of asking the apparently simple— even simpleminded—question. He asks Gertrude Stein if she has a definite philosophy. This nets him some splendid Stein:

"A writer must always try to have a philosophy and he should also have a psychology and a philology and many other things. Without a philosophy and a psychology and all these various other things he is not really worthy of being called a writer. I agree with Kant and Schopenhauer and Plato and Spinoza and that is quite enough to be called a philosophy. But then of course a philosophy is not the same thing as a style . . ."

Later Prokosch and friend lie in wait for a style as incarnated by James Joyce at Sylvia Beach's bookshop. Incidentally, it is the friend who is ravished by Stein and Joyce. At this point, Prokosch is still as interested in tennis as in literature; but he has read *Ulysses* and Mrs. Woolf, and when the reluctant lion is trapped over tea in the shop's back room, he asks Joyce what he thinks of Virginia Woolf and is told that

she married her wolfish husband purely in order to change her name. Virginia Stephen is not a name for an exploratory authoress. I shall write a book some day about the appropriateness of names. Geoffrey Chaucer has a ribald ring, as is proper and correct, and Alexander Pope was inevitably Alexander Pope . . . and Shelley was very Percy and very Bysshe.

When confronted with the "stream of consciousness," Joyce's response is sour: "When I hear the word 'stream' uttered with such a revolting primness, what I think of is urine and not the contemporary novel. And besides, it isn't new, it is far from the *dernier cri*. Shakespeare used it continually, much too much in my opinion, and there's *Tristram Shandy,* not to mention the *Agamemnon* . . ."

Prokosch was a good tennis player; at squash, he was a champion. Suddenly, one hears the somewhat surprising voice of Bill Tilden, who had written, *"Never* change a winning game, and *always* change a losing one,"* a maxim that must be reversed when applied to art. "One day I finally cornered Bill Tilden . . ." Prokosch got the master to autograph one of his books on tennis. Tilden had also written two novels, which Prokosch had read. Tilden dismisses them as "perfect trash. I always yearned to become a novelist. But I didn't have it in me. Just rubbish, that's all they are." But for Tilden—and the young Prokosch—tennis was an art form, too. Unhappily, the Tilden that Prokosch met was at the end of his career: "My legs are giving way. Will the last act be tragic?"

For Prokosch there were two golden ages, divided by the war: Cambridge at the end of the thirties and Rome at the end of the forties. He seems to have enjoyed his literary success without ever having taken on the persona of the great author. Also, surprisingly, Dr. Prokosch has never taught school; never sought prizes or foundation grants; never played at literary politics. He seems to have been more interested in the works or voices of others than in himself as a person (as opposed to himself as a writer), a characteristic that tends to put him outside contemporary American literature; and contemporary American literature, sensing this indifference to the games careerists play, extruded him entirely from the canon. He was like no one else, anyway. He had always been a kind of expatriate at a time when the drums of America First had begun to beat their somewhat ragged martial tattoo. Finally, he was dedicated to literature in a way hard for his contemporaries to grasp as they pretended to be boxers or bullfighters—not to mention bullshitters, Zelda Fitzgerald's nice phrase for the huge hollow Hemingway who had set the tone for a generation that only now is beginning to get truly lost. Hail, Amnesia!

Prokosch went his own way; and listened to his voices. At Cambridge he invites an ancient don to tea. The old man tells him, "You are rather naïve to have written a masterpiece. I agree with the critics. *The Asiatics is* a little masterpiece. But is your air of simplicity just a part of your cunning, or is your cunning just an aspect of your inner simplicity?" Although this is the sort of self-serving conversation that memoirists are prone to include to show how much the famous admired them, I quote the exchange because Prokosch seldom gets this personal about himself; he keeps tributes to his genius at a delicate minimum. Prokosch has no response other than "Both, maybe." To which Housman (yes, it was he; later to become famous as the TV spokesperson for a Los Angeles bank) replied, "In every American there is an air of incorrigible innocence, which seems to conceal a diabolical cunning." Prokosch broods on Housman; on Eliot; on beauty . . . and on Auden.

Beauty, first. The absolutely relative or relatively absolute nature of beauty was not as firmly established in those prewar days as it is now. It was generally agreed then that beauty was good; and that the good is hard to achieve. "Of this wisdom," wrote Walter Pater, "the poetic passion, the desire of beauty, the love of art for art's sake has most; for it comes to you professing frankly to give nothing but the highest quality to your moments as they pass, simply for those moments' sake." In a way, this is incontrovertible; but the way that Pater put what Prokosch echoes is not our present way. Today all abstract nouns are questioned save those abstractions that are used to measure the ones that have gone out of fashion. We signal and we sign; we structure and we deconstruct; and for a long time a good deal of the century's philosophy has been a division of logic. Although Prokosch's idea of beauty in art is very old-fashioned indeed, the way in which he himself deploys his own art is a formidable reminder that beauty, no matter by what sign or name acknowledged, can be a fact whose refutation is a highly risky business even for the most confident literary bureaucrat.

The voice of Auden is the most significant in Prokosch's memoirs. Auden was his almost exact contemporary. By the time that Prokosch had published his first volume of poems (after the two celebrated novels), Auden was already the most famous young poet in English. From the beginning Prokosch acknowledged not only Auden's mastery but his own indebtedness to him. This is a rare thing for a contemporary to do: When it comes to envy and malice, our century's poets make even the dizziest of American novelists appear serene and charitable.

Prokosch had fallen under Auden's spell long before they finally met in New York City at the Yale Club. Auden had just arrived from England. "He wore a pin-striped suit, a wrinkled shirt, and a checkered tie. I had the impression that he had tried to look tidy for the Yale Club. His thick unruly hair was parted far on the right. There was a wart on his right cheek and he cocked his head to the right, so that his body as well as his mind seemed to tilt into the asymmetrical." Auden asks Prokosch to propose him for American citizenship. Prokosch says he would be delighted. They talk of Delmore Schwartz's new book, *In Dreams Begin Responsibilities*. "Auden listened inquisitively and nodded his head politely. He seemed, by some secret antennalike instinct, to be appraising all the strengths and all the weaknesses in Delmore Schwartz." But at the mention of Dylan Thomas "he looked irritable and queasy" while a reference to Prokosch's recent book of poems, *The*

*Carnival,* and its debt to *early* Auden, appeared to trouble Auden with "the ambivalence of my admiration and his politeness was fringed with little tentacles of hostility."

And I suddenly realized that there were four of us at the table: two speakers and two listeners who were hiding behind the speakers, each with his own hidden attitudes and doubts and suspicions. And abruptly, as we glanced across the table uneasily, we were engulfed in a silence of mutual shyness and distrust.

I said, "Tell me, Wystan. Why did you decide to escape to America?"

"*Escape!* What in the world makes you think it was an escape? It was not an escape. And what's more, it was not a *decision.* It was an instinct, a desire. Please don't try to intellectualize. One has impulses and instincts. There was no yearning to escape. And there was nothing that remotely resembled a decision!"

Although Prokosch tells us nothing of his own private life, he does describe a Turkish bath in Forty-second Street where "I was repelled by the cockroaches and the smell of secretions but intrigued by the atmosphere of silence and cunning.

"As I sat in the steam room I caught sight of Wystan Auden. He looked like a naked sea beast as he prowled through the steam, and his skin looked phosphorescent under the damp electric bulb." Auden's voice is now from a nightmare. "He rambled on wildly, as though secretly distraught." He compares the steam room to Kafka; talks of Dostoevsky: "All is focused on obsession. All this vice all around us, there's a touch of lunacy, isn't there? It's so mad and ridiculous in its Dostoevskyan fashion. 'To extreme sickness,' said Pascal, 'one must apply extreme remedies.' " Very clever, of course, but what did he mean by *extreme remedies*?

He clutched at the marble slab, as though seized with a fit of dizziness, then faded into the steam like a fog-bound vessel.

Years later Prokosch sees Auden, alone at a café in Venice. Prokosch begins:

"I've been to see the de Chiricos."

"Ah, you've been to see the de Chiricos," said Auden remotely.

"They were very disappointing," I said, blowing a smoke ring.

"Oh, I see. They were *disappointing,* " said Auden sarcastically.

"Almost sinisterly so," I muttered, half-imploringly.

"Indeed. Were they really? Almost *sinisterly* so!" He perked up a bit. His teeth protruded slightly.

I had an unerring knack for always saying the wrong thing to Auden. Whatever I wanted to say, however simple or sincere, the moment I opened my mouth it sounded gauche, vapid, insolent.

He seemed somehow to revel in this air of mutual embarrassment. He seemed to swell up into a sleek, didactic majesty.

I said, "Venice has changed."

"Venice," he snorted, "is constantly changing. With all that sky and water, how can it keep from changing incessantly?"

"I used to think of Tiepolo whenever I thought of Venice."

"Of Tiepolo. How interesting. So it reminded you of Tiepolo?"

"But I now think of Tintoretto. It has a beard, like Tintoretto."

"A beard. Yes. I see. Like Tintoretto. How very amusing."

Perhaps he was drunk. Impossible to be sure. He had already started on his desolate journey downward. The wrinkles were deepening, the pouches were thickening. The eyelids looked scaly and shifty, reptilian. Even the eyes were no longer the old Auden eyes, which used to be quick and alert as hummingbirds. They had turned into eyes that seemed to gloat over a malady, to brood over some accumulating inner calamity.

"Tintoretto," he said, with an accusatory precision. He seemed to ponder over the word, to linger over its contours. He cocked his head a little, as though looking for a new perspective. His hair was very tousled and his fingernails were purple. He stared across the piazza with an air of agitation.

And for an instant I caught that old familiar whiff of a festering unhappiness. . . . There was something almost regal in this massive, drunken misery. I felt almost reconciled to this grim, penultimate Auden. I yearned to cry out, "Come, let's drop all this pretense! Let's be friends after all! Let's forgive and forget!"

But I couldn't bring myself to say it. He slumped back in his chair. He seemed to catch on the wing this momentary impulse in me and all of a sudden he seemed to be listening to a voice in the distance and the folds of his face took on a ruinous splendour. This quick, molten beauty was the last glimpse I had of him. It was like a quick shaft of lightning on a war-shattered landscape.

I said, "Well, goodbye. It was nice to see you, Wystan."

"Yes. Of course. Tintoretto. It's odd about Tintoretto . . . ."

I must say it takes guts to record such a scene at one's expense.

The Santayana voice that Prokosch records is not at all the voice that I heard. The old man says to Prokosch, "One must always, without necessarily being a pessimist, be prepared for the worst. For the end of what we call our Western civilization—I include the Athenian—and all that grandeur of Christian romanticism."

His head sagged a little. His eyes began to water. His voice rose imperceptibly, as though for a final effort. "We are sailing ever deeper into the dark, uncharted waters. The lights in the lighthouses are beginning to go out. Is there anything to guide us? Is there anyone worth listening to? I wake up in the middle of the night and I'm cold with terror. . . ."

I fear that my Santayana was a stoic like me, and I could not imagine him cold with terror at the thought of civilization's end. Even at eighty-five, the clear black eyes did not water but shone as bright and as hard as obsidian. When I said to him, with youthful despair, that the world had never been in so terrible a state, Santayana could not have been more brisk, or chilling. "My own lifetime has been spent in a longer period of peace and security than that of almost anyone I could conceive of in the European past." When I spoke with horror and revulsion of the possibility that Italy . . . *bella Italia* . . . might go communist in the next month's election, Santayana looked positively gleeful. "Oh, let them! Let them try it! They've tried everything else, so why not communism? After all, who knows what new loyalties will emerge as they become part of a—of a wolf pack." I was sickened and revolted by his sangfroid, by his cynicism, by his, yes, blancmange. I was also much amused by his response to my sad comment on the speed with which literary reputations were lost in Amnesia. "It would be insufferable," he said swiftly, "if they were not." Could *he* have heard time's winged wastebasket hovering near?

Among Prokosch's voices there are some marvelously comical ones, including Lady Cunard and Hemingway in deadly combat for the mucho-macho drawing-room championship award. An exchange between Edith Sitwell and Edmund Wilson is also splendid. It is 1948 or 1949. The Sitwells are being lionized by *tout* New York.

The butler slid past with a tray of boiled shrimps. Edmund Wilson approached the sofa with a glass in his hand. He plucked a shrimp from the tray and dipped it in the mayonnaise. He held it in the air as he sipped his whisky. I watched with frozen horror as the shrimp slid from its toothpick and gracefully landed on Miss Sitwell's coiffure. But Miss Sitwell ignored it and continued with serenity.

"It is always the incantatory element which basically appeals to me . . . ."

" 'The Hollow Men' is pure incantation," said Edmund Wilson. He kept peering at the shrimp with a scrupulous curiosity. "I heard Eliot read it aloud once. It was a marvel of rhythmicality."

"Even in Dryden," said Miss Sitwell, "there is a sense of abracadabra . . . ."

I kept staring at the shrimp with a feverish fascination. It lay poised on Miss Sitwell like an amulet of ivory. I visualized it in terms of the Victorian, the Elizabethan, the Gothic. I suddenly began rather to like Edith Sitwell.

I suddenly began rather to admire Frederic Prokosch twenty years ago when he visited me on the Hudson River where I lived. I took him to a party attended by a number of hicks and hacks and hoods from a nearby outpost of Academe. Naturally, they regarded Prokosch with contempt. They knew that he had once been famous in Amnesia but they had forgotten why. Anyway, Auden had won. And Auden had said that there can only be one poet per epoch.

A great deal was said about poetry; and some of it was said by poets—teacher-poets, true, but poets nevertheless; winners of prizes ("They got more prizes now than they got poets": Philip Rahv, circa 1960, Amnesia). Prokosch was entirely ignored. But he listened politely as the uses of poetry in general and of the classics in particular were brought into question. Extreme positions were taken. Finally, one poet-teacher pulled the chain, as it were, on all of Western civilization: The classics, as such, were totally irrelevant. For a moment, there was a blessed silence. Then Prokosch began to recite in Latin a passage from Virgil; and the room grew very cold and still. "It's Dante," a full professor whispered to a full wife.

When Prokosch had finished, he said mildly, "Those lines are carved in marble in the gardens of the Villa Borghese at Rome. I used to look at them every day and I'd think, that is what poetry is, something that can be carved in marble, something that can still be beautiful to read after so many centuries."

Now in his seventy-fifth year, Prokosch ends his memoir with: "I live in a valley below Grasse in a cottage enclosed by cypresses. Behind me loom the hills where the walls are perched in the sunlight. Below me flows the cold green canal of the Siagne. Every morning I look at the dew which clings to the olive trees and I wonder what strange new excitement the day will hold for me. . . . My voyage is at its end. I think how glorious to grow old!" But "then I sit by the window and drink a cup of coffee and labor once again in my ceaseless struggle to produce a masterpiece."

So he is still at work, writing, as he ends. "I am no longer afraid of loneliness or suffering or death. I see the marvelous faces of the past gathering around me and I hear once again the murmuring of voices in the night." One must have created for oneself a very good day indeed to have so beautiful a prospect of the night.

*The New York Review of Books*
May 12, 1983

# 40
## •
# PROFESSOR V. NABOKOV

Professor Vladimir Nabokov's beautiful memoir *Speak Memory* has now been succeeded by *Strong Opinions*—a collection of press clippings in which he has preserved for future classes what looks to be every interview granted during the last decade. Plainly he has not taken to heart Turgenev's "Never try to justify yourselves (whatever libelous stories they may tell about you). Don't try to explain a misunderstanding, don't be anxious, yourselves, either to say or hear 'the last word.' "

Alas, the Black Swan of Swiss-American letters has a lot of explaining to do (no singing, however: we need the swan for many a future summer). In addition to the bubbling interviews, Professor Nabokov recounts the many misunderstandings between him and the French publisher of *Lolita,* between him and the critics of his translation of Pushkin's *Eugene Onegin,* between him and various adversaries in the form of Letters to the Editor (by slyly omitting the pretext for each letter, he creates a loony Kafka-like mood). Included, too, are examples of his own bookchat: Sartre's *La Nausée* "belongs to that tense-looking but really very loose type of writing, which has been popularized by many second-raters—Barbusse, Céline, and so forth." Finally, he gives us several meticulous portraits of those butterflies he murdered ("with an expert nip of its thorax") during his celebrated tours of America's motels.

Professor Nabokov's answers to the questions posed him by a dozen or so interviewers are often amusing, sometimes illuminating, and always—after the third or fourth performance—unbearable in their repetitiveness. Never again do I want to read that he writes in longhand with a hard pencil while standing at a lectern until he tires and sits or lies down, that he writes on Bristol cards which are lined on only one side so that he will not mistake a used card for a fresh card. Reading and rereading these descriptions, one understands why he thinks Robbe-Grillet a great writer.

Admittedly, interviewers are always eager to know how a writer writes (*what* he writes holds less magic for them). But the Swan of Lac Léman in the course of what he admits has been a good deal of editing might have spared us so many repetitions. "I demanded of my students the passion of science and the patience of poetry." Superb—but only the first time. ("Aphoristicism is a symptom of arteriosclerosis.") And of course the synoptic interviews tell and retell the sacred story of all that was lost by the noble family of "squires and soldiers" (perhaps descended from Genghis Khan) in the Russian revolution, and of their heir's hegira (Germany, England, America) and metamorphosis at Cornell from "lean lecturer into full professor," from obscure Russian emigré novelist into the creator of *Lolita,* considered by Isherwood to be the best travel book ever written about America.

Professor Nabokov's public appearances and occasional commentaries are always looked forward to because he likes to attack celebrated writers. Hemingway and Conrad are, essentially, "writers of books for boys." "I cannot abide Conrad's souvenir-shop style, bottled ships and shell necklaces of romanticist clichés." Nor can he abide Mann's "asinine *Death in Venice* or Pasternak's melodramatic and vilely written *Zhivago* or Faulkner's corn-cobby chronicles" . . . while at Cornell, "I remember the delight of tearing apart *Don Quixote,* a cruel and crude old book . . ." or "that awful Monsieur Camus," or "the not quite first-rate Eliot . . . and definitely second-rate Pound." Or "the so-called 'realism' of old novels, the easy platitudes of Balzac or Somerset Maugham, or D. H. Lawrence . . ." The Professor does admit to admiring Borges, Salinger (J. D., not Pierre), Updike, and at one point he pays a nice tribute to several other *New Yorker* writers while *"My* greatest masterpieces of twentieth-century prose are, in this order, Joyce's *Ulysses,* Kafka's *Transformations,* Biely's *Petersburg* and the first half of Proust's fairy tale in search of lost time." Class dismissed.

*Strong Opinions* reminds one to what extent the author is still very much a part of the American academic machine. Certainly the best bit

of material in this ragbag of a book is a description of giving an examination to a large class at Cornell on a winter's day. Although sensibly stern
about "the symbolism racket in schools [which] attracts computerised
minds but destroys plain intelligence as well as poetical sense," Nabokov
himself has become just the sort of writer the racketeers most like to
teach. Not only is his prose full of trilingual puns and word-play but "as
I just like composing riddles with elegant solutions," there are bound
to be symbols galore and much, much more beneath those Tartar arbors,
amongst those Scythian mists.

The best of the interviews are the ones with Alfred Appel, Jr.—plainly
a Nabokovian invention—the "Jr." is one giveaway. Another is that Mr.
Appel's questions are often longer and wittier than the Professor's answers. Can this mean that an intellectual comedy team is being discreetly tried out in these pages? A brand-new Stravinsky and Craft?
Certainly, teacher provides pupil with the most elegant *cache-cache* as
well as *cache-sexe.* Periodically, the Professor is obliged to note that he
himself is not *repeat* not attracted to those very young girls who keep
cropping up in his work. ("Lewis Carroll liked little girls. I don't.") At
these moments, our proud Black Swan becomes an uneasy goose, fearful
of being cooked by Cornell's board of regents.

Despite occasional pleasures, this is not a book for those who admire
Nabokov's novels. But for students who will write about him in American universities, it is probably useful to have all this twaddle in one
volume. For myself, I am rereading *Transparent Things,* that perfect
radiogram of found objects, precisely set in the artist's own Time. If only
for this lovely work, Nabokov will never be forced to echo an earlier
American culture hero who wrote, sadly:

Yet do I find it perceptible—here to riot in understatement—that I, who
was once a leading personage in and about those scanty playgrounds of
human interest which we nickname literature seem now to have become,
for all practical results, unheard-of thereabouts.

Readers who can correctly identify the author of the above passage will
be given a letter of introduction to Professor V. Nabokov, Palace Hotel,
Montreux, Vaud, Switzerland.

*The Observer*
May 12, 1974

# 41

## PAUL BOWLES'S STORIES

"Carson McCullers, Paul Bowles, Tennessee Williams are, at this moment at least, the three most interesting writers in the United States." A third of a century has passed since I wrote that sentence in a piece on contemporary American writing.

Later, when I reprinted those words, I felt obliged to add: "This was written in 1952. McCullers was a good and fashionable novelist of the day (I cannot say that I have any great desire to read her again). Paul Bowles was as little known then as he is now. His short stories are among the best ever written by an American. Tennessee Williams, etc. . . ." All in all, I still see no reason not to support my youthful judgment of Paul Bowles. As a short-story writer, he has had few equals in the second half of the twentieth century. Obvious question: If he is so good, why is he so little known?

Great American writers are supposed not only to live in the greatest country in the world (the United States, for those who came in late), but to write about that greatest of all human themes: *the American experience.* From the beginning of the Republic, this crude America First-ism has flourished. As a result, there is a strong tendency to misrepresent or undervalue our three finest novelists: Henry James (who lived in England), Edith Wharton (who lived in France), Vladimir Nabokov

(who lived in Switzerland, and who wasn't much of an American anyway despite an unnatural passion for our motels, so lyrically rendered
in *Lolita*).

Paul Bowles has lived most of his life in Morocco. He seldom writes
about the United States. On the other hand, he has shrewd things to say
about Americans confronted with strange cultures and . . . strange
selves.

Born in 1911, Bowles was brought up in New York City and New
England. He attended the University of Virginia. When he was seventeen, the Paris-based avant-garde magazine *transition* published some of
his poems. Bowles went to Paris, met Gertrude Stein, was influenced by
the Surrealists. He quit school to become a writer. Except for Poe, his
writing derives not from the usual Anglo-American tradition but from
such "exotics" as Valéry, Roussel, Gide and, of course, the expatriate
Miss Stein. Later, he was to put to his own uses oral Mexican and
Moroccan folklore; he listened as much as he read.

I suspect that Bowles's apparent foreignness has limited the number
of doctoral theses that ought by now to have been devoted to one whose
art far exceeds that of . . . well, name the great American writers of our
day (a list that was as different yesterday as it will be tomorrow). For
the American academic, Bowles is still odd man out; he writes as if *Moby
Dick* had never been written. Odder still, he is also a distinguished
composer of music. In fact, he supported himself for many years by
writing incidental music for such Broadway plays as *The Glass Menagerie*. It is curious that at a time when a number of serious critics have
expressed the hope that literature might one day take on the attributes
of the "highest" of all the arts, music, Bowles has been composing music
as well as writing prose. I am certain that the first critic able to deal both
with his music and his writing will find that Bowles's life work has been
marvelous in a way not accessible to those of us who know only one or
the other of the two art forms. Only Anthony Burgess knows enough
to do him justice.

In 1972, Paul Bowles wrote a memoir called *Without Stopping*. For
those able to read between the lines, the book was pleasurable. For
anyone else, it must have sounded a bit like Julius Caesar's account of
the wars in Gaul. Although there is a good deal of information about
various commanders and troop movements, we don't learn much about
what the subject had in mind. But there are interesting asides, and the
best sort of memoir is entirely to one side of the mere facts of a life.

We learn that Bowles originally wanted to be a writer, not a composer. But at a progressive school he had shown an aptitude for mathematics, cousin-german to music. Nevertheless, he preferred to arrange words rather than notes upon a page until Gertrude Stein read his poems. "She sat back and thought a moment. Then she said: 'Well, the only trouble with all this is that it isn't poetry.' " She found his images false; did not think much of his attempt to write in the Surreal manner, "without conscious intervention." Later, she asked him if he had rewritten the poems. When he said no, "She was triumphant. 'You see,' she cried. 'I told you you were no poet. A real poet, after one conversation, would have gone upstairs and at least tried to recast them, but you haven't even looked at them.' " Bowles stopped writing. He turned to music.

Between 1929 and 1945 he made a name as a composer. He married the odd, brilliant Jane Bowles. She was a writer. He was a composer. Together and separately, they were much admired. During the late thirties and forties they became central figures in the transatlantic (and Pan-American) world of the arts. Although unknown to the general public, the Bowleses were famous among those who were famous; and in some mysterious way the art grandees wanted, if not the admiration of the Bowleses (seldom bestowed), their tolerance.

They lived in Mexico (the unknown Tennessee Williams made a pilgrimage to their house in Acapulco); they lived in New York, sharing a house with W. H. Auden and Benjamin Britten. After the Second War they moved for good to Tangier where Paul Bowles still lives. Jane Bowles died in Spain in 1973.

In the spring of 1945, Charles Henri Ford asked Bowles to edit an issue of the magazine *View*. The subject was Central and South American culture. Bowles translated a number of Spanish writers; and wrote some texts of his own. In the course of "reading some ethnographic books with texts from the Arapesh or from the Tarahumara given in word-for-word translation . . . the desire came to me to invent my own myths, adopting the point of view of the primitive mind." He resorted to "the old Surrealist method of abandoning conscious control and writing whatever words came from the pen." The first of these stories was written "one rainy Sunday"; it is called "The Scorpion."

The story was well received, and Bowles went on writing. "The subject matter of the myths soon turned from 'primitive' to contemporary. . . . It was through this unexpected little gate that I crept back into the land of fiction writing. Long ago I had decided that the world was too complex for me ever to be able to write fiction; since I failed to understand life, I would not be able to find points of reference which the hypothetical reader might have in common with me." He did not entirely proceed through that small gate until he wrote "A Distant Episode" and found that if life was no more understandable to him than before, prose was. He now possessed the art to depict his dreams.

During the next thirty years Paul Bowles wrote thirty-nine short stories. They were published originally in three volumes: *The Delicate Prey*, 1950; *The Time of Friendship*, 1967; *Things Gone and Things Still Here*, 1977. Even before the first collection was published, three of the stories caused a great stir in the literary world. "Pages from Cold Point," "The Delicate Prey," and "A Distant Episode" were immediately recognized as being unlike anything else in our literature. I have just reread the three stories, with some nervousness. After all these years, I wondered if they would still "work." In my youth I had admired D. H. Lawrence's novels. Now, I deeply dislike them. I was relieved to find that Bowles's art is still as disturbing as ever. I was surprised to note how the actual stories differ from my memory of them. I recalled a graphic description of a sixteen-year-old boy's seduction of his father on a hot summer night in Jamaica. Over the years, carnal details had built up in my memory like a coral reef. Yet on rereading "Pages from Cold Point," nothing (and everything) happens. In his memoirs Bowles refers, rather casually, to this story as something he wrote aboard ship from New York to Casablanca: "a long story about a hedonist . . ." It is a good deal more than that. Both "The Delicate Prey" and "A Distant Episode" create the same sense of strangeness and terror that they did the first time I read them. "The Delicate Prey" turns on a Gidean *acte gratuit*: The slicing off of the boy's penis is not only like the incident on the train in *Les Caves du Vatican* but also presages the driving of a nail through a skull in Bowles's novel *Let It Come Down.* "A Distant Episode" seems to me to be more than ever emblematic of the helplessness of an overcivilized sensibility (the professor's) when confronted with an alien culture. Captured by North African nomads, his tongue cut out, he is made into a clown, a toy. He is used to make his captors laugh. He *appears* to accept his fate. Something harsh is glimpsed in the lines of a story that is now plainer in its reverberations than it was when written. But then it is no longer news to anyone that the floor to this ramshackle civilization that we have built cannot bear much longer our weight. It was Bowles's genius to suggest the horrors which lie beneath that floor, as fragile, in its way, as the sky that shelters us from a devouring vastness.

The stories fall into rough categories. First: locale. Mexico and North Africa are the principal settings. Landscape is all-important in a Bowles story. Second: how the inhabitants of alien cultures regard the creatures of our civilized world, as in "Under the Sky." Bowles goes even further in a beautiful story called "The Circular Valley" where human life is depicted as it must appear to the anima of a place. This spirit inhabits at will those human beings who visit its valley; feeds on their emotions; alters them during its occupancy. Third: the stories of transference. In "You Are Not I" a madwoman becomes her sane sister. In "Allal," a boy exchanges personality with a snake. The intensity of these stories makes them more like waking dreams than so many words on a page. Identity is transferred in such a way that one wonders which, finally, is which? and what is what? The effect is rather like the Taoist story of the man who dreamed that he was a butterfly. When "he woke up with a start, he did not know whether he was Chuang Chou who had dreamed that he was a butterfly, or whether he was a butterfly dreaming that he was Chuang Chou. Between Chuang Chou and the butterfly there must be some distinction. This is what is called the transformation of things."

There are a number of more or less realistic stories that deal with the plain incomprehension of Americans in contact with the natives of Mexico, North Africa, Thailand. One of the most amusing is "You Have Left Your Lotus Pods on the Bus." An American goes on an excursion with some Buddhist priests. The day is filled with splendid misunderstandings. There is the man at the back of a crowded bus who never stops screaming. He is ignored by everyone except the American who wonders why no one shuts him up. At the end, the priests tell him that the "madman" is an employee of the bus company giving necessary warnings and advice to the driver.

In several stories white ladies respond not-so-ambiguously to dark-skinned youths. Bowles notes the sadism that sexual frustration can cause ("At Paso Rojo"). But where the ordinary writer would leave it at that Bowles goes deeper into the human case and, paradoxically, he achieves his greatest effects when he concentrates entirely on surfaces. Although he seldom describes a human face, he examines landscape with the precision of a geologist. Bowles himself seems like one of those bright sharp-eyed birds that flit from story to story, staring with eyes that do not blink at desert, hills, sky. He records weather with all the solemnity of a meteorologist. He looks closely at food. As for his human characters, he simply lets them reveal themselves through what they say or do not say. Finally, he is a master of suggesting anxiety (Are all the traveler's checks lost or just mislaid?) and dread (Will this desert prove to be the setting for a very special death?). Story after story turns on flight. It is no accident that Bowles called his memoir (with pride?) *Without Stopping.*

Four stories were written to demonstrate that by using "kif-inspired motivations, the arbitrary would be made to seem natural, the diverse elements could be fused, and several people would automatically become one." These pieces strike me as entirely uninhabited, and of no interest. Yet in other stories (inspired perhaps by smaller doses of kif) he does demonstrate the essential oneness of the many as well as the interchangeability not only of personality but of all things. As Webster saw the skull beneath the skin, so Bowles has glimpsed what lies back of our sheltering sky . . . an endless flux of stars so like those atoms which make us up that in our apprehension of this terrible infinity, we experience not only horror but likeness.

Introduction to *Collected Stories of Paul Bowles*
(Santa Rosa, California: Black Sparrow Press, 1983)

# 42

---
◆
---

## TENNESSEE WILLIAMS: SOMEONE TO LAUGH AT THE SQUARES WITH

I

Although poetry is no longer much read by anyone in freedom's land, biographies of those American poets who took terrible risks not only with their talents but with their lives, are often quite popular; and testimonies, chockablock with pity, terror and awe, provide the unread poet, if not his poetry, with a degree of posthumous fame. Ever since Hart ("Man overboard!") Crane dove into the Caribbean and all our hearts, the most ambitious of our poets have often gone the suicide route:

There was an unnatural stillness in the kitchen which made her heart skip a beat then she saw Marvin, huddled in front of the oven; then she screamed: the head of the "finest sestina-operator of the Seventies" [*Hudson Review,* Spring 1970] had been burned to a crisp.

If nothing else, suicide really *validates,* to use lit-crit's ultimate verb, the life if not the poetry; and so sly Marvin was able to die secure in the knowledge that his emblematic life would be written about and that readers who would not have been caught dead, as it were, with the work of the finest sestina-operator of the seventies will now fall, like so many hyenas, on the bio-bared bones of that long agony his life: high school valetudinarian. Columbia. The master's degree, written with heart's blood (on Rimbaud in *transition*). The awakening at Bread Loaf, and the stormy marriage to Linda. Precocious—and prescient—meteoric success of "On First Looking Into Delmore Schwartz's Medicine Cabinet" (*Prairie Schooner,* 1961). The drinking. The children. The pills. Pulitzer lost; Pulitzer regained. Seminal meeting with Roethke at the University of Iowa in an all-night diner. What conversation! Oh, they were titans then. But—born with one skin too few. All nerves; jangled sensibility. Lithium's failure is Lethe's opportunity. Genius-magma too radioactive for leaden human brain to hold. Oh! mounting horror as, one by one, the finest minds of a generation snuff themselves out in ovens, plastic bags, the odd river. Death and then—triumphant transfiguration as A Cautionary Tale.

By and large, American novelists and playwrights have not had to kill themselves in order to be noticed: There are still voluntary readers and restless playgoers out there. But since so many American writers gradually drink themselves to death (as do realtors, jockeys, and former officers of the Junior League), these sodden buffaloes are now attracting the sort of Cautionary Tale-spinner that usually keens over suicide-poets. Although the writer as actor in his time is nothing new, and the writer as performing self has been examined by Richard Poirier as a phenomenon ancillary to writer's writing, for the first time the self now threatens to become the sole artifact—to be written about by others who tend to erase, in the process, whatever writing the writer may have written.

Scott Fitzgerald, that most self-conscious of writers, made others conscious of himself and his crack-up through the pages known as *The Crack-Up.* Ever since then, American journalists and academics have used him as our paradigmatic Cautionary Tale on the ground that if you are young, handsome, talented, successful, and married to a beautiful woman, you will be destroyed because your life will be absolutely unbearable to those who teach and are taught. If, by some accident of fate, you are *not* destroyed, you will have a highly distressing old age like Somerset Maugham's, which we will describe in all its gamy incontinent horror. There is no winning, obviously. But then the Greeks knew that. And the rest is—Bruccoli. Today the writer need not write his life. Others will do it for him. But he must provide them with material; and a gaudy descent into drink, drugs, sex, and terminal name-dropping.

As Tennessee Williams's powers failed (drink/drugs/age), he turned himself into a circus. If people would not go to his new plays, he would see to it that they would be able to look at him on television and read about him in the press. He lived a most glamorous crack-up; and now that he is dead, a thousand Cautionary Tales are humming along the electrical circuits of a thousand word processors en route to the electrical circuits of thousands upon thousands of brains already overloaded with tales of celebrity-suffering, the ultimate consolation—and justification—to those who didn't make it or, worse, didn't even try.

In 1976, I reviewed Tennessee Williams's *Memoirs.* We had been friends from the late forties to the early sixties; after that, we saw very little of each other (drink/drugs), but I never ceased to be fond of what I called the Glorious Bird. Readers of my review, who have waited, I hope patiently, to find out Tennessee's reaction should know that when next we met, he narrowed his cloudy blue eyes and said, in tones that one of these biographers would call "clipped," "When your review appeared my book was number five on the nonfiction best-seller list of *The New York Times.* Within two weeks of your review, *it was not listed at all.*"

I last saw him three or four years ago. We were together on a televised Chicago talk show. He was in good form, despite a papilla on the bridge of his nose, the first sign, ever, of that sturdy rubbery body's resentment of alcohol. There were two or three other guests around a table, and the host. Abruptly, the Bird settled back in his chair and shut his eyes. The host's habitual unease became panic. After some disjointed general chat, he said, tentatively, "Tennessee, are you asleep?" And the Bird replied, eyes still shut, "No, I am not asleep but sometimes I shut my eyes when I am bored."

Two testimonials to the passion and the agony of the life of Tennessee Williams have just been published. One is a straightforward biography of the sort known as journeyman; it is called *The Kindness of Strangers* (what else?) by Donald Spoto. The other is *Tennessee: Cry of the Heart* (whose heart?) by a male sob sister who works for *Parade* magazine.

The first book means to shock and titillate in a *responsible* way (drink, drugs, "wildly promiscuous sex"); that is, the author tries, not always successfully, to get the facts if not the life straight. The second is a self-serving memoir with a Capotean approach to reality. In fact, I suspect that Crier of the Heart may indeed be the avatar of the late Caravaggio of gossip. If so, he has now taken up the fallen leper's bell, and we need not ask ever for whom it tolls.

Crier tells us that he lived with Williams, from time to time, in the seventies. He tells us that Williams got him on the needle for two years, but that he bears him no grudge. In turn, he "radicalized" Williams during the Vietnam years. Each, we are told, really and truly hated the rich. Yet, confusingly, Crier is celebrated principally for his friendships with not one (1) but two (2) presidential sisters, Pat Kennedy Lawford and the late Ruth Carter Stapleton. He is also very much at home in counterrevolutionary circles: "A year before Tennessee died, I visited Mrs. Reagan at the White House and we had a long conversation alone in the Green Room after lunch. She asked about Tennessee, and Truman Capote, among others . . ." Oh, to have been a fly on that Green wall! But then when it comes to the rich and famous, Crier's style alternates between frantic to tell us the very worst and vatic as he cries up what to him is plainly the only game on earth or in heaven, Celebrity, as performed by consenting adults in Manhattan.

Since most of Crier's references to me are wrong, I can only assume that most of the references to others are equally untrue. But then words like *true* and *false* are irrelevant to this sort of venture. It is the awful plangency of the Cry that matters, and this one's a real hoot, as they used to say on the Bird Circuit.

On the other hand, responsible Mr. Spoto begins at the beginning, and I found interesting the school days, endlessly protracted, of Thomas Lanier Williams (he did not use the name Tennessee until he was twenty-eight). The first twenty years of Williams's life provided him with the characters that he would write about. There is his sister, Rose, two years older than he, who moved from eccentricity to madness. There is the mother, Edwina, who gave the order for Rose's lobotomy, on the best medical advice, or so she says; for Rose may or may not have accused the hard-drinking father, Cornelius, at war with sissy son, Tom, and relentlessly genteel wife, of making sexual advances to her, which he may or may not have made. In any case, Tom never ceased to love Rose, despite the blotting out of her personality. Finally, there was the maternal grandfather, the Reverend Dakin; and the grandmother, another beloved Rose, known as Grand.

In 1928, the Reverend Dakin took the seventeen-year-old Williams to Europe. Grandson was grateful to grandfather to the end, which did not come until 1955. Many years earlier, the reverend gave his life savings to unkind strangers for reasons never made clear. The Bird told me that he thought that his grandfather had been blackmailed because of an encounter with a boy. Later, the reverend burned all his sermons on the lawn. In time, Tennessee's sympathies shifted from his enervating mother to his now entirely absent father. These are the cards that life dealt Williams; and he played them for the rest of his life. He took on no new characters, as opposed to male lovers, who tend either to appear in his work as phantoms or as youthful versions of the crude father, impersonated, much too excitingly, by Marlon Brando.

A great deal has been made of Williams's homosexual adventures; not least, alas, by himself. Since those who write about him are usually more confused about human sexuality than he was, which is saying a lot, some instruction is now in order.

Williams was born, 1911, in the heart of the Bible belt (Columbus, Mississippi); he was brought up in St. Louis, Missouri, a town more southern than not. In 1919, God-fearing Protestants imposed Prohibition on the entire United States. Needless to say, in this world of fierce Christian peasant values anything pleasurable was automatically sin and to be condemned. Williams may not have believed in God but he certainly believed in sin; he came to sex nervously and relatively late—in his twenties; his first experiences were heterosexual; then he shifted to homosexual relations with numerous people over many years. Although he never doubted that what he liked to do was entirely natural, he was obliged to tote the usual amount of guilt of a man of his time and place and class (lower-middle-class WASP, southern-airs-and-graces division). In the end, he suffered from a sense of otherness, not unuseful for a writer.

But the guilt took a not-so-useful turn: He became a lifelong hypochondriac, wasting a great deal of psychic energy on imaginary illnesses. He was always about to die of some dread inoperable tumor. When I first met him (1948), he was just out of a Paris hospital, and he spoke with somber joy of the pancreatic cancer that would soon cause him to fall from the perch. Years later I discovered that the pancreatic cancer for which he had been hospitalized was nothing more than a half-mile or so of homely tapeworm. When he died (not of "an unwashed grape" but of suffocation caused by the inhaling of a nasal-spray top), an autopsy was performed and the famous heart ("I have suffered a series of cardiac seizures and arrests since my twelfth year") was found to be in fine condition, and the liver that of a hero.

Just as Williams never really added to his basic repertory company of actors (Cornelius and Edwina, Reverend Dakin and Rose, himself and Rose), he never picked up much information about the world during his half-century as an adult. He also never tried, consciously at least, to make sense of the society into which he was born. If he had, he might have figured out that there is no such thing as a homosexual or a heterosexual person. There are only homo- or heterosexual acts. Most people are a mixture of impulses if not practices, and what anyone does with a willing partner is of no social or cosmic significance.

So why all the fuss? In order for a ruling class to rule, there must be arbitrary prohibitions. Of all prohibitions, sexual taboo is the most useful because sex involves everyone. To be able to lock up someone or deprive him of employment because of his sex life is a very great power indeed, and one seldom used in civilized societies. But although the United States is the best and most perfect of earth's societies and our huddled masses earth's envy, we have yet to create a civilization, as opposed to a way of life. That is why we have allowed our governors to divide the population into two teams. One team is good, godly, straight; the other is evil, sick, vicious. Like the good team's sectarian press, Williams believed, until the end of his life, in this wacky division. He even went to an analyst who ordered him to give up both writing and sex so that he could be transformed into a good-team player. Happily, the analyst did not do in the Bird's beak, as Freud's buddy Fliess ruined the nose of a young lady, on the ground that only through breaking the nose could onanism be stopped in its vile track. Also, happily, the Bird's anarchy triumphed over the analyst. After a troubling session on the couch, he would appear on television and tell Mike Wallace all about the problems of his analysis with one Dr. Kubie, who not long after took down his shingle and retired from shrinkage.

Both *The Glass Menagerie* and *A Streetcar Named Desire* opened during that brief golden age (1945–1950) when the United States was everywhere not only regnant but at peace, something we have not been for the last thirty-five years. At the beginning, Williams was acclaimed by pretty much everyone; only *Time* magazine was consistently hostile, suspecting that Williams might be "basically negative" and "sterile," code words of the day for fag. More to the point, *Time*'s founder, Henry Luce, had been born in China, son of a Christian missionary. "The greatest task of the United States in the twentieth century," he once told me, "will be the Christianization of China." With so mad a proprietor, it is no wonder that Time-Life should have led the press crusade against fags in general and Williams in particular.

Although Williams was able to survive as a playwright because he was supported by the drama reviewers of *The New York Times* and *Herald Tribune,* the only two newspapers that mattered for a play's success, he was to take a lot of flak over the years. After so much good-team propaganda, it is now widely believed that since Tennessee Williams liked to have sex with men (true), he hated women (untrue); as a result, his women characters are thought to be malicious caricatures, designed to subvert and destroy godly straightness.

But there is no actress on earth who will not testify that Williams created the best women characters in the modern theater. After all, he never ceased to love Rose and Rose, and his women characters tended to be either one or the other. Faced with contrary evidence, the anti-fag brigade promptly switch to their fallback position. All right, so he didn't hate women (as real guys do—the ball-breakers!) but, worse, far worse, *he thought he was a woman.* Needless to say, a biblical hatred of women intertwines with the good team's hatred of fags. But Williams never thought of himself as anything but a man who could, as an artist, inhabit any gender; on the other hand, his sympathies were always with those defeated by "the squares"; or by time, once the sweet bird of youth is flown. Or by death, "which has never been much in the way of completion."

Finally, in sexual matters (the principal interest of the two Cautionary Tales at hand), there seems to be a double standard at work. Although the heterosexual promiscuity of Pepys, Boswell, Byron, Henry Miller, and President Kennedy has never *deeply* upset any of their fans, Williams's ("feverish") promiscuity quite horrifies Mr. Spoto, and even Crier from the Heart tends to sniffle at all those interchangeable pieces of trade. But Williams had a great deal of creative and sexual energy; and he used both. Why not? And so what?

Heart's Crier describes how I took Williams to meet another sexual athlete (good-team, natch), Senator John F. Kennedy. Crier quotes the Bird, who is speaking to Mrs. Pat Lawford, Kennedy's sister and Crier's current friend: "Gore said he was invited to a lunch by Mr. Kennedy and would I like to come along? Of course I did, since I greatly admired your brother. He brought such vitality to our country's life, such hope and great style. He made thinking fashionable again." Actually, the Bird had never heard of Kennedy that day in 1958 when we drove from Miami to Palm Beach for lunch with the golden couple, who had told me that they lusted to meet the Bird. He, in turn, was charmed by them.

"Now tell me again," he would ask Jack, repeatedly, "what you are. A governor or a senator?" Each time, Jack, dutifully, gave name, rank, and party. Then the Bird would sternly quiz him on America's China policy, and Jack would look a bit glum. Finally, he proposed that we shoot at a target in the patio.

While Jackie flitted about, taking Polaroid shots of us, the Bird banged away at the target; and proved to be a better shot than our host. At one point, while Jack was shooting, the Bird muttered in my ear, "Get that ass!" I said, "Bird, you can't cruise our next president." The Bird chuckled ominously: "They'll never elect those two. They are much too attractive for the American people." Later, I told Jack that the Bird had commented favorably on his ass. He beamed. "Now, that's *very* exciting," he said. But, fun and games to one side, it is, of course, tragic that both men were, essentially, immature sexually and so incapable of truly warm *mature* human relations. One could weep for what might have been.

Crier from the Heart has lots and lots of scores to settle in the course of his lament and he brings us bad news about all sorts of famous people who may have offended him. Certainly, he wears if not his heart his spleen on his sleeve. Mary Hemingway confessed to him that she and her husband Ernest were "never lovers. Mr. Hemingway was beyond that by then." Bet you didn't know that! As for the rich whom he and Tennessee so radically hate, they are finally incarnated not by the Rockefellers or by the Mellons but by a couple of hard-working overachievers called De la Renta, whose joint fortune must be a small fraction of the Bird's. To be fair, Crier has his compassionate side. A piece of trade had no money, and Tennessee was passed out. So Crier took the Bird's checkbook and "wrote out a check for six hundred dollars made out to cash, and took it downstairs to the hotel desk and had it cashed. I went back upstairs, handed Chris the money, and kissed him goodbye.

"It was the only time I ever forged Tennessee's name to a check, and I do not regret it." For such heroic continence, *canaille oblige.*

### 2

Thirty-seven years ago, in March 1948, Tennessee Williams and I celebrated his thirty-seventh birthday in Rome, except that he said that it was his thirty-*fourth* birthday. Years later, when confronted with the fact that he had been born in 1911 not 1914, he said, serenely, "I do not choose to count as part of my life the three years that I spent working for a shoe company." Actually, he spent ten months, not three years, in the shoe company, and the reason that he had changed his birth date was to qualify for a play contest open to those twenty-five or under. No matter. I thought him very old in 1948. But I was twenty-two in the spring of *annus mirabilis* when my novel *The City and the Pillar* was a best seller (Mr. Spoto thinks the book was published later) and his play, *A Streetcar Named Desire,* was taking the world by storm, as it still does.

I must say I was somewhat awed by Tennessee's success. Of course, he went on and on about the years of poverty but, starting with *The Glass Menagerie* (1944), he had an astonishingly productive and successful fifteen years: *Summer and Smoke* (1947), *The Rose Tattoo* (1951), *Cat on a Hot Tin Roof* (1955), *Suddenly Last Summer* (1958), *Sweet Bird of Youth* (1959). But even at that high moment in Rome, the Bird's eye was coldly realistic. "Baby, the playwright's working career is a short one. There's always somebody new to take your place." I said that I didn't believe it would happen in his case, and I still don't. The best of his plays are as permanent as anything can be in the age of Kleenex.

All his life, Tennessee wrote short stories. I have just finished reading the lot of them, some forty-six stories. The first was written when Tom was seventeen—a sister avenges her brother in lush prose in even lusher Pharaonic Egypt ("The Vengeance of Nitocris")—and published in *Weird Tales.* The last is unpublished. "The Negative" was written when Tennessee was seventy-one; he deals, as he so often came to do, with a poet, losing his mind, art; at the end, "as he ran toward this hugely tolerant receiver, he scattered from his gentleman's clothes, from their pockets, the illegibly scribbled poetry of his life."

To my mind, the short stories, and not *Memoirs,* are the true memoir of Tennessee Williams. Whatever happened to him, real or imagined, he turned into prose. Except for occasional excursions into fantasy, he sticks pretty close to life as he experienced or imagined it. No, he is not a great short-story writer like Chekhov but he has something rather more rare than mere genius. He has a narrative tone of voice that is wholly convincing. In this, he resembles Mark Twain, a very different sort of writer (to overdo understatement); yet Hannibal, Missouri, is not all that far from St. Louis, Missouri. Each is best at comedy and each was always uneasy when not so innocently abroad. Tennessee loved to sprinkle foreign phrases throughout his work, and they are *always* wrong.

·  ·  ·

Tennessee worked every morning on whatever was at hand. If there was no play to be finished or new dialogue to be sent round to the theater, he would open a drawer and take out the draft of a story already written and begin to rewrite it. I once found him revising a short story that had just been published. "Why," I asked, "rewrite what's already in print?" He looked at me, vaguely; then he said, "Well, obviously it's not finished." And went back to his typing.

In Paris, he gave me the story "Rubio y Morena" to read. I didn't like it. So fix it, he said. He knew, of course, that there is no fixing someone else's story (or life) but he was curious to see what I would do. So I reversed backward-running sentences, removed repetitions, eliminated half those adjectives and adverbs that he always insisted do their work in pairs. I was proud of the result. He was deeply irritated. "What you have done is remove my *style,* which is all that I have."

Tennessee could not possess his own life until he had written about it. This is common. To start with, there would be, let us say, a sexual desire for someone. Consummated or not, the desire ("something that is made to occupy a larger space than that which is afforded by the individual being") would produce reveries. In turn, the reveries would be written down as a story. But should the desire still remain unfulfilled, he would make a play of the story and then—and this is why he was so compulsive a working playwright—he would have the play produced so that he could, at relative leisure, like God, rearrange his original experience into something that was no longer God's and unpossessable but *his.* The Bird's frantic lifelong pursuit of—and involvement in— play productions was not just ambition or a need to be busy; it was the only way that he ever had of being entirely alive. The sandy encounters with his first real love, a dancer, on the beach at Provincetown and the dancer's later death ("an awful flower grew in his brain") instead of being forever lost were forever his once they had been translated to the stage where living men and women could act out his text and with their immediate flesh close at last the circle of desire. "For love I make characters in plays," he wrote; and did.

I had long since forgotten why I called him the Glorious Bird until I reread the stories. The image of the bird is everywhere in his work. The bird is flight, poetry, life. The bird is time, death: "Have you ever seen the skeleton of a bird? If you have you will know how completely they are still flying." In "The Negative" he wrote of a poet who can no longer assemble a poem. "Am I a wingless bird?" he writes; and soars no longer.

Although the Bird accepted our "culture's" two-team theory, he never seriously wanted to play on the good team, as poor Dr. Kubie discovered on prime-time television. He went right on having sex; he also went right on hating the "squares" or, as he put it, in the story "Two on a Party" (1954), where Billy (in life the poet Oliver Evans) and Cora (Marion Black Vaccaro) cruise sailors together:

It was a rare sort of moral anarchy, doubtless, that held them together, a really fearful shared hatred of everything that was restrictive and which they felt to be false in the society they lived in and against the grain of which they continually operated. They did not dislike what they called "squares." They loathed and despised them, and for the best of reasons. Their existence was a never-ending contest with the squares of the world, the squares who have such a virulent rage at everything not in their book.

The squares had indeed victimized the Bird but by 1965, when he came to write *The Knightly Quest,* he had begun to see that the poor squares' "virulent rage" is deliberately whipped up by the rulers in order to distract them from such real problems as, in the sixties, the Vietnam War and Watergate and Operation Armageddon then—and now—under way. In this story, Tennessee moves Lyndon Johnson's America into a near future where the world is about to vanish in a shining cloud; and he realizes, at last, that the squares have been every bit as damaged and manipulated as he; and so he now writes an elegy to the true American, Don Quixote, an exile in his own country: "His castles are immaterial and his ways are endless and you do not have to look into many American eyes to suddenly meet somewhere the beautiful grave lunacy of his gaze." Also, Tennessee seems to be trying to bring into focus the outlandish craziness of a society which had so wounded him. Was it possible that he was not the evil creature portrayed by the press? Was it possible that they are wrong about *everything*? A light bulb switches on: "All of which makes me suspect that back of the sun and way deep under our feet, at the earth's center, are not a couple of noble mysteries but a couple of joke books." Right on, Bird! It was a nice coincidence that just as Tennessee was going around the bend (drink, drugs, and a trip to the bin in 1969) the United States was doing the same. Suddenly, the Bird and Uncle Sam met face to face in *The Knightly Quest.* Better too late than never. Anyway, he was, finally, beginning to put the puzzle together.

"I cannot write any sort of story," said Tennessee to me, "unless there is at least one character in it for whom I have physical desire."

In story after story there are handsome young men, some uncouth like Stanley Kowalski; some couth like the violinist in "The Resemblance Between a Violin Case and a Coffin." Then, when Tennessee produced *A Streetcar Named Desire,* he inadvertently smashed one of our society's most powerful taboos (no wonder Henry Luce loathed him): He showed the male not only as sexually attractive in the flesh but as an object for something never before entirely acknowledged by the good team, the lust of women. In the age of Calvin Klein's steaming hunks, it must be hard for those under forty to realize that there was ever a time when a man was nothing but a suit of clothes, a shirt and tie, shined leather shoes, and a gray, felt hat. If he was thought attractive, it was because he had a nice smile and a twinkle in his eye. In 1947, when Marlon Brando appeared on stage in a torn sweaty T-shirt, there was an earthquake; and the male as sex object is still at our culture's center stage and will so remain until the likes of Boy George redress, as it were, the balance. Yet, ironically, Tennessee's auctorial sympathies were not with Stanley but with his "victim" Blanche.

I have never known anyone to complain as much as the Bird. If he was not dying of some new mysterious illness, he was in mourning for a dead lover, usually discarded long before the cancerous death, or he was suffering from the combination of various cabals, real and imagined, that were out to get him. Toward the end, he had personified the ringleaders. They were a Mr. and Mrs. Gelb, who worked for *The New York Times.* Because they had written a book about Eugene O'Neill, the Bird was convinced that the Gelbs were using the *Times* in order to destroy him so that they could sell more copies of their book about O'Neill, who would then be America's *numero uno* dramatist. Among Crier's numerous errors and inventions is the Eugene O'Neill letter, "the only one he ever wrote to Tennessee," who "read it to me, first explaining that he had received it after the opening of *The Glass Menagerie. . . .* It was a very moving and a very sad letter, and I don't know what became of it." The letter was written not after *Menagerie* but *Streetcar,* and Tennessee never read it to Crier or to anyone else because neither Tennessee nor I, in Rome 1948, could make head or tail of it. O'Neill was suffering from Parkinson's disease; the handwriting was illegible. The Bird and I had a running gag over the years that would begin, "As Eugene O'Neill wrote you . . ." Except for O'Neill, the Bird's sharp eye saw no dangerous competition. Once, at a function, where the guests were asked to line up alphabetically, Thornton Wilder approached the Bird and said, "I believe Wilder comes before Williams." To which the Bird responded, *"Only* in the alphabet."

I did not see much of him in the last years. I don't recall when he got into the habit of taking barbiturates (later, speed; and worse). He certainly did his mind and body no good; but he was tough as they come, mind and body. The current chroniclers naturally emphasize the horrors of the last years because the genre requires that they produce A Cautionary Tale. Also, since the last years are the closest to us, they give us no sense at all of what he was like for most of his long life. Obviously, he wasn't drunk or drugged all that much because he lived to write; and he wrote, like no one else.

I remember him best one noon in Key West during the early fifties (exact date can be determined because on every jukebox "Tennessee Waltz" was being mournfully sung by Patti Page). Each of us had finished work for the day. We met on South Beach, a real beach then. We made our way through sailors on the sand to a terraced restaurant where the Bird sat back in a chair, put his bare feet up on a railing, looked out at the bright blue sea, and, as he drank his first and only martini of the midday, said, with a great smile, "I like my life."

*The New York Review of Books*
June 13, 1985

# 43
· 

# *THE DEATH OF MISHIMA*

A white silky beach just south of Madras. Blue sea full of sharks, blue sky full of clouds like egret plumes. Nearby, half in the water, half on the beach, the gray-violet pyramid of a Hindu temple gradually dissolving as the sea with each century rises. In the foreground, the body of a man, headless, armless, with only one leg whose flesh stops at the knee. Below the knee, a bright beautiful white bone around which a rope has been knotted. The angle of the bone indicates that the man's legs and arms had been tied together behind him. Coolly, I become coroner. Speculate sagely on the length of time the man has been dead. Draw my companions' attention to the fact that there is not a drop of blood left in the body: at first glance we thought it a scarecrow, a bundle of white and gray rags—then saw real muscles laid bare, ropy integuments, the shin bone, and knew someone had been murdered, thrown into the sea alive. But who? And why? Definitely not Chinese, I decide (not only am I at heart a coroner—redundancy—but I am also a geographer of Strabo's school).

I am interrupted by the arrival of a small Tamil girl resembling the late Fanny Brice. She glares at the corpse. "Not nice, not nice at all!" She shakes her head disapprovingly, hopes we won't get a wrong impression of India. As we do our best to reassure her, we are joined by a friend with a newspaper: Yukio Mishima has committed *seppuku* (the proper word for hara-kiri) in the office of Japan's commanding general, his head was then hacked from his body by an aide. . . . We read the bloody details with wonder. Such is the power of writing (to those addicted to reading) that the actual corpse at our feet became less real than the vivid idea of the bodyless head of Mishima, a man my exact contemporary, whose career in so many ways resembled my own, though not to the degree that certain writers of bookchat in the fifties thought.

Tokyo. Unbeautiful but alive and monstrously, cancerously growing, just as New York City—quite as unbeautiful—is visibly dying, its rot a way of life. That will be Tokyo's future, too, but for the moment the mood is one of boom. Official and mercantile circles are euphoric. Elsewhere, unease.

I meet with a leader of the Left currently giving aid to those GIs who find immoral their country's murder of Asiatics. He is not sanguine about Japan. "We don't know who we are since the war. The break with the old culture has left us adrift. Yet we are still a family."

The first thing the traveler in Japan notices is that the people resemble each other, with obvious variations, much the way members of a family do, and this sense of a common identity was the source of their power in the past: all children of an emperor who was child of the sun. But the sun no longer rises for Japan—earth turns, in fact—and the head of the family putters about collecting marine specimens while his children are bored with their new prosperity, their ugly cities, their half-Western, half-Japanese culture, their small polluted islands.

I ask the usual question: what do the Japanese think of the Americans? The answer is brisk. "Very little. Not like before. I was just reading an old Osaka newspaper. Fifty years ago a girl writes that her life ambition is to meet a Caucasian, an American, and become his mistress. All very respectable. But now there is a certain . . . disdain for the Americans. Of course Vietnam is part of it." One is soon made aware in Tokyo of the Japanese contempt not only for the American imperium but for its cultural artifacts. Though not a zealous defender of my country, I find goading its Tokyo detractors irresistible, at least in literary matters. After all, for some decades now, Japan's most popular (and deeply admired) writer has been W. Somerset Maugham.

We spoke of Mishima's death and the possibility of a return to militarism. Two things which were regarded as one by the world press. But my informant saw no political motive in Mishima's death. "It was a personal gesture. A dramatic gesture. The sort of thing *he* would do.

You know he had a private army. Always marching around in uniform. Quite mad. Certainly he had no serious political connections with the right wing."

Mishima's suicide had a shattering effect on the entire Japanese family. For one thing, he was a famous writer. This meant he was taken a good deal more seriously by the nation (family) than any American writer is ever taken by those warring ethnic clans whose mutual detestation is the essential fact of the American way of life. Imagine Paul Goodman's suicide in General Westmoreland's office as reported by *The New York Times* on page 22. "Paul Goodman, writer, aged 59, shot himself in General Westmoreland's office as a protest to American foreign policy. At first, General Westmoreland could not be reached for comment. Later in the day, an aide said that the General, naturally, regretted Mr. Goodman's action, which was based upon a 'patent misunderstanding of America's role in Asia.' Mr. Goodman was the author of a number of books and articles. One of his books was called *Growing Up Absurd*. He is survived by . . ." An indifferent polity.

But Mishima at forty-five was Japan's apparent master of all letters, superb jack of none. Or in the prose of a Knopf blurb writer,

He began his brilliantly successful career in 1944 by winning a citation from the Emperor as the highest-ranking honor student at graduation from the Peers' School. In 1947 he was graduated from Tokyo Imperial University School of Jurisprudence. Since his first novel was published, in 1948, he has produced a baker's dozen of novels, translations of which have by now appeared in fifteen countries; seventy-four short stories; a travel book; and many articles, including two in English (appearing in *Life* and *Holiday*). About ten films were made from his novels. *The Sound of Waves* (1956) was filmed twice, and one of Ishikawa's masterpieces, *Enjo,* was based on *The Temple of the Golden Pavillion* (1959). Also available in English are the novels *After the Banquet* (1963) and *The Sailor Who Fell from Grace with the Sea* (1965), and *Five Modern Nō Plays* (1957).
He has acted the title role in a gangster film, and American television audiences have seen him on "The Twentieth Century" and on Edward R. Murrow's "Small World." Despite a relentless work schedule, Mr. Mishima has managed to travel widely in the United States and Europe. His home is in Tokyo, with his wife and two children.

The range, variety, and publicness of the career sound ominously familiar to me. Also each of us might be said by those innocent of literature to have been influenced (as a certain "news" magazine gaily

wrote of Mishima) "by Proust and Gide." The fact that Proust and Gide
resembled one another not at all (or either of us) is irrelevant to the
"news" magazine's familiar purpose—the ever-popular sexual smear
job which has so long made atrocious the American scene.

The American press, by and large, played up two aspects of the
suicide: Mishima's homosexuality and his last confused harangue to
the troops, demanding a return to militarism and ancient virtue. The
Japanese reaction was more knowledgeable and various than the
American. It was also occasionally dotty. Professor Yozo Horigome of
Tokyo University found "a striking resemblance" between Mishima's
suicide and the death of Thomas à Becket, as reported by T. S. Eliot!
Apparently the good professor had been working up some notes on
Eliot and so absorbed was he in his task that any self-willed death
smacked of high jinks at Canterbury Cathedral. Taruho Inagaki
thought that by extraverting his narcissism, Mishima could not continue as writer or man. Inagaki also observed, somewhat mysteriously,
that since Mishima lacked "nostalgia," his later work tended to be
artificial and unsatisfactory.

Professor Taku Yamada of Kanazawa University compared Mishima's suicide to that of an early nineteenth-century rebel against the
Shogunate—a virtuous youth who had been influenced (like Mishima)
by the fifteenth-century Chinese scholar Wang Yang-ming, who believed that "to know and to act are one and the same." The Japanese,
the professor noted, in adapting this philosophy to their own needs,
simplified it into a sort of death cult with the caveat "one is not afraid
of the death of body, but fears the death of mind." Yamada seems to
me to be closest to the mark, if one is to regard as a last will and
testament Mishima's curious apologia *Sun and Steel,* published a few
months before his death.

The opening sentences set the tone:

Of late, I have come to sense within myself an accumulation of all kinds
of things that cannot find adequate expression via an objective artistic form
such as the novel. A lyric poet of twenty might manage it, but I am twenty
no longer.

Right off, the obsession with age. In an odd way, writers often predict
their own futures. I doubt if Mishima was entirely conscious when he
wrote *Forbidden Colors* at the age of twenty-five that he was drawing
a possible portrait of himself at sixty-five: the famous, arid man of letters

Shunsuké (his first collected edition was published at forty-five) "who hated the naked truth. He held firmly to the belief that any part of one's talent . . . which revealed itself spontaneously was a fraud." The old writer amuses himself during his last days by deliberately corrupting a beautiful youth (unhappily, the aesthetic influence of *Dorian Gray* is stronger here than that of *Les Liaisons Dangereuses*) whose initials are—such is the division even at twenty-five in Yukio Mishima—Y. M. The author is both beautiful blank youth and ancient seducer of mind. At the end the youth is left in limbo, heir to Shunsuké who, discreetly, gratefully, kills himself having used Y. M. to cause considerable mischief to others.

Mishima's novels are pervaded with death. In an early work, *Thirst for Love* (1950), a young widow reflects that "it was an occult thing, that sacrificial death she dreamed of, a suicide proffered not so much in mourning for her husband's death as in envy of that death." Later, in *Forbidden Colors,* "Suicide, whether a lofty thing or lowly, is rather a suicide of thought itself; in general, a suicide in which the subject does not think too much does not exist." Not the most elegant of sentences. The translator A. H. Marks usually writes plain American English with only an occasional "trains shrilling" or women "feeling nauseous." Yet from Mr. Marks's prose it is hard to determine whether or not Mishima's writing possesses much distinction in the original. I found Donald Keene's rendering of the dialogue of Mishima's Nō plays unusually eloquent and precise, the work of a different writer, one would say; or is it (heart sinking) simply the distinguished prose of a different translator who has got closer to the original? Unable to read Japanese, I shall never know. Luckily, United Statesmen have no great interest in language, preferring to wrestle with Moral Problems, and so one may entirely ignore the quality of the line (which is all that a writer has of his own) in order to deal with his Ideas, which are of course the property of all, and usually the least interesting thing about him.

Mishima refers to *Sun and Steel* as "confidential criticism." He tells us how he began his life as one besotted with words. And although he does not say so directly, one senses from his career (fame at nineteen, a facility for every kind of writing) that things were perhaps too easy for him. It must have seemed to him (and to his surprisingly unbitter contemporaries) that there was nothing he could not do in the novel, the essay, the drama. Yet only in his reworking of the Nō plays does he appear to transcend competence and make (to a foreign eye) literature. One gets the impression that he was the sort of writer who is reluctant to take the next hard step after the first bravura mastery of a form. But then he was, he tells us, aware from the beginning of "two contradictory tendencies within myself. One was the determination to press ahead loyally with the corrosive function of words, to make that my life's work. The other was the desire to encounter reality in some field where words should play no part."

This is the romantic's traditional and peculiar agony. There is no internal evidence that Mishima read D. H. Lawrence (his rather insistent cultural references consist of hymns in the Winckelmann manner to Greek statuary and the dropping of names like Pater, Beardsley, Poe, Baudelaire, De Sade), but one recognizes a similar tension in Mishima's work. The fascination with the bodies of others (in Mishima's case the young male with a "head like a young bull," "rows of flashing teeth"— sometimes it seems that his ideal is equipped with more than the regulation set of choppers—"wearing sneakers"), and the vain hope of somehow losing oneself in another's identity, fusing two bodies into something new and strange. But though homosexual encounters are in themselves quite as exciting as heterosexual encounters (more so, claim the great pederasts whose testimony echoes down the ages), it is not easy to build a universal philosophy on a kind of coupling that involves no procreative mystery—only momentary delight involving, if one is so minded, the enactment of ritual, the imposition of fantasy, the deliberate act of imagination without which there is no such thing as love or its philosophy, romanticism.

To judge from Mishima's writing, his love ritual was a complex one, and at the core of his madness. He quickly tired of the promiscuity which is so much easier for the homosexualist than for the heterosexualist. More to the point, Mishima could not trick himself into thinking, as Lawrence could, that a total surrender to the dark phallic god was a man's highest goal. Mishima was too materialistic, too flesh-conscious for that. As for his own life, he married, had two children. But apparently sought pleasure elsewhere. A passage from one of the novels sounds as if taken from life. Mishima describes the bedding of a new husband and wife.

Yuichi's first night had been a model of the effort of desire, an ingenious impersonation that deceived an unexperienced buyer. . . . On the second night the successful impersonation became a faithful impersonation of an impersonation. . . . In the dark room the two of them slowly became four people. The intercourse of the real Yuichi with the boy he had made Yasuko into, and the intercourse of the makeshift Yuichi—imagining he could love a woman—with the real Yasuko had to go forward simultaneously.

One looks forward to the widow Mishima's memoirs.

In *Sun and Steel* Mishima describes the flowering of his own narcissism (a noun always used in a pejorative sense by the physically ill-favored) and his gradual realization that flesh is all. What is the "steel" of the title? Nothing more portentous than weight lifting, though he euphemizes splendidly in the French manner. Working on pecs and lats, Mishima found peace and a new sense of identity. "If the body could achieve perfect, nonindividual harmony, then it would be possible to shut individuality up forever in close confinement." It is easy to make fun of Mishima, particularly when his paean to steel begins to sound like a brochure for Vic Tanney, but there is no doubt that in an age where there is little use for the male body's thick musculature, the deliberate development of that body is as good a pastime as any, certainly quite as legitimate a religion as Lawrence's blood consciousness, so much admired in certain literary quarters.

To Mishima the body is what one is; and a weak sagging body cannot help but contain a spirit to match. In moments of clarity (if not charity) Mishima is less stern with the soft majority, knows better. Nevertheless, "bulging muscles, a taut stomach and a tough skin, I reasoned, would correspond respectively to an intrepid fighting spirit. . . ."

Why did he want this warrior spirit? Why did he form a private army of dedicated ephebi? He is candid.

Specifically, I cherished a romantic impulse toward death, yet at the same time I required a strictly classical body as its vehicle; a peculiar sense of destiny made me believe that the reason why my romantic impulse toward death remained unfulfilled in reality was the immensely simple fact that I lacked the necessary physical qualifications.

There it is. For ten years he developed his body in order to kill it ritually in the most public way possible.

This is grandstanding of a sort far beyond the capacity of our local product. Telling Bobby Kennedy to go fuck himself at the White House is trivial indeed when compared to the high drama of cutting oneself open with a dagger and then submitting to decapitation before the army's chief of staff.

It should be noted, however, that Japanese classicists were appalled.

"So vulgar," one of them told me, wincing at the memory. "*Seppuku* must be performed according to a precise and elegant ritual, *in private,* not" (a shudder) "in a general's office with a dozen witnesses. But then Mishima was entirely Westernized." I think this is true. Certainly he was devoted to French nineteenth-century writing, preferring Huysmans to Flaubert. In fact, his literary taste is profoundly corny, but then what one culture chooses to select from another is always a mysterious business. Gide once spoke to me with admiration of James M. Cain, adding, quite gratuitously, that he could not understand why anyone admired E. M. Forster.

Yet Mishima's passion for physical strength has no counterpart in Western letters. Few of the bourgeois inky men who created Western literature ever believed that the beauty of the sword was:

. . . in its allying death not with pessimism and impotence but with abounding energy, the flower of physical perfection and the will to fight. Nothing could be farther removed from the principle of literature. In literature, death is held in check yet at the same time used as a driving force; strength is devoted to the construction of empty fictions; life is held in reserve, blended to just the right degree with death, treated with preservatives, and lavished on the production of works of art that possess a weird eternal life. Action—one might say—perishes with the blossom. Literature is an imperishable flower. And an imperishable flower, of course, is an artificial flower. Thus to combine action and art is to combine the flower that wilts and the flower that lasts forever . . .

It is often wise (or perhaps compassionate is the better word) to allow an artist if not the last the crucial say on what he meant to make of himself and his life. Yet between what Mishima thought he was doing and what he did there is still confusion. When I arrived in Japan journalists kept asking me what I thought of his death. At first I thought they were simply being polite. I was vague, said I could not begin to understand an affair which seemed to me so entirely Japanese. I spoke solemnly of different cultures, different traditions. Told them that in the West we kill ourselves when we can't go on the way we would like to: a casual matter, really—there is no *seppuku* for us, only the shotgun or the bottle. But now that I have read *Sun and Steel* and a dozen of Mishima's early works, some for the first time, I see that what he did was entirely idiosyncratic. Here then, belatedly, the coroner's report on the headless body in the general's office.

Forty-five is a poignant time for the male, particularly for one who has been acutely conscious of his own body as well as those of others. Worshiping the flesh's health and beauty (American psychiatrists are particularly offended by this kind of obsession) is as valid an aesthetic—even a religion—as any other, though more tragic than most, for in the normal course half a life must be lived within the ruin of what one most esteemed. For Mishima the future of that body he had worked so hard to make worthy of a classic death (or life) was somber. Not all the sun and steel can save the aging athlete.

Yet Mishima wanted a life of the flesh, of action, divorced from words. Some interpreted this to mean that he dreamed of becoming a sort of warlord, restoring to Japan its ancient military virtues. But I think Mishima was after something much simpler: the exhaustion of the flesh in physical exercise, in bouts of love, in such adventures as becoming a private soldier for a few weeks in his middle age or breaking the sound barrier with a military jet.

Certainly Mishima did not have a political mind. He was a Romantic Artist in a very *fin de siècle* French way. But instead of deranging the senses through drugs, Mishima tried to lose his conscious mind (his art) through the use and worship of his own flesh and that of others. Finally, rather than face the slow bitter dissolution of the incarnate self, he chose to die. He could not settle for the common fate, could not echo the healthy dryness of the tenth-century poet (in the *Kokinshū*) who wrote: "If only when one heard / that old age was coming / one could bolt the door / and refuse to meet him!" The Romantic showman chose to die as he had lived, in a blaze of publicity.

Now for some moralizing in the American manner. Mishima's death is explicable. Certainly he has prepared us, and himself, for it. In a most dramatic way the perishable flower is self-plucked. And there are no political overtones. But what of the artificial flowers he left behind? Mishima was a writer who mastered every literary form, up to a point. Reading one of his early novels, I was disturbed by an influence I recognized but could not place right off. The book was brief, precise, somewhat reliant on *coups de théâtre,* rather too easy in what it attempted but elegant and satisfying in a conventional way like . . . like Anatole France, whom I had not read since adolescence. *Le Lys Rouge,* I wrote in the margin. No sooner had I made this note than there appeared in the text the name Anatole France. I think this is the giveaway. Mishima was fatally drawn to what is easy in art.

Technically, Mishima's novels are unadventurous. This is by no means a fault. But it is a commentary on his art that he never made anything entirely his own. He was too quickly satisfied with familiar patterns and by no means the best. Only in his reworking of the Nō plays does Mishima, paradoxically, seem "original," glittering and swift in his effects, like Ibsen at the highest. What one recalls from the novels are simply fleshly obsessions and sadistic reveries: invariably the beloved youth is made to bleed while that sailor who fell from grace with the sea (the nature of this grace is never entirely plain) gets cut to pieces by a group of pubescent males. The conversations about art are sometimes interesting but seldom brilliant (in the American novel there are no conversations about art, a negative virtue, but still a virtue).

There is in Mishima's work, as filtered through his translators, no humor, little wit; there is irony, but of the W. Somerset Maugham variety . . . things are not what they seem, the respectable are secretly vicious. Incidentally, for those who think that Japanese culture is heavy, portentous, bloody, and ritual-minded (in other words, like Japanese samurai films), one should point out that neither of the founders of Japanese prose literature (the Lady Murasaki and Sei-Shōnagon) was too profound for wit. In Sei-Shōnagon's case quite the contrary.

As Japan's most famous and busy writer, Mishima left not a garden but an entire landscape full of artificial flowers. But, Mishima notwithstanding, the artificial flower is quite as perishable as the real. It just makes a bigger mess when you try to recycle it. I suspect that much of his boredom with words had to do with a temperamental lack of interest in them. The novels show no particular development over the years and little variety. In the later books, the obsessions tend to take over, which is never enough (if it were, the Marquis de Sade would be as great as the enemies of art claim).

Mishima was a minor artist in the sense that, as Auden tells us, once the minor artist "has reached maturity and found himself he ceases to have a history. The major artist, on the other hand, is always re-finding himself, so that the history of his works recapitulates or mirrors the history of art." Unable or unwilling to change his art, Mishima changed his life through sun, steel, death, and so became a major art-figure in the only way—I fear—our contemporaries are apt to understand: not through the work, but through the life. Mishima can now be ranked with such "great" American novelists as Hemingway (who never wrote a good novel) and Fitzgerald (who wrote only one). So maybe their books weren't so good but they sure had interesting lives, and desperate last days. Academics will enjoy writing about Mishima for a generation or two. And one looks forward to their speculations as to what he might have written had he lived. Another *A la recherche du temps perdu*? or *Les caves du Vatican*? Neither, I fear. My Ouija board has already spelled out what was next on the drawing board: *Of Human Bondage*.

Does any of this matter? I suspect not. After all, literature is no longer of very great interest even to the makers. It may well be that that current phenomenon, the writer who makes his life his art, is the most useful of all. If so, then perhaps Mishima's artificial flowers were never intended to survive the glare of sun and steel or compete with his own fleshly fact, made bloody with an ax. What, after all, has a mask to confess except that it covers a skull? All honor then to a man who lived and died the way he wanted to. I only regret we never met, for friends found him a good companion, a fine drinking partner, and fun to cruise with.

*The New York Review of Books*
June 17, 1971

# 44

·

# SCIASCIA'S ITALY

Since World War II, Italy has managed, with characteristic artistry, to create a society that combines a number of the least appealing aspects of socialism with practically all the vices of capitalism. This was not the work of a day. A wide range of political parties has contributed to the invention of modern Italy, a state whose vast metastasizing bureaucracy is the last living legacy anywhere on earth of the house of Bourbon (Spanish branch). In fact, the allegedly defunct Kingdom of the Two Sicilies has now so entirely engulfed the rest of the peninsula that the separation between Italian state and Italian people is nearly perfect.

Although the Italian treasury loves the personal income tax quite as much as other treasuries, any attempt to collect tax money is thwarted not only by the rich (who resemble their counterparts in the land of the free and the home of the tax accountant), but by nearly everyone else. Only those unfortunate enough to live on fixed incomes (e.g., industrial workers, schoolteachers) are trapped by the withholding tax, Zio Sam's sly invention. Since many Italians are either not on a payroll or, if they are, have a second job, they pay little or no personal tax to a state which is then obliged to raise money through a series of value-added and sales taxes. Needless to say, the treasury is often in deficit, thanks not only to the relative freedom from taxation enjoyed by its numerous entrepre-

neurs (capitalist Italy) but also to the constant drain on the treasury of
the large state-owned money-losing industrial consortia (socialist Italy).

Last year one fourth of the national deficit went to bail out state-
controlled industries. As a result, the Communist Party of Italy is
perhaps the only Communist Party anywhere on earth that has proposed, somewhat shyly, the return of certain industries to the private
sector of the economy. As the former governor of the Bank of Italy,
Guido Carli, put it: "The progressive introduction of socialistic elements
into our society has not made us a socialist society. Rather, it has
whittled down the space in which propulsive economic forces can operate."

The Italians have made the following trade-off with a nation-state
which none of them has ever much liked: if the state will not interfere
too much in the lives of its citizens (that is, take most of their money
in personal taxes), the people are willing to live without a proper postal
service, police force, medical care—all the usual amenities of a European industrialized society. But, lately, the trade-off has broken down.
Italy suffers from high inflation, growing unemployment, a deficit of
some $50 billion. As a result, there are many Italians who do not in the
least resemble Ms. Wertmuller's joyous, life-enhancing, singing waiters.
Millions of men and women have come to hate the house of Bourbon
in whose stifling rooms they are trapped. Therefore, in order to keep
from revolution a large part of the population, the government has
contrived an astonishing system of pensions and welfare assistance.

In a country with a labor force of 20.5 million people, 13.5 million
people are collecting pensions or receiving welfare assistance. Put another way, while the state industries absorb about 5 percent of Italy's
GDP or $9.5 billion, the pensioners get 11 percent or $25.2 billion a year.

The shrewd *condottiere* who control Italy realize that the state must,
from time to time, placate with milk from her dugs those babes that a
malign history has left in her lupine care.

Ten years ago, in the Sicilian town of Caltanissetta, a forty-eight-year-
old schoolteacher and clerk in the state granary was given a pension for
life. As a result, the part-time writer Leonardo Sciascia became not only
a full-time writer but, recently, he has become a political force . . . well,
no, not exactly a force (individuals, as such, exert little force in Italy's
Byzantine politics) but, rather, a voice of reason in a land where ideology has always tended to take the place of ideas. In the last election,
Sciascia stood as a candidate for the Radical Party. The fact that the
Radicals nearly quintupled their delegation in the parliament can be

attributed, at least in part, to Sciascia's ability to make plain the obvious. After Marco Panella, the Radical Party's unusual leader (one is tired of calling him charismatic), Sciascia is now one of the few literary political figures who is able to illuminate a prospect that cannot be pleasing to anyone, Marxist or Christian Democrat or neither.

Elected to the national parliament last spring, Sciascia opted to go to the European parliament instead. "Sicilians," he muttered, "gravitate either to Rome or to Milan. I like Milan."* Presumably, Strasbourg is an acceptable surrogate for Milan. Actually, Sciascia is unique among Sicilian artists in that he never abandoned Sicily for what Sicilians call "the continent." Like the noble Lampedusa, he has preferred to live and to work in his native Sicily. This means that, directly and indirectly, he has had to contend all his life with the Mafia and the Church, with fascism and communism, with the family, history. During the last quarter century, Sciascia has made out of his curious Sicilian experience a literature that is not quite like anything else ever done by a European— because Sicily is not part of Europe?—and certainly unlike anything done by a North American.

To understand Sciascia, one must understand when and where he was born and grew up and lived. Although this is true of any writer, it is crucial to the understanding of someone who was born in Sicily in 1921 (the year before Mussolini marched on Rome); who grew up under fascism; who experienced the liberation of Sicily by Lucky Luciano, Vito Genovese, and the American army; who has lived long enough to see the consumer society take root in Sicily's stony soil.

Traditionally, Sicily has almost always been occupied by some foreign power. During Sciascia's youth the Sicilians despised fascism because it was not only an alien form of government (what continental government is not alien to the Sicilians?) but a peculiarly oppressive alien government. The fascists tried to *change* the Sicilians. Make them wear uniforms. Conform them to the Duce's loony pseudo-Roman norm. Although Mussolini himself paid little attention to the island, he did manage to get upstaged in the piazza of Piano dei Greci by the capo of the local mafia, one Don Ciccio Cuccia. Aware that appearance is everything and substance nothing, Mussolini struck back at Don Ciccio (he put him in jail), at the Mafia in general (he sent down an efficient

*This was said in an interview given to *Il Messaggero.* All other quotations—not from his books—are taken from a series of conversations that Sciascia had with the journalist Marcelle Padovani and collected in a volume called *La Sicilia come Metafora* (Mondadori, 1979). The un-beautiful English translations are by me.

inspector named Mori who did the Mafia a good deal of damage post-1924), at Piano dei Greci (Mussolini changed the name Greci to Albanese . . . more Roman).

By the time that Sciascia was fourteen years old, Mussolini was able to announce—almost accurately—that he had broken the back of the Mafia. Pre-Mori, ten people were murdered a day in Sicily; post-Mori, only three were murdered a week. Meanwhile, Inspector Mori was trying to change the hearts and minds of the Sicilians. In a moment of inspiration, he offered a prize to the best school-boy essay on how to combat the Mafia. Although there were, predictably, no entries at the time, Sciascia has been trying ever since to explain to Inspector Mori how best to combat or cope with the Mafia, with Sicily, with the family, history, life.

"I spent the first twenty years of my life in a society which was doubly unjust, doubly unfree, doubly irrational. In effect, it was a non-society Society. La Sicilia, the Sicily that Pirandello gave us a true and profound picture of. And Fascism. And both in being Sicilian and living under fascism, I tried to cope by seeking within myself (and outside myself only in books) the ways and the means. In solitude. What I want to say is that I know very well that in those twenty years I ended up acquiring a kind of 'neurosis from reasoning.' "

Sciascia's early years were spent in the village of Racalmuto, some twenty-two kilometers from Agrigento. As a clerk's son, Sciascia was destined to be educated. When he was six, the teacher assured the class that "the world envied fascism and Mussolini." It is not clear whether or not the child Sciascia was ever impressed by the party line, but he certainly disliked the *balilla,* a paramilitary youth organization to which he was assigned. Fortunately, at the age of nine, "a distant relative was appointed the local leader of the *balilla.* " Influence was used and "I was relieved of my obligations" because "in Sicily the family has its vast ramifications. . . . The family is the main root of the Mafia, which I know well. But that one time I was the willing beneficiary."

Meanwhile, like most writers-to-be, the young Sciascia read whatever he could. He was particularly attracted to the eighteenth-century writers of the Enlightenment. If he has a precursor, it is Voltaire. Predictably, he preferred Diderot to Rousseau. "Sicilian culture ignored or rejected romanticism until it arrived from France under the name of realism." Later, Sciascia was enchanted—and remains enchanted—by Sicily's modern master, Pirandello. As a boy, "I lived inside Pirandello's world, and Pirandellian drama—identity, the relativeness of things—

was my daily dream. I almost thought that I was mad." But, ultimately, "I held fast to reason," as taught by Diderot, Courier, Manzoni.

Although Sciascia is a Pirandellian as well as a man of the Enlightenment, he has a hard clarity, reminiscent of Stendhal. At the age of five, he saw the sea: "I didn't like it, and I still don't like it. Sicilians don't like the sea, even those who live on its shores. For that matter, the majority of Sicilian towns have been built with their backs to the sea, ostentatiously. How could islanders like the sea which is capable only of carrying their men away as emigrants or bringing in invaders?"

Immediately after the war, the revived Mafia and their traditional allies (or clients or patrons) the landowners were separatists. When the government of the new Italian republic offered Sicily regional autonomy, complete with a legislature at Palermo, the Mafia's traditional capital, landowners and mafiosi became fervent Italians and the separatist movement failed. But then, it was doomed in 1945 when the United States refused (unkindly and probably unwisely) to fulfill the dream of innumerable Sicilians by annexing Sicily as an American state. In those innocent days, who knew that before the twentieth century had run its dismal course the Mafia would annex the United States? A marvelous tale still in search of its Pirandello.

Although everyone agreed that Sicily's only hope was industrialization, the Mafia fought industrialization because industry meant labor unions and labor unions (they thought naïvely) are not susceptible to the usual pressures of the honorable society which does and does not exist, rather like the Trinity. The first battle between Mafia and industrialization occurred when Sciascia was twenty-three. The communists and socialists held a meeting in the piazza of Villalba. Authority challenged, the local capo ordered his thugs to open fire. Legal proceedings dragged on for ten years, by which time the capo had died a natural death.

What happened at Villalba made a strong impression on Sciascia. Sometimes, in his work, he deals with it directly and realistically; other times, he is oblique and fantastic. But he has never *not,* in a symbolic sense, dealt with this business. Even *Todo Modo* (1974) was an attempt to analyze those forces that opposed one another on a September day in 1944, in a dusty piazza, abruptly loud with guns.

Today the Mafia thrives in Sicily. Gangs still extort money from citrus growers through control of water sources as well as through what once looked to be a permanent veto on refrigeration, a situation that has made Sicilian oranges noncompetitive in Europe. Mafia gangs control dockworkers, the sale of contraband, construction permits, etc. Meanwhile,

as Sciascia has described more than once, those continentals who come
to Sicily as prosecutors and police inspectors soon learn that the true
lover of justice must love death, too. Many of Sciascia's tales have, at
their heart, thanatophilia. Lately, he has extended the geographical
range of his novels. All Italy is now in the process of being Sicilianized.
But then, ever since World War II, Sicilians have been over-represented
in the country's police and judiciary in rather the same way that, post
Civil War, American Southerners took control of the Congress and the
military and, until recently, had a lock on each. Also, with the influx
of Sicilian workers to the northern cities (not to mention to the cities
of the United States, Canada, Australia) the Mafia mentality has been
exported with a vengeance.

What is the Mafia mentality? What is the Mafia? What is Sicily? When
it comes to the exploration of this particular hell, Leonardo Sciascia is the
perfect Virgil. As we begin our descent, he reminds us that like most
Mediterranean societies Sicily is a matriarchy. The father-god of the
conquering Aryans has never had much attraction for Mediterranean
peoples. Effigies of the original Great Goddess of the Mediterranean can
still be seen all over Sicily; and as the idol simpers at the boy-baby
clutched in one hand, the other hand is depicted free to stir the life-giving
*minestra*—or wield a knife.

D. H. Lawrence once described an exchange he had with an old
woman in a Sicilian church. Why, he wanted to know, was the tortured
figure of Jesus always shown in such vivid, such awful detail? Because,
said the old woman firmly, he was unkind to his mother. The sea at the
center of the earth is the sea of the mother, and this blood-dark sea is
at the heart of Sciascia's latest novel *Candido*: the story of a Sicilian
who, during an American air raid in 1943, was born to a mother whom
he was to lose in childhood to another culture; thus making it possible
for him to begin a journey that would remove him from the orbit of the
mother-goddess.

Sciascia has made an interesting distinction between what he calls the
"maternal man" (someone like Robert Graves who serves the Great
Goddess?) and the "paternal man." Although "I spent my infancy and
adolescence surrounded by women, with my aunts and 'mothers' . . . I
became a rather 'paternal' man. Many Sicilians are like me: they have
hostile relations with their fathers during their youth and then, as if
they've just seen themselves in a looking glass, they correct their attitude, realize that they *are* their fathers. They are destined to become
them." For Sciascia,

many wrongs, many tragedies of the South, have come to us from the women, above all when they become mothers. The Mezzogiorno woman has that *terrible* quality. How many crimes of honor has she provoked, instigated or encouraged! Women who are mothers, mothers-in-law. They are capable of the worst kinds of wickedness just in order to make up for the vexations they themselves were subjected to when they were young, as part of a terrifying social conformism. "Ah, yes," they seem to be saying, "you're my son's wife? Well, he's worth his weight in gold!"

These women are elements of violence, of dishonesty, of abuse of power in Southern society, even though some of that ancient power was reduced when the American troops landed in Sicily during the last war. And so it is that Candido (the character in my book) loses his mother at the moment of the arrival in Palermo of U.S. soldiers. If that event dealt a hard blow to the matriarchy, it also introduced "consumerism," a taste for modern gadgets, possessions, a house. . . . From the moment that they began building new housing in Sicily, the sons (and the daughters-in-law) began to leave the old tyrannical hearths of their mothers, thus undermining, in part, the ancient power structure.

After the bombardment, the child is named, "surreally," Candido: neither parent has ever heard of Voltaire. The town is occupied by the American army and Captain John H. (for Hamlet) Dykes becomes, in effect, the mayor. Candido's lawyer-father asks the American to dinner, and Candido's mother falls in love with him. Sourly, surreally, the father comes to believe that Dykes is the blond Candido's father even though the child was conceived nine months before the arrival in Sicily of the Americans. Nevertheless, in the father's mind, Candido is always "the American."

As a result of the April 18, 1948 election (when knowledgeable authorities told me to flee Italy because the Communists would win and there would be—what else?—"a blood bath"), the Christian Democrat Party doubled its vote and Candido's fascist grandfather, the General, was elected to parliament while the General's aide-de-camp, a local nobleman, was also elected, but on the Communist ticket. Nicely, the two ex-fascists work in tandem. Meanwhile, Candido's mother has divorced his father and gone to live with her American lover in Helena, Montana. Candido is left behind.

Sciascia's Candido is a serene, not particularly wide-eyed version of Voltaire's Candide. In fact, this Sicilian avatar is a good deal cleverer than the original. As a boy, "His games—we can try to define them only approximately—were like crossword puzzles which he would play with things. Adults make words cross, but Candido made things cross." One of the things that he makes cross . . . cross the shining river, in fact . . . is his lawyer-father who has assisted in the cover-up of a murder. When Candido overhears a discussion of the murder, he promptly tells his schoolmates the true story. As a result of the boy's candor, the father commits suicide and Candido, now known as "the little monster," goes to live with the General. At no point does Candido feel the slightest guilt. Pondering his father's death, he begins to arrange an image in his mind "of a man who adds up his whole life and arrives at a sum indicating that it would be right for him to put a bullet through his head."

It is now time for Dr. Pangloss to make his entrance, disguised as the Archpriest Lepanto. Highly civilized priests keep recurring in Sciascia's work, although he confesses that "I have never met one."

The Archpriest and the boy spar with each another. "Up to a point, the Archpriest also was convinced that he was a little monster . . . whereas Candido had discovered that the Archpriest had a kind of fixed idea, rather complicated but reducible, more or less, to these terms: all little boys kill their fathers, and some of them, sometimes, kill even Our Father Who is in Heaven." Patiently, Candido sets out to disabuse the Archpriest: "he had not killed his father, and he knew nothing, nor did he want to know anything, about that other Father."

Sciascia's themes now begin to converge. The mother has abandoned the son, a very good thing in the land of the Great Goddess (who would be Attis, who Pan could be?); the father has killed himself because of Candido's truthfulness or candor when he made cross the thing-truth with the thing-*omertà;* now the Heavenly Father, or Aryan sky-god, is found to be, by Candido, simply irrelevant. Plainly, Candido is a monster. He is also free. He becomes even freer when he inherits money and land. But when he cultivates his own land for the good of his tenant farmers, they know despair. When a parish priest is murdered (with the regularity of a Simenon, Sciascia produces his murders), Candido and the Archpriest decide to assist the inspector of police. When, rather cleverly, they apprehend the murderer, everyone is in a rage. They—not the killer—have broken the code. A theologian is called in by the local bishop and an inquiry is held into the Archpriest's behavior. It is decided that he must

step down as Archpriest: he could not continue to fulfill that office if all the faithful now disapproved of him, even despised him. "And further," the learned theologian said, "not that truth may not be beautiful, but at times it does so much harm that to withhold it is not a fault but a merit."

In handing the theologian his resignation, the Archpriest, now archpriest no longer, said, in a parodying, almost lilting voice, " 'I am the way, the truth, and the life,' but sometimes I am the blind alley, the lie, and death."

With that, the moral education of Candido is complete. On the other hand, that of Dr. Pangloss has just begun. The Archpriest—now Don Antonio—becomes a militant communist. To an extent, Candido goes along with Don Antonio. But he is not one to protest too much. He cannot be a protestant if only because he "was utterly averse to believing that there were any sins other than lying and seeking the pain and humiliation of others."

The political education of Candido—as opposed to moral—begins in early manhood. Like so many educated Italians of that time, he regards communism as a replacement for a church that has not only failed but in the land of the Great Goddess never truly taken hold. Candido likes the writings of Gramsci; finds Marx boring; as for Lenin, "he had come to picture Lenin as a carpenter atop a scaffolding who had worn himself out hitting the same nails on the head, but all of his efforts had not prevented some nails from being poorly set or going in crooked." (I am not always enchanted by the translation of Adrienne Foulke.) Although Candido believes that "to be a Communist was, in a word, almost a fact of nature" because "capitalism was bearing man toward dissolution," he much prefers the imaginative writers to the contorted Machiavellianism of the communist theoreticians: " 'Zola and Gorki, they talk about things that used to be, and it's as if they were talking about things that came later. Marx and Lenin talk about things that would happen, and it's as if they were talking about things that are no longer.' "

But Candido becomes a member of the Communist Party even though he is more repelled than not by its sacred texts (excepting, always, Gramsci). Acting on principle, Candido offers his own land for a hospital but because of the usual collusion between the *condottiere* of the left and the right, another piece of land is bought by the community and the *condottiere* make their profit. Candido is thrown out of the Communist Party. In due course, after he is done out of his fortune by his own family, he goes off with his cousin Francesca to Turin, "a more and more sullen city. . . . The North and the South of Italy settled there; they sought crazily to avoid each other and, at the same time, to strike out at each other; both were bottled up in making automobiles, a superflu-

ous necessity for all, a necessary superfluity for all." Just before the
young couple move on to Paris, Candido says to Francesca, "Do you
know what our life is, yours and mine? It's a dream dreamed in Sicily.
Perhaps we're still there, and we are dreaming."

In Paris, at the Brasserie Lipp (August 1977), Candido runs into the
long-mislaid mother and her husband, Mr. Dykes. Don Antonio is also
there: he is now as doctrinaire a Communist as he had been a Roman
Catholic. Predictably, the Americans have little to say to the Sicilians.
But Don Antonio does ask former Captain Dykes: "How did you manage, only a few days after you had arrived in our town, to choose our
worst citizens for public service?" Dykes is offhand: he had been given
a list. Yes, he had suspected that the people on the list were mafiosi,
"But we were fighting a war. . . ."

When Candido's mother, rather halfheartedly, proposes that Candido
visit America, Candido is polite. For a visit, perhaps. " 'But as for living
there, I want to live here. . . . Here you feel that something is about to
end and something is about to begin. I'd like to see what should come
to an end come to its end.' Embracing him once again, his mother
thought, He's a monster." Mother and son part, presumably forever.

Rather drunk, Don Antonio has, once again, missed the point to what
Candido has been saying. Don Antonio says that "here," meaning
France, "something is about to end, and it's beautiful. . . . At home,
nothing ends, nothing ever ends." On the way back to his hotel, Don
Antonio salutes the statue of Voltaire as "our true father!" But Candido
demurs; and the book's last line is: " 'Let's not begin again with the
fathers,' he said. He felt himself a child of fortune, and happy." *Magari,*
as the Italians say.

I am not sure just what it is that makes Sciascia's novels unique. Where
"serious" American writers tend to let the imagination do the work of the
imagination, Sciascia prefers to invent for us a world quite as real as any
that Dreiser ever dealt with, rendered in a style that is, line by line, as
jolting as an exposed electrical wire. I suppose, as a Pirandellian, Sciascia
is letting a very real world imagine *him* describing it.

*Candido* is bracketed by two political events: one of importance to
Sciascia, the other to the world as well as Sciascia. From time to time,
Italian political parties will propose for election a sympathetic non-party
member, preferably a *"technico"* (usually, an economist who has
managed to jam the central computer of a major bank) or a *"per-
sonaggio,"* a celebrated man like Sciascia. One year before *Candido* was
written, pensioner Sciascia was a Communist Party candidate for the

Palermo city council. "My 'debut' was solicited by the local [party] leaders as an event destined to have consequences at the local level."

Sciascia accepted the Communist nomination for city councilor with a certain Candide-like innocence. Like most Italians of his generation, he is a man of the left. Unlike most Italians, Sciascia is a social meliorist. As a public man, he has an empirical streak which is bound to strike as mysterious most politically minded Italians. Sciascia has ideas but no ideology in a country where political ideology is everything and political ideas unknown. Sciascia's reasons for going on the city council are straightforward. Grave problems faced Palermo, "in certain quarters there was no water, whole neighborhoods lacked sewers and roads, and the restoration . . . the rehabilitation of the historic center presented all sorts of problems," but "during the eighteen months that I served on the city council, not once did anyone talk about water or any other urgent problems. . . ."

Sciascia was also shocked to find that the council seldom met before nine in the evening; then, around midnight, when people were yawning, a bit of business was done. Finally, Sciascia was wised up,

off the record, thanks to the benevolence of a socialist councilman who spelled the whole thing out to me in real terms, clearly: thus, I was able to understand how the Communists and the Christian Democrats did business together and I was less than pleased. . . . Aware that my presence in the bosom of the city council was inopportune and useless, and that the possibility of a row between me and the party that had put me there seemed more and more likely, it was obvious that I'd have to quit. I wanted to go without slamming the door, but that wasn't possible.

There was a good deal of fuss when Sciascia quit the council in 1975. But though he may, personally, have found the experience "inopportune and useless," he was able to make good use of it in *Candido*: when Candido tries to give the city land for a hospital, he discovers that nothing can ever be given in a society where everything is bought and sold, preferably twice over.

Sciascia entered Italian political history in the wake of the kidnapping and murder by terrorists of Aldo Moro, the president of the Christian Democrat party. More than anyone else, Moro was responsible for the tentative coming together of left and right in what the Communists like to call the "historic compromise" between Christ and Marx, in what Moro himself used to call, with a positively Eisenhowerian gift for demented metaphor, "the inevitable convergence of parallel lines."

Moro was kidnapped by a mysterious entity known as the Red Brigades. Whoever they were or are, their rhetoric is Marxist. If Italy was shocked by the Moro kidnapping, the intellectuals were traumatized. Since Italy's intellectuals are, almost to a man, Marxists, this was the moment of truth. Moro was the leader of the party that serves the Agnellis, the Pope, and the American (somewhat fractured) hegemony. If the leader of this party is really being tried by a *truly* revolutionary Marxist court, well. . . . Although any communist party is a party of revolution, the Italian party long ago dropped its "to the barricades" rhetoric, preferring to come to power through the ballot box. Until the Moro affair, the Communist Party was prospering. In the previous election they had got well over their usual 30 percent of the vote and it looked as if a coalition government was possible. Christ and Marx were, if not at the altar, getting their prenuptial blood tests. But, suddenly, prenuptial blood tests turned to bloodletting. Why, asked a number of political commentators, are the intellectuals silent?

Eventually, Italy's premier man of letters, Alberto Moravia, admitted to a feeling of "sorrowing extraneousness" while the young Turks at *Lotta Continua* (a radical newspaper of the left) proclaimed: "Neither Red Brigades nor the state." But the real polemic began when it came time to try a number of Red Brigadeers in Turin. So many potential jurors received death threats that sixteen refused to serve. When Eugenio Montale said that he "understood" their fear, Italo Calvino took him to task. "The state," said Calvino, "is all of us." Calvino chose to cling to what Taoists call "the primal unity." So did the Communist Party. Contemptuous of Montale's unease, the Communist leader Giorgio Amendola declared: "Civil courage has never been in great supply among Italian intellectuals."

With that Sciascia went into action. "I intervened," he said later, "because of Calvino's article, in which he expressed embarrassment and concern when Montale said that he 'understood' the sixteen citizens of Turin who refused to be jurors. I felt that I ought to contribute to the debate: I, too, understood the sixteen citizens, just as I understood Montale . . . even I might have declined the honor and the burden of being a juror. What guarantee, I asked, does this state offer when it comes to the protection of those citizens who put themselves at risk by becoming jurors? What guarantee against theft, abuse of power, injustice? None. The impunity that covers crimes committed against the general public and the general good was worthy of a South American regime." As for the Red Brigades: "All my life, everything that I've thought and written makes it clear that I cannot take the side of the Red Brigades."

Sciascia then turned on Amendola. "For him the state must be a sort of mythical and metaphysical entity. . . ." Sciascia's own view of the state is less exalted: a state is a system of well-coordinated services. "But when those services are inadequate or lacking then one must repair them or make something new. If this is not done, then one is defending nothing but corruption and inefficiency under the pretext that one is defending the state." As for Amendola (and, presumably, the Communist Party), he "was simply animated by the desire for an authoritarian state . . . and from a visceral aversion to non-conforming writers."

Ultimately, Sciascia has taken the line that "the Italian Communist Party has become a precise mirror-image of the Christian Democrat Party." Consequently, "one can only make two hypotheses: either the Communist Party has not the capacity to make a valid opposition, and Italians have credited the party with qualities that it never had, or the Italian party is playing the game 'the worse things are the better' or 'to function least is to function best.' . . . These two parties seem to be intertwined and interchangeable not only in their existence today but in their future."

Now, in 1979, Sciascia has moved toward new perceptions if not, necessarily, realities. To the statement, "We cannot *not* be socialist" (the famous paraphrase of Croce's "we cannot *not* be Christians"), he replies that things have changed as "it is plain that, at the level of collective humanity, socialism has known failures even more serious than those of Christianity." For Italian intellectuals of Sciascia's generation, this is a formidable heresy. But he goes even further. Contemplating those who speak of Marxism with a human face, he responds, "I respect their position, but I retain the idea that 'an authentic Marxism' is a utopia within a utopia, a dream, an illusion." Nevertheless, he cannot be anti-communist. This is the dilemma that faces any Italian who takes politics seriously. To the question: what would you like to see happen next? Sciascia replied, perhaps too simply, "The creation of a social democratic party." But then, less simply, he acted upon his own words, and stood for parliament in the Radical Party interest. Like a growing number of Italians, Sciascia finds appealing a party which compensates for its lack of ideology with all sorts of ideas. In the last election, the party tripled its vote.

Although the Radical Party stands for such specific things as liberalized laws on abortion, divorce, drugs, sex, as well as the cleaning up of the environment and the removal of Italy from NATO (something the Communist Party has not mentioned since 1976), the party is constantly being denounced for representing nothing at all. But then, for most Italians, a political party is never a specific program, it is a flag, a liturgy, the sound of a trombone practicing in the night.

"Remember," Sciascia said to Marcelle Padovani, "what Malraux said of Faulkner? 'He has managed to intrude Greek tragedy into the detective story.' It might be said of me that I have brought Pirandellian drama to the detective story!" Often disguised as detective stories, Sciascia's novels are also highly political in a way quite unlike anything that has ever been done in English. While the American writer searches solemnly for his identity, Sciascia is on the trail of a murderer who, invariably, turns out to be not so much a specific character as a social system. That Mafia, which Americans find so exciting and even admirable, is for Sciascia the evil consequence of a long bad history, presided over by The Kindly Ones. Whenever (as in *Il Giorno della Civetta,* 1961)* one of Sciascia's believers in justice confronts the Mafia (which everyone says—in the best Pirandellian manner—does not exist), he is not only defeated, but, worse, he is never understood. Particularly if, like Captain Bellodi from Parma, he regards "the authority vested in him as a surgeon regards the knife: an instrument to be used with care, precision, and certainty; a man convinced that law rests on the idea of justice and that any action taken by the law should be governed by justice." Captain Bellodi was not a success in Sicily.

A decade later, in *Il Contesto,* † Sciascia again concerns himself with justice. But now he has moved toward a kind of surrealism. Sometimes the country he writes about is Italy; sometimes not. A man has gone to prison for a crime that he did not commit. When he gets out of prison, he decides to kill off the country's judges. When Inspector Rogas tries to track down the killer, he himself is murdered. In a splendid dialogue with the country's Chief Justice, Inspector Rogas is told that "the only possible form of justice, of the administration of justice, could be, and will be, the form that in a military war is called decimation. One man answers for humanity. And humanity answers for the one man."

Although moral anarchy is at the basis of this ancient society, Sciascia himself has by no means given up. The epigraphs to *Il Contesto* are very much to the point. First, there is a quotation from Montaigne: "One

*Published by Knopf in 1964 as *Mafia Vendetta.*
†Published by Harper & Row in 1973 as *Equal Danger.*

must do as the animals do, who erase every footprint in front of their lair." Then a response from Rousseau: "O Montaigne! You who pride yourself on your candor and truthfulness, be sincere and truthful, if a philosopher can be so, and tell me whether there exists on earth a country where it is a crime to keep one's given word and to be clement and generous, where the good man is despised and the wicked man honored." Sciascia then quotes Anonymous: "O Rousseau!" One has a pretty good idea who this particular Anonymous is.

It is Sciascia's self-appointed task to erase the accumulated footprints (history) in front of the animal's lair (Sicily, Italy, the world). The fact that he cannot undo the remembered past has not prevented him from making works of art or from introducing a healthy skepticism into the sterile and abstract political discourse of his country. No other Italian writer has said, quite so bluntly, that the historic compromise would lead to "a regime in which, finally and enduringly, the two major parties would be joined in a unified management of power to the preclusion of all alternatives and all opposition. Finally, the Italians would be tranquil, irresponsible, no longer forced to think, to evaluate, to choose."

Rather surprisingly, Sciascia seems not to have figured out what the historic compromise ultimately signifies. When he does, he will realize that Italy's two great unloved political parties are simply the flitting shadows of two larger entities. As any Voltairean knows, the Vatican and the Kremlin have more in common than either has with the idea of a free society. Once each realizes that the other is indeed its logical mate, Sciascia will be able to write his last detective story, in which the murder will be done with mirrors. Meanwhile, he continues to give us all sorts of clues; reminds us that criminals are still at large; demonstrates that life goes on *todo modo*.

*The New York Review of Books*
October 25, 1979

# 4 5
·

## CALVINO'S NOVELS

Between the end of the Second World War in 1945 and the beginning of the Korean War in 1950, there was a burst of creative activity throughout the American empire as well as in our client states of Western Europe. From Auden's *Age of Anxiety* to Carson McCullers's *Reflections in a Golden Eye* to Paul Bowles's *The Sheltering Sky* to Tennessee Williams's *A Streetcar Named Desire* to Tudor's ballets and to Bernstein's enthusiasms, it was an exciting time. The cold war was no more than a nip in the air while the junior senator from Wisconsin was just another genial pol with a drinking problem and an eye for the boys. In that happy time the young American writer was able to reel in triumph through the old cities of Europe—the exchange rate entirely in his favor.

Twenty-six years ago this spring I arrived in Rome. First impressions: Acid-yellow forsythia on the Janiculum. Purple wisteria in the Forum. Chunks of goat on a plate in a trattoria. Samuel Barber at the American Academy, talking Italian accurately. Harold Acton politely deploring our barbarous presence in *his* Europe. Frederic Prokosch at Doney's, eating cakes. Streets empty of cars. Had there been traffic of any kind, Tennessee Williams would have been planted long since in the Protestant cemetery, for he drove a jeep although "I am practically *blind* in one eye," he would say proudly, going through the occasional red light, treating sidewalk and street as one.

I visited George Santayana in his hospital cell at the Convent of the Blue Nuns. He wore a dressing gown; Lord Byron collar open at the withered neck; faded mauve waistcoat. He was genial; made a virtue of his deafness. "*I* will talk. You will listen." A sly smile; black glittering eyes—he looked exactly like my grandmother gone dramatically bald.

"Have you met my young *new* friend Robert Lowell?" I said no. "He will have a difficult life. To be a Lowell. From Boston. A Catholic *convert.*" The black eyes shone with a lovely malice. "And a poet, too! Oh, dear. Now tell me who is a Mr. Edmund Wilson? He came to see me. I think that he must be very important. In fact, I believe he *said* that he was very important. You sent me a book, he said. I said that I had not. He said but you did, and got very angry. I tried to tell him that I do not *send* books. But later I recalled that when we were rescued by the American army—and how *glad* we were to see you!" A fond glance at me (one still wore khakis, frayed army belt). "A major, a very forceful man, came to see me, with a number of my books. He stood over me and *made* me sign them . . . for this one, for that one. I was terrified and did as he requested. Perhaps one of those books was for Mr. Wilson."

The only books in Santayana's cell were his own—and a set of Toynbee's recently published history, which he was reading characteristically; that is, he first broke (or foxed) the spine of the book and undid the sections; then, as he finished reading each section, he would throw it in the wastebasket. "Some sort of preacher, I should think," he said of Toynbee. "But the footnotes are not entirely worthless."

Santayana signed a copy of *The Middle Span* for me; he wrote "from" before his name. "I almost never do that," he said. An appraising look. "You look younger than you are because your head is somewhat small in proportion to your body." That was in 1948, when the conquering Americans lived in Rome and Paris and strolled streets as yet uncrowded with automobiles or with the billion or so human beings who have since joined us.

In that far-off time, the people one met talked about novels and novelists the way they now talk of movies and directors. Young people today think that I am exaggerating. But novelists mattered then and the Italian novel, in particular, was having a fine flowering. Yet the American writers in Rome and Paris saw little of their counterparts. For one thing, the Italians were just getting around to reading Dos Passos and

Steinbeck—the generation that had gone untranslated during the Fascist era. Also, few Italian writers then (or now) spoke or read English with any ease while the American writers then (though not so much now) proudly spoke no language but English.

I do remember in 1948 coming across a book by Italo Calvino. An Italian Calvin, I said to myself, fixing permanently his name in my memory. Idly, I wondered what a man called Italo Calvino would write about. I glanced at his first novel, *Il sentiero dei nidi di ragno* (1947). Something about partisans in Liguria. A fellow war novelist. No, I thought; and put it down. I did note that he was two years older than I, worked for the publisher Einaudi, lived in Turin.

During the last year, I have read Calvino straight through, starting with the book I only glanced at in 1948, now translated as *The Path to the Nest of Spiders*.

Calvino's first novel is a plainly told, exuberant sort of book. Although the writing is conventional, there is an odd intensity in the way Calvino sees things, a closeness of scrutiny much like that of William Golding. Like Golding he knows how and when to occupy entirely, with all senses functioning, landscape, state of mind, act. In *The Spire* Golding makes the flawed church so real that one smells the mortar, sees the motes of dust, fears for the ill-placed stones. Calvino does the same in the story of Pin, a boy living on the Ligurian coast of Italy, near San Remo (although Calvino was brought up in San Remo, he was actually born in Cuba, a detail given by none of his American publishers; no doubt in deference to our recent attempted conquest of that unfortunate island).

Pin lives with his sister, a prostitute. He spends his days at a low-life bar where he amuses with songs and taunts the grown-ups, a race of monsters as far as he is concerned, but he has no other companions, for "Pin is a boy who does not know how to play games, and cannot take part in the games either of children or grownups." Pin dreams, however, of "a friend, a real friend who understands him and whom he can understand, and then to him, and only to him, will he show the place where the spiders have their lairs."

It's on a stony little path which winds down to the torrent between earthy grassy slopes. There, in the grass, the spiders make their nests, in tunnels lined with dry grass. But the wonderful thing is that the nests have tiny doors, also made of dried grass, tiny round doors which can open and shut.

This sort of precise, quasi-scientific observation keeps Calvino from the sort of sentimentality that was prevalent in the forties, when wise children learned compassion from a black mammy as she deep-fried chitlins and Jesus in equal parts south of the Mason-Dixon line.

Pin joins the partisans in the hills above the Ligurian coast. I have a suspicion that Calvino is dreaming all this, for he writes like a bookish, near-sighted man who has mislaid his glasses: objects held close-to are vividly described but the middle and far distances of landscape and war tend to blur. It makes no difference, however, for the dreams of a near-sighted young man at the beginning of a literary career can be more real to the reader than the busy reportage of those journalist-novelists who were so entirely there and, seeing it all, saw nothing.

Although Calvino manages to inhabit the skin of the outraged and outrageous child, his men and women are almost always shadowy. Later in his career, Calvino will eliminate men and women altogether as he re-creates the cosmos. Meanwhile, as a beginning, he is a vivid, if occasionally clumsy, writer. Two thirds of the way through the narrative he shifts the point of view from Pin to a pair of commissars who would have been more effective had he observed them from outside. Then, confusingly, he shifts again, briefly, into the mind of a traitor who is about to be shot. Finally, he returns to Pin just as the boy finds the longed-for friend, a young partisan called Cousin who takes him in hand not only literally but, presumably, for the rest of the time Pin will need to grow up. Calvino's last paragraphs are almost always jubilant—the sort of cheerful codas that only a deep pessimist about human matters could write. But then Calvino, like one of Pin's friends, Red Wolf, "belongs to the generation brought up on strip cartoons; he has taken them all seriously and life has not disproved them so far."

In 1952 Calvino published *The Cloven Viscount,* one of the three short novels he has since collected under the title *Our Ancestors.* They are engaging works, written in a style somewhat like that of T. H. White's Arthurian novels. The narrator of *The Cloven Viscount* is, again, an orphan boy. During a war between Austria and Turkey (1716) the boy's uncle Viscount Medardo was cloven from pate to crotch by a cannonball. Saved by doctors on the battlefield, the half Viscount was sent home with one leg, one arm, one eye, half a nose, mouth, etc. En route, Calvino pays homage (ironic?) to Malaparte ("The patch of plain they were crossing was covered with horses' carcasses, some supine with hooves to the sky, others prone with muzzles dug into the earth"—a nice reprise of those dead horses in *The Skin*).

The story is cheerfully, briskly told. The half Viscount is a perfect bastard and takes pleasure in murder, fire, torture. He burns down part of his own castle, hoping to incinerate his old nurse Sebastiana; finally, he packs her off to a leper colony. He tries to poison his nephew. He never stops slashing living creatures in half. He has a thing about halfness.

"If only I could have every thing like this," said my uncle, lying face down on the rocks, stroking the convulsive half of an octopus, "so that everyone could escape from his obtuse and ignorant wholeness. I was whole and all things were natural and confused to me, stupid as the air; I thought I was seeing all and it was only the outside rind. If you ever become a half of yourself, and I hope you do for your own sake, my boy, you'll understand things beyond the common intelligence of brains that are whole. You'll have lost half of yourself and of the world, but the remaining half will be a thousand times deeper and more precious."

I note that the publisher's blurb would have us believe that this is "an allegory of modern man—alienated and mutilated—this novel has profound overtones. As a parody of the Christian parables of good and evil, it is both witty and refreshing." Well, at least the book is witty and refreshing. Actually the story is less Christian than a send-up of Plato and his ideas of the whole.

In due course the other half of the Viscount hits town; this half is unbearably good and deeply boring. He, too, is given to celebrating halfness because "One understands the sorrow of every person and thing in the world at its own incompleteness. I was whole and did not understand. . . ." A charming young girl named Pamela (homage to Richardson) is beloved by both halves of the Viscount; but she has serious reservations about each. "Doing good together is the only way to love," intones the good half. To which the irritable girl responds, "A pity. I thought there were other ways." When the two halves are finally united, the resulting whole Viscount is the usual not very interesting human mixture. In a happy ending, he marries Pamela. But the boy-narrator is not content. "Amid all this fervor of wholeness, [I] felt myself growing sadder and more lacking. Sometimes one who thinks himself incomplete is merely young."

*The Cloven Viscount* is filled with many closely observed natural images like "The subsoil was so full of ants that a hand put down anywhere came up all black and swarming with them." I don't know which was written first, *The Cloven Viscount* (1952) or "The Argentine Ant," published in *Botteghe Oscure* (1952), but Calvino's nightmare of an ant-infested world touched on in the novel becomes the subject of "The Argentine Ant" and I fear that I must now trot out that so often misused word "masterpiece." Or, put another way, if "The Argentine Ant" is not a masterpiece of twentieth-century prose writing, I cannot think of anything better. Certainly it is as minatory and strange as anything by Kafka. It is also hideously funny. In some forty pages Calvino gives us "the human condition," as the blurb writers would say, in spades. That is, the human condition *today*. Or the dilemma of modern man. Or the disrupted environment. Or nature's revenge. Or an allegory of grace. Whatever . . . But a story is, finally, what it tells and no more.

Calvino's first sentence is rather better than God's "in the beginning was the word." God (as told to Saint John) has always had a penchant for cloudy abstractions of the sort favored by American novelists, heavyweight division—unlike Calvino, who simply tells us what's what: "When we came to settle here we did not know about the ants." No nonsense about "here" or "we." *Here* is a place infested with ants and *we* are the nuclear family: father, mother, child. No names.

"We" have rented a house in a town "where our Uncle Augusto used to hang out. Uncle Augusto rather liked the place, though he did say, 'You should see the ants over there . . . they're not like the ones here, those ants. . . .' But we paid no attention at the time." As the local landlady Signora Mauro shows the young couple about the house they have just rented from her, she distracts their attention from the walls with a long dissertation on the gas meter. When she has gone, the baby is put to bed and the young couple take a stroll outside. Their next-door neighbor is spraying the plants in his garden with a bellows. The ants, he explains, "as if not wanting to make it sound important."

The young couple return to their house and find it infested with ants. The Argentine ants. The husband-narrator suddenly recalls that this country is known for them. "It comes from South America," he adds, helpfully, to his distraught wife. Finally, they go to bed without "the feeling we were starting a new life, only a sense of dragging on into a future full of new troubles."

The rest of the story deals with the way that the others in the valley cope with the ants. Some go in for poisons; others make fantastic contraptions to confuse or kill the insects while for twenty years the Argentine Ant Control Corporation's representative has been putting out

molasses ostensibly to control (kill) the ants but many believe that this
is done to *feed* the ants. The frantic young couple pay a call on Signora
Mauro in her dim palatial drawing room. She is firm; ants do not exist
in well-tended houses, but from the way she squirms in her chair it is
plain that the ants are crawling about under her clothes.

Methodically, Calvino describes the various human responses to The
Condition. There is the Christian Scientist ignoring of all evidence; the
Manichaean acceptance of evil; the relentless Darwinian faith that genetic superiority will prevail. But the ants prove indestructible and the
story ends with the family going down to the seaside where there are
no ants; where

The water was calm, with just a slight continual change of color, blue and
black, darker farthest away. I thought of the expanses of water like this, of
the infinite grains of soft sand down there at the bottom of the sea where
the currents leave white shells washed clean by the waves.

I don't know what this coda means. I also see no reason for it to mean.
A contrast has been made between the ant-infested valley and the cool
serenity of mineral and of shell beneath the sea, that other air we can
no longer breathe since our ancestors chose to live upon the land.

In 1956 Calvino edited a volume of Italian fables, and the local critics
decided that he was true heir to Grimm. Certainly the bright, deadly
fairy tale attracts him and he returned to it with *The Baron in the Trees*
(1957). Like the other two tales in the trilogy, the story is related in the
first person; this time by the eponymous baron's brother. The year is
1767. The place Liguria. The Baron is Cosimo Piovasco di Rondò, who
after an argument at dinner on June 15 decides to live in the trees. The
response of family and friends to this decision is varied. But Cosimo is
content. Later he goes in for politics; deals with Napoleon himself;
becomes legend.

Calvino has now developed two ways of writing. One is literally
fabulous. The other makes use of a dry, rather didactic style in which
the detail is as precisely observed as if the author were writing a manual
for the construction of a solar heating unit. Yet the premises of the
"dry" stories are often quite as fantastic as those of the fairy tales.*

---

*I have not read *La speculazione edilizia* (1957). From the description of it in
*Dizionario della letteratura italiana contemporanea,* it is a general indictment of
Italy's postwar building boom and of the helplessness of the intellectual Quinto
Anfossi to come to terms with "cement fever."

"Smog" was published in 1958, a long time before the current preoccupation with man's systematic destruction of the environment. The narrator comes to a large city to take over a small magazine called *Purification.* The owner of the magazine, Commendatore Cordà, is an important manufacturer who produces the sort of air pollution that his magazine would like to eliminate. Cordà has it both ways and his new editor settles in nicely. The prevailing image of the story is smog: gray dust covers everything; nothing is ever clean. The city is very like the valley of the Argentine ants but on a larger scale, for now a vast population is slowly strangling in the fumes of its industry, of the combustion engine.

Calvino is finely comic as he shows us the publisher instructing his editor in how to strike the right tone. "We are not utopians, mind you, we are practical men." Or, "It's a battle for an ideal." Or, "There will not be (nor has there ever been) any contradiction between an economy in free, natural expansion and the hygiene necessary to the human organism . . . between the smoke of our productive factories and the green of our incomparable natural beauty. . . ." Finally, the editorial policy is set. "We are one of the cities where the problem of air pollution is most serious, but at the same time we are the city where most is being done to counteract the situation. At the same time, you understand!" By some fifteen years, Calvino anticipated Exxon's double-talk ads on American television.

This is the first of Calvino's stories where a realistic affair takes place between a man and a woman—well, fairly realistic. We never know how the elegant and wealthy Claudia came to meet the narrator or what she sees in him; yet, periodically, she descends upon him, confuses him ("to embrace her, I had removed my glasses"). One day they drive out of the city. The narrator comments on the ugliness of the city and the ubiquitous smog. Claudia says that "people have lost the sense of beauty." He answers, "Beauty has to be constantly invented." They argue; he finds everything cruel. Later, he meets a proletarian who is in arms against Cordà. The narrator admires the worker Omar, admires "the stubborn ones, the tough ones." But Calvino does not really *engage,* in Sartre's sense. He suspects that the trap we are in is too great for mere politics to spring.

The narrator begins to write about atomic radiation in the atmosphere; about the way the weather is changing in the world. Is there a connection? Even Cordà is momentarily alarmed. But then life goes on, for is not Cordà himself "the smog's master? It was he who blew it out constantly over the city," and his magazine was "born of the need to give those working to produce the smog some hope of a life that was not all smog, and yet, at the same time, to celebrate its power."

The story's coda resembles that of "The Argentine Ant." The narrator goes to the outskirts of the city where the women are doing laundry. The sight is cheering. "It wasn't much, but for me, seeking only images to retain in my eyes, perhaps it was enough."

The next year Calvino switched to his other manner. *The Nonexistent Knight* is the last of the Our Ancestors trilogy though it comes first chronologically, in the age of Charlemagne. Again a war is going on. We are not introduced to the narrator until page 34—Sister Theodora is a nun in a convent who has been assigned to tell this story "for the health of the soul." Unfortunately, the plot is giving her a good deal of trouble because "we nuns have few occasions to speak with soldiers. . . . Apart from religious ceremonies, triduums, novenas, gardening, harvesting, vintaging, whippings, slavery, incest, fires, hangings, invasions, sacking, rape and pestilence, we have had no experience."

Sister Theodora does her best with the tale of Agiluf, a knight who does not exist. What does exist is a suit of white armor from which comes the voice of Agiluf. He is a devoted knight in the service of Charlemagne who thinks him a bit much but graciously concedes, "for someone who doesn't exist, you seem in fine form." Since Agiluf has no appetites or weaknesses, he is the perfect soldier and so disliked by all. As for Agiluf, "people's bodies gave him a disagreeable feeling resembling envy, but also a stab of pride of contemptuous superiority." A young man (an older version of Pin, of the cloven Viscount's nephew) named Raimbaut joins the army to avenge his father's death. Agiluf gives him dull advice. There are battles. General observations. "What is war, after all, but this passing of more and more dented objects from hand to hand?" Then a meeting with a man who confuses himself with things outside himself. When he drinks soup, he becomes soup; thinks he is soup to be drunk in turn: "the world being nothing but a vast shapeless mass of soup in which all things dissolved."

Calvino now strikes a theme which will be developed in later works. The confusion between "I"/"it"; "I"/"you"; the arbitrariness of naming things, of categorizing, and of setting apart, particularly when "World conditions were still confused in the era when this book took place. It was not rare then to find names and thoughts and forms and institutions that corresponded to nothing in existence. But at the same time the world was polluted with objects and capacities and persons who lacked any name or distinguishing mark."

A triangle occurs. Raimbaut falls in love with a knight who proves to be a young woman, Bradamante. Unfortunately, *she* falls in love with Agiluf, the nonexistent knight. At this point there is rather too much plot for Sister Theodora, who strikes the professional writer's saddest note. "One starts off writing with a certain zest, but a time comes when the pen merely grates in dusty ink, and not a drop of life flows, and life is all outside, outside the window, outside oneself, and it seems that never more can one escape into a page one is writing, open out another world, leap the gap."

But the teller finally gets a grip on the tale; closes the gap. Knightly quests are conducted, concluded. Agiluf surrenders his armor and ceases to be; Raimbaut is allowed to inhabit the armor. Bradamante has vanished, but with a fine *coup de théâtre* Sister Theodora reveals to us that *she* is Bradamante, who is now rushing the narrative to its end so that she can take the beloved white armor in her arms: aware that it now contains the young and passionate Raimbaut, her true love. "That is why my pen at a certain point began running on so. I rush to meet him. . . . A page is good only when we turn it and find life urging along. . . ."

With the completion of the trilogy, Calvino took to his other manner and wrote "The Watcher," the most realistic of his stories and the most overtly political. The narrator has a name, Amerigo Ormea. He is a poll watcher in Turin for the Communist party during the national election of 1953. Amerigo's poll is inside the vast "Cottolengo Hospital for Incurables." Apparently the mad and the senile and even the comatose are allowed to vote ("hospitals, asylums and convents had served as great reservoirs of votes for the Christian Democrat party"). Amerigo is a serene observer of democracy's confusions, having "learned that change, in politics, comes through long and complex processes"; he also confesses that "acquiring experience had meant becoming slightly pessimistic."

In the course of the day, Amerigo observes with fine dispassion the priests and nuns as they herd their charges into the polling booths that have been set up inside the hospital. Despite the grotesqueries of the situation, Amerigo takes some pleasure in the matter-of-factness of the voting, for "in Italy, which had always bowed and scraped before every form of pomp, display, sumptuousness, ornament, this seemed to him finally the lesson of an honest, austere morality, and a perpetual, silent revenge on the Fascists . . . ; now they had fallen into dust with all their gold fringe and their ribbons, while democracy, with its stark ceremony of pieces of paper folded over like telegrams, of pencils given to callused or shaky hands, went ahead."

But for the watcher boredom eventually sets in; it is a long day. "Amerigo felt a yearning need for beauty, which became focused in the thought of his mistress Lia." He contemplates Lia in reverie. "What is this need of ours for beauty? Amerigo asks himself." Apparently Calvino has not advanced much beyond the last dialogue in "Smog." He contemplates the perfection of classical Greece but recalls that the Greeks destroyed deformed children, redundant girls. Obviously placing beauty too high in the scale of values is "a step toward an inhuman civilization, which will then sentence the deformed to be thrown off a cliff."

When another poll watcher remarks to Amerigo that the mad all must recognize one another in Cottolengo, he slips into reverie: "They would remember that humanity could be a different thing, as in fables, a world of giants, an Olympus. . . . As we do: and perhaps, without realizing it, we are deformed, backward, compared to a different, forgotten form of existence. . . ." What is human, what is real?

Calvino's vision is usually presented in fantastic terms but now he becomes unusually concrete. Since he has elected to illuminate an actual time and place (Italy between 1945 and the election of 1953), he is able to spell it out. "In those years the Italian Communist party, among its many other tasks, had also assumed the position of an ideal liberal party, which had never really existed. And so the bosom of each individual communist could house two personalities at once: an intransigent revolutionary and an Olympian liberal." Amerigo's pessimism derives from the obvious fact that the two do not go together. I am reminded of Alexander Herzen's comment about the Latins: they do not want liberty, they want to sue for liberty.

Amerigo goes home to lunch (he has a maid who cooks and serves! Written in 1963 about the events of 1953, this is plainly a historical novel). He looks for a book to read. "Pure literature" is out. "Personal literature now seemed to him a row of tombstones in a cemetery; the literature of the living as well as of the dead. Now he sought something else from books: the wisdom of the ages or simply something that helped to understand something." He takes a stab at Marx's *Youthful Writings*. "Man's universality appears, practically speaking, in that same universe that makes all nature man's *inorganic body*. . . . Nature is man's *inorganic body* precisely because it is not his human body." Thus genius turns everything into itself. As Marx invented *Kapital* from capitalism, so Calvino turns a passage of Marx into Calvino himself: the man who drinks soup is the soup that drinks him. Wholeness is all.

Fortified with this reassuring text, Amerigo endures a telephone conversation with Lia. It is the usual quibbling conversation between Calvino protagonist and Calvino mistress. She tells him that she is pregnant. "Amerigo was an ardent supporter of birth control, even though his party's attitude on the subject was either agnostic or hostile. Nothing shocked him so much as the ease with which people multiply, and the more hungry and backward, the more they keep having children. . . ." In the land of Margaret Sanger this point of view is not exactly startling, but for an Italian communist a dozen years ago, the sense of a world dying of too many children, of too much "smog" was a monstrous revelation. At this point, Amerigo rounds on both the Bible and Marx as demented celebrators of human fecundity.

Amerigo returns to the hospital; observes children shaped like fish and again wonders at what point is a human being human. Finally the day ends; the voting is done. Amerigo looks out over the complex of hospital buildings and notes that the reddish sun appeared to open "perspectives of a city that had never been seen." Thus the Calvino coda strikes its first familiar chord. Laughing women cross the courtyard with a cauldron, "perhaps the evening soup. Even the ultimate city of imperfection has its perfect hour, the watcher thought, the hour, the moment, when every city is the City." In Italian the plural for the word "city" is also the singular.

Most realistic and specific of Calvino's works, "The Watcher" has proved (to date) to be the last of the "dry" narratives. In 1965 Calvino published *Cosmicomics*: twelve brief stories dealing in a fantastic way with the creation of the universe, man, society. Like Pin's young friend who decided that life indeed resembles the strip cartoon, Calvino has deployed his complex prose in order to compose in words a super strip cartoon narrated by Qfwfq whose progress from life inside the first atom to mollusk on the earth's sea floor to social-climbing amphibian to dinosaur to moon-farmer is told in a dozen episodes that are entirely unlike anything that anyone else has written since, well, let us say Lucian.

"At Daybreak" is the story of the creation of the universe as viewed by Qfwfq and his mysterious tribe consisting of a father, mother, sister, brother, Granny, as well as acquaintances—formless sentiencies who inhabit the universal dust that is on the verge of becoming the nebula which will contain our solar system. Where and who *they* are is, literally, obscure, since light has not yet been invented. So "there was nothing to do but wait, keep covered as best we could, doze, speak out now and then to make sure we were all still there; and, naturally, scratch ourselves; because—they can say what they like—all those particles spinning around had only one effect, a troublesome itching." That itch starts to change things. Condensation begins. Also, confusion: Granny loses her cushion, "a little ellipsoid of galactic matter." Things clot; nickel is formed; members of the tribe start flying off in all directions. Suddenly the condensation is complete and light breaks. The sun is now in its place and the planets begin their orbits "and, above all, it was deathly hot."

As the earth starts to jell, Qfwfq's sister takes fright and vanishes inside the planet and is not heard from again "until I met her, much later, at Canberra in 1912, married to a certain Sullivan, a retired railroad man, so changed I hardly recognized her."

The early Calvino was much like his peers Pavese and Vittorini—writers who tended to reflect the realistic storytelling of Hemingway and Dos Passos. Then Calvino moved to Paris, where he found his own voice or voices and became, to a degree, infected by the French. Since the writing of *Our Ancestors* and the three stories that make up *The Watcher,* Calvino has been influenced, variously, by Barthes and the semiologists, by Borges and by the now old New Novel. In *Cosmicomics* these influences are generally benign, since Calvino is too formidable and original an artist to be derailed by theoreticians or undone by the example of another creator. Nevertheless the story "A Sign in Space" comes perilously close to being altogether too reverent an obeisance to semiology.

As the sun takes two hundred million years to revolve around the galaxy, Qfwfq becomes obsessed with making a sign in space, something peculiarly his own to mark his passage as well as something that would impress anyone who might be watching. His ambition is the result of a desire to think because "to think something had never been possible, first because there were no things to think about, and second because signs to think of them by were lacking, but from the moment there was that sign, it was possible for someone thinking to think of a sign, and therefore that one, in the sense that the sign was the thing you could think about and also the sign of the thing thought, namely, itself." So he makes his sign ("I felt I was going forth to conquer the only thing that mattered to me, sign and dominion and name . . .").

Unfortunately, a spiteful contemporary named Kgwgk erases Qfwfq's sign and replaces it with his own. In a rage, Qfwfq wants "to make a new sign in space, a real sign that would make Kgwgk die of envy." So, out of competitiveness, art is born. But the task of sign-making is becoming more difficult because the world "was beginning to produce an image of itself, and in everything a form was beginning to correspond to a function" (a theme from *The Nonexistent Knight*) and "in this new sign of mine you could perceive the influence of our new way of looking at things, call it style if you like. . . ."

Qfwfq is delighted with his new sign but as time passes he likes it less and less, thinks it is a bit pretentious, old-fashioned; decides he must erase it before his rival sees it (so writers revise old books or make new ones that obliterate earlier works—yes, call it style if you like). Finally, Qfwfq erases the inadequate sign. For a time he is pleased that there is nothing in space which might make him look idiotic to a rival—in this, he resembles so many would-be writers who contrive to vanish into universities and, each year, by not publishing that novel or poem, increase their reputations.

But doing nothing is, finally, abhorrent to the real artist: Qfwfq starts to amuse himself by making *false* signs, "to annoy Kgwgk . . . notches in space, holes, stains, little tricks that only an incompetent creature like Kgwgk could mistake for signs." So the artist masochistically mocks his own art, shatters form (the sign) itself, makes jokes to confuse and exploit 57th Street. But then things get out of hand. To Qfwfq's horror, every time he passes what he thinks was one of his false signs, there are a dozen other signs, all scribbled over his.

Finally, everything was now so obscured by a crisscross of meaningless signs that "world and space seemed the mirror of each other, both minutely adorned with hieroglyphics and ideograms" including the badly inked tail of the letter *R* in an evening newspaper joined to a thready imperfection in the paper, one among the eight hundred thousand flakings of a tarred wall in the Melbourne docks. . . . In the universe now there was no longer a container and a thing contained, but only a general thickness of signs superimposed and coagulated."

Qfwfq gives up. There is no longer a point of reference "because it was clear that, independent of signs, space didn't exist and perhaps had never existed." So the story concludes; and the rest is the solipsism of art. To the old debate about being and non-being, Calvino adds his own vision of the multiplicity of signs which obliterates *all* meaning. Too many names for a thing is like no name for a thing; therefore, no thing, nothing.

"How Much Shall We Bet?" continues the theme. At the beginning Qfwfq "bet that there was going to be a universe, and I hit the nail on the head." This was the first bet he won with Dean (k)yK. Through the ages the two continue to make bets and Qfwfq usually wins because "I bet on the possibility of a certain event's taking place, whereas the Dean almost always bet against it."

Qfwfq kept on winning until he began to take wild leaps into the future. "On February 28, 1926, at Santhia, in the Province of Vercelli—got that? At number 18 in Via Garibaldi—you follow me? Signorina Giuseppina Pensotti, aged twenty-two, leaves her home at quarter to six in the afternoon; does she turn right or left?" Qfwfq starts losing. Then they begin to bet about characters in unwritten novels . . . will Balzac make Lucien de Rubempré kill himself at the end of *Les illusions perdues*? The Dean wins that one.

The two bettors end up in charge of vast research foundations which contain innumerable reference libraries. Finally, like man's universe itself, they begin to drown in signs and Qfwfq looks back nostalgically to the beginning, "How beautiful it was then, through that void, to draw lines and parabolas, pick out the precise point, the intersection between space and time when the event would spring forth, undeniable in the prominence of its glow; whereas now events come flowing down without interruption, like cement being poured, one column next to the other . . . a doughy mass of events without form or direction, which surrounds, submerges, crushes all reasoning."

In another story the last of the dinosaurs turns out to be Qfwfq, who meets and moves in with the next race. The New Ones don't realize that he is one of their dread enemies from the past. They think him remarkably ugly but not unduly alien. Qfwfq's attitude is like that of the protagonist in William Golding's *The Inheritors* except that in Calvino's version the last of the Old Ones merges with the inheritors. Amused, Qfwfq listens to the monstrous, conflicting legends about his race, tribute to the power of man's imagination, to the words he uses, to the signs he recognizes.

Finally, "I knew that the more the Dinosaurs disappear, the more they extend their dominion, and over forests far more vast than those that cover the continents: in the labyrinth of the survivors' thoughts." But Qfwfq was not at all sentimental about being the last dinosaur and at the story's end he left the New Ones and "travelled through valleys and plains. I came to a station, caught the first train, and was lost in the crowd."

In "The Spiral," the last of the *Cosmicomics*, Qfwfq is a mollusk on a rock in the primeval sea. The theme is again *in ovo omnes*. Calvino describes with minuteness the sensations of the mollusk on the rock, "damp and happy. . . . I was what they call a narcissist to a slight extent; I mean I stayed there observing myself all the time, I saw all my good points and all my defects, and I liked myself for the former and for the latter; I had no terms of comparison, you must remember that, too." Such was Eden. But then the heat of the sun started altering things; there were vibrations from another sex; there were eggs to be fertilized: love.

In response to the new things, Qfwfq expresses himself by making a shell which turns out to be a spiral that is not only very good for defense but unusually beautiful. Yet Qfwfq takes no credit for the beauty: "My shell made itself, without my taking any special pains to have it come out one way rather than another." But then the instinctive artist in the mollusk asserts itself: "This doesn't mean that I was absent-minded during that time; I applied myself instead, to the act of secreting. . . ." Meanwhile, *she,* the beloved, is making *her* shell, identical with his.

Ages pass. The shell-Qfwfq is on a railroad embankment as a train passes by. A party of Dutch girls looks out the window. Qfwfq is not startled by anything, for "I feel as if, in making the shell, I had also made the rest." But one new element has entered the equation. "I had failed to foresee one thing: the eyes that finally opened to see us didn't belong to us but to others." So dies Narcissus. "They developed eyes at our expense. So sight, *our* sight, which we were obscurely waiting for, was the sight that the others had of us."

But the artist who made the spiral-shaped shell is not to be outdone by miscalculation or by fate. Proudly he concludes: "All these eyes were mine. I had made them possible; I had had the active part; I furnished them the raw material, the image." Again the gallant coda, for fixed in the watcher's eye is not only the fact of the beautiful shell that *he* made but also "the most faithful image of her" who had inspired the shell and was the shell: thus male and female are at last united in the retina of a stranger's eye.

In 1967, Calvino published more of Qfwfq's adventures in *Time and the Hunter.* For the most part they are engaging cartoons, but one is disconcerted to encounter altogether too many bits of Sarraute, of Robbe-Grillet, of Borges (far too much of Borges) incorporated in the prose of what I have come to regard as a true modern master. On page 6 occurs "viscous"; on page 11 "acid mucus." I started to feel queasy: these are Sarraute words. I decided that their use was simply a matter of coincidence. But when, on page 29, I saw the dread word "magma"

I knew that Calvino has been too long in Paris, for only Sarrautistes use "magma," a word the great theoretician of the old New Novel so arbitrarily and uniquely appropriated from the discipline of science. Elsewhere in the stories, Robbe-Grillet's technique of recording the minutiae of a banal situation stops cold some of Calvino's best effects.

"The Chase," in fact, could have been written by Robbe-Grillet. This is not a compliment. Take the beginning:

That car chasing me is faster than mine; inside there is one man, alone, armed with a pistol, a good shot. . . . We have stopped at a traffic signal, in a long column. The signal is regulated in such a way that on our side the red light lasts a hundred and eighty seconds and the green light a hundred and twenty, no doubt based on the premise that the perpendicular traffic is heavier and slower.

And so on for sixteen pages, like a movie in slow motion.

The theory behind this sort of enervating prose is as follows, since to write is to describe, with words, why not then describe words themselves (with other words)? Or, glory be! words describing words describing an action of no importance (the corner of that room in Robbe-Grillet's *Jalousie*). This sort of "experiment" has always seemed to me to be of more use to students of language than to readers of writing. On his own and at his best, Calvino does what very few writers can do: he describes imaginary worlds with the most extraordinary precision and beauty (a word he has single-handedly removed from that sphere of suspicion which the old New Novelists maintain surrounds all words and any narrative).

In *Cosmicomics* Calvino makes it possible for the reader to inhabit a meson, a mollusk, a dinosaur; makes him for the first time see light ending a dark universe. Since this is a unique gift, I find all the more alarming the "literariness" of *Time and the Hunter.* I was particularly put off by the central story "t zero," which could have been written (and rather better) by Borges.

With a bow and arrow, Qfwfq confronts a charging lion. In his head he makes an equation: Time zero is where he Qfwfq is; where the Lion-o is. All combinations of a series which may be finite or infinite pass through Qo's head, exactly like the man before the firing squad in Borges's celebrated story. Now it is possible that these stories will appeal to minds more convergent than mine (students of mathematics, engineers, Young Republicans are supposed to think convergently while novelists, gourmets, and non-Christian humanists think divergently) but to me this pseudo-scientific rendering of a series of possibilities is deeply boring.

But there are also pleasures in this collection. Particularly "The Origin of the Birds." "Now these stories can be told better with strip drawings than with a story composed of sentences one after the other." So the crafty Calvino by placing one sentence after another *describes* a strip cartoon and the effect is charming even though Qfwfq's adventure among the birds is not really a strip cartoon but the description of a cartoon *in words.*

The narrator's technique is like that of *The Nonexistent Knight.* He starts to draw a scene; then erases it the way Sister Theodora used to eliminate oceans and forests as she hurried her lovers to their inevitable rendezvous. Calvino also comes as close as any writer can to saying that which is sensed about creation but may not be put into words or drawn in pictures.

"I managed to embrace in a single thought the world of things as they were and of things as they could have been, and I realized that a single system included all." In the arms of Or, the queen of the birds, Qfwfq begins to *see* that "the world is single and what exists can't be explained without . . ." But he has gone too far. As he is about to say the unsayable, Or tries to smother him. But he is still able to blurt out, "There's no difference. Monsters and non-monsters have always been close to one another! What hasn't been continues to be. . . ." At that point, the birds expel him from their paradise; and like a dreamer rudely awakened, he forgets his vision of unity. "(The last strip is all photographs: a bird, the same bird in close-up, the head of the bird enlarged, a detail of the head, the eye. . . .)" It is the same eye that occurs at the end of *Cosmicomics,* the eye of—cosmic consciousness for those who recall that guru of a past generation, Dr. Richard M. Bucke.

Calvino ends these tales with his own *The Count of Monte Cristo.* The problem he sets himself is how to get out of Château d'If. Faria keeps making plans and tunneling his way through an endless, exitless fortress. Dantès, on the other hand, broods on the nature of the fortress as well as on the various drafts of the novel that Dumas is writing. In some drafts, Dantès will escape and find a treasure and get revenge on his enemies. In other drafts, he suffers a different fate. The narrator contemplates the possibilities of escape by considering the way a fortress (or a work of art) is made. "To plan a book—or an escape—the first thing to know is what to exclude." This particular story is Borges at his very best and, taking into account the essential unity of the multiplicity of all things, one cannot rule out that Calvino's version of *The Count of Monte Cristo* by Alexandre Dumas is indeed the finest achievement of Jorge Luis Borges as imagined by Italo Calvino.

Calvino's seventh and latest novel (or work or meditation or poem), *Invisible Cities,* is perhaps his most beautiful work. In a garden sit the aged Kublai Khan and the young Marco Polo—Tartar emperor and Venetian traveler. The mood is sunset. Prospero is holding up for the last time his magic wand: Kublai Khan has sensed the end of his empire, of his cities, of himself.

Marco Polo, however, diverts the emperor with tales of cities that he has seen within the empire and Kublai Khan listens, searches for a pattern in Marco Polo's Cities and memory, Cities and desire, Cities and signs, Thin Cities, Trading Cities, Cities and eyes, Cities and names, Cities and the dead, Cities and the sky, Continuous Cities, Hidden Cities. The emperor soon determines that each of these fantastic places is really the same place.

Marco Polo agrees: " 'Memory's images, once they are fixed in words, are erased,' Polo said." " 'Perhaps I am afraid of losing Venice all at once, if I speak of it, or perhaps, speaking of other cities, I have already lost it, little by little.' " Again the theme of multiplicity and wholeness, "when every city," as Calvino wrote at the end of "The Watcher," "is the City."

Of all tasks, describing the contents of a book is the most difficult and in the case of a marvelous creation like *Invisible Cities,* perfectly irrelevant. I shall spare myself the labor; noting, however, that something new and wise has begun to enter the Calvino canon. The artist seems to have made a peace with the tension between man's idea of the many and of the one. He could now, if he wanted, stop.

Yet Calvino is obliged to go on writing just as his Marco Polo goes on traveling because

he cannot stop; he must go on to another city, where another of his pasts awaits him, or something perhaps that had been a possible future of his and is now someone else's present. Futures not achieved are only branches of the past: dead branches.

"Journeys to relive your past?" was the Khan's question at this point, a question which could also have been formulated: "Journeys to recover your future?"

And Marco's answer was: "Elsewhere is a negative mirror. The traveler recognizes the little that is his, discovering the much he has not had and will never have."

Later, after more descriptions of his cities, Kublai Khan decides that "the empire is nothing but a zodiac of the mind's phantasms."

"On the day when I know all the emblems," he asked Marco, "shall I be able to possess my empire, at last?"

And the Venetian answered, "Sire, do not believe it. On that day you will be an emblem among emblems."

Finally, Kublai Khan recognizes that all cities are tending toward the concentric circles of Dante's hell.

He said: "It is all useless, if the last landing place can only be the infernal city, and it is there that, in ever-narrowing circles, the current is drawing us."

And Polo said: "The inferno of the living is not something that will be; if there is one, it is what is already here, the inferno where we live every day, that we form by being together. There are two ways to escape suffering it. The first is easy for many: accept the inferno and become such a part of it that you can no longer see it. The second is risky and demands constant vigilance and apprehension; seek and learn to recognize who and what, in the midst of the inferno, are not inferno, then make them endure, give them space."

During the last quarter century Italo Calvino has advanced far beyond his American and English contemporaries. As they continue to look for the place where the spiders make their nests, Calvino has not only found that special place but learned how himself to make fantastic webs of prose to which all things adhere. In fact, reading Calvino, I had the unnerving sense that I was also writing what he had written; thus does his art prove his case as writer and reader become one, or One.

*The New York Review of Books*
May 30, 1974

# 46

·

# *CALVINO'S DEATH*

On the morning of Friday, September 20, 1985, the first equinoctial storm of the year broke over the city of Rome. I awoke to thunder and lightning; and thought I was, yet again, in the Second World War. Shortly before noon, a car and driver arrived to take me up the Mediterranean coast to a small town on the sea called Castiglion della Pescáia where, at one o'clock, Italo Calvino, who had died the day before, would be buried in the village cemetery.

Calvino had had a cerebral hemorrhage two weeks earlier while sitting in the garden of his house at Pineta di Roccamare, where he had spent the summer working on the Charles Eliot Norton lectures that he planned to give during the fall and winter at Harvard. I last saw him in May. I commended him on his bravery: He planned to give the lectures in English, a language that he read easily but spoke hesitantly, unlike French and Spanish, which he spoke perfectly; but then he had been born in Cuba, son of two Italian agronomists; and had lived for many years in Paris.

It was night. We were on the terrace of my apartment in Rome; an overhead light made his deep-set eyes look even darker than usual. Italo gave me his either-this-or-that frown; then he smiled, and when he smiled, suddenly, the face would become like that of an enormously bright child who has just worked out the unified field theory. "At

Harvard, I shall stammer," he said. "But then I stammer in every language."

Unlike the United States, Italy has both an educational system (good or bad is immaterial) and a common culture, both good and bad. In recent years Calvino had become the central figure in Italy's culture. Italians were proud that they had produced a world writer whose American reputation began, if I may say so, since no one else has, when I described all of his novels as of May 30, 1974 in *The New York Review of Books.* By 1985, except for England, Calvino was read wherever books are read. I even found a Calvino coven in Moscow's literary bureaucracy, and I think that I may have convinced the state publishers to translate more of him. Curiously, the fact that he had slipped away from the Italian Communist party in 1957 disturbed no one.

Three weeks short of Calvino's sixty-second birthday, he died; and Italy went into mourning, as if a beloved prince had died. For an American, the contrast between them and us is striking. When an American writer dies, there will be, if he's a celebrity (fame is no longer possible for any of us), a picture below the fold on the front page; later, a short appreciation on the newspaper's book page (if there is one), usually the work of a journalist or other near-writer who has not actually read any of the dead author's work but is at home with the arcana of gossipy "Page Six"; and that would be that.

In Calvino's case, the American newspaper obituaries were perfunctory and incompetent: The circuits between the English departments, where our tablets of literary reputation are now kept, and the world of journalism are more than ever fragile and the reception is always bad. Surprisingly, *Time* and *Newsweek,* though each put him on the "book page," were not bad, though one thought him "surrealist" and the other a "master of fantasy"; he was, of course, a true realist, who believed "that only a certain prosaic solidity can give birth to creativity: fantasy is like jam; you have to spread it on a solid slice of bread. If not, it remains a shapeless thing, like jam, out of which you can't make anything." This homely analogy is from an Italian television interview, shown after his death.

*The New York Times,* to show how well regarded Calvino is in these parts, quoted John Updike, our literature's perennial apostle to the middlebrows* (this is not meant, entirely, unkindly), as well as Marga-

---

*Although the three estates, high-, middle-, and lowbrow, are as dead as Dwight Macdonald, their most vigorous deployer, something about today's literary scene,

ret Atwood (a name new to me), Ursula K. Le Guin (an estimable sci-fi writer, but what is she doing, giving, as it were, a last word on one of the most complex of modern writers?), Michael Wood, whose comment was pretty good, and, finally, the excellent Anthony Burgess, who was not up to his usual par on this occasion. Elsewhere, Mr. Herbert Mitgang again quoted Mr. Updike as well as John Gardner, late apostle to the lowbrows, a sort of Christian evangelical who saw Heaven as a paradigmatic American university.

Europe regarded Calvino's death as a calamity for culture. A literary critic, as opposed to theorist, wrote at length in *Le Monde,* while in Italy itself, each day for two weeks, bulletins from the hospital at Siena were published, and the whole country was suddenly united in its esteem not only for a great writer but for someone who reached not only primary schoolchildren through his collections of folk and fairy tales but, at one time or another, everyone else who reads.

After the first hemorrhage, there was a surgical intervention that lasted many hours. Calvino came out of coma. He was disoriented: He thought that one of the medical attendants was a policeman; then he wondered if he'd had open-heart surgery. Meanwhile, the surgeon had become optimistic, even garrulous. He told the press that he'd never seen a brain structure of such delicacy and complexity as that of Calvino. I thought immediately of the smallest brain ever recorded, that of Anatole France. The surgeon told the press that he had been obliged to do his very best. After all, he and his sons had read and argued over *Marcovaldo* last winter. The brain that could so puzzle them must be kept alive in all its rarity. One can imagine a comparable surgeon in America: Only last Saturday she had kept me and my sons in stitches; now I could hardly believe that I was actually gazing into the fabulous brain of Joan Rivers! On the other hand, the admirer of Joan Rivers might have saved Calvino; except that there was no real hope, ever. In June he had had what he thought was a bad headache; it was the first stroke. Also, he came from a family with a history of arterial weakness. Or so it was said in the newspapers. The press coverage of Calvino's final days resembled nothing so much as that of the recent operation on the ancient actor that our masters have hired to impersonate a president, the sort of subject that used to delight Calvino—the Acting President, that is.

---

combined with Calvino's death, impels me to resurrect the terms. Presently, I shall demonstrate.

. . .

As we drove north through the rain, I read Calvino's last novel, *Palomar*. He had given it to me on November 28, 1983. I was chilled—and guilty—to read for the first time the inscription: "For Gore, these last meditations about Nature, Italo." *Last* is a word artists should not easily use. What did this "last" mean? Latest? Or his last attempt to write about the phenomenal world? Or did he know, somehow, that he was in the process of "Learning to be dead," the title of the book's last chapter?

I read the book. It is very short. A number of meditations on different subjects by one Mr. Palomar, who is Calvino himself. The settings are, variously, the beach at Castiglion della Pescáia, the nearby house in the woods at Roccamare, the flat in Rome with its terrace, a food specialty shop in Paris. This is not the occasion to review the book. But I made some observations and marked certain passages that seemed to me to illuminate the prospect.

Palomar is on the beach at Castiglion: he is trying to figure out the nature of waves. Is it possible to follow just one? Or do they all become one? *E pluribus unum* and its reverse might well sum up Calvino's approach to our condition. Are we a part of the universe? Or is the universe, simply, us thinking that there is such a thing? Calvino often writes like the scientist that his parents were. He observes, precisely, the minutiae of nature: stars, waves, lizards, turtles, a woman's breast exposed on the beach. In the process, he vacillates between macro and micro. The whole and the part. Also, tricks of eye. The book is written in the present tense, like a scientist making reports on that ongoing experiment, the examined life.

The waves provide him with suggestions but no answers: Viewed in a certain way, they seem to come not from the horizon but from the shore itself. "Is this perhaps the real result that Mr. Palomar is about to achieve? To make the waves run in the opposite direction, to overturn time, to perceive the true substance of the world beyond sensory and mental habits?" But it doesn't quite work, and he cannot extend "this knowledge to the entire universe." He notes during his evening swim that "the sun's reflection becomes a shining sword on the water stretching from shore to him. Mr. Palomar swims in that sword . . ." But then so does everyone else at that time of day, each in the same sword which is everywhere and nowhere. "The sword is imposed equally on the eye of each swimmer; there is no avoiding it. 'Is what we have in common precisely what is given to each of us as something exclusively his?' " As

Palomar floats he wonders if he exists. He drifts now toward solipsism: "If no eye except the glassy eye of the dead were to open again on the surface of the terraqueous globe, the sword would not gleam any more." He develops this, floating on his back. "Perhaps it was not the birth of the eye that caused the birth of the sword, but vice versa, because the sword had to have an eye to observe it at its climax." But the day is ending, the windsurfers are all beached, and Palomar comes back to land: "He has become convinced that the sword will exist even without him."

In the garden at Roccamare, Palomar observes the exotic mating of turtles; he ponders the blackbird's whistle, so like that of a human being that it might well be the same sort of communication. "Here a prospect that is very promising for Mr. Palomar's thinking opens out; for him the discrepancy between human behavior and the rest of the universe has always been a source of anguish. The equal whistle of man and blackbird now seems to him a bridge thrown over the abyss." But his attempts to communicate with them through a similar whistling leads to "puzzlement" on both sides. Then, contemplating the horrors of his lawn and its constituent parts, among them weeds, he precisely names and numbers what he sees until "he no longer thinks of the lawn: he thinks of the universe. He is trying to apply to the universe everything he has thought about the lawn. The universe as regular and ordered cosmos or as chaotic proliferation." The analogy, as always with Calvino, then takes off (the jam on the bread) and the answer is again the many within the one, or "collections of collections."

Observations and meditations continue. He notes, "Nobody looks at the moon in the afternoon, and this is the moment when it would most require our attention, since its existence is still in doubt." As night comes on, he wonders if the moon's bright splendor is "due to the slow retreat of the sky, which, as it moves away, sinks deeper and deeper into darkness or whether, on the contrary it is the moon that is coming forward, collecting the previously scattered light and depriving the sky of it, concentrating it all in the round mouth of its funnel." One begins now to see the method of a Calvino meditation. He looks; he describes; he has a scientist's respect for data (the opposite of the surrealist or fantasist). He wants us to see not only what he sees but what we may have missed by not looking with sufficient attention. It is no wonder that Galileo crops up in his writing. The received opinion of mankind over the centuries (which is what middlebrow is all about) was certain that the sun moved around the earth but to a divergent highbrow's mind, Galileo's or Calvino's, it is plainly the other way around. Galileo applied the scientific methods of his day; Calvino used his imagination. Each either got it right or assembled the data so that others could understand the phenomenon.

In April 1982, while I was speaking to a Los Angeles audience with George McGovern, Eugene McCarthy, and the dread physical therapist Ms. Fonda-Hayden, "the three 'external' planets, visible to the naked eye . . . are all three 'in opposition' and therefore visible for the whole night." Needless to say, "Mr. Palomar rushes out on to the terrace." Between Calvino's stars and mine, he had the better of it; yet he wrote a good deal of political commentary for newspapers. But after he left the Communist party, he tended more to describe politics and its delusions than take up causes. "In a time and in a country where everyone goes out of his way to announce opinions or hand down judgments, Mr. Palomar has made a habit of biting his tongue three times before asserting anything. After the bite, if he is still convinced of what he was going to say, he says it." But then, "having had the correct view is nothing meritorious; statistically, it is almost inevitable that among the many cockeyed, confused or banal ideas that come into his mind, there should also be some perspicacious ideas, even ideas of genius; and as they occurred to him, they can surely have occurred also to somebody else." As he was a writer of literature and not a theorist, so he was an observer of politics and not a politician.

Calvino was as inspired by the inhabitants of zoos as by those of cities. "At this point Mr. Palomar's little girl, who has long since tired of watching the giraffes, pulls him toward the penguins' cave. Mr. Palomar, in whom penguins inspire anguish, follows her reluctantly and asks himself why he is so interested in giraffes. Perhaps because the world around him moves in an unharmonious way, and he hopes always to find some pattern to it, a constant. Perhaps because he himself feels that his own advance is impelled by uncoordinated movements of the mind, which seem to have nothing to do with one another and are increasingly difficult to fit into any pattern of inner harmony."

Palomar is drawn to the evil-smelling reptile house. "Beyond the glass of every cage, there is the world as it was before man, or after, to show that the world of man is not eternal and is not unique." The crocodiles, in their stillness, horrify him. "What are they waiting for, or what have they given up waiting for? In what time are they immersed? . . . The

thought of a time outside our existence is intolerable." Palomar flees to
the albino gorilla, "sole exemplar in the world of a form not chosen, not
loved." The gorilla, in his boredom, plays with a rubber tire; he presses
it to his bosom by the hour. The image haunts Palomar. " 'Just as the
gorilla has his tire, which serves as tangible support for a raving, word-
less speech,' he thinks, 'so I have this image of a great white ape. We
all turn in our hands an old, empty tire through which we would like
to reach the final meaning, at which words do not arrive.' " This is the
ultimate of writers' images; that indescribable state where words are
absent not because they are stopped by the iron bars of a cage at the zoo
but by the limitations of that bone-covered binary electrical system
which, in Calvino's case, broke down on September 19, 1985.

Suddenly, up ahead, on a hill overlooking the sea, is Castiglion della
Pescáia. To my left is the beach where Palomar saw but sees no longer
the sword of light. The sea has turned an odd disagreeable purple color,
more suitable to the Caribbean of Calvino's birth than the Mediterranean. The sky is overcast. The air is hot, humid, windless (the headline
of today's newspaper, which has devoted six pages to Calvino's life and
work: CATACLISMA IN MESSICO). I am forty minutes early.

The cemetery is on a hill back of the town which is on a lower hill.
We park next to a piece of medieval wall and a broken tower. I walk
up to the cemetery which is surrounded by a high cement wall. I am
reminded of Calvino's deep dislike of cement. In one of his early books,
*La Speculazione Edilizia,* he described how the building trade had
managed, in the 1950s, to bury the Italian Riviera, his native Liguria,
under a sea of "horrible reinforced cement"; "*il boom,*" it was called.
To the right of the cemetery entrance a large section of wall has been
papered over with the same small funeral notice, repeated several hundred times. The name "Italo Calvino," the name of Castiglion della
Pescáia, "the town of Palomar," the sign says proudly; then the homage
of mayor and city council and populace.

Inside the cemetery there are several walled-off areas. The first is a
sort of atrium, whose walls are filled with drawers containing the dead,
stacked one above the other, each with a photograph of the occupant,
taken rather too late in life to arouse much pity as opposed to awe. There
are plastic flowers everywhere and a few real flowers. There are occasional small chapels, the final repository of wealthy or noble families.
I have a sense of panic: They aren't going to put Italo in a drawer, are
they? But then to the right, at the end of the atrium, in the open air,

against a low wall, I see a row of vast floral wreaths, suitable for an American or Neapolitan gangster, and not a drawer but a new grave, the size of a bathtub in a moderately luxurious hotel. On one of the wreaths, I can make out the words *Senato* and *Communist . . .* , the homage of the Communist delegation in the Italian Senate. Parenthetically, since Italy is a country of many political parties and few ideologies, the level of the ordinary parliamentarian is apt to be higher than his American or English counterpart. Moravia sits in the European Parliament. Sciascia was in the chamber of deputies. Every party tries to put on its electoral list a number of celebrated intellectual names. The current mayor of Florence was, until recently, the head of the Paris Opéra: According to popular wisdom, anyone who could handle that can of worms can probably deal with Florence.

Over the wall, the purple sea and red-tiled whitewashed houses are visible. As I gaze, moderately melancholy, at Palomar country, I am recognized by a journalist from Naples. I am a neighbor, after all; I live at nearby Ravello. Among the tombs, I am interviewed. How had I met Calvino? A few drops of warm rain fall. A cameraman appears from behind a family chapel and takes my picture. The state television crew is arriving. Eleven years ago, I say, I wrote a piece about his work. Had you met him *before* that? Logrolling is even more noticeable in a small country like Italy than it is in our own dear *New York Times*. No, I had not met him when I wrote the piece. I had just read him, admired him; described (the critic's only task) his work for those who were able to read me (the critic's single aim). Did you meet him later? Yes, he wrote me a letter about the piece. In Italian or English? Italian, I say. What did he say? What do you think he said? I am getting irritable. He said he liked what I'd written.

Actually, Calvino's letter had been, characteristically, interesting and tangential. I had ended my description with "Reading Calvino, I had the unnerving sense that I was also writing what he had written; thus does his art prove his case as writer and reader become one, or One." This caught his attention. Politely, he began by saying that he had always been attracted by my "mordant irony," and so forth, but he particularly liked what I had written about him for two reasons. The first, "One feels that you have written this essay for the pleasure of writing it, alternating warm praise and criticism and reserve with an absolute sincerity, with freedom, and continuous humor, and this sensation of pleasure is irresistibly communicated to the reader. Second, I have always thought it would be difficult to extract a unifying theme from my books, each so different from the other. Now you—exploring my works as it should be done, that is, by going at it in an unsystematic way, stopping here and there; sometimes aimed directly without straying aside; other times, wandering like a vagabond—have succeeded in giving a general sense to all I have written, almost a philosophy—'the whole and the many,' etc.—and it makes me very happy when someone is able to find a philosophy from the productions of my mind which has little philosophy." Then Calvino comes to the point. "The ending of your essay contains an affirmation of what seems to me important in an absolute sense. I don't know if it really refers to me, but it is true of an ideal literature for each one of us: the end being that every one of us must be, that the writer and reader become one, or One. And to close all of my discourse and yours in a perfect circle, let us say that this One is All." In a sense, the later Palomar was the gathering together of the strands of a philosophy or philosophies; hence, the inscription "my last meditations on Nature."

I let slip not a word of this to the young journalist. But I do tell him that soon after the letter I had met Calvino and his wife, Chichita, at the house of an American publisher, and though assured that there would be no writers there but us, I found a room ablaze with American literary genius. Fearful of becoming prematurely One with them, I split into the night.

Two years ago, when I was made an honorary citizen of Ravello, Calvino accepted the town's invitation to participate in the ceremony, where he delivered a splendid discourse on my work in general and on *Duluth* in particular. Also, since Calvino's Roman flat was on the same street as mine (we were separated by—oh, the beauty of the random symbol!—the Pantheon), we saw each other occasionally.

For the last year, Calvino had been looking forward to his fall and winter at Harvard. He even began to bone up on "literary theory." He knew perfectly well what a mephitic kindergarten our English departments have become, and I cannot wait to see what he has to say in the five lectures that he did write. I had planned to arm him with a wonderfully silly bit of lowbrow criticism (from *Partisan Review*) on why people just don't like to read much anymore. John Gardner is quoted with admiration: " 'In nearly all good fiction, the basic—all but inescapable—plot form is this: a central character wants something, goes after it despite opposition (perhaps including his own doubts), and so arrives

at a win, lose or draw.' " For those still curious about high-, middle-,
and lowbrow, this last is the Excelsior of lowbrow commercialites,
written in letters of gold in the halls of the Thalberg Building at MGM
but never to be found in, say, the original *Partisan Review* of Rahv and
Dupee, Trilling and Chase. The *PR* "critic" then quotes "a reviewer"
in *The New York Times* who is trying to figure out why Calvino is
popular. "If love fails, they begin again; their lives are a series of new
beginnings, where complications have not yet begun to show themselves. Unlike the great Russian and French novelists [this is pure
middlebrow: *Which* novelists, dummy? Name names, make your case,
*describe*], who follow their characters through the long and winding
caverns [!] of their lives, Calvino just turns off the set after the easy
beginning and switches to another channel." This sort of writing has
given American bookchat a permanently bad name. But our *PR* critic,
a woman, this year's favored minority (*sic*), states, sternly, that all this
"indeterminacy" is not the kind of stuff real folks want to read. "And
Calvino is popular, if at all, among theorists, consumers of 'texts' rather
than of novels and stories." I shall now never have the chance to laugh
with Calvino over this latest report from the land to which Bouvard and
Pécuchet emigrated.

At the foot of cemetery hill, a van filled with police arrives. Crowds
are anticipated. The day before, the president of the republic had come
to the Siena hospital to say farewell. One can imagine a similar scene
in the United States. High atop the Tulsa Tower Hospital, the Reverend
Oral Roberts enters the hushed room. "Mr. President, it's all over. *He*
has crossed the shining river." A tear gleams in the Acting President's
eye. "The last roundup," he murmurs. The tiny figure at his side, huge
lidless eyes aswim with tears, whispers, "Does this mean, no more
Harlequin novels?" The Acting President holds her close. "There will
always be Harlequins, Mommie," he says. "But they won't be the same.
Not without Louis L'Amour."

Now several hundred friends of Calvino, writers, editors, publishers,
press, local dignitaries fill up the cemetery. I hold Chichita's hand a long
moment; she has had, someone said, two weeks of coming to terms not
so much with death as with the nightmare of dying.

The last chapter of *Palomar* begins, "Mr. Palomar decides that from
now on he will act as if he were dead, to see how the world gets along
without him." So far, not too good, I thought. Mexico City has fallen
down and his daughter is late to the burial. On the plus side, there is

no priest, no service, no words. Suddenly, as a dozen television cameras switch on, the dark shiny wooden box, containing Calvino, appears in the atrium. How small the box is, I think. Was he smaller than I remember? Or has he shrunk? Of course, he is dead but, as he wrote, "First of all, you must not confuse being dead with not being, a condition that occupies the vast expanse of time before birth, apparently symmetrical with the other, equally vast expanse that follows death. In fact, before birth we are part of the infinite possibilities that may or may not be fulfilled; whereas, once dead, we cannot fulfill ourselves either in the past (to which we now belong entirely but on which we can no longer have any influence) or in the future (which, even if influenced by us, remains forbidden to us)."

With a crash, the pallbearers drop the box into the shallow bathtub. Palomar's nose is now about four inches beneath the earth he used to examine so minutely. Then tiles are casually arranged over the coffin; and the box is seen no more. As we wait for the daughter to arrive, the heat is disagreeable. We look at one another as though we are at a party that has refused to take off. I recognize Natalia Ginzburg. I see someone who looks as if he ought to be Umberto Eco, and is. "A person's life consists of a collection of events, the last of which could also change the meaning of the whole . . ." I notice, in the crowd, several dozen young schoolchildren. They are fans of Calvino's fairy tales; plainly, precocious consumers of "texts" and proto-theorists. Then daughter and buckets of cement arrive simultaneously. One of the masons pours cement over the tiles; expertly, he smooths the viscous surface with a trowel. Horrible cement. "Therefore Palomar prepares to become a grouchy dead man, reluctant to submit to the sentence to remain exactly as he is; but he is unwilling to give up anything of himself, even if it is a burden." Finally, the cement is flush with the ground; and that's that.

I am standing behind Chichita, who is very still. Finally, I look up from the gray oblong of fresh cement and there, staring straight at me, is Calvino. He looks anguished, odd, not quite right. But it is unmistakably Mr. Palomar, witnessing his own funeral. For one brief mad moment we stare at each other; then he looks down at the coffin that contains not himself but Italo. The man I thought was Italo is his younger brother, Floriano.

I move away, before the others. On the drive back to Rome, the sun is bright and hot; yet rain starts to fall. Devil is beating his wife, as they say in the South. Then a rainbow covers the entire eastern sky. For the Romans and the Etruscans, earlier inhabitants of the countryside through which we are driving, the rainbow was an ominous herald of coming change in human affairs, death of kings, cities, world. I make a gesture to ward off the evil eye. Time can now end. But " 'If time has to end, it can be described, instant by instant,' Palomar thinks, 'and each instant, when described, expands so that its end can no longer be seen.' He decides that he will set himself to describing every instant of his life, and until he has described them all he will no longer think of being dead. At that moment he dies." So end "my last meditations on Nature," as Calvino and Nature are now one, or One.

*The New York Review of Books*
November 21, 1985

# 47

## *MONTAIGNE*

"In every work of genius," wrote Emerson, "we recognize our own rejected thoughts; they come back to us with a certain alienated majesty." After four centuries, Montaigne's curious genius still has that effect on his readers and, time and again, one finds in his self-portrait one's own most brilliant *aperçus* (the ones that somehow we forgot to write down and so forgot) restored to us in his essays—attempts—to assay—value—himself in his own time as well as, if he was on the subject, all time, if there is such a thing.

For thirty years I have kept Donald M. Frame's translation of *The Complete Works of Montaigne* at, if not bedside, hand. There are numerous interlocking Olympic circles on the maroon binding where glasses were set after I had written some no longer decipherable commentary in the margin or, simply, "How true!" I never actually read all of *The Complete Works,* but I did read here and there, and I reread favourite essays rather more than I ever tried to read the famous "Apology for Raymond Sebond," who needed, I used to think, neither apology nor indeed memorial. But the generation of the twenty-first century is now in place, and to celebrate its entry into the greenhouse there is a new translation of *The Complete Essays of Montaigne* by M. A. Screech who, years ago, so ably—even sternly—led me through Rabelais.

It has taken me one month to read every one of the 1,269 pages.

(Montaigne, III 8: "I have just read through at one go Tacitus's *History* [something which rarely happens to me, it is twenty years since I spent one full hour at a time on a book]. . . .") I enjoyed comparing Screech with Frame. Where Frame is sonorous and euphemistic, Screech is sharp and up-to-date, as readers of his *Montaigne and Melancholy* (1983) might suspect. Although my nature inclines me to enrol Montaigne in the relativist school of Lucretius and the Epicureans, thus making him proto-Enlightenment, Screech firmly nails Montaigne within the Roman Catholic Church of his day, beleaguered as it was by the Reformation, which took the form of civil war in France between Catholics and Protestants, an ideological, that is pointless, war of the crude sort that has entertained us for so much of our own science-ridden century.

Michel Eyquem was born in 1533 at his father's estate, Montaigne, east of Bordeaux. A family of fish and wine merchants, the Eyquems were minimally ennobled by the acquisition of Montaigne, which gave them their "de." The mother's family were Spanish Jewish, presumably long since converted. When schism came, Michel, his parents, two brothers and a sister remained Catholic, while one brother and two sisters became Protestant. By the 1560s, there was an out-and-out civil war that continued to Michel's death in 1592. The Montaigne family remained on amiable terms not only with the Catholic court at Paris but with that Protestant sovereign of nearby Navarre who so proverbially celebrated a Mass in order to become King Henry IV of France.

Montaigne's education was odd but useful. As his tutor spoke no French, Latin became his first language, spoken and written, until he was six. Then he went on to spend seven years at a Latin school, where he was immersed in the Roman classics; but little Greek. He also learned the agreed-upon French of the day, as well as Gascon dialect. He was more or less trained to be a soldier, a lawyer, an estate manager and what used to be called a "gentleman," a category that no longer exists in our specialized time. As such, Montaigne naturally hated lying, and it was his essay on the subject that first drew me to him years ago. "Lying is an accursed vice. It is only our words which bind us together and make us human. If we realized the horror and weight of lying, we would see that it is more worthy of the stake than other crimes. . . . Once let the tongue acquire the habit of lying and it is astonishing how impossible it is to make it give it up" (I 8). As one who has been obliged to spend a lifetime in diverse liar-worlds (worlds where the liar is often most honoured when he is known to be lying and getting away with it), I find Montaigne consoling.

Montaigne's father became Mayor of Bordeaux, while his son spent thirteen years in the city's legal council. It was during this period that he met a fellow public servant, Etienne de La Boëtie. Each was to become the other's other self. "If you press me to say why I loved him, I feel that it can only be expressed by replying 'Because it was him: because it was me.' . . . We were seeking each other before we set eyes on each other . . ." (I 28). Their relationship was an intense dialogue on every possible subject. De La Boëtie inclined to stoicism. He had written against tyranny. He died young.

Montaigne's letter to his father on de La Boëtie's last days is rather like that of Ammianus Marcellinus on the death of the Emperor Julian, something of a hero to Montaigne if not to the Holy Office. (Letter to father: "He gave up the ghost at about three o'clock on the Wednesday morning, August 18th, 1563, after living 32 years, nine months, and 17 days. . . .")

Certainly, we are all in poor de La Boëtie's debt for dying, because Montaigne was never to find another soulmate and so, in due course, after marriage, children, the inheritance of the estate, "In the year of Christ 1571, at the age of thirty-eight, on the last day of February, his birthday, Michel de Montaigne, long weary of the servitude of the court and of public employment . . .", retired to Montaigne, where he then began to make attempts at understanding everything, which meant, principally, the unknowable (so Socrates thought) self. In the absence of a friend to talk to or an Atticus to write to, Montaigne started writing to himself about himself and about what he had been reading which became himself. He made many attempts to try—*essayer*—to find his form. "If I had somebody to write to I would readily have chosen it as the means of publishing my chatter. . . . Unless I deceive myself my achievement then would have been greater" (I 40). At first, he wrote short memoranda—how to invest a city, or what one is to make of a certain line of Seneca. Later, he settled for the long essay that could be read in an hour. He did a lot of free-associating, as "all subjects are linked to each other" (III 5). Essentially, he wrote as a man of action, involved in the world both locally and nationally. He was personally esteemed by Catherine de Medici, Henry III, Marguerite de Valois and Henry of Navarre, who twice visited him at Montaigne and would, as King of France, have made him a counsellor had the essayist not made one final attempt to understand death—life by dying.

The greatest action of this man of action was to withdraw to his library in order to read and think and write notes to himself that eventually became books for the world:

At home I slip off to my library (it is on the third storey of a tower); it is easy for me to oversee my household from there. I am above my gateway and have a view of my garden, my chicken-run, my backyard and most parts of my house. There I can turn over the leaves of this book or that, a bit at a time without order or design. Sometimes my mind wanders off, at others I walk to and fro, noting down and dictating these whims of mine. . . . My library is round in shape, squared off only for the needs of my table and chair: as it curves round, it offers me at a glance every one of my books ranged on five shelves all the way along. It has three splendid and unhampered views and a circle of free space sixteen yards in diameter (III 3).

Montaigne seems to have read every Latin author extant; he was also much intrigued with contemporary stories of the Americas and other exotic places where cannibals and realms of gold coexisted. Much of his writing starts with a quotation that sets him to ruminating on his own, buttressed by more quotations, making a sort of palimpsest. If nothing else, he was a superb arranger of other men's flowers. He was particularly drawn to biographical anecdote, and it was lucky for him that not long after he settled in his tower room, Bishop Jacques Amyot published a French translation of Plutarch, who quickly became Montaigne's most useful source and touchstone. In fact, one wonders what the essays would have been like without Plutarch. Would Montaigne have found so attractive those human titans, Alexander and Caesar? Or those paradigms of human virtue, Epaminondas and Cato the Younger?

Among the thousand books on the five shelves, Montaigne returns most often to Lucretius and Seneca. He reveres Homer, but he is happiest with those two worldly writers who appeal to his own worldliness. The first because of his sense of the diversity—even relativity—of things, the second as a wise counsellor, not only in the conduct of a life at home but at a dangerous court. He turns often to Cicero, but he is vaguely disapproving of the vanity of that politician, ever avid, especially in retirement, for glory. Cicero "said he wanted to use his withdrawal and his repose from affairs of state to gain life ever-lasting through his writings" (I 39). Then Montaigne, slyly, quotes Persius: "Does *knowing* mean nothing to you, unless somebody else knows that you know it?"

I thought of a chat with Robert Lowell at my Hudson river house forty years ago. Somehow, we had got on to the subject of Julius Caesar's character. I mentioned Cicero's letter to Atticus on how unnerving it was to have Caesar as a house guest. "But," said Lowell, "remember how pleased Cicero was when Caesar praised his consulship." Of course, each of us wanted the other to know that *he* had read the letter and that, if nothing else, we held, in common, a small part of the classical heritage—so etiolated! so testeronish! so Eurocentric!—that Montaigne had spent his life in communion with. I wonder what a poet and a novelist would have in common to talk about nowadays. After all, a shared knowledge of old books was probably the largest part of the "loving friendship" between Étienne and Montaigne. Today they would share— what? Robert Altman's films?

Montaigne disliked pedants. He notes that in his local dialect they are called *Lettreferits*—word-struck. He himself is after other game than words or "words about words": "scribbling seems to be one of the symptoms of an age of excess" (III 9). "We work merely to fill the memory, leaving the understanding and the sense of right and wrong. . . . Off I go, rummaging about in books for sayings which please me—not so as to store them up (for I have no storehouses) but so as to carry them back to the book, where they are no more mine than they were in their original place. We only know, I believe, what we know now: 'knowing' no more consists in what we once knew than in what we shall know in the future" (I 24). He frets about his poor memory. "I am so outstanding a forgetter that, along with all the rest, I forget even my own works and writings. People are constantly quoting me to me without my realising it" (II 17). This is a bit swank. But writers often forget what they have written, since the act of writing is a letting go of a piece of one's mind, and so an erasure. Montaigne's first two volumes of essays were published in 1580: he was forty-seven. Eight years later, he revised the first two volumes and published a third. From the beginning, he was accepted as a classic in the Roman sense, or as a writer *utile-doux,* as the French styled the great works.

Montaigne was much concerned with his body and believed Sebond's proposition that man is a marriage between soul and body. He hated doctors, a family tradition to which he not only adhered but attributed the long lives in the male line (he himself was dead at sixty, rather younger than father and grandfather). He feared kidney stones, which tortured his father and, finally, himself. To cure "the stone," he visited spas everywhere and took the baths: "I reckon that bathing in general is salubrious and I believe that our health has suffered . . . since we lost the habit. . . . we are all the worst for having our limbs encrusted and our pores blocked up with filth" (II 37). Of himself, "my build is a little below the average. This defect is not only ugly but unbecoming, especially in those who hold commands . . ." (II 17), but "my build is tough and thick-set, my face is not fat but full, my complexion is between the jovial and the melancholic. . . . Skill and agility I have never had . . . except at running (at which I was among the average)."

He records without despair or even pride that he has almost no gifts for music, dancing, tennis, wrestling, and none at all for swimming, fencing, vaulting and jumping.

My hand is so clumsy that I cannot even read my own writing, so that I prefer to write things over again rather than to give myself the trouble of disentangling my scribbles. . . . That apart, I am quite a good scholar! I can never fold up a letter neatly, never sharpen a pen, never carve passably at table, nor put harness on horse, nor bear a hawk properly nor release it, nor address hounds, birds or horses. My bodily endowments are, in brief, in close harmony with my soul's. There is no agility, merely a full firm vigour, but I can stick things out.

Like his father, he wore mostly black and white. "Whether riding or walking I have always been used to burdening my hand with a cane or stick, even affecting an air of elegance by leaning on it with a distin- guished look on my face" (II 25).

He deplored the codpieces of the previous generation, which drew attention to and exaggerated the unmentionables. He had had sex at so early an age that he could not recall just when. Like Abraham Lincoln, he contracted syphilis ("a couple of light anticipatory doses") (III 3). For this vileness, American universities would erase him from the canon, if they could, since no great man has ever had syphilis or engaged in same-sexuality. On Greek love, Montaigne understood exactly what Achilles and Patroclus were up to in the sack and he found their activi- ties "rightly abhorrent to our manners" on the novel ground that what was not equal in body-mind could not be love, much less "perfect love." The man chose not another man but a boy for his looks. It was Mon- taigne's view that true love, sexual or not, meant the congruence of two men as equals. This was the highest form of human relationship. He does note that "male and female are cast in the same mould: save for education and custom the difference between them is not great" (III 6). Theoretically, if a woman was educated as a man and met her male equal, this could be the "perfect love": but he gives no examples. Odd, since Plutarch had filled him in on Aspasia and Pericles. But then he did not place Pericles very high; thought him a tricky orator. Of course, he had not read Thucydides.

On "Some Lines of Virgil," he has a good time with sex, as both necessity and madness. "The genital activities of mankind are so natural, so necessary and so right: what have they done to make us never dare to mention them without embarrassment . . . ? We are not afraid to utter the words 'kill,' 'thief,' or 'betray' " (III 5). Yet "The whole movement of the world tends and leads towards copulation. It is a substance infused through everything; it is the centre—towards which all things turn." He comments on the uncontrollability—and unreliability—of the male member. "Every man knows . . . that he has a part of his body which often stirs, erects, and lies down again without his leave. Now such passive movements which only touch our outside cannot be called ours" (II 6). (Screech thinks that Montaigne never read Augustine's *Confessions.*) Montaigne notes priapic cults in other lands and times. Finally, all in all, he favours arranged marriages: "A good marriage (if there be such a thing) rejects the company and conditions of Cupid; it strives to reproduce those of loving friendship" (III 5). Incidentally, nowhere does Montaigne mention his wife. There is one reference to his daughter Léonor, and a mysterious panegyric to a sort of adopted daughter that, Screech thinks, may have been written by herself in a posthumous edition, which gives rise to the agreeable notion that there may have been some sort of Ibsen plot unfolding in old Périgord. Rousseau thought that Montaigne ought to have told us a lot more about his private life, but then Rousseau was no gentleman.

On politics, Montaigne was deeply but not dully conservative. That is, he did not, figuratively or literally, believe in witches:

I abhor novelty, no matter what visage it presents, and am right to do so, for I have seen some of its disastrous effects. That novelty (the wars of religion) which has for so many years beset us is not solely responsible, but one can say with every likelihood that it has incidentally caused and given birth to them all. . . . Those who shake the State are easily the first to be engulfed in its destruction. The fruits of dissension are not gathered by the one who began it: he stirs and troubles the water for other men to fish in (I 23).

A nice presage of France's revolution two centuries later, though not particularly applicable to the American adventure that actually turned the whole world upside down. But in the midst of a civil war over religion, the absolutist must appear more than usually monstrous: "There is a great deal of self-love and arrogance in judging so highly of

your opinions that you are obliged to disturb the public peace in order
to establish them" (I 23). Plainly, he was not the sort of conservative
who would have admired that radical British prime minister who, for
a decade, so strenuously disturbed the death-like peace of those sunnily
arid North Sea islands.

Montaigne was very much school of the-devil-we-know: "Not as a
matter of opinion but of truth, the best and most excellent polity for each
nation is the one under which it has been sustained. Its form and its
essential advantages depend upon custom. It is easy for us to be displeased with its present condition; I nevertheless hold that to yearn for
an oligarchy in a democracy or for another form of government in a
monarchy is wrong and insane" (III 9). He regarded any fundamental
change as "the cure of illness by death. . . . My own contemporaries here
in France could tell you a thing or two about that!"

Since I want Montaigne on my side in the great task of reworking my
own country's broken-down political system, I must invoke him—like
Scripture—in another context. "The most desirable laws are those
which are fewest, simplest and most general. I think moreover that it
would be better to have none at all than to have them in the profusion
as we do now. . . . When King Ferdinand sent colonies of immigrants
to the Indies he made the wise stipulation that no one should be included
who had studied jurisprudence, lest law suits should pullulate in the
New World" (III 13), causing endless faction and altercation. Since *our*
New World is entirely paralysed by lawyers hired by pullulating pollu-
ters of politics as well as of environment and put in place to undo many
thousands of laws made by other lawyers, I cannot think Montaigne
would be so cruel as *not* to want us to rid ourselves of such a government, but I suppose he would echo, mockingly, his young contemporary
Shakespeare's final solution for lawyers, while suggesting that it might
do us Americans a world of good if each took a course or two in torts
and malfeasances since, from the beginning, we were intended to be a
lawyerly republic and must not change.

Common sense is a phrase, if not a quality, much revered in the bright
islands of the North Sea. Montaigne is often accused of possessing this
rare quality, but what most strikes me in his meanderings is the *uncom-
monness* of his sense. He turns a subject round and round and suddenly
sees something that others had not noticed. He is also inclined to humour, usually of the dead-pan sort: "Herodotus tells us of a certain
district of Libya where men lie with women indiscriminately, but where,
once a child can toddle, it recognizes its own father out of the crowd,

natural instinct guiding its first footsteps. There are frequent mistakes, I believe . . ." (II 8).

Of literary style, he wrote: "I want things to dominate, so filling the thoughts of the hearer that he does not even remember the words. I like the kind of speech which is simple and natural, the same on paper as on the lip; speech which is rich in matter, sinewy, brief and short" (I 26). As for "the French authors of our time. They are bold enough and proud enough not to follow the common road; but their want of invention and their power of selection destroy them. All we can see is some wretched affectation of novelty, cold and absurd fictions which instead of elevating their subject batter it down" (III 5). He delighted in Boccaccio, Rabelais and the *Basia* of Johannes Secundus. Of poets, he put Virgil highest, especially the *Georgics;* then Lucretius, Catullus and Horace. He finds Aesop interestingly complex. "Seneca is full of pithy phrases and sallies; Plutarch is full of matter. Seneca inflames you and stirs you: Plutarch is more satisfying and repays you more. Plutarch leads us: Seneca drives us" (II 10). He seems to be looking ahead at our own scribbling time when he writes, "There are so many ways of taking anything, that it is hard for a clever mind *not* to find in almost any subject something or other which appears to serve his point, directly or indirectly. That explains why an opaque, ambiguous style has been so long in vogue" (II 12).

From 1581 to 1585, Montaigne served as Mayor of Bordeaux: "People say that my period of office passed without trace or mark. Good!" In 1582, the Pope dealt him a grievous blow by replacing the Julian calendar with the Gregorian, which lopped eleven days off everyone's life. "Since I cannot stand novelty even when corrective, I am constrained to be a bit of a heretic in this case" (III 10). He enjoyed his fame as a writer but noted "that in my own climate of Gascony they find it funny to see me in print; I am valued the more, the farther from home knowledge of me has spread . . ." (III 2). In the Frame translation, there is a "How true" in the margin next to what could be the mark of a tear, if it did not still smell of whisky. In a variation on Aesop, he notes, "A hundred times a day when we go mocking our neighbour we are really mocking ourselves; we abominate in others those faults which are most manifestly our own, and with a miraculous lack of shame and perspicacity, are astonished by them" (III 8). Perhaps this universal failing is why "I study myself more than any other subject. That is my metaphysics; that is my physics" (III 13).

In a comment on Montaigne's most celebrated essay, "On the Education of Children," Sainte-Beuve remarked that "he goes too far, like a child of Aristippus who forgets Adam's fall." He is *"simply* Nature . . . Nature in all its Grace-less completeness." The clarity—charity, too—with which he saw his world has made him seem a precursor of the age of Enlightenment, even that of Wordsworth. But Screech does not allow us so easily to appropriate him to our secular ends, and Montaigne's Epicurean stoicism is more than balanced by his non-questioning—indeed defence—of the traditional faith. For him, his translation of the *Theologia Naturalis* of Raymond Sebond was to be regarded as a prophylactic against the dread Luther.

Incidentally, Screech's own translation is as little ambiguous as possible; it is also demotic. Where Frame writes "ruminating," Screech writes "chewing over," "frenzied" becomes "raging mad," "loose-boweled" becomes "squittering," a word that I was obliged to look up—"to void thin excrement." We are all in Screech's debt for giving us back a word so entirely useful that no critic's portmanteau should ever again be without it. On the other hand, Frame's "this bundle of so many disparate pieces is being composed" becomes the perhaps less happy phrase "all the various pieces of this faggot are being bundled together . . ."

"The writer's function is not without arduous duties. By definition, he cannot serve those who make history; he must serve those who are subject to it." Montaigne would not have agreed with Albert Camus. In a sense, Montaigne is writing for the rulers (Henry IV was particularly taken by his essay "On High Rank as a Disadvantage"). Educate the rulers, and they will not torment their subjects. But Montaigne's political interests are aside from his main point, the exploration of self. Once he had lost Étienne, he was all he had; so he wrote a book about himself. "I am most ignorant about myself. I marvel at the assurance and confidence everyone has about himself, whereas there is virtually nothing that I *know* I know. . . . I think that I am an ordinary sort of man, except in considering myself to be one. . . . That I find my own work pardonable is not so much for itself or its true worth as from a comparison with others' writings which are worse—things which I can see people taking seriously" (II 17).

Vanity of any sort amuses him. Even the great Julius Caesar is ticked off: "Observe how Caesar spreads himself when he tells us about his ingenuity in building bridges and siege-machines; in comparison, he is quite cramped when he talks of his professional soldiering, his valour or the way he conducts his wars. His exploits are sufficient proof that he was an outstanding general: he wants to be known as something else rather different: a good engineer" (I 17).

Montaigne begins his essays (first thought of as *rhapsodies*—confused medleys) with a pro forma bow to Cicero–Plato: "Cicero says that philosophizing is nothing other than getting ready to die. That is because study and contemplation draw our souls somewhat outside ourselves keeping them occupied away from the body, a state which both resembles death and which forms a kind of apprenticeship for it; or perhaps it is because all the wisdom and argument in the world eventually come down to one conclusion which is to teach us not to be afraid of dying" (I 20). In this way "all the labour of reason must be to make us live well."

Montaigne's reigning humour may have been melancholic, but he is hardly morbid in his musings on that good life which leads to a good death. He is a true stoic, despite occasional obeisance to the Holy Spirit, a post-Platonic novelty now running down. He is even a bit sardonic: "Everybody goes out as though he had just come in. Moreover, however decrepit a man may be, he thinks he still has another twenty years." But "I have adopted the practice of always having death not only in my mind but on my lips. There is nothing I inquire about more readily than how men have died: what did they say? How did they look?" Like me, when he read a biography, he first skipped to the end to see how its subject died. As his book—and life—proceed, he is more than ever aware of the diversity within the unity of things and the inability to know very much of what came before us because, "Great heroes lived before Agamemnon. Many there were: yet none is lamented, being swept away unknown into the long night."

After the arrival of kidney stones, Montaigne occasionally strikes a bleak note: "I am on the way out: I would readily leave to one who comes later whatever wisdom I have learnt about dealing with the world. . . . At the finish of every task the ending makes itself known. My world is over: my mould has been emptied; I belong entirely to the past" (III 10). But before self-pity could spread her great fluffy wings, he then makes a joke about being cruelly robbed of eleven days of life by the Pope's new calendar. Meanwhile, "Time and custom condition us to anything strange: nevertheless, the more I haunt myself and know myself the more my misshapenness amazes me and the less I understand myself" (III 11). Finally, "We confuse life with worries about death, and death with worries about life. One torments us; the other terrifies us" (III 12). Yet,

If we have not known how to live, it is not right to teach us how to die, making the form of the end incongruous with the whole. If we have known how to live steadfastly and calmly we shall know how to die the same way. . . . death is indeed the ending of life, but not therefore its end: it puts an end to it, it is its ultimate point: but it is not its objective. Life must be its own objective, its own purpose. . . . Numbered among its other duties included under the general and principal heading, *How to Live,* there is the sub-section, *How to Die.*

Thus, Montaigne firmly reverses the Cicero–Plato notion that "to philosophize is to learn how to die" and enjoins us to meditate not on unknowable, irrelevant death but on life which can be known, at least in part. Sixteen years of observing himself and reading and rereading the thousand books in the round library had convinced him not only that life was all there is but that "Each man bears the entire form of man's estate" (III 2). At the end, Montaigne had met himself at last; and everyone else, too. On September 13, 1592, he died in bed while listening to Mass. What one would give to know what he said, how he looked, just before he, too, entered the long night.

Meanwhile, Screech now replaces Frame at my bedside. Anglophones of the next century will be deeply in his debt. Despite his insistence on the Catholicism of Montaigne, the good Screech does note that Montaigne uses the word Fortune—in the sense of fate—350 times. That is satisfying.

*The Times Literary Supplement*
June 26, 1992

# STATE
# OF
# THE
# UNION

# 48

## THE TWELVE
## CAESARS

Tiberius, Capri. Pool of water. Small children . . . So far so good. One's laborious translation was making awful sense. Then . . . Fish. Fish? The erotic mental image became surreal. Another victory for the Loeb Library's sly translator, J. C. Rolfe, who, correctly anticipating the prurience of schoolboy readers, left Suetonius' gaudier passages in the hard original. One failed to crack those intriguing footnotes not because the syntax was so difficult (though it was not easy for students drilled in military rather than civilian Latin) but because the range of vice revealed was considerably beyond the imagination of even the most depraved schoolboy. There was a point at which one rejected one's own translation. Tiberius and the little fish, for instance.

Happily, we now have a full translation of the text, the work of Mr. Robert Graves, who, under the spell of his Triple Goddess, has lately been retranslating the classics. One of his first tributes to her was a fine rendering of *The Golden Ass;* then Lucan's *Pharsalia;* then the *Greek Myths,* a collation aimed at rearranging the hierarchy of Olympus to afford his Goddess (the female principle) a central position at the expense of the male. (Beware Apollo's wrath, Graves: the "godling" is more than front man for the "Ninefold Muse-Goddess.") Now, as a diversion, Mr. Graves has given us *The Twelve Caesars* of Suetonius in a good, dry, no-nonsense style; and, pleasantly enough, the Ancient Mother of Us All is remarkable only by her absence, perhaps a subtle criticism of an intensely masculine period in history.

Gaius Suetonius Tranquillus—lawyer and author of a dozen books, among them *Lives of Famous Whores* and *The Physical Defects of Mankind* (What was that about?)—worked for a time as private secretary to the Emperor Hadrian. Presumably it was during this period that he had access to the imperial archives, where he got the material for *The Twelve Caesars,* the only complete book of his to survive. Suetonius was born in A.D. 69, the year of the three Caesars Galba, Otho, Vitellius; and he grew up under the Flavians: Vespasian, Titus, Domitian, whom he deals with as contemporaries. He was also close enough in time to the first six Caesars to have known men who knew them intimately, at least from Tiberius on, and it is this place in time which gives such immediacy to his history.

Suetonius saw the world's history from 49 B.C. to A.D. 96 as the intimate narrative of twelve men wielding absolute power. With impressive curiosity he tracked down anecdotes, recording them dispassionately, despite a somewhat stylized reactionary bias. Like his fellow historians from Livy to the stuffy but interesting Dion Cassius, Suetonius was a political reactionary to whom the old Republic was the time of virtue and the Empire, implicitly, was not. But it is not for his political convictions that we read Suetonius. Rather, it is his gift for telling us what we want to know. I am delighted to read that Augustus was under five feet seven, blond, wore lifts in his sandals to appear taller, had seven birthmarks and weak eyes; that he softened the hairs of his legs with hot walnut shells, and liked to gamble. Or to learn that the droll Vespasian's last words were: "Dear me, I must be turning into a god." ("Dear me" being Graves for "*Vae.*") The stories, true or not, are entertaining, and when they deal with sex, startling, even to a post-Kinseyan.

Gibbon, in his stately way, mourned that of the twelve Caesars only Claudius was sexually "regular." From the sexual opportunism of Julius Caesar to the sadism of Nero to the doddering pederasty of Galba, the sexual lives of the Caesars encompassed every aspect of what our post-medieval time has termed "sexual abnormality." It would be wrong, however, to dismiss, as so many commentators have, the wide variety of Caesarean sensuality as simply the viciousness of twelve abnormal men. They were, after all, a fairly representative lot. They differed from us—and their contemporaries—only in the fact of power, which made it possible for each to act out his most recondite sexual fantasies. This is the psychological fascination of Suetonius. What will men so placed do? The answer, apparently, is anything and everything. Alfred Whitehead once remarked that one got the essence of a culture not by those things which were said at the time but by those things which were *not* said, the underlying assumptions of the society, too obvious to be stated. Now it is an underlying assumption of twentieth-century America that human beings are either heterosexual or, through some arresting of normal psychic growth, homosexual, with very little traffic back and forth. To us, the norm is heterosexual; the family is central; all else is deviation, pleasing or not depending on one's own tastes and moral preoccupations. Suetonius reveals a very different world. His underlying assumption is that man is bisexual and that given complete freedom to love—or, perhaps more to the point in the case of the Caesars, to violate—others, he will do so, going blithely from male to female as fancy dictates. Nor is Suetonius alone in this assumption of man's variousness. From Plato to the rise of Pauline Christianity, which tried to put the lid on sex, it is explicit in classical writing. Yet to this day Christian, Freudian and Marxian commentators have all decreed or ignored this fact of nature in the interest each of a patented approach to the Kingdom of Heaven. It is an odd experience for a contemporary to read of Nero's simultaneous passion for both a man and a woman. Something seems wrong. It must be one or the other, not both. And yet this sexual eclecticism recurs again and again. And though some of the Caesars quite obviously preferred women to men (Augustus had a particular penchant for Nabokovian nymphets), their sexual crisscrossing is extraordinary in its lack of pattern. And one suspects that despite the stern moral legislation of our own time other human beings are no different. If nothing else, Dr. Kinsey revealed in his dogged, arithmetical way that we are all a good deal less predictable and bland than anyone had suspected.

One of the few engaging aspects of the Julio-Claudians was authorship. They all wrote; some wrote well. Julius Caesar, in addition to his account of that famed crusade in Gaul, wrote an *Oedipus.* Augustus wrote an *Ajax,* with some difficulty. When asked by a friend what his *Ajax* had been up to lately, Augustus sighed: "He has fallen not on his sword, but wiped himself out on my sponge." Tiberius wrote an *Elegy on the Death of Julius Caesar.* The scatterbrained Claudius, a charmingly dim prince, was a devoted pedant who tried to reform the alphabet. He was also among the first to have a serious go at Etruscan history. Nero of course is remembered as a poet. Julius Caesar and Augustus were distinguished prose writers; each preferred plain old-fashioned Latin. Augustus particularly disliked what he called the "Asiatic" style, favored by, among others, his rival Marc Antony, whose speeches he found imprecise and "stinking of farfetched phrases."

Other than the fact of power, the twelve Caesars as men had little in common with one another. But that little was significant: a fear of the knife in the dark. Of the twelve, eight (perhaps nine) were murdered. As Domitian remarked not long before he himself was struck down: "Emperors are necessarily wretched men since only their assassination can convince the public that the conspiracies against their lives are real." In an understandable attempt to outguess destiny, they studied omens, cast horoscopes, and analyzed dreams (they were ingenious symbolists, anticipating Dr. Freud, himself a Roman buff). The view of life from Palatine Hill was not comforting, and though none of the Caesars was religious in our sense of the word, all inclined to the Stoic. It was Tiberius, with characteristic bleakness, who underscored their dangerous estate when he declared that it was Fate, not the gods, which ordered the lives of men.

Yet what, finally, was the effect of absolute power on twelve representative men? Suetonius makes it quite plain: disastrous. Caligula was certifiably mad. Nero, who started well, became progressively irrational. Even the stern Tiberius' character weakened. In fact, Tacitus, in covering the same period as Suetonius, observes: "Even after his enormous experience of public affairs, Tiberius was ruined and transformed by the violent influence of absolute power." Caligula gave the game away when he told a critic, "Bear in mind that I can treat anyone exactly as I please." And that cruelty which is innate in human beings, now given the opportunity to use others as toys, flowered monstrously in the Caesars. Suetonius' case history (and it is precisely that) of Domitian is particularly fascinating. An intelligent man of some charm, trained to govern, Domitian upon succeeding to the Principate at first contented himself with tearing the wings off flies, an infantile pastime which gradually palled until, inevitably, for flies he substituted men. His favorite game was to talk gently of mercy to a nervous victim; then, once all fears had been allayed, execute him. Nor were the Caesars entirely unobjective about their bizarre position. There is an oddly revealing letter of Tiberius to the Senate which had offered to ensure in advance ratification of all his future deeds. Tiberius declined the offer: "So long as my wits do not fail me, you can count on the consistency of my behavior;

but I should not like you to set the precedent of binding yourselves to approve a man's every action; for what if something happened to alter that man's character?" In terror of their lives, haunted by dreams and omens, giddy with dominion, it is no wonder that actual insanity was often the Caesarean refuge from a reality so intoxicating.

The unifying *Leitmotiv* in these lives is Alexander the Great. The Caesars were fascinated by him. The young Julius Caesar sighed enviously at his tomb. Augustus had the tomb opened and stared long at the conqueror's face. Caligula stole the breastplate from the corpse and wore it. Nero called his guard the "Phalanx of Alexander the Great." And the significance of this fascination? Power for the sake of power. Conquest for the sake of conquest. Earthly dominion as an end in itself: no Utopian vision, no dissembling, no hypocrisy. I knock you down; now *I* am king of the castle. Why should young Julius Caesar be envious of Alexander? It does not occur to Suetonius to explain. He assumes that *any* young man would like to conquer the world. And why did Julius Caesar, a man of first-rate mind, want the world? Simply, to have it. Even the resulting Pax Romana was not a calculated policy but a fortunate accident. Caesar and Augustus, the makers of the Principate, represent the naked will to power for its own sake. And though our own society has not much changed from the Roman (we may point with somber pride to Hitler and Stalin), we have, nevertheless, got so into the habit of dissembling motives, of denying certain dark constants of human behavior, that it is difficult to find a reputable American historian who will acknowledge the crude fact that a Franklin Roosevelt, say, wanted to be President merely to wield power, to be famed and to be feared. To learn this simple fact one must wade through a sea of evasions: history as sociology, leaders as teachers, bland benevolence as a motive force, when finally, power *is* an end to itself, and the instinctive urge to prevail the most important single human trait, the necessary force without which no city was built, no city destroyed. Yet many contemporary sociologists and religionists turned historians will propose, quite seriously: If there had not been a Julius Caesar then the *Zeitgeist* would have provided another like him, even though it is quite evident that had this particular Caesar not existed no one would have dared invent him. World events are the work of individuals whose motives are often frivolous, even casual. Had Claudius not wanted an easy conquest so that he might celebrate a triumph at Rome, Britain would not have been conquered in A.D. 44. If Britain had not been colonized in the first century . . . the chain of causality is plain.

One understands of course why the role of the individual in history is instinctively played down by a would-be egalitarian society. We are, quite naturally, afraid of being victimized by reckless adventurers. To avoid this we have created the myth of the ineluctable mass ("other-directedness") which governs all. Science, we are told, is not a matter of individual inquiry but of collective effort. Even the surface storminess of our elections disguises a fundamental indifference to human personality: if not this man, then that one; it's all the same; life will go on. Up to a point there is some virtue in this; and though none can deny that there is a prevailing grayness in our placid land, it is certainly better to be non-ruled by mediocrities than enslaved by Caesars. But to deny the dark nature of human personality is not only fatuous but dangerous. For in our insistence on the surrender of private will ("inner-directedness") to a conception of the human race as some sort of virus in the stream of time, unaffected by individual deeds, we have been made vulnerable not only to boredom, to that sense of meaninglessness which more than anything else is characteristic of our age, but vulnerable to the first messiah who offers the young and bored some splendid prospect, some Caesarean certainty. That is the political danger, and it is a real one.

Most of the world today is governed by Caesars. Men are more and more treated as things. Torture is ubiquitous. And, as Sartre wrote in his preface to Henri Alleg's chilling book about Algeria, "Anybody, at any time, may equally find himself victim or executioner." Suetonius, in holding up a mirror to those Caesars of diverting legend, reflects not only them but ourselves: half-tamed creatures, whose great moral task it is to hold in balance the angel and the monster within—for we are both, and to ignore this duality is to invite disaster.

1952
(published in *The Nation,* 1959)

# *SEX AND THE LAW*

In 1963, H. L. A. Hart, Oxford Professor of Jurisprudence, gave three lectures at Stanford University. In these lectures (published by the Stanford University Press as *Law, Liberty and Morality*) Professor Hart attempted to answer an old question: Is the fact that certain conduct is by common standards immoral a sufficient cause to punish that conduct by law? A question which leads him to what might be a paradox: "Is it morally permissible to enforce morality as such? Ought immorality as such to be a crime?" Philosophically, Professor Hart inclines to John Stuart Mill's celebrated negative. In *On Liberty,* Mill wrote, "The only purpose for which power can rightfully be exercised over any member of a civilized community against his will is to prevent harm to others"; and to forestall the arguments of the paternally minded, Mill added that a man's own good, either physical or moral, is not sufficient warrant. He cannot rightfully be compelled to do or forbear because it will be better for him to do so, because it will make him happier, because in the opinions of others, to do so would be wise or even right.

Now it would seem that at this late date in the Anglo-American society, the question of morality and its relation to the law has been pretty much decided. In general practice, if not in particular statute, our society tends to keep a proper distance between the two. Yet national crisis may, on occasion, bring out the worst in the citizenry. While our boys were Over There, a working majority of the Congress decided that drink was not only bad for morals but bad for health. The result was Prohibition. After a dozen years of living with the Great Experiment, the electorate finally realized that moral legislation on such a scale is impossible to enforce. A lesson was learned and one would have thought it unlikely that the forces which created the Volstead Act could ever again achieve a majority. But today strange things are happening in the American Empire, as well as in the Kingdom across the water where Professor Hart detects a revival of what he calls "legal moralism," and he finds alarming certain recent developments.

In the days of the Star Chamber, to conspire to corrupt public morals was a common-law offense. Needless to say, this vague catchall turned out to be a useful instrument of tyranny and it was not entirely abandoned in England until the eighteenth century. Now it has been suddenly revived as a result of the 1961 case *Shaw v. Director of Public Prosecutions.* Shaw was an enterprising pimp who published a magazine called *Ladies Directory,* which was just that. Despite this useful contribution to the gallantry of England, Shaw was found guilty of three offenses: publishing an obscene article, living on the earnings of prostitutes, and conspiring to corrupt public morals. The last offense delighted the legal moralists. There was much satisfied echoing of the eighteenth-century Lord Mansfield's statement, "Whatever is *contra bonos mores et decorum* the principles of our laws prohibit and the King's Court as the general censor and guardian of the public morals is bound to restrain and punish." As a result of the decision against Mr. Shaw, the possibilities of banning a book like *Lady Chatterley's Lover* on the imprecise grounds that it will corrupt public morals (themselves ill-defined) are endless and alarming. Though various American states still retain "conspiring to corrupt" statutes, they are largely cherished as relics of our legal origins in the theocratic code of Oliver Cromwell. The last serious invoking of this principle occurred in 1935 when the Nazis solemnly determined that anything was punishable if it was deserving of punishment according "to the fundamental conceptions of penal law and sound popular feeling."

Defining immorality is of course not an easy task, though English judges and American state legislatures seem not to mind taking it on. Lord Devlin, a leader of the legal moralists, has said that "the function of the criminal law is to enforce a moral principle and nothing else." How does Lord Devlin arrive at a moral principle? He appeals to the past. What is generally said to be wrong is wrong, while "a recognized

morality is as necessary to society's existence as a recognized government." Good. But Lord Devlin does not acknowledge that there is
always a considerable gap between what is officially recognized as good
behavior and what is in actual fact countenanced and practiced. Though
adultery in England is thought to be morally wrong, there are no statutes under which a man may be punished for sleeping with someone
else's wife. Adultery is not a legal offense, nor does it presumably arouse
in the public "intolerance, indignation, and disgust," the three emotions
which Lord Devlin insists are inevitably evoked by those acts which
offend the accepted morality. Whenever this triad is present, the law
must punish. Yet how is one to measure "intolerance, indignation, and
disgust"? Without an appeal to Dr. Gallup, it would be difficult to
decide what, if anything, the general public really thinks about these
matters. Without a referendum, it is anyone's guess to what degree
promiscuity, say, arouses disgust in the public. Of course Lord Devlin
is not really arguing for this sort of democracy. His sense of right and
wrong is based on what he was brought up to believe was right and
wrong, as prescribed by church and custom.

In the realm of sexual morals, all things take on a twilight shade. Off
and on for centuries, homosexuality has aroused the triple demon in the
eyes of many. But a majority? It would be surprising if it did, knowing
what we now know about the extent—if not the quality—of human
sexual behavior. In any case, why should homosexual acts between
consenting adults be considered inimical to the public good? This sort
of question raises much heat, and the invoking of "history." According
to Lord Devlin, "the loosening of moral bonds is often the first stage of
[national] disintegration." Is it? The periods in history which are most
admired by legal moralists tend to be those vigorous warlike times when
a nation is pursuing a successful and predatory course of military expansion, such as the adventures of the Spartans and Alexander, of Julius
Caesar and Frederick of Prussia. Yet a reading of history ought to
convince Lord Devlin that these militaristic societies were not only
brutish and "immoral" by any standard but also startlingly homosexual.
Yet what was morally desirable in a clean-limbed Spartan army officer
is now punished in Leicester Square. Obviously public attitudes have
changed since those vigorous days. Does that then mean that laws
should alter as old prejudices are replaced by new? In response to public
opinion, the Emperor Justinian made homosexuality a criminal offense
on the grounds that buggery, as everyone knew, was the chief cause of
earthquakes.

With the decline of Christianity, western moralists have more and more used the state to punish sin. One of Lord Devlin's allies, J. G. Stephen, in *Liberty, Equality, Fraternity,* comes straight to the point. Referring to moral offenders, he writes, "The feeling of hatred and the desire of vengeance are important elements to human nature which ought, in such cases, to be satisfied in a regular public and legal manner." There is the case not only for capital punishment but for public hangings, all in the name of the Old Testament God of vengeance. Or as Lord Goddard puts it, "I do not see how it can be either non-Christian, or other than praiseworthy, that the country should be willing to avenge crime." Yet Mr. Stephen also realizes that for practical purposes "you cannot punish anything which public opinion as expressed in the common practice of society does not strenuously and unequivocally condemn. To be able to punish a moral majority must be overwhelming." But is there such a thing as moral majority in sexual matters? Professor Hart thinks not. "The fact that there is lip service to an official sexual morality should not lead us to neglect the possibility that in sexual, as other matters, there may be a number of mutually tolerant moralities, and that even where there is some homogeneity of practice and belief, offenders may be viewed not with hatred or resentment, but with amused contempt or pity."

In the United States the laws determining correct human behavior are the work of the state legislatures. Over the years these assemblies have managed to make a complete hash of things, pleasing no one. The present tangled codes go back to the founding of the country. When the Cromwells fell, the disgruntled Puritans left England for Holland (not because they were persecuted for their religious beliefs but because they were forbidden to persecute others for *their* beliefs). Holland took them in, and promptly turned them out. Only North America was left. Here, as lords of the wilderness, they were free to create the sort of quasi-theocratic society they had dreamed of. Rigorously persecuting one another for religious heresies, witchcraft, sexual misbehavior, they formed that ugly polity whose descendants we are. As religious fundamentalists, they were irresistibly drawn to the Old Testament God at his most forbidding and cruel, while the sternness of St. Paul seemed to them far more agreeable than the occasional charity of Jesus. Since adultery was forbidden by the Seventh Commandment and fornication was condemned in two of St. Paul's memos, the Puritans made adultery and fornication criminal offenses even though no such laws existed in England, before or after Cromwell's reign. As new American states were formed, they modeled their codes on those of the original states. To this day, forty-three states will punish a single act of adulterous intercourse, while twenty-one states will punish fornications between unmarried people. In no other western country is fornication a criminal offense. As for adultery, England, Japan, and the Soviet Union have no such statutes. France and Italy will punish adultery under special conditions (e.g., if the man should establish the mistress in the family home). Germany and Switzerland punish adultery only if a court can prove that a marriage has been dissolved because of it.

In actual practice, the state laws are seldom invoked, although two hundred and forty-two Bostonians were arrested for adultery as recently as 1948. These statutes are considered "dead-letter laws" and there are those who argue that since they are so seldom invoked, why repeal them? One answer came in 1917 when a number of racketeers were arrested by the Federal government because they had taken girl friends to Florida, violating the Mann Act as well as the local fornication-adultery statutes. This case (*Caminetti* v. *U.S.*) set a dangerous precedent. Under a busy Attorney General, the "dead-letter laws" could be used to destroy all sorts of dissidents, villainous or otherwise.

Rape is another offense much confused by state laws. During the thirties, out of 2,366 New York City indictments for rape, only eighteen percent were for forcible rape. The remaining eighty-two percent were for statutory rape, a peculiar and imprecise crime. For instance, in Colorado it is statutory rape if intercourse takes place between an unmarried girl under eighteen and a man over eighteen. In practice this means that a boy of nineteen who has an affair with a consenting girl of seventeen is guilty of statutory rape. All the girl needs to do is to accuse her lover of consensual relations and he can be imprisoned for as long as fifty years. There are thousands of "rapists" serving time because, for one reason or another, they were found guilty of sexual intercourse with a willing partner.

In nearly every state fellatio, cunnilingus, and anal intercourse are punished. Not only are these acts forbidden between men, they are forbidden between men and women, within as well as without wedlock. As usual, the various state laws are in wild disarray. Ohio deplores fellatio but tolerates cunnilingus. In another state, sodomy is punished with a maximum twenty-year sentence, while fellatio calls for only three years, a curious discrimination. Deviate sexual acts between consenting adults are punished in most states, with sentences running from three years to life imprisonment. Of the other countries of the West, only the Federal German Republic intrudes itself upon consenting adults.

Elsewhere in the field of moral legislation, twenty-seven states forbid sexual relations and/or marriage between the white race and its "inferiors": blacks, American Indians, Orientals. And of course our narcotics laws are the scandal of the world. With the passage in 1914 of the Harrison Act, addiction to narcotics was found to be not the result of illness or bad luck but of sin, and sin must of course be punished by the state. For half a century the Federal government has had a splendid time playing cops and robbers. And since you cannot have cops without robbers, they have created the robbers by maintaining that the sinful taking of drugs must be wiped out by law. As a result, the government's severity boosts the price of drugs, makes the game more desperate for addicts as well as pushers, and encourages crime which in turn increases the payroll of the Narcotics Bureau. This lunatic state of affairs could exist only in a society still obsessed by the idea that the punishing of sin is the responsibility of the state. Yet in those countries where dope addiction is regarded as a matter for the doctor and not the police, there can be no criminal traffic in drugs. In all of England there are 550 drug addicts. In New York City alone there are 23,000 addicts.

Theoretically, the American separation of church and state should have left the individual's private life to his conscience. But this was not to be the case. The states promptly took it upon themselves to regulate the private lives of the citizens, flouting, many lawyers believe, the spirit if not the letter of the Constitution. The result of this experiment is all around us. One in eight Americans is mentally disturbed, and everywhere psychiatry flourishes. Our per capita acts of violence are beyond anything known to the other countries of the West. Clearly the unique attempt to make private morality answerable to law has not been a success. What to do?

On April 25, 1955, a committee of the American Law Institute presented a Model Penal Code (tentative draft No. 4) to the Institute, which was founded some forty years ago "to promote the clarification and simplification of the law and its better adaptation to social needs." This Code represented an attempt to make sense out of conflicting laws, to remove "dead-letter laws" which might, under pressure, be used for dark ends, and to recognize that there is an area of private sexual morality which is no concern of the state. In this the Code echoed the recommendation of the British Wolfenden Report, which said: "Unless a deliberate attempt is to be made by society, acting through the agency of the law, to equate the sphere of crime with that of sin, there must remain a realm of private morality and immorality which is, in brief and crude terms, not the law's business."

The drafters of the Code proposed that adultery and sodomy between consenting adults be removed from the sphere of the law on the grounds that "the Code does not attempt to use the power of the state to enforce purely moral or religious standards. We deem it inappropriate for the government to attempt to control behavior that has no substantial significance except as to the morality of the actor. Such matters are best left to religious, educational and other influences." The Committee's recommendation on adultery was accepted. But on sodomy, Judge John J. Parker spoke for the legal moralists: "There are many things that are denounced by the criminal civil code in order that society may know that the state disapproves. When we fly in the face of public opinion, as evidenced by the code of every state in this union, we are not proposing a code which will commend itself to the thoughtful." Judge Parker was answered by Judge Learned Hand, who said, "Criminal law which is not enforced practically is much worse than if it was not on the books at all. I think homosexuality is a matter of morals, a matter very largely of taste, and it is not a matter that people should be put in prison about." Judge Hand's position was upheld by the Institute.

As matters now stand, only the state of Illinois has attempted to modify its sex laws. As of 1962 there is no longer any penalty in Illinois for the committing of a deviate sexual act. On the other hand, an "open and notorious" adulterer can still be punished with a year in prison and fornication can be punished with six months in prison. So it is still taken for granted that the state has the right to regulate private behavior in the interest of public morality.

One postwar phenomenon has been the slowness of the liberal community to respond to those flaws in our society which might be corrected by concerted action. It would seem to me that a change in the legal codes of the fifty American states might be an interesting occupation for the liberally inclined. As the laws stand, they affect nearly everyone; implemented, they would affect millions. Originally, the United States made a brave distinction between church and state. But then we put within the legal province of the states that which was either the concern of religion or of the moral conscience of the individual. The result has caused much suffering. The state laws are executed capriciously and though in time they may fade away, without some organized effort they could continue for generations. In fact, there are signs today that the legal conservatives are at work strengthening these laws. In Florida the administration has distributed an astonishing pamphlet denouncing homosexualists in terms of seventeenth-century grandeur. In Dallas a stripper named Candy Barr was given an unprecedented fifteen-year prison term, ostensibly because she was found with marijuana in her possession but actually because she was a sinful woman. In the words of a Dallas lawyer (Warren Leslie in *Dallas, Public and Private*), the jury was "showing the world they were in favor of God, heaven, and sending to hell-fire a girl who violated their sense of morality."

In these lowering days, there is a strong movement afoot to save society from sexual permissiveness. Guardians of the old-time virtue would maintain what they believe to be the status quo. They speak of "common decency" and "accepted opinion." But do such things really exist? And if they do, are they "right"? After all, there is no position so absurd that you cannot get a great many people to assume it. Lord Maugham, a former Lord Chancellor (where do they find them?), was convinced that the decline of the Roman Empire was the result of too frequent bathing. Justinian *knew* there was a causal link between buggery and earthquakes, while our grandparents, as Professor Steven Marcus recently reminded us, believed that masturbation caused insanity. I suspect that our own faith in psychiatry will seem as touchingly quaint to the future as our grandparents' belief in phrenology seems now to us. At any given moment, public opinion is a chaos of superstition, misinformation, and prejudice. Even if one could accurately interpret it, would that be a reason for basing the law upon a consensus?

Neither Professor Hart nor the legal moralists go that far. The conservatives are very much aware that they are living in an age of "moral decline." They wish to return to a stern morality like that of Cato or of Calvin. Failing that, they will settle for maintaining existing laws, the harsher the better. Professor Hart, on the other hand, believes that between what the law says people ought to do in their private lives and what they in fact do, there is a considerable division. To the degree that such laws ought, ideally, to conform with human practice, he is a democrat. In answering those who feel that despite what people actually do, they ought not to do it, he remarks that this may be true, yet "the use of legal punishment to freeze into immobility the morality dominant at a particular time in a society's existence may possibly succeed, but even where it does it contributes nothing to the survival of the animating spirit and formal values of social morality and may do much harm to them."

There is some evidence that by fits and starts the United States is achieving a civilization. Our record so far has not been distinguished, no doubt because we had a bad beginning. Yet it is always possible to make things better—as well as worse. Various groups are now at work trying to make sense of the fifty state codes. New York and California are expected to have improved codes by the end of this decade. But should there be a sudden renewal of legal moralism, attempts to modify and liberalize will fail. What is needed, specifically, is a test case before the Supreme Court which would establish in a single decision that "sin," where it does not disturb the public order, is not the concern of the state. This conception is implicit in our Constitution. But since it has never been tested, our laws continue to punish the sinful as though the state were still an arm of Church Militant. Although a Great Society is more easily attained in rhetoric than in fact, a good first step might be the removal from our statute books of that entirely misplaced scarlet letter.

*Partisan Review*
Summer 1965

# 50
—— ◆ ——

# SEX IS
# POLITICS

"But surely you do not favor the publishing of pornography?" When you hear someone say do not instead of don't, you know that you are either in court or on television. I was on television, being interviewed by two men—or persons, as they say nowadays. One was a conservative, representing the decent opinion of half a nation. One was a reactionary, representing the decent opinion of half a nation.

"Of course, I favor the publishing of—"

"You *favor* pornography?" The reactionary was distressed, appalled, sickened.

"I said the *publishing* of pornography, yes. . . ."

"But what's the difference? I mean between being in favor of publishing pornography and pornography?"

The conservative was troubled. "Whether or not I personally like or dislike pornography is immaterial." Television is a great leveler. You always end up sounding like the people who ask the questions. "The freedom to publish *anything* is guaranteed by the First Amendment to the Constitution. That is the law. Whether you or I or anyone likes what is published is"—repetition coming up. I was tired—"is, uh, immaterial. The First Amendment guarantees us the right to say and write and publish what we want. . . ."

Before I could make the usual exemptions for libel and for the reporting of troop movements during wartime and for that man or person who
falsely yells fire in a crowded theatre (all absolutes are relative beneath
the sun), the conservative struck. "But," he said, eyes agleam with what
looked to be deep feeling but was actually collyrium, "the founders of
the United States"—he paused, reverently; looked at me, sincerely;
realized, unhappily, that I was staring at the lacing to his hairpiece (half
the men who appear on television professionally are bald; why?). Nervously, he touched his forehead, and continued—"of America intended
freedom of speech only for . . . uh, politics."

"But sex is politics," I began . . . and ended.

I got two blank stares. I might just as well have said that the Pelagian
heresy will never take root in south Amish country. Neither the conservative nor the reactionary had ever heard anyone say anything like that
before and I knew that I could never explain myself in the seven remaining in-depth minutes of air time. I was also distracted by that toupee.
Mentally, I rearranged it. Pushed it farther back on his head. Didn't like
the result. Tried it lower down. All the while, we spoke of Important
Matters. I said that I did not think it a good idea for people to molest
children. This was disingenuous. My secret hero is the late King Herod.

Sex is politics.

In the year or two since that encounter on television, I have been
reminded almost daily of the fact that not only is sex politics but sex
both directly and indirectly has been a major issue in this year's election.
The Equal Rights Amendment, abortion, homosexuality are hot issues
that affect not only the political process but the private lives of millions
of people.

The sexual attitudes of any given society are the result of political
decisions. In certain militaristic societies, homosexual relationships
were encouraged on the ground that pairs of dedicated lovers (Thebes'
Sacred Legion, the Spartan buddy system) would fight more vigorously
than reluctant draftees. In societies where it is necessary to force great
masses of people to do work that they don't want to do (building
pyramids, working on the Detroit assembly line), marriage at an early
age is encouraged on the sensible ground that if a married man is fired,
his wife and children are going to starve, too. That grim knowledge
makes for docility.

Although our notions about what constitutes correct sexual behavior
are usually based on religious texts, those texts are invariably interpreted
by the rulers in order to keep control over the ruled. Any sexual or

intellectual or recreational or political activity that might decrease the amount of coal mined, the number of pyramids built, the quantity of junk food confected will be proscribed through laws that, in turn, are based on divine revelations handed down by whatever god or gods happen to be in fashion at the moment. Religions are manipulated in order to serve those who govern society and not the other way around. This is a brand-new thought to most Americans, whether once or twice or never bathed in the Blood of the Lamb.

Traditionally, Judaeo-Christianity approved of sex only between men and women who had been married in a religious ceremony. The newly-weds were then instructed to have children who would, in turn, grow up and have more children (the Reverend Malthus worried about this inverted pyramid), who would continue to serve the society as loyal workers and dutiful consumers.

For the married couple, sexual activity outside marriage is still a taboo. Although sexual activity before marriage is equally taboo, it is more or less accepted if the two parties are really and truly serious and sincere and mature . . . in other words, if they are prepared to do their duty by one day getting married in order to bring forth new worker-consumers in obedience to God's law, which tends to resemble with suspicious niceness the will of the society's owners.

Fortunately, nothing human is constant. Today civil marriages out-number religious marriages; divorce is commonplace; contraception is universally practiced, while abortion is legal for those with money. But our rulers have given ground on these sexual-social issues with great reluctance, and it is no secret that there is a good deal of frustration in the board rooms of the republic.

For one thing, workers are less obedient than they used to be. If fired, they can go on welfare—the Devil's invention. Also, the fact that most jobs men do women can do and do do has endangered the old patriarchal order. A woman who can support herself and her child is a threat to marriage, and marriage is the central institution whereby the owners of the world control those who do the work. Homosexuality also threatens that ancient domination, because men who don't have wives or children to worry about are not as easily dominated as those men who do.

At any given moment in a society's life, there are certain hot buttons that a politician can push in order to get a predictably hot response. A decade ago, if you asked President Nixon what he intended to do about unemployment, he was apt to answer, "Marijuana is a halfway house to something worse." It is good politics to talk against sin—and don't worry about non sequiturs. In fact, it is positively un-American—even

Communist—to discuss a real issue such as unemployment or who is stealing all that money at the Pentagon.

To divert the electorate, the unscrupulous American politician will go after those groups not regarded benignly by Old or New Testament. The descendants of Ham are permanently unpopular with white Americans. Unhappily for the hot-button pusher, it is considered bad taste to go after blacks openly. But code phrases may be used. Everyone knows that "welfare chiseler" means nigger, as does "law and order." The first on the ground that the majority of those on welfare are black (actually, they are white); the second because it is generally believed that most urban crimes are committed by blacks against whites (actually they are committed by jobless blacks against other blacks). But poor blacks are not the only target. Many Christers and some Jews don't like poor white people very much, on the old Puritan ground that if you're good, God will make you rich. This is a familiar evangelical Christian line, recently unfurled by born-again millionaire Walter Hoving. When he found himself short $2,400,000 of the amount he needed to buy Bonwit Teller, Mr. Hoving "opened himself up to the Lord," who promptly came through with the money. "It was completely a miracle." Now we know why the rich are always with us. God likes them.

Jews are permanently unpopular with American Christers because they are forever responsible for Jesus' murder, no matter what those idolatrous wine-soaked Roman Catholics at the Second Vatican Council said. It is true that with the establishment of Israel, the Christers now have a grudging admiration for the Jew as bully. Nevertheless, in once-and-twice-born land, it is an article of faith that America's mass media are owned by Jews who mean to overthrow God's country. Consequently, "mass media" is this year's code phrase for get the kikes, while "Save Our Children" means get the fags.

But politics, like sex, often makes for odd alliances. This year, militant Christers in tandem with militant Jews are pushing the sort of hot buttons that they think will strengthen the country's ownership by firming up the family. Apparently, the family can be strengthened only by depriving women of equal status not only in the marketplace but also in relation to their own bodies (Thou shalt not abort). That is why the defeat of the Equal Rights Amendment to the Constitution is of great symbolic importance.

Family Saviors also favor strong laws designed, ostensibly, to curtail pornography but actually intended to deny freedom of speech to those that they dislike.

Now, it is not possible for a governing class to maintain its power if there are not hot buttons to push. A few months ago, the "Giveaway of the Panama Canal" issue looked as though it were going to be a very hot button, indeed. It was thought that if, somehow, American manhood could be made to seem at stake in Panama, there was a chance that a sort of subliminal sexual button might be pushed, triggering throughout the land a howl of manly rage, particularly from ladies at church receptions: American manhood has never been an exclusively masculine preserve. But, ultimately, American manhood (so recently kneed by the Viet Cong) did not feel endangered by the partial loss of a fairly dull canal, and so that button jammed.

The issue of Cuban imperialism also seemed warm to the touch. Apparently, Castro's invincible troops are now on the march from one end of Africa to the other. If Somalia falls, Mali falls; if Mali falls. . . . No one cares. Africa is too far away, while Cuba is too small and too near to be dangerous.

In desperation, the nation's ownership has now gone back to the tried-and-true hot buttons: save our children, our fetuses, our ladies' rooms from the godless enemy. As usual, the sex buttons have proved satisfyingly hot.

But what do Americans actually think about sex when no one is pressing a button? Recently, *Time* magazine polled a cross section of the populace. Not surprisingly, 61 percent felt that "it's getting harder and harder to know what's right and what's wrong these days." Most confused were people over 50 and under 25. Meanwhile, 76 percent said that they believed that it was "morally wrong" for a married man to be unfaithful to his wife, while 79 percent thought it wrong for a woman to cheat on her husband.

Sexual relations between teenagers were condemned by 63 percent while 34 percent felt that a young man should be a virgin on his wedding night or afternoon. Nevertheless, what people consider to be morally objectionable does not seem to have much effect on what they actually do: 55 percent of unmarried women and 85 percent of unmarried men admit to having had sex by the age of 19 . . . no doubt, while jointly deploring teenage immorality. A worldly 52 percent think it is *not* morally wrong for an unmarried couple to live together.

Forty-seven percent thought that homosexual relations were morally wrong; 43 percent thought that they were all right: 10 percent didn't know. Yet 56 percent "would vote for legislation guaranteeing the civil rights of homosexuals." Although a clear majority thought that fags should be allowed to serve in the Army, run for office, live where they choose, Anita Bryant has done her work sufficiently well to deny them the right to teach school (48 percent against, 44 percent for) or be ministers (47 percent against, 44 percent for).

Pornography continues to be the hottest of buttons: seventy-four percent want the government to crack down on pornographers. Meanwhile, 76 percent think that that old devil permissiveness "has led to a lot of things that are wrong with the country these days."

Finally, 70 percent thought that "there should be no laws, either Federal or state, regulating sexual practice." Either this can be interpreted as a remarkable demonstration of live and let live (an attitude notoriously not shared by the current Supreme Court) or it can be nothing more than the cynical wisdom of our people who know from experience that *any* area the government involves itself in will be hopelessly messed up.

Despite the tolerance of the 70 percent, some 20 percent to 40 percent of the population are moral absolutists, according to the Kinsey Institute's soon-to-be-published *American Sexual Standards.* Fiercely, these zealots condemn promiscuity, adultery, homosexuality, masturbation, long hair and fluoride. Out there in the countryside (and in cities such as St. Paul and Wichita), they are the ones who most promptly respond to the politician who pushes a sex button in order to . . . what? Create an authoritarian society? Keep the workers docile within the confines of immutable marriage? Punish sin? Make money? Money! There is a lot of money out there on the evangelical Christian circuit and much of it is tax-exempt.

In the fall of 1977, the journalist Andrew Kopkind visited Bensenville, Illinois, in the heart of the heart of the country, in order to study those roots of grass that are now not only as high as an elephant's eye but definitely swaying to the right. *Save the Family* is this year's rallying cry. Since hardly anyone ever openly questions the value of the family in human affairs, any group that wants to save this allegedly endangered institution is warmly supported.

But to the zealots of what Kopkind calls the New Right, saving the family means all sorts of things not exactly connected with the nuclear family. Kopkind discovered that Family Saviors support "the death penalty, Laetrile, nuclear power, local police, Panama Canal, saccharin, FBI, CIA, defense budget, public prayer and real-estate growth."

Family Saviors view darkly "busing, welfare, public-employee unions, affirmative action, amnesty, marijuana, communes, gun control, pornography, the 55-mph speed limit, day-care centers, religious ecumenism, sex education, car pools and the Environmental Protection Agency." Kopkind believes that those attitudes are fairly spontaneous. He is probably right—up to a point. To get Americans to vote constantly against their own interests, however, requires manipulation of the highest order, and it starts at birth in these remarkably United States and never ends.

Until recently, it had not occurred to anyone that a profamily movement might be politically attractive. Our demagogues usually concentrate on communism versus Americanism. But Nixon's jaunts to Peking and Moscow diminished communism as an issue. Those trips also served to remind Americans that we are a fragile minority in a world where the majority is Marxist. Although communism is still a button to be pressed, it tends to tepidity.

On the other hand, to accuse your opponent of favoring any of those vicious forces that endanger the family is to do him real harm. In the past 18 months, Family Saviors have been remarkably effective. They have defeated equal-rights ordinances for homosexualists in Dade County, St. Paul, Wichita, Eugene; obliged the House of Representatives to reverse itself on an anti-abortion bill; stalled (for a time) the Equal Rights Amendment, and so on. Sex is the ultimate politics and very soon, one way or another, every politician is going to get—as it were—into the act.

Officially, our attitudes toward sex derive from the Old and New Testaments. Even to this day, Christian fundamentalists like to say that since every single word in the good book is absolutely true, every one of God's injunctions must be absolutely true, every one of God's injunctions must be absolutely obeyed if we don't want the great plains of the republic to be studded with pillars of salt or worse. Actually, even the most rigorously literal of fundamentalists pick and choose from Biblical texts. The authors of Leviticus proscribe homosexuality—and so do all good Christers. But Leviticus also proscribes rare meat, bacon, shellfish, and the wearing of nylon mixed with wool. If Leviticus were to be obeyed in every instance, the garment trade would collapse.

The authors of the Old and New Testaments created not only a religious anthology but also a political order in which man is woman's eternal master (Jewish men used to pray, "I thank thee, Lord, that thou hast not created me a woman"). The hatred and fear of women that runs through the Old Testament (not to mention in the pages of our justly admired Jewish novelists) suggests that the patriarchal principle so carefully built into the Jewish notion of God must have been at one time opposed to a powerful and perhaps competitive matriarchal system. Whatever the original reasons for the total subordination of woman to man, the result has been an unusually ugly religion that has caused a good deal of suffering not only in its original form but also through its later heresy, Christianity, which in due, and ironic, course was to spin off yet another heresy, communism.

The current wave of Christian religiosity that is flowing across the republic like an oil slick has served as a reminder to women that they must submit to their husbands. This is not easy, as twice-born Anita Bryant admits. She confesses to a tendency to "dump her garbage" all over her husband and master and employee, Bob Green. But she must control herself: "For the husband is the head of the wife, even as Christ is the head of the Church" (Ephesians 5:23). Anita also knows that because of woman's disobedience, the prototypes of the human race were excluded from the Garden of Eden.

Brooding on the Old Testament's dislike of women, Freud theorized that an original patriarchal tribe was for a time replaced by a matriarchal tribe that was then overthrown by the patriarchal Jews: the consequent "re-establishment of the primal father in his historic rights was a great step forward." This speculative nonsense is highly indicative of the way that a mind as shrewd and as original as Freud's could not conceive of a good (virtuous?) society that was not dominated by man the father.

"What do women want?" Freud once asked, plaintively. Well, Sigmund, they want equality with men. But that equality was not acceptable either to the authors of the Old Testament or to Freud himself. Today, almost 3,000 years after Moses came down from Sinai, women are approaching equality with men in the United States. But the war against woman's equality still goes on; at the moment, it is being conducted in the name of The Family.

The New Testament's Christ is a somewhat milder figure than the Jehovah of the Old Testament. Yet one is very much the son of the other, and so, presumably, nothing basic was supposed to change in the relations between the sexes. In fact, at one point, Jesus displays a positively Portnoyesque exasperation with the traditional Jewish mother. "Woman," he says to Mary, "what art thou to me?" Mary's no doubt lengthy answer has not been recorded.

As a Jew, Jesus took seriously the Ten Commandments. But he totally confused the whole business of adultery by saying that even to entertain so much as a Carter-like lust for a woman is the equivalent of actually committing adultery. Jesus also went on record as saying that whores had as good a chance of getting to heaven as IRS men. It is possible that he meant this as a joke. If so, it is the only joke in the New Testament.

To an adulteress, Jesus said, "Neither do I condemn thee," before suggesting that she stop playing around. Jesus had nothing to say about homosexuality, masturbation or the Equal Rights Amendment; but he did think the absolute world of eunuchs (Matthew 19:10–12). Finally, Jesus believed that the world was about to end. "But I tell you of a truth, there are some standing here, who shall not taste of death, till they see the kingdom of God" (Luke 9:27). As far as we can tell, the world did not end in the first century A.D., and all those standing there died without having seen the kingdom.

A few years later, Saint Paul had his vision on the road to Damascus. "Both Jews and gentiles all are under sin," he—what is that best-seller verb?—shrilled. Since Paul was also convinced that the world was about to end, he believed that man must keep himself ritually pure for the day of judgment, and ritual purity required a total abstention from sex. For those who could not remain heroically chaste (to "abide even as I"), Paul rather sourly agreed that "it is better to marry than to burn"—burn with lust, by the way, not hell-fire, as some primitive Christers like to interpret that passage.

Paul also advised married men to live with their wives "as though they had none. . . . For the form of this world is passing away." Although this world's form did not pass away, Paul's loathing of sexuality did not pass away, either. As a result, anyone brought up in a Christian-dominated society will be taught from birth to regard his natural sexual desires as sinful, or worse.

A state of constant guilt in the citizenry is a good thing for rulers who tend not to take very seriously the religions that they impose on their subjects. Since marriage was the only admissible outlet for the sexual drive, that institution was used as a means of channeling the sexual drive in a way that would make docile the man, while the woman, humanly speaking, existed only as the repository of the sacred sperm (regarded as a manifestation of the Holy Ghost).

Woman was commanded to serve and obey her husband as totally as he, in turn, served and obeyed his temporal, Bible-quoting master. If one had set out deliberately to invent a religion that would effectively enslave a population, one could not have done much better than Judaeo-Christianity.

Curiously enough, Paul is the only Old or New Testament maven to condemn lesbianism, an activity that Queen Victoria did not believe existed and Jesus ignored. But Paul knew better. Why, even as he spoke, Roman ladies were burning "in their lust one toward another . . . !" Whenever Paul gets onto the subject of burning lust, he shows every sign of acute migraine.

Now, what is all this nonsense really about? Why should natural sexual desires be condemned in the name of religion? Paul would have said that since judgment day was scheduled for early next year, you should keep yourself ritually clean and ritual cleanliness amongst the Jews involved not only sexual abstinence but an eschewal of shellfish. But Paul's hatred of the flesh is somewhat hard to understand in the light of Jesus' fairly relaxed attitude. On the other hand, Paul's dislike of homosexuality is a bit easier to understand (though never properly understood by American Christers). It derives from the Old Testament book Leviticus, the so-called Holiness Code.

Homosexual relations between heroes were often celebrated in the ancient world. The oldest of religious texts tells of the love between two men, Gilgamesh and Enkidu. When Enkidu died, Gilgamesh challenged death itself in order to bring his lover back to life. In the *Iliad,* Gilgamesh's rage is echoed by Achilles when *his* lover Patroclus dies before the walls of Troy. So intense was the love between the heroes David and Jonathan that David noted in his obituary of Jonathan, "Thy love to me was wonderful, passing the love of women." Elsewhere in the Old Testament, the love that Ruth felt for Naomi was of a sort that today might well end in the joint ownership of a ceramics kiln at Laguna Beach. Why, then, the extraordinary fuss about homosexuality in Leviticus?

Leviticus was written either during or shortly after the Jewish exile in Babylon (586–538 B.C.). The exile ended when Persia's Great King Cyrus conquered Babylon. Tolerant of all religions Cyrus let the Jews go home to Jerusalem, where they began to rebuild the temple that had been destroyed in 586. Since it was thought that the disasters of 586 might have been averted had the Jews been a bit more straitlaced in their deportment, Leviticus was drafted. It contained a very stern list of dos and don'ts. Adultery, which had been proscribed by Moses, was now not only proscribed but the adulterers were to be put to death, while "If a man . . . lie with mankind, as he lieth with a woman, both of them have committed an abomination" and must be put to death.

What is all this about? In earlier days, Jonathan and David were much admired. Was their celebrated love for each other an abomination? Obviously not. The clue to the mystery is the word abomination, which derives from the Hebrew word *to'ebah,* meaning idolatrous. At the time of Leviticus (and long before), the Great Goddess was worshiped throughout the Middle East. She had many names: Cybele, Astarte, Diana, Anahita. Since the Jews thought that the Great Goddess was in direct competition with their Great God, they denounced her worshipers as idolatrous, or *to'ebah,* or abominable; and particularly disapproved of the ritual sex associated with her worship. Many of Cybele's admirers castrated themselves for her glory while male and female prostitutes crowded the temple precincts, ready for action.

In Babylon, every respectable woman was obliged to go at least once in a lifetime to the temple and prostitute herself to the first pilgrim who was willing to pay her. According to Herodotus, ill-favored women were obliged to spend an awful lot of time at the temple, trying to turn that reluctant trick which would make them blessed in the eyes of the goddess.

No doubt, many Jews in Babylon were attracted, if not to the goddess's worship, to the sexual games that went on in her temples. Therefore, the authors of Leviticus made it clear that any Jew who went with a male or female temple prostitute was guilty of an idolatrous or abominable act in the eyes of the Great God Jehovah—a notoriously jealous god by his own admission. As a result, the abominations in Leviticus refer *not* to sexual acts as such but to sexual acts associated with the cult of the Great Goddess.

Elsewhere in the Old Testament, Sodom was destroyed not because the inhabitants were homosexualists but because a number of local men wanted to gang-rape a pair of male angels who were guests of the town. That was a violation of the most sacred of ancient taboos: the law of hospitality. Also, gang rape, whether homosexual or heterosexual, is seldom agreeable in the eyes of any deity.

Human beings take a long time to grow up. This fact means that the tribe or the family or the commune is obliged to protect and train the young in those skills that will be needed for him to achieve a physical maturity whose sole purpose seems to be the passing on to a new generation of the sacred DNA code. The nature of life is more life. This is not very inspiring, but it is all that we know for certain that we have. Consequently, our religio-political leaders have always glorified the tribe or the family or the state at the expense of the individual. But societies change and when they do, seemingly eternal laws are superseded. Flat earth proves to be a sphere. Last year's wisdom is this year's folly.

In an overpopulated world, the Biblical injunction to be fruitful and multiply is less and less heeded. Thanks to increased automation and incontinent breeding, every industrial society in the world now has more workers than it needs. Meanwhile, housing has become so expensive that it is no longer possible for three generations of a family to live in the same house, the ideal of most Christers and strict Jews. Today the nuclear family consists of a boy for you and a girl for me in a housing development . . . hardly an ideal setting for either children or parents.

At this point, it would seem sensible to evolve a different set of arrangements for the human race. Certainly, fewer families would mean fewer children, and that is a good thing. Those who have a gift for parenthood (an infinitely small minority) ought to be encouraged to have children. Those without the gift ought to be discouraged. People would still live in pairs if that pleased them, but the social pressure to produce babies would be lifted.

Unhappily, the thrust of our society is still Judaeo-Christian. As a result, the single American male and the working woman are second-class citizens. A single man's median income is $11,069, while his married brother's income is $14,268 and his working sister's salary is $9,231. This is calculated discrimination. Plainly, it is better to marry than to be ill-paid.

After tax reform, this year's major political issue is Save the Family. Predictably, the Christers have been gunning for women's libbers and fags, two minorities that appear to endanger the family. Not so predictably, a number of Jews are now joining in the attack. This is odd, to say the least. Traditionally, Jews tend to a live-and-let-live attitude on the sensible ground that whenever things go wrong in any society where Jews are a minority, they will get it in the neck. So why make enemies? Unfortunately, Jewish tolerance has never really extended to homosexuality, that permanent abomination. Fag-baiting by American Jewish journalists has always been not only fashionable but, in a covert way, antigoyim.

Eighteen years ago, the busy journalist Alfred Kazin announced that homosexuality was a dead end for a writer. Apparently, fags couldn't make great literature. Today he is no longer quite so certain. In a recent issue of *Esquire,* Kazin accepted the genius of Gertrude Stein, but he could not resist mocking her lesbianism; he also felt it necessary to tell us that she was "fat, queer-looking," while her lover Alice B. Toklas was equally ugly. Although Kazin can accept—barely—the genius of an occasional fag writer, he detests what he calls "the gay mob." He is distressed that "homosexuality is being politicized and is becoming a social fact and a form of social pressure. Does the increasing impatience on all sides with the family, the oldest human institution, explain the widespread growth or emergence of homosexuality amidst so much anxiety about overpopulation?" This is one of those confused rhetorical questions whose answer is meant to be implicit in the polemical tone.

Actually, there is no such thing as a homosexual person, any more than there is such a thing as a heterosexual person. The words are adjectives describing sexual acts, not people. Those sexual acts are entirely natural; if they were not, no one would perform them. But since Judaism proscribes the abominable, the irrational rage that Kazin and his kind feel toward homosexualists has triggered an opposing rage. Gay militants now assert that there is something called gay sensibility, the outward and visible sign of a new kind of human being. Thus madness begets madness.

I have often thought that the reason no one has yet been able to come up with a good word to describe the homosexualist (sometimes known as gay, fag, queer, etc.) is because he does not exist. The human race is divided into male and female. Many human beings enjoy sexual relations with their own sex; many don't; many respond to both. This plurality is the fact of our nature and not worth fretting about.

Today Americans are in a state of terminal hysteria on the subject of sex in general and of homosexuality in particular because the owners of the country (buttressed by a religion that they have shrewdly adapted to their own ends) regard the family as their last means of control over those who work and consume. For two millennia, women have been treated as chattel, while homosexuality has been made to seem a crime, a vice, an illness.

In the *Symposium,* Plato defined the problem: "In Ionia and other places, and generally in countries which are subject to the barbarians [Plato is referring to the Persians, who were the masters of the Jews at the time Leviticus was written], the custom [homosexuality] is held to be dishonorable; loves of youths share the evil repute in which philosophy and gymnastics are held, because they are inimical to tyranny; the interests of rulers require that their subjects should be poor in spirit and that there should be no strong bond of friendship or society among them, which love, above all other motives, is likely to inspire, as our Athenian tyrants learned by experience; for the love of Aristogeiton and the constancy of Harmodius had a strength which undid their power." This last refers to a pair of lovers who helped overthrow the tyrants at Athens.

To this, our American Jews would respond: so what else would you expect from an uncircumcised Greek? While our American Christers would remind us of those scorching letters that Saint Paul mailed to the residents of Corinth and Athens.

Although the founders of our republic intended the state to be entirely secular in its laws and institutions, in actual fact, our laws are a mishmash of Judaeo-Christian superstitions. One ought never to be surprised by the intolerant vehemence of our fundamentalist Christers. After all, they started the country, and the seventeenth-century bigot Cotton Mather is more central to their beliefs than the eighteenth-century liberal George Mason, who fathered the Bill of Rights. But it is odd to observe Jews making common cause with Christian bigots.

I have yet to read anything by a Christer with an IQ above 95 that is as virulent as the journalist Joseph Epstein's statement (in *Harper's* magazine): "If I had the power to do so, I would wish homosexuality off the face of this earth. I would do so because I think that it brings infinitely more pain than pleasure to those who are forced to live with it," etc. Surely, Epstein must realize that if the word Jewry were substituted for homosexuality, a majority of American Christers would be in full agreement. No Jew ought ever to mention the removal of any minority "from the face of the earth." It is unkind. It is also unwise in a Christer-dominated society where a pogrom is never *not* a possibility.

In a recent issue of *Partisan Review,* what I take to be a Catskill hotel called the Hilton Kramer wants to know why the New York intellectuals are not offering the national culture anything "in the way of wisdom about marriage and the family, for example? Anything but attacks, and often vicious attacks, on the most elementary fealties of family life?"

The hotel is worried that for the nation at large, the New York intellectual world is represented in the pages of *The New York Review of Books* "by the likes of Gore Vidal and Garry Wills." I assume that the hotel disapproves of Wills and me because we are not Jewish. The hotel then goes on to characterize me as "proselytizing for the joys of buggery." Needless to say, I have never done such a thing, but I can see how to a superstitious and ill-run hotel anyone who has worked hard to remove consenting sexual relations from the statute books (and politics) must automatically be a salesman for abominable vices, as well as a destroyer of the family and an eater of shellfish.

Finally, dizziest of all, we have the deep thoughts of Norman Podhoretz, the editor of *Commentary,* a magazine subsidized by the American Jewish Congress. In the Sixties, Podhoretz wrote a celebrated piece in which he confessed that he didn't like niggers. Now, in the Seventies, he has discovered that he doesn't like fags, either—on geopolitical rather than rabbinical grounds.

In an article called "The Culture of Appeasement" (again in *Harper's*), Podhoretz tells us that the Vietnam caper had a bad effect on Americans because we now seem not to like war at all. Of course, "The idea of war has never been as natural or as glamorous to Americans as it used to be to the English or the Germans or the French." Podhoretz obviously knows very little American history. As recently as Theodore Roosevelt, war was celebrated as the highest of all human activities. Sadly, Podhoretz compares this year's United States to England in the Thirties when, he assures us, a powerful homosexual movement made England pacifist because the fags did not want beautiful (or even ugly?) boys killed in the trenches.

Aside from the fact that quite as many faggots like war as heterosexualists (Cardinal Spellman, Senator Joe McCarthy, General Walker), the argument makes no sense. When the English were ready to fight Hitler, they fought. As for Vietnam, if we learned anything from our defeat so far from home, it was that we have no right to intervene militarily in the affairs of another nation.

But Podhoretz is not exactly disinterested. As a publicist for Israel, he fears that a craven United States might one day refuse to go to war to protect Israel from its numerous enemies. Although I don't think that he has much to worry about, it does his cause no good to attribute our country's alleged pacifism to a homosexual conspiracy. After all, that is the sort of mad thinking that inspired Hitler to kill not only 6,000,000 Jews but also 600,000 homosexualists.

In the late Sixties and early Seventies, the enemies of the Equal Rights Amendment set out to smear the movement as lesbian. All sorts of militant right-wing groups have since got into the act: the Ku Klux Klan, the John Birch Society, the Committee for the Survival of a Free Congress, Phyllis Schlafly's Eagle Forum, The Conservative Caucus, and dozens of other like-minded groups. Their aim is to deny equal rights to women through scare tactics. If the amendment is accepted, they warn us that lesbians will be able to marry each other, rape will be common, men will use women's toilets. This nonsense has been remarkably effective.

But then, as The Conservative Caucus's Howard Phillips told *The New Republic* with engaging candor, "We're going after people on the basis of their hot buttons." In the past year, the two hot buttons have proved to be sexual: ERA and gay rights legislation. Or "Save the Family" and "Save Our Children."

Elsewhere in the badlands of the nation, one Richard Viguerie is now the chief money raiser for the powers of darkness. In 1977, Viguerie told the *Congressional Quarterly,* "I'm willing to compromise to come to power. There aren't 50 percent of the people that share my view, and I'm willing to make concessions to come to power." That has a familiar Nuremberg ring.

Viguerie is said to have at least 10,000,000 names and addresses on file. He sends out mailings and raises large sums for all sorts of far-right political candidates and organizations. But Viguerie is not just a hustler. He is also an ideologue. "I have raised millions of dollars for the conservative movement over the years and I am not happy with the results. I decided to become more concerned with how the money is spent." He is now beginning to discuss the creation of a new political party.

Among groups that Viguerie works for and with is Gun Owners of America. He also works closely with Phyllis Schlafly, who dates back to Joe McCarthy and Barry Goldwater; currently, she leads the battle against the ERA. Another of Viguerie's clients is Utah's Senator Orrin Hatch, a proud and ignorant man who is often mentioned as a possible candidate for president if the far right should start a new political party.

Viguerie has vowed that "the organized conservative community is going to put in many times more than 3,000,000 [*sic*]. . . . I want a massive assault on Congress in 1978. I don't want any token efforts. We now have the talent and resources to move in a bold, massive way. I think we can move against Congress in 1978 in a way that's never been conceived of."

"Move against Congress." That sounds like revolution. Anyway, it will be interesting to see whether or not Congress will be overwhelmed in November; to see whether or not those children will actually be saved; to see whether or not fealty will be sworn by all right-thinking persons to the endangered family.

*Playboy*
January 1979

# 51
·

# POLICE
# BRUTALITY

For some time now our leaders, both demagogic and honest, have been telling us to rouse ourselves to greater purpose, national and private. Walter Lippmann suggests that the United States behaves like a society which thinks it is complete, with no more to accomplish; that, for better or worse, we are what we are, and the only danger to our comfort is external. President Kennedy's exhortations to self-sacrifice are becoming ever more urgent, even shrill. Yet his critics point out that he has not done much to show us how we might best serve our society. To which the answer of the Administration, at least privately, is that until Americans understand those things that threaten us, both from without and within, any presidential program demanding the slightest sacrifice would be demolished by Congress and the jingo press. After all, things do look all right if you don't look too carefully, and no one can accuse us of ever looking carefully at an unpleasant sight, whether it is Soviet superiority in space or chronic unemployment at home. Now, I don't want to add my voice to the general keening. American society has many virtues which we should never underestimate. By fits and starts, we are attaining a civilization and, barring military accident, we shall certainly attain one before the Soviets. "Be the First into Civilization!" Now *there's* a slogan for the two competitors.

Yet for those who are puzzled at how to respond to Presidential cries for action, vigor and moving-aheadness, I propose that there are certain very practical things we can do in a society that is by no means complete. I might add that those professional patriots who trumpet that this is the new Eden and only traitors would change it or downgrade it are declaring, of course, that the society is closed and therefore decadent and soon to fall. I vote No to "perfection," and Yes to change and survival. Most of us spend too much time solving international problems at cocktail parties, rather than dealing with those things which we might affect and change, the tying up of the loose ends in our own society. There are many of them, ranging from the abolition of capital punishment to school integration. On either of those great matters any citizen can be usefully engaged. He can also be useful in social and moral legislation, where there is much work to be done. As for civil liberties, anyone who is not vigilant may one day find himself living, if not in a police state, at least in a police city. Now I will tell a horror story which has haunted me for several months, something that, I am told, is common but which I witnessed for the first time, reacting as deeply as the writer in Angus Wilson's novel *Hemlock and After*.

I was in Washington for a few days last spring. At about ten o'clock in the evening of my last day in town, I took a taxicab to the Union Station. It was a mild, drizzly night. Traffic in the side streets near Pennsylvania Avenue was tied up. My cab was stopped in front of the YMCA, a large building a half-block from the Old State Department and two blocks from the White House. The sidewalk was deserted. As we sat there, out of the building marched four men, wearing light raincaps with upturned brims and trench coats. There were two men with them. One was well dressed, perhaps sixty; he wore a white raincoat. The other was young and thin and shabby, and he wore no raincoat. I watched as this odd company moved seven or eight yards along the sidewalk toward the traffic light, which was now red. In front of a deserted shop, the trench-coats stopped and methodically began to beat up the two men with them. I sat there stunned. There had been no provocation. As suddenly and pointlessly as a nightmare, the attack began; and there, right in front of me on the black wet sidewalk, the older man lay as two men kicked him, while the other two shoved the young man into the doorway of the shop and began to beat him across the face.

The cab driver, an old Negro, said, "I hate to see anybody do that to another man. I do." The light was now green, but I told him to wait.

I got out and crossed to the nearest trench-coat. He was, at the moment, disengaged. He had been working the younger man over and he now stood a few feet away, breathing hard. I asked him who he was and what he was doing. He turned on me and I have never seen such a savage, frightening little face. It was plump, flushed, with popping eyes; the face of a young pig gone berserk. He began to scream at me to get out of there or I'd be arrested. Threats and obscenities poured out of him in one long orgiastic breath. I looked away and saw that the older man was now on his stomach, trying to shield his head from the kicks of the men standing over him. His raincoat was streaked with mud. The younger man was silent, except for the whacking noise his face made when it was struck— first left, then right, like a punching bag. In my hardest voice I said: "You're going to be the one in trouble if you don't tell me who you are." The dark one came over to me at this point; he showed me his detective's badge, and suggested I get lost. Then he returned to his sport. The plump one was now longing (and I do not exaggerate by using a verb of judgment) to get back to the man in the doorway. But before he could, I asked him for his name. He started to curse again, but a look from his companion stopped him. He gave me his name and then with a squeal leaped on the man in the doorway and began hitting him, making, as he did, obscene gasping noises.

I stood there dumbly wondering what to do. Right in front of me, two men were being knocked about by four men who were, quite simply, enjoying their work. I was also witness to the fact that the victims had *not* resisted arrest, which would of course be the police explanation of what had happened. Cravenly, I got back into the cab. I asked my driver if he would be a witness with me. He shook his head sadly. "I don't want no trouble. This is a mighty dirty town."

At Union Station I telephoned the *Washington Post* and talked to the night editor. I gave him my name. Yes, he knew who I was. Yes, the story interested him. I gave him the detective's name, which I had thought was probably false. He said no, there was such a man. I gave him the cab driver's license number, in case the driver changed his mind. Then the editor asked me what I intended to do about it. I shouted into the receiver, "This is your town. Your scandal. Your newspaper. *You* do something about it, I'm catching a train." He asked if they could use my name. I said of course, and hung up.

But that was the end of it.

I got back to New York to read that a Southern editor had written an editorial attacking the John Birch Society. In the course of his editorial, he quoted the F.B.I. as saying that the Birchers were "irresponsible." Some hours *before* the editorial was published, two men from the F.B.I. arrived at the editor's office and asked him on what authority he could quote the F.B.I. as terming the Birch Society "irresponsible." The editor's sources were not, as it turned out, reliable. But then the editor, quite naturally, asked how it was that the F.B.I. knew the contents of his editorial before it was published. He got no answer.

Now the point to these two stories is that here is something we *can* do: guard our own liberties. We may not be able to save Laos; but we can, as individuals, keep an eye on local police forces, even if it means, as some have proposed, setting up permanent committees of appeal in every city to hear cases of police brutality, or to consider infractions of our freedom to speak out in the pursuit of what our founders termed happiness—two rights always in danger, not only at the local but at the Federal level.

*Esquire*
August 1961

# 52

## PORNOGRAPHY

The man and the woman make love; attain climax; fall separate. Then she whispers, "I'll tell you who I was thinking of if you'll tell me who you were thinking of." Like most sex jokes, the origins of this pleasant exchange are obscure. But whatever the source, it seldom fails to evoke a certain awful recognition, since few lovers are willing to admit that in the sexual act to create or maintain excitement they may need some mental image as erotic supplement to the body in attendance. One perverse contemporary maintains that when he is with A he thinks of B and when he is with B he thinks of A; each attracts him only to the degree that he is able simultaneously to evoke the image of the other. Also, for those who find the classic positions of "mature" lovemaking unsatisfactory yet dare not distress the beloved with odd requests, sexual fantasy becomes inevitable and the shy lover soon finds himself imposing mentally all sorts of wild images upon his unsuspecting partner, who may also be relying on an inner theater of the mind to keep things going; in which case, those popular writers who deplore "our lack of communication today" may have a point. Ritual and magic also have their devotees. In one of Kingsley Amis's fictions, a man mentally conjugates Latin verbs in order to delay orgasm as he waits chivalrously for his partner's predictably slow response. While another considerate lover (nonfictional) can only reduce tempo by thinking of a large loaf of sliced white bread, manufactured by Bond.

Sexual fantasy is as old as civilization (as opposed to as old as the race), and one of its outward and visible signs is pornographic literature, an entirely middle-class phenomenon, since we are assured by many investigators (Kinsey, Pomeroy, et al.) that the lower orders seldom rely upon sexual fantasy for extra-stimulus. As soon as possible, the uneducated man goes for the real thing. Consequently he seldom masturbates, but when he does he thinks, we are told, of *nothing at all.* This may be the last meaningful class distinction in the West.

Nevertheless, the sex-in-the-head middle classes that D. H. Lawrence so despised are not the way they are because they want deliberately to be cerebral and anti-life; rather they are innocent victims of necessity and tribal law. For economic reasons they must delay marriage as long as possible. For tribal reasons they are taught that sex outside marriage is wrong. Consequently the man whose first contact with a woman occurs when he is twenty will have spent the sexually most vigorous period of his life masturbating. Not unnaturally, in order to make that solitary act meaningful, the theater of his mind early becomes a Dionysian festival, and should he be a resourceful dramatist he may find actual lovemaking disappointing when he finally gets to it, as Bernard Shaw did. One wonders whether Shaw would have been a dramatist at all if he had first made love to a girl at fourteen, as nature intended, instead of at twenty-nine, as class required. Here, incidentally, is a whole new line of literary-psychological inquiry suitable for the master's degree: "Characteristics of the Onanist as Dramatist." Late coupling and prolonged chastity certainly help explain much of the rich dottiness of those Victorians whose peculiar habits planted thick many a quiet churchyard with Rose La Touches.

Until recently, pornography was a small cottage industry among the grinding mills of literature. But now that sex has taken the place of most other games (how many young people today learn bridge?), creating and packaging pornography has become big business, and though the high courts of the American Empire cannot be said to be very happy about this state of affairs, they tend to agree that freedom of expression is as essential to our national life as freedom of meaningful political action is not. Also, despite our governors' paternalistic bias, there are signs that they are becoming less intolerant in sexual matters. This would be a good thing if one did not suspect that they may regard sex as our bread and circuses, a means of keeping us off the political streets, in bed and out of mischief. If this is so, we may yet observe the current President in his mad search for consensus settling for the consensual.

Among the publishers of pornography ("merchants of smut," as they say at the FBI), Maurice Girodias is uniquely eminent. For one thing, he is a second-generation peddler of dirty books (or "d.b.'s," as they call them on Eighth Avenue). In the 1930s his English father, Jack Kahane, founded the Obelisk Press in Paris. Among Kahane's authors were Anaïs Nin, Lawrence Durrell, Cyril Connolly, and of course Henry Miller, whose books have been underground favorites for what seems like a century. Kahane died in 1939 and his son, Maurice Girodias (he took his mother's name for reasons not given), continued Kahane's brave work. After the war, Girodias sold Henry Miller in vast quantities to easily stimulated GIs. He also revived *Fanny Hill.* He published books in French. He prospered. Then the terror began. Visionary dictatorships, whether of a single man or of the proletariat, tend to disapprove of irregular sex. Being profoundly immoral in public matters, dictators compensate by insisting upon what they think to be a rigorous morality in private affairs. General de Gaulle's private morality appears to have been registered in his wife's name. In 1946 Girodias was prosecuted for publishing Henry Miller. It was France's first prosecution for obscenity since the trial of *Madame Bovary* in 1844. Happily, the world's writers rallied to Miller's defense, and since men of letters are taken solemnly in France, the government dropped its charges.

In a preface to the recently published *The Olympia Reader,* Girodias discusses his business arrangements at length; and though none of us is as candid about money as he is about sex, Girodias does admit that he lost his firm not as a result of legal persecution but through incompetence, a revelation that gives him avant-garde status in the new pornography of money. Girodias next founded the Olympia Press, devoted to the creation of pornography, both hard and soft core. His adventures as a merchant of smut make a nice story. All sorts of writers, good and bad, were set to work turning out books, often written to order. He would think up a title (e.g., *With Open Mouth*) and advertise it; if there was sufficient response, he would then commission someone to write a book to go with the title. Most of his writers used pseudonyms. Terry Southern and Mason Hoffenberg wrote *Candy* under the name of Maxwell Kenton. Christopher Logue wrote *Lust* under the name of Count Palmiro Vicarion, while Alex Trocchi, as Miss Frances Lengel, wrote *Helen and Desire.* Girodias also published Samuel Beckett's *Watt,* Vladimir Nabokov's *Lolita,* and J. P. Donleavy's *The Ginger Man;* perversely, the last three authors chose not to use pseudonyms.

Reading of these happy years, one recalls a similar situation just after the Second War when a number of New York writers were commissioned at so many cents a page to write pornographic stories for a United States Senator. The solon, as they say in smutland, never actually met the writers but through a go-between he guided their stories: a bit more flagellation here, a touch of necrophilia there. . . . The subsequent nervous breakdown of one of the Senator's pornographers, now a celebrated poet, was attributed to the strain of not knowing which of the ninety-six Senators he was writing for.*

In 1958 the Fourth French Republic banned twenty-five of Girodias's books, among them *Lolita*. Girodias promptly sued the Ministry of the Interior and, amazingly, won. Unfortunately, five months later, the General saw fit to resume the grandeur of France. De Gaulle was back; and so was Madame de Gaulle. The Minister of the Interior appealed the now defunct Fourth Republic's decision and was upheld. Since then, censorship has been the rule in France. One by one Girodias's books, regardless of merit, have been banned. Inevitably, André Malraux was appealed to and, inevitably, he responded with that elevated double-talk which has been a characteristic of what one suspects will be a short-lived Republic. Girodias is currently in the United States, where he expects to flourish. Ever since our Puritan republic became a gaudy empire, pornography has been a big business for the simple reason that when freedom of expression is joined with the freedom to make a lot of money, the dream of those whose bloody footprints made vivid the snows of Valley Forge is close to fulfillment and that happiness which our Constitution commands us to pursue at hand.

*The Olympia Reader* is a collection of passages from various books published by Maurice Girodias since 1953. Reading it straight through is a curiously disjointed experience, like sitting through a program of movie trailers. As literature, most of the selections are junk, despite the presence of such celebrated contemporary figures as Nabokov, Genet and Queneau; and of the illustrious dead, Sade and Beardsley.

Pornography is usually defined as that which is calculated to arouse sexual excitement. Since what arouses X repels Y, no two people are apt to respond in quite the same way to the same stimulus. One man's meat, as they say, is another man's poison, a fact now recognized by the American judiciary, which must rule with wearisome frequency on obscenity. With unexpected good sense, a judge recently observed that since the books currently before him all involved ladies in black leather

*David Ignatius Walsh (Dem., Mass.).

with whips, they could not be said to corrupt the generality, since a taste for being beaten is hardly common and those who are aroused by such fantasies are already "corrupted" and therefore exempt from laws designed to protect the young and usual. By their nature, pornographies cannot be said to proselytize, since they are written for the already hooked. The worst that can be said of pornography is that it leads not to "antisocial" sexual acts but to the reading of more pornography. As for corruption, the only immediate victim is English prose. Mr. Girodias himself writes like his worst authors ("Terry being at the time in acute financial need . . .") while his moral judgments are most peculiar. With reverence, he describes his hero Sir Roger Casement (a "superlative pederast," whatever that is) as "politically confused, emotionally unbalanced, maudlin when depressed and absurdly naïve when in his best form; but he was exceptionally generous, he had extraordinary courage and a simple human wisdom which sprang from his natural goodness." Here, Mr. Girodias demonstrates a harmony with the age in which he lives. He may or may not have described Sir Roger accurately, but he has certainly drawn an accurate portrait of the Serious American Novelist, 1966.

Of the forty selections Mr. Girodias has seen fit to collect, at least half are meant to be literature in the most ambitious sense, and to the extent that they succeed, they disappoint; Beckett's *Watt,* Queneau's *Zazie,* Donleavy's *The Ginger Man* are incapable of summoning up so much as the ghost of a rose, to appropriate Sir Thomas Browne's handsome phrase. There is also a good deal of Henry Miller, whose reputation as a pornographer is largely undeserved. Though he writes a lot about sex, the only object he seems ever to describe is his own phallus. As a result, unless one lusts specifically for the flesh of Henry Miller, his works cannot be regarded as truly edifying. Yet at Miller's best he makes one irritably conscious of what it is like to be inside his skin, no mean feat . . . the pornographic style, incidentally, is contagious: the stately platitude, the arch paraphrase, the innocent line which starts suddenly to buck with unintended double meanings.

Like the perfect host or madam, Mr. Girodias has tried to provide something for everyone. Naturally there is a good deal of straightforward heterosexual goings-on. Mr. Girodias gives us several examples, usually involving the seduction of an adolescent male by an older woman. For female masochists (and male sadists) he gives us *Story of O.* For homosexual sadists (and masochists) *The Gaudy Image.* For negrophiles (and phobes) *Pinktoes,* whose eloquent author, Chester

Himes, new to me, has a sense of humor which sinks his work like a stone. For anal eroticists who like science fiction there are passages from William Burroughs's *Naked Lunch* and *The Soft Machine.* For devotees of camp, new to the scene, the thirty-three-year-old *The Young and Evil* by Charles Henri Ford and Parker Tyler is a pioneer work and reads surprisingly well today. Parenthetically, it is interesting to note the role that clothes play in most of these works, camp, kinky, and straight. Obviously, if there is to be something for everyone, the thoughtful entrepreneur must occasionally provide an old sock or pair of panties for the fetishist to get, as it were, his teeth into. But even writers not aiming at the fetishist audience make much of the ritual taking off and putting on of clothes, and it is significant that the bodies thus revealed are seldom described as meticulously as the clothes are.

Even Jean Genet, always lyric and vague when celebrating cock, becomes unusually naturalistic and detailed when he describes clothes in an excerpt from *The Thieves' Journal.* Apparently when he was a boy in Spain a lover made him dress up as a girl. The experiment was a failure because "Taste is required . . . I was already refusing to have any. I forbade myself to. Of course I would have shown a great deal of it." Nevertheless, despite an inadequate clothes sense, he still tells us far more about the *travesti manqué* than he ever tells us about the body of Stilitano for whom he lusted.

In most pornography, physical descriptions tend to be sketchy. Hard-core pornographers seldom particularize. Inevitably, genitals are massive, but since we never get a good look at the bodies to which they are attached, the effect is so impersonal that one soon longs to read about those more modest yet entirely tangible archetypes, the girl and boy next door, two creatures far more apt to figure in the heated theater of the mind than the voluptuous grotesques of the pulp writer's imagination. Yet by abstracting character and by keeping his human creatures faceless and vague, the pornographer does force the reader to draw upon personal experience in order to fill in the details, thereby achieving one of the ends of all literary art, that of making the reader collaborator.

As usual, it is the Marquis de Sade (here represented by a section from *Justine*) who has the most to say about sex—or rather the use of others as objects for one's own pleasure, preferably at the expense of theirs. In true eighteenth-century fashion, he explains and explains and explains. There is no God, only Nature, which is heedless of the Good as well as of the Bad. Since Nature requires that the strong violate the weak and since it is demonstrably true that Nature made women weak and men strong, therefore . . . and so on. The Marquis's vision—of which so much has been made in this century—is nothing but a rather simple-minded Manicheism, presented with more passion than logic. Yet in his endless self-justification (un-Natural this: Nature never apologizes, never explains) Sade's tirades often strike the Marlovian note: "It is Nature that I wish to outrage. I should like to spoil her plans, to block her advance, to halt the course of the stars, to throw down the globes that float in space—to destroy everything that serves her, to protect everything that harms her, to cultivate everything that irritates her—in a word to insult all her works." But he stops considerably short of his mark. He not only refused to destroy one of her more diverting creations, himself, but he also opposed capital punishment. Even for a French *philosophe,* Sade is remarkably inconsistent, which is why one prefers his letters to his formal argument. Off duty he is more natural and less Natural. While in the Bastille he described himself as possessing an "extreme tendency in everything to lose control of myself, a disordered imagination in sexual matters such as has never been known in this world, an atheist to the point of fanaticism—in two words there I am, and so once again kill me or take me like that, because I shall never change." Latter-day diabolists have tried to make of his "disordered imagination in sexual matters" a religion and, as religions go, it is no more absurd than that of the crucified tripartite man-god. But though Nature is indeed nonhuman and we are without significance except to ourselves, to make of that same indifferent Nature an ally in behavior which is, simply, harmful to human society is to be singularly vicious.

Yet it is interesting to note that throughout all pornography, one theme recurs: the man or woman who manages to capture another human being for use as an unwilling sexual object. Obviously this is one of the commonest of masturbatory daydreams. Sade's originality was to try, deliberately, to make his fantasies real. But he was no Gilles de Rais. He lacked the organizational sense, and his actual adventures were probably closer to farce than to tragedy, more Charlie Chaplin trying to drown Martha Raye than Ilse Koch castrating her paramours at Buchenwald. Incidentally, it is typical of our period that the makers of the play *Marat/Sade* were much admired for having perversely reduced a splendid comic idea to mere tragedy.

Mr. Girodias's sampler should provide future sociologists with a fair idea of what sex was like at the dawn of the age of science. They will no doubt be as amused as most of us are depressed by the extent to which superstition has perverted human nature (not to mention thwarted Nature). Officially the tribal norm continues. The family is the central unit of society. Man's function is to impregnate woman in order to make children. Any sexual act that does not lead to the making of a child is untribal, which is to say antisocial. But though these assumptions are still held by the mass of human society in the West, the pornographers by what they write (as well as by what they omit to mention) show that in actual fact the old laws are not only broken (as always) but are being questioned in a new way.

Until this generation, even nonreligious enemies of irregular sexuality could sensibly argue that promiscuity was bad because it led to venereal disease and to the making of unwanted babies. In addition, sex was a dirty business since bodies stank and why should any truly fastidious person want to compound the filth of his own body's corruption with that of another? Now science has changed all that. Venereal disease has been contained. Babies need not be the result of the sexual act ("I feel so happy and safe now I take the pill"), while improved bathing facilities together with the American Mom's relentless circumcision of boys has made the average human body a temptingly hygienic contraption suitable for all sorts of experiment. To which the moralists can only respond: Rome born again! Sexual license and excessive bathing, as everyone knows, made the Romans effete and unable to stand up to the stalwart puritan savages from the German forests whose sacred mission was to destroy a world gone rotten. This simplistic view of history is a popular one, particularly among those who do not read history. Yet there *is* a basic point at issue and one that should be pondered.

Our tribal standards are an uneasy combination of Mosaic law and the warrior sense of caste that characterized those savage tribesmen who did indeed engulf the world of cities. The contempt for people in trade one still finds amongst the Wasp aristocracy, the sense of honor (furtive but gnawing), the pride in family, the loyalty to class, and (though covert) the admiration for the military virtues and physical strength are all inherited not from our civilized predecessors who lived in the great cities but from their conquerors, the wandering tribesmen, who planted no grain, built no cities, conducted no trade, yet preyed successfully upon those who did these contemptible, unmanly things. Today of course we are all as mixed in values as in blood, but the unstated assumption that it is better to be physically strong than wise, violent than gentle, continent than sensual, landowner or coupon clipper than shopkeeper, lingers on as a memorial to those marauding tribes who broke into history at the start of the Bronze Age and whose values are with us still, as the Gallup Poll attested recently, when it revealed that the President's war in Vietnam is most popular in the South, the most "tribal" part of the United States. Yet the city is the glory of our race, and today in the West, though we are all city dwellers, we still accept as the true virtue the code of our wild conquerors, even though our actual lives do not conform to their laws, nor should they, nor should we feel guilty because they don't.

In ten thousand years we have learned how to lengthen human lives but we have found no way to delay human puberty. As a result, between the economics of the city and the taboos of the tribe we have created a monstrous sexual ethic. To mention the most notorious paradox: It is not economically convenient for the adolescent to marry; it is not tribally correct for him to have sex outside of marriage. Solutions to this man-made problem range from insistence upon total chastity to a vague permissiveness which, worriedly, allows some sexuality if those involved are "sincere" and "mature" and "loving." Until this generation, tribal moralists could argue with perfect conviction that there was only one correct sexual equation: man plus woman equals baby. All else was vice. But now that half the world lives with famine—and all the world by the year 2000, if Pope Paul's as yet unborn guests are allowed to attend (in his unhappy phrase) the "banquet of life"—the old equation has been changed to read: man plus woman equals baby equals famine. If the human race is to survive, population will have to be reduced drastically, if not by atomic war then by law, an unhappy prospect for civil liberties but better than starving. In any case, it is no longer possible to maintain that those sexual acts which do not create (or simulate the creation of) a child are unnatural; unless, to strike the eschatological note, it is indeed Nature's will that we perish through overpopulation, in which case reliable hands again clutch the keys of Peter.

Fortunately, the pornographers appear to be on the side of survival. They make nothing of virginity deflowered, an important theme for two thousand years; they make nothing of it for the simple reason we make little of it. Straightforward adultery no longer fascinates the pornographer; the scarlet letter has faded. Incest, mysteriously, seldom figures in current pornographies. This is odd. The tribal taboo remains as strong as ever, even though we now know that when members of the same family mate the result is seldom more cretinous or more sickly than its parents. The decline of incest as a marketable theme is probably due to today's inadequate middle-class housing. In large Victorian houses with many rooms and heavy doors, the occupants could be mysterious and

exciting to one another in a way that those who live in rackety developments can never hope to be. Not even the lust of a Lord Byron could
survive the fact of Levittown.

Homosexuality is now taken entirely for granted by pornographers
because we take it for granted. But though there is considerable awareness nowadays of what people actually do, the ancient somewhat ambivalent hostility of the tribe persists; witness *Time* magazine's recent
diagnosis of homosexuality as a "pernicious sickness" like influenza or
opposing the war in Vietnam. Yet from the beginning, tribal attitudes
have been confused on this subject. On the one hand, nothing must be
allowed to deflect man the father from his procreative duty. On the other
hand, man the warrior is more apt than not to perform homosexual acts.
What was undesirable in peace was often a virtue in war, as the Spartans
recognized, inventing the buddy system at the expense of the family
unit. In general, it would seem that the more warlike the tribe, the more
opportunistic the sexual response. "You know where you can find your
sex," said that sly chieftain Frederick the Great to his officers, "—in the
barracks." Of all the tribes, significantly, the Jews alone were consistently opposed not only to homosexuality but to any acknowledgment of
the male as an erotic figure (cf. II Maccabees 4:7–15). But in the great
world of pre-Christian cities, it never occurred to anyone that a homosexual act was less "natural" than a heterosexual one. It was simply a
matter of taste. From Archilochus to Apuleius, this acceptance of the
way people actually are is implicit in what the writers wrote. Suetonius
records that of his twelve emperors, eleven went with equal ease from
boys to girls and back again without Suetonius ever finding anything
remarkable in their "polymorphous perverse" behavior. But all that, as
Stanley Kauffmann would say, happened in a "different context."

Nevertheless, despite contexts, we are bisexual. Opportunity and
habit incline us toward this or that sexual object. Since additional children are no longer needed, it is impossible to say that some acts are
"right" and others "wrong." Certainly to maintain that a homosexual
act in itself is antisocial or neurotic is dangerous nonsense, of the sort
that the astonishing Dr. Edmund Bergler used to purvey when he
claimed that he would "cure" homosexuals, as if this was somehow
desirable, like changing Jewish noses or straightening Negro hair in
order to make it possible for those who have been so altered to pass more
easily through a world of white Christians with snub noses.

Happily, in a single generation, science has changed many old assumptions. Economics has changed others. A woman can now easily

support herself, independent of a man. With the slamming of Nora's door, the family ceased to be the essential social unit. Also, the newly affluent middle class can now pursue other pleasures. In the film *The Collector,* a lower-class boy captures an educated girl and after alternately tormenting and boring her, he says balefully, "If more people had more time and money, there would be a lot more of this." This got an unintended laugh in the theater, but he is probably right. Sexual experiment is becoming more open. A placid Midwestern town was recently appalled to learn that its young married set was systematically swapping wives. In the cities, group sex is popular, particularly among the young. Yet despite the new freedoms that the pornographers reflect (sadly for them, since their craft must ultimately wither away), the world they show, though closer to human reality than that of the tribalists, reveals a new illness: the powerlessness that most people feel in an overpopulated and overorganized society.

The sado-masochist books that dominate this year's pornography are not the result of a new enthusiasm for the *vice anglais* so much as a symptom of helplessness in a society where most of the male's aggressive-creative drive is thwarted. The will to prevail is a powerful one, and if it is not fulfilled in work or in battle, it may find an outlet in sex. The man who wants to act out fantasies of tying up or being tied up is imposing upon his sex life a power drive which became socially undesirable once he got onto that escalator at IBM that will take him by predictable stages to early retirement and the medically prolonged boredom of sunset years. Solution of this problem will not be easy, to say the least.

Meanwhile, effort must be made to bring what we think about sex and what we say about sex and what we do about sex into some kind of realistic relationship. Indirectly, the pornographers do this. They recognize that the only sexual norm is that there is none. Therefore, in a civilized society law should not function at all in the area of sex except to protect people from being "interfered with" against their will.

Unfortunately, even the most enlightened of the American state codes (Illinois) still assumes that since adultery is a tribal sin it must be regarded as a civil crime. It is not, and neither is prostitution, that most useful of human institutions. Traditionally, liberals have opposed prostitution on the ground that no one ought to be forced to sell his body because of poverty. Yet in our Affluency, prostitution continues to flourish for the simple reason that it is needed. If most men and women were forced to rely upon physical charm to attract lovers, their sexual lives would be not only meager but in a youth-worshiping country like America painfully brief. Recognizing this state of affairs, a Swedish psychologist recently proposed state brothels for women as well as for men, in recognition of the sad biological fact that the middle-aged woman is at her sexual peak at a time when she is no longer able to compete successfully with younger women. As for the prostitutes themselves, they practice an art as legitimate as any other, somewhere between that of masseur and psychiatrist. The best are natural healers and, contrary to tribal superstition, they often enjoy their work. It is to the credit of today's pornographer that intentionally or not, he is the one who tells us most about the extraordinary variety of human sexual response. In his way he shows us as we are, rather like those Fun House mirrors which, even as they distort and mock the human figure, never cease to reflect the real thing.

*The New York Review of Books*
March 31, 1966

# 53

·

# DOC REUBEN

*Everything you always wanted to know about sex\**
Explained by David Reuben, M.D.
*\*But were afraid to ask*

The title of the current number-one nonfiction best seller is cute as a
bug's ear, and we know what Freud thought of those who were cute
about sex. ("Very uptight"—Sigmund Freud, M.D.). If a jocose approach to sexual matters is a mask for unease, then David Reuben, M.D.
("currently in private psychiatric practice in San Diego, California"), is
in a state of communicable panic and I would be most unwilling to have
him privately practice psychiatry on me, even in San Diego, the Vatican
of the John Birch Society.

David Reuben, M.D., is a relentlessly cheery, often genuinely funny
writer whose essential uncertainty about sex is betrayed by a manner
which shifts in a very odd way from night-club comedian to reform
rabbi, touching en route almost every base except the scientific. Essentially he is a moralist, expressing the hang-ups of today's middle-aged,
middle-class urban American Jews, hang-ups which are not (as I shall
attempt to show) necessarily those of the gentile population or, for that
matter, of the rising generation of American Jews.

Yes, I am going to talk about class and race-religion, two unmentionables in our free land, and I am going to make a case that Jewish family
patterns, sexual taboos, and superstitions are often very different from
those of the rest of the population, black, white, and yellow, Roman
Catholic, Protestant and Moslem. For gentile readers much of the
charm of *Portnoy's Complaint* was its exoticism. And despite those
ecumenical reviewers who insist that *everyone's* mother is a Jewish
mother, the truth is that Mrs. Portnoy was the result of a specific set
of historical circumstances, not applicable to anyone else, including the
next generation of American Jews, if we are to believe in her child
Alexander's rebellion. Certainly his son (assuming he has not entirely
wasted his posterity) will probably resemble next-door neighbor George
Apley III rather more than father or grandfather.

I mention Alexander Portnoy because David Reuben, M.D., is his
contemporary and they have a good deal in common. But where Portnoy's creator is a highly talented artist often able to view objectively the
prejudices and tribal taboos of his mother's ghetto culture, Dr. Reuben
is still very much in her thrall. Essentially he is not a man of science
but a moderately swinging rabbi who buttresses his prejudices with
pious quotations from the Old Testament (a single reference to the New
Testament is inaccurate); surprisingly, the only mental therapist he
mentions is Freud—in order to set him straight.

But then Dr. Reuben seems not to have been affected at all by the
discipline of science. He explodes with snappy generalities ("All children at the time of puberty develop pimples") and opinions ("All prostitutes hate men") and statistics which he seems to have made up
("Seventy to eighty percent of Americans engage in fellatio and cunnilingus"). He makes no attempt to prove anything; he merely states his
prejudices and enthusiasms as though they were in some way self-
evident. It is possible that his advice to middle-aged, middle-class Jewish
heterosexuals is useful, but they make up a very small part of the
population he now wants to convert to his notions of "mature" sexuality. Certainly a white Protestant will find much of what he has to say
inscrutable, while a black will no doubt regard him as something from
outer space (that is to say, suburbia) and yet another good reason for
replacing Jerusalem with Mecca.

At two points Dr. Reuben is at odds with Moses. He thinks Onan was
quite a guy, and his lonely practice particularly useful in toning up those
of our senior citizens whose wheelchairs will not accommodate two
people; and he has a positively Updikean enthusiasm for cunnilingus.

Dr. Reuben would like everyone to indulge in this chivalrous practice—except women, of course: Lesbianism is "immature." He is also sufficiently American to believe that more of everything is best. At times he sounds not unlike the late Bruce Barton extolling God as a super-salesman. "Success in the outside world breeds success in the inside world of sex," sermonizes Dr. Reuben. "Conversely, the more potent a man becomes in the bedroom, the more potent he is in business." Is God a super-salesman? You bet!—and get this—*God eats it, too!*

On those rare occasions when Dr. Reuben is not proselytizing, he can be most instructive, particularly when he describes what happens to the body during orgasm (I assume he is correct about the plumbing), and as he lists all the things that take place between the first thought of sex (D. H. Lawrence, apparently, was wrong: sex is all in the head) and final emission, the male reader is certain to be impotent for the next twenty-four hours ("You will never again," said Leo Tolstoi wickedly, "step on a crack without thinking of a white bear"). Dr. Reuben also has a good plan for eliminating venereal disease by a mass inoculation of the entire population, which he only slightly spoils by suggesting that we use "our gigantic Civil Defense network," which was set up for "just such a mass medical program (in case of bacteriological warfare). This would be a wonderful opportunity for a dry run which might pay off in case of a real war." Well, he does live in San Diego.

Dr. Reuben is also a liberal on abortion, and informative on the subject of contraceptives. He finds something a bit wrong with all the present methods and suspects that the eventual solution will be a morning-after pill for women—as a Jewish patriarch he believes that woman, the lesser vessel, should bear the responsibility. He is also filled with wonderful lore, some of which I hope is true. Want to know the best nonmedical contraceptive? "Coca-Cola. Long a favorite soft drink, it is, coincidentally, the best douche available. A Coke contains carbolic acid which kills the sperm and sugar which explodes the sperm cells . . . The six-ounce bottle is just the right size for one application." Yes, but won't it rot her teeth?

Between mature guys and gals, anything goes (though anal penetration of the gal leaves Doc a bit queasy). Male impotence and female frigidity he recognizes as hazards, but psychiatry, he is quick to point out, will work wonders. He is a remorseless self-advertiser. Every few pages he gives us a commercial with brisk dialogue and characters named Emily who suffer from frigidity until . . . But let's listen in on Emily and her doctor after some months of treatment. Is Emily frigid now? Lordy no! Emily is fucking like a minx. "I'm happy to say, Doctor, this is just a social call. I wanted to tell you how happy I am. I don't know what it's done for other people but psychiatry did what Mother Nature couldn't do—it made a woman out of me!" Music up and out.

Or take the case of Joni, the beautiful airline stewardess who couldn't achieve the big O no matter how hard she (he) tried. After being told that the values she had learned as a girl on a farm in Iowa (Christian puritanism) were not applicable to a flying bunny, she was able in a matter of months to write her doctor "at Christmastime" (when, presumably, all thoughts flow toward the orgasm), "I may have been a stewardess, but I really 'won my wings' in the psychiatrist's office." To one who locates psychiatry somewhere between astrology and phrenology on the scale of human gullibility, the cold-blooded desire to make money by giving one's fellows (at best) obvious advice and (at worst) notions even sillier than the ones that made them suffer smacks of *Schadenfreude.*

Along with testimonials to the efficacy of his art, Dr. Reuben has a good deal to say about many subjects, and since he never attempts to prove anything, his opinions must be taken as just that. Some examples. "Orgasm among nymphomaniacs is as rare as orgasm among prostitutes." To which any liberal arts professor would scribble in the margin, "prove." For Dr. Reuben's instruction, the only bona fide nymphomaniac I ever went to bed with promptly produced a splendid series of orgasms of the variety known as "skimming." In fact, she enjoyed having orgasms so much that she thought it fun to have sex with a lot of different people, thus betraying her immaturity. Three point two times a week year in and year out with the same mature and loving mate ought to have been quite enough for the saucy shiksa.

Then there is Smiling Jack, who suffers from premature ejaculation. Why? *Because he wants to punish women.* "The smile is characteristic of men with premature ejaculation—they are all profusely apologetic but their regrets have a hollow ring." Fast comer, wipe that smile off your face before you stretch out on Dr. Reuben's couch.

"Blind girls become particularly adept at secret masturbation. They . . ." No. You had better read this section for yourself. At least the author had the courtesy to wait until Helen Keller was dead before rushing into print with the news. Then "The chap who pays to see two ladies perform homosexually also has his problems, as do the father and son who patronize the same hustler." A breath-taking non sequitur, as usual unprovable and also, as usual, an echo of Mosaic law: Thou shalt not look upon thy father's nakedness.

The looniest of Dr. Reuben's folklore is "Food seems to have a mysterious fascination for homosexuals. Many of the world's greatest chefs have been homosexuals." (Who? I'm really curious. Not Brillat-Savarin, not Fanny Farmer.) "Some of the country's best restaurants are run by homosexuals" (Those two at Twenty One?). "Some of the fattest people are homosexuals" (King Farouk? Orson Welles? President Taft?). "The exact reason is complex. . . ." It certainly is, since there is no evidence one way or the other. But if there were, Dr. Reuben had best find himself a friendly shrink because he makes at least eight references in his book to the penis as food, usually "limp as a noodle"; in fact, food is seldom far from the good doctor's mind when he contemplates genitalia—no doubt for a very complex reason (when I met him three years ago in San Diego he was round as a . . . well, butterball; since then, according to the dustjacket photo, he has "matured" and lost weight).

But Reuben the folklorist is nothing compared to Reuben the statistician. "At least seventy-five to eighty-five percent of [prostitutes'] clients want to have their penises sucked." "Ninety-nine percent of johns refuse to wear condoms [with prostitutes]." "Only about one tenth of [aging] females choose celibacy." "Chronic or repeated impotence probably affects about thirty to forty percent of men at any given time." And of course those 70 to 80 percent of men who engage in cunnilingus. Since two can play these games, I shall now open my own private files to the public. Right off, 92 percent of those men who get cancer of the tongue have practiced cunnilingus from once to 3309 times in their lives. Those who practice fellatio, however, are not only better dressed but will take at least one long trip in the coming year. Ninety-six percent of those who practice sixty-nine (for Dr. Reuben's heteros a must) periodically complain of a sense of suffocation. Finally, all major American novelists after forty occasionally have orgasm without a full erection. Further statistics on this poignant condition will be revealed as soon as I have heard from Saul, Vladimir and Mary.

In favor of contraception, abortion, masturbation, oral sex between male and female, Dr. Reuben is up-to-date and a source of comfort to his reformed congregation (though the orthodox must be grimly looking about for some useful anathema to lob his way). On circumcision he is orthodox—nature wanted the glans penis covered but Jehovah knew better (our rabbi quotes from both Genesis and Exodus to support this profitable—for doctors—mutilation); on prostitution he is orthodox but tries not to be; on homosexuality he is Mosaic—it is a bad business strictly for immature freaks. Bisexuality does not exist for reasons he and his mentor the late Dr. Bergler never quite give, though they have a lot of opinions which, in their confident American way, they present as facts.

Parenthetically, the collapse of responsible commentary in the United States is as noticeable in a pseudoscience like psychiatry as it is, say, in literary criticism. No one need *prove* anything; simply state private opinion as public fact, preferably in lurid terms. It is now a national characteristic and part of the general cretinizing effect certain dour biologists (accused, accurately, of elitism) regard as a concomitant of promiscuous breeding and overpopulation.

To his credit, Dr. Reuben realizes the practical uses and pleasures of prostitution, an arrangement necessary to the well-being of many millions of men (and women) since the dawn of money, and he is forced to admit that most of the usual arguments against it are not only hypocritical but inaccurate. Nevertheless, looking up from his well-thumbed Old Testament, he is obliged to remind us that " 'harlots' are mentioned forty-four times in the Bible, 'whores' and 'whore mongers' are featured fifty-three times, and committing 'whoredoms' is mentioned eight times."

He then makes his only allusion to the New Testament. Apparently "[it] began where the Old Testament left off and commenced a religious campaign against prostitution which took on all the attributes of a Crusade. . . ." As J. C.'s numerous readers know, his only reference to prostitution was a proposal that the fallen Mary Magdalene be shown charity. Even St. Paul was not a pornophobe; he was a chiliast who believed the day of judgment was at hand and so thought it wise to keep oneself in a state of ceremonial purity—in other words, no sex of any kind (even mature); but if such continence was unbearable then "it is better to marry than to burn."

It should be noted that in matters of history (excepting always Old Testament studies) and etymology Dr. Reuben is usually wrong. He tells us that the word pornography "comes from two Greek words, *pornos,* meaning dirty, and *graphos,* meaning words." *Graphos* of course means "writing" not "words." *Pornos* does not mean "dirty"; it means "harlot." Though I do not think Dr. Reuben has any Greek, if he did it would be a marvelous tribute to the unconscious mind that he confuses "harlot" with "dirty." He also thinks that homosexual sadists "filled the ranks of Hitler's Gestapo and SS." After the purge of Ernst Roehm and his friends in 1934, only banal heterosexual sadists were recruited by the Gestapo and SS. By 1940 homosexualists were being carted off to concentration camps along with Jews, gypsies, and communists. The text is full of misprints (as if anyone cares), bad grammar, misspellings (on page 142 "syphillitic").

While acknowledging the Old Testament's harsh line on prostitution, our cruise director finds peculiarly contemptible the moralizing of those "ministers and moral educators who couldn't be farther removed from practical knowledge of the subject if they lived on the moon." Although Dr. Reuben is robust in his attacks on Protestant clergymen, neither Roman Catholic priest nor Jewish rabbi is ever noted as a hypocritical enemy of life. Obviously Dr. Reuben knows a militant minority when he sees one. But though he is right in blaming a good deal of what is wrong with our sexual ethos on the Protestant founders, he ought, in all fairness, to note that later arrivals haven't been much help either.

To Dr. Reuben's credit, he puts at rest the myth that prostitutes are wicked people because they spread venereal disease. Of 4700 women arrested for prostitution in New York City (1966), 619 had gonorrhea and only four had syphilis. Not a bad record considering their line of work and the harassment they are subject to. He also reminds us that where prostitution is legal, sex crimes diminish. Finally, "most girls become prostitutes because they like it." But then he can't leave that reasonable opinion alone (those 105 Old Testament cracks about "whores" obviously prey on him). Two paragraphs later we are told that "in prostitution no one's happy." Then Dr. Reuben erupts in a torrent of tribal wisdom worthy of any Baptist divine working out of the Oral Roberts Tabernacle. "All prostitutes have at least one thing in common—they hate men." They are doomed to this sad state unless "some dramatic change like psychiatric treatment intervenes." Unexpectedly "their genitals are usually in better condition than those of the average woman." But unfortunately (for men) "the majority of prostitutes are female homosexuals in their private lives."

This, incidentally, is a beloved post-Freudian myth, quite unproven but perennially exciting to men who want to believe that the women they rent deeply hate them and only go to bed with them because they lack money. It is the ultimate charade in the power fantasy which drives so many men (you are tied up and helpless, my proud beauty), including homosexualists who try, not always vainly, to make that one "totally" heterosexual male either because he needs money or must yield to physical force. To say that all female prostitutes are really Lesbians is to succumb to a pleasant if rather silly daydream.

But then Dr. Reuben the rabbi sooner or later does in Dave the swinger. Harlots must, finally, suffer for their evil ways; therefore few "achieve orgasm even in the privacy of their own bedrooms" (a slightly confusing statement: where do they work? They can't all be represented by Al Fresco), but then how can they be expected to have mature orgasms when the only source of "love for a prostitute is her pimp . . . who provides her with what little emotional warmth he is capable of"? Value judgment. Prove. But then there is no superstition about prostitutes that Dr. Reuben does not offer us as "scientific" fact. Mrs. Portnoy would be proud of Alexander's nice contemporary, particularly when he tells us that the relationship between prostitute and customer is simply "masturbation in a vagina" (a slight contradiction since earlier he told us that 75 to 85 percent of the johns are blown).

Although none of this is provable one way or the other (the nice thing about a pseudoscience like psychiatry is that one can pose any hypothesis upon which to build if not a science a religion), and assuming that a good deal of commercial sex is a kind of joyless masturbation, one is tempted to point out that the same is true of marriage in which, as time passes, the man (and now women are beginning to make the same confession) is constantly forced to rely on inner newsreels in order to make love to a body that no longer excites him yet because of law and tribal custom he must pretend to respond to for thirty or forty or, if Dr. Reuben is counseling him, seventy years of mature sexuality.

In the course of "proving" that a majority of prostitutes are Lesbians and so (naturally) unhappy, Dr. Reuben reveals the bedrock upon which all his superstitions finally rest. "Just as one penis plus one penis equals nothing, one vagina plus another vagina still equals zero." There it is. Dr. Reuben believes in what Roman Catholics term "natural law"— everything is created for a *single* natural purpose. Penis plus vagina equals continuation of the species. Unfortunately the big natural lawyer in the sky slightly confused matters by combining our divine instruments of conception with those of excretion, a source of chagrin and shame to the perennial puritan. Our genitals have always done double duty and cannot be said strictly to have only one sacred function from which all else is deviation, wicked or not, depending on who is doing the moralizing.

Yet from Moses to Freud (despite his discontents) to Dr. Reuben, Judaeo-Christian doctrine has been remarkably unchanging. Man and woman are joined together in a special covenant to bring into the world children; and as it has been since the Bronze Age, so shall it be not only in our Age of Plastic but for all time to come. Those who transgress this law shall be punished, if not with death by stoning then with a mild rash due to neurosis brought on by immature (that is, unholy) attitudes.

It is not an overstatement to say that a belief in this ancient covenant has made a hell of Western man's life on earth (try to find a hotel room in which to make love in any American state; a few seedy places exist but by and large the entire society is resolutely determined to keep from carnal knowledge of one another those not joined together by the Jewish/Christian God). Worse, the ancient covenant's injunction to be fruitful and multiply (Dr. Reuben surprisingly omits this text. It is Genesis I:28) has now brought the human race to what may well be a most unpleasant coda as too many people destroy not only the biosphere which supports us but the society which sustains us.

On the subject of homosexuality, Dr. Reuben tries to be a good sport. Yet at heart he is angry with the homosexualist who perversely refuses to enter into a penis-vagina relationship. It would be so easy to straighten him out. If he would only visit "a psychiatrist who knows how to cure homosexuality, he has every chance of becoming a happy, well-adjusted heterosexual." I wonder if Dr. Reuben might be got up on a charge of violating the fair advertising practices act—on the ground that no such psychiatrist exists. It is true that the late Dr. Bergler enjoyed announcing "cures," but since no one knows what a homosexualist is (as opposed to a homosexual act), much less what the psychic life (as opposed to the sex life) of any of his patients was like, his triumphs must be taken on faith.

However, it should be noted that anyone so disturbed by society's condemnation of his natural sexual instinct that he would want to pervert it in order to conform would, no doubt, be a candidate for some kind of "conversion" at the hands of a highly paid quack. Yet to change a man's homosexual instinct is as difficult (if not impossible) as changing a man's heterosexual instinct, and socially rather less desirable since it can hardly be argued, as it used to be—the clincher, in fact, of the natural lawyers—that if everyone practiced homosexuality the race would die out. The fact of course is that not everyone would, at least exclusively, and the race currently needs no more additions.

As a religious rather than a scientific man, Dr. Reuben believes that there is something wicked (he would say sick) about the homosexual act. Therefore those who say they really enjoy it must be lying. He also believes implicitly a set of old queens' tales that any high school boy in Iowa (if not the Bronx) could probably set him straight on. "Most homosexuals at one time or another in their lives act out some aspect of the female role." Aside from his usual inability to define anything (what is a male role? a female role?), he seems to mean that a man who enjoys relations with his own sex is really half a man, a travesty of woman.

This is not the case. The man involved in a homosexual act is engaged in a natural male function; he is performing as a man, and so is his partner. That there are men who think of themselves as women is also a fact, as the visitor to any queer bar will have noticed (those Bette Davis types are with us from Third Avenue to Hong Kong), but they are a tiny minority, not unlike those odd creatures who think of themselves as 100 percent he-men on the order of Lyndon Johnson, another small and infinitely more depressing minority, which of course includes the thirty-sixth President.

Dr. Reuben is also horrified by what he thinks to be the promiscuity of all homosexualists. But then "homosexuals thrive on danger," he tells us, and of course their "primary interest is the penis, not the person." As usual no evidence is given. He takes as fact the prejudices of his race-religion-country, and, most important, as I shall point out, class. Reading him on homosexuality, I was reminded of the lurid anti-Semitic propaganda of the thirties: All Jews love money. All Jews are sensualists with a penchant for gentile virgins. All Jews are involved in a conspiracy to take over the financial and cultural life of whatever country they happen to be living in. Happily, Dr. Reuben is relatively innocent of making this last charge. The Homintern theory, however, is a constant obsession of certain journalists and crops up from time to time not only in the popular press but in the pages of otherwise respectable literary journals. Fag-baiting is the last form of minority baiting practiced at every level of American society.

Dr. Reuben tends to gloss over the social pressures which condition the life of anyone who prefers, occasionally or exclusively, the company of his own sex. Homosexualists seldom settle down to cozy mature domesticity for an excellent reason: society forbids it. Two government workers living together in Washington, D.C., would very soon find themselves unemployed. They would be spied on, denounced secretly, and dismissed. Only a bachelor entirely above suspicion like J. Edgar Hoover can afford to live openly with another man. In any case, homosexual promiscuity differs from heterosexual only in the atmosphere of fear in which the homosexualist must operate. It is a nice joke if a Louisiana judge is caught in a motel with a call girl. It is a major tragedy if a government official with a family is caught in a men's room.

For someone like Dr. Reuben who believes that there is no greater sin than avoidance of "heterosex—penis and vagina," two men who do live together must, somehow, be wretched. "Mercifully for both of them, the life expectancy of their relationship together is brief." Prove? I wrote for the tenth time in the margin. But we are beyond mere empiricism. We are now involved in one of the major superstitions of our place and time and no evidence must be allowed to disturb simple faith.

Dr. Kinsey (dismissed by Dr. Reuben as a mere biologist) did try to find out what is actually going on. Whatever Kinsey's shortcomings as a researcher, he revealed for the first time the way things are. Everyone is potentially bisexual. In actual practice a minority never commits a homosexual act, others experiment with their own sex but settle for heterosexuality, still others swing back and forth to a greater or lesser degree, while another minority never gets around to performing the penis-vagina act. None of this is acceptable to either Dr. Bergler or Dr. Reuben because they *know* that there is no such thing as bisexuality. Therefore Dr. Kinsey's findings must be discredited. To the rabbinical mind, any man who admits to having enjoyed sexual relations with another man must be, sadly, consigned to the ranks of Sodom. That the same man spends the rest of his sex life in penis-vagina land means nothing because, having enjoyed what he ought not to have enjoyed, his relations with women are simply playacting. Paradoxically, in the interest of making money, the mental therapists are willing to work with any full-time homosexualist who has never had a penis-vagina relationship because deep down they know he does not enjoy men no matter what he says. This is the double standard with a vengeance.

Driving through Wyoming, a Jewish friend of mine picked up a young cowhand and had sex with him. Dr. Reuben will be pleased to note that my friend was, as usual, guilt-ridden; so much so that the boy finally turned to his seducer and with a certain wonder said, "You know, you guys from the East do this because you're sick and we do it because we're horny." My friend has never recovered from this insight into that polymorphic goyisher world best revealed some years ago in Boise, Idaho, where a number of businessmen were discovered frolicking with the local high school boys. Oddly enough (to the innocent), as husbands and fathers, the businessmen were all long-time homesteaders in penis-vagina land. So what were they up to? Bisexuality? No, it does not exist. Evidence dismissed, just as all accounts of other cultures are also unacceptable. Turks, Greeks, Moslems . . . Well, as one critic likes to say, that is another context (disgusting lot is what he means). I would suggest, however, that a recent book by Brian W. Aldiss, *The Hand-Reared Boy,* be admitted as evidence.

Mr. Aldiss is an English heterosexual—well, he *pretends* to be one, has wife and children—and he tells us in fascinating detail what it was like to go to a second-rate public school just before the Second World War. Admittedly all Americans think all Englishmen are fags, so I daresay this interesting account of a seventeen-year-old who has full sexual relationships with other boys as well as a mature penis-vagina relationship with a girl will be dismissed on the ground that seventeen is a man for all practical purposes, and so he could not do both whole-heartedly. Yet he did. In this Mr. Aldiss tends to resemble his American counterparts, a world obviously alien to the Dr. Reubens, who cannot accept the following simple fact of so many lives (certainly my own): that it is possible to have a mature sexual relationship with a woman on Monday, and a mature sexual relationship with a man on Tuesday, and perhaps on Wednesday have both together (admittedly you have to be in good condition for this).

Now I am sure that Dr. Reuben would not like for 100-percent heterosexualists to be advised on their behavior by 100-percent homosexualists, so may I, diffidently, suggest that until Dr. Reuben has had a full and mature relationship with a man, he ought not to speak of what he does not know. Finally, realizing that at the deepest level, no rabbi can take this sort of blunt talk from a foreskinned dog (Bernard Malamud's loving phrase), I suggest that he read that grandest of Anti-Rabbis, Paul Goodman. He will learn a lot about the naturalness of bisexuality, and in a Jewish context.

It is ironic (and dismaying) that Dr. Reuben's collection of tribal taboos and reactionary nostrums should be popular just when the entire concept of the family is undergoing a radical revision. Population continues to double at shorter and shorter intervals. Famine is now chronic in half the world. If the race is to continue, we must limit human breeding by law. That is the simple fact of our present condition. Once we have acted to regulate population (I am assuming that this will be done: mass suicide is not a characteristic of our race), most people will not have children to raise. Without children, there will be no reason for men and women to enter into lifetime contracts with one another and marriage, as we have known it, will be at an end. Certainly that curious institution is already in a state of advanced decay in America, witness the underlying theme of all the how-to sex books (including Dr. Reuben's): how to stay sexually interested in your mate long after nature has ceased to make either of you attractive to the other.

Needless to say, even if all governments were to act promptly to limit population, marriage would not end at once or (in some forms) ever entirely vanish, but once it ceases to be the central fact of our society, to that extent women will be for the first time in recorded history freed from a particularly debasing relationship in which they are relentlessly conditioned by the Dr. Reubens to be brainless, enticing bunnies whose reward for making a good home in which to raise their husbands' children through a series of wonderful orgasms. The most startling thing about the women's liberation movement is not its ferocity (and ghastly rhetoric) but the fact that it took so long to surface. It is certainly true that women are half-citizens even in the relatively liberated West. From birth they are programmed by the tribalists to serve men, raise children, and be (if they are interested in True Maturity) geishas, as we are told by "J" (a pseudonym for Dr. Reuben? Or for the sly Professor James Moran?) in *The Sensuous Woman,* a volume every bit as fatuous as Dr. Reuben's compendium of tribal taboos. "J" sees woman's job as not only how to get HIM in the sack but how to keep him excited, a job she admits is not easy within marriage since ardor sooner or later flags. Nevertheless, by unexpectedly redoing the bedroom in sexy shades, a new hair style, exotic perfumes, ravishing naughty underwear, an unexpected blow job with a mouth full of cream of wheat, *somehow* a girl who puts her mind to it can keep him coming back for more year after year after year. As far as I know, no one in tribal lore has ever asked the simple question: Why bother? Why not move on?

Finally, it is to be hoped that with the reduction of population by law and the consequent abandoning of the family unit, men and women will be able for the first time to confront one another as equals, no longer resorting to the sick game in which the man thinks the woman means to trap him into a legal arrangement and the woman thinks she is wrong not to want to capture him and sign herself up for a lifetime of dull subservience. In any case, new things are happening as yet undreamed of in the office of David Reuben, M.D. We are coming either to a better understanding of our sexual nature, or to the race's end. Certainly, either is preferable to the way things are.

*The New York Review of Books*
June 4, 1970

# WOMEN'S LIBERATION: FEMINISM AND ITS DISCONTENTS

Every schoolboy has a pretty good idea of what the situation was down at Sodom but what went on in Gomorrah is as mysterious to us as the name Achilles took when he went among women. Or was. Thanks to Eva Figes, author of *Patriarchal Attitudes,* we now know what Gomorrheans are up to. Miss Figes quotes from an eighth-century Palestinian midrash which tries to explain the real reason for the Flood (one of the better jokes in the Old Testament). Apparently passage on the Ark was highly restricted. "Some authorities say that according to God's orders, if the male lorded it over the female of his own kind, both were admitted but not otherwise."

The Founding Father had strong views on the position of woman (under the man) and one of the few mistakes he ever admitted to was the creation of Lilith as a mate for Adam. Using the same dust as his earthly replica . . . but let us hear it in his own words, rabbinically divined in the fifth century.

Adam and Lilith never found peace together; for when he wished to lie with her, she took offense at the recumbent posture he demanded. "Why must I lie beneath you?" she asked. "I also was made from dust, and am therefore your equal." Because Adam tried to compel her obedience by force, Lilith, in a rage, uttered the magic name of God, rose into the air and left him.

The outcast Lilith is still hanging about the *Zeitgeist,* we are told, causing babies to strangle in their sleep, men to have wet dreams, and Kate Millett, Betty Friedan, Germaine Greer, and Eva Figes to write books.

The response to *Sexual Politics, Feminine Mystique,* etcetera, has been as interesting as anything that has happened in our time, with the possible exception of Richard Nixon's political career. The hatred these girls have inspired is to me convincing proof that their central argument is valid. Men do hate women (or as Germaine Greer puts it: "Women have very little idea of how much men hate them") and dream of torture, murder, flight.

It is no accident that in the United States the phrase "sex and violence" is used as one word to describe acts of equal wickedness, equal fun, equal danger to that law and order our masters would impose upon us. Yet equating sex with violence does change the nature of each (words govern us more than anatomy), and it is quite plain that those who fear what they call permissiveness do so because they know that if sex is truly freed of taboo it will lead to torture and murder because that is what *they* dream of or, as Norman Mailer puts it, "Murder offers us the promise of vast relief. It is never unsexual."

There has been from Henry Miller to Norman Mailer to Phyllis Schafly a logical progression. The Patriarchalists have been conditioned to think of women as, at best, breeders of sons; at worst, objects to be poked, humiliated, killed. Needless to say, their reaction to Women's Liberation has been one of panic. They believe that if women are allowed parity with men they will treat men the way men have treated women and that, even they will agree, has not been very well or, as Cato the Censor observed, if woman be made man's equal she will swiftly become his master.

Patriarchalists know that women are dangerously different from men, and not as intelligent (though they have their competencies: needlework, child-care, detective stories). When a woman does show herself to be superior at, say, engineering, Freud finessed that anomaly by reminding us that since she is a bisexual, like everyone else, her engineering skill simply means that she's got a bit too much of the tomboy in her, as W. C. Fields once remarked to Grady Sutton on a similar occasion.

Women are not going to make it until the Patriarchalists reform, and that is going to take a long time. Meanwhile the current phase of the battle is intense and illuminating. Men are on the defensive, shouting names; they think that to scream "dyke" is enough to make the girls burst into tears, but so far they have played it cool. Some have even admitted to a bit of dyking now and then along with warm mature heterosexual relationships of the deeply meaningful fruitful kind that bring much-needed children into the world ("Good fucks make good babies"—N. Mailer). I love you Marion and I love you too, Marvin. The women are responding with a series of books and position papers that range from shrill to literature. In the last category one must place Eva Figes who, of the lot, is the only one whose work can be set beside John Stuart Mill's celebrated review of the subject and not seem shoddy or self-serving.

In effect, the girls are all writing the same book. Each does a quick biological tour of the human body, takes on Moses and St. Paul, congratulates Mill, savages Freud (that mistake about vaginal orgasm has cost him glory), sighs over Marx, roughs up the Patriarchalists, and concludes with pleas for child-care centers, free abortions, equal pay, and—in most cases—an end to marriage. These things seem to be well worth accomplishing. And even the enemy are now saying that of course women should be paid the same as men for the same work. On that point alone Women's Lib has already won an important battle because, until recently, the enemy was damned if a woman was going to be paid as much as he for the same job.

Figes begins her short, elegant work with an attempt to define masculine and feminine. Is there any real difference between male and female other than sexual gear? Figes admits to the systematic fluctuation of progesterone levels during the woman's menstrual cycle and pregnancy, and these fluctuations make for "moods," which stop with menopause. Yet Figes makes a most telling point when she observes that although there is little or no hormonal difference between girls and boys before puberty, by the age of four or five boys are acting in a very different manner from girls. Since there is no hormonal explanation for this, the answer is plainly one of indoctrination.

What Figes is saying and what anyone who has ever thought with any seriousness about the human estate knows is that we are, or try to be, what our society wants us to be. There is nothing innate in us that can be called masculine or feminine. We have certain common drives involving survival. Yet our drive toward procreation, oddly enough, is not as powerful as our present-day obsession with sex would lead us to believe.

Of all mammals, man is the only one who must be taught how to mate. In open societies this is accomplished through observation but in a veiled, minatory, Puritan society, sex is a dirty secret, the body shameful, and making love a guilty business, often made dreadful through plain ignorance of what to do. Yet the peripheral male and female roles are carefully taught us. A little girl is given a doll instead of a chemistry set. That she might not like dolls, might prefer a chemistry set, will be the start of a nice neurosis for her, a sense of guilt that she is not playing the part society wants her to play. This arbitrary and brutal shaping of men and women has filled the madhouses of the West, particularly today when the kind of society we still prepare children for (man outside at work, woman at home with children) is no longer the only possibility for a restless generation.

Figes quotes Lévi-Strauss. "Men do not act as members of a group, in accordance with what each feels as an individual; each man feels as a function of the way in which he is permitted or obliged to act. Customs are given as external norms before giving rise to internal sentiments, and these non-sentiment norms determine the sentiments of individuals as well as the circumstances in which they may, or must, be displayed." One sees this in our society's emphasis on what Hemingway called "grace under pressure," or that plain old-fashioned patriotism which so often means nothing more than persuading a man to kill a man he does not know. To get him to do this the society must with its full weight pervert the normal human instinct not to kill a stranger against whom he has no grudge.

This kind of conditioning is necessary for the maintenance of that acquisitive, warrior society to which we belong, a society which now appears to be cracking up in the United States, to the despair of the Patriarchalists, not to mention those financial interests whose profits depend upon the exploitation and conquest of distant lands and markets. Concentrating on social pressures, Figes has written a book concerned with those external norms "which give rise to internal sentiments, with the organization of emotions into sentiments."

For those who like to remind the girls that no woman wrote anything in the same class as *Paradise Lost* or painted anything like the Sistine Chapel or composed *Don Carlos* (in the novel the girls hold their own), Figes observes that women were not expected to do that sort of thing and so did not. It is easy for a talented boy to be a sculptor because there are other males whom he can identify with and learn from. But society does everything to discourage a girl from making the attempt; and so she stifles as best she can whatever secret yearning she might have to shape stone, and gets on with the dishes.

In recent years, however, women have begun to invade fields traditionally assigned to men. Eventually, the boys will have to face the fact that the arts and sciences are not masculine or feminine activities, but simply human ones. Incidentally, all the girls have a go at one Otto Weininger, a nineteenth-century *philosophe* who at twenty-three wrote a book to prove that women were incapable of genius, then killed himself. The girls tend unkindly to cackle over that.

Figes does the obligatory chapters on Moses and St. Paul, those proud misogynists whose words have caused so much misery down the millennia. The hatred of women that courses through both Old and New Testaments is either lunatic or a mask for something else. What were the Patriarchs so afraid of? Is Robert Graves right after all? Was there really a Great Mother cult the Patriarchs destroyed? Were the attacks on woman political in origin? to discredit the Great Mother and her priestesses? We shall never know.

Perhaps it is simply guilt. People don't like their slaves very much. Women were—and in some cases still are—slaves to men, and attempts to free slaves must be put down. Also, as Figes puts it, "Human beings have always been particularly slow to accept ideas that diminish their own absolute supremacy and importance." For men, "like all people who are privileged by birth and long tradition, the idea of sharing could only mean giving up."

According to Figes, "The rise of capitalism is the root cause of the modern social and economic discrimination against women, which came to a peak in the last century." She remarks upon the degree of equality women enjoyed in Tudor times. From Portia to Rosalind, women existed as people in their own right. But with the simultaneous rise of Puritanism and industry, woman was more and more confined to the home—when she was not exploited in the factories as a cheap source of labor. Also, the Puritan tide (now only beginning to ebb) served to remind man that woman was unclean, sinful, less than he, and the cause of his fall. It was in those years that Patriarchalism was born, emigrated to America, killed Indians, enslaved blacks, conned women with sonorous good manners to get them into the wilderness, then tried to dominate them but never quite succeeded: a woman in a covered wagon with a rifle on her lap is going to be a formidable opponent, as the American woman has proved to be, from Daisy Miller to Kate Millett (a name James would have savored, weakly changing "i" to "a").

What does the American woman want? is the plaintive cry. Doesn't she kill off her husbands with mantis-abandon, inherit the money, become a Mom to Attis-like sons, dominate primary education (most

American men are "feminized" in what they would regard as the worst sense of that word by being brought up almost entirely by women and made to conform to American female values which are every bit as twisted as American male values)?

Yet the American woman who seems to have so much is still very much a victim of patriarchal attitudes—after all, she is made to believe that marriage is the most important thing in life, a sentiment peculiarly necessary to a capitalist society in which marriage is still the employer's best means of controlling the employee. The young man with a child and pregnant wife is going to do as he is told. The young man or woman on his own might not be so tractable. Now that organized religion is of little social significance, the great corporations through advertising (remember "Togetherness"?) and hiring policies favor the married, while looking with great suspicion on the bachelor who might be a Commie Weirdo Fag or a Pro-Crypto dyke. As long as marriage (and Betty Friedan's *Feminine Mystique*) are central to our capitalism (and to its depressing Soviet counterpart) neither man nor woman can be regarded as free to be human.

"In a society where men have an overriding interest in the acquisition of wealth, and where women themselves have become a form of property, the link between sexuality and money becomes inextricable." This is grim truth. Most men buy their wives, though neither party would admit to the nature of the transaction, preferring such euphemisms as Marvin is a good provider and Marion is built. Then Marion divorces Marvin and takes him to the cleaners, and he buys with whatever is left a younger model. It is money, not sex, that Puritans want. After all, the English word for "coming" used to be "spending": you spend your seed in the woman's bank and, if the moon is right, nine months later you will get an eight-pound dividend.

Needless to say, if you buy a woman you don't want anyone else using her. To assure your rights, you must uphold all the taboos against any form of sex outside marriage. Figes draws an interesting parallel between our own society and the Mainus, as reported by Margaret Mead.

There was such a close tie between women and property that adultery was always a threat to the economic system. These people devalued sex, were prudish, and tended to equate the sex act with the excretory functions and, perhaps most significant of all, had commercial prostitution which is rare in primitive societies.

Rousseau is briskly dealt with by the girls: his rights of man were just that, for men. He believed women "should reign in the home as a minister reigns in the state, by contriving to be ordered to do what she wants." Darwin? According to Figes, "Darwin was typically a creature of his age in seeing the class and economic struggles as a continuation of the evolutionary one." In this struggle woman was *hors de combat.* "The chief distinction in the intellectual powers of the two sexes is shown by man attaining to a higher eminence, in whatever he takes up, than woman can attain, etc." Schopenhauer found woman "in every respect backward, lacking in reason and true morality . . . a kind of middle step between the child and the man, who is the true human being."

Figes finds a link between anti-feminism and anti-Semitism. It is called Nietzsche. "Man should be trained for war and woman for the recreation of the warrior: all else is folly." Like the effeminate Jews, women subvert the warrior ideal, demanding sympathy for the poor and the weak. Hitler's reaction to this rousing philosophy has not gone unnoticed.

Like her fellow polemicists, Figes is at her most glittering with Freud . . . one almost wrote "poor Freud," as Millett calls him. Apparently Freud's gravest limitation was an inability to question the status quo of the society into which he was born. Politically, he felt that "it is just as impossible to do without control of the mass by a minority as it is to dispense with coercion in the work of civilization. For the masses are lazy and unintelligent."

To Freud, civilization meant a Spartan denial of pleasure in the present in order to enjoy solvency and power in middle age. Unhappily, the main line of Freudian psychoanalysis has served well the status quo by insisting that if one is not happy with one's lot, a better adjustment to society must be made because society is an unalterable fact, not to be trifled with or changed. Now, of course, every assumption about the rights of society as opposed to those of the individual is in question, and Freud's complacency seems almost as odd to us as his wild notion that clitoral excitement was a wicked (immature) thing in a grown woman, and the longer she resisted making the transfer from the tiny pseudo-penis to the heavenly inner space of the vagina (Erik Erikson is not in the girls' good books either) the sicker she would become.

One would like to have been a fly on the wall of that Vienna study as one woman after another tearfully admitted to an itch that would not go away, despite the kindly patriarch's attempts to get to the root of the problem. It is a nice irony that the man who said that anatomy is destiny took no trouble to learn woman's anatomy. He did *know* that the penis was the essential symbol and fact of power and primacy; otherwise (and his reasoning was circular) why would girls envy boys' having penises? Why would little boys suffer from fears of castration if they did not instinctively know that the penis is a priceless sign of God the Father, which an envious teeth-lined cunt might want to snap off? Figes's response to Freud's circle is reasonable.

In a society not sexually repressive little boys would be unlikely to develop castration fears; in a society where all the material rewards did not go to those endowed with penises there would be no natural envy of that regalia.

The Patriarchs' counterattack is only now gathering momentum. So far Figes appears to be unknown to United Statesmen, but Millett has been attacked hereabouts with a ferocity usually reserved for major novelists. She should feel important. The two principal spokesmen to weigh in so far are Norman Mailer and Irving Howe. Mailer's answer to Millett ("The Prisoner of Sex" in *Harper's*) gave the impression of being longer than her book *Sexual Politics.* Part of this is due to a style which now resembles H. P. Lovecraft rather more than the interesting, modest Mailer of better days. Or as Emma Cockburn (excellent name for a Women's Libber) pointed out, Mailer's thoughts on sex read like three days of menstrual flow.

Mailer begins by reminding the reader who he is. This is cunning and necessary in a country with no past. We learn of marriages, children, prizes (the Nobel is almost at hand), the great novel he will one day write, the rejection of *Time*'s offer to put him on the cover which Millett then gets for, among other things, attacking him. His credits given, he counterattacks, says she writes like a tough faggot, a literary Mafiosa, calls her comrade and commissar. He then makes some excellent points on her disingenuous use of quotations from Miller and Lawrence (she has a tendency to replace those qualifying phrases which make the Patriarchs seem human with three dots).

But Mailer's essential argument boils down to the following points. Masturbation is bad and so is contraception because the whole point to sex between man and woman is conception. Well, that's what the Bible says, too. He links homosexuality with evil. The man who gives in to his homosexual drives is consorting with the enemy. Worse, not only does he betray moral weakness by not fighting those drives but he is a coward for not daring to enter into competition with other Alpha males for toothsome females. This is dizzy but at least a new thought. One of the many compliments Mailer has tendered the Patriarchs over the years is never having succumbed to whatever homosexual urges they might have had. Now, to his shock, instead of getting at least a Congressional Medal of Honor for heroism, he sees slowly descending upon his brow an unmistakable dunce cap. All that hanging about boxers, to no good end!

Finally, Mailer's attitude toward woman is pretty much that of any VFW commander in heartland America. He can never understand that a woman is not simply a creature to be used for breeding (his "awe" at the thought of her procreative function is blarney), that she is as human as he is, and that he is dangerous to her since did not the Lord thy God say, "In sorrow thou shalt bring forth children. And thy desire shall be thy husband. And he shall rule over thee." Which brings us to Figes's remark, "We cannot be iconoclasts, we cannot relinquish the old gods because so much has been sacrificed to them."

Irving Howe's tone is apoplectic. He *knows* what the relations between men and women ought to be and no Millett is going to change his mind or pervert other women if he can do anything about it—which is to write a great deal on the subject in a magazine piece called "The Middle Class Mind of Kate Millett." Astonishingly enough, the phrase "middle class" is used in a pejorative sense, not the most tactful thing to do in a middle-class country. Particularly when one is not only middle class oneself but possessed of a brow that is just this side of high.

Anyway, Howe was aroused enough to address to her a series of *ad hominem* (*ad hysteram?*) insults that are startling even by the vicious and mindless standards of New York bookchat writing. Millett is "squalid," "feckless," "morally shameful," a failed scholar, a female impersonator, and so on. But Howe is never able to take on the essential argument of the girls. Men have enslaved women, made them second-rate citizens, made them hate themselves (this to me is the worst of all . . . I'm a man's woman, says the beauty complacently, I don't like other women; meaning, I don't like myself), and now that woman is beginning to come alive, to see herself as the equal of man, Rabbi Howe is going to strike her down for impertinence, just as the good Christian knows that "it is shameful for women to speak in church."

Howe has always had an agreeable gift for literary demolition and his mind, though hardly of the first quality, is certainly good by American academic standards. But now watch him tie himself in a knot. Millett makes the point, as Figes does, that the Nazis were anti-woman and pro-family. Woman was breeder, man was warrior. Now Irving doesn't want the Nazis to be so "sensible," so much like himself. He writes:

The comedy of all this is that Miss Millett prints, at one point, a footnote quoting from a book by Joseph Folsom. "The Nazis have always wanted to strengthen the family as an instrument of the state. *State interest is always paramount.* Germany does not hesitate to turn a husband against a wife or children against parents when political loyalty is involved." (Emphasis added.) Miss Millett prints this footnote but clearly does not understand it: otherwise she would recognize how completely it undermines her claim that in the totalitarian countries the "sexual counterrevolution" consisted in the reinforcement of the family.

This passage would make a good test question for a class in logic. Find where Howe misses or distorts the point to the Folsom footnote. Point one: the Nazis strengthened the family yet put the state first. All agreed? What does this mean? It means that, on occasion, Nazis would try to turn members of a family against one another *"when political loyalty is involved."* (Emphasis added.) O.K.? Well, class, how many people are politically subversive in any country at any time? Not many, alas; therefore Millett's point still stands that the Nazis celebrated old-time family virtues except in cases of suspected subversion.

Howe's piece is full of this sort of thing and I can only assume that his usually logical mind has been unhinged by all these unnatural girls. Howe ends with a celebration of the values of his immigrant parents in the Depression years. Apparently his mother was no more a drudge than his father (but why in a good society should either be a drudge?), and they were happy in the old-time Mosaic, St. Pauline, Freudian way, and . . . well, this hymn to tribal values was rather better sung by the judge in the movie version of *Little Murders.*

Those who have been treated cruelly will treat others cruelly. This seems to be a fact of our condition. The Patriarchs have every reason to be fearful of woman's revenge should she achieve equality. He is also faced with the nightmare (for him) of being used as a sexual object or, worse, being ignored (the menacing cloud in the middle distance is presently no larger than a vibrator). He is fighting back on every front.

Take pornography. Though female nudes have been usually acceptable in our Puritan culture, until recently the male nude was unacceptable to the Patriarchs. After all, the male—any male—is a stand-in for

God, and God wears a suit at all times, or at least jockey shorts. Now, thanks to randy Lilith, the male can be shown entirely nude but, say the American censors, never with an erection. The holy of holies, the totem of our race, the symbol of the Patriarchs' victory over the Great Mother must be respected. Also, as psychologists point out, though women are not as prone to stimulus through looking at pictures as men (is this innate or the result of conditioning?), they are more excited by pictures of the male erect than of the male at ease. And excitement of course is bad for them, gives them ideas, makes them insatiable; even the ancient Greeks, though freer in sexual matters than we, took marriage seriously. As a result, only unmarried girls could watch naked young men play because young girls ought to be able to look over a field which married women had better not know about.

Today we are witnessing the breakup of patterns thousands of years old. The patriarchal response is predictable: if man on top of woman has been the pattern for all our known history, it must be right. This of course was the same argument he made when the institution of slavery was challenged. After all, slavery was quite as old an institution as marriage. With the rejection of the idea of ownership of one person by another at the time of our Civil War, Women's Lib truly began. If you could not own a black man, you could not own a woman either. So the war began. Needless to say, the forces of reaction are very much in the saddle (in every sense), and women must fight for their equality in a system which wants to keep them in manageable family groups, buying consumer goods, raising future consumers, until the end of time—or the world's raw resources, which is rather closer at hand.

Curiously enough, not even Figes senses what is behind this new restiveness, this new desire to exist not as male or female but as human. It is very simple: we are breeding ourselves into extinction. We cannot feed the people now alive. In thirty-seven years the world's population will double unless we have the "good luck" to experience on the grandest scale famine, plague, war. To survive we must stop making babies at the current rate, and this can only be accomplished by breaking the ancient stereotypes of man the warrior, woman the breeder. The patriarchal roar is that of our tribal past, quite unsuitable, as the old Stalinists used to say, to new necessities.

Figes feels that a change in the economic system will free women (and men) from unwanted roles. I have another idea. Free the sexes first and the system will have to change. There will be no housewife to be conned into buying things she does not need. But all this is in the future. The present is the battleground, and the next voice you hear will be that of a patriarch, defending his attitudes—on a stack of Bibles.

*The New York Review of Books*
July 22, 1971

# 5 5
·
# PINK TRIANGLE
# AND YELLOW STAR

A few years ago on a trip to Paris, I read an intriguing review in *Le Monde* of a book called *Comme un Frère, Comme un Amant,* a study of "Male Homosexuality in the American Novel and Theatre from Herman Melville to James Baldwin," the work of one Georges-Michel Sarotte, a Sorbonne graduate and a visiting professor at the University of Massachusetts. I read the book, found it interesting; met the author, found him interesting. He told me that he was looking forward to the publication of his book in the United States by Anchor Press/Double-day. What sort of response did I think he would have? I was touched by so much innocent good faith. There will be no reaction, I said, because no one outside of the so-called gay press will review your book. He was shocked. Wasn't the book serious? scholarly? with an extensive bibliography? I agreed that it was all those things; unfortunately, schol-arly studies having to do with fags do not get reviewed in the United States (this was before the breakthrough of Yale's John Boswell, whose ferociously learned *Christianity, Social Tolerance and Homosexuality* obliged even the "homophobic" *New York Times* to review it intelli-gently). If Sarotte had written about the agony and wonder of being female and/or Jewish and/or divorced, he would have been extensively reviewed. Even a study of black literature might have got attention

(Sarotte is beige), although blacks are currently something of a nonsubject in these last days of empire.

I don't think that Professor Sarotte believed me. I have not seen him since. I also have never seen a review of his book or of Roger Austen's *Playing the Game* (a remarkably detailed account of American writing on homosexuality) or of *The Homosexual as Hero in Contemporary Fiction* by Stephen Adams, reviewed at much length in England and ignored here, or of a dozen other books that have been sent to me by writers who seem not to understand why an activity of more than casual interest to more than one-third of the male population of the United States warrants no serious discussion. That is to say, no serious *benign* discussion. All-out attacks on faggots are perennially fashionable in our better periodicals.

I am certain that the novel *Tricks* by Renaud Camus (recently translated for St. Martin's Press by Richard Howard, with a preface by Roland Barthes) will receive a perfunctory and hostile response out there in bookchat land. Yet in France, the book was treated as if it were actually literature, admittedly a somewhat moot activity nowadays. So I shall review *Tricks*. But first I think it worth bringing out in the open certain curious facts of our social and cultural life.

The American passion for categorizing has now managed to create two nonexistent categories—gay and straight. Either you are one or you are the other. But since everyone is a mixture of inclinations, the categories keep breaking down; and when they break down, the irrational takes over. You *have* to be one or the other. Although our mental therapists and writers for the better journals usually agree that those who prefer same-sex sex are not exactly criminals (in most of our states and under most circumstances they still are) or sinful or, officially, sick in the head, they must be, somehow, evil or inadequate or dangerous. The Roman Empire fell, didn't it? because of the fags?

Our therapists, journalists, and clergy are seldom very learned. They seem not to realize that most military societies on the rise tend to encourage same-sex activities for reasons that should be obvious to anyone who has not grown up ass-backward, as most Americans have. In the centuries of Rome's great military and political success, there was no differentiation between same-sexers and other-sexers; there was also a lot of crossing back and forth of the sort that those Americans who *do* enjoy inhabiting category-gay or category-straight find hard to deal with. Of the first twelve Roman emperors, only one was exclusively heterosexual. Since these twelve men were pretty tough cookies, rigorously trained as warriors, perhaps our sexual categories and stereotypes are—can it really be?—false. It was not until the sixth century of the empire that same-sex sex was proscribed by church and state. By then, of course, the barbarians were within the gates and the glory had fled.

Today, American evangelical Christians are busy trying to impose on the population at large their superstitions about sex and the sexes and the creation of the world. Given enough turbulence in the land, these natural fascists can be counted on to assist some sort of authoritarian— but never, never totalitarian—political movement. Divines from Santa Clara to Falls Church are particularly fearful of what they describe as the gay liberation movement's attempt to gain "special rights and privileges" when all that the same-sexers want is to be included, which they are not by law and custom, within the framework of the Fourteenth Amendment. The divine in Santa Clara believes that same-sexers should be killed. The divine in Falls Church believes that they should be denied equal rights under the law. Meanwhile, the redneck divines have been joined by a group of New York Jewish publicists who belong to what they proudly call "the new class" (né arrivistes), and these lively hucksters have now managed to raise fag-baiting to a level undreamed of in Falls Church—or even in Moscow.

In a letter to a friend, George Orwell wrote, "It is impossible to mention Jews in print, either favorably or unfavorably, without getting into trouble." But there are times when trouble had better be got into before mere trouble turns into catastrophe. Jews, blacks, and homosexualists are despised by the Christian and Communist majorities of East and West. Also, as a result of the invention of Israel, Jews can now count on the hatred of the Islamic world. Since our own Christian majority looks to be getting ready for great adventures at home and abroad, I would suggest that the three despised minorities join forces in order not to be destroyed. This seems an obvious thing to do. Unfortunately, most Jews refuse to see any similarity between their special situation and that of the same-sexers. At one level, the Jews are perfectly correct. A racial or religious or tribal identity is a kind of fact. Although sexual preference is an even more powerful fact, it is not one that creates any particular social or cultural or religious bond between those so-minded. Although Jews would doubtless be Jews if there was no anti-Semitism, same-sexers would think little or nothing at all about their preference if society ignored it. So there *is* a difference between the two estates. But there is no difference in the degree of hatred felt by the Christian majority for Christ-killers and Sodomites. In the German concentration camps, Jews wore yellow stars while homosexualists wore pink triangles. I was present when Christopher Isherwood tried to make this point to a young Jewish movie producer. "After all," said Isherwood, "Hitler killed six hundred thousand homosexuals." The young man was not impressed. "But Hitler killed six *million* Jews," he said sternly. "What are you?" asked Isherwood. "In real estate?"

Like it or not, Jews and homosexualists are in the same fragile boat, and one would have to be pretty obtuse not to see the common danger. But obtuseness is the name of the game among New York's new class. Elsewhere, I have described the shrill fag-baiting of Joseph Epstein, Norman Podhoretz, Alfred Kazin, and the Hilton Kramer Hotel. *Harper's* magazine and *Commentary* usually publish these pieces, though other periodicals are not above printing the odd exposé of the latest homosexual conspiracy to turn the United States over to the Soviet Union or to structuralism or to Christian Dior. Although the new class's thoughts are never much in themselves, and they themselves are no more than spear carriers in the political and cultural life of the West, their prejudices and superstitions do register in a subliminal way, making mephitic the air of Manhattan if not of the Republic.

A case in point is that of Mrs. Norman Podhoretz, also known as Midge Decter (like Martha Ivers, *whisper* her name). In September of last year, Decter published a piece called "The Boys on the Beach" in her husband's magazine, *Commentary.* It is well worth examining in some detail because she has managed not only to come up with every known prejudice and superstition about same-sexers but also to make up some brand-new ones. For sheer vim and vigor, "The Boys on the Beach" outdoes its implicit model, *The Protocols of the Elders of Zion.*

Decter notes that when the "homosexual-rights movement first burst upon the scene," she was "more than a little astonished." Like so many new-class persons, she writes a stilted sort of genteel-gentile prose not unlike—but not very like, either—*The New Yorker* house style of the 1940s and 50s. She also writes with the authority and easy confidence of someone who knows that she is very well known indeed to those few who know her.

Decter tells us that twenty years ago, she got to know a lot of pansies at a resort called Fire Island Pines, where she and a number of other new-class persons used to make it during the summers. She estimates that 40 percent of the summer people were heterosexual; the rest were not. Yet the "denizens, homosexual and heterosexual alike, were predominantly professionals and people in soft marginal businesses—lawyers, advertising executives, psychotherapists, actors, editors, writers, publishers, etc." Keep this in mind. Our authoress does not.

Decter goes on to tell us that she is now amazed at the recent changes in the boys on the beach. Why have they become so politically militant—and so ill groomed? "What indeed has happened to the homosexual community I used to know—they who only a few short years ago [as opposed to those manly 370-day years] were characterized by nothing so much as a sweet, vain, pouting, girlish attention to the youth and beauty of their bodies?" Decter wrestles with this problem. She tells us how, in the old days, she did her very best to come to terms with her own normal dislike for these half-men—and half-women, too: "There were also homosexual women at the Pines, but they were, or seemed to be, far fewer in number. Nor, except for a marked tendency to hang out in the company of large and ferocious dogs, were they instantly recognizable as the men were." Well, if I were a dyke and a pair of Podhoretzes came waddling toward me on the beach, copies of Leviticus and Freud in hand, I'd get in touch with the nearest Alsatian dealer pronto.

Decter was disturbed by "the slender, seamless, elegant and utterly chic" clothes of the fairies. She also found it "a constant source of wonder" that when the fairies took off their clothes, "the largest number of homosexuals had hairless bodies. Chests, backs, arms, even legs were smooth and silky. . . . We were never able to determine just why there should be so definite a connection between what is nowadays called their sexual preference [previously known to right-thinking Jews as an abomination against Jehovah] and their smooth feminine skin. Was it a matter of hormones?" Here Decter betrays her essential modesty and lack of experience. In the no doubt privileged environment of her Midwestern youth, she could not have seen very many gentile males without their clothes on. If she had, she would have discovered that gentile men tend to be less hairy than Jews except, of course, when they are not. Because the Jews killed our Lord, they are forever marked with hair on their shoulders—something that no gentile man has on *his* shoulders except for John Travolta and a handful of other Italian-Americans from the Englewood, New Jersey, area.

It is startling that Decter has not yet learned that there is no hormonal difference between men who like sex with other men and those who like sex with women. She notes, "There is also such a thing as characteristic homosexual speech . . . it is something of an accent redolent of small towns in the Midwest whence so many homosexuals seemed to have migrated to the big city." Here one detects the disdain of the self-made

New Yorker for the rural or small-town American. "Midwest" is often a code word for the flyovers, for the millions who do not really matter. But she is right in the sense that when a group chooses to live and work together, they do tend to sound and look alike. No matter how crowded and noisy a room, one can always detect the new-class person's nasal whine.

Every now and then, Decter does wonder if, perhaps, she is generalizing and whether this will "no doubt in itself seem to many of the uninitiated a bigoted formulation." Well, Midge, it does. But the spirit is upon her, and she cannot stop because "one cannot even begin to get at the truth about homosexuals without this kind of generalization. They are a group so readily distinguishable." Except of course, when they are not. It is one thing for a group of queens, in "soft, marginal" jobs, to "cavort," as she puts it, in a summer place and be "easily distinguishable" to her cold eye just as Jewish members of the new class are equally noticeable to the cold gentile eye. But it is quite another thing for those men and women who prefer same-sex sex to other-sex sex yet do not choose to be identified—and so are not. To begin to get at the truth about homosexuals, one must realize that the majority of those millions of Americans who prefer same-sex sex to other-sex sex are obliged, sometimes willingly and happily but often not, to marry and have children and to conform to the guidelines set down by the heterosexual dictatorship.

Decter would know nothing of this because in her "soft, marginal" world, she is not meant to know. She does remark upon the fairies at the Pines who did have wives and children: "They were for the most part charming and amusing fathers, rather like favorite uncles. And their wives . . . drank." This dramatic ellipsis is most Decterian.

She ticks off Susan Sontag for omitting to mention in the course of an essay on camp "that camp is of the essence of homosexual style, invented by homosexuals, and serving the purpose of domination by ridicule." The word "domination" is a characteristic new-class touch. The powerless are always obsessed by power. Decter seems unaware that all despised minorities are quick to make rather good jokes about themselves before the hostile majority does. Certainly Jewish humor, from the Book of Job (a laff-riot) to pre-*auteur* Woody Allen, is based on this.

Decter next does the ritual attack on Edward Albee and Tennessee Williams for presenting "what could only have been homosexual relationships as the deeper truth about love in our time." This is about as true as the late Maria Callas's conviction that you could always tell a Jew because he had a hump at the back of his neck—something Callas herself had in dromedarian spades.

Decter makes much of what she assumes to be the fags' mockery of the heterosexual men at the Pines: "Homosexuality paints them [hetero-sexuals] with the color of sheer entrapment," while the fags' "smooth and elegant exteriors, unmussed by traffic with the detritus of modern family existence, constituted a kind of sniggering reproach to their striving and harried straight brothers." Although I have never visited the Pines, I am pretty sure that I know the "soft marginal" types, both hetero and homo, that hung out there in the 1960s. One of the most noticeable characteristics of the self-ghettoized same-sexer is his perfect indifference to the world of the other-sexers. Although Decter's blood was always at the boil when contemplating these unnatural and imma-ture half-men, they were, I would suspect, serenely unaware of her and her new-class cronies, solemnly worshiping at the shrine of The Family.

To hear Decter tell it, fags had nothing to complain of then, and they have nothing to complain of now: "Just to name the professions and industries in which they had, and still have, a significant presence is to define the boundaries of a certain kind of privilege: theatre, music, letters, dance, design, architecture, the visual arts, fashion at every level—from head, as it were, to foot, and from inception to retail—advertising, journalism, interior decoration, antique dealing, publish-ing . . . the list could go on." Yes. But these are all pretty "soft, marginal" occupations. And none is "dominated" by fags. Most male same-sexers are laborers, farmers, mechanics, small businessmen, schoolteachers, firemen, policemen, soldiers, sailors. Most female same-sexers are wives and mothers. In other words, they are like the rest of the population. But then it is hard for the new-class person to realize that Manhattan is not the world. Or as a somewhat alarmed Philip Rahv said to me after he had taken a drive across the United States, "My God! There are so many of them!" In theory, Rahv had always known that there were a couple of hundred million gentiles out there, but to see them, in the flesh, unnerved him. I told him that I was unnerved, too, particularly when they start showering in the Blood of the Lamb.

Decter does concede that homosexualists have probably not "estab-lished much of a presence in basic industry or government service or in such classic [new-classy?] professions as doctoring and lawyering but then for anyone acquainted with them as a group the thought suggests itself that few of them have ever made much effort in these directions."

Plainly, the silly billies are too busy dressing up and dancing the hully-gully to argue a case in court. Decter will be relieved to know that the percentage of same-sexers in the "classic" activities is almost as high, proportionately, as that of Jews. But a homosexualist in a key position at, let us say, the Department of Labor will be married and living under a good deal of strain because he could be fired if it is known that he likes to have sex with other men.

Decter knows that there have always been homosexual teachers, and she thinks that they should keep quiet about it. But if they keep quiet, they can be blackmailed or fired. Also, a point that would really distress her, a teacher known to be a same-sexer would be a splendid role model for those same-sexers that he—or she—is teaching. Decter would think this an unmitigated evil because men and women were created to breed; but, of course, it would be a perfect good because we have more babies than we know what to do with while we lack, notoriously, useful citizens at ease with themselves. That is what the row over the schools is all about.

Like most members of the new class, Decter accepts without question Freud's line *(Introductory Lectures on Psychoanalysis)* that "we actually describe a sexual activity as perverse if it has given up the aim of reproduction and pursues the attainment of pleasure as an aim independent of it." For Freud, perversion was any sexual activity involving "the abandonment of the reproductive function." Freud also deplored masturbation as a dangerous "primal affliction." So did Moses. But then it was Freud's curious task to try to create a rational, quasi-scientific basis for Mosaic law. The result has been not unlike the accomplishments of Freud's great contemporary, the ineffable and inexorable Mary Baker Eddy, whose First Church of Christ Scientist he was able to match with *his* First Temple of Moses Scientist.

Decter says that once faggots have "ensconced" themselves in certain professions or arts, "they themselves have engaged in a good deal of discriminatory practices against others. There are businesses and professions [which ones? She is congenitally short of data] in which it is less than easy for a straight, unless he makes the requisite gesture of propitiation to the homosexual in power, to get ahead." This, of course, was Hitler's original line about the Jews: they had taken over German medicine, teaching, law, journalism. Ruthlessly, they kept out gentiles; lecherously, they demanded sexual favors. "I simply want to reduce their numbers in these fields," Hitler told Prince Philip of Hesse. "I want them proportionate to their overall number in the population." This was the early solution; the final solution followed with equal logic.

In the 1950s, it was an article of faith in new-class circles that television had been taken over by the fags. Now I happen to have known most of the leading producers of that time and, of a dozen, the two who were interested in same-sex activities were both married to women who . . . did not drink. Neither man dared mix sex with business. Every now and then an actor would say that he had not got work because he had refused to put out for a faggot producer, but I doubt very much if there was ever any truth to what was to become a bright jack-o'-lantern in the McCarthy *Walpurgisnacht.*

When I was several thousand words into Decter's tirade, I suddenly realized that she does not know what homosexuality is. At some level she may have stumbled, by accident, on a truth that she would never have been able to comprehend in a rational way. Although to have sexual relations with a member of one's own sex is a common and natural activity (currently disapproved of by certain elements in this culture), there is no such thing as a homosexualist any more than there is such a thing as a heterosexualist. That is one of the reasons there has been so much difficulty with nomenclature. Despite John Boswell's attempts to give legitimacy to the word "gay," it is still a ridiculous word to use as a common identification for Frederick the Great, Franklin Pangborn and Eleanor Roosevelt. What makes some people prefer same-sex sex derives from whatever impulse or conditioning makes some people prefer other-sex sex. This is so plain that it seems impossible that our Mosaic-Pauline-Freudian society has not yet figured it out. But to ignore the absence of evidence is the basis of true faith.

Decter seems to think that yesteryear's chic and silly boys on the beach and today's socially militant fags are simply, to use her verb, "adopting" what she calls, in her tastefully appointed English, a lifestyle. On the other hand, "whatever disciplines it might entail, heterosexuality is not something adopted but something accepted. Its woes—and they have of course nowhere been more exaggerated than in those areas of the culture consciously or unconsciously influenced by the propaganda of homosexuals—are experienced as the woes of life."

"Propaganda"—another key word. "Power." "Propitiation." "Domination." What *does* the new class dream of?

Decter now moves in the big artillery. Not only are fags silly and a nuisance but they are, in their unrelenting hatred of heterosexualists, given to depicting them in their plays and films and books as a bunch of klutzes, thereby causing truly good men and women to falter—even question—that warm, mature heterosexuality that is so necessary to keeping this country great while allowing new-class persons to make it materially.

Decter is in full cry. Fags are really imitation women. Decter persists in thinking that same-sexers are effeminate, swishy, girlish. It is true that a small percentage of homosexualists are indeed effeminate, just as there are effeminate heterosexualists. I don't know why this is so. No one knows why. Except Decter. She believes that this sort "of female imitation pointed neither to sympathy with nor flattery of the female principle." Yet queens of the sort she is writing about tend to get on very well with women. But Decter can only cope with two stereotypes: the boys on the beach, mincing about, and the drab political radicals of gay liberation. The millions of ordinary masculine types are unknown to her because they are not identifiable by voice or walk and, most important, because they have nothing in common with one another except the desire to have same-sex relations. Or, put the other way around, since Lyndon Johnson and Bertrand Russell were both heterosexualists, what character traits did *they* have in common? I should think none at all. So it is with the invisible millions—now becoming less invisible—of same-sexers.

But Decter knows her Freud, and reality may not intrude: "The desire to escape from the sexual reminder of birth and death, with its threat of paternity—that is, the displacement of oneself by others—was the main underlying desire that sent those Fire Island homosexuals into the arms of other men. Had it been the opposite desire—that is, the positive attraction to the manly—at least half the boutiques, etc.," would have closed. Decter should take a stroll down San Francisco's Castro Street, where members of the present generation of fags look like off-duty policemen or construction workers. They have embraced the manly. But Freud has spoken. Fags are fags because they adored their mothers and hated their poor, hard-working daddies. It is amazing the credence still given this unproven, unprovable thesis.

Curiously enough, as I was writing these lines, expressing yet again the unacceptable obvious, I ran across Ralph Blumenthal's article in *The New York Times* (August 25), which used "unpublished letters and growing research into the hidden life of Sigmund Freud" to examine "Freud's reversal of his theory attributing neurosis in adults to sexual seduction in childhood." Despite the evidence given by his patients, Freud decided that their memories of molestation were "phantasies." He then appropriated from the high culture (a real act of hubris) Oedipus the King, and made him a complex. Freud was much criticized for this theory at the time—particularly by Sandor Ferenczi. Now, as we learn more about Freud (not to mention about the sexual habits of Victorian Vienna as reported in police records), his theory is again under attack. Drs. Milton Klein and David Tribich have written a paper titled "On Freud's Blindness." They have studied his case histories and observed how he ignored evidence, how "he looked to the child and only to the child, in uncovering the causes of psychopathology." Dr. Karl Menninger wrote Dr. Klein about these findings: "Why oh why couldn't Freud believe his own ears?" Dr. Menninger then noted, "Seventy-five per cent of the girls we accept at the Villages have been molested in childhood by an adult. And that's today in Kansas! I don't think Vienna in 1900 was any less sophisticated."

In the same week as Blumenthal's report on the discrediting of the Oedipus complex, researchers at the Kinsey Institute reported (*The Observer,* August 30) that after studying 979 homosexualists ("the largest sample of homosexuals—black and white, male and female—ever questioned in an academic study") and 477 heterosexualists, they came to the conclusion that family life has nothing to do with sexual preference. Apparently, "homosexuality is deep-rooted in childhood, may be biological in origin, and simply shows in more and more important ways as a child grows older. It is not a condition which therapy can reverse." Also, "homosexual feelings begin as much as three years before any sort of homosexual act, undermining theories that homosexuality is learned through experience." There goes the teacher-as-seducer-and-perverter myth. Finally, "Psychoanalysts' theories about smothering mum and absent dad do not stand investigation. Patients may tend to believe that they are true because therapists subtly coach them in the appropriate memories of their family life."

Some years ago, gay activists came to *Harper's,* where Decter was an editor, to demonstrate against an article by Joseph Epstein, who had announced, "If I had the power to do so, I would wish homosexuality off the face of the earth." Well, that's what Hitler had the power to do in Germany, and did—or tried to do. The confrontation at *Harper's* now provides Decter with her theme. She tells us that one of the demonstrators asked, "Are you aware of how many suicides you may be responsible for in the homosexual community?" I suspect that she is leaving out the context of this somewhat left-field *cri de coeur.* After all, homosexualists have more to fear from murder than suicide. I am sure that the actual conversation had to do with the sort of mischievous effect that Epstein's Hitlerian piece might have had on those fag-baiters who read it.

But Decter slyly zeroes in on the word "suicide." She then develops a most unusual thesis. Homosexualists hate themselves to such an extent that they wish to become extinct either through inviting murder or committing suicide. She notes that in a survey of San Francisco's homosexual men, half of them "claimed to have had sex with at least five hundred people." This "bespeaks the obliteration of all experience, if not, indeed, of oneself." Plainly Decter has a Mosaic paradigm forever in mind and any variation on it is abominable. Most men—homo or hetero—given the opportunity to have sex with 500 different people would do so, gladly; but most men are not going to be given the opportunity by a society that wants them safely married so that they will be docile workers and loyal consumers. It does not suit our rulers to have the proles tomcatting around the way that our rulers do. I can assure Decter that the thirty-fifth president went to bed with more than 500 women and that the well-known . . . but I must not give away the secrets of the old class or the newly-middle-class new class will go into shock.

Meanwhile, according to Decter, "many homosexuals are nowadays engaged in efforts at self-obliteration . . . there is the appalling rate of suicide among them." But the rate is not appreciably higher than that for the rest of the population. In any case, most who do commit—or contemplate—suicide do so because they cannot cope in a world where they are, to say the least, second-class citizens. But Decter is now entering uncharted country. She also has a point to make: "What is undeniable is the increasing longing among the homosexuals to do away with themselves—if not in the actual physical sense then at least spiritually—a longing whose chief emblem, among others, is the leather bars."

So Epstein will not be obliged to press that button in order to get rid of the fags. They will do it themselves. Decter ought to be pleased by this, but it is not in her nature to be pleased by anything that the same-sexers do. If they get married and have children and swear fealty to the family gods of the new class, their wives will . . . drink. If they live openly with one another, they have fled from woman and real life. If they pursue careers in the arts, heteros will have to be on guard against vicious covert assaults on heterosexual values. If they congregate in the fashion business the way that Jews do in psychiatry, they will employ only those heterosexuals who will put out for them.

Decter is appalled by the fag "takeover" of San Francisco. She tells us about the "ever deepening resentment of the San Francisco straight

community at the homosexuals' defiant displays and power ['power'!]
over this city," but five paragraphs later she contradicts herself: "Having
to a very great extent overcome revulsion of common opinion, are they
left with some kind of unappeased hunger that only their own feelings
of hatefulness can now satisfy?"

There it is. *They are hateful.* They know it. That is why they want
to eliminate themselves. "One thing is certain." Decter finds a lot of
certainty around. "To become homosexual is a weighty act." She still
has not got the point that one does not choose to have same-sex impulses; one simply has them, as everyone has, to a greater or lesser
degree, other-sex impulses. To deny giving physical expression to those
desires may be pleasing to Moses and Saint Paul and Freud, but these
three rabbis are aberrant figures whose nomadic values are not those of
the thousands of other tribes that live or have lived on the planet.
Women's and gay liberation are simply small efforts to free men and
women from this trio.

Decter writes, "Taking oneself out of the tides of ordinary mortal
existence is not something one does from any longing to think oneself
ordinary (but only following a different 'life-style')." I don't quite grasp
this sentence. Let us move on to the next: "Gay Lib has been an effort
to set the weight of that act at naught, to define homosexuality as
nothing more than a casual option among options." Gay lib has done
just the opposite. After all, people are what they are sexually not
through "adoption" but because that is the way they are structured.
Some people do shift about in the course of a life. Also, most of those
with same-sex drives do indeed "adopt" the heterosexual life-style because they don't want to go to prison or to the madhouse or become
unemployable. Obviously, there *is* an option but it is a hard one that
ought not to be forced on any human being. After all, homosexuality
is only important when made so by irrational opponents. In this, as in
so much else, the Jewish situation is precisely the same.

Decter now gives us not a final solution so much as a final conclusion:
"In accepting the movement's terms [hardly anyone has, by the way],
heterosexuals have only raised to a nearly intolerable height the costs
of the homosexuals' flight from normality." The flight, apparently, is
deliberate, a matter of perverse choice, a misunderstanding of daddy, a
passion for mummy, a fear of responsibility. Decter threads her clichés
like Teclas on a string: "Faced with the accelerating round of drugs,
S-M and suicide, can either the movement or its heterosexual sympa-
thizers imagine they have done anyone a kindness?"

Although the kindness of strangers is much sought after, gay liberation has not got much support from anyone. Natural allies like the Jews are often virulent in their attacks. Blacks in their ghettos, Chicanos in their barrios, and rednecks in their pulpits also have been influenced by the same tribal taboos. That Jews and blacks and Chicanos and rednecks all contribute to the ranks of the same-sexers only increases the madness. But the world of the Decters is a world of perfect illogic.

Herewith the burden of "The Boys on the Beach": since homosexualists choose to be the way they are out of idle hatefulness, it has been a mistake to allow them to come out of the closet to the extent that they have, but now that they are out (which most are not), they will have no choice but to face up to their essential hatefulness and abnormality and so be driven to kill themselves with promiscuity, drugs, S-M and suicide. Not even the authors of *The Protocols of the Elders of Zion* ever suggested that the Jews, who were so hateful to them, were also hateful to themselves. So Decter has managed to go one step further than the *Protocols'* authors; she is indeed a virtuoso of hate, and thus do pogroms begin.

*Tricks* is the story of an author—Renaud Camus himself—who has twenty-five sexual encounters in the course of six months. Each of these encounters involves a pick-up. Extrapolating from Camus's sexual vigor at the age of 35, I would suspect that he has already passed the 500 mark and so is completely obliterated as a human being. If he is, he still writes very well indeed. He seems to be having a good time, and he shows no sign of wanting to kill himself, but then that may be a front he's keeping up. I am sure that Decter will be able to tell just how close he is to OD'ing.

From his photograph, Camus appears to have a lot of hair on his chest. I don't know about the shoulders, as they are covered, modestly, with a shirt. Perhaps he is Jewish. Roland Barthes wrote an introduction to *Tricks*. For a time, Barthes was much admired in American academe. But then, a few years ago, Barthes began to write about his same-sexual activities; he is now mentioned a bit less than he was in the days before he came out, as they say.

Barthes notes that Camus's book is a "text that belongs to literature." It is not pornographic. It is also not a Homosexual Novel in that there are no deep, anguished chats about homosexuality. In fact, the subject is never mentioned; it just is. Barthes remarks, "Homosexuality shocks less [well, he is—or was—French], but continues to be interesting; it is still at that stage of excitation where it provokes what might be called feats of discourse [see "The Boys on the Beach," no mean feat!]. Speaking of homosexuality permits those who aren't to show how open, liberal, and modern they are; and those who are to bear witness, to assume responsibility, to militate. Everyone gets busy, in different ways, whipping it up." You can say that again! And Barthes does. But with a nice variation. He makes the point that you are never allowed *not* to be categorized. But then, "say 'I am' and you will be socially saved." Hence the passion for the either/or.

Camus does not set out to give a panoramic view of homosexuality. He comments, in *his* preface, on the variety of homosexual expressions. Although there is no stigma attached to homosexuality in the French intellectual world where, presumably, there is no equivalent of the new class, the feeling among the lower classes is still intense, a memento of the now exhausted (in France) Roman Catholic Church's old dirty work ("I don't understand the French Catholics," said John Paul II). As a result, many "refuse to grant their tastes because they live in such circumstances, in such circles, that their desires are not only for themselves inadmissible but inconceivable, unspeakable."

It is hard to describe a book that is itself a description, and that is what *Tricks* is—a flat, matter-of-fact description of how the narrator meets the tricks, what each says to the other, where they go, how the rooms are furnished, and what the men do. One of the tricks is nuts; a number are very hairy—the narrator has a Decterian passion for the furry; there is a lot of anal and banal sex as well as oral and floral sex. *Frottage* flows. Most of the encounters take place in France, but there is one in Washington, D.C., with a black man. There is a good deal of comedy, in the Raymond Roussel manner.

*Tricks* will give ammunition to those new-class persons and redneck divines who find promiscuity every bit as abominable as same-sex relations. But that is the way men are when they are given freedom to go about their business unmolested. One current Arab ruler boasts of having ten sexual encounters a day, usually with different women. A diplomat who knows him says that he exaggerates, but not much. Of course, he is a Moslem.

The family, as we know it, is an economic, not a biological, unit. I realize that this is startling news in this culture and at a time when the economies of both East and West require that the nuclear family be, simply, God. But our ancestors did not live as we do. They lived in packs for hundreds of millennia before "history" began, a mere 5,000 years ago. Whatever social arrangements human society may come up with in the future, it will have to be acknowledged that those children who are needed should be rather more thoughtfully brought up than they are today and that those adults who do not care to be fathers or mothers should be let off the hook. This is beginning, slowly, to dawn. Hence, the rising hysteria in the land. Hence, the concerted effort to deny the human ordinariness of same-sexualists. A recent attempt to portray such a person sympathetically on television was abandoned when the Christers rose up in arms.

Although I would never suggest that Truman Capote's bright wit and sweet charm as a television performer would not have easily achieved for him his present stardom had he been a *hetero*sexualist, I do know that if he had not existed in his present form, another would have been run up on the old sewing machine because that sort of *persona* must be, for a whole nation, the stereotype of what a fag is. Should some macho film star like Clint Eastwood, say, decide to confess on television that he is really into same-sex sex, the cathode tube would blow a fuse. That could never be allowed. That is all wrong. That is how the Roman Empire fell.

There is not much *angst* in *Tricks.* No one commits suicide—but there is one sad story. A militant leftist friend of Camus's was a teacher in the south of France. He taught 14-year-old members of that oldest of all the classes, the exploited laborer. One of his pupils saw him in a fag bar and spread the word. The students began to torment what had been a favorite teacher. "These are little proles," he tells Camus, "and Mediterranean besides—which means they're obsessed by every possible macho myth, and by homosexuality as well. It's all they can think about." One of the boys, an Arab, followed him down the street, screaming "Faggot!" "It was as if he had finally found someone onto whom he could project his resentment, someone he could hold in contempt with complete peace of mind."

This might explain the ferocity of the new class on the subject. They know that should the bad times return, the Jews will be singled out yet again. Meanwhile, like so many Max Naumanns (Naumann was a German Jew who embraced Nazism), the new class passionately supports our ruling class—from the Chase Manhattan Bank to the Pentagon to the Op-Ed page of *The Wall Street Journal*—while holding in fierce contempt faggots, blacks (see Norman Podhoretz's "My Negro Problem and Ours," *Commentary,* February 1963), and the poor (see Midge Decter's "Looting and Liberal Racism," *Commentary,* September 1977). Since these Neo-Naumannites are going to be in the same gas chambers as the blacks and the faggots, I would suggest a cease-fire and a common front against the common enemy, whose kindly voice is that of Ronald Reagan and whose less than kindly mind is elsewhere in the boardrooms of the Republic.

*The Nation*
November 14, 1981

# 56

## THE BIRDS
## AND THE
## BEES

Recently, while assembling forty years of bookchat, I noted with some alarm—even guilt—that I had never really explained sex. True, I have demonstrated that sex is politics and I have noted that the dumb neologisms, homo-sexual and hetero-sexual, are adjectives that describe acts but never people. Even so, I haven't spelled the whole thing out. So now, before reading skills further atrophy, let me set the record straight, as it were.

First, the bad news: Men and women are *not* alike. They have different sexual roles to perform. Despite the best efforts of theologians and philosophers to disguise our condition, there is no point to us, or to any species, except proliferation and survival. This is hardly glamorous, and so to give Meaning to Life, we have invented some of the most bizarre religions that . . . alas, we have nothing to compare ourselves to. We are biped mammals filled with red sea water (reminder of our oceanic origin), and we exist to reproduce until we are eventually done in by the planet's changing weather or a stray meteor.

Men and women are dispensable carriers, respectively, of seeds and eggs; programmed to mate and die, mate and die, mate and die. One can see why "love" was invented by some artist who found depressing the dull mechanics of our mindless mission to be fruitful and multiply.

Apparently, the first human societies were tribal—extended families. Then the prenuclear family was invented. Skygods were put in place— jealous ones, too. The monotheistic religions from which we continue to suffer are fiercely grounded on the only fact that we can be certain of: Man plus Woman equals Baby. This, for many, is *the* Natural Law. Inevitably, if unnaturally, natural lawyers thought up marriage and monogamy and then, faced with the actual nature of the male and the female, they created numerous sexual taboos in order to keep the population in line so that the senior partners in the earthly firm could keep the rest of us busy building expensive pyramids to the glory of the Great Lawyer in the Sky.

But as a certain Viennese novelist and classics buff, Sigmund ("It's all in the vagina, dear") Freud, noted, all those fierce do's and don'ts have created discontents, not to mention asthma and date rape. In fact, everything that the Book (from which come Judaism, Christianity, Islam) has to say about sex is wrong. Of course, practically everything the Book has to say about everything else, including real estate, is wrong too, but today's lesson is sex.

The male's function is to shoot semen as often as possible into as many women (or attractive surrogates) as possible, while the female's function is to be shot briefly by a male in order to fertilize an egg, which she will lay nine months later. Although there is nothing anywhere in the male psyche that finds monogamy natural or normal (the scientific search for monogamous, exclusively heterosexual mammals has been sadly given up, while our feathery friends—those loving doves, too—have let the natural lawyers down), the monogamous concept is drilled into the male's head from birth because, in the absence of those original tribal support systems that we discarded for the Book, someone must help the woman during gravidity and the early years of baby rearing.

If one starts with the anatomical difference, which even a patriarchal Viennese novelist was able to see was destiny, then one begins to understand why men and women don't get on very well within marriage, or indeed in any exclusive sort of long-range sexual relationship. *He* is designed to make as many babies as possible with as many different women as he can get his hands on, while *she* is designed to take time off from her busy schedule as astronaut and role model to lay an egg and bring up the result. Male and female are on different sexual tracks, and that cannot be changed by the Book or any book. Since all our natural instincts are carefully perverted from birth, it is no wonder that we tend to be, if not all of us serial killers, killers of our own true nature.

It is a fact that, like any species, our only function is replication. It is a fact that even the dullest and most superstitious of us now suspects that we may have overdone the replicating. Five and a half billion people now clutter a small planet built for two. Simply to maintain the breeders in the United States we have managed to poison all our water. Yes, *all* of it. When I was told this by a member of the Sierra Club, I asked, so what do we drink? And he said, well, some of it's less poisoned than the rest. Despite the fulminations of the Sky Lawyer's earthly representatives, some effort is being made to limit population. But the true damage is already done, and I would not bet the farm on our species continuing in rude health too far into the next century. Those who would outlaw abortion, contraception and same-sex while extolling the family and breeding are themselves the active agents of the destruction of our species. I would be angrier if I had a high opinion of the species, but I don't, and so I regard with serenity Pope and Ayatollah as the somehow preprogrammed agents of our demise, the fate of every species. Hordes of furious lemmings are loose among us; and who would stay them, particularly if they have the Book to throw?

But while we are still here, I suggest a change in attitude among those few capable of rational thought. Let us accept the demonstrable fact that the male has no exclusive object in his desire to shoot. Instead of hysteria, when he wants to shoot with another shootist, he should be encouraged in an activity that will not add another consumer to the population. The woman who decides not to lay that egg should be encouraged, if so minded, to mate with another woman. As it is, a considerable portion of the population, despite horrendous persecution, does just that, and they should be considered benefactors by everyone, while the breeders must be discouraged though, of course, not persecuted.

*The Day America Told the Truth* is a recent book in which a cross section of the population expressed its ignorance on many issues and confessed to some of its most dreadful deeds and reveries. Since 91 percent of the population admit to telling lies habitually, I can't think why the authors should take too seriously the lies new-minted for them; but then lies often illustrate inadvertent truths. A majority of men and women like oral sex (as the passive partner, presumably). Next in popularity was sex with a famous person. Plainly being blown by George or Barbara Bush would be the ultimate trip for our huddled masses.

Although the authors list twenty-three sexual fantasies (such as sex in a public—pubic?—place), they do not ask about same-sex fantasies, which tells us where they are, as we say in pollster land, coming from. But in what people do do, they report that 17 percent of the men and 11 percent of the women practice same-sex. This strikes me as low—even mendacious. It is true that in the age of AIDS both sexes are very nervous about same-sex or even other-sex, but not, surely, in experimental youth. In the prewar Southern town of Washington, D.C., it was common for boys to have sex with one another. It was called "messing around," and it was no big deal. If the boy became a man who kept on messing around, it was thought a bit queer—sexual exclusivity *is* odd and suggests obsession—but no big deal as long as he kept it quiet. If he didn't, our natural lawyers would do their best to deprive him of his inalienable rights. In any case, I don't think the folks have changed all that much since 1948, when 37 percent of the men told Dr. Kinsey that they had messed around in those years.

Certainly, women today are more candid about their preference for other women. Although this "preference" has been noted for millenniums, it was thought by shootists to be simply a coming together of two unhappy wives for mutual solace. Instead, there seems to have been a strong sexual element all along. But then a pair of egg-layers will have more in common (including a common genetic programming for nurturing) than they will ever have with a shootist, who wants to move on the second he's done his planting—no nurturing for him, no warm, mature, caring relationship. He isn't built for it. His teats may have a perky charm but they are not connected to a dairy. He can fake a caring relationship, of course, but at great cost to his own nature, not to mention battered wife and abused little ones. The fact that couples may live together harmoniously for decades is indeed a fact, but such relationships are demonstrations not of sexuality but of human comity—I dare not use the word "love," because the 91 percent who habitually lie do so about love.

Unfortunately, the propaganda to conform is unrelenting. In a charming fable of a movie, *Moonstruck,* a middle-aged woman discovers that her husband is having an affair with another woman. As the wife is a loving, caring, warm, mature person in love with her husband, why on earth would he stray from her ancient body, which is ever-ready to receive his even greater wreck of a biped? Why do men chase women? Why do they want more than one woman? She asks everyone in sight and no one can think of an answer until she herself does: *Men fear death,* she says—something that, apparently, women never do. Confronted with this profound insight, the husband stops seeing the other woman.

Whether or not he loses the fear of death is unclear. This is really loony. It is true that sex/death are complementary: No sex, no birth for the unlucky nonamoeba; once born, death—that's our ticket. Meanwhile, fire at will.

When people were few and the environment was hostile, it is understandable that we should have put together a Book about a Skygod that we had created in our own image—a breathtaking bit of solipsism, but why not? The notion is comforting, and there were no Book reviewers at the time of publication, while later ones, if they wrote bad Book reviews, were regularly condemned to death by natural lawyers employing earthly hit men, as Salman Rushdie can testify. Then our Skygod told us to multiply in a world that he had put together just for us, with dominion over every living thing. Hence the solemn wrecking of a planet that, in time, will do to us what we have done to it.

Meanwhile, "the heterosexual dictatorship," to use Isherwood's irritable phrase, goes on its merry way, adding unwanted children to a dusty planet while persecuting the virtuous nonbreeders. Actually, the percentage of the population that is deeply enthusiastic about other-sex is probably not much larger than those exclusively devoted to same-sex—something like 10 percent in either case. The remaining 80 percent does this, does that, does nothing; settles into an acceptable if dull social role where the husband dreams of Barbara Bush while pounding the old wife, who lies there, eyes shut, dreaming of Barbara too. Yes, the whole thing is a perfect mess, but my conscience is clear. I have just done something more rare than people suspect—stated the obvious.

*The Nation*
October 28, 1991

# 57

# HOW TO FIND
# GOD AND
# MAKE MONEY

Both *Publishers Weekly* and *Christian Bookseller* agree that 1978 will be a "bumper year" for evangelical literature. Particularly popular is the first-person confession of a washed-up or caught-up-with celebrity who has found God. Rinsed in the Blood of the Lamb, the redeemed celebrity is presented with what looks to be a real book, bearing a personalized dust jacket—that is, he will be credited with having written a memoir composed by someone else. Sinwise, mis-labeling is less than deadly; it is also big business. Celebrity-sinner books are sold by the millions through hundreds of bookstores and dozens of book clubs that cater to fundamentalist Christians. Last year over $600 million worth of "Christian books" were sold in the United States.

If the redeemed and revived celebrity can so much as tote a tune (Pat Boone, Anita Bryant), there are countless stops not only along but above and below the Bible Belt where large audiences will pay to observe a reborn celebrity. For those who cannot sing songs, a patter of penitence will do. *Ci-devant* revolutionary, rapist, and couturier Eldridge Cleaver's repentance number is a heart-warming crowd-pleaser wherever chiggers burrow and Jesus saves.

Watergate criminals are also in demand. When the inspiring Charles Colson (author of *Born Again*) and the inspired Jeb S. Magruder (author of *An American Life*) confess to all sorts of small sins and crimes not unlike those that Shakespeare's Cardinal Wolsey sang of in *his* final aria, the audience is able to enjoy if not pity and awe a certain amount of catharsis.

*Christian Bookseller* reports on some new good books: "Master's Press announced a first print run of 300,000 copies of its spring release, *Looking Good,* the biography of Freddie Prinze by Mary Pruetzel, the late comedian's mother. . . . Mrs. Pruetzel's purpose in writing Freddie's biography is to spare other young hopefuls the tragic fate which befell her son." Celebrity, sex, drugs, suicide—*as told by a Mother!* Not only will Master's Press be in the chips this year, but any young and hopeful Puerto Rican Magyar who wants to be a comic will know what to look out for en route to the next presidential Inaugural Eve Gala.

Also scheduled for 1978 is *Christ and the Media* by Malcolm Muggeridge. According to *Christian Bookseller* this "English radio and television personality who became a Christian late in life, is pessimistic about the present and future influence of television on human morality. He observes that television station owners, producers, writers and performers—like the films—operate under no established code of moral values. They are free to create their own morality as they go along." Plainly, this is a bad thing. Plainly, an established code would be a good thing and Harold M. Voth, M.D., might be just the man to come up with one.

Dr. Voth's latest book is *The Castrated Family,* a "critical assessment of the women's movement, gay liberation, unisex, open marriage and role blurring . . . phenomena [that] are destroying the American family." Ann Landers thinks that "Dr. Voth has said a mouthful," while from far-off Monte Carlo H.S.H. Princess Grace hopes that the book "will be read as widely as possible."

*Thank God I Have Cancer!* by Clifford Oden has best seller written all over it. Arlington House tells us that "When Rev. Oden learned he had cancer eight years ago he turned to God in prayer. He asked God to show him how to cope. Now he is living proof that cancer can be controlled by natural means—without surgery, without radiation or chemotherapy." Meanwhile, Alba Books gives us *Sexuality Summary* by W. F. Allen. "A clear treatment of four problem areas: homosexuality, abortion, contraception and premarital sex." Since a great many of the new books deal with these four problem areas, it is obvious that Evangelical Christians want those areas cleaned up, *and quick.*

According to the *National Catholic Register* Harold J. Brown's *The*

*Reconstruction of the Republic* shows us how this can be done. "Prof. Brown makes a telling criticism of government without Christianity, and does not spare even the Constitution, which omits the name of God. In the process he exposes the fallacies of welfarism and the Equal Rights Amendment. A meaty volume that requires study and action." The word "action" reminds us of those of our Roman Catholics who dislike the American Constitution and its beautiful appendage the Bill of Rights. Yet if the Inventors had been so unkind and superstitious as to work *their* God into the fabric of the Constitution, the United States would have been a stern and illiberal Protestant republic from which Roman Catholics might very well have been excluded. Fortunately, the Inventors tended to deism, and so were able to eliminate deity from our secular republic.

One of the busiest of the religio-publishers is Christian Herald Books, located at 40 Overlook Drive, Chappaqua, NY 10514. Christian Herald publishes books about missionaries in the Amazon jungle ("larger than life true adventures") as well as "triumphant encounters with the Divine" and of course retold Old Testament stories about the likes of Hagar ("a powerful novel of love, conflict and faith"). Christian Herald also owns at least four book clubs if, as I suspect, "Christian Book Club for Today's Woman," "Family Bookshelf," "Farm Journal Family Bookshelf," and "Grit Family Bookshelf" are all tentacles to the Christian Herald octopus. A deduction gleaned from a close analysis of the club advertisements: *each operates out of 40 Overlook Drive.* Further analysis reveals that the president of one of the clubs is Fenwick Loomer; his editor is Evelyn Bence. Mr. Loomer is also president of a second club but in this enterprise Ms. Bence's job is filled by Gary Sledge (remember that name). A third club is managed by Douglas Andrews; a fourth by Frank Cummings. Assuming that each of these names represents a different person, we have some idea of the shadowy conclave up there on Overlook Drive.

To date, Christian Herald has not hit the really big time. That is, none of its books has sold more than one million copies. But they are definitely fighting the good fight, and doing the Lord's work. If they have yet to sell more than two million copies of a book like *I've Got to Talk to Somebody, God,* by the dread Marjorie Holmes (whose *Two from Galilee* I once reviewed), they have at least been able to put into fiery orbit a celebrity-sinner book called *This Too Shall Pass* written by Mrs. Bert (LaBelle) Lance, "with Gary Sledge" (editor of Family Bookshelf).

Properly speaking, LaBelle is neither a celebrity nor a sinner even though she was much photographed and written about during the early years of the Carter administration or, to be precise, months. Since devotees of the celebrity-sinners are interested not in her but in Bert, LaBelle's dark glory is entirely of the reflected kind. She has committed no lurid crimes; as for her sins, I am sure that they add up to nothing more than a twinge or two of pride at being married to a guy as swell as Bert Lance. Certainly, the magazine *Christian Life* ("The Wonderful Way of Living") thinks the world of both Bert and LaBelle; so much so, that the cover story of the April issue is devoted to "The Lance Ordeal: Let God Have the Burden." The author of this sympathetic account is Wesley J. Pippert, who reveals to us "The secret of the Lance's [*sic*] strength during public scrutiny."

The Pippert account of the agony of the Lances makes almost as good reading as the adjacent article, "Exercising Your Authority Over Satan." Apparently, Satan can be defeated not only by Faith but by the repetition of sacred texts guaranteed to undo the wicked incantations of those who walk up and down and all about this great republic, peddling abortion, contraception, and the Equal Rights Amendment. Ultimately, the writer tells us, "the battle will be won or lost according to which side uses its mouths right." Among the bad-mouthers are the residents of the Moslem world where "the powers of darkness have expressed themselves . . . through those Islamic chants. And let me say in all love, without being controversial, for in some ways Islam is a good religion, it just has one problem: its god is the devil."

Apropos Islam, it should be noted that earlier this year Bert tried to obtain control of Financial General Bankshares, Inc., a $2.2 billion holding company that owns banks in four states. Bert's associates in this caper (currently halted by order of the Federal District Court of the District of Columbia) are—aside from LaBelle—such devil-worshipers as Sheikh Kamal Adham, Faisal Saud Al-Fulaij, Sheikh Sultan Bin Azid Al-Nahyan, Sheikh Mohammed Bin Zaid Al-Nahyan, Abdullah Darwaish, and the Pakistani financial wizard Agha Hassen Abedi, who recently paid off Bert's $3.4 million bank loan, simply because he liked the cut of Bert's Twice-Born jib.

*Christian Life* identifies Wesley J. Pippert as "a professional news correspondent with UPI"; he is also "an approved supply pastor with the United Methodist Church" whose special concern "as a Christian reporter is how the mass media can better handle the moral aspects of public issues." Although Rev. Pippert is in no doubt about the moral correctness of Bert Lance, he tends to hurry through the events that caused Bert to resign as budget director last fall. A year ago last January

Bert "reported [to the Senate Finance Committee] assets of $7.9 million and debts of $5.3 million. He also agreed to sell 190,000 shares of stock in the National Bank of Georgia, Atlanta, in which he held controlling interest." Four months later, "there were news reports that a surge in the prime rate and the pay-cut Lance had taken were hindering his ability to keep up the interest payments on his debts."

As a Christian reporter and supply pastor, Rev. Pippert finds nothing wrong in any of this. In fact, if the increase in the prime rate was in any way attributable to Bert's policies then that would be a definite plus for Bert Lance, Fiscal Conservative. Another plus is that pay cut. Yet the money that Bert saved the American taxpayer would not have made much of a dent in interest payments he was obliged to make on $5.3 million worth of loans.

"Lance had been accused of permitting $450,000 in overdrafts by himself and his family at the family-owned bank in Calhoun," etc. There were new hearings. Although Bert handled himself well, The Mass Media would not let up. Finally, "His eyes welling, President Carter went on nationwide television to announce his friend's resignation. . . . Then the Lances flew home to Georgia. . . . Despite his sense of peace, Lance had serious questions about what had happened. 'It's important we not lose the freedom of the presumption of innocence,' he told this reporter." Bert turned a cold eye on The Mass Media. " 'God has a laser beam that's a whole lot stronger than that other laser beam,' he said in a reference to the beam of the television camera."

When Rev. Pippert asked LaBelle to confirm whether or not the Lances' lavish $2 million fifty-room-plus Atlanta home was for sale, she said that it was not. After all, " 'We were not on the verge of bankruptcy, but if we were, who cares?' This was typical of lovely, long-haired Mrs. Lance. A talk with her does not dwell on the material world for long. Inevitably conversation with her turns to the spiritual, for that's where her heart is."

Bert's heart is very much in the same place. "Lance led the White House Bible study," Rev. Pippert tells us, "but prefers not to talk about it."

"That's something that's very personal to everyone over there. I sort of took a pledge with that group that we really wouldn't talk about it. We got together on a very personal basis."

Lance did say that Carter, who had a conflict at that hour, expressed a desire to come.

Lance also did considerable lay speaking to religious groups.

Now Rev. Wesley J. Pippert gives way to Mr. Gary Sledge of 40 Overlook Drive. LaBelle has a tale to unfold and unfold it she does ("with
Gary Sledge") in the pages of *This Too Shall Pass*. Between the two of
them they manage to illuminate the Bert Lance Continuing Scandal not
at all. Nevertheless, many good things are said—indeed, good news is
everywhere spread, for the book is dedicated to the Lances' old family
friend "the Glory of God through his Son Jesus Christ."

The prologue is datelined "Calhoun, Ga." First sentence: "This too
shall pass." When (and if) "this" passes, "hopefully we grow wiser,
more patient, more loving." LaBelle tells us that not only has she been
going through a pretty awful time lately but "Let me just list the human
afflictions that have touched my life: alcoholism, drugs, broken homes,
suicide, death, violence, serious illness, car accidents, jailings, homosexuality, murder, adultery, runaway children." Sly Mr. Sledge knows that
television series are usually shot in series of thirteen. Each of LaBelle's
thirteen human afflictions would make for at least one powerful episode
in a high-rated series.

But after this scorching teaser, LaBelle neglects to Tell All. No doubt
on the ground that we are all so used to suicide, murder, and runaway
children in our daily lives from television. Instead, LaBelle zeroes in on
something truly hated and feared out there on the circuit, The Mass
Media. As a Christian, LaBelle *tries* to forgive the press. If she fails, . . .
well, it is the effort that counts and if Jesus does not want LaBelle for
a sunbeam at the end of life's journey, it will not have been for want of
her (and Mr. Sledge's) trying.

"Our family is not so different from any other. But I'd like you to walk
with me down the Lance road of life, if only to illustrate how wonderful
is the Lord on whom we rely." Actually, the Lances are quite a bit
different from most people. For one thing, they have managed to acquire
a whole lot of money real fast. For another, Bert was for many years
a chief adviser and lender of money to what may prove to be our most
mysterious president. Nevertheless, the fact that Carter and Lance in
tandem were for a time allowed to preside over the republic's affairs does
indeed illustrate the loony sense of humor as well as true mystery of our
Lord and His ways.

LaBelle begins at a high moment: the morning of the day that Bert
is going to talk to the president about resigning as director of the Office
of Management and Budget. For months the scandal has been breaking
all around them. LaBelle is aroused from a . . . what else, Mr. Sledge?
"fitful sleep" by "laughter and many loud voices and the sound of

shuffling feet." Whose laughter? whose feet? The Mass Media are outside in the street. "We were under seige [*sic*], as we had been throughout September."

Bert brings her breakfast in bed. Things look bad. Bert leaves for the White House. LaBelle dares not look at *The Washington Post* because "recently there had been a story on the front page . . . about my brother Banks' death two years before. The writer implied that our family's financial situation was rocky, that Bert was somehow responsible, and that this was the reason my brother had taken his own life. All that was untrue."

According to LaBelle, Beverly Banks David committed suicide "when his high expectations for himself were not realized, he felt unreasonable guilt or failure." This is dignified reticence. We are given no revelations of the sort promised in the prologue. Yet there is evidence that, wittingly or unwittingly as Mr. Sledge might say, LaBelle's brother had been very much involved in Bert's shenanigans at the National Bank of Georgia. In fact, according to the SEC, thirteen months *after* the death of Beverly Banks David, his bank account was $73,401 overdrawn, presumably by the Holy Ghost.

Later that afternoon, Bert comes home, having "played tennis with President Carter. . . . He looked exhausted. . . . I could see the suppressed anger in his face, the tiredness and the letting go. . . . Then at supper in the garden, we asked God to give us wisdom and strength and to show us his [LaBelle knows God too well to capitalize the pronoun] will. . . . God was not far off. He was near. We talked to him intimately and often." Actually, it was Jimmy Carter who was far off by now, sweating ice over the so-called Lance Affair.

Like the stern Nixon women of an earlier epoch, LaBelle was against resignation. But Bert had had it. He was going to resign even though "I had a dream about what could be accomplished in this job." The first Kuwaiti Mutual Fund? The first International Bank of Georgia and Abu Dhabi? Dreams, dreams. . . .

The next day LaBelle hightailed it over to the White House to put the arm on Jimmy. "The President was very cordial, very gracious. . . . He always is a friend to everyone in our family on a person-to-person basis, despite the formalities of his office. I think the President believes strongly that Christ's love and concern can only be shown in this way." But Jimmy was concerned about that old devil The Mass Media. "He spoke honestly about his public relations problem caused by Bert's name being in the news so long." Although LaBelle *knew* that she was filled to the brim with Christ when she told Jimmy that Bert should remain in office, Jimmy was every bit as filled with Christ when he came to the conclusion that Bert should get his ass out of town.

Like Saint Jerome battling with the pagan shade of Cicero, LaBelle and Mr. Sledge wrestle with this exquisite theological problem. "I knew that the President had presented his views in the light of faith. He, just as Bert and I, had prayed about this situation and each of us reached different conclusions—but each of us had come to realize the profound love in Christ we shared." Thus LaBelle papers over the inexplicable plurality of Truth.

Since Jimmy and LaBelle can't both be right, she surrenders if not to the Holy Ghost to the Gallup Poll: "I have often learned [that] God's purpose and my intentions are not always the same. Yet everything comes in his own time!" A striking image, worthy of Ecclesiastes. Back at the house ("I was suddenly tired"), LaBelle dealt compassionately with The Mass Media at the door. Then, "I went back to the TV but only the afternoon game shows were on, so I turned off the set and read a daily devotional book."

The rest of *This Too Shall Pass* is a somewhat mechanical ghosted story of LaBelle's family and early life, marriage and motherhood, riches and heartbreak, and above all a steadfast Faith. Inevitably, she falls from a horse; inevitably, she is told that she "must remount with dignity." Daddy owned the Calhoun bank while Bert's father had been president of Young Harris, a small Methodist college in northeast Georgia. As a child, Bert had experienced "an exciting mix of intellectual conversation and theological discussion." Then he moved to Calhoun where he went to school with LaBelle, who "had a dream. I wanted to be an actress on Broadway or in the movies. See Hollywood and the Pacific Ocean." But, luckily, she chose to "think and work for Christ. The Christian road is a hard one, but it is the most rewarding road." And so it proved to be for Bert and LaBelle.

LaBelle did not go with Bert to an outdoor political barbecue, attended by "a young state senator named Carter. . . . Bert was attracted initially by Jimmy's forthright approach and community conscience." Apparently, they were as alike as two black-eyed peas in a pod. Each had so much in common with the other: "Concern for progress in Georgia . . . raised in a small town . . . strong commitment to public service . . . boyhood dreams of going to sea . . . both were involved in agribusiness, Jimmy as a farmer and warehouser of peanuts, Bert as the financial underwriter . . . born-again Christians." Civil rights? LaBelle passes on that one. Martin Luther King is not a name to conjure with amongst those who read this sort of inspirational Christian literature.

In due course, Jimmy becomes governor; he appoints Bert head of the Bureau of Transportation. Bert donates his salary to charity. When "Jimmy had hopes of higher office . . . [Bert] presented Jimmy with a set of small medals of all the states, saying he now had dominion over one—someday he hoped he would have dominion over all." As soon as Jimmy's term of office ended, he proceeded to seek dominion over all the states while Bert stayed home and tried to dominate Georgia. "We announced Bert's candidacy [for governor] at a party held out at Lancelot, at which Bert spoke from the bed of an old wagon. . . ." Bert lost. Jimmy won.

Bert was offered the big job at Management and Budget. Should he take it? He agonizes with LaBelle: " 'It would mean a dramatic cut in salary,' Bert said. 'But it's a matter of duty. A citizen owes something to his country. I can't turn my back on a nation that's given us so much. In a free society we all must pay the "rent." ' " The dream . . . always the dream!

The Lances join the Carters in Washington. LaBelle was soon "encircled by new friends and prayer partners. Shortly after we got settled in Georgetown, I invited Cabinet wives to join me in a prayer group which met at our house." LaBelle also "taught a Bible class for senior citizens at the Dumbarton Avenue Methodist Church. . . ."

Then, on May 23, *Time* magazine struck. Something about irregular bank loans. LaBelle was impervious at first: "I knew Bert would never do anything illegal." But The Mass Media had tasted blood. They did not let up until they had sent Bert and LaBelle back to Calhoun, their finances tangled but their faith in God more resolute than ever. The Lances were also bucked up by the president, who promptly sent them abroad as "co-chairmen of the Friendship Force—America's people-to-people outreach to other nations. Rosalynn Carter is the very active honorary chairman."

That's all LaBelle has to say about this organization. *Christian Life* is a bit more explicit. Apparently, this "non-profit, non-government organization designed to promote world peace through friendships" was invented by Rev. Wayne Smith of Decatur, Georgia. "The exchanges last about ten days. . . . Once there, the ambassadors stay in guest homes, live, work and share with their hosts" for eight days. Each "ambassador" shells out $250 for an "embassy" of ten days, but can that possibly cover the costs of the trip? If it doesn't, who pays? But then, whatever the Lances get mixed up in tends to be mysterious—like the Lord Himself.

Has it come to this? Franz Joseph would mutter, as he gazed down at the mob of shouting dress extras below his window at Schönbrunn palace in Burbank, California. Cut to the hunting lodge at old-world Mayerling. Sulky Crown Prince Rudolf wonders, what does it all mean? as he draws a bead on LaBelle . . . I mean Maria Vetsera. Slow dissolve to the funeral cortege, to the grieving Franz Joseph, to Hitler riding through the streets of Vienna.

Rhetorical questions never get answered either in Golden Age movies or in modern-day United States. At most, grand juries, congressional committees, district courts sometimes manage to extract a few pale perjuries from the odd scapegoat. Presumably, this will happen in the case of Bert Lance when he goes before a grand jury in Atlanta to answer charges of criminal misapplication of bank funds. Three federal agencies are also on his tail for assorted crimes while his secret attempt to take over Financial General Bankshares, Inc. has been temporarily stopped by a federal judge. Will Bert be found guilty? And if so, of what is he actually guilty?

With some pride, the Inventor-owners of the United States announced that their republic would be "a government of laws and not of men." The world applauded. It never occurred to any Enlightenment figure in the eighteenth century that law was not preferable to man. The republic was then given to lawyers to govern. Predictably, lawyers make laws, giving work to other lawyers. As a result of two centuries of law-making every aspect of an American's life has either been prescribed for or proscribed by laws that even as they are promulgated split amoeba-like to create more laws. The end to this Malthusian nightmare of law metastasized is nowhere in sight.

Plaintively, Bert acknowledged this state of affairs in his last appearance before the Senate. He maintained that he had not really broken any law, while desperately signaling to the senators that if you were to obey every dumb law on the statute books you could do no business at all. The senator-lawyers would doubtless have been more understanding if their client-constituents had not been watching them on television.

One rationale for the necessity of new laws is the need to protect that vague entity known to lawyers as the public, to corporations as the consumer. Yet each virtuous law promptly creates counterlaws designed to serve those special interests that do not have at heart the public's interest. As a result virtually any polluter of rivers, corrupter of politicians, hustler of snake-oil who can afford expensive legal counsel is able to sail with the greatest of ease through the legislative chambers and courtrooms of the republic. This is the way that we are now, and that is the way we have always been. Nevertheless, from time to time, the system of ownership requires a sacrificial victim to show that the system truly works and that no one is above the law—except those who are.

What sustains a system that is plainly unjust if not illegal? The Lance affair suggests an answer. One third of the American population claim to be twice-born Christians. Although redemption is big on the evangelical Christian circuit, punishment of sinners is even bigger. To the fundamentalist Christian mind, evil is everywhere and every day is a lovely day, as John Latouche's lyric goes, for an *auto-da-fé*. According to hard-core white fundamentalists, Jews are forever guilty of the murder of our Lord. As children of Ham, blacks are eternally inferior to whites. The Pauline injunction that slaves obey their masters still applies in the sense that those without money must serve those with money, for money is the most tangible sign of God's specific love. Sexual activity outside marriage must be punished by law in the here-and-now as well as by God in eternity. The unremitting rage of the fundamentalist Christian against so many varieties of sin is the source of innumerable laws that have bred, in turn, other laws of the sort that now enmesh Bert Lance, the Georgia Laocoön.

Bert is now being sacrificed by his own kind, and he still can't believe it. When Bert and LaBelle inveigh against The Mass Media, they are sending out distress signals in Twice-Born Code. The Mass Media means Jews. Surely the Christers will rally to the defense of an innocent man traduced by those elders of Zion who have gained control of the nation's television and press in order to destroy the moral fiber of God's own country. But code phrases can no longer save Bert's bacon. Like Nixon, he got caught. And like Nixon he must be made to suffer by those for whom the infliction of pain is not only a Christian duty but an abiding pleasure.

It says a good deal for Jimmy Carter's essential decency or timidity or both that he has not yet put together a populist (and popular) Christian crusade to "save" those whose very birth and deeds are offensive to the God of the Twice-Born. But should he ever be so minded, there are more than enough laws already on the books to help him in his holy task.

Fortunately, Jimmy's friends Bert and LaBelle have the consolation of Holy Scripture in their dark hours. As the grand jury convenes in

Atlanta, Bert is certain to turn to Luke 11:52: "Woe to you lawyers! For you have taken away the key of knowledge; you did not enter yourselves, and you hindered those who were entering."

*The New York Review of Books*
June 29, 1978

# 58

### RICH KIDS

*Privileged Ones* is the fifth and last of Robert Coles's *Children of Crisis* series. In four earlier volumes Dr. Coles interviewed a wide range of American children—Eskimos, Appalachians, migrant workers. Now he deals with the children of what he calls "The Well-Off and the Rich in America."

  Dr. Coles is a professional child psychiatrist ("There are, after all, only a few hundred such men and women in the country"); he is currently at Harvard. According to the publisher, he has written twenty-four books. Except for *Children of Crisis,* I cannot say that I really know his work. From time to time I see articles by him; whenever I do, I feel a warm glow. I like thee, Dr. Coles, I know not why. Perhaps it is because I am interested in many of his large subjects (economic injustice, children, Middle America). Certainly, I admire his uninhibited liberalism; his obvious compassion for those he deals with. The fact that I seldom actually finish reading anything that he writes probably has to do with my own perhaps irrational conviction that Dr. Coles's heart is so entirely in all the right places (mouth, boots, upon the sleeve) that nothing he has to say will ever surprise me despite the fact that he has traveled far and reasonably wide because "One hopes; one hopes against hope that somehow it will make a little difference; only a little, but still some, if people mostly unknown to almost all of us get better known to more of us." This generous sentiment is from the preface to the penultimate volume *Eskimos, Chicanos, Indians.* Yet no matter how far afield Dr. Coles goes, he is seldom able to tell us anything that we did not already know.

I suspect that this gift for inducing *déjà vu* may very well be the most subtle form of teaching. Where Plato makes us think by asking questions, Dr. Coles makes us *feel* by giving answers—in the form of monologues attributed to various children, an enjoyable if somewhat questionable technique (even Dr. Coles is disturbed by a form of "narrative that excludes myself as much as possible, and brings [the reader] directly to the children. . . . I may well have made a mistake, given the limitations of words, not to mention my own shortcomings").

*Children of Crisis* is a work of high seriousness, and a great deal of labor if not work has gone into the compilation of so many interviews with so many children over so many years. The persona of Dr. Coles is truly attractive . . . and it is the persona that one is most conscious of while reading him. Thanks no doubt to "the limitations of words" he is present, like God, in every aspect of his creation and, unlike God, he must be a most agreeable companion for a child, causing a minimum of that sort of dislocation Lévi-Strauss notes in *Tristes tropiques*: the moment that the anthropologist appears on the scene a pristine culture ceases, by definition, to be what it was and becomes something else again in order to accommodate the researcher-invader and his preconceptions.

Dr. Coles is attractively modest; he does not claim to know all the questions—as opposed to answers. In a sense, *Children of Crisis* could be called *The Education of Robert Coles.* Although he has a strong if oddly undefined sense of the way the world ought to be, he knows perfectly well that he is apt to impose his own world view on the children he talks to. In fact, the most beguiling aspect of his work is the pains that he takes not to do what, of course, he cannot help doing: expressing through the children his outrage at a monstrously unjust society. As a result, we get to know a lot about the mind (or feelings) of Dr. Coles. This is no bad thing. On the other hand, the children he interviewed during the last twenty years are somewhat shadowy.

In *Privileged Ones* Dr. Coles talks to the children of the rich. As he describes his method of work, he worries whether or not the phrase "children of crisis" really applies to them. The original "crisis" of the earlier studies was the integration of America's public schools and its effect on not-rich children. In theory, the rich don't have to worry about integrated public schools if they don't want to; their children can always go elsewhere. Finally (and rightly, I think), Dr. Coles thinks that the "crisis" does include the squire's children (Dr. Coles's approach is not unlike Horatio Alger's, whose cast of characters always included a "purse-proud" squire's son who treats badly poor pluck-and-luck Luke, who eventually works hard and makes money and has the satisfaction of one day condescending to his old enemy who has lost all his money). It was a black parent who told Dr. Coles that the rich are the people he should be talking to because "they own us" (this was in New Orleans). A sensible observation; and suggestion.

Dr. Coles set about the work at hand in his usual way. "I do *not* interview children with tests, tape-recorders, questions. I call upon them as a visitor and eventually, one hopes, a friend." How he comes to meet them is somewhat mysterious. He tells us, "In 1960 I started visiting regularly five quite well-to-do New Orleans families. . . . These were not the 'first' families of New Orleans, but they were far from the last in rank." He tells us that he had been so much with the victims of our economic system that he felt "ill at ease" with the New Orleans bourgeoisie, although they were "my own kind." So Saint Francis must have felt whenever he stopped off in Assisi to visit the folks, only to find them still busy netting and eating those very same little birds he liked to chat with. Yet Dr. Coles is able to give the rich almost the same compassionate attention that he gave the less "advantaged" (his verb) families.

I never came to their parents as a stranger, suddenly at the door with a brazenly insistent set of inquiries. I met these upper-income families as an outgrowth of work that often they had good reason to know about: as growers and plantation owners; as important citizens.

This does not explain very much. For instance, was Dr. Coles ever called in professionally? Several of the children he talked to had already had dealings with that somber eminence known as "the school psychologist." Were they difficult children? And did the parents turn to Dr. Coles? If so, did they know what *he* was doing?

The most extraordinary omission in this work is the parents. Although we hear a good deal about them at secondhand through the children, Dr. Coles seldom records his own impression of the parents. As a result, his Privileged Ones often sound like voices in one of Beckett's enervating plays—literally unrelated to any recognizable world. He does warn us that his method requires, "at times, not only changes of

name and place of residence, but the substantial alteration of other
significant information. The point has been to struggle for representative
accounts. I have not hesitated, at times, to condense remarks drastically
or to draw upon the experiences of several children in the interest of a
composite picture." I am afraid that the result not only makes the
children sound all alike (Dr. Coles has no ear for the way people speak),
but since we are given so little precise data about any of the families,
there is a flat sameness of tone as well as of subject. Dr. Coles's education (like that of Henry Adams) starts with certain things already absolutely known and contrary data is either excluded or made to fit certain
preconceptions.

What are Dr. Coles's absolutes? At the start, he makes clear "my
political sympathies, my social and economic views. . . . I worked for
years in the South and SNCC and CORE, the civil rights movement."
He reminds us that the first volume of the series was the result of the
crisis brought on by the integration of Mississippi schools and that the
second volume dealt with the perpetual crisis (exploitation) of migrant
workers: "I dedicated a book I wrote on Erik H. Erikson's psychoana-
lytic work to Cesar Chavez." Also, "I have written an assortment of
muckraking articles in connection with the social, racial, and economic
problems of the South," etc. Finally, "My heroes—of this century, at
least—are James Agee and George Orwell, Walker Percy and Flannery
O'Connor, Simone Weil and Georges Bernanos, William Carlos Williams, and Dorothy Day—none of them great admirers of this nation's
upper-income, propertied families."

Although I have not read every work by the writers named, I have
read something of each and I think that one can safely say that Bernanos
never had a word to say about America's propertied families. Flannery
O'Connor was interested not in class but in grace. Walker Percy is a
southern aristocrat who has not shown, to date, any leveling social
tendencies. No doubt Orwell deplored our "well-off and rich families"
as he did their British equivalents, but he did not write about them.
Neither Simone Weil nor William Carlos Williams, M.D., seems quite
relevant. Dorothy Day obviously contributed to Dr. Cole's education as
did, I fear, James Agee, whose early ersatz-Biblical style has not had a
good influence on Dr. Coles's over-fluent prose. Like so many good-
hearted, soft-headed admirers of the Saint James (Agee) version of
poverty in America, *Let Us Now Praise Famous Men,* Dr. Coles is
enthralled by the windy, woolly style of the saint, unaware that the only
numinous presence in that book is Walker Evans, whose austere photo-

graphs are so at odds with Agee's tumescent (the pornographers have stolen "turgid"; we'll never get it back) text.

In any case, somehow or other, Dr. Coles got to talk to a number of nicely "advantaged" children in, variously, Alaska, New Mexico, New Orleans, a San Antonio barrio, an Atlanta black ghetto, "north of Boston," "west of Boston," and "well north of Boston" (the last three phrases reverberate for the Massachusetts-bred author in much the same way that Combray and Balbec did for Proust). The geographic range is wide, and interesting. Once Dr. Coles got to know the children (aged, roughly, six to eleven or twelve at first encounter), he would encourage them to draw pictures for him. The pictures are included in the book and I am sure that they reveal a good deal about the artists.

Since Dr. Coles gives the impression of being a thoroughly nice man, the children were probably as candid as he thinks they were. Rather sweetly, he admits that he liked *them* even though, with his credentials (Cesar Chavez, Georges Bernanos, Walker Percy), he feared that he might be put off by their advantaged-ness. I am sure that they liked him, too. But then it is not possible to dislike an author who dedicates a book: "To America's children, rich and well-off as well as poor, in the hope that some day, one day soon, all boys and girls everywhere in the world will have a decent chance to survive, grow, and affirm themselves as human beings." Plainly, Bishop Coles will not rest easy as long as a single child on this earth is obliged to negate himself as a vegetable or mineral.

The American vice is explanation. This is because there is so little conversation (known as "meaningful dialogue" to the explainers) in the greatest country in the history of the greatest world in the Milky Way. Dr. Coles is a born explainer and prone to loose rhetoric; given his "credentials," this is as it should be. But it is somewhat disturbing to find that most of the children are also great explainers. Admittedly, Dr. Coles is homogenizing their characters and prose in the interests of "representativeness" and "compositiveness"; as a result, not only do they sound like him, they also come through as a batch of born-explainers, faithfully reflecting the explanatory style of parents, teachers, television commercials.

But despite the grimly didactic tendencies of our future rulers, the kids themselves are often interesting; particularly when Dr. Coles gets down to facts. In an excellent early chapter called "Comfortable, Comfortable Places," Dr. Coles gives us a sharp look at the way the rich live nowadays. He describes the air-conditioned ranch houses in the South-

west, the Georgian and Colonial manors west and north and well north
of Boston, the Gothic mansions in New Orleans's Garden District. He
has a gift for the expensive detail. He notes the almost universal desire
of the rich to live in the country (hangover from the days of the British
Ascendancy?). They acquire ranches, farms, estates; go richly native.
Pools, tennis courts, stables are taken for granted. For many parents a
life "without golf . . . would be unbearable, even hard to imagine."
Although Dr. Coles describes the obsession that the rich have with
sports, he does not analyze the significance of the games that they play,
and oblige their children to play. He seems to think that sports are
indulged in either for the sake of health or to show off wealth (the private
golf course, the ski run).

In the case of the new rich (his usual subject), expensive sports may
indeed be a sign of status. But for the old rich, games are a throwback
to a warrior heritage, real or imagined. A competence with weapons and
horses was a necessity for the noble. Later, when such things were of
no use to desk-bound magnates, horses, weapons, games continued to
exert an atavistic appeal. Also, as late as my own youth, it was taken
for granted that since making a living was not going to be much of a
problem or even (in some cases) a necessity, the usual hard round of
money-making with all its excitements and insecurities was not to be
one's lot. Therefore, time must be filled—hence, games. Certainly physical activity is better than drinking, gambling, lechery . . . the traditional
hazards of great families, not to mention fortunes.

As a child, at each birthday or Christmas, I came to dread the
inevitable tennis racquet, Winchester rifle, skis: these objects were presented to me in much the same way that the pampered dog in the
television commercial is tempted with every sort of distasteful dog food
until, finally, he goes up the wall when given The Right Brand. In any
case, The Right Brand proved to be books . . . not proper sustenance
for the growing boy of forty years ago; or even today, if Dr. Coles's
findings are correct. I don't believe a single child whom he talked to
mentions a book to him (did he mention any books to them?). But
television is noted. And sports. And school. And parents. And servants.
Servants!

Dr. Coles notes that in the South the servants are black; in the North
they are sometimes black, but more usually (in the houses of the true
nobles) white. Dr. Coles records what the children have to say about
servants. But he does not probe very deeply. He does not seem to
understand to what extent, prepuberty, "privileged children" are

brought up not by parents but by servants. Governesses, nannies, mademoiselles (our spelling) are still very much a part of the scene even in the age of the baby-sitter, and they can be more important to the child than his parents. Although Dr. Coles records a good deal of what the children have to say about the people who work in the house or around the place, he is not (except in one case) sensitive to the deep and complex relationships that exist between, say, nurse and child. But then Dr. Coles is after different game: the attitude of the rich child toward economic inferiors.

Dr. Coles is good at showing the subtle and not-so-subtle ways in which class lines are drawn by parents and toed by children. One must never be rude or unkind to those less fortunate. Above all, one must never embarrass (recurring word) the lower orders by asking them to dinner or by going to visit their house (or "home," as Dr. Coles would say—a word seldom used by the nobles). Incidentally, all schoolteachers and most doctors are counted as plebes. This news will come as a particular jolt to our medicos, who are not only well-to-do but when espied on a dim day on a green fairway might pass for upper class.

The last time that I saw W. H. Auden, he announced, apropos nothing at all, "*I* am upper middle class. My father was a doctor. In England that is upper middle class." Like the Baron de Charlus enumerating his titles for the benefit of Madame Verdurin, Auden discoursed for ten minutes on the social importance of his family. As an old corsair in the class wars, I waited for him to pause; then raised the Jolly Roger. I told him that in my youth we were tended by Washington's "leading society physician" (the Homeric epithet always put before his name in the city's social columns). He would come to our house in not-so-nearby Virginia. Dressed in morning coat and striped trousers, he would dispense aspirin (and morphine to the family junkie); then, if the company at table was not too grand, he would be *invited for lunch*. Auden received this bit of cutlass-work with the bland announcement, "*I* am upper middle class." And repeated himself, word for word.

Dr. Coles notes a significant difference between rich and poor children. The poor tend to live in a long unchanging present while the rich have a future to look forward to. For the rich there is always "next year" when they will go to Switzerland to ski or to the West Indies to scuba-dive. Early on, rich children are trained to think of themselves as having a certain "entitlement" (Dr. Coles's not so bad synonym for "privilege"—from the Latin for "private law") to a way of life that despite numerous perils and often onerous obligations is bound to be satisfactory and worthwhile. Unlike the present-trapped poor, each child of privilege is acutely conscious of his own specialness. Dr. Coles defines this self-consciousness most elegantly: "With none of the . . . children I have worked with" (well, disregard those two inelegant "withs") "have I heard such a continuous and strong emphasis put on the 'self.' In fact, other children rarely if ever think about themselves in the way children of well-to-do and rich parents do—with insistence, regularity, and, not least, out of a learned sense of obligation. These privileged ones are children who live in homes with many mirrors. They have mirrors in their rooms, larger mirrors in adjoining bathrooms. . . ." *Mirrored Ones* or *Reflected Ones* might have been an even better title than *Privileged Ones.* At his best, Dr. Coles is himself something of a mirror, with fun-house tendencies.

Certain themes emerge from these monologues. The collapse of the financial order in the early Thirties made a lasting impression on the parents of these children. The Depression convinced them of the essential fragility of what is now known as the consumer society. Menaced, on the one hand, by labor unions and, on the other, by the federal government, even the richest American family feels insecure. It is fascinating that this unease . . . no, paranoia (somehow or other *they* will ruin us) still persists after so many years of prosperity for the rich. But then, the privileged had a number of frights in the Thirties. One of my first memories was the march on Washington of war veterans in 1932. Demanding bonuses for having served in World War I, they were nicknamed Boners. I thought them Halloween skeletons. Then I saw them at the Capitol. They looked like comic-strip hobos. But there was nothing comic about the rocks that they heaved at my grandfather's car. In due course, General MacArthur and his corps of photographers sent the Boners home; nevertheless, we *knew* that one day they would come back and kill us all. Like Cavafy's urbanites, we waited with a certain excitement for the barbarians to return and sack the city.

Dr. Coles's children also fear the Boners. Only now they are called communists or liberals, blacks or Chicanos; and the federal government is in league with them. Worse, the Boners are no longer encamped outside the city; they have occupied the city. All streets are dangerous now. Apartment houses are fortresses; and even the suburbs and exurbs are endangered by "them," and (recurrent theme) there is nowhere to go. Although some of Dr. Coles's children talk of France and England as relative paradises (curious, the fascination with Europe), most are fatalistic. As an Alaskan girl puts it, "I hear Daddy tell Mom that he feels like taking all his money out of the bank and getting a compass and spinning it, and wherever it ends up pointing to, we would go there. But if it pointed straight north, we couldn't go to live near the North Pole." Meanwhile the son of a Boston banker reports that, "It's hard to trust the help these days." He worries about the house being robbed: "Someone tips off the crooks." As for Boston, his mother "doesn't like to walk even a block in the city when it gets dark. . . ."

Dr. Coles's principal interest is how the rich regard the poor. This is a good subject. But one wishes that he was a bit less direct and on target in his approach. After all, there are a lot of ways to come at the subject. For instance, many of the children are pubescent or even adolescent; yet sex is hardly mentioned. Now the question of sexual role is every bit as political, in the true sense, as conditioned attitudes toward money, class, and race. Dr. Coles nowhere deals with the *idea* of the family ("fealty" to which is so excitedly sworn by certain childless lowbrow moralists). For instance, what do the young girls he talked to think of motherhood? Most of the girl children (*genus* privileged) that I know are adamant about *not* having children. They believe that the planet is overcrowded, that resources are limited, that the environment is endangered. Their vehemence is often startling—if, perhaps, short-lived. Dr. Coles notes none of this. But then *his* "crisis" was racial integration.

Except for one anecdote about a New Orleans girl who liked to contemplate a nearby cemetery, wondering "who 'those people' were," death is hardly present in these tales. Although Dr. Coles handles with delicacy the New Orleans girl's "morbidity," he seems not to have been interested in what the other children had to say on a subject of enormous concern to children. The moment that a child comprehends not only the absoluteness but the inevitability of his own death, he is obliged, for better or worse, to come to terms with how best to live in the world. For a rich child to whom all things seem possible, the knowledge of death often brings on a vastation not unlike the one that helped to propel to enlightenment the uniquely over-advantaged Prince Siddhartha.

But if death is absent in Dr. Coles's testaments, God is all over the place. Since Dr. Coles has so generalized the families that he writes about, it is hard to tell just what their actual beliefs are. I would guess that none is Jewish or Roman Catholic. I would assume that the southern or southwestern families are Protestant with fundamentalist tendencies of the twice-born variety. West, north, and well north of Boston, the rich tend to belong to the highly refined Episcopal Church where talk of God is considered bad taste. Yet I was startled by how many of

Dr. Coles's families say grace before meals; go to church; refer to God. I never heard grace said at table in any house that I visited as a child. Yet God and religion mean so much to so many of Dr. Coles's families that I can't help thinking he himself is enthralled by that tripartite deity whose sense of fun has made sublunary life so strenuous and odd.

In describing a disaster dream, "My father asked God to spare us," says a girl with a pair of alcoholic parents. A New Mexico boy wonders if Indians "pray to the same God his parents ask him to beseech before going to sleep. His parents are Presbyterians, attend church with their children every Sunday, and encourage in them prayer at the table and upon retiring." The son of a black entrepreneur notes his father's appeals to God to forgive him if he has wronged anyone in the course of making money. A southern girl notes that "Christ didn't want people to look down on the poor. . . ." The *good* poor, that is. One child is critical of his father's treatment of migrant labor; he is regarded with some unease by his family as "a believing Christian." I suspect that Dr. Coles may himself be a believing Christian (like Bernanos, O'Connor, Weil, et al.). If he is, it is possible that he has exaggerated the importance of religion in the lives of the families that he deals with. But I propose this only tentatively. After all, a recent poll assured us that one-third of the American population (mostly unrich) claims to be twice-born.

According to Dr. Coles's research, the children of the rich (poor, too, but in a different way) pass through an altruistic phase at about the age of ten or eleven. They become aware not only of injustice but of hypocrisy. They question seriously the ancient parental injunction: do as I say, not as I do. Thanks to television, an unexpected agent of revolution, a white child can watch a black child being menaced by a mob (thus compassion begins), while television serials like "The Adventures of Robin Hood" can have a positively subversive effect. After all, to rob the rich in order to give to the poor is not entirely unlike what he has been taught in Sunday School. Eventually, there is a showdown between parent and child. "Robin Hood" is replaced by "Gilligan's Island" and all's right with the world—for the time being, anyway. Predictably, parents get a good deal of help from schoolteachers who also have a stake in maintaining things as they are. Dr. Coles's children are uncommonly shrewd when it comes to analyzing their teachers. They know that the teachers are terrified of saying anything that might distress the parents. The children also know when a teacher does get out of line, there is hell to pay: the subject of one of Dr. Coles's best tales.

The stories that comprise *Privileged Ones* seem to me to belong more to moral literature than to science. I assume that psychology still pretends to be a science. Dr. Coles has used conversations with actual children in order to write a series of short stories. Since the author is the least disinterested of men, these stories are essentially polemical and so, to my mind, entirely honorable if not exactly "scientific." Dr. Coles's mind tends to the political and the moral rather than to the abstract or the empirical. He believes that the economic system by which this country maintains its celebrated standard of living (for a few) is eminently unfair. Millions of men, women, and children are financially exploited in order to support one percent of the population in opulence and the rest in sufficient discomfort to keep them working at jobs that they dislike in order to buy things that they do not need in order to create jobs to make money to be able to buy, etc. This is not a just society. It may not last much longer. But for the present, the children of the rich are as carefully conditioned to the world as it is as are those of the poor.

In story after story, Dr. Coles shows a child at the moment he becomes aware of the problems of those who work his father's mine, or harvest his father's crops. Then he is enlightened. He is told that the world is a cruel place where big fish eat little fish and Daddy is a big fish. Family and teachers unite; convince the child that there is not much he can do now—or, perhaps, ever. The world is as it is. Perhaps, later, something might be done. Just wait. Meanwhile. . . . But the waiting is not long. Metamorphosis is at hand. Parents and teachers know that the principal agent of social conformity is puberty. As Old Faithful DNA triggers, on schedule, certain hormones, the bright outward-looking compassionate ten-year-old becomes like everyone else. Or sixteen equals cynicism equals a car.

From the cradle, our economic rulers-to-be are imbued with a strong sense of what they are entitled to, which is, technically speaking, 25 percent of the wealth of the United States. To make sure that they will be able to hold on to this entitlement, most of the boys and one of the girls want to be—what else?—lawyers. Dr. Coles keens: "it is unfair that a few be so very privileged and that the overwhelming majority be either hard-pressed or barely able to make do." He also worries that his own social-meliorizing views might have colored these stories because "one has to distinguish between social criticism and psychological observation." I can't think why. At least not in the case of Robert Coles. Whatever pretensions he may have as a scientific observer, he is essentially a moralist and, in these interesting stories, he has shown how the ruling class of an unjust society perpetuates itself through the indoctrination of its young.

Unfortunately, Dr. Coles does nothing much with his material. He is hortatory; good-hearted; vague. Were he less timid, he might have proposed a kind of socialism as partial solution to the "crisis." But like those collusive schoolteachers he writes about and resembles, he keeps within the familiar framework of a political system which is itself not only in crisis but the crisis. Although Dr. Coles's notes on contemporary children are in themselves of no particular urgency, they might one day serve as useful appendices to some yet to be written synthesizing work in which our peculiar society is looked at plain from an economic or political or (why not?) religious point of view.

*The New York Review of Books*
February 9, 1978

# 59
## *DRUGS*

It is possible to stop most drug addiction in the United States within a very short time. Simply make all drugs available and sell them at cost. Label each drug with a precise description of what effect—good and bad—the drug will have on the taker. This will require heroic honesty. Don't say that marijuana is addictive or dangerous when it is neither, as millions of people know—unlike "speed," which kills most unpleasantly, or heroin, which is addictive and difficult to kick.

For the record, I have tried—once—almost every drug and liked none, disproving the popular Fu Manchu theory that a single whiff of opium will enslave the mind. Nevertheless many drugs are bad for certain people to take and they should be told why in a sensible way.

Along with exhortation and warning, it might be good for our citizens to recall (or learn for the first time) that the United States was the creation of men who believed that each man has the right to do what he wants with his own life as long as he does not interfere with his neighbor's pursuit of happiness (that his neighbor's idea of happiness is persecuting others does confuse matters a bit).

This is a startling notion to the current generation of Americans. They reflect a system of public education which has made the Bill of Rights, literally, unacceptable to a majority of high school graduates (see the annual Purdue reports) who now form the "silent majority"—a phrase which that underestimated wit Richard Nixon took from Homer who used it to describe the dead.

Now one can hear the warning rumble begin: if everyone is allowed to take drugs everyone will and the GNP will decrease, the Commies will stop us from making everyone free, and we shall end up a race of Zombies, passively murmuring "groovie" to one another. Alarming thought. Yet it seems most unlikely that any reasonably sane person will become a drug addict if he knows in advance what addiction is going to be like.

Is everyone reasonably sane? No. Some people will always become drug addicts just as some people will always become alcoholics, and it is just too bad. Every man, however, has the power (and should have the legal right) to kill himself if he chooses. But since most men don't, they won't be mainliners either. Nevertheless, forbidding people things they like or think they might enjoy only makes them want those things all the more. This psychological insight is, for some mysterious reason, perennially denied our governors.

It is a lucky thing for the American moralist that our country has always existed in a kind of time-vacuum: we have no public memory of anything that happened before last Tuesday. No one in Washington today recalls what happened during the years alcohol was forbidden to the people by a Congress that thought it had a divine mission to stamp out Demon Rum—launching, in the process, the greatest crime wave in the country's history, causing thousands of deaths from bad alcohol, and creating a general (and persisting) contempt among the citizenry for the laws of the United States.

The same thing is happening today. But the government has learned nothing from past attempts at prohibition, not to mention repression.

Last year when the supply of Mexican marijuana was slightly curtailed by the Feds, the pushers got the kids hooked on heroin and deaths increased dramatically, particularly in New York. Whose fault? Evil men like the Mafiosi? Permissive Dr. Spock? Wild-eyed Dr. Leary? No.

The Government of the United States was responsible for those deaths. The bureaucratic machine has a vested interest in playing cops and robbers. Both the Bureau of Narcotics and the Mafia want strong laws against the sale and use of drugs because if drugs are sold at cost there would be no money in it for anyone.

If there was no money in it for the Mafia, there would be no friendly playground pushers, and addicts would not commit crimes to pay for the next fix. Finally, if there was no money in it, the Bureau of Narcotics would wither away, something they are not about to do without a struggle.

Will anything sensible be done? Of course not. The American people are as devoted to the idea of sin and its punishment as they are to making money—and fighting drugs is nearly as big a business as pushing them. Since the combination of sin and money is irresistible (particularly to the professional politician), the situation will only grow worse.

*The New York Times*
September 26, 1970

# 60

## THE FOUR GENERATIONS OF THE ADAMS FAMILY

The Inventors of the United States decided that there would be no hereditary titles in God's country. Although the Inventors were hostile to the idea of democracy and believed profoundly in the sacredness of property and the necessary dignity of those who owned it, they did not like the idea of king, duke, marquess, earl. Such a system of hereditary nobility was liable to produce aristocrats who tended to mix in politics (like the egregious Lord North) instead of politically responsible burghers.

But the Inventors were practical men and the federal constitution that they assembled in 1787 was an exquisite machine that, with a repair here and a twist there, has gone on protecting the property of the worthy for two hundred years while protecting in the Bill of Rights (that sublime afterthought) certain freedoms of speech and assembly which are still unknown even now to that irritable fount of America's political and actual being, old Europe. The Inventors understood human greed and self-interest. Combining brutal cynicism with a Puritan sense of virtue, they used those essential drives to power the machinery of the state.

Certainly none wanted to change the way people were. "As to political reformation in Europe or elsewhere," wrote conservative Inventor John Jay in 1796, "I confess that . . . I do not amuse myself with dreams about an age of reason. I am content that little men should be as free as big ones and have and enjoy the same rights, but nothing strikes me as more absurd than projects to stretch little men into big ones, or shrink big men into little ones. . . . We must take men and measures as they are, and act accordingly." That is the very voice of the American Inventors: conservative, commonsensical, and just—within (as opposed to the age of) reason.

At the Constitutional Convention in Philadelphia a few romantics fought a losing battle to make Washington king and to create a peerage using the odd title "margrave." The matter was then settled, the Inventors thought, once and for all. Government would be by the best people in order to forward the best interests of the country's owners. They might have invented the word "meritocracy" had they not had the same prejudice against neologisms that they had against new men.

But although America's "best" people were not to have titles, they did have names; they also acquired fortunes which they passed on to sons and to grandsons and to great-grandsons. As a result, the history of the American republic is the history of certain families, of names that are now every bit as awesome as titles.

First among the country's political families are the Adamses. In four successive generations the Adams family produced not only two presidents but a number of startlingly brilliant men and women, culminating in the country's only major historian, Henry Adams, the bright light of the fourth and the last splendid generation that ended with the death of Henry's brother Brooks Adams in 1927.

To try to understand the Adamses one must begin by placing them. The first Adams to come to America was a copy-hold farmer in Somerset, on land belonging to the Lord of the Manor of Barton St. David. For reasons unknown, this Henry Adams, with wife and nine children, emigrated to Boston in 1636. Possible sign of character? Of proto-Puritanism? Most English emigrants of that period preferred the balmy West Indies to the cold arduousness of New England.

Ten years later, Adams died, leaving a comfortable property. The next two generations produced dim but increasingly prosperous farmers. In the third generation, church deacon John Adams performed that obligatory act of all families destined to distinguish themselves. He committed hypergamy by marrying Susanna Boylston of Brookline, Massachusetts. The Boylstons were distinguished physicians and for an Adams to consort with a Boylston was very much a step up in that little world. Their first child was John Adams (born October 30, 1735); and with him the family entered history, remaining at the center of national and sometimes world affairs for nearly two centuries.

John Adams was a small plump man, fierce of face and brusque of manner, and very much unlike everyone else. Although he was a true child of the bleak New England countryside and mind, he was a good deal more complicated than any of the other Inventors, saving Jefferson. Adams kept, intermittently, a diary; he composed some chaotic fragments of autobiography; and he copied out most of his letters. Adams thought a very great deal about himself and of himself, and much of his worrying is now available in the many yards of microfilm that record his papers.

At the age of forty-four John Adams scrutinized his own character: "There is a Feebleness and a Languor in my Nature. My Mind and Body both partake of this Weakness." Like so many valetudinarians, John Adams suffered good health until the age of ninety-one. "By my Physical Constitution I am but an ordinary Man. The Times alone have destined me to Fame—and even these have not been able to give me much." Note the irritability; the sense that fate—or something—does not properly value him. This will be one of the family's important recurring motifs. "Yet some great Events, some cutting Expressions, some mean Hypocrisies, have at Times, thrown this Assemblage of Sloth, Sleep, and littleness into Rage a little like a Lion."

John Adams could not be better described. He was indeed born at the right time and in the right place, and at great moments he was more than a little like a lion. But he was also a Puritan. He worried about his vanity. When his legal career started to flourish, he wrote, "What is the end and purpose of my studies, journeys, labours . . . ? Am I grasping at money or scheming for power? Am I planning the illustration of my family or the welfare of my country? These are great questions. . . . Which of these lies nearest my heart?"

The answer of course is that all these things can dwell in reasonable harmony within the same great bosom. But only a New England Puritan would fret so. Certainly one does not find in Franklin, Jefferson or Washington any of the cold-eyed self-scrutiny that the first and all the subsequent Adamses turned upon themselves. Happily, the Adamses were not uncritical of others. In fact, a certain censoriousness is very much the family style. John Adams managed to quarrel hugely with Franklin, Jefferson, and, disastrously, with the co-leader of his own party Alexander Hamilton. He was also wary of the cold, self-loving, and self-satisfied grandeur of his predecessor in the office of first magistrate, George Washington.

In the New England slang of the day, Adams was "saucy." He was also prone to nervous breakdowns ("my Fidgets"). Peter Shaw* writes that "Adams suffered from a constantly rising temper at *anticipated* enmity. But when attacked directly he rarely took offense." Despising popularity, Adams required universal applause for his good works. Yet laurel wreaths tended to give him headaches for "Good Treatment makes me think I am admired, beloved and my own Vanity will be indulged in me. So I dismiss my Gard and grow weak, silly, vain, conceited, ostentatious. But a Check, a frown, a sneer, a Sarcasm . . . makes me more careful and considerate." Or, as Mr. Shaw puts it, "The truth was that from the beginning he courted not popularity but unpopularity as a mark of distinction."

The facts of John Adams's early career are unremarkable. He attended Harvard; studied law; was admitted to the bar in 1758 at Boston. Had the English Ministry not managed entirely to outrage its American colonies, John Adams would be known today, if at all, as a sharp New England lawyer who kept a diary not so good as Pepys's. As it was, by the age of thirty-six, he had the largest law practice in the colony. He owned a house at Braintree near Boston, and he commuted between the private practice of law and public life. "Farewell Politicks," he writes time and again. But with the American Revolution it was farewell to private life for thirty years.

"The year 1765 has been the most remarkable Year of my Life. That enormous Engine, fabricated by the British Parliament, for battering down all the Rights and Liberties of America, I mean the Stamp Act, has raised and spread, thro the whole Continent, a Spirit that will be recorded to our Honour, with all future Generations."

Adams was one of those chosen to present the objections of the people of Massachusetts to the taxes levied on them by the faraway Ministry at London. When selected by his fellow citizens, Adams wondered how it was that someone "unknown as I am" should have been thrust into history. Obviously some "secret invisible Laws of Nature" were at work. This is to be one of the family's principal themes, ultimately expressed in Henry Adams's theory of history.

Adams enjoyed describing the pathetic departure for Philadelphia of the Massachusetts delegates, "all destitute of Fortune, four poor Pilgrims, proceeded in one coach." Actually they were splendidly accompanied by two armed white servants and four blacks in livery.

But no matter how or why John Adams was chosen by the *Zeitgeist*

*The Character of John Adams* (University of North Carolina Press, 1976).

to lead, he more than any other Inventor prepared the way intellectually and rhetorically for Revolution, as we like to call the slow separation of the colonies from England. "I grounded my Argument on the Invalidity of the Stamp Act, it not being in any sense our Act, having never consented to it." Or, "No taxation without representation." With that mighty line, the United States were born as a political entity and in the two hundred years since that noble genesis the government of our states has blithely taxed other peoples from the far-off Filipinos to the nearby residents of the District of Columbia without for a moment allowing *them* representation.

Adams was a member of the Continental Congress from 1774 to 1778. By seconding the nomination of the Virginian George Washington as commander-in-chief, he ensured Washington's selection. Alas. From that moment on Adams tended to regard Washington rather the way Baron Frankenstein was to regard *his* handiwork. At forty, Adams toyed with the idea of winning glory as a soldier; but decided that he was "too old, and too much worn with fatigues of study in my youth." Yet he was three years younger than Washington; but then Washington had never fatigued himself with books.

In November 1777 Adams was bored with the Congress. But Congress was not bored with Adams. He was sent in February 1778 to France, to join the other American representatives there, chief among them Benjamin Franklin. Adams admitted that Franklin was "a great genius, a great wit, a great humorist, a great satirist, and a great politician." After all, Adams happened to be none of those things and did not value them. But he did doubt if Franklin was "a great philosopher, a great moralist, and a great statesman . . ." like John Adams.

He also deeply envied Franklin's charm and universal popularity ("I expect soon to see a proposition to name the 18th Century, the Franklinian Age"). He also found Franklin dissipated, lazy, and Frenchified. More in sorrow than in anger, Franklin observed that Adams was "in some things, absolutely out of his senses."

Adams took with him to Europe his ten-year-old son John Quincy, a future diplomat and president. The education of John Quincy Adams was to be the most superb of any of the American presidents, and consequently absolutely crippling. He was too brilliant and too addicted to toil; he knew too many languages, books, nations, political and philosophical systems to be able to preside with any grace or tolerance over the dingy republic of his day. But in late eighteenth-century Europe the boy was wide-eyed and impressionable. The world was his.

In due course, John Adams was chosen to negotiate the peace with England. After seven dreadful years Washington had finally blundered not into a clear-cut American victory over the English but into a situation where a nervous and weary Ministry at London wanted to cut its losses in America. Summarily, the English abandoned their former colonies and went home.

For three successive generations each head of the Adams family was, in a sense, made by England, for each was American minister at London during a crisis and each did his job satisfactorily, if sometimes tactlessly. Or as Sir John Temple noted of John Adams, "He is the most ungracious man I ever saw."

Negotiations with the English themselves were not as difficult for Adams as getting on with his two American co-negotiators Franklin and Jay: "the one malicious, the other, I think honest. . . . Franklin's cunning will be to divide us; to this end he will provoke, he will insinuate, he will intrigue, he will maneuver." As it turned out, Franklin was not all that bad and Jay was brilliant. Meanwhile, the fourteen-year-old John Quincy Adams left the school he was attending at The Hague and went off to be secretary to the American minister at St. Petersburg. The education was proceeding uniquely well. John Quincy now spoke French, Dutch, German; knew Latin and Greek.

In 1785 John Adams was appointed first American minister to England. By then Adams had been joined by his wife Abigail. In marrying the daughter of the noted Reverend William Smith and the very grand Elizabeth Quincy, Adams had, like his father, committed the obligatory act of hypergamy and his children were now related to *everyone* in Massachusetts.

The sharp-tongued Abigail was a devoted wife and a fine letter writer. Exactly a century ago, Charles Francis Adams edited some three hundred of the letters his grandparents wrote to each other. Now *The Book of Abigail and John*\* has just been published. This selection of letters between husband and wife is a good deal more lively than the demure 1876 arrangement. While Adams fretted about politics and history, Abigail was the efficient manager of the household and the farm. She had a first-rate mind and resented her own lack of education. In 1776, she wrote wistfully, "I always had a fancy for a closet with a window which I could peculiarly call my own." But she was, like it or not, farm-

---

\**Selected Letters of the Adams Family, 1762–1784,* edited by L. H. Butterfield et al. (Harvard University Press, 1975).

manager, wife, mother. Although the eldest son John Quincy Adams was, from the beginning, a paragon, the second son Charles took to drink and died at thirty, while a daughter married not too well. But Abigail's principal interest was her prickly husband and their marriage was happy.

Abigail's political judgment was often shrewd. Rightly suspicious of Jefferson and the Virginians, she wondered whether or not these slave owners could truly possess a "passion for Liberty" when they "have been accustomed to deprive their fellow creatures of theirs." Yet she did her best to keep smooth relations between John Adams and Jefferson.

In 1788 Adams returned home where he was much admired for his labors in England. Everyone quoted his prescription for the new republic, "a government of laws and not of men." But like his descendants, Adams could never *not* express himself. In a lengthy treatise on the various American state constitutions, he made it plain that the country ought to be governed by "the rich, the well-born and the able." But the poor, the ill-born, and the incompetent, that is to say the majority, disliked this bold elitism, and Adams was to suffer to the end of his career gibes accusing him of being in favor of monarchy and aristocracy.

Democracy, Adams believed, was "the most ignoble, unjust and detestable form of government." The other Inventors agreed. But then, early on, they had a great fright. Before the separation from England only men of property could vote in Massachusetts. After independence, only men of property could vote in Massachusetts; but the property qualifications were doubled. A number of former soldiers led by one Daniel Shays revolted. Shays's Rebellion was quickly put down. In the process, the Inventors came to the conclusion that a relatively strong federal constitution was needed to make thirteen loosely allied states into a single nation with the sort of powers that would discourage rebellion and protect property. Carefully, they limited the franchise to some 700,000 propertied adult males. Out of a total population of 3,250,000, slaves, indentured servants, and convicts comprised nearly a third of the total. The Inventors also devised an Electoral College to choose president and vice president. As expected, George Washington was unanimously elected president while the man who got the second most votes in the College became vice president. On April 21, 1789, John Adams began the first of two terms as vice president.

Adams was much misunderstood during this period. Although he had never been a lover of Demos, he was not in favor of aristocracy. Yet, according to Mr. Shaw, "he forged an enduring reputation as a champion of aristocracy by the manner in which he opposed himself to it:

namely by warning that aristocrats were dangerous because superior."
Also, he did himself harm when "Apparently unaware of the new
prestige of equality, he defended the people while emphasizing their
inferiority." Thus was laid the curse upon the house of Adams.

Nicknamed "His Rotundity," Adams presided over the Senate, and
waited his turn to replace Washington. That turn almost never came,
thanks to Alexander Hamilton. In many ways the most brilliant as well
as the most unstable of the Inventors, Hamilton was magically beguiling
when he chose to be, particularly with doting older men like George
Washington. During the eight years of Washington's presidency, Secretary of the Treasury Hamilton was, in effect, the actual ruler of the
United States. Hamilton's preeminence did not please his senior the vice
president. Because of an untidy private life, foreign birth, and a personality calculated to make the ill-born froth with Jacobin sentiments,
Hamilton was never himself a candidate for president. But he did his
best to make Adams's elevation not the natural thing it ought to have
been but a complicated near-miss. Adams defeated Jefferson by only
three votes.

In 1875, that glorious crook, contender for the presidency, and nobody's fool James G. Blaine was firmly opposed to the idea of nominating for president John Adams's grandson Charles Francis Adams.
Blaine was firm: both President John Adams and his son President John
Quincy Adams had each managed to kill his party. The Republican
party of 1875 might be defeated and still survive, said Blaine, "but if it
should win with Adams it would never live again." In one sense, this
was very much a bum rap for the Adamses since their parties were, in
any case, deteriorating. Yet it is true that their overwhelming *amour-
propre* was such that they were hopeless when it came to the greasy art
of survival in American politics. Although they were sly enough to rise
to the top, they were never sufficiently adhesive to stay there.

John Adams began his presidency in a sour mood. He had nearly been
robbed of the office by Hamilton. At the inaugural, Washington got all
the attention: "He seemed to enjoy a triumph over me." The man he
trusted least, the head of the Republican party, Thomas Jefferson, was
vice president. Nevertheless, Adams decided to do his best to transcend
faction, and so made the fatal mistake of retaining George Washington's
cabinet. This group of second-raters was for the most part loyal to
Alexander Hamilton, now practicing law at New York and dreaming
of one day leading a great army into Mexico and South America in order
to make himself another Bonaparte.

But for Hamilton to raise a great army he needed a war. After much intrigue, Hamilton nearly maneuvered the United States into a war with France (one issue: Talleyrand had suggested that to keep the peace a bribe might be in order; virtuous United Statesmen were outraged). The Republican party under Jefferson was not only pro-French but opposed to standing armies, taxes, and all the accouterments of that nation-state which Hamilton saw as inevitable and desirable. Although Adams did his best to maintain the peace, Hamilton orchestrated the war-scare so skillfully that Adams was obliged to call Washington out of retirement to take charge of a mobilization.

Ever obedient to the beloved Hamilton, Washington insisted that Adams make Hamilton the ranking major-general of the army. Overwhelmed by *force majeure* from Mount Vernon, Adams gave way. Hamilton could now attend cabinet meetings; organize the coming war with France; and plan the eventual conquest of Latin America. But Adams was not without cunning. He continued to play up to the jingoes while quietly preparing an accommodation with France. Shortly before the election of 1800, the president's own minister to France made peace.

Finished as a party leader, Hamilton felt obliged to damage if not destroy Adams. With that creative madness for which he was noted, Hamilton wrote a "secret" attack on the president while, quixotically, proposing that of course he be re-elected. Aaron Burr got a copy of Hamilton's pamphlet and published it, fatally splitting the Federalist party. Even so, had Burr not carried New York State for Jefferson and himself, Adams would have been re-elected. As it was, Adams spent his last days in office at the new and dreadful "city" of Washington, creating Federalist judges. The most significant act of John Adams's presidency was the appointment of John Marshall to be chief justice. More than any other Inventor, the conservative Marshall defined the United States and shaped its Constitution.

During the war-scare, the infamous Alien and Sedition Acts were passed by a panicky Congress, and Adams had the bad sense to sign them. In effect, they suspended freedom of speech "in the national interest," as the Nixonians used to say. Historians have tended to be overwhelmed by this blot on the Adams administration; yet hardly any historian, retrospectively, much minds the fact that the sainted Lincoln suspended habeas corpus during the Civil War. Actually, it was not the high-handed attitude toward civil rights that harmed the Federalists but, as John Quincy Adams wrote, "The [creation of] the army was the first decisive symptom of a schism in the Federal Party itself, which accomplished its final overthrow and that of the administration."

Nevertheless, Adams continued to feel guilty about having signed into law measures designed to curtail free speech and assembly. A decade later he blamed the Alien and Sedition Acts on Hamilton. "Congress, however, adopted both these measures." Then he trims. After all, they were "War measures" and "I knew there was need enough of both, and therefore I consented to them." Abigail was a good deal firmer. Referring to an offensive editor, "In any other Country [he] and all his papers would have been seazd and ought to be here, but Congress are dilly dallying about passing a Bill enabling the President to seize suspisious Persons and their papers."

Refusing to remain in Washington for the inauguration of his successor Thomas Jefferson, Adams went home to Massachusetts where he lived for another twenty-six years, eating too much, reading Cicero, following with delighted apprehension his son's rise in the world. Although he wanted his son to succeed, the Puritan in John Adams insisted that noble failure was the only grace to be longed for. In 1808, he wrote, "Happy will you be if you can be turned out as your Father has been. . . ." But in 1825, John Quincy Adams became the president. His father wrote Jefferson, with whom he had become reconciled, "He appeared to be almost as much your boy as mine."

Summing up his own career, Adams wrote, "I cannot repent of anything I ever did conscientiously and from a sense of duty. I never engaged in public affairs for my own interest, pleasure, envy, jealousy, avarice, or ambition, or even the desire of fame." Excepting "pleasure" and perhaps "avarice," Adams listed his own peculiar faults. Yet he was by no means an opportunist. In fact, he believed that his best act as president was the one that cost him re-election: "I desire no other inscription over my gravestone than: 'Here lies John Adams, who took upon himself the responsibility of the peace with France in the year 1800.' "

On the mantelpiece of the dining room at the White House is carved a line from one of Adams's letters to his wife, "May none but honest and wise men ever rule under this roof."

When John Adams ceased to be president, his son John Quincy Adams was thirty-three years old and the ablest of America's diplomats. In 1791 John Quincy was in London, helping John Jay negotiate a treaty. Although John Quincy was now too grand to stoop to hypergamy, he did manage to bring into the family a new type. Louisa Johnson was the daughter of the American consul general at London. Mr. Johnson was a feckless Marylander married to an Englishwoman. Brought up in

Europe, Louisa was "charming, like a Romney portrait," according to her grandson Henry Adams, "but among her many charms that of being a New England woman was not one." Louisa did not take to Boston or Braintree ("Had I stepped into Noah's Ark, I do not think I could have been more utterly astonished"). Happily, the old President took to her. She also made John Quincy a good wife; but then great men seldom make bad marriages.

Nevertheless, in a recent biography of John Quincy Adams,* Marie B. Hecht (who annoyingly refers to her subject as "Johnny") suggests that the marriage must have been rather hard-going for the Europeanized Louisa, who once confided to her son Charles Francis that the Adams men were "peculiarly harsh and severe with their women." Frequent miscarriages, bouts of fainting and illness were to be Louisa's revenge. But her husband never varied from his view that "political subserviency and domestic influence must be the lot of women. . . ." Also, to be fair, he was as hard and severe with himself as he was with others.

John Quincy disliked the idea of holding diplomatic posts under his father. Uncharacteristically, Washington himself wrote to the new president John Adams, expressing the hope "that you will not withhold merited promotion from Mr. John (Quincy) Adams because he is your son." So John Quincy Adams was posted American minister to Prussia 1797–1801. He then returned to Boston ostensibly to practice law but actually to become the president. He served as a commissioner in bankruptcy until removed by President Jefferson (who later, disingenuously, denied any knowledge of this petty act against the son of his predecessor). After service in the Massachusetts state legislature, John Quincy was sent to the United States Senate in 1803. As senator, he showed a complete independence of party, supporting Jefferson's Embargo Act. Consequently "the Republicans trampled upon the Federalists, and the Federalists trampled upon John Quincy Adams."

Personally, John Quincy was esteemed but not much liked. He himself liked neither political party: "between both, I see the impossibility of pursuing the dictates of my own conscience, without sacrificing every prospect, not merely of advancement, but even of retaining that character and reputation I have enjoyed. Yet my own choice is made, and if I cannot hope to give satisfaction to my country, I am at least determined to have the approbation of my own reflections."

*John Quincy Adams: A Personal History of an Independent Man* (Macmillan, 1972).

But presently John Quincy gave satisfaction both to country and self. After losing his seat in the Senate, he served four years as President Madison's minister to Russia during the War of 1812. Czar Alexander took to John Quincy and kept open Russian ports to American shipping. In 1812 John Quincy Adams was appointed one of the commissioners to make peace with England, the meetings to be held at Ghent.

Among the other four commissioners were the brilliant Albert Gallatin, Geneva-born secretary of the treasury to Jefferson, and the rising Kentucky lawyer and quadrennial presidential candidate Henry Clay. They shared the same house in Ghent. Clay wanted to sit up all night and gamble while Adams liked to go to bed at nine; wild oats seem never to have been planted (at least visibly) in the garden of any Adams. John Quincy particularly avoided actresses "because," he writes in old age, "the first woman I ever loved was an actress, but I never spoke to her, and I think I never saw her off the stage. . . . Of all the ungratified longings that I ever suffered, that of being acquainted with her, merely to tell her how much I adored her, was the most intense." At the time this Laura and Petrarch were each fourteen years old. The Puritan must suffer or he is not good.

Clay had been as responsible as any American leader for the 1812 war with England (he particularly wanted to annex Canada); consequently, he was quite willing to prolong the war in order "to make us a warlike people." But John Quincy was not a war-lover; he also knew that the English Ministry was unhappy with a war that could not be won, particularly at a time when not only had Castlereagh managed to antagonize both Russia and Prussia but Lord Liverpool's Government was being much criticized for imposing a property tax in order to prosecute a far-off war. On December 24, 1814, the treaty of Ghent was signed. Two weeks later, a wild Tennessee backwoodsman named Andrew Jackson won a mighty victory over English troops at New Orleans. The fact that the war was already over made the victory no less sweet for the humiliated Americans, and the political star of Jackson was now in the ascendant.

Like his father before him, John Quincy Adams was appointed minister to England. For two years the Adamses lived at Ealing; they were pressed for money, which was just as well for they were not much sought after by London society. For one thing, Americans of any kind were less than the vogue; for another, Adamses can never be in vogue. But John Quincy's eye was as sharp as ever. Of Castlereagh he wrote, "His manner was cold, but not absolutely repulsive." He did enjoy Holland House and what intellectual company came his way. Yet he was eager to go home. He feared expatriation—taking on "an European disposition" and then, returning home, "a stranger in his own country." Meanwhile, his son Charles Francis Adams was initiated to the glories and miseries of the English public school, where being an American was not a passport to gentle treatment.

For some time John Quincy had been a Republican. As early as 1802, he wrote his brother Tom: "I concur with you in the opinion that the cause of federalism is irretrievable." The old Federalist party had indeed fallen apart. Everyone was now a Republican of one sort or another. The Western leader of the party was Henry Clay, closely pressed by Andrew Jackson. John Quincy himself was not a man of locality: "My system of politics more and more inclines to strengthen the union and the government." Yet when he heard an American jingo say, as a toast, "Our country, right or wrong," John Quincy responded severely: "I disclaim all patriotism incompatible with the principles of eternal justice." As far as we know, it never occurred to any Adams of the Four Generations that there might be no such thing as eternal justice. The first Adams believed in the Puritan God. The second was equally devout (until the very end). In the last generations overt religion vanished almost entirely from their voluminous letters and diaries; nevertheless, the idea of eternal justice, of moral right, of some essential and binding law to the universe never ceased to order their lives.

President Monroe appointed John Quincy to be his secretary of state, at that time the second most important office in the land and the surest way to the presidency. The eight years that John Quincy served President Monroe were known as the era "of good feelings." It was indeed a tribute to John Quincy's pronounced excellence that he was given the post; for Monroe was a Virginian and the Virginians had governed the United States from the beginning: Washington, Jefferson, Madison, and Monroe dominated the nation for thirty-six years with only one break, the four years that John Adams of Massachusetts was president.

John Quincy was not delighted with cabinet life: "There is a slowness, want of decision, and a spirit of procrastination in the President, which perhaps arouses more from his situation than his personal character." Experiencing flak from the ambitious Clay and his other rivals for the presidency Jackson and Crawford, John Quincy wrote: "My office . . . makes it for the interest of all the partisans of the candidates for the next Presidency . . . to decry me as much as possible." "Always complain, but superbly explain" could be the Adams family motto.

Although John Quincy was generally admired for his intellectual brilliancy and hard work—certainly he was our best secretary of state—he was filled with the usual Adams misgivings. When he gave a reception, he was certain that no one would come. He was afraid of either talking too much or too little. The ladies of the family worried about his shabby appearance. Watery of eye, tremulous of hand, he grew fat, and flatulent. He feared—but finally dared—to eat a peach. With quiet satisfaction, he confided to his diary: "I am a man of reserved, cold, austere and forbidding manners. . . ." He was prone to such solitary pleasures as swimming in the Potomac River, wearing nothing but a black swimming cap and green goggles. Much of the time he was bored by the politicians he had to deal with. But when he was stimulated intellectually, he could be eloquent.

During this period, General Andrew Jackson was on the rampage in the Spanish Floridas, hanging people right and left, including two Englishmen. Yet John Quincy did his best to defend Jackson (a man of whom Jefferson wrote: Now he is *really* crazy!). In the process Adams helped formulate what is known as the Monroe Doctrine—that no European power may interfere in the Western hemisphere while no American government will interfere in Europe. This proud doctrine is still, theoretically, in force although it ceased to have any meaning when the United States went to war with the Central Powers in 1917.

Jackson's filibuster-capers appealed hugely to the electorate and in 1824, under the system of the Electoral College, Jackson received 99 votes for president; Adams, 84; Crawford, 41; Clay, 37. Since no candidate had the required majority, the election went into the House of Representatives for decision. Rightly, Clay feared Jackson, the hero of New Orleans, more than he did John Quincy. Clay gave his support to John Quincy Adams, who became president in February 1825. Clay was then appointed secretary of state. Everyone cried "Foul," and John Quincy was held to be corrupt by all Jackson men and a good many disinterested worthies as well.

Now, once again, there was a President Adams; and he proved to be every bit as wounded in his *amour-propre,* as bitter as the first Adams who wrote from Massachusetts: "My dear son, Never did I feel so much solemnity as upon this occasion. The multitude of my thoughts, and the intensity of my feelings are too much for a mind, like mine, in its 90th year."

The administration of John Quincy Adams proved to be even more of a disaster than that of his father. Jackson and his allies were rightly indignant at losing an election in which Jackson had, after all, got the most votes; they also regarded as corrupt the alliance between John Quincy and Clay. Nor did the new president very much like or understand the country he presided over. For one thing, democracy had made a sudden advance with universal suffrage—that is, any free man over twenty-one could now vote. The rule by "the best" was ended once and for all.

John Quincy saw what was coming but he meant to hold the line, and his first inaugural address was a challenge to the democrats: "While foreign nations, less blessed with that freedom which is power than ourselves" (obligatory gesture to Demos) "are advancing with gigantic strides in the career of public improvements, are we to slumber in our indolence or fold up our arms and proclaim to the world that we are *palsied by the will of our constituents?*" There sounded for the last time *ex cathedra presidentis* the voice of the original Inventors of the nation.

John Quincy had great plans to foster education, science, commerce, civil service reform; but his projects were too rigorous and too unpolitical to be accepted. For instance, the United States had not one astronomical station while in Europe there were 130 "lighthouses of the sky." This happy phrase was received with perfect derision by the mob. It was plain that John Quincy was not suited to lead a quasi-democracy. He was too intelligent, too unyielding, too tactless. He also found hard to bear the inanities of political attack (he was supposed to have supplied a lecherous Russian nobleman with an innocent American girl). Needless to say, Jackson swamped him in the next election. The Jackson slogan was prophetic of the era: "Jackson who can fight, and Adams who can write."

But John Quincy saw the future more clearly than most of the mob-pleasing politicians. Of slavery he wrote privately in 1820, it is "an outrage upon the goodness of God." But at the time he stayed clear of the subject because he saw that any challenge to the slave-owning states would lead to the dissolution of the Union. In 1837, after President Jackson's savage treatment of the Creeks and Cherokees, John Quincy wrote: "We have done more harm to the Indians since our Revolution than had been done to them by the French and English nations before. . . . These are crying sins for which we are answerable before a higher Jurisdiction."

"Three days more, and I shall be restored to private life . . . I go into it with a combination of parties and of public men against my character and reputation such as I believe never before was exhibited. . . ." Pure Adams, the self-pity; but not so far off the mark.

Like his father, John Quincy Adams refused to attend the inaugural of his successor. Back in Massachusetts, he started to put his father's papers in order but this bookish task bored him. He was not cut out for libraries and retirement. To the horror of his son Charles Francis Adams, John Quincy "demeaned" himself and went back to Washington as a mere representative to Congress, where he served in the House until his death seventeen years later. As Emerson rather unexpectedly wrote, "Mr. Adams chose wisely and according to his constitution, when, on leaving the presidency, he went into Congress. He is no literary old gentleman, but a bruiser, and he loves the *mélée*. . . . He is an old *roué* who cannot live on slops, but must have sulphuric acid in his tea."

Certainly John Quincy Adams's most useful period was the last when he was obliged to enter the hurly-burly at something of a disadvantage. For one thing, his voice was weak, his manner tentative: "It is so long since I was in the habit of speaking to a popular assembly, and I am so little qualified by nature for an extemporaneous orator, that I was at the time not a little agitated by the sound of my own voice." But he persisted, fighting and eventually winning the battle to admit those petitions against slavery that the House would not for years entertain. He helped create the Smithsonian Institution. He denounced the American conquest of Mexico which added Texas and California to the empire. Then, in the midst of a debate, he collapsed on the floor of the House; he was taken to the Speaker's chambers. On February 23, 1848, he died. Final words: "This is the last of earth. I am composed."

The Third Generation was on the rise. Charles Francis Adams had commited hypergamy in the sense that he was the first Adams to marry a lot of money in the shape of Abigail Brooks, who, according to one of her children, took a "constitutional and sincere pleasure in the forecast of evil. She delighted in the dark side of anticipation." Four of her sons were to be remarkable in the next generation: John Quincy II, Charles Francis II, Henry, and Brooks. Like all the Adamses the sons were voluminous writers and Henry was a writer of genius even though his brother Charles wrote rather better prose. Their father also wrote copiously or, as his son Charles observed glumly, while writing his father's biography: "He took to diary writing early, and he took to it bad." Mark Twain apologized to William Dean Howells for using "three words where one would answer—a thing I am always trying to guard against. I shall become as slovenly a writer as Charles Francis Adams if I don't look out. . . ."

It is during the Fourth Generation that the high moral style of the early and the puissant Adamses is now tinged with irony, that necessary weapon of the powerless. There was to be no more life at the very top for the family but there were still good, even great things to be done.

Of his father Charles Francis Adams, Henry wrote, "[his] memory was hardly above the average; his mind was not bold like his grandfather's or restless like his father's, or imaginative, or oratorical—still less mathematical; but it worked with singular perfection. . . . Within its range it was a model." The range included diplomacy and the by now inevitable family post of minister at London. Charles Francis was minister during the difficult years 1861–1868 when a powerful movement in England favored the Confederacy for reasons both sentimental and practical. The despised colonies of four-score years before had now become a predatory and dangerous empire, filling up the North American continent and threatening, by its existence, the British Empire. The vision of the United States split into two countries brought roses to many a cheek both on the government and the opposition benches.

Adams went about his work of keeping England neutral with that coolness which had caused a political associate to describe him as "the greatest Iceberg in the Northern Hemisphere." Or as this solemn gelidity himself put it: "My practice has been never to manifest feeling of any kind, either of elation or of depression. In this, some Englishmen have taken occasion to intimate that I have been thought quite successful."

Paradoxically, much of the pro-Southern sentiment in England came from those who abominated the peculiar institution of slavery. Although they disapproved of the slave-holding South, they saw Lincoln as a ruthless despot, trying to hold together by force a union that was constitutionally based on the right of any state to leave that union when it chose. Lincoln was never, to say the least, devoted to the abolition of slavery; and not until the third year of the war to preserve the union did he free the slaves in the Confederacy (slaves were not freed in those states that had not seceded). Consequently Charles Francis was forced to listen to much sharp criticism from high-minded anti-slave Englishmen while his son Henry (acting as the minister's secretary) was denounced in the street for Lincoln's wickedness by Thackeray.

The chief crisis in Anglo-American relations during Charles Francis's ministry was the *Alabama* affair. The *Alabama* was a formidable warship built at Liverpool for the South. Charles Francis maintained that if the English allowed such a ship to be built and armed, they automatically ceased to be neutral. Foreign Secretary Lord John Russell asked for proof of the ship's ultimate use. When this was provided, the attorney general supported Charles Francis and recommended that the ship be seized. But by then the *Alabama* had sailed. The American minister then proceeded to keep careful count of each ship sunk by the *Alabama* in the course of the war and later saw to it that England paid the bill.

When another ship destined for the Confederacy was ready to go to sea and Lord John seemed unwilling to stop it, Charles Francis played the diplomat's ultimate card: "it would be superfluous in me to point out to your lordship that this is war." Three days later Lord John seized the Southern warships.

Now the focus shifts to the Fourth Generation. Henry Adams in his autobiography writes a good deal about his formative years in London as his father's secretary. Although there is little doubt that Henry inherited the family passion to be the first in the nation, it was already plain to him that the plutocratic-democracy was not apt to take well to one with such an "education." The age of the robber barons was now in full swing. Shysters like Jay Gould and Jim Fisk controlled the economic life of the country, buying and selling members of Congress—and presidents, too. Although Henry's father was, from time to time, mentioned for president, no one ever took very seriously this brilliant, cold man who spoke French better than English.

Of the four sons of Charles Francis only John Quincy II got into elective politics. And failed. Just as he failed to get out from under the weight of the family's intellectual tradition by, among other things, abandoning "the vile family habit of preserving letters."

The second son Charles Francis II was a marvelous scribbler; also, a man of action. After examining in detail the misdeeds of the railroad tycoons (published in a volume called *Chapters of Erie,* with several essays by his brother Henry), he himself became a railroad tycoon and president of the Union Pacific. The next brother, Henry, was to write the finest of American histories as well as one of our few good political novels. The youngest brother, Brooks, was also a writer very much in the Adams (by now) highly pessimistic vein. In fact, it is he who rather gives the game away with the title he chose for a posthumous edition of some of his brother Henry's essays, *The Degradation of the Democratic Dogma.*

I cannot remember when I was not fascinated by Henry Adams. I was brought up in Washington; belonged to a political family; and used often to pass the site of the house where Adams had lived in Lafayette Park, just opposite the White House.

Once I asked Eleanor Roosevelt if she had known Henry Adams, who died in 1918. "Oh, yes! He was such a kind man, so good with the children. They would crawl all over him when he sat in his victoria. He was very . . . tolerant. But," and she frowned, "we did *not* agree politically. I remember the first time we went to his house. My Franklin had just come to Washington" (as assistant secretary of the navy) "and I of course was very shy then and could never get the courage to speak up, particularly with someone so much older. Well, my Franklin made some remark about President Wilson, about how well he was doing. And Mr. Adams just laughed at him and pointed toward the White House and said, 'Young man, it doesn't make the slightest difference who lives in that house, history goes on with or without the president.' Well, I just couldn't keep quiet. 'Mr. Adams,' I said, 'that is a very terrible thing to say to a young man who wants to go into politics and be of use to other people.' Oh, I made quite a speech."

"And what did Mr. Adams say?"

"I can't remember. I think he just laughed at me. We were always good friends."

So the great Adams line ended with a theory of history that eliminated Carlyle's hero and put in its stead something like Hegel's "course of the divine life." Yet one can see from the beginning the family's dependency on fate, on some inscrutable power at work in the universe which raised men up or cut them down, and guided nations. At the beginning this was, plainly, the work of the Puritan God. Later, when that god failed, it was simply energy or "the Dynamo," as Henry Adams called those "secret invisible Laws of Nature" that hurl this petty race through time and spinning space.

There was more than a degree of sourness in Henry's old age; after all, he was living across the park from the White House where grandfather and great-grandfather had presided. As compensation, his beautiful memoir is filled with a good deal of mock humility, confessions of "failure," and a somewhat overwrought irony. "I like [Henry]," wrote Henry James, "but suffer from his monotonous, disappointed pessimism. . . . However, when the poor dear is in London, I don't fail to do what I can."

But, politically, Henry Adams was not without influence; his best friend and next-door neighbor was that most literary of secretaries of state John Hay, while Adams himself was always at the center of the capital's intellectual life. Invitations to his house were much sought after; yet he "called on no one and never left a card." Henry James in a short story set in Washington describes a distinguished figure based on Henry Adams. As the character draws up a guest list for a party, he says, finally, wearily: "Well, why not be vulgar? Let us ask the President."

Henry Adams was remarkably prescient about the coming horrors; like his mother he anticipated the worst. Before the First World War, he prophesied the decline of England and France, and the rise of the United States, Russia and Germany. But in the long run, he felt that Germany was too small a power "to swing the club." Ultimately, he saw the world in two blocs: the east dominated by Russia; the west dominated by the United States. He also predicted that should Russia and China ever come together "the result will be a single mass which no amount of force could possibly deflect." He predicted that this great mass would be both socialist and despotic; and its only counterbalance would be an "Atlantic combine," stretching from "the Rocky Mountains on the west to the Elbe on the east." Henry Adams always used what influence he had to try to persuade the various American administrations to bring Russia into our sphere of influence.

The last days of Henry Adams were spent trying to understand the forces that control history. He wanted an equivalent in history to Einstein's never-to-be-found unified field theory. The best Henry Adams could come up with was a chapter of the memoir called "A Dynamic Theory of History"; and it was not enough. Finally, Adams abandoned history altogether. "I don't give a damn what happened," he wrote, "what I want to know is why it happened—never could find out—stopped writing history."

How would John Adams have responded to such despair? In his college diary he copied out *Contemptu Famae, Contemni Virtutem,* which he translated as "A Contempt of Fame generally begets or accompanies a Contempt of Virtue." And then he adds: "Iago makes the reflection that Fame is but breath, but vibrated Air, an empty sound. And I believe Persons of his Character are most inclined to feel and express such an Indifference about fame." No Adams was ever, to himself, truly famous and so all Adamses thought themselves used poorly by fate. But then from the beginning they set themselves intellectual and moral standards that no one could live up to. With Puritan vigor they positively insisted on noble failure in a society that has always been devoted to easy, crass success. So let us, late in the day as it is, praise such famous men.

*The New York Review of Books*
March 18 and April 1, 1976

---

# FIRST NOTE ON
# ABRAHAM LINCOLN

In "Patriotic Gore," Edmund Wilson wrote, "There are moments when one is tempted to feel that the cruelest thing that has happened to Lincoln since he was shot by Booth has been to fall into the hands of Carl Sandburg." The late Mr. Sandburg was a public performer of the first rank ("Ker-oh-seen!" he crooned in one of the first TV pitches for the jet-engine—ole banjo on his knee, white hair mussed by the jet-stream), a poet of the second rank (who can ever forget that feline-footed fog?) and a biographer of awesome badness. Unfortunately, the success of his four-volume *Abraham Lincoln: The War Years* was total. In the course of several million clumsily arranged words, Sandburg managed to reduce one of the most interesting and subtle men in world history to a cornball Disneyland waxwork rather like . . . yes, Carl Sandburg himself.

The real Lincoln is elsewhere. He is to be found, for those able to read old prose, in his own writings. According to Lincoln's law partner William Herndon: "He was the most continuous and severest thinker in America. He read but little and that for an end. Politics was his Heaven and his Hades metaphysics." Lincoln read and reread Shakespeare; he studied Blackstone's legal commentaries. And that was about it. Biographies bored him; he read no novels. Yet, somehow (out of continuous and severe thinking?), he became a master of our most difficult language, and the odd music to his sentences is unlike that of anyone else—with the possible exception of Walt Whitman on a clear unweepy day.

The principal source for Lincoln's pre-presidential life is Herndon. For eighteen years they were close friends as well as colleagues; they traveled the circuit together in Illinois; they shared an office in Springfield. After Lincoln was murdered, Herndon began to collect every bit of information that he could find about his fallen friend. Unlike most obscure associates of the great, Herndon was not interested in cutting Lincoln down to valet-size; or even to cash in. In fact, Herndon generously gave to any and every biographer not only his personal recollections of Lincoln but the notes that he had compiled during his long investigation of Lincoln's somewhat murky antecedents. Since Lincoln was said to have been illegitimate, Herndon talked to those who had known his mother, Nancy Hanks, and her husband, Thomas Lincoln. Herndon was told by an eyewitness that Thomas (viewed at the old swimming hole) dramatically lacked a number of those parts that are necessary for propagation. After studying all the evidence, Herndon decided that Thomas must have started out fully equipped and so was able to father Abraham off Nancy Hanks who was, according to Lincoln himself, illegitimate: "the daughter of a Virginia grandee." Romantics have often suggested that John C. Calhoun was Nancy's father. But if Lincoln knew who his real grandfather was, he never told Herndon.

The Sandburg–Mount Rushmore Lincoln is a solemn gloomy cuss, who speaks only in iambic pentameter, a tear forever at the corner of his eye—the result, no doubt, of being followed around by the Mormon Tabernacle Choir, which keeps humming "The Battle Hymn of the Republic" behind him while the future ambassador Shirley Temple Black curls up in his lap. The official Lincoln is warm, gentle, shy, modest . . . everything a great man is supposed to be in Sandburg-land but never is in life. As Lincoln's secretary John Hay put it: "No great man is ever modest. It was his intellectual arrogance and unconscious assumption of superiority that men like Chase and Sumner could never forgive."

The actual Lincoln was cold and deliberate, reflective and brilliant. In private life, he had no intimates except Herndon—and their relationship ended when he became president. In family life Lincoln was most forbearing of Mary Todd—a highly intelligent woman who went mad—and he spoiled his sons. That was the extent of the private Lincoln. The rest was public.

Honest Abe the rail-splitter was the creation of what must have been the earliest all-out PR campaign for a politician. Lincoln was born poor; but so were a great many successful lawyers in his part of the world. By the time he was elected president, he was a well-to-do lawyer, representing the railroad interests as well as the common man. From the beginning, Lincoln knew he was going to be, somehow, great. "His ambition," wrote Herndon, "was a little engine that knew no rest."

Herndon has his biases. He disliked Mary Todd and he tends to exaggerate her bad temper while pushing the story of Lincoln's love for Anne Rutledge, a highly dubious business. Usually, when Herndon repeats secondhand stories, he says that they are just that. When he speaks with firsthand knowledge, he is to be trusted.

It will come as a terrible shock to many of those who have been twice-born in the capacious bosom of Jesus to learn that Lincoln not only rejected Christianity but wrote a small book called "Infidelity" (meaning lack of faith in God). Lincoln "read his manuscript to Samuel Hill, his employer (who) said to Lincoln: 'Lincoln, let me see your manuscript.' Lincoln handed it to him. Hill ran it in a tin-plate stove, and so the book went up in flames. Lincoln in that production attempted to show that the Bible was false: first on the grounds of reason, and, second, because it was self-contradictory; that Jesus was not the son of God any more than any man." Later, in the presidency, pressure was brought on Lincoln to start putting God into his speeches. At the beginning, he did so in the vague sense of the Almighty or heaven. Later, there is a good deal of God in the speeches but no mention of Jesus. At heart, Lincoln was a fatalist, a materialist of the school of Democritus and Lucretius.

Devotees of the Mount Rushmore school of history like to think that the truly great man is a virgin until his wedding night; and a devoted monogamist thereafter. Apparently, Lincoln was indeed "true as steel" to Mary Todd even though, according to Herndon, "I have seen women make advances and I have seen Lincoln reject or refuse them. Lincoln had terrible strong passions for women, could scarcely keep his hands off them, and yet he had honor and a strong will, and these enabled him to put out the fires of his terrible passion." But in his youth he was seriously burned by those fires. In the pre-penicillin era syphilis was epidemic—and, usually, incurable. According to Herndon: "About the year 1835–36 Mr. Lincoln went to Beardstown and during a devilish passion had connection with a girl and caught the disease. Lincoln told me this. . . ." Later, after a long siege, Lincoln was cured, if he was cured, by a Dr. Daniel Drake of Cincinnati.

Herndon suspected that Lincoln might have given Mary Todd syphilis. If he had, that would have explained the premature deaths of three Lincoln children: "Poor boys, they are dead now and gone! I should like to *know* one thing and that is: What caused the death of these children? I have an opinion which I shall never state to anyone." So states to everyone Herndon. The autopsy on Mary Todd showed a physical deterioration of the brain consistent with paresis. If Lincoln had given his wife syphilis and if he had, inadvertently, caused the death of his children, the fits of melancholy are now understandable—and unbearably tragic.

The public Lincoln has been as mythologized as the private Lincoln. As a congressman, he had opposed the 1846 war with Mexico—a nasty business, started by us in order to seize new territories. In a speech that was to haunt him thirteen years later, he declared, "Any people anywhere being inclined and having the power have the right to rise up and shake off the existing government, and form a new one that suits them better. . . . Any portion of such people that can may revolutionize and make their own so much of the territory as they inhabit." When the South chose to follow Congressman Lincoln's advice, President Lincoln said they could not go. When confronted with his 1848 declaration, he remarked, rather lamely, "You would hardly think much of a man who is not wiser today than he was yesterday."

Although a small part of the country in 1860 (and all of the Mount Rushmoreites since) took it for granted that the main issue of the Civil War was the abolition of slavery, the actual issue was the preservation of the Union. Lincoln took the position that the South could not leave the Union. When the southern states said that they had every right to go, Lincoln shifted the argument to a positively mystical level: the Union was an absolute, to be preserved at all costs. As for slavery: "If slavery is not wrong, then nothing is wrong," he said. But: "If I can save the Union without freeing any slaves, I will do that. If I can save the Union by freeing some and leaving others alone, I will do that."

As it was, in the third year of his administration, he freed all the slaves in the states that had rebelled but he maintained slavery in the border states that had remained loyal to the Union. This did not go down very well in the world. But Lincoln knew what he was doing: First, the Union; then abolition.

Early in Lincoln's administration he acquired land in Central America for the newly freed blacks. "Why," he said to a black delegation, "should the people of your race be colonized, and where? Why should they leave this country? This is, perhaps, the first question for proper consideration. You and we are different races. We have between us a broader difference than exists between almost any other two races. Whether it is right or wrong I need not discuss; but this physical difference is a great disadvantage to us both, as I think. Your race suffers very greatly, many of them, by living among us, while ours suffers from your presence. In a word, we suffer on each side. If this is admitted, it affords a reason, at least, why we should be separated." Although Lincoln was at his dialectical best, the blacks did not want to leave a country which, as slaves, they had helped to build. Lincoln had no further solution to the problem.

The real Lincoln was a superb politician. He knew when to wait; when to act. He had the gift of formulating, most memorably, ideas whose time had, precisely, on the hour, as it were, come. He could also balance opposites with exquisite justice. As the war was ending, he said, "Neither party expected for the war the magnitude or the duration which it has already attained. Neither anticipated that the cause of the conflict might cease with, or even before, the conflict itself should cease. Each looked for an easier triumph, and a result less fundamental and astounding. Both read the same Bible, and pray to the same God; and each invokes his aid against the other. It may seem strange that any man should dare to ask a just God's assistance in wringing their bread from the sweat of other men's faces; but let us judge not, that we be not judged. The prayers of both could not be answered—that of neither has been answered fully. . . ."

As for himself: "I feel a presentiment that I shall not outlast the rebellion. When it is over, my work is done." The work was done; and so was he. But for a century Lincoln's invention, the American nation-state, flourished. Now, as things begin to fall apart, Lincoln's avatar will have his work cut out for him, repairing that memorial we have so fecklessly damaged, the Union—or finding something better to put in its place.

*The Los Angeles Times*
February 8, 1981

# 62

## *LINCOLN, LINCOLN, AND THE PRIESTS OF ACADEME*

### I

In the beginning, there was the spoken word. The first narrations concerned the doings of gods and kings, and these stories were passed on from generation to generation, usually as verse in order to make memorizing easier. Then, mysteriously, in the fifth century B.C. all the narratives were written down, and literature began. From Greece to Persia to India to China, there was a great controversy. Could a narrative be possessed that had been committed to writing rather than to memory? Traditionalists said no; modernists said yes. The traditionalists lost. Now, twenty-five hundred years later, there is a similar crisis. Modernists believe that any form of narration and of learning can be transmitted through audiovisual means rather than through the, now, traditional written word. In this controversy I am, for once, a conservative to the point of furious reaction.

In any case, we are now obliged to ask radical questions. What is the point to writing things down other than to give directions on how to operate a machine? Why tell stories about gods and kings or, even, men and women?

Very early, the idea of fame—eternal fame—afflicted our race. But fame for the individual was less intense at the beginning than for one's tribe. Thucydides is often read as a sort of biographer of Pericles when, indeed he was writing the biography, to misuse the word, of their city, Athens. It is the idea of the city that the writer wants us to understand not the domestic affairs of Pericles, which he mentions only as civic illustrations. Love had not yet been discovered as opposed to lust. Marriage was not yet a subject except for comedy (Sophocles did not care who got custody of the children, unless Medea killed them; or they were baked in a pie). For more than two millennia, from Homer to Aeschylus to Dante to Shakespeare to Tolstoi, the great line of our literature has concerned itself with gods, heroes, kings, in conflict with one another and with inexorable fate. Simultaneously, all 'round each story, whether it be that of Prometheus or of a Plantagenet prince, there is a people who need fire from heaven or land beyond the sea. Of arms and of the man, I sing, means just that. Of the people then and now, of the hero then and his image now, as created or re-created by the poet. From the beginning, the bard, the poet, the writer was a most high priest to his people, the custodian of their common memory, the interpreter of their history, the voice of their current yearnings.

All this stopped in the last two centuries when the rulers decided to teach the workers to read and write so that they could handle machinery. Traditionalists thought this a dangerous experiment. If the common people knew too much, might they not overthrow their masters? But the modernists, like John Stuart Mill, won. And, in due course, the people—proudly literate—overthrew their masters. We got rid of the English while the French and the Russians—ardent readers—shredded their ancient monarchies. In fact, the French—who read and theorize the most—became so addicted to political experiment that in the two centuries since our own rather drab revolution they have exuberantly produced one Directory, one Consulate, two empires, three restorations of the monarchy, and five republics. That's what happens when you take writing too seriously. Happily, Americans have never liked reading all that much. Politically ignorant, we keep sputtering along in our old Model T, looking wistfully every four years for a good mechanic.

Along with political change—the result of general literacy and the printing press—the nature of narrative began to fragment. High literature concerned itself, most democratically, with the doings of common folk. Although a George Eliot or a Hardy could make art out of these simple domestic tales, in most hands crude mirrors of life tend to be duller than Dumas, say, and, paradoxically, less popular. Today's serious novel is apt to be a carefully written teacherly text about people who teach school and write teacherly texts to dwindling classes. Today's popular novel, carelessly, recklessly composed on—or by—a machine, paradoxically has taken over the heroes and kings and gods, and places them in modern designer clothes amongst consumer dreams beyond the dreams of Sheherazade.

This is a strange reversal. The best writers tend to write, in a highly minimal way, of the simple and the dull, while the worst give us whirlwind tours of the house—I mean home—of Atreus, ripping every skeleton from its closet, and throwing back every Porthault sheet. The fact that this kind of bad writing is popular is not because the reading public—an endangered minority—cherishes bad writing for its own sake but because the good writers fail to interest them. As a result, everything is now so totally out of whack that the high academic bureaucrats have dropped literature, with some relief, and replaced it with literary theory, something that one needs no talent to whip up. As a result, in twenty years, enrollment in American English departments has been cut by more than half. Writers and writing no longer matter much anywhere in freedom's land. Mistuh Emerson, he dead. Our writers are just entertainers, and not all that entertaining either. We have lost the traditional explainer, examiner, prophet.

So what am I up to? If nothing else, I continue, endlessly, to explain, to examine, to prophesy, particularly in the six novels* where I deal with the history of the United States from the beginning to now. The fact that there is still a public eager to find out who we are and what we did ought to encourage others to join me but, by and large, the universities have made that impossible. They have established an hegemony over every aspect of literature—except the ability to make any. They have also come to believe that a serious novelist deals only with what he knows and since our educational system is what it is he is not apt to know much about anything; and since our class system is uncommonly rigid he is not going to have much chance to find out about any world other than the one he was born into—and the school he went to. Certainly, he will never, like his predecessors, be able to deal with his nation's rulers. They prefer the shadows. Mary McCarthy recently listed all the things that cannot be put into a serious novel—from sunsets to a hanging to a cabinet meeting. Also, to be fair, though our political life is entirely devoid of politics, it is so vivid with personalities and the stuff of bad

*Burr; Lincoln; 1876; Empire; Hollywood/Washington, D.C.

fiction that one can hardly expect the novelist to compete with the journalist.

One of the absolutes of bookchat land is that the historical novel is neither history nor a novel. On the other hand, a literal record of a contemporary murder is, triumphantly, a novel. This is what I call "the Capote confusion," his monument. Actually, there is no such thing as The Novel as opposed to novels. No one can say what a novel ought to be. But history is something else. Although I try to make the agreed-upon facts as accurate as possible, I always use the phrase "agreed upon" because what we know of a figure as recent, say, as Theodore Roosevelt is not only not the whole truth—an impossibility anyway—but the so-called facts are often contradicted by other facts. So one must select; and it is in selection that literature begins. After all, with *whose* facts do you agree? Also, in a novel, as opposed to a literal history, one can introduce made-up characters who can speculate on the motives of the real people. How real are the real people? Do I have them say what they really said, or am I, like Shakespeare, reinventing them? For those of you ablaze with curiosity regarding the difference between Shakespeare and me, I'll give you an example.

There is in Washington, D.C., my native city and often subject, a South Korean newspaper called the *Washington Times.* This paper is owned by the Moonies and its political line is, baroquely, fascist. Now let's watch one of their employees in action. The first scene of a recent book of mine, *Empire,* takes place in England, at a country house that has been rented for the summer of 1898 by Henry Adams and Senator Don Cameron for the use of their friend John Hay, our ambassador. All those present at a lunch that I describe were actually there, including Henry James, an old friend of Hay and of Adams, who was living at nearby Rye. Confronted with such a scene, the hostile reviewer—who writes only of what *he* knows—often shouts name-dropper. But how is it possible to tell the story of John Hay without mentioning the fact that as Lincoln's secretary, he got to meet Lincoln? The South Korean reviewer does the ritual attack on me: I hate my native land because I deplore the National Security State. Because I deplore our imperial adventures, I am an *isolationist.* He tells us, "Henry James and Henry Adams figure in *Empire,* neither of them believably, alas . . . for their main function is to serve as spokesmen for Mr. Vidal's isolationism. 'You speak of the laws of history and I am no lawyer,' says the Vidalized James. 'But I confess to misgivings. How can we, who honestly cannot govern ourselves, take up the task of governing others? Are we to govern the Philippines from Tammany Hall?' Neither in style nor in substance does this mini-editorial sound even remotely like the Master." That is very magisterial indeed. Plainly, a James scholar. But let's look at what the Master actually wrote apropos the Spanish-American war. In a letter, he remarks on his "deep embarrassment of thought—of imagination. I have hated, I have almost loathed it." James also spoke most sardonically of the exportation of Tammany and King Caucus to the newly acquired Philippines, "remote countries run by bosses." My South Korean critic did not quote easily the harshest of the Vidalized Henry James's remarks: "The acquisition of an empire civilized the English. That may not be a law but it is a fact. . . . But what civilized them might very well demoralize us even further." That's about as anti-imperial—or "isolationist"—as you can get. Now did the real Henry James ever say so un-American a thing? Yes, he did, when he confided to his nephew Harry: "Expansion has so made the English what they are—for good or for ill, but on the whole for good—that one doesn't quite feel one's way to say for one's country 'No—I'll have none of it.' Empire has educated the English. Will it only demoralize us?" Now you see how I have "my" James say, in substance, precisely what the original said. I do condense and rearrange, something a biographer must never do but a novelist must do. If the James of *Empire* is not credible then he himself would not be credible to a jingo on a Washington newspaper, who also tells us, basking in his ignorance, that no young woman—like my invented Caroline—could have taken over a Washington newspaper and made a success of it. But less than twenty years later one Eleanor Patterson, whom I knew very well, did just that and published the earlier *Washington Times-Herald.* As for America's perennially venal press, the *Washington Times* reviewer will be stunned to hear Henry James, in real life, blame the newspapers for the despicable war with Spain because of "the horrible way in which they envenomize all dangers and reverberate all lies." Like Mark Twain and William Dean Howells he was, incredibly, an "isolationist" with a contempt for the popular press. So, as you can see, I do not invent my literary ancestors. If anything, they invented me.

I have mentioned agreed-upon facts as the stuff of history. But if it is impossible to take seriously the press of one's own time, why should the historian treat old newspaper cuttings as unimpeachable primary sources? For instance, I am now writing about Warren Harding. One of the few quotations of Harding that I have known all my life was what he said, after his unlikely nomination for president, "We drew to a pair of deuces, and filled." This strikes absolutely the right note for the agreed-upon Harding that our canting society requires: a sleazy poker-playing, hard-drinking, womanizing nonentity put in office by cynical Republican bosses. Yet the journalist Mark Sullivan was with Harding before, during, and after the 1920 convention. In *Our Times* he quotes the poker phrase; then, in a footnote, he says this sort of phrase was not characteristic of Harding, who had a considerable sense of his own dignity. Apparently, Sullivan, who could have asked Harding at any time during the next three years if he had made this remark, never did. Instead he tells us that maybe Harding said it when he was "off balance" from excitement. "Or he may never have said it—it may have been some reporter's conception of what he ought to say." There we have it. In effect, the press invents us all; and the later biographer or historian can only select from the mass of crude fictions and part-truths those "facts" that his contemporaries are willing to agree upon.

Where many English Department hustlers now favor literary theory over literature, the workaday bureaucrats of the History Departments are solemnly aware that *their* agreed-upon facts must constitute—at least in the short term—a view of the republic that will please their trustees. Since all great Americans are uniquely great, even saints, those who record the lives of these saints are hagiographers. This is quite a big solemn business, not unlike the bureaucracy of some huge advertising firm, handling a hallowed account like Ivory soap. A major bureaucrat is Comar Vann Woodward, Sterling Professor of History Emeritus at Yale. A southerner, he noticed, many years ago, that blacks were people. This Newtonian revelation brought him tenure; and landed him many important accounts.

Like so many academic bureaucrats the Sterling Professor is highly protective of his turf; he does not want the untenured loose in the field. Sadly, he noted in the *New York Review,* regarding my novel *Lincoln,* that the "book was extravagantly praised by both novelists and historians—a few of the latter at least. Some of the foremost Lincoln scholars do not share these views. After listing numerous historical blunders and errors of the novel, Richard N. Current, a leading Lincoln biographer, declares that " 'Vidal is wrong on big as well as little matters. He grossly distorts Lincoln's character and role in history.' " Woodward gives no examples of these distortions. He does tell us that "Roy P. Basler, editor of *The Collected Works of Abraham Lincoln,* estimates that 'more than half of the book could never have happened as told by Vidal.' " Apparently, Woodward believes that it is sufficient merely to assert. He does not demonstrate, doubtless because he is innocent of the text in question; so he cites, vaguely, other assertions.

The late Vladimir Nabokov said that when anyone criticized his art, he was indifferent. That was their problem. But if anyone attacked his scholarship, he reached for his dictionary. After reading Woodward, I took the trouble to read the two very curious little essays that he cites. What case do they make? Is half the book all wrong; and Lincoln himself grossly distorted? Although I do my own research, unlike so many professors whose hagiographies are usually the work of those indentured servants, the graduate students, when it comes to checking a finished manuscript, I turn to Academe. In this case professor David Herbert Donald of Harvard, who has written a great deal about the period which the Sterling Professor, as far as I recall, has not written about at all. Once the book was written, I employed a professional researcher to correct dates, names, and even agreed-upon facts.

Professor Richard N. Current fusses, not irrelevantly, about the propriety of fictionalizing actual political figures. I also fuss about this. But he has fallen prey to the scholar-squirrels' delusion that there is a final Truth revealed only to the tenured few in their footnote maze; in this he is simply naïve. All we have is a mass of more or less agreed-upon facts about the illustrious dead, and each generation tends to rearrange those facts according to what the times require. Current's text seethes with resentment, and I can see why. "Indeed, Vidal claims to be a better historian than any of the academic writers on Lincoln ('hagiographers,' he calls them)." Current's source for my unseemly boasting is, God help us, the Larry King radio show, which lasts several hours from midnight on, and no one is under oath for what he says during—in my case—two hours. On the other hand, Larry King, as a source, is about as primary as you can get.

Now it is true that I have been amazed that there has never been a first-rate biography of Lincoln, as opposed to many very good and—yes, scholarly—studies of various aspects of his career. I think one reason for this lack is that too often the bureaucrats of Academe have taken over the writing of history and most of them neither write well nor, worse, understand the nature of the men they are required to make saints of. In the past, history was the province of literary masters—of Gibbon, Macaulay, Burke, Locke, Carlyle and, in our time and nation, Academe's bête noire, Edmund Wilson. In principle, it would be better if English teachers did not write novels and history teachers did not write history. After all, teaching is a great and essential profession, marvelously ill-practiced in our country as was recently demonstrated when half of today's college freshmen could not locate on an unmarked map of the world, the United States. Obviously, there are fine academic historians (to whom I am indebted) but the Donalds, McPhersons, and Foners are greatly outnumbered by—the others.

Then, zeroing in on my chat with Larry King, Current writes that

by denying there is any real basis for Vidal's intimation that Lincoln had syphilis [Stephen] Oates "shows," according to Vidal, "that, . . . Mr. Oates is not as good a historian as Mr. Vidal."

First, I like Current's slippery "any real basis" for Lincoln's syphilis. No, there is no existing Wassermann report or its equivalent. But there is the well-known testimony of William Herndon, Lincoln's law partner, that Lincoln told him that he had contracted syphilis in his youth and that it had "hung" to him." This is a primary source not to be dismissed lightly yet Mr. Oates was quoted in the press as saying that there was never any evidence that Lincoln had had syphilis, ignoring Lincoln's own words to Herndon. It was *Newsweek,* not I, who said that Mr. Vidal is a better historian than Mr. Oates. I have no opinion in the matter as I've never read Oates except on the subject of me, where he is bold and inaccurate.

Current finds my trust in Herndon naïve; and quotes Professor Donald on Herndon as being important largely because of "the errors that he spread." But Donald was referring to Herndon's haphazard researches into Lincoln's family and early life, conducted after Lincoln's death. I am not aware that Donald or anyone—except a professional hagiographer—could doubt Herndon when he says that Lincoln himself told him something. For the record, Donald's actual words: "Herndon stands in the backward glance of history, mythmaker and truthteller."

Current has literary longings; he frets over my prose. I spell "jewelry" and "practice" in the English manner and speak of a house *in* Fourteenth Street instead of *on* Fourteenth Street. It was not until H. L. Mencken, in 1919, that an attempt was made to separate the American language from the English; and even then, many writers ignored and still ignore the Sage of Baltimore. Since *Burr* and *1876* were written in the first person, as if by an American early in the last century, I used those locutions that were then common to agreed-upon American speech. For consistency's sake, I continued them in *Lincoln.* As for myself, neither in prose nor in life would I say that someone lived on

Fourteenth Street, though in the age of Reagan I have detected quite a few people living on rather than in streets. I also note that two novels I've been rereading follow my usage: *The Great Gatsby,* 1925, *The Last Puritan,* 1936. Current wins only one small victory: I use the word *trolley* in 1864 when the word did not surface until the 1890s. But his other objections are not only trivial but wrong. He says Charles Sumner was struck with a "cane" not, as I say, a "stick"; then and now the words are interchangeable, at least in Senator Sumner's circles. He also trots out the tired quibble over the origin of "hooker." For the purposes of a Civil War novel it is enough to give General Hooker the credit because the whores in Marble Alley, back of what is now the Washington Post Office, were commonly known as Hooker's Division. According to Partridge's *Dictionary of Slang,* the only British meaning we have for the word at that time is a watch-stealer or pickpocket.

Current then fires off a series of statements that I have written such and such. And such and such is not true. This is dizzy even by contemporary American university standards. For instance, "Ulysses S. Grant had not failed in 'the saddlery business.'" That he had failed is an offhand remark I attribute (without footnote) to a contemporary. The truth? At thirty-seven Grant had failed at every civilian job he had put his hand to, obliging him to become a clerk in his father's firm, Grant & Perkins, which "sold harnesses and other leather goods . . . providing new straps for old saddles" (William McFeely's *Grant*), and the business was run not by failure Grant but by his younger brother Orvil. Current is also outraged by a reference to Lincoln's bowels, whose "frequency," he tells us, "cannot be documented." But, of course, they can. "Truth-teller" Herndon tells us that Lincoln was chronically constipated and depended on a laxative called blue-mass. Since saints do not have bowels, Current finds all this sacrilegious; hence "wrong."

Now there is no reason why Current, master of our language though he is, should understand how a novel—even one that incorporates actual events and dialogue—is made. The historian-scholar, of course, plays god. He has his footnotes, his citations, his press clippings, his fellow scholar-squirrels to quote from. If he lacks literary talent, he then simply serves up the agreed-upon facts as if they were the Truth, and should he have a political slant—and any American schoolteacher is bound to, and most predictable it is—the result will emerge as a plaster saint, like that dead effigy of Jefferson by Dumas Malone and his legion of graduate students.

Although a novel *can* be told as if the author is God, often a novel is told from the point of view of one or more characters. For those of us inclined to the Jamesian stricture, a given scene ought to be observed by a single character, who can only know what he knows, which is often less than the reader. For someone with no special knowledge of—or as yet interest in—Grant, the fact that harnesses and *other* leather goods were sold along with saddles by the failure Grant is a matter of no interest. The true scholar-squirrel, of course, must itemize everything sold in the shop. This is the real difference between a novel and a biography. But though I tend in these books more to history than to the invented, I am still obliged to dramatize my story through someone's consciousness. But when it comes to a great mysterious figure like Lincoln, I do not enter his mind. I only show him as those around him saw him at specific times. This rules out hindsight, which is all that a historian, by definition, has; and which people in real life, or in its imitation the novel, can never have.

Current is a master of the one-line unproved assertion. Here are some of what he calls my false "contentions." "As early as April 1861 Lincoln was thinking of emancipation as possibly justifiable as 'a military necessity.' " I looked up the scene in the novel and found that it was not Lincoln but the abolitionist Sumner who was thinking along those lines; Lincoln himself was noncommittal. Then "Vidal pictures Lincoln as an ignoramus in regard to public finance. He makes him so stupid as to think Secretary of the Treasury Chase personally signed every greenback, and so uninformed as to have 'no idea what the greenbacks actually represented.' " This is nicely—deliberately?—garbled. It is not Chase that Lincoln thinks signs the greenbacks but the treasurer, Lucius Crittenden; this provided a famous scene in Carl Sandburg's hagiography, on which I do an ironical variation.

Current tells us that I go along with the "innuendo" that Stanton "masterminded the assassination." If he had actually read the book, he would have been able to follow almost every turn to Booth's assassination plot, in which Stanton figures not at all; had he got to the end of the book, he would have heard Hay make fun of those who believed that Stanton had any connection with the murder of the man to whom he owed everything. Next I "intimate" that there was a second plot afoot, involving "Radical Republicans in Congress." There was indeed a second plot, to be found in Pinkerton's Secret Service files. But no one knows who masterminded it. At one point the Democratic leader, August Belmont, was thought involved.

Next, I propose the following outrage: that "Lincoln excluded Union-held areas from the Emancipation Proclamation" as a favor to "pro-Union slaveholders." Yet it is a fact that seven counties in and around Norfolk, Virginia, and several Louisiana parishes were allowed to maintain slavery while slavery was banned in the rest of the South. Why did Lincoln do this? He needed Unionist votes in Congress, and one belonged to a Louisiana congressman. After all, Lincoln was never an abolitionist; he was a Unionist, and as he most famously said, if he could preserve the Union only by maintaining slavery, he would do so. Apparently, saints don't make deals.

By and large, Current's complaints range from the trivial to the pointless. Does he find me wrong on anything of consequence? Yes, he does. And I think it is the whole point to his weird enterprise. Current tells us that "there is no convincing evidence" for Vidal's contention that "as late as April 1865 [Lincoln] was still planning to colonize freed slaves outside the United States." This is a delicate point in the 1980s, when no national saint can be suspected of racism. I turned to one of my authorities for this statement; and realized that I may have relied on suspect scholarship. Here is the passage I used:

Lincoln to the last seemed to have a lingering preference for another kind of amendment, another kind of plan. He still clung to his old ideas of postponing final emancipation, compensating slaveholders, and colonizing freedmen. Or so it would appear. As late as March of 1865, if the somewhat dubious Ben Butler is to be believed, Lincoln summoned him to the White House to discuss with him the feasibility of removing the colored population of the United States.

This is from a book called *The Lincoln Nobody Knows* (p. 230) by Richard N. Current. So either Current is as wrong about this as he is about me, or he is right and between March and April 15, 1865, when Lincoln departed this vale of tears, the President changed his mind on the colonizing of slaves. If he did, there is no record known to me—or, I suspect, to anyone else.

What is going on here is a deliberate revision by Current not only of Lincoln but of himself in order to serve the saint in the 1980s as opposed to the saint at earlier times when blacks were still colored, having only just stopped being Negroes. In colored and Negro days the saint might have wanted them out of the country, as he did. But in the age of Martin Luther King even the most covertly racist of school boards must agree that a saint like Abraham Lincoln could never have wanted a single black person to leave freedom's land much less bravery's home. So all the hagiographers are redoing their plaster images and anyone who draws attention to the discrepancy between their own past crudities and their current falsities is a very bad person indeed, and not a scholar, and probably a communist as well.

Roy P. Basler, Woodward's other "authority," is given to frantic hyperbole. He declares Sandburg's *Lincoln* a "monumental achievement." Well, it's a monument all right—to a plaster saint, of the sort that these two professional hagiographers are paid to keep dusted. Basler finds my *Lincoln* the "phoniest historical novel I have ever had the pleasure of reading." Well, there may be *one* phony bit, the Crittenden signature story, which I got from Basler's monumental biographer Sandburg. Basler should have at least liked that. Also, "more than half the book could never have happened as told." Unfortunately, he doesn't say which half. If I knew, we could then cut it free from the phony half and publish the result as Basler's Vidal's *Lincoln.*

Like Current, Basler gets all tangled up in misread or misunderstood trivia. He goes on at great length that it was not the Reverend James Smith whom Lincoln appointed consul in Scotland but his son Hugh. Well, the son, Hugh, was appointed consul on June 10, 1861; then died; and the father was appointed, later, in his place. Basler says that Mary Todd's scene with General Ord's wife "is histrionically exaggerated out of all proportion to the recorded facts." But it conforms with those recorded facts given by Justin G. and Linda Levitt Turner's standard *Mary Todd Lincoln: Her Life and Letters.* He is also most protective of the saint. For instance, every saint is a kind and indulgent yet gently stern father, devoted to his children who worship him. But Lincoln's oldest son, Robert, did not much like his father.

Basler gets all trembly as he writes,

When Vidal has Robert Lincoln say to Hay about his father, "He hates his past. He hates having been a scrub. . . . He wanted me to be what he couldn't be," I find no excuse. Robert did admit that he and his father had never been close after he was grown, and he may have felt neglected, but for him to speak thus is beyond comprehension.

But he did speak thus, to Senator Thomas Pryor Gore of Oklahoma, my grandfather, who often talked to me about Robert's bleak attitude toward his father, who, having sent his son to Exeter and Harvard in order to move him up in the world, then found that he had a son with whom he had not much in common. I myself attended Exeter four score years after Robert, and memories of Lincoln were still vivid; and well-described not long ago in the alumni bulletin: how Lincoln spoke at the Academy shortly after Cooper Union, and enthralled the boys. But not Robert.

Basler is also protective of the only recently beatified, by Academe, Walt Whitman. (This miracle was accomplished by making Walt Whitman homoerotic rather than homosexual.) "Consider," he rails, "the three pages [actually one and a half] that he devotes to a fictional interview with Secretary of the Treasury, Salmon P. Chase, looking for a job." Basler correctly notes that a Mr. Trowbridge presented a letter to Chase from Emerson, asking that Whitman be given a job. I have Whitman delivering the letter. Basler is stern. "Anyone who knows about Whitman would recognize that presenting the letter in person . . . is wholly false to Whitman's character at this time of his life, and his conversation with Chase is entirely what Vidal might have said, but not Whitman." If Whitman had thought a meeting with Chase would have got him a job he would have done so because, as he wrote of himself then, "I was pulling eminent wires in those days."

As for Whitman's dialogue with Chase, I quite fancied it. He describes the decorations of the Capitol and how "not in one's flightiest dreams has there been so much marble and china, gold and bronze, so many painted gods and goddesses." Whitman compares the Capitol—favorably—but fatally for the teetotaler Chase—to Taylor's saloon in New York. I took this particular passage from Whitman's *Democratic Vistas,* as anyone immersed in the Whitman style—or mine for that matter—would know. Literary criticism is not, perhaps, Basler's strong suit. Actually, I needed the encounter to fill in my portrait of Chase, who, exactly as I described, detested Whitman as the author of a "very bad book," which he had not read; then, being an autograph collector, Chase kept the Emerson letter; then, being a jittery man on the subject of public rectitude, he turned the letter over to the Treasury archive. This is not too bad for a page and a half—of agreed-upon facts, used to illuminate the character not of Whitman but of Chase.

Basler like Current is eager to bring the saint into the mainstream of today's political superstition. Both are appalled whenever I mention his scheme for colonizing the ex-slaves. Both deny that he ever had anything but love and admiration for blacks, who were, he believed, in every way his equals, once slavery was past. "The one thing I most resented," writes Basler, "is the perpetuation of 'Lincoln's unshaken belief that the colored race was inferior to the white. . . .' I have never found any such categorical avowal in anything Lincoln wrote or was reported to have said." The slippery adjective here is "categorical." Yet Basler himself wrote in *The Lincoln Legend* (pp. 210–211), "[Lincoln] never contemplated with any degree of satisfaction the prospect of a free negro race living in the same country with a free white race." Not even I have dared go so far as to suggest that I have ever had any way of knowing what Lincoln may or may not have *contemplated*! In any case, Basler, like Current, is revising himself.

Actually, Lincoln's views of blacks were common to his time and place but, as he was an uncommon man, he tried to transcend them, as he did in a speech in Peoria, in 1854: "My first impulse," he said rather daringly for that year, "would be to free all slaves and send them to Liberia." He then lists all the objections that others would later make to him. He finally throws in the towel when he asks: "Free them and make them politically and socially our equals? Our own feelings would not admit of it, and if mine would, we well know that those of the great mass of whites will not."

It is my radical view that Americans are now sufficiently mature to be shown a Lincoln as close to the original as it is possible for us so much later in time to get. Since the race war goes on as fiercely as ever in this country, I think candor about blacks and whites and racism is necessary. It was part of Lincoln's greatness that, unlike those absolute abolitionists, the Radical Republicans, he foresaw the long ugly confrontation, and tried to spare future generations by geographically separating the races. The fact that his plan was not only impractical but inadvertently cruel is beside the point. He wanted to *do* something; and he never let go the subject, unless of course he had a vision in the last two weeks of his life, known only to Current, who has chosen not to share it.

Recently, an excellent academic historian, Theodore S. Hamerow, published a book called *Reflections on History and Historians*. It was reviewed in *The New York Times* by an English history don, Neil McKendrick. Here is what two professionals have to say of the average American history teacher. As presented by Hamerow, he is "cynical." I quote now from McKendrick: "He is also mean-minded, provincial and envious. We hear verdict after verdict condemning, in the words of one academic, 'the wretched pedantry, the meanness of motive, the petty rancors of rivalry, the stultifying provincialism.' " But then "most professors of history do little research and less publishing and there are statistical tables to prove it. What little is produced is seen as 'coerced productivity,' mainly a parade of second-hand learning and third-rate opinions." Thus, the high professional academics view their run-of-the-mill colleagues.

Recently in *The New York Times* Herbert Mitgang took me to task, indirectly, when he wrote: "Several revisionist academics have advanced the incredible theory that Lincoln really wanted the Civil War, with its 600,000 casualties, in order to eclipse the Founding Fathers and insure his own place in the pantheon of great presidents." Now there is no single motive driving anyone but, yes, that is pretty much what I came to believe, as Lincoln himself got more and more mystical about the Union, and less and less logical in his defense of it, and more and more appalled at all the blood and at those changes in his country, which, he confessed—with pride?—were "fundamental and astounding." The Lincoln portrayed by me is based on a speech he made in 1838 at the Young Men's Lyceum in Springfield. He began by praising the Founding Fathers and their republic; then he went on:

This field of glory is harvested, and the crop is already appropriated. But new reapers will arise, and they too will seek a field. It is to deny what the history of the world tells us is true to suppose that men of ambitions and talents will not continue to spring up amongst us. And when they do, they will as naturally seek the gratification of their ruling passions as others have done before them. The question, then, is can that gratification be found in supporting and maintaining an edifice that has been erected by others? Most certainly it cannot.

Thus Lincoln warns us against Lincoln.

Towering genius disdains a beaten path. It seeks regions unexplored. . . . It denies that it is glory enough to serve under any chief. It scorns to tread in the path of any predecessor however illustrious. It thirsts and burns for distinction; and, if possible, it will have it, whether at the expense of emancipating slaves or enslaving free men.

Nothing that Shakespeare ever invented was to equal Lincoln's invention of himself and, in the process, us. What the Trojan War was to the

Greeks, the Civil War is to us. What the wily Ulysses was to the Greeks, the wily Lincoln is to us—not plaster saint but towering genius, our nation's haunted and haunting re-creator.

*The New York Review of Books*
April 28, 1988

2

It's savory scholar-squirrel stew time again! Or, to be precise, one scholar-squirrel (Current Redux in a letter to *The New York Review of Books*) and one plump publicist-pigeon for the pot. So, as the pot boils and I chop this pile of footnotes fine, let me explain to both pigeon and the no doubt bemused readers of these pages why it was that *The New York Times,* the Typhoid Mary of American journalism, should have wanted to discredit, one week before airing, the television dramatization of my book on Abraham Lincoln. The publicist (a caption-*and*-text writer for two Civil War picture books that he shrewdly guesses I've never looked at) tells us that "the *Times* did not assign me to 'bloody' the mini-series . . . but to measure its faithfulness to history," etc. This begs the question: Why, if the *Times* were so uncharacteristically concerned with faithfulness to fact of any kind, should they select him, a nonhistorian, whose current job, he told me, disarmingly, is that of publicist for the admirable Mario Cuomo? I suspect that he was chosen because a publicist will give an editor exactly what he wants. In any case, my own long history with *The New York Times* does, in a curious way, illuminate not only this peculiar dispute but the rather more interesting nature of history itself.

In 1946 my first novel was published. A war novel, it was praised by the daily book reviewer of the *Times,* one Orville Prescott, whose power to "make or break" a book was then unique; and now unimaginable. I was made. Then, in 1948, two books were published within weeks of each other. First, *The City and the Pillar* by me; then *Sexual Behavior in the Human Male* by Dr. Alfred C. Kinsey, et al. In my novel, I found the love affair between two ordinary American youths to be a matter-of-fact and normal business. Dr. Kinsey then confirmed, statistically, that more than a third of the American male population had performed, at least once, a vile and abominable act against nature. Since the generation of American males that he was studying had just won the last great war that our sissy republic ever was to win (as R. M. Nixon would say, I mean "sissy" in the very best sense of that word), it was unthinkable that . . . The polemic began; and goes on.

At the time, Orville Prescott told my publisher, Nicholas Wreden of E. P. Dutton, that he would never again read much less review a book by me. The *Times* then refused to advertise either my book or the Kinsey report. True to Prescott's word, my next five novels were not reviewed in the daily *Times* or, indeed, in *Time* or *Newsweek.* In freedom's land what ought not to be is not and must be blacked out. I was unmade. For ten years I did television, theater, movies; then returned to the novel.

The war goes on, though with less spirit than in the old days when the Sunday editor of the *Times,* Lester Markel, canvassed five writers, among them my friend Richard Rovere, to see if one would "bloody" *The Best Man,* a play that their autonomous daily reviewer had liked. Finally, Douglass Cater wrote a mildly dissenting piece, which was duly published. Simultaneously, a writer was assigned to "bloody" my campaign for Congress in New York's Twenty-ninth District, a polity usually unnoticed by *The New York Times;* and then . . . and then . . . Anyway, we need not believe the publicist when he says that he was not engaged to "bloody" the television *Lincoln.* Of course he was; and I fell into the trap.

The publicist wrote to tell me that he was writing about the television *Lincoln* and the problems of dramatized history. Since I had nothing to do with the production, I thought that the *Times* might be playing it straight. Plainly, I had lost my cunning. I was interviewed on the telephone. He asked me if I read historical novels. I said, almost never. I'm obliged to read history. A few moments later he said, "As you never read history . . ." I realized then that I'd been had yet again by the foxy old *New York Times.* I remarked upon the mysteriousness of history. Quoted Henry Adams's famous summing up on the "why" and the "what." The publicist got the quotation right but attributed it to Thoreau.

The headline of *The New York Times* story:

## A FILTERED PORTRAIT OF LINCOLN
## COMES TO THE SMALL SCREEN.

Filtered is meant to indicate some sort of bias. A second headline was set up in type reminiscent of the *National Enquirer:*

THE PRODUCERS OF THE MINISERIES
ADAPTED IT FROM GORE VIDAL'S NOVEL,
A WORK ALREADY FAULTED BY HISTORIANS.

That was the best—and pretty good, too—that the *Times* could do to scare off viewers. The publicist's story was dim. There was no mention of those historians who had praised *Lincoln*. The caption writer found many things "troubling"; none of any consequence, except Lincoln's attitude toward blacks.

The publicist tells us that "Lincoln hardly made" a shady bargain with Salmon P. Chase "to win his support for his 1864 reelection campaign, by offering him in return the job of chief justice." I don't recollect the phrase *shady bargain* in either book or drama. But if the publicist does not understand Lincoln's devious game with Chase then he doesn't understand politics in general or Lincoln in particular. Although Lincoln had ended Chase's dream of being the Republican nominee that year, Chase could still have made trouble. Chase was also one of the few men in public life whom Lincoln genuinely disliked. In the summer of 1864, Chase, who had resigned as Lincoln's secretary of the treasury, was making overtures to the Democratic party: "This . . . might mean much," he wrote, "if the Democrats would only cut loose from slavery and go for freedom. . . . *If they would do that, I would cheerfully go for any man they might nominate.*"[*] Aware of Chase's conniving, Lincoln confided to his secretary, John Hay, "What Chase ought to do is to help his successor through his installation . . . ; go home without making any fight and wait for a good thing hereafter, such as a vacancy on the Supreme Bench or some such matter."[†]

Lincoln played a lovely game with Chase; he even got him to stump Indiana and Ohio for him. He hinted to Chase's friends that Chase was under serious consideration for the chief justiceship, which my publicist-critic thinks impossible because the chief justice was still alive. Unknown to the caption writer, the chief justice, Roger B. Taney, was eighty-seven years old that summer and poorly. The new president was bound to make the appointment. So there was a lot of maneuvering, by the dark of the moon, on Lincoln's part to put Chase, in his daughter's

[*]See Robert B. Warden, *An Account of the Private Life and Public Services of Salmon Portland Chase* (Cincinnati, 1874), p. 627.
[†]Tyler Dennett, ed., *Lincoln and the Civil War in the Diaries and Letters of John Hay* (New York: Dodd, Mead, 1939), p. 203.

phrase, "on the shelf." In exchange for not rocking the boat (supporting McClellan, say) Chase became chief justice after Taney's death, which was after the election. Was Chase chosen because he was the best man for the job? No, he was not. Politics is bargains and their shadiness depends entirely on which side of the street you happen to be standing.

The publicist's confusions about Lincoln and slavery and what I am supposed to have written are simply hortatory. He seems to think that I think that Lincoln was "desperately seeking a way to renege on Emancipation while at the same time spearheading the Thirteenth Amendment that abolished slavery." This is OK for *The New York Times* but not for a responsible paper. Neither I nor the dramatizers ever suggested that he wanted to renege, desperately or not, on Emancipation. It will also come as news to any Lincoln scholars that the saint "spearheaded" the Thirteenth Amendment. He favored it. The spear-carriers were abolitionists, Radical Republicans. But Lincoln and the blacks is the crux of all this nonsense, and I shall address the question in due course.

From the tone of Professor Richard N. Current's letter I fear that I may have hurt his feelings. In a covering letter to the editors of *The New York Review of Books,* he refers to my "personal attack" on him. As Current is as unknown to me as Lincoln was to him in his book *The Lincoln Nobody Knows,* I could hardly have been personal. I thought my tone in the last exchange sweetly reasonable if necessarily disciplinary. I am sorry he finds "hysterical" my "diatribe." What I was obliged to do in his case was to take, one by one, his flat assertions that such-and-such as written by me (often it wasn't) was untrue; and so great does he feel his emeritus weight that that was that.

Finally, about halfway through I gave up answering him. Now he is at it again. He tells us that I have "pretended" to be a scholar-squirrel; I give the impression (false it would seem) that I have visited libraries and looked at old newspapers, etc. Now, in the case of *Lincoln,* I have relied heavily on the diaries of John Hay and Salmon P. Chase since I observe Lincoln from the viewpoint of each. Current seems to think that I could not possibly have read these diaries despite internal evidence to the contrary. As for old newspapers, I used a reporter's shorthand version of the Gettysburg Address, which differs somewhat from the official text. But, by and large, I have always relied heavily on the work of *scholars* in my reflections on American history and, in a way, I have become their ideal reader because I have no professional ax to grind, no tenure to seek, no prizes or fellowships to win.

How does a scholar differ from a scholar-squirrel? The squirrel is a careerist who mindlessly gathers little facts for professional reasons. I don't in the least mind this sort of welfare for the "educated" middle class. They must live, too. But when they start working in concert to revise history to suit new political necessities, I reach for my ancient Winchester.

Current tells us that "[Vidal] implied that he was a greater Lincoln authority than Stephen B. Oates or any other academic historian except David Herbert Donald." As I pointed out in the last exchange, it was *Newsweek* that found me to be (in reference to Lincoln's alleged syphilis) a better historian than Mr. Oates, whom I have never read. I do not "imply" (Current has a guardhouse lawyer's way with weasel-words) that I am a better historian than anyone. This is the sort of thing that obsesses academic careerists. Scholar-squirrels spend their lives trying to be noted and listed and graded and seeded because such rankings determine their careers. Those of us engaged in literature and, perhaps, in history as well don't think in such terms. We also don't go on Pulitzer Prize committees to give a friend a prize which, in due course, when he is on the committee, he will give us for our squirrelings.

Current feels that I "grossly distort" Lincoln by showing him "as ignorant of economics, disregardful of the Constitution, and unconcerned with the rights of blacks." Even a casual reading of *Lincoln* shows that I spend quite a lot of time demonstrating the President's concern with the rights of blacks, and where and how they should be exercised. Disregardful of the Constitution? No other president until recent years has shown so perfect a disregard for that document in the guise of "military necessity." The chief justice himself thought the president so disregardful that he hurled the Constitution at his head. Lincoln just ducked; and the corpus of one Mr. Merryman of Baltimore was not delivered up for trial, as the chief justice had ordered. I should like Current to demonstrate (elsewhere, please) Lincoln's mastery of economics. Meanwhile, I highly recommend *Lincoln's Preparation for Greatness* by Paul Simon (yes, the Illinois senator),* where he records Lincoln's activities in the state House of Representatives. During four terms, Lincoln and eight other school-of-Clay legislators, known as "the long Nine," nearly bankrupted the state with a "Big Improvements" bill that took Illinois forty-five years to pay off. The story about Lincoln's

*Paul Simon, *Lincoln's Preparation for Greatness: The Illinois Legislative Years* (University of Oklahoma Press, 1965).

confusions over who signed the greenbacks occurs in Sandburg; and is public domain.* I'm sorry if Current finds my last "screed" somewhat "maundering" but there are a limited number of ways of saying "false" without actually using the word.

Current, lord of language, wants Lincoln to be Will Rogers, all folksy and homey. But Lincoln's own language resounds with what Current calls "Briticisms." Lincoln's prose was drenched in Shakespeare. Of course, H. L. Mencken was not the first to try to separate American English from English. But in our country, he has been the prime instigator. Finally, prose is all a matter of ear. A word like *screed,* for instance, is now used only by the semiliterate when they want to sound highfalutin, usually in the course of a powerful letter to the editor.

We shall go no further into the word *hooker* other than to observe that a word, in different contexts, picks up additional meanings. A copperhead is a snake is a traitor is a Democrat, depending on the year the word is used and the user. One authority gives a New York origin for *hooker.* In Washington, in the Civil War, General Hooker's name added new resonance. Another authority says the word comes from the verb *to hook,* as the whores in London hooked arms with potential customers as a means of introduction.

Current affects not to understand what I mean by "agreed-upon facts" as the stuff of history. He would like the reader to think that I invent something and get someone to agree to it. The point to my long disquisition on *The New York Times* is to show that one cannot trust *any* primary source. If the *Times* says that I said Thoreau wrote something that Henry Adams actually wrote, my "error" becomes a fact because the *Times* is a primary source for scholar-squirrels—scholars, too. To take at face value any newspaper story is to be dangerously innocent. But one can't challenge everything that has ever been printed. So, through weariness and ignorance, there is a general consensus, which then becomes what I call an "agreed-upon" fact. We all decide not to worry it. Yet in two standard biographies of John Hay, though the writers agree upon the year of his birth, each gives a different natal month. I have also found that whenever I do make a mistake in writing about history, it is usually because I have followed an acknowledged authority who turns out wrong.

*Carl Sandburg, *Abraham Lincoln: The War Years* (New York: Harcourt, Brace, 1939), Volume I.

On Emancipation and the exemption of certain areas for political reasons: Lincoln maintained slavery in the slave states within the Union and freed those in the Confederacy. Current is more than usually confused here. He thinks Lincoln maintained slavery in "liberated" or "restored" sections of Louisiana because the Union controlled these counties and no political necessity was involved. Like so many hagiographers, Current refuses to face the fact that before Lincoln became a saint he was a superb politician. He did nothing without political calculation. He was also a master of telling different people different things, causing no end of trouble for later worshipers who can't deal with all the contradictions. Emancipation was as much a political as a military necessity for Lincoln. For instance, when Lincoln appointed the pro-slavery Edward Stanly governor of occupied North Carolina, it was with the understanding that Lincoln would *not* interfere with slavery in the states. When the Emancipation Proclamation was issued, according to one professor of history,

Stanly went to Washington intending to resign. After several talks with Lincoln, however, Stanly was satisfied. He returned to his job, but first he called at the office of James C. Welling, editor of the *National Intelligencer*. Welling wrote in his diary: "Mr. Stanly said that the President had stated to him that the proclamation had become a civil necessity to prevent the Radicals from openly embarrassing the government in the conduct of the war."

So Lincoln speaks with forked tongue in this passage from Richard N. Current's *The Lincoln Nobody Knows.* * Personally, I'd not have let this agreed-upon fact sail so easily by. Wouldn't Stanly lie to Welling, to explain his behavior? Or might Welling have misunderstood what Stanly said Lincoln said? Or, unthinkable thought, could Lincoln have lied to Stanly? Current accepts too readily a story highly discreditable to the Great Emancipator he would now have us worship in all his seamless integrity.

Here comes Grant again. One thing about Current, he knows not defeat. I "asserted that Ulysses S. Grant 'had gone into the saddlery business, where he had attractively failed.'" The "assertion" in the novel was John Hay's, in an idle moment, about a man he knew nothing much of

*New York: McGraw-Hill (1958), p. 227.

in 1862. Triumphantly, Current now writes, "The point is that Grant had never gone into the saddlery, harness, or leather-goods business and therefore could not have failed at it. He was only an employee." This is the sort of thing that gives mindless pedantry a bad name. Even in Current's super-American English, it is possible to fail at a job by being fired or being carried if your father owns the place. "At thirty-seven Grant had to go back [home] and admit that he was still a failure: the boy who could not bargain for a horse had become a man who could not bring in a crop of potatoes or collect a batch of bills. It was humiliating."* After a year as a clerk, under the managership of his younger brother, Grant was saved by the war and, as he himself wrote, "I never went into our leather store after the meeting" (where he got his command), "to put up a package or do other business."

But note the Current technique throughout this supremely unimportant business. He zeroes in on an idle remark by someone who knows nothing about Grant other than his failure in civilian life, most recently in leather goods. The man who said it is a character living in history not looking back on it. Current seems to think that I should supply the indifferent Hay with the full and absolute knowledge of Grant's affairs that a scholar-squirrel could find out but a contemporary stranger could hardly have known. Owing to Current's uneasy grasp of any kind of English he seems to think that to fail at a business means you must own the business and go broke. That's one meaning. But you can also fail by losing your job or by being tolerated as a hopeless employee by your family. Current wonders why I don't answer more of his charges. They are almost all of them as specious as this.

One of the signs of obsession is an inability to tell the difference between what matters and what does not. The obsessed gives everything the same weight. Current juggles words this way and that to try to "prove" what is often pointless and unprovable. There *is* an issue here but he can't focus on it. The issue is Lincoln and the blacks. The United States was then and is now a profoundly racist society that pretends not to be and so requires the likes of Current to disguise the American reality from the people, while menacing the society's critics, most successfully, it should be noted, within the academy where the squirrels predominate. I shall indulge Current on two minor points and then get to what matters.

Lincoln's bowels. This occupies a few lines in my book. It is necessary

*William S. McFeely, *Grant: A Biography* (New York: Norton, 1981), p. 64.

to mention the subject because one of Booth's conspirators tried to poison Lincoln's laxative, which was made up at Thompson's drugstore; whether or not prescription clerk David Herold actually poisoned the medicine is not agreed upon.* Current thinks that constipation is a central theme to the book, the Emancipator as Martin Luther. Herndon tells us: "Mr. Lincoln had an evacuation, a passage, about once a week, ate blue mass. Were you to read his early speeches thoroughly and well, you could see his, then, coarse nature, his materialism, etc." That's all. Since Herndon shared an office with Lincoln for seventeen years there is no reason for this subject not to have been mentioned. After all, many of Lincoln's famed funny stories concerned the outhouse. Current should read them. Also, Current might have given some thought to the sentence after constipation—Lincoln's early "coarse nature, his materialism"; this is provocative.

But Current is now prey to obsession: "Vidal would have us believe that every time Lincoln defecated he reported it to Herndon." I would not have anyone believe such a thing since Herndon in my book makes no mention of Lincoln's bowels, a subject of interest only to the putative poisoners. I fear Current is now sailing right round the bend. He claims that I said on NBC's *Today* show (he seems to be watching rather too much TV) that Lincoln definitely gave Mary Todd syphilis and that she had died of paresis that had affected the brain. He quotes me as saying that one is not "under oath" on television so that one can presumably tell lies. When I say I'm not under oath, I mean that I'm free to speculate on matters that cannot be proven. I would not write that Lincoln gave his wife syphilis, but I can certainly, in conversation, give an opinion. Since my book stops in 1865 and Mary Todd didn't die until 1882, I never tried to "prove" the subject. But years ago a doctor friend in Chicago told me that an autopsy had been performed on Mrs. Lincoln (but only on the head, an odd procedure even then) and that the brain was found to have physically deteriorated, ruling out mere neurosis, the usual explanation for her behavior. I didn't write about this and have never followed it up. If Current can tear himself away from the Larry King show, he might have a go at it.

As for Lincoln's syphilis, I use the words Herndon himself used: "About the year 1835–36 Mr. Lincoln went to Beardstown and during a devilish passion had connection with a girl and caught the disease

---

*Louis J. Weichmann, *A True History of the Assassination* (New York: Vintage, 1977), p. 44.

[syphilis]. Lincoln told me this. . . . About the year 1836–37 Lincoln moved to Springfield. . . . At this time I suppose that the disease hung to him and, not wishing to trust our physicians, he wrote a note to Doctor Drake." Since there is no reason for Herndon to lie about this, I suppose we should all agree upon it as a fact. But since no saint has ever had syphilis, Herndon is a liar and so the consensus finds against him. I don't much admire this sort of thing. Current, historian and master of the American language, now reveals another facet to a protean nature that nobody knows: Current, diagnostician:

If Vidal had the slightest concern for truth, he could easily have learned from such a reference as *The Merck Manual of Diagnosis and Therapy* that Mrs. Lincoln's symptoms and those of a paretic do not correspond.

This is a brave leap in the dark and, once again, Current, the Mr. Magoo of the History Department, lands on his face. From the *Merck Manual*:

General paresis or demential paralytica generally affects patients in their 40s and 50s. The onset is usually insidious and manifested by behavior changes. It also may be present with convulsions or epileptic attacks and there may be aphasia or a transient hemiparesis. Changes in the patient include irritability, difficulty in concentration, memory deterioration, and defective judgment. Headaches and insomnia are associated with fatigue and lethargy. The patient's appearance becomes shabby, unkempt, and dirty; emotional instability leads to frequent weeping and temper tantrums; neurasthenia, depression, and delusions of grandeur with lack of insight may be present.

This exactly describes Mrs. Lincoln's behavior as reported by contemporaries and by such sympathetic biographers as Ruth Painter Randall and the Turners.* I am in Current's debt for leading me to this smoking, as it were, gun. But where, I wonder, is the autopsy report? Could Robert Lincoln have destroyed all copies? Has Walter Reed collected it in its great presidential net?

Current admits to changing his mind about Lincoln in the course of many years of squirreling. But although he no longer holds to his views

*Ruth Painter Randall, *Mary Lincoln: Biography of a Marriage* (New York: Little, Brown, 1953); Justin G. Turner and Linda Levitt Turner, eds., *Mary Todd Lincoln: Her Life and Letters* (New York: Knopf, 1972).

on Lincoln and the blacks as presented in *The Lincoln Nobody Knows*
(a book, he'll be relieved to know, I never took very seriously, largely
because of the megalomaniacal title in which he has inserted himself),
he does find, as do I, disconcerting the way that Lincoln lovers (no hater
would be allowed tenure anywhere in bravery's home) keep changing
the image to conform to new policies. When the civil rights movement
took off in the sixties, uppity blacks toyed with the notion that Lincoln
was a honkie (Julius Lester, in *Look Out, Whitey!*, etc.). Immediately
the agreed-upon facts of earlier times (colonize the freed slaves, reim-
burse the slave owners, etc.) had to be papered over and a new set of
agreed-upon facts were hurried into place, so that LaWanda Cox could
deliver a new verdict: "There is no mistaking the fact that by 1865
Lincoln's concern for the future of the freed people was directed to their
condition and rights at home, rather than abroad."*

This is the new line, and I have no particular quarrel with it. But
certain hagiographers are now pretending that Lincoln was *never* serious about colonization, which is a falsification of the record. In Lincoln's second annual message to Congress (December 1, 1862) he said:
"I cannot make it better known than it is, that I strongly favor colonization." Certainly for the first two years of his administration Lincoln was
mad on the subject. Gradually, he *seems* to have let the notion go
because of the logistical impossibility of shipping out three or four
million people who were less than enthusiastic about a long sea voyage
to the respective wilds of Haiti, Panama, Liberia.

Current says that he "did not . . . state it as my opinion . . . that
Lincoln remained a colonizationist." That was wise, because no one
knows. I don't give my personal view either though I did note (but did
not write) that usually when Lincoln started in on the necessity of
reimbursing the slave owners, colonization was seldom far behind: the
two seemed twinned in his head. The revisionists now admired by
Current maintain that the only evidence that Lincoln at the end was still
pondering colonization is Ben Butler's testimony that the president
mentioned it to him some time after February 3, 1865. I found most
intriguing Mark E. Neely, Jr.'s case that Lincoln could not have talked
to Butler at the time that Butler says he did because Butler had written
Secretary of War Stanton a letter assuring him that he had stayed in
New York until March 23, in conformance with War Department policy

*LaWanda Cox, *Lincoln and Black Freedom: A Study in Presidential Leadership*
(University of South Carolina Press, 1981), p. 23.

that forbade officers from visiting the capital without permission.* This is a scholarly not squirrelly finding. But if one is to factor out Butler as a crucial witness because he is a liar, why believe the letter to Stanton? If Dan Sickles and other general officers slipped into town without permission, why not the irrepressible Butler? My point is that when one decides a source is apt to be untrue (Herndon, Butler, *The New York Times*), how does one choose what to believe—if anything—from the discredited source?

I understand the politics behind the current (no pun) revisionists but I think they rather overdo it. One dizzy squirrel claims that after 1862, Lincoln discarded the idea of colonization with indecent haste. Yet July 1, 1864, John Hay writes, "I am glad the President has sloughed off that idea of colonization."† For obvious reasons, the revisionists never quote the next sentence. "I have always thought it a hideous & barbarous humbug & the thievery of Pomeroy and Kock have about converted him to the same belief." This sounds a lot more tentative than the revisionists would like us to believe. Perhaps they will now have to establish that Hay is untrustworthy.

In any event, when the black separatist movement starts up in the next decade, new revisionists will supersede the present lot, and Butler's probity will be rehabilitated and Lincoln the colonizer reestablished.

On the dust jacket, between the title *Lincoln* and my name there is a one-inch-high caveat: *A Novel.* I tell the story of Lincoln's presidency from the imagined points of view of his wife, of E. B. Washburne, John Hay, Salmon P. Chase, and, marginally, David Herold, one of the conspirators. I never enter Lincoln's mind and, unlike the historian or biographer, I do not make magisterial judgments or quibble with others in the field. The five points of view were dictated, in the case of Hay and Chase, because they kept diaries, skimpily I fear, but many of their letters are available. What I aimed to achieve was balance. Hay admired Lincoln, Chase hated him, Mary Todd loved him, and so on. Each sees him in a different way, under different circumstances.

I am also reflecting upon the nature of fact as observed in fiction, and, indeed, fiction in fact. That is why the scholar-squirrels fascinate me much more than the scholars because they are like barometers, ever

---

*Mark E. Neely, Jr., "Abraham Lincoln and Black Colonization: Benjamin Butler's Spurious Testimony," *Civil War History,* Vol. XXV (March 1979), pp. 77–83.
†*Diaries and Letters of John Hay,* p. 203.

responsive to any change in the national weather. This bad period in American history has been, paradoxically, a good period for American history writing. There have never been so many intelligent biographies (yes, they are often written in academe but not by the squirrels) and interesting historians. But pure history, if such a thing could be, is flawed because "history will never reveal to us what connections there are, and at what times, between . . ." For the novelist it is the imagining of connections that brings life to what was. Finally, "History," as Tolstoi also observed, "would be an excellent thing if only it were true." Perhaps, in the end, truth is best imagined, particularly if it is firmly grounded in the disagreed- as well as agreed-upon facts.

*The New York Review of Books*
*August 18, 1988*

## 3

Every now and then, the Lincoln priests issue lists of "errors" that I am supposed to have made in my book, *Lincoln* [1984], a narrative that follows with perhaps uncomfortable closeness the progress of the "actual" Lincoln, so unlike their protean deity whose shape they must keep altering, to accommodate changes in our political weather.

Today's list of "errors" is the work of a very high priest indeed, Don E. Fehrenbacher, professor emeritus at Stanford. As layman, he is a pretty good historian (*The Dred Scott Case: Its Significance in American Law and Politics* [1978]), but when he dons canonicals, he is transfigured (*Prelude to Greatness,* or "Mormon Tabernacle Choir, here I come"). Because Fehrenbacher published his sermon not in a journal but in a book (*The Historian's* [sic] *Lincoln,* edited by Gabor S. Boritt), I am most indebted to the editors of these innocent pages for allowing me to set the record straight. This time, the "errors" are actually kind of fun, on the order of, "Vidal claims that George Washington, not John Hancock, was the first American president." Herewith Fehrenbacher's "errors" in sequence.

First: "Vidal has Lincoln say 'I was in New Orleans once' (instead of twice)." Several years ago, when this "error" was first announced at Gettysburg, a number of historians present (names will be provided during pre-trial deposition) laughed on the ground that "if that's all he can find wrong . . ." In conversation, Lincoln says that he was in New Orleans once, the way that I might say that I was in New York City once and witnessed a mugging. I would not feel obliged to list all other visits to that exciting city, nor would Lincoln when the subject of his remarks was not the Crescent City and himself as tourist but slavery.

Second: Again, Fehrenbacher quibbles, Vidal "declares that the Taylor administration offered Lincoln no government appointment other than the secretaryship of the Oregon territory (ignoring the governorship of Oregon also offered)." If Fehrenbacher were an attentive reader, he would note that *I* do not "declare" anything. I am inside the mind of John Hay. He is meditating—not declaring—on Lincoln's career at the time of their arrival in Washington in 1861. Fehrenbacher seems not to realize that every known bit of information on every subject mentioned cannot be used in a narrative meant to be read as opposed to taught. Happily, every good historian or biographer knows this. Unhappily, they are scarce in freedom's land.

Third: I am in "error" (actually it is not I but Seward) when I noted that Douglas won re-election " 'decisively' (instead of narrowly) in 1858." For Lincoln, this election looked to be a decisive end to his political career. I do not know whether or not Fehrenbacher has ever been a candidate in a state-wide senatorial contest, but I was (1982) and so was Lincoln (1858), and I can tell you, firsthand, that no matter how many votes you get, the adverb that springs to mind, in defeat, is "decisively."

Fourth: I am supposedly in error when I put "a statue of Jefferson in Lafayette Park." I did not put a statue there. I "put" the statue where it was—on the north lawn of the White House where it dominated the view of Lafayette Park from John Nicolay's bedroom, which was my context. Although Fehrenbacher is not alone in being unaware that such a statue existed and was where I said it was from 1847 to 1873, he is again in error.

Fifth: I am supposedly in error when I refer to Robert E. Lee as "the rebel commander" as of June 1861. But he was made commanding general of Virginia's forces in April 1861, and as I am describing a scene at Lee's Arlington, Virginia, house, surely he would be "the rebel commander" for those present, McDowell and staff.

Fehrenbacher suggests it might be "fair" to assume that I have simply been making the sort of errors (having made none) that any sloppy nonacademic might make. He now brings out bell, book, and candle because he fears that I may have gone beyond mere error to "literary invention" in order to . . . He dares not say what. Examples of possible "literary inventions":

Sixth: Apparently, it is a literary invention for me to say that Elihu

B. Washburne was one of "Lincoln's frequent companions on the judicial circuit." This is sloppy reading. I do not use the word "frequent" or "companion." I do write, from the point of view of Washburne, that "many times" he heard Lincoln tell his stories among lawyers on the circuit. From Gaillard Hunt's *Israel, Elihu and Cadwallader Washburne* (New York, 1925), 228: "Elihu Washburne knew Abraham Lincoln from the time that he first went to Illinois but he was not thrown with him intimately until both were attending the session of the Supreme Court of Illinois at Springfield in the winter of 1843–44. In the library of the court in the evenings the lawyers were wont to gather for social purposes and there Washburne heard Lincoln tell his amusing stories surrounded by congenial friends." This is the authority for my absolutely inconsequential and *non*-invented point that, before 1861, Washburne had known Lincoln as a fellow lawyer in Illinois, and he had heard him tell his stories. Neither Fehrenbacher nor I have any idea when or where, on circuit or in Springfield, Washburne first met Lincoln.

Seventh: Fehrenbacher is appalled when I cause Lincoln as president-elect to carry "an elaborate file of papers in his hat." Fehrenbacher has again misread my text. On a visit to Springfield, years earlier, S. P. Chase (I am writing from *his* point of view) noticed that Lincoln ("the president-to-be," not "elect") carried papers in his top hat. This is a standard Lincoln story of the Herndon-Sandburg (not to mention John Ford!) sort and perfectly apposite where I place it, which is long before Lincoln was elected president. Fehrenbacher misread the phrase "president-to-be" as "president-elect."

Eighth: Fehrenbacher objects when I picture "Mary Lincoln as having been in love with Lyman Trumbull." Again, I am not writing in the person of an anxious academic seeking promotion but from the point of view of someone *not* myself. I have entered Mrs. Lincoln's mind and am trying to re-create the nature of her well-documented madness. For the record, Trumbull was indeed a member of her pre-marriage social circle (several biographies of Mary Todd Lincoln, including *Mary Todd Lincoln: Her Life and Letters,* by Justin G. Turner and Linda Levitt Turner [New York, 1973, p. 73], place Trumbull as one of the members of Mary Todd's "coterie"), and if she had not at least flirted with him, she would have been out of character.

Ninth: I "retail dubious testimony (such as Herndon's maggoty speculation that Lincoln contracted syphilis . . .)." This is a pretty maggoty twisting of the facts. It was not Herndon's "speculation" that Lincoln might have had syphilis. It was Lincoln's own word to Herndon that he had indeed contracted syphilis. Lincoln gave Herndon the time, the place, a doctor's name, all recorded by Herndon in a letter to Jesse W. Weik of January 1891. Although Herndon's researchers into Lincoln's past (Ann Rutledge, etc.) are a mess, it is a very foolhardy scholar indeed who rejects anything that Herndon says Lincoln himself told him. Incidentally, can one imagine a European historian ignoring the syphilis of, say, Lincoln's great contemporary and closest equivalent, Bismarck?

Tenth: Finally, Fehrenbacher thinks that I incline to the "outmoded interpretation" that Lincoln "deliberately adopted [a] strategy calculated to lose the senatorial contest with Douglas in order to win the presidency two years later." Since I am as aware of the "in" and the "out" of Lincoln modes as Fehrenbacher, I give to the ancient Francis Blair the "outmoded" notion that Lincoln had tricked Douglas into the fatal Freeport response. When Blair confronts *my* Lincoln with this, he responds, "Do you really think I plan so far ahead?" Despite some ambiguity, my Lincoln is, here, very much à la mode.

There we have my "errors" or tendentious literary inventions. The errors are either clumsy quibbles or nonexistent. There are no literary inventions. I have not set out to prove that Stanton murdered Lincoln or any of the usual bees-in-the-bonnet amateur speculations or illuminations. I suspect that most of my teacherly critics either did not read the book but gave to others that onerous task or, worse, cannot read a complex book at all. Proof? I should have thought it plain that for all the pleasure I take in the Lincoln persona, I regard that statesman's blood-and-iron response to the withdrawal of the Southern states as a very great evil; hence, his tragedy; ours, too. But no academic turf-defender has so far confronted my truly unacceptable heresy.

In order to protect the latest Lincoln model, Fehrenbacher, *et al.,* want to create the illusion that I cannot read sources as well as they can. This is . . . "Hubristic" hovers on my portable's rim but, modestly, I pull back and murmur that any fool, Fehrenbacher or I, can assemble the facts of any case.

What is done with the facts is what matters.

As a novelist (and, yes, historian), I am now in the odd position of sticking to the known facts of Lincoln's career while academic historians are constantly revising the national icon in order, currently, to persuade blacks that Lincoln never really and truly favored colonizing the ex-slaves. To do this, Ben Butler must be declared a liar and John Hay

ignored. The first is fun to do; the second impossible; the whole enterprise specious.

Of course, there is a problem with historical fictions or fictionalized
histories, and I tend to be on the side, if not of the paid propagandists
for our corporate way of life, of those historians whose teeth are set on
edge by the fantasies of the talented E. L. Doctorow or the wistful
musings of the author of *Roots.* For a people as poorly educated as
Americans (take a bow, teachers), it is a mistake to play any sort of game
with agreed-upon facts. Certainly, it is hardly wise, in what looks to be
a factual account, to have Harry Houdini chat with Walt Whitman
aboard the *Titanic,* or whatever. Fantasy, as such, must be clearly
labeled, even for our few remaining voluntary readers. I trust I am, in
this, as reactionary as any turf-protecting bureaucrat of academe.

I set my fictions within history. Imagined characters intersect with
historical ones. The history is plainly history. Fiction fiction. Admittedly, I am not well disposed toward the National Security State that
pays for academe's icon-dusters, and one cannot blame them for hurt
feelings. Even so, the surrender of academe to the imperial paymaster
is an ongoing scandal in our affairs, while the lack of any sort of
independent intellectual life in the country explains why there is no
American Gibbon or Macaulay (forget Thucydides) and why, to come
to the point, after more than a century of incontinent publishing, there
is no halfway decent biography of Abraham Lincoln.

*The American Historical Review*
February 1991

# LAST NOTE
# ON LINCOLN

Once, at the Library of Congress in Washington, I was shown the contents of Lincoln's pockets on the night that he was shot at Ford's Theater. There was a Confederate bank note, perhaps acquired during the President's recent excursion to the fallen capital, Richmond; a pocket knife; a couple of newspaper cuttings (good notices for his administration); and two pairs of spectacles. It was eerie to hold in one's hand what looked to be the same spectacles that he wore as he was photographed reading the Second Inaugural Address, the month before his murder. One of the wire "legs" of the spectacles had broken off and someone, presumably Lincoln himself, had clumsily repaired it with a piece of darning wool. I tried on the glasses: he was indeed farsighted, and what must have been to him the clearly printed lines, "let us strive on to finish the work we are in; to bind up the nation's wounds," was to my myopic eyes a gray quartz-like blur.

Next, I was shown the Bible which the President had kissed as he swore his second oath to preserve, protect, and defend the Constitution of the United States; the oath that he often used, in lieu of less spiritual argument, to justify the war that he had fought to preserve the Union. The Bible is small and beautifully bound. To the consternation of the custodian, I opened the book. The pages were as bright and clear as the day that they were printed; in fact, they stuck together in such a way as to suggest that no one had ever even riffled them. Obviously the book had been sent for at the last moment; then given away, to become a treasured relic.

Although Lincoln belonged to no Christian church, he did speak of the "Almighty" more and more often as the war progressed. During the Congressional election of 1846, Lincoln had been charged with "infidelity" to Christianity. At the time, he made a rather lawyerly response. To placate those who insist that presidents must be devout monotheists (preferably Christian and Protestant), Lincoln allowed that he himself could never support "a man for office, whom I knew to be an open enemy of, and scoffer at, religion." The key word, of course, is "open." As usual, Lincoln does not lie—something that the Jesuits maintain that no wise man does—but he shifts the argument to his own advantage and gets himself off the atheistical hook much as Thomas Jefferson had done almost a century earlier.

Last, I was shown a life mask, made shortly before the murder. The hair on the head has been tightly covered-over; the whiskers greased. When the sculptor Saint-Gaudens first saw it, he thought it was a *death* mask, so worn and remote is the face. I was most startled by the smallness of the head. In photographs, with hair and beard, the head had seemed in correct proportion to Lincoln's great height. But this vulpine little face seems strangely vulnerable. The cheeks are sunken in. The nose is sharper than in the photographs, and the lines about the wide thin mouth are deep. With eyes shut, he looks to be a small man, in rehearsal for his death.

Those who knew Lincoln always thought it a pity that there was never a photograph of him truly smiling. A non-user of tobacco, he had splendid teeth for that era, and he liked to laugh, and when he did, Philip Hone noted, the tip of his nose moved like a tapir's.

Gertrude Stein used to say that U. S. Grant had the finest American prose style. The general was certainly among our best writers but he lacked music (Gertrude lacked it too, but she did have rhythm). Lincoln deployed the plain style as masterfully as Grant; and he does have music. In fact, there is now little argument that Lincoln is one of the great masters of prose in our language and the only surprising aspect of so demonstrable a fact is that there are those who still affect surprise. Partly, this is due to the Education Mafia that has taken over what little culture the United States has and, partly, to the sort of cranks, who maintain that since Shakespeare had little Latin and less Greek, and did not keep company with kings, he could never have written so brilliantly of kings and courts, and so not he but some great lord had written the plays in his name.

For all practical purposes, Lincoln had no formal education. But he studied law, which meant reading not only Blackstone (according to Jeremy Bentham, a writer "cold, reserved and wary, exhibiting a frigid pride") but brooding over words in themselves and in combination. In those days, most good lawyers, like good generals, wrote good prose; if they were not precisely understood, a case or a battle might be lost.

William Herndon was Lincoln's law partner in Springfield, Illinois, from 1844 to February 18, 1861, when Lincoln went to Washington to be inaugurated president. Herndon is the principal source for Lincoln's prepresidential life. He is a constant embarrassment to Lincoln scholars because they must rely on him; yet since Lincoln is the national deity, they must omit a great deal of Herndon's testimony about Lincoln. For one thing, Lincoln was something of a manic-depressive, to use current jargon. In fact, there was a time when, according to Herndon, Lincoln was *"as 'crazy as a loon' in this city in 1841."* Since this sort of detail does not suit the history departments, it is usually omitted or glossed over, or poor Herndon is accused of telling lies.

The Lincoln of the hagiographers is forever serene and noble in defeat as well as in victory. With perfect hindsight, Lincoln priest Don E. Fehrenbacher maintains that it was immediately apparent that the Lincoln–Douglas contest had opened wide the gates of political opportunity for Lincoln. Actually, after Lincoln's defeat by Douglas for the US Senate, he was pretty loon-like for a time; and he thought that the gates of political opportunity had slammed shut for him. Lincoln's friend, Henry C. Whitney, in a letter to Herndon, wrote:

I shall never forget the day—January 6, 1859—I went to your office and found Lincoln there alone. He appeared to be somewhat dejected—in fact I never saw a man so depressed. I tried to rally his drooping spirits . . . but with ill success. He was simply steeped in gloom. For a time he was silent . . . blurting out as he sank down: "Well, whatever happens I expect everyone to desert me now, but Billy Herndon."

Despite the busyness of the Lincoln priests, the rest of us can still discern the real Lincoln by entering his mind through what he wrote, a seductive business, by and large, particularly when he shows us unexpected views of the familiar. Incidentally, to read Lincoln's letters in holograph is revelatory; the writing changes dramatically with his mood. In the eloquent, thought-out letters to mourners for the dead, he writes a clear firm hand. When the governor of Massachussetts, John A. Andrew, in the summer of 1862, wrote that he could not send troops because his paymasters were incapable of "quick work," Lincoln replied, "Please say to these gentlemen that if they do not work quickly I will make quick work of them. In the name of all that is reasonable, how long does it take to pay a couple of regiments?" The words tumble from Lincoln's pen in uneven rows upon the page and one senses not only his fury but his terror that the city of Washington might soon fall to the rebels.

Since 1920 no American president has written his state speeches; lately, many of our presidents seem to experience some difficulty in reading aloud what others have written for them to say. But until Woodrow Wilson suffered a stroke, it was assumed that the chief task of the first magistrate was to report to the American people, in their Congress assembled, upon the state of the union. The president was elected not only to execute the laws but to communicate to the people his vision of the prospect before us. As a reporter to the people, Lincoln surpassed all presidents. Even in his youthful letters and speeches, he is already himself. The prose is austere and sharp; there are few adjectives and adverbs; and then, suddenly, sparks of humor.

Fellow Citizens—It will be but a very few words that I shall undertake to say. I was born in Kentucky, raised in Indiana and lived in Illinois. And now I am here, where it is my business to care equally for the good people of all the States. . . . There are but few views or aspects of this great war upon which I have not said or written something whereby my own opinions might be known. But there is one—the recent attempts of our erring brethren, as they are sometimes called—to employ the negro to fight for them. I have neither written nor made a speech on that subject, because that was their business, not mine; and if I had a wish upon the subject I had not the power to introduce it, or make it effective. The great question with them was, whether the negro, being put into the army, would fight for them. I do not know, and therefore cannot decide. They ought to know better than we. I have in my lifetime heard many arguments why the negroes ought to be slaves; but if they fight for those who would keep them in slavery it will be a better argument than any I have yet heard. He who will fight for that ought to be a slave. They have concluded at last to take one out of four of the slaves, and put them in the army; and that one out of the four who will fight to keep the others in slavery ought to be a slave himself unless he is killed in a fight. While I have often said that all men ought to be free, yet

I would allow those colored persons to be slaves who want to be; and next to them those white persons who argue in favor of making other people slaves. I am in favor of giving an opportunity to such white men to try it on for themselves.

Also, as a lawyer on circuit, Lincoln was something of a "stand-up comedian," able to keep an audience laughing for hours as he appeared to improvise his stories; actually, he claimed no originality as "I am a re-tailer."

Lincoln did not depend very much on others for help when it came to the writing of the great papers. Secretary of State William Seward gave him a line or two for the coda of the First Inaugural Address, while the poetry of Shakespeare and the prose of the King James version of the Bible were so much in Lincoln's blood that he occasionally slipped into iambic pentameter.

The Annual Message to Congress, December 1, 1862, has echoes of Shakespeare's *Julius Caesar* and *Macbeth* (ominously, Lincoln's favorite play):

We can not escape history. We of this Congress and this administration will be remembered in spite of ourselves. No personal significance, or insignificance, can spare one or another of us. The fiery trial through which we pass will light us down, in honor or dishonor, to the latest generation.

A few years earlier, at Brown University, Lincoln's young secretary, John Hay, wrote a valedictory poem. Of his class's common memories, "Our hearts shall bear them safe through life's commotion / Their fading gleam shall light us to our graves." But, of course, Macbeth had said long before Hay, "And all our yesterdays have lighted fools / The way to dusty death."

Of Lincoln's contemporaries, William Herndon has given us the best close-up view of the man that he had shared an office with for seventeen years.

What was it like to be in the audience when Lincoln made a speech? What did he really look like? What did he sound like? To the first question we have the photographs: but they are motionless. He was six feet four, "more or less stoop-shouldered," wrote Herndon. "He was very tall, thin, and gaunt. . . . When he first began speaking, he was shrill, squeaking, piping, unpleasant; his general look, his form, his pose, the color of flesh, wrinkled and dry, his sensitiveness, and his momentary diffidence, everything seemed to be against him." Then, "he gently and gradually warmed up . . . voice became harmonious, melodious, musical, if you please, with face somewhat aglow. . . . Lincoln's gray eyes would flash fire when speaking against slavery or spoke volumes of hope and love when speaking of liberty, justice and the progress of mankind."

Of Lincoln's politics, Herndon wrote, he "was a conscientious conservative; he believed in Law and Order. See his speech before Springfield Lyceum in 1838." This speech is indeed a key to Lincoln's character, for it is here that he speaks of the nature of ambition and how, in a republic that was already founded, a tyrant might be tempted to reorder the state in his own image. At the end Lincoln himself did just that. There is a kind of terrible Miltonian majesty in his address to the doubtless puzzled young men of the Springfield Lyceum. In effect, their twenty-nine-year-old contemporary was saying that, for the ambitious man, it is better to reign in hell than serve in Heaven.

In the end whether or not Lincoln's personal ambition undid him and the nation is immaterial. He took a divided house and jammed it back together. He was always a pro-Union man. As for slavery, he was averse, rather than adverse, to the institution but no Abolitionist. Lincoln's eulogy on Henry Clay (July 6, 1852) is to the point. Of Clay, Lincoln wrote,

As a politician or statesman, no one was so habitually careful to avoid all sectional ground. Whatever he did, he did for the whole country. . . . Feeling as he did, and as the truth surely is, that the world's best hope depended on the continued union of the States, he was ever jealous of, and watchful for, whatever might have the slightest tendency to separate them.

He supports Clay's policy of colonizing the blacks elsewhere; today any mention of Lincoln's partiality for this scheme amuses black historians and makes many of the white ones deal economically with the truth.

Eight years later, the eulogist, now the President, promptly made war on those states that had chosen to depart the Union on the same high moral ground that Lincoln himself had so eloquently stated at the time of the Mexican War in 1848: "Any people anywhere, being inclined and having the power, have the right to rise up, and shake off the existing government, and form a new one that suits them better." Lawyer Lincoln would probably have said, rather bleakly, that the key phrase here was "and having the power." The Confederacy did not have the power; six hundred thousand men died in the next four years; and the Confederacy was smashed and Lincoln was murdered.

In a sense, we have had three republics. The first, a loose confederation of former British colonies, lasted from 1776 to 1789 when the first Congress under the Constitution met. The second republic ended April 9, 1865, with the South's surrender. In due course Lincoln's third republic was transformed (inevitably?) into the national security state where we have been locked up for forty years. A fourth republic might be nice.

In any event, for better or worse, we still live in the divided house that Lincoln cobbled together for us, and it is always useful to get to know through his writing not the god of the establishment-priests but a literary genius who was called upon to live, rather than merely to write, a high tragedy. I can think of no one in literary or political history quite like this essential American writer.

*The New York Review of Books*
August 15, 1991

# 64

---------------- • ----------------

# PRESIDENT AND
# MRS. U. S. GRANT

Some years ago a friend remarked to a brand-new President's wife (a woman of unique charm, wit, sensibility, and good grooming) that there was no phrase in our language which so sets the teeth on edge as "First Lady."

"Oh, how true!" said that lady, after the tiniest of pauses. "I keep telling the operators at the White House not to call me that, but they just love saying 'First Lady.' And of course Mrs. E + + + + + + + +r always insisted on being called that."

According to one Ralph Geoffrey Newman, in a note to the recently published *The Personal Memoirs of Julia Dent Grant,* "the term 'First Lady' became a popular one after the *Lady in the Land* . . . December 4, 1911." The phrase was in use, however, as early as the Ladyhood of Mrs. Rutherford B. ("Lemonade Lucy") Hayes.

Martha Washington contented herself with the unofficial (hence seldom omitted) title "Lady" Washington. Mrs. James Monroe took a crack at regal status, receiving guests on a dais with something suspiciously like a coronet in her tousled hair. When twenty-four-year-old Miss Julia Gardiner of Gardiners Island became the doting wife of senior citizen John Tyler, she insisted that his tottering arrivals and departures be accompanied by the martial chords of "Hail to the Chief."

Mary Todd Lincoln often gave the impression that she thought she was Marie Antoinette.

It is curious that a Johnny-come-fairly-lately republic like the United States should so much want to envelop in majesty those for the most part seedy political hacks quadrennially "chosen" by the people to rule over them. As the world's royalties take to their bicycles—or to their heels—the world's presidents from Giscard to Leone to our own dear sovereign affect the most splendid state.

It would seem to be a rule of history that as the actual power of a state declines, the pageantry increases. Certainly the last days of the Byzantine empire were marked by a court protocol so elaborate and time-consuming that the arrival of the Turks must have been a relief to everyone. Now, as our own imperial republic moves gorgeously into its terminal phase, it is pleasant and useful to contemplate two centuries of American court life, to examine those personages who have lived in the White House and borne those two simple but awful titles "The President," "The First Lady" and, finally, to meditate on that peculiarly American religion, President-worship.

The Eighteenth President Ulysses Simpson Grant and his First Lady Julia Dent Grant are almost at dead center of that solemn cavalcade which has brought us from Washington to Ford, and in the process made a monkey of Darwin. Since 1885 we have had Grant's own memoirs to study; unfortunately, they end with the Civil War and do not deal with his presidency. Now Julia Dent Grant's memoirs have been published for the first time and, as that ubiquitous clone of Parson Weems Mr. Bruce Catton says in his introduction, she comes through these pages as a most "likeable" woman. "No longer is she just Mrs. Grant. Now she has three dimensions."

From her own account Julia Dent Grant does seem to have been a likeable, rather silly woman, enamored of First Ladyhood (and why not?), with a passion for clothes. If photographs are to be trusted (and why should they be when our Parson Weemses never accept as a fact anything that might obscure those figures illuminated by the high noon of Demos?), Julia was short and dumpy, with quite astonishingly crossed eyes. As divinity in the form of First Ladyhood approached, Julia wanted to correct with surgery nature's error but her husband very nicely said that since he had married her with crossed eyes he preferred her to stay the way she was. In any case, whatever the number of Julia's dimensions, she is never anything but Mrs. Grant and one reads her only to find out more about that strange enigmatic figure who proved to be one of our country's best generals and worst presidents.

Grant was as much a puzzle to contemporaries as he is to us now. To Henry Adams, Grant was "pre-intellectual, archaic, and would have seemed so even to the cave-dwellers." Henry Adams's brother had served with Grant in the war and saw him in a somewhat different light. "He is a man of the most exquisite judgment and tact," wrote Charles Francis Adams. But "he might pass well enough for a dumpy and slouchy little subaltern, very fond of smoking." C. F. Adams saw Grant at his best, in the field; H. Adams saw him at his worst, in the White House.

During Grant's first forty years of relative failure, he took to the bottle. When given command in the war, he seems to have pretty much given up the booze (though there was a bad tumble not only off the wagon but off his horse at New Orleans). According to Mr. Bruce Catton, "It was widely believed that [Grant], especially during his career as a soldier, was much too fond of whiskey, and that the cure consisted in bringing Mrs. Grant to camp; in her presence, it was held, he instantly became a teetotaler. . . . This contains hardly a wisp of truth." It never does out there in Parson Weems land where all our presidents were good and some were great and none ever served out his term without visibly growing in the office. One has only to listen to Rabbi Korff to know that this was true even of Richard M. Nixon. Yet there is every evidence that General Grant not only did not grow in office but dramatically shrank.

The last year of Grant's life was the noblest, and the most terrible. Dying of cancer, wiped out financially by a speculator, he was obliged to do what he had always said he had no intention of doing: write his memoirs in order to provide for his widow. He succeeded admirably. The two volumes entitled *Personal Memoirs of U. S. Grant* earned $450,000; and Julia Grant was able to live in comfort for the seventeen years that she survived her husband. Now for the first time we can compare Grant's memoirs with those of his wife.

With the instinct of one who knows what the public wants (or ought to get), Grant devoted only thirty-one pages to his humble youth in Ohio. The prose is Roman—lean, rather flat, and, cumulatively, impressive. Even the condescending Matthew Arnold allowed that Grant had "the high merit of saying clearly in the fewest possible words what had to be said, and saying it, frequently, with shrewd and unexpected turns of expression." There is even a quiet wit that Grant's contemporaries were not often allowed to see: "Boys enjoy the misery of their contemporaries, at least village boys in that day did" (this is known as the Eisenhower qualification: is it taught at West Point? in order to confuse the press?), "and in later life I have found that all adults are not free from this peculiarity."

The next 161 pages are devoted to West Point and to Grant's early career as a professional army officer. Grant's eyes did not fill with tears at the thought of his school days on the banks of the Hudson. In fact, he hated the Academy: "Early in the session of the Congress which met in December, 1839, a bill was discussed abolishing the Military Academy. I saw this as an honorable way to obtain a discharge . . . for I was selfish enough to favor the bill." But the Academy remained, as it does today, impregnable to any Congress.

On graduation, Second Lieutenant Grant was posted to Jefferson Barracks, St. Louis, where, he noted, "too many of the older officers, when they came to command posts, made it a study to think what orders they could publish to annoy their subordinates and render them uncomfortable."

Grant also tells us, rather casually, that "At West Point I had a classmate . . . F. T. Dent, whose family resides some five miles west of Jefferson Barracks. . . ." The sister of the classmate was Julia Dent, aged seventeen. According to Grant, visits to the Dent household were "enjoyable." "We would often take long walks, or go on horseback to visit the neighbors. . . . Sometimes one of the brothers would accompany us, sometimes one of the younger sisters."

In May 1844, when it came time to move on (the administration was preparing an interdiction or incursion of Mexico), Grant writes: "before separating [from Julia] it was definitely understood that at a convenient time we would join our fortunes. . . ." Then Grant went off to his first war. Offhandedly, he gives us what I take to be the key if not to his character to his success: "One of my superstitions had always been when I started to go any where, or to do anything, not to turn back, or stop until the thing intended was accomplished." This defines not only a certain sort of military genius but explains field-commander Grant who would throw wave after wave of troops into battle, counting on superior numbers to shatter the enemy while himself ignoring losses.

When Henry Adams met Grant at the White House, he came away appalled by the torpor, the dullness of the sort of man "always needing stimulants, but for whom action was the highest stimulant—the instinct of fight. Such men were forces of nature, energies of the prime. . . ." This was of course only partly true of Grant. Unlike so many American jingoes, Grant did not like war for its own bloody self or conquest for conquest's sake. Of the administration's chicanery leading up to the invasion of Mexico, he wrote with hard clarity, "I was bitterly opposed to the measure, and to this day regard the war, which resulted, as one of the most unjust ever waged by a stronger against a weaker nation. . . . It was an instance of a republic following the bad example of European monarchies, in not considering justice in their desire to acquire additional territory."

Grant also had a causal sense of history that would have astonished Henry Adams had he got to know the taciturn and corrupted, if not corrupt, president. Of the conquest of Mexico and the annexation of Texas, Grant wrote, "To us it was an empire and of incalculable value; but it might have been obtained by other means. The Southern rebellion was largely the outgrowth of the Mexican War. Nations, like individuals, are punished for their transgressions. We got our punishment in the most sanguinary and expensive war of modern times." If Grant's law still obtains, then the only hope for today's American is emigration.

The Grant of those youthful years seems most engaging (but then we are reading his own account). He says firmly, "I do not believe that I ever would have the courage to fight a duel." He was probably unique among military commanders in disliking dirty stories while "I am not aware of ever having used a profane expletive in my life; but I would have the charity to excuse those who may have done so, if they were in charge of a train of Mexican pack mules. . . ."

Grant saw right through the Mexican war, which "was a political war, and the administration conducting it desired to make party capital of it." Grant was also very much on to the head of the army General Scott, who was "known to have political aspirations, and nothing so popularizes a candidate for high civil positions as military victories." It takes one, as they say, to know another.

Mark Twain published Grant's memoirs posthumously, and one wonders if he might have added a joke or two. Some possible Twainisms: "My regiment lost four commissioned officers, all senior to me, by steamboat explosions during the Mexican war. The Mexicans were not so discriminating. They sometimes picked off my juniors." The cadence of those sentences reveals an expert sense of music-hall timing. When a Mexican priest refused to let Grant use his church during an engagement, Grant threatened the priest with arrest. Immediately, the man "began to see his duty in the same light that I did, and opened the door, though he did not look as if it gave him any special pleasure to do so." But whether or not Twain helped with the jokes, it must be remembered that the glum, often silent, always self-pitying president was capable, when he chose, of the sharp remark. Told that the brilliant but inordinately vain *littérateur* Senator Charles Sumner did not believe in the Bible, Grant said, "That's only because he didn't write it."

The Mexican war ended, and "On the twenty-second of August, 1848, I was married to Miss Julia Dent Grant, the lady of whom I have before spoken." With that Caesarian line, the lady appears no more in the two volumes dedicated to the fighting of the Civil War. Now Julia's memoirs redress the balance.

In old age, Julia put pen to paper and gave her own version of her life and marriage, but for one reason or another she could never get the book published. Now, at last, her memoirs are available, suitably loaded with a plangent introduction by Mr. Catton ("they shared one of the great, romantic, beautiful loves of all American history"), a note by R. G. Newman on "The First Lady as an Author," and a foreword and notes by J. Y. Simon. The notes are excellent and instructive.

In her last years Julia was not above hawking her manuscript to millionaire acquaintances; at one point she offered the manuscript to book-lover Andrew Carnegie for $125,000. Just why the book was never published is obscure. I suspect Julia wanted too much money for it; also, as she wrote in a letter, the first readers of the text thought it "*too* near, *too* close to the private life of the Genl for the public, and I thought this was just what was wanted." Julia was right; and her artless narrative does give a new dimension (if not entirely the third) to one of the most mysterious (because so simple?) figures in our history.

"My first recollections in life reach back a long way, more than three-score years, and ten now. We, my gentle mother and two little brothers, were on the south end of the front piazza at our old home, White Haven." Julia sets us down firmly in Margaret Mitchell country. "Life seemed one long summer of sunshine, flowers, and smiles to me and to all at that happy home." Mamma came from "a large eastern city," and did not find it easy being "a western pioneer's wife." The darkies were happy as can be (this was slave-holding Missouri) and "I think our people were very happy. At least they were in mamma's time, though the young ones became somewhat demoralized about the beginning of the Rebellion, when all the comforts of slavery passed away forever."

Julia was obviously much indulged. "Coming as I did to the family after the fourth great boy, I was necessarily something of a pet. . . . It was always 'Will little daughter like to do this?' 'No!' Then little daughter did not do it." I suspect that little daughter's alarmingly crossed eyes may have made the family overprotective. She herself seems unaware of any flaw: "Imagine what a pet I was with my three, brave, handsome brothers." She was also indulged in school where she was good in philosophy (what could that have been?), mythology, and history, but "in every other branch I was below the standard, and, worse still, my indifference was very exasperating." Although Julia enjoys referring to herself as "poor little me," she sounds like a pretty tough customer.

Enter Lieutenant Grant. Julia's description of their time together is considerably richer than that of the great commander. "Such delightful rides we all used to take!" So far her account tallies with his. But then, I fear, Julia falls victim to prurience: "As we sat on the piazza alone, he took his class ring from his finger and asked me if I would not wear it. . . . I declined, saying, 'Oh, no, mamma would not approve . . . !' " "I, child that I was, never for a moment thought of him as a lover." He goes. "Oh! how lonely it was without him." "I remember he was kind enough to make a nice little coffin for my canary bird and he painted it yellow. About eight officers attended the funeral of my little pet." When Grant came back to visit, Julia told him "that I had named one of my new bedstead posts for him." Surely the good taste of the editor might have spared us this pre-Freudian pornography. In any case, after this shocker, Julia was obliged to marry Grant . . . or "Ulys" as she called him.

"Our station at Detroit is one pleasant memory . . . gay parties and dinners, the fêtes champêtres. . . . Our house was very snug and convenient: two sitting rooms, dining room, bedroom, and kitchen all on the first floor." (And all of this on a captain's pay.) Julia's especial friend that winter was the wife of Major John H. Gore. Together they gave a fancy dress ball on a Sunday, invoking the wrath of the Sabbatarians. But the girls persisted and Mrs. Gore came as the Sultana of Turkey while "I, after much consideration, decided upon the costume of the ideal tambourine girl. . . . Ulys called me 'Tambourina' for a long time afterwards."

But then Grant left the army; and the descent began. "I was now to commence," he wrote, "at the age of thirty-two, a new struggle for our support." Like most professional army men Grant was fitted for no work of any kind save the presidency and that was not yet in the cards. "My wife had a farm near St. Louis, to which we went, but I had no means to stock it." Nevertheless, "I managed to keep along very well until 1858, when I was attacked by fever and ague." Perhaps he was; he was also attacked by acute alcoholism.

But the innumerable clones of Parson Weems tend to ignore any blemish on our national heroes. And Julia does her part, too. She writes, "I have been both indignant and grieved over the statement of pretended personal acquaintances of Captain Grant at this time to the effect that he was dejected, low-spirited, badly dressed, and even slovenly." "Low-spirited" is a nice euphemism for full of spirits. Julia had the Southern woman's loyalty to kin: protect at all costs and ignore the unpleasant. She even goes beyond her husband's dour record, declaring, "Ulys was really very successful at farming . . . and I was a splendid farmer's wife."

Julia's family loyalty did not extend to Ulys's folks. Although Ulys and the Dent family could do no wrong, the Grants were generally exempted from her benign policy. In fact, Julia loathed them. "I was joyous at the thought of not going to Kentucky, for the Captain's family, with the exception of his mother, did not like me. . . . we were brought up in different schools. They considered me unpardonably extravagant, and I considered them inexcusably the other way and may, unintentionally, have shown my feelings." There were also political disagreements between the two families as the Civil War approached. The Dents were essentially Southern, and Julia "was a Democrat at that time (because my father was). . . . I was very much disturbed in my political sentiments, feeling that the states had a right to go out of the Union if they wished to." But she also thought that the Union should be preserved. "Ulys was much amused at my enthusiasm and said I was a little inconsistent when I talked of states' rights."

With the coming of the Civil War, the lives of the Grants were never again to be private. Rapidly he rose from Illinois colonel (they had moved to Galena) to lieutenant general in command of the Union forces. The victories were splendid. Julia had anxious moments, not to mention innumerable prophetic dreams which she solemnly records.

At one point, separated from the General, "I wept like a deserted child . . . Only once again in my life—when I left the White House—did this feeling of desertion come over me." There were also those unremitting base rumors. Why, "The report went out," on some crucial occasion, "that General Grant was not in the field, that he was at some dance house. The idea! Dear Ulys! so earnest and serious; he never went to a party of any kind, except to take me." Julia's usual euphemism for the drunken bouts was "he was ill." And she always helped him get well.

Grant was not above making fun of her. Julia: "Ulys, I don't like standing stationary washstands, do you?" Ulys: "Yes, I do; why don't you?" Julia: "Well, I don't know." Ulys: "I'll tell you why. You have to go to the stand. It cannot be brought to you."

Midway through the war, some Southern friends were talking of "the Constitution, telling me the action of the government was unconstitutional. Well, I did not know a thing about this dreadful Constitution and told them so. . . . I would not know where to look for it even if I wished to read it. . . . I was dreadfully puzzled about the horrid old Constitution." She even asked her father: "Why don't they make a new Constitution since this is such an enigma—one to suit the time." I suspect Julia was pretty much reflecting her husband's lifelong contempt for a Constitution that he saw put aside in the most casual way by Abraham Lincoln, who found habeas corpus incompatible with national security. But although neither Grant nor Julia was very strong on the Bill of Rights, she at least had a good PR sense. When "General Grant wrote that obnoxious order expelling the Jews from his lines for which he was so severely reprimanded by the federal Congress—the General said deservedly so, as he had no right to make an order against any special sect."

In triumph, Julia came east after Ulys assumed command of the armies. Julia was enchanted by the White House and President Lincoln, in that order. Mrs. Lincoln appears to have been on her worst behavior and Julia has a hard time glossing over a number of difficult moments. On one occasion, Julia plumped herself down beside the First Lady. Outraged, Mrs. Lincoln is alleged to have said, "How dare you be seated, until I invite you?" Julia denies that this ever happened. But she does describe a day in the field when Mrs. Lincoln was upset by a mounted lady who seemed to be trying to ride beside President Lincoln. As one reads, in the vast spaces between the lines of Julia's narrative, it would seem that Mrs. Lincoln went absolutely bananas, "growing more and more indignant and not being able to control her wrath. . . ." But, fortunately, Julia was masterful—"I quietly placed my hand on hers"—and was soothing.

Later, when the presidential yacht was in the James River, close to Grant's headquarters, Julia confesses that "I saw very little of the presidential party now, as Mrs. Lincoln had a good deal of company and seemed to have forgotten us. I felt this deeply and could not understand it. . . . Richmond had fallen; so had Petersburg. All of these places were visited by the President and party, and I, not a hundred yards from them, was not invited to join them."

Despite the dresses, the dreams, the self-serving silly-little-me talk, Julia has a sharp eye for detail; describing Richmond, the last capital of the Confederacy, she writes: "I remember that all the streets near the public buildings were covered with papers—public documents and letters, I suppose. So many of these papers lay on the ground that they reminded me of the forest leaves when summer is gone."

Although Grant ignores such details he is shrewd not only about his colleagues but about his former colleagues, the West Pointers who led the Confederate army. He writes of Jefferson Davis with whom he had served in Mexico: "Mr. Davis had an exalted opinion of his own military genius. . . . On several occasions during the war he came to the relief of the Union army by means of his superior *military genius.*" Grant also makes the Cromwellian assertion: "It is men who wait to be selected, and not those who seek, from whom we may always expect the most efficient service."

Although never a Lincoln man in politics, Grant came to like the President, and would listen respectfully to Lincoln's strategic proposals, refraining from pointing out their glaring flaws. Grant also took seriously Secretary of War Stanton's injunction never to tell Lincoln his plans in advance because the President is "so kind-hearted, so averse to refusing anything asked of him, that some friend would be sure to get from him all he knew." Lincoln was plainly aware of this defect because he "told me he did not want to know what I proposed to do."

At about this time the press that was to be Grant's constant, lifelong *bête noire,* began to get on his nerves. *The New York Times* was a particular offender; grimly, Grant remarked on that portion of the press which "always magnified rebel successes and belittled ours." In fact, "the press was free up to the point of treason."

Grant had great respect for the Confederate army, and in retrospect lauded the Fabian tactics of General J. E. Johnston on the ground that "anything that could have prolonged the war a year beyond the time that it did finally close, would probably have exhausted the North to such an extent that they might then have abandoned the contest and agreed to a separation." Because "the South was a military camp, controlled absolutely by the government with soldiers to back it . . . the war could have been protracted, no matter to what extent the discontent reached. . . ." One suspects that if Grant had been the president, he would have shut down the press, sent Congress home, and made the North an armed camp.

Grant had much the same lifelong problem with the "horrid old Constitution" that Julia had. Magisterially, he writes, "The Constitution was not framed with a view to any such rebellion as that of 1861–5. While it did not authorize rebellion it made no provision against it. Yet the right to resist or suppress rebellion is as inherent as the right of self defense. . . ." Accepting this peculiar view of that intricate document, Grant noted with some satisfaction that "the Constitution was therefore in abeyance for the time being, so far as it in any way affected the progress and termination of the war." During Grant's presidency, the Constitution was simply an annoyance to be circumvented whenever possible. Or as he used to say when he found himself, as president, blocked by mere law: "Let the law be executed."

On that day when lilacs in the dooryard bloomed, Julia was in Washington preparing to go with Grant to Philadelphia. At noon, a peculiar-looking man rapped on her door. " 'Mrs. Lincoln sends me, Madam, with her compliments, to say she will call for you at exactly eight o'clock to go to the theater.' To this, I replied with some feeling (not liking either the looks of the messenger or the message, thinking the former savored of discourtesy and the latter seemed like a command), 'You may return with my compliments to Mrs. Lincoln and say I regret that as General Grant and I intend leaving the city this afternoon, we will not, therefore, be here. . . .' "

It is nice to speculate that if Mrs. Lincoln had asked Julia aboard the yacht that day in the James River, there might never have been a Grant administration. Julia has her own speculation: "I am perfectly sure that he [the messenger], with three others, one of them [John Wilkes] Booth himself, sat opposite me and my party at luncheon."

That night in Philadelphia they heard the news. "I asked, 'This will make Andy Johnson President, will it not?' 'Yes,' the General said, 'and for some reason, I dread the change.' " Nobly, Julia did her duty: "With my heart full of sorrow, I went many times to call on dear heart-broken Mrs. Lincoln, but she could not see me."

After commanding the armies in peacetime and behaving not too well during that impasse between President Johnson and Secretary of War Stanton which led to Johnson's impeachment, Grant was himself elected president. Although, unhappily, Grant's own memoirs stop with the war, Julia's continue gaily, haphazardly, and sometimes nervously through that gilded age at whose center these two odd little creatures presided.

Until our own colorful period, nothing quite like the Grant administration had ever happened to the imperial republic. In eight years almost everyone around Grant was found to be corrupt from his first vice president Colfax to his brother-in-law to his private secretary to his secretary of war to his minister to Great Britain; the list is endless. Yet the people forgave the solemn little man who had preserved the Union and then proposed himself to a grateful nation with the phrase "Let us have peace."

Grant was re-elected president in 1872, despite a split in the Republican party: the so-called Liberal Republicans supported Horace Greeley as did the regular Democrats. Although the second term was even more scandalous than the first, the Grants were eager for yet a third term. But the country was finally fed up with Grantism. In the centennial summer of 1876, at the Philadelphia exhibition, President Grant had the rare experience of being booed in public. Julia does not mention the booing. But she does remember that the Empress of Brazil was asked to start the famous Corliss engine, while "I, the wife of the President of the United States—I, the wife of General Grant—was there and was not invited to assist at this little ceremony. . . . Of this I am quite sure: if General Grant had known of this intended slight to his wife, the engine never would have moved with his assistance."

Nevertheless, after four years out of office General and Mrs. Grant were again eager to return to the White House, to "the dear old house. . . . Eight happy years I spent there," wrote Julia, "so happy! It still seems as much like home to me as the old farm in Missouri, White Haven." But it looked rather different from the farm or, for that matter, from the way the White House has usually looked. By the time Mrs. Grant had finished her refurbishments, the East Room was divided into three columned sections and filled with furniture of ebony and gold. Julia was highly pleased with her creation; in fact, "I have visited many courts and, I am proud to say, I saw none that excelled in brilliancy the receptions of President Grant."

Except for a disingenuous account of the secretary of war's impeachment (his wife "Puss" Belknap was a favorite of Julia's), the First Lady herself hardly alludes to the scandals of those years. On the other hand, Julia describes in rapturous detail her trip around the world with Ulys. In London dinner was given them by the Duke of Wellington at Apsley House. "This great house was presented to Wellington by the government for the single [sic] victory at Waterloo, along with wealth and a noble title which will descend throughout his line. As I sat there, I thought, 'How would it have been if General Grant had been an Englishman—I wonder, I wonder?' "

So did Grant. Constantly. In fact, he became obsessed by the generos-

ity of England to Marlborough and to Wellington and by the niggardli-
ness of the United States to its unique savior. It is possible that Grant's
corruption in office stems from this resentment; certainly, he felt that
he had every right to take expensive presents from men who gained
thereby favors. Until ruined by a speculator-friend of his son, Grant
seems to have acquired a fortune; although nowhere near as large as that
of the master-criminal Lyndon Johnson, it was probably larger than that
of another receiver of rich men's gifts, General Eisenhower.

Circling the globe, the vigorous Grant enjoyed sightseeing and Julia
enjoyed shopping. There was culture, too: at Heidelberg "we remained
there all night and listened with pleasure to Wagner or Liszt—I cannot
remember which—who performed several of his own delightful pieces
of music for us." (It was Wagner.) "Of course, we visited the Taj and
admired it as everyone does. . . . Everyone says it is the most beautiful
building in the world, and I suppose it is. Only I think that everyone
has not seen the Capitol at Washington!" It is no accident that General
Grant's favorite book was *Innocents Abroad*. After nearly two years,
Maggie and Jiggs completed the grand tour, and came home with every
hope of returning to the "dear old house" in Washington.

A triumphal progress across the States began on the West Coast (it
was Grant's misfortune never to have become what he had wanted to
be ever since his early years in the army, a Californian). Then they
returned to their last official home, Galena, Illinois, "To Galena, dear
Galena, where we were at home again in reality," writes Julia. Then
"after a week's rest, we went to Chicago." The Grants were effete
Easterners now, and Galena was no more than a place from which to
regain the heights. "We were at Galena when the Republican Convention met at Chicago . . . I did not feel that General Grant would be
nominated. . . . The General would not believe, but I saw it plainly."
Julia was right, and James A. Garfield was nominated and elected.

Galena was promptly abandoned for a handsome house in New York
City's East 66th Street. The Grants' days were halcyon until that grim
moment when Grant cried out while eating a peach: he thought that
something had stung him in the throat. It was cancer. The Grants were
broke, and now the General was dying. Happily, various magnates like
the Drexels and the Vanderbilts were willing to help out. But Grant was
too proud for overt charity. Instead he accepted Mark Twain's offer to
write his memoirs. And so, "General Grant, commander-in-chief of
1,000,000 men, General Grant, eight years President of the United
States, was writing, writing of his own grand deeds, recording them that

he might leave a home and independence to his family." On July 19, 1885, Grant finished the book, "and on the morning of July the twenty-third, he, my beloved, my all, passed away, and I was alone, alone."

In *Patriotic Gore* Edmund Wilson writes: "It was the age of the audacious confidence man, and Grant was the incurable sucker. He easily fell victim to their [*sic*] trickery and allowed them to betray him into compromising his office because he could not believe that such people existed." This strikes me as all wrong. I think Grant knew exactly what was going on. For instance, when Grant's private secretary General Babcock was indicted for his part in the Whisky Ring, the President, with Nixonian zeal, gave a false deposition attesting to Babcock's character. Then Grant saw to it that the witnesses for the prosecution would not, as originally agreed, be granted exemption for testifying. When this did not inhibit the United States Attorney handling the suit, Grant fired him in mid-case: obstruction of justice in spades.

More to the point, it is simply not possible to read Grant's memoirs without realizing that the author is a man of first-rate intelligence. As president, he made it his policy to be cryptic and taciturn, partly in order not to be bored by the politicians (and from the preening Charles Sumner to the atrocious Roscoe Conkling it was an age of insufferable megalomaniacs, so nicely described by Henry Adams in *Democracy*) and partly not to give the game away. After all, everyone was on the take. Since an ungrateful nation had neglected to give him a Blenheim palace, Grant felt perfectly justified in consorting with such crooks as Jim Fisk and Jay Gould, and profiting from their crimes.

Neither in war nor in peace did Grant respect the "horrid old Constitution." This disrespect led to such bizarre shenanigans as Babcock's deal to buy and annex to the United States the unhappy island of Santo Domingo, the Treasury's money to be divvied up between Babcock and the Dominican president (and, perhaps, Grant, too). Fortunately, Grant was saved from this folly by cabinet and Congress. Later, in his memoirs, he loftily justifies the caper by saying that Santo Domingo would have been a nice place to put the former slaves.

Between Lincoln and Grant the original American republic of states united in free association was jettisoned. From the many states they forged one union, a centralized nation-state devoted to the acquisition of wealth and territory by any means. Piously, they spoke of the need to eliminate slavery but, as Grant remarked to Prince Bismarck, the real struggle *"in the beginning"* was to preserve the Union, and slavery was a secondary issue. It is no accident that although Lincoln was swift to go to war for the Union, he was downright lackadaisical when it came to Emancipation. Much of the sympathy for the South among enlightened Europeans of that day was due to the fierce arbitrariness of Lincoln's policy to deny the states their constitutional rights while refusing to take a firm stand on the moral issue of slavery.

In the last thirty-four years, the republic has become, in many ways, the sort of armed camp that Grant so much esteemed in the South. For both Lincoln and Grant it was *e pluribus unum* no matter what the price in blood or constitutional rights. Now those centripetal forces they helped to release a century ago are running down and a countervailing force is being felt: *ex uno plures*.

But enough. In this bicentennial year, as the benign spirit of Walt Disney ranges up and down the land, let us look only to what was good in Ulysses S. Grant. Let us forget the corrupted little president and remember only the great general, the kind and exquisitely tactful leader, the Roman figure who, when dying, did his duty and made the last years of his beloved goose of a wife comfortable and happy.

*The New York Review of Books*
September 18, 1975

---◆---

# THEODORE ROOSEVELT:
# AN AMERICAN SISSY

In Washington, D.C., there is—or was—a place where Rock Creek crosses the main road and makes a ford which horses and, later, cars could cross if the creek was not in flood. Half a hundred years ago, I lived with my grandparents on a wooded hill not far from the ford. On summer days, my grandmother and I would walk down to the creek, careful to avoid the poison ivy that grew so luxuriously amid the crowded laurel. We would then walk beside the creek, looking out for crayfish and salamanders. When we came to the ford, I would ask her to tell me, yet again, what happened when the old President Roosevelt—not the current President Roosevelt—had come riding out of the woods on a huge horse just as two ladies on slow nags had begun a slow crossing of the ford.

"Well, suddenly, Mr. Roosevelt screamed at them, 'Out of my way!' " My grandmother imitated the president's harsh falsetto. "Stand to one side, women. *I am the President.*" What happened next? I'd ask, delighted. "Oh, they were both soaked to the skin by his horse's splashing all over them. But then, the very next year," she would say with some satisfaction, "*nice* Mr. Taft was the president." Plainly, there was a link in her mind between the Event at the Ford and the change in the presidency. Perhaps there was. In those stately pre-personal days you did not call ladies women.

The attic of the Rock Creek house was filled with thousands of books on undusted shelves while newspapers, clippings, copies of the *Congressional Record* were strewn about the floor. My grandmother was not a zealous housekeeper. There was never a time when rolled-up Persian rugs did not lie at the edge of the drawing room, like crocodiles dozing. In 1907, the last year but one of Theodore Roosevelt's administration, my grandfather came to the Senate. I don't think that they had much to do with each other. I found only one reference to TR—as he was always known—on the attic floor. In 1908, when Senator Gore nominated William Jennings Bryan for president, he made an alliterative aside, "I much prefer the strenuosity of Roosevelt to the sinuosity of Taft."

Years later I asked him why he had supported Bryan, a man who had never, in my grandfather's own words, "developed. He was too famous too young. He just stopped in his thirties." So why had he nominated Bryan for president? Well, at the time there were reasons: he was vague. Then, suddenly, the pale face grew mischievous and the thin, straight Roman mouth broke into a crooked grin. "After I nominated him at Denver, we rode back to the hotel in the same carriage and he turned to me and said, 'You know, I base my political success on just three things.' " The old man paused for dramatic effect. What were they? I asked. "I've completely forgotten," he said. "But I do remember wondering why he thought he was a success."

In 1936, Theodore Roosevelt's sinuous cousin Franklin brought an end to my grandfather's career in the Senate. But the old man stayed on in Rock Creek Park and lived to a Nestorian age, convinced that FDR, as he was always known, was our republic's Caesar while his wife, Eleanor, Theodore's niece, was a revolutionary. The old man despised the whole family except Theodore's daughter Alice Longworth.

Alice gave pleasure to three generations of our family. She was as witty—and as reactionary—as Senator Gore; she was also deeply resentful of her distant cousin Franklin's success while the canonization of her own first cousin Eleanor filled her with horror. "Isn't Eleanor no-ble," she would say, breaking the word into two syllables, each hummed reverently. "So very, *very* good!" Then she would imitate Eleanor's buck teeth which were not so very unlike her own quite prominent choppers. But Alice did have occasional, rare fits of fairness. She realized that what she felt for her cousins was "Simply envy. *We* were the President Roosevelt family. But then along came the Feather Duster," as she habitually referred to Franklin, "and we were forgotten." But she was exaggerating, as a number of new books attest, not to mention that once beautiful Dakota cliff defaced by the somber Gutzon Borglum with the faces of dead pols.

It is hard for Americans today to realize what a power the Roosevelts exerted not only in our politics but in the public's imagination. There had been nothing like them since the entirely different Adamses and there has been nothing like them since—the sad story of the Kennedys bears about as much resemblance to the Roosevelts as the admittedly entertaining and cautionary television series *Dallas* does to Shakespeare's chronicle plays.

From the moment in 1898 when TR raced up Kettle Hill (incorrectly known as San Juan) to April 12, 1945, when Franklin Roosevelt died, the Roosevelts were at the republic's center stage. Also, for nearly half that fifty-year period, a Roosevelt had been president. Then, as poignant coda, Eleanor Roosevelt, now quite alone, acted for seventeen years as conscience to a world very different from that of her uncle TR or even of FDR, her cousin-husband.

In the age of the condominium and fast foods, the family has declined not only as a fact but as a concept. Although there are, presumably, just as many Roosevelts alive today as there were a century ago, they are now like everyone else, scattered about, no longer tribal or even all of the same class. Americans can now change class almost as fast—downward, at least—as they shift from city to city or job to job. A century ago, a member of the patriciate was not allowed to drop out of his class no matter how little money he had. He might be allowed to retire from the world, like TR's alcoholic brother Elliott, in order to cultivate his vices, but even Elliott remained very much a part of the family until death—not his own kind—declassed him.

As a descendant of Theodore Roosevelt said to David McCullough, author of *Mornings on Horseback,* "No writer seems to have understood the degree to which [TR] was part of a clan." A clan that was on the rise, socially and financially, in nineteenth-century New York City. In three generations the Roosevelts had gone from hardware to plate glass to land development and banking (Chemical). By and large, the Roosevelts of that era were a solemn, hardworking, uninspired lot who, according to the *New York World,* had a tendency "to cling to the fixed and the venerable." Then, suddenly, out of this clan of solid burghers erupted the restless Theodore and his interesting siblings. How did this happen? *Cherchez la mère* is the usual key to the unexpected—for good or ill—in a family's history.

During Winston Churchill's last government, a minister found him
in the Cabinet room, staring at a newspaper headline: one of his daughters had been arrested, yet again, for drunkenness. The minister said
something consoling. Churchill grunted. The minister was then inspired
to ask: "How is it possible that a Churchill could end up like this?" To
which the old man replied: "Do you realize just *what* there was between
the first Duke of Marlborough and *me*?" Plainly, a genetic disaster area
had been altered, in Winston's case, by an American mother, Jennie
Jerome, and in Theodore Roosevelt's case by a southern mother, named
Mittie Bulloch, a beautiful, somewhat eccentric woman whom everyone
delighted in even though she was not, to say the least, old New York.
Rather, she was proudly southern and told her sons exciting stories of
what their swashbuckling southern kin had done on land and sea. In
later life, everyone agreed that Theodore was more Bulloch than Roosevelt just as his cousin Franklin was more Delano—or at least *Sara
Delano*—than Roosevelt.

Mr. McCullough's book belongs to a new and welcome genre: the
biographical sketch. Edmund Wilson in *Patriotic Gore* and Richard
Hofstadter in *The American Political Tradition* were somewhat specialized practitioners of this art but, by and large, from Plutarch to Strachey, it has been more of a European than an American genre. Lately,
American biography has fallen more and more into the hands not of
writers but of academics. That some academics write very well indeed
is, of course, perfectly true and, of course, perfectly rare. When it comes
to any one of the glorious founders of our imperial republic, the ten-
volume hagiography is now the rule. Under the direction of a tenured
Capo, squads of graduate students spend years assembling every known
fact, legend, statistic. The Capo then factors everything into the text,
like sand into a cement mixer. The result is, literally, monumental, and
unreadable. Even such minor figures as Ernest Hemingway and Sinclair
Lewis have been accorded huge volumes in which every letter, telegram,
drunken quarrel is memorialized at random. "Would *you* read this sort
of book?" I asked Mark Schorer, holding up his thick life of Sinclair
Lewis. He blinked, slightly startled by my bad manners. "Well," he said
mildly, politely, "I must say I never really *liked* Lewis's work all that
much."

Now, as bright footnotes to the academic texts, we are offered such
books as Otto Friedrich's *Clover* and Jean Strouse's *Alice James*. These
sketches seem to me to belong to literature in a way that Schorer's
*Sinclair Lewis* or Dumas Malone's *Jefferson and His Time* do not—the

first simply a journeyman compilation, the second a banal hagiography (with, admittedly, extremely valuable footnotes). In a sense, the reader of Malone et al. is obliged to make his own text out of the unshaped raw material while the reader of Strouse or Friedrich is given a finished work of literature that supplies the reader with an idiosyncratic view of the subject. To this genre *Mornings on Horseback* belongs: a sketch of Theodore Roosevelt's parents, brothers and sisters, wife, and self until the age of twenty-eight. Mr. McCullough has done a good swift job of sketching this family group.

Unfortunately, he follows in the wake not of the usual dull, ten-volume academic biography of the twenty-sixth president but of the first volume of Edmund Morris's *The Rise of Theodore Roosevelt.* This is bad luck for Mr. McCullough. Morris's work is not only splendid but covers the same period as Mr. McCullough, ending some years later with the death of McKinley. Where Mr. McCullough scores is in the portrait of the family, particularly during Theodore's youth. Fortunately, there can never be too much of a good thing. Since Morris's work has a different, longer rhythm, he does not examine at all closely those lesser lives which shaped—and explain, somewhat—the principal character.

Theodore Roosevelt, Senior, was a man of good works; unlike his wife Mittie. "She played no part in his good works, and those speculations on life in the hereafter or the status of one's soul, speculations that appear in Theodore's correspondence . . . are not to be found in what she wrote. She was not an agnostic exactly," writes McCullough, but at a time when the church was central to organized society she seems more than slightly indifferent or, as her own mother wrote, "If she was only a Christian, I think I could feel more satisfied."

Mittie's lack of religion was to have a lasting effect on her grand-daughter Eleanor, the future Mrs. Franklin Delano Roosevelt. In 1870 Mittie placed her eldest child, Anna—known as Bamie—in Les Ruches, a girls' school at Fountainebleau. The school's creator was Mlle. Marie Souvestre, "a woman of singular poise and great culture, but also an outspoken agnostic . . . as brief as Bamie's time there would be, Mlle. Souvestre's influence would carry far." Indeed it did. In the next generation Bamie's niece Eleanor was also sent to school with Mlle. Souvestre, now removed to Allenwood in England. One of Mlle. Souvestre's teachers was Dorothy Bussy, a sister of Lytton Strachey and the pseudonymous as well as eponymous author of *Olivia* by Olivia, a story of *amitiés particulières* in a girls' school.

Bamie was not to marry until she was forty, while Eleanor's dislike of heterosexuality was lifelong ("*They* think of nothing else," she once said to me, grimly—and somewhat vaguely, for she never really said exactly who "they" were); it would seem that Mlle. Souvestre and her school deserve a proper study—before M. Roger Peyrefitte gets to it. Certainly, Eleanor had learned Mlle. Souvestre's lesson well: this world is the one that we must deal with and, if possible, improve. Eleanor had no patience with the other-worldly. Neither had her uncle TR. In a letter to Bamie, the future president says that he is marrying for a second time—the first wife had died. As a highly moral man, he is disgusted with himself. So much so that "were I sure there were a heaven my one prayer would be I might never go there, lest I should meet those I loved on earth who are dead."

A recurrent theme in this family chronicle is ill health. Bamie had a disfiguring curvature of the spine. Elliott had what sounds like epileptic fits. Then, at thirty-four, he was dead of alcoholism, in West 102nd Street, looked after by a mistress. Theodore, Junior's general physical fragility was made intolerable by asthma. Mr. McCullough has done a good deal of research into asthma, that most debilitating and frightening of nervous afflictions. "Asthma is repeatedly described as a 'suppressed cry for the mother'—a cry of rage as well as a cry for help." Asthmatics live in constant terror of the next attack, which will always seem to be—if indeed it is not—terminal.

Parenthetically, I ran into the Wise Hack not long ago—in the lobby of the Beverly Hills Hotel. Where else? He is now very old, very rich: he owns a lot of Encino. Although he will no longer watch a movie made after 1945, he still keeps an eye on "the product." He knows all the deals. "One funny thing," he said, wheezing from emphysema—not asthma. "You know, all these hotshot young directors they got now? Well, every last one of them is a fat sissy who likes guns. And every last one of them has those thick glasses and the asthma." But before I could get him to give me the essential data, as Mrs. Wharton used to say, he had been swept into the Polo Lounge by the former managing editor of *Liberty*.

I must say that I thought of the Wise Hack's gnomic words as I read Mr. McCullough's account of TR's asthma attacks, which usually took place on a Sunday "which in the Victorian era was still the Lord's day . . . the one day of the week when the head of the household was home from work. . . ." Sunday also involved getting dressed up and going to church, something TR did not like. On the other hand, he enjoyed everyone's attention once the attacks had ended. Eventually, father and son came under the spell of a Dr. Salter, who had written that "organs are made for action, not existence; they are made to *work,* not to be; and when they *work* well, they can *be* well." You must change your life, said Rilke's Apollo. And that is what the young TR did: he went to a gymnasium, became an outdoorsman, built up his fragile body. At Harvard he was five foot eight inches tall and weighed one hundred twenty-five pounds. In later life, he was no taller but he came to weigh more than two hundred pounds; he was definitely a butterball type, though a vigorous one. He also wore thick glasses; liked guns.

Unlike the sissies who now make violent movies celebrating those who kill others, Theodore was a sissy who did not know that he was one until he was able to do something about it. For one thing, none of the Roosevelt children was sent to school. They were tutored at home. The boys seemed not to have had a great deal to do with other boys outside their own tribe. When Theodore went to Harvard, he was on his own for the first time in his life. But even at Harvard, Mittie would not allow him to room with other boys. He had an apartment in a private house; and a manservant. At first, he was probably surprised to find that he was unpopular with the other students; but then he was not used to dealing with those he did not know. He was very much a prig. "I had a headache," he writes in his diary, aged eleven, "and Conie and Ellie made a tremendous noise playing at my expense and rather laughed when I remonstrated."

At Harvard, he was very conscious of who was and who was not a gentleman. "I stand 19th in the class. . . . Only one gentleman stands ahead of me." He did not smoke; he got drunk on only one occasion—when he joined the Porcellian Club; he remained "pure" sexually. He was a lively, energetic youth who spoke rapidly, biting off his words as if afraid there would not be enough breath for him to say what he wanted to say. Properly bespectacled and gunned since the age of thirteen, he shot and killed every bird and animal that he could; he was also a fair taxidermist. Toward the end of his Harvard career, he was accepted as what he was, a not unattractive New York noble who was also rich; his income was $8,000 a year, about $80,000 in today's money. In his last two years at Harvard "clothes and club dues . . . added up to $2,400, a sum the average American family could have lived on for six years."

In later years, Theodore was remembered by a classmate as "a joke . . . active and enthusiastic and that was all," while a girl of his generation said "he was not the sort to appeal at first." Harvard's President Eliot, who prided himself on knowing no one, remembered Theodore as "feeble" and rather shallow. According to Mr. McCullough, he made "no lasting male friendships" at Harvard, but then, like so many men of power, he had few attachments outside his own family. During the early part of his life he had only one friend—Henry Cabot (known as La-de-dah) Lodge, a Boston aristo-sissy much like himself.

The death of his father was a shattering experience; and the family grew even closer to one another than before. Then Theodore fell in love and added a new member to the clan. When TR met Alice Lee, she was seventeen and he was nineteen. "See that girl," he said to Mrs. Robert Bacon at a party. "I am going to marry her. She won't have me, but I am going to have *her.*" Have her he did. "Alice," said Mrs. Bacon years later, "did not want to marry him, but she did." They were married October 27, 1880, on Theodore's twenty-second birthday. They lived happily ever after—for four years. Alice died of Bright's disease, shortly after giving birth to their daughter; a few hours earlier, in the same house, Mittie had died of typhoid fever. The double blow entirely changed Theodore's life. He went west to become a rancher, leaving little Alice with his sister Bamie. That same year Elliott also became a father when his wife, Anna Hall, gave birth to Eleanor.

In 1876, as General Grant's second administration fell apart in a storm of scandal and the winds of reform gathered force, New York State's great lord of corruption, Senator Roscoe Conkling, observed with characteristic sour wit: "When Dr. Johnson defined patriotism as the last refuge of a scoundrel, he ignored the enormous possibilities of the word reform." Since good Republicans like Theodore Roosevelt, Senior, could not endure what was happening to their party and country, they joined together to cleanse party, country.

As a member of the New York delegation to the Republican convention at Cincinnati, Theodore, Senior, helped deny both Conkling and James G. Blaine, another lord of corruption, the nomination for president. After a good deal of confusion the dim but blameless Rutherford B. Hayes was nominated. Although Hayes was not exactly *elected* president, he became the president as a result of the Republican Party's continued mastery of corruption at every level of the republic.

The new president then offered Theodore, Senior, the Collectorship of the Port of New York, a powerhouse of patronage and loot that had been for some years within Conkling's gift. And so it remained: thanks to Conkling's efforts in the Senate, Theodore, Senior, was denied the Collectorship. A week after this rejection, he wrote his son at Harvard to say that, all in all, he was relieved that he was not to be obliged to "purify our Customhouse." Nevertheless, he was glad that he had fought the good fight against the "machine politicians" who "think of nothing higher than their own interests. I fear for your future. We cannot stand so corrupt a government for any great length of time." This was the last letter from father to son. Two months later Theodore, Senior, was dead of cancer, at the age of forty-six.

Although TR worshipped his father, he does not seem to have been particularly interested in the politics of reform. During the Collectorship battle, he had wanted to be a naturalist; later he thought of writing, and began to compose what proved to be, or so one is told, a magisterial study of the early years of the American navy, *The Naval War of 1812*. He also attended Columbia Law School until 1881, when he got himself elected to the New York State Assembly. He was twenty-three years old; as lively and bumptious as ever.

Much had been made of what a startling and original and noble thing it was for a rich young aristo to enter the sordid politics of New York State. Actually, quite a number of young men of the ruling class were going into politics, often inspired by fathers who had felt, like Theodore, Senior, that the republic could not survive so much corruption. In fact, no less a grandee than the young William Waldorf Astor had been elected to the Assembly (1877) while, right in the family, TR's Uncle Rob had served in Congress, as a Democrat. There is no evidence that Theodore went into politics with any other notion than to have an exciting time and to rise to the top. He had no theory of government. He was, simply, loyal to his class—or what he called, approvingly, "our kind." He found the Tammany politicians repellent on physical and social as well as political grounds.

To TR's credit, he made no effort at all to be one of the boys; quite the contrary. He played the city dude to the hilt. In Albany, he arrived at his first Republican caucus, according to an eyewitness, "as if he had been ejected by a catapult. He had on an enormous great ulster . . . and he pulled off his coat; he was dressed in full dress, he had been to dinner somewhere. . . ." Even then, his high-pitched voice and upper-class accent proved to be a joy for imitators, just as his niece Eleanor's voice—so very like his—was a staple of mimics for fifty years. To the press, he was known, variously, as a "Jane-Dandy," "his Lordship," "Oscar Wilde," "the exquisite Mr. Roosevelt." He sailed above these epithets. He was in a hurry to . . . do what?

Mr. McCullough quotes Henry James's description of a similar char-

acter in *The Bostonians* (published five years after Theodore's entry into
politics): "He was full of purpose to live . . . and with a high success;
to become great, in order not to be obscure, and powerful not to be
useless." In politics, it is character rather than ideas that makes for
success; and the right sort of character combined with high energy can
be fairly irresistible. Although TR was the most literary of our post–
Civil War presidents, he had a mind that was more alert to fact than
to theory. Like his father, he was against corruption and machine politicians, and that was pretty much that—until he met Samuel Gompers,
a rising young trade unionist. Gompers took the dude around the tenements of New York City; showed him how immigrants were forced to
live, doing such sweated labor as making cigars for wealthy firms. TR
had planned to oppose a bill that the Cigarmaker's Union had spon-
sored, outlawing the manufacture of cigars "at home." After all, TR was
a laissez-faire man; he had already opposed a minimum wage of $2.00
a day for municipal workers. But the tour of the tenements so shocked
the dude that he supported the Cigar Bill.

TR also began to understand just how the United States was governed. Predictably, he found the unsavory Jay Gould at the center of
a web that involved not only financiers but judges and newspaper pro-
prietors and, to his horror, people that he knew socially. He describes
how a kindly friend of the family, someone whom he referred to as a
"member of a prominent law firm," explained the facts of life to him.
Since *everyone,* more or less openly, did business with the likes of Jay
Gould, TR was advised to give up "the reform play" and settle down
as a representative member of the city's ruling—as opposed to governing—class. This was the sort of advice that was guaranteed to set him
furiously in motion. He had found, at last, the Horatio-at-the-bridge role
that he had been looking for. He took on the powers that be; and he
coined a famous phrase, "the wealthy criminal class." Needless to say,
he got nowhere in this particular battle, but by the time he was twenty-
six he had made a national name for himself, the object of the exercise.
He had also proven yet again that he could take it, was no sissy, had
what Mark Sullivan was to call "a trait of ruthless righteousness."

In 1884, TR was a delegate to the Republican convention where, once
again, James G. Blaine was a candidate. Like his father before him, TR
joined the reformers; and together they fought to eliminate Blaine; but
this time the gorgeous old trickster finally got the nomination, only to
lose the election to Grover Cleveland. But by the time Cleveland was
elected, the young widower and ex-assemblyman was playing cowboy

in the Dakota Badlands. Just before TR disappeared into the wilderness, he made what was to be the most important decision of his career. In 1884 the reform Republicans deserted Blaine much as the antiwar Democrats were to abandon Hubert Humphrey in 1968. But TR had already made up his mind that he was going to have a major political career and so, cold-bloodedly, he endorsed Blaine: "I have been called a reformer but I am a Republican." For this show of solidarity with the Grand Old Party, he lost the decent opinion of the reformers and gained the presidency. He might have achieved both, but that would have required moral courage, something he had not been told about.

Give a sissy a gun and he will kill everything in sight. TR's slaughter of the animals in the Badlands outdoes in spades the butcheries of that sissy of a later era, Ernest Hemingway. Elks, grizzly bears, blacktail bucks are killed joyously while a bear cub is shot, TR reports proudly, "clean through . . . from end to end" (the Teddy bear was yet to be invented). "By Godfrey, but this is fun!" TR was still very much the prig, at least in speech: "He immortalized himself along the Little Missouri by calling to one of his cowboys, 'Hasten forward quickly here!'" Years later he wrote: "There were all kinds of things of which I was afraid at first, ranging from grizzly bears to 'mean' horses and gunfighters; but by acting as if I was not afraid I gradually ceased to be afraid."

There is something strangely infantile in this obsession with dice-loaded physical courage when the only courage that matters in political or even "real" life is moral. Although TR was often reckless and always domineering in politics, he never showed much real courage, and despite some trust-busting, he never took on the great ring of corruption that ruled and rules in this republic. But then, he was born a part of it. At best, he was just a dude with the reform play. Fortunately, foreign affairs would bring him glory. As Lincoln was the Bismarck of the American states, Theodore Roosevelt was the Kaiser Wilhelm II, a more fortunate and intelligent figure than the Kaiser but every bit as bellicose and conceited. Edith Wharton described with what pride TR showed her a photograph of himself and the Kaiser with the Kaiser's inscription: "President Roosevelt shows the Emperor of Germany how to command an attack."

I once asked Alice Longworth just why her father was such a war-lover. She denied that he was. I quoted her father's dictum: "No triumph of peace is quite as great as the supreme triumph of war." A sentiment to be echoed by yet another sissy in the next generation: *"Meglio un giorno da leone che cento anni da pecora."* "Oh, well," she said, "that's the way they all sounded in those days." But they did not all sound that way. Certainly Theodore, Senior, would have been appalled, and I doubt if Eleanor really approved of Uncle Teddy's war-mongering.

As president, TR spoke loudly and carried a fair-sized stick. When Colombia wouldn't give him the land that he needed for a canal, he helped invent Panama out of a piece of Colombia; and got his canal. He also installed the United States as the policeman of the Western Hemisphere. In order to establish an American hegemony in the Pacific, TR presided over the tail-end of the slaughter of more than half a million Filipinos who had been under the illusion that after the Spanish-American War they would be free to set up an independent republic under the leadership of Emilio Aguinaldo. But TR had other plans for the Philippines. Nice Mr. Taft was made the governor-general and one thousand American teachers of English were sent to the islands to teach the natives the sovereign's language.

Meanwhile, in the aftermath of the Boxer Rebellion, TR's "open-door policy" to China had its ups and downs. In 1905 the Chinese boycotted American goods because of American immigration policies, but the United States was still able to establish the sort of beachhead on the mainland of Asia that was bound to lead to what TR would have regarded as a bully fine war with Japan. Those of us who were involved in that war did not like it all that much.

In 1905, the world-famous Henry James came, in triumph, to Washington. He was a friend of Secretary of State John Hay and of Henry Adams. "Theodore Rex," as James called the president, felt obliged to invite the Master to the White House even though TR had denounced James as "effete" and a "miserable little snob"—it takes one to know one—while James thought of TR as "a dangerous and ominous Jingo." But the dinner was a success. James described the president as a "wonderful little machine . . . quite exciting to see. But it's really like something behind a great plate-glass window on Broadway." TR continued to loathe "the tone of satirical cynicism" of Henry James and Henry Adams while the Master finally dismissed the president as "the mere monstrous embodiment of unprecedented and resounding noise."

Alice Longworth used to boast that she and her father's viceroy Taft were the last Westerners to be received by the Dowager Empress of China. "We went to Peking. To the Forbidden City. And there we were taken to see this strange little old lady standing at the end of a room.

Well, there was no bowing or scraping for us. So we marched down the room just behind the chamberlain, a eunuch, like one of those in that book of yours, *Justinian,* who slithered on his belly toward her. After he had announced us, she gave him a kick and he rolled over like a dog and slithered out." What had they talked about? She couldn't recall. I had my impression that she rather liked the way the empress treated her officials.

In the years before World War II, Alice was to be part of a marital rectangle. The heart having its reasons, Alice saw fit to conduct a long affair with the corrupt Senator William Borah, the so-called lion of Idaho, who had once roared, "I'd rather be right than president," causing my grandfather to murmur, "Of course, he was neither." In 1940, when the poor and supposedly virtuous Borah died, several hundred thousand dollars were found in his safety deposit box. Where had the money come from? asked the press. "He was my friend," said Senator Gore, for public consumption, "I do not speculate." But when I asked him who had paid off Borah, the answer was blunt. "The Nazis. To keep us out of the war." Meanwhile, Alice's husband, the Speaker of the House Nicholas Longworth, was happily involved with Mrs. Tracy (another Alice) Dows.

Rather late in life, Alice Longworth gave birth to her only child. In *The Making of Nicholas Longworth,* by Longworth's sister Clara de Chambrun, there is a touching photograph of Longworth holding in his arms a child whose features are unmistakably those of a lion's cub. "I should have been a grandmother, not a mother," Alice used to say of her daughter. But then, she had as little maternal instinct toward her only child as TR had had paternal instinct for her. When Nicholas Longworth died in 1931, Alice Dows told me how well Alice Longworth had behaved. "She asked me to go with her in the private train that took Nick back to Ohio. Oh, it was very moving. Particularly the way Alice treated me, as if *I* was the widow, which I suppose I was." She paused; then the handsome, square-jawed face broke into a smile and she used the Edwardian phrase: "Too killing."

When Alice Dows died she left me a number of her books. Among them was *The Making of Nicholas Longworth,* which I have just read. It is a loving, quite uninteresting account of what must have been a charming, not very interesting man. On the page where Alice Dows makes her appearance "one evening at Mrs. Tracy Dows's home . . . ," she had placed a four-leaf clover—now quite faded: nice emblem for a lucky lot.

In the electronic era, letter-writing has declined while diaries are kept only by those ill-educated, crazed, lone killers who feel obliged to report, in clinical detail, just how crazed and solitary they are as they prepare to assassinate political leaders. Except for Christopher Isherwood, I can think of no contemporary literary figure who has kept, for most of a lifetime, a journal. *The Diaries of Anaïs Nin* were, of course, her fiction. Fortunately, the preelectronic Roosevelts and their friends wrote countless letters and journals and books, and Mr. McCullough has done a good job of selection; one is particularly grateful for excerpts from the writings of Elliott Roosevelt, a rather more natural and engaging writer than his industrious but not always felicitous older brother. Mr. McCullough's own style is easy to the point of incoherence. "The horse he rode so hard day after day that he all but ruined it," sounds more like idle dictation than written English. But, all in all, he has succeeded in showing us how a certain world, now lost, shaped the young Theodore Roosevelt. I think it worth noting that Simon and Schuster has managed to produce the worst set of bound galleys that I have ever read. There are so many misspellings that one has no sense of TR's own hit-or-miss approach to spelling, while two pages are entirely blank.

Now that war is once more thinkable among the thoughtless, Theodore Roosevelt should enjoy a revival. Certainly, the New Right will find his jingoism appealing, though his trust-busting will give less pleasure to the Honorable Society of the Invisible Hand. The figure that emerges from the texts of both Mr. McCullough and Mr. Morris is both fascinating and repellent. Theodore Roosevelt was a classic American sissy who overcame—or appeared to overcome—his physical fragility through "manly" activities of which the most exciting and ennobling was war.

As a politician-writer, Theodore Roosevelt most closely resembles Winston Churchill and Benito Mussolini. Each was as much a journalist as a politician. Each was a sissy turned showoff. The not unwitty Churchill—the most engaging of the lot—once confessed that if no one had been watching him he could quite easily have run away during a skirmish in the Boer War. Each was a romantic, in love with the nineteenth-century notion of earthly glory, best personified by Napoleon Bonaparte, whose eagerness to do in *his* biological superiors led to such a slaughter of alpha-males that the average French soldier of 1914 was markedly shorter than the soldier of 1800—pretty good going for a fat little fellow, five foot four inches tall—with, to be fair, no history of asthma.

As our dismal century draws to a close, it is fairly safe to say that no matter what tricks and torments are in store for us, we shall not see *their* like again. Faceless computer analysts and mindless cue-card readers will preside over our bright noisy terminus.

*The New York Review of Books*
August 13, 1981

# 66

• ——

# *ELEANOR*
# *ROOSEVELT*

*Nicholas and Alexandra.* Now *Eleanor and Franklin.* Who's next for the tandem treatment? *Dick and Pat*? *J. Edgar and Clyde*? Obviously there is a large public curious as to what goes on in the bedrooms of Winter Palace and White House, not to mention who passed whom in the corridors of power. All in all, this kind of voyeurism is not a bad thing in a country where, like snakes, the people shed their past each year ("Today nobody even remembers there *was* a Depression!" Eleanor Roosevelt exclaimed to me in 1960, shaking her head at the dullness of an audience we had been jointly trying to inspire). But though Americans dislike history, they do like soap operas about the sexual misbehavior and the illnesses—particularly the illnesses—of real people in high places: "Will handsome, ambitious Franklin ever regain the use of his legs? Tune in tomorrow."

The man responsible for the latest peek at our masters, off-duty and on, is Joseph Lash. A journalist by trade, a political activist by inclination, an old friend of Eleanor Roosevelt as luck would have it (hers as well as his), Mr. Lash has written a very long book. Were it shorter, it would have a smaller sale but more readers. Unfortunately, Mr. Lash has not been able to resist the current fashion in popular biography: he puts in everything. The Wastebasket School leaves to the reader the task of arranging the mess the author has collected. Bank balances, invitations to parties, funerals, vastations in the Galerie d'Apollon—all are presented in a cool democratic way. Nothing is more important than anything else. At worst the result is "scholarly" narrative; at best, lively soap opera. No more does prophet laurel flower in the abandoned Delphi of Plutarch, Johnson, Carlyle, Strachey: Ph.D. mills have polluted the sacred waters.

Objections duly noted, I confess that I found *Eleanor and Franklin* completely fascinating. Although Mr. Lash is writing principally about Eleanor Roosevelt, someone I knew and admired, I still think it impossible for anyone to read his narrative without being as moved as I was. After all, Eleanor Roosevelt was a last (*the* last? the *only*?) flower of that thorny Puritan American conscience which was, when it was good, very, very good, and now it's quite gone things are horrid.

A dozen years ago, Mrs. Roosevelt asked me to come see her at Hyde Park. I drove down to Val-Kill cottage from where I lived on the Hudson. With some difficulty, I found the house. The front door was open. I went inside. "Anybody home?" No answer. I opened the nearest door. A bathroom. To my horror, there in front of the toilet bowl, stood Eleanor Roosevelt. She gave a startled squeak. "Oh, *dear!*" Then, resignedly, "Well, now you know *everything.*" And she stepped aside, revealing a dozen gladiolas she had been arranging in the toilet bowl. "It does keep them fresh." So began our political and personal acquaintance.

I found her remarkably candid about herself and others. So much so that I occasionally made notes, proud that I alone knew the truth about this or that. Needless to say, just about every "confidence" she bestowed on me appears in Mr. Lash's book and I can testify that he is a remarkably accurate recorder of both her substance and style. In fact, reading him is like having her alive again, hearing that odd, fluting yet precise voice with its careful emphases, its nervous glissade of giggles, the great smile which was calculated not only to avert wrath but warn potential enemies that here was a lioness quite capable of making a meal of anyone.

Then there were those shrewd, gray-blue eyes which stared and stared at you when you were not looking at her. When you did catch her at it, she would blush—even in her seventies the delicate gray skin would grow pink—giggle, and look away. When she was not interested in someone she would ask a polite question; then remove her glasses, which contained a hearing aid, and nod pleasantly—assuming she did not drop into one of her thirty-second catnaps.

The growing up of Eleanor Roosevelt is as interesting to read about as it was, no doubt, hard to have lived through. Born plain. Daughter of an alcoholic father whom she adored. Brought up by a sternly religious maternal grandmother in a house at Tivoli, New York, some thirty miles north of Hyde Park, where her cousin Franklin was also growing up, a fatherless little boy spoiled by his mother, the dread Sara Delano, for forty years the constant never-to-be-slain dragon in Eleanor's life.

Long after the death of Mrs. James (as Sara Delano Roosevelt was known to the Valley), Eleanor would speak of her with a kind of wonder and a slight distention of the knotty veins at her temples. "Only once did I ever *openly* quarrel with Mrs. James. I had come back to Hyde Park to find that she had allowed the children to run wild. Nothing I'd wanted done for them had been done. 'Mama,' I said" (accent on the second syllable, incidentally, in the French fashion), " 'you are *impossible*!' " "And what did she say?" I asked. "Why, nothing." Mrs. Roosevelt looked at me with some surprise. "You see, she was a grande dame. She never noticed *anything* unpleasant. By the next day she'd quite forgotten it. But of course I couldn't. I forgive . . ." One of her favorite lines, which often cropped up in her conversation as well as—now—in the pages of Mr. Lash's book, "but I *never* forget."

But if Mrs. James was to be for Eleanor a life's antagonist, her father was to be the good—if unlikely—angel, a continuing spur to greatness, loved all the better after death. Elliott Roosevelt was charming and talented (many of his letters are remarkably vivid and well-written) and adored by everyone, including his older brother Theodore, the President-to-be. Elliott had everything, as they say; unfortunately, he was an alcoholic. When his drinking finally got out of control, the family sent him south; kept him away from Eleanor and her young brother Hall (himself to be an alcoholic). During these long absences, father and daughter exchanged what were, in effect, love letters, usually full of plans to meet. But when those rare meetings did take place, he was apt to vanish and leave her sitting alone at his club until, hours later, someone remembered she was there and took her home.

Yet in his letters, if not in his life, Elliott was a Puritan moralist—with charm. He wanted his daughter, simply, to be good. It is hard now to imagine what being good is, but to that generation there was not much ambiguity about the word. As Eleanor wrote in 1927, in a plainly autobiographical sketch,

She was an ugly little thing, keenly conscious of her deficiencies, and her father, the only person who really cared for her, was away much of the time;

but he never criticized her or blamed her, instead he wrote her letters and stories, telling her how he dreamed of her growing up and what they would do together in the future, but she must be truthful, loyal, brave, well-educated, or the woman he dreamed of would not be there when the wonderful day came for them to fare forth together. The child was full of fears and because of them lying was easy; she had no intellectual stimulus at that time and *yet she made herself as the years went on into a fairly good copy of the picture he painted.*

As it turned out, Eleanor did not fare forth with her father Elliott but with his cousin Franklin, and she was indeed all the things her father had wanted her to be, which made her marriage difficult and her life work great.

In 1894, Elliott died at 313 West 102nd Street, attended by a mistress. The ten-year-old Eleanor continued to live in the somber house at Tivoli, her character forming in a way to suggest that something unusual was at work. The sort of world she was living in could hardly have inspired her to write, as she did at fourteen:

Those who are ambitious & make a place & a name in the great world for themselves are nearly always despised & laughed at by lesser souls who could not do as well & all they do for the good of men is construed into wrong & yet they do the good and they leave their mark upon the ages & if they had had no ambition would they have ever made a mark?

This was written in the era of Ward McAllister, when the best circles were still intent on gilding the age with bright excess. Eleanor was already unlike others of her class and time.

The turning point—the turning on—of her life occurred at Allenswood, an English school run by the formidable Mlle. Souvestre, a free-thinker (doubtless shocking to Eleanor, who remained a believing Christian to the end of her days) and a political liberal. Readers of *Olivia* know the school through the eyes of its author, Dorothy Bussy—a sister of Lytton Strachey. Allenswood was a perfect atmosphere in which to form a character and "furnish a mind." The awkward withdrawn American girl bloomed, even became popular. Some of Eleanor's essays from this period are very good. On literature:

"The greatest men often write very badly and all the better for them. It is not in them that we look for perfect style but in the secondary writers (Horace, La Bruyère)—one must know the masters by heart, adore them, try to think as they do and then leave them forever. For technical instruction there is little of profit to draw from the learned and polished men of genius."

So exactly did Flaubert speak of Balzac (but it is unlikely that Eleanor could have read that report of dinner Chez Magny). She perfected her French, learned Italian and German, and became civilized, according to the day's best standards.

Nearly eighteen, Eleanor returned to America. It was 1902: a time of great hope for the Republic. Uncle Theodore was the youngest President in history. A reformer (up to a point), he was a bright example of the "right" kind of ambition. But Tivoli was no more cheerful than before. In fact, life there was downright dangerous because of Uncle Vallie, a splendid alcoholic huntsman who enjoyed placing himself at an upstairs window and then, as the family gathered on the lawn, opening fire with a shotgun, forcing them to duck behind trees (in the forties there was a young critic who solemnly assured us that America could never have a proper literature because the country lacked a rich and complex class system!). It is no wonder that Eleanor thought the Volstead Act a fine thing and refused to serve drink at home for many years.

Eleanor came out, as was expected, and suffered from what she considered her ungainly appearance. Yet she was much liked, particularly by her cousin Franklin (known to *their* cousin Alice as "The Feather Duster": "You know, the sort of person you wouldn't ask to dinner, but for afterward"). During this period, Eleanor's social conscience was stirring. She worked at a settlement house where she not only saw how the poor lived but met a generation of women reformers, many of them also active in the suffragette movement. Eleanor was a slow convert to women's rights. But a convert she became. Just as she was able to change her prejudices against Jews and blacks (she was once attacked by the NAACP for referring to the colored, as they were then known, as "darkies").

Franklin began to court her. The letters he wrote her she destroyed— no doubt, a symbolic act when she found him out in adultery. But her letters remain. They are serious (she had been nicknamed "Granny"); they are also ambitious. For a young man who had made up his mind that he would rise to the top of the world she was a perfect mate. It is a sign of Franklin's genius—if that is the word—that even in his spoiled and callow youth he had sense enough to realize what Eleanor was all about.

The marriage ceremony was fine comedy. The bride and groom were entirely overshadowed by Uncle Ted. Eleanor was amused, Franklin not. Mr. Lash misses—or omits—one important factor in the marriage. For all of Eleanor's virtues (not immediately apparent to the great world which Franklin always rather liked) she was a catch for one excellent reason: she was the President's niece, and not just your average run-of-the-mill President but a unique political phenomenon who had roused the country in a way no other President had since Jackson. I suspect this weighed heavily with Franklin. Certainly when it came time for him to run for office as a Democrat, many Republicans voted for him simply because his name was Roosevelt and he was married to the paladin's niece.

As the world knows, Franklin and Eleanor were a powerful political partnership. But at the personal level, the marriage must never have been happy. For one thing, Eleanor did not like sex, as she confided in later years to her daughter. Franklin obviously did. Then there was his mother. The lives of the young couple were largely managed by Mrs. James, who remained mistress of the house at Hyde Park until she died. It is poignant to read a note from Eleanor to Franklin after the old lady's death in 1941, asking permission to move furniture around—permission generally not granted, for the place was to remain, as long as Franklin lived (and as it is now), the way his mother wanted it—and the most God-awful Victorian taste it is. But surroundings never meant much to any of the family, although Mrs. Roosevelt once told me how "Mr. Truman showed me around the White House, which he'd just redone, and he was so proud of the upstairs which looked to me *exactly* like a Sheraton Hotel!"

Franklin went to the State Senate. Eleanor learned to make speeches—not an easy matter because her voice was high, with a tendency to get out of control. Finally, she went to a voice coach. "You must tell President Kennedy. The exercises did wonders for my voice." A giggle. "Yes, I know, I don't sound *very* good but I was certainly a lot worse before, and Mr. Kennedy does need help because he talks much too fast and too high for the average person to understand him."

I remarked that in the television age it was quite enough to watch the speaker. She was not convinced. One spoke to the people in order to *educate* them. That was what politics was all about, as she was among the last to believe.

It is startling how much is known at the time about the private lives of the great. My grandfather Senator Gore's political career ended in 1936 after a collision with President Roosevelt ("This is the last relief check you'll get if Gore is reelected" was the nice tactic in Oklahoma), but in earlier times they were both in the liberal wing of the Democratic party and when Franklin came to Washington as Assistant Secretary of the Navy under Wilson, he was on friendly terms with the Senator. Washington was a small town then and everyone knew all about everyone else's private life. Not long ago Alice Longworth managed to startle even me by announcing, at a dinner party: "Daisy Harriman told me that every time she was alone with Senator Gore he would pounce on her. I could never understand why he liked her. After all, he was *blind*. But then Daisy always smelled nice."*

Meanwhile, the Gores were keeping track of the Roosevelts. Franklin fell in love with Eleanor's young secretary, Lucy Mercer, and they conducted an intense affair (known to everyone in Washington except Eleanor who discovered the truth in the tried-and-true soap opera way: innocently going through her husband's mail when he was ill). Senator Gore used to say, "What a trial Eleanor must be! She waits up all night in the vestibule until he comes home." I never knew exactly what this meant. Now Mr. Lash tells us "the vestibule story." Angry at her husband's attentions to Lucy at a party, Eleanor went home alone but because Franklin had the keys, she spent much of the night sitting on the stoop.

Later, confronted with proof of Franklin's adultery, Eleanor acted decisively. She would give him a divorce but, she pointed out, she had five children and Lucy would have to bring them up. Lucy, a Catholic, and Franklin, a politician-on-the-make, agreed to cool it. But toward the end of his life they began to see each other again. He died with Lucy in the room at Warm Springs and Eleanor far away. Eleanor knew none of this until the day of her husband's death. From what she later wrote about that day, a certain amount of normal grief seems not to have been present.

When Franklin got polio in 1921, Eleanor came into her own. On his behalf, she joined committees, kept an eye on the political situation, pursued her own good works. When the determined couple finally arrived at the White House, Eleanor became a national figure in her own right. She had her own radio program. She wrote a syndicated column for the newspapers. She gave regular press conferences. At last she was loved, and on the grandest scale. She was also hated. But at fourteen she

*My sister responded to this story by reminding Mrs. Longworth of a certain peculiar episode in the Governor's office at Albany between TR and a lady. Mrs. Longworth was not amused.

had anticipated everything ("It is better to be ambitious & do something than to be unambitious & do nothing").

Much of what Mr. Lash writes is new to me (or known and forgotten), particularly Eleanor's sponsorship of Arthurdale, an attempt to create a community in West Virginia where out-of-work miners could each own a house, a bit of land to grow things on, and work for decent wages at a nearby factory. This was a fine dream and a bureaucratic catastrophe. The houses were haphazardly designed, while the factory was not forthcoming (for years any industrialist who wanted to be invited to the White House had only to suggest to Eleanor that he might bring industry to Arthurdale). The right wing of course howled about socialism.

The right wing in America has always believed that those who have money are good people and those who lack it are bad people. At a deeper level, our conservatives are true Darwinians and think that the weak and the poor ought to die off, leaving the spoils to the fit. Certainly a do-gooder is the worst thing anyone can be, a societal pervert who would alter with government subsidy nature's harsh but necessary way with the weak. Eleanor always understood the nature of the enemy: she was a Puritan, too. But since she was Christian and not Manichaean, she felt obliged to work on behalf of those dealt a bad hand at birth. Needless to say, Franklin was quite happy to let her go about her business, increasing his majorities.

"Eleanor has this state trooper she lives with in a cottage near Hyde Park." I never believed that one but, by God, here the trooper is in the pages of Mr. Lash. Sergeant Earl R. Miller was first assigned to the Roosevelts in Albany days. Then he became Eleanor's friend. For many years she mothered him, was nice to his girlfriends and wives, all perfectly innocent—to anyone but a Republican. It is a curious fact of American political life that the right wing is enamored of the sexual smear. Eleanor to me: "There are actually people in Hyde Park who knew Franklin all his life and said that he did not have polio but the sort of disease you get from not living the *right* sort of life."

The left wing plays dirty pool, too, but I have no recollection of their having organized whispering campaigns of a sexual nature against Nixon, say, the way the right so often does against liberal figures. Knowing Eleanor's active dislike of sex as a subject and, on the evidence of her daughter, as a fact, I think it most unlikely she ever had an affair with anyone. But she did crave affection, and jealously held on to her friends, helped them, protected them—often unwisely. Mr. Lash describes most poignantly Eleanor's grief when she realized that *her* friend Harry Hopkins had cold-bloodedly shifted his allegiance to Franklin.

Eleanor was also faced with the President's secretary and *de facto* wife Missy Le Hand ("Everybody knows the old man's been living with her for years," said one of the Roosevelt sons to my father who had just joined the subcabinet. My father, an innocent West Pointer, from that moment on regarded the Roosevelt family arrangements as not unlike those of Ibn Saud). Yet when Missy was dying, it was Eleanor who would ring her up. Franklin simply dropped her. But then Missy was probably not surprised. She once told Fulton Oursler that the President "was really incapable of a personal friendship with anyone."

Mr. Lash writes a good deal about Eleanor's long friendship with two tweedy ladies, Marion Dickerman and Nancy Cook. For years Eleanor shared Val-Kill cottage with them; jointly they ran a furniture factory and the Todhunter School, where Eleanor taught until she went to the White House. The relationship of the three women seems unusually tangled, and Mr. Lash cannot do much with it. Things ended badly with an exchange of letters, filled with uncharacteristic bitterness on Eleanor's side. If only the author of *Olivia* could have had a go at that subject.

In a sense Eleanor had no personal life after the White House years began. She was forever on the go (and did not cease motion during the long widowhood). She suffered many disappointments from friends and family. I remember her amused description of Caroline Kennedy and what a good thing it was that the two Kennedy children would still be very young when they left the White House because, she frowned and shook her head, "It is a terrible place for young people to grown up in, continually flattered and—*used.*"

I was with her the day the news broke that a son had married yet again. While we were talking, he rang her and she smiled and murmured, over and over, "Yes, dear . . . yes, I'm very happy." Then when she hung up, her face set like stone. "You would think that he might have told his mother *first,* before the press." But that was a rare weakness. Her usual line was "people are what they are, you can't change them." Since she had obviously begun life as the sort of Puritan who thought people not only could but must be changed, this later tolerance was doubtless achieved at some cost.

When I was selected as Democratic-Liberal candidate for Congress, Eleanor (I called her Mrs. R) was at first cool to the idea—I had known her slightly all my life (she had liked my father, detested my grandfather). But as the campaign got going and I began to move up in the polls and it suddenly looked as if, wonder of wonders, Dutchess County might go Democratic in a congressional election for the first time in fifty years (since Franklin's senatorial race, in fact), she became more and more excited. She joined me at a number of meetings. She gave a tea at Val-Kill for the women workers in the campaign. Just as the women were leaving, the telephone rang. She spoke a few minutes in a low voice, hung up, said good-by to the last of the ladies, took me aside for some political counsel, was exactly as always except that the tears were streaming down her face. Driving home, I heard on the radio that her favorite granddaughter had just been killed.

In later years, though Eleanor would talk—if asked—about the past, she was not given to strolls down memory lane. In fact, she was contemptuous of old people who lived in the past, particularly those politicians prone to the Ciceronian vice of exaggerating their contribution to history, a category in which she firmly placed that quaint Don Quixote of the cold war, Dean Acheson. She was also indifferent to her own death. "I remember Queen Wilhelmina when she came to visit during the war" (good democrat that she was, nothing royal was alien to Eleanor) "and she would sit under a tree on the lawn and commune with the dead. She would even try to get *me* interested in spiritualism but I always said: Since we're going to be dead such a long time anyway it's rather a waste of time chatting with all of them *before* we get there."

Although a marvelous friend and conscience to the world, she was, I suspect, a somewhat unsatisfactory parent. Descendants and their connections often look rather hard and hurt at the mention of her. For those well-placed by birth to do humanity's work, she had no patience if they were—ultimate sin—unhappy. A woman I know went to discuss with her a disastrous marriage; she came away chilled to the bone. These things were to be borne.

What did Eleanor feel about Franklin? That is an enigma, and perhaps she herself never sorted it out. He was complex and cold and cruel (so many of her stories of life with him would end, "And then I *fled* from the table in tears!"). He liked telling her the latest "Eleanor stories"; his sense of fun was heavy. A romantic, Mr. Lash thinks she kept right on loving him to the end (a favorite poem of the two was E. B. Browning's "Unless you can swear, 'For life, for death,'/Oh, fear to call it loving!"). But I wonder. Certainly he hurt her mortally in their private relationship; worse, he often let her down in their public partnership. Yet she respected his cunning even when she deplored his tactics.

I wonder, too, how well she understood him. One day Eleanor told me about something in his will that had surprised her. He wanted one side of his coffin to be left open. "Well, we hadn't seen the will when he was buried and of course it was too late when we did read it. But what *could* he have meant?" I knew and told her: "He wanted, physically, to get back into circulation as quickly as possible, in the rose garden." She looked at me as if this were the maddest thing she had ever heard.

I suspect the best years of Eleanor's life were the widowhood. She was on her own, no longer an adjunct to his career. In this regard, I offer Mr. Lash an anecdote. We were four at table: Mrs. Tracy Dows, Mrs. Roosevelt, her uncle David Gray (our wartime Ambassador to Ireland), and myself. Eleanor began: "When Mr. Joe Kennedy came back from London, during the war . . ." David Gray interrupted her. "Damned coward, Joe Kennedy! Terrified they were going to drop a bomb on him." Eleanor merely grinned and continued. "Anyway he came back to Boston and gave that *unfortunate* interview in which he was . . . well, somewhat *critical* of us."

She gave me her teacher's smile, and an aside. "You see, it's a very funny thing but whatever people say about us we almost always hear. I don't know *how* this happens but it does." David Gray scowled. "Unpleasant fellow, that Joe. Thought he knew everything. Damned coward." I said nothing, since I was trying to persuade Eleanor to support the wicked Joe's son at the Democratic convention; something she could not, finally, bring herself to do.

"Well, *my* Franklin said, 'We better have him down here'—we were at Hyde Park—'and see what he has to say.' So Mr. Kennedy arrived at Rhinecliff on the train and I met him and took him straight to Franklin. Well, ten minutes later one of the aides came and said, 'The President wants to see you right away.' This was unheard of. So I *rushed* into the office and there was Franklin, white as a sheet. He asked Mr. Kennedy to step outside and then he said, and his voice was *shaking,* 'I never want to see that man again as long as I live.' " David Gray nodded: "Wanted us to make a deal with Hitler." But Eleanor was not going to get into that. "Whatever it was, it was *very* bad. Then Franklin said, 'Get him out of here,' and I said, 'But, dear, you've invited him for the weekend, and we've got guests for lunch and the train doesn't leave until two,' and Franklin said, 'Then you drive him around Hyde Park and put him on that train,' and I did and it was the most dreadful four hours of my life!" She laughed. Then, seriously: "I wonder if the *true* story of Joe Kennedy will ever be known."

To read Mr. Lash's book is to relive not only the hopeful period in

American life (1933–40) but the brief time of world triumph (1941–45). The book stops, mercifully, with the President's death and the end of Eleanor and Franklin (Mr. Lash is correct to put her name first; of the two she was greater). Also, the end of . . . what? American innocence? Optimism? From 1950 on, our story has been progressively more and more squalid. Nor can one say it is a lack of the good and the great in high places: they are always there when needed. Rather the corruption of empire has etiolated the words themselves. Now we live in a society which none of us much likes, all would like to change, but no one knows how. Most ominous of all, there is now a sense that what has gone wrong for us may be irreversible. The empire will not liquidate itself. The lakes and rivers and seas will not become fresh again. The arms race will not stop. Land ruined by insecticides and fertilizers will not be restored. The smash-up will come.

To read of Eleanor and Franklin is to weep at what we have lost. Gone is the ancient American sense that whatever is wrong with human society can be put right by human action. Eleanor never stopped believing this. A simple faith, no doubt simplistic—but it gave her a stoic serenity. On the funeral train from Georgia to Washington: "I lay in my berth all night with the window shade up, looking out at the countryside he had loved and watching the faces of the people at stations, and even at the cross-roads, who came to pay their last tribute all through the night. The only recollection I clearly have is thinking about 'The Lonesome Train,' the musical poem about Lincoln's death. ('A lonesome train on a lonesome track/Seven coaches painted black/A slow train, a quiet train/Carrying Lincoln home again . . .'). I had always liked it so well—and now this was so much like it."

I had other thoughts in 1962 at Hyde Park as I stood alongside the thirty-third, the thirty-fourth, the thirty-fifth, and the thirty-sixth Presidents of the United States, not to mention all the remaining figures of the Roosevelt era who had assembled for her funeral (unlike the golden figures in Proust's last chapter, they all looked if not smaller than life smaller than legend—so many shrunken March of Time dolls soon to be put away). Whether or not one thought of Eleanor Roosevelt as a world ombudsman or as a chronic explainer or as a scourge of the selfish, she was like no one else in her usefulness. As the box containing her went past me, I thought, well, that's that. We're really on our own now.

*The New York Review of Books*
November 18, 1971

# 67
·

# H. L. MENCKEN
# THE JOURNALIST

## I

After politics, journalism has always been the preferred career of the ambitious but lazy second-rater. American exceptions to mediocrity's leaden mean: from column A, there was Franklin D. Roosevelt; from column B, H. L. Mencken.

Although Henry Louis Mencken was a magazine editor *(The Smart Set, American Mercury),* a literary critic, an expositor of Nietzsche, and a school-of Samuel Johnson compiler of *The American Language,* he never ceased to be a journalist for the *Sunpapers* in his hometown of Baltimore, where he was born in 1880 and where he died in 1956. From 1906 to 1948, he was connected with the Baltimore *Sun,* as a columnist, feature writer, editor. He was the most influential journalist of his day; he was also the wittiest.

As a working journalist, Mencken's lifelong subject was nothing less than Freedom's land and Bravery's home, the United States where flourished such gorgeous clowns as Calvin Coolidge, and "The Great Croon of Croons," Franklin D. Roosevelt, the not-so-great Great Commoner, William Jennings Bryan, and many, many others. But if only God could have invented such a cast, it was Mencken who proved to be God's most attentive and appreciative drama critic. It was Mencken who described the show. He revelled in absurdity; found no bonnet entirely bee-less. He loved the national bores for their own sweet sake.

As he contemplated the meagre lives of our dull presidents, he wrote: "There comes a day of public ceremonial, and a chance to make a speech ... A million voters with IQs below 60 have their ears glued to the radio. It takes four days' hard work to concoct a speech without a sensible word in it. Next a dam must be opened somewhere. Four dry Senators get drunk and make a painful scene. The Presidential automobile runs over a dog. It rains."

American journalism's golden (a kinder adjective than "yellow") age coincided with Mencken's career; that is, from century's turn to mid-century's television. During this period, there was still a public educational system and although Mencken often laughs at the boobs out there, the average person could probably get through a newspaper without numb lips. Today, half the American population no longer reads newspapers: plainly, they are the clever half.

For Mencken, the old-time journalist, or "newsie," was a combination of François Villon and Shane. He was "wildcattish." He was freelance, a knight for hire. In 1927, Mencken was already looking back nostalgically to the time when a journalist "used to make as much as a bartender or a police sergeant," now "he makes as much as the average doctor or lawyer, and his wife, if he has one, maybe has social ambitions." Today, of course, the "journalist" is often paid movie-star prices for movie-star appearances on television or along the lecture circuit, and he needs no wife to inspire him to a cozy lunch *à deux* with Nancy Reagan or Barbara Bush.

Mencken did acknowledge that, even then, some journalists liked to mingle with the wealthy and the powerful but, for him, there was always a greater fascination in those lower depths where dwell bartenders and police sergeants.

Mencken's ideal popular paper for that vast public which "gets all its news by listening" (today one would change "listening" to "staring"— at television), would be "printed throughout, as First Readers are printed, in words of one syllable. It should avoid every idea that is beyond the understanding of a boy of ten" on the ground that "all ideas are beyond them. They can grasp only events. But they will heed only those events that are presented as drama with one side clearly right and the other clearly wrong. They can no more imagine neutrality than they can imagine the fourth dimension." Thus, Mencken anticipates not only the television news programme but the television political campaign with its combative thirty-second spot commercials and sound-bites. Movies were already showing the way, and Mencken acknowledged the wisdom of the early movie magnates whose simple-minded screened *agons* had made them rich. Unfortunately, once rich, they pined for culture, against which Mencken sternly warns with his famous injunction: "No one in this world, so far as I know—and I have researched the records for years, and employed agents to help me—has ever lost money by underestimating the intelligence of the great masses of the plain people. Nor has anyone ever lost public office thereby."

Today, Mencken's boisterous style and deadpan hyperboles are very difficult even for "educated" Americans to deal with, and Sanskrit to the generality. Although every American has a sense of humour—it is his birthright and encoded somewhere in the Constitution—few Americans have ever been able to cope with wit or irony and even the simplest jokes often cause unease, especially today when every phrase must be examined for covert sexism, racism, ageism.

American character (which does and does not exist) fascinated Mencken, who observed, in 1918, that the universal image of Uncle Sam the money-grubber was mistaken. "The character that actually marks off the American is not money-hunger at all; it is what might be called, at the risk of misunderstanding, social aspiration." For the American, money plays only a part in moving upward "to break down some barrier of caste, to secure the acceptance of his betters." "Unlike Europe, no one has a station," [so far as he knows, of course: Class is a national dirty secret] "unless he makes it for himself." Of course Mencken lived in simpler times. For the American of 1918 "There is always something just behind him and tantalizing him, menacing him and causing him to sweat."

Mencken quotes Wendell Phillips: "More than any other people, we Americans are afraid of one another." Mencken acknowledges this truth, and he puts it down to the desire to conform, which means howling with the rest of the mindless pack as it careens from nowhere to nowhere in pursuit of such instant-enemies of the week as Gaddafi, Noriega, Saddam, put in place by our packmeisters, successively, like that mechanical rabbit used to keep racing dogs on course. For this sense of collective security, the individual must sacrifice himself in order "to belong to something larger and safer than he is," and he can "work off steam within prudent limits. Beyond lie the national taboos. Beyond lies true independence and the heavy penalties that go therewith."

A century earlier, that shrewd passerby, Tocqueville, also noted the force of the majority on the individual to conform. But Mencken was obliged to live a lifetime in such a society and so, unlike the French penologist, he can present data from inside the slammer: "The taboos that I have mentioned are extraordinarily harsh and numerous. They stand around nearly every subject that is genuinely important to man: they hedge in free opinion and experimentation on all sides. Consider, for example, the matter of religion. It is debated freely and furiously in almost every country in the world save the United States," but here the critic is silenced. "The result is that all religions are equally safeguarded against criticism, and that all of them lose vitality. We protect the status quo, and so make steady war upon revision and improvement."

In August 1925, Mencken meditated on how Europeans view Americans, and how they noted "our growing impatience with the free play of ideas, our increasing tendency to reduce all virtues to the single one of conformity, our relentless and all pervading standardization . . . Europe doesn't fear our military or economic prowess, rather it is Henry Ford that gives them the shivers . . . By Americanization it means Fordization—and not only in industry but also in politics, art and even religion." Nor is this simply the spontaneous power of public opinion; it is the deliberate power of the state brought into play. "No other nation of today is so rigorously policed. The lust to standardize and regulate extends to the most trivial minutia of private life."

At the time that Mencken wrote this alcohol had been prohibited by law to the American people, as well as almost every form of sex, disturbing reading matter, and so on. Mencken also adverts to the Scopes trial of that year, whose verdict forbade the teaching of Darwin's theory of evolution in the schools of Christian Tennessee. This trial convinced thoughtful Europeans that Americanism was "a conspiracy of dull and unimaginative men, fortuitously made powerful, against all the ideas and ideals that seem sound to their betters," leading the Europeans to suspect "that a nation cherishing such notions and feelings, and with the money and the men to enforce them, deserved to be watched very carefully."

2

As a first-generation American, Mencken liked playing the vaudeville German, with a passion for beer, Brahms, German culture. "My grandfather made a mistake when he came to America, and I have always lived in the wrong country." Like so many *echt*-Americans, Mencken deeply resented the British. Not only did he share in the tribal dislike of Teuton for Anglo but he resented the ease with which the Brits manipulated American politics in their favour at the time of the two world wars. During the first world war, Mencken's pro-Germanism got him banned from the *Sun*. But despite Mencken's somewhat stagy dislike of Brits, socialism, radicals, the "Anglo-maniacal" Woodrow Wilson, and the reformers Franklin and Eleanor Roosevelt, he tended to make very good *patriotic* sense of American politics.

Mencken notes that from the start of the republic, "Setting aside religion, [politics] was literally the only concern of the people. All men of ability and ambition turned to it for self-expression." This is wondrously wise and an echo of Pericles's comment that the man who thinks politics not his business has no business. In the 18th and early 19th centuries, politics drew "the best literary talent into its service—Franklin, Jefferson and Lincoln may well stand as examples—it left the cultivation of belles lettres to women and second-rate men." Now, of course, the second-rate have taken over politics. As for beautiful letters . . .

Mencken's alarm at our system's degradation was in no way based upon a starry-eyed notion of the revered but always circumvented Constitution. Although that long-ignored primer says that only Congress may declare war, President Bush has only recently confided to us that "we have fought 204 wars of which only five were declared," so put that in your peace pipe and smoke it! Mencken would not have been startled. For him, "All government, in its essence, is organized exploitation, and in virtually all of its existing forms it is the implacable enemy of every industrious and well-disposed man." This must have got a good chuckle from the Baltimore burgher over his breakfast of chipped beef and scrapple.

Mencken continues. Government "invades his liberty and collars his money in order to protect him, but in actuality, it always makes a stiff profit on the exchange. This profit represents the income of the professional politicians, nine-tenths of whom are professional rogues." That was then. The rogues are smoother now and often endearing on television. They are also no longer paid for by such chickenfeed as kickbacks on city contracts. Rather, they are the proud employees of the bankers and the military industrial procurers who have bought them their offices, both square and oval. But though we are worse off than in Mencken's day, he was at least able to give one cheer for the Constitution, or at least for the idea of such a document, as a kind of stoplight: "So far you may go, but no further. No matter what excuse or provocation, you may not invade certain rights, or pass certain kinds of laws."

Inevitably, Mencken's journalism is filled with stories of how our enumerated rights are constantly being evaded or struck down because it is the reflexive tactic of the politicians "to invade the Constitution stealthily, and then wait to see what happens. If nothing happens they go on more boldly; if there is a protest they reply hotly that the Constitution is worn out and absurd, and that progress is impossible under the dead hand. This is the time to watch them especially."

Mencken also notes that in the first decade of this century there was "a sudden change . . . Holes began to be punched in the Bill of Rights, and new laws of strange and often fantastic shape began to slip through them. The hysteria of the late war completed the process. The espionage act enlarged the holes to great fissures. Citizens began to be pursued into their houses, arrested without warrants, and jailed without any form of trial. The ancient writ of habeas corpus was suspended: the Bill of Rights was boldly thrown overboard."

Although the extent of the decadence of the democratic process at our end of the century was unknown if not unsuspected to Mencken at his, he knew enough of history and its engine, entropy, to know that "no government, of its own motion, will increase its own weakness, for that would mean to acquiesce in its own destruction . . . governments, whatever their pretensions otherwise, try to preserve themselves by holding the individual down . . . Government itself, indeed, may be reasonably defined as a conspiracy against him. Its one permanent aim, whatever its form, is to hobble him sufficiently to maintain itself." As a self-styled "Presbyterian Tory" (with Manichean tendencies), Mencken regarded attempts at reform as doomed while the thought of any Utopian system bettering things caused him deep distress because to create Utopia you would have to enslave more and more people in order to better— while worsening—their lot.

Curiously enough, of all those good and bad Americans who shuddered at the sudden sharp wind from the east known as communism, Mencken, as early as 1930, figured that there was no way that communism could ever set up shop within our alabaster cities, much less take sickle to our fruited plains. Mencken's reasoning is exquisitely sound: "That Americans, in the mass, have anything properly described as keen wits is surely far from self-evident. On the contrary, it seems likely that, if anything, they lie below the civilised norm." Incidentally, for several decades I have been trying to convince Europe that Americans are not innately stupid but merely ignorant and that with a proper educational system, et cetera. But the more one reads Mencken, the more one eyes, suspiciously, the knuckles of his countrymen, looking to see callouses from too constant a contact with the greensward.

Mencken believes Americans to be more gullible than most people, dwelling as we do in "the home of freak economic schemes" (often, alas, contagious) and "the happy hunting ground of the most blatant and absurd sort of charlatans in politics." From this intimate knowledge of the American "mind," Mencken thought that Americans, as lovers of "the bizarre and the irrational would embrace communism with joy, just as multitudes of them, in a previous age, embraced free silver. But, as everyone knows, they will have none of it." Mencken concedes the attraction of Utopias to the foreign-born and educated Americans but "two-thirds of the native-born Communists that I have encountered are so plainly *mashuggah* that it would be flattery to call them stupid."

Mencken gives two reasons for the failure of communism/socialism to take root in the United States. The first is that Americans have long since been vaccinated by the likes of Bryan and Roosevelt (TR) against this sort of virus: in effect, the folks had been there before and they are aware of so "gross" a social and economic solution. Mencken's second reason strikes me as not only true but inspired. Americans were more sensitive to "the concrete debacle in Russia" because "they probably felt themselves, in a subtle and unconscious way, to be nearer to the Russians than any Europeans. Russia was not like Europe, but it was strangely like America. In the same way the Russians were like Americans. They, too, were naturally religious and confiding; they, too, were below the civilized average in intelligence; and they, too, believed in democracy, and were trying to give it a trial."

For Mencken, communist literature was "as childish as the literature of Christian Science" while communism itself "will probably disappear altogether when the Russian experiment comes to a climax, and Bolshevism either converts itself into a sickly imitation of capitalism or blows up with a bang. The former seems more likely." This is pretty good for 1930.

As Mencken thought all government bad, it follows that he was a Jeffersonian who believed that the least we had of a bad thing the better. As "an incurable Tory in politics," he was congenitally anti-liberal, though "I always give heed to them politely, for they are at least free men." Surprisingly, he has respectful words for Emma Goldman and

Alexander Berkman, victims of Federal persecution (it is not taught in our schools that once upon a time, at the behest of the Secretary of Labor, foreign-born Americans could be deported, without due process). Mencken finds the two radicals "extremely intelligent—[and] once their aberrant political ideals are set aside they are seen to be very sharp wits. They think clearly, unsentimentally and even a bit brilliantly. They write simple, glowing and excellent English." Mencken confesses that he cannot understand how they can believe so childishly in the proletariat, but "the fact that a human brain of high amperage, otherwise highly efficient, may have a hole in it is surely not a secret. All of us, in our several ways, are illogical, irrational, almost insane." Mencken's tolerance for the bees aswarm in the bonnets of others was very great if the swarm be honest and its honey pure.

The state as hostile tropism is Mencken's central philosophic notion as a journalist. Whether the state is used to deport or imprison people for their ideas or the colour of their skin (as in the case of the Nisei) or simply to harass citizens who drink whisky, he was that malevolent state's hard critic. He illuminates our marvelous bill of rights, no sooner promulgated than struck with the first of those sets of alien and sedition acts that continue, in one form or another, to this day. He is very funny about the Noble Experiment to prohibit alcohol (1919–33) which made the United States the world's joke-nation, a title still unceded.

As for America's once triumphant mass-production of the automobile, he notes that this achievement promptly became a pretext for the persecution of the citizenry by creating "a body of laws which fills two courtrooms to suffocation every day (in Baltimore), and keeps three judges leaping and tugging like fire-engine horses. The situation is made more intoxicating by the fact that nine-tenths of the criminals are persons who would not otherwise fall into their toils—that the traffic regulations tap whole new categories of victims . . . The ideal of the *polizei,* at all times and everywhere, is to get their hands upon every citizen at least once a day." Today the tobacco smoker is at risk. Tomorrow, who knows who will fall victim to the state's endless sense of fun?

### 3

Like all good writers, Mencken is a dramatist, at his best when he shows us the ship of state in motion on high seas while his character studies of the crew of this ship of fools still give delight though every last one now lies full fathom five. Ding dong dell.

As a reporter Mencken covered many political conventions from 1904 to 1948. As a Baltimore *Sun* columnist, he wrote about national politics whenever the spirit moved or, indeed, shoved him. In 1925, he was amused, as always, by the collapse yet again of the Liberals and their journals: "*The Nation* gradually abandons Liberalism for libertarianism. *The New Republic* hangs on, but is obviously not as vigorous and confident as it used to be." Mencken delights in "Dr Coolidge," Liberalism's natural enemy. But then "A politician has no actual principles. He is in favor of whatever seems to him to be popular at the moment." Even so, Coolidge "believes naturally in Law Enforcement—by lawful means if possible: if not, by any means at hand, lawful or lawless . . . he actually got his first considerable office . . . by posturing as a fascist of the most advanced type." This was in 1919 when governor Coolidge of Massachusetts broke the Boston police strike and became famous.

But Coolidge is only an engaging character actor in a drama whose star throughout is William Jennings Bryan (Democratic candidate for president 1896, 1900, 1908—spokesman or person for Free Silver and the common person—or man). Bryan had become famous and popular and dangerous to the status quo when he put together a huge coalition of poor farmers and poorer labourers and, in their interest, spoke against the rich and their gold standard. Bryan gave the country's ownership its first big scare since the rebellion of Daniel Shays. Alas, Mencken was not at the convention in '96 when with a single speech ("You shall not crucify mankind upon a cross of gold!"), Bryan got the nomination at the age of thirty-six and as his friend and ally, my grandfather, used to say, "He never learned anything else ever again in his life."

As much as Mencken despised Bryan, the demagogue, he is moderately touched by Bryan's appearance at the 1904 convention "in his familiar alpaca coat and his old white string tie," looking "weak and haggard" (he was suffering from pneumonia) until he started to speak and brought down the house, yet again. Four years later he would be the doomed nominee: four years after that, Wilson made him his secretary of state, a post he resigned when he saw that the Administration was moving toward war, an act of principle that Mencken rather meanly does not credit in a man he calls "the magnificent job-seeker."

At the end, Mencken was present in Dayton, Tennessee, for the Scopes trial where the old man seemed "maleficent" to Mencken when he spoke for supersitition and the literal interpretation of the Bible. Bryan and the Bible won the day, but Bryan himself was dead a few weeks later, killed, my grandmother always said, by an ungovernable passion for "chicken and rice and gravy."

For Mencken, Bryan is the *id*—to use Freudian jargon—of American politics: the ignorant, religious, underclass leader whose fateful and dramatic climax came in the trial to determine whether or not we are descended from monkeys. Herbert Hoover is the *ego;* he also represents the British interest, forever trying to draw the great stupid republic into their wars and combinations. Calvin Coolidge is a near-fascist clown, whose career is "as appalling and as fascinating as a two-headed boy." Warren G. Harding is the master of a glorious near-English in which "the relations between word and meaning have long since escaped him"; Harding's style "reminds me of a string of wet sponges; it reminds me of tattered washing on the line: it reminds me of stale bean soup, of college yells, of dogs barking idiotically through endless nights. It is so bad that a sort of grandeur creeps into it." Mencken's descriptions of these wondrous clowns are still a delight because, though the originals are long since erased from the collective "memory" of the United States of Amnesia, the types persist. "I am not," Mencken observes demurely at one point, when blood is on the walls, "a constructive critic."

For Mencken "the best of [politicians] seem to be almost as bad as the worst. As private citizens they are often highly intelligent and realistic men, and admirable in every way." But because of the superstitious mass, they are not allowed to make sense. "When they accomplish anything, it is usually by accident." Even of his sometimes hero, Al Smith, he deplored his speeches but then, "like all habitual orators, he plainly likes to make speeches, no matter how dull the subject or hot the hall."

Mencken is quite aware that behind the diverting spectacle of our politics stands the ownership of the country, Business. He understands the general preference of the Business-boss for the Lawyer-employee in politics. Partly it is because "A lawyer practicing his craft under Anglo-Saxon jurisprudence becomes a pedant almost inevitably. The system he follows is expressly designed to shut out common sense," which is just as well because "Big Business, in America, is almost wholly devoid of anything even poetically describable as public spirit. It is frankly on the make . . . Big Business was in favor of Prohibition, believing that a sober workman would make a better slave than one with a few drinks in him. It was in favor of all the gross robberies and extortions that went on in the [First] war," and profited by the curtailment of civil liberties and so on. Coolidge was their man; so was Herbert Hoover, "the perfect self-seeker . . . His principles are so vague that even his intimates seem unable to put them into words . . . He knows who his masters are, and he will serve them."

Mencken is also aware that there is a small but constant resistance to the "masters," but he gives the resistance little aid or comfort. Essentially, he is on the side of Business if not Businessmen because "business is the natural art of the American people." He pities those with "believing minds" who would follow this or that demagogue, and he lived long enough to attend the 1948 convention of the Progressive Party where Henry Wallace picked up the banner marked Nay; but Mencken was put off not so much by the poignant, plaintive "nay" as he was by the colouring of the letters, red.

Even so, the Tory Mencken understood the roots of radicalism. Although "it is assumed that men become radicals because they are naturally criminal, or because they have been bribed by Russian gold," what actually moves them "is simply the conviction that the Government they suffer under is unbearably and incurably corrupt . . . The notion that a radical is one who hates his country is naive and usually idiotic. He is, more likely, one who likes his country more than the rest of us, and is thus more disturbed than the rest of us when he sees it debauched. He is not a bad citizen turning to crime; he is a good citizen driven to despair." But Mencken himself is no radical because "I believe that all government is evil, and that trying to improve it is largely a waste of time. But that is certainly not the common American view . . . When they see an evil they try to remedy it—by peaceful means if possible, and if not, then by force." Yet, paradoxically, Mencken can also write that "history . . . is the upward struggle of man, out of darkness and into light," presumably a struggle with ooze alone.

Eventually, Franklin Delano Roosevelt would appear to be the answer to the radicals' dream and Mencken regarded him, at the beginning, with a cold but not disapproving eye as FDR metamorphosed from a John the Baptist for Al Smith to the Christ himself, or the national *super-ego*. With some pleasure, Mencken described the Democratic convention that nominated FDR for vice-president, largely because he bore the name of a famous Republican president. Also, he was chosen to "perfume the ticket." As "leader of the anti-Tammany Democrats in New York," he could be counted on "to exorcise the Tammany split from the party." Finally, "he is a civilized man and safely wet."

When FDR's turn came at Chicago 1932, Mencken wrote, "I can recall no candidate of like importance who ever had so few fanatics whooping for him." But Mencken allowed that FDR was good on radio, and he smiled a lot. By the 1940 convention, Mencken was hostile not only to the New Deal but to the approaching war. To Mencken 1940 looked like a re-run of 1916 when Wilson had campaigned as "the man who kept us out of war." Politics being nothing if not imitative of what has worked before, he glumly observed that "Roosevelt himself has promised categorically, on at least a dozen occasions, to keep out of the war, and with the most pious and eye-rolling solemnity" even though "his foreign policy . . . has been unbrokenly devious, dishonest and dishonorable. Claiming all the immunities of a neutral, he has misled the country into countless acts of war, and there is scarcely an article of international law that he has not violated." But Roosevelt won the election. And the war came.

Roosevelt's opponent in the election of 1940 was Wendell Willkie, an eloquent "barefoot boy," as they called him, "from Wall Street," with a Hoosier accent and considerable demagogic skills. Just before he was nominated, I shook his limp hand, and he glared at me with blind eyes in a white sweating face and croaked, "Ah'd be a lah-er if ah sed ah diduhn wanna be Prez Nigh Stays." The only occasion where I gazed as Mencken gazed upon the same political spectacle was the Republican convention at Philadelphia where Wilkie was nominated. This was in June, 1940, and I was guide to my blind grandfather, former Senator T. P. Gore. A Democrat, TPG was not about to miss any convention that might be fun. On a hot evening, we rode to the convention hall in a streetcar with former vice-president Charles G. Dawes, a bright, crickety little man, wearing a white straw hat. At the hall, the heat was dreadful. Young women gave out palmetto fans with "Fan for Van" written on them; thus, the great moose of Michigan, Senator Arthur H. Vandenberg, majestically hurled himself into the ring. Senator Robert A. Taft was also a candidate. He was even then known as "Mr Conservative." Twelve years later, when he was denied the nomination in favour of D. D. Eisenhower, he let slip the terrible truth that no Republican can be nominated for president without the permission of the Chase Manhattan Bank.

We sat in the bleachers to stage left of the podium where stood the former president, Herbert Hoover, face like a rosy marshmallow. Carefully, I described the scene for my blind grandfather; he had entered political history not only as the first senator from the new state of Oklahoma but as the orator who had started the longest demonstration ever recorded at any convention (for Bryan, at Denver, 1908). TPG was one of the few speakers that Mencken could endure, noting that in 1928, when he "rose to second the nomination of his old friend, Senator Reed, there was humor in his brief speech, and also a very impressive earnestness. He won the crowd instantly and got a great round of applause. No other rhetorician came near his mark . . ."

Hoover "stood before the mike like a schoolboy reciting a piece, and seldom varied his intonation or made a gesture." Mencken brings it all alive to me a half-century later though he finds Hoover paler than I did but then I had never seen the President before—or since. I was deeply impressed by Hoover's rigid gravitas. But my grandfather, whose wit and politics were not unlike Mencken's, after listening to the ovation for the ex-president, said, "Hoover's the only man here who doesn't know that he's finished."

As the galleries chanted, "We want Willkie," I became addicted to the convention as then practised, and it is ironic that in 1968, thanks to some television "debates" with a right-wing publicist, I should have helped preside over the transformation of the party conventions from the comings-together of the nation's tribes to a series of low-rated TV specials. No one can now say, with Mencken, "Me, I like [conventions] because they amuse me. I never get tired of the show . . . so unimaginably exhilarating and preposterous that one lives a gorgeous year in an hour."

**4**

Currently, any use of the word "race" in the United States is considered an *a priori* proof of the user's racism. Abstract nouns are now subject to close scrutiny to make sure that the noun's deployer is not a racist or sexist or ageist or bigot. Meanwhile, any word or phrase that might cause distress must undergo erasure while euphemism (the E- or is it the U- or Eu-word?) is the order of the day as "body bag" suddenly becomes, in Pentagonese, "human remains pouch" since "pouch" is a resolutely cheery word, suggesting cute marsupials Down Under while "bag" is a downer, as in "bag lady." Munich, appeasement, Hitler. A babble of words that no one understands now fills the airwaves, and language loses all meaning as we sink slowly, mindlessly, into herstory rather than history because most rapists are men, aren't they?

Mencken is a nice antidote. Politically, he is often right but seldom correct by today's stern standards. In a cheery way, he dislikes most minorities and if he ever had a good word to say about the majority of his countrymen, I have yet to come across it. Recently, when his diaries were published, it was discovered that He Did Not Like the Jews, and that he had said unpleasant things about them not only as individuals but In General, plainly the sign of a Hitler-Holocaust enthusiast. So shocked was everyone that even the *New York Review of Books*'s unofficial de–anti-Semitiser, Garry Wills (he salvaged Dickens, barely), has yet to come to his aid, with An Explanation. But in Mencken's private correspondence, he also snarls at black Americans, Orientals, Britons, women and WASPs, particularly the clay-eating Appalachians whom he regarded as sub-human. But private irritability is of no consequence when compared to what really matters, public action.

Far from being an anti-Semite, Mencken was one of the first journalists to denounce the persecution of the Jews in Germany at a time when *The New York Times,* say, was notoriously reticent. On November 27, 1938, Mencken writes (Baltimore *Sun*), "It is to be hoped that the poor Jews now being robbed and mauled in Germany will not take too seriously the plans of various politicians to rescue them." He then reviews the various schemes to "rescue" the Jews from the Nazis who had not yet announced their own final solution.

To the British proposal that the Jews be admitted to British Guiana, Teutonophile Mencken thinks that the *Ostjuden might* hack it in British Guiana but not the German Jews as "they constitute an undoubtedly superior group . . . Try to imagine a German-Jewish lawyer or insurance man, or merchant, or schoolmaster [in] a place where the climate is that of a Turkish Bath . . ." Tanganyika he thought marginally better but still pretty bad, at least "as good as the worst parts of Mexico." He then suggests that Canada could "absorb 100,000 or even 200,000 with ease, and they would be useful acquisitions, especially in the western prairie populations, which are dominated today by a low-grade of farmers, without any adequate counterbalance of a competent middle class." Today Mencken could not write this because the Farmers' Anti-Defamation League of Saskatchewan would be offended, and his column banned in Canada. "Australia, now almost as exclusive as Sing Sing, which it somewhat resembles in population, could use quite as many [Jews] as Canada and New Zealand." The Australian government would, today, file a protest; and Mencken's column would be banned.

Then Mencken gets down to business: "The American plan for helping the refugees is less openly brutal than the British plan, but almost as insulting to them, and even more futile." After many official and unofficial condemnations of Germany, including "the Hon. Mr Roosevelt's declaration that he could scarcely believe that such things could occur in a Twentieth Century civilization," the President is still not willing to relax the immigration laws or do anything "that might cause him political inconvenience." Mencken finds such "pecksniffery . . . gross and disgusting . . . and I hope that American Jews will not be fetched by it." Mencken also notes how the "Aframerican press" found amazing Roosevelt's solicitousness for German Jews, so unlike his complaisance to the ongoing crimes against black Americans.

Mencken concludes: "There is only one way to help the refugees, and that is to find places for them in a country in which they can really live. Why shouldn't the United States take in a couple of hundred thousand of them, or even all of them?" He notes two popular objections. One, there is already a lot of unemployment in the United States, to which he responds that it is unlikely the Jewish immigrants will either loaf or be incompetent. Two, there is anti-Semitism of the sort then being fanned by the Ku Klux Klan but, as he observes, "not many Jews are likely to go to Mississippi or Arkansas."

I am certain that those who wish to will be able to find anti-Semitism in Mencken's proposal to admit all Jewish refugees. Certainly he *generalizes* about Jews. (How does he know that they don't *all* want to go to Mississippi?) But then perhaps the whole message is code; certainly the remark about Jewish "efficiency" is a classic blood libel.

As of 1934, Mencken was moderately impressed by Eretz Israel and agreeably condescending to the Arabs, who "breed like flies but die in the same way." Mencken was generally approving of the European Jewish settlers, though he predictably cast a cold eye on the collectivist farms and kibbutzim. Of one of them, he wrote, presciently, "It was founded in 1921, and is still in the first flush of its success. Will it last? Probably not. As soon as its present kindergartners grow up they will begin to marry outside, and then there will be quarrels over shares, and it will no doubt go the way of Brook Farm, Amana and all the other predecessors." Mencken thought that there was only a 50–50 chance of the Jewish plantation in Palestine enduring. "On the one hand [Eretz Israel] is being planted intelligently and shows every sign of developing in a healthy manner. But on the other hand there are the Arabs—and across the Jordan there is a vast reservoir of them, all hungry, all full of enlightened self-interest. Let some catastrophe in world politics take the British cops away, and the Jews who now fatten on so many lovely farms will have to fight desperately for their property and their lives." The catastrophe came right on schedule in the form of Hitler and of such professional Jewish terrorists as Begin and Shamir.

One of the few groups that Americans are fairly free to denounce, after the Arabs, are the Japanese. Mencken was almost alert to "the yellow peril." (I use quotes to forestall the usual letters accusing me of hating all Orientals along with Mencken, when neither did nor does.) In 1939, Mencken was thinking seriously about Japan. As there is no public memory in the United States, let me remind the reader that since the Japanese victory over Russia in 1904, the United States had been preparing for a war with Japan in order to establish who would be *numero uno* not only in the Pacific but in Asia.

By 1939, Japan was busy conquering China, having acquired Korea and Manchuria, and the Nippon imperial eye was set on the southeast Asian oil fields, at the time in the hands of two "local" Asiatic powers, the British and the Dutch.

As a "racist," Mencken blithely generalized about race, a real no-no in today's world where each and every one of the five billion people on our common crowded planet is a treasured and unique creation, sharing nothing at all with anyone else except, maybe, the Big Fella—I mean Big Gal—in the Sky. But generalize he did, something no longer allowed in freedom's land. Mencken writes: "The Japanese, judged by Western eyes, are an extremely homely people, and no doubt the fact has a good deal to do with their general unpopularity." Mencken thought that they look both "sinister and ludicrous," not an encouraging or likable combination. "They look, taking one with another, like Boy Scouts with buck teeth, wearing horn-rimmed spectacles . . . I have never met a Caucasian who professed any affection for the Japs, though there are not a few white fans for the scenery," etc. Already guilty of Racist Generalizing, Mencken proceeds, sickeningly, to grade *all* Japanese: "They are a people of very considerable talents, and will have to be reckoned with in the future history of the human race. They have long since got past the stage of sitting respectfully at the feet of the West . . . In all the fields of human endeavor save theology, politics and swine justice they are showing the way to their ofay mentors. They have made important durable contributions to knowledge in each and every one of the exact sciences, and they have taken such a lead in trade and industry that the only way left to beat them is to murder them." But even this solution, particularly favoured by England, won't be easy because they have "a considerable knack for war."

As "nearly all white men dislike the Japs and like the Chinese," Mencken tried to give an accurate impression of our soon-to-be great adversary and, as I gaze out over the Hollywood hills towards Japanese Universal Pictures, our eventual conquerors. But accuracy in reporting

on Pacific matters is always difficult because the American press have
always given us a view of the Japanese that "is seldom accurate and not
always honest," to say the least. As of 1939, China and Chiang Kai-shek
were, as always, on the brink of victory but, somehow, Japan always
won and, as Mencken remarked, "The Japs, in truth, had as sound a
mandate to clean up China as the United States have had to clean up
Cuba." Or Mexico, Nicaragua, Salvador, Panama, Grenada, not to
mention Korea, Vietnam, Cambodia, Iran and Iraq.

Three years later, the Japs, heavily provoked, sank the American fleet
at Pearl Harbor and the great race war was on with Round One (with
guns) going to the white race (1945) and Round Two (with computers)
going to the yellow race (1990). Mencken was particularly good—that
is, prophetic—on American skulduggeries south of the border where he
often visited and duly noted our eerie inability to do anything honest or
even intelligent whether in Cuba or Haiti or in dealing with Nicaragua's
Sandino.

Like Puck, Mencken found most mortals fools. He showed us odd
glimpses of the vacuous Duke of Windsor and his Baltimore lady as well
as of Rudolph Valentino whom he once entertained in what must have
been an unusually alcoholic session for a young Italian. Mencken commiserated with the assault by the press on the lad's manhood and he
shed a public tear at the beauty's demise not long after.

In literary matters, Mencken was a shield to the-meat-and-potatoes
of naturalism-realism, a sounder diet than one of, shall we say, frozen
fish? He was a champion of Dreiser; a foe of censorship. He was good
on Conrad but at sea with James and insensitive to Wharton. He knew
cooking and provided a sound recipe for "shore soup," the crab-based
glory of the eastern shore of Maryland. He was passionate about music.
Disliked jazz but admired "Aframerican" musicians. Interested in architecture, he was appalled by the ugliness of American cities except for
San Francisco where "There is nothing European about the way life is
lived; the color is all Asiatic" because it is so happily cut off from "the
rest of the dun and dour Republic." He described the average person's
way of life in New York as that of a "sardine in a can" while the grass
in the so-called parks "looks like embalmed sauerkraut." He hated
chiropractors. He was amazed, as an editor, to find that graduates of
West Point write the best English. He took a bitter pride in "the love
of ugliness [that] is apparently inherent in the American people. They
cherish and venerate the unspeakable."

Matthew Arnold wrote that a "style is the saying in the best way what you have to say. The what you have to say depends on your age." Mencken certainly said what he had to say about the age that he had been assigned to. When asked why, if he can find nothing to "revere" in the United States, he lived there, he replied, "Why do men go to zoos?"

Religion as generally practised by the Americans of his day, he saw as a Great Wall of China designed to keep civilization out while barbarism might flourish within the gates. He himself was a resolute breacher of the Great Wall, and to the extent that some civilization has got through, he is one of the few Americans that we can thank. Plainly, so clear and hard a writer would not be allowed in the mainstream press of today, and those who think that they would like him back would be the first to censor and censure him.

As for Mencken himself, he wrote his own epitaph in 1921 for *Smart Set*: "If, after I depart this vale, you ever remember me and have thought to please my ghost, forgive some sinner and wink your eye at some homely girl." I realize that he has viciously used the G-word and, even worse, the long-since banned H-word. But there he is. And here we are, lucky we.

Originally published as the Foreword to *The Impossible H. L. Mencken: a Selection of his Best Newspaper Stories,* edited by Marion Elizabeth Rodgers, Doubleday/Anchor Books, 1991.

# 6 8

## PARANOID
## POLITICS

Of the many words with which the mental therapists have enriched our
language, "paranoia" is one of the most used if not useful. According
to authority, a paranoiac is one who suffers from delusions of persecution or grandeur. Everyone, of course, has paranoid tendencies. In fact,
a sizable minority of the people in the world maintain sanity by focusing
their fears and sense of outrage upon some vague enemy usually referred
to simply as "them." Once the source of distress has been identified as
the Jews or the Communists or the Establishment, the moderate paranoiac is then able to function normally—until the magic word is said,
as in that famous vaudeville sketch where mention of the town Kokomo
makes mad the timid comic, who begins ominously to intone: "Then
slowly I turned . . ."

If the poet of the paranoid style is Kafka, one of its best contemporary
critics is Professor Richard Hofstadter, whose new book illuminates
various aspects of a style which has always flourished in God's country,
possibly because the North American continent was meant, literally, to
be God's country, a haven for seventeenth-century Protestant fundamentalists who did not understand, as Hölderlin so sweetly put it, what
a sin it is "to make the state a school of morals. The state has always
been made a hell by man's wanting to make it his heaven." Into this

heaven, *they* came: the secular-minded eighteenth-century skeptics who proceeded to organize the United States along freethinking lines. Since then, the paranoid style has been a constant in the affairs of the American Republic. Though it originated with Christian fundamentalists, who could not bear to see their heaven made hell by a national majority which now includes those very elements that caused them to flee the old world in the first place, the style is by no means peculiar to them. Western farmers denouncing Eastern banks, Jews trying to censor the film of *Oliver Twist,* uneasy heterosexuals fearful of a homosexual take-over—all demonstrate that the paranoid style has at one time or another been the preferred manner of nearly every one of the groups that comprise the nation, and in a most engaging essay Professor Hofstadter traces the main line of this illness from the persecution of the Bavarian Illuminati in the eighteenth century to the current obsession with the Communist conspiracy.

It is ironic that a nation which has never experienced a *coup d'état* should be so obsessed with the idea of conspiracy. From the John Birchers who regard General Eisenhower as a crypto-Communist to those liberals who find it thrilling to believe that Lyndon Johnson was responsible for Kennedy's murder, paranoid delusions afflict millions. Knowing this, even the most responsible of politicians finds it difficult not to play upon the collective madness of the electorate.

There is a power somewhere so organized, so subtle, so watchful, so inter-locked, so complete, so pervasive that they had better not speak above their breath when they speak in condemnation of it.

Although this sounds like Joseph McCarthy at his most eloquent, it is actually Woodrow Wilson at his least responsible, warning against "the special interests" (that what he was warning against might indeed exist to some degree is irrelevant; it is the manner in which he exploits the fears of the electorate that gives away the game).

According to Professor Hofstadter, the paranoid style is popular not only with that minority which is prone "to secularize a religiously derived view of the world," but also from time to time with the great majority which has never had any clear sense of national identity. For the American there is no motherland or fatherland to be shared with others of his tribe, for the excellent reason that he has no tribe; all that he holds in common with other United Statesmen is something called "the American way of life," an economic system involving the constant purchase of consumer goods on credit to maintain a high standard of living involving the constant purchase, etc. But though this materialistic, even sybaritic ethos does far less damage in the world than old-fashioned tribalism, it fails to satisfy all sorts of atavistic yearnings. A man might gladly give his life for a totem like the flag or the Cross, but who would give so much as a breath for a washing machine not yet paid for?

As a result, not only are the paranoid stylists of both Left and Right appalled by the soullessness of American society, but a good many nonparanoids are equally concerned by the lack of "national purpose," a phrase whose innocent implication is that a human society is like a factory with a quota to be met. Among the simple, this absence of traditional identity has let some strange obsessions flourish, particularly today when the national majority is made up of third-generation citizens uncertain of just what's expected of them. Not unnaturally, those of a passionate and idealistic nature are driven to displays of one hundred percent Americanism, ranging from frequent hand-on-heart pledges of allegiance to the country's proto–Op-art flag to the joyous persecution of those suspected of being un-American (the only other society to have such a concept was Nazi Germany).

Analyzing the identity crisis, as the mental therapists would say, Professor Hofstadter makes a distinction between what he terms status politics and interest politics. In times of economic or military distress (that is to say, "normal" times), people vote their economic interests, and new deals are possible. But when the voters are affluent, they feel free to vote not their interests but their prejudices. The election of 1928 was such a time, and in an orgy of anti-Romanism the majority chose Herbert Hoover over Al Smith. Three years ago, when all seemed to be going smoothly for the nation, the Republicans nominated Barry Goldwater, quite aware that not only was he the most radical politician in the country (Supreme Court decisions are not, he declared, "necessarily the law of the land") but also the most consistent morally. Fiercely militant in the holy war against world Communism ("we will never reconcile ourselves to the Communist possession of power of any kind in any part of the world"), he was even more emphatic in his desire to repeal a hundred years of social legislation in order to create a society in which every man has the inalienable right *not* to give a sucker an even break. The fact that by living the "wrong" sort of economic life the United States had become incredibly rich did not disturb him; as a status politician he spoke for virtue, and the millions that heeded him were quite willing (or so they thought) to sacrifice their material prosperity in order to gain spiritual health by obeying the "natural law" of the marketplace.

According to Professor Hofstadter, those going up or down the social scale are the most prone to paranoia. When white Anglo-Saxon Protestants lose status, they often suspect a conspiracy aimed at depriving them of their ancient primacy, while Irish Catholics, moving up, are often disappointed to find that their new riches do not entitle them to more of a say in the governing of the country, and so suspect the Protestant old guard or the Jews of conspiring to deny them dignity. Religious (as well as ethnic) prejudices often decide the way these people vote. Since Americans lack an agreed-upon class system, status tends to originate in race and religion.

The fact that each of Professor Hofstadter's essays was written for an occasion other than the present ought to have inspired him to make some sort of link from piece to piece. Unfortunately, he has not made the effort, even though the paranoid style would have provided a fine common denominator. Nevertheless, he is interesting on such subjects as "Cuba, the Philippines and Manifest Destiny": skillfully, he gives the background to the Spanish-American War, and shows how the paranoid style helped make possible the war, which gave birth to the American empire.

Like most empires, this one was the result of trouble at home. With the settling of California, the frontier shut down and there was no place new to go, a matter of poignant concern to a nomadic and adventurous people. Then came the depression of '93. To those of faint heart, the last best hope of earth appeared to be fading fast. At such times the shrewd politician can usually be counted upon to obscure domestic crises with foreign pageants. Or, as Henry Cabot Lodge confided to a friend, "Should there be a war, we will not hear much of the currency question in the election." Between Lodge's practicality and Theodore Roosevelt's vision of empire ("All the great masterful races have been fighting races. No triumph of peace is quite as great as the supreme triumphs of war!"), history required a war. But who was there to fight? Fortunately, Cuba wanted to be free of Spain; and so the United States, a Goliath posing as David, struck down Spain, a David hardly able to pose at all, and thus was Cuba freed to become a client state, the Philippines conquered and occupied, and westward the course of empire flowed. The Pacific Ocean, at first thought to be the end of the road, proved to be a new frontier whose end is not yet in sight, though it is heartening to know that downtown Hanoi is currently off limits.

The American empire began in a blaze of rhetoric, much of it paranoid. Witness Senator Albert J. Beveridge:

God has been preparing the English-speaking and Teutonic peoples for a thousand years [to be] master organizers of the world. He has made us adepts in government that we may administer government among savages and senile peoples.

Even thoughtful commentators felt that though "we risk Caesarism, Caesarism is preferable to anarchy." And so, to avoid anarchy (and socialism), the United States chose empire, and contrary to the famous witticism, empires are the deliberate creation of an adroit presence—not absence—of mind. Franklin Roosevelt, in his way, was quite as imperial as his cousin Theodore. Beneath a genuine high-mindedness (puzzling to foreigners who find the American nonparanoid style either hypocritical or unrealistic), American leaders have unconsciously accepted the "English-speaking, Teutonic" role of world conquerors for the world's good. With the result that the Americans are in this age the barbarian horde, as the English were in the last century.

Happily enough, it would also appear that the United States is destined to be the last empire on earth (in the best if not the apocalyptic sense), and there are now stirrings within the camp of the Great Khan at Washington to the effect that new necessities do not always require military force. Barring unexpected catastrophe, the hordes may soon achieve, if not peace, an uneasy stasis which one hopes should endure until the human race begins the infection of other worlds. For more and more do we resemble a proliferating virus, destructive of other organisms, incapable of arresting itself, and so destined—manifestly!—to prevail or vanish furiously in space and time.

*New Statesman*
January 13, 1967

# 69

# *WHAT ROBERT MOSES*
# *DID TO*
# *NEW YORK CITY*

"When coming up from Richmond by the night train, Mr. Laurence Oliphant, myself, and many more, arrived at Acquia Creek about one o'clock; the passage thence to Washington takes four hours; and as we were much fatigued, and had only these four hours for rest, we begged that the key of our berths might be given to us at once. 'I'll attend to you when I'm through,' was the only answer we could get; and we waited—a train of ladies, young folks, gentlemen—until the man had arranged his affairs, and smoked his pipe, more than an hour. Yet not one word was said, except by Mr. Oliphant and myself. The man was in office; excuse enough in American eyes for doing as he pleased. This is the kind of circle in which they reason; take away his office, and the man is as good as we are; all men are free and equal; add office to equality, and he rises above our heads. More than once I have ventured to tell my friends that this habit of deferring to law and lawful authority, good in itself, has gone with them into extremes, and would lead them, should they let it grow, into the frame of mind for yielding to the usurpation of any bold despot who may assail their liberties, like Caesar, in the name of law and order!"

This little sermon occurs in a book called *New America* published in 1867 by an Englishman named William Hepworth Dixon. Since Mr.

Dixon was a journalist of absolutely no distinction, one must take very seriously what he says because he only records the obvious. After a year among us it was plain to him that in the name of law and order Americans are quite capable of building themselves a prison and calling it Happy Acres or Freedom Park and to reach this paradise all you have to do is take your first left at the Major Deegan Expressway out of New York; then your second right just past Hawthorne Circle and so on up the Taconic State Parkway to where the Caesarian spirit of Robert Moses will lead you into the promised land.

For thirty or forty years I have seen the name Robert Moses on the front pages of newspapers or attached to articles in that graveyard of American prose the Sunday *New York Times Magazine* section. But I never had a clear idea just who he was because I never got past that forbiddingly dull title Parks Commissioner. I associated him with New York City and I lived upstate. I now realize what a lot I have missed, thanks to someone called Robert A. Caro whose life of Moses has not only taken me a month to read (there are 1,246 pages) but not once—uniquely—did I find myself glumly riffling the pages still to be read at the back.

To begin at the beginning: The United States has always been a corrupt society. Periodically, "good" citizens band together and elect to office political opportunists who are presented to the public as *non-politicians*. Briefly, things appear to be clean. But of course bribes are still given; taken. Nothing ever changes nor is there ever going to be any change until we summon up the courage to ask ourselves a simple if potentially dangerous question: Is the man who gives a bribe as guilty as the man who takes a bribe?

For decades Vice President-designate Nelson Rockefeller has used his family's money to buy and maintain the Republican party of the State of New York while his predecessor but one, Spiro Agnew, was busy taking money from various magnates who wanted favors done—men who differ from the Rockefellers only in degree. Yet the Agnews are thought to be deeply wicked (if found out) while no sign of Cain ever attaches itself to their corrupters. It is a curious double standard—rather like those laws that put the hooker in jail for selling her ass while letting the john go free with a wink. But then we are a godly people and, as Scripture hath it, it is better to give than to receive. Blessed then are the Kennedys and the Rockefellers who buy directly or indirectly the votes of the poor and the loyalty of their leaders in order that public office might be won, and personal vanity hugely served.

"The fact is New York politics were always dishonest—long before my time." So testified Boss Tweed a hundred years ago. "There never was a time when you couldn't buy the Board of Aldermen. A politician in coming forward takes things as they are. This population is too hopelessly split up into races and factions to govern it under universal suffrage, except by the bribery of patronage, or corruption." This is elegantly put. As far as we know, Robert Moses did not take money for himself like Tweed or Agnew. He was more ambitious than that. Wanting power, Moses used the people's money to buy, as it were, the Board of Aldermen over and over again for forty-four years during which time, if Mr. Caro is to be believed, he was, without peer, the fount of corruption in the state.

Mr. Caro starts his long story briskly. At Yale Moses was eager to raise money for the undergraduate Minor Sports Association. To get money, Moses planned to go to an alumnus interested only in the swimming team and con him into thinking that his contribution would go not to the association but to the swimmers. The captain of the team demurred. "I think that's a little bit tricky, Bob. I think that's a little bit smooth. I don't like that at all." Furious, Moses threatened to resign from the team. The resignation was promptly accepted. There, *in ovo,* was the future career: the high-minded ends (at least in Moses's own mind) as represented by the Minor Sports Association; the dishonest means to attain those ends; the fury at being crossed; the threat of resignation which, in this instance, to his amazement, was accepted. For decades that threat of resignation brought presidents, governors, and mayors to their knees until Nelson Rockefeller turned him out—by which time Moses was approaching eighty and no longer the killer he had been.

Robert Moses came from a well-to-do German Jewish family, very much at home in turn-of-the-century New York City. Apparently mother and grandmother were arrogant, intelligent, domineering women. I think Mr. Caro goes on a bit too much about how like grandmother and mother Moses is. Yet it is interesting to learn that his mother abandoned Judaism for Ethical Culture and that her son was never circumcised or bar-mitzvahed. Later he was to deny that he was a Jew at all.

From Yale Moses went to Oxford where he succumbed entirely to the ruling-class ethos of that glamorous place. For young Moses the ruling class of Edwardian England was the most enlightened the world had ever known, and its benign but firm ordering of the lower orders at home and the lesser breeds abroad ought, he believed, to be somehow transported to our own notoriously untidy, inefficient, and corrupt land. Moses's Ph.D. thesis *The Civil Service of Great Britain* reveals its author as non-liberal, to say the least. Fearful that ignorant workers might organize unions and behave irresponsibly, he sternly proposed "the remorseless exercise of the executive power of suppression and dismissal to solve this problem."

Moses returned to New York, wanting to do good. He saw himself as a proto-mandarin whose education, energy and intelligence made him peculiarly suited to regulate the lives of those less fortunate. But pre-1917 New York was still the New York of Boss Tweed. The unworldly Moses did not realize that if you want to build a new slum for the teeming masses or create a playground for the not-so-teeming but deserving middle classes you must first buy the Board of Aldermen. Now this is never a difficult thing to do. In fact, these amiable men will give you as much money as you want to do almost anything you want to do (assuming that the loot is on hand) *if* you in turn will give them a slice of that very same money.

In the old days this was done in a straightforward way: the tin box full of cash (although one fairly recent mayor eccentrically insisted on money being delivered to him at Gracie Mansion in pillowcases). But as the years passed and the IRS began to cast an ever-lengthening shadow across the land, politicians became wary. They set up law offices (sometimes in the back bedroom of a relative's house) where "legal fees" from the city or the builder could be collected. Or they became associated with public relations firms: "fees" from the city or the contractors would then be laundered for personal use in much the same way that a now famous contribution to Nixon's re-election campaign surfaced as a pair of diamond earrings dangling from the pretty ears of the First Criminal's moll.

Robert Moses's early years as a reformer in New York City were not happy. He joined something called the Bureau of Municipal Research, an instrument for reform—neither the first nor the last. He annoyed his fellow reformers with his imperious ways; his formidable intelligence; his impatience. Then at the end of 1918, the goddess from the machine descended to earth and put him on the path to power. The name of the goddess was Belle Moskowitz. Although a reformer, Belle was a superb politician who had early on seen the virtues of one Al Smith, a Tammany vulgarian whom everyone misunderstood and, more seriously, underestimated. Belle brought Moses and Smith together. They were made for each other. And rose together.

The writing of legislation is perhaps the highest art form the United States has yet achieved, even more original and compelling than the television commercial. In tortured language, legislators rob the people of their tax money in order to enrich themselves and their friends. As an assemblyman from the city, Al Smith had become a power at Albany by the unusual expedient of reading all the bills that were introduced. Lacking education but not shrewdness, Smith very soon figured out who was getting the cash and why. An honest man (relatively speaking), Smith used his knowledge of bill-drafting to gain power over the other legislators; also, from time to time, he was able to blackmail them into occasionally doing something for the ridiculous masses who had elected them.

As a result of these gratuitous acts of kindness, Smith became governor of New York. In the process, governor's aide Robert Moses became a positive Leonardo of bill-drafting. One of his earliest masterpieces (equal to the *Virgin with St. Anne and St. John* or the *Turtle Oil Cosmetic two-minute TV spot*) was the State Reconstruction Commission. Masterfully, Moses rearranged the structure of the state, giving his friend Smith more power than any governor had ever before exercised. Moses also saw to it that he himself got full credit for this masterwork even though there were many apprentices in his atelier and at least one other master—the future historian Charles A. Beard whom Moses later accused of plagiarism when, in fact, Beard was using his own unacknowledged material from the commission report. Artists!

If Robert Moses had not taken a house at Babylon, Long Island, the history of New York City might have been very different. Going from the city to Babylon and back again, Moses began to think about public parks and beaches, about diversions for the worthy middle classes of the city. After all, the age of the automobile was in its bright morning; and no one then living could have foreseen its terrible evening. Like most right-minded men of the day, Moses thought that anyone who owned a car ought to have a nearby park or beach to go to; those without cars were obviously not worthwhile and ought to stay home. As the automobile was the labarum in whose sign Moses would conquer, so the idea of mass transit was to be the perennial dragon to be slain whenever it threatened to invade any of his demesnes. Meanwhile, Long Island was full of empty beaches, promising sand bars, unspoiled woods. How to appropriate all this natural beauty for the use of the car owners?

Until 1923, the parks of New York State were run by sleepy patroons who simply wanted to conserve wildlife for future generations. The patroons did not mind responsible campers and hikers wandering about their woods and lakes but they certainly did not want great highways to crisscross the wilderness or tons of cement to be poured over meadows in order to make shuffleboards, restaurants, and comfort stations for millions of visitors; nor did they think that every natural stream or pond ought to be rearranged by someone with a degree in civil engineering.

Unhappily for the patroons, Moses now had a Dream. He went to work to realize it. Exercising his formidable art, he drafted *A State Park Plan for New York.* Parks would be used for recreation as well as conservation. Parks would be reorganized into one system. The presidency of the Long Island State Park Commission would go to Moses; term of office—six years, longer than the governor's term. There are those who think that this bill was Moses's greatest masterpiece, even more compelling than the bill that set up the Triborough Authority. Certainly Moses displayed in its drafting a new maturity, as well as a mastery of every type of ambiguity. But I leave to Mr. Caro the task of being Walter Pater to this Gioconda. Enough to say that the principal joker in the bill was the use of an unrepealed 1884 law that gave the state the right to "appropriate" land "by simply walking on it and telling the owner he no longer owned it." This was power.

Jones Beach and other parks were connected with highways to the city and transformed into playgrounds. In the process a lot of people were "remorselessly" kicked off their land. But there are people and people. At first Moses wanted to put a parkway through the North Shore Long Island estates of such nobles as Stimson, Winthrop, Mills, and Otto Kahn. The lords objected and so, partly because Mr. Kahn was on good terms with Moses and partly because the other nobles owned the Republican party which controlled the state legislature, the parkway was diverted to a stretch of land inhabited by farmers who had no clout. The farmers were driven from their land.

Although Moses was always a profound conservative who only seemed to be liberal because he had a Dream about parks and highways, he was not above using the press to blast the "rich golfers" who stood athwart the people's right of way. Early on, Moses demonstrated a genius for publicity. Knowing that the New York press thrives on personal attacks, he gave them plenty. He also enjoyed the full support of *The New York Times* because he had managed to persuade one Iphigene Sulzberger that he was as interested in conservation as she was. For decades, with the connivance of the press, Moses was able to slander as "Pinkos" and "Commies" his many enemies. Also, the corrupter of others was careful to keep dossiers on those he had corrupted. But then to realize his Dream of an America covered with highways and of wilderness tamed to resemble fun fairs, Moses was remorseless since you cannot, he would observe, make an omelette with unbroken eggs (a line much used in those days by supporters of Hitler and Mussolini). He also liked to crow: "Nothing I have ever done has been tinged with legality."

The perfect public servant made only one serious error during this period. In 1934 he was Republican candidate for governor of New York against the incumbent Herbert Lehman. During the campaign Moses's contempt for all of the people all of the time was so open, so pure, so unremitting that he made Coriolanus seem like Hubert Humphrey. Even the docile press which had worked so hard to create a liberal image for Moses was appalled by the virulence of his *ad hominem* attacks on Governor Lehman—a decent man with whom Moses had always had good relations.

Suddenly his friend the governor was "a miserable, snivelling type of man . . . contemptible." Moses also charged that Lehman "created most of the state deficit." Actually, Lehman had reduced the deficit to almost zero. But then Moses has always had a Hitlerian capacity for the lie so big that it knocks the truth out of the victim who knows that his denial will never be played as big in the press as the lie itself. Then Moses called Lehman "a liar"—a word, one politician remarked, never before used in a gubernatorial campaign. Eventually, the Mutual Broadcasting System refused to broadcast Moses's speeches unless the Republican party insured the network against libel. Moses's defeat was so thorough that he never again offered himself to the public except in controlled interviews conducted by admiring journalists. Soon he was a hero again with his parks, highways, beaches. Was he not incorruptible?

From time to time Mr. Caro feels that he ought to explain *why* Moses is what he is and his narrative is occasionally marred by vulgar Freudianisms in the Leon Edel manner. This is a pity because the chief interest of biography is not *why* men do what they do, which can never be known unless one turns novelist the way Freud did when he wrote *Leonardo,* but what they do. One does not want a theory explaining Moses's celebrated vindictiveness when examples of that vindictiveness are a matter of interesting record. For instance, after a run-in with Mayor Jimmy Walker, Moses tore down the Casino in Central Park because Walker had patronized it; yet the building itself was a charming relic of the previous century and the people's property. Prematurely, he razed a yacht club because the members "were rude to me." Shades of Richard Nixon! Petty revenge was certainly behind his desire to remove the

Battery's most famous landmark—the Aquarium in the old fort known as Castle Garden. Fortunately Eleanor Roosevelt got her husband the president to save the fort itself through a Byzantine process involving the War Department.

This was FDR's only victory over Moses. The two men despised each other; they were also somewhat alike. As an admiring biographer of the president wrote, sadly, FDR had "a capacity for vindictiveness which could be described as petty." When an earlier move against Moses failed, Roosevelt was criticized for pettiness by a friend. The great man's response was plaintive: "Isn't the president of the United States entitled to one personal grudge?"

In 1939 the Triborough Bridge was opened and the Moses empire was at its zenith. The bridge was—and is—a huge moneymaker. Money from those toll booths goes to an Authority and the Authority (as adapted by Robert Moses) is the supreme example of his dark art. The Authority is responsible to no one except those who hold its bonds. As a result, with Triborough money, Moses was now in a position to reward directly those who helped him and damage those who hurt him.

Mr. Caro quotes one city official as saying of Moses, "He gave everybody involved in the political set-up in this city whatever it was that they wanted." Tammany, Republicans, reformers, Fusionists . . . it made no difference. Either they were paid off through their law and insurance offices, their public relations and building firms, or they were attacked through the press, and hounded from office like Stanley Isaacs, the honest borough president of Manhattan.

Moses's achievement, according to Mr. Caro, "was to replace graft with benefits that could be derived with legality from a public works project." After all, the Authority had every right to hire someone's uncle to be a PR consultant just as the Authority was able to spend $500,000 a year on insurance premiums, a windfall for the insurers because, according to Moses's aide George Spargo, the Authority never filed or collected a claim during its first eighteen years. All perfectly legal and all perfectly corrupt. But who was to know? The books of the Authority could only be audited after a complaint by those who held the bonds of the Authority, and the trustee for those bond-holders was the Chase Manhattan Bank, the Rockefeller family's cosa nostra. Since the Authority was a great success, the bank was not curious about its inner workings.

From Triborough headquarters on Randall's Island, Moses presided over city and state. By the time the Second World War ended, he was uniquely powerful because the city, as usual, was broke and the only money available for building was either from the federal government or from the Triborough Authority, whose millions Moses could spend as he pleased—and it pleased him to cover as much of Manhattan as possible with cement while providing himself with a lavish way of life that included private yachts and a court theater at Jones Beach where his very own minstrel Guy Lombardo made a lot of money grinding out the sweetest music this side of coins clinking in toll booths. Why steal money to have a sumptuous life when you can openly use the public money to live gorgeously? Yet during all these years the press, led by the ineffable *New York Times,* praised Moses for his incorruptibility.

At one time or another most of the mayors and governors Moses dealt with wanted to get rid of him; none dared. Moses was a god to the press and a master to the legislature. Finally, he alone had the money with which to create those public works that mayors must be able to point to with pride just before election time. To keep the irascible Mayor La Guardia happy, Moses built dozens of playgrounds and swimming pools (there was a pool *near* Harlem) so that the mayor could dash about greeting the kiddies and bragging. It was heady stuff. In time, however, the overreacher overreaches, and one now begins to read Mr. Caro's text like a Greek tragedy, aware rather earlier than was usual at the Dionysos Theater of the hero's Tragic Flaw. Never having known just how Moses fell from power, I was glad that I could read the last sections of the book like a mystery novel: who would get him? and what would be the murder weapon?

The building of the Cross-Bronx Expressway might be the point where Moses found himself at the three roads, to maintain the classical analogy. He was then all-conquering and all-spending: after the Second World War he built more than $2 billion worth of roads within the city. To do this, he expropriated thousands of buildings, not all of them slums, and evicted tens of thousands of people who were left to fend for themselves. Moses's elevated highways shadowed and blighted whole neighborhoods. The inner city began to rot, die. But no one could stop Moses for he had yet another Dream: exodus from the city to the suburbs but only by car, for there were to be no busses or trains on his expressways—just more and more highways for more and more cars, creating more and more traffic jams, while the once thriving railroads that had served the city went bankrupt, lingering on as derelict ghosts of what had been, fifty years before, a splendid mass transit system.

In 1952 East Tremont was a lower-middle-class Jewish neighborhood in the Bronx, reasonably content and homogeneous. Moses wanted his Cross-Bronx Expressway to go straight through the most populous part of East Tremont, razing 159 buildings and evicting 1,530 families. Alarmed, the people of this non-slum organized to save their homes. They prepared maps that showed how easy it would be to build an alternative route which would involve tearing down no more than six buildings. Except for the *World-Telegram* and the *Post,* the press ignored the matter. At first the politicians were responsive; but then, one by one, they succumbed to pressure and the community was duly destroyed. But Moses was now hated by the powerless millions who neither read nor are written about by *The New York Times.*

By the late fifties, however, even the newspaper of record was concerned about the lack of mass transport. City planners wanted Moses to put at the center of his expressways what Mr. Caro unhappily refers to as "a subway running at ground level." This would have made the city more escapable for the poor as well as for the car owners. It was also proposed that a train on the Van Wyck Expressway would get travelers from Pennsylvania Station to the airport at Idlewild in sixteen minutes. But Moses refused to listen. Criticism became more intense as the traffic jams increased. The city became more desperate and congested. Moses's answer: build more roads. When told that "the automobiles required to transport the equivalent of one trainload of commuters use about four acres of parking space in Manhattan," Moses spoke of huge skyscrapers filled with cars; he even built one but it was not practical at the price.

For Moses Long Island was now the promised land for the deserving middle class. "Figure out what sort of people you want to attract into Nassau County," he admonished. "By that I mean people of what standards, what income levels and what capacity to contribute to the source of local government. . . . Nassau should always be largely residential and recreational." This is as unmistakable an appeal as any ever made by Nixon-Agnew to the not-so-silent bigots of the heartland.

But now the master of corruption was growing insolent and careless from too much victory. A non-slum neighborhood on the West Side was marked for destruction by the Mayor's Slum Clearance Committee, chaired by Moses. The condemned six square blocks comprised 338 buildings worth $15 million. For $1 million the city sold the entire neighborhood to a group headed by Samuel Caspert, "a Democratic clubhouse figure" who was required to raze the area by 1954 in order to create something called Manhattantown. But politician Caspert and his friends were in no hurry. By October 1954, 280 buildings were still standing, and the tenants were paying rents to the Caspert cabal. The Senate Banking and Currency Committee thought this odd and began hearings. But Moses's perennial mouthpiece, the famed judge and friend of presidents Sam Rosenman, skillfully protected the Caspert gang and the scandal blew over.

In 1956 came the battle of the Tavern-on-the-Green. Moses wanted to expand the Tavern's parking lot, removing in the process a bosky dell beloved of the affluent mothers of Central Park West. As usual, Moses won: at least before the injunctions arrived, the trees were bulldozed. But the West-siders stopped the parking lot, giving Moses a good deal of bad personal publicity in the process. Since the New York press is geared almost entirely to personalities, the real issue was ignored except by the *World-Telegram,* whose reporters saw fit to investigate Moses's connection with the manager of the Tavern-on-the-Green. During a four-year period the Tavern's gross income was $1,786,000, of which, thanks to Moses, the city got only $9,000 for the rental of a building that was city property. In exchange for this gift to the manager, Moses was able to use the Tavern as a private dining room.

But now two paladins appear on the scene, the journalists Gene Gleason and Fred Cook. They began a series of exposés in *World-Telegram.* Who was giving whose money to whom and for what? Eventually even *The New York Times* got interested in the corruption of the city, the exploitation of the poor, the lunatic set of priorities that had for decades put cars before people.

Pressure was put on Wagner to fire Moses. But Wagner could do nothing for, as Mr. Caro puts it, "the whole Democratic machine, the leaders of all five county organizations, on which Wagner depended, were on Moses's payroll." Those coins from the toll booths of the Triborough had bought the city's government.

In the end Moses was brought down not by the press or the reformers but by the true owner of the American republic, the family Rockefeller as personified by Nelson, who had begun his quest for the presidency in 1958 by spending a lot of the family's money to become New York's governor. Moses now confronted an arrogance equal to his own; a remorselessness quite as complete; and resources that were infinite. The two were bound to be enemies. After all, Rockefeller supported mass transit; liked to build things to celebrate himself; fancied parks; wanted no trouble or competition from the likes of Moses.

After a spat, on November 28, 1962, Moses sent the governor one of his many letters of resignation . . . carefully hedged with "tentatives" and "perhapses." With indecent briskness, Rocky accepted "with regret" Moses's resignation from the Long Island Park Commission. The governor then turned over the job to one of his brothers. Moses had a final brief orgy in the press. On the front page of the ever-loyal *New York Times,* he attacked the governor for nepotism. But, uncharacteristically, Moses ignored O. W. Holmes's famed advice—he had struck at a prince and not killed him. This was unwise. But perhaps Moses had deluded himself that he was as great a lord. Was he not still head of the Triborough Bridge and Tunnel Authority as well as creator of the World's Fair? No matter. The roof had begun to fall in.

Moses was never as interested in the New York World's Fair of 1964–65 as he was in the park that would succeed the fair. In setting up the fair, he managed, as usual, to offend a great many people, among them the representatives of the various European governments who decided to have nothing to do with the rude Mr. Moses. The result was a World's Fair without the world's involvement, and a series of breathtaking financial scandals that Mr. Caro has recorded with more than usual detail. All told, Moses had about $1 billion to play with while putting together the fair, and $1 billion can buy all sorts of loyalties and power in the land. The fair itself lost money.

By 1965 the Moses empire had shrunk to the Triborough Authority. The new mayor, John Lindsay, decided to get rid of Moses five years before the end of Moses's term. In a final bravura performance at Albany, Moses handed the mayor his beautiful head. Moses remained. But the end was near.

The sovereign at Albany desperately needed money to build things. The treasury of the Authority contained $110 million in cash and securities to which was added each year another $30 million. Rockefeller proposed to merge the Triborough with his own creature, the MTA (Metropolitan Commuter Transportation Authority). It should be noted that for all of Rockefeller's antagonism to Moses the man, he has never ceased to emulate Moses the power broker. According to Mr. Caro, "Rockefeller had created several giant 'public authorities' that were bastards of the genre because their revenue bonds would be paid off not out of their own revenues but out of the general revenues of the state."

Recently (September 2) *Time* magazine wrote an affectionate story on Vice President-designate Rockefeller. With a wry editorial smile, *Time* concedes that "Rockefeller was an expensive governor . . . as the budget kept rising, from $2 billion when he took office to $8.6 when he left, he devised a novel way of paying for his programs. Rather than going to balky state legislatures or to the voters, who might turn him down, he set up a host of quasi-independent agencies—the Metropolitan Transportation Authority, the Urban Development Corporation, the Housing Finance Agency—that issued bonds on their own initiative and repaid them with fees collected from users of the facilities that were constructed. 'The greatest system ever invented!' he exclaimed." Next to the sales tax, it *is* the greatest—until the taxpayer gets the bill. But long before that day of reckoning the governor moved on—and is now moving up. Terrific! Dubonnet on the rocks. Venezuela. Museum of Modern Art. Attica. Hiya, fella!

Preparing for the showdown with Rockefeller, Moses did what might have been the most useful work of his career. He sat down and figured out what Rockefeller's various Authorities would eventually cost the state. The figures were staggering. For instance, the MTA's bond issue for $2.5 billion would eventually cost the taxpayers $1 billion in interest. But Moses's addition and multiplication were never published. The Rockefeller machine had begun to move against him. In 1967, Rockefeller arranged for Chase Manhattan (headed by his brother David) to blow the whistle on the Triborough Authority. The bank wanted a look at the Authority's books, a dangerous business if things were not in order, but necessary if the bonds were to be retired preparatory to merger. Thomas E. Dewey was hired as the bank's counsel.

Mr. Caro seems to think that if Moses had put up a fight, he might have staved off—or delayed—the merger with MTA. Certainly had he the public interest at heart, Moses ought to have revealed his arithmetic to a grateful nation. But, somehow, Moses was conned. He made no demur to the merger, and Chase Manhattan dropped its suit against the Authority. The merger went through and Moses found himself on the new payroll as a nonconsulted consultant, with a car and driver. And that was the end of the line.

Last August 27, Moses released a 3,500-word attack on Mr. Caro's book through a public relations outfit named Edward V. O'Brien. So suspicious has Mr. Caro made me of PR firms that I want to know *which* O'Brien is Edward V. (the one on page 1,089 of *The Power Broker*?) and has he ever done any work for the city or the Triborough? For old times' sake *The New York Times* gave fair space to Moses's attack. According to the King Lear of Jones Beach, Mr. Caro's book contains "hundreds of careless errors. Many charges are downright lies." But Moses does not mention any errors or lies except to deny that he ever had an affair with ex-Representative Ruth Pratt. Here I think Moses is on strong ground. The biographer of a living person ought never to address himself to the private life of his subject—particularly if the subject is someone like Moses whose *public* life is not only fascinating in itself but continues to affect us all. I did not enjoy reading about Moses's alcoholic wife or about the feud with his only brother Paul (whom Moses refers to, curiously, as "a brother of mine, now dead," as if there were hundreds of brothers to choose from and Mr. Caro, maliciously, picked the wrong one to interview).

Moses does confess that he may have been a bit rough at times in his career, again quoting his favorite cliché about eggs and omelettes. He also says that he personally favors mass transit but argues, disingenuously, that he did nothing about it because he was never in charge of mass transit—as if that was the point to his lifelong obstruction. He is still a lover of the automobile: "We live in a motorized civilization." Energy crisis, unlivable cities, pollution—none of these things has altered his proud Dream. But rather than make the obvious point that a man of eighty-six is now out-of-date, one ought instead to regard with a degree of awe his stamina and his continuing remorseless brilliance.

Finally, in looking back over all that Robert Moses has done to the world we live in and, more important, the way that he did it by early mastering the twin arts of publicity and of corruption, one sees in the design of his career a perfect blueprint for that inevitable figure, perhaps even now standing in the wings of the Republic, rehearsing to himself such phrases as "law and order," "renewal and reform," "sacrifice and triumph," the first popularly elected dictator of the United States.

*The New York Review of Books*
October 17, 1974

# 70

CONGLOMERATES

In 1966 Edmund Wilson wrote in his journal (published as *Upstate*):

Fred Dupee, who now lives on the Hudson, had invited a new neighbor, an IBM tycoon. The subject of Vietnam arose and the tycoon asked Dorothea Straus for her opinion on the subject. Dorothea made the tactful reply that she took the war question so seriously that she would rather not talk about it. The tycoon said something invidious about her being Jewish. Dwight Macdonald became inflamed, and the tycoon offered to sock him in the jaw . . .

As second-hand stories go this is about par. Actually the threat to Macdonald was made before Mrs. Straus was dismissed by the tycoon as a mere Jewess (and so a Commie) while the *New Yorker*'s own Diderot "responded" to the threat of a sock in the jaw with a fit of giggles. Final correction: the tycoon was employed by ITT, and according to Anthony Sampson's new book,* he is today one of the six top executives of a vast conglomerate that owns everything from tasteless Wonderbread to most of the lousy telephone systems in Europe. At the

*The Sovereign State of ITT (Stein and Day, 1973).

time, I wondered how the Jewess-baiter could hold a job of importance in any firm anywhere. As the party crumbled, I asked several guests: What is—or are—ITT? No one knew. That was an innocent age.

Mr. Sampson has now turned his attention to the multinational conglomerates in general and to International Telephone and Telegraph in particular and, predictably, he views with alarm the way these nomadic holding companies have transformed themselves into sovereign states able to treat with nation states from a position of strength—witness, the current dealings between ITT and the pack of woolly lambs that presently gambol in the shadows of the Kremlin's onion domes.

ITT was invented by one Sosthenes Behn in 1920. A Virgin Islander of Danish-French extraction, Colonel Behn was curiously well-situated to be an international businessman, turning a buck wherever possible. The fact that the Colonel got on better with dictators than he did with democrats was not necessarily a sign of bad character: serious businessmen have always preferred paying off one man or his son-in-law to buying half a thousand members of a Congress the way they must do in Washington, DC, say—not to mention subsidizing the key figures of a permanent and ever-expanding bureaucracy.

When Peron took over ITT's telephone system in Argentina, the caudillo of the pampas made a gentlemanly settlement of the sort Castro (not exactly your average fanatic democrat) refused to make, causing Colonel Behn's successor Harold Geneen to present the exiled dictator Batista with a golden telephone—presumably for old times' sake.

After Hitler came to power, Colonel Behn increased his holdings in Germany to include 28 percent of Focke-Wulf, which manufactured Luftwaffe bombers. When war came, Colonel Behn saw no conflict of interest: like the Pope he regarded himself as belonging to all sinners. In fact, the Colonel had a pleasant meeting with Hitler in 1938 (apparently, the Führer was nicely groomed with the manners, thank heaven, of a gentleman), and ITT was allowed to keep its German holdings. Two years later Goering arranged the acquisition of ITT's local holdings "in exchange [for] the mysterious and prosperous company General Anilin and Film Corporation (GAF), an offshoot of the I.G. Farben cartel . . . seized by the United States Treasury Department" in 1942. Mr. Sampson leaves the unsavory story at this point. His readers might be amused to know that two decades later Attorney General R. F. Kennedy settled the matter of GAF's ownership with a fifty-fifty split between the Swiss group which claimed the company and the Justice Department which maintained that the company belonged to the US on the ground that it had been simply a cover for the Nazi I.G. Farben. Kennedy was inclined to be generous because, as Victor Navasky (*Kennedy Justice*) put it, "the Kennedys had appointed a number of family friends to various positions in and around the company."

Mr. Sampson takes us on a swift and generally entertaining—that is to say, chilling—tour of ITT's present horizon which is the great globe itself: Avis Cars, Sheraton Hotels, Levitt towns, and now the third largest insurance company in the world; cash in-flow is very important for a business which is in the business not of making things but of making money. I suspect that much of the nervousness the conglomerates excite in the American puritan's bosom is not so much their brutal devotion to making money as their indifference to the things that they are required to make in order to make the money. Of peripheral interest are the potato chips, rental cars, dog food, insurance. What matters to Geneen (an accountant) are loans, interest rates, currency fluctuations, corporate mergers, and the avoidance of paying taxes on profits anywhere on earth. According to Senator E. Kennedy, ITT—the eighth largest American company—paid no federal American tax in 1971.

In some detail Mr. Sampson describes ITT's attempted takeover of ABC, the third American television network. To the government ITT spoke glowingly of all the money that they would put into the network; to others they spoke coolly of what they intended to take out of it. Their lobbying was, as always, thorough; so too was their intimidation of their critics. One *New York Times* reporter discovered that the company was collecting a dossier on her private life. The Justice Department finally stopped the merger on the ground that ABC did not need ITT's financing. It was also felt that the network's news programs would be affected because of ITT's "close and confidential relation with foreign governments." But it was a close call for network freedom of speech which is, of course, no more than the heady freedom to paraphrase the demure editorials of *The Washington Post* and *The New York Times*.

During the last few years Geneen has taken a tack quite different from that of Colonel Behn. Instead simply of trying to get on with whatever government happens to be in charge of a country where he wants to make money, Geneen is now attempting to create the sort of governments that would be obliged to get on with him. So began the sinister comedy in Chile that involved not only Geneen but John McCone, a former head of the CIA and now an ITT director. Fearing that Allende's election as president would mean nationalization of ITT's telephone holdings in Chile, Geneen offered at least a million dollars to the CIA to help defeat Allende. As far as we know, the CIA sat that one out and Allende was duly elected.

ITT then set about acquiring the Hartford Insurance Company, the biggest caper in their history thus far and as all major heists nowadays seem to do, it involved the 37th president whose eccentric notions of law (ignore it) and order (impose it) have to date been contained not by the Constitution or by the Congress or by the press but by his own eerie and rather touching propensity to fuck up.

Nixon wanted the Republican convention to be held in San Diego, his "lucky city." San Diego was not thrilled. Money would be needed, the city fathers said. In another part of the swamp Geneen was having trouble with the antitrust-buster Richard McLaren at the Justice Department. McLaren also wanted to take the case to the Supreme Court in order to clarify once and for all the antitrust laws. Attorney General Mitchell (now under indictment) and Vice President Agnew (still at large)* were both well-disposed to Geneen. Words were spoken on ITT's behalf; letters written. But McLaren soldiered on. Then a light went on in Geneen's head: donate through ITT's Sheraton hotel chain $400,000 to the Republicans for their San Diego convention and . . . The offer was made. The offer was accepted. The trust suit against ITT was swiftly settled out of court, and to everyone's surprise, ITT was allowed to keep their most precious acquisition, Hartford. McLaren left the Department of Justice to become a federal judge.

Unfortunately for the funsters, ITT's Washington lobbyist Dita Beard wrote a memo giving the game away. Promptly, she went into the hospital (with a weak heart). In disguise (red wig, a voice modulator), novelist–CIA agent–presidential burglar E. Howard Hunt arrived from the White House with orders to get Dita in line. No doubt intimidated by the red wig, the altered voice, she recanted: the memo was a forgery, she said, or sort of. A year later E. Howard Hunt was arrested at the Watergate break-in and. . . . No, no. Enough. Linkage is all, as Nixon's Metternich would say.

Mr. Sampson ends his book with the nice irony of Geneen publicly deploring the collapse of the "free" world as Latin America goes Marxist while, simultaneously, putting together what promises to be a super deal with Moscow. Mr. Sampson comes to no precise conclusion. There is evidence that companies which are taken over by conglomerates

---

*This was written before Agnew's crimes came to light. How did I know? Ah . . .

usually become inefficient (when they are not simply gutted of their assets and discarded). It is also true that Geneen's crusading fervor and vigor is something new under the corporate sun. Instead of being embarrassed by all the dirty tricks he had been caught at, he takes the high line that in order to maintain the Western world's prosperity his is the only way and if the United States and Western Europe are to compete with a corporate nation-state like Japan, say, then more not less ITT is necessary.

Mr. Sampson tells us that he wrote this book at "high speed." I wish he had not. There are sentences which the elegant author of *The New Europeans* ought not to have allowed to wriggle onto the page ("Her relations were especially strained with Bill Merriam, a sociable aristocrat of 60 who had once been a friend of the Jack Kennedys, but who was much less adept at politics than her"). Those bracketing "hers" are Mid-Atlantic at its most refined.

Mr. Sampson ought to redo his book post-Watergate, if there should ever be such an era. For instance, two months ago, the Justice Department reopened the business of the Hartford merger because, according to Attorney General Richardson "the ITT inquiry has begun to overlap with the Watergate investigation." Will Mr. Sampson be obliged by events to call his sequel *Sovereign Empire*? I think not. I have a feeling that like the joyous Cornfeld's paper pyramid, ITT, too, will pass, taking the currency of the Western world with it in a replay of 1929. So, puritans, take heart. We may be at the end of that paper money which has been for our rulers a puzzling and currently alarming fiat for their much loved barbarous metal; and for the poor, as someone once said, their blood. Absolute purity will then require us to return to the delights and challenges of barter, and to real things.

*New Statesman*
July 20, 1973

# 71

## *EDMUND WILSON,*
## *TAX DODGER*

"Between the year 1946 and the year 1955, I did not file any income tax returns."

With that blunt statement, Edmund Wilson embarks on a most extraordinary polemic.* He tells us why he did not pay his taxes. Apparently he had never made much money. He was generally ignorant of the tax laws. In 1946, when his novel *Memoirs of Hecate County* was published, his income doubled. Then the book was suppressed by court order and the income stopped. While all this was going on, he was much distracted by a tangled private life. So what with one thing and another, Mr. Wilson never got around to filing a return.

"It may seem naïve, and even stupid, on the part of one who had worked for years on a journal which specialized in public affairs (the *New Republic*) that he should have paid so little attention to recent changes in the income tax laws . . ." It does indeed seem naïve and stupid, and one cannot help but think that our premier literary critic (who among other great tasks of illumination explained Marxian economics to a generation) is a bit of a dope. But with that harsh judgment out of the way, one can only admire his response to the American bureaucracy.

*The Cold War and the Income Tax* (1963).

Mr. Wilson originally owed $20,000 in unpaid taxes. With interest and fines, the $20,000 became $60,000. The Internal Revenue Service then went into action, and Mr. Wilson learned at first hand just how much power the IRS exerts. Royalties, trust funds, bank accounts can be attached; automobiles may be seized and sold at auction. Nothing belongs to the victim until the case is settled. Meanwhile, his private life is ruthlessly invaded in order to discover if he is of criminal intent (and therefore willfully bilking the nation of its rightful revenue). In Mr. Wilson's case, much was made of the fact that he had been married four times (a sign of unstable temperament); that he had written, Heaven help him, *books*! In a passage of exquisite irony, Mr. Wilson describes how one of the agents was put to work reading the master's complete *oeuvre* in order to prove that his not paying taxes was part of a sinister design to subvert a great nation. Did they find anything? Yes. In a journalistic piece, Mr. Wilson seemed to admire a man who had, among other crimes, not paid a Federal tax.

Even more unpleasant than the bureau's legitimate investigation was the unrelenting impertinence of the investigators. Why did Mr. Wilson spend six dollars to buy a cushion for his dog to sleep on? Why did he keep three places to live when the investigator (who earned a virtuous $7,500 a year) needed only one place to live in? Why was Mr. Wilson's daughter in a private school? Even worse than this sort of harassment was the inefficiency and buck-passing of the bureau. No one seemed able to make a decision. Regional office A had no idea what regional office B had decided. Then, just as progress was about to be made, a new investigator would be assigned the case and everyone had to go back to "Start." Kafka inevitably comes to mind; also, the bureaucracy of the Soviet Union which Mr. Wilson once contrasted—to his regret—unfavorably with our own.

After describing his own particular predicament, Mr. Wilson then discusses the general question of the income tax and the free society. He records in detail the history of the tax since the 1913 Constitutional amendment which made it legal (in 1895 the Supreme Court had ruled that President Lincoln's wartime tax on personal income was unconstitutional). Inexorably, the Federal tax has increased until today we pay more tax than we did during the Second World War. And there is no end in sight.

Mr. Wilson then asks a simple question: Why must we pay so much? He notes the conventional answer: Since the cold war, foreign aid, and defense account for seventy-nine percent of all Federal expenditures, putting the nation in permanent hock to that economic military complex

President Eisenhower so movingly warned us against after a lifetime's loyal service to it. There is of course some consolation in the fact that we are not wasting our billions weakening the moral fiber of the American yeoman by building him roads and schools, or by giving him medical care and decent housing. In public services, we lag behind all the industrialized nations of the West, preferring that the public money go not to the people but to big business. The result is a unique society in which we have free enterprise for the poor and socialism for the rich. This dazzling inequity is reflected in our tax system where the man on salary pays more tax than the man who lives on dividends, who in turn pays more tax than the wheeler-dealer who makes a capital-gains deal.

How did we get into this jam? Admittedly, the Soviet is a formidable enemy, and we have been well advised to protect ourselves. Empires traditionally must buy not only weapons but allies, and we are, like it or not, an empire. But there is no evidence that we need spend as much as we do spend on atomic overkill, on foreign aid, on chemical and bacteriological warfare (we are now reactivating at great expense diseases that the human race has spent centuries attempting to wipe out).

Mr. Wilson is excellent at describing the mad uses to which our tax money is being put ($30 billion to get a man on the moon is lunacy), but he seems not to be aware of the original policy behind the cold war. It was John Foster Dulles's decision to engage the Soviet in an arms race. Dulles figured, reasonably enough, that the Soviet economy could not endure this sort of competition. It was also believed that even if they should achieve military parity, their people, hungering for consumer goods, would revolt. This policy was successful for a time. But it worked as much hardship on our free society as it did on their closed one. We have become a garrison state, frightened of our own government and bemused by a rhetoric in which all is appearance, nothing reality. Or, as Mr. Wilson puts it:

The truth is that the people of the United States are at the present time dominated and driven by two kinds of officially propagated fear: fear of the Soviet Union and fear of the income tax.

These two terrors have been adjusted so as to complement one another and thus to keep the citizen of our free society under the strain of a double pressure from which he finds himself unable to escape—like the man in the old Western story who, chased into a narrow ravine by a buffalo, is confronted with a grizzly bear. If we fail to accept the tax, the Russian buffalo will butt and trample us, and if we try to defy the tax, the Federal bear will crush us.

Is there a way out? Mr. Wilson is not optimistic. Opponents of the income tax tend to be of the Far Right, where they fear the buffalo even more than they do the bear. There is nothing quite so engaging in our public life today as to hear Barry Goldwater tell us how we can eventually eliminate the graduated income tax *while* increasing military expenditures. Also, the militant conservative, though he will go to the barricades to keep a Federal dollar from filtering down to a state school, sees nothing wrong with Federal billions subsidizing a corporation in which he owns stock. As for the politicians, they tend to be too much part of the system to try and change it. The most passionate Congressional budget cutter will do all that he can to get Federal money for his own district. Between the pork barrel and the terrible swift sword, Pentagon, Congress, and industry are locked together, and nothing short of a major popular revolt can shatter their embrace.

Mr. Wilson discusses in some detail various attempts made by individuals (mostly pacifists) to thwart the IRS. But the results have not been happy. The line between Thoreau and Poujade is a delicate one. Yet it is perfectly clear that it must one day be drawn if the United States is not to drift into a rigid Byzantine society where the individual is the state's creature (yes, liberals worry about this, too), his life the property of a permanent self-perpetuating bureaucracy, frozen in some vague never-ending cold war with an enemy who is merely a reflection of itself.

Edmund Wilson's personal conclusion is a sad one. He points out that at the age of sixty-eight he can never hope to pay the government what he owes. According to his settlement with the IRS, everything that he makes over a certain amount goes automatically toward settling the debt. On principle, he hopes to keep his income below the taxable level. More to the point, as a result of his experience with the New America, "I have finally come to feel that this country, whether or not I live in it, is no longer any place for me." That is a stunning indictment of us all. Edmund Wilson is our most distinguished man of letters. He has always been (though the bureaucrats may not know it) something of a cultural America Firster. To lose such a man is a warning signal that our society is approaching that shadow line which, once crossed, means an end to what the makers of the country had hoped would be a place in which happiness might be usefully pursued. Yet Mr. Wilson's grim pamphlet may be just the jolt we need. Not since Thomas Paine has the drum of polemic sounded with such urgency through the land, and it is to be hoped that every citizen of the United States will read this book.

*Book Week*
November 3, 1963

# 72
·

# *PRESIDENT*
# *KENNEDY*

Until last month (March, 1961), I had not been at the White House since 1957, when I was asked to compose a speech for President Eisenhower.*

At that time the White House was as serene as a resort hotel out of season. The corridors were empty. In the various offices of the Executive (wings contiguous to the White House proper) quiet gray men in waist-coats talked to one another in low-pitched voices.

The only color, or choler, curiously enough, was provided by President Eisenhower himself. Apparently his temper was easily set off; he scowled when he stalked the corridors; the Smile was seldom in evidence. Fortunately, Eisenhower was not at the White House often enough to disturb that tranquility which prevailed, no matter what storms at home, what tragedies abroad.

Last month I returned to the White House (a defeated Democratic politician, full of pluck) to find the twentieth century, for good or ill, installed. The corridors are filled with eager youthful men, while those not young are revitalized.

As Secretary of Commerce Luther Hodges (at sixty-two the oldest member of the Cabinet) remarked: "There I was a few months ago,

*Never delivered.

thinking my life was over. I'd retired to a college town. Now . . . well, that fellow in there" (he indicated the President's office) "he calls me in the morning, calls me at noon, calls me at night: *Why don't we try this? Have you considered that?* Then to top it all he just now asks me: *Where do you get your suits from?* I tell you I'm a young man again."

In the White House press room reporters are permanently gathered. Photographers are on constant alert and television cameramen stand by, for news is made at all hours.

The affection of the press for Kennedy is a phenomenon, unique in presidential politics. There is of course the old saw that he was a newspaperman himself (briefly, for INS) and also that he is a bona fide intellectual (on the other hand, the working press is apt to be anti-intellectual); but, finally, and perhaps more to the point, Kennedy is candid with the press in a highly personal way. He talks to journalists easily. There is no pomp; there is little evasion in his manner; he involves them directly in what he is doing. His wit is pleasingly sardonic.

Most important, until Kennedy, it was impossible for anyone under fifty (or for an intellectual of any age) to identify himself with the President. The intellectual establishment of the country opted for "alienation," the cant word of the 1940s and 1950s, and even those who approved of this or that president's deeds invariably regarded the men set over us by the electorate as barbarians (Truman's attack on modern painting, Roosevelt's breezy philistinism, Eisenhower's inability to express himself coherently on any subject).

For twenty years the culture and the mind of the United States ignored politics. Many never voted; few engaged in active politics. Now everything has changed. From Kenneth Galbraith to Robert Frost the intellectual establishment is listened to and even, on occasion, engaged to execute policy.*

Close to, Kennedy looks older than his photographs. The outline is slender and youthful, but the face is heavily lined for his age. On the upper lip are those tiny vertical lines characteristic of a more advanced

---

*Alas. The intellectual establishment can take a great deal of credit for the attempted conquest of Asia and the subsequent collapse of America's imperial pretension. The end may be a good if serendipitous thing. Unfortunately, to achieve it, the Bundys and the Goodwins and the Rostows helped shatter those fragile balances which made the Republic, on good days, a place to take pride in. If Kennedy had devoted more time to sex and less to speed-reading the memos of the clerks, he might still be alive, a small matter, not to mention the large matter of saving the lives of those hundreds of thousands of Asiatics and Americans who died to make Harvard Yard Palatine Hill.

age. He is usually tanned from the sun, while his hair is what lady novelists call "chestnut," beginning to go gray. His eyes are very odd. They are, I think, a murky, opaque blue, "interested," as Gertrude Stein once said of Hemingway's eyes, "not interesting"; they give an impression of flatness, while long blond eyelashes screen expression at will. His stubby boy fingers tend to drum nervously on tables, on cups and glasses. He is immaculately dressed; although, disconcertingly, occasional white chest hairs curl over his collar.

The smile is charming even when it is simulated for the public. Franklin Roosevelt set an unhappy tradition of happy warriors, and ever since his day our politicians are obliged to beam and grin and simper no matter how grave the occasion. Recently, at a public dinner, I had a thoughtful conversation with Harry Truman. He was making a particularly solemn point when suddenly, though his tone did not change, his face jerked abruptly into a euphoric grin, all teeth showing. I thought he had gone mad, until I noticed photographers had appeared in the middle distance.

As for Kennedy's personality, he is very much what he seems. He is withdrawn, observant, icily objective in crisis, aware of the precise value of every card dealt him. Intellectually, he is dogged rather than brilliant.

Over the years I've occasionally passed books on to him, which I thought would interest him (including such arcana as Byzantine economy). Not only does he read them but he will comment on what he's read when I see him next (our meetings are casual, at long intervals, and I am happy to say that I have no influence).

After his defeat for the Vice-Presidential nomination in 1956, he was amused when I suggested that he might feel more cheerful if every day he were to recite to himself while shaving the names of the vice-presidents of the United States, a curiously dim gallery of minor politicians. Also, somewhat mischievously, I suggested that he read *Coriolanus* to see if he might find Shakespeare's somewhat dark view of democracy consoling. Mrs. Kennedy and he read it aloud one foggy day at Hyannisport. Later he made the point with some charm that Shakespeare's knowledge of the democratic process was, to say the least, limited.

On another occasion, I gave him the manuscript of a play of mine (*The Best Man*) whose setting was a nominating convention for the Presidency. He read the play with interest; his comments were shrewd. I recall one in particular, because I used it.

"Whenever," he said, "a politician means to give you the knife at a convention, the last thing he'll say to you, as he leaves the room, is:

'Now look, Jack, if there's *anything* I can do for you, you just let me know!' That's the euphemism for 'You're dead.' "

Kennedy's relationships tend to be compartmentalized. There are cronies who have nothing to do with politics whom he sees for relaxation. There are advisers whom he sees politically but not socially. The only occasion where personal friendship and public policy appear to have overlapped was in his appointment of the perhaps not distinguished Earl Smith (our envoy to Cuba at the time of the Batista debacle) as ambassador to Switzerland. The Swiss, who were acting for the United States in Havana, complained loudly. To save the President embarrassment, Smith withdrew. With chilling correctness, Kennedy is reported to have called in the Swiss Ambassador to Washington and given him a lesson in international diplomacy (i.e. you do not criticize publicly an ambassadorial appointment without first apprising the Chief of State privately). The ambassador left the White House shaken and bemused. Immediately afterwards, an aide entered the President's office to find him beaming. "That was very satisfying," he said.

Kennedy is unique among recent Presidents in many ways. For one thing, he has ended (wistfully, one hopes forever) the idea that the presidency is a form of brevet rank to be given a man whose career has been distinguished in some profession other than politics or, if to a politician, one whose good years are past, the White House being merely a place to provide some old pol with a golden Indian summer.

Yet the job today is literally killing, and despite his youth, Kennedy may very well not survive. A matter, one suspects, of no great concern to him. He is fatalistic about himself. His father recalls with a certain awe that when his son nearly died during the course of a spinal operation he maintained a complete serenity: if he was meant to die at that moment he would die and complaint was useless.

Like himself, the men Kennedy has chosen to advise him have not reached any great height until now. They must prove themselves *now*. Government service will be the high point of their lives, not an agreeable reward for success achieved elsewhere. Few men have the energy or capacity to conduct successfully two separate careers in a lifetime, an obvious fact ignored by most presidents in their search, often prompted by vanity or a sense of public relations, for celebrated advisers.

Nearly half the electorate was eager to find Kennedy and his regime "intellectual," given to fiscal irresponsibility and creeping socialism. (There is, by the way, despite the cries of demagogues, no operative Left in the United States. We are divided about evenly between conservatives and reactionaries.) But now, having experienced his Administration, it is evident even to the most suspicious of the Radical Right that Kennedy is not an adventurous reformer of the body politic, if only because this is not the time for such a reformation, and he knows it.

Essentially, he is a pragmatist with a profound sense of history, working within a generally liberal context. Since the United States is in no immediate danger of economic collapse, and since there is no revolutionary party of Left or Right waiting to seize power, our politics are firmly of the Center. The problems of the nation are a lagging economic growth, which under an attentive Administration can be corrected, and foreign affairs, where the United States *vis-à-vis* Russia remains a perhaps insoluble problem, but one to which Kennedy is addressing himself with a commendable lack of emotion.

Perhaps Kennedy's most unusual gift is an objectivity which extends to himself. He can discuss his own motives with a precision not usual in public men, who tend to regard themselves tenderly and according to the rhetoric of the day.

Before the primaries last spring, when his main opponent for the nomination was the attractively exuberant Senator Hubert Humphrey, Kennedy remarked privately that the contest was really one of temperaments, of "images," and though he confessed he did not have the Senator's passion for liberal reform, he did not think that was what the country in its present mood wanted or needed. Kennedy admitted to being less interesting and less dramatic than Humphrey, but for this time and place he felt he himself would prove more appealing, a correct if unflattering self-estimate.

Kennedy is certainly the most accessible and least ceremonious of recent presidents. After last month's conference with the Canadian Prime Minister, the two men appeared in front of the White House for the usual television statement. Kennedy said his few words. Then he turned to the Prime Minister and said: "Now you make your statement while I go back to the office and get your coat." And the Prime Minister made his statement and the President got his coat for him.

A few days later, when Eleanor Roosevelt came to see him at the White House, he insisted that she allow him to show her her old home. As they were about to leave his office, he motioned for her to precede him through the door.

Mrs. Roosevelt drew back. "No," she said. "You go first. You are the president."

He laughed. "I keep forgetting." With her lovely, deliberate blandness, she replied, "But you must *never* forget."

Perhaps the most distressing aspect of the last Administration was

President Eisenhower's open disdain of politics and his conviction that "politician" was a dirty word. This tragic view is shared even now by the majority of the American electorate, explaining the General's continuing appeal.* Time and again during those years one used to hear: "O.K., so he is a lousy president, but thank God he's not a politician!"

Kennedy, on the other hand, regards politics as an honorable, perhaps inevitable, profession in a democracy. Not only is he a master of politics, but he also takes a real pleasure in power. He is restless; he wants to know everything; he wanders into other people's offices at odd hours; he puts in a ten-hour office day; he reads continuously, even in the bathtub.

Most interesting of all, and the greatest break with tradition, have been his visits to the houses of friends in Washington, many of them journalists. Ever since the first protocol drawn up for George Washington, the president seldom goes visiting and never returns calls. Kennedy has changed that. He goes where he pleases; he talks candidly; he tries to meet people who otherwise might never get to him through the elaborate maze of the White House, in which, even during the most enlightened Administration, unpleasant knowledge can be kept from the president.

Inevitably, a president is delivered into the hands of an inner circle which, should he not be a man of considerable alertness and passion, tends to cut him off from reality. Eisenhower was a classic case. It was painfully evident at press conferences that he often had no knowledge of important actions taken by the government in his name; worse still, he was perhaps the only president not to read newspapers. The result was that when crises occurred, despite good intentions, he was never sufficiently aware of the nature of any problem to have a useful opinion as to its solution.

Only by constant study and getting about can a president be effective. As Harry Truman once remarked, despite the great power of the office, it is remarkably difficult to get anything done. "You tell 'em what you want and what happens? Nothing! You have to tell 'em five times."

Most presidential staffs inevitably take advantage of their president, realizing that in the rush of any day's business he will make many decisions and requests which he cannot possibly follow up. Kennedy, however, has already shown an unusual ability to recall exactly what he requested on any subject, and the impression he gives is of a man who means to be obeyed by his staff.

*Ike wasn't so wrong.

"He is deliberately drawing all the threads of executive power to himself," remarked one adviser. The cumbersome staff system of the Eisenhower Administration has been abandoned in favor of highly personal relationships between President and advisers. No one's function is ever clearly defined. The president moves men from project to project, testing them, extracting new points of view.

Not only is this a useful way of getting the most out of his staff, but it also ensures, rather slyly, Kennedy's own unique position at the center of the web of power: he alone can view and manipulate the entire complex of domestic and international policy. No one in his Administration may circumvent him, because none can master more than a part of the whole.

This ultimate knowledge of the whole is power, and, finally, the exercise of power is an art like any other. There is no doubt of John Kennedy's mastery of that art. He is a rare combination of intelligence, energy and opportunism. Most important, he is capable of growth. He intends to be great.

What he will accomplish depends largely upon his ability to rally the bored and cynical Western world, to fire the imagination of a generation taught never to think of "we" but only of "I." There are fragile signs (the warm response to the Peace Corps) and favorable omens (popular approbation reflected in polls) that a torpid society has at last been stirred by its youthful leader. If true, it is in the nick of time. Civilizations are seldom granted a second chance.

London *Sunday Telegraph*
April 9, 1961

I liked Kennedy personally to the end. But I did not like his presidency from the day he invaded Cuba to the last month of his life when he turned hot the cold war in Vietnam. Kennedy misplayed his cards from the beginning. Khrushchev frightened him at Vienna. Because Republicans would always suspect a Democratic president of being not only a nigger-lover but a fellow traveler, Kennedy's response was predictable. Secretly, I think he thought war was fun.

# 73
·

# THE MANCHESTER
# BOOK

At any given moment only a handful of people are known to almost everyone in the world. Mr. and Mrs. Richard Burton, the Kennedys . . . and the list is already near its end. There are of course those who enjoy reading about Sir Winston Churchill and General de Gaulle, but their fans are relatively few. Interest in Lyndon Johnson the Man (as opposed to the Warrior) is alarmingly slight; in fact, of the world's chiefs of state, only the enigmatic Mao Tse-tung can be said to intrigue the masses. There is something perversely gratifying in the fact that in an age of intense gossip and global publicity so few people are known to both the alert Malaysian and the average American. Things were different of course in the small world of Europe's Middle Ages. Numerous heroes were much sung about, while everyone was imbued with the Christian ethos. As a result, painters had a subject, scholars had something to argue about, poets had a point of departure. But the idea of Christendom died in Darwin's study, and now perhaps the only thing that we may all be said to hold in common is Bobby and Teddy and Jackie, and the memory of the dead President. Is it enough?

William Manchester thinks so, and his testament, *The Death of a President,* is very much a work of love, even passion. As we learned in the course of his notorious agony last year, the sun set for him when

John Kennedy died. Happily, the sun has since risen and Mr. Manchester can now take satisfaction in knowing that he too is part of history, a permanent footnote to an administration which is beginning to look as if it may itself be simply a glamorous footnote to that voluminous text the Age of Johnson. But whether or not Camelot will continue to exert its spell (and perhaps, like Brigadoon, rematerialize), Mr. Manchester has written a book hard to resist reading, despite its inordinate length. The narrative is compelling even though one knows in advance everything that is going to happen. Breakfast in Fort Worth. Flight to Dallas. Governor Connally. The roses. The sun. The friendly crowds. The Governor's wife: "Well, you can't say Dallas doesn't love you, Mr. President." And then one hopes that for once the story will be different—the car swerves, the bullets miss, and the splendid progress continues. But each time, like a recurrent nightmare, the handsome head is shattered. It is probably the only story that everyone in the world knows by heart. Therefore it is, in the truest sense, legend, and like all legends it can bear much repetition and reinterpretation. In classical times, every Greek playgoer knew that sooner or later Electra would recognize Orestes, but the manner of recognition varied significantly from teller to teller.

Mr. Manchester's final telling of the death of Kennedy is most moving; it is also less controversial than one had been led to believe by those who read the original manuscript and found the portrait of President Johnson unflattering. According to the current text, Johnson seems a bit inadequate but hardly villainous. The Kennedys, on the other hand, blaze with light; the author's love is apparent on every page. That love, however, did his writing little service, for the prose of the book is not good—the result, no doubt, of the strain under which the author was compelled to work. Certainly the style shows none of the ease which marked his first book on Kennedy, nor is there any trace of that elegance with which he once portrayed H. L. Mencken. Yet the crowded, overwritten narrative holds. Mr. Manchester is perhaps too haughty in his dismissal of the plot theory, and altogether too confident in analyzing Oswald's character ("In fact, he was going mad"). Nevertheless, if the best the detractors of the book can come up with is a photograph proving that, contrary to what Mr. Manchester has written, a number of Kennedy courtiers did indeed attend the swearing-in of the new President, then it is safe to assume that he has apparently accomplished what he set out to do: describe accurately what happened at Dallas, and immediately after.

Apparently. For there is a certain mystery about the origins of the book. It is known that the Kennedys approached Mr. Manchester and asked him to write the "official" version of the assassination. But in this age of image-making, politicians are never motivated simply. Whatever the moment's purpose, everything must serve it. Certainly nothing must get out of hand, as the Kennedys know better than anyone, for they were stung once before by a writer. Preparing for 1960, they gave Professor James MacGregor Burns a free hand to write what, in effect, was to be a campaign biography of John Kennedy. The result was a work of some candor which still remains the best analysis of the thirty-fifth President's character, but the candor which gave the book its distinction did not at all please its subject or his family. References to Joe Kennedy's exuberant anti-Semitic outbursts combined with a shrewd analysis of John Kennedy's ambivalent attitude toward McCarthy caused irritation. Therefore the next writer must be tractable. The starry-eyed Mr. Manchester seemed made to order: he was willing to swear loyalty; more important, he was willing to sign agreements. With some confidence, Launcelot and Guinevere confided to him the task of celebrating the fallen hero.

The comedy began. Right off, there was the matter of President Johnson. Whatever Mr. Manchester's original feelings about Johnson, he could not have spent all those hours communing with members of the exiled court and not get the sense of what a disaster it was for the country to have that vulgar, inept boor in Jack's place. The Kennedys have always been particularly cruel about Johnson, and their personal disdain is reflected and magnified by those around them, particularly their literary apologists, of whom Mr. Manchester was now one. When at last he submitted his work to the family, they proved too great and too sensitive to read it for themselves. Instead friends were chosen to vet the contents of the book. The friends found the anti-Johnson tone dangerous in the political context of the moment. They said so, and Mr. Manchester obediently made changes.

But Mr. Manchester's true ordeal did not begin until Richard Goodwin, a former aide to President Johnson, read the manuscript and found fault. He alarmed Mrs. Kennedy with tales of how what she had said looked in cold print. As a result, she threatened to sue if large cuts were not made. Some were made. Some were not. At last the publishers grew weary: the text could not be further altered. To their amazement, Mrs. Kennedy brought suit against them; meanwhile, in communicating her displeasure to Mr. Manchester, she reminded him that so secure was she in the pantheon of American heroines, no one could hope to cross her and survive—"unless I run off with Eddie Fisher," she added drolly. Needless to say, Mrs. Kennedy had her way, as the world knows.

It is now reasonable to assume that Mr. Manchester is not the same man he was before he got involved with the Kennedys. But though one's sympathy is with him, one must examine the matter from the Kennedy point of view. They are playing a great and dangerous game: they want the presidency of the United States and they will do quite a lot to obtain it. By reflecting accurately their view of Johnson, Mr. Manchester placed in jeopardy their immediate political future. Put simply, they do not want, in 1967, to split fatally the Democratic Party. Unhappily for them, Mr. Manchester's sense of history did not accommodate this necessary fact; nevertheless, since he was, in their eyes, a "hired" writer, he must tell the story their way or not at all. As it turned out, he did pretty much what they wanted him to do. But, in the process of publicly strong-arming Mr. Manchester and the various publishers involved, the Kennedys gave some substance to those "vicious" rumors (so often resorted to by polemicists) that they are ruthless and perhaps not very lovable after all. As a result, Mr. Manchester's contribution to history may prove not to be the writing of this took so much as being the unwitting agent who allowed the innocent millions an unexpected glimpse of a preternaturally ambitious family furiously at work manipulating history in order that they might rise.

It was inevitable that sooner or later popular opinion would go against this remarkable family. In nature there is no raising up without a throwing down. It does not take a particularly astute political observer to detect the public's change of mood toward the Kennedys. Overt ambition has always caused unease in the Republic, while excessive busyness makes for fatigue. Since our electorate is as easily alarmed as it is bored, political ascent has always been hazardous, and the way strewn with discarded idols. Mrs. Kennedy, in particular, is a victim of the public's fickleness; undeserving of their love, she is equally undeserving of their dislike. But then it is a most terrible thing to live out a legend, and one wonders to what extent the Kennedys themselves understand just what was set in motion for them by their father's will that they be great. Theirs is indeed *the* story of our time, and, if it did nothing else, the noisy quarrel with Mr. Manchester made vivid for everyone not only their arrogance but their poignancy. They are unique in our history, and the day they depart the public scene will be a sad one; for not only will we have lost a family as much our own as it is theirs, we shall have also lost one of the first shy hints since Christianity's decline that there may indeed be such a thing as fate, and that tragedy is not merely a literary form of little relevance in the age of common men but a continuing fact of the human condition, requiring that the overreacher be struck down and in his fall, we, the chorus, experience awe, and some pity.

*Book Week*
April 9, 1967

# 74

## *THE HOLY FAMILY*

From the beginning of the Republic, Americans have enjoyed accusing the first magistrate of kingly ambition. Sometimes seriously but more often derisively, the president is denounced as a would-be king, subverting the Constitution for personal ends. From General Washington to the present incumbent, the wielder of power has usually been regarded with suspicion, a disagreeable but not unhealthy state of affairs for both governor and governed. Few presidents, however, have been accused of wanting to establish family dynasties, if only because most presidents have found it impossible to select a successor of any sort, much less promote a relative. Each of the Adamses and the Harrisons reigned at an interval of not less than a political generation from the other, while the two Roosevelts were close neither in blood nor in politics. But now something new is happening in the Republic, and as the Chinese say, we are living "in interesting times."

In 1960, with the election of the thirty-fifth President, the famous ambition of Joseph P. Kennedy seemed at last fulfilled. He himself had come a long way from obscurity to great wealth and prominence; now his eldest surviving son, according to primogeniture, had gone the full distance and become president. It was a triumph for the patriarch. It was also a splendid moment for at least half the nation. What doubts one may have had about the Kennedys were obscured by the charm and intelligence of John F. Kennedy. He appeared to be beautifully on to himself; he was also on to us; there is even evidence that he was on to the family, too. As a result, there were few intellectuals in 1960 who were not beguiled by the spectacle of a president who seemed always to be standing at a certain remove from himself, watching with amusement his own performance. He was an ironist in a profession where the prize usually goes to the apparent cornball. With such a man as chief of state, all things were possible. He would "get America moving again."

But then mysteriously the thing went wrong. Despite fine rhetoric and wise commentary, despite the glamor of his presence, we did not move, and if historians are correct when they tell us that presidents are "made" in their first eighteen months in office, then one can assume that the Kennedy administration would never have fulfilled our hopes, much less his own. Kennedy was of course ill-fated from the beginning. The Bay of Pigs used up much of his credit in the bank of public opinion, while his attempts at social legislation were resolutely blocked by a more than usually obstructive Congress. In foreign affairs he was overwhelmed by the masterful Khrushchev and not until the Cuban missile crisis did he achieve tactical parity with that sly gambler. His administration's one achievement was the test-ban treaty, an encouraging footnote to the cold war.

Yet today Kennedy dead has infinitely more force than Kennedy living. Though his administration was not a success, he himself has become an exemplar of political excellence. Part of this phenomenon is attributable to the race's need for heroes, even in deflationary times. But mostly the legend is the deliberate creation of the Kennedy family and its clients. Wanting to regain power, it is now necessary to show that once upon a time there was indeed a Camelot beside the Potomac, a golden age forever lost unless a second Kennedy should become the president. And so, to insure the restoration of that lovely time, the past must be transformed, dull facts transcended, and the dead hero extolled in films, through memorials, and in the pages of books.

The most notorious of the books has been William Manchester's *The Death of a President.* Hoping to stop Jim Bishop from writing one of his ghoulish *The Day They Shot* sagas, the Kennedys decided to "hire" Mr. Manchester to write their version of what happened at Dallas. Unfortunately, they have never understood that treason is the natural business of clerks. Mr. Manchester's use of Mrs. Kennedy's taped recollections did not please the family. The famous comedy of errors that

ensued not only insured the book's success but also made current certain
intimate details which the family preferred for the electorate not to
know, such as the President's selection of Mrs. Kennedy's dress on that
last day in order, as he put it, "to show up those cheap Texas broads,"
a remark not calculated to give pleasure to the clients of Neiman-
Marcus. Also, the family's irrational dislike of President Johnson came
through all too plainly, creating an unexpected amount of sympathy for
that least sympathetic of magistrates. Aware of what was at stake, Mrs.
Kennedy tried to alter a book which neither she nor her brothers-in-law
had read. Not since Mary Todd Lincoln has a president's widow been
so fiercely engaged with legend if not history.

But then, legend-making is necessary to the Kennedy future. As a
result, most of the recent books about the late president are not so much
political in approach as religious. There is the ritual beginning of the
book which is the end: the death at Dallas. Then the witness goes back
in time to the moment when he first met the Kennedys. He finds them
strenuous but fun. Along with riotous good times, there is the constant
question: How are we to elect Jack president? This sort of talk was in
the open after 1956, but as long ago as 1943, according to *The Pleasure
of His Company,* Paul B. Fay, Jr., made a bet that one day Jack would
be JFK.

From the beginning the godhead shone for those who had the eyes
to see. The witness then gives us his synoptic version of the making of
the President. Once again we visit cold Wisconsin and dangerous West
Virginia (can a young Catholic war hero defeat a Protestant accused of
being a draft dodger in a poor mining state where primary votes are
bought and sold?) From triumph to triumph the hero proceeds to the
convention at Los Angeles, where the god is recognized. The only
shadow upon that perfect day is cast, significantly, by Lyndon B. Johnson. Like Lucifer he challenged the god at the convention, and was
struck down only to be raised again as son of morning. The deal to make
Johnson vice-president still causes violent argument among the new
theologians. Pierre Salinger in *With Kennedy* quotes JFK as observing
glumly, "The whole story will never be known, and it's just as well that
it won't be." Then the campaign itself. The great television debates
(Quemoy and Matsu) in which Nixon's obvious lack of class, as classy
Jack duly noted, did him in—barely. The narrowness of the electoral
victory was swiftly erased by the splendor of the inaugural ("It all began
in the cold": Arthur M. Schlesinger, Jr., *A Thousand Days*). From this
point on, the thousand days unfold in familiar sequence and, though

details differ from gospel to gospel, the story already possesses the quality of a passion play: disaster at Cuba One, triumph at Cuba Two; the eloquent speeches; the fine pageantry; and always the crowds and the glory, ending at Dallas.

With Lucifer now rampant upon the heights, the surviving Kennedys are again at work to regain the lost paradise, which means that books must be written not only about the new incarnation of the Kennedy godhead but the old. For it is the dead hero's magic that makes legitimate the family's pretensions. As an Osiris-Adonis-Christ figure, JFK is already the subject of a cult that may persist, through the machinery of publicity, long after all memory of his administration has been absorbed by the golden myth now being created in a thousand books to the single end of maintaining in power our extraordinary holy family.

The most recent batch of books about JFK, though hagiographies, at times cannot help but illuminate the three themes which dominate any telling of the sacred story: money, image-making, family. That is the trinity without which nothing. Mr. Salinger, the late President's press secretary, is necessarily concerned with the second theme, though he touches on the other two. Paul B. Fay, Jr., (a wartime buddy of JFK and Under Secretary of the Navy) is interesting on every count, and since he seems not to know what he is saying, his book is the least calculated and the most lifelike of the ones so far published. Other books at hand are Richard J. Whalen's *The Founding Father* (particularly good on money and family) and Evelyn Lincoln's *My Twelve Years with John F. Kennedy,* which in its simple way tells us a good deal about those who are drawn to the Kennedys.

While on the clerical staff of a Georgia Congressman, Mrs. Lincoln decided in 1952 that she wanted to work for "someone in Congress who seemed to have what it takes to be President"; after a careful canvass, she picked the Representative from the Massachusetts Eleventh District. Like the other witnesses under review, she never says *why* she wants to work for a future president; it is taken for granted that anyone would, an interesting commentary on all the witnesses from Schlesinger (whose *A Thousand Days* is the best political novel since *Coningsby*) to Theodore Sorensen's dour *Kennedy.* Needless to say, in all the books there is not only love and awe for the fallen hero who was, in most cases, the witness's single claim to public attention, but there are also a remarkable number of tributes to the holy family. From Jacqueline (Isis-Aphrodite-Madonna) to Bobby (Ares and perhaps Christ-to-be) the Kennedys appear at the very least as demigods, larger than life. Bobby's hard-working staff seldom complained, as Mr. Salinger put it, "because we all knew that Bob was working just a little harder than we were." For the same reason "we could accept without complaint [JFK's] bristling temper, his cold sarcasm, and his demands for always higher standards of excellence because we knew he was driving himself harder than he was driving us—despite great and persistent physical pain and personal tragedy." Mrs. Lincoln surprisingly finds the late President "humble"—doubtless since the popular wisdom requires all great men to be humble. She refers often to his "deep low voice" [*sic*], "his proud head held high, his eyes fixed firmly on the goals—sometimes seemingly impossible goals—he set for himself and all those around him." Mr. Schlesinger's moving threnody at the close of *his* gospel makes it plain that we will not see JFK's like again, at least not until the administration of Kennedy II.

Of the lot, only Mr. Fay seems not to be writing a book with an eye to holding office in the next Kennedy administration. He is garrulous and indiscreet (the Kennedys are still displeased with his memoirs even though thousands of words were cut from the manuscript on the narrow theological ground that since certain things he witnessed fail to enhance the image, they must be apocryphal). On the subject of the Kennedys and money, Mr. Fay tells a most revealing story. In December, 1959, the family was assembled at Palm Beach; someone mentioned money, "causing Mr. [Joseph] Kennedy to plunge in, fire blazing from his eyes. 'I don't know what is going to happen to this family when I die,' Mr. Kennedy said. 'There is no one in the entire family, except Joan and Teddy, who is living within their means. No one appears to have the slightest concern for how much they spend.'" The tirade ended with a Kennedy sister running from the room in tears, her extravagance condemned in open family session. Characteristically, Jack deflected the progenitor's wrath with the comment that the only "solution is to have Dad work harder." A story which contradicts, incidentally, Mr. Salinger's pious "Despite his great wealth and his generosity in contributing all of his salaries as Congressman, Senator and President to charities, the President was not a man to waste pennies."

But for all the founding father's grumbling, the children's attitude toward money—like so much else—is pretty much what he wanted it to be. It is now a familiar part of the sacred story of how Zeus made each of the nine Olympians individually wealthy, creating trust funds which now total some ten million dollars per god or goddess. Also at the disposal of the celestials is the great fortune itself, estimated at a hundred, two hundred, three hundred, or whatever hundred millions of dollars, administered from an office on Park Avenue, to which the Kennedys send their bills, for we are told in *The Founding Father,* "the childhood habit of dependence persisted in adult life. As grown men and women the younger Kennedys still look to their father's staff of accountants to keep track of their expenditures and see to their personal finances." There are, of course, obvious limitations to not understanding the role of money in the lives of the majority. The late President was aware of this limitation and he was forever asking his working friends how much money they made. On occasion, he was at a disadvantage because he did not understand the trader's mentality. He missed the point to Khrushchev at Vienna and took offense at what, after all, was simply the boorishness of the marketplace. His father, an old hand in Hollywood, would have understood better the mogul's bluffing.

It will probably never be known how much money Joe Kennedy has spent for the political promotion of his sons. At the moment, an estimated million dollars a year is being spent on Bobby's behalf, and this sum can be matched year after year until 1972, and longer. Needless to say, the sons are sensitive to the charge that their elections are bought. As JFK said of his 1952 election to the Senate, "People say 'Kennedy bought the election. Kennedy could never have been elected if his father hadn't been a millionaire.' Well, it wasn't the Kennedy name and the Kennedy money that won that election. I beat Lodge because I hustled for three years" (quoted in *The Founding Father*). But of course without the Kennedy name and the Kennedy money, he would not even have been a contender. Not only was a vast amount of money spent for his election in the usual ways, but a great deal was spent in not so usual ways. For instance, according to Richard J. Whalen, right after the pro-Lodge Boston *Post* unexpectedly endorsed Jack Kennedy for the Senate, Joe Kennedy loaned the paper's publisher $500,000.

But the most expensive legitimate item in today's politics is the making of the image. Highly paid technicians are able to determine with alarming accuracy just what sort of characteristics the public desires at any given moment in a national figure, and with adroit handling a personable candidate can be made to seem whatever the times require. The Kennedys are not of course responsible for applying to politics the techniques of advertising (the two have always gone hand in hand), but of contemporary politicians (the Rockefellers excepted) the Kennedys alone possess the money to maintain one of the most remarkable self-publicizing machines in the history of advertising, a machine which for a time had the resources of the Federal government at its disposal.

It is in describing the activities of a chief press officer at the White House that Mr. Salinger is most interesting. A talented image maker, he was responsible, among other things, for the televised press conferences in which the President was seen at his best, responding to simple questions with careful and often charming answers. That these press conferences were not very informative was hardly the fault of Mr. Salinger or the President. If it is true that the medium is the message and television is the coolest of all media and to be cool is desirable, then the televised thirty-fifth President was positively glacial in his effectiveness. He was a natural for this time and place, largely because of his obsession with the appearance of things. In fact, much of his political timidity was the result of a quite uncanny ability to sense how others would respond to what he said or did, and if he foresaw a negative response, he was apt to avoid action altogether. There were times, however, when his superb sense of occasion led him astray. In the course of a speech to the Cuban refugees in Miami, he was so overwhelmed by the drama of the situation that he practically launched on the spot a second invasion of that beleaguered island. Yet generally he was cool. He enjoyed the game of pleasing others, which is the actor's art.

He was also aware that vanity is perhaps the strongest of human emotions, particularly the closer one comes to the top of the slippery pole. Mrs. Kennedy once told me that the last thing Mrs. Eisenhower had done before leaving the White House was to hang a portrait of herself in the entrance hall. The first thing Mrs. Kennedy had done on moving in was to put the portrait in the basement, on aesthetic, not political grounds. Overhearing this, the President told an usher to restore the painting to its original place. "The Eisenhowers are coming to lunch tomorrow," he explained patiently to his wife, "and that's the first thing she'll look for." Mrs. Lincoln records that before the new Cabinet met, the President and Bobby were about to enter the Cabinet room when the President "said to his brother, 'Why don't you go through the other door?' The President waited until the Attorney General entered the Cabinet room from the hall door, and then he walked into the room from my office."

In its relaxed way Mr. Fay's book illuminates the actual man much better than the other books if only because he was a friend to the President, and not just an employee. He is particularly interesting on the early days when Jack could discuss openly the uses to which he was being put by his father's ambition. Early in 1945 the future President told Mr. Fay how much he envied Fay his postwar life in sunny California while "I'll be back here with Dad trying to parlay a lost PT boat and a bad back into a political advantage. I tell you, Dad is ready right now and can't understand why Johnny boy isn't 'all engines full ahead.' " Yet the exploitation of son by father had begun long before the war. In 1940 a thesis written by Jack at Harvard was published under the title *Why England Slept,* with a foreword by longtime, balding family friend Henry Luce. The book became a best seller and (Richard J. Whalen tells us) as Joe wrote at the time in a letter to his son, "You would be surprised how a book that really makes the grade with high-class people stands you in good stead for years to come."

Joe was right of course and bookmaking is now an important part of the holy family's home industry. As Mrs. Lincoln observed, when JFK's collection of political sketches "won the Pulitzer prize for biography in 1957, the Senator's prominence as a scholar and statesman grew. As his book continued to be a best seller, he climbed higher up on public-opinion polls and moved into a leading position among Presidential possibilities for 1960." Later Bobby would "write" a book about how he almost nailed Jimmy Hoffa; and so great was the impact of this work that many people had the impression that Bobby had indeed put an end to the career of that turbulent figure.

Most interesting of all the myth-making was the creation of Jack the war hero. John Hersey first described for *The New Yorker* how Jack's Navy boat was wrecked after colliding with a Japanese ship; in the course of a long swim, the young skipper saved the life of a crewman, an admirable thing to do. Later they were all rescued. Since the officer who survived was Ambassador Kennedy's son, the story was deliberately told and retold as an example of heroism unequaled in war's history. Through constant repetition the simple facts of the story merged into a blurred impression that somehow at some point a unique act of heroism had been committed by Jack Kennedy. The last telling of the story was a film starring Cliff Robertson as JFK (the President had wanted Warren Beatty for the part, but the producer thought Beatty's image was "too mixed up").

So the image was created early: the high-class book that made the grade; the much-publicized heroism at war; the election to the House of Representatives in 1946. From that point on, the publicity was constant and though the Congressman's record of service was unimpressive, he himself was photogenic and appealing. Then came the Senate, the marriage, the illnesses, the second high-class book, and the rest is history. But though it was Joe Kennedy who paid the bills and to a certain extent managed the politics, the recipient of all this attention was meanwhile developing into a shrewd psychologist. Mr. Fay quotes a letter written him by the new Senator in 1953. The tone is jocular (part of the charm of Mr. Fay's book is that it captures as no one else has the preppish side to JFK's character; he was droll, particularly about himself, in a splendid W. C. Fields way): "I gave everything a good deal of thought. I am getting married this fall. This means the end of a promising political career, as it has been based up to now almost completely on the old sex appeal." After a few more sentences in this vein the groom-to-be comes straight to the point. "Let me know the general reaction to this in the Bay area." He did indeed want to know, like a romantic film star, what effect marriage would have on his career. But then most of his life was governed, as Mrs. Lincoln wrote of the year 1959, "by the public-opinion polls. We were not unlike the people who check their horoscope each day before venturing out." And when they did venture out, it was always to create an illusion. As Mrs. Lincoln remarks in her guileless way: after Senator Kennedy returned to Washington from a four-week tour of Europe, "it was obvious that his stature as a Senator had grown, for he came back as an authority on the current situation in Poland."

It is not to denigrate the late President or the writers of his gospel that neither he nor they ever seemed at all concerned by the bland phoniness of so much of what he did and said. Of course politicians have been pretty much the same since the beginning of history, and part of the game is creating illusion. In fact, the late President himself shortly after Cuba Two summed up what might very well have been not only his political philosophy but that of the age in which we live. When asked whether or not the Soviet's placement of missiles in Cuba would have actually shifted the balance of world power, he indicated that he thought not. "But it would have politically changed the balance of power. It would have appeared to, and appearances contribute to reality."

From the beginning, the holy family has tried to make itself appear to be what it thinks people want rather than what the realities of any situation might require. Since Bobby is thought by some to be ruthless, he must therefore be photographed as often as possible with children, smiling and happy and athletic, in every way a boy's ideal man. Politically, he must *seem* to be at odds with the present administration without ever actually taking any important position that President Johnson does not already hold. Bobby's Vietnamese war dance was particularly illustrative of the technique. A step to the Left (let's talk to the Viet Cong), followed by two steps to the Right, simultaneously giving "the beards"—as he calls them—the sense that he is for peace in Vietnam while maintaining his brother's war policy. Characteristically, the world at large believes that if JFK were alive there would be no war in Vietnam. The mythmakers have obscured the fact that it was JFK who began our active participation in the war when, in 1961, he added to the six hundred American observers the first of a gradual buildup of American troops, which reached twenty thousand at the time of his assassination. And there is no evidence that he would not have persisted in that war, for, as he said to a friend shortly before he died, "I have to go all the way with this one." He could not suffer a second Cuba and hope to maintain the appearance of Defender of the Free World at the ballot box in 1964.

The authors of the latest Kennedy books are usually at their most interesting when they write about themselves. They are cautious, of course (except for the jaunty Mr. Fay), and most are thinking ahead to Kennedy II. Yet despite a hope of future preferment, Mr. Salinger's self-portrait is a most curious one. He veers between a coarse unawareness of what it was all about (he never, for instance, expresses an opinion of the war in Vietnam), and a solemn bogusness that is most putting off. Like an after-dinner speaker, he characterizes everyone ("Clark Clifford, the brilliant Washington lawyer"); he pays heavy tribute to his office staff; he praises Rusk and the State Department, remarking that "JFK had more effective liaison with the State Department than any President in history," which would have come as news to the late President. Firmly Mr. Salinger puts Arthur Schlesinger, Jr., in his place, saying that he himself never heard the President express a lack of confidence in Rusk. Mr. Salinger also remarks that though Schlesinger was "a strong friend" of the President (something Mr. Salinger, incidentally, was not), "JFK occasionally was impatient with their [Schlesinger's memoranda] length and frequency." Mrs. Lincoln also weighs in on the subject of the historian-in-residence. Apparently JFK's "relationship with Schlesinger was never that close. He admired Schlesinger's brilliant mind, his enormous store of information . . . but Schlesinger was never more than an ally and assistant."

It is a tribute to Kennedy's gift for compartmentalizing the people in his life that none knew to what extent he saw the others. Mr. Fay was an after-hours buddy. Mrs. Lincoln was the girl in the office. Mr. Salinger was a technician and not a part of the President's social or private or even, as Mr. Salinger himself admits, political life. Contrasting his role with that of James Hagerty, Mr. Salinger writes, "My only policy duties were in the information field. While Jim had a voice in deciding what the administration would do, I was responsible only for presenting that decision to the public in a way and at a time that would generate the best possible reception." His book is valuable only when he discusses the relations between press and government. And of course when he writes about himself. His 1964 campaign for the Senate is nicely told and it is good to know that he lost because he came out firmly for fair housing on the ground that "morally I had no choice—not after sweating out Birmingham and Oxford with John F. Kennedy." This is splendid but it might have made his present book more interesting had he told us something about that crucial period of sweating out. Although he devotes a chapter to telling how he did not take a fifty-mile hike, he never discusses Birmingham, Oxford, or the black revolution.

All in all, his book is pretty much what one might expect of a PR man. He papers over personalities with the reflexive and usually inaccurate phrase (Eisenhower and Kennedy "had deep respect for each other"; Mrs. Kennedy has "a keen understanding of the problems which beset mankind"). Yet for all his gift at creating images for others, Mr. Salinger seems not to have found his own. Uneasily he plays at being U.S. Senator, fat boy at court, thoughtful emissary to Khrushchev. Lately there has been a report in the press that he is contemplating writing a novel. If he does, Harold Robbins may be in the sort of danger that George Murphy never was. The evidence at hand shows that he has the gift. Describing his divorce from "Nancy, my wife of eight years," Mr. Salinger manages in a few lines to say everything. "An extremely artistic woman, she was determined to live a quieter life in which she could pursue her skills as a ceramicist. And we both knew that I could not be happy unless I was on the move. It was this difference in philosophies, not a lack of respect, that led to our decision to obtain a divorce. But a vacation in Palm Springs, as Frank Sinatra's guest, did much to revive my spirits."

Mr. Fay emerges as very much his own man, and it is apparent that he amused the President at a level which was more that of a playmate escorting the actress Angie Dickinson to the Inaugural than as serious companion to the prince. Unlike the other witnesses, Mr. Fay has no pretensions about himself. He tells how "the President then began showing us the new paintings on the wall. 'Those two are Renoirs and that's a Cézanne,' he told us. Knowing next to nothing about painters or paintings, I asked, 'Who are they?' The President's response was predictable, 'My God, if you ask a question like that, do it in a whisper or wait till we get outside. We're trying to give this administration a semblance of class.' " The President saw the joke; he also saw the image which must at all times be projected. Parenthetically, a majority of the recorded anecdotes about Kennedy involve keeping up appearances; he was compulsively given to emphasizing, often with great charm, the division between how things must be made to seem, as opposed to the way they are. This division is noticeable, even in the censored version of Mr. Manchester's *The Death of a President.* The author records that when Kennedy spoke at Houston's coliseum, Jack Valenti, crouched below the lectern, was able to observe the extraordinary tremor of the President's hands, and the artful way in which he managed to conceal them from the audience. This tension between the serene appearance and that taut reality add to the poignancy of the true legend, so unlike the Parson Weems version Mrs. Kennedy would like the world to accept.

Money, image, family: the three are extraordinarily intertwined. The origin of the Kennedy sense of family is the holy land of Ireland, priest-ridden, superstitious, clannish. While most of the West in the nineteenth century was industrialized and urbanized, Ireland remained a famine-ridden agrarian country, in thrall to politicians, homegrown and British, priest and lay. In 1848, the first Kennedy set up shop in Boston, where the Irish were exploited and patronized by the Wasps; not unnaturally, the Irish grew bitter and vengeful and finally asserted themselves at the ballot box. But the old resentment remained as late as Joe Kennedy's generation and with it flourished a powerful sense that the family is the only unit that could withstand the enemy, as long as each member remained loyal to the others, "regarding life as a joint venture between one generation and the next." In *The Fruitful Bough,* a privately printed cluster of tributes to the Elder Kennedy (collected by Edward M. Kennedy) we are told, in Bobby's words, that to Joe Kennedy "the most important thing . . . was the advancement of his children . . . except for his influence and encouragement, my brother Jack might not have run for the Senate in 1952." (So much for JFK's comment that it was his own "hustling" that got him Lodge's seat.)

The father is of course a far more interesting figure than any of his sons if only because his will to impose himself upon a society which he felt had snubbed him has been in the most extraordinary way fulfilled. He drove his sons to "win, win, win." But never at any point did he pause to ask himself or them just what it was they were supposed to win. He taught them to regard life as a game of Monopoly (a family favorite):

you put up as many hotels as you can on Ventnor Avenue and win. Consequently, some of the failure of his son's administration can be ascribed to the family philosophy. All his life Jack Kennedy was driven by his father and then by himself to be first in politics, which meant to be the president. But once that goal had been achieved, he had no future, no place else to go. This absence of any sense of the whole emerged in the famous exchange between him and James Reston, who asked the newly elected President what his philosophy was, what vision did he have of the good life. Mr. Reston got a blank stare for answer. Kennedy apologists are quick to use this exchange as proof of their man's essentially pragmatic nature ("pragmatic" was a favorite word of the era, even though its political meaning is opportunist). As they saw it: give the President a specific problem and he will solve it through intelligence and expertise. A "philosophy" was simply of no use to a man of action. For a time, actual philosophers were charmed by the thought of an intelligent young empiricist fashioning a New Frontier.

Not until the second year of his administration did it become plain that Kennedy was not about to do much of anything. Since his concern was so much with the appearance of things, he was at his worst when confronted with those issues where a moral commitment might have informed his political response not only with passion but with shrewdness. Had he challenged the Congress in the Truman manner on such bills as Medicare and Civil Rights, he might at least have inspired the country, if not the Congress, to follow his lead. But he was reluctant to rock the boat, and it is significant that he often quoted Hotspur on summoning spirits from the deep: any man can summon, but will the spirits come? JFK never found out; he would not take the chance. His excuse in private for his lack of force, particularly in dealing with the Congress, was the narrow electoral victory of 1960. The second term, he declared, would be the one in which all things might be accomplished. With a solid majority behind him, he could work wonders. But knowing his character, it is doubtful that the second term would have been much more useful than the first. After all, he would have been constitutionally a lame duck president, interested in holding the franchise for his brother. The family, finally, was his only commitment and it colored all his deeds and judgment.

In 1960, after listening to him denounce Eleanor Roosevelt at some length, I asked him why he thought she was so much opposed to his candidacy. The answer was quick: "She hated my father and she can't stand it that his children turned out so much better than hers." I was startled at how little he understood Mrs. Roosevelt, who, to be fair, did not at all understand him, though at the end she was won by his personal charm. Yet it was significant that he could not take seriously any of her political objections to him (e.g., his attitude to McCarthyism); he merely assumed that she, like himself, was essentially concerned with family and, envying the father, would want to thwart the son. He was, finally, very much his father's son even though, as all the witnesses are at pains to remind us, he did not share that magnate's political philosophy— which goes without saying, since anyone who did could not be elected to anything except possibly the Chamber of Commerce. But the Founding Father's confidence in his own wisdom ("I know more about Europe than anybody else in this country," he said in 1940, "because I've been closer to it longer") and the assumption that he alone knew the absolute inside story about everything is a trait inherited by the sons, particularly Bobby, whose principal objection to the "talking liberals" is that they never know what's really going on, as he in his privileged place does but may not tell. The Kennedy children have always observed our world from the heights.

The distinguished jurist Francis Morrissey tells in *The Fruitful Bough* a most revealing story of life upon Olympus. "During the Lodge campaign, the Ambassador told [Jack and me] clearly that the campaign . . . would be the toughest fight he could think of, but there was no question that Lodge would be beaten, and if that should come to pass Jack would be nominated and elected President. . . . In that clear and commanding voice of his he said to Jack, 'I will work out the plans to elect you President. It will not be any more difficult for you to be elected President than it will be to win the Lodge fight . . . you will need to get about twenty key men in the country to get the nomination for it is these men who will control the convention. . . .' "

One of the most fascinating aspects of politician-watching is trying to determine to what extent any politician believes what he says. Most of course never do, regarding public statements as necessary noises to soothe the electorate or deflect the wrath of the passionate, who are forever mucking things up for the man who wants decently and normally to rise. Yet there are cases of politicians who have swayed themselves by their own speeches. Take a man of conservative disposition and force him to give liberal speeches for a few years in order to be elected and he will, often as not, come to believe himself. There is evidence that JFK often spellbound himself. Bobby is something else again. Andrew Kopkind in *The New Republic* once described Bobby's career as a series of "happenings": the McCarthy friend and fellow traveler of one year emerges as an intense New York liberal in another, and between these two happenings there is no thread at all to give a clue as to what the man actually thinks or who he really is. That consistency which liberals so furiously demanded of the hapless Nixon need not apply to any Kennedy.

After all, as the recent gospels point out, JFK himself was slow to become a liberal, to the extent he ever was (in our society no working politician can be radical). As JFK said to James MacGregor Burns, "Some people have their liberalism 'made' by the time they reach their late twenties. I didn't. I was caught in crosscurrents and eddies. It was only later that I got into the stream of things." His comment made liberalism sound rather like something run up by a tailor, a necessary garment which he regrets that he never had time in his youth to be fitted for. Elsewhere (in William Manchester's *Portrait of a President*) he explains those "currents and eddies." Of his somewhat reactionary career in the House of Representatives he said, "I'd just come out of my father's house at the time, and these were the things I knew." It is of course a truism that character is formed in one's father's house. Ideas may change but the attitude toward others does not. A father who teaches his sons that the only thing that matters is to be first, not second, not third, is obviously (should his example be followed) going to be rewarded with energetic sons. Yet it is hardly surprising that to date one cannot determine where the junior Senator from New York stands on such a straightforward issue (morally if not politically) as the American adventure in Vietnam. Differing with the President as to which cities ought to be bombed in the North does not constitute an alternative policy. His sophisticated liberal admirers, however, do not seem in the least distressed by his lack of a position; instead they delight in the *uses* to which he has put the war in Vietnam in order to embarrass the usurper in the White House.

The cold-blooded jauntiness of the Kennedys in politics has a remarkable appeal for those who also want to rise and who find annoying—to the extent they are aware of it at all—the moral sense. Also, the success of the three Kennedy brothers nicely makes hash of the old American belief that by working hard and being good one will deserve (and if fortunate, receive) promotion. A mediocre Representative, an absentee Senator, through wealth and family connections, becomes the president while his youngest brother inherits the Senate seat. Now Bobby is about to become RFK because he is Bobby. It is as if the United States had suddenly reverted to the eighteenth century, when the politics of many states were family affairs. In those days, if one wanted a political career in New York one had best be born a Livingston, a Clinton, or a Schuyler; failing that, one must marry into the family, as Alexander Hamilton did, or go to work for them. In a way, the whole Kennedy episode is a fascinating throwback to an earlier phase of civilization. Because the Irish maintained the ancient village sense of the family longer than most places in the West and to the extent that the sons of Joe Kennedy reflect those values and prejudices, they are an anachronism in an urbanized nonfamily-minded society. Yet the fact that they are so plainly not of this time makes them fascinating; their family story is a glamorous continuing soap opera whose appeal few can resist, including the liberals, who, though they may suspect that the Kennedys are not with them at heart, believe that the two boys are educable. At this very moment beside the river Charles a thousand Aristotles dream of their young Alexanders, and the coming heady conquest of the earth.

Meanwhile, the source of the holy family's power is the legend of the dead brother, who did not much resemble the hero of the books under review. Yet the myth that JFK was a philosopher-king will continue as long as the Kennedys remain in politics. And much of the power they exert over the national imagination is a direct result of the ghastliness of what happened at Dallas. But though the world's grief and shock were genuine, they were not entirely for JFK himself. The death of a young leader necessarily strikes an atavistic chord. For thousands of years the man-god was sacrificed to ensure with blood the harvest, and there is always an element of ecstasy as well as awe in our collective grief. Also, Jack Kennedy was a television star, more seen by most people than their friends or relatives. His death in public was all the more stunning because he was not an abstraction called The President, but a man the people thought they knew. At the risk of *lèse-divinité*, however, the assassination of President Nixon at, let us say, Cambridge by what at first was thought to be a member of the ADA but later turned out to be a dotty Bircher would have occasioned quite as much national horror, mourning, and even hagiography. But in time the terrible deed would have been forgotten, for there are no Nixon heirs.

Beyond what one thinks of the Kennedys themselves, there remains the large question: What sort of men ought we to be governed by in the coming years? With the high cost of politics and image-making, it is plain that only the very wealthy or those allied with the very wealthy can afford the top prizes. And among the rich, only those who are able to please the people on television are Presidential. With the decline of the religions, the moral sense has become confused, to say the least, and intellectual or political commitments that go beyond the merely expedient are regarded with cheerful contempt not only by the great operators themselves but also by their admirers and, perhaps, by the electorate itself. Also, to be fair, politicians working within a system like ours can never be much more than what the system will allow. Hypocrisy and self-deception are the traditional characteristics of the middle class in any place and time, and the United States today is the paradigmatic middle-class society. Therefore we can hardly blame our political gamesmen for being, literally, representative. Any public man has every right to try and trick us, not only for his own good but, if he is honorable, for ours as well. However, if he himself is not aware of what he is doing or to what end he is playing the game, then to entrust him with the first magistracy of what may be the last empire on earth is to endanger us all. One does not necessarily demand of our leaders passion (Hitler supplied the age with quite enough for this century) or reforming zeal (Mao Tse-tung is incomparable), but one does insist that they possess a sense of community larger than simply personal power for its own sake, being first because it's fun. Finally, in an age of supercommunications, one must have a clear sense of the way things are, as opposed to the way they have been made to seem. Since the politics of the Kennedys are so often the work of publicists, it is necessary to keep trying to find out just who they are and what they really mean. If only because should *they* be confused as to the realities of Cuba, say, or Vietnam, then the world's end is at hand.

At one time in the United States, the popular wisdom maintained that there was no better work for a man to do than to set in motion some idea whose time had not yet arrived, even at the risk of becoming as unpopular as those politicians JFK so much admired in print and so little emulated in life. It may well be that it is now impossible for such men to rise to the top in our present system. If so, this is a tragedy. Meanwhile, in their unimaginative fierce way, the Kennedys continue to play successfully the game as they found it. They create illusions and call them facts, and between what they are said to be and what they are falls the shadow of all the useful words not spoken, of all the actual deeds not done. But if it is true that in a rough way nations deserve the leadership they get, then a frivolous and apathetic electorate combined with a vain and greedy intellectual establishment will most certainly restore to power the illusion-making Kennedys. Holy family and bedazzled nation, in their faults at least, are well matched. In any case, the age of the commune in which we have lived since the time of Jackson is drawing to a close and if historical analogies are at all relevant, the rise of the *signori* is about to begin, and we may soon find ourselves enjoying a strange new era in which all our lives and dreams are presided over by smiling, interchangeable, initialed gods.

*Esquire*
April 1967

# 75

# BARRY GOLDWATER:
## A CHAT

Julius Caesar stood before a statue of Alexander the Great and wept, for Alexander at twenty-nine had conquered the world and at thirty-two was dead, while Caesar, a late starter of thirty-three, had not yet subverted even his own state. Pascal, contemplating this poignant scene, remarked rather sourly that he could forgive Alexander for wanting to own the earth because of his extreme youth, but Caesar was old enough to have known better.

I suggest, with diffidence, that Pascal did not entirely understand the nature of the politician; and the inner mechanism of a Caesar is no different in kind from that of an Alfred M. Landon. The aim of each is power. One would achieve it through military conquest, the other through what it pleases us to call the democratic process. It is natural for men to want power. But to seek power actively takes a temperament baffling to both the simple and the wise. The simple cannot fathom how any man would dare presume to prevail, while the wise are amazed that any reasonable man would *want* the world, assuming he could get it.

Suspended then between simplicity and wisdom, self-delusion and hard practicality, is the operative politician. He is not at all like other men, though he must acquire as protective coloration the manners of his society, join in its rituals (Caesar, the atheist, was a solemn high priest and our own Calvin Coolidge wore an Indian war bonnet), exploit its prejudices and anticipate its hungers.

Like his predecessors, an American politician in the midtwentieth century must conform to certain conventions. He must be gregarious (or seem to be), candid (but never give the game away), curious about people (otherwise, he would find his work unendurable). An American politician must not seem too brainy. He must put on no airs. He must smile often but at the same time appear serious. Most disagreeable of all, according to one ancient United States Senator, wise with victory, "is when you got to let some s.o.b. look you straight in the eye and think he's making a fool of you. Oh, that is gall and wormwood to the spirit!" Above all, a politician must not sound clever or wise or proud.

Finally, the politician must have that instinctive sense of occasion which is also the actor's art. To the right challenge he must have the right response. He is, in the purest sense, an opportunist. He must be an accurate barometer to the weather of his time. He must know the phases of the political moon and the hour of the tides. He must be ready at a moment's notice to seize that prize which is the game's reward, power. He must know in the marrow of his bones when it is right to make the large effort. For example, at the Democratic convention of 1956 the Vice-Presidential nomination was unexpectedly thrown open to the floor. The young Senator from Massachusetts went for the prize. The moment was wrong but the move was right. In a car on his way to the convention the day of the voting, John Kennedy was heard muttering grimly to himself, "Go, go, go!" When to go, when to stay; that is the art.

Even those who write knowledgeably about politics tend to make certain fundamental errors. They look for subtle motives where there are none. They believe there is a long-range plan of war when there is seldom anything more than quick last-minute deployments of troops before unscheduled battle. In a society like ours, politics is improvisation. To the artful dodger rather than the true believer goes the prize.

The junior Senator from Arizona, Barry Goldwater, is a politician of some grace and skill who at this moment is studying the political sky for omens, waiting for a sign in which to conquer. His moment may come in the Presidential election of 1964, or of 1968 or never. There is every evidence that he is, this year, a divided man, uncertain how to proceed. His sense of occasion is keen; his sense of history is practical. He knows perfectly well that his views are at variance with the majority views of his time. To do great deeds, to take the prize, he must, paradoxically, surrender many of those positions he has so firmly taken in his reaction to a society he neither likes nor, many feel, understands. Yet, again paradoxically, his entire celebrity is due to his appealingly cranky rejection of those positions the majority reveres. In short, he is loved for those very attitudes which a majority of the electorate does not accept.

Goldwater's success is phenomenal considering that he is only a second-term Senator with no significant legislation to his name. He comes from a politically unimportant state. By his own admission he is not a profound thinker. His success in Arizona was due not only to his charm and hard campaigning in a state usually Democratic but also to the popularity of his family, one of the oldest in the state, whose business, Goldwater's department stores, is to Arizona what Macy's is to New York.

It is a clue to Goldwater's recent success that he was primarily a salesman in the family business (his one creative contribution was the invention and promotion of men's shorts decorated with large red ants in the pants) and he considers his role at the moment as salesman for the conservative point of view, which is not necessarily the Republican view. But, spokesman for the majority of his party or not, bumper stickers with GOLDWATER IN '64 are beginning to appear around the country (as well as a few GOLDWATER IN 1864 stickers).

Goldwater's path to higher office is strewn with many hazards, not all of his own making. His father was Jewish (the family name originally was Goldwasser), yet he is an Episcopalian. Since he favors right-to-work laws and limitations on unions, organized labor is against him. Personally, he sees nothing wrong with Negro and white children together in the same schools. But he opposes any Federal interference with the rights of the Southern states to maintain segregation, even in the face of the recent Supreme Court decision. Goldwater has about as much chance of getting the Negro vote, according to one Tennessee politician, as "a legless man in a pants-kicking contest." Reluctantly, Goldwater realizes that Social Security is here to stay—it is too late to take it away—but he does think the program should be voluntary and certainly not enlarged to include medical care for the aged or anything else. He favors breaking off diplomatic relations with the Russians; he wants to present them wherever possible with a take-it-or-leave-it, peace-or-war attitude which many thoughtful conservatives who approve his domestic program find disquietingly like brinkmanship. In his own party he is blocked not only by Nelson Rockefeller but by Richard Nixon.

As if all these difficulties, inherent and assumed, were not enough, he is now seriously endangered by his admirers. Like most radicals of Right or Left, he is attractive to every sort of extremist. His most compromising support comes from the mysterious John Birch Society, whose beleaguered "Founder" (a title last used by the creator of Hollywood's Forest Lawn Cemetery), Robert Welch, is firmly convinced that forty million Americans are Communists, including such unexpected conspirators as Milton and Dwight D. Eisenhower. Stubbornly, Goldwater has refused to repudiate the Birch Society, a stand which has led one Republican leader to say, "That's the end of Barry."

Yet, despite great handicaps, Goldwater is perhaps the country's most popular politician, after Kennedy. He gets enormous crowds wherever he goes. They are enthusiastic and—hopeful sign—they include many young people. He has caught on as a personality even if his policies have not. It is common to hear, "O.K., so a lot of his ideas are cockeyed, but at least he tells you where he stands. He isn't afraid to speak up, the way the others are." That many of Goldwater's ideas are in a state of flux and that many of his positions are quite as obscure as those of any other politician does not penetrate. Once a man's "image," good or ill, is set in the public's mind, he can contradict himself every day and still be noted for consistency.

Yet Goldwater *is* something new on the scene. He is perhaps the first American politician who, though spokesman for an unpopular minority, finds himself personally popular for reasons irrelevant to his politics. He is forgiven by admirers when he speaks against the $1.25 minimum wage, union activities or the Supreme Court's power to integrate schools. So what? He's a nice guy, and nice guys are not dangerous. He is also sincere, a vague quality far more admired by the lonely crowd than competence or intelligence.

Barry Goldwater's office is on the fourth floor of the old Senate Office Building. The corridors are marble with high ceilings and enormous doors which tend to dwarf not only visitors but Senators. There is an air of quiet megalomania which is beguiling in its nakedness.

Behind the great mahogany door with its sign MR. GOLDWATER, ARIZONA is the outer office: wooden paneling, a view through large windows of the Capitol grounds. I was greeted by the Senator's secretary, Mrs. Coerver. She is small, amiable, gray, with that somewhat fixed smile politicians and their aides develop. (One smile is a vote gained, maybe. One frown is a vote lost, definitely.) "The Senator will see you in just a moment." She beamed.

I approached this meeting with curiosity. For one thing, since his book, *The Conscience of a Conservative,* Goldwater's fundamentalist ideas about the Constitution and society had undergone changes. When the Presidential virus attacks the system there is a tendency for the patient in his fever to move from the Right or the Left to the Center where the curative votes are, where John Kennedy now is. Other observers of Goldwater had also detected a perceptible shift to the Center. Further shifts would depend entirely on whether the patient took a turn for the White House. I wanted, simply, to take his temperature as of that day, for like all illnesses the Presidential virus has its own peculiar ebb and flow. At night in the company of good friends the fever blazes. In a cold dawn on the way to an airport to speak in some far-off town the virus is at its lowest point: To hell with it! thinks the patient, almost cured.

Also, I wanted to get an impression of character. I have often thought and written that if the United States were ever to have a Caesar, a true subverter of the state, (1) he would attract to himself all the true believers, the extremists, the hot-eyed custodians of the Truth; (2) he would oversimplify some difficult but vital issue, putting himself on the side of the majority, as Huey Long did when he proclaimed every man a king and proposed to divvy up the wealth; (3) he would not in the least resemble the folk idea of a dictator. He would not be a hysteric like Hitler. Rather, he would be just plain folks, a regular guy, warm and sincere, and while he was amusing us on television storm troopers would gather in the streets.

Now I have put the case extremely only because in recent months there has been an unusual rash of extremist groups like the John Birch Society, reminding us that there is a totalitarian potential in this country just as there is in every country. Fortunately, barring military or economic disaster, none of these groups is apt to come to much without a leader who could appeal personally to a majority. It seemed to me that Goldwater was perhaps such a man: (1) He has already attracted many extremists, and he has not denied them; (2) he oversimplifies a great many issues (getting "tough" with the Russians is fine and getting rid of the income tax is fine, too, but toughness costs money; where will it come from?); (3) he is exactly the sort of charming man whom no one would suspect of Caesarism, least of all himself.

Barry Goldwater entered Mrs. Coerver's office in his shirt sleeves and said, "Come on in." At the door to his own office he turned to a departing interviewer and said, finishing some earlier thought: "You know, of all the untrue things they write, the wildest one is how I'm a millionaire. I've been called that now so many times I'm beginning to feel like I ought to live like one." Chuckling at his own hyperbole (he is a millionaire; he does live like one), he led me to his office. The large desk was catercornered so that the light from the windows was in the visitor's face. Beside the desk was a bookcase containing, among other works, a leather-bound set of the speeches of Barry Goldwater. On the mantel of the fireplace was a bust of Lincoln. In the far corner of the room stood three flags. One of them was the Senator's own flag: he is a brigadier general in the Air Force Reserve. On the walls were photographs of the Arizona landscape, as beautiful and empty as a country of the moon.

We sat and looked at each other a moment. At fifty-two, he is lean and obviously in fine condition. The hair is gray. The eyes are small, alert, dark blue; the face tanned from a recent trip home. The nose is pleasantly crooked. The nostrils are odd, visible only when he tilts his head back, like the small neatly round punctures in a child's rubber mask. The mouth is wide and thin-lipped, the jaw square. The smile is attractive but when his face is in repose there is an unexpected hardness, even harshness. Neither of us, I noticed, was very good at looking straight at the other. Simultaneously, each looked away. I looked out the window. Goldwater examined his brigadier general's flag (for those who believe the old saw that an honest man must have a direct gaze, I refer them to a contemporary's report that the shiftiest-eyed man he had ever met was Thomas Jefferson).

I began compassionately: "You must get awfully tired of being interviewed." He smiled. "It's repetitive, but . . ," His voice trailed off. It is a good voice for politics, light but earnest, with a slight rural accent of the sort made familiar by television Westerns.

I had debated whether to bring a tape recorder. I knew that Goldwater had a small wrist-watch recorder which he used gleefully to disconcert others as well as to protect himself from misquotation. I decided to take notes instead. On a small pad of paper I had written a few topics. First, the John Birch Society. Recently Goldwater had said that "a great many fine people" were members, including "Republicans, liberal Democrats, conservatives," and he thought it would cause considerable political embarrassment if they were attacked en masse. He had also implied that besides the two known Birchers in Congress, Representatives Edgar Hiestand and John Rousselot, both Republicans of California, there were others. In one interview, however, he suggested that Robert Welch resign. Later he denied he had said this. I asked him how well he knew Welch. He frowned thoughtfully.

"Well, I've known Bob Welch five, maybe six years. But I didn't really get to him until that summit business, you know, when we all tried to keep Eisenhower from meeting Khrushchev. Welch and I worked together then. Of course all that stuff of his about Eisenhower being a Communist and so on was silly. Fact, I told him when he gave me that book of his [*The Politician*] to read, I said: 'Unless you can prove every one of those statements about people being Communists is true, you better go destroy every single copy of that book.' "

"Do you think Welch should resign as head of the society?"

The answer was quick: "I do. Just the other day I sent somebody over to the Library of Congress to get me the bylaws of the Birch Society, and I was disturbed about this dictatorial thing, how he personally can chuck people out any time he pleases. I didn't like it."

"What did you mean when you said there were liberal Democrats in the Birch Society?"

"Because there are. There're all kinds of people in that group. I know. I've met 'em and a nicer-looking bunch you never saw. That thirty- to forty-five-year-old group you want in politics. They're thoughtful people and they're concerned. But don't get the idea they're all conservatives because they're fighting Communism. A lot of people are fighting Communism who aren't conservative." I had the impression he wanted it made clear that his own conservative position was one thing and the fight against Communism was another thing. Most conservatives regard the two as synonymous. Goldwater does ordinarily, but this day I felt he was preparing a possible escape hatch.

I asked him if he knew of any members of Congress who belonged to the society, other than the two Californians. He paused. Then he said, "No." It was a slow, thoughtful "no," hard to interpret. Then: "You know, I don't really know that much about those people."

I asked him if he approved of their methods, as outlined in Welch's *Blue Book*. "Never read it. I don't know." It seemed to me strange that he would read the bylaws and *The Politician* yet not read the *Blue Book*, which contains not only the bylaws but a ten-point program on how to expose and discourage "Communists."

I mentioned some of Welch's gambits: infiltrating school boards and library boards, getting "mean and dirty" with known liberals, encouraging students to spy on teachers.

Goldwater interrupted. No, he didn't like that, of course. "In fact, I've always been in favor of teaching Communism in schools. Show the kids what we're up against. Naturally I'd want a good course in American history to balance it. After all, the only way you're going to beat

Communism is with a better idea, like Nero and the Christians . . . you know? He couldn't stamp 'em out, because there was that idea they had. Well, that's what we've got to have."

Goldwater had been against Federal aid to education. First, he is not convinced any aid is needed. Second, he feels that to give money to the states is an invasion of states' rights. Recently he testified before a House Education subcommittee in the interests of a bill of his own which he said would solve the whole problem. He proposed giving property owners a rebate on their Federal income tax up to one hundred dollars, the amount to represent what the property owner had paid in local school taxes. Even Goldwater's admirers found this solution baffling. His exchange with Representative John Brademas in committee had a good deal of unconscious humor in it.

Brademas asked Goldwater why he had proposed a bill to answer a problem which he did not believe existed. Soon both men were lost in a maze of: "I said 'if.' Well, if there is a problem, which I don't believe, then here's the answer. . . . All right, but if there is *not* a problem, then why propose . . . ?"

In the course of his testimony, Goldwater unexpectedly came out for minimum academic standards to be set by the Federal government for the entire country. Brademas pointed out the contradiction: to set such standards and requirements would mean government intervention of the most extreme sort. Goldwater saw no contradiction: the government's minimum standards would not be compulsory; they would be "guide lines." He felt, too, that although Federal aid to education was unconstitutional, *if* there was to be such aid parochial and private schools should be included.

I teased Goldwater about his exchange with Brademas. He laughed. He then repeated his position: There was no problem, and it was growing less. He quoted statistics. . . . Neither of us listened. I had touched a familiar button. He was responding as he had many times before.

I was amused during the Nixon-Kennedy debates by those who were astonished at the wide range of knowledge displayed by the two men, at their "mastery" of detail. Actually, neither was asked a question he had not already answered on an average of a dozen times a day for months. After such rehearsal any politician can discuss a number of subjects with what seems encyclopedic detail. It is a trick of the trade but a dangerous one, for answering the same questions over and over interferes with thought. Goldwater finished his statistics and waited for me to press the next button.

Not wanting to get him on a familiar track, I thought quickly, a little desperately. I wanted a general subject. The idea of the presidency occurred to me. What would *he* do if he were president? Goldwater had once said to a journalist that, all in all, he preferred the Senate to the White House because as a Senator he could speak his mind, "where if you're president you can't. You got to be cautious and watch what you say." When the journalist asked Goldwater what he had been saying as a Senator that he would not feel free to say as president, he had looked baffled and finally said, "Well, damned if I know."

On the word "president" I noticed a faint flush of the fever. His eyes glittered. He sat back in his chair. "If I was president," he began with a new weight and authority, "I'd move slowly, cautiously at first. You'd have to feel your pathway. Not that my ideas are new ideas. No, they're old, old ideas."

Then he talked of government farm supports. In the campaign, he had demanded "prompt and final termination of all subsidy." But he has changed. He would still eliminate supports, but gradually. I mentioned that only about half of the nation's farmers are needed to grow most of our food. Without supports a lot of people would be thrown on the labor market—in addition to the five million already unemployed. This, I suggested, was a real crisis. He agreed. They would have to be absorbed gradually. But how? Well, management and labor would get together (*without* the government) and set up a joint program to retrain and reallocate displaced people, "Not just farmers either, anybody who's been displaced by mechanization, and so on," and to sponsor "basic research for new gadgets—you know, for a lot of things like that we need."

Could labor and management be relied upon to do the job without some urging from the government? He thought they could. "Of course back in the 1920s management was pretty stupid, but I think they've come of age now, lot of fine new people at the top. The day of those self-made men, the founders, all that's over. In fact, labor's at the same place today management was in the 1920s. All those labor leaders, they're the same type of self-made man ran big business in the old days."

I asked him about his quarrel with Reuther. ("I would rather have Jimmy Hoffa stealing my money than Walter Reuther stealing my freedom.") He shook his head. "It's not personal. I just don't believe labor should be in politics." I was about to ask him what he thought of management in politics (the N.A.M., the Chamber of Commerce) when we were interrupted. A visiting lawyer was outside. He would like to shake the Senator's hand. He was ushered in.

The lawyer was a pleasant-looking, somewhat tense young man who

was in Washington for the American Bar Association's antitrust conference. Goldwater came around from behind his desk. He smiled warmly.
They shook hands. The young lawyer said in a voice shaking with
emotion, "I just wanted you to know, Senator, there are a lot of people
over in that Justice Department who better get off their fud and realize
we've got some states that can do the job." Goldwater was sympathetic.
I turned away, embarrassed. Two conservatives had met and I felt their
intensity, their oneness. They spoke in their own shorthand and they
knew the enemy.

I made notes while they talked. I wondered idly if I should ask
Goldwater what he liked to eat and whether or not he wore pajamas and
if he liked movies. I have always enjoyed reading those interviews which
are made up of an incredible amount of minutiae; like coral islands they
rise bit by bit out of the sea of personality, formed of dead facts. Absently, with what I hoped was the eye of a naturalist-novelist, I began
to record the objects on his desk: a large transparent plastic duck mysteriously containing a small metal elephant, all mounted rather disagreeably on a penholder. Next to the duck was a clipping from a Hartford
newspaper whose editorial began, *Well, What About Goldwater?* On the
wall behind the desk hung a number of small photographs. There was
one of Nixon, smiling, with a long inscription which I was too far away
to read. There was a similar photograph of Eisenhower, also smiling,
also inscribed. Why are politicians so happy when on view? "Always
smiling," I wrote neatly on the pad. Then the young lawyer shook hands
again. Goldwater smiled. I smiled. The photographs smiled. Only the
young lawyer did not smile. He knew the Republic was in danger. He
left. Goldwater and I put our smiles away and resumed the interview.

I had been told that the one question which made him uncharacteristically edgy was: Who wrote his book, *The Conscience of a Conservative*?
I asked it. He frowned. "That's what wrote it," he said, somewhat
irrelevantly. He ran his hand across the row of leather-bound books.
"My speeches. The book's nothing but a selection from speeches, from
a lot of the things I've been saying for years. After all, I've written four
books, a lot of magazine articles, my column."

I had been told that among his literary ghosts were Steve Shadegg and
L. Brent Bozell. I started to ask him about them but decided not to. It
was cruel. It was pointless. We live in an age of ghosts: singers whose
high notes are ghosted by others; writers whose works are created by
editors; actors whose performances are made out of film by directors.
Why should one harry politicians for not writing their own books and

speeches? Few have the time or the talent. In any case the work published must necessarily reflect the views of its "author."

I was ready to drop the subject, but Goldwater was not. He told me he was planning another book. He was going on a cruise with his wife in the fall. While traveling, he would write the first draft. Then he would go over it carefully for "improvement in expression. Then after that I'll submit it to an author . . . I mean publisher." I suspect that Goldwater knows even less about Freud than I do, which is little, but we both know a Freudian slip when we hear one. The dark eyes darted anxiously in my direction. Had I caught the slip? I had.

He talked about conservatism. "Bunch of us got together after the convention and we all agreed we'd never heard such conservative speeches get so much applause, and then they go and accept that platform which 95 percent of them were against." He sighed. "I don't know. What's wrong with the word 'conservative' anyway? Must be something." He said he had been impressed by the British Conservatives' comeback in 1951. They had got out and sold the party to the young people. This was his own plan. He would sell conservatism wherever he could, preferably to the young and uncommitted. "Of course the Conservative Party in England is about like the New Deal was here."

I asked him his impression of Kennedy. "Well, I guess I know him about as well as anybody around here. I like him. Of course we disagree on a lot of things. He thinks the government should do a lot more for people than I do." He mused about the campaign. He had advised against Nixon's television debates with Kennedy. "Funny, when my sister saw the first one, she said, 'Why, that Kennedy isn't so young!' And I knew then and there that was it. Of course, on sheer debating points Nixon took Kennedy every time. Anybody who knows about these things could see that. Especially on Quemoy and Matsu. Boy, if *I* had been debating Kennedy, I sure would have jazzed him all over the lot—Berlin, Laos, everything!"

I commented that Nixon had been a victim of his own legend. He had been pictured by both admirers and enemies as a rough infighter, a merciless debater, a ruthless killer, yet in the campaign and in the television debates it was quite clear that of the two, Kennedy was by far the tougher fighter. Goldwater nodded. "I warned Nixon about that a long time ago when the real mistake was made, 'way back there in California in that Senate election. You see, Nixon was sold by these people on putting himself over as a real gut fighter. They figured it would do him good against Helen Gahagan Douglas. So they built him up tough and mean, when of course he wasn't, when all he ever did was just tell the truth about that woman. The whole thing about him being so mean was nothing but publicity. So I told him: 'You wait and see, when you get to running for President and you start getting rough, the way you *got* to, they'll jump on you and say it's the old Nixon.' And they did. And then he'd pussyfoot." Goldwater shook his head sadly.

We talked about medical care for the aged to be paid through Social Security. The Senator was against it. He said that at the Arizona hospital of which he was a director, only one elderly person had been unable to pay. He had also seen a poll from western Florida where the elderly people had voted firmly against Federal aid. I suggested that those who could afford to retire to Arizona and Florida might be comfortably off. He said no, their average income was about $300 a month. Anyway, people ought to look after themselves either through their own foresight or through help from their families. Failing that, indigence should be handled the way it has always been: at the local level, by charities and so on.

I suggested that with taxes as high as they are, and longer life expectancies, there would be more rather than fewer programs for state and Federal aid in the coming years. He agreed. That was why he felt the whole tax structure had to be overhauled. And though he no longer favors repealing the graduated income tax, as he suggested in his book, he did feel that taxes on business should be reduced and greater allowance made for depreciation. "I told Jack Kennedy: you could be President for life if you'd just lift some of those taxes so that businessmen—and I know hundreds of 'em—would have some incentive to get new machinery, to overhaul their plants, to *really* start producing."

Publicly, no American politician can admit that we have anything to learn from the experiments of any other society. The ritual dialogue between office seeker and electorate is one of mutual congratulation, and to suggest that perfection has another home is treasonable. But privately our more conscientious legislators do ponder other countries' penal reforms, medical programs, educational methods. From his book and speeches I suspected Goldwater had done little or no homework. He was firmly against socialized medicine, but he seemed to know nothing about how it worked in Scandinavia, West Germany, England.

Goldwater was honest. No, he didn't know much about European socialism. "But I did meet this Norwegian doctor, matter of fact her name was Goldwater, which is how she happened to get in touch with me. She said the thing *seemed* to work all right, but that being assured of a certain income every month from the government kept her from feeling any real urge to study harder—you know, keep up at her profession. There was no incentive." I asked him if he thought that the desire to be good was entirely economic in origin. He said of course it was. I then asked him to explain how it was that two people as different as ourselves worked hard, though in neither case was money the spur. He was startled. Then he murmured vaguely and slipped away from the subject.

I asked him what he felt about some of his more oddball admirers. Goldwater became suddenly cautious. The quick, easy responses were replaced by a slow, careful measuring of words. He knew, he said, of some 250 organizations either conservative or anti-Communist. He admitted it was often difficult to figure out who was what. "Every invitation I get to speak, I have to check it for this and check it for that, make absolutely sure they're O.K. You never know what you may be getting into. Some are first-rate, like this fellow in New Orleans, Ken Courtney. He publishes a magazine down there. He's quite a guy." He asked on the phone for the magazine's name. I mentioned the Young Americans for Freedom, an organization founded by those who had been involved in the Youth for Goldwater movement at the Chicago convention. He approved of them highly, especially of "What's his name—Gaddy? Caddy, that's right. Nice kid, a real savvy guy with a lot on the ball."

Mrs. Coerver entered. "The magazine's called *Independent American,* and his name is Kent, not Ken, Courtney." She left.

More than once, Goldwater has complained that though the Republican Party's leaders are conservative they invariably choose liberal or moderate candidates to run for President on the false (to him) premise that a true conservative could never win. I asked him, Why not start a third party?

Goldwater sat up briskly. "If I thought it would work, I might. But I don't know . . . third parties never get off the ground in this country. There was Teddy Roosevelt, and there was . . ." He shook his head. "No, I don't see it. For one thing, conservatism is pretty divided. Suppose I started a party. Then somebody would come along and say, 'Well, look here, you're not *my* kind of conservative,' and then he'd go off and start *his* party and you'd end up like France. That's the trouble with the conservatives. They've got this all-or-nothing attitude." He sighed. "Why, I got booed in New York when I said if it was between Rockefeller and Harriman I'd be for Rockefeller. I tried to explain how at least Rockefeller was a Republican and you got your foot in the door. . . . No. A political party can only start around a strong individual." He looked past me at the bust on the mantelpiece; his jaw had set. "Like Lincoln. The people were there looking for a party, looking for this strong individual. And there he was and that's how the Republican Party started. A strong individual."

The next question was obvious. Was Goldwater that "strong individual"? Could he lead his people out of the wilderness? Were there enough of them to allow him to re-create that dream of Eden which conservatives evoke whenever they recall the bright simple days of our old agrarian Republic? But I let it go. Neither of us knew the answer. He had his hopes, and that was enough.

I rose to go. He walked me to the door. We exchanged impieties, each about his own political party, then said good-by.

"Ignorant but shrewd" was the verdict of one colleague of Goldwater. "He's read very little. He has no knowledge of economics. He's completely outside the world of ideas. Even his passion for the Constitution is based upon a misunderstanding of its nature." I am not sure I would agree that Goldwater's ignorance of ideas is necessarily relevant to his ability or his capacity for growth.

I was impressed by his charm, which, even for a politician, is considerable. More than that, in his simplifying of great issues Goldwater has a real appeal for a nation which is not at all certain about its future either as a society or as a world power. Up and down the land there are storm warnings. Many look nervously for shelter, and Goldwater, in the name of old-time virtue and ruggedness and self-reliance, offers them refuge beneath the venerable great roof of the Constitution. True or not, his simplifications are enormously appealing and, who knows, in a time of crisis he might seize the prize.

But I make no predictions. I would only recommend to Goldwater Cicero's warning to a fellow political adventurer, in a falling year of the Roman Republic: "I am sure you understand the political situation into which you have . . . no, not stumbled, but stepped; for it was by deliberate choice and by no accident that you flung your tribunate into the very crisis of things; and I doubt not that you reflect how potent in politics is opportunity, how shifting the phases, how incalculable the issues of events, how easily swayed are men's predilections, what pitfalls there are and what insincerity in life."

*Life*
June 9, 1961

This interview received a great deal of attention. Henry Luce complimented the editor, adding that he never again wanted to see a piece like that in *Life*.

# 76

# THE TWENTY-NINTH
# REPUBLICAN CONVENTION

The dark blue curtains part. As delegates cheer, the nominee walks toward the lectern, arms loose, shoulders somewhat rigid like a man who. . . . No, as Henry James once said in quite a different but no less dramatic context, it cannot be done. What is there to say about Richard M. Nixon that was not said eight years ago? What is there to say that he himself did not say at that memorable "last" press conference in Los Angeles six years ago? For some time he has ceased to figure in the conscious regions of the mind, a permanent resident, one had thought, of that limbo where reside the Stassens and the Deweys and all those other ambitious men whose failures seemed so entirely deserved. But now, thanks to two murders in five years, Richard Nixon is again a presidential candidate. No second acts to American careers? Nonsense. What is lacking are decent codas. At Miami Beach, we were reminded that no politician can ever be written off this side of Arlington.

The week before the convention began, various Republican leaders met at the Fontainebleau Hotel to write a platform, knowing that no matter what wisdom this document might contain it would be ignored by the candidate. Nevertheless, to the extent issues ever intrude upon the making of Presidents, the platform hearings do give publicity to different points of view, and that is why Ronald Reagan took time from his busy schedule as Governor of California to fly to Miami Beach in order to warn the platform committee of the dangers of crime in the streets. The Governor also made himself available to the flower of the national and international press who sat restively in a windowless low-ceilinged dining room of the Fontainebleau from two o'clock to two-thirty to "just a short wait, please, the Governor is on his way," interviewing one another and trying to look alert as the television cameras, for want of a candidate, panned from face to face. At last, His Excellency, as Ivy Baker Priest would say, entered the room, flanked by six secret servicemen. As they spread out on either side of him, they cased us narrowly and I knew that simply by looking into my face they could see the imaginary gun in my pocket.

Ronald Reagan is a well-preserved not young man. Close-to, the painted face is webbed with delicate lines while the dyed hair, eyebrows, and eyelashes contrast oddly with the sagging muscle beneath the as yet unlifted chin, soft earnest of wattle-to-be. The effect, in repose, suggests the work of a skillful embalmer. Animated, the face is quite attractive and at a distance youthful; particularly engaging is the crooked smile full of large porcelain-capped teeth. The eyes are interesting: small, narrow, apparently dark, they glitter in the hot light, alert to every move, for this is enemy country—the liberal Eastern press who are so notoriously immune to that warm and folksy performance which Reagan quite deliberately projects over their heads to some legendary constituency at the far end of the tube, some shining Carverville where good Lewis Stone forever lectures Andy Hardy on the virtues of thrift and the wisdom of the contract system at Metro-Goldwyn-Mayer.

The questions begin. Why don't you announce your candidacy? Are you a candidate? Why do people feel you will take votes away from George Wallace? Having answered these questions a hundred times before, the actor does not pause to consider his responses. He picks up each cue promptly, neatly, increasing the general frustration. Only once does the answer-machine jam. "Do you *want* to be President?" The room goes silent. The smile suddenly looks to have been drawn in clay, fit for baking in a Laguna kiln. Then the candidate finds the right button. He pushes it. We are told what an honor it is for any citizen to be considered for the highest office on earth. . . . We stop listening; he stops listening to himself.

"Governor, even though you're not a candidate, you must know that there is a good deal of support for you. . . ." The questioner's irony is suitably heavy. Reagan's lips purse—according to one biographer this is a sign he is displeased; there was a good deal of lip-pursuing during the conference not to mention the days to come. "Well," he speaks through pursed lips, "I'd have to be unconscious not to know what was going on but. . . ." As he continues the performance, his speech inter-larded with "my lands" (for some reason Right Wingers invariably talk like Little Orphan Annie), I recalled my last glimpse of him, at the Cow Palace in San Francisco four years ago. The Reagans were seated in a box, listening to Eisenhower. While Mrs. Reagan darted angry looks about the hall (displeased at the press?), the star of Death Valley Days was staring intently at the speaker on the platform. Thus an actor prepares, I thought, and I suspected even then that Reagan would some day find himself up there on the platform: as the age of television progresses, the Reagans will be the rule, not the exception. "Thank you, Governor," said a journalist, and everyone withdrew, leaving Ronald Reagan with his six secret servicemen—one black, a ratio considerably better than that of the convention itself where only two percent could claim Africa as motherland.

Seventy-second Street Beach is a gathering place for hustlers of all sexes. With some bewilderment, they watch one of their masters, the Chase Manhattan Bank made flesh—sweating flesh—display his wounds to the sandy and the dull, a Coriolanus but in reverse, one besotted with the vulgar. In shirt-sleeves but firmly knotted tie, Nelson Aldrich Rock-efeller stands on a platform crowded with officials and aides (most seriously crowded by the Governor of Florida, Claude Kirk, who wears a bright orange sports jacket and a constant smile for his people, who regard him, the few who know who he is, with bright loathing). Ordinar-ily Rockefeller's face is veal-white, as though no blood courses beneath that thick skin. But now, responding to the lowering day, he has turned a delicate conch pink. What is he saying? "Well, let's face it, there's been some disagreement among the pollsters." The upper class tough boy accent (most beautifully achieved by Montgomery Clift in *The Heiress*) proves effective even down here where consonants are disdained and vowels long. Laughter from the audience in clothes, bewildered looks from the hustlers in their bathing suits. "Like, man, who *is* it?"

"But now Harris and Gallup have agreed that I can beat. . . ." Rockefeller quotes at length from those polls which are the oracles of our day, no, the very gods who speak to us of things to come. Over and over again, he says, "Let's face it," a phrase popular twenty years ago, particularly among girls inclined to alcoholism ("the Governor drinks an occasional Dubonnet on the rocks before dinner," where did I read that?). Beside him stands his handsome wife, holding a large straw hat and looking as if she would like to be somewhere else, no loving Nancy Reagan or loyal Pat Nixon she. The convention is full of talk that there has been trouble between them. Apparently. . . . One of the pleasures of American political life is that, finally, only personalities matter. Is he a nice man? Is she happy with him? What else should concern a sovereign people?

Rockefeller puts down the polls, takes off his glasses, and starts to attack the Administration. "Look at what they're doing," he says with a fine vehemence. "They're *exhilarating* the war!" But although Rockefeller now sounds like a peace candidate, reprising Bobby Kennedy and Eugene McCarthy, he has always been devoted to the war in Vietnam and to the principle underlying it: American military intervention wherever "freedom is endangered." Consequently—and consistently—he has never found any defense budget adequate. Two years ago at a dinner in New York, he was more hawk than Johnson as he told us how the Viet Cong were coldbloodedly "shooting little mayors" (the phrase conjured up dead ponies); mournfully, he shook his head, "Why can't they learn to fight fair?" Nevertheless, compared to Nixon and Reagan, Rockefeller is positively Lincolnesque. All of us on 72nd Street Beach liked him, except perhaps the hustlers wanting to score, and we wished him well, knowing that he had absolutely no chance of being nominated.

By adding the third character to tragedy, Sophocles changed the nature of drama. By exalting the chorus and diminishing the actors, television has changed entirely the nature of our continuing history. Watching things as they happen, the viewer is a part of events in a way new to man. And never is he so much a part of the whole as when things do not happen, for, as Andy Warhol so wisely observed, people will always prefer to look at something rather than nothing; between plain wall and flickering commercial, the eyes will have the second. As hearth and fire were once center to the home or lair so now the television set is the center of modern man's being, all points of the room converge upon its presence and the eye watches even as the mind dozes, much as our ancestors narcotized themselves with fire.

At Miami Beach television was everywhere: in the air, on the streets, in hotel lobbies, on the convention floor. "From gavel to gavel" the networks spared us nothing in the way of empty speeches and mindless interviews, but dull and uninformative as the events themselves were, something rather than nothing was being shown and the eye was diverted while the objects photographed (delegates et al.) reveled in the exposure even though it might be no more than a random shot of a nose being picked or a crotch rearranged. No matter: for that instant the one observed existed for all his countrymen. As a result the delegates were docile beyond belief, stepping this way and that as required by men with wired helmets and handmikes which, like magic wands, could confer for an instant total recognition.

The fact that television personalities so notoriously took precedence over the politicians at Miami Beach was noted with sour wonder by journalists who have begun to fear that their rendering of events into lines of linear type may prove to be as irrelevant an exercise as turning contemporary literature into Greek. The fact that in a hotel lobby it was Eric Sevareid not John Tower who collected a crowd was thought to be a sign of the essential light-mindedness of the electorate. Yet Sevareid belongs to the country in a way few politicians ever do. Only Ronald Reagan among the politicians at Miami exerted the same spell, and for the same reason: he is a bona fide star of the Late Show, equally ubiquitous, equally mythic.

Miami Beach is a rich sandbar with a drawbridge, and in no sense part of the main. The televised convention made it even more remote than it is. So locked were we all in what we were doing that Miami's black riots on Wednesday went almost unnoticed. There are those who thought that the Republicans deliberately played down the riots, but that is too Machiavellian. The fact is no one was interested. For those involved in creating that formidable work of television art, the 29th Republican convention, there was only one important task, creating suspense where none was. Everyone pretended that Reagan and Rockefeller could stop Nixon on the first ballot and so persuasive is the medium that by continually acting as if there might be a surprise, all involved came to believe that there would be one.

Even Nixon who should have known better fell victim to the collective delusion. On Tuesday he made his deal with Thurmond: no candidate for Vice-President displeasing to the South. Yet there was never, we now know, any danger of the Southern delegations switching to Reagan, despite the actor's enormous appeal to them. After all, how could they not love a man who had campaigned for a segregationist Southern politician (Charlton Lyons of Louisiana), who had denounced the income tax as "Marxist," and federal aid to education as "a tool of tyranny," and welfare as an "encouragement to divorce and immorality," and who generally sounded as if he wouldn't mind nuking North Vietnam and maybe China, too? He was their man but Nixon was their leader.

By the time the balloting began on Wednesday night, it was all over. There were of course idle pleasures. Everett Dirksen prowling from camera to camera, playing the part of a Senator with outrageous pleasure. Strom Thurmond, High Constable of the South, staring coldly at the delegates with stone catfish face. John Lindsay of New York, slyly separating his elegant persona from any words that he might be called upon to say. The public liked Lindsay but the delegates did not. They regarded him with the same distaste that they regard the city of which he is mayor, that hellhole of niggers and kikes and commies, of dope and vice and smut. . . . So they talk among themselves, until an outsider approaches; then they shift gears swiftly and speak gravely of law and order and how this is a republic not a democracy.

A lady from Vermont read the roll of the States as though each state had somehow grievously offended her. Alabama was plainly a thorn to be plucked, while Alaska was a blot upon the Union. She did achieve a moment of ribald good humor when she asked one state chairman *which* Rockefeller his state was voting for. But long before the Yankee virago had got to Wisconsin it was plain that Nixon was indeed "the one" as the signs had proclaimed, and immediately the Medium began to look in on the hotel suites, to confront the losers, hoping for tears, and reveal the winner, hoping for . . . well, *what* do you hope for with Nixon?

The technician. Once nominated Nixon gravely explained how he had pulled it off. He talked about the logistics of campaigning. He took us backstage. It was a nice background briefing, but nothing more. No plans for the ghettos, no policy for Asia, just political maneuvering. He did assure us that he would select "a candidate for Vice President who does not divide this country." Apparently he would have a free hand because "I won the nomination without paying any price or making any deals." The next day of course he revealed the nature of his deal with the Southerners and the price he must now pay for their support: Spiro Agnew of Maryland. Despite the howls of the party liberals and the total defection of the blacks, Nixon had probably done the wise thing.

Thursday was the big day. Agnew was proposed, opposed, nominated. A lumbering man who looks like a cross between Lyndon Johnson and

Juan Perón, his acceptance speech was thin and ungrammatical; not surprisingly, he favored law and order. Adequate on civil rights when he became governor, Agnew behaved boorishly to the black establishment of Baltimore in the wake of riots last spring. This made him acceptable to Thurmond. Even so, all but the most benighted conservatives are somewhat concerned by Agnew's lack of experience. Should Nixon be elected and die, a man with only one year's experience as governor of a backward border state would become Emperor of the West. Though firm with niggers, how would he be on other issues? No one knows, including the candidate himself whose great virtue, in his own eyes, "is that I try to be credible—I want to be believed. That's one of the most priceless assets." So it is. So it is.

Nixon is now on stage, ready to accept for a second time his party's nomination. He is leaner than in the past. In a thickly made-up face, the smile is not unappealing, upper lip slightly hooked over teeth in the Kennedy manner. With his jawline collapsing in a comforting way, the middle-aged Nixon resembles the average voter who, we are told, is a gray-colored forty-seven-year-old. The candidate swings neatly to left, hands raised, two forefingers of each hand making the victory salute. Arms drop. Slide step to right. Arms again extended above head as hands make salute. Then back to center stage and the lectern. The television camera zooms in on the speech: one can see lines crossed out, words added; the type is large, the speech mercifully short.

Nixon begins. The voice is deep and slightly toneless, without regional accent, like a radio announcer's. We have been told that he wrote his own script. It is possible. Certainly every line was redolent of the man's strange uncharm. He spoke of Eisenhower ("one of the greatest Americans of our time—or of any time") who was watching them from his hospital bed. "His heart is with us!" the candidate exclaimed, reminding us inadvertently that that poor organ was hardly the General's strongest contribution to the moral crusade the times require. No matter, "let's win this one for Ike!" (A rousing echo of *Knute Rockne,* a film in which the youthful Ronald Reagan had been most affecting.) Nixon next paid careful tribute to his Republican competitors, to the platform and, finally, to Spiro Agnew "a statesman of the first rank who will be a great campaigner." He then drew a dark picture of today's America, ending with "did we come all this way for this?" Despite the many hours of literary labor, Nixon's style was seldom felicitous; he was particularly afflicted by "thisness": "This I say is the real voice of America. And in this year 1968 this is. . . ." The real voice of America, needless to say, is Republican; "the forgotten Americans—the nonshouters, the non-demonstrators"; in short, the nonprotesting white Protestants, who must, he enjoined, commit themselves to the truth, "to see it like it is, and to tell it like it is," argot just slightly wrong for now but to Nixon "tell it like it is" must sound positively raunchy, the sort of thing had he been classy Jack Kennedy he might have heard at Vegas, sitting around with the Clan and their back-scratchers.

Solemnly Nixon addressed himself to Vietnam. His administration would "bring to an honorable end the war." How? Well, "after an era of confrontation, the time has come for an era of negotiation." But in case that sounded like dangerous accommodation he quickly reminded us that since the American flag is spit on almost daily around the world, it is now "time we started to act like a great nation." But he did not tell us *how* a great nation should act. Last January, he said that the war will end only when the Communists are convinced that the U.S. "will use its immense power and is not going to back down." In March he said, "There is no alternative to the continuation of the war in Viet-nam." It is of course never easy to determine what if anything Nixon means. When it was revealed that his recent support of public housing was not sincere but simply expedient (his secret remarks to a Southern caucus had been taped), no one was surprised. "He just had to say that," murmur his supporters whenever he contradicts himself, and they ad-mire him for it. After all, his form of hypocrisy is deeply American: if you can't be good, be careful. Significantly, he was most loudly ap-plauded when he struck this year's favorite Republican note: *Remember the Pueblo.* "The United States has fallen so low that a fourth rate military power like North Korea [can] hijack a United States naval vessel. . . ." Quite forgotten were his conciliatory words of last spring: "If the captured American Intelligence spy ship violated North Korean waters, the United States has no choice but to admit it."

Nixon next praised the courts but then allowed that some of them have gone "too far in weakening the peace forces as against the criminal forces." Attacks on the judiciary are surefire with Republicans. Witness the old Nixon five years after the Supreme Court's 1954 decision on the integration of schools: "the Administration's position has not been, is not now, and should not be immediate total integration." Like Barry Goldwater he tends to the radical belief that the Supreme Court's deci-sions "are not, necessarily, the law of the land." Happily, once the present Attorney General is replaced, it will be possible to "open a new front against the filth peddlers and the narcotics peddlers who are corrupting the lives of our children." As for the forty million poor, they can take heart from the example of past generations of Americans who were aided not by government "but because of what people did for themselves." Those small inequities that now exist in the American system can be easily taken care of by "the greatest engine of progress ever developed in the history of man—American private enterprise." The poor man who wants "a piece of the action" (Vegas again) is very apt to get it if the streets are orderly and enough tax cuts are given big business.

If Nixon's reputation as the litmus-paper man of American politics is deserved, his turning mauve instead of pink makes it plain that the affluent majority intend to do nothing at all in regard to the black and the poor and the aged, except repress with force their demonstrations, subscribing finally not so much to the bland hortatory generalities of the platform and the acceptance speech but to the past statements of the real Nixon who has said (1) "If the conviction rate was doubled in this country, it would do more to eliminate crime in the future than a quadrupling of the funds for any governmental war on poverty." (2) "I am opposed to pensions in any form, as it makes loafing more attractive to [*sic*] working." (3) To tie health care to social security "would set up a great state program which would inevitably head in the direction of herding the ill and elderly into institutions whether they desire this or not." Echo of those Republicans in 1935 who declared that once Social Security was law "you won't have a name any longer, only a number." Most ominous of all, the candidate of the military-industrial complex has no wish to decrease the military budget. Quite the contrary. As recently as last June he was warning us that "the United States has steadily fallen behind the Soviet Union in the levelling of its spending on research and development of advance systems to safeguard the nation." In short, there is no new Nixon, only the old Nixon experimenting with new campaigning techniques in response, as the Stalinists used to say, to new necessities. Nixon concluded his speech on a note of self-love. Most viewers thought it inappropriate: since no one loves him, why should he? To his credit, he sounded slightly embarrassed as he spoke of the boy from Whittier—a misfire but worth a try.

Friday. On the plane to New York. John Lindsay remarks, "Awful as it was, he made a vote-getting speech." He is probably right. Nixon has said in the past that no Republican can hope to get the black vote, so why try for it? Particularly when the principal danger to Nixon's candidacy is George Wallace, in the North as well as the South. Nixon is also perfectly aware of a little-known statistic: the entire black vote plus the entire vote of whites under twenty-five is slightly less than one-fourth of the total electorate. Since Nixon has no chance of attracting either category, he has, by selecting Agnew, served notice that he is the candidate of that average forty-seven-year-old voter who tends to dislike and fear the young and the black and the liberal; in fact, the more open Nixon is in his disdain of this one-fourth of a nation, the more pleasing he will seem to the remaining three-fourths who want a change, any change, from Johnson-Humphrey as well as some assurance that the dissident forces at work in American life will be contained. The great technician has worked out a winning combination and, barring the (obligatory?) unexpected, it is quite likely that it will pay off and Richard Milhous Nixon will become the 37th President of the United States.

*The New York Review of Books*
September 12, 1968

# 77

# POLITICAL
# MELODRAMAS

Recently *The New York Times* noted that, once again, the television viewer would be able to watch "Gore Vidal's political melodrama *The Best Man.*" Over the years I have become so familiar with this listing that I no longer wonder why I am irritated by it. No longer, that is, until Watergate. I realize now that my distress was always with the word "melodrama." *The Best Man* was first written as a realistic play about two men at a political convention, fighting one another for the presidential nomination of their party.

In 1959 when I wrote the play, the Democratic rivals for the nomination were Adlai Stevenson (who was being smeared as a homosexual— and an indecisive one to boot), John F. Kennedy (who was being smeared as an altogether too active heterosexual as well as the glad beneficiary of his wealthy father's ability to buy elections) and the majority leader of the Senate, Lyndon Johnson (who was known to take cash for any political services rendered). In the background was Harry S Truman, whose campaign for election in 1948 nearly ended before it began. Unable to pay for the train in which he was to whistle-stop the country, giving hell to the rich, Truman turned to his crony Louis Johnson and asked for money quick. Johnson got the money from the "China Lobby," and ever after the grateful President loyally served the cause of Chiang Kai-shek. All of this was common knowledge to most of us who were involved in the life and politics of Washington, DC.

When I based the character of the wicked candidate in the play on Richard Nixon, I thought it would be amusing if liberal partisans were to smear unjustly that uxorious man as a homosexual. I was promptly condemned by a conservative columnist who said that my plot was absurdly melodramatic since no man could rise to any height in American politics if he were thought to be a fag. Yet this same columnist used to delight in making coy allusions in print to Stevenson's lack of robustness.

The noble, if waffling, character in the play was based on Adlai Stevenson. I thought it might be interesting if he were to have undergone some mild psychiatric therapy which the bad guy could seize upon as a sign of mental instability, maintaining solemnly that no one who had ever been to a psychiatrist ought to have access to the arrows that our imperial eagle-ensign holds in its claw—much less the eagle's sprig of laurel. This time a liberal pundit said that it was simply not possible for anyone who had undergone "serious" psychotherapy to be considered for high office. So, no doubt, thought the hapless McGovern when he took as his running mate shock-treated Senator Thomas Eagleton.

When faced with a moral issue most American commentators simply ignore it—or as Elaine May said to Mike Nichols in one of their skits, "I like a moral issue so much more than a real issue." Journalists who know quite as much or more than I about American politics seem never able to deal in print with the actual issues raised as opposed to the occasional muck raked. They black out because, well, the institution of the presidency must be preserved while the sanctity of Congress and the Supreme Court. . . . In other words, don't give away the game because we're all in this together, making a pretty good living out of USA, Inc. To describe the way things really are is to be a shit and we know what happens to shits: they are flushed away. Unfortunately, to complete this out-of-control metaphor, the waters of the Republic are now befouled from too much flushing, and we are poisoned when we drink.

In 1967 I published a novel called *Washington, D.C.* The narrative began in the Roosevelt era and ended as dawn struck the towers of Camelot. I invented two senators: one old-style, one new-style. Hoping to be president in 1940, my old senator raised money by doing the wrong kind of favor for a lobbyist. Since the senator was essentially a moral man (brought up on McGuffey's Eclectic Reader), he was literally demoralized by his crime, and fell. The young senator was very much in the Kennedy tradition and so was able to take without a second thought anything that was not nailed down because that's the way you play the game around here: that's what the word "pragmatism" means. At the end of the book it was fairly plain that he was presidential material. Across the land there was a chorus of distress from writers of book-chat as well as from political camp-followers. The author was traducing famous and honorable men, not to mention the greatest society the world had ever seen. Why was the writer such a shit? Because, God help us, he was filled with envy! Apparently anyone who criticizes anything or anyone in the land of the free does so because he is envious—proving, I suppose that this peculiar emotion must indeed be a prevailing national trait.

J. K. Galbraith wrote one of the few favorable reviews of *Washington, D.C.,* but even that lovable old cynic saw fit to admonish me in person: "You know things are not that bad in politics." I looked at him with, as they say in popular fiction, wonder. Surely Ken must have heard the funny story told by a Kennedy relation who, on his way to West Virginia, stopped at a barber's to have his hair cut and then hurried off, leaving behind his bag filled with dollars to be paid to the honest yeomen of West Virginia in exchange for their support of the family's candidate. Also, when I ran for Congress as a Democrat in 1960, I caught some Republicans buying votes. I wanted to prosecute but was dissuaded by a leader of my party. "If you nail them here, they'll nail us somewhere else in the state."

Last spring I felt obliged to offer my countrymen yet another glimpse of their masters in a play called *An Evening With Richard Nixon.* All of Nixon's dialogue in this entertainment was taken from his actual speeches and press conferences. The effect was properly devastating but, alas, the envious author was found guilty of having, this time, drawn attention to those small lapses which we are taught from childhood to paper over. ("If you can't be good be careful" is an American maxim.) Even the British drama reviewer for *The New York Times* was shaken by the unfair way I had treated a man whom he referred to with true reverence as "our President."

Was it ever thus? Yes. I fear the United States has always been a nation of ongoing hustlers from the prisons and disaster-areas of old Europe. Our grand British heritage is now wearing thin but still can be observed in our racism as well as in the spontaneous hypocrisy with which our public men respond to inconvenient disclosures and the self-serving rhetoric that swirls about them in time of crisis like squid's ink. The brilliant Alexander Hamilton was almost certainly corrupt during his years at the Treasury—his right-hand man went to jail. Hamilton was also a British secret agent, as was Benjamin Franklin. Jefferson's commanding general of the American army, James Wilkinson, was a Spanish agent (for political reasons the President protected him and thus condoned treason). Andrew Jackson's appointment of his Tammany friend Sam Swartwout to the collectorship of the Port of New York helped undermine the Jacksonian "revolution" (such as it was) because the President's political heir, Van Buren, was brought down, in part, by Swartwout's theft of more than $1 million from the port.

Growing up in the Washington house of my grandfather, Senator T. P. Gore of Oklahoma, I was intimately aware of the Teapot Dome scandal. My grandfather had once written a brief for one of the oil barons in the case. Although I do not think that my grandfather was on the take (senator from an oil state, he died poor), he was certainly unwise and for at least one troublesome election he was known irreverently as "Teapot Gore." When the poor but eloquent tribune of the people Senator William Borah (the lion of Idaho) died, several hundred thousand dollars were found in his safety deposit box. "He was my friend," said Senator Gore gravely to the press, "I do not speculate." In private, my grandfather was fairly certain that the money was from Hitler. Borah was a devoted isolationist and not above taking money from those whose interests he would have furthered anyway.

Last year a remarkable book was published in the United States, *Washington Pay-Off* by Robert N. Winter-Berger. At first hand, the author, a former lobbyist, described how the Speaker of the House of Representatives, John McCormack, rented space in his Capitol office to a master criminal named Nathan Voloshen. From the Speaker's office a team of influence-peddlers sold favors to innumerable clients. Eventually they were busted by US Attorney Robert Morgenthau. Voloshen went to jail. The Speaker was persuaded to retire from Congress. This horror story was one of several carefully detailed by Mr. Winter-Berger; each involved some of our most celebrated public men.

Needless to say, the book did not please the owners of the United States, a loose consortium that includes the editors of *The New York Times* and *The Washington Post,* the television magnates, the Rockefellers, Kennedys, ITT, IBM, etc. Winter-Berger's exposés were largely ignored by the press and television. The book did become a best seller but never became what it should have been, a subject for national debate. Intrigued by the silence the book had aroused, I rang Robert Morgenthau and asked him if he thought Winter-Berger a reliable witness (in the high Whittaker Chambers sense of the word). Morgenthau said that, all in all, the text was accurate. If so, the following scene was drawn from life.

Early in Johnson's reign, the President appears in the Speaker's office. Unaware that Winter-Berger is also in the room, the President denounces his former aide, Bobby Baker, who is under indictment. "John, that son of a bitch is going to ruin me. If that cocksucker talks, I'm going to land in jail." Thus, characteristically, spoke the emperor of the West, the scourge of Asia and shield to ungrateful Europe, the sole wielder of the arrows and the laurel. The Speaker draws Johnson's attention to the cowering Winter-Berger. The President wants to know if the witness is "all right." Winter-Berger swears loyalty to his sovereign, and listens raptly as LBJ outlines a plan to stay out of the clink. A message must be got to Baker: "I will give him a million dollars if he takes the rap."

Recently Bobby Baker left prison and it is said that he, too, may write a book. If he does, I suspect that a quorum of that senate whose secretary he was may yet convene itself in Lewisburg Federal Penetentiary. For my British readers who are now reeling in disbelief from line to line of this cheery report: yes, we do have laws of libel in the United States but they are less strict than yours. Even so, the scene with Johnson in the Speaker's office was published while the former President was still alive and capable of bringing action against publisher and author. He did neither.

I have nothing to add to the unfolding scandals of Watergate except to note that what has so far been revealed is only the tip of not an iceberg but a glacier. As a professional political melodramatist, however, I am struck by the tameness of my work. Like Clive, when I consider my opportunities I am impressed by my restraint.

During the last few days the owners of the United States have been telling us that to preserve the Republic everyone must now support a chastened Nixon and make it possible for him to govern. Why? To continue the devastation of Cambodia and Laos? The erosion of civil liberties? The stockpiling of redundant arms? The control of wages but not of profits? The curtailing of all programs that might make the poor less desperate?

I cannot for the life of me see the value of continuing this administration another day in office. More to the point, I do not think that the American system in its present state of decadence is worth preserving. The initial success of the United States was largely accidental. A rich almost empty continent was occupied and exploited by rapacious Europeans who made slaves of Africans and corpses of Indians in the process. They created a Venetian-style republic based on limited suffrage and dedicated to the sacredness of property. Now the land is no longer rich enough to support the pretensions of the inhabitants. Institutions that once worked well enough for the major stockholders are no longer adequate to bear the burden of all our mistakes. Yet I am certain that a majority of my countrymen would like things to continue pretty much as they are. If they do, then their only hope is the prompt impeachment and dismissal of this president. A ritual scapegoat is needed to absolve our sins and Nixon has obligingly put his head on the block. Certainly to allow him to go free makes us all accomplices. It also brings to a swift end the brief, and by the world no doubt unlamented, American imperium.

*New Statesman*
May 4, 1973

# THE ART
# AND ARTS OF
# E. HOWARD HUNT

From December 7, 1941, to August 15, 1973, the United States has been
continuously at war except for a brief, too little celebrated interregnum.
Between 1945 and 1950 the empire turned its attention to peaceful pursuits and enjoyed something of a golden or at least for us not too brazen
an age. The arts in particular flourished. Each week new genius was
revealed by the press; and old genius decently buried. Among the new
novelists of that far-off time were Truman Capote (today a much loved
television performer) and myself. Although we were coevals (a word
that the late William Faulkner thought meant evil at the same time as),
we were unlike: Capote looked upon the gorgeous Speed Lamkin as a
true tiger in the Capotean garden where I saw mere lambkin astray in
my devouring jungle.

The one thing that Capote and I did have in common was a need for
money. And so each of us applied to the Guggenheim Foundation for
a grant; and each was turned down. Shocked, we compared notes.
Studied the list of those who had received grants. "Will you just look,"
moaned Truman, "at those *ahh*-full pee-pull they keep giving *muh*-nee
to!" Except for the admirable Carson McCullers who got so many grants
in her day that she was known as the conductress on the gravy train,
the list of honored writers was not to our minds distinguished. Typical

of the sort of novelist the Guggenheims preferred to Capote and me in
1946 was twenty-eight-year-old (practically middle-aged) Howard Hunt,
author of *East of Farewell* (Random House, 1943); a novel described by
the publishers as "probably the first novel about this war by an American who actually helped fight it." The blurb is unusually excited. Apparently, H.H. "grew up like any other American boy" (no tap-dancing on
a river boat for him) "going to public schools and to college (Brown
University, where he studied under I.J. Kapstein)."

A clue. I slip into reverie. Kapstein will prove to be my Rosebud. The
key to the Hunt mystery. But does Kapstein still live? Will he talk? *Or
is he afraid?* I daydream. "Hunt . . . E. Howard Hunt . . . ah, yes. Sit
down, Mr. . . . uh, Bozell? Forgive me . . . this last stroke seems to have
. . . Where were we? Howie. Yes. I must tell you something of the
Kapstein creative writing method. I require the tyro pen-man to copy
out in longhand some acknowledged world masterpiece. Howie copied
out—if memory serves—*Of Human Bondage.*"

But until the Kapstein Connection is made, I must search the public
record for clues. The dust jacket of H.H.'s first novel tells us that he
became a naval ensign in May 1941. "There followed many months of
active duty at sea on a destroyer, on the North Atlantic patrol, protecting
the life-line to embattled England. . . ." That's more like it. My eyes shut:
the sea. A cold foggy day. Slender, virile H.H. arrives (by kayak?) at a
secret rendezvous with a British battleship. On the bridge is Admiral Sir
Leslie Charteris, K.C.B.: it's Walter Pidgeon, of course. "Thank God,
you got through. I never thought it possible. There's someone particularly wants to thank you." Then out of the fog steps a short burly figure;
the face is truculent yet somehow indomitable (no, it's not Norman
Mailer). In one powerful hand he holds a thick cigar. When He speaks,
the voice is the very voice of human freedom and, yes, dignity. "Ensign
Hunt, seldom in the annals of our island story has this our embattled yet
still mightily sceptered realm owed to but one man . . ."

H.H. is a daydreamer and like all great dreamers (I think particularly
of Edgar Rice Burroughs) he stirs one's own inner theater into productions of the most lurid sort, serials from which dull fact must be rigorously excluded—like the Random House blurb. "In February 1942,
Howard Hunt was detached from his ship and sent to Boston." Now if
the dates given on the jacket are accurate, he served as an ensign for no
more than nine months. So how many of those nine months could he
have spent protecting England's embattled life-line? H.H.'s naval career
ends when he is "sent to Boston, to take treatment for an injury in a

naval hospital." This is worthy of the Great Anti-Semanticist Nixon himself. Did H.H. slip a disk while taking a cholera shot down in the dispensary? *Who's Who* merely records: "Served with USNR, 1940–42."

I turn for information to Mr. Tad Szulc, H.H.'s principal biographer and an invaluable source of reference. According to Mr. Szulc, H.H. worked for the next two years "as a movie script writer and, briefly, as a war correspondent in the Pacific." *Who's Who* corroborates: "Movie script writer, editor March of Time (1942–43); war corr. Life mag. 1942." Yet one wonders what movies he wrote and what stories he filed, and from where.

*Limit of Darkness* (Random House, 1944) was written during this period. H.H.'s second novel is concerned with a naval air squadron on Guadalcanal in the Solomons. Was H.H. actually on Guadalcanal or did he use as source book Ira Wolfert's just published *Battle for the Solomons*? Possible clue: the character of war correspondent Francis H. O'Bannon . . . not at first glance a surrogate for H.H., who never casts himself in his books as anything but a Wasp. O'Bannon is everything H.H. detests—a low-class papist vulgarian who is also—what else?— "unhealthily fat and his jowls were pasty." The author contrasts him most unfavorably with the gallant Wasps to whom he dedicates the novel: "The Men Who Flew from Henderson."

They are incredibly fine, these young chaps. They ought to be, with names like McRae, Cordell, Forsyth, Lambert, Lewis, Griffin, Sampson, Vaughan, Scott—not a nigger, faggot, kike, or wop in the outfit. Just real guys who say real true simple things like "a guy who's fighting just to get back to the States is only half fighting. . . ." A love scene: " 'Oh, Ben, if it only would stop.' She put her face into the hollow of his shoulder. 'No,' he said. . . . 'We haven't killed enough of them yet or burned their cities or bombed them to hell the way we must. When I put away my wings I want it to be for good—not just for a few years.' " A key motif in the H.H. *oeuvre:* the enemy must be defeated once and for all so that man can live at peace with himself in a world where United Fruit and ITT know what's best not only for their stockholders but for their customers as well.

An academic critic would doubtless make something of the fact that since the only bad guy in the book is a fat, pasty Catholic newspaperman, H.H. might well be reproaching himself for not having flown with the golden gallant guys who gave so much of themselves for freedom, to get the job done. In their numinous company, H.H. may very well have *felt* like an overweight Catholic—and all because of that mysteri-

ous accident in the naval hospital; in its way so like Henry James's often
alluded to but never precisely by the Master named disability which
turned out to have been—after years of patient literary detective
work—chronic constipation. Academic critics are not always wrong.

The actual writing of *Limit of Darkness* is not at all bad; it is not at
all good either. H.H. demonstrates the way a whole generation of writers ordered words upon the page in imitation of what they took to be
Hemingway's technique. At best Hemingway was an artful, careful
writer who took a good deal of trouble to master scenes of action—the
hardest kind of writing to do—while his dialogue looks most attractive
on the page. Yet unwary imitators are apt to find themselves (as in *Limit
of Darkness*) slipping into aimless redundancies. Wanting to Heming-
wayize the actual cadences of Wasp speech as spoken by young fliers,
H.H. so stylizes their voices that one character blends with another.
Although Hemingway worked with pasteboard cutouts, too, he was
cunning enough to set his dolls against most stylishly rendered landscapes; he also gave them vivid things to do: the duck that got shot was
always a real duck that really got shot. Finally, the Hemingway trick
of repeating key nouns and proper names is simply not possible for other
writers—as ten thousand novels (including some of Hemingway's own)
testify.

In H.H.'s early books, which won for him a coveted (by Capote and
me) Guggenheim grant, there is a certain amount of solemnity if not
seriousness. The early H.H. liked to quote from high-toned writers like
Pliny and Louis MacNeice as well as from that *echt* American Wasp
William Cullen Bryant—whose radical politics would have shocked
H.H. had he but known. But then I suspect the quotations are not from
H.H.'s wide reading of world literature but from brief random inspec-
tions of *Bartlett's Familiar Quotations.*

H.H.'s fliers are conservative lads who don't think much of Roosevelt's Four Freedoms. They fight to get the job done. That's all. Old
Glory. H.H. is plainly dotty about the Wasp aristocracy. One of the
characters in *Limit of Darkness* is almost unhinged when he learns that
a girl he has met went to Ethel Walker. Had H.H. not chosen a life of
adventure I think he might have made a good second string to John
O'Hara's second string to Hemingway. H.H. has the O'Hara sense of
irredeemable social inferiority which takes the place for so many Irish-
American writers of original sin; he also shares O'Hara's pleasure in
listing the better brand-names of this world. Even on Guadalcanal we
are told of a pipe tobacco from "a rather good New Zealand leaf."

By 1943 H.H. was a promising author. According to *The New York Times,* "*East of Farewell* was a fine realistic novel, without any doubt the best sea story of the war." Without any doubt it was probably the *only* sea story of the war at that point but the *Times* has its own dread style to maintain. Now a momentous change in the daydreamer's life. With *Limit of Darkness* in the works at Random House, H.H. (according to *Who's Who*) joined the USAF (1943–46); and rose to the rank of first lieutenant. It would seem that despite "the injury in a naval hospital" our hero was again able to fight for human dignity, this time in the skies.

But according to Mr. Szulc what H.H. really joined was not the Air Force but the Office of Strategic Services, a cloak-and-dagger outfit whose clandestine activities probably did not appreciably lengthen the war. "As a cover, he was given the rank of Air Corps Lieutenant." Mr. Szulc tells us that H.H. was sent to China to train guerrillas behind the Japanese lines. Curiously enough, I have not come across a Chinese setting in any of H.H.'s novels. Was he ever in China? One daydreams. " 'Lieutenant Hunt reporting for duty, General.' The haggard face with the luminous strange eyes stared at him through the tangled vines. 'Lieutenant Hunt?' Wingate's voice was shrill with awe. 'Until today, no man has ever hacked his way through that living wall of slant-eyed Japanese flesh . . . !' "

In 1946, H.H. returned to civilian life and wrote what is probably his most self-revealing novel, *Stranger in Town* (Random House, 1947). This must have been very nearly the first of the returned-war-veteran novels, a genre best exemplified by Merle Miller's *That Winter;* reading it, I confess to a certain nostalgia.

Handsome, virile young Major Fleming returns to New York City, a glittering Babylon in those days before the writing appeared on Mayor Lindsay's wall. Fleming has a sense of alienation (new word in 1947). He cannot bear the callous civilian world which he contrasts unfavorably with how it was for us back there in the Pacific in our cruddy foxholes with the frigging sound of mortars overhead and our buddies dying—for what? How could any black-marketing civilian spiv know what war was really like?

Actually, none of *us* knew what it was like either since, as far as my investigations have taken me, no novelist of the Second World War or returned-veteran-from-the-war novelist ever took part in any action. Most were clerks in headquarter companies or with *Yank* or *Stars and Stripes;* one cooked. H.H. may have *observed* some of the war as a correspondent and, perhaps, from behind the lines in China, but no foxhole ever held him, no wolf ever fed him, no vastation overwhelmed him in the Galleria at Naples. But the daydreamer of course is always there. And how!

The book is dedicated to two dead officers (Wasp), as well as to "The other gallant young men who did not return." Only a book reviewer whose dues were faithfully paid up to the Communist party could keep a tear from his eye as he read that line. Then the story. It is early 1946. Major Fleming checks into the elegant Manhattan flat of his noncombatant brother who is out of town but has given him the flat and the services of a worthy black retainer who could have played De Lawd in *Green Pastures.* A quick résumé of Fleming's career follows.

Incidentally, each of H.H.'s narratives is periodically brought to a halt while he provides the reader with highly detailed capsule biographies written in *Who's Who* style. H.H. plainly enjoys composing plausible (and implausible) biographies for his characters—not to mention for himself. In *Contemporary Authors,* H.H. composed a bio for one of his pseudonyms, Robert Dietrich, taking ten years off his age, putting himself in the infantry during Korea, awarding himself a Bronze Star and a degree from Georgetown. A quarter century later when the grandmother-trampler and special counselor to the President Charles W. Colson wanted documents invented and history revised in the interest of Nixon's re-election, he turned with confidence to H.H. He knew his man—and fellow Brown alumnus.

As Fleming orders himself champagne and a luxurious meal ending with baked Alaska (for one!), we get the bio. He has been everywhere in the war from "Jugland" (Yugoslavia?) to the Far East. He remembers good meals in Shanghai and Johnny Walker Black Label. Steak. Yet his memories are bitter. He is bitter. He is also edgy. "I can't go around for the rest of my life like somebody out of the Ministry of Fear."

Fleming is an artist. A sculptor. H.H. conforms to that immutable rule of bad fiction which requires the sensitive hero to practice the one art his creator knows nothing about. We learn that Fleming's old girl friend has married someone else. This is a recurrent theme in the early novels. Was H.H. jilted? Recipient of a Dear John letter? Get cracking, thesis-writers.

The civilian world of New York, 1946, annoys Fleming ("maybe the Far East has spoiled me for America"). He is particularly enraged by demobilization. "Overseas, the nineteen-year-old milksops were bleeding for their mothers, and their mothers were bleeding for them, and the army was being demobilized, stripped of its powers. . . . He had had faith in the war until they partitioned Poland again. . . . Wherever Russia moved in, that part of the world was sealed off." Fleming has a suspicion that he is not going to like what he calls "the Atomic Age." But then, "They trained me to be a killer. . . . Now they'll have to undo it."

At a chic night club, Fleming meets the greasy Argentine husband of his old flame; he beats him up. It seems that Fleming has never been very keen about Latins. When he was a schoolboy at Choate (yes, Choate), he met an Italian girl in New York. She took him home and got his cherry. But "she smelled of garlic, and the sheets weren't very clean, and after it was all over when I was down on the street again, walking home, I thought that I never wanted to see her again." Ernest would have added rain to that sentence, if not to the scene.

The themes that are to run through H.H.'s work and life are all to be found in *Stranger in Town.* The sense that blacks and Latins are not quite human (Fleming is moderately attracted to a "Negress" but fears syphilis). The interest in pre-war jazz: Beiderbecke and Goodman. A love of fancy food, drink, decor; yet whenever the author tries to strike the elegant worldly note, drapes not curtains tend to obscure the view from his not so magic casements, looking out on tacky lands forlorn. Throughout his life's work there is a constant wistful and, finally, rather touching identification with the old American patriciate.

There is a rather less touching enthusiasm for war. "An atom bomb is just a bigger and better bomb," while "the only justification for killing in war is that evil must be destroyed." Although evil is never exactly defined, the killers for goodness ought to be left alone to kill in their own way because "if I hired a man to do a dirty job for me, I wouldn't be presumptuous enough to specify what weapons he was to use or at what hour. . . ." Toward the end of the book, H.H. strikes a minatory anti-communist note. Fleming denounces pacifists and a "new organiza-tion called the Veterans Action Council" whose "ideals had been a paraphrase of the Communist manifesto." Apparently these veterans prefer to follow the party line which is to disarm the U.S. while Russia arms. A few years later when Joe McCarthy got going, this was a standard line. But it was hot stuff in 1945, and had the book-chat writers of the day like Orville Prescott and Charles Poore not hewed so closely to the commie line *Stranger in Town* would have been much read. As it was, the book failed. Too avant-garde. Too patriotic.

The gullible *Who's Who* now tells us that H.H. was a "screen writer, 1947–48; attaché Am Embassy, Paris, France, 1948–49." But Mr. Szulc knows better. Apparently H.H. joined the CIA "early in 1949, and after a short period in Washington headquarters, he was sent to Paris for nearly two years. Now for a cover, he called himself a State Department reserve officer." But the chronology seems a bit off.

According to the blurb of a John Baxter novel, the author [H.H.] "worked as a screen writer until Hollywood felt the impact of TV. 'When unemployed screen writer colleagues began hanging themselves aboard their yachts,' Baxter joined the Foreign Service." I slip into reverie. I am with Leonard Spigelgass, the doyen of movie writers at MGM. "Lenny, do you remember E. Howard Hunt alias John Baxter alias Robert Dietrich alias . . ." Lenny nods; a small smile plays across his handsome mouth. "Howie never got credit on a major picture. Used to try to peddle these foreign intrigue scripts. He was hipped on assassination, I recall. Poor Howie. Not even Universal would touch him." But I fear that like Pontius Pilate in the Anatole France story, Lenny would merely say, "E. Howard Hunt? I do not recall the name. But let me tell you about Harry Essex . . ." If H.H. *was* in Hollywood then he is, as a writer, unique. Not one of his books that I have read uses Hollywood for background. This is superhuman continence considering how desperate for settings a man who writes nearly fifty books must be.

*Who's Who* puts H.H. in Paris at the Embassy in 1948. Mr. Szulc puts him there (and in the CIA) early 1949. Actually H.H. was working for the Economic Cooperation Administration at Paris in 1948 where he may have been a "black operator" for the CIA. With H.H. the only facts we can rely on are those of publication. *Maelstrom* appeared in 1948 and *Bimini Run* in 1949. *The Herald Tribune* thought that *Maelstrom* was a standard thriller-romance while *Bimini Run* was dismissed as "cheap, tawdry" ( it is actually pretty good). That was the end. H.H. had ceased to be a contender in the big literary sweepstakes which currently features several young lions of that day grown mangy with time's passage but no less noisy.*

In 1949, at popular request, the novelist Howard Hunt hung up the jock until this year when he reappeared as E. Howard Hunt, author of *The Berlin Ending*. Simultaneous with the collapse of his career as a serious author, his attempts at movie writing came to nothing because of "the impact of TV." Too proud to become part of our Golden Age of television, H.H. joined the CIA in 1948 or 1949, a period in which his alias Robert Dietrich became an agent for the IRS in Washington.

*My friends Irwin Shaw and James Jones were told by a helpful journalist that I was referring to them. Actually, I was thinking of Norman Mailer and myself.

In Paris, H.H. met Dorothy Wetzel, a pretty girl herself given to daydreaming: she claimed to be a full-blooded Cherokee Indian to the consternation of her family; she may or may not have been married to a Spanish count before H.H. One reasonably hard fact (ritually denied) is that she was working as a secretary for the CIA in Paris when she met H.H. They were married in 1949 and had four children; their marriage appears to have been idyllically happy despite the fact that they were rather alike in temperament. A relative recalls that as a girl Dorothy always had her nose in a book—a bad sign, as we know. She also believed in the war against evil, in the undubiousness of the battle which at the end of her life last December seemed to be going against the good.

From Paris the two CIA employees moved on to Vienna where they lived a romantic life doing whatever it is that CIA agents do as they defend the free world, presumably by confounding the commies. According to *Who's Who,* H.H. was transferred to the American Embassy in Mexico City in 1950. Latin America was a natural field for H.H. (with the Guggenheim money he had gone for a year to Mexico to learn Spanish). Also, in Latin America the struggle between good and evil might yet be resolved in good's favor. Europe was old; perhaps lost. John Baxter's *A Foreign Affair* (1954) describes H.H.'s life in those days and his settling views. *A Foreign Affair* also marks the resumption of H.H.'s literary career and the beginning of what one must regard as the major phase of his art. Between 1953 and 1973, H.H. was to write under four pseudonyms over forty books.

Three years in Mexico City. Two years in Tokyo. Three years at Montevideo (as consul, according to *Who's Who;* actually he was CIA station chief). During this decade 1950–60, H.H. created Gordon Davis who wrote *I Came to Kill* (Fawcett, 1954). In 1957 H.H. gave birth to Robert Dietrich who specialized in thrillers, featuring Steve Bentley, formerly of the CIA and now a tax consultant. Steve Bentley first appears in *Be My Victim* (1957). It is interesting that the Bentley stories are set in Washington, DC, a city which as far as I can judge H.H. could not have known at all well at the time. According to Mr. Szulc, H.H. was briefly at CIA headquarters in 1949; otherwise he was abroad until the 1960s. Presumably the city whose symbol was one day to be Watergate always had a symbiotic attraction for him.

From the number of books that H.H. began to turn out, one might suspect that he was not giving his full attention to the work of the CIA. Nevertheless, in 1954, H.H. found time to assist in the overthrow of the liberal government of Jacobo Arbenz in Guatemala.

H.H. has now published *Give Us This Day,* his version of what *really* happened at the Bay of Pigs. He also tells us something about the Guatemala adventure where he had worked under a Mr. Tracy Barnes who was "suave and popular . . . a product of Groton, Yale, and Harvard Law. Through marriage he was connected to the Rockefeller clan. . . ." Incidentally, both the OSS and its successor the CIA of the early cold war were manned by fun-loving American nobles. Considering H.H.'s love of the patriciate, it is not impossible that his principal motive in getting into the cloak-and-dagger game was to keep the best company. The hick from western New York who had gone not to Harvard but to Brown, who had not fought in the Second War but worked behind the lines, who had failed as a serious novelist found for himself in the CIA a marvelous sort of club where he could rub shoulders with those nobles whose *savoir-faire* enthralled him. After all, social climbing is one of the most exciting games our classless society has to offer.

But as Scott Fitzgerald suspected, the nobles are not like those who would serve them on the heights. They are tough eggs who like a good time whether it is playing polo or murdering enemies of the state. They take nothing seriously except their pleasures and themselves. Their admirers never understand this. Commie-hunting which is simply fun for the gamesters became for their plebian friend a holy mission. And so it is the true believer H.H. who is in the clink today while his masters are still at large, having good times. Of course they make awful messes, as Fitzgerald noted; luckily the Howies of this world are there to clean up after them.

In recruiting H.H. for the Bay of Pigs, Barnes expected to use him as "on that prior operation—Chief of Political Action . . . to assist Cuban exiles in overthrowing Castro." This means that H.H. had worked with Guatemalan right-wingers in order to remove Arbenz. "The nucleus of the project was already in being—a cadre of officers I had worked with against Arbenz. This time, however, all trace of US official involvement must be avoided, and so I was to be located not in the Miami area, but in Costa Rica." Later in the book we learn that "the scheduled arrival of Soviet arms in Guatemala had determined the date of our successful anti-Arbenz effort." Arms which the American government had refused to supply.

During a meeting with President Idigoras of Guatemala (who was giving aid, comfort, and a military base to the anti-Castro forces) H.H. "thought back to the period before the overthrow of Colonel Arbenz when CIA was treating with three exiled leaders: Colonel Castillo Armas, Dr. Juan Cordova Cerna, and Colonel Miguel Idigoras Fuentes. As a distinguished and respected jurist, Cordova Cerna had my personal vote as provisional president . . ." But H.H. was not to be a kingmaker this time. Castillo Armas was chosen by the golden gamesters, only to be "assassinated by a member of the presidential bodyguard in whose pocket was found a card from Radio Moscow. . . ." They always carry cards—thank God! Otherwise how can you tell the bad from the good guys?

One studies the book for clues to H.H.'s character and career; day-dreams are always more revelatory than night dreams. As I have noted, H.H. chose Washington, DC, as setting for the Robert Dietrich thrillers starring Steve Bentley. Although he could not have known the city well in the fifties, he writes knowledgeably of the broken-down bars, the seedy downtown area, the life along the wharfs—but of course low-life scenes are the same everywhere and I can't say that I recognize my home city in his hard-boiled pages.

Here is Georgetown. "In early Colonial times it was a center of periwigged fashion and Federalist snobbery that lasted a hundred years. For another eighty the close-built dwellings settled and tottered apart until only Negroes would live there, eight to a room. Then for the last twenty-five years, the process reversed. The New Deal's flood of bureau-crats claimed Georgetown as its own. . . . On the fringes huddle morose colonies of dikes and nances, the shops and restaurants have names that are ever so quaint, and sometimes it seemed a shame that the slaves had ever left." The narrator, Steve Bentley, is a tough guy who takes pride in the fact that Washington has "per capita, more rape, more crimes of violence, more perversion, more politicians, more liquor, more good food, more bad food . . . than any other city in the world. A fine place if you have enterprise, durability, money, and powerful friends." It also helps to have a good lawyer.

The adventures of Steve Bentley are predictable: beautiful girl in trouble; a murder or two. There is a great deal of heavy drinking in H.H.'s novels; in fact, one can observe over the years a shift in the author's attitude from a devil-may-care-let's-get-drunk-and-have-a-good-time preppishness to an obsessive need for the juice to counteract the melancholy of middle age; the hangovers, as described, get a lot worse, too. Mr. Szulc tells us that in real life H.H. had been known to tipple and on at least one occasion showed a delighted Washington party his CIA credentials. H.H.'s taste in food moves from steak in the early books (a precious item in wartime so reminiscent of today's peacetime arrangements) to French wine and lobster. As a student of H.H., I was pleased to learn that H.H. and his fellow burglars dined on lobster the night of the Watergate break-in. I think I know who did the ordering.

It is a curious fact that despite American right-wingers' oft-declared passion for the American Constitution they seem always to dislike the people's elected representatives. One would think that an enthusiasm for the original republic would put them squarely on the side of a legislature which represents not the dreaded people but those special and usually conservative interests who pay for elections. But there is something about a congressman—any congressman—that irritates the American right-winger and H.H. is no exception.

*Angel Eyes* (Dell, 1961) is typical. Beautiful blonde calls on Steve Bentley. Again we get his philosophy about Washington. "A great city. . . . All you need is money, endurance, and powerful friends." The blonde has a powerful friend. She is the doxie of "Senator Tom Quinby. Sixty-four if he was a day, from a backwoods, hillbilly state that featured razorback hogs, turkey-neck sharecroppers, and contempt for Civil Rights. . . . A prohibitionist and a flag-waving moralizer." One suspects a bit of deceit in the course of the Steve Bentley thrillers. They are not as heavily right-wing and commie-baiting as the Howard Hunt or John Baxter or Gordon Davis works, while some of the coloreds are actually OK guys in Steve Bentley's book. All the more reason, however, to find odd the contempt for a tribune of the people whose political views (except on prohibition) must be close to H.H.'s own.

I suspect that the root of the problem is, simply, a basic loathing of democracy, even of the superficial American sort. The boobs will only send boobs to Congress unless a clever smooth operator like Representative Lansdale in *End of a Stripper* manages to buy an election in order to drive the country, wittingly or unwittingly, further along the road to collectivism. It would be much simpler in the world of Steve Bentley not to have elections of any kind.

Steve doesn't much cotton to lady publishers either. "Mrs. Jay Redpath, otherwise known as Alma Ward" (or Mrs. Philip Graham, otherwise known as Kay Meyer) makes an appearance in *Angel Eyes,* and hard as nails she is. But Steve masters the pinko spitfire. He masters everything, in fact, but Washington itself with its "muggers and heroin pushers and the whiteslavers and the faggotry. . . . This town needs a purifying rain!" Amen to that, Howie.

In 1960 H.H. published three Dietrich thrillers. In 1961 H.H. published two Dietrich thrillers. In 1962 there was no Dietrich thriller. But as John Baxter, H.H. published *Gift for Gomala* (Lippincott, 1962). The dates are significant. In 1961 H.H. was involved in the Bay of Pigs and so, presumably, too busy to write books. After the Bay of Pigs, he dropped Robert Dietrich and revived John Baxter, a straight if rather light novelist who deals with the not-so-high comedy of Kennedy Washington.

H.H. begins his apologia for his part in the Bay of Pigs with the statement that "No event since the communization of China in 1949 has had such a profound effect on the United States and its allies as the defeat of the US-trained Cuban invasion brigade at the Bay of Pigs in April, 1961. Out of that humiliation grew the Berlin Wall, the missile crisis, guerrilla warfare throughout Latin America and Africa, and our Dominican Republic intervention. Castro's beachhead triumph opened a bottomless Pandora's box of difficulties . . ." This is the classic reactionary's view of the world, uncompromised by mere fact. How does one lose China if one did not possess China in the first place? And what on earth did Johnson's loony intervention in the Dominican Republic really have to do with our unsuccessful attempt to overthrow Castro?

H.H. deplores the shortness of the national memory for America's disgrace twelve years ago. He denounces the media's effort to make JFK seem a hero for having pulled back from the brink of World War III. Oddly, he remarks that "The death of Jack Ruby and worldwide controversy over William Manchester's book for a time focused public attention on events surrounding the assassination of John Fitzgerald Kennedy. Once again it became fashionable to hold the city of Dallas collectively responsible for his murder. Still, and let this not be forgotten, Lee Harvey Oswald was a partisan of Fidel Castro, and an admitted Marxist who made desperate efforts to join the Red Revolution in Havana. In the end he was an activist for the Fair Play for Cuba Committee." Well, this is what H.H. and a good many like-minded people want us to believe. But is it true? Or special pleading? Or a cover story? A pattern emerges.

H.H.'s memoir is chatty. He tells how in 1926 his father traced an absconding partner to Havana and with an army Colt .45 got back his money. "Father's intervention was direct, illegal, and effective." Years later his son's Cuban work proved to be indirect and ineffective; but at least it was every bit as illegal as Dad's. Again one comes up against the paradox of the right-wing American who swears by law and order yet never hesitates to break the law for his own benefit. Either law and order is simply a code phrase meaning get the commie-weirdo-fag-nigger-lovers or H.H.'s Nixonian concept of law and order is not due process but vigilante.

As H.H. tells us how he is brought into the Cuban adventure, the narrative reads just like one of his thrillers with the same capsule biographies, the same tight-lipped asides. "I'm a career officer. I take orders and carry them out." It appears that ex-President Figueres offered to provide the anti-Castro Cubans with a base in Costa Rica (the same Figueres sheltered Mr. Vesco). But the Costa Rican government decided not to be host to the patriots so H.H. set up his Cuban government-in-exile in Mexico City, resigning from the Foreign Service (his cover). He told everyone he had come into some money and planned to live in Mexico. Privately, he tells us, he was dedicated to getting rid of the "blood-soaked gang" in Havana by shedding more blood.

This was the spring and summer of 1960 and Kennedy and Nixon were running for president. Since Kennedy's denunciations of the commie regime ninety miles off the coast of Florida were more belli-cose than Nixon's, the exiled Cubans tended to be pro-Kennedy in the election. But not H.H. He must have known even then that JFK was a communist at heart because his chief support came from the pinko elements in the land. H.H. also had a certain insight into the new President's character because "JFK and I were college contempo-raries" (what he means is that when Jack was at Harvard Howie was at Brown) "and I had met him at a Boston debut" (of what?) "where he was pointed out to me. . . . I freely confess not having discerned in his relaxed lineaments the future naval hero, Pulitzer laureate, Sena-tor, and President."

Meanwhile H.H. is stuck with his provisional government in Mexico and he was "disappointed. For Latin American males their caliber was about average; they displayed most Latin faults and few Latin virtues." In other words, shiftless but not musical. What can an associate member of the Wasp patriciate and would-be killer of commies do but grin and bear it and try to make a silk purse or two of his Latin pigs' ears?

In 1960 Allen Dulles received the top team for a briefing on the proposed liberation of Cuba. H.H. was there and tells us of the plan to drop paratroopers at "Santa Clara, located almost in Cuba's geographic center" while "reinforcing troops would land by plane at Santa Clara and Trinidad . . . on the southern coast." Assuming that Castro's troops would be in the Havana area, the Brigade would "march east and west, picking up strength as they went." There would also be, simultaneously, a fifth column to "blow up bridges and cut communications." But "let me underscore that neither during this nor other meetings was it asserted that the underground or the populace was to play a decisive role in the campaign." H.H. goes on to explain that the CIA operation was to be essentially military and he admits, tacitly, that there would probably be no great uprising against Castro. This is candid but then H.H. wants no part of *any* revolution. At one point he explains to us correctly that the American revolution was not a class revolution but a successful separation of a colony from an empire. "Class warfare, therefore, is of foreign origin."

The Kennedy administration did not inspire H.H. with confidence. Richard Goodwin, Arthur Schlesinger, Jr., Chester Bowles "all had a common background in Americans for Democratic Action—the ADA." In H.H.'s world to belong to ADA is tantamount to membership in the Communist party. True to form, the White House lefties started saying that the Castro revolution had been a good thing until betrayed by Castro. This Trotskyite variation was also played by Manolo Ray, a liberal Cuban leader H.H. found as eminently shallow and opportunistic as the White House found noble. H.H. had his hands full with the Consejo or government-to-be of Cuba.

Meanwhile, troops were being trained in Guatemala. H.H. made a visit to their secret camp and took a number of photographs of the Brigade. Proud of his snaps, he thought they should be published in order to "stimulate recruiting"; also, to show the world that members of the Consejo were getting on well with the Brigade, which they were not.

At this point in time (as opposed to fictional points out of time), aristocratic Tracy Barnes suggested that H.H. meet Arthur Schlesinger, Jr., at the White House where Camelot's historian was currently "pounding out" the White Paper on Cuba for Jack the King. Arthur the historian "was seated at his desk typing furiously, a cigarette clinging to his half-open mouth, looking as disorderly as when we had first met in Paris a decade before." Although H.H.'s style is not elegant he seldom comes up with an entirely wrong word; it is particularly nice that in the monster-ridden cellar of his brain the word "disorderly" should have surfaced instead of "disheveled" for are not all ADA'ers enemies of law'n'order and so *dis*orderly?

During this meeting, H.H. learns that Dean Rusk has vetoed the seizure from the air of Trinidad because the world would then know that the US was deeply implicated in the invasion. (The word "incursion" had not yet been minted by the empire's hard-working euphemists.) Then the supreme master of disorder appeared in the historian's office. Said Adlai Stevenson to aristocratic Tracy Barnes, " 'Everything going well, Tracy?' and Barnes gave a positive response. This exchange is important for it was later alleged that Stevenson had been kept in the dark about invasion preparations."

Later, waiting in the press secretary's office, "I sat on Pamela Turnure's desk until the getaway signal came and we could leave the White House unobserved, much like President Harding's mistress." This is Saint-Simon, as told to Harold Robbins.

D-Day. "I was not on the beachhead, but I have talked with many Cubans who were." Shades of the war novelists of a quarter century before! "Rather than attempt to write what has been written before, it is enough to say that there were no cowards on the beach, aboard the assault ships or in the air." But the Bay of Pigs was a disaster for the free world and H.H. uses the word "betrayal." As the sun set on the beachhead which he never saw, "only vultures moved." Although safe in Washington, "I was sick of lying and deception, heartsick over political compromise and military defeat." Fortunately, H.H.'s sickness with lying and deception was only temporary. Ten years later Camelot would be replaced by Watergate and H.H. would at last be able to hit the beach in freedom's name.

At least two other Watergate burglars were involved with the Bay of Pigs caper. "Co-pilot [of a plane that dropped leaflets over Havana] was an ex-Marine named Frank Fiorini," who is identified in a footnote: "Later, as Frank Sturgis, a Watergate defendant." That is H.H.'s only reference to Sturgis/Fiorini.* On the other hand, he tells us a good deal about Bernard "Bernie" L. Barker, "Cuban-born US citizen. First man in Cuba to volunteer after Pearl Harbor. Served as USAF Captain/ Bombardier. Shot down and spent eighteen months in a German prison camp." H.H. tells us how Bernie was used by the CIA to infiltrate the Havana police so "that the CIA could have an inside view of Cuban antisubversive operations." Whatever that means. Bernie was H.H.'s assistant in Miami during the pre-invasion period. He was "eager, efficient, and completely dedicated." It was Bernie who brought Dr. Jose Miró Cardona into H.H.'s life. Miró is a right-wing "former president of the Cuban bar" and later head of the Cuban revolutionary council. He had also been, briefly, Castro's prime minister.

*The hero of *Bimini Run* is called Sturgis.

Bernie later became a real estate agent in Miami. Later still, he was to recruit two of his employees, Felipe de Diego and Eugenio P. Martinez, for duty as White House burglars. According to Barker, de Diego had conducted "a successful raid to capture Castro government documents," while Martinez made over "300 infiltrations into Castro Cuba." At the time of Watergate Martinez was still on the CIA payroll.

*Give Us This Day* is dedicated "To the Men of Brigade 2506." The hero of the book is a very handsome young Cuban leader named Artime. H.H. prints a photograph of this glamorous youth with one arm circling the haunted-eyed author-conspirator. It is a touching picture. No arm, however, figuratively speaking, ever encircles the equally handsome Augustus of the West. H.H. is particularly exercised by what he believes to have been Kennedy's tactic "to whitewash the New Frontier by heaping guilt on the CIA." H.H. is bitter at the way the media played along with this "unparalleled campaign of vilification and obloquy that must have made the Kremlin mad with joy." To H.H., the real enemy is anyone who affects "to see communism springing from poverty" rather than from the machinations of the men in the Kremlin.

"On December 29, 1962, President Kennedy reviewed the survivors of the Brigade in Miami's Orange Bowl. Watching the televised ceremony, I saw Pepe San Román give JFK the Brigade's flag" (Footnote: "Artime told me the flag was a replica, and that the Brigade feeling against Kennedy was so great that the presentation nearly did not take place") "for temporary safekeeping. In response the President said, 'I can assure you that this flag will be returned to this Brigade in a free Havana.'" H.H. adds sourly, "One wonders what time period he had in mind."

*Who's Who* tells us that H.H. was a consultant with the Defense Department 1960–65. Mr. Szulc finds this period of H.H.'s saga entirely murky. Apparently H.H. became personal assistant to Allen Dulles after the Bay of Pigs. Mr. Szulc also tells us that in 1963 the American ambassador to Spain refused to accept H.H. as deputy chief of the local CIA station because of H.H.'s peculiar activities as station chief for Uruguay in 1959. After persuading that country's president Nardone to ask Eisenhower to keep him *en poste* in Uruguay, H.H. then tried to overthrow the same President Nardone without telling the American ambassador. It was this tactless treatment of the *ambassador* that cost H.H. the Spanish post.

One of H.H.'s friends told Mr. Szulc, "This is when Howard really began losing touch with reality."* In *Give Us This Day* H.H. tells us how

*The New York Times Magazine,* June 3, 1973, p. 11.

he tried to sell Tracy Barnes on having Castro murdered. Although H.H. gives the impression that he failed to persuade the CIA to have a go at killing the Antichrist, columnist Jack Anderson has a different story to tell about the CIA. In a column for January 25, 1971, he tells us that an attempt was made to kill Castro in March 1961, a month before the invasion. Castro was to be poisoned with a capsule in his food. Capsule to be supplied by one John Roselli—a Las Vegas mobster who was eager to overthrow Castro and re-open the mob's casinos. Also involved in the project was a former FBI agent Robert Maheu, later to be Howard Hughes's viceroy at Las Vegas.

It is known that Castro did become ill in March. In February–March 1963, the CIA again tried to kill Castro. Anderson wonders, not illogically, if Castro might have been sufficiently piqued by these attempts on his life to want to knock off Kennedy. This was Lyndon Johnson's theory. He thought the Castroites had hired Oswald. The Scourge of Asia was also distressed to learn upon taking office that "We had been operating a damned Murder, Inc., in the Caribbean." Since it is now clear to everyone except perhaps Earl Warren that Oswald was part of a conspiracy, who were his fellow conspirators? Considering Oswald's strenuous attempts to identify himself with Castro, it is logical to assume that his associates had Cuban interests. But which Cubans? Pro-Castro or anti-Castro?

I think back on the evidence Sylvia Odio gave the FBI and the Warren Commission's investigators.* Mrs. Odio was an anti-Castro, pro-Manolo Ray Cuban exile who two months before the assassination of President Kennedy was visited in her Dallas apartment by three men. Two were Latins (Mexican, she thought, they weren't the right color for Cubans). The third, she maintained, was Oswald. They said they were members of her friend Manolo Ray's organization and one of them said that their companion Oswald thought Kennedy should have been shot after the Bay of Pigs. If Mrs. Odio is telling the truth, then whoever was about to murder Kennedy may have wanted the left-wing anti-Castro group of Manolo Ray to get the credit.†

*Warren Commission *Hearings,* Vols. XI:369–381 and XXVI:834–838; see also National Archives: Commission Document No. 1553.
†The Warren Commission and the FBI never satisfactorily identified Mrs. Odio's visitors. Just before the Report was finished, the FBI reported to the Warren Commission that one Loran Eugene Hall, "a participant in numerous anti-Castro activities," had recalled visiting her with two other men, one of them, William Seymour, resembling Oswald. But after the Report appeared the FBI sent the Commission a report that Hall had retracted his story and that Mrs. Odio could not identify Hall or Seymour as the men she had seen. (See Richard H. Popkin,

During this period Oswald's behavior was odd but not, necessarily, as official chroniclers maintain, mad. Oswald was doing his best to become identified publicly with the Fair Play for Cuba Committee as well as setting himself up privately as a sort of Soviet spy by writing a mysterious "fact"-filled letter to the Soviet Embassy. That the Russians were genuinely mystified by his letter was proved when they turned it over to the American government after the assassination. Also, most intriguingly, Oswald visited Mexico City in September 1963, where H.H. was acting chief of the CIA station. Finally, Osward's widow tells us that he took a pot-shot at the reactionary General Walker, the sort of thing a deranged commie would do. Was he then simply a deranged commie? The right-wing Cubans and their American admirers certainly want us to think so.

After the murder of the President, one of those heard from was Frank Fiorini/Sturgis, who was quoted in the Pompano Beach, Florida, *Sun-Sentinel* to the effect that Oswald had been in touch with Cuban Intelligence the previous year, as well as with pro-Castroites in Miami, Mexico City, New Orleans. A Mrs. Marjorie Brazil reported that she had heard that Oswald had been in Miami demonstrating in front of the office of the Cuban Revolutionary Council headed by our old friend Dr. Miró Cardona. A sister of one Miguel Suarez told nurse Marjorie Heimbecker who told the FBI that JFK would be killed by Castroites. The FBI seems eventually to have decided that they were dealing with a lot of wishful thinkers.

Finally, Fiorini/Sturgis denied the story in the *Sun-Sentinel;* he said that he had merely speculated with the writer on some of the gossip that was making the rounds in Miami's anti-Castro Cuban community. The gossip, however, tended to be the same: Oswald had killed Kennedy, on orders from Castro or from those of his admirers who thought that the murder of an American president might in some way save the life of a Cuban president.

Yet the only Cuban group that would be entirely satisfied by Kennedy's death would be the right-wing enemies of Castro who held

---

*The Second Oswald* [Avon, 1967], pp. 75–80.) Hall had already been brought to the Commission's attention in June 1964, under the names of "Lorenzo Hall, *alias* Lorenzo Pascillio." The FBI heard in Los Angeles that Hall and a man called Jerry Patrick Hemming had pawned a 30.06 rifle, which Hall redeemed shortly before the assassination with a check drawn on the account of the "Committee to Free Cuba." Hemming was identified in 1962 as one of the leaders of Frank Sturgis's anti-Castro brigade. (See Warren Commission Document 1179:296–298 and Hans Tanner, *Counter Revolutionary Brigade* [London, 1962], p. 127.)

Kennedy responsible for their humiliation at the Bay of Pigs. To kill him would avenge their honor. Best of all, setting up Oswald as a pro-Castro, pro-Moscow agent, they might be able to precipitate some desperate international crisis that would serve their cause. Certainly Castro at this date had no motive for killing Kennedy, who had ordered a crackdown on clandestine Cuban raids from the United States—of the sort that Eugenio Martinez is alleged so often to have made.

I suspect that whoever planned the murder must have been astonished at the reaction of the American establishment. The most vengeful of all the Kennedys made no move to discover who really killed his brother. In this, Bobby was a true American: close ranks, pretend there was no conspiracy, do not rock the boat—particularly when both Moscow and Havana seemed close to nervous breakdowns at the thought that they might be implicated in the death of the Great Prince. The Warren Report then assured the nation that the lone killer who haunts the American psyche had struck again. The fact that Bobby Kennedy accepted the Warren Report was proof to most people (myself among them) that Oswald acted alone. It was not until several years later that I learned from a member of the family that although Bobby was head of the Department of Justice at the time, he refused to look at any of the FBI reports or even speculate on what might have happened at Dallas. Too shaken up, I was told.*

Fortunately, others have tried to unravel the tangle. Most intriguing is Richard H. Popkin's theory that there were two Oswalds.† One was a bad shot; did not drive a car; wanted the world to know that he was pro-Castro. This Oswald was caught by the Dallas police and murdered on television. The other Oswald was seen driving a car, firing at a rifle range, perhaps talking to Mrs. Odio; he was hired by . . . ? I suspect we may find out one of these days.

In 1962, H.H. published *A Gift for Gomala* as John Baxter. This was an attempt to satirize the age of Camelot. Lippincott suggests that it is "*must* reading for followers of Reston, Alsop and Lippmann who are looking for comic relief." One would think that anyone who tried to follow all three of those magi would be beyond comic relief. The tale is clumsy: a black opportunist dresses up as a representative from a new African nation and tries to get a loan from Congress; on the verge of

---

*We now know that Bobby was terrified that a thorough investigation would reveal the numerous Kennedy attempts to murder Castro.
†Popkin, *The Second Oswald* (Avon, 1967).

success, Gomala ceases to exist. Like Evelyn Waugh, H.H. thinks African republics are pretty joky affairs but he gives us no jokes.

For about a year during this period (1965–66) H.H. was living in Spain. Whether or not he was working for the CIA is moot. We do know that he was creating a new literary persona: David St. John, whose specialty is thrusting a CIA man named Peter Ward into exotic backgrounds with a bit of diabolism thrown in.

As Gordon Davis, H.H. also wrote *Where Murder Waits,* a book similar in spirit to *Limit of Darkness.* In the early work H.H. daydreams about the brave lads who flew out of Henderson, often to death against the foe. In *Where Murder Waits* H.H.'s dream self hits the beach at the Bay of Pigs, that beach where, finally, only vultures stirred. Captured, the hero spends nine months in the prisons of the archfiend Castro. Once again: Expiation for H.H.—in dreams begins self-love.

It is curious that as H.H. moves out of the shadows and into the glare of Watergate his books are more and more open about his political obsessions. *The Coven,* by David St. John, is copyrighted 1972. In July of 1971, on the recommendation of Charles W. ("If you have them by the balls their hearts and minds will follow") Colson, H.H. was hired by the White House and became a part-time criminal at $100 a day. Zeal for his new masters informs every page of *The Coven.* The villain is the hustling handsome rich young Senator Vane with "a big appeal to the young and disadvantaged" (i.e., commies)—just like Jack-Bobby-Teddy. The description of Mrs. Vane makes one think irresistibly (and intentionally) of Madame Onassis—not to mention Harold Robbins, Jacqueline Susann, and the horde of other writers who take such people and put them in books thinly revealed rather than disguised.

"The Vanes are legally married to each other and that's about all. Their private lives are separate. He's a terror among the chicks, and she gets her jollies from the artists, writers and beach boy types Vane gets public grants for." She also seduces her narrator. "I had seen a hundred magazine and newspaper photographs of her cutting ribbons, first-nighting, fox-hunting at Warrenton, and empathizing with palsied kids. . . ." But, as H.H. reminds us, "only a fool thinks there's any resemblance between a public figure's public image and reality." Fortunately the narrator is able to drive the Vane family out of public life (they are prone to taking off their clothes at orgies where the devil is invoked). H.H. believes quite rightly that the presidency must never go to devil-worshipers who appeal to the young and disadvantaged.

The chronology of H.H.'s life is a tangle until 1968 when he buys

Witches Island, a house at Potomac, Maryland (his wife went in for horses). On April 30, 1970, the new squire retired from the CIA under a cloud—he had failed too often. But H.H. had a pension; he also had a lively new pseudonym David St. John; his wife Dorothy had a job at the Spanish Embassy. But H.H. has always needed money so he went to work for Robert R. Mullen and Company, a PR firm with links to the Republican party and offices not only a block from the White House but across the street from the Committee to Re-elect the President.

Mullen represented Howard Hughes in Washington. H.H. knew his way around the Hughes operation—after all, Hughes's man in Las Vegas was Robert Maheu, whose contribution to Cuban affairs, according to Jack Anderson,* was to "set up the Castro assassination" plot in 1961, and whose contribution to Nixon was to funnel $100,000 to Bebe Rebozo in 1970. But Hughes sacked Maheu late in 1970. In 1971 H.H. found a second home at the White House, assigned with G. Gordon Liddy to "the Room 16 project" where the administration prepared its crimes.

Room 16 marks the high point of H.H.'s career; his art and arts were now perfected. Masterfully, he forged; he burglarized; he conspired. The Shakespeare of the CIA had found, as it were, his Globe Theatre. Nothing was beyond him—including tragedy. According to *Newsweek*, John Dean told Senate investigators that H.H. "had a contract" from "low-level White House officials" to murder the president of Panama for not obeying with sufficient zeal the American Bureau of Narcotics directives. "Hunt, according to Dean, had his team in Mexico before the mission was aborted."†

As the world now knows, on the evening of June 16, 1972, H.H. gave a splendid lobster dinner to the Watergate burglars and then sent Bernie Barker and his Cubans into battle to bug the offices of the Democratic party because H.H. had been told by G. Gordon Liddy "that Castro funds were going to the Democrats in hopes that a rapproachement with Cuba would be effected by a successful Democratic presidential candidate." H.H. has also said (*Time*, August 27, 1973) that his own break-in of the office of Daniel Ellsberg's psychiatrist was an attempt to find out whether Ellsberg "might be a controlled agent for the Sovs."

One daydreams: "Dr. Fielding, I have these terrible headaches. They started just after I met my control Ivan and he said, 'Well, boychick,

*Japan Times,* January 23, 1971.
†*Newsweek,* June 18, 1973, p. 22.

it's been five years now since you signed on as a controlled agent. Now I guess you know that if there's one thing we Sovs hate it's a non-producer so . . .' Dr. Fielding, I hope you're writing all this down and not just staring out the window like last time."

Now for the shooting of George Wallace. It is not unnatural to suspect the White House burglars of having a hand in the shooting. But suspicion is not evidence and there is no evidence that H.H. was involved. Besides, a good CIA man would no doubt have preferred the poison capsule to a gunshot . . . slipping ole George the sort of slow but lethal dose that Castro's powerful gut rejected. In an AP story this summer, former CIA official Miles Copeland is reported to have said that "senior agency officials are convinced Senator Edward Muskie's damaging breakdown during the presidential campaign last year was caused by convicted Watergate conspirator E. Howard Hunt or his henchman spiking his drink with a sophisticated form of LSD."*

When Wallace ran for president in 1968, he got 13 percent of the vote; and Nixon nearly lost to Humphrey. In May 1972, 17 percent favored Wallace for president in the Harris poll. Wallace had walked off with the Michigan Democratic primary. Had he continued his campaign for president as an independent or as a Democrat in states where he was not filed under his own party, he could have swung the election to the Democrats, or at least denied Nixon a majority and sent the election to the House.

"This entire strategy of ours," Robert Finch said in March 1972, "depends on whether George Wallace makes a run on his own." For four years Nixon had done everything possible to keep Wallace from running; and failed. "With Wallace apparently stronger in the primaries in 1972 than he had been before," Theodore White observed, "with the needle sticking at 43 percent of the vote for Nixon, the President was still vulnerable—until, of course, May 15 and the shooting. Then it was all over."†

Wallace was shot by the now familiar lone assassin—a demented (as usual) busboy named Arthur Bremer. Then on June 21, 1973, the headline in the *New York Post* was HUNT TELLS OF ORDERS TO RAID BREMER'S FLAT.

According to the story by Bob Woodward and Carl Bernstein, H.H. told the Senate investigators that an hour after Wallace was shot, Colson

*AP dispatch, London, August 17, 1973.
†*The Making of the President, 1972* (Atheneum, 1973), p. 238.

ordered him to fly to Milwaukee and burglarize the flat of Arthur H. Bremer, the would-be assassin—in order to connect Bremer somehow with the commies? Characteristically, the television senators let that one slip by them. As one might expect, Colson denied ordering H.H. to Milwaukee for any purpose. Colson did say that he had talked to H.H. about the shooting. Colson also said that he had been having dinner with the President that evening. Woodward and Bernstein's "White House source" said, "The President became deeply upset and voiced concern that the attempt on Wallace's life might have been made by someone with ties to the Republican Party or the Nixon campaign." This, Nixon intuited, might cost him the election.*

May 15, 1972, Arthur H. Bremer shot George Wallace, governor of Alabama, at Laurel, Maryland; easily identified as the gunman, he was taken into custody. Nearby in a rented car, the police found Bremer's diary (odd that in the post-Gutenberg age Oswald, Sirhan, and Bremer should have all committed to paper their *pensées*).

According to the diary, Bremer had tried to kill Nixon in Canada but failed to get close enough. He then decided to kill George Wallace. The absence of any logical motive is now familiar to most Americans, who are quite at home with the batty killer who acts alone in order to be on television, to be forever entwined with the golden legend of the hero he has gunned down. In a nation that worships psychopaths, the Oswald-Bremer-Sirhan-Ray figure is to the general illness what Robin Hood was to a greener, saner world.

Bremer's diary is a fascinating work—of art? From what we know of the twenty-two-year-old author he did not have a literary turn of mind (among his effects were comic books, some porno). He was a television baby, and a dull one. Politics had no interest for him. Yet suddenly—for reasons he never gives us—he decides to kill the President and starts to keep a diary on April 4, 1972.

According to Mr. Szulc, in March 1972, H.H. visited Dita ("call me Mother") Beard in Denver. Wearing a red wig and a voice modulator, H.H. persuaded Dita to denounce as a forgery the memo she had written linking ITT's pay-off to the Republican party with the government's subsequent dropping of the best part of its antitrust suit against the conglomerate. In May, H.H. was installing the first set of bugs at the Democratic headquarters. His movements between April 4 and May 15 might be usefully examined—not to mention those of G. Gordon Liddy, et al.

*New York Post,* June 21, 1973, reprinting a *Washington Post* story.

For someone who is supposed to be nearly illiterate there are startling literary references and flourishes in the Bremer diary. The second entry contains "You heard of *One Day in the Life of Ivan Dynisovich*? Yesterday was my day." The misspelling of Denisovich is not bad at all. Considering the fact that the name is a hard one for English-speaking people to get straight, it is something of a miracle that Bremer could sound the four syllables of the name correctly in his head. Perhaps he had the book in front of him but if he had, he would not have got the one letter wrong.

The same entry produces more mysteries. "Wallace got his big votes from Republicans who didn't have any choice of candidates on their own ballot. Had only about $1055 when I left." This is the first and only mention of politics until page 45 when he describes his square clothes and haircut as "just a disguise to get close to Nixon."

One reference to Wallace at the beginning; then another one to Nixon a dozen pages later. Also, where did the $1,055 come from? Finally, a minor psychological point—Bremer refers to some weeds as "taller than me 5′6″. I doubt if a neurotic twenty-two-year-old would want to remind himself on the page that he is only 5′6″ tall. When people talk to themselves they seldom say anything so obvious. On the other hand, authors like this sort of detail.

Popular paperback fiction requires a fuck scene no later than a dozen pages into the narrative. The author of the diary gives us a good one. Bremer goes to a massage parlor in New York (he has told the diary that he is a virgin—Would he? Perhaps) where he is given an unsatisfying hand-job. The scene is nicely done and the author writes correctly and lucidly until, suddenly, a block occurs and he can't spell anything right—as if the author suddenly remembers that he is meant to be illiterate.

One of these blocks occurs toward the end of the massage scene when the girl tells Bremer that she likes to go to "wo-gees." This is too cute to be believed. Every red-blooded American boy, virgin or not, knows the word "orgy." Furthermore, Bremer has been wandering around porno bookstores on 42nd Street and the word "orgy" occurs almost as often in his favored texts as "turgid." More to the point, when an illiterate is forced to guess at the spelling of a word he will render it phonetically. I cannot imagine that the girl said anything that sounded like "wo-gee." It is as if the author had suddenly recalled the eponymous hard-hat hero of the film *Joe* (1970) where all the hippies got shot so satisfyingly and the "g" in orgy was pronounced hard. On this page, as though to emphasize Bremer's illiteracy, we get "spair" for "spare," "enphaais" for "emphasis," and "rememmber." Yet on the same page the diarist has no trouble spelling "anticipation," "response," "advances."

The author of the diary gives us a good many random little facts—seat numbers of airplanes, prices of meals. He does not like "hairy hippies." A dislike he shares with H.H. He also strikes oddly jarring literary notes. On his arrival in New York, he tells us that he forgot his guns which the captain then turned over to him, causing the diarist to remark "Irony abounds." A phrase one doubts that the actual Arthur Bremer would have used. As word and quality, irony is not part of America's demotic speech or style. Later, crossing the Great Lakes, he declares "Call me Ismal." Had he read *Moby Dick*? Unlikely. Had he seen the movie on the Late Show? Possibly. But I doubt that the phrase on the sound track would have stayed in his head.

The diary tells us how Bremer tried to kill Nixon. The spelling gets worse and worse as Bremer becomes "thruorly pissed off." Yet suddenly he writes, "This will be one of the most closely read pages since the Scrolls in those caves." A late April entry records, "Had bad pain in my left temple† just in front† about it." He is now going mad as all the lone killers do, and refers to "writing a *War + Peace.*"

More sinister: "saw 'Clockwork Orange' and thought about getting Wallace all thru the picture—fantasing my self as the Alek on the screen. . . ." This is a low blow at highbrow sex 'n' violence books and flicks. It is also—again—avant-garde. Only recently has a debate begun in England whether or not the film *Clockwork Orange* may have caused unbalanced youths to commit crimes (clever youths now tell the Court with tears in their eyes that it was the movie that made them bash the nice old man and the Court is thrilled). The author anticipated that ploy all right—and no matter who wrote the diary we are dealing with a true author. One who writes, "Like a novelist who knows not how his book will end—I have written this journal—what a shocking surprise that my inner character shall steal the climax and destroy the author and save the anti-hero from assasination!" Only one misspelling in that purple patch. But "as I said befor, I Am A Hamlet." It is not irony that abounds so much in these pages as professional writing.

May 8, Bremer is reading *R.F.K. Must Die!* by Robert Blair Kaiser. Like his predecessor he wants to be noticed and then die because "suicide is a birth right." But Wallace did not die and Bremer did not die. He is now at a prison in Baltimore, awaiting a second trial. If he lives to be re-examined, one wonders if he will tell us what company he kept during the spring of 1972, and whether or not a nice man helped him to write his diary, as a document for the ages like the scrolls in those caves.

Lack of originality has marked the current administration's general style (as opposed to the vivid originality of its substance; witness, the first magistrate's relentless attempts to subvert the Constitution). Whatever PR has worked in the past is tried again. Goof? Then take the blame yourself—just like JFK after the Bay of Pigs. Caught with your hand in the till? Checkers time on the tube and the pulling of heartstrings.

Want to assassinate a rival? Then how about the Dallas scenario? One slips into reverie. Why not set up Bremer as a crazy who wants to shoot Nixon (that will avert suspicion)? But have him fail to kill Nixon just as Oswald was said to have failed to kill *his* first target, General Walker. In midstream have Bremer—like Oswald—shift to a different quarry. To the real quarry. Make Bremer, unlike Oswald, apolitical. Too heavy an identification with the Democrats might backfire. Then—oh, genius!—let's help him to write a diary to get the story across. (Incidentally, the creation of phony documents and memoirs is a major industry of our secret police forces. When the one-man terror of the Southeast Asian seas, Lieutenant Commander Marcus Aurelius Arnheiter, was relieved of his command, the Pentagon put him to work writing the "memoirs" of a fictitious Soviet submarine commander who had defected to the Free World.)*

The White House's reaction to the Watergate burglary was the first clue that something terrible has gone wrong with us. The elaborate and disastrous cover-up was out of all proportion to what was, in effect, a small crime the administration could have lived with. I suspect that our rulers' state of panic came from the fear that other horrors would come to light—as indeed they have. But have the horrors ceased? Is there something that our rulers know that we don't? Is it possible that during the dark night of our empire's defeat in Cuba and Asia the American story shifted from cheerful familiar farce to Jacobean tragedy—to murder, chaos?

*The New York Review of Books*
December 13, 1976

*The Arnbeiter Affair* by Neil Sheehan (Random House, 1971).

# 79
·

# *AN AMERICAN PRESS*
# *LORD*

Shortly after Richard Nixon was chosen to bring us together, he announced that he would write each of the many thousands of Americans listed in *Who's Who* a letter requesting guidance. Although everyone would get the same letter, Nixon did want to make one thing very clear: he himself would add a personal postscript complimenting the recipient for his particular contribution to the American imperium. On tender hooks, as the late Alfalfa Bill Murray would say, I waited for my letter. What word of praise would Nixon have for the author of *The Best Man?* The suspense was exquisite. At last the letter arrived. *Office of the President-Elect* (a nostalgic moment as I recalled 1960's joke: the President-Erect) *Richard M. Nixon, Washington, D.C.* was the heading. Under this my name and address; then nothing until the bold signature *Richard Nixon.* Thus did the wittiest administration in American history begin.

Now, a year later, it is plain to almost everyone that Nixon's sense of fun is the most remarkable thing about him, even more appealing than his ability to hear what the silent say (a typical Nixon joke, incidentally, quite lost on ponderous liberals). If he has not yet made America (love it or leave it) one great Laugh-in, the fault's not his but ours, as Max Lerner might put it. He has done his best. From the unveiling on television's prime time of Spiro Agnew (our very own Greek Colonel) to the running commentaries of Martha and John Mitchell (the Allen and Burns of the Nixon Network), he has proved a master entrepreneur as well as source of a thousand jokes, many too subtle for the solemn race history requires him to preside over.

For instance, hardly anyone suspected that something funny was up when Nixon appointed Walter Annenberg as ambassador to England. Yet any student of Nixon mischief ought to have known that he would somehow manage to apple-pie the bed of Harold Wilson's Socialist government, which had sent as ambassador to Washington (in anticipation of a Humphrey administration), one John Freeman, former *New Statesman* editor who had written unkindly of Nixon in 1960. That's just the sort of thing Dick remembers as he surveys those crises which make up his past with an eye to fixing any wagon that ever ran over him: but with sly rather than vindictive wit; with the boffo laugh, not the mean curse.

Before Annenberg was appointed, lovers of Nixon wit were making up lists of possible ambassadors. Dean Acheson? His bland dismissals of postwar England were a high qualification. Claire Boothe Luce? Always good for a wisecrack. H. L. Hunt? This was my choice. A distinguished anti-Commie, he carries his lunch about with him in a used brown paper bag. But then came the news that Walter Annenberg had been inked.

Nothing was known of Annenberg except that he published a couple of bad newspapers in Philadelphia (no great laughing matter) and his father Mo had gone to the clink in the thirties for tax evasion (an event which forced my right-wing Washington family to overcome their anti-Semitism long enough to acknowledge that, Jew or not, Mo was busted because he had the guts to stand up to the Antichrist FDR). But one prison sentence does not a Nixon joke make. There had to be more to Annenberg than his father's ill luck. Yet a first look at him revealed nothing remarkable (that is to say risible). Very rich. Powerful in Pennsylvania politics. Gave a lot of money to Nixon's campaign (how much is a mystery). Was a friend to Dick in the dark days. All in all, a perfectly unqualified appointee on the order of the late Joe Kennedy. Could it be that Funny Dick had let us down?

Two months later when Annenberg presented his credentials to the Queen of England the world realized that Nixon had done it again. He had, very simply, launched the most brilliant clown since the late Bert Lahr. But as every impresario knows, it is not enough to book a clown into a palace; infinite care must be taken to show the comic at his best. Although Nixon is not known to have initiated the BBC's coverage of Annenberg's meeting with the Queen, I am sure that the CIA had a hand in it. The performances were much too outrageous for the BBC; the comedy too carefully polished.

Annenberg appears at palace and forgets to remove a funny hat; footmen force him to (early Chaplin this); then he is briefed on how to begin the long march to the throne. "We start," he is told sternly, "with our left foot." Starting with the right foot, he approaches the Queen. With that graciousness for which she is insufficiently paid, Britannic Majesty asks if he is living at the embassy. Little does she know she is playing straight to a Nixon joke. Like many Americans who inherit money and evade school, Annenberg has not an easy way with the President's, much less the Queen's, English (Nixon must have auditioned Annenberg a dozen times before he signed him up). At first startled by the difficulty of the question, Annenberg gives a great Bert Lahr *Uhhh.* Then, laboriously, he constructs the following answer (like all great acts, this one improves with each airing): "We're in the embassy residence, subject, of course, to some of the discomfiture as a result of a need for, uh, elements of refurbishing and rehabilitation." Then a perfectly timed reaction shot of the Queen looking as if a cigar has just exploded in her face. Back in Washington Dick must have been on the floor as he watched her try to maneuver her way out of *that* one.

Untoppable as the premier seg was, Annenberg followed up almost immediately with a speech to the Pilgrims (a group of Americanophile English). In Eddie Mayhoff fashion, he attacked American students as revolutionaries, while praising his friend Ronald Reagan for magisterial restraint. The British were overwhelmed. Nixon had more than paid Wilson back for the appointment of Freeman to Washington, paid him in full with funny money.

But enough of what everyone knows. What is the real Walter Annenberg like? The face behind the successful clown's mask? Like Chaplin, Lahr, Keaton, there must be a heartache, a suppurating wound to go with that comic bow. Just as curiosity seemed never to be satisfied, Mr. Gaeton Fonzi offers us *Annenberg: A Biography of Power,* a book which Morris Ernst believes "should be read by everyone interested in the First Amendment. Very few authors have the temerity to comment on the giants of the mass media." Senior editor of *Philadelphia Magazine,* Mr. Fonzi spent two years raking Philadelphia's muck in order to set in proper context what I take to be the late William Claude Dukinfield's spiritual heir, a true Allegheny carbon in the rough. The result is a devastating account of the misuse of media for private and vindictive ends, as well as a fascinating exposé of the relationship between big money and big politics, a familiar corruption no less disturbing for being, once again, documented.

Mr. Fonzi's study is in two parts. The first is devoted to Mo, founder of the publishing dynasty; the second to Walter's expansion of the business in order to achieve that high respectability his father too had dreamed of but lost when the Feds caught up with him.

Shortly after his release from prison in 1942, Mo died, leaving Walter controlling interest in Triangle Publications, Inc., which owned Philadelphia's *Inquirer* and *Daily News.* Ownership of these two newspapers made Walter, automatically, a power in the land; in fact, they proved to be the making of the ambassador. Once made, he no longer needed them and so they were sold for $55 million, winning Mr. Fonzi's praise: "I believe Walter Annenberg's finest contribution to American journalism was revealed on October 28, 1969. That was the day it was announced he was selling the Philadelphia *Inquirer* and *Daily News* to the John S. Knight Chain."

But Annenberg still owns *TV Guide* (largest weekly circulation of any periodical in the world), *Seventeen,* a dozen radio and television stations, seven cable television companies, and the basis of old Mo's fortune, the *New York Morning Telegraph.* On his own, Walter is the largest stockholder in Penn Central Transportation Co., and an important stockholder in both the Girard Trust Bank and Campbell's Soup Co. Until his translation to what the State Department persists in calling the Court of St. James, he was an active director in these enterprises.

The section on Mo is no doubt of some interest in trying to understand Walter, a task which intrigues Mr. Fonzi as much as it bores me. The Walter Annenbergs are clear as a sheet of cellophane and we need beard no minotaurs in pursuit of hidden rosebuds. He is what he seems. So was Mo, who started the *Morning Telegraph* (a racing sheet), which naturally brought him into close contact with the underworld of gambling or, as Harold Ickes nicely said, "Mo comes from the world and from the lawless tradition commonly associated with Al Capone."

This blast was the result of Mo's attacks on Harold Ickes's master, Christendom's right arm. Originally, as publisher of the Miami *Daily News,* Mo had been a dedicated New Dealer but with the sale of the *News* and the acquisition of the *Inquirer,* he promptly became a dedicated Republican. It was quite simple: wherever he was, he wanted to get in with the gentry. Since the Philadelphia gentry were Republican, Mo became more Republican than the Pews. But in spite of gangster connections, tax evasion on a grand scale, and opportunistic politics, Mo seems to have been, even to Mr. Fonzi, an agreeable monster who— important point in a demos-praising time—mingled genially with his employees. Not so the heir.

Walter dropped out of school as soon as he could; a shy youth who stammered, he "was extremely sensitive about his withered right ear, through which he cannot hear." Nice sentence. Try another preposition; it still sounds funny. Mr. Fonzi's prose style . . . no, not a word about style. Sufficient to say, demos is well served by Mr. Fonzi.

Not taken seriously by his father, Walter idolized him (was it ever otherwise in popular biography?), felt the shame of his imprisonment more than anyone, blamed everything on Roosevelt and the liberal establishment and, not unnaturally, wanted to compensate, to rise to a high place in the national hierarchy. Mr. Fonzi's crude character analysis makes one almost sympathize with Walter. After all, he is a classic American type. At one remove from the European ghetto, the hero makes up his mind to be accepted by the Wasp establishment, which not only looks down on him, his profession, his religion, his manner, but locked up his father. So he gives money to charities (that is the way you get to meet socially important people if you have nothing to recommend you but money). Collects pictures (same motive). And gives money to politicians. Through inspired ignorance, Walter put his money on that onyx-hued horse Richard Nixon; as a result, he got a diplomatic appointment much to his liking (it has been said but not proved that Walter raised several million dollars for Nixon's campaign with the understanding that he be made ambassador to England).

Mr. Fonzi's attempts at psychology are of no great interest. What fascinates, however, is his description of Walter Annenberg's use of the press and television to dominate Philadelphia. It is a remarkakly ugly story.

To everyone's surprise, Walter proved a better businessman than his father. In founding *TV Guide,* he outdid all his father's works. But business in itself was always a means to an end: acceptance by the Main Line and a place among the magnates of that empire he so deeply loves and so passionately defends. To achieve this, he drove his associates hard. Wide-eyed, Mr. Fonzi tells us of heart attacks, breakdowns, betrayals, as though we ought to be outraged at the way Walter used men, drove them beyond their endurance. But this is simplistic: no one is ever driven unless he wants to be. Just as each masochist finds his sadist, so the proto-ulcer is sure to find its emotional trigger.

From a commercial point of view Walter was an excellent publisher. The *Inquirer*'s Sunday edition carried more comic strips than any paper in the country; therefore it sold well. Walter must take credit for the paper's healthy circulation as well as for the eccentricity of its editorial policy and the unreliability of its reporting. Very early on, he began to use his papers and television stations as a means to punish those he disliked and praise those who could advance him socially. Most publishers do this in subtle ways; but Walter was not subtle, and that is the theme to Mr. Fonzi's study . . . the blatant misuse of the power of the press for personal ends.

To begin with, there was a shit list. Certain people could not be mentioned. Usually the politicians on the list were local liberals, and Walter's motives were understandable if dishonorable. But there were all sorts of other people whose names could not be mentioned. From the world of show business, Imogene Coca, Zsa Zsa Gabor, and Dinah Shore all managed somehow to offend Walter. At the height of Dinah Shore's popularity, her program was listed in *TV Guide* without her name. Then, often as not, the ban would be lifted as inscrutably as it had been imposed. Recently the ambassador told an English lady that he was faced with a great problem in public relations. He wanted to invite a dear friend to come and stay at the embassy but because of the unfair way the press had treated her, he didn't dare. The English woman wondered who it could be: Mary McCarthy? Margaret Mead? Madalyn O'Hair? No, said the ambassador, Zsa Zsa Gabor.

Mr. Fonzi makes considerable hay out of the indictment of the *Inquirer*'s top reporter as a blackmailer who belonged to an extortion ring which shook down local businessmen. No doubt a bad business and proof that Walter did not run a tight ship, but he can hardly be blamed for the corruption of an employee in a city where corruption is a way of life. Far worse is the way Walter used the power of his newspapers and television stations to harm others. In 1964 *Holiday* published a piece on Philadelphia, amiably remarking upon Walter's social rise. Overreacting as usual, Walter immediately ordered a story on the imminent collapse of *Holiday*'s publisher, Curtis. Not satisfied with the first story, he had it rewritten, made tougher, and himself wrote the lead. Disliking Ralph Nader, he saw to it that a speech in Philadelphia by the national ombudsman was not mentioned in the *Inquirer*. Thinking that he had been snubbed at a party given by Nubar Gulbenkian, Walter ordered a reporter to write a story "exposing" that jolly oil man. These are examples of capriciousness, idle malice, and relentless triviality. Now for the conflict of interest.

Out of the blue, Walter ordered a story which would "knock the hell out of" one Matthew Fox. The reporter charged with the assignment was puzzled. Why? What was Walter's motive? Fox was a wheeler-dealer, with no Philadelphia interests. But—and the picture came into focus—Fox was deeply involved in California's pay television experiment. Walter opposed pay television not only because it was un-American (as did the networks) but, more specifically, because if Fox's people issued their own listings it would harm *TV Guide*. To the reporter's credit, he wrote a piece so deliberately scurrilous that the *Inquirer*'s lawyers killed it.

Walter's most notorious intervention in politics came in 1966 when Milton Shapp ran for governor of Pennsylvania. Aside from being a Democrat, Shapp had a number of other serious demerits in Walter's eyes. He owned an interest in a cable television firm in direct conflict with Triangle; worse, he had managed to stop Walter from slipping through the city council a motion to grant Triangle exclusive CATV rights for the city. Finally (and the reason Walter gave for the virulence of his opposition), Shapp "made his objection to the merger of the Pennsylvania and New York Central railroads one of the principal campaign issues." This was too much for good Philadelphian Walter. "I had a sympathetic view toward Mr. Shapp long before the campaign," he said, "but then he used the Pennsylvania Railroad as his *schtick* . . . one of the great American corporations . . . chairman of the board . . . personal friend of mine . . ."

It was too much. Consequently the *Inquirer* outdid itself in what a political observer at the time termed "character assassination." Every trick in the book was used, including what is sometimes referred to as *"The Best Man* caper"; hint that the candidate is not right in the head. An *Inquirer* reporter asked Shapp if it was true that he'd sue should the paper print that he'd ever been in a mental home. Having never been in a loony bin, Shapp quite naturally said, yes, he would sue. Next day's headlines: SHAPP DENIES EVER HAVING BEEN IN A MENTAL HOME. After the campaign the general public learned that the largest individual stockholder in the Pennsylvania Railroad was Walter Annenberg.

Mr. Fonzi records with zest a dozen other peculiar uses Walter made of his newspapers and television stations. For instance, he would not allow WFIL-TV to show the ABC documentary *The Political Demise of Richard Nixon* (Walter wasn't so dumb, come to think of it) because a minute or two was devoted to Alger Hiss's view of his nemesis. Then Walter suppressed in his newspapers the national uproar over Hiss's having been allowed to appear on television since Hiss was, in Walter's phrase, "a convicted treasonable spy." Fortunately for Walter, perjurer Hiss did not sue. When Martin Luther King came to town, a reporter was instructed to ask him, "Is it true the ultimate aim of your campaign is interracial marriage?" When a local politician named Musmanno died, Walter (who liked him) wanted to include in the obituary that his death had been hastened by a row with Senator Joseph Clark (whom Walter loathed). And so on and on.

But though it is good to show the corruption of the press under an ambitious, ignorant, and malicious owner, one cannot help wondering what Mr. Fonzi finds so startling. The media in America exist only to serve the financial interests of their owners. That is the way things are and have always been. For sheer breathtaking character assassination the pious Henry Luce did more harm than a dozen crude Walters mucking about in a sad city where, from time to time, nearly everyone is for sale or at least rent (it is sad to note that one of Philadelphia's few admirable politicians, Richardson Dilworth, belonged to a law firm retained by Walter and so he never . . .)

But the pure of heart can take some consolation in the fact that newspapers in America are less and less read. A recent Gallup Poll caused much clucking in the press: apparently 45 percent thought the press biased. How could the good people be so suspicious of the American press, which (because it is American) has to be the world's best, serving the Bill of Rights with lonely fervor? Yet the real surprise was that 37 percent are so stupid as to think that the press is objective. They are the real suckers, and we know what sort of break an earlier Philadelphia clown would have given them.

The case of Walter Annenberg has its touching side. Had he not been born with money he might have found a happy niche for himself as a sales manager in some small firm where his crudeness and lack of civilization would have been a virtue. As it was, an heir to power with a drive for respectability, he had the accidental luck to befriend a future President and so found himself one day facing a mildly contemptuous Senate committee which knew perfectly well (if he did not) that he had no business being an ambassador to anywhere.

Senator Fulbright handled the occasion with many mumbled asides (not all repeated by Mr. Fonzi) to the effect that it really made no

difference what the Senate thought of a President's diplomatic appointments, since they were almost always consented to. He did wonder if
Walter had given any money to Nixon's campaign. A firm "no" from
the ambassador-designate. Later Walter admitted that, well, his wife
had. Asked whether or not he had tried to link Musmanno's death with
Senator Clark's "persecution," he lied and said "no." He was confirmed.

It is usual for this sort of book to end upon the hortatory note: if only
we join together and force the newspapers to be objective, all will again
be well. It is to Mr. Fonzi's credit that he tells his sad story simply for
its own sake. There is nothing to be done about Walter except defeat the
jokester who appointed him and boycott all Triangle publications. The
first is possible; the second . . . so what? In any case, as one who loves
wit and the appositeness of things, I cannot help but feel Mr. Fonzi is
too melodramatic and, finally, unjust. It is altogether right that Walter
Annenberg should represent not only the present administration but the
nation which elected it. Birds of a feather, as they say; and what birds!
Eagles, no less, and like the predatory American eagle, near to extinction as a result of our poisoned environment.

*The New York Review of Books*
April 9, 1970

# H. HUGHES

Is Howard R. Hughes the most boring American? Admittedly, the field is large; over two hundred million of us are in competition. Yet on the strength of an old associate's recent memorial, I am inclined to give Hughes the benefit of the belief I have long held that the more money an American accumulates the less interesting he himself becomes. Certainly there is not much you can do with the fact of someone else's fortune except stare at all those naughts upon the page. Then, naughts aside, Hughes the actual man emanates a chloroform quite his own: the high droning voice, the catatonic manner, the absence of all humor (a characteristic of the very rich American, but here quintessential), the lack of interest in the human, the preoccupation with machinery (yet he is "a lousy engineer," according to my father, a long-time aviator acquaintance, and "a menace as a flier"), the collecting of beautiful and famous women to no vivid end (although feisty Ava Gardner did knock him out with an ashtray), and, of course, the grim eating habits (dinner is always a steak with peas, followed by vanilla ice cream and cookies).

The best thing about Hughes has been his withdrawal from the world—for this, if nothing else, he ought not only to have been honored but encouraged by a grateful nation. Yet even in the shadows of his cloistered motels, the inept tycoon insists on pulling strings, making a mess of TWA, a disaster of RKO, a shambles of vice in Las Vegas, all the while creating the largest unworkable plywood plane in the world at a cost to the taxpayers of twenty-two million dollars. There is something peculiarly inhuman even about his incompetence. At least John D. Rockefeller gave out dimes and drank mother's milk (from other people's mothers, that is). Why then contemplate Howard Hughes? Because he is involved in politics and even a cursory glance at his career is a chilling reminder of the nation's corruption at every level.

In 1925, Noah Dietrich was engaged by the nineteen-year-old Howard Hughes to run the business Hughes had inherited from his father (the manufacturer of a special kind of drill much favored by Texas oil men). The handsome young heir had moved to Hollywood where the girls and the boys and the movies were. Aware that he knew nothing about money, Hughes hired Mr. Dietrich, a certified public accountant, to look after his affairs. This profitable association lasted until 1957, when Mr. Dietrich, feeling the shadows lengthen, asked for some stock and a few capital gains to supplement the large salary on which he was forced to pay a large tax. Hughes promptly let him go. If Mr. Dietrich is a bitter man, the book *Howard, the Amazing Mr. Hughes* (by Noah Dietrich and Bob Thomas) does not reveal it. Every page radiates octogenarian serenity—the CPA at Colonus. Nevertheless, despite the sunny manner, Mr. Dietrich and Mr. Thomas, his prose stylist (as such workers are called in *Youngblood Hawke*), have managed to give us a highly detailed and most plausible portrait of what is apparently an honest-to-God American shit.

In Hollywood Hughes produced a number of pictures. Those in which he took no "creative" part sometimes made money (like Milestone's *Two Arabian Knights*); those he himself worked on invariably lost money, including the renowned *Hell's Angels* (the aesthetic value of these works will not be dealt with here). Incidentally, during the first thirty years of his association with Dietrich, Hughes made only one visit to the Hughes Tool Company. As a result, the company was a great success, producing the money Hughes promptly lost on movie-making, on a color process for films, on a new kind of automobile, on the career of Miss Jane Russell (a lifelong search for the perfect set of boobs ended abruptly for Howard in a dentist's office when Nurse Russell suddenly made her appearance carrying a tray of pliers). For an American bore of major standing, Hughes demonstrated, from the beginning, an attractive talent for failure which almost—but not quite—catapults him into the ranks of the human.

"My first objective is to become the world's number one golfer. Second, the top aviator, and third I want to become the world's most famous motion picture producer. Then, I want you to make me the richest man in the world." So spoke the young Faust to Mr. Dietrich, his eager counter-Faust. For a very rich young man the realization of such simple dreams ought to have been an easy matter. Unfortunately, Hughes's golf was not all that good; as a flier, he was the Icarus of an entire generation of aviators; while the movies he produced brought him only publicity. Mr. Dietrich did make him very rich, but not as rich as J. P. Getty.

It would seem, on the evidence of this memoir, that Hughes was never interested in money or movies or airplanes or women. What did absorb him was tinkering with bits of machinery or celluloid. Hour after hour, day after day, he would concentrate totally (and to no ultimate purpose) on a carburetor or the editing of a zoom shot. Detail work was his narcotic. But attempts to relate the details of the work to some larger unit like an automobile or a finished film (or a love affair?) were quite beyond him, as even devotees of *The Outlaw* must admit.

Mr. Dietrich gives us a bit of character analysis, but not much. This is wise. The point to Hughes is that he is what he seems: a simple, uneducated man, interested in machinery. He apparently never liked anyone very much, man or woman. Suffering from hereditary deafness, he went into retirement because it was difficult for him to hear conversations at parties (he can hear perfectly on an altered telephone and so prefers to conduct his business at long distance). Since his family is not long lived, he has become frightened of the germ and its carrier, people. "Everyone carries germs around with them. I want to live longer than my parents, so I avoid germs." Living alone, with only servants to look after him, he has developed a somewhat solipsistic turn of mind, given to night fears—not only of germs, death, betrayal, but of monsters like the ones he watches so avidly on *The Late, Late Show* coming to kidnap him, to eat him up.

The interesting part of Mr. Dietrich's book begins during the war. Over the years, Hughes had managed to offend a number of important generals (Hap Arnold, the army air force's commander, was turned away at the door to the Hughes plant). In the interest of landing war contracts, Hughes decided to corrupt the generals and their masters, the politicians. Why not? All businessmen dealing with the government do—or try to. Hughes hired an amiable man-about-town called Johnny Meyer, who "certainly knew how to please the tired politician or general, and he was lavish with hotel suites, fancy dinners, champagne, and caviar, not to mention $100-per-night beauties. You'd be surprised how many senators, governors and generals partook of his largesse."

I think Mr. Dietrich exaggerates the surprise of those of us born under the dread sign of the unshredded Dita Beard. What we really want to know is not how our masters behave in the sack but what deals they make in the office. "Despite his obviousness Johnny Meyer produced results for the Hughes enterprise." The most important VIP that he snared was Elliott Roosevelt. Parenthetically, when my father became Roosevelt's Director of Air Commerce (1933–1936), young Elliott told him, "Everyone else in the family's got their man in the Administration. Well, you're going to be mine." Thus from an early age, Elliott showed a great interest in the future of aviation, and worked hard to give America that mastery of the skies she has so long held.

The air force procurement brass was anti-Hughes, particularly General Echols. But air force Brigadier General Roosevelt managed to turn them all around, obtaining for Hughes a contract for one hundred F-11 plywood fighters at $700,000 apiece. Meanwhile, the actress to whom Johnny Meyer had introduced Elliott became his wife—benignly, Hughes paid for both wedding and honeymoon.

Meyer was also working on Major General Bennett Meyers in Materiel, Maintenance, and Distribution. This general had a passion for money unusual even in a military man sworn to defend capitalism. He wanted "to buy government bonds on margin and turn over a quick profit." To accomplish this, Hughes was to lend the general $200,000 "on a short-term, no-interest loan." As it turned out, Hughes's lawyer in Washington aborted the scheme and General Meyers eventually ended up in the clink.

During this period, Hughes was not always himself. Dietrich recalls a telephone conversation in which his employer repeated the same sentence thirty-three times. When this dysfunction was drawn to his attention, Hughes allowed that his doctor was also concerned, and promptly vanished for six months, to return in 1947 ready for his finest hour.

Senator Owen Brewster of Maine, dreaming of the Vice-Presidency as Maine men tend to do during those long hard winters Down East, decided he needed some publicity. What better target than the eccentric young millionaire, flyer, and stud-consort of sinful lascivious Hollywood stars and broads? Forthwith, Brewster summoned Hughes before a Senate committee in order to show the foul ways in which clean-limbed West Pointers, golden Presidential sons, selfless tribunes of the people had been tempted by Johnny Meyer, booze, and women, women, women.

But Senator Brewster had met his match. The inarticulate Hughes suddenly found his voice. Masterfully, he defended himself, often disingenuously, but then a Congressional committee is not exactly the *Bocca della Verita*. Luckily for Hughes, the senator from Maine was a . . . well, enthusiast for Pan American Airways, even though Pan American made no stops in Maine. Suddenly the alleged corrupter of public virtue turned on Senator Brewster and said, "I specifically charge that during luncheon at the Mayflower Hotel in Washington in the week beginning February 10, 1947, in the suite of Senator Brewster, the senator told me in so many words that if I would agree to merge TWA with Pan Am and go along with this community airline bill, there would be no further hearing in this matter." The career of Senator Brewster was at an end. Not only did he not become Tom Dewey's running mate in 1948, but when he came up for reelection to the Senate in 1952, Hughes gave $60,000 to his opponent. Brewster was defeated.

During the late 1940s and throughout the 1950s, Howard's political contributions ran between $100,000 and $400,000 a year. He financed Los Angeles councilmen and county supervisors, tax assessors, sheriffs, state senators and assemblymen, district attorneys, governors, congressmen and senators, judges—yes, and Vice Presidents and Presidents, too. Besides cash, Howard was liberal in providing airplanes for candidates.

In 1944 a fine comedy took place at the Biltmore Hotel in Los Angeles. Hughes and his lawyer went around to the suite of the candidate for Vice-President, Harry S Truman. Hughes sent the lawyer in to see Truman, with an envelope containing $12,500. Brooding in the outer room, Hughes began to worry that Truman might give the lawyer the credit for the cash. Hughes barged into the politician's presence "and said bluntly, 'I want you to know, Mr. Truman, that is *my* money Mr. McCarthy is giving you.' Truman managed to laugh off Howard's lack of diplomacy. . . ." Ho ho ho all the way to the White House.

For those who are curious as to how large sums of money are got physically into the hands of politicians, Mr. Dietrich is most illuminating. In fact, revelatory.

I asked Trippe (president of Pan Am) how he managed to wield so much influence in Washington—the Pan American lobby was enormously effective, and not only with Senator Brewster. "Well, you know," he confided, "the law says nothing at all about contributions from *foreign* corporations. We have a subsidiary in South America that takes an intense interest in our US elections."

From that moment, Hughes Tool of Canada dispersed three to four hundred thousand dollars a year to American politicians, and it was all legal.

Most notorious of the Hughes loans was to Richard Nixon's brother Don. Apparently Don has two passions: money and food, which he was able to combine in a Whittier, California restaurant starring the Nixon-burger. In 1956, shortly after Richard Nixon was re-elected Vice-President, he got in touch with Hughes's political lawyer and told him that brother Don needed $205,000. Now Mr. Dietrich was a good Republican who had supported the Eisenhower-Nixon crusade for decency. He was as appalled as Hughes was delighted. "Let 'em have it," said Hughes. After all, $205,000 is not much to buy a Vice-President—particularly when the pro for the quid (yes, wicked partisans do take a sequential view of life) was nothing less than saving Howard Hughes from having to pay taxes.

Prior to the loan, Hughes had been trying to set up a tax-exempt medical foundation with himself as sole trustee. The IRS had twice refused him a tax exemption. Then the loan was made to Donald Nixon, through his mother, the saintly Quaker woman Hannah. As collateral, she put up a lot in Whittier valued at $13,000. Hannah then popped $165,000 into Don's company. No one seems to know what happened to the rest of the loan. A few months later the Howard Hughes Medical Foundation was exempted from taxes by the IRS.

Alarmed by these shenanigans, Mr. Dietrich went to Washington on his own to talk sense to Richard Nixon. "He was extremely cordial and showed me around his office, pointing out mementos of his visits to foreign lands" (the verisimilitudinous touch which authenticates). "Then we sat down for a serious talk." Mr. Dietrich talked turkey. " 'If this loan becomes public information, it could mean the end of your political career. And I don't believe that it can be kept quiet.' He [Nixon] responded immediately, perhaps having anticipated what I had said. 'Mr. Dietrich,' he said, 'I have to put my relatives ahead of my career.' Nothing further was said about the subject." Not long after, Don's restaurant failed and the Nixonburger was history.

In 1957 Mr. Dietrich ceased to be privy to Howard Hughes's political donations and so his inside narrative is fifteen years out of date. Are bribes still being paid? We do not know. But we do know that Hughes Aircraft is the Pentagon's twelfth largest contractor, and 90 percent of its $750,000,000 annual sales are to the government. This company, incidentally, is the one entirely owned by the tax-exempt Howard Hughes Medical Institute whose great task is to do research around the country on various diseases, with particular emphasis on the heart. As in most successful Hughes enterprises, the living legend has little to do with the company's management.

Political corruption has been with us since the first congress sat at Philadelphia, and there is nothing to be done about it as long as we are what we are. In fact, as election costs mount the corruption will tend to be institutionalized by the small group of legislators and bankers, generals and industrialists who own and govern the United States, Inc. But it does not take great prescience to realize that they are playing a losing game. As the polity becomes more and more conscious of the moral nullity at the center of American life, there will develop not the revolutionary situation dreamed of in certain radical circles but, rather, a deep contempt for the nation and its institutions, an apathy bound to be exploited by clever human engineers. In the name of saving the environment and restoring virtue, they will continue the dismantling of an unloved and unhonored republic. But then republics are social anomalies, as Thomas Jefferson must have suspected when he claimed to see, off there in the distance, no larger than a Federalist's head, the minatory shape of the despot's crown.

*The New York Review of Books*
April 20, 1972

# RICHARD NIXON:
## NOT THE BEST MAN'S
## BEST MAN

Of all my literary inventions, Richard Nixon is the most nearly autonomous. Like all great literary creations—Beowulf, Gargantua, Little Nell—one does not know what on earth he might do next. When I first invented him as a character called Joe Cantwell in the play and later the movie *The Best Man,* I thought to myself, There! I have done it. For at least a generation I have fixed on the page—or, in this case, on the stage and upon some strips of celluloid—a splendid twentieth-century archetype. But little did I suspect that my invention would suddenly take on a life of its own and that I would be forced to return again and again to this astonishing protean creature whose genius it is to be always the same.

My last major effort was in 1972, when *An Evening with Richard Nixon* was produced on Broadway. But this time my invention did an end run around me, as he would put it in his jock jargon. When the play opened, most of the press had decided to support Nixon's Committee to Re-Elect the President (the acronym was CREEP—remember?), and my revelations about shoe boxes filled with money and break-ins and illegal spying and other high capers were not only premature but they were the one thing that no American journalist can abide—bad taste. In fact, so bad was my taste that an apostle of good taste at *The New*

*York Times* (a paper that is good taste incarnate—and utter refinement, too) said that I had said "mean and nasty things about our President." The apostle was English and did not know that although the sovereign of his native islands is called Our Queen, the emperor of the West is known to us aficionados as The Goddamned President.

Needless to say, I cannot stop following the adventures of my invention . . . *my* invention! He is ours in a way that the queen is not England's, because she was invented by history, while Nixon made himself up, with a lot of help from all of us. As individuals, the presidents are accidental; but as types, they are inevitable and represent, God help us, us. We are Nixon; he is us.

Although hypocrisy has been the name of the American game for most of this century, Nixon's occasional odd bursts of candor are often stunning. Of General Eisenhower, whose despised (by Ike) vice president he was, Nixon wrote in *Six Crises:* "Eisenhower was a far more complex and devious man than most people realized"—a truth not generally known even now. Then comes the inimitable Nixon gloss: Eisenhower was complex and devious "in the best sense of those words."

The Machiavelli of Whittier, California, often says what he means when he means to say something quite different, and that is why one cannot stop listening to him. In Nixon we are able to observe our faults larger than life. But we can also, if we try, see in this huge, dusty mirror our virtues as well. So the time has now come for us to regard the thirty-seventh president in the light, if not of eternity, of the twentieth century, now drawing to its unmourned close.

Currently, in a series of books signed with Nixon's name, he himself is trying to rearrange his place in that long cavalcade of mediocrity—and worse—that has characterized the American presidency since the death of Franklin Roosevelt.

Nixon's chroniclers have their work cut out for them, because he is simply too gorgeous and outsize an American figure for any contemporary to put into a clear perspective. To understand Nixon's career you would have to understand the United States in the twentieth century, and that is something that our educational, political, and media establishments are not about to help us do. After all: no myth, no nation. They have a vested interest in maintaining our ignorance, and that is why we are currently stuck with the peculiar notion that Nixon just happened to be the one bad apple in a splendid barrel. The fact that there has not been a good or serious president since Franklin Roosevelt is ignored, while the fact that Nixon was corrupt some of the time, and complex and devious all of the time, is constantly emphasized in order to make him appear uniquely sleazy—and the rest of us just grand. Yet Nixon is hardly atypical. Certainly his predecessor, Lyndon Johnson, far surpassed Nixon when it came to mendacity and corruption. But the national myth requires, periodically, a scapegoat; hence Nixon's turn in the barrel.

Actually, corruption has been more the rule than the exception in our political life. When Lincoln was obliged to appoint a known crook as secretary of war, he asked a congressman from the appointee's state if he thought that the new cabinet minister would actually steal in office. "Well," said the congressman thoughtfully, "I don't think he'd steal a red-hot stove."

Neither personally nor auctorially did I feel sorry for Nixon during the days of Watergate and his resignation. After all, he was simply acting out his Big Loser nature, and, in the process, he turned being a Big Loser into a perfect triumph by managing to lose the presidency in a way bigger and more original than anyone else had ever lost it before. That takes gumption. No, I only began to feel sorry for him when the late, much-dreaded Fawn M. Brodie, a certifiable fool (of the dead only the truth), wrote one of her pseudo-psychobiographies of him and plowed him under as if he were a mere Thomas Jefferson (a previous victim of her somber art) in pursuit of mulatto nymphets. Enough is enough, I said to myself; do not inflict this Freudian horseshit on Nixon—*my* Nixon.

So let us now praise an infamous man who has done great deeds for his country. The clatter you just heard is that of knives falling on the floor of the American pantheon, where now, with slow and mechanical and ever-so-slightly-out-of-sync tread, the only great president of the last half of the twentieth century moves toward his rightful niche. Future historians—and with some thanks to Nixon, there may even be future historians—will look to Nixon as the first president who acted upon the not-exactly-arcane notion that the United States is just one country among many countries and that communism is an economic and political system without much to recommend it at the moment and with few voluntary adherents.

Simultaneously Nixon realized that coexistence with the Soviet Union is the only game that we can safely play. Nixon also saw the value of exploiting the rift between Russia and China.

In a book called *Leaders,* Nixon praises de Gaulle, from whom he learned two lessons. First, power accrues to the ruler whose actions are unpredictable. Although this tactic might work at a local level for the leader of a minor country, such a system of unexpectedness on the part of the emperor of the West could send what is known euphemistically as the Wrong Signal to the emperor of the East, in which case there would never be enough shovels to protect us from the subsequent nuclear rain. The second—more practical—lesson was in de Gaulle's view that nations are nations, and while political systems come and go, national interests continue for millennia. Like every good and bad American, Nixon knows almost no history of any kind. But he was quick to pick up on the fact that the Russians and the Chinese each have a world view that has nothing at all to do with communism, or whatever happens to be the current official name for Heaven's Mandate.

Nixon proceeded to do the unexpected. He buried the hatchet with the Son of Heaven, Mao, by going to see him—as is proper for the Barbarian from beyond the Four Seas if he wishes to enjoy the patronage of the Lord of the Middle Kingdom. Then, from this position of strength, Nixon paid a call on the Czar of all the Russians, whose mouth, to say the least, was somewhat ajar at what Nixon had done in China. With one stroke, Nixon brought the world's three great powers (all nuclear) into the same plane of communication. There was no precedent for what he had done. Kennedy worshipers point to Kennedy's celebrated we-are-all-in-this-together speech at American University; but Kennedy was a genuine war lover in a way that Nixon was not, despite his locker-room-macho imitation of what he took to be Kennedy's genuine locker-room macho. Actually, neither one ever qualified for the team; they were just a standard pair of weaklings.

Although Nixon is the one who will be remembered for ending, four years too late, the Vietnam War, he is currently obliged to share some of the glory with a curious little man called Henry Kissinger. In the war of the books now going on between Nixon and Kissinger, Kissinger is trying hard to close the fame gap. The Kissinger books give the impression that while Nixon was holed up in the Executive Office Building, swilling martinis and listening to the emetic strains of Richard Rodgers's score for *Victory at Sea,* the American Metternich was leading the free world out of the Valley of the Shadow. But, ultimately, a Kissinger is just a Kissinger, something the burglar uses to jimmy a lock. While Nixon allowed the Vietnam War to drag on for four years, hoping that something would turn up, Kissinger did as he was told.

Even so, if the Kissinger books are to be believed, he was a lot tougher than Nixon when it came to dealing with Hanoi. After the election of

'72, Kissinger tells us, "basically, [Nixon] now wanted the war over on almost any terms. . . . He had a horror of appearing on television to announce that he was beginning his new mandate by once again expanding the war." But Kissinger was made of sterner stuff. Although he praised (to Nixon's face) the Christmas bombing of North Vietnam, he was taking a tougher line than Nixon in negotiations despite "Nixon's brooding disquietude with my new-found celebrity. . . ." Also, Kissinger, being Kissinger, did not want the press to think that he had concurred in the brutal bombing. "I did not indicate to any journalist that I had opposed the decision to use B-52s," he tells us firmly, then adds, "but I also did little to dampen the speculation, partly in reaction to the harassment of the previous weeks, partly out of a not very heroic desire to deflect the assault from my person."

Meanwhile, Nixon quotes from his diary at the time the decision to bomb was made: "Henry talked rather emotionally about the fact that this was a very courageous decision. . . ." Later, when the war ran out of gas, the diarist reports: ". . . I told [Kissinger] that the country was indebted to him for what he had done. It is not really a comfortable thing for me to praise people so openly. . . . On the other hand, Henry expects it. . . . He, in turn, responded that without my having the, as he puts it, courage to make the difficult decision of December 18th, we would not be where we are today."

The unsatisfactory end to the most unsatisfactory and pointless war in American history will be, like Kissinger himself, a footnote to a presidency that will be remembered for the bold initiative to China combined with a degree of détente with the Soviet Union.

Today we are all of us in Nixon's debt for seizing an opportunity (*ignore his motives: the world is governed by deeds, not motives*) in order to make sense of close to one third of a century of dangerous nonsense.

Finally, I am happy to say that the ever-restless householder of Saddle River, New Jersey, continues to surprise. In the spring of last year he addressed a fund-raising event at the Disneyland Hotel, in Orange County, California. For the right-wingers present, he was obliged to do a bit of the Russians-are-coming; then he made absolute sense.

"The Soviet Union needs a deal," Nixon said. "And we should give them one. But for a price." Noting that the West has a five-to-one edge in economic power over the Soviets, Nixon said that this advantage should be used as an "economic lever." Because "simply to have a program that would lead to a balance of nuclear terror is not enough. We must try to add to that a new dimension of the use of America's and the free world's economic power as both a carrot and a stick." Predictably, the press did not pick up on any of this, but history will; and since we are all of us Nixon and he is us, the fact that he went to Peking and Moscow in order to demonstrate to all the world the absolute necessity of coexistence proves that there is not only good in him but in us as well—hope, too.

*Esquire*
December 1983

# HOMAGE TO
# DANIEL SHAYS

To govern is to choose how the revenue raised from taxes is spent. So far so good, or bad. But some people earn more money than others. Should they pay proportionately more money to the government than those who earn less? And if they do pay more money are they entitled to more services than those who pay less or those who pay nothing at all? And should those who pay nothing at all because they have nothing get anything? These matters are of irritable concern to our rulers, and of some poignancy to the rest.

Although the equality of each citizen before the law is the rock upon which the American Constitution rests, economic equality has never been an American ideal. In fact, it is the one unmentionable subject in our politics, as the Senator from South Dakota recently discovered when he came up with a few quasi-egalitarian tax reforms. The furious and enduring terror of communism in America is not entirely the work of those early cold warriors Truman and Acheson. A dislike of economic equality is something deep-grained in the American Protestant character. After all, given a rich empty continent for vigorous Europeans to exploit (the Indians were simply a disagreeable part of the emptiness, like chiggers), any man of gumption could make himself a good living. With extra hard work, any man could make himself a fortune, proving that he was a better man than the rest. Long before Darwin the American ethos was Darwinian.

The vision of the rich empty continent is still a part of the American unconscious in spite of the Great Crowding and its attendant miseries; and this lingering belief in the heaven any man can make for himself through hard work and clean living is a key to the majority's prevailing and apparently unalterable hatred of the poor, kept out of sight at home, out of mind abroad.

Yet there has been, from the beginning, a significant division in our ruling class. The early Thomas Jefferson had a dream: a society of honest yeomen, engaged in agricultural pursuits, without large cities, heavy industry, banks, military pretensions. The early (and the late) Alexander Hamilton wanted industry, banks, cities, and a military force capable of making itself felt in world politics. It is a nice irony that so many of today's laissez-faire conservatives think that they descend from Hamilton, the proponent of a strong federal government, and that so many liberals believe themselves to be the heirs of the early Jefferson, who wanted little more than a police force and a judiciary. Always practical, Jefferson knew that certain men would rise through their own good efforts while, sadly, others would fall. Government would do no more than observe this Darwinian spectacle benignly, and provide no succor.

In 1800 the Hamiltonian view was rejected by the people and their new President Thomas Jefferson. Four years later, the Hamiltonian view had prevailed and was endorsed by the reelected Jefferson. "We are all Hamiltonians now!" he might have exclaimed had he the grace of the Thirty-Seventh President, whose progress from moth to larva on so many issues gives delight. Between 1800 and 1805 Jefferson had seen to it that an empire *in posse* had become an empire *in esse*. The difference between Jefferson I and Jefferson II is reflected in the two inaugural addresses.

First Inaugural: "a wise and frugal government, which shall restrain men from injuring one another, which shall leave them otherwise free to regulate their own pursuit of industry and improvement, and shall not take from the mouth of labor the bread it has earned. This is the sum of good government. . . ." In other words, no taxes beyond a minimal levy in order to pay for a few judges, a postal service, small executive and legislative bodies.

Second Inaugural: Jefferson II was now discussing the uses to which taxes might be put (once the national debt was paid off, oh Presidential chimera!), "*In time of peace,* to rivers, canals, roads, arts, manufactures, education, and other great objects within each State. *In time of war*—if injustice, *by ourselves*" (those italics, irresistibly, mine) "or others, must sometimes produce war. . . . War will be but a suspension of useful works. . . ." The idea of the rich empty continent best exploited by men unbugged by a central government had now been succeeded by the notion that government ought to pitch in and help with those roads and schools, but of course that's going to take money, so taxes must be raised to pay for these good things which benefit us all equally, don't they?

It is significant that nothing more elevated than greed changed the Dr. Jekyll of Jefferson I into the Mr. Hyde of Jefferson II. Like his less thoughtful countrymen, Jefferson could not resist a deal. Subverting the Constitution he had helped create, Jefferson bought Louisiana from Napoleon, acquiring its citizens without their consent; he then proceeded to govern them as if they had been conquered, all the while secretly—comically—maneuvering, by hook or by crook, to bag the Floridas. The author of the Declaration of Independence was quite able to forget the unalienable rights of anyone whose property he thought should be joined to our empire—a word which crops up frequently and unselfconsciously in his correspondence.

In the course of land-grabbing, Jefferson II managed to get himself into hot water with France, England, and Spain simultaneously, a fairly astonishing thing to do considering the state of politics in Napoleonic Europe. But then war is bound to result if you insist on liberating vast tracts of land from colonial nations as well as from home-grown Indians (they were equal to whites, Jefferson thought, in spite of their bad habits, but different from the hopeless black races which had started out white but then, in the unwholesome African climate, contracted a form of leprosy; enlightened optimists like Jefferson's friend the learned Dr. Rush were certain that advanced dermatology would one day restore to these dark peoples their lost prettiness). The result of this finagling was a series of panicky appropriations for the navy and the creation of the American military machine which in the last fiscal year cost us honest yeomen 75.8 billion dollars out of a total of 126 billion dollars paid in personal and corporate income taxes. Forever forgotten was the wisdom of Jefferson I: "Sound principles will not justify our taxing the industry of our fellow citizens to accumulate treasure for wars to happen we know not when, and which might not perhaps happen but from the temptation offered by that treasure."

It is a tribute to the Protestant passion for wanting always to appear to be doing good (particularly when one is robbing the till) that Americans have been constitutionally incapable (*double entendre* intended) of recognizing the truth about themselves or anyone else. Mixing his metaphors, celebrating the empire electric, appealing to the god Demos whose agent he thought himself to be, Jefferson II so clouded over our innate imperialism that we cannot to this day recognize the nature of American society, even as our bombs murder strangers (admittedly leprous) 8,000 miles away. Fortunately, the empire has taken such a shellacking in the last few years that critics (not yet loved) are being listened to at last, and it is now unlikely that even a yeomanry so constantly and deliberately misinformed from kindergarten days to wrap-up time in the Forest Lawn Slumber Room will ever allow another president the fun of destroying someone else's country in the name of Jefferson I self-determination. As the empire falls apart, things may yet come together again in a good—or at least more realistic—way.

To make sense of our situation a simple question must be asked. Why do we allow our governors to take so much of our money and spend it in ways that not only fail to benefit us but do great damage to others as we prosecute undeclared wars—which even our brainwashed majority has come to see are a bad proposition because of the cost of maintaining a vast military machine, not to mention a permanent draft of young men (an Un-American activity if there ever was one) in what is supposed to be peacetime? Whether he knows it or not, the middle-income American is taxed as though he were living in a socialist society. But for the money he gives the government he gets almost nothing back. He does pay for a lot of military hardware, and his congressman will point to all the jobs "defense" (that happy euphemism) contracts bring to his district, as if the same federal money could not create even more jobs doing things that need doing as well as benefiting directly the man who paid the taxes in the first place. Ultimate irony, the middle American still tends to believe that he is living in a Jefferson I society when, in fact, he has been for some decades in a Jefferson II world, allowing an imperial-minded elite to tax him in order to wage a holy war against something called communism.

Fortunately, there are now signs that they don't make suckers like that any more. The taxpayers' revolt has begun. A dislike of all politicians is in the land. Word is out that the rich don't pay as much, proportionately, to maintain their empire as do the middle-income people. They hate socialism and communism and all the things good people are supposed to hate, but they are also beginning to wonder just why they have to give up so much of their income to fight those very same Commies Nixon likes to dine with in Peking and Moscow.

The fact is that our present governors are not very bright, and this may be our salvation. In 1968 they absent-mindedly gave us a president whose schizophrenic behavior and prose style ("This is *not* an invasion of Cambodia") is creepily apparent to even the most woolly-headed yeoman. Now three new books provide useful information about the small group who own the United States, how our economic and foreign policies are manipulated, how members of Congress are bought, how presidential candidates are selected and financed.

The mold that cast the mind of C. Wright Mills was not broken at his flesh's departure. Another such mind was promptly cast and labeled G. William Domhoff (those first initials and middle names are reminiscent of a generation of three-named Episcopalian clergymen). A Mills disciple, Domhoff has published *Who Rules America?* (1967) and *The Higher Circle* (1970). The subjects of those books are exactly what their titles suggest. Domhoff has now written another illuminating treatise called *Fat Cats and Democrats: The Role of the Big Rich in the Party of the Common Man.*

Domhoff's thesis is straightforward. The country is governed by a small elite which knows pretty much what it is up to and coordinates its various moves in foreign affairs and the economy. Most academics dispute this theory. They tend to be Jefferson I types who believe that the United States is a pluralist society filled with all sorts of dominations and powers constantly balancing and checking one another. To them, anyone who believes that an elite is really running the show is paranoid. But as the late Delmore Schwartz once said with the weary lucidity of his own rich madness, "Paranoids have real enemies, too." Admittedly, it is difficult at first to accept the proposition that the owners of the country also rule it and that the electorate is nothing but a quadrennial chorus whose function is to ratify with hosannahs one or the other of two presidential candidates carefully picked for them by rulers who enjoy pretending that ours is really government of, by, and for the you-know-who. In the same manner, Tiberius always respectfully consulted a Senate to whose irrelevant ranks his heir nicely added a racehorse.

Domhoff's style does not command admiration. His manner is disconcertingly gee whiz. He is given to easy liberal epithets like "Godforsaken Mississippi" yet forced to admit that except on the subject of race, the proud folk down there are populist to the core, and populist is the thing to be this year. But if one is not put off by the somewhat slap-dash manner, Domhoff has seen and measured the tip of an iceberg which most of the other passengers on the US *Titanic* have not noticed. He also does his best to figure out what lies beneath the water.

Domhoff's method is to examine those committees and advisory councils, federal and private, that do the actual work of making foreign and economic policy (something like three-quarters of the federal budget has to do with military and foreign aid expenditures—control the spending of that three-quarters and the US is your thing). He then studies the men who serve on these committees. Notes what schools they went to, what banks they work for (most are lawyers or lawyer-bankers), what political contributions they make. He also records the overlapping that goes on, or "linkage" as the American Metternich would say.

In 1968, for instance, 51 of 284 trustees and honorary trustees of the Committee for Economic Development were also members of the Council on Foreign Relations, while 126 were members of the National Council of the Foreign Policy Association. Or as Domhoff puts it,

Policy formation is the province of a bipartisan power elite of corporate rich [Rockefeller, Mellon] and their career hirelings [Nixon, McNamara] who work through an interlocking and overlapping maze of foundations, universities and institutes, discussion groups, associations and commissions. Political parties are only for finding interesting and genial people [usually ambitious middle-class lawyers] to ratify and implement these policies in such a way that the under classes feel themselves to be, somehow, a part of the governmental process. Politics is not exactly the heart of the action but it is nice work—if you can afford to campaign for it.

If Domhoff's thesis is even partly true (and at least one skeptic is persuaded that it is) much of the malaise one detects among intelligent members of the Senate and House is understandable. It is not so much the removal of power from the Hill to the White House (a resourceful Congress can still break a president if they want, or at least bring him to heel); rather, it is the knowledge or suspicion that the legislative branch reflects not the electorate but the elite who pay for congressional campaigns and are duly paid off with agreeable tax laws and military procurement and foreign aid bills passed at the dark of the moon. There is a constant if gentle tugging of the reins—perhaps Caligula had the right idea about what a proper senator should be. "We don't seem to matter at all," said one East Coast senator to me some years ago. "And

I don't know why. We're every bit as bright or brighter than the Borah–La Follette group. But we're just . . . well, nothing." Domhoff agrees and tells us why.

In *Fat Cats and Democrats,* Domhoff describes our rulers. Year in, year out, "About one percent of the population—a socially interacting upper class whose members go to prep schools, attend debutante balls, join exclusive clubs, ride to hounds and travel all over the world for business or pleasure—will continue to own 60 percent to 70 percent of all privately held corporate wealth and receive 24 percent of the national income." Domhoff tends to be a bit wide-eyed about the life-style of the nobles but, barring those riders to hounds, he seldom indulges in the sort of solemn generality recently dished up by a sociologist who discovered that most American banking is controlled by the Wasps (true) and that the Wasps at the top of the banking hierarchy have larger and fleshier ears than those farther down (true?).

Domhoff accepts the Ferdinand Lundberg formulation that there is only one political party in the United States and that is the Property Party, whose Republican wing tends to be rigid in maintaining the status quo and not given to any accommodation of the poor and the black. Although the Democratic wing shares most of the basic principles (that is to say, money) of the Republicans, its members are often shrewd enough to know that what is too rigid will shatter under stress. The Democrats have also understood for some time the nature of the American empire. While the Republicans indulge in Jefferson I rhetoric and unrealities, including isolationism, the Democrats have known all along that this is a Jefferson II world. As Dean Acheson put it in 1947, "You must look to foreign markets." As early as 1928 a distinguished member of the Republican wing of the Property Party saw its limitations. After all, Averell Harriman was involved in German zinc mines, Polish iron mines, and Soviet manganese. "I thought Republican isolationism was disastrous." And just before the 1929 crash, he switched.

But essentially the two wings of the Property Party are more alike than not. Witness the bipartisan foreign policy which the elite hammered out twenty-five years ago over the dead bodies of the Republican faithful. The Property Party has known from the beginning how and when to reconcile its two wings in order to survive. After all, according to Domhoff,

The American Constitution was carefully rigged by the noteholders, land speculators, rum runners, and slave holders who were the Founding Fathers, so that it would be next to impossible for upstart dirt farmers and indebted masses to challenge the various forms of private property held by these well read robber barons. Through this Constitution, the over-privileged attempted to rule certain topics out of order for proper political discussion. To bring these topics up in polite company was to invite snide invective, charges of personal instability, or financial ruin.

In other words, don't start a political party in opposition to the Property Party. From Henry Wallace's Progressive Party, so viciously smeared by the liberal ADA, to today's sad attempt to field a People's Party, those who wish to promote economic equality should not be surprised to have their heads handed to them, particularly by a "free" press which refuses to recognize any alternative to the way things are.

Property is power, as those Massachusetts veterans of the revolution discovered when they joined Captain Daniel Shays in his resistance to the landed gentry's replacement of a loose confederation of states with a tax-levying central government. The veterans thought that they had been fighting a war for true independence. They did not want London to be replaced by New York. They did want an abolition of debts and a division of property. Their rebellion was promptly put down. But so shaken was the elite by the experience that their most important (and wealthiest) figure grimly emerged from private life with a letter to Harry Lee. "You talk of employing influence," wrote George Washington, "to appease the present tumults in Massachusetts. I know not where that influence is to be found, or if attainable, that it would be a proper remedy for the disorders. *Influence* is no *government.* Let us have one by which our lives, liberties and properties will be secured or let us know the worst at once." So was born the Property Party and with it the Constitution of the United States. We have known the "best" for nearly 200 years. What would the "worst" have been like?

The rulers of the country are, according to Domhoff, 80 percent to 90 percent Republican. For the most part they are not isolationist. They know that money is to be made overseas either from peace or war, from the garrison state and its attendant machismo charms. Who then supports the Democratic wing? Labor is responsible for 20 percent to 25 percent of the party's financing. Racketeers from 10 percent to 15 percent—obviously certain areas like New York, Chicago, and Las Vegas interest these entrepreneurs more than, say, the Good Government League of Bangor, Maine. Around 15 percent is contributed by the "little man." The rest comes from the fat cats. Who are they? And why do they give money to the wrong wing of the Property Party?

Domhoff rather coldbloodedly divides these perverse investors into two groups. Sentimental liberals—usually from rich families, reacting against Dad's Republicanism, and status seekers among new-money Jews and Catholics with some Texas oilmen thrown in. Yet the margin of action, like that of debate, is deliberately limited by the conservative as well as the reactionary wing of the Property Party. Or as Domhoff puts it, the elite Republicans "must accommodate the reactionaries just enough to keep them from forming an ultra-conservative party, just as it is the task of the wealthy moderate Democrats to assimilate or crush any sanguine liberals who try to stray through the left boundary of the sacred two-party system."

An uneasy alliance of Jewish bankers and Texas oilmen has financed most of the Democratic Party. Yet this Jewish-cowboy axis (Domhoff's phrase), powerful and rich though it is, represents only a small, moderately lunatic fringe to the sturdy fabric of the ruling class. They are the sports who give us Democratic presidential candidates guaranteed to speak of change and different deals while altering nothing. But then how could they change anything and still get the money to buy television spots?

Interestingly enough, Domhoff does not think that the Nixon Southern strategy has a chance of working at the congressional or local level. The South tends to be hawkish and racist—two chords the incumbent Property Party manager knows how to pluck. But the South is not about to support a party which is against federal spending. Nine Rehnquists would not be anywhere near enough to counterbalance the Southward flow of money from Treasury through the conduit of Southern Democratic Congressional leaders who have employed the seniority system to reverse that bad trip at the Appomattox Courthouse. They govern the House in tandem with machine Democrats from the North. Each takes in the other's washing. The Northerners get a few housing bills out of the Southerners, who in turn are granted military bases and agricultural subsidies. Both groups are devoted to keeping the Property Party prosperous and the money where it belongs, in the hands of the elite. Southern Democrats are not about to join with Nixon's true-blue Republicans in turning off federal aid.

At the congressional level, one can see how the elite works even more clearly than at the presidential level, where enthusiasm for attractive candidates often blinds even the sharpest critic (not to mention, very often, the candidate himself) to the charade being enacted by the Property Party. It is in the House and the Senate that the day-by-day dirty work is done, and Bella Abzug gives a splendid account *(Bella!)* of her two years in the House, trying to represent her constituents and her conscience, to the amusement of a genial body of corrupt politicians whose votes are all too often for sale to the highest bidder, usually in the form of cash in white envelopes, if Robert N. Winter-Berger's astonishing book *The Washington Pay-Off* is to be believed. With these two books, one ideological, the other muckraking, the bankruptcy of the House of Representatives has been duly filed.

Bella Abzug was elected from Lower Manhattan to end the war, gain equal rights for women and blacks, and generally be herself, serving the unpropertied. A bright lawyer as well as a formidable self-publicist, she immediately struck the fancy of the press (when they get her full range, she will be dropped—tense?). All in all, Abzug rather likes the floor managers of the Property Party. They are good fun and she always knows where she stands with them. "The men in the Club here are very charming to me," which they can afford to be since "they have all the power." They even "like to be entertained a bit. I don't mean in a ha-ha funny way, but in an interesting way." It is the liberals for whom she has real contempt. They have fallen for "the old crap, the anaesthesia of the liberals: If you want to get along, you've got to go along . . . very little men." They would rather fight one another for such posts as House Majority leader than unite to keep a reactionary from continuing in that job.

For five years (1964 to 1969) Mr. Winter-Berger was a Washington lobbyist, engaged in getting favors done for a wide range of people. Nathan Voloshen was his principle contact. This extraordinary man had known Representative John W. McCormack since 1945. In 1962, McCormack became Speaker of the House and Voloshen's "public relations" career soared. For use of the Speaker's opulent office in the Capitol, Voloshen paid McCormack $2,500 a month rent, a small amount considering the address. As clients came and went, the Speaker would assure them, "Nat can take care of that for you. Nat's my dear friend and I will do anything I can for him. Any friend of Nat's is a friend of mine." In one form or another, this speech is the ancient Washington formula to indicate that things will be done if you pay the price.

Eventually, Voloshen and company were nabbed by the embarrassingly honest Property Party maverick, US Attorney Robert Morgenthau. Voloshen pleaded guilty. At the trial of one of Voloshen's henchmen,

McCormack pleaded ignorance which, according to the 1925 House Code of Ethics Act, made him innocent. Rather ludicrously, on the stand,

McCormack said: "I am not an inquiring fellow." Actually, if ever a man always knew precisely what was going on around him it was John McCormack.

Mr. Winter-Berger also tells us that he was present in the Speaker's office when Lyndon Johnson sailed in and, thinking the Speaker was alone, began a tirade with, "John, that son of a bitch is going to ruin me. If that cocksucker talks, I'm gonna land in jail." Apparently the President did not want his former Senate aide, Bobby Baker, to contest certain charges brought against him. "I will give him a million dollars if he takes the rap," said Johnson.

It is no wonder that most newspapers and magazines have refused to review this book and that many bookstores will not sell it. The fear is not of libel. Something much more elemental is involved. If the corruption and greed of the men the Property Party has placed in the Congress and the White House become common knowledge, the whole rotten business could very well collapse and property itself would be endangered. Had there actually been a two-party system in the United States, the incoming President would have taken advantage of such an extraordinary scandal in the Democratic ranks. Instead, Nixon moved swiftly to remove Robert Morgenthau from office. If there is one thing Nixon understands, it is dominoes. Or as Mr. Winter-Berger puts it,

At the time, Voloshen said to me: "Mitchell is afraid that if any of the Congressmen are found guilty, the whole public image of the Congress would be destroyed." Voloshen also told me about the proviso which Attorney General Mitchell added to his offer to drop the case against Frenkil [Voloshen's pal]: House Speaker John McCormack would have to resign from Congress. Knowing how much McCormack loved his job and his life in the world of politics, I didn't think such a powerful man would go along. But in fact he did.

Yet the personal enrichment of congressmen and their friends is small potatoes compared to the way the great corporations use the government and its money for their own ends. The recent ITT comedy was just one example—and hardly investigated by the Property Party men in the Senate. The press also plays its supporting role. Mr. Winter-Berger notes that the Bobby Baker scandal became big news with suspicious slowness. "Having been filed in the court records, information about the suit should have been available immediately to any newspaper reporter, but it took the Washington *Post* three days to find out about it and break the story." This was September 12, 1963. *The New York Times* did not think this news fit to print until October 5, and then buried it on page 19. Not until Bobby Baker resigned three days later, did he make the front page of the *Times.*

But then, as Domhoff has remarked, few substantive matters are considered fit for open discussion in our society. Every president is honest because he is our president and we are honest. An occasional congressman may fall from grace because there are always a few rotten apples in every barrel, but the majority are straightshooters. The Congress represents all the interests of the people, at least district by district and state by state. *The New York Times* will always call the shots if there is any funny business anywhere. Just as they will always support the best "liberal" candidate (Abzug has a nice horror story about how the *Times* killed a piece on her because it was too favorable). These threadbare myths sustain us. But for how much longer?

After the burning of Newark, the elite wondered, some more reluctantly than others, what might be next for burning if they did not appear to pay off the poor and/or black. To the amazement of the innocent, the Nixon Administration came up with a family income plan for the poor which was favored (fathered?) by the Council for Economic Development. The council then set out to sell the plan to the Right Wing. Predictably, Ronald Reagan was opposed because of a "philosophical antipathy" which he thought reflected the prejudices of his constituency. A number of the council's leaders swiftly materialized in San Francisco and proceeded to instruct the public in the virtues of the plan. They stressed that not only businessmen but *experts* favored it. Even Democrats thought it sound. Gently chiding Reagan, they sold the program to California's media and public in a bipartisan way. The Property Party has no intention of actually putting this plan into effect, of course, but at least they now have something nice to talk about when the poor are restive. The fact that McGovern acts as if he might implement the plan has caused alarm.

Recently (June 18) one of the CED's members, Herbert Stein, now chairman of the President's Council of Economic Advisers, gave us the elite's latest view of McGovern's tax reforms. "All such plans count on the willingness of the non-poor to give money to the poor. There has to be such willingness because the non-poor greatly outnumber the poor and dominate the political process." Elegant sophistry. The not-so-poor do outnumber the poor but if the not-so-poor who are nicked heavily

by taxes were to join with the poor they would outnumber the elite by
99 to 1. The politician who can forge that alliance will find himself, at
best, the maker of a new society; at worst, in a hole at Arlington.

To maintain its grip on the nation, the Property Party must keep
actual issues out of political debate. So far they have succeeded marvelously well. Faced with unemployment, Nixon will oppose abortion.
Inflation? Marijuana is a halfway house to something worse. The bombing of North Vietnam? Well, pornographers are using the mailing lists
of Cub Scouts. Persuading the people to vote against their own best
interests has been the awesome genius of the American political elite
from the beginning.

It will be interesting to see what happens to George McGovern.
Appealing to the restive young, he came up with a number of tax
reforms which threatened to alter the foundation of the Property Party.
The result was a terrible squawking from the Alsops and the Restons.
We were told that McGovern is the Goldwater of the left (a good joke
since Goldwater represented the reactionary country club minority
while McGovern would represent the not-so-poor to poor majority), but
then any hack journalist knows that his ink-drugged readers will not
stand for pot, abortion, amnesty. Now that McGovern is the candidate
they have decided that he is, thank God, a pragmatist (i.e. a Property
Party opportunist) and so will move where the votes are and where you
can bet your sweet ass the Sulzbergers and Schiffs, the Luces and Gra-
hams are.

With each passing day, McGovern will more and more come to
resemble a Property Party candidate. This is fair enough, if not good
enough. But what happens when he is elected? Then we will know—too
late, I fear—to what extent he was simply exploiting the people's deep
inchoate hatred of the Property Party in order to become that Party's
loyal manager. This would be sad because 1972 could have been the year
for a counterparty or for a transformation of the Democratic wing of
the Property Party. But barring catastrophe (in the form of home-grown
apple-pie fascism), the early response to McGovern (and Wallace, too)
is the first indication we have had that there now exists a potential
American majority willing to see its best interests served not through
the restrictive Constitution of the elite but through the egalitarian vision
of Daniel Shays and his road not taken—yet.

*The New York Review of Books*
August 10, 1972

# 83

---•---

# THE STATE
# OF THE UNION:
# 1975

"How can you say such awful things about America when *you live in Italy*?" Whenever I go on television, I hear that plangent cry. From vivacious Barbara Walters of the *Today* show (where I was granted six minutes to comment on last November's elections) to all the other vivacious interviewers across this great land of ours, the question of my residency is an urgent matter that must be mentioned as soon as possible so that no one will take seriously a single word that that awful person has to say about what everybody knows is not only the greatest country in the history of the world but a country where vivacious Barbara Walters et al. can make a very pretty penny peddling things that people don't need. "So if you no liva here," as sly fun-loving Earl Butz might say, "you no maka da wisecracks."

Usually I ignore the vivacious challenge: the single statement on television simply does not register; only constant repetition penetrates . . . witness, the commercials. Yet on occasions, when tired, I will rise to the bait. Point out that I pay full American income tax—50 percent of my earned income contributes to the support of the Pentagon's General Brown, statesman/soldier and keen student of the Protocols of the Elders of Zion. Remind one and all that I do spend a good part of my time in the land of the free, ranging up and down the countryside for months at a time discussing the state of the union with conservative audiences (no use talking to the converted), and in the process I manage to see more of the country than your average television vivacity ever does. In fact, I know more about the relative merits of the far-flung Holiday Inns than anyone who is not a traveling salesman or a presidential candidate.

Last fall I set out across the country, delivering pretty much the same commentary on the state of the union that I have been giving for several years, with various topical additions, subtractions. In one four-week period I gave fifteen lectures, starting with the Political Union at Yale and then on to various colleges and town forums in New York, New Jersey, West Virginia, Nebraska, Missouri, Michigan, Washington, Oregon, California . . .

October 29. Bronxville, New York. A woman's group. Ten-thirty in the morning in a movie house where Warhol's *Frankenstein* was playing. Suitable, I decide. In the men's room is a life-size dummy of a corpse that usually decorates the lobby. Creative management.

Fairly large audience—five, six hundred. Very conservative—abortion equals euthanasia. Watergate? What about Chappaquiddick? Our dialectic would not cause Plato to green with Attic envy.

I stack the cards of my text on the lectern. Full light on me. Audience in darkness. Almost as restful as the creative stillness of a television studio. I feel an intimacy with the camera that I don't with live audiences. Had I played it differently I might have been the electronic Norman Thomas, or George Brent.

I warn the audience: "I shall have to refer to notes." Actually, I read. Could never memorize anything. No matter how many times I give the same speech, the words seem new to me . . . like Eisenhower in 1952: "If elected in November," the Great Golfer read dutifully from a text plainly new to him. "I will go to . . . *Korea?*" The voice and choler rose on the word "Korea." No one had told him about the pledge. But go to Korea he did, resentfully.

I reassure the audience that from time to time I will look up from my notes, "in order to give an air of spontaneity." Get them laughing early. And often. Later the mood will be quite grim out there as I say things not often said in this great land of ours where the price of freedom is eternal discretion.

For some minutes, I improvise. Throw out lines. Make them laugh. I've discovered that getting a laugh is more a trick of timing than of true wit (true wit seldom provokes laughter; rather the reverse). I tell them that although I mean to solve most of the problems facing the United States in twenty-seven minutes—the time it takes to read my prepared text (question time then lasts half an hour, longer if one is at a college and speaking in the evening), I will not touch on the number one problem facing the country—the failing economy (this is disingenuous: politics is the art of collecting and spending money and everything I say is political). "I leave to my friend Ken Galbraith the solving of the depression." If they appear to know who Galbraith is, I remark how curious it is that his fame is based on two books, *The Liberal Hour,* published just as the right-wing Nixon criminals hijacked the presidency, and *The Affluent Society,* published shortly before we went broke. Rueful laughter.

I begin the text. Generally the light is full in one's eyes while the lectern is so low that the faraway words blur on my cards. I crouch; squint. My heart sinks as flash bulbs go off and cameras click: my second chin is not particularly noticeable when viewed straight on but from below it has recently come to resemble Hubert Humphrey's bull-frog swag. Do I dare to wear a scarf? Or use metal clamps to tuck the loose skin up behind the ears like a certain actress who appeared in a television play of mine years ago? No. Let the flesh fall to earth in full public view. Soldier on. Start to read.

"According to the polls, our second principal concern today is the breakdown of law and order. Now, to the right wing, law and order is often just a code phrase meaning 'get the niggers.' To the left wing it often means political oppression. When we have one of our ridiculous elections—ridiculous because they are about nothing at all except personalities—politicians declare a war on crime which is immediately forgotten after the election."

I have never liked this beginning and so I usually paraphrase. Shift lines about. Remark that in the recent Presidential election (November 7, 1972) 45 percent of the people chose not to vote. "They aren't apathetic, just disgusted. There is no choice."

Sometimes, if I'm not careful, I drift prematurely into my analysis of the American political system: there is only one party in the United States, the Property party (thank you, Dr. Lundberg, for the phrase) and it has two wings: Republican and Democrat. Republicans are a bit stupider, more rigid, more doctrinaire in their laissez-faire capitalism than the Democrats, who are cuter, prettier, a bit more corrupt—until recently (nervous laugh on that)—and more willing than the Republicans to make small adjustments when the poor, the black, the anti-imperialists get out of hand. But, essentially, there is no difference between the two parties. Those who gave Nixon money in '68 also gave money to Humphrey.

Can one expect any change from either wing of the Property party? No. Look at McGovern. In the primaries he talked about tax reform and economic equality . . . or something close to it. For a while it looked as if he was nobly preparing to occupy a long box at Arlington. But then he was nominated for president and he stopped talking about anything important. Was he insincere in the primaries? I have no idea. I suspect he was just plain dumb, not realizing that if you speak of economic justice or substantial change you won't get the forty million dollars a Democratic candidate for president needs in order to pay for exposure on television where nothing of any real importance may be said. Remember Quemoy? and her lover Matsu?

Once I get into this aria, I throw out of kilter the next section. Usually I do the Property party later on. Or in the questions and answers. Or not at all. One forgets. Thinks one has told Kansas City earlier in the evening what, in fact, one said that morning in Omaha.

Back to law and order.

"An example: roughly eighty percent of police work in the United States has to do with the regulation of our private morals. By that I mean, controlling what we drink, eat, smoke, put into our veins—not to mention trying to regulate with whom and how we have sex, with whom and how we gamble. As a result, our police are among the most corrupt in the Western world."

Nervous intake of breath on this among women's groups. Some laughter at the colleges. Glacial silence at Atlantic City. Later I was told, "We've got a lot of very funny sort of element around here . . . you know, from Philadelphia, originally. Uh . . . like Italian." I still don't know quite what was meant.

"Not only are police on the take from gamblers, drug pushers, pimps, but they find pretty thrilling their mandate to arrest prostitutes or anyone whose sexual activities have been proscribed by a series of state legal codes that are the scandal of what we like to call a free society. These codes are very old of course. The law against sodomy goes back fourteen hundred years to the Emperor Justinian, who felt that there should be such a law because, as everyone knew, sodomy was a principal cause of earthquake."

"Sodomy" gets them. For elderly, good-hearted audiences I paraphrase; the word is not used. College groups get a fuller discussion of

Justinian and his peculiar law, complete with quotations from Procopius. California audiences living on or near the San Andreas fault laugh the loudest—and the most nervously. No wonder.

"Cynically one might allow the police their kinky pleasures in busting boys and girls who attract them, not to mention their large incomes from the Mafia and other criminal types, *if* the police showed the slightest interest in the protection of persons and property, which is why we have hired them. Unhappily for us, the American police have little interest in crime. If anything, they respect the criminal rather more than they do the hapless citizen who has just been mugged or ripped off.

"Therefore, let us remove from the statute books all laws that have to do with *private* morals—what are called victimless crimes. If a man or woman wants to be a prostitute that is his or her affair. It is no business of the state what we do with our bodies sexually. Obviously laws will remain on the books for the prevention of rape and the abuse of children, while the virtue of our animal friends will continue to be protected by the S.P.C.A."

Relieved laughter at this point. He can't be serious . . . or is he?

"Let us end the vice squad. What a phrase! It is vice to go to bed with someone you are not married to or someone of your own sex or to get money for having sex with someone who does not appeal to you—incidentally, the basis of half the marriages of my generation."

Astonished laughter at this point from middle-aged women . . . and by no means women liberationists. I speak only to, as far as I am able, conservative middle-class audiences off the beaten track—Parkersburg, West Virginia; Medford, Oregon; Longview, Washington. If the women respond well, I improvise; make a small play: "Marvin may not be handsome but he'll be a *good provider* . . . and so Marion walks down the aisle a martyr to money." Encouraging that "nice" women are able to acknowledge their predicament openly. I got no such response five years ago.

"Let us make gambling legal. Those who want to lose their money gambling should have every right to do so. The principal objectors to legalized gambling are the Mafia and the police. *They* will lose money. Admittedly a few fundamentalist Christians will be distressed by their neighbors' gambling, but that is a small price to pay for the increased revenue to the cities, states and federal government, not to mention a police force which would no longer be corrupted by organized crime.

"All drugs should be legalized and sold at cost to anyone with a doctor's prescription."

Intake of breath at this point. Is *he* a drug addict? Probably. Also, varying degrees of interest in the subject, depending on what part of the country you are in. Not much interest in Longview because there is no visible problem. But the college towns are alert to the matter as are those beleaguered subs close to the major urbs.

"For a quarter of a century we have been brainwashed by the Bureau of Narcotics, a cancer in the body politic that employs many thousands of agents and receives vast appropriations each year in order to play cops and robbers. And sometimes the cops we pay for turn out to be themselves robbers or worse. Yet for all the legal and illegal activities of the Bureau the use of drugs is still widespread. But then if drugs were entirely abolished thousands of agents would lose their jobs, and that would be unthinkable."

Around in here I take to discussing the findings of one doctor who had recently appeared on television warning of the perils of pot. Apparently too much pot smoking will enlarge the breasts of young males (Myra Breckinridge would have had a lot to say on this subject but I may not) while reducing their fertility. I say, "Isn't this *wonderful*?" using a Nixon intonation; and recommend that we get all the males in the country immediately on pot. The women laugh happily; a sort of pill for the male has always been their dream. Equality at last.

I play around with the idea of Southern senators doing television commercials, pushing the local product: "Get your high with Carolina Gold." I imitate Strom Thurmond, puffing happily.

"How would legalization work? Well, if heroin was sold at cost in a drugstore it would come to about fifty cents a fix—to anyone with a doctor's prescription. Is this a good thing? I hear the immediate response: Oh, God, every child in America will be hooked. But will they? Why do the ones who get hooked get hooked? They are encouraged to take drugs by the pushers who haunt the playgrounds of the cities. But if the drugs they now push can be bought openly for very little money then the pushers will cease to push.

"Legalization will also remove the Mafia and other big-time drug dispensers from the scene, just as the repeal of Prohibition eliminated the bootleggers of whisky forty years ago."

I feel I'm going on too long. My personal interest in drugs is slight. I've tried opium, hashish, cocaine, LSD, and pot, and liked none of them except cocaine, which leaves you (or at least me) with no craving for more. Like oysters. If in season, fine. Otherwise, forget them. Pot and opium were more difficult for me because I've never smoked cigarettes and so had to learn to inhale. Opium made me ill; pot made me drowsy.

"The period of Prohibition—called the noble experiment—brought on the greatest breakdown of law and order the United States has known until today. I think there is a lesson here. Do not regulate the private morals of people. Do not tell them what they can take or not take. Because if you do, they will become angry and antisocial and they will get what they want from criminals who are able to work in perfect freedom because they have paid off the police.

"Obviously drug addiction is a bad thing. But in the interest of good law and good order, the police must be removed from the temptation that the current system offers them and the Bureau of Narcotics should be abolished.

"What to do about drug addicts? I give you two statistics. England with a population of over fifty-five million has eighteen hundred heroin addicts. The United States with over two hundred million has nearly five hundred thousand addicts. What are the English doing right that we are doing wrong? *They* have turned the problem over to the doctors. An addict is required to register with a physician who gives him at controlled intervals a prescription so that he can buy his drug. The addict is content. Best of all, society is safe. The Mafia is out of the game. The police are unbribed, and the addict will not mug an old lady in order to get the money for his next fix."

Eleanor Roosevelt maintained that you should never introduce more than one "new" thought per speech. I'm obviously not following her excellent advice. She also said that if you explain things simply and in proper sequence people will not only understand what you are talking about but, very often, they will begin to realize the irrationality of some of their most cherished prejudices.

One of the reasons I took the trouble to spell out at such length the necessity of legalizing drugs was to appeal not to the passions of my audience, to that deeply American delight in the punishing of others so perfectly exploited by Nixon-Agnew-Reagan, but to appeal to their common sense and self-interest. If you *give* an addict his drugs, he won't rob you. The police won't be bribed. Children won't be hooked by pushers. Big crime will wither away. Some, I like to think, grasp the logic of all this.

"I worry a good deal about the police because traditionally they are the supporters of fascist movements and America is as prone to fascism as any other country. Individually, no one can blame the policeman. He is the way he is because Americans have never understood the Bill of

Rights. Since sex, drugs, alcohol, gambling are all proscribed by various religions, the states have made laws against them. Yet, believe it or not, the United States was created entirely separate from any religion. The right to pursue happiness—as long as it does not impinge upon others— is the foundation of our state. As a modest proposal, this solution to the problem of law and order is unique: *it won't cost a penny.* Just cancel those barbarous statutes from our Puritan past and the police will be obliged to protect us—the job they no longer do.

"Meanwhile, we are afflicted with *secret* police of a sort which I do not think a democratic republic ought to support. In theory, the FBI is necessary. For the investigation of crime. But in all the years that the FBI has been in existence the major criminals—the Mafia, Cosa Nostra—have operated freely and happily. Except for the busting of an occasional bank robber or car thief, the FBI has not shown much interest in big crime. Its time has been devoted to spying on Americans whose political beliefs did not please the late J. Edgar Hoover, a man who hated Commies, blacks and women in more or less that order."

This generally shocked the audience and never got a laugh. Needless to say, my last lecture was given before the FBI's scrutiny of "dissidence" became public; not to mention the CIA's subsequent admission that at least ten thousand Americans are regularly spied upon by that mysterious agency whose charter is to subvert wicked foreigners not lively homebodies.

"The FBI has always been a collaborating tool of reactionary politicians. The Bureau has also had a nasty talent for amusing presidents with lurid dossiers on the sex lives of their enemies.

"I propose that the FBI confine its activities to *organized* crime and stop pretending that those who are against undeclared wars like Vietnam or General Motors or pollution want to overthrow the government and its Constitution with foreign aid. Actually, in my lifetime, the only group of any importance that has come near to overthrowing the Constitution was the Nixon administration."

A number of cheers on this. When I am really wound up I do a number of Nixon turns. I have the First Criminal's voice down . . . well, pat. I do a fair Eisenhower, and an excellent FDR. Am working on Nelson Rockefeller right now. No point to learning Ford.

"So much, as General Eisenhower used to say, for the domestic front. Now some modest proposals for the future of the American empire. At the moment things are not going very well militarily. Or economically. Or politically.

"At the turn of the century we made our bid for a world empire. We provoked a war with Spain. We won it and ended up owning the Spanish territories of Cuba and the Philippines. The people of the Philippines did not want us to govern them. So we killed three million Filipinos, the largest single act of genocide until Hitler."

Much interest in this statistic. Taken from Galloway and Johnson's book, *West Point: America's Power Fraternity*. Recently I got a letter from a Filipino scholar who has been working on the subject. She says that no one will ever know the exact number killed because no records were kept. But whole towns were wiped out, every man, woman and child slaughtered. The American army does admit that perhaps a quarter million were killed during the "mopping up." The spirit of My Lai is old with us.

"The first and second world wars destroyed the old European empires, and created ours. In 1945 we were the world's greatest power, not only economically but militarily—we alone had the atom bomb. For five years we were at peace. Unfortunately those industries that had become rich during the war *combined* with the military—which had become powerful—and together they concluded that it was in the best interest of the United States to maintain a vast military establishment.

"Officially this was to protect us from the evil Commies. Actually it was to continue pumping federal money into companies like Boeing and Lockheed and keep the Pentagon full of generals and admirals while filling the pork barrels of congressmen who annually gave the Pentagon whatever it asked for, *with* the proviso that key military installations and contracts be allocated to the home districts of senior congressmen."* Tough sentence to say. Never did get it right.

"Nobody in particular was to blame. It just happened. To justify our having become a garrison state, gallant Harry Truman set about deliberately alarming the American people. The Soviet was dangerous. We must have new and expensive weapon systems. To defend the free world. And so the cold war began. The irony is that the Soviet was not dangerous to us *at that time*. Millions of their people had been killed in the war. Their industries had been shattered. Most important, they did not have atomic weapons and we did.

"So, at the peak of our greatness, we began our decline."

Absolute silence at this point.

---

*I notice that I am cannibalizing earlier pieces. Later, on page 1021, I describe the National Security State.

"Instead of using the wealth of the nation to improve the lot of our citizens, we have been wasting over a third of the federal budget on armaments and on the prosecution of open and secret wars. We have drafted men into the Army in peacetime, something the founders of this country would have been appalled at. We have been, in effect, for thirty-three years a garrison state whose main purpose has been the making of armaments and the prosecution of illegal wars—openly as in Vietnam and Cambodia, secretly as in Greece and Chile. Wherever there is a choice between a military dictatorship—like Pakistan—and a free government—like India—we support the dictator. And then wonder why we are everywhere denounced as hypocrites.

"This is not good for character. This is not good for business. We are running out of raw materials. Our currency is worth less and less. Our cities fall apart. Our armed forces have been, literally, demoralized by what we have done to them in using them for unjust ends.

"In a third of a century the only people who have benefited from the constant raid on our treasury and the sacrifice of our young men have been the companies that are engaged in making instruments of war— with the connivance of those congressmen who award the contracts and those generals who, upon early retirement, go to work for those same companies.

"What to do? A modest and obvious proposal: cut the defense budget. It is currently about a quarter of the national budget—eighty-five billion eight hundred million dollars. Unhappily both Ford and Rockefeller are loyal servants of the Pentagon. *They* will never cut back. They will only increase a military budget that is now projected for the end of the decade to cost us one hundred fourteen billion dollars a year. This is thievery. This is lunacy.

"Conservative estimates say that we can cut the budget by ten percent and still make the world free for ITT to operate in. I propose we aim to cut it by two thirds in stages over the next few years. I propose also a reduction of conventional forces. We need maintain no more than an army, navy, air force of perhaps two hundred thousand highly trained technicians whose task would be to see that anyone who tried to attack us would be destroyed.

"A larger army only means that we are bound to use it sooner or later. To attack others. We have learned that from experience. Generals like small wars because there is a lot of money being spent and, of course, they get promoted. I might be more tolerant of their not unnatural bias *if* they could actually *win* a war, but that seems beyond their capacity.

They prefer a lot of activity; preferably in an undeveloped country blasting gooks from the air.

"I would also propose phasing out the service academies. And I was born in the cadet hospital at West Point where my father was an instructor."

To relieve the tension that has started to build, I wander off the track. Describe how I was delivered by one Major Snyder. Later Ike's doctor. "It's only gas, Mamie," he is supposed to have said to Mrs. Eisenhower when the President was having his first heart attack.

"The academies have created an un-American military elite that has the greatest contempt for the institutions of this country, for democratic institutions anywhere. Over the years West Point graduates have caused grave concern. On two occasions in the last century the academy was nearly abolished by Congress. I do not think, despite the virtues of an Omar Bradley, say, that the system which has helped lock us into a garrison state ought to continue."

Often, at this point, I recall an evening at my family's house shortly after the second war began. A group of West Point generals took some pleasure in denouncing that Jew Franklin D. Rosenfeld who had got us into the war on the wrong side. We ought to be fighting the Commies not Hitler. But then FDR was not only a kike, he was sick in the head—and not from polio but from syphilis. Anyway, everything could be straightened out—with just one infantry brigade they would surround the White House, the Capitol, remove the Jew . . .

My lecture tour ended just as General Brown made his memorable comments on international Jewry and its fifth column inside the United States. I've since heard from several people who said they'd not believed my story until General Brown so exuberantly confirmed what I'd been saying.

"The motto of the academy is 'Duty, Honor, Country.' Which is the wrong order of loyalties. Worse, the West Point elite has created all around the world miniature West Points. Ethiopia, Thailand, Latin America are studded with academies whose function is to produce an elite not to fight wars—there are no wars in those parts of the world— but to *limit* democracy.

"West Point also trains many of these past and future oligarchs—like the present dictator of Nicaragua, Somoza. Retired West Pointers also do profitable business in those nations that are dominated by West Point–style elites.

"Finally, the best result of ceasing to be a garrison state would be economic. Until the energy crisis, the two great successes in the world today were Japan and Germany and they have small military establishments. The lesson is plain: no country needs more military power than it takes to deter another nation from attacking it.

"Now none of these proposals is of much use if we do not reduce our population. The US is now achieving a replacement rate of population. This is a startling and encouraging reduction of population but there are still too many of us and we ought to try by the next century to reduce our numbers by half. The problem is not lack of room. In area we have a big country, though we are gradually covering the best farmland with cement and poisoning the lakes and rivers.

"The problem is our way of living. With six percent of the world's population we use forty percent of the world's raw resources. This unnatural consumption is now ending. We are faced with shortages of every kind and we will have to change the way we live whether we want to or not.

"Obviously fewer Americans means less consumption and more for everybody. How do we stop people from breeding? First, by not constantly brainwashing the average girl into thinking that motherhood must be her supreme experience. Very few women are capable of being good mothers; and very few men of being good fathers. Parenthood is a gift, as most parents find out too late and most children find out right away."

This never fails to please.

"More radically, I would say that no one ought to have a child *without* permission from the community. A sort of passport must be issued to the new citizen. How these passports will be allotted I leave to the wisdom of the democracy. Perhaps each girl at birth might be given the right to have one child with the understanding that if she decided to skip the hard work of motherhood she could pass that permission on to a woman who wanted two or three or four children.

"For those who gasp and say that this is interfering with man's most sacred right to add as many replicas of himself as he likes to the world, let me point out that society does not let you have more than one husband or wife at a time, a restriction which I have heard no conservative complain of, even though any Moslem would find it chilling, and Mrs. Richard Burton would find it square."

Mrs. Burton is thrown in, cheaply, to reduce the tension that is mounting. Most members of the audience believe that the right to have as many children as they want is absolute; and to limit population by law seems a terrible imposition. Yet most of them take for granted that the government has the right to control most aspects of our private lives (remember the legendary prisoner of Alcatraz who served time for going down on his wife?).

During the question-and-answer period someone always says that I have contradicted myself. On the one hand, I would allow free drugs, prostitution, gambling, and all sorts of wickedness while, on the other, I would restrict the right to have children—well, isn't that interfering with people's private lives?

The answer is obvious: adding a new citizen to a country is a public not a private act, and affects the whole community in a way that smoking pot or betting on horses does not. After all, the new citizen will be around a long time after his parents have departed. Doesn't it then make sense that if there is insufficient space, food, energy, the new citizen ought not to be born?

"In an age of chronic and worsening shortages, I would propose that all natural resources—oil, coal, minerals, water—be turned over to the people, to the government."

Two years ago when I made this proposal, the response was angry. The dread word "communism" was sounded. Now hardly anyone is much distressed. Even die-hard conservatives have fallen out of love with the oil industry.

"But since none of us trusts our government to do anything right— much less honest—national resources should be a separate branch of the government, coequal with the other three but interconnected so that Congress can keep a sharp eye on its funding and the courts on its fairness. The president, any president, on principle, should be kept out of anything that has to do with the economy.

"Much of today's mess is due to Johnson's attempt to conquer Asia without raising taxes, and to Nixon's opportunistic mucking about with the economy at election time. These presidential ninnies should stick to throwing out baseballs, and leave important matters to serious people."

At this point, without fail, a hot-eyed conservative will get to his feet and say that it is ridiculous to nationalize anything since it is not possible for a government agency to operate efficiently or honestly.

I then ask: Isn't this a democratic society? and aren't those who do the government's work not an abstract enemy to be referred to as "them" but simply ourselves? Are you trying to say that we are, deep down, a nation of crooked fuck-ups? (Naturally, I euphemize.)

The point still does not penetrate. So I shift ground. Agree that the

United States was founded by the brightest people in the country—and we haven't seen them since. Nice laugh. Tension relaxes a bit.

I agree that most people who go into government are second-raters. The bright ones go into the professions or into money-making. This flatters the audience. I suggest that we ought to "change our priorities." Businesslike phrase. Perhaps our schools should train a proper civil service. Train people who prefer payment in honor rather than in money. England, France, Scandinavia attract bright people into government despite low salaries.

This deeply disturbs the audience. First, you must never say that another country handles anything better than we do. Second, although the word "honor" makes no picture at all in the American head, "money" comes on as a flashing vivid green—for *go*.

Someone then says that socialist Sweden is a failure because everybody commits suicide, the logic being that a society without poverty will be so boring that death is the only way out. When I tell them that fewer Swedes commit suicide than Americans (we falsify statistics; they don't) they shake their heads. *They know.*

The next questioner says that England's National Health Service is a flop. This is not true but he would have no way of knowing since the newspapers he reads reflect the AMA's dark view of socialized medicine. Incidentally, England is always used as an example of what awful things will happen to you when you go socialist.

I point out that England's troubles are largely due to the energy crisis and an ancient unsolved class war. I mention England's successful nationalization of steel some years ago. I might as well be speaking Greek. The audience has no way of knowing any of these things. Year after year, the same simple false bits of information are fed them by their rulers and they absorb them, like television commercials.

I do find curious and disturbing the constant hatred of government which is of course a hatred of themselves. Do these "average" Americans know something that I don't? Is the world really Manichaean? Perhaps deep down inside they really believe we *are* all crooked fuckups, and murderous ones, too (thank you, Lieutenant Calley, President Johnson). After all, the current national sport is shoplifting. For once, I am probably too optimistic about my country.

"Now those who object to nationalizing our resources in the name of free enterprise must be reminded that the free enterprise system ended in the United States a good many years ago. Big oil, big steel, big agriculture avoid the open marketplace. Big corporations fix prices among themselves and thus drive out of business the small entrepreneur.

Also, in their conglomerate form, the huge corporations have begun to challenge the very legitimacy of the state.

"For those of you who are in love with Standard Oil and General Motors and think that these companies are really serving you, my sympathy. I would propose, however, that the basic raw resources, the true wealth of the country, be in our hands, not in theirs. We would certainly not manage our affairs any worse than they have.

"As for the quality of our life, well, it isn't much good for most people because most people haven't got much money. Four point four percent own most of the United States. To be part of the four point four you must have a net worth of at least sixty thousand dollars."

This projected figure is from the IRS and I find it hard to believe. Surely individual net worth must be higher. In any case, recent figures show that most of the country's ownership is actually in the hands of one percent with, presumably, a higher net capital.

"This gilded class owns twenty-seven percent of the country's real estate. Sixty percent of all corporate stock, and so on. They keep the ninety-five point six percent from rebelling by the American brand of bread and circuses: whose principal weapon is the television commercial. From babyhood to grave the tube tells you of all the fine things you ought to own because other people (who are nicer-looking and have better credit ratings than you) own them.

"The genius of our ruling class is that it has kept a majority of the people from ever questioning the inequity of a system where most people drudge along, paying heavy taxes for which they get *nothing* in return while ITT's taxes in 1970 diminished, despite increased earnings."

For any Huey Long in embryo, I have a good tip: suggest that we stop paying taxes until the government gives us something in return for the money we give it.

"We got freedom!" vivacious Barbara Walters positively yelled into my ear during our six minutes on the *Today* show. To which the answer is you don't have freedom in America if you don't have money and most people don't have very much, particularly when what they do make goes to a government that gives nothing back. I suppose vivacious Barbara meant that the people are free to watch television's God-awful programming which they pay for when they buy those overpriced shoddy goods the networks advertise.

"I would propose that no one be allowed to inherit more than, let us say, a half million dollars, while corporate taxes obviously must be higher.

"We should also get something back for the money we give the

government. We should have a national health service, something every
civilized country in the world has. Also, improved public transport.
Also, schools which do more than teach conformity. Also, a cleaning
of the air, of the water, of the earth before we all die of the poisons let
loose by a society based on greed.

"Television advertising should be seriously restricted if not eliminated. Although the TV commercial is the only true art form our society
has yet contrived, the purpose of all this beauty is sinister—to make us
want to buy junk we don't need by telling us lies about what is being
sold.

"Obviously, the bright kids know that what is being sold on the screen
is a lot of junk but that is corruption, too, because then everyone who
appears on the screen is also thought to be selling junk and this is not
always true, even at election time.

"Fascism is probably just a word for most of you. But the reality is
very much present in this country. And the fact of it dominates most
of the world today. Each year there is less and less freedom for more
and more people. Put simply, fascism is the control of the state by a
single man or by an oligarchy, supported by the military and the police.
This is why I keep emphasizing the dangers of corrupt police forces, of
uncontrolled *secret* police, like the FBI and the CIA and the Bureau of
Narcotics and the Secret Service and Army counterintelligence and the
Treasury men—what a lot of sneaky types we have, spying on us all.

"From studying the polls, I would guess that about a third of the
American people at any given moment would welcome a fascist state.
This is because we have never been able to get across in our schools what
the country was all about. I suspect that the reason for this failure is the
discrepancy between what we were meant to be—a republic—and what
we are—a predatory empire—is so plain to children that they regard
a study of our Constitution as just another form of television commercial and just as phony. This is sad. Let us hope it is not tragic. The means
exist to set things right."

Now for the hopeful note, struck tinnily, I fear. But the last "solution" I offer is a pretty good one.

"In the end we may owe Richard Nixon a debt of gratitude. Through
his awesome ineptitude we have seen revealed the total corruption of our
system. From the Rockefellers and the Kennedys who buy elections—
and people—to the Agnews and Nixons who take the money from those
who buy, we are perfectly corrupt. What to do?

"How do we keep both the corrupting Kennedys and Rockefellers as
well as the corrupted Nixons and Agnews *out* of politics?

"I propose that no candidate for any office be allowed to buy space on television or in any newspaper or other medium. This will stop cold the present system where presidents and congressmen are bought by corporations and gangsters. To become president you will not need thirty, forty, fifty million dollars to smear your opponents and present yourself falsely on TV commercials.

"Instead television (and the rest of the media) would be required by law to provide prime time (and space) for the various candidates.

"I would also propose a four-week election period as opposed to the current four-year one. Four weeks is more than enough time to present the issues. To show us the candidates in interviews, debates, *un*controlled encounters in which we can actually see who the candidate really is, answering tough questions, his record up there for all to examine. This ought to get a better class into politics."

There is about as much chance of getting such a change in our system approved by Congress as there is of replacing the faces on Mt. Rushmore with those of Nixon and company. After all, the members of the present Congress got there through the old corrupt route and, despite the occasional probity of an individual member, each congressman is very much part of a system which now makes it impossible for anyone to be elected president who is not beholden to those interests that are willing to give him the millions of dollars he needs to be a candidate.

Congress's latest turn to the screw is glorious: when paying income tax, each of us can now give a dollar to the Presidential Election Campaign Fund. This means that the two major parties can pick up thirty million dollars apiece from the taxpayers while continuing to receive, under the counter, another thirty or so million from the milk, oil, insurance, etc., interests.

"Since Watergate, no one can say that we don't know where we are or who we are or what sort of people we have chosen to govern us. Now it remains to be seen if we have the power, the will to restore to the people a country which—to tell the truth—has never belonged to the ninety-five point six percent but certainly ought to, as we begin our third—and, let us hope not, terminal—century."

I ended the series with a noon lecture at a college in Los Angeles . . . not UCLA. They told me this so often that now I've forgotten what the school was actually called. No matter. They have doubtless forgotten what I've said. In a sense, I've forgotten too. The act of speaking formally (or informally, for that matter) is rather like the process of writing: at the moment it is all-absorbing and one is absolutely concentrated. Then the great eraser in one's brain mercifully sweeps away what was said, written.

But impressions of audiences do remain with me. The young appear to have difficulty expressing themselves with words. Teachers tell me that today's students cannot read or write with any ease (having read the prose of a good many American academics, I fear that the teachers themselves have no firm purchase on our beautiful language).

Is television responsible? Perhaps. Certainly if a child does not get interested in reading between six and thirteen he will never be able to read or write (or speak) well and, alas, the pre-pubescent years are the years of tube addiction for most American children.

Naturally that small fraction of one percent which will maintain the written culture continues, as always, but they must now proceed without the friendly presence of the common reader who has become the common viewer, getting his pleasure and instruction from television and movies. A new kind of civilization is developing. I have no way of understanding it.

As I re-do these notes, I am troubled by the way that I responded to the audiences' general hatred of any government. Yes, *we* are the government—but only in name. I realize that I was being sophistical when I countered their cliché that our government is dishonest and incompetent with that other cliché: *you* are the government.

Unconsciously, I seem to have been avoiding the message that I got from one end of the country to the other: we hate this system that we are trapped in but we don't know who has trapped us or how. We don't know what our cage really looks like because we were born in it and have nothing to compare it to but if anyone has the key to the lock then where the hell is he?

Most Americans lack the words, the concepts that might help them figure out what has happened; and it is hardly their fault. Simple falsities have been drummed into their heads from birth (socialism = Sweden = suicide) so that they will not rebel, not demand what is being withheld them . . . and that is not Nixon's elegant "a piece of the action" but justice. Social justice.

The myth of upward social mobility dies hard; but it dies. Working-class parents produce children who will be working-class while professional people produce more professionals. Merit has little to do with one's eventual place in the hierarchy. We are now locked into a class system nearly as rigid as the one that the Emperor Diocletian impressed upon the Roman empire.

Yes, I should have said, our rulers *are* perfectly corrupt but they are not incompetent: in fact, they are extremely good at exercising power over those citizens whom they have so nicely dubbed "consumers." But the consumers are not as dopey as they used to be and when they have to listen to exhortations from old-style Americans like myself, telling them *they* are the government and so can change it (underlying message: this bad society is what you dumb bastards deserve), they respond with the only epithets they can think of, provided them for generations by their masters: it's the Commies, pinkos, niggers, foreigners, it's *them* who have somehow screwed it all up.

But the consumers still have no idea who the enemy are, no idea who really is tearing the place apart. No one has dared tell them that the mysterious *they* are the rich who keep the consumers in their places, consuming things that are not good for them, and doing jobs they detest. Witness, the boredom and fury of the younger workers on the Detroit assembly lines; no doubt made more furious—if not bored—by the recent mass firings, as the depression deepens.

Not since Huey Long has a major political leader come forward and said we are going to redistribute the wealth of the country. We are going to break up the great fortunes. We are going to have a just society whose goal will be economic equality. And we can do this without bloody revolution (although knowing the clever resourcefulness of our rulers, I suspect it will be a terrible time—Attica on a continental scale).

True revolution can only take place when things fall apart in the wake of some catastrophe—a lost war, a collapsed economy. We seem headed for the second. If so, then let us pray that that somber, all-confining Bastille known as the consumer society will fall, as the *first* American revolution begins. It is long overdue.

*Esquire*
May 1975

# 84

# THE STATE
# OF THE UNION:
## 1980

Five years and two presidents ago, I presented in the pages of *Esquire* my own State of the Union Address, based on a chat I'd been giving in various parts of the republic. Acting as a sort of shadow president, I used to go around giving a true—well, Heisenberg's uncertainty principle being what it is, a *truer* report on the state of the union than the one we are given each year by that loyal retainer of the Chase Manhattan Bank, the American president, who is called, depending on the year, Johnson, Nixon, Ford, Carter. Although the presidents now come and go with admirable speed, the bank goes on forever, constantly getting us into deeper and deeper trouble of the sort that can be set right—or wrong—only by its man in the Oval Office. One of the bank's recent capers has got the Oval One and us into a real mess. The de-Peacock-Throned King of Kings wanted to pay us a call. If we did not give refuge to the Light of the Aryans (Banksman David Rockefeller and Banksman Henry Kissinger were the tactical officers involved), the heir of Cyrus the Great would take all his money out of the bank, out of Treasury bonds, out of circulation in North America. Faced with a choice between loss of money and loss of honor and good sense, Banksman Carter chose not to lose money. As a result, there will probably be a new president come November. But whether it is this Banksman or that, Chase Manhattan will continue to be served and the republic will continue to be, in Banksman Nixon's elegant phrase, shafted.

In 1973, Banksman D. Rockefeller set up something called the Trilateral Commission in order to bring together politicians on the make (a tautology if there ever was one) and academics like Kissinger, the sort of gung-ho employee who is always eager to start a war or to improve the bank's balance sheet. Not long after the Trilateral Commission came into being, I started to chat about it on television. Although I never saw anything particularly sinister in the commission itself (has any commission ever *done* anything?), I did think it a perfect symbol of the way the United States is ruled. When Trilateral Commission member Carter was elected president after having pretended to be An Outsider, he chose his vice-president and his secretaries of state, defense, and treasury, as well as the national security adviser, from Chase Manhattan's commission. I thought this pretty bold—even bald.

To my amazement, my warnings were promptly heeded by, of all outfits, the American Right, a group of zanies who ought deeply to love the bank and all its works. Instead, they affect to fear and loathe the Trilateral Commission on the ground that it is, somehow or other, an integral part of that international monolithic atheistic godless communist conspiracy that is bent on forcing honest American yeomen to get up at dawn and walk to work for the state as abortionists and fluoride dispensers. Needless to say, although the American right wing is a good deal stupider than the other fragile political wings that keep the republic permanently earthbound, their confusion in this matter is baffling. The bank is very much their America.

Although there has never been a left wing in the United States, certain gentle conservatives like to think of themselves as liberals, as defenders of the environment, as enemies of our dumber wars. I would think that they'd have seen in the bank's Trilateral Commission the perfect symbol of why we fight our dumber wars, why we destroy the environment. But not a single gentle liberal voice has ever been raised against the bank. I suppose this is because too many of them work for the Bank. . . . I shall now use the word Bank (capitalized, naturally) as a kind of shorthand not just for the Chase Manhattan but also for the actual ownership of the United States. To quote from my earlier State of the Union message: "Four point four percent own most of the United States. . . . This gilded class owns 27 percent of the country's real estate. Sixty percent of all corporate stock, and so on." The Bank is the Costa Nostra of the 4.4 percent. The United States government is the Cosa Nostra of the Bank.

For more than a century, our educational system has seen to it that 95.6 percent of the population grow up to be docile workers and consumers, paranoid taxpayers, and eager warriors in the Bank's never-ending struggle with atheistic communism. The fact that the American government gives back to the citizen-consumer very little of the enormous revenues it extorts from him is due to the high cost of what the Bank—which does have a sense of fun—calls freedom. Although most industrial Western (not to mention Eastern European) countries have national health services, the American taxpayer is not allowed this amenity because it would be socialism, which is right next door to godless communism and free love, followed by suicide in the long white Swedish night. A major part of our country's revenue must always go to the Pentagon, which then passes the money on to those client states, industries, and members of Congress with which the Bank does business. War is profitable for the Bank. Health is not.

Five years ago, incidentally, I said: "The defense budget is currently about a quarter of the national budget—$85 billion. . . . [It] is now projected for the end of the decade to cost us $114 billion. This is thievery. This is lunacy." The requested defense budget for the first year of our brand-new decade is $153.7 billion, which is still thievery, still lunacy—and highly inflationary to boot. But since the defense budget is at the heart of the Bank's system of control over the United States, it can never be seriously reduced. Or, to put it another way, cut the defense budget and the Bank will start to die.

Since my last State of the Union Address, the election law of 1971 has come into its ghastly own. The first effect of the law was to give us the four-year presidential campaign. The second treat we got from it was the presidency of Banksman Jimmy Carter. It is now plain that anyone who can get elected president under the new ground rules ought not to be allowed to take office.

For once, even the dullest of the Bank's depositors is aware that something is wrong. Certainly, there have never been quite so many demonstrably dim Banksmen running for president as there are in 1980. Part of this is historical: not since the country's bright dawn have first-rate people gone into politics. Other countries take seriously their governance. Whatever one might think of the politics of Giscard d'Estaing and Helmut Schmidt, each is a highly intelligent man who is proud to hold a place in government—unlike his American equivalent, who stays out of politics because the Bank fears the superior man. As a result, the contempt in which Carter is held by European and Japanese leaders is not so much the fault of what I am sure is a really swell Christian guy as it is due to the fact that he is intellectually inferior to the other leaders. They know history, economics, geography. He doesn't—and neither do his rivals. The Bank prefers to keep the brightest Americans hidden away in the branch offices. The dull and the docile are sent to Congress and the White House.

I don't know any thoughtful person who was not made even more thoughtful by the recent Canadian election. The new prime minister was not popular. He made mistakes. In the course of a half-hour vote of no confidence, the government fell. There was a nine-and-a-half-week campaign that cost about $60 million. At its end, the old prime minister was back. In a matter of weeks there had been a political revolution. If the United States had had a parliamentary system last April, we would have been relieved of Jimmy Carter as chief of government after his mess in the Iranian desert. But he is still with us, and the carnival of our presidential election goes on and on, costing tens of millions of dollars, while the candidates smile, shake hands, and try to avoid ethnic jokes and the demonstration of any semblance of intelligence. Although the economy is in a shambles and the empire is cracking up, the political system imposed upon us by the Bank does not allow any candidate to address himself seriously to any issue. I know that each candidate maintains, in some cases accurately, that he has superb position papers on all the great issues; but no one pays any attention—further proof that the system doesn't work. After all, since the Bank owns the media, the Bank is able to decide who and what is newsworthy and just how much deeptalk its depositors can absorb. Plainly, the third American republic is drawing to a close, and we must now design for ourselves a fourth republic, a democratic society not dedicated to war and the Bank's profits. Third republic? Fourth republic? What am I talking about? Let me explain.

The first American republic began with the revolution in 1776 and ended with the adoption of the Constitution in 1788. The first republic was a loose confederation of thirteen autonomous states. The second republic was also a fairly loose affair until 1861, when the American Bismarck, Abraham Lincoln, took the mystical position that no state could ever leave the Union. When the southern states disagreed, a bloody war was fought in order to create "a more perfect [sic] union." At war's end, our third and most imperial republic came into existence. This republic was rich, belligerent, hungry for empire. This republic's master was the Bank. This republic became, in 1945, the world's master.

Militarily and economically, the third American republic dominated the earth. All should then have been serene: the mandate of Heaven was plainly ours. Unfortunately, the Bank made a fatal decision. To keep profits high, it decided to keep the country on a permanent wartime footing. Loyal Banksman Harry S Truman deliberately set out to frighten the American people. He told us that the Soviet Union was on the march while homegrown Reds were under every bed—all this at a time when the United States had atomic weapons and the Russians did not, when the Soviet Union was still in pieces from World War II and we were incredibly prosperous.

Those who questioned the Bank's official line were called commies or soft on communism. Needless to say, in due course, the Soviet Union did become the powerful enemy that the Bank requires in order to keep its control of the third republic. The business of our third republic is war, or defense, as it's been euphemistically called since 1949. As a result, of the thirty-five years since the end of World War II, the United States has managed to be at war (hot and cold) for thirty; and if the Bank has its way, we shall soon be at war again, this time on a really large scale. But then, as Banksman Grover Cleveland so presciently observed almost a century ago, "the United States is not a country to which peace is necessary."

There comes a time, however, when the waging of war is too danger-ous even for Banksmen. There also comes a time when the crude politics of getting the people to vote against their own interests by frightening them with the Red Menace simply doesn't work. We are now in such a time. Clearly, a new sort of social arrangement is necessary.

The fact that half of those qualified to vote don't vote in presidential elections is proof that the third republic is neither credible nor truly legitimate. The fact that the Bank's inspired invention, the so-called two-party system (which is really one single Banksparty), is now col-lapsing is further proof that the fourth republic will require political parties that actually represent the various groups and classes in the country and do not simply serve the Bank. By breaking out of the two-party system this year, Banksman John Anderson has demon-strated in the most striking way that, like the Wizard of Oz, the two-party system never existed.

The time has come to hold another constitutional convention. Those conservatives known as liberals have always found this notion terrifying, because they are convinced that the powers of darkness will see to it that the Bill of Rights is abolished. This is always a possibility, but sometimes it's best to know the worst all at once rather than to allow those rights to be slowly taken away from us by, let us say, the present majority of the Supreme Court, led by Banksman Burger.

In the development of a new Constitution, serious attention should be paid to the Swiss political arrangement. Its cantonal system is something that might work for us. The United States could be divided into autonomous regions: northern California, Oregon, and Washington would make a fine Social Democratic society, while the combined states of Texas, Arizona, and Oklahoma could bring back slavery and the minstrel show. There ought to be something for everybody to choose from in the United States, rather than the current homogenized overcentralized state that the Bank has saddled us with. The Swiss constitution has another attractive feature: the citizens have the right to hold a referendum and rescind, if they choose, a law. No need for a Howard Jarvis to yodel in the wilderness: the Jarvis Effect would be institutionalized.

Ideally, the fourth republic should abandon the presidential system for a parliamentary one. The leader of a majority in Congress would form the government. Out of respect for the rocks at Mount Rushmore, we would retain the office of president, but the president would be a figurehead and not what he is today—a dictator who is elected by half of half the people from a very short list given them by the Banksparty.

One aspect of our present patchwork Constitution that should be not only retained but strengthened is that part of the First Amendment which says "Congress shall make no law respecting an establishment of religion, or prohibiting the free exercise thereof"—which, according to Justice Hugo Black, "means at least this: Neither a state nor the Federal Government can . . . pass laws which aid one religion, aid all religions, or prefer one religion over another. Neither can [they] force nor influence a person to go to or remain away from church against his will or force him to profess a belief or disbelief in any religion." This is clearcut. This is noble. This has always been ignored—even in the two pre-Bank republics. Religion, particularly the Judaeo-Christian variety, is hugely favored by the federal government. For one thing, the revenues of every religion are effectively tax-exempt. Billions of dollars are taken in by the churches, temples, Scientological basements, and Moonie attics, and no tax need be paid. As a result, various fundamentalist groups spend millions of dollars propagandizing over the airwaves, conducting savage crusades against groups that they don't like, mixing in politics. Now, a church has as much right as an individual to try to persuade others that its way is the right way, but not even the Bank is allowed to advertise without first doing its duty as a citizen and paying (admittedly too few) taxes.

The time has come to tax the income of the churches. After all, they are essentially money-making corporations that ought to pay tax at the same rate secular corporations do.* When some of the Founders proposed that church property be tax-exempt, they meant the little white church house at the corner of Elm and Main—not the $25-billion portfolio of the Roman Catholic Church, nor the even weirder money-producing shenanigans of L. Ron Hubbard, a science fiction writer who is now the head of a wealthy "religion" called Scientology, or of that peculiar Korean gentleman who may or may not be an agent of Korean intelligence but who is certainly the boss of a "religion" that takes in many millions of tax-free dollars a year.

Here are two comments *not* to be found in any American public-school book. Thomas Jefferson: "The day will come when the mystical generation of Jesus, by the Supreme Being as his father, in the womb of a virgin, will be classed with the fable of the generation of Minerva in the brain of Jupiter." John Adams (in a letter to Jefferson): "Twenty times, in the course of my late reading, have I been on the point of breaking out. 'This would be the best of all possible worlds, if there was no religion in it.'" But since the Bank approves of most religions ("Slaves, obey thy masters" is an injunction it finds irresistible), superstition continues to flourish. On the other hand, if we were to tax the various denominations, a good many religions would simply wither away, on the ground that they had ceased to be profitable to their managers.

During the 1960 presidential campaign, Richard Nixon referred to John Kennedy's Catholicism six times in practically a single breath; he then said, piously, that he did not think religion ought to play any part in any political election—unless, maybe, *the candidate had no religion* (and Nixon shuddered ever so slightly). As the First Criminal knew only too well, religion is the most important force not only in American politics but in world politics, too. Currently, the ninth-century Imam at Qom is threatening an Islamic holy war against Satan America. Currently, the fifth-century-B.C. prime minister of Israel is claiming two parcels of real estate because an ancient text says that Jews once lived there. Currently, the eleventh-century Polish pope is conducting a series

*Or did, pre-Reagan.

of tours in order to increase his personal authority and to shore up a church whose past excesses caused so much protest that a rival Protestant church came into being—and it, in turn, hates . . .

Religion is an endless and complicated matter, and no one in his right mind can help agreeing with John Adams. Unfortunately, most of the world is not in its right mind; and the Bank can take some credit for this. For years, relations were kept tense between poor American whites and poor blacks (would you let your sister marry one?), on the ground that if the two groups ever got together in a single labor union, say, they could challenge the Bank's authority. Religion is also the basis of those laws governing personal conduct that keep the prisons overcrowded with people who get drunk, take dope, gamble, have sex in a way that is not approved by the holy book of a Bronze Age nomad tribe as reinterpreted by a group of world-weary Greeks in the first centuries of the last millennium.

The thrust of our laws at the beginning of the country—and even now—is to make what these religions regard as sin secular crimes to be punished with fines and prison terms. The result? Last year the United States shelled out some $4 billion to keep 307,000 sinners locked up. Living conditions in our prisons are a famous scandal. Although the National Advisory Commission on Criminal Justice Standards and Goals declared in 1973 that "prisons should be repudiated as useless for any purpose other than locking away people who are too dangerous to be allowed at large in a free society," there are plans to build more and more prisons to brutalize more and more people who are, for the most part, harmless. In much of Scandinavia, even vicious criminals are allowed a degree of freedom to work so that they can lead useful lives, turning over a part of the money that they earn to their victims. At present, at least five American states are experimenting with a compensatory system. All agree that the new way of handling so-called property offenders is a lot cheaper than locking them up at a cost that, in New York State, runs to $26,000 a year—more than enough to send a lively lad to Harvard, where he will soon learn how to commit his crimes against property in safe and legal ways.

But since the Bank is not happy with the idea of fewer prisons, much less with the idea of fewer crimes on the books, the Bank has now come up with something called the Omnibus Crime Bill. This has been presented in the Senate by Banksman Kennedy as S. 1722 and in the House of Representatives by Banksman the Reverend Robert F. Drinan as H.R. 6233. Incidentally, Banksman Drinan will presently give up his seat in the House at the order of the Polish pope, who says that he does not want his minions in politics, which is nonsense. A neo-fascist priest sits as a deputy in the Italian Parliament, just across the Tiber from the Vatican. Father Drinan, alas, is liberal. He does not favor the Right to Life movement. On the other hand, he is a loyal Banksman—hardly a conflict of interest, since the Vatican has an account with the Bank, administered until recently by Michele Sindona, a master criminal.

The point of these two bills is as simple as the details are endlessly complex: the Bank wants more power to put in prison those people who challenge its authority. At the moment it looks as if this repressive legislation will become law, because, as Republican Senator James A. McClure has pointed out, the Omnibus Crime Bill is now "a law unto itself, a massive re-creation whose full implications are known only by its prosecutorial draftsmen (in the Justice Department)." Some features:

If, during a war, you should advise someone to evade military service, to picket an induction center, to burn a draft card, *you* can go to jail for five years while paying a fine of $250,000 (no doubt lent you by the bank at 20 percent).

If, as a civilian, you speak or write against a war in such a way that military authorities think you are inciting insubordination, you can get up to ten years in prison or pay a fine of $250,000, or both. If, as a civilian, you write or speak against a war or against conditions on a military installation, and if the Bank is conducting one of its wars at the time (according to the bill—by omission—a war is not something that Congress declares anymore), you can get ten years in prison and pay the usual quarter-million-dollar fine. If the Bank is not skirmishing some place, you can go to jail for only five years while forking out a quarter mill.

If you break a federal law and tell your friendly law enforcer that you did not break that federal law, and if he has corroboration from another friendly cop that you did, you have made a False Oral Statement to a Law Enforcement Officer, for which you can get two years in the slammer after paying the customary quarter mill.

Anyone who refuses to testify before a grand jury, court, or congressional committee, even though he has claimed his constitutional (Fifth Amendment) right against self-incrimination, can be imprisoned if he refuses to exchange his constitutional right to remain silent for a grant of *partial* immunity from prosecution.

The Bank's deep and abiding love of prison requires that alternatives to prison not be encouraged. According to a 1978 Congressional Research Service report, this bill (then S. 1437), enacted and enforced, would add anywhere from 62.8 to 92.8 percent to our already over-crowded federal prisons. The Bank's dream, plainly, is to put all its dissident depositors either in prison or, if they're young enough, into the army, where they lose most of their civil rights.

Needless to say, the press gets it in the chops. If you're a newspaper-man and you refuse to identify your sources for a story, you are Hinder-ing Law Enforcement, for which you can get the usual five and pay the usual quarter. If you receive documentary proof that the government is breaking the law or that its officials are corrupt, you may be guilty of Defrauding the Government, and you can get the old five and pay a quarter. On the other hand, if you are a public servant who blows the whistle on government corruption or criminality, you can get only two and pay a quarter: the Bank has a certain compassion for apostate tellers.

Finally, a judge will have the right to put any person accused of any crime in prison before he has been tried, and that same judge can then deny the accused bail for any reason that appeals to him. This provision means the end of the basis of our legal system: you are innocent until you are proved guilty. According to the *Los Angeles Times:* "What is contemplated in S. 1722 is a fundamental reordering of the relationship between the people and the government, with the dominant emphasis placed on the power of the government. . . . Under the proposed radical revisions of federal criminal law now before Congress, we would be less free and ultimately less secure." But (at this writing) this huge, complex assault on our liberties continues to sail through the Congress, guided by Banksman Kennedy and Popesman Drinan, and it looks fairly cer-tain to pass.*

Plainly, there is panic in the boardroom of the Bank. A number of things have started to go wrong all at once. Since energy will soon be in short supply to all the world, the third republic will be particularly hard hit, because the Bank is not capable of creating alternatives to the conventional unrenewable (and so highly profitable) sources of energy, any more than the Bank was able to anticipate the current crisis of small car versus gas-guzzler, something that consumer-depositors had figured out some time ago when they demonstrated a preference for small economic models by buying foreign cars.

*The bill was defeated in the fall of 1980 by the lame-duck Congress. Like Dracula, it is sure to rise again.

The empire is cracking up because the Banksmen have never had a very clear world view. On the one hand, they are superb pragmatists. They will do business with Mao, Stalin, Franco, the Devil, if profits can be made that way. On the other hand, simultaneously, they must continue to milk this great cow of a republic; and the only way they know to get their hands on our tax dollars is to frighten us with the menace of godless communism, not easily done when you're seen to be doing business quite happily with these godless predators. The final madness occurred when Banksman Nixon went to Peking and Moscow in search of new accounts (which he got on terms unfavorable to us) while continuing to rail against those two ruthless, inexorable enemies of all that we hold dear. This sort of schizophrenia has switched off the public and made our government a source of wonder and despair to its allies.

When Banksman Nixon was audited and found wanting, the Bank itself came under scrutiny of a sort that it is not used to. Lowly consumer-depositors now speak of a national "crisis of confidence." The ordinarily docile media have even revealed a few tips of the iceberg—no, glacier—that covers with corruption our body politic.

Now the masters of the third republic are striking back. They are loosening the CIA's leash, which had been momentarily shortened (or so they told us). They have also come up with a new charter for the FBI that is now before the Senate (S. 1612). In testimony before the Judiciary Committee, law professor emeritus T. I. Emerson of Yale was highly critical of the new powers given the FBI. "The natural tendency of any system of law enforcement," he testified, "is to formulate its doctrines, train its personnel, and utilize its machinery to support social stability and thwart social change." Among the features of the new charter that Emerson found dangerous was the right to initiate an investigation where there is a suspicion, in the agency's eyes, that a person "will engage" in illegal activity. This means that anyone is a potential target of the FBI because anyone might somehow, someday, do something illegal. The FBI also wants access to the financial records of political associations—an invasion of political as well as personal freedom. Finally, the new charter will pretty much remove the agency from any outside scrutiny. In so doing, it will create something that our pre-Bank republics refused to countenance: a centralized national police force. Well, as that wily old fox Benjamin Franklin once hinted, sooner or later every republic becomes a tyranny.

For 169 years, from the halls of Montezuma to the shores of Tripoli, the United States was a military success, able to overlook the odd scalped general or the White House that the British so embarrassingly burned to the ground in 1814. With considerable dash, we tore a chunk of land away from Mexico (which the Mexicans are now, sensibly, filling up again); next, we killed a million or so Filipinos (no one has ever determined just how many) in order to establish ourselves as a regnant Pacific power at the beginning of this century; but then, after we got through two world wars in fine shape, something started to go wrong. In fact, since 1945 nothing has gone right for us. The war in Korea was a draw. The war in Vietnam was a defeat. Our constant meddling in the affairs of other countries has made us not only widely hated but, rather more serious, despised. Not unlike the Soviet Union, our opposite number, we don't seem able to maintain our helicopters properly or to gauge in advance the world's reactions to our deeds or to have sufficient intelligence to know when to make a run for it and when to stand still. What's wrong?

Those born since World War II have been taught to believe that the CIA has always been an integral part of American life. They don't know that the agency is only thirty-three years old, that it is essentially illegal not only in its activities (overthrowing a Chilean president here, an Iranian prime minister there) but also in its charter. The Constitution requires that "a regular Statement and Account of the Receipts and Expenditures of all Public Money shall be published from time to time." The CIA does no such thing: it spends billions of dollars a year exactly as it pleases. Although forbidden by law to operate inside the United States, the CIA has spied on American citizens at home, in merry competition with numerous other intelligence agencies whose single interest is the control of the American people in the name of freedom. Most Americans have heard of the FBI and the Treasury men and the Secret Service (though few Americans have a clear idea of what they actually do or of how much money they spend). On the other hand, hardly anyone knows about the National Security Agency, a miniature CIA run by the Defense Department. It has been estimated that in 1975, the NSA employed 20,000 civilians, used between 50,000 and 100,000 military personnel, and had a budget of $1 billion. Needless to say, the NSA is quite as illegal as the CIA—more so, in fact. The CIA was chartered, messily but officially, by Congress; but the NSA was created secretly by presidential directive in 1952, and Congress has never legalized the agency.

All good Americans want the budget balanced, and the liquidation of the CIA and the NSA would probably save anywhere from $10 billion to

$20 billion a year. For those who are terrified that we won't have enough information about our relentless and godless enemy, the State Department is a most expensive piece of machinery whose principal purpose is—or was—the gathering of information about all the countries of the world. For underground, James Bond stuff, we should rely on the organization that was so useful to us when we were successful: army intelligence. Meanwhile, as a free society—the phrase no longer has much humor in it—we ought not to support tens of thousands of spies, secret agents, and dirty-tricksters, on the practical ground that a rich, lawless, and secret agency like the CIA could, with no trouble at all, take over the United States—assuming that it has not already done so.

The Bank hopes to maintain its power through the perpetuation of that garrison state it devised for us after World War II. This can be done only by involving the country in a series of small wars that will keep tax money flowing from the citizens to the Treasury to the Pentagon to the secret agencies and, eventually, to the Bank. Meanwhile, to stifle criticism, the Bank has ordered an all-out attack on the civil liberties of the people. There is little doubt that, from Banksman Kennedy to Banksman Thurmond, the entire political spectrum in the United States (which is always a single shade of green, just like the money) will work to take away as many of our traditional freedoms as it can. Happily, the Bank's marvelous incompetence, which gave us Nixon and Carter and is now offering (at this writing) Reagan or Bush "versus" Carter or Kennedy, is of a kind that is bound to fail. For one thing, everyone knows that small wars have a way of escalating; and though Banksmen Nixon and Bush view with what looks like equanimity World War III, the rest of the world—including, with luck, an aroused American citizenry—may call a halt to these mindless adventures for private profit. Finally, Anderson's candidacy *could* pull the plug on the two-party-system-that-is-really-one-party apparatus that has kept the Bank in power since the 1870s.*

Meanwhile, a new constitutional convention is in order. The rights guaranteed by the Founders in the old Constitution should be reinforced; the presidential form of government should be exchanged for a more democratic parliamentary system; the secret agencies should be abolished; the revenues of the country should go to create jobs, educational and health systems, alternative forms of energy, and so on. All

---

*"I believe in the two-party system," said Mr. Anderson in the course of his campaign, nicely pulling the plug on himself.

those things, in fact, that the Bank says we can never afford. But I am sure that what countries less rich than ours can do, we can do.

Where will the money come from? Abolish the secret agencies, and gain at least $20 billion a year. Cut the defense budget by a third, and gain perhaps $50 billion. Tax the thousand and one religions, and get untold billions more. Before you know it, the chief financial support of a government become gross and tyrannous will no longer be the individual taxpayer, that perennial patsy, but the Bank, whose entry into receivership will be the aim of the fourth, the good, the democratic republic that we must start to create sometime between now and 1984.

*Esquire*
August 1980

# 85
#### ◆
# THE REAL
# TWO-PARTY
# SYSTEM

In the United States there are two political parties of equal size. One is the party that votes in presidential elections. The other is the party that does not vote in presidential elections. This year the party that votes is divided into four parts: the Democratic, Republican, Libertarian and Citizens—and a number of fragments, including the independent candidacy of Republican John Anderson. Forty-eight percent of the party that votes are blue-collar or service workers; the rest tend to be white, middle-class and over twenty-one years old. Seventy-five percent of the party that does not vote are blue-collar or service workers in combination with most of the eighteen-to-twenty-year-olds—whatever their estate.

Presidential elections are a bit like the Grammy Awards, where an industry of real interest to very few people honors itself fulsomely [correct use of this adverb] on prime-time television. Since the party that does not vote will never switch on, as it were, the awards ceremony, the party that does vote has to work twice as hard to attract attention, to get a rating.

As a result, media-men, -women and -persons analyze at length and in bright shallow the three principal candidates of the one party. To read, hear and watch the media-types, one would think that the election really mattered. Grave subjects are raised: Will Ronald Reagan get us into a war with the forests once he has unilaterally zapped the trees in order to stop the pollution of Mount St. Helens? Will Jimmy Carter be able to balance the budget as he keeps, simultaneously, the interest rates high for the bankers and low for the homeowners? Will John Anderson ever again debate anyone on prime-time television, other than Regis Philbin, who is not national? These are the great issues in the year of our Lord 1980.

And it is the year of our Lord, in spades. Once- and twice-born Christians haven't been on such a rampage since World War I when they managed to add an amendment to the Constitution making it a crime for Americans to drink alcohol. Ironically, the Christers seemed to have turned away from their own twice-born Carter and twice-born Anderson. They prefer once-born Reagan (presumably, the rest of him is with the Lord), because Reagan is against Satan as represented by rights for women and homosexualists—two groups that get a bad press in the Old Testament, and don't do much better in the New. In fact, every candidate of the party that votes is being forced this year to take a stand on abortion, and if the stand should be taken on law and not on the Good Book, the result can be very ugly indeed for the poor politician because abortion is against God's law: "Thou shalt not kill." Since this commandment is absolute, any candidate who favors abortion must be defeated as a Satanist. On the other hand, any candidate who does not favor capital punishment must be defeated as permissive. In the land of the twice-born, the life of the fetus is sacred; the life of the adult is not.

Were the United States in less trouble, this election would be treated the way it deserves to be treated—like the Grammy Awards: those who are amused by such trivia will tune in; the rest will not. But the next president—even though he will simply be a continuation of the previous president ("clones" was the apt word used to describe Reagan and Carter by clone Kennedy) will have to face: 1) A nation whose per-capita income has dropped to ninth in the world; 2) A working population whose real discretionary income (money you get to spend out of what you earn) has declined 18 percent since 1973; 3) An industrial plant with the lowest productivity growth rate in the Western world—yes, we've sunk below England; 4) Double-digit inflation and high unemployment that, according to the latest Nobel prize person for economics, will go on into the foreseeable future; 5) A federal budget of some $600 billion, of which 75 percent can never be cut back (service on the national debt, Social Security, congressionally mandated programs, entitlements); 6) A mindlessly wasteful military establishment whose clients in Congress and in the press can always be counted on to yell, "the Russians are coming," when it is appropriations time on the Hill. And so the military budget grows while our military capacity, by some weird law of inverse ratio, decreases. The national debt increases.

The party that votes (to which I no longer belong) is now offering for our voting pleasure a seventy-year-old clone (if you're born in 1911, you are now in your seventieth not sixty-ninth year) whose life has been spent doing what a director tells him to do: Hit the mark, Ronnie! He has now played so many parts that his confusions and distortions of fact are even more surrealist than those of Carter, and need not be repeated here. There is no reason to assume that Reagan's administration would be any different from that of Carter any more than Reagan's administration as governor of California was much different from that of Brown, Senior—or Junior. The party that votes knows what it is doing when it comes to giving awards on the big night. Also, the magnates who control the party that votes are now acting upon Machiavelli's advice to the Prince: to gain perfect control over the state, keep the people poor and on a wartime footing. Between the extortion racket of the IRS and the bottomless pit of the Pentagon, this is happening.

What to do? A vote for Carter, Reagan or Anderson is a vote against the actual interests of the country. But for those who like to vote against their interests, I would pass over the intelligent but unadventurous Anderson as well as the old actor who knows nothing of economics ("Parity?"), foreign affairs ("Well, I've met the King of Siam"), geography ("Pakistan?"), history ("Fascism was really the basis of the New Deal") and return to office the incoherent incumbent on the ground that he cannot get it together sufficiently to start a war or a Lincoln-Douglas debate. But this is to be negative. To be affirmative—for a compulsive voter, that is: vote for the Citizens or Libertarian parties; each actually means something, like it or not.

Finally, if I may speak *ex cathedra,* as a leading—which is to say following (we're all the same)—member of the party that does not vote, I would suggest that those of you who are accustomed to vote join us in the most highly charged political act of all: not voting. When two-thirds—instead of the present half—refuse to acknowledge the presidential candidates, the election will lack all legitimacy. Then we shall be in a position to invoke Article Five of the Constitution and call a new constitutional convention where, together, we can devise new political arrangements suitable for a people who have never, in 193 years, been truly represented.

*The Los Angeles Times*
October 26, 1980

# 8 6

·

# THE SECOND
# AMERICAN
# REVOLUTION

Future generations, if there are any, will date the second American Revolution, if there is one, from the passage of California's Proposition 13 in 1978, which obliged the managers of that gilded state to reduce by more than half the tax on real estate. Historically, this revolt was not unlike the Boston Tea Party, which set in train those events that led to the separation of England's thirteen American colonies from the crown and to the creation, in 1787, of the First Constitution. And in 1793 (after the addition of the Bill of Rights) of the Second Constitution. And in 1865 of the Third Constitution, the result of those radical alterations made by the Thirteenth, Fourteenth, and Fifteenth amendments. Thus far we have had three Constitutions for three quite different republics. Now a Fourth Constitution—and republic—is ready to be born.

The people of the United States (hereinafter known forever and eternally as We) are deeply displeased with their government as it now malfunctions. Romantics who don't read much think that all will be well if we would only return, somehow, to the original Constitution, to the ideals of the founders, to a strict construction of what the Framers (nice word) of the First Constitution saw fit to commit to parchment during the hot summer of 1787 at Philadelphia. Realists think that an odd amendment or two and better men in government (particularly in the

Oval Office, where too many round and square pegs have, in recent years, rattled about) would put things right.

It is taken for granted by both romantics and realists that the United States is the greatest country on earth as well as in the history of the world, with a government that is the envy of the lesser breeds just as the life-style of its citizens is regarded with a grinding of teeth by the huddled masses of old Europe—while Africa, mainland Asia, South America are not even in the running. Actually, none of the hundred or so new countries that have been organized since World War II has imitated our form of government—though, to a nation, the local dictator likes to style himself the president. As for being the greatest nation on earth, the United States's hegemony of the known world lasted exactly five years: 1945 to 1950. As for being envied by the less fortunate (in a *Los Angeles Times* poll of October 1, 1980, 71 percent of the gilded state's citizens thought that the United States had "the highest living standard in the world today"), the United States has fallen to ninth place in per-capita income while living standards are higher for the average citizen in more than eight countries.

Although this sort of information is kept from the 71 percent, they are very much aware of inflation, high taxes, and unemployment. Because they know that something is wrong, Proposition 13, once a mere gleam in the eye of Howard K. Jarvis, is now the law in California and something like it has just been enacted in Massachusetts and Arkansas. Our ancestors did not like paying taxes on their tea; we do not like paying taxes on our houses, traditionally the only form of capital that the average middle-class American is allowed to accumulate.

Today, thanks to the efforts of the National Taxpayers Union, thirty state legislatures have voted in favor of holding a new constitutional convention whose principal object would be to stop the federal government's systematic wrecking of the economic base of the country by requiring, somewhat naïvely, a balanced federal budget and, less naïvely, a limitation on the federal government's power to print money in order to cover over-appropriations that require over-borrowing, a process (when combined with a fifteen-year decline in industrial productivity) that has led to double-digit inflation in a world made more than usually dangerous by the ongoing chaos in the Middle East from which the West's oil flows—or does not flow.

Even the newspapers that belong to the governing establishment of the republic are beginning to fret about that national malaise which used to trouble the thirty-ninth Oval One. Two years ago, *The New York*

*Times* printed three articles, more in sorrow than in anger, on how, why, where, when did it all go wrong? "The United States is becoming increasingly difficult to govern," the *Times* keened, "because of a fragmented, inefficient system of authority and procedures that has developed over the last decade and now appears to be gaining strength and impact, according to political leaders, scholars and public interest groups across the country."

Were this not an observation by an establishment newspaper, one would think it a call for a Mussolini: "difficult to govern . . . inefficient system of authority. . . ." Surely, We the People govern, don't we? This sort of dumb sentiment is passed over by the *Times,* which notes that "the national political parties have continued to decline until they are little more than frameworks for nominating candidates and organizing Congress and some state legislatures." But this is all that our political parties have ever done (honorable exceptions are the first years of the Republican party and the only years of the Populists). The Framers did not want political parties—or factions, to use their word. So what has evolved over the years are two pieces of electoral machinery devoted to the acquiring of office—and money. Since neither party represents anything but the interests of those who own and administer the country, there is not apt to be much "choice" in any election.

Normally, *The New York Times* is perfectly happy with any arrangement of which the *Times* is an integral part. But a series of crazy military adventures combined with breathtaking mismanagement of the economy (not to mention highly noticeable all-out corruption among the politicos) has thrown into bright relief the failure of the American political system. So the thirty-ninth Oval One blames the people while the people blame the lousy politicians and wish that Frank Capra would once more pick up the megaphone and find us another Gary Cooper (*not* the second lead) and restore The Dream.

Serious establishment types worry about the Fragmentation of Power. "Our political system has become dominated by special interests," said one to the *Times,* stars falling from his eyes like crocodile tears. After all, our political system is—and was—the invention of those special interests. The government has been from the beginning the *cosa nostra* of the few and the people at large have always been excluded from the exercise of power. None of our rulers wants to change this state of affairs. Yet the heirs of the Framers are getting jittery; and sense that something is going wrong somewhere. But since nothing can ever be their fault, it must be the fault of a permissive idle electorate grown fat (literally) before our eyes, which are television. So give the drones less wages; more taxes; and put them on diets.

But the politician must proceed warily; if he does not, that 71 percent which has been conned into thinking that they enjoy the highest standard of living in the world might get suspicious. So for a while the operative word was "malaise" in political circles; and no effort was made to change anything. Certainly no one has recognized that the principal source of all our problems is the Third Constitution, which allows the big property owners to govern pretty much as they please, without accountability to the people or to anyone else, since for at least a century the Supreme Court was perhaps the most active—even reckless—part of the federal machinery, as we shall demonstrate.

There is more than the usual amount of irony in the fact that our peculiar Constitution is now under siege from those who would like to make it either more oppressive (the Right-to-Lifers who want the Constitution to forbid abortion) or from those sly folks who want to make more and more money out of their real estate shelters. But no matter what the motive for change, change is now very much in the air; and that is a good thing.

This autumn, the counsel to the president, Mr. Lloyd N. Cutler, proposed some basic changes in the Constitution.* Although Mr. Cutler's approach was tentative and highly timid (he found no fault at all with the Supreme Court—because he is a partner in a Washington law firm?), he does think that it is impossible for a president to govern under the present Constitution because the separation of powers has made for a stalemate between executive and legislative branches. Since "we are not about to revise our own Constitution so as to incorporate a true parliamentary system," he proceeded to make a number of suggestions that would indeed give us a quasi-parliamentary form of government— president, vice president, and representative from each congressional district would all be elected at the same time for a four-year term (Rep. Jonathan Bingham has such a bill before the House); half the Cabinet to be selected from the Congress where they would continue to sit—and answer questions as in England; the president would have the power, once in his term, to dissolve the Congress and hold new elections—and the Congress would have the power, by a two-thirds vote, to call for a new presidential election; et cetera. Mr. Cutler throws out a number of other notions that would involve, at most, amendments to the Constitu-

*Foreign Affairs, Fall 1980.

tion; he believes that a new constitutional convention is a "non-starter" and so whatever change that is made must originate in the government as it now is even though, historically, no government has ever voluntarily dissolved itself.

Mr. Cutler also suffers from the malaise syndrome, contracted no doubt while serving in the Carter White House: "The public—and the press—still expect the President to govern. But the President cannot achieve his overall program, and the public cannot fairly blame the President because he does not have the power to legislate and execute his program." This is perfect establishment nonsense. The president and the Congress together or the president by himself or the Supreme Court on its own very special power trip can do virtually anything that they want to do as a result of a series of usurpations of powers that have been taking place ever since the Second Constitution of 1793.

When a president claims that he is blocked by Congress or Court, this usually means that he does not want to take a stand that might lose him an election. He will then complain that he is stymied by Congress or Court. In 1977, Carter could have had an energy policy *if* he had wanted one. What the president cannot get directly from Congress (very little if he knows how to manage those princes of corruption), he can often obtain through executive order, secure in the knowledge that the House of Representatives is not apt to exercise its prerogative of refusing to fund the executive branch: after all, it was nearly a decade before Congress turned off the money for the Vietnam war. In recent years, the presidents have nicely put Congress over a barrel through the impounding of money appropriated for projects displeasing to the executive. Impounded funds combined with the always vast Pentagon budget and the secret revenues of the CIA give any president a plump cushion on which to rest his Pharaonic crook and flail.

Obviously, a president who does not respect the decent opinion of mankind (namely, *The New York Times*) can find himself blocked by the Court and impeached by Congress. But the Nixon misadventure simply demonstrated to what extremes a president may go before his money is turned off—before the gates of Lewisberg Federal Penitentiary, like those to Hell or Disneyland, swing open.

Carter could have given us gas rationing, disciplined the oil cartels, encouraged the development of alternative forms of energy. He did none of those things because he might have hurt his chances of reelection. So he blamed Congress for preventing him from doing what he did not want to do. This is a game that all presidents play—and Congress, too.

Whenever the Supreme Court strikes down a popular law which Congress has been obliged to enact against its better judgment, the Supreme Court gets the blame for doing what the Congress wanted to do but dared not. Today separation of powers is a useful device whereby any sin of omission or commission can be shifted from one branch of government to another. It is naïve of Mr. Cutler to think that the president he worked for could not have carried out almost any program *if he had wanted to.* After all, for eight years Johnson and Nixon prosecuted the longest and least popular war in American history by executive order. Congress's sacred and exclusive right to declare war was ignored (by Congress as well as by the presidents) while the Supreme Court serenely fiddled as Southeast Asia burned. Incidentally, it is startling to note that neither Congress nor the Court has questioned the *principle* of executive order, even in the famous steel seizure case.

What *was* the original Constitution all about? I mean by this, what was in the document of 1787 as defended in the Federalist Papers of 1787–1788 by Madison, Hamilton, and Jay. Currently, Ferdinand Lundberg's *Cracks in the Constitution* is as good a case history of that Constitution (and its two successors) as we are apt to get this troubled season. Lundberg is the latest—if not the last—in the great line of muckrakers (TR's contemptuous phrase for those who could clean with Heraclean zeal the national stables which he, among others, had soiled) that began with Steffens and Tarbell. Luckily for us, Lundberg is still going strong.

The father of the country was the father if not of the Constitution of the convention that met in May 1787, in Philadelphia. Washington had been troubled by the civil disorders in Massachusetts in particular and by the general weakness of the original Articles of Confederation in general. From Mount Vernon came the word; and it was heard—and obeyed—all around the states. Quick to respond was Washington's wartime aide Alexander Hamilton, who knew exactly what was needed in the way of a government. Hamilton arrived at Philadelphia with a scheme for a president and a senate and a supreme court to serve for life—while the state governors would be appointed by the federal government.

Although neither John Adams nor John Jay was present in the flesh at Philadelphia, Jay's handiwork, the constitution of New York State (written with Gouverneur Morris and R. J. Livingston), was on view as was that of John Adams, who wrote nearly all of the Massachusetts state constitution; these two charters along with that of Maryland were the basis of the convention's final draft, a curious document which in its separation of powers seemed to fulfill not only Montesquieu's cloudy theories of separation of powers but, more precisely, was a mirror image of the British tripartite arrangement of crown, bicameral legislature, and independent judiciary. Only the aged Franklin opted for a unicameral legislature. But the other Framers had a passion for England's House of Lords; and so gave us the Senate.

Lundberg discusses at some length just who the Framers were and where they came from and how much money they had. The state legislatures accredited seventy-four men to the convention. Fifty-five showed up that summer. About half drifted away. Finally, "no more than five men provided most of the discussion with some seven more playing fitful supporting roles." Thirty-three Framers were lawyers (already the blight had set in); forty-four were present or past members of Congress; twenty-one were rated rich to very rich—Washington and the banker Robert Morris (soon to go to jail where Washington would visit him) were the richest; "another thirteen were affluent to very affluent"; nineteen were slave owners; twenty-five had been to college (among those who had *not* matriculated were Washington, Hamilton, Robert Morris, George Mason—Hamilton was a Columbia dropout). Twenty-seven had been officers in the war; one was a twice-born Christian—the others tended to deism, an eighteenth-century euphemism for agnosticism or atheism.

All in all, Lundberg regards the Framers as "a gathering of routine politicians, eyes open for the main chance of a purely material nature. . . . What makes them different from latter-day politicians is that in an age of few distractions, many—at least twenty—were readers to varying extents in law, government, history and classics."

Lundberg does not accept the traditional American view that a consortium of intellectual giants met at Philadelphia in order to answer once and for all the vexing questions of how men are to be governed. Certainly, a reading of the Federalist Papers bears out Lundberg. Although writers about the Constitution like to mention Locke, Hume, Montesquieu and the other great savants of the Enlightenment as godfathers to the new nation, Montesquieu is quoted only four times in the Federalist Papers; while Hume is quoted just once (by Hamilton) in a passage of ringing banality. Locke is not mentioned. Fans of the Framers can argue that the spirit of Locke is ever-present; but then non-fans can argue that the prevailing spirit of the debate is that of the never-mentioned but always felt Hobbes. There is one reference each to

Grotius, Plato, and Polybius. There are three references to Plutarch (who wrote about great men) and three to Blackstone (who showed the way to greatness—or at least the higher solvency—to lawyers). God is mentioned three times (in the Thank God sense) by Madison, a clergyman's son who had studied theology. Jesus, the Old and New Testaments, abortion, and women's rights are not alluded to. The general tone is that of a meeting of the trust department of Sullivan and Cromwell.

Lundberg quotes Merrill Jensen as saying, "Far more research is needed before we can know, if ever, how many men actually voted for delegates to the state conventions [which chose the Framers]. An old guess that about 160,000 voted—that is, not more than a fourth or fifth of the total adult (white) male population—is probably as good as any. About 100,000 of these men voted for supporters of the Constitution and about 60,000 for its opponents." It should be noted that the total population of the United States in 1787 was about 3,000,000, of which some 600,000 were black slaves. For census purposes, each slave would be counted as three fifths of a person within the First Republic.

The Framers feared monarchy and democracy. In order to prevent the man who would be king from assuming dictatorial powers and the people at large from seriously affecting the business of government, the Framers devised a series of checks and balances within a tripartite government that would, they hoped (none was very optimistic: they were practical men), keep the people and their passions away from government and the would-be dictator hedged 'round with prohibitions.

In the convention debates, Hamilton took on the romantic notion of the People: "The voice of the people has been said to be the voice of God; and however generally this maxim has been quoted and believed, it is not true in fact. The people are turbulent and changing; they seldom judge or determine right. Give therefore to [the rich and wellborn] a distinct, permanent share in the government." The practical old Tory Gouverneur Morris took the same view, though he expressed himself rather more serenely than the fierce young man on the make: "The rich will strive to establish their dominion and enslave the rest. They always did. They always will. The proper security against them is to form them into a separate interest." Each was arguing for a Senate of lifetime appointees, to be chosen by the state legislatures from the best and the richest. It is curious that neither envisioned political parties as the more natural way of balancing economic interests.

Since Hamilton's dark view of the human estate was shared rather more than less by the Framers ("Give all power to the many, they will oppress the few. Give all power to the few, they will oppress the many"), the House of Representatives was intended to be the principal engine of the tripartite government. Like the British Parliament, the House was given (in Hamilton's words) "The exclusive privilege of originating money bills. . . . The same house will possess the sole right of instituting impeachments; the same house will be the umpire in all elections of the President. . . ." And Hamilton's ultimate defense of the new Constitution (*Federalist Paper* No. 60) rested on the ingenious way that the two houses of Congress and the presidency were chosen: "The House of Representatives . . . elected immediately by the people, the Senate by the State legislatures, the President by electors chosen for that purpose by the people, there would be little probability of a common interest to cement these different branches in a predilection for any particular class of electors."

This was disingenuous: the electoral franchise was already so limited in the various states that only the propertied few had a hand in electing the House of Representatives and the state legislatures. Nevertheless, this peculiar system of government was a success in that neither the mob nor the dictator could, legally at least, prevail. The turbulent "democratic" House would always be reined in by the appointed senators in combination with the indirectly elected president and his veto. The Constitution gave the oligarch, to use Madison's word, full possession of the government—the object of the exercise at Philadelphia. Property would be defended, as George Washington had insisted that it should be. Since Jefferson's teeth were set on edge by the word property, the euphemism "pursuit of happiness" had been substituted in the Declaration of Independence. Much pleased with this happy phrase, Jefferson recommended it highly to the Marquis de Lafayette when he was Rights of Man-ing it in France.

The wisest and shrewdest analysis of how the House of Representatives would evolve was not provided by the would-be aristo Hamilton but by the demure James Madison. In *Federalist Paper* No. 59, Madison tried to set at ease those who feared that popular gathering in whose horny hands had been placed the national purse. Madison allowed that as the nation increased its population, the House would increase its membership. But, said he with perfect candor and a degree of complacency, "The people can never err more than in supposing that by multiplying their representatives beyond a certain limit they strengthen the barrier against the government of the few. Experience will forever admonish them that . . . they will counteract their own views by every addition to their representatives. The countenance of the government may become more democratic, but the soul that animates it will be more oligarchic" because "the greater the number composing [a legislative assembly] the fewer will be the men who will in fact direct their proceedings." Until the present—and temporary—breakdown of the so-called lower House, this has proved to be the case.

By May 29, 1790, the Constitution had been ratified by all the states. The need for a bill of rights had been discussed at the end of the convention but nothing had been done. Rather than call a second convention, the Bill of Rights was proposed—and accepted—as ten amendments to the new Constitution. A principal mover for the Bill of Rights was George Mason of Virginia, who had said, just before he left Philadelphia, "This government will set out [commence] a moderate aristocracy: it is at present impossible to foresee whether it will, in its operation, produce a monarchy, or a corrupt, tyrannical [oppressive] aristocracy: it will most probably vibrate some years between the two, and then terminate in the one or the other." The words in brackets were supplied by fellow Virginian—and notetaker—Madison. As the ancient Franklin observed brightly, sooner or later every republic becomes a tyranny. They liked reading history, the Framers.

But the wild card in the federal apparatus proved not to be the predictable Congress and the equally predictable presidency whose twistings and turnings any reader of Plutarch might have anticipated. The wild card was the Supreme Court.

Lundberg calls attention to the following language of Article III of the Constitution.

"The Supreme Court shall have appellate jurisdiction, both as to law and fact, *with such exceptions, and under such regulations as the Congress shall make.*"

The preceding twelve words [he continues] are emphasized because they are rarely alluded to in discussions about the Court. They bring out that, under the Constitution, the Supreme Court is subject to regulation by Congress, which may make exceptions among the types of cases heard, individually or by categories. Congress, in short, is explicitly empowered by the Constitution to regulate the Court, not *vice versa.*

Certainly, the Court was never explicitly given the power to review acts of Congress. But all things evolve and it is the nature of every organism to expand and extend itself.

In 1800, the outgoing Federalist President John Adams made a last-minute appointment to office of one William Marbury. The incoming Republican President Jefferson ordered his secretary of state Madison to deny Marbury that office. Marbury based his right to office on Section 13 of Congress's Judiciary Act of 1789. Federalist Chief Justice John Marshall responded with marvelous cunning. In 1803 (*Marbury v. Madison*) he found unconstitutional Section 13, the work of Congress; therefore, the Court was unable to go forward and hear the case. The partisan Jefferson was happy. The equally partisan Marshall must have been secretly ecstatic: he had set a precedent. In passing, as it were, Marshall had established the right of the Supreme Court to review acts of Congress.

The notion of judicial review of the Executive or of Congress was not entirely novel. Hamilton had brought up the matter in 1787 (*Federalist Paper* No. 78). "In a monarchy [the judiciary] is an excellent barrier to the despotism of the prince; in a republic it is a no less excellent barrier to the encroachments and representations of the representative body." But the other Framers did not accept, finally, Hamilton's view of the Court as a disinterested umpire with veto power over the legislative branch. Yet Hamilton had made his case most persuasively; and he has been much echoed by subsequent upholders of judicial review.

Hamilton believed that the judiciary could never be tyrannous because it lacked real power; he does admit that "some perplexity respecting the rights of the courts to pronounce legislative acts void because contrary to the Constitution, has arisen from an imagination that the doctrine would imply a superiority of the judiciary to the legislative power. It is urged that the authority which can declare the acts of another void must necessarily be superior to the one whose acts must be declared void." Since this is true and since the Constitution that Hamilton is defending does *not* give judicial review to the Supreme Court, Hamilton does a most interesting dance about the subject. The Constitution is the "fundamental law" and derives from the people. If the legislative branch does something unconstitutional it acts against the people and so a disinterested court must protect the people from their own Congress and declare the act void.

Nor does this conclusion by any means suppose a superiority of the judicial to the legislative power. It only supposes that the power of the people is superior to both, and that where the will of the legislature, declared in its statutes, stands in opposition to that of the people, declared in the Constitution, the judges ought to be governed by the latter rather than the former.

This is breathtaking, even for Hamilton. He has now asserted that a court of life appointees (chosen from the rich and wellborn) is more interested in the rights of the people than the House of Representatives, the only more or less democratically elected branch of the government. But Hamilton is speaking with the tongue of a prophet who knows which god he serves. The future in this, as in so much else, was what Hamilton had envisaged, constitutional or not. Characteristically, by 1802, he had dismissed the Constitution as "a frail and worthless fabric."

Marshall was most sensitive to the charge of judicial usurpation of congressional primacy; and during the rest of his long tenure on the bench, he never again found an act of Congress unconstitutional. But Marshall was not finished with republic-shaping. Although he shared the Framers' passion for the rights of property, he did not share the admittedly subdued passion of certain Framers for the rights of the citizens. In 1833, Marshall proclaimed (speaking for a majority of his Court in *Barron* v. *City of Baltimore*) that the Bill of Rights was binding only upon the federal government and not upon the states. In order to pull off this caper, Marshall was obliged to separate the amendments from the Constitution proper so that he could then turn to Article VI, Paragraph 2, where it is written that this Constitution (pre–Bill of Rights) "shall be the supreme law of the land . . . any thing in the Constitution or laws of any state to the contrary not withstanding." Apparently, the first ten amendments were not an integral part of "this Constitution."

The result of Marshall's decision was more than a century of arbitrary harassment of individuals by sheriffs, local police, municipal and state governing bodies—to none of whom the Bill of Rights was held to apply. As for the federal government, the Supreme Court was only rarely and feebly willing to enforce the rights of citizens against it. It is startling to think that the Supreme Court did not seriously begin to apply the Bill of Rights to the states until the 1930s despite the Fourteenth Amendment (1868), which had spelled out the rights of citizens. Gradually, over the last thirty years, an often grudging court has doled out to the people of the United States (including Mr. Brown) most of those rights which George Mason had wanted them to have in 1793.

Fifty-four years after *Marbury* v. *Madison,* the Supreme Court found a second act of Congress unconstitutional. In order to return property to its owner (the slave Dred Scott to his master Dr. Emerson), the Supreme Court declared unconstitutional the Missouri Compromise; and made inevitable the Civil War. It was ironic that the Court which Hamilton had so Jesuitically proposed as a defender of the people

against a wicked legislature should, in its anxiety to protect property of
any kind, have blundered onto a stage where it had neither competence
nor even provenance. (Article IV: "The Congress shall have power to
dispose of and make all needful rules and regulations respecting the
territory or other property belonging to the United States. . . .") But the
wild card had now been played. Judicial review was a fact. The Court
was now ready—give or take a Civil War or two—to come into its
unconstitutional own.

In 1864, the Court struck down the income tax, denying Congress its
absolute power to raise revenue; and not until the passage of the Sixteenth Amendment (1913) did Congress get back its right, in this instance, to raise taxes—which it can never *not* have had, under the
Constitution. But as Lundberg says, "The Court had gained nearly
eighteen years of tax-free bliss for its patrons although it was shown to
be out of harmony with the thinking of the country as well as that of
the framers, previous courts, and legal scholars—and the Constitution."

From March 9, 1865 (when the management of the reigning Republican party became almost totally corrupt), to 1970, ninety acts of Congress were held void in whole or in part. Most of these decisions involved
property, and favored large property owners. As of 1970, the Court had
also managed to overrule itself 143 times. Plainly, the Constitution that
the justices keep interpreting and reinterpreting is a more protean document than the Framers suspected. "The trouble with the Constitution
of the United States," wrote the *London Chronicle* a century ago, "is
that nobody has ever been able to find out what it means." Or, put
another way, since everybody knows what it means, much trouble must
be taken to distort the meaning in order to make new arrangements for
the protection of property.

Lundberg takes the position that, by and large, the Court's behavior
is the result of a tacit consensus among the country's rulers: that two
percent of the population—or one percent, or sixty families, or those
*active* members of the Bohemian Club owns most of the wealth of a
country that is governed by the ruler's clients in the three branches of
government. On those occasions when their Congress is forced by public
opinion to pass laws that they do not want enacted, like the income tax
of 1864, they can count either on their president's veto or on the Court's
invocation of the Constitution to get Congress off the hook. The various
courts are so devised, Lundberg writes, as to "rescue the legislatures and
executives from their own reluctant acts."

Except for the passing of the Sixteenth Amendment, Congress has made only two serious attempts to reclaim its constitutional primacy over the Court (as opposed to a lot of unserious attempts). The first was in 1868. The House Judiciary Committee, fearful that the Court would strike down a number of reconstruction acts, reported a bill requiring that two thirds of a court's judges must concur in any opinion adverse to the law. This bill passed the House but died in the Senate. In the same year, the House did manage to pass a law (over presidential veto) to limit certain of the Court's appellate powers. On March 19, 1869, the Court unanimously bowed to Congress, with a sideswipe to the effect that although the Constitution did vest them with appellate powers, the clause that their powers were conferred "with such exceptions and under such Regulations as Congress shall make" must be honored.

This is one of the few times that Congress has asserted directly its constitutional primacy over a Court that for the next seventy years took upon itself more and more the powers not only to review any and all acts of Congress but to make law itself, particularly when it came to preventing the regulation of corporations or denying rights to blacks. During the last forty years, although the Court has tended to stand aside on most economic matters and to intervene on racial ones, the Court's record of self-aggrandizement has been equaled only by that of the Johnny-come-lately wild card, the president.

The first fifteen presidents adjusted themselves to their roomy constitutional cage and except for an occasional rattling of the bars (the Alien and Sedition Acts) and one break-out (the Louisiana Purchase) they were fairly docile prisoners of Article II. In 1860, the election of the sixteenth president caused the Union to collapse. By the time that Abraham Lincoln took office, the southern states had organized themselves into what they called a confederacy, in imitation of the original pre-Constitution republic. As Lincoln himself had declared in 1847, any state has the moral and, implicitly, constitutional right to govern itself. But permissive Congressman Lincoln was not stern President Lincoln. Firmly he put to one side the Constitution. On his own authority, he levied troops and made war; took unappropriated money from the Treasury; suspended habeas corpus. When the aged Chief Justice Taney hurled the Constitution at Lincoln's head, the president ducked and said that, maybe, all things considered, Congress ought now to authorize him to do what he had already done, which Congress did.

Lincoln's constitutional defense for what he had done rested upon the oath that he had sworn to "preserve, protect and defend the Constitution" as well as to see to it "that the law be faithfully executed." Lincoln proved to be a satisfactory dictator; and the Union was preserved. But the balances within the constitution of the Second Republic had been forever altered. With the adoption of the Thirteenth, Fourteenth, and Fifteenth Amendments extending the vote to blacks (and, by 1920, to women and, by 1970, to eighteen- to twenty-year-olds) while ensuring, yet again, that no state can "deprive any person of life, liberty, or property without the process of law; nor deny to any person within its jurisdiction the equal protection of the laws," the Bill of Rights was at last, officially at least, largely applicable to the people who lived in the states that were again united.

Needless to say, the Supreme Court, often witty if seldom wise, promptly interpreted the word "person" to mean not only a human being but a corporate entity as well. During the next fifty years, the Court continued to serve the propertied interests against any attack from the other branches of government while ignoring, as much as possible, the rights of actual persons. Any state that tried to curb through law the excesses of any corporation was sure to be reminded by the Court that it had no such right.

But the Third Republic had been born; the electorate had been expanded; and civil rights were on the books if not engraved in letters of fire upon the hearts of the judiciary. Although the presidents pretty much confined themselves to their constitutional duties, the memory of Lincoln was—and is—a constant stimulus to the ambitious chief magistrate who knows that once the nation is at war his powers are truly unlimited, while the possibilities of personal glory are immeasurable.

At the turn of the century Theodore Roosevelt nicely arranged a war for his president, McKinley, who did not particularly want one. In 1917 Wilson arranged a war which neither Congress nor nation wanted. Since then the presidents have found foreign wars irresistible. With the surrender of Japan in 1945, the last official war ended. But the undeclared wars—or "police actions"—now began with a vengeance and our presidents are very much on the march. Through secret organizations like the CIA, they subvert foreign governments, organize invasions of countries they do not like, kill or try to kill foreign leaders while spying, illegally, on American citizens. The presidents have fought two major wars—in Korea and Vietnam—without any declaration of war on the part of Congress.

Finally, halfway through the executive's war in Vietnam, the sluggish venal Congress became alarmed—not to mention hurt—at the way they had been disregarded by Johnson Augustus. The Senate Committee on Foreign Relations began to ask such questions as, by what inherent right does a president make war whenever he chooses? On March 8, 1966, the president (through a State Department memorandum) explained the facts of life to Congress: "since the Constitution was adopted there have been at least 125 instances in which the President has ordered the armed forces to take action or maintain positions abroad without obtaining prior Congressional authorization, starting with the 'undeclared war' with France (1798–1800). . . ." Congress surrendered as they had earlier when the inexorable Johnson used a murky happening in the Tonkin Bay to ensure their compliance to his war. It was not until many thousands of deaths later that Congress voted to stop funds for bombing the Indochinese.

How did the president break out of his cage? The bars were loosened by Lincoln, and the jimmy that he used was the presidential oath, as prescribed by the Constitution: "I do solemnly swear that I will faithfully execute the Office of President of the United States, and will to the best of my ability, preserve, protect, and defend the Constitution of the United States." Lincoln put the emphasis on the verb "defend" because he was faced with an armed insurrection. Later presidents, however, have zeroed in on the verb "execute"—as broad a verb, in this context, as any president on the loose could wish for. From this innocuous-seeming word have come the notions of inherent executive power and executive privilege, and that astonishing fact with which we have been obliged to live for half a century, the executive order.

Congress and Court can be bypassed by an executive order except on very odd occasions such as Truman's unsuccessful seizure of the steel mills. When Wilson's request to arm merchant American ships was filibustered to death by the Senate in 1917, Wilson issued an executive order, arming the ships. Later, still on his own, Wilson sent troops to Russia to support the czar; concluded the armistice of 1918; and introduced Jim Crow to Washington's public places. In 1936 Franklin Roosevelt issued a secret executive order creating what was later to become, in World War II, the OSS, and then in peacetime (sic) the CIA. This vast enterprise has never been even moderately responsive to the Congress that obediently funds it. The CIA is now the strong secret arm of the president and no president is about to give it up.

For all practical purposes the Third Republic is now at an end. The president is a dictator who can only be replaced either in the quadrennial election by a clone or through his own incompetency, like Richard

Nixon, whose neurosis it was to shoot himself publicly and repeatedly in, as they say, the foot. Had Nixon not been helicoptered out of the White House, men in white would have taken him away. The fact that we are living in an era of one-term presidents does not lessen, in any way, the formidable powers of the executive.

The true history of the executive order has yet to be written. As of December 31, 1975, the presidents had issued 11,893 executive orders. The Constitution makes no allowances for them. In fact, when an order wages war or spends money, it is unconstitutional. But precedents can always, tortuously, be found for the president to "execute his office." In 1793, Washington proclaimed that the United States was neutral in the war between England and France, in contravention of the treaty of 1778 which obliged the United States to come to France's aid. In 1905 the Senate declined to approve a treaty that Theodore Roosevelt wanted to make with Santo Domingo. Ever brisk and pugnacious, TR made an agreement on his own; and a year later the Senate ratified it. In 1940 Franklin Roosevelt gave England fifty destroyers that were not his to give. But three years earlier, the Supreme Court had validated the principle of the executive *agreement* (*U.S.* v. *Belmont*); as a result, the executive agreement and the executive order are now for the usurper president what judicial review has been for the usurper Court.

Law by presidential decree is an established fact. But, as Lundberg notes, it is odd that there has been no effective challenge by Congress to this usurpation of its powers by the executive. Lundberg quotes the late professor Edward S. Corwin of Princeton, a constitutional scholar who found troubling the whole notion of government by decree: "It would be more accordant," wrote Corwin in *Court Over Constitution,* "with American ideas of government by law to require, before a purely executive agreement to be applied in the field of private rights, that it be supplemented by a sanctioning act of Congress. And that Congress, which can repeal any treaty as 'law of the land or authorization' can do the same to executive agreements would seem to be obvious." Obvious— but ignored by a Congress more concerned with the division of the contents of the pork barrel than with the defense of its own powers.

Between a president ruling by decrees, some secret and some not, and a Court making policy through its peculiar powers of judicial review, the Congress has ceased to be of much consequence. Although a number of efforts were made in the Congress during the Fifties to put the president back in his cage and to deflect the Court from its policymaking binges, nothing substantive was passed by a Congress which, according to Lundberg, "is no more anxious to restrict the president than it is to restrict the Supreme Court. Congress prefers to leave them both with a free hand, reserving the right at all times to blame them if such a tactic fits the mood of the electorate." When Congress rejected Carter's energy program, it was not blocking a president who might well have got around it with an executive order. Congress was simply ducking responsibility for a gasoline tax just as the president had ducked it by maliciously including them in the process. Actually, Congress does, from time to time, discipline presidents, but it tends to avoid collisions with the principle of the executive order when wielded by the lonely Oval One. So does the Supreme Court. Although the Court did stop President Truman from seizing the steel mills in the course of the Korean (by executive order) War, the Court did not challenge the principle of the executive order per se.

Since the main task of government is the collection of money through taxes and its distribution through appropriations, the blood of the Third Republic is the money-labor of a population which pays taxes to support an executive establishment of some ten million people if one includes the armed forces. This is quite a power base, as it includes the Pentagon and the CIA—forever at war, covertly or overtly, with monolithic communism. "Justice is the end of government," wrote Madison (*Federalist Paper* No. 52). "It is the end of civil society. It ever has been and ever will be pursued until it is obtained, or until liberty be lost in the pursuit." Time to start again the hard pursuit.

It was the wisdom of Julius Caesar and his heir Octavian to keep intact the ancient institutions of the Roman republic while changing entirely the actual system of government. The new dynasty reigned as traditional consuls, not as kings. They visited regularly their peers in the Senate— in J.C.'s case once too often. This respect for familiar forms should be borne in mind when We the People attend the second constitutional convention. President, Senate, House of Representatives must be kept as familiar entities just as their actual functions must be entirely altered.

Thomas Jefferson thought that there should be a constitutional convention at least once a generation because "laws and institutions must go hand in hand with the progress of the human mind. As that becomes more developed, more enlightened, as new discoveries are made, new truths disclosed, and manners and opinions change with the change of circumstances, institutions must advance also, and keep pace with the times. We might as well require a man to wear still the coat which fitted him as a boy, as a civilized society to remain ever under the regimen of their barbarous ancestors." Jefferson would be amazed to see how the boy's jacket of his day has now become the middle-aged man's strait-jacket of ours. The amended Constitution of today is roomier than it was, and takes into account the national paunch; but there is little freedom to move the arms because, in Herder's words, "The State is happiness for a group" and no state has ever, willingly, spread that happiness beyond the group which controls it. The so-called "iron law of oligarchy," noted by James Madison, has always obtained in the United States.

Ten years ago Rexford Guy Tugwell, the old New Dealer, came up with Version XXXVII of a constitution that he had been working on for some years at the Center for the Study of Democratic Institutions at Santa Barbara. Tugwell promptly makes the mistake that Julius Caesar and family did not make. Tugwell changes names, adds new entities. Yet the old unwieldy tripartite system is not really challenged and the result is pretty conventional at heart because "I believe," said Tugwell, explaining his new arrangements, "in the two-party system." One wonders why.

The Framers wanted no political parties—or factions. It was their view that all right-minded men of property would think pretty much alike on matters pertaining to property. To an extent, this was—and is—true. Trilateral Commissions exist as shorthand symbols of this meeting of minds and purses. But men are hungry for political office. Lincoln felt that if the United States was ever destroyed it would be by the hordes of people who wanted to be office-holders and to live for nothing at government expense—a vice, he added dryly, "from which I myself am not free."

By 1800 there were two political parties, each controlled by a faction of the regnant oligarchy. Today, despite close to two centuries of insurrections and foreign wars, of depressions and the usurpations by this or that branch of government of powers not accorded, there are still two political parties, each controlled by a faction of the regnant oligarchy. The fact that the country is so much larger than it was makes for an appearance of variety. But the substance of the two-party system or non-system is unchanged. Those with large amounts of property control the parties which control the state which takes through taxes the people's money and gives a certain amount of it back in order to keep docile the populace while reserving a sizable part of tax revenue for the oligarchy's use in the form of "purchases" for the defense department, which is the unnumbered, as it were, bank account of the rulers.

As Walter Dean Burnham puts it, "The state is primarily in business to promote capital accumulation and to maintain social harmony and legitimacy." But expensive and pointless wars combined with an emphasis on the consumption of goods at the expense of capital creation has called into question the legitimacy of the oligarchy's government. Even the dullest consumer has got the point that no matter how he casts his vote for president or for Congress, his interests will never be represented because the oligarchy serves only itself. It should be noted that this monomania can lead to anomalies. In order to buy domestic tranquillity, Treasury money in the form of transfer-payments to the plebes now accounts for some 70 percent of the budget—which cannot, by law, be cut back.

In the 1976 presidential election, 45.6 percent of those qualified to vote did not vote. According to Burnham, of those who did vote, 48.5 percent were blue-collar and service workers. Of those who did not vote, 75 percent were blue-collar and service workers. The pattern is plain. Nearly 70 percent of the entire electorate are blue-collar and service workers. Since only 20 percent of this class are unionized, natural interest requires that many of these workers belong together in one party. But as 49 percent of the electorate didn't vote in 1980, the "two-party system" is more than ever meaningless and there is no chance of a labor party—or of any party other than that of the status quo.

The regnant minority is genuinely terrified of a new constitutional convention. They are happier with the way things are, with half the electorate permanently turned off and the other half mildly diverted by presidential elections in which, despite a semblance of activity, there is no serious choice. For the last two centuries the debate has been going on as to whether or not the people can be trusted to govern themselves. Like most debates, this one has been so formulated that significant alternative ideas are excluded at the start. "There are nations," said Herzen, "but not states." He saw the nation-state as, essentially, an evil—and so it has proved most of the time in most places during this epoch (now ending) of nation-states which can be said to have started, in its current irritable megalomaniacal form, with Bismarck in Germany and Lincoln in the United States.

James Madison's oligarchy, by its very nature, cannot and will not share power. We are often reminded that some 25 percent of the population are comprised of (in Lundberg's words) "the super-annuated, the unskilled, the immature of all ages, the illiterate, the improvident propagators, the mentally below par or disordered" as well as "another 25 percent only somewhat better positioned and liable at any turn or whirligig of circumstances to find themselves in the lower category." As Herzen, in an unhappy mood, wrote, "Who that respects the truth would ask the opinion of the first man he meets? Suppose Columbus or Copernicus had put to the vote the existence of America or the movement of the earth?" Or as a successful movie executive, in a happy mood, once put it: "When the American public walks, its knuckles graze the ground."

The constant search for external enemies by the oligarchy is standard stuff. All dictators and ruling groups indulge in this sort of thing, reflecting Machiavelli's wisdom that the surest way to maintain one's power over the people is to keep them poor and on a wartime footing. We fought in Vietnam to contain China, which is now our Mao-less friend; today we must have a showdown with Russia, in order to. . . . One has already forgotten the basis for the present quarrel. No. Arms race. That's it. They are outstripping us in warheads, or something. On and on the propaganda grinds its dismal whine. Second to none. Better to die in Afghanistan than Laguna. We must not lose the will. . . .

There are signs that the American people are beginning to tire of all of this. They are also angry at the way that their money is taken from them and wasted on armaments—although they have been sufficiently conned into thinking that armaments are as good as loafers on welfare and bureaucrats on the Treasury teat are bad. Even so, they believe that too much is being taken away from them; and that too little ever comes back.

Since Lundberg began his career as an economist, it is useful to quote him at length on how the oligarchy operates the economy—acting in strict accordance with the letter if not the spirit of the three constitutions.

The main decision that Congress and the President make that is of steady effect on the citizenry concerns appropriations—that is, how much is to be spent up to and beyond a half-trillion dollars and what for. The proceeds are supposed to come from taxes but here, in response to citizen sensitivity, the government tends to understate the cost. Because the government has taken to spending more than it takes in, the result is inflation—a steady rise in the prices of goods and services.

The difference between what it spends and what it takes in the government makes up by deviously operating the money-printing machine, so that the quantity of money in circulation exceeds the quantity of goods and services. Prices therefore tend to rise and money and money-values held by citizens decline in purchasing value. . . .

All that the government has been doing in these respects is strictly constitutional. For the Constitution empowers it, first, to lay taxes without limit (Article I, Section 8, Paragraph 1). It is empowered in the very next paragraph to borrow money on the credit of the United States—that is, the taxpayers—also without limit. . . . As to inflation, Paragraph 5 empowers the government, through Congress and the President, not only to coin money but to "regulate the value thereof." In other words, under the Constitution a dollar is worth whatever Congress and the President determine it to be by their fiscal decisions, and for nearly three decades officials, Republican and Democratic alike, have decreed that it be worth less. . . .

When Congress and president over-appropriate, the Treasury simply prints

. . . short-term notes and bonds and sends these over to the Federal Reserve Bank, the nation's central bank. In receipt of these securities, the Federal Reserve simply credits the Treasury with a deposit for the total amount. The Treasury draws checks against these deposits. And these checks are new money. Or the Treasury may simply offer the securities for sale in the open market, receiving therefore the checks of buyers.

Since there is no legal way to control either president or Congress under the current system, it is inevitable that there would be a movement for radical reform. The National Taxpayers Union was organized to force the federal government to maintain a balanced budget. In order to accomplish this, it will be necessary to change the Constitution. So the National Taxpayers Union has called for a new constitutional convention. To date, thirty state legislatures have said yes to that call. When thirty-four state legislatures ask for a new convention, there will be one. As Professor Gerald Gunther of Stanford Law School recently wrote:

The convention delegates would gather after popular elections—elections where the platforms and debates would be outside congressional control, where interest groups would seek to raise issues other than the budget, and where some successful candidates would no doubt respond to those pressures. Those convention delegates could claim to be legitimate representatives of the people. And they could make a plausible—and I believe correct—argument that a convention is entitled to set its own agenda. . . .*

*"Constitutional Roulette: The Dimensions of the Risk" in *The Constitution and the Budget,* edited by W. S. Moore and Rudolph G. Penner (American Enterprise Institute for Public Policy Research, Washington and London, 1980).

Those who fear that Milton Friedman's cheerful visage will be swiftly hewn from Dakota rock underestimate the passion of the majority not to be unemployed in a country where the gap between rich and poor is, after France, the greatest in the Western world. Since the welfare system is the price that the white majority pays in order to exclude the black minority from the general society, entirely new social arrangements will have to be made if that system is to be significantly altered.

Predictably, the oligarchs and their academic advisers view with alarm any radical change. The Bill of Rights will be torn to shreds, they tell us. Abortion will be forbidden by the Constitution while prayers will resonate in the classrooms of the Most Christian Republic. The oligarchs think that the people are both dangerous and stupid. Their point is moot. But we do know that the oligarchs are a good deal more dangerous to the polity than the people at large. Predictions that civil rights would have a rocky time at a new convention ignore the reality that the conglomeration of groups attending it will each have residual ethnic, ideological, religious, and local interests whose expression they will not want stifled. It is by no means clear that civil liberties would be submerged at a new convention; and there is no reason why the delegates should not decide that a Supreme Court of some sort should continue to act as protector of the Bill of Rights—a better protector, perhaps, than the court that recently separated a Mr. Snepp from his royalties.

The forms of the first three republics should be retained. But the presidency should be severely limited in authority, and shorn of the executive order and the executive agreement. The House of Representatives should be made not only more representative but whoever can control a majority will be the actual chief of government, governing through a cabinet chosen from the House. This might render it possible for the United States to have, for the first time in two centuries, real political parties. Since the parliamentary system works reasonably well in the other industrially developed democracies, there is no reason why it should not work for us. Certainly our present system does not work, as the late election demonstrated.

Under a pure parliamentary system the Supreme Court must be entirely subservient to the law of the land, which is made by the House of Representatives; and judicial review by the Court must join the executive order on the junk-heap of history. But any parliamentary system that emerged from a new constitutional convention would inevitably be a patchwork affair in which a special niche could, and no doubt would, be made for a judicial body to protect and enforce the old Bill of Rights. The Senate should be kept as a home for wise men, much like England's House of life-Lords. One of the Senate's duties might be to study the laws of the House of Representatives with an eye to their constitutionality, not to mention rationality. There should be, at regular intervals, national referenda on important subjects. The Swiss federal system provides some interesting ideas; certainly their cantonal system might well be an answer to some of our vexing problems—particularly, the delicate matter of bilingualism.

The present Constitution will be two hundred years old in 1987—as good a date as any to finish the work of the second constitutional convention, which will make possible our Fourth Republic, and first— ah, the note of optimism!—civilization.

*The New York Review of Books*
February 5, 1981

# 87

# RONNIE AND NANCY:
# A LIFE IN PICTURES

I

I first saw Ronnie and Nancy Reagan at the Republican convention of
1964 in San Francisco's Cow Palace. Ronnie and Nancy (they are called
by these names throughout Laurence Leamer's book *Make-Believe: The
Story of Nancy and Ronald Reagan*) were seated in a box to one side
of the central area where the cows—the delegates, that is—were whooping it up. Barry Goldwater was about to be nominated for president.
Nelson Rockefeller was being booed not only for his communism but
for his indecently uncloseted heterosexuality. Who present that famous
day can ever forget those women with blue-rinsed hair and leathery
faces and large costume jewelry and pastel-tinted dresses with tasteful
matching accessories as they screamed "Lover!" at Nelson? It was like
a TV rerun of *The Bacchae,* with Nelson as Pentheus.

I felt sorry for Nelson. I felt sorry for David Brinkley when a number
of seriously overweight Sunbelt Goldwaterites chased him through the
kitchens of the Mark Hopkins Hotel. I felt sorry for myself when I, too,
had to ward off their righteous wrath: I was there as a television commentator for Westinghouse. I felt sorry for the entire media that day as
fists were actually shaken at the anchorpersons high up in the eaves of

the hall. I felt particularly sorry for the media when a former president named Eisenhower, reading a speech with his usual sense of discovery, attacked the press, and the convention hall went mad. At last Ike was giving it to those commie-weirdo-Jew-fags who did not believe in the real America of humming electric chairs, well-packed prisons, and kitchens filled with every electrical device that a small brown person of extranational provenance might successfully operate at a fraction of the legal minimum wage.

As luck would have it, I stood leaning on the metal railing that enclosed the boxed-in open place where, side by side, Ronnie and Nancy were seated watching Ike. Suddenly, I was fascinated by them. First, there was her furious glare when someone created a diversion during Ike's aria. She turned, lip curled with Bacchantish rage, huge unblinking eyes afire with a passion to kill the enemy so palpably at hand—or so it looked to me. For all I know she might have been trying out new contact lenses. In any case, I had barely heard of Nancy then. Even so, I said to myself: There is a lot of rage in this little lady. I turned then to Ronnie. I had seen him in the flesh for a decade or so as each of us earned his mite in the Hollyjungle. Ronnie was already notorious for his speeches for General Electric, excoriating communists who were, apparently, everywhere. I had never actually spoken to him at a party because I knew—as who did not?—that although he was the soul of amiability when not excoriating the international monolithic menace of atheistic godless communism, he was, far and away, Hollywood's most grinding bore—Chester Chatterbox, in fact. Ronnie never stopped talking, even though he never had anything to say except what he had just read in the *Reader's Digest,* which he studied the way that Jefferson did Montesquieu. He also told show-biz stories of the sort that overexcites civilians in awe of old movie stars, but causes other toilers in the industry to stampede.

I had heard that Reagan might be involved in the coming campaign. So I studied him with some care. He was slumped in a folding chair, one hand holding up his chins; he was totally concentrated on Eisenhower. I remember thinking that I had made the right choice in 1959 when we were casting *The Best Man,* a play that I had written about a presidential convention. An agent had suggested Ronald Reagan for the lead. We all had a good laugh. He is by no means a bad actor, but he would hardly be convincing, I said with that eerie prescience which has earned me the title the American Nostradamus, as a presidential candidate. So I cast Melvyn Douglas, who could have made a splendid president in real life had his career not been rejuvenated by the play's success, while the actor whom I had rejected had no choice but to get himself elected president. I do remember being struck by the intensity with which Reagan studied Eisenhower. I had seen that sort of concentration a thousand times in half-darkened theatres during rehearsals or Saturday matinees: The understudy examines the star's performance and tries to figure how it is done. An actor prepares, I said to myself: Mr. Reagan is planning to go into politics. With his crude charm, I was reasonably certain that he could be elected mayor of Beverly Hills.

In time all things converge. The campaign biography and the movie star's biography are now interchangeable. The carefully packaged persona of the old-time movie star resembles nothing so much as the carefully packaged persona of today's politician. Was it not inevitable that the two would at last coincide in one person? That that person should have been Ronald Reagan is a curiosity of more than minor interest. George Murphy had broken the ice, as it were, by getting elected to the Senate from California.

Since Mr. Leamer is as little interested in politics and history as his two subjects, he is in some ways an ideal chronicler. He loves the kind of gossip that ordinary folks—his subjects and their friends—love. He takes an O'Haran delight in brand names while the "proper" names that are most often seen in syndicated columns ravish him. On the other hand, he is not very interested in the actual way politics, even as practiced by Ronnie, works. Although Reagan's eight years as governor of California are of some interest, Leamer gets through the-time-in-Sacramento as quickly as possible, with only one reference to Bob Moretti, the Democratic speaker of the assembly who, in effect, ran the state while Ronnie made his speeches around state, country, world on the dangers of communism. When in town, Ronnie played with his electric trains (something omitted by Mr. Leamer). On the other hand, there are twenty-four references to "wardrobe" in the index. So, perhaps, Mr. Leamer has got his priorities right after all. In any case, he never promised us a Rosebud.

Leamer begins with the inaugural of the fortieth president. First sentence: "On a gilded California day, Ronald and Nancy Reagan left their home for the last time." That is *echt Photoplay* and there is much, much more to come. Such lines as: "She had begun dating him when he thought he would never love again." You know, I think I will have some of those Hydrox cookies after all. "Unlike many of his backers, Ronnie was no snob. He believed that everybody should have his shot at this great golden honeypot of American free enterprise." The Golden Horde now arrives in Washington for the inaugural. "Ostentatious," growled that old meanie Barry Goldwater, nose out of joint because the man who got started in politics by giving The Speech for him in 1964 kept on giving The Speech for himself, and so, sixteen years and four wonderful presidents later, got elected Numero Uno.

Leamer tells us about their wardrobes for the great day. Also, "as a teenager and a young woman, [Nancy] had had her weight problems, but now at fifty-nine [Leamer finks on Nancy: Long ago she sliced two years off her age] she was a perfect size six. Her high cheekbones, huge eyes, delicate features and extraordinary attention to appearance made her lovelier than she had ever been." According to the testimony of the numerous ill-reproduced photographs in the book, this is quite true. The adventures simply of Nancy's nose down the years is an odyssey that we *Photoplay* fans would like to know a lot more about. At first there is a bulb on the tip; then the bulb vanishes but there is a certain thickness around the ridge; then, suddenly, retroussé triumph!

The inaugural turns out to be a long and beautiful commercial to Adolfo, Blass, Saint Laurent, Galanos, De la Renta, and Halston. At one point, Ronnie reads a poem his mother had written; there were "tears in his eyes." During the ceremonies, Ronnie said later, "It was so hard not to cry during the whole thing." But then Ronnie had been discovered, groomed, and coiffed, by the brothers Warner, who knew how to produce tears on cue with Max Steiner's ineffable musical scores. So overwhelming was Maestro Steiner that at one point, halfway up the stairs to die nobly in *Dark Victory,* Bette Davis suddenly stopped and looked down at the weeping director and crew and said, "Tell me now. Just who is going up these goddamned stairs to die? Me or Max Steiner?" She thought the teary music a bit hard on her thespian talents. No, I don't like the Oreos as much as the Hydrox but if that's all there is . . .

"As her husband spoke . . . her eyes gleamed with tears," while "the Mormon Tabernacle choir brought tears to his eyes." Tears, size sixes, Edwards-Lowell furs, Jimmy and Gloria Stewart, Roy Rogers and Dale Evans, new noses and old ideas, with charity toward none . . . then a final phone call to one of Nancy's oldest friends who says: "Oh, Nancy, you aren't a movie star now, not the biggest movie star. You're the star of the whole world. The biggest star of all." To which Nancy answers,

"Yes, I know, and it scares me to death." To which, halfway around the world, at Windsor Castle, an erect small woman of a certain age somewhat less than that of Nancy is heard to mutter, "What is all this shit?"

Mr. Leamer's book is nicely organized. After "A Gilded Dawn," he flashes back to tell us Nancy's story up until she meets Ronnie (who thought he would never love again); then Mr. Leamer flashes back and tells us Ronnie's story up until that momentous meeting. Then it is side by side into history. Curiously enough Nancy's story is more interesting than Ronnie's because she is more explicable and Mr. Leamer can get a grip on her. Ronnie is as mysterious a figure as ever appeared on the American political stage.

Nancy's mother was Edith Luckett, an actress from Washington, D.C. She worked in films and on the stage: "Edith's just been divorced from a rich playboy who's not worth the powder to blow him up." There is a lot of fine period dialogue in *Make-Believe*. Edith's father was a Virginian who worked for the old Adams Express Company where, thirty-one years earlier, John Surratt had worked; as you will recall, Surratt was one of the conspirators in the Abraham Lincoln murder case. Mr. Leamer tactfully omits this ominous detail.

Edith's marriage to Ken Robbins, "a handsome stage-door johnny . . . from a far better family than Edith's," is skimpily, even mysteriously, described by Mr. Leamer. Where did they meet? When and where were they married? Where did they live? All we are told is that "when Ken entered the service in 1917, he and Edith were newlyweds. But he had his duties and she had her career. . . . Ken had been released from the army in January 1919. Edith had tried to keep the marriage going with her twenty-three-year-old husband [with her career? his duties?], but all she had to show for it was a baby, born on July 6, 1921, in New York City. Ken hadn't even been there." After two years of dragging Nancy around with her ("using trunks as cradles," what else?) Edith parked baby with her older sister, Virginia, in Maryland, while Ken went to live with his mother in New Jersey. So when were Edith and Ken divorced? It does not help that Mr. Leamer constantly refers to Ken as Nancy's "natural father."

Nancy was well looked after by her aunt; she was sent to Sidwell Friends School in Washington, some four years before I went there. Mr. Sidwell was an ancient Quaker whose elephantine ears were filled with hair while numerous liver spots made piebald his kindly bald head. I used to talk to him occasionally: *Never once did he mention Nancy Robbins.*

Meanwhile, Edith had found Mr. Right, Loyal Davis, M.D., F.A.C.S., a brain surgeon of pronounced reactionary politics and a loathing of the lesser breeds, particularly those of a dusky hue. The marriage of Edith and Loyal (I feel I know them, thanks to Mr. Leamer) seems to have been happy and, at fourteen, Nancy got herself adopted by Mr. Davis and took his name. Nancy Davis now "traveled at the top of Chicago's social world." She was a school leader. Yearbook: "Nancy's social perfection is a constant source of amazement. She is invariably becomingly and suitably dressed. She can talk, and even better listen intelligently . . ." Thus was child begetter of the woman and First Lady-to-be. Destiny was to unite her with a man who has not stopped talking, according to his associates and relatives, for threescore years at least.

Nancy went to Smith and to deb parties. She herself had a tea-dance debut in Chicago. She had beaux. She was a bit overweight, while her nose was still a Platonic essence waiting to happen. A friend of her mother's, ZaSu Pitts, gave Nancy a small part in a play that she was bringing to Broadway. From an early age, Nancy had greasepaint in her eyes. The play opened on Broadway unsuccessfully but Nancy stayed on. She modeled, looked for work (found it in *Lute Song*), dated famous family friends, among them Clark Gable, who after a few drinks would loosen his false teeth, which were on some sort of peg and then shake his head until they rattled like dice. I wonder if he ever did that for Nancy. Can we ever really and truly know *anyone*? The Oreos are stale.

Hollywood came Nancy's way in the form of Benny Thau, a vice president of MGM. Nancy had a "blind date" with him. In 1949 Thau was a great power at the greatest studio. He got Nancy a screen test, and a contract. By now Nancy was, as Mr. Leamer puts it,

dating Benny Thau. Barbara, the pretty teen-age receptionist, saw Nancy frequently. Many years later she remembered that she had orders that on Sunday morning Nancy was to be sent directly into Benny Thau's suite. Barbara nodded to Miss Davis as she walked into the vice-president's office; nodded again when she left later.

No wonder Nancy thinks the ERA is just plain silly.

.   .   .

Now Mr. Leamer cuts to the career of Ronnie ("Dutch") Reagan. This story has been told so much that it now makes no sense at all. Dixon, Illinois. Father drank (Irish Catholic). Mother stern (Protestant Scots-Irish); also, a fundamentalist Christian, a Disciple of Christ. Brother Neil is Catholic. Ronnie is Protestant. Sunday School teacher. Lifeguard. Eureka College. Drama department. Debating society. Lousy grades. Lousy football player but eager to be a successful jock (like Nixon and Ike *et al.* . . . What would happen if someone who could really play football got elected President?). Imitates radio sportscasters. Incessantly. Told to stop. Gets on everyone's nerves. Has the last laugh. Got a job as . . . sportscaster. At twenty-two. Midst of depression. Gets better job. Goes west. Meets agent. Gets hired by Warner Brothers as an actor. Becomes, in his own words, "the Errol Flynn of the B's."

Mr. Leamer bats out this stuff rather the way the studio press departments used to do. He seems to have done no firsthand research. Dutch is a dreamer, quiet (except that he talks all the time, from puberty on), unread and incurious about the world beyond the road ahead, which was in his case a thrilling one for a boy at that time: sportscaster at twenty-two and then film actor and movie star.

Mr. Leamer might have done well to talk to some of the California journalists who covered Reagan as governor. I was chatting with one last year, backstage in an Orange County auditorium. When I said something to the effect how odd it was that a klutz like Reagan should ever have been elected president, the journalist then proceeded to give an analysis of Reagan that was far more interesting than Mr. Leamer's mosaic of *Photoplay* tidbits. "He's not stupid at all. He's ignorant, which is another thing. He's also lazy, so what he doesn't know by now, which is a lot, he'll never know. That's the way he is. But he's a perfect politician. He knows exactly how to make the thing work for him."

I made some objections, pointed to errors along the way, not to mention the storms now gathering over the republic. "You can't look at it like that. You see, he's not interested in politics as such. He's only interested in himself. Consider this. Here is a fairly handsome ordinary young man with a pleasant speaking voice who first gets to be what he wants to be and everybody else then wanted to be, a radio announcer [equivalent to an anchorperson nowadays]. Then he gets to be a movie star in the Golden Age of the movies. Then he gets credit for being in the Second World War while never leaving L.A. Then he gets in at the start of television as an actor and host. Then he picks up a lot of rich friends who underwrite him politically and personally and get him elected governor twice of the biggest state in the union and then they get him elected president, and if he survives he'll be reelected. The point is that here is the only man I've ever heard of who got everything that he ever wanted. That's no accident."

I must say that as I stepped out onto the stage to make my speech, I could not help but think that though there may not be a God there is quite possibly a devil, and we are now trapped in the era of the Dixon, Illinois, Faust.

One thing that Mr. Leamer quickly picks up on is Ronnie's freedom with facts. Apparently this began quite early. "Dutch had been brought up to tell the truth; but to him, facts had become flat little balloons that had to be blown up if they were to be seen and sufficiently appreciated." In Hollywood he began a lifelong habit of exaggerating not only his own past but those stories that he read in the *Reader's Digest* and other right-wing publications. No wonder his aides worry every time he opens his mouth without a script on the TelePrompTer to be read through those contact lenses that he used, idly, to take out at dinner parties and suck on.

By 1938 Ronnie was a featured player in *Brother Rat.* He was and still is an excellent film actor. The notion that he was just another Jon Hall is nonsense. For a time he was, in popularity with the fans, one of the top five actors in the country. If his range is limited that is because what he was called on to do was limited. You were a type in those days, and you didn't change your type if you wanted to be a star. But he did marry an actress who was an exception to the rule. Jane Wyman did graduate from brash blonde wisecracker to "dramatic" actress (as Mr. Leamer would say). After the war, she was the bigger star. The marriage fell apart. Natural daughter Maureen and adopted son Michael could not hold them together. Plainly, Jane could not follow Ronnie's sage advice. "We'll lead an ideal life if you'll just avoid doing one thing: Don't think." Never has there been such a perfect prescription for success in late-twentieth-century American political life.

But war clouds were now gathering over the Hollywood Hills. Five months after Pearl Harbor was attacked, Ronnie, though extremely nearsighted, was available for "limited service." To much weeping and gorge-rising, Ronnie went not overseas but over to Culver City where he made training films for the rest of the war. *Modern Screen* headline: BUT WHEN RONNIE WENT RIDING OFF TO BATTLE, HE LEFT HIS HEART BEHIND HIM! *Photoplay:* I WON'T BE DOING THESE PICTURES. UNCLE SAM HAS CALLED ME . . . AND I'M OFF TO THE WAR.

Ronnie was now known for two important roles, one as the doomed

"Gipper" in *Knute Rockne, All American* and the other as the playboy whose legs are sawed off ("Where's the rest of me?") in *King's Row.* As Ronnie's films moved once again B-ward, he moved toward politics. Originally, he had been a New Deal liberal, or something. Actually his real political activity was with the Screen Actors Guild where, by and large, in those days at least, first-rate working actors were seldom to be found giving much time to meetings, much less to becoming its president, as Reagan did.

When the McCarthy era broke upon America, Ronnie took a stern anticommie line within his own union. In 1951 in *Fortnight,* he wrote that "several members of Congress are known Communists" and as one whose reviews had not been so good lately, he went on to add that though good American newspapers were attacking "dirty Reds" their publishers didn't know that they were employing "drama and book critics who . . . were praising the creative efforts of their little 'Red Brothers' while panning the work of all non-Communists."

Ronnie then went to work vetting (or, as it was called then, "clearing") people in the movies who might be tainted with communism. This was done through the Motion Picture Industry Council. The witch hunt was on, and many careers were duly ruined. Ronnie believed that no commie should be allowed to work in the movies and that anyone who did not cooperate with his council or the House Committee on Un-American Activities (in other words, refused to allow the committee to ask impertinent questions about political beliefs) should walk the plank. To this day, he takes the line that there was never a blacklist in Hollywood except for the one that commies within the industry drew up in order to exclude good Americans from jobs. Ronnie has always been a very sincere sort of liar.

As luck would have it, Nancy Davis cropped up on one of the nonexistent blacklists. Apparently there was another possibly pinker actress named Nancy Davis in lotusland. She asked a producer what to do; he said that Reagan could clear her. Thus, they met . . . not so cute, as the Wise Hack would say. It was the end of 1949. They "dated" for two years. Plainly, she loved this bona fide movie star who never stopped talking just as she could never stop appearing to listen (what her stepfather Dr. Davis must have been like at the breakfast table can only be imagined). But the woman who had launched the marriage of Ronnie and Janie, Louella Parsons, the Saint Simon of San Simeon as well as of all movieland, could not understand why that idyllic couple had split up. She described in her column how "one of the lovely girls Ronnie seemed interested in for a while told me he recently said to her, 'Sure, I like you. I like you fine. But I think I've forgotten how to fall in love.' I wonder—do those embers of the once perfect love they shared still burn deep with haunting memories that won't let them forget?" If the popcorn isn't too old, we can pop it. But no salt and use oleomargarine.

Apparently, the embers had turned to ash. After two years, thirty-year-old Nancy married the forty-one-year-old Ronnie in the company of glamorous Mr. and Mrs. William Holden who posed, beaming, beside their new best friends at a time when they were their own new worst friends for, according to Mr. Leamer, as they posed side by side with the Reagans, "The Holdens weren't even talking to one another."

Nancy's career is now one of wifedom and motherhood and, of course, listening. Also, in due course, social climbing. She was born with a silver ladder in her hand, just like the rest of us who went to Sidwell Friends School. Naturally, there were problems with Ronnie's first set of children. Ronnie seems not to have been a particularly attentive father, while Nancy was an overattentive mother to her own two children. But she took a dim view of Ronnie's first litter. The Reagans settled on Pacific Palisades. Ronnie's movie career was grinding to an end; he was obliged to go to Las Vegas to be a gambling casino "emcee." As there were no commies working for the trade papers by then, the reviews were good.

2

The year 1952 is crucial in Reagan's life. The Hollywood unions had always taken the position that no talent agency could go into production on a regular basis since the resulting conflict of interest would screw agency clients. Eventually, federal law forbade this anomaly. But thirty years ago there was a tacit agreement between agencies and unions that, on a case-by-case basis, an occasional movie might be produced by an agency. The Music Corporation of America represented actor Ronald Reagan. Within that vast agency, one Taft Schreiber looked after Ronald Reagan's declining career. At the end of Reagan's term as president of the Screen Actors Guild, he did something unprecedented.

On July 3, 1952, after a series of meetings, Ronnie sent a letter to MCA granting the agency the blanket right to produce films.

Within a few years, MCA was a dominant force in show business. In
television, the forty or so shows that Revue Productions produced each
week far surpassed the output of other programming suppliers.

Now for the payoff:

Later that year [1954], Taft Schreiber . . . told Ronnie about a possible role
introducing a new weekly television anthology series, "The GE Theater"
. . . Schreiber owed his position as head of MCA's new Revue Productions
to a SAG decision in which Ronnie played an instrumental role,

and so on.

For eight years, Ronnie was GE's host and occasional actor; he also
became the corporate voice for General Electric's conservative viewpoint. During Reagan's tours of the country, he gave The Speech in the
name of General Electric in particular and free enterprise in general.
Gradually, Reagan became more and more right wing. But then if his
principal reading matter told him that the Russians were not only
coming but that their little Red brothers were entrenched in Congress
and the school libraries and the reservoirs (fluoride at the ready), he
must speak out. Finally, all this nonsense began to alarm even GE.
When he started to attack socialism's masterpiece, the TVA (a GE client
worth 50 million a year to the firm), he was told to start cooling it, which
he did. Then, "In 1962, pleading bad ratings, GE canceled the program."
   During this period, Reagan was not only getting deeper and deeper
into the politics of the far right, but he and Nancy were getting to know
some of the new-rich Hollywood folk outside show biz. Car dealers such
as Holmes Tuttle and other wheeler-dealers became friends. The wives
were into conspicuous consumption while the husbands were into
money and, marginally, conservative politics which would enable them
to make more money, pay less tax, and punish the poor. Thanks to
Ronnie's brother Neil, then with an advertising agency that peddled
Borax, the future leader of Righteous Christendom became host to
Borax's television series, *Death Valley Days.* That same year Ronnie
attended the Cow Palace investiture of Barry Goldwater.
   "In late October, Goldwater was unable to speak at the big $1,000-a-
plate fund raiser at the Ambassador Hotel in Los Angeles. . . . Holmes
Tuttle asked Ronnie to pinch-hit." Tuttle sat next to wealthy Henry
Salvatori, Goldwater's finance chairman. Tuttle suggested that they run

Ronnie for governor of California in 1966. Salvatori didn't think you could run an actor against an old political pro like the Democratic incumbent Pat Brown. But when Ronnie went national with The Speech on television, Ronnie was in business as a politician, and his friends decided to finance a Reagan race. To these new-rich Sunbelters, "Politicians and candidates, even Ronnie, were an inferior breed. 'Reagan doesn't have great depth,' Salvatori admits, 'but I don't know any politician who does. He's not the most intelligent man who ever was, but I've never met a politician with great depth. I don't know of any politician who would be smart enough to run my business, but Reagan just might.' " There it all is in one nut's shell.

The rest is beginning now to be history. "In the spring of 1965, forty-one rich businessmen formed 'The Friends of Ronald Reagan.' " For fifty thousand dollars a year, they hired a public-relations firm that specialized in political campaigns to groom Ronnie. California politics were carefully explained to him and he was given a crash course in the state's geography, which he may have flunked. He often had no idea where he was, or, as a supporter remarked to Leamer, "once, he didn't know a goddamn canal and where it went. Another time, he was standing in the Eagle River and didn't know where the hell he was," etc. But he had his dream of the city on the hill and he had The Speech and he had such insights as: the graduated income tax was "spawned by Marx as the prime essential of the socialistic state."

Alas, Mr. Leamer is not interested in Reagan's two terms as governor. He is more interested in Nancy's good grooming and circle of "best dressed" friends; also, in the way her past was falsified: "Nancy Davis Reagan was born in Chicago, the only daughter of Dr. and Mrs. Loyal Davis," said a campaign biography. Although Nancy had denied seeing her "natural" father after her adoption, she had indeed kept in touch for a time; but when he was dying in 1972 and her natural cousin tried to get through to her, there was no response. Mr. Leamer goes on rather too much about Nancy's wealthy girlfriends and their clothes as well as her wealthy *cavaliere servente* Jerome Zipkin who has known everyone from my mother to W. Somerset Maugham. "Maugham's biographer, Ted Morgan, thinks the British author may have patterned Elliot Templeton, a snobbish character in *The Razor's Edge*, on his American friend." Since *The Razor's Edge* was published in 1944, when Mr. Zipkin was still under thirty, it is most unlikely that that exquisite Anglophile American snob (and anti-Semite) could have been based on the charming Mr. Zipkin. Actually, for those interested in such trivia, the character was based on Henry de Courcey May, a monocled figure of my youth, much visible at Bailey's Beach in Newport, Rhode Island; although this exquisite was adored by our mothers, we little lads were under orders never to be alone with nice Mr. May—or not-so-nice Mr. Maugham for that matter. But once, on the train from Providence, Mr. May . . . But that is for Mr. Leamer's next book.

In a bored way, Mr. Leamer rushes through the governorship, using familiar Reagan boiler plate: the highest taxes in the state's history, and so on. He skirts around the most interesting caper of all, the ranch that Reagan was able to acquire through the good offices of MCA. When some details of this transaction were reported in the press, I was at a health spa near San Diego where Jules Stein and his wife (lifelong friends, as Mr. Leamer would say) were also taking the waters. When I asked Jules about the ranch caper, he got very nervous indeed. "What exactly did they print?" he asked. I told him. "Well," he said, "I didn't know anything about that. It was Schreiber who looked after Ronnie." By then Schreiber was dead.

Mr. Leamer tells us more than we want to know about the Reagan children. There seems to be a good deal of bitterness in a family that is closer to that of the Louds than to Judge Hardy's. But this is par for the course in the families of celebrities in general, and of politicians in particular. A ballet-dancer son with his mother's nose did not go down well. A daughter who decided to run for the Senate (and support the ERA) did not go down well either. So in 1982 Ronnie and his brother, Neil, helped to defeat Maureen, which was a pity since she would have been a more honorable public servant than her father. Apparently he has now had second thoughts or something; he has appointed her consultant "to improve his image among women." The family seems a lot creepier than it probably is simply because Reagan, a divorced man, has always put himself forward as the champion of prayer in the schools, and monogamy, and God, and a foe of abortion and smut and pot and the poor.

Mr. Leamer races through the political life: Ronnie sets out to replace Ford as president but instead is defeated in the primaries of 1976. Mr. Leamer finds Ronnie a pretty cold fish despite the professional appearance of warmth. When one of Ronnie's aides, Mike Deaver, lost out in a power struggle within the Reagan campaign, he was banished; and Ronnie never even telephoned him to say, "How are tricks?"

As he did in his own family, Ronnie stood above the squabble. Indeed four years before, when Ronnie had been choking on a peanut, Deaver had saved his life.

For God's sake, Leamer, dramatize! as Henry James always told us to do. When and how did that peanut get into his windpipe? Where were they? Was it the Heimlich maneuver Deaver used?

In 1980 Reagan took the nomination from Bush, whom he genuinely dislikes, if Mr. Leamer is correct. Reagan then wins the presidency though it might be more accurate to say that Carter lost it. Nancy woos Washington's old guard, the Bright Old Things as they are dubbed, who were at first mildly charmed and then more and more bemused by this curious couple who have no interest at all in talking about what Washington's BOT have always talked about: power and politics and history and even, shades of Henry Adams and John Hay, literature and art. Henry James was not entirely ironic when he called Washington "the city of conversation." Ronnie simply bends their ears with stories about Jack Warner while Nancy discusses pretty things.

Mr. Leamer gets quickly through the politics to the drama: the shooting of Ronnie, who was more gravely injured than anyone admitted at the time. By now, Mr. Leamer is racing along: "Unknown to [Nancy's] staff . . . she was accepting dresses and gowns from major designers as well as jewels from Bulgari and Harry Winston." Seven pages later: "Unknown to Nancy's staff, much of this jewelry didn't belong to her; it had been 'borrowed' for an unspecified period from the exclusive jeweler to be part of a White House collection." Nancy wriggled out of all this as best she could, proposing to give her dresses to a museum while suggesting a permanent White House collection of crown jewels for future first ladies. Conspicuous consumption at the White House has not been so visible since Mrs. Lincoln's day. But at least old Abe paid out of his own pocket for his wife's "flub dubs."

The most disturbing aspect of *Make-Believe* is that Ronnie not only is still the president but could probably be reelected. Almost as an afterthought, Mr. Leamer suddenly reveals, in the last pages of his book, the true Reagan problem, which is now a world problem:

What was so extraordinary was Ronnie's apparent psychic distance from the burden of the presidency. He sat in cabinet meetings doodling. Unless held to a rigid agenda, he would start telling Hollywood stories or talk about football in Dixon. Often in one-on-one conversations Ronnie seemed distracted or withdrawn: "He has a habit now," his brother, Neil, said. "You might be talking to him, and it's like he's picking his fingernails, but he's not. And you know then he's talking to himself."

"If people knew about him living in his own reality, they wouldn't believe it," said one White House aide. "There are only ten to fifteen people who know the extent, and until they leave and begin talking, no one will believe it."

Of all our presidents, Reagan most resembles Warren Harding. He is handsome, amiable, ignorant; he has an ambitious wife (Mrs. Harding was known as the Duchess). But in the year 1983 who keeps what brooch from Bulgari is supremely unimportant. What is important is that in a dangerous world, the United States, thanks to a worn-out political system, has not a president but an indolent cue-card reader, whose writers seem eager for us to be, as soon as possible, at war. To the extent that Reagan is aware of what is happening, he probably concurs. But then what actor, no matter how old, could resist playing the part of a wartime president? even though war is now the last worst hope of earth; and hardly make-believe.

Mr. Leamer's *Make-Believe* will be criticized because it is largely a compendium of trivia about personalities. Unfortunately, there is no other book for him to write—unless it be an updated version of *Who Owns America?*

*The New York Review of Books*
September 29, 1983

# 88

·

# ARMAGEDDON?

**I**

As the curtain falls on the ancient Acting President and his "Administration," it is time to analyze just what this bizarre episode in American history was all about. When Ronald Reagan's career in show business came to an end, he was hired to impersonate, first, a California governor and then an American president who would reduce taxes for his employers, the southern and western New Rich, much of whose money came from the defense industries. There is nothing unusual in this arrangement. All recent presidents have had their price tags, and the shelf life of each was short. What *was* unusual was his employers' cynical recognition that in an age of television one must steer clear of politicians who may not know how to act president and go instead for the best actor available for the job, the one who can read with warm plausibility the commercials that they have written for him.

Now it is quite possible to find an actor who does understand politics. Orson Welles and Gregory Peck come to mind; but would they have been sufficiently malleable? The producers were not about to experiment. They selected an actor who has never shown the slightest interest in actual politics as opposed to the mechanics of political elections in the age of television. That is why Reagan's economic and foreign policies have never made the slightest sense to anyone who knows anything about either. On the other hand, there is evidence that, unlike his wealthy sponsors, he has a sense of mission that, like Jesus', is not of this world.

The Great Obfuscator has come among us to dispense not only good news for the usual purposes of election but Good News. Reagan is nothing so mundane as an American president. Rather, he is here to prepare us for the coming war between the Christ and the Antichrist. A war, to be specific, between the United States and Russia, to take place in Israel. Hence, the mysterious and irrelevant, to most of us, exhortations about prayer in the schools, abortion, drugs, evil empires, and, mostly lately, the encroaching "sea of darkness." Hence, the military buildup that can never, ever cease until we have done battle for the Lord. Hence, the evangelical tone which makes the priestly eloquence of the late Woodrow Wilson sound like the current mayor of New York City. Hence, the perfect indifference to the disintegration of the American economy, educational system, industrial infrastructure; and, finally, really finally, the all-out one-time-only investment in a nuclear war to end all wars and Evil itself. This world is simply a used-up Kleenex, as Reagan's secretary of the interior, James Watt, acknowledged when he scorned the environmentalists with the first hint of what was in the works: "I do not know," he said to Congress in 1981, "how many future generations we can count on before the Lord returns." So why conserve anything, if Judgment Day is at hand?

For those, and I am one, who have been totally mystified by this president's weird indifference to the general welfare at home and the preservation of peace abroad, the most plausible answer has now been given in a carefully documented and deeply alarming book called *Prophecy and Politics: Militant Evangelists on the Road to Nuclear War.* The Texas-born author, Grace Halsell, comes from a fundamentalist Christian family. She has been for many years a working journalist, the author of seven books, a speechwriter for the dread Lyndon Johnson, and a longtime student of the twice-born Christians and their current president.

According to Halsell's interpretation and synthesis of facts available to all, the old actor has been rehearsing for some time the part of the Great Anarch who lets the curtain fall on the late great planet earth, as prophesied in the Good Book and in that even Better Book, *The Late Great Planet Earth* by an ex-riverboat captain, Hal Lindsey, whose account of the ultimate showdown between Christ and Antichrist was much admired by Ronald Reagan as well as by the eighteen million other Christian fundamentalists who bought the book in the 1970s and who believe that we are living in the penultimate Dispensation. The what? Let me explain.

Let us begin not with the Old Testament sky-god but with one Clyde Ingerson Scofield, who was born in Michigan in 1843. Scofield had an innate end-of-the-world bent which was reinforced by an Anglo-Irish divine named John Nelson Darby, who "taught that God had two plans and two groups of people with whom to work. Israel was God's kingdom here on earth and the Church (Christianity) was God's heavenly kingdom." According to Scofield/Darby, the sky-god has divided history into seven seven-year plans, or "Dispensations." During each Dispensation, God relates to man in a different way. Obviously, this particular sky-god is highly bureaucratic, even Leninist in his approach. Although Scofield was easily able to identify seven Dispensations in scripture, others could not. Eager to shed light, Mr. Scofield then sat down and rewrote the Bible so that we could all share in the Bad News. In 1909, he published the first *Scofield Reference Bible.* Since then many millions of copies have been (and are being) sold of his mock Bible.

Essentially, the Scofield exegesis is both Manichean (material world evil, spirit good; therefore, man cannot live at peace, is flawed, doomed) and Zoroastrian (Ahura Mazda, the wise Lord, defeats the evil Ahriman at the end of "the time of long dominion"). During the last but one Dispensation, Christ will defeat the Antichrist at Armageddon, fifty-five miles north of Tel Aviv. Just before the battle, the Church will be wafted to Heaven and all the good folks will experience "Rapture," as Scofield calls it. The wicked will suffer horribly. Then after seven years of "burying the dead" (presumably there will be survivors), God returns, bringing Peace and Joy and the Raptured Ones.

The gospel according to Scofield is preached daily by such American television divines as Jerry Falwell, Pat Robertson, Jimmy Swaggart, Jim Bakker, *et al.,* and according to a Yankelovich poll (1984), 39 percent of the American people believe in the death of earth by nuclear fire; and Rapture. Among the 39 percent is Ronald Reagan, as we shall see.

In 1985, Grace Halsell went on a Falwell Old Time Gospel Hour Tour of the Holy Land. If any of the good Christians on this tour expected to gaze upon Bethlehem and Nazareth where their God's son was born and lived, they were doomed to disappointment. These trips have only one purpose: to raise money for Falwell and Israel, under the guise of preparing the pilgrims for the approaching Armageddon. At Halsell's request, her group finally met one nervous taciturn local Christian. Moslems were ignored. On the other hand, there were constant briefings by Israelis on their military might.

The Falwell indoctrination is, relentlessly, the imminent end of the world, the ambiguity of the role of the Jews (*why* won't they convert?), and the importance of the state of Israel whose invention in 1948 and victories in 1967 were all foretold, most excitingly, by Scofield: exciting because Dispensationalists can never be sure *which* Dispensation they happen to be living in. Is this the one that will end in Armageddon? If so, when will the seven years be up and the fireworks start? In 1982, poor Pat Robertson got out on a limb when he thought that Israel's invasion of Lebanon was the beginning of the longed-for end; rapturously, Pat declared on television: "The whole thing is in place now, it can happen at any time. . . . But by fall, undoubtedly something like this will happen which will fulfill Ezekiel." Happily for us, unhappily for Pat, 1982 wasn't the year. But I reckon if we all pray hard enough the end's bound to come real fast.

As Halsell and group gaze upon Armageddon, an innocent rural countryside, one of her companions fills her in on *the meaning of it all.* Reverently, he quotes St. John: "And he gathered them together into a place called in the Hebrew tongue Armageddon." When she inquires what this neutral sentence has to do with a final battle between Christ and Antichrist, she gets a barrage of Bronze-age quotes: "The cities of the nation fell . . . and every island fled away and the mountains were not found." Apparently, the Euphrates then dries up and the Antichrist himself (you guessed it, Gorbachev) crosses into Israel to do battle with the Lord, who comes down from Heaven, with "a great shout" (played by Charlton Heston—once again Ronald Reagan is, in Jack Warner's phrase, the star's "best friend"). The Lord and the Americans win hands down, thanks to SDI and the B-I bomber and the Fourteenth Regiment cavalry from Des Moines, Iowa, and a number of Republican elephants who happen to have strayed onto the field, trumpeting free enterprise, as the Lord requires.

Dispensationalists delight in the horror of this crucial (pun intended) battle, as predicted so gloatingly by Ezekiel: "Torrential rains and hailstone, fire and brimstone . . . a great shaking in the land . . . every kind of terror." But it is sly prescient old Zechariah, eye glued to that Bronze-age crystal ball, who foretells atomic weapons: "Their flesh shall consume away while they stand upon their feet, and their eyes shall consume away in their holes, and their tongue shall consume away in their mouth."

What about the Jews? asked Halsell. Since they won't be with Gorbachev (a.k.a. Gog and Magog), what happens to them? The answer is stern: "Two-thirds of all the Jews living here will be killed . . ." She asks, why, if the Jews are *His* chosen people, as the Dispensationalists believe? The answer glows with charity: "He's doing it mainly for his ancient people, the Jews. . . . He devised a seven-year Tribulation period mainly to purge the Jews, to get them to see the light and recognize Christ as their Savior. . . . Don't you see? God wants them to bow down before His only son, who is our Lord Jesus Christ." Anyway, forget the Jews because many, many other people will also be exterminated so that Christ may come again, *in peace*. Just why Jesus' Dad should have chosen nuclear war as the means of universal peace is as rare and impenetrable a mystery as the Trinity itself.

Although the three religions (Judaism, Christianity, and Islam) of the Book, as Moslems call the Old Testament, are alike in a common worship of a highly primitive sky-god (rejected by the more civilized Hindus, Buddhists, and Confucians) and variously adapted to different times, peoples, and climates, only Fundamentalist Christianity in our century has got so seriously into the end-of-the-world game, or Rapture, as it is described by the Dispensationalists who believe . . .

But why am *I* telling you this? Let Jerry Falwell, the millionaire divine of Lynchburg, Virginia, explain it to you as he did to the journalist Bob Scheer in the *Los Angeles Times* (March 4, 1981): "We believe that Russia, because of her need of oil—and she's running out now [no, she's not, Jerry]—is going to move in the Middle East, and particularly Israel because of their hatred of the Jew [so where's the oil there, Jerry?] and that it is at that time when all hell will break out. And it is at that time when I believe there will be some nuclear holocaust on this earth. . . ." Falwell then does the obligatory mishmash from Apocrypha—and the wild "real" thing, too: Russia "will be ultimately totally destroyed," he tells us. When Scheer says that if that happens the whole world will be destroyed, Falwell spells out the Dispensationalist doctrine: "No, not the whole world, because then our Lord is coming back to the earth. First, he comes to take the Church out [plainly, Falwell was never in the army—for us "to take out" means destroy; he means lift up, save]. Seven years later, after Armageddon, this terrible holocaust, He's coming back to this very earth so it won't be destroyed, and the Church is coming with him [up, down; out, in—the vertiginous Church], to rule and reign with

Christ on the earth for a thousand years. . . ." A joyous millennium of no abortion, no sodomy, no crack, no Pure Drug and Food Act, no civil rights, but of schools where only prayers are said, and earth proved daily flat.

"We believe," says Falwell, "we're living in those days just prior to the Lord's coming." When Scheer asks for an expected time of arrival, Falwell assures him that although the Lord has warned them not to give dates, he himself has a hunch: "I do not think we have fifty years left. I don't think my children will live their full lives out. . . ." So we are now in the penultimate seven-year Dispensation, which will end with Armageddon.

Scheer suggests that after the nuclear weapons we drop on Russia and the ones they drop on us, the great planet earth will be very late indeed. But Falwell *knows* that there will be survivors, in addition to the taken-out Church. Personally, he has no fear of the nuclear holocaust because, as he said to Halsell's group, with a grin, "You know why I'm not worried? I ain't gonna be here."

**2**

Halsell notes: "A Nielsen survey released in October 1985 shows that 61 million Americans (40 percent of all regular viewers) listen to preachers who tell them that we can do nothing to prevent a nuclear war in our lifetime." But do the 61 million actually believe what they hear? I suspect that they probably do on the ground that so little other information gets to them. They are not book readers (the United States has dropped to twenty-fourth place among book-reading nations); the public educational system has been allowed to deteriorate as public money goes mostly to defense; while television news is simply entertainment and the principal entertainer (until the latest Iran scandal) is a professional actor who knows very little about anything other than his necessary craft, which is to sell emotions—and Armageddon. But, again, does the salesman believe in the product that he sells? Halsell thinks that he does.

On September 20, 1970, an evangelical Christian, George Otis, and several like-minded folk visited Reagan when he was governor of California. They spoke rapturously of Rapture. Then, according to Otis, they all joined hands in prayer and Otis prophesied Reagan's coming election to the presidency. According to Otis (*Visit with a King*) Reagan's arms "shook and pulsated" during this prophecy. The next summer (June 29, 1971) Reagan asked Billy Graham to address the California legislature; afterward, at lunch, Reagan asked Graham, "Well, do you believe that Jesus Christ is coming soon, and what are the signs of his coming if that is the case?" Graham did not beat about this burning bush. "The indication," he said, "is that Jesus Christ is at the very door."

Later in 1971 Governor Reagan attended a dinner where he sat next to James Mills, the president of the California state senate. Mills was so impressed by the dinner conversation that he wrote it all down immediately afterward, but published it much later (*San Diego Magazine,* August 1985), *pro bono publico,* if a bit late.

After the main course, the lights dimmed and flaming bowls of cherries jubilee were served. No doubt inspired by the darkness and the flames, Reagan suddenly asked, out of right field, if Mills had read "the fierce Old Testament prophet Ezekiel." Mills allowed that he had (after all, you don't get elected to the California State Senate if you say no); as it turned out, he did know Ezekiel. Then, "with firelit intensity," Reagan began to talk about how Libya had now gone communist, just as Ezekiel had foretold, and "that's a sign that the day of Armageddon isn't far off." When Mills reminded him that Ethiopia was also due to go over to Satan and he couldn't, somehow, see the Emperor Haile Selassie turning pinko or allowing the Reds to take over his country in order to make war "on God's Chosen People," Reagan agreed "that everything hasn't fallen into place yet. But there is only that one thing left that has to happen. The Reds have to take over Ethiopia." Mills thought this unlikely. Reagan thought it inevitable: "It's necessary to fulfill the prophecy that Ethiopia will be one of the ungodly nations that go against Israel." As it turned out, Reagan was right on target. Three years later Ethiopia went communist, or something very like it.

Mills was particularly impressed by Reagan's manner, which is usually amiable to the point of goofiness: Now he was "like a preacher [talking] to a skeptical college student." Reagan then told Mills: "All of the other prophecies that had to be fulfilled before Armageddon have come to pass. In the thirty-eighth chapter of Ezekiel it says God will take the children of Israel from among the heathen when they'd been scattered and will gather them again in the promised land. That has finally come about after 2,000 years. For the first time ever, everything is in place for the battle of Armageddon and the Second Coming of Christ."

When Mills said that the Bible clearly states that men will never have the fun of knowing just *when* this awesome event will take place, Reagan replied, "Everything is falling into place. It can't be too long now. Ezekiel says that fire and brimstone will be rained upon the enemies of God's people. That must mean that they will be destroyed by nuclear weapons . . . Ezekiel tells us that Gog, the nation that will lead all of the other powers of darkness ['sea of darkness,' he moaned just after he plunged into Irangate] against Israel, will come out of the north. What other powerful nation is to the north of Israel? None. But it didn't seem to make much sense before the Russian revolution, when Russia was a Christian country. Now it does, now that Russia has become communistic and atheistic, now that Russia has set itself against God. Now it fits the description perfectly." So you thought there would be an arms deal with the Soviet Union? A cutback of nuclear weapons? Not on, literally, our lives. To stop the arms race would be to give the victory to Gog.

Mills's conversation took place fifteen years ago. Nine years later, the nemesis of Gog was elected president. If he survives, Constitutionally or constitutionally, he now has two more years to see us on our way to, if not actually *into,* glory. Until recently, one could not imagine any American president with a sense of history openly expressing religious views that are so opposed to the spirit of the founders of the United States. Jefferson had a low opinion of religious—as opposed to ethical—Christianity, and no friendly view of the pre-Scofield Old Testament, while the non-Christian Lincoln's appeals to the Almighty were as vague as Confucius's ritual hymns to Heaven. The American republic was created by men of Enlightenment, who had little or no use for sky-god systems; certainly they would have regarded the Scofield-Falwell-Reagan sky-god as a totem more suitable for dull Neanderthals rather than for us neo-Cro-Magnons.

But Reagan knows nothing about Jefferson, and history is not his bag. On the other hand, "I was fortunate," he told TV evangelist Jim Bakker. "I had a mother who planted a great faith in me. . . .' " Garry Wills, in his recent book *Reagan's America,* tells us a great deal about Nelle Reagan who "was baptized in Tampico (Illinois), as a Disciple of Christ, by total immersion . . . on Easter Sunday, 1910." She was a great influence on her son, who taught Sunday School and then attended Drake University, a Disciples' college. With mounting horror, one realizes that he may not be what all of us had hoped (even prayed), a hypocrite. Until Reagan's recent misfortunes, he had not the United States but Armageddon on his mind.

During the presidential race of 1980, Reagan told Jim Bakker of the

PTL network: "We may be the generation that sees Armageddon," while a writer for *The New York Times* reported that Reagan (1980) told a Jewish group that "Israel is the only stable democracy we can rely on as a spot where Armageddon could come." Apparently, the god of Ezekiel has a thing about the necessity of stable democratic elections *prior* to sorting out the Elect just before the Bang.

Although most American right-wingers are anti-Semites, the Armageddonists need a strong Israel in order to fulfil prophecy. So TV-evangelicals, Pentagon ("Those are the *real* anti-Semites," former Austrian Chancellor Bruno Kreisky muttered in my ear last October at Frankfurt), and right-wing politicians like Richard Nixon are all dedicated supporters of Israel. Sensibly and cynically, the Israelis exploit this religious madness.

Halsell reports that in October 1983, President Reagan told an Israeli lobby leader, Tom Dine, "You know, I turn back to your ancient prophets [Dine runs a home for retired ancient prophets where you can be denounced by the prophet of your choice] in the Old Testament, and I find myself wondering if we're the generation that's going to see that come about. I don't know if you noticed any of those prophecies lately, but believe me, they certainly describe the times we're going through." This was the year that Reagan decided to alert the nation to Gog. On March 8, 1983 he declared, "They [the Soviet Union] are the focus of evil in the modern world." Later, "I believe that communism is another sad, bizarre chapter in human history *whose last pages even now are being written* [my italics]." The old Acting President seems not to mind our approaching fiery fate. But then, of course, he's been saved, as he told George Otis. So, like Falwell, he ain't gonna be here either at the end.

3

The fifteenth of February, 1987, proved to be a bright sunny day in Hell, where I had come with nine hundred worthies from several dozen countries, to listen to Satan himself, Gorbachev, who spoke thoughtfully of the absolute necessity of abolishing all nuclear weapons on the ground that the fact of their existence endangers the human race. Plainly, the Lord of the Flies has not read the Good Book. If he had, he would know that this planet is just a staging area for that glorious place in the sky where, free of abortion and contraception and communism, the chosen will swirl about in the cosmic dust, praising the Lord for all eternity. In fact, not only did Gorbachev not seem to know the Truth that Reagan adheres to (so unlike mere irksome truth telling), he even suggested to us that this planet may be the only one that could support a human race. It would be, he said, a pity to lose everything through war or, more likely, accident. Then, to everyone's amazement, Gorbachev mentioned Chernobyl by name, breaking the first law of the TV politician—never acknowledge failure. Since Hitler's invasion, nothing has alarmed the Russians more than Chernobyl's fallout, which is everywhere, including the village where I live in southern Italy: There is cesium 137 at the bottom of my garden. Gorbachev owned up to the whole mess, something our Acting President would never do . . . indeed has not, specifically, done.

On April 10, 1986, in order to preserve freedom for all men everywhere, the Acting President ordered a resumption of underground nuclear testing. The test's code name was Mighty Oak; the place, Nevada. Several weeks before Chernobyl, Mighty Oak came a cropper. Some sort of unanticipated explosion went wrong. When nongovernment analysts duly noted increased radiation in the spring zephyrs, they were told by the Department of Energy that all was well. Then, on May 7, the department admitted that the level of the radioactive inert gas xenon 133 had been detected fifty miles from the site, at 550 picocuries per cubic meter. Of course things were, as always, worse in Russia. Now we learn that of our last six nuclear underground tests, three have made the atmosphere more than ever poisonous through mishap. In August 1986, Gorbachev announced a moratorium on such tests. But Reagan chooses to ignore the moratorium and stands tall.

As I stared at the stocky round-faced little man addressing us, I tried to imagine any American politician making as straightforward and intelligent an address to the likes of Trudeau and Galbraith, Milos Forman and Berio (needless to say the American press ignored the substance of the speech and zeroed in on the charismatic presence of one Yoko Ono). The only direct reference that Lucifer made to the Archangel from Warner Brothers concerned something that Reagan had said to him in Geneva: If the earth were ever to be invaded by Martians, the United States and the Soviet Union would, of course, be joint allies in a common cause. Gorbachev sighed: "I told the president that it was, perhaps, premature to prepare for such an invasion but as we had a common enemy right now, nuclear weapons, why couldn't we unite to get rid of them?" But the planter of Mighty Oaks was not to be seduced.

How could he be? Nearly every major politician in the United States is paid for by what is known as "the defense industry." That is why close to 90 percent of the government's income is wasted on "defense."

Ordinarily, American conservatives (known, amusingly, as liberals) would have stopped this destruction of the economy and endangerment of life itself by the radical right (known, yet another thigh slapper, as conservatives). But things began to go awry with the invention of Israel. Many American conservatives decided that, for them, Israel comes first and so they chose to make common cause with the anti-Semitic but pro-Israel Jesus Christers, who lust for rapture.

Two years ago, Irving Kristol justified this shift in a house organ of the American Jewish Committee. Kristol noted that when the Jews were new to the American scene they "found liberal opinion and liberal politicism more congenial in their attitudes, more sensitive to Jewish concerns." So they voted for the liberal paladin, Franklin D. Roosevelt and his heirs. But now, Kristol writes, "is there any point in Jews hanging on, dogmatically and hypocritically, to their opinions of yesteryear when it is a new era we are confronting?" Because of Israel, "we are constrained to take our allies where and how we find them." Finally, "If one had informed American Jews fifteen years ago that there was to be a powerful revival of Protestant fundamentalism as a political as well as religious force, they would surely have been alarmed, since they would have assumed that any such revival might tend to be anti-Semitic and anti-Israel. But the Moral Majority is neither." But, of course, the Moral Majority is deeply anti-Semitic and will always remain so because the Jews killed our Lord (proving that no good deed ever goes unpunished: Were not those first-century Jews simply fulfilling The Divine Plan?), and the Jesus Christers are pro-Israel for reasons that have nothing to do with the Jews who are—except for exactly 144,000—going to get it along with the commies, at Armageddon.

Currently, there is little open debate in the United States on any of these matters. The Soviet Union must be permanently demonized in order to keep the money flowing to the Pentagon for "defense," while Arabs are characterized as subhuman terrorists. Israel may not be criticized at all (ironically, the press in Israel is far more open and self-critical than ours). We do have one token Palestinian who is allowed an occasional word in the press, Professor Edward Said, who wrote (*Guardian,* December 21, 1986): since the "1982 Israeli invasion of Lebanon . . . it was felt by the Zionist lobby that the spectacle of ruthless Israeli power on the TV screen would have to be effaced from memory

by the strategy of incriminating the media as anti-Semitic for showing
these scenes at all." A wide range of Americans were then exuberantly
defamed, including myself (see page 1017, "A Cheerful Response").

I wondered, as I listened to Gorbachev, if he had any notion of the
forces arrayed against him in the United States. Obviously, he is aware
of the Israeli lobby, but that is something that he can come to terms
with: Neither the Israelis nor the Russians are interested in suicide. But
the Dispensationalists are quite another matter. By accident, the producers of that one-time hit-show the United States of America picked for
the part of president a star with primitive religious longings. We cannot
blame them. How could they have known? They thought that he was
giving all that money to defense simply to reward them for giving him
the lead, which he was doing, in part; but he was also responding to
Ezekiel, and the glory of the coming end.

On the other hand, Gorbachev said that because he believes in life,
the nuclear arms race will end because this is the only world that we
have. We applauded. He paused. Then, with perfect timing, he said, "I
had expected warmer applause on that line." We gave it to him. He
laughed. The speech was soon over.

I said to Norman Mailer, "I think there should be a constitutional
amendment making it impossible for anyone to be president who believes in an afterlife." Mailer said, "Well, that rules me out." I was
astonished and said so. "If there isn't an afterlife," he said, "then what's
the point to all this?" Before I could answer, he said, "All right, all right.
I know what you're going to say. There is no point." A pride of exotic
bishops separated us.

Yes, that is what I would have said, and because there is no cosmic
point to the life that each of us perceives on this distant bit of dust at
galaxy's edge, all the more reason for us to maintain in proper balance
what we have here. Because there is nothing else. No thing. This is it.
And quite enough, all in all.

*The Observer* (London)
November 15, 1987
(But written as of March 1987)

# 8 9

·

# THE DAY
# THE AMERICAN EMPIRE
# RAN OUT OF GAS

On September 16, 1985, when the Commerce Department announced that the United States had become a debtor nation, the American Empire died. The empire was seventy-one years old and had been in ill health since 1968. Like most modern empires, ours rested not so much on military prowess as on economic primacy.*

After the French Revolution, the world money power shifted from Paris to London. For three generations, the British maintained an old-fashioned colonial empire, as well as a modern empire based on London's primacy in the money markets. Then, in 1914, New York replaced London as the world's financial capital. Before 1914, the United States had been a developing country, dependent on outside investment. But with the shift of the money power from Old World to New, what had been a debtor nation became a creditor nation and central motor to the world's economy. All in all, the English were well pleased to have us take their place. They were too few in number for so big a task. As early as the turn of the century, they were eager for us not only to help them

*In *The Guardian* (November 20, 1987) Frank Kermode wrote: "I happened to hear Vidal expound this thesis in a New York theater, to a highly ribald and incredulous, though doubtless very ignorant audience. . . ." Since then, my thesis has been repeated by others so many times that it is now conventional wisdom.

out financially but to continue, in their behalf, the destiny of the Anglo-Saxon race: to bear with courage the white man's burden, as Rudyard Kipling not so tactfully put it. Were we not—English and Americans—all Anglo-Saxons, united by common blood, laws, language? Well, no, we were not. But our differences were not so apparent then. In any case, we took on the job. We would supervise and civilize the lesser breeds. We would make money.

By the end of the Second World War, we were the most powerful and least damaged of the great nations. We also had most of the money. America's hegemony lasted exactly five years. Then the cold and hot wars began. Our masters would have us believe that all our problems are the fault of the Evil Empire of the East, with its satanic and atheistic religion, ever ready to destroy us in the night. This nonsense began at a time when we had atomic weapons and the Russians did not. They had lost twenty million of their people in the war, and eight million of them before the war, thanks to their neoconservative Mongolian political system. Most important, there was never any chance, then or now, of the money power shifting from New York to Moscow. What was—and is—the reason for the big scare? Well, the Second War made prosperous the United States, which had been undergoing a depression for a dozen years, and made very rich those magnates and their managers who govern the republic, with many a wink, in the people's name. In order to maintain a general prosperity (and enormous wealth for the few) they decided that we would become the world's policeman, perennial shield against the Mongol hordes. We shall have an arms race, said one of the high priests, John Foster Dulles, and we shall win it because the Russians will go broke first. We were then put on a permanent wartime economy, which is why close to two thirds of the government's revenues are constantly being siphoned off to pay for what is euphemistically called defense.

As early as 1950, Albert Einstein understood the nature of the rip-off. He said, "The men who possess real power in this country have no intention of ending the cold war." Thirty-five years later, they are still at it, making money while the nation itself declines to eleventh place in world per capita income, to forty-sixth in literacy and so on, until last summer (not suddenly, I fear) we found ourselves close to two trillion dollars in debt. Then, in the fall, the money power shifted from New York to Tokyo, and that was the end of our empire. Now the long-feared Asiatic colossus takes its turn as world leader, and we—the white race—have become the yellow man's burden. Let us hope that he will treat us more kindly than we treated him.* In any case, if the foreseeable future is not nuclear, it will be Asiatic, some combination of Japan's advanced technology with China's resourceful landmass. Europe and the United States will then be, simply, irrelevant to the world that matters, and so we come full circle: Europe began as the relatively empty uncivilized Wild West of Asia; then the Western Hemisphere became the Wild West of Europe. Now the sun has set in our West and risen once more in the East.

The British used to say that their empire was obtained in a fit of absentmindedness. They exaggerate, of course. On the other hand, our modern empire was carefully thought out by four men. In 1890 a U.S. Navy captain, Alfred Thayer Mahan, wrote the blueprint for the American imperium, *The Influence of Sea Power Upon History, 1660–1783*. Then Mahan's friend, the historian-geopolitician Brooks Adams, younger brother of Henry, came up with the following formula: "All civilization is centralization. All centralization is economy." He applied the formula in the following syllogism: "Under economical centralization, Asia is cheaper than Europe. The world tends to economic centralization. Therefore, Asia tends to survive and Europe to perish." Ultimately, *that* is why we were in Vietnam. The amateur historian and professional politician Theodore Roosevelt was much under the influence of Adams and Mahan; he was also their political instrument, most active not so much during his presidency as during the crucial war with Spain, where he can take a good deal of credit for our seizure of the Philippines, which made us a world empire. Finally, Senator Henry Cabot Lodge, Roosevelt's closest friend, kept in line a Congress that had a tendency to forget our holy mission—our manifest destiny—and ask, rather wistfully, for internal improvements.

From the beginning of our republic we have had imperial longings. We took care—as we continue to take care—of the indigenous population. We maintained slavery a bit too long even by a cynical world's tolerant standards. Then, in 1846, we produced our first conquistador, President James K. Polk. After acquiring Texas, Polk deliberately started a war with Mexico because, as he later told the historian George Bancroft, we had to acquire California. Thanks to Polk, we did. And that is why to this day the Mexicans refer to our southwestern states as "the occupied lands," which Hispanics are now, quite sensibly, filling up.

*Believe it or not, this plain observation was interpreted as a racist invocation of "the Yellow Peril"!

The case against empire began as early as 1847. Representative Abraham Lincoln did not think much of Polk's war, while Lieutenant Ulysses S. Grant, who fought at Veracruz, said in his memoirs, "The war was an instance of a republic following the bad example of European monarchies, in not considering justice in their desire to acquire additional territory." He went on to make a causal link, something not usual in our politics then and completely unknown now: "The Southern rebellion was largely the outgrowth of the Mexican War. Nations, like individuals, are punished for their transgressions. We got our punishment in the most sanguinary and expensive war of modern times."

But the empire has always had more supporters than opponents. By 1895 we had filled up our section of North America. We had tried twice—and failed—to conquer Canada. We had taken everything that we wanted from Mexico. Where next? Well, there was the Caribbean at our front door and the vast Pacific at our back. Enter the Four Horsemen—Mahan, Adams, Roosevelt, and Lodge.

The original republic was thought out carefully, and openly, in *The Federalist Papers:* We were not going to have a monarchy and we were not going to have a democracy. And to this day we have had neither. For two hundred years we have had an oligarchical system in which men of property can do well and the others are on their own. Or, as Brooks Adams put it, the sole problem of our ruling class is whether to coerce or to bribe the powerless majority. The so-called Great Society bribed; today coercion is very much in the air. Happily, our neoconservative Mongoloids favor only authoritarian and never totalitarian means of coercion.

Unlike the republic, the empire was worked out largely in secret. Captain Mahan, in a series of lectures delivered at the Naval War College, compared the United States with England. Each was essentially an island state that could prevail in the world only through sea power. England had already proved his thesis. Now the United States must do the same. We must build a great navy in order to acquire overseas possessions. Since great navies are expensive, the wealth of new colonies must be used to pay for our fleets. In fact, the more colonies acquired, the more ships; the more ships, the more empire. Mahan's thesis is agreeably circular. He showed how small England had ended up with most of Africa and all of southern Asia, thanks to sea power. He thought that we should do the same. The Caribbean was our first and easiest target. Then on to the Pacific Ocean, with all its islands. And, finally, to China, which was breaking up as a political entity.

Theodore Roosevelt and Brooks Adams were tremendously excited by this prospect. At the time Roosevelt was a mere police commissioner in New York City, but he had dreams of imperial glory. "He wants to be," snarled Henry Adams, "our Dutch-American Napoleon." Roosevelt began to maneuver his way toward the heart of power, sea power. With Lodge's help, he got himself appointed assistant secretary of the navy, under a weak secretary and a mild president. Now he was in place to modernize the fleet and to acquire colonies. Hawaii was annexed. Then a part of Samoa. Finally, colonial Cuba, somehow, had to be liberated from Spain's tyranny. At the Naval War College, Roosevelt declared, "To prepare for war is the most effectual means to promote peace." How familiar that sounds! But since the United States had no enemies as of June 1897, a contemporary might have remarked that since we were already at peace with everyone, why prepare for war? Today, of course, we are what he dreamed we would be, a nation armed to the teeth and hostile to everyone. But what with Roosevelt was a design to acquire an empire is for us a means to transfer money from the Treasury to the various defense industries, which in turn pay for the elections of Congress and president.

Our turn-of-the-century imperialists may have been wrong, and I think they were. But they were intelligent men with a plan, and the plan worked. Aided by Lodge in the Senate, Brooks Adams in the press, Admiral Mahan at the Naval War College, the young assistant secretary of the navy began to build up the fleet and look for enemies. After all, as Brooks Adams proclaimed, "war is the solvent." But war with whom? And for what? And where? At one point England seemed a likely enemy. There was a boundary dispute over Venezuela, which meant that we could invoke the all-purpose Monroe Doctrine (the invention of John Quincy Adams, Brooks's grandfather). But as we might have lost such a war, nothing happened. Nevertheless, Roosevelt kept on beating his drum: "No triumph of peace," he shouted, "can equal the armed triumph of war." Also: "We must take Hawaii in the interests of the white race." Even Henry Adams, who found T.R. tiresome and Brooks, his own brother, brilliant but mad, suddenly declared, "In another fifty years . . . the white race will have to reconquer the tropics by war and nomadic invasion, or be shut up north of the 50th parallel." And so at century's end, our most distinguished ancestral voices were not prophesying but praying for war.

An American warship, the *Maine,* blew up in Havana harbor. We held Spain responsible; thus, we got what John Hay called "a splendid little war." We would liberate Cuba, drive Spain from the Caribbean. As for the Pacific, even before the *Maine* was sunk, Roosevelt had ordered Commodore Dewey and his fleet to the Spanish Philippines— just in case. Spain promptly collapsed, and we inherited its Pacific and Caribbean colonies. Admiral Mahan's plan was working triumphantly.

In time we allowed Cuba the appearance of freedom while holding on to Puerto Rico. Then President William McKinley, after an in-depth talk with God, decided that we should also keep the Philippines, in order, he said, to Christianize them. When reminded that the Filipinos were Roman Catholics, the president said, Exactly. We must Christianize them. Although Philippine nationalists had been our allies against Spain, we promptly betrayed them and their leader, Emilio Aguinaldo. As a result it took us several years to conquer the Philippines, and tens—some say hundreds—of thousands of Filipinos died that our empire might grow.

The war was the making of Theodore Roosevelt. Surrounded by the flower of the American press, he led a group of so-called Rough Riders up a very small hill in Cuba. As a result of this proto-photo opportunity he became a national hero, governor of New York, McKinley's running mate and, when McKinley was killed in 1901, president.

Not everyone liked the new empire. After Manila, Mark Twain thought that the stars and bars of the American flag should be replaced by a skull and crossbones. He also said, "We cannot maintain an empire in the Orient and maintain a republic in America." He was right, of course. But as he was only a writer who said funny things, he was ignored. The compulsively vigorous Roosevelt defended our war against the Philippine population, and he attacked the likes of Twain. "Every argument that can be made for the Filipinos could be made for the Apaches," he explained, with his lovely gift for analogy. "And every word that can be said for Aguinaldo could be said for Sitting Bull. As peace, order and prosperity followed our expansion over the land of the Indians, so they will follow us in the Philippines."

Despite the criticism of the few, the Four Horsemen had pulled it off. The United States was a world empire. And one of the horsemen not only got to be president, but for his pious meddling in the Russo-Japanese conflict our greatest apostle of war was awarded the Nobel Peace Prize. One must never underestimate Scandinavian wit.

Empires are restless organisms. They must constantly renew themselves; should an empire start leaking energy, it will die. Not for nothing were the Adams brothers fascinated by entropy. By energy. By force.

Brooks Adams, as usual, said the unsayable. "Laws are a necessity," he declared. "Laws are made by the strongest, and they must and shall be obeyed." Oliver Wendell Holmes, Jr., thought this a wonderful observation, while the philosopher William James came to a similar conclusion, which can also be detected, like an invisible dynamo, at the heart of the novels of his brother Henry.

According to Brooks Adams, "The most difficult problem of modern times is unquestionably how to protect property under popular governments." The Four Horsemen fretted a lot about this. They need not have. We have never had a popular government in the sense that they feared, nor are we in any danger now. Our only political party has two right wings, one called Republican, the other Democratic. But Henry Adams figured all that out back in the 1890s. "We have a single system," he wrote, and "in that system the only question is the price at which the proletariat is to be bought and sold, the bread and circuses." But none of this was for public consumption. Publicly, the Four Horsemen and their outriders spoke of the American mission to bring to all the world freedom and peace, through slavery and war if necessary. Privately, their constant fear was that the weak masses might combine one day against the strong few, their natural leaders, and take away their money. As early as the election of 1876 socialism had been targeted as a vast evil that must never be allowed to corrupt simple American persons. When Christianity was invoked as the natural enemy of those who might limit the rich and their games, the combination of cross and dollar sign proved—and proves—irresistible.

During the first decade of our disagreeable century, the great world fact was the internal collapse of China. Who could pick up the pieces? Britain grabbed Kowloon; Russia was busy in the north; the Kaiser's fleet prowled the China coast; Japan was modernizing itself and biding its time. Although Theodore Roosevelt lived and died a dedicated racist, the Japanese puzzled him. After they sank the Russian fleet, Roosevelt decided that they were to be respected and feared even though they were our racial inferiors. For those Americans who served in the Second World War, it was an article of faith—as of 1941 anyway—that the Japanese could never win a modern war. Because of their slant eyes, they would not be able to master aircraft. Then they sank our fleet at Pearl Harbor.

Jingoism aside, Brooks Adams was a good analyst. In the 1890s he wrote: "Russia, to survive, must undergo a social revolution internally and/or expand externally. She will try to move into Shansi Province,

richest prize in the world. Should Russia and Germany combine . . ."
That was the nightmare of the Four Horsemen. At a time when simpler
folk feared the rise of Germany alone, Brooks Adams saw the world
ultimately polarized between Russia and the United States, with China
as the common prize. American maritime power versus Russia's landmass. That is why, quite seriously, he wanted to extend the Monroe
Doctrine to the Pacific Ocean. For him, "war [was] the ultimate form
of economic competition."

We are now at the end of the twentieth century. England, France, and
Germany have all disappeared from the imperial stage. China is now
reassembling itself, and Confucius, greatest of political thinkers, is again
at the center of the Middle Kingdom. Japan has the world money power
and wants a landmass; China now seems ready to go into business with
its ancient enemy. Wars of the sort that the Four Horsemen enjoyed are,
if no longer possible, no longer practical. Today's conquests are shifts
of currency by computer and the manufacture of those things that
people everywhere are willing to buy.

I have said very little about writers because writers have figured very
little in our imperial story. The founders of both republic and empire
wrote well: Jefferson and Hamilton, Lincoln and Grant, T.R. and the
Adamses. Today public figures can no longer write their own speeches
or books, and there is some evidence that they can't read them either.

Yet at the dawn of the empire, for a brief instant, our *professional*
writers tried to make a difference. Upton Sinclair and company attacked
the excesses of the ruling class. Theodore Roosevelt coined the word
"muckraking" to describe what they were doing. He did not mean the
word as praise. Since then a few of our writers have written on public
themes, but as they were not taken seriously, they have ended by not
taking themselves seriously, at least as citizens of a republic. After all,
most writers are paid by universities, and it is not wise to be thought
critical of a garrison state which spends so much money on so many
campuses.

When Confucius was asked what would be the first thing that he
would do if he were to lead the state—his never-to-be-fulfilled dream—
he said *rectify the language.* This is wise. This is subtle. As societies grow
decadent, the language grows decadent, too. Words are used to disguise,
not to illuminate, action: You liberate a city by destroying it. Words are
used to confuse, so that at election time people will solemnly vote
against their own interests. Finally, words must be so twisted as to

justify an empire that has now ceased to exist, much less make sense. Is rectification of our system possible for us? Henry Adams thought not. In 1910 he wrote: "The whole fabric of society will go to wrack if we really lay hands of reform on our rotten institutions." Then he added, "From top to bottom the whole system is a fraud, all of us know it, laborers and capitalists alike, and all of us are consenting parties to it." Since then, consent has grown frayed; and we have become poor, and our people sullen.

To maintain a thirty-five-year arms race it is necessary to have a fearsome enemy. Not since the invention of the Wizard of Oz have American publicists created anything quite so demented as the idea that the Soviet Union is a monolithic, omnipotent empire with tentacles everywhere on earth, intent on our destruction, which will surely take place unless we constantly imitate it with our war machine and secret services.

In actual fact, the Soviet Union is a Second World country with a First World military capacity. Frighten the Russians sufficiently and they might blow us up. By the same token, as our republic now begins to crack under the vast expense of maintaining a mindless imperial force, we might try to blow them up. Particularly if we had a president who really was a twice-born Christian and believed that the good folks would all go to heaven (where they were headed anyway) and the bad folks would go where *they* belong.

Even worse than the not-very-likely prospect of a nuclear war—deliberate or by accident—is the economic collapse of our society because too many of our resources have been wasted on the military. The Pentagon is like a black hole; what goes in is forever lost to us, and no new wealth is created. Hence, our cities, whose centers are unlivable; our crime rate, the highest in the Western world; a public education system that has given up . . . you know the litany.

There is now only one way out. The time has come for the United States to make common cause with the Soviet Union. The bringing together of the Soviet landmass (with all its natural resources) and our island empire (with all its technological resources) would be of great benefit to each society, not to mention the world. Also, to recall the wisdom of the Four Horsemen who gave us our empire, the Soviet Union and our section of North America combined would be a match, industrially and technologically, for the Sino-Japanese axis that will dominate the future just as Japan dominates world trade today. But where the horsemen thought of war as the supreme solvent, we now know that war is worse than useless. Therefore, the alliance of the two great powers of the Northern Hemisphere will double the strength of each and give us, working together, an opportunity to survive, economically, in a highly centralized Asiatic world.*

*The Nation*
January 11, 1986

*The suggestion that the United States and the USSR join forces set alarm bells ringing in Freedom's Land. The Israel lobby, in particular, attacked me with such ferocity that I felt obliged to respond, cheerily. (See the following essay.)

# 90

### • ###

# A CHEERFUL
# RESPONSE

Recently, Norman Mailer and I chatted together at the Royale Theatre in New York, under the auspices of PEN American Center. Part of what I said was reprinted in *The Nation* on January 11, 1986. I gave a bit of a history lesson about our empire's genesis, and I brooded on its terminus last fall, when Tokyo took over from New York as the world's economic center.

My conclusion: For America to survive economically in the coming Sino-Japanese world, an alliance with the Soviet Union is a necessity. After all, the white race is a minority race with many well-deserved enemies, and if the two great powers of the Northern Hemisphere don't band together, we are going to end up as farmers—or, worse, mere entertainment—for the more than one billion grimly efficient Asiatics.*

As expected, that wonderful, wacky couple, Norman (Poddy) Podhoretz and his wife, Midge Decter, checked in. The Lunts of the right wing (Israeli fifth column division), they are now, in their old age, more and

---

*Again, I was attacked as a racist, invoking the "Yellow Peril." Simultaneously, the Japanese premier announced that the United States was a failure because there were too many inferior races in our heterodox land, while one of his cabinet ministers predicted that, in the next century, the United States would be Japan's farm, and Western Europe its boutique.

more like refugees from a Woody Allen film: *The Purple Prose of West End Avenue.*

Poddy was the first to respond. He is the editor of *Commentary* (circulation 55,000 and allegedly falling; paid for by the American Jewish Committee). He is best known—and by me loved—for his autobiographical "novel," *Making It,* in which he tells us that he has made it because he has become editor of *Commentary* and might one day be a guest at the White House, as he has already been a guest of Huntington Hartford in Nassau. Over the years, Poddy has, like his employers, the AJC, moved from those liberal positions traditionally occupied by American Jews (and me) to the far right of American politics. The reason for that is simple. In order to get Treasury money for Israel (last year five billion dollars), pro-Israel lobbyists must see to it that America's "the Russians are coming" squads are in place so that they can continue to frighten the American people into spending enormous sums for "defense," which also means the support of Israel in its never-ending wars against just about everyone. To make sure that nearly two thirds of the federal budget goes to the Pentagon and Israel, it is necessary for the pro-Israel lobbyists to make common cause with our lunatic right. Hence, the virulent propaganda.

Poddy denounced Mailer and me in the pages of the *New York Post.* According to him, we belong to that mindless majority of pinko intellectuals who actually think that the nation spends too much on the Pentagon and not enough on, say, education. Since sustained argument is not really his bag, he must fall back on the *ad hominem* attack, a right-wing specialty—and, of course, on our flag, which he wears like a designer caftan because "the blessings of freedom and prosperity are greater and more widely shared [here] than in any country known to human history." Poddy should visit those Western European countries whose per capita income is higher than ours. All in all, Poddy is a silly billy.

Significantly, the one Yiddish word that has gained universal acceptance in this country is *chutzpah.* Example: In 1960, Mr. and Mrs. Podhoretz were in upstate New York where I used to live. I was trying out a play at the Hyde Park Playhouse; the play was set during the Civil War. "Why," asked Poddy, "are you writing a play about, of all things, the Civil War?" I explained to him that my mother's family had fought for the Confederacy and my father's for the Union, and that the Civil War was—and is—to the United States what the Trojan War was to the Greeks, the great single tragic event that continues to give resonance to our Republic.

"Well, to me," said Poddy, "the Civil War is as remote and as irrelevant as the War of the Roses." I realized then that he was not planning to become an "assimilated American," to use the old-fashioned terminology; but, rather, his first loyalty would always be to Israel. Yet he and Midge stay on among us, in order to make propaganda and raise money for Israel—a country they don't seem eager to live in. Jewish joke, circa 1900: A Zionist is someone who wants to ship other people off to Palestine.

Midge was next to strike. But before she launched her attack, in something called *Contentions,* she put on her thinking cap and actually read what I wrote. I give her high marks for that. Unfortunately, she found my history lesson hard going. But then, like most of our Israeli fifth columnists, Midge isn't much interested in what the *goyim* were up to before Ellis Island. She also likes the *ad hominem* attack. When I noted that our writers seldom speak out on matters of war and peace because so many of them are paid for by universities that receive money from the garrison state, Midge tartly retorted, "*He,* after all, is not paid by a university but by those great centers of independence, the film companies." Since my last Hollywood film, *The Best Man,* was made in 1964, I have been "paid" by that American public that buys my books about the American past, a subject of no demonstrable interest to Midge and Poddy and their friends.

Midge was amazed by my description of how we seized territories from Mexico, including California; annexed Hawaii and Puerto Rico and, of course, the Philippines, where we slaughtered between 100,000 and 200,000 of the inhabitants. Interesting note: American imperialists froth if the figures for those murdered are ever in excess of 60,000 men, women, and children, the acceptable statistical minimum for genocide. Then Midge, with that magisterial gooniness that marks her polemical style, told us, "that three of these conquered territories are now states of the United States, and a fourth an independent republic, is evidently beside the point—as, we cannot resist remarking . . ."

Oh, Midge, resist. Resist! Don't you get the point? We stole other people's land. We murdered many of the inhabitants. We imposed our religion—and rule—on the survivors. General Grant was ashamed of what we did to Mexico, and so am I. Mark Twain was ashamed of what we did in the Philippines, and so am I. Midge is not because in the Middle East another predatory people is busy stealing other people's land in the name of an alien theocracy. She is a propagandist for these predators (paid for?), and that is what all this nonsense is about.

Since spades may not be called spades in freedom's land, let me spell
it all out. In order to get military and economic support for Israel, a
small number of American Jews,* who should know better, have made
common cause with every sort of reactionary and anti-Semitic group in
the United States, from the corridors of the Pentagon to the TV studios
of the evangelical Jesus Christers. To show that their hearts are in the
far-right place, they call themselves neoconservatives and attack the
likes of Mailer and me, all in the interest of supporting the likes of
Sharon and Greater Israel as opposed to the Peace Now Israelis whom
they disdain. There is real madness here; mischief too.

"Well, one thing is clear in all this muddle," writes Midge, adrift in
her tautological sea, "Mr. Vidal does not like his country." Poor Midge.
Of course I like my country. After all, I'm its current biographer. But
now that we're really leveling with each other, I've got to tell you I don't
much like your country, which is Israel.

Although there is nothing wrong with being a lobbyist for a foreign
power, one is supposed to register with the Justice Department. Also,
I should think that tact would require a certain forbearance when it
comes to the politics of the host country. But tact is unknown to the
Podhoretzes. Joyously they revel in the politics of hate, with plangent
attacks on blacks and/or fags and/or liberals, trying, always, to outdo
those moral majoritarians who will, as Armageddon draws near, either
convert all the Jews, just as the Good Book says, or kill them.

All in all, the latest Podhoretz diatribes have finally convinced me
that the time has come for the United States to stop all aid not only to
Israel but to Jordan, Egypt, and the rest of the Arab world. The Middle
Easterners would then be obliged to make peace, or blow one another
up, or whatever. In any case, we would be well out of it. After all, the
theological and territorial quarrels of Israel and Islam are as remote to
225 million Americans as—what else?—the Wars of the Roses.

*The Nation*
March 22, 1986

---

*This sentence has since been carefully revised by publicists like W. Safire and M.
Peretz and C. Krauthammer to mean "all Jews," thus demonstrating my "virulent"
anti-Semitism. Well, ours is a sectarian society.

# 91

# THE NATIONAL
# SECURITY STATE

Every now and then, usually while shaving, I realize that I have lived through nearly one third of the history of the United States, which proves not how old I am but how young the Republic is. The American empire, which started officially in 1898 with our acquisition of the Philippines, came to a peak in the year 1945, while I was still part of that army which had won us the political and economic mastery of two hemispheres. If anyone had said to me then that the whole thing would be lost in my lifetime, I would have said it is not possible to lose so much so quickly without an atomic catastrophe, at least. But lose it we have.

Yet, in hindsight, I can see that our ending was implicit in our beginning. When Japan surrendered, the United States was faced with a choice: Either disarm, as we had done in the past, and enjoy the prosperity that comes from releasing so much wealth and energy to the private sector, or maintain ourselves on a full military basis, which would mean a tight control not only over our allies and such conquered provinces as West Germany, Italy, and Japan but over the economic—which is to say the political—lives of the American people. As Charles E. Wilson, a businessman and politician of the day, said as early as 1944, "Instead of looking to disarmament and unpreparedness as a safeguard against war, a thoroughly discredited doctrine, let us try the opposite: full preparedness according to a continuing plan."

The accidental president, Harry Truman, bought this notion. Although Truman campaigned in 1948 as an heir to Roosevelt's New Deal, he had a "continuing plan." Henry Wallace was onto it, as early as: "Yesterday, March 12, 1947, marked a turning point in American history, [for] it is not a Greek crisis that we face, it is an American crisis. Yesterday, President Truman . . . proposed, in effect, America police Russia's every border. There is no regime too reactionary for us provided it stands in Russia's expansionist path. There is no country too remote to serve as the scene of a contest which may widen until it becomes a world war." But how to impose this? The Republican leadership did not like the state to be the master of the country's economic life while, of the Democrats, only a few geopoliticians, like Dean Acheson, found thrilling the prospect of a military state, to be justified in the name of a holy war against something called communism in general and Russia in particular. The fact that the Soviet Union was no military or economic threat to us was immaterial. It must be made to appear threatening so that the continuing plan could be set in motion in order to create that National Security State in which we have been living for the past forty years.*

What is the National Security State? Well, it began, officially, with the National Security Act of 1947; it was then implemented in January 1950 when the National Security Council produced a blueprint for a new kind of country, unlike anything that the United States had ever known before. This document, known as NSC-68 for short, and declassified only in 1975, committed—and still, fitfully, commits—us to the following program: First, never negotiate, ever, with Russia. This could not last forever; but the obligatory bad faith of U.S.-U.S.S.R. meetings still serves the continuing plan. Second, develop the hydrogen bomb so that when the Russians finally develop an atomic bomb we will still not have to deal with that enemy without which the National Security State cannot exist. Third, rapidly build up conventional forces. Fourth, put through a large increase in taxes to pay for all of this. Fifth, mobilize the entire American society to fight this terrible specter of communism. Sixth, set up a strong alliance system, directed by the United States (this

*For those interested in the details, I recommend H. R. Shapiro's *Democracy in America,* the only political history of the United States from British shires to present deficits. Needless to say, this masterly work, fourteen years in the making, is published privately by Manhattan Communication, 496 LaGuardia Place, Suite 406, New York, NY 10012. The present volume is only half the whole and lacks scholarly apparatus (index, bibliography) but not scholarship.

became NATO). Seventh, make the people of Russia our allies, through propaganda and CIA derring-do, in this holy adventure—hence the justification for all sorts of secret services that are in no way responsible to the Congress that funds them, and so in violation of the old Constitution.

Needless to say, the blueprint, the continuing plan, was not openly discussed at the time. But, one by one, the major political players of the two parties came around. Senator Arthur Vandenburg, Republican, told Truman that if he really wanted all those weapons and all those high taxes to pay for them, he had better "scare hell out of the American people." Truman obliged, with a series of speeches beginning October 23, 1947, about the Red Menace endangering France and Italy; he also instituted loyalty oaths for federal employees; and his attorney general (December 4, 1947) published a list of dissident organizations. The climate of fear has been maintained, more or less zealously, by Truman's successors, with the brief exception of Dwight Eisenhower, who in a belated fit of conscience at the end of his presidency warned us against the military-industrial complex that had, by then, established permanent control over the state.

The cynicism of this coup d'etat was breathtaking. Officially we were doing nothing but trying to preserve freedom for ourselves and our allies from a ruthless enemy that was everywhere, monolithic and all-powerful. Actually, the real enemy were those National Security Statesmen who had so dexterously hijacked the country, establishing military conscription in peacetime, overthrowing governments that did not please them, and finally keeping all but the very rich docile and jittery by imposing income taxes that theoretically went as high as 90 percent. That is quite an achievement in a country at peace.

We can date from January 1950 the strict governmental control of our economy and the gradual erosion of our liberties, all in order to benefit the economic interest of what is never, to put it tactfully, a very large group—defense spending is money but not labor intensive. Fortunately, all bad things must come to an end. Our huge indebtedness has made the maintenance of the empire a nightmare; and the day Japan stops buying our Treasury bonds, the troops and the missiles will all come home to a highly restless population.

Now that I have defined the gloomy prospect, what solutions do I have? I shall make five proposals. First, limit presidential election campaigns to eight weeks. That is what most civilized countries do, and all democratic ones are obliged to do. Allow no paid political ads. We might then entice that half of the electorate which never votes to vote.

Second, the budget: The press and the politicians constantly falsify the revenues and the disbursements of the federal government. How? By wrongly counting Social Security contributions and expenditures as a part of the federal budget. Social Security is an independent, slightly profitable income-transferring trust fund, which should be factored out of federal revenue and federal spending. Why do the press and the politicians conspire to give us this distorted view of the budget? Because neither they nor their owners want the public to know how much of its tax money goes for a war that does not exist. As a result Federal Reserve chairman Alan Greenspan could say last March, and with a straight face, that there are only two options for a serious attack on the deficit. One is to raise taxes. The other is to reduce the entitlement programs like Social Security and Medicare. He did not mention the defense budget. He did not acknowledge that the so-called entitlements come from a special fund. But then, he is a disciple of Ayn Rand.

In actual fact, close to 90 percent of the disbursements of the federal government go for what is laughingly known as "defense." This is how: In 1986 the gross revenue of the government was $794 billion. Of that amount, $294 billion were Social Security contributions, which should be subtracted from the money available to the National Security State. That leaves $500 billion. Of the $500 billion, $286 billion go to defense; $12 billion for foreign arms to our client states; $8 billion to $9 billion to energy, which means means, largely, nuclear weapons; $27 billion for veterans' benefits, the sad and constant reminder of the ongoing empire's recklessness; and, finally, $142 billion for interest on loans that were spent, over the past forty years, to keep the National Security State at war, hot or cold. So, of 1986's $500 billion in revenue, $475 billion was spent on National Security business. Of that amount, we will never know how much was "kicked back" through political action committees and so-called soft money to subsidize candidates and elections. Other federal spending, incidentally, came to $177 billion in 1986 (guarding presidential candidates, cleaning the White House), which was about the size of the deficit, since only $358 billion was collected in taxes.

It is obvious that if we are to avoid an economic collapse, defense spending must be drastically reduced. But it is hard to reduce a budget that the people are never told about. The first politician who realizes why those politicians who appear to run against the government always win, could not only win himself but be in a position to rid us of the National Security State—which is what people truly hate. "Internal

Improvements" was the slogan of Henry Clay's popular movement. A neo-Clayite could sweep the country if he wanted seriously to restore the internal plant of the country rather than invade Honduras or bob expensively about the Persian Gulf or overthrow a duly elected government in Nicaragua while running drugs (admittedly, the CIA's only margin of profit).

Third, as part of our general retrenchment, we should withdraw from NATO. Western Europe is richer and more populous than America. If it cannot defend itself from an enemy who seems to be falling apart even faster than we are, then there is nothing that we, proud invaders of Grenada, can effectively do. I would stop all military aid to the Middle East. This would oblige the hardliners in Israel to make peace with the Palestinians. We have supported Israel for forty years. No other minority in the history of the United States has ever extorted so much Treasury money for its Holy Land as the Israeli lobby, and it has done this by making a common cause with the National Security State. Each supports the other. I would have us cease to pay for either.

Fourth, we read each day about the horrors of drug abuse, the murder of policemen, the involvement of our own government in drug running, and so on. We are all aware that organized crime has never been richer nor the society more demoralized. What is the solution? I would repeal every prohibition against the sale and use of drugs, because it is these prohibitions that have caused the national corruption, not to mention most of the addiction. Since the American memory has a span of about three days, I will remind you that in 1919 alcohol was prohibited in the United States. In 1933 Prohibition was repealed because not only had organized crime expanded enormously but so had alcoholism. What did not work then does not work now. But we never learn, which is part of our national charm. Repeal would mean that there is no money for anyone in selling drugs. That's the end of the playground pusher. That's the end of organized crime, which has already diversified and is doing very nicely in banking, films, and dry cleaning. Eventually, repeal will mean the end of mass drug addiction. As there will always be alcoholics, there will always be drug addicts, but not to today's extent. It will be safe to walk the streets because the poor will not rob you to pay for their habit.

Fifth, two years ago I described how the American empire ended the day the money power shifted from New York to Tokyo and we became, for the first time in seventy-one years, a debtor nation. Since then, we have become the largest debtor country in history. I suggested a number of things that might be done, some of which I've again mentioned. But, above all, I see our economic survival inextricably bound up with that of our neighbor in the Northern Hemisphere, the Soviet Union. Some sort of alliance must be made between us so that together we will be able to compete with Japan and, in due course, China. As the two klutzes of the north, each unable to build a car anyone wants to drive, we deserve each other. In a speech at Gorbachev's anti-nuclear forum in Moscow, I quoted a Japanese minister of trade who said that Japan would still be number one in the next century. Then, tactlessly he said that the United States will be Japan's farm and Western Europe its boutique. A Russian got up and asked, "What did he say about us?" I said that they were not mentioned but, if they did not get their act together, they would end up as ski instructors. It is my impression that the Russians are eager to be Americans, but, thanks to the brainwashing of the National Security State's continuing plan, Americans have a built-in horror of the Evil Empire, which the press and the politicians have kept going for forty years. Happily, our National Security State is in the red, in more ways than one. Time for a change?

*The Nation*
June 4, 1988

### N. B.

Shortly before I gave this talk to the National Press Club, I spoke to the American-Arab Anti-Discrimination League in Washington (March 13, 1988). I used the same text, giving the history of the National Security State. Then instead of suggesting some things that might be done to help free ourselves from our masters, I addressed the thousand Arab-Americans on problems of specific interest to them. In the audience was the most dreaded of *The New Republic*'s secret agents, code name: Weasel, who, despite a shoulder-length gray fright wig, was easily identified by his tiny ruby-red rabid eyes. Later he characterized my remarks on the National Security State as "cheap patrician rant"—whatever that is; I've never heard a patrician rant the way I do, and at such cost: He characterized what follows not, surprisingly, as "anti-Semitic" but as "nativist," and accused me of now cheating the Arabs as I had once cheated the Jews. This is plainly code, meant to be understood only by the initiate. The Weasel knows. Here is what I said.

It has been my fate—or, perhaps, function—to give warnings long before the politicians and the press are able to absorb them. After all, they are in place to give a rosy view of the National Security State, and they give good value for their salaries. Since I'm not paid, I can ruminate; and share my findings.

I am here today because I said much of what I've said just now in New York City at the Royale Theatre, on January 11, 1986. I also passed on the news that the American empire had officially died the previous year when we became, after seventy-one years, a debtor nation, and the money power had gone from New York to Tokyo. I was predictably attacked by the press that serves the National Security State. I was also attacked by those simple Jesus Christers who have been taught all their lives to fear and loathe communism, whatever it may be, and I was also attacked by that not-so-simple Israel lobby which never ceases to demonize the Soviet Union in order to make sure that half the federal revenue goes to defense, out of which the state of Israel, the lobby's sole preoccupation, is financed. I was promptly attacked by that small group of Israel Firsters, who call themselves neoconservatives. I hated my country, they said, because I had criticized that National Security State in which, like a prison, we have all been obliged to live—and go broke—for forty years.

I responded to my critics with characteristic sweetness, turning the other fist as is my wont. I said that as much as I hated what our rulers have done to my country, it was not us, the country, who were at fault. I then added, while we're on the subject of our respective homelands, I'm not so keen about yours, which is Israel. Until then, no one had really challenged the lobby in so public a way. Congress and president and press are all more or less bought or otherwise intimidated by this self-described "sexy" lobby. While the sins and errors of Israel are openly debated in Israel itself, there has been only fearful silence in bravery's home and freedom's land. Well, I lanced the boil. Naturally, I was called an anti-Semite, usually with the adjective "frenzied" or "virulent" attached.

Now, at the risk of hurting more feelings, I must tell you that I regard monotheism as the greatest disaster ever to befall the human race. I see no good in Judaism, Christianity, or Islam—good people, yes, but any religion based on a single . . . well, frenzied and virulent god, is not as useful to the human race as, say, Confucianism, which is not a religion but an ethical and educational system that has worked pretty well for twenty-five hundred years. So you see I am ecumenical in my dislike for the Book. But, like it or not, the Book is there; and because of it people die; and the world is in danger.

Israel had the bad luck to be invented at a moment in history when the nation-state was going out of style. These two clumsy empires, the Soviet Union and the United States are now becoming unstuck. Only by force can the Soviets control their Armenians and Moslems and Mongols, and only by force can we try to control a whole series of escalating race wars here at home, as well as the brisk occupation of the southern tier of the United States by those Hispanics from whom we stole land in 1847. The world, if we survive, will be one not of nations but of *inter*national cartels, of computerized money hurtling between capitals, of countries making what contributions they can to a more or less homogeneous world economy. Simultaneously, armies and flags and centralized administration will give way to a regionalism that is interdependent with everyone else on earth.

Is this possible? Well, Switzerland is a splendid small-scale model of what the world could be. Four languages, four races, four sets of superstitions about one another—all live most harmoniously in a small area where they make a fortune out of those of us who haven't learned that we are living in a post–national security world. When we finally stop giving to Israel the money that Japan so reluctantly lends us, peace will have to be made. If a cantonal system is set up, some areas of Palestine will be Orthodox Jewish; others Shiite Moslem; others secular Jewish and/or Moslem and/or Christian. In any event, the Great Bronze Age realtor in the sky will finally have to accept that none of those desirable rental properties between the Nile and the Euphrates can ever again include in the lease a discrimination clause.

So what shall we celebrate this joyous Sunday? The slow but highly visible collapse, due to bankruptcy, of the National Security Council-68 state and its ramshackle empire. Once we Americans are free of this dangerous state and its imperial burden we may not have heaven on earth, but we will certainly have lessened the current hell, and got *our* country back.

# 92

---------------------- ♦ ----------------------

## CUE THE GREEN GOD, TED

There has not been a political debate in the United States since the one that ended with the Japanese attack on Pearl Harbor. From September 1939 to December 7, 1941, the ruling class of the United States was split between those who would join the Allies in their war against Hitler and those who would stay out. For three years there was fierce argument in Congress, the press, the schools. At my school, Exeter, there was a sharp division between the isolationists, known as America Firsters, and the interventionists. True to the populist tradition in which I was brought up, I was isolationist. Then, or as Lincoln once so bleakly put it, *and the war came;* and I enlisted in the Army, age 17.

Since the victory of 1945, the United States, as befits the leader of something called "the free world," has fought open and unsuccessful wars in Korea and Vietnam; and relatively covert wars in Cambodia, Laos, the Caribbean, Central America, Africa, Chile, the Middle East, etc. In almost every case, our overwhelming commitment to freedom, democracy and human rights has required us to support those régimes that would deny freedom, democracy and human rights to their own people. We justify our affection for fascist (or, to be cozy, authoritarian) régimes because each and every one of them is a misty-eyed convert to our national religion, which is anti-communism. Then, once our dictator is in place, we echo Andy Hardy: Hey, kids, let's put on an election! And so, in the presence of cold-eyed avatars of Tammany and Daley, our general on the spot does.

To their credit, our rulers don't often bore us with tortured rationalisations or theological nit-picking. They don't have to. Since we have no political parties and no opposition media, there is always a semblance of "consensus" for these wars. Congress funds the Pentagon, which then responds to the National Security State's directives to overthrow an Arbenz here or a Sihanouk there or—why not?—devastate a neutral country like Cambodia to show how tall we can stand in all our marvellously incredible credibility. Voices of dissent are either blacked out or marginalised, while known apostates of the national religion are either demonised or trivialised. Meanwhile, no one has noticed that the National Security State, in its zeal to bring the national religion to all nations, has now deprived us of our original holy text—our Old Testament—the Constitution.

Every war that we have fought since 1945 has been by executive (or National Security Council) order. Since only Congress may declare war, these wars have all been in violation of the Constitution. To the House of Representatives was assigned, uniquely, the power of the purse. But, in thrall to those religious wars that we forever fight, our debts are now so great that Congress dares not prepare a proper budget. So the power of the purse has been replaced by a ridiculous formula, involving a blind arbitrary cutting of the budget should Federal waste exceed a certain arbitrary figure. Although the most militant of our national religionists enjoy calling themselves conservatives, they have not managed to conserve either the letter or the spirit of the Constitution.

For some time knowledgeable foreigners have found it difficult to talk about much of anything to Americans because we appear to know so little about much of anything. History of any kind is a closed book to us. Geography is no longer taught in most public schools. Foreign languages make everyone's head ache—anyway, *they* all know English. As for politics, that's simple: it's either *us* (what the silver-tongued felon Spiro Agnew, or his wordsmith William Safire, so memorably dubbed "the greatest nation in the country") or *them*—foreigners who envy us our vast choice of detergents, our freedom to repeat as loudly as we want the national prayers, our alabaster cities to which, we tell ourselves, they can't wait to emigrate. On the other hand, the average American, when it comes to his own welfare, is very shrewd indeed. He knows that we are in an economic decline and that our quality of life, though better than that of Russia (all that really matters, our priests hum softly) is noticeably lousy. But the reasons for our decline are never made clear because the corporate ownership of the country has absolute control of the pulpit—'the media'—as well as of the schoolroom.

David Hume's celebrated *Of the First Principles of Government* (1758) has never been more to the point than now:

Nothing appears more surprising to those who consider human affairs with a philosophical eye than the easiness with which the many are governed by the few, and the implicit submission with which men resign their own sentiments and passions to those of their rulers. When we inquire by what means this wonder is effected, we shall find that, as Force is always on the side of the governed, the governors have nothing to support them but opinion. It is, therefore, on opinion only that government is founded, and this maxim extends to the most despotic and most military governments as well as to the most free and most popular.

The corporate grip on opinion in the United States is one of the wonders of the Western world. No First World country has ever managed to eliminate so entirely from its media all objectivity—much less dissent. Of course, it is possible for any citizen with time to spare, and a canny eye, to work out what is actually going on, but for the many there is no time, and the network news is the only news even though it may not be news at all but only a series of flashing fictions intended, like the avowed commercials, to keep docile huddled masses, keep avid for products addled consumers.

I seldom watch television. But when I do set out to twirl the dial, it is usually on Sunday, when our corporate rulers address us from their cathode pulpit. Seedy Washington journalists, sharp-eyed government officials who could not dispose of a brand-new car in Spokane, think-tank employees, etiolated from too long residence 'neath flat rocks, and always, always, Henry Kissinger, whose destruction of so many Asians and their once-charming real estate won him a prize for peace from the ironists of northern Europe. The level of the chat on those programmes is about as low as it is possible to get without actually serving the viewers gin. The opinion expressed ranges from conservative to reactionary to joyous neofascist. There is even, in William Safire, an uncloseted anti-Gentile.

I was once placed between two waxworks on a programme where one of the pair was solemnly identified as a "liberal"; appropriately, he

seemed to have been dead for some time, while the conservative had all
the vivacity of someone on speed. For half an hour it is the custom of
this duo to "crossfire" clichés of the sort that would have got them
laughed out of the Golden Branch Debating Society at Exeter. On air,
I identified the conservative as a liberal and vice versa. The conservative
fell into the trap. "No, no!" he hyperventilated. "I'm the conservative!"
(What on earth they think these two words mean no one will ever
know.) It was the liberal who got the point; from beyond, as it were, the
tomb he moaned, "He's putting us on."

I have been involved in television since the early 1950s, when it ceased
to be a novelty and became the principal agent for the simultaneous
marketing of consumer goods and of National Security State opinion.
Although I thought I knew quite a bit about the ins and outs of the
medium, I now know a lot more, thanks to Ben H. Bagdikian's *The
Media Monopoly* and *Manufacturing Consent,* a study of "the political
economy of the mass media," by Edward S. Herman and Noam
Chomsky. These two studies demonstrate exactly how the few manipulate opinion. To begin with: the average American household keeps the
set throbbing seven hours a day. This means the average American has
watched 350,000 commercials by age 17. Since most opinion is now
controlled by twenty-nine corporations—due to be at least one fewer if
Time-Warner or Paramount-Time or, most chilling of all, Nation-Time
comes to pass—one can then identify those twenty-nine CEOs as a sort
of politburo or college of cardinals, in strict charge of what the people
should and should not know. They also select the Presidents and the
Congresses or, to be precise, they determine what the politicians may
talk about at election time—that famed agenda that never includes the
interesting detail that, in peacetime, more than two thirds of the Federal
revenue goes to war. Although AIDS can be discussed as a means of
hitting out at unpopular minorities, the true epidemic can never be
discussed: the fact that every fourth American now alive will die of
cancer. This catastrophe is well kept from the public by the tobacco
companies, the nuclear power companies (with their bungled waste
disposal) and other industries that poison the earth so that corporate
America may enjoy the freedom to make money without the slightest
accountability to those they are killing.

The invention of the talk show on television was, at first, a most
promising development. Admittedly, no one very radical would ever be
allowed on, but a fair range of opinion could be heard, particularly as
the Vietnam war began to go bad. On the original *Today* show, Hugh

Downs and I would talk off and on for an hour as news, weather, commercials floated lazily by us. But Hazel Bishop, an obscure lipstick company, changed all that. The firm began running commercials not linked to specific programmes and it was soon determined that the thirty-second commercial duplicates exactly the attention span of the average viewer. Therefore, no in-depth interview can last for more than seven minutes; three minutes is considered optimum. Recently, I found myself confronting the amiable Pat Sajak. I was all set to do what I think of as my inventing-the-wheel-in-seven-minutes (why what's wrong is wrong and what to do) when my energy level crashcd. I did say that if you wanted to know what the ownership of the country wants you to know, tune in to *Nightline* and listen to Ted Koppel and his guests. The effect of this bit of information must have been surreal. Since no voices other than those of the national consensus are heard, how could a viewer know that there are any other viewpoints?

I was made aware of the iron rules in 1968, when William F. Buckley, Jr., and I had our first live chat on ABC at the Republican Convention in Miami Beach. I was billed as the conservative; he as the pro-crypto—or was it the other way around? Anyway, we were hired to play the opinion game in order to divert the audience from the issues. Buckley Junior's idea of a truly deep in-depth political discussion is precisely that of corporate America's. First, the Democrat must say that the election of a Republican will lead to a depression. Then the Republican will joyously say, Ah Hah, but the Democrats always lead us into war! After a few minutes of this, *my* attention span snapped. I said that there was no difference at all between the two parties because the same corporations paid for both, usually with taxpayers' money, tithed, as it were, from the faithful and then given to "defence," which in turn passes it on to those candidates who will defend the faith. With that bit of news for the national audience, I revealed myself not only as an apostate to the national religion; I came close to revealing what I really am: a dedicated anti-anticommunist, a category far more vile to the true believer than a mere communist. Although my encounters with Buckley Junior got ABC its highest ratings, I was seen no more at election times. Last year, Peter Jennings proposed to ABC that, for old times' sake, it might be a good idea to have me on. "No," he was told. "He'll just be outrageous."

In 1972 the future Supreme Court Justice Lewis Powell wrote to the US Chamber of Commerce proposing that they "buy the top academic reputations in the country to add credibility to corporate studies and give business a stronger voice on the campuses." One wonders, stronger than what? But the advice was taken. Also, as corollary, keep off prime-time television those who do not support corporate America. During the 1960s and early 1970s I used, once a year, to do a "state of the union" analysis on David Susskind's non-network, non–prime-time television programme. Many people watched. In the summer before the 1976 presidential election, Susskind wanted to produce a series of one-hour interviews with the twenty or so leading candidates of the two parties. For one hour I would question each candidate about politics, history, economics—whatever came up. Since I favoured no candidate and nei-ther party, I could not be said to be partisan. Public Broadcasting System agreed that this sort of programme was precisely why PBS had been founded and funded. All the candidates, save President Ford, affected delight. As we prepared for the first programme, the head of PBS affiliate WNET, Jay Iselin, cancelled the series without explana-tion. Then the intrepid producer Hillard Elkins took over. He had "a good relationship" with Home Box Office, which was "hungry for prod-uct." HBO manifested delight in having its hunger so cheaply sated. Then, just before the first taping, Andrew Heiskell, the overall *capo* of Time-Life-HBO, cancelled us. In due course, I was advised that it was not in the national (that is, corporate) interest for so many *expensive* presidential candidates to be questioned by me in a—what was the phrase?—"nonstructured format." Now, of course, with the megacor-porate ownership of the media becoming more and more concentrated in fewer and fewer hands, structure is total, indeed totalitarian, and the candidates can no longer be discerned through the heavy blizzard of thirty-second spots.

Currently, the principal dispenser of the national religion is Ted Koppel, a very smooth bishop indeed. Fairness & Accuracy In Report-ing—noble, doomed enterprise—had a study made of just who appeared as Koppel's guests during a forty-month period from 1985 to 1988. White male Establishment types predominated. Henry Kissinger (Koppel's guru and a longtime cardinal in the national security state's curia) and Alexander Haig (by his own admission, in one of many moments of confusion at the White House, "a vicar") each appeared fourteen times, the maximum for any guest. Yet the Cardinal's views on almost any subject are already known to anyone who might be interested in looking at *Nightline,* while Haig's opinions have never interested anybody in the course of a long busy career climbing ladders so that he could be close to those with power—in order to be close to them. The next two champ guests, weighing in at twelve appearances each, were the mendacious Elliott Abrams (Koppel assumes that although Abrams will lie to Congress, he won't lie to Koppel) and Jerry Falwell, a certified voice of God whose dolorous appearance suggests a deep, almost personal grief that the Thirteenth and Fourteenth Amendments to the Constitution are not yet repealed. Most of the other guests are hired guns for the National Security state.

The Koppel explanation for this bizarre repertory company is that, well, they are the folks who are running the country and so that's why they're on. Well, yes, Ted, that *is* why they're on, but there are other more interesting and more learned—even disinterested—voices in the land and, in theory, they should be heard, too. But theory is not practice in bravery's home. Of semi-dissenters, only Jesse Jackson and Studs Terkel have been honoured with solo interviews with the bishop, who insists, by the way, that the guest face not him but a camera in another room, preferably in another city, with an earphone but no monitor. Good television one-upmanship.

To my amazement, just before Mikhail Gorbachev spoke at the United Nations, on December 7, 1988, I was asked to contribute a tiny pre-recorded (and thus easily edited) cameo. I suppose that I was asked because I had attended Gorbachev's famous antinuclear forum in Moscow two years earlier. I spoke to a camera. I predicted, accurately, that Gorbachev would say that Russia was unilaterally disarming, and that we were now dangerously close to peace. To the question What will the United States do without The Enemy?—a pretty daring question from those whose livelihood depends on the demonising of Russia and Communism—I said that, thanks to television, a new demon can be quickly installed. Currently, the Arabs are being thoroughly demonized by the Israel lobby while the Japanese are being, somewhat more nervously, demonized by elements of the corporate state. But neither will do as a long-term devil because the Arabs are too numerous (and have too much oil) while the Japanese will simply order us to stop it; should we disobey them, they will buy the networks and show us many hours of the soothing tea ceremony. I suggested that the new devil will be the threat to our ecosphere, and the new world god, Green. None of this was used, of course, but a man who writes Russians-Are-Coming thrillers was shown, frowning with intense anguish at, What, *what*! does it all mean? Because you godda be real careful with these guys. Fine show, Ted.

. . .

The unloved American empire is now drifting into history on a sea of red ink, as I predicted in *The Nation* on January 11, 1986 ("The Day the American Empire Ran Out of Gas"), to the fury of the few and the bewilderment of the many. Thanks to money wasted in support of the national religion, our quality of life is dire, and although our political institutions work smoothly for the few, the many hate them; hence the necessity of every corporate candidate for president to run against the government, which is, of course, the corporate state—good fun. In due course, something on the order of the ethnic rebellions in the Soviet Union or even of the people's uprising in China will take place here. Too few have ripped off too many for too long. Opinion can no longer disguise the contradiction at the heart of conservative-corporate opinion. The corporate few are free to do what they will to customers and environment while the many are losing their freedoms at a rapid rate. The Supreme Court, the holy office of the national religion, in upholding the principle of preventive detention got rid of due process two years ago, and now the Court is busily working its way through the Bill of Rights, producing, as it goes, a series of bright, crackling *autos-da-fé.*

Significantly, our prison population is now among the world's largest. Certainly, it is right up there, per capita, with the Soviet Union and the Republic of South Africa. Now the few are proposing that if the war budget is to be, tragically, reduced, the army camps—perfect symbolism—can be used to house our criminal population, particularly weak-fibred drug users. Thus do the few now declare open war on the many, as millions of citizens are now liable to mandatory blood, urine and lie-detector tests, while an electronic bracelet has been invented that will make it possible to track its wearer wherever he goes. Theoretically, half a nation can now monitor the movements of the other half. Better we enslave ourselves, the priests chant, than *they* do.

Lately, the language of government, always revealing, grows more and more fierce and commanding (due to so many wars lost? so much money wasted?), and military metaphors abound as czars lead all-out wars on drugs. Yet, at the risk of causing both offence and embarrassment among even the not-so-faithful, I feel obliged to say that I do not accept the authority of any state—much less one founded as was ours upon the free fulfillment of each citizen—to forbid me, or anyone, the use of drugs, cigarettes, alcohol, sex with a consenting partner or, if one is a woman, the right to an abortion. I take these rights to be absolute and should the few persist in their efforts to dominate the private lives of the many, I recommend force as a means of changing their minds. In this, I echo Jefferson.

Meanwhile, let us hope that opinion will respond to recent events. For instance, despite millions of dollars spent in the last presidential election on trying—successfully—to obscure every political issue while demonstrating—unsuccessfully—that there was a dramatic difference between Dukakis and Bush, 50 percent of the American electorate refused to vote. When a majority boycotts a political system, its days are numbered. The many are now ready for a change. The few are demoralised. Fortunately, the Messiah is at hand: the Green God. Everyone on earth now worships him. Soon there will be a worldwide Green movement, and the establishment of a worldwide state, which the few will take over, thus enslaving us all while forgetting to save the planet. That is the worst-case scenario. The best? Let the many create a *new* few.

*The Nation*
August 7–14, 1989

# 93

# GODS & GREENS

For three days, at a long green baize-covered table littered with microphones and translators' headsets, Graham Greene and I sat side by side in a conference room of the Kosmos Hotel in Moscow. Facing us, several hundred members of the cultural section of Gorbachev's international conference on nuclear disarmament. One look at this hanging jury and that one-time engineering student, Norman Mailer, fled to the science section. Hour after hour, Greene and I listened to long speeches, usually delivered in flawed or, most chillingly, in flawless French.

As we did not break for lunch until noon, Graham would start to get a bit edgy around eleven o'clock. On the third day, he muttered in my ear, "I have a flask. Dare I . . . ?" Since Gorbachev was currently engaged in his doomed battle against vodka, I said we must show solidarity, in public. "But why not drop a paper on the floor, reach down for it, and take a swig?" He shook his head sadly (I use this tired adverb because Greene is hostile to the adverb and I in love with it): "I might not come back up again."

At noon we went from conference to a room bright with television lights. The world's journalists, east and west, were all on hand and at their pert prettiest. Greene and I were promptly interviewed by a number of television journalists, many from exotic lands. At lunch, a bottle

of vodka between our plates, Graham observed, "I never do television."
As he had clocked at least a dozen appearances in three days, I asked
myself, aloud, as the French say, what did he mean by "never"? "But
this is the East. That doesn't count. I don't live here," he said. "But in
the West I don't want people to know my face."

When I remarked that his face was perhaps the best known of any
of the world's writers, the familiar pale face—like an adolescent boy's
left out too long in a great cold—turned pink, and we changed the
subject. But then, as we ate pale February watermelon from Georgia,
he said, "You like to go on television, don't you?" I said, yes, I did—very
much, in fact. Why? Because how else could I talk politics and history
and religion to the general public without the smothering intervention
of a print-journalist bent on re-creating one to conform to his publisher's
prejudices? This interested him. "Then you don't talk about your
work?" I said that as I assume no one is interested in anyone's writing,
I only talk about what interests the viewer—and me. The grey-yellow
eyes blinked (what about a "thoughtfully," Graham?). Then he said, "I
saw Anthony Burgess on French television." Graham frowned. There
had been some sort of a chill between the two neighbours on the Côte
d'Azur, and as I enjoy each, I have never inquired the reason. What,
then, did Burgess talk about? Graham shuddered with true horror; then
he whispered, "He talked about *his* books."

Two years later, I was asked if I would chat for 30 minutes into a
television camera. Subject? Anything. Naturally, given so much freedom, I could think of nothing. Then the day, as it always does, came.
On April 13, 1989, a television crew arrived at my house in Ravello
(province of Salerno, Italy), and I still had no text. I would ramble, I
decided. See what, if anything, was in my head other than the fact that
my father had been born on this day, 94 years ago. I panicked. Had I
been thinking about anything lately, or merely thinking that I was
thinking? What most disturbed me? That was easy. There had been no
rain all winter. This had never happened before. In Salerno water was
being rationed. Environment. Yes. But how to do it without every eye
glazing over as the familiar statistics sound, merry as a leper's bell?

I take the camera into my confidence. Say where we are—on a balcony 400 metres above the Tyrrhenian sea. I live part of the year in Italy,
part in Los Angeles. I am not a tax exile (this always astonishes the
British who do not know that every American must pay full tax to his
beloved country no matter where he lives or makes his living). I am also
not a political exile—yet. On that note, a gust of wind topples the

electrical equipment, and we retreat to my work room. I start over. When in doubt, grab *The Oxford Book of Greek Verse* (after all, we are in Magna Graecia). Quote Lucian: "The world is fleeting; all things pass away;/Or is it we that pass and they that stay?" I say that the first line is now the correct one. We are killing our green world and everything will pass away. Question: what ought we to do so that they will stay?

Our lives are dominated by symbols of our own making. Once we had invented time by differentiating one year from another, we became in thrall to the notion of the decade, the century, the millennium. Every twenty years the middle-aged celebrate the decade of their youth. Hence the current preoccupation with the Sixties, while the elderly dote upon the Forties or even the Thirties.

But these arbitrary groupings mean nothing at all except in a subjective way. Nevertheless, such is the force of habit, we are now faced, most dramatically, with not only the century's end but with the end of the second Christian millennium. As the first joyous millennium was drawing to a close, the end of the world was regularly announced, as a sort of marker to celebrate the thousand years that had gone by since a sky-god had chosen unwisely to become a man who was then put to death, all the while predicting that the world would end within the lifetime of many of his contemporaries. Millennial fever is a bit like the madness of those citizens of Cavafy's Hellenic city who lived in terror of the Barbarians whose coming would destroy them. But the Barbarians never came. Possibly because the citizens themselves *were* the Barbarians and, in their waiting, they destroyed themselves within their own high gates.

Now, two millennia later, we are once again talking of final things. First eye-glazer: there are five billion people on a very small planet. At least four of those billions are too many, but which four? That is when the enlightened start talking of planned parenthood, while the dark souls contemplate with ecstasy the four horsemen cantering into view.

But if the four or whatever billions were to vanish or simply be unborn, what about the planet itself? Although the signs of disaster have been clearly visible for more than a generation, no one has thought to do much of anything to purify the water and the air, and to shut, if possible, those two great holes in the polar skies. Only a world crisis can focus our rulers' attention. This year's skewed harvests may do the trick.

David Hume once observed that all power is with the governed because they are many while the governors are few. How then do the few control the many? Through Opinion, as expressed from the pulpit and in the classroom. Today we can add that terrible word—media.

In my lifetime and country I have watched our governors manipulate Opinion with the greatest of ease. Certain races, arbitrary categories of human beings, political systems are demonised or trivialised on a daily and unrelenting basis. These are the carefully crafted subliminal *opinionated* messages that hiss through the airways and into the minds of everyone from the first switching on of the cathode tube to the last TV supper when the light goes out.

At a time of imperial crisis, Americans demonised the Germans and the Japanese. Then, once they were safely enclosed within our empire, we demonised the Russians and something called communism which was particularly evil because it was godless, while everyone knows that we have more than enough sky-god for two.

The present crisis is due not so much to the actual crisis—the destruction of the environment—but to a realignment of official enemies. Opinion is changing rapidly in every country. After the Second World War, the American empire decreed that the three conquered countries were not to maintain military establishments. As a result, Japan and Germany, unencumbered by military pretensions, now lead the world's economy while Italy is doing very well indeed. For almost half a century America's client states in western Europe have depended on American nuclear power to protect them from godless communism and brute Russia. Thanks to all those trillions of dollars spent to keep at bay phantom Barbarians, the United States has ceased to be the world's preeminent economic and industrial power. Worse, the Soviet Union has perversely lost all interest in playing Lucifer to America's nuclear god, and so by simply opting out of our peculiar version of Paradise Lost we are bereft of a beloved enemy.

Desperate attempts are being made to rally the American people and their European clients—soon to be non-clients—by redemonising the Japanese. During the Second World War, I was assigned to the Pacific Theatre, as our Japanese war was called. We were regularly briefed on the inhumanity of the Japanese.

Currently, another American candidate for demonisation is the one billion Muslims in general and the Arabs in particular. Since America's Israel lobby controls American foreign policy in the Middle East, and since terrorist elements within Israel now control the Israeli government, we shall see Arabs more and more depicted as sub-human killers, never so happy as when blowing up a school. But, again, I don't think that the Muslims will make a suitable enemy. For one thing, there are too many of them. For another, they control too much of the world's oil supply. Finally, if the more thoughtful elements within Israel fail to make peace now, the Japanese may not give the Americans the money that they then give to Israel for its wars. So, let us rule out the Japanese and the Arabs as demons to be used to frighten the governed. What is left? Just us—the human race which is now breeding like a virus under optimum conditions.

Think of earth as a living organism that is being attacked by billions of bacteria whose numbers double every forty years. Either the host dies, or the bacteria die, or both die. That seems to be what we are faced with. The Reverend Malthus is often revived in order to show how wrong he was with his formula that population increases in a geometrical ratio, food in an arithmetical one; hence, the first must outgrow the second. So far it has not, but in order to feed so many, the damage to air, earth and water has been catastrophic. Until recently any attempt to recognise that we are all at risk has been ignored by our rulers because to acknowledge that things are wrong would hurt their short-term profits.

Governments are in place so that the few can take advantage of the many whom they control through Opinion. This explains the fierce tone of coercion assumed by the few when they give orders to the many. If ours were openly totalitarian societies, everything could then be justified in the name of the State or of the leader or of the all-powerful party of the people from which the actual people are excluded. But in the northern so-called democracies, we pretend that we are liberal societies where the many govern themselves and the few put down their plough, as it were, from time to time, to go to Washington or to Westminster.

The sad truth is that we live not in liberal democracies but in quasi-totalitarian patriarchies. This has been a gradual evolution since the eighteenth century's partial enlightenment. So great now is the indoctrination in the United States and so vast the ignorance due to the—calculated?—collapse of the general school system, that America's high school graduates when shown the Bill of Rights, unidentified, sternly reject all its guaranteed freedoms.

But then, paradoxically, despite our "inalienable rights," we have always accepted, in principle, the right of the State to intervene in our private lives. It is taken for granted that we are allowed only one husband or wife at a time and always of the opposite sex. It is considered fitting and proper that the Government may seize the children of anyone, except the rich, and incarcerate them in schools where they learn very little, except how to become docile workers and eager consumers. Although the few are also obliged to send their children to school—expensive schools where they do learn a good deal more than the many—their children are even more fiercely indoctrinated than those of the many in Opinion.

Where then does the battle—let us be warlike—to save the green planet fit in? In theory, it is the one cause that everyone on earth supports. In practice, those who profit by destroying rivers and forests are not going to do much of anything until something vividly goes wrong. Now the climate is changing—vividly. The next battle-plan will be an attempt to coordinate all efforts in order to reverse the greenhouse effect. This will mean demonising some of our governors.

But they are shrewd enough to adapt to new necessities. Note the speed with which the "mostest" ever British Prime Minister became the Lady Greensleeves. Thus far our own Bush is not yet ablaze (he belongs to the oil industry as well as to "defence") but he will come around—and when the world's various fews all agree, we shall then end up with that most terrible of all utopias, a world government. There may be no alternative.

But let us anticipate the perils. After two thousand years of history, it is fairly evident that once the few have total charge of the many, they will forget to preserve the environment, and we shall perish as slaves rather than as what we are now, demi-slaves. It is not wise ever to be optimistic when it comes to the human race. Prometheus stole fire from Heaven so that we could cook not only dinner but one another. We create; we destroy. Balance is what we have always needed. Know thyself. Everything in moderation. Man is near, Heaven is far. Do unto others as you would have them do unto you. This last sentence everyone knows in the West as the words of Jesus. But five hundred years before Jesus, Confucius said exactly the same thing.

I suggest that those who create Opinion must address themselves—and us their victims—to a new way of looking at life. To a new religious sense that differs drastically from the truly terrible religions that we have suffered from for two millennia. Monotheism is easily the greatest disaster to befall the human race. By nature, the sky-god is totalitarian. You will have no other god but he. You will kill those who refuse to worship him, and you are free to destroy the earth because he has instructed us "to be fruitful and multiply, and replenish the Earth, and subdue it; and have dominion over every living thing that moveth upon the Earth." In today's context, the instruction is madness and its single god—Judaic, Christian, Islamic—is one of immaculate evil.

It is time for us in the West to look to more subtle religions and ethical systems, particularly those of China and India. Here there are many gods. There, there are no gods. For the Buddha, we are not here except to be gone from here. For Confucius, harmony within the State is all. When asked what happens after death, Confucius said, since we know so little of life why ask about death of which we know nothing? He thought there was a golden mean and, through education and right conduct, it could be achieved in public as well as in private life.

The technology now exists to change dramatically everyone's way of looking at the world, past, present and future. One has only to think of Gorbachev's first four years in power. Seventy years of demonizing the Soviet Union was expertly undone by his masterful use of television and all the teacherly arts. The few can now create, rapidly, new Opinion so that we can make a proper marriage with the planet instead of an incontinent rape, in the name of dominion.

But, if I may give some advice to the Greens of the world, do not allow our totalitarian-minded governors in the West to coopt your movement. Start with the many. Let them convert the few. Meanwhile, the clock is ticking. The new millennium is at hand.

Let me note that just as I finished my chat to the camera on the Sahelian drought that has befallen southern Italy, it started to rain cats and dogs and we have had the wettest summer in years. Let us give thanks to the protean Green God.

*The Observer*
August 27, 1989

## 94

# PATRIOTISM

What is patriotism now, and how do we get rid of it, and what do we put in its place, if anything? The word is politically incorrect, of course. Patria-pater-father. So where is Mom? Didn't she help Dad turn the American wilderness into a cement desert bright with golden arches? Didn't she help Dad kill those pesky redskins? Anyway, whose patria are we talking about? The so-called Indians are the original Americans whose homeland European invaders stole. My own family settled on Cherokee land in South Carolina and on Chickasaw land in Mississippi. In due course, the remnants of dozens of tribes were finally dumped in what is now Oklahoma, a place none of us wanted any part of until the oil started to gush at the Osage reservation, and my Mississippi-born grandfather made a state out of the last worst hope of the Choctaws, Sioux, Seminoles, et al.

Certainly, it is very hard for most Americans to be patriotic when there is no agreed-upon country to cherish, only warring tribes and, over all, a National Security State to keep the lid on—$300 billion a year for law and order. There is one nation for a black, one for a boat-person, a third for a Cherokee, and milk and honey for that one-fifth of the population with money. What we are now witnessing is not so much the disintegration of the United States (less dramatic than that of the Soviet

Union but no less inexorable) as the brand-new realization that we are never going to integrate in order to form a more perfect nation-state of the sort that Bismarck and Lincoln dreamed of. There is a flight from the center everywhere. Simultaneously, there is a centripetal movement toward the creation of a single world state in order to preserve, protect and defend the human race—from itself. The world state will be a tyrannous one unless the tribes assert themselves within the framework of what will be not a nation-state but, ideally, an organization to monitor the weather, the food supply, the (*Ora Pro Nobis, Pater Sancte*) population.

On July 4, the Descendants of Robert Kay will hold an annual reunion in South Carolina. Who was Robert Kay? A descendant himself of English farmers who came to Virginia in the seventeenth century, he bought land (1791) in what is now Anderson County, South Carolina. He has many descendants and I am one of them. So is my fifth cousin, Jimmy Carter (all right, all right, it could have been Gerald Ford). I won't be there this year but last year I attended the Gore family reunion in Mississippi. At the last moment cousin Albert (Al) Gore (Jr.) and his button-cute wife, Tipper, sent word that a fundraiser took precedence over kin. I found this candor endearing. The cousinage did not.

I knew no one at the gathering but I was at home. Who would not be when confronted with 200 variations of one's own nose and elephantine ears? These clan reunions that are taking place all over the country are not a WASP phenomenon. Blacks have been searching out their roots for some time while the original "Americans" have never ceased to honor their tribal ghosts, just about all that we have left them. Hispanics now live in blithe unassimilated enclaves in what Mexicans still refer to as the Occupied Lands, seized by us from Mexico. Meanwhile, American Jews gaze raptly upon their recently exhumed "homeland," half a world away from North America, and though most of them sensibly refuse to go there to live, they allow the rest of us to finance (officially at a cost thus far of over $50 billion) this land that other Jews have occupied.

Is it any wonder that, in the absence of an agreed-upon nation, our many tribes are unfurling their standards and casting ever wider the webs of kinship for mutual support and defense against the state that no one loves? If the Vice President and Secretary of Defense chose not to fight for their country in Vietnam, why should *anyone* fight for their country? Suddenly, all our turkeys are coming home to roost; and the skies are dark with their unlovely wings while the noise of their gobbling makes hideous Sunday television.

As there was, famously, no there there in Gertrude Stein's Oakland, so there is no here here, and to try to do something about it is to misread the times that we live in. We can do nothing at all. Jefferson foresaw the eventual degradation of our system and he suggested that we hold a constitutional convention once a generation. But neither our rulers nor their hapless critics will allow such a thing. ("You see, *they* will take away the Bill of Rights"; plainly, it is more seemly to allow the Supreme Court to take it away.)

So, center-less, we now begin to fall apart. Meanwhile, the clans are gathering. If the state be bad, then each tribe must protect itself, and we shall exchange the world of Jefferson for that of Hobbes. In due course, the *idea* of the nation-state may become as obsolete as the nation-state, in fact, already is. Russia is more mirror of us—or we of it—than either cares to admit. In any case, it will be the collapse of the world's already skewed economy that will make for great change, not the firing of a patriot's gun at some National Security Fort.

From the one, many. That could be our happy fate in a single, interdependent world, with no flags to burn, no guns to be shot in anger, no—*dare* I propose so dangerous a proposition?—taxation without representation? In short, a new world *dis*order. Freedom, justice for all. CNN, too. *In hoc signo . . .*

*The Nation*
July 15–22, 1991

# MONOTHEISM AND
# ITS DISCONTENTS

The word "radical" derives from the Latin word for root. Therefore, if you want to get to the root of *any*thing you must be radical. It is no accident that the word has now been totally demonized by our masters, and no one in politics dares even to use the word favorably, much less track any problem to its root. But then a ruling class that has been able to demonize the word "liberal" is a master at controlling—indeed stifling—any criticism of itself. "Liberal" comes from the Latin *liberalis,* which means pertaining to a free man. In politics, to be liberal is to want to extend democracy through change and reform. One can see why that word had to be erased from our political lexicon.

Meanwhile, the word "isolationist" has been revived to describe those who would like to put an end to the national security state that replaced our Republic a half-century ago while extending the American military empire far beyond our capacity to pay for it. The word was trotted out in the presidential election of 1992 to describe one Pat Buchanan, who was causing great distress to the managers of our national security state by saying that America must abandon the empire if we are ever to repair the mess at home. Also, as a neo-isolationist, Buchanan must be made to seem an anti-Semite. This is not hard to do. Buchanan is a classic Archie Bunker type, seething with irrational prejudices and resentments, whose origin I'll get to presently.

The country is now dividing, as it did a half-century ago, between those who think that America comes first versus those who favor empire and the continued exertion of force everywhere in the name of democracy, something not much on display here at home. In any case, as the whole world is, more or less, a single economic unit in which the United States is an ever smaller component, there are no isolationists today. But the word games go on and the deliberate reversals of meaning are always a sign that our corporate masters are worried that the people are beginning to question their arrangements. Many things are now coming into focus. *The New York Times* promptly dismissed Buchanan as a minor irritant, which was true, but it ignored his potentially major constituency—those who now believe that it was a mistake to have wasted, since 1950, most of the government's revenues on war.

Another candidate, Jerry Brown, alarmed the *Times* even more than Buchanan did. There was the possibility that he could be elected. More important, he might actually change our politics in the sense of who pays for whom. In a sudden frenzy, the *Times* compared him to Perón—our Jerry?—a dangerous demagogue whose "sharp-edged anger . . . resonates among a variety of Americans." Plainly, the ownership of the country is frightened that the current hatred of politicians, in general, may soon be translated into a hatred of that corporate few who control the many through Opinion, as manufactured by the *Times,* among others.

Now to the root of the matter. The great unmentionable evil at the center of our culture is monotheism. From a barbaric Bronze Age text known as the Old Testament, three antihuman religions have evolved—Judaism, Christianity and Islam. These are sky-god religions. They are, literally, patriarchal—God is the omnipotent father—hence the loathing of women for 2,000 years in those countries afflicted by the sky-god and his earthly male delegates. The sky-god is a jealous god, of course. He requires total obedience from everyone on earth, as he is in place not just for one tribe but for all creation. Those who would reject him must be converted or killed for their own good. Ultimately, totalitarianism is the only sort of politics that can truly serve the sky-god's purpose. Any movement of a liberal nature endangers his authority and that of his delegates on earth. One God, one King, one Pope, one master in the factory, one father-leader in the family at home.

The founders of the United States were not enthusiasts of the sky-god. Many, like Jefferson, rejected him altogether and placed man at the center of the world. The young Lincoln wrote a pamphlet *against* Christianity, which friends persuaded him to burn. Needless to say, word got around about both Jefferson and Lincoln and each had to cover his tracks. Jefferson said that he was a deist, which could mean anything or nothing, while Lincoln, hand on heart and tongue in cheek, said he could not support for office anyone who "scoffed" at religion.

From the beginning, sky-godders have always exerted great pressure in our secular republic. Also, evangelical Christian groups have traditionally drawn strength from the suppressed. African slaves were allowed to organize heavenly sky-god churches, as a surrogate for earthly freedom. White churches were organized in order to make certain that the rights of property were respected and that the numerous religious taboos in the New and Old Testaments would be enforced, if necessary, by civil law. The ideal to which John Adams subscribed—that we would be a nation of laws, not of men—was quickly subverted when the churches forced upon everyone, through supposedly neutral and just laws, their innumerable taboos on sex, alcohol, gambling. We are now indeed a nation of laws, mostly bad and certainly antihuman.

Roman Catholic migrations in the last century further reinforced the Puritan sky-god. The Church has also put itself on a collision course with the Bill of Rights when it asserts, as it always has, that "error has no rights." The last correspondence between John Adams and Thomas Jefferson expressed their alarm that the Jesuits were to be allowed into the United States. Although the Jews were sky-god folk, they followed Book One, not Book Two, so they have no mission to convert others; rather the reverse. Also, as they have been systematically demonized by the Christian sky-godders, they tended to be liberal and so turned not to their temple but to the A.C.L.U. Unfortunately, the recent discovery that the sky-god, in his capacity as realtor, had given them, in perpetuity, some parcels of unattractive land called Judea and Samaria has, to my mind, unhinged many of them. I hope this is temporary.

In the First Amendment to the Constitution the Founders made it clear that this was not to be a sky-god nation with a national religion like that of England, from whom we had just separated. It is curious how little understood this amendment is—yes, everyone has a right to worship any god he chooses but he does *not* have the right to impose his beliefs on others who do not happen to share in his superstitions and taboos. This separation was absolute in our original Republic. But the sky-godders do not give up easily. During the Civil War, they actually got the phrase "In God We Trust" onto the currency, in direct violation of the First Amendment, while "Under God" was added to the Oath of Allegiance under Eisenhower.

Although many of the Christian evangelists feel it necessary to convert everyone on earth to their primitive religion, they have been prevented—so far—from forcing others to worship as they do, but they *have* forced—most tyrannically and wickedly—their superstitions and hatreds upon all of us through the civil law and through general prohibitions. So it is upon that account that I now favor an all-out war on the monotheists.

Let us dwell upon the evils they have wrought. The hatred of blacks comes straight from their Bad Book. As descendants of Ham (according to Redneck divines), blacks are forever accursed, while Saint Paul tells the slaves to obey their masters. Racism is in the marrow of the bone of the true believer. For him, black is forever inferior to white and deserves whatever ill fortune may come his way. The fact that some monotheists can behave charitably means, often, that their prejudice is at so deep a level that they are not aware it is there at all. In the end, this makes any radical change of attitude impossible. Meanwhile, welfare has been the price the sky-godders were willing to pay to exclude blacks from their earthly political system. So we must live—presumably forever—with a highly enervating race war, set in train by the One God and his many hatreds.

Patriarchal rage at the thought of Woman ever usurping Man's place at the helm, in either home or workplace, is almost as strong now as it ever was, while the ongoing psychopathic hatred of same-sexuality has made the United States the laughingstock of the civilized world. After all, in most of the First World, monotheism is weak. Where it is weak or nonexistent, private sexual behavior has nothing at all to do with those not involved, much less with the law. At least when the Emperor Justinian, a sky-god man, decided to outlaw sodomy, he had to come up with a good *practical* reason, which he did. It is well known, Justinian declared, that buggery is a principal cause of earthquakes, and so must be prohibited. But our sky-godders, always eager to hate, still quote Leviticus, as if that loony text had anything useful to say about anything except, perhaps, the inadvisability of eating shellfish in the Jerusalem area.

We are now, slowly, becoming alarmed at the state of the planet. For a century, we have been breeding like a virus under optimum conditions, and now the virus has begun to attack its host, the earth. The lower atmosphere is filled with dust, we have just been told from our satellites in space. Climate changes; earth and water are poisoned. Sensible people grow alarmed; sky-godders are serene, even smug. The planet is just a staging area for heaven. Why bother to clean it up? Did not the sky-god tell his slaves to "be fruitful and multiply, and replenish the earth, and subdue it, and have dominion . . . over every living thing that moveth upon the earth." Well, we did just like you told us, massa. We've used everything up. We're ready for heaven now. Or maybe Mars will do.

Ordinarily, as a descendant of the eighteenth-century Enlightenment, which shaped our Republic, I would say live and let live and I would try not to "scoff"—to use Lincoln's verb—at the monotheists. But I am not allowed to ignore them. They won't let me. They are too busy. They have a divine mission to take away our rights as private citizens. We are forbidden abortion here, gambling there, same-sex almost everywhere, drugs, alcohol in a dry county. Our prisons are the most terrible and the most crowded in the First World. Our death-row executions are a source of deep disgust in civilized countries, where more and more we are regarded as a primitive, uneducated and dangerous people. Although we are not allowed, under law, to kill ourselves or to take drugs that the good folk think might be bad for us, we are allowed to buy a handgun and shoot as many people as we can get away with.

Of course, as poor Arthur (There Is This Pendulum) Schlesinger Jr. would say, these things come in cycles. Every twenty years liberal gives way to conservative, and back again. But I suggest that what is wrong now is not cyclic but systemic. And our system, like any system, is obeying the second law of thermodynamics. Everything is running down; and we are well advanced along the cold, dusty road to entropy. I don't think much of anything can be done to halt this progress under our present political-economic system. We lost poor Arthur's pendulum in 1950 when our original Constitution was secretly replaced with the apparatus of that national security state, which still wastes most of our tax money on war or war-related matters. Hence deteriorating schools, and so on.

Another of our agreed-upon fantasies is that we do not have a class system in the United States. The Few who control the Many through Opinion have simply made themselves invisible. They have convinced us that we are a classless society in which anyone can make it. Ninety percent of the stories in the pop press are about winners of lotteries or poor boys and girls who, despite adenoidal complaints, become over-night millionaire singers. So there is still hope, the press tells the folks, for the 99 percent who will never achieve wealth no matter how hard they work. We are also warned at birth that it is not polite to hurt people's feelings by criticizing their religion, even if that religion may be damaging everyone through the infiltration of our common laws.

Happily, the few cannot disguise the bad times through which we are all going. Word is spreading that America is now falling behind in the civilization sweepstakes. So isn't it time to discuss what we all really think and feel about our social and economic arrangements?

Although we may not discuss race other than to say that Jesus wants each and every one of us for a sunbeam, history is nothing more than the bloody record of the migration of tribes. When the white race broke out of Europe five hundred years ago, it did many astounding things all over the globe. Inspired by a raging sky-god, the whites were able to pretend that their conquests were in order to bring the One God to everyone, particularly those with older and subtler religions. Now the tribes are on the move again. Professor Pendulum is having a nervous breakdown because so many different tribes are now being drawn to this sweet land of liberty and, thus far, there is no indication that any of the new arrivals intends ever to read *The Age of Jackson.* I think the taking in of everyone can probably be overdone. There may not be enough jobs for very many more immigrants, though what prosperity we have ever enjoyed in the past was usually based on slave or near-slave labor.

On the other hand, I think Asians and Hispanics are a plus culturally, and their presence tends to refocus, somewhat, the relentless white versus black war. Where I *am* as one with friend Pendulum is that the newcomers must grasp certain principles as expressed in the Declaration of Independence and the Bill of Rights. Otherwise, we shall become a racially divided totalitarian state enjoying a Brazilian economy.

To revert to the unmentionable, religion. It should be noted that religion seemed to be losing its hold in the United States in the second quarter of this century. From the Scopes trial in '25 to the repeal of Prohibition in '33, the sky-godders were confined pretty much to the backwoods. Then television was invented and the electronic pulpit was soon occupied by a horde of Elmer Gantrys, who took advantage of the tax exemption for religion. Thus, out of greed, a religious revival has been set in motion and the results are predictably poisonous to the body politic.

It is usual, on the rare occasions when essential problems are addressed, to exhort everyone to be kinder, gentler. To bring us together, O Lord, in our common humanity. Well, we have heard these exhortations for a couple of hundred years and we are further apart than ever. So instead of coming together in order that the many might be one, I say let us separate so that each will know where he stands. From the *one, many,* and each of us free of the sky-god as secular lawgiver. I preach, to put it bluntly, confrontation.

Whether Brown and Buchanan knew it or not, they were revealing two basic, opposing political movements. Buchanan speaks for the party of God—the sky-god with his terrible hatred of women, blacks, gays, drugs, abortion, contraception, gambling—you name it, he hates it. Buchanan is a worthy peddler of hate. He is also in harmony not only with the prejudices and superstitions of a good part of the population but, to give him his due, he is a reactionary in the good sense—reacting against the empire in favor of the old Republic, which he mistakenly thinks was Christian.

Brown speaks for the party of man—feminists can find another noun if they like. Thomas Paine, when asked *his* religion, said he subscribed only to the religion of humanity. There now seems to be a polarizing of the country of a sort that has never happened before. The potential fault line has always been there, but whenever a politician got too close to the facts of our case, the famed genius of the system would eliminate him in favor of that mean which is truly golden for the ownership, and no one else. The party of man would like to re-establish a representative government firmly based upon the Bill of Rights. The party of God will have none of this. It wants to establish, through legal prohibitions and enforced taboos, a sky-god totalitarian state. The United States ultimately as prison, with mandatory blood, urine and lie-detector tests and with the sky-godders as the cops, answerable only to God.

For once, it's all out there, perfectly visible, perfectly plain for those who can see. For the first time in 140 years, we now have the outline of two parties. Each knows the nature of its opposite, and those who are wise will not try to accommodate or compromise the two but will let them, at last, confront each other.

Jefferson's famous tree of liberty is all that we have ever really had. Now, for want of nurture—the blood of tyrants and of patriots—it is dying before our eyes. Of course, the sky-god never liked it. But some of us did—and some of us do. So, perhaps, through facing who and what we are, we may achieve a nation not under God but under man—or should I say our common humanity?

*The Nation*
July 13, 1992

# STATE
# OF
# BEING

# AT HOME IN
# WASHINGTON, D. C.

Like so many blind people my grandfather was a passionate sightseer, not to mention a compulsive guide. One of my first memories is driving with him to a slum in southeast Washington. "All this," he said, pointing at the dilapidated red brick buildings, "was once our land." Since I saw only shabby buildings and could not imagine the land beneath, I was not impressed.

Years later I saw a map of how the District of Columbia had looked before the district's invention. Georgetown was a small community on the Potomac. The rest was farmland, owned by nineteen families. I seem to remember that the Gore land was next to that of the Notleys—a name that remains with me since my great-grandfather was called Thomas Notley Gore. (A kind reader tells me that the landowning Notleys were located elsewhere in Maryland.) Most of these families were what we continue to call—mistakenly—Scots-Irish. Actually, the Gores were Anglo-Irish from Donegal. They arrived in North America at the end of the seventeenth century and they tended to intermarry with other Anglo-Irish families—particularly in Virginia and Maryland.

George Washington not only presided over the war of separation from Great Britain (*revolution* is much too strong a word for that confused and confusing operation) but he also invented the federal republic whose original constitution reflected his powerful will to create the sort of government which would see to it that the rights of property will be forever revered. He was then congenial, if not controlling, party to the deal that moved the capital of the new republic from the city of Philadelphia to the wilderness not far from his own Virginia estate.

When a grateful nation saw fit to call the capital-to-be Washington City, the great man made no strenuous demur. Had he not already established his modesty and republican virtue by refusing the crown of the new Atlantic nation on the ground that to replace George III with George I did not sound entirely right? Also, and perhaps more to the point, Washington had no children. There would be no Prince of Virginia, ready to ascend the rustic throne at Washington City when the founder of the dynasty was translated to a higher sphere.

Although Washington himself did not have to sell or give up any of his own land, he did buy a couple of lots as speculation. Then he died a year before the city was occupied by its first president-in-residence, John Adams. The families that had been dispossessed to make way for the capital city did not do too badly. The Gores who remained sold lots, built houses and hotels, and became rich. The Gores who went away—my grandfather's branch—moved to the far west, in those days, Mississippi. It was not until my grandfather was elected to the Senate in 1907 that he was able to come home again—never to leave until his death in 1949.

Although foreign diplomats enjoy maintaining that Washington is—or was—a hardship post, the British minister in 1809, one Francis James Jackson, had the good sense to observe: "I have procured two very good saddle horses, and Elizabeth and I have been riding in all directions round the place whenever the weather has been cool enough. The country has a beautifully picturesque appearance, and I have nowhere seen finer scenery than is composed by the Potomac and the woods and hills about it; yet it has a wild and desolated air from being so scantily and rudely cultivated, and from the want of population. . . . So you see we are not fallen into a wilderness,—so far from it that I am surprised no one should before have mentioned the great beauty of the neighborhood. The natives trouble themselves but little about it; their thoughts are chiefly of tobacco, flour, shingles, and the news of the day." *Plus ça change.*

Twenty years ago, that well-known wit and man-about-town, John F. Kennedy, said, "Washington perfectly combines southern efficiency with northern charm." I think that this was certainly true of the era when he and his knights of the Round Table were establishing Camelot amongst the local chiggers. By then too many glass buildings were going up. Too many old houses were being torn down or allowed to crumble. Too many slums were metastasizing around Capitol Hill. Also, the prewar decision to make an imperial Roman—literally, Roman—capital out of what had been originally a pleasant Frenchified southern city was, in retrospect, a mistake.

When such Roman palaces as the Commerce Department were being built, I can remember how we used to wonder, rather innocently, if these huge buildings could ever be filled up with people. But a city is an organism like any other and an organism knows its own encodement. Long before the American empire was a reality, the city was turning itself into New Rome. While the basilicas and porticoes were going up, one often had the sense that one was living not in a city that was being built but in a set of ruins. It is curious that even in those pre-nuclear days many of us could imagine the city devastated. Was this, perhaps, some memory of the War of 1812 when the British burned Capitol and White House? Or of the Civil War when southern troops invaded the city, coming down Seventh Street Road?

"At least they will make wonderful ruins," said my grandfather, turning his blind eyes on the Archives Building; he was never a man to spend public money on anything if he could help it. But those Piranesi blocks of marble eventually became real buildings that soon filled up with real bureaucrats, and by the end of the Second World War Washington had a real world empire to go with all those (to my eyes, at least) bogus-Roman sets.

Empires are dangerous possessions, as Pericles was among the first to point out. Since I recall pre-imperial Washington, I am a bit of an old Republican in the Ciceronian mode, given to decrying the corruption of the simpler, saner city of my youth. In the twenties and thirties, Washington was a small town where everyone knew everyone else. When school was out in June, boys took off their shoes and did not put them on again—at least outside the house—until September. The summer heat was—and is—Egyptian. In June, before Congress adjourned, I used to be sent with car and driver to pick up my grandfather at the Capitol and bring him home. In those casual days, there were few guards at the Capitol—and, again, everyone knew everyone else. I would wander on to the floor of the Senate, sit on my grandfather's desk if he wasn't ready to go, experiment with the snuff that was ritually allotted each senator; then I would lead him off the floor. On one occasion, I came down the aisle of the Senate wearing nothing but a bathing suit. This caused a good deal of amusement, to the blind man's bewilderment. Finally, the vice president, Mr. Garner—teeth like tiny black pearls and a breath that was all whisky—came down from the chair and said, "Senator, this boy is nekkid." Afterward I always wore a shirt on the Senate floor—but never shoes.

I date the end of the old republic and the birth of the empire to the invention, in the late thirties, of air conditioning. Before air conditioning, Washington was deserted from mid-June to September. The president—always Franklin Roosevelt—headed up the Hudson and all of Congress went home. The gentry withdrew to the northern resorts. Middle-income people flocked to Rehoboth Beach, Delaware or Virginia Beach, which was slightly more racy. But since air conditioning and the Second World War arrived, more or less at the same time, Congress sits and sits while the presidents and their staffs never stop making mischief at the White House or in "Mr. Mullett's masterpiece," the splendid old State, War and Navy building, now totally absorbed by the minions of President Augustus. The Pentagon—a building everyone hated when it was being built—still gives us no great cause to love either its crude appearance or its function, so like that of a wasp's nest aswarm.

Now our Roman buildings are beginning to darken with time and pigeon droppings while the brutal glass towers of the late twentieth century tend to mask and dwarf them. But here and there in the city one still comes across shaded streets and houses; so many relics of lost time—when men wore white straw hats and suits in summer while huge hats decorated the ladies (hats always got larger just before a war) and one dined at Harvey's Restaurant, where the slow-turning ceiling-fans and tessellated floors made the hottest summer day seem cool even though the air of the street outside was ovenlike and smelled of jasmine and hot tar, while nearby Lafayette Park was a lush tropical jungle where one could see that Civil War hero, Mr. Justice Oliver Wendell Holmes, Jr., stroll, his white moustaches unfurled like fierce battle pennants. At the park's edge our entirely own and perfectly unique Henry Adams held court for decades in a house opposite to that Executive Mansion where grandfather and great-grandfather had reigned over a capital that was little more than a village down whose muddy main street ran a shallow creek that was known to some even then as—what else?—the Tiber.

*The New York Review of Books*
April 29, 1982

## 9 7

—————— ◆ ——————

# ON FLYING

I was twice footnote to the history of aviation. On July 7, 1929, still on the sunny side of four years old, I flew in the first commercially scheduled airliner (a Ford trimotor) across the United States, from New York to Los Angeles in forty-eight hours. Aviation was now so safe that even a little child could fly in comfort. I remember only two things about the flight: the lurid flames from the exhaust through the window; then a sudden loss of altitude over Los Angeles, during which my eardrums burst. Always the trouper, I was later posed, smiling, for the rotogravure sections of the newspapers, blood trickling from tiny lobes. Among my supporting cast that day were my father, the assistant general manager of the company (Transcontinental Air Transport), his great and good friend, as the never great, never good *Time* magazine would say, Amelia Earhart, as well as Anne Morrow Lindbergh, whose husband Charles was my pilot.* Both Lindbergh and Amelia had been hired by the line's promoter, one C. M. Keys (not even a footnote now but then known as

*A recent investigation of a certain newspaper of record shows that, contrary to family tradition, I was *not* on the first flight. I made my first cross-country flight a few months later, at the age of four. In any case, I am still a triumphant footnote: the first child ever to cross the country by air-rail.

the czar of aviation), to publicize TAT, popularly known as "The Lindbergh Line."

My second moment of footnotehood occurred in the spring of 1936, when I was—significantly—on the sunny side of eleven. I was picked up at St. Albans School in Washington, D.C., by my father, Eugene L. Vidal, director of the Bureau of Air Commerce (an appointee of one Franklin D. Roosevelt, himself mere tinkling prelude to Reagan's heavenly choir). FDR wanted to have a ministry of aviation like the European powers; and so the Bureau of Air Commerce was created.

On hot spring mornings Washington's streets smelled of melting asphalt, and everything was a dull tropical green. The city was more like a Virginia county seat than a world capital. Instead of air conditioning, people used palmetto fans. As we got into my implausibly handsome father's plausible Plymouth, he was mysterious, while I was delighted to be liberated from school. I wore short trousers and polo shirt, the standard costume of those obliged to pretend that they were children a half-century ago. What was up? I asked. My father said, You'll see. Since we were now on the familiar road to Bolling Field, I knew that whatever was up, it was probably going to be us. Ever since my father— known to all as Gene—had become director in 1933, we used to fly together nearly every weekend in the director's Stinson monoplane. Occasionally he'd let me take the controls. Otherwise, I was navigator. With a filling-station road map on my bony knees, I would look out the window for familiar landmarks. When in doubt, you followed a railroad line or a main highway. Period joke: A dumb pilot was told to follow the Super Chief no matter what; when the train entered a tunnel, so did the pilot. End of joke.

At Bolling Field, I recognized the so-called Hammond flivver plane. Gene had recently told the press that a plane had been developed so safe that anyone could fly it and so practical that anyone who could afford a flivver car could buy it—in mass production, that is. At present, there was only the prototype. But it was my father's dream to put everyone in the air, just as Henry Ford had put everyone on the road. Since 1933, miles of newsprint and celluloid had been devoted to Gene Vidal's dream—or was it folly?

We had been up in the Hammond plane before, and I suppose it really was almost "foolproof," as my father claimed. I forget the plane's range and speed but the speed was probably less than a hundred miles an hour. (One pleasure of flying then: sliding the window open and sticking out your hand, and feeling the wind smash against it.) As a boy, the actual flying of a plane was a lot simpler for me than building one of those model planes that the other lads were so adept at making and I all thumbs in the presence of balsa wood, paper, and glue—the Dionysiac properties of glue were hardly known then. But those were Depression years, and we Americans a serious people. That is how we beat Hitler, Mussolini, and Tojo.

Next to the Hammond, there was a Pathé newsreel crew, presided over by the familiar figure of Floyd Gibbons, a dark patch covering the vacancy in his florid face where once there had been an eye that he had lost—it was rumored—as a correspondent in the war to make the world safe for democracy. Since my father appeared regularly in newsreels and *The March of Time,* a newsreel crew was no novelty. At age seven, when asked what my father did, I said, He's in the newsreels. But now, since I had been taken so mysteriously out of class, could it be . . . ? I felt a premonitory chill.

As we drove on to the runway (no nonsense in those days when the director came calling), Gene said, "Well, you want to be a movie actor. So here's your chance." He was, if nothing else, a superb salesman. Jaded when it came to flying, I was overwhelmed by the movies. Ever since Mickey Rooney played Puck in *A Midsummer Night's Dream,* I had wanted to be a star, too. What could Rooney do that I couldn't? Why was I at St. Albans, starting Latin, when I might be darting about the world, unconfined by either gravity or the director's Stinson? "I'll put a girdle round about the earth in forty minutes!" Rooney had croaked. Now I was about to do the same.

As we parked, Gene explained that I was to take off, circle the field once, and land. After I got out of the plane, I would have to do some acting. Floyd Gibbons would ask me what it was like to fly the flivver plane, and I was to say it was just like driving a bicycle. I told Gene that it was a lot harder than riding a bicycle. He told me to keep to the script.

My earlier footnotehood was clear-cut. I was indeed the first child to cross the country by air. But now I was a challenger. In 1927, one Jack Chapman, aged eleven, had soloed. Since there had been so much public complaint (suppose he had gone and killed a cow?), my father's predecessor had made it the law that no one under sixteen years of age could solo. Now here I was a few months younger than Chapman had been in 1927, ready to break the prepubescent record. But the law said that I could not fly unattended. Ordinarily, my father—true pioneer—would have ignored this sort of law. But the director of Air Commerce could not—at least in front of *Pathé News of the Week*—break a law that he was sworn to uphold.

As I stood by the door to the plane, staring glassy-eyed at the cobra-camera, a long discussion took place. How was I to solo (thus proving that the Hammond flivver was if not foolproof boyproof) and yet not break the 1927 law? Floyd Gibbons proposed that my father sit behind me. But Gene said, no. He was already so familiar a figure in the Trans-Luxes of the Republic that the audience would think that he had done the flying. Finally, Fred Geisse, an official of the bureau (and, like me, a nonpilot), got in first and crouched behind the pilot's seat. The cameras started to turn. With a slight but lovable Rooneyesque swagger, I climbed aboard.

Recently, I saw some footage from the newsreel. As I fasten my seat belt, I stare serenely off into space, not unlike Lindbergh-Earhart. I even looked a bit like the god and goddess of flight who, in turn, looked spookily like each other. I start up the engine. I am still serene. But as I watched the ancient footage, I recalled suddenly the terror that I was actually feeling. Terror not of flying but of the camera. This was my big chance to replace Mickey Rooney. But where was my script? My director? My talent? Thinking only of stardom, I took off. With Geisse behind me kindly suggesting that I keep into the wind (that is, opposite to the way that the lady's stocking on the flagpole was blowing), I circled the field not once but twice and landed with the sort of jolt that one of today's jet cowboys likes to bring to earth his DC-10.

The real terror began when I got out of the plane and stood, one hand on the door knob, staring into the camera. Gibbons asked me about the flight. I said, Oh, it wasn't much, and it wasn't, either. But I was now suffering from terminal stage fright. As my voice box began to shut down, the fingers on the door knob appeared to have a life of their own. I stammered incoherently. Finally, I gave what I thought was a puckish Rooneyesque grin which exploded on to the screen with all the sinister force of Peter Lorre's *M.* In that final ghastly frame, suddenly broken off as if edited by someone's teeth in the cutting room, my career as boy film star ended and my career as boy aviator was launched. I watched the newsreel twice in the Belasco Theater, built on the site of William Seward's Old Club House. Each time, I shuddered with horror at that demented leer which had cost me stardom. Yet, leer notwithstanding, I was summer-famous; and my contemporaries knew loathing. The young Streckfus Persons (a.k.a. Truman Capote) knew of my exploit.

"Among other things," Harper Lee writes of the boy she based on Capote, "he had been up in a mail plane seventeen times, he had been to Nova Scotia, he had seen an elephant, etc." In the sixties, when I introduced Norman Mailer to my father, I was amazed how much Mailer knew of Gene's pioneering.

I record this trivia not to try to regain my forever-lost feetnotehood but to try to recall the spirit of the early days of aviation, a spirit itself now footnote to the vast air and aerospace industries of today. In Anthony Sampson's *Empires of the Sky,* only a dozen pages are devoted to the first quarter-century of American aviation. There are also three times as many references to something called Freddie Laker as there are to Lindbergh. Well, *sic transit* was always the name of the game, even now when the focus is on space itself. Finally, I am put in mind of all this by a number of recent books on aviation, of which the most intriguing and original is *The Winged Gospel* by Joseph J. Corn, in which the author recalls the quasi-religious fervor that Americans experienced when men took to the air and how, for a time, there was "a gospel of flight," and Gene Vidal was its "high priest."* Flight would make men near-angels, it was believed; and a peaceful world one.

## 2

Ever since the development of the balloon in eighteenth-century France, so-called "lighter-than-air craft" were a reality. Heavier-than-air craft were considered mad inventors' dreams until the brothers Orville and Wilbur Wright created the first heavier-than-air plane and flew it at Kitty Hawk, North Carolina, on December 17, 1903. Curiously enough, it took five years before the press could figure out exactly *what* it was that they had done. At that time the world was full of inventors like the Wright brothers; but the others were either inventing lighter-than-air craft such as the dirigible, or experimenting with gliders. Only a few certified nuts believed in the practicality of heavier-than-air craft. One of these "crackpots" was Henry Adams's friend at the Smithsonian Institution, Dr. S. P. Langley, and he was on much the same theoretical tack as the Wright brothers. But they left earth first.

It was not until Orville Wright flew a plane at Fort Myer outside Washington in the presence of five thousand people that the world

*Joseph J. Corn, *The Winged Gospel: America's Romance with Aviation, 1900–1950* (London: Oxford University Press, 1984).

realized that man had indeed kicked gravity and that the sky was only the beginning of no known limit. Like so many of the early airship makers, the Wright brothers were bicycle mechanics. But then the bicycle itself had been a revolutionary machine, adding an inch or two to the world's population by making it possible for boys to wheel over to faraway villages where taller (or shorter) girls might be found. At least in the days when eugenics was a science that was the story. Other bicycle manufacturers soon got into the act, notably Glenn H. Curtiss, who was to be a major manufacturer of aircraft.

Although the first generation of flyers believed that airplanes would eventually make war unthinkable, the 1914–18 war did develop a new glamorous sort of warfare, with Gary Cooper gallantly dueling Von Stroheim across the bright heavens. By 1918 the American government had an airmail service. In 1927 the twenty-five-year-old Lindbergh flew the Atlantic and became, overnight, the most famous man on earth, the air age beautifully incarnate. In 1928 Amelia Earhart flew the Atlantic and took her place in the heavens as yin to Lindbergh's yang.

It is hard to describe to later generations what it was like to live in a world dominated by two such shining youthful deities. Neither could appear in public without worshipers—no other word—storming them. Yet each was obliged to spend a lot of time not only publicizing and selling aircraft but encouraging air transport. Of the two, Lindbergh was the better paid. But, as a deity, the commercial aspect was nothing to him, he claimed, and the religion all. On the other hand, Earhart's husband, the publisher and publicist George Palmer Putnam (known as G.P.), worked her very hard indeed. The icons of the air age were big business.

*Time* magazine, September 28, 1931:

To Charles Townsend Ludington, socialite of Philadelphia, $8,000 might be the price of a small cabin cruiser such as he sails on Biscayne Bay. . . . But the $8,073.61 profit which showed on a balance sheet upon [his] desk last week was as exciting to him as a great fortune. It was the first year's net earning of the Ludington Line, plane-per-hour passenger service between New York, Philadelphia and Washington.

As practically sole financiers of the company [Nicholas and Charles Townsend] Ludington might well be proud. But they would be the first to insist that all credit go to two young men who sold them the plan and then made it work: brawny, handsome Gene Vidal, West Point halfback of

1916–20, one-time Army flyer; and squint-eyed, leathery Paul ("Dog") Collins, war pilot, old-time airmail pilot.

*Time* style still exerts its old magic, while *Time* checkers are, as always, a bit off—my father graduated from West Point in 1918. An all-American halfback, he also played quarterback. But he *was* one of the first army flyers and the first instructor in aeronautics at West Point. Bored with peacetime army life and excited by aviation, he quit the army in 1926. Already married to the "beauteous" (*Time* epithet) Nina Gore, daughter of "blind solon" (ditto) Senator T. P. Gore, he had a year-old son for whom *Time* had yet to mint any of those Lucite epithets that, in time (where "All things shall come to pass," Ecclesiastes), they would.

New airlines were cropping up all over the country. After 1918, anyone who could nail down a contract from the postmaster general to fly the mail was in business. Since this was the good old United States, there was corruption. Unkind gossips thought that an army flyer whose father-in-law was a senator would be well placed to get such a contract. But during the last years of President Hoover, Senator Gore was a Democrat; and during the first term of President Roosevelt, he was an enemy of the New Deal. Gore was no help at all to Gene. But anyone who could fly was automatically in demand at one or another of the small airlines that carried (or did not carry) the mail.

In 1929, C. M. Keys combined a couple of airlines and started Transcontinental Air Transport, or TAT. For a quarter million dollars cash, Keys hired, as a sort of consultant, Charles Lindbergh; he also gave the Lone Eagle shrewd advice on how to avoid income tax. Thus, TAT was dubbed "The Lindbergh Line." Keys was perhaps the first true hustler or robber baron in American aviation: "He had been an editor of *The Wall Street Journal* and had worked with Walter Hines Page on the old *World's Work;* Keys was also an important aviation promoter. He got into the manufacturing end of the industry during the war and eventually won control of Curtiss Aeroplane & Motor Company. . . ." In other words, a businessman who "got control" of companies; who bought and sold them. TAT also acquired ex–airmail flyer Paul Collins and Gene Vidal.

Like most of the early airlines, TAT was a combined air-rail service. Passenger planes did not fly at night or over the turbulent Alleghenys. On a TAT transcontinental flight, the passengers left New York by rail in the evening; then, in Columbus, Ohio, they boarded a Ford trimotor (eight passengers maximum) and flew to Waynoka, Oklahoma. Here they transferred to the Santa Fe railroad for an overnight haul to Clovis, New Mexico, where another plane flew them into Los Angeles—or Burbank, to be precise. It is a tribute to the faith of the air-gospellers that they truly believed that this grueling two-day journey would, in time, be preferable to the comforts of a Pullman car. Interestingly enough, many descendants of the original railroad barons were immediately attracted to aviation, and names like Harriman and Whitney and Vanderbilt crop up on the boards of directors. These young men were prescient. By the end of the Second War, the railroads that had dominated American life since the Civil War, buying not only politicians but whole states, would be almost entirely superseded by civil aviation and the Teamsters union. But the railroad lords suffered not at all; they simply became airlords.

The transition was hardly overnight. In TAT's eighteen months of service, the line lost $2,750,000. There were simply not enough customers at sixteen cents a mile; also, more important, there was no mail contract.

TAT's headquarters were at St. Louis, and my only memory of the summer of 1929 (other than bleeding eardrums) was of city lights, as seen from a downtown hotel window. For anyone interested in period detail, there were almost no colored lights then. So, on a hot airless night in St. Louis, the city had a weird white arctic glow. Also, little did I suspect as I stared out over the tropical city with its icy blinking signs, that a stone's throw away, a youth of eighteen, as yet unknown to me and to the world, Thomas Lanier Williams, was typing, typing, typing into the night, while across the dark fields of the Republic . . .

Paul Collins describes the end of TAT (*Tales of an Old Air-Faring Man*):

About Christmastime 1929 all the St. Louis executives were called to a meeting in New York including Joseph Magee, the general manager; Gene Vidal, his assistant; Luke Harris, Jack Herlihy, and me. We were introduced in Mr. Keyes's [*sic*] office to one Jack Maddux, President of Maddux Airlines, an operation that flew from Los Angeles to San Francisco. . . . Mr. Keyes [*sic*] stated that a merger had been effected between TAT and Maddux.

The ineffable Keys then waited until the assembled management of TAT had returned to St. Louis, where they were all fired.

Simultaneously, the Great Depression began. Small airlines either merged or died. Since a contract to fly the mail was the key to survival, the postmaster general, one Walter F. Brown, was, in effect, the most powerful single figure in aviation. He was also a political spoilsman of considerable energy. In principle, he wanted fewer airlines; and those beholden to him. As of 1930, United Air Lines carried all transcontinental mail. But Brown decided that, in this case, there should be two transcontinental carriers: one would have the central New York–Los Angeles route; the second the southern Atlanta–Dallas–Los Angeles route. As befitted a Herbert Hoover socialist, Brown did not believe in competitive bidding. The southern route would go to Brown-favored American Airlines and the central route to an airline yet to be created but already titled Transcontinental and Western Air, today's Trans World Airlines.

Brown then forced a merger between TAT (willing) and Western Air Express (unwilling). But as neither flew the mail, Brown's promise of a federal contract for the combined operation did the trick. Since Brown was not above corporate troilism, a third airline, a shy mouse of a company called Pittsburgh Aviation Industries Corporation (PAIC), became a member of the wedding. How on earth did such a mouse get involved with two working airlines? Well, there were three Mellons on PAIC's board of directors, of whom the most active was Richard, nephew of Andrew, former secretary of the treasury. The nobles missed few tricks in the early days of aviation. As it turned out, the first real boss of TWA was a PAIC man, Richard W. Robbins. And so, on August 25, 1930, TWA was awarded the central airmail route even though its competitor, United, had made a lower bid. There was outcry, but nothing more. After all, the chief radio engineer for TWA was the president's twenty-eight-year-old son, Herbert Hoover, Jr. In those days, Hoover socialism was total; and it was not until his successor, Franklin D. Roosevelt, that old-fashioned capitalism was restored.

During all this, Gene Vidal had retreated to Senator Gore's house in Rock Creek Park, Washington, D.C. Certain that he had learned enough about the airline business to start one, he convinced the brothers Ludington that a regular New York–Philadelphia–Washington service was practical. He also came up with the revolutionary notion that the planes would fly "every hour on the hour": New York to Washington round trip was twenty-three dollars. When the Ludingtons insisted that costs be kept to a minimum, Gene, ever ingenious, said, "We'll operate at forty cents a mile, taking only a livable salary. Anything under forty cents, we'll agree to take in stock." The Ludingtons were charmed.

In September 1930, the Ludington Line began regular service. Tickets were sold in railway terminals. Gene personally built the first counter in Washington, using two crates with a board across. Everything was ad hoc. On one occasion, in Philadelphia, passengers from New York to Washington were stretching their legs while passengers from Washington to New York were doing the same. Then each group was shepherded into the wrong plane and the passengers to Washington went back to New York and those to New York back to Washington.

What to serve for lunch? My mother, always dieting, decided that consommé was bound to be popular. Fortunately, in those less litigious times, the first batch of badly scalded passengers gallantly did not sue. Later, hard-boiled eggs and saltine crackers made the sort of lunch that stayed down longest. As the passengers dined, and the plane lurched, and the smell of exhaust filled the cabin, cylindrical cardboard ice-cream containers were tactfully passed around. The fact that what was supposed to contain ice cream was used, instead, for vomit was my first metaphysical experience, an intimation of the skull beneath the skin. During the Second War, as first mate of an army ship in the Aleutians, I would grimly stuff our shaky passengers with crackers and hard-boiled eggs; and it is true: They do stay down longest.

At the end of the first year, the Ludington Line showed the profit duly noted by *Time.* As organizer and general manager, my father persuaded Amelia Earhart to become a vice president; he also hired Felix Du Pont to be the agent in Washington. He persuaded Herbert Hoover to light up the Washington monument at dusk because, sooner or later, a plane was bound to hit it. On the other hand, he ignored the mandatory fire drills at the Washington terminal on the sensible ground that "We have a real fire," as one of his mechanics put it, "most every day." Between New York and Washington, he put up twenty-four billboards. Slowpoke passengers on the Pennsylvania railroad could read, at regular intervals, "If you'd flown Ludington, you'd have been there." Were it not for Hoover socialism, so successful and busy a passenger airline would have got a mail contract. But Postmaster General Brown chose to give the franchise to Eastern Air Transport, who were eager to carry the mail at eighty-nine cents a mile versus Ludington's twenty-five cents. But that has always been the American way; who dares question it? The

Ludingtons lost heart; and in February 1933 they sold out to Eastern—
even though Hoover socialism had been rejected at the polls and there
was now a new president, eager to restore prosperity with classic capital-
istic measures.

Franklin Roosevelt was something of an aviation freak and, thanks in
part to some backstage maneuvering on the part of Amelia Earhart and
her friend Eleanor Roosevelt, Eugene L. Vidal became the director of the
Bureau of Air Commerce at the age of thirty-eight. He was a popular
figure not only in aviation circles but with the press. Henry Ladd Smith
wrote: "Gene Vidal had fared so badly at the hands of Postmaster
General Brown and the Republican administration that there was a
certain poetic justice in his appointment. . . ." But Smith felt that there
was more honor than power in the job. The bureau was divided into three
parts and Vidal "had all the responsibilities that go with the title, but few
of the powers. Unhappy Mr. Vidal took all the blame for mistakes, but he
had to share credit with his two colleagues. . . ." I don't think Gene felt
all that powerless, although he certainly took a good deal of blame.
Mainly he was concerned with, in Mr. Corn's words,

the dream of wings for all . . . in November 1933 [he] announced that the
government would soon spend half a million dollars to produce a "poor
man's airplane." The machine would sell for $700. . . . He planned to launch
the project with a grant from Harold Ickes's Public Works Administration
(PWA), one of the numerous government agencies established in the depression to battle unemployment.

Although a lot of out-of-work engineers and craftsmen would be
employed, Ickes saw nothing public in private planes, and Gene was
obliged to use his power to buy planes for the bureau's inspectors. He
ordered five experimental prototypes. The results were certainly
unusual. There was one plane whose wings could be folded up; you
could then drive it like an automobile. Although nothing came of this
hybrid, its overhead rotor was the precursor of the helicopter, still
worshiped as a god by the Vietnamese. Finally, there was the Hammond
Y-1, which I was to fly.

Along with the glamor of flight, there was the grim fact that planes
often crashed and that the bodies of the passengers tended to be un-
pretty, whether charred or simply in pieces strewn across the landscape.
Knute Rockne, Grace Moore, Carole Lombard died; and at least half
of the people I used to see in my childhood would, suddenly, one day,

not be there. "Crashed" was the word; nothing more was said. As director, Gene was obliged to visit the scenes of every major accident, and he had gruesome tales to report. One survivor sued the bureau because the doctor at the scene of the accident refused to replace in his scrotal sac the testicles that lay nearby.

In 1934 the Democratic senator Hugo Black chaired a Senate committee to investigate the former Republican postmaster general Brown's dealings with the airlines. Black's highly partisan committee painted Brown even darker than he was. Yes, he had played favorites in awarding mail contracts but no one could prove that he—or the Grand Old Party—had in any specific way profited. Nevertheless, Jim Farley, the new postmaster general, charged Brown with "conspiracy and collusion" while the president, himself a man of truly superhuman vindictiveness, decided to punish Brown, the Republican party, and the colluded-with airlines.

What could be more punitive—and dramatic—than the cancellation of all U.S. airmail contracts with private companies? Since the army had flown the mail back in 1918, let them fly the mail now. The president consulted the director of Air Commerce, who told him that army flyers did not have the sort of skills needed to fly the mail. After all, he should know; he was one. Undeterred, the president turned to General Benjamin D. Foulois, the chief of the air corps, who lusted for appropriations as all air corps chiefs do; and the general said, of course, the air corps could fly the mail.

On February 9, 1934, by executive order, the president canceled all airmail contracts; and the Army flew the mail. At the end of the first week, five army pilots were dead, six critically injured, eight planes wrecked. One evening in mid-March, my father was called to the White House. As Gene pushed the president's wheelchair along the upstairs corridor, the president, his usual airy self, said, "Well, Brother Vidal, we seem to have a bit of a mess on our hands." Gene always said, "I found that 'we' pretty funny." But good soldiers covered up for their superiors. What, FDR wondered, should they do? Although my father had a deep and lifelong contempt for politicians in general ("They tell lies," he used to say with wonder, "even when they don't have to") and for Roosevelt's cheerful mendacities in particular, he did admire the president's resilience: "He was always ready to try something new. He was like a good athlete. Never worry about the last play. Only the next one." Unfortunately, before they could extricate the administration from the mess, Charles Lindbergh attacked the president; publicly, the Lone Eagle held FDR responsible for the dead and injured army pilots.

Roosevelt never forgave Lindbergh. "After that," said Gene, "he would always refer to Slim as 'this man Lindbergh,' in that condescending voice of his. Or he'd say '*your* friend Lindbergh,' which was worse." Although Roosevelt was convinced that Lindbergh's statement was entirely inspired by the airlines who wanted to get back their airmail contracts, he was too shrewd a politician to get in a shooting match with the world's most popular hero. Abruptly, on April 20, 1934, Postmaster General Farley let the airlines know that the Post Office was open to bids for mail contracts because, come May, the army would no longer fly the mail. It was, as one thoughtful observer put it, the same old crap game, with Farley not Brown as spoilsman.

In 1935, "lifelong bachelor" (as *Time* would say) Senator Bronson Cutting was killed in an air crash. He was a popular senator (survived to this day by his estimable niece, Iris Origo) and the Senate promptly investigated. My father was grilled at length.

The bureau was accused of wasting time and money in a futile effort to develop a "flivver plane" for the masses. . . . Vidal himself did not fare so badly. The committee rebuked him mildly and reported that he appeared "lacking in iron," but since Vidal was hardly in the position to enforce orders, perhaps even this accusation was unfair.

My father's affection for politicians was not increased by the Senate hearings. But the real prince of darkness had now entered his life, Juan Trippe, and a lifelong struggle began. Even after I was grown, at the Maidstone Club in East Hampton, I used to observe the two men, who never exactly *not* spoke to each other and yet never did speak.

Juan Trippe was a smooth-looking man with very dark eyes. Grandson of a bank robber, as Gene liked to recall, Trippe had gone to Yale; got into the airline business in 1926, backed by two Yale friends, C. V. Whitney and William Rockefeller (what on earth do the rich *do* nowadays?). While Lindbergh was officially associated with my father and the Ludington Line, Slim was also being wooed by Trippe, who had acquired a small Florida–Cuba airline called Pan American. By 1931, Trippe had replaced Keys as the principal robber baron of the airways. Unlike Keys, he was wonderfully well connected socially and politically. For Pan American's original board, he managed to collect not only a

Whitney but a Mellon son-in-law, David Bruce, and Robert Lehman. During Black's investigation of Brown, Trippe had been caught disguising his profits in what is now standard conglomerate procedure but in those sweet days was fraud; worse, Trippe was a Republican. But smoothness is all, and, in due course, Trippe charmed Farley and Gene; and, for a time, the sly president.

Trippe's ambitions for Pan American were worldwide. He already had South America; he now wanted the Pacific and China; the Atlantic and Europe. But he would need considerable help from the administration to get the routes nailed securely down. Smoothly, he invited the director of the Bureau of Air Commerce to tour South America. A good time was had by all and, en route, Gene collected a number of exotic decorations from various exotic presidents. Then, back in Washington, Trippe presented Gene with a long list of requests. The guileless director explained to his recent host that the law required *competitive* bidding and that the United States, unlike old Europe, did not have "chosen instruments." Naturally, if Pan American wanted to enter in competition with other airlines . . .

Trippe took his revenge. He went to his friend William Randolph Hearst—no longer a Roosevelt enthusiast—and together they orchestrated a press campaign against Gene Vidal, Jim Farley and FDR—in that order. It is my impression that Lindbergh may have sided with Trippe. There is a curious photograph in *The Chosen Instrument.* * My father is at the center, speaking into a microphone. Trippe is smoothly obsequious to his right, while Igor Sikorsky and Lindbergh are also present. The caption: "Attending the delivery of the Sikorsky S-42 in May 1934," followed by the names of all those present except for the director, whose endorsement was the point to the photograph. Thanks in part to Trippe's inspired press campaign, Gene quit the government in 1937, and the bureau was broken up. The Civil Aeronautics Board was then created; on January 1, 1985 it, too, ended, a victim of Reaganism.

Although Trippe got most of the world, he never forgave Gene. Some years later, when my father was put up for membership in Philadelphia's Racquet Club, Trippe tried to blackball him because Gene's father's name was Felix. "A *Jewish* name," said Juan, smoothly. Those were racist days. When my father pointed out that in our section of *Romano-Rhaetia,* Felix is a common Christian name, he inadvertently revealed

*Marylin Bender and Selig Altschul, *The Chosen Instrument* (New York: Simon and Schuster, 1982).

the family's darkest secret. Upon arrival (1848) in the Great Protestant Republic, the Roman Catholic Vidals had promptly turned Protestant. Obviously, during the Republic's high noon, no mass was worth exclusion from the Racquet Club, against whose windows were pressed so many wistful Kennedy and Lee (born Levy) noses. Recently, a journalist told me that while interviewing Trippe, he noticed the old man was reading one of my books. When the journalist told him that the author was Gene Vidal's son, Trippe shook his head with wonder. "My, my," he said. "Hard to believe, isn't it?" Oh, there were real shits in those days.

## 3

I have no memory of Lindbergh. But Amelia Earhart was very much a part of my life. She wrote poetry and encouraged me to write, too. She had a beautiful speaking voice, which I am sure I would have recognized during the war if she had really been, as certain fabulists believe, Tokyo Rose, a captive of the Japanese. Since she usually dressed as a boy, it was assumed that she had what were then called Sapphic tendencies. I have no idea whether or not she did but I do know that she wore trousers because she thought her legs were ugly; and if she were truly Sapphic, I doubt that she would have been so much in love with my father. She had milk-white eyelashes.

In the fall of 1936, Amelia, Gene, and I went to the Army–Navy game at West Point. On the way back, as her fans peered excitedly into our train compartment, she described how she planned to fly around the world, following, more or less, the equator. I asked her what part of the flight worried her the most. "Africa," she said. "If you got forced down in those jungles, they'd never find you." I said that the Pacific looked pretty large and wet to me. "Oh, there are always islands," she said. Then she asked Gene: "Wouldn't it be wonderful to just go off and live on a desert island?" He rather doubted it. Then they discussed just *how* you could survive; and what would you do if there was no water? and if there was no water, you would have to make a sun-still and extract salt from sea water and how was that done? As we approached Grand Central Station, I suddenly decided that I wanted a souvenir of Amelia. Shortly before she left on her flight around the world, she sent me the blue-and-white checked leather belt that she often wore. She gave my father her old watch. She also made a new will, as she usually did before a dangerous flight. She left Gene her California house, on condition that if he didn't want it (he didn't), he would give it to her mother, something she did not trust G.P., her husband, to do.*

Although my father was as fond of conspiracy theories as any other good American, he rejected most of the notions that still circulate about Amelia's last flight. Of course, he was at a disadvantage: He knew something about it. When Amelia's plane vanished on July 2, 1937, somewhere between Lae, New Guinea, and Howland Island in the Pacific—where there are all those islands—the president sent the navy to look for her. He also asked Gene to help out and act as a sort of coordinator. If Amelia had been on a spy mission for the American government, as is still believed in many quarters,† the commander in chief hadn't been told about it. Years later, Eleanor Roosevelt used to talk a lot about Amelia. When I asked her if she had ever been able to find out anything, she said no. More to the point, since Mrs. Roosevelt had been devoted to Amelia, if there *had* been a secret mission, Mrs. Roosevelt would have certainly revealed it after the war and demanded all sorts of posthumous recognition for her friend. But Mrs. Roosevelt was certain that there had been no spy mission; on the other hand, she—like my father—thought there *was* something fishy about the whole business.

Shortly before Amelia left the States, she told my father that since she would have to take a navigator with her, she was going to hire Fred Noonan, formerly Pan American's chief navigator. Gene was alarmed: Noonan was a drunk. "Take anyone but Noonan," he said. "All right then," said Amelia, "why not you?" To Gene's surprise she wasn't joking. Although Gene had recently divorced my mother and G.P. was simply Amelia's manager, Gene's affection for Amelia was not equal to her love for him. "I'm not that good a navigator," he said. She then hired Noonan, who swore he was forever off the sauce. The flight began.

From India, Amelia rang G.P. and Gene together. She reported "personnel trouble": code for Noonan's drinking. Gene advised her to stop the flight. But she chose to keep on. Amelia rang again; this time from New Guinea. "Personnel trouble" had delayed her next hop—to

---

*G.P. managed to suppress Amelia's final will; my father didn't inherit the California property. I don't know what became of Amelia's mother.

†For a gorgeously off-the-wall "search" for Amelia, read *Amelia Earhart Lives,* by Joe Klaas (New York: McGraw-Hill, 1970). Apparently, in the sixties, she was alive and well and living in New Bedford; she who had so deeply hated Rye.

Howland Island. This time both Gene and G.P. told her to abandon the flight. But she thought "personnel" might be improving. She was wrong. The night before they left Lae, Noonan was drunk; worse, he had had only forty-five minutes' sleep. When they took off, he was still drunk.

Gene's theory of what happened is this: Amelia was going through a disagreeable early menopause; she deeply disliked her husband; she hated the publicness of her life and she was, at some romantic level, quite serious about withdrawing to a desert island—symbolically if not literally. Years earlier, she had made a number of conditions when she allowed G.P. to marry her. The marriage was to be, as they called it then, "open." Also, "I may have to keep some place where I can go to be by myself now and then, for I cannot guarantee to endure at all times the confinements of even an attractive cage." Finally, Gene thought it unlikely that even a navy so sublimely incompetent that, four years later, it would allow most of its fleet to be sunk at Pearl Harbor, would ever have engaged such a nervy lady to spy on Japan, while *she* would have pointed out that a pioneer circumnavigation of the globe was quite enough for one outing.

According to Gene, there were only two mysteries. One of Amelia's last radio messages was, "742 from KHAQQ: We must be on you but we cannot see you. Gas is running low. Been unable to reach you by radio. Flying at one thousand feet. One half-hour's gas left." Gene said that this was not a true report. She had a good deal more than a half-hour's gas left. Why did she lie? The second mystery was that of the radio frequency. Amelia's last message was at 8:46 A.M.; after that, some fourteen minutes passed with her frequency still coming in strong at what is known as "maximum 5." "Then," said Gene, "the frequency didn't break off, the way it does when you crash. Someone switched it off." So what happened? It was Gene's hunch that she had indeed found an island—and landed. "But what about Fred Noonan?" I asked. "He sounds even worse than G.P." Gene's response was grim: "If Amelia wanted to get rid of him, she'd have got rid of him. Hit him over the head with one of his bottles. She was like that."

Over the years, there were many stories of a white woman sighted on this or that island. The only intriguing one, according to G.P., was from a Russian sailor whose ship had passed a small island on which a white woman signaled them; she was wearing nothing except a man's drawers. "The funny thing is," said G.P. to my father, "she always wore my shorts when she flew, but I wore boxer shorts, and the sailor said this woman was wearing those new jockey shorts." Gene never told G.P. that for some years Amelia had been wearing Gene's "new jockey shorts." In any event, the ship had not stopped; and no one ever followed up.

Four years before Amelia's last flight, she and Gene started what became Northeast Airlines, with Paul Collins as president. Although Gene was never very active in the airline, he remained a director to the end of his life. According to Mr. Corn, Vidal never gave up his dream "of mass-produced personal planes, and in private life began experiments with molded plywood, a material he thought appropriate for the purpose." This is true enough, except that he also experimented, more successfully, with fiberglass. But by the time he died in 1969, the world was far too full of people even to dream of filling the skies with private planes in competition with military aircraft and the planes of those airlines, three of which he had had a hand in founding. I do know that he found modern civil aviation deeply boring; and though he shared the general ecstasy when a man got to the moon, the gospel of flight that he and Lindbergh and Earhart preached was by then a blurred footnote to the space age, where technology is all and, to the extent that there is a human aspect to space, it involves team players with the right stuff. Neil Armstrong first stepped on the moon but it was Werner von Braun and a cast of thousands who put him there. Mr. Armstrong did not fly to the moon; and for all his personal pluck and luck, he is already perceived as a footnote, a name for Trivial Pursuit.

It was different on December 17, 1934, when my father asked all the nation's pilots "to take off at 10.30 in the morning and to stay in the air for half an hour. They would thus be aloft at the precise time at which, thirty-one years earlier, Orville Wright had also been airborne. The response to Vidal's call was impressive . . . an estimated 8,000 aircraft participated in the ritual."*

Today it is marvelous indeed to watch on television the rings of Saturn close and to speculate on what we may yet find at galaxy's edge. But in the process, we have lost the human element; not to mention the high hope of those quaint days when flight would create "one world."

*Corn, *The Winged Gospel*, p. 64.

Instead of one world, we have "star wars," and a future in which dumb, dented human toys will drift mindlessly about the cosmos long after our small planet's dead.

*The New York Review of Books*
January 17, 1985

# 98

# WEST POINT

On the table at which I write is a small silver mug with a square handle; it is inscribed to *Eugene L. Vidal, Jr., October 3, 1925*—a gift from the West Point football team to its mascot, which that year was not a mule but me. I drank milk from the cup for a good many years and from the look of the rim did a bit of teething on it, too.

I have no early memory of West Point. Apparently I was born in the cadet hospital on a Saturday morning because my mother had decided to stay on the post and go to a football game. I was delivered not by an obstetrician but by one Major Howard Snyder who happened to be officer of the day at the cadet hospital. Later, as surgeon general of the army, he looked after President Eisenhower ("Just indigestion, Mamie," he was reported to have said when she rang him in the middle of the night with news of the Great Golfer's first tussle with the Reaper. "Give him some bicarbonate"). More than thirty years later I visited General Snyder at his office in the basement of the White House. He recalled my birth; was still angry at my mother for not having gone to a civilian hospital; was most protective of his old friend the President. "Tough South German peasant. There's nothing at all wrong with him, you know, except this really nasty temper. That's what'll kill him." Then the inevitable question, "Why didn't *you* go to the Point?" A member of a

West Point family had chosen *not* to join the Long Gray Line. Something wrong there.

At the time of my birth Eugene L. Vidal, *Sr.,* was known as Gene Vidal to the world of jocks—and to just about everybody else in the country for in those days college athletes were like rock stars (Scott Fitzgerald's apostrophe to Princeton's Hobe Baker is plainly tribute to a god). Class of 1918 at West Point, G.V. was an All-American quarterback; he is still regarded as the best all-around athlete in the history of the Academy, moving with equal ease from track to basketball to football to rugby (learned in one afternoon); a master of every sport except the one invented by Abner Doubleday (West Point 1842). "Baseball is the favorite American sport because it's so slow," G.V. used to say. "Any idiot can follow it. And just about any idiot can play it." After graduation, he came back to the Point as football coach; he was also the first instructor in aeronautics.

Shortly after I was born, G.V. resigned from the army (he found it boring) and went into civil aviation. But, as with most West Pointers of his generation, the links between him and the Academy proved to be unbreakable. Although his disposition was ironic, his style deflationary, his eye for the idiocies of the military sharp, he took some pride in being not only a part of the history of the Point but also a sort of icon for those graduates who came to prominence in the Second War.

The Eisenhowers, Groveses, Stratemeyers, Ridgways and Taylors created the American world empire; they also gave us the peacetime draft, a garrison state, and the current military debacle in Southeast Asia. With the best will in the world (and with the blessing of their civilian masters to whom the cold war was good business), these paladins have in the quarter century since Hiroshima wasted lives and money while treating with contempt the institutions of the republic. Now the game is changing—the army, too. Currently the West Pointers are fighting for a permanent draft. Otherwise, they tell us, we will have an "unrepresentative" (i.e., black) military establishment. But these same officers never objected to the prewar army, which was redneck and every bit as dumb as the coming black army because nobody smart (black or white) is going to be an enlisted man in the American army if he can help it.

I was less than a year old when my parents moved into the Washington house of my mother's father, Senator T. P. Gore (where I was put to bed in a bureau drawer). Like a number of high-powered cadets Gene Vidal was hypergamous. Yet, as a boy growing up in Madison, South

Dakota, he was not particularly ambitious, as far as one can tell—which is not much: he had no memory for the past, his own or that of the family. He was so vague, in fact, that he was not certain if his middle initial "L" stood for Louis, as he put on my birth certificate, or for Luther. It was Luther. At fourteen I settled the confusion by taking my grandfather's name Gore.

As it turned out, the congressman from South Dakota was ambitious enough for two. After watching G.V. play football at the University of South Dakota, the congressman said, "How would you like an appointment to West Point?" "And where," answered my father with his usual charm and inability to dissemble, "is West Point? And what is there?" He was promptly appointed; thus ended his dream of becoming a barber because barbers seemed to have a lot of free time. Apparently in a town like Madison there was no one very interesting to emulate. Certainly G.V.'s father Felix was no model. Felix had been an engineer on whatever railroad it is that goes through South Dakota; for reasons unknown, he got off at Madison one day and went into the coal business.

Felix's father had been born in Feldkirch, Austria, of Romanic stock (descendants of the Roman legionnaires who settled Rhaetia in the first century).* A hypergamous adventurer and phony MD, Eugen Fidel Vidal married Emma de Traxler Hartmann of Lucerne, Switzerland— an heiress until she married him and got herself disinherited. "A *real* countess," my aunt used to say with wonder. In 1848 the unhappy couple came to Wisconsin where the Gräfin was promptly deserted by her husband. She brought up five children by translating American news stories for German, French, and Italian newspapers. She had every reason to be bitter; and was bitter. I go into all this family history because it has a good deal to do with the kind of men who went to West Point in those days.

Athlete. Lapsed Roman Catholic. The meager prairie background, somewhat confused by a family tradition of exciting wars (the Traxlers and Hartmanns had been professional soldiers for several hundred years). Then West Point and the companionship of men like himself. In the class three years ahead of G.V. were Bradley and Eisenhower (Ike was known as the "Swedish Jew"—my father as "Tony the Wop"); while in the class of 1918 were Mark Clark, Leslie Groves, and Lucius

*A certain venerable vendor of American book-chat thought it preposterous that I should claim descent from the Romans. But the Romanic Vidals were originally called Vitalis and from Trieste north to Friuli and to Vorarlberg, Roman monuments bear witness to our ubiquitousness.

Clay (who once persuaded me to write a speech for his friend President Eisenhower on the virtues—if any—of integration: the speech was not delivered). Among those my father taught was the grand architect of our empire's Syracusan adventure in Southeast Asia, the Alcibiades of counterinsurgency, Maxwell Taylor.

These men had a good deal in common even before they were put into the pressure cooker on the Hudson. Most came from rural backgrounds; from lower-middle-class families; certainly they were not representative of the country's ruling class. In this century our nobles have not encouraged their sons to go to West Point. There were also no blacks at the Academy and few, if any, Jews or Roman Catholics. West Point was a very special sort of place.

According to K. Bruce Galloway and Robert Bowie Johnson, Jr. (*West Point: America's Power Fraternity*),* "The Military Academy offers an ideology, not an education, and because of this and the uniform, the graduates find themselves anointed with access to America's ruling elite." The authors take a dark view of the Academy and its graduates, and they tend to see conspiracy where there is often only coincidence. For instance:

By 1933 President Roosevelt had created the position of Director of Aeronautics . . . and appointed Eugene L. Vidal (W.P. 1918) as first director. Vidal had to deal immediately with the controversy over the place of aviation in—where else?—military affairs. He survived that problem, only to be faced with the airmail scandals of 1933 and 1934. . . . In the years following, West Point control of civil aeronautics lapsed only temporarily.

Galloway and Johnson would be more nearly right if they simply said that all West Pointers tend to look out for one another. In 1943 (aged seventeen) I enlisted as a private in the army and was assigned to a much publicized Training Program, which promptly collapsed. Aware that I was about to be shunted off to an infantry outfit that was soon to contribute a number of half-trained eighteen-year-olds to be butchered on the Rhine, I signaled to the nonexistent but very real West Point Protective Association. I was promptly transferred to the Air Force. I do not in the least regret this use of privilege and would do it again; but privilege comes from the Latin words meaning "private law," and even in a would-be canting democracy like ours there ought to be only public laws.

*Simon and Schuster, 1973.

*Duty, Honor, Country.* That is the motto of West Point. It is curious that no one until recently seems to have made much of an ominous precedence that makes the nation the third loyalty of our military elite. Duty comes first. But duty to what? Galloway and Johnson are plain: the officer class. Or as a veteran instructor at the Point puts it, "In my system of values West Point comes first, the Army second, and the country comes third."

Honor. Galloway and Johnson are particularly interesting on the origins of West Point's honor system. The Academy's true founding father, Sylvanus Thayer, was a passionate admirer of Bonaparte; he also found good things in the Prussian system. Although the United States did not seem to have much need for an officer caste when he took charge of the Academy in 1817 (of course the British had burned down Washington a few years earlier but that sort of thing doesn't happen very often), Thayer set about creating a four-year hell for the young men sent to him from all over the country. They were kept constantly busy; treated like robots; given an honor system which, simply put, required them to spy on one another.

This sort of system is always diabolic and usually effective, particularly in an environment like West Point where, according to Colonel L.C. West of the Judge Advocate General Corps, "at a tender age, the West Point Cadet learns that military rules are sacred and in time readily accepts them as a substitute for integrity. As he progresses through his military career, the rules remain uppermost in his code of honor. In fact, his 'honor' is entwined with the rules and so long as he obeys the rules, whatever their content, or whatever manner of man or fool may have written them, his honor is sound." This explains the ease with which these self-regarding young men whose honor is, officially, not to lie, cheat or steal (or go to the bars in Highland Falls) can with such ease cover up a massacre like My Lai or, like General Lavelle, falsify bombing reports, invent military victories in order to help one another get decorations and promotions—not to mention take bribes from those large corporations whose manufacture of expensive weaponry absorbs so much of the military budget.

Country. To the West Pointer loyalty to the United States comes after loyalty to the Academy and to himself. Over the years this lack of patriotism has not gone entirely unnoticed. In fact, ever since the Academy was founded there have been critics of Thayer's military elite and its separateness from the rest of the country. According to the third superintendent, Alden Partridge (W.P. 1806), the Academy was "mo-

narchial, corrupt and corrupting . . . a palpable violation of the constitution and laws of the country, and its direct tendency to introduce and
build up a privileged order of the very worst class—a military aristocracy—in the United States."

In 1830 Tennessee's show-biz congressman Davy Crockett introduced
a bill to shut down the Academy while in 1863 another bill in Congress
also proposed abolition. Speaking for the later measure, the radical
Republican Senator B.F. Wade of Ohio declared: "I do not believe that
there can be found on the whole face of the earth . . . any institution
that has turned out as many false, ungrateful men as have emanated
from this institution."

For more than a century West Pointers have returned the compliment. They do not like civilians, while their contempt for politicians is
as nearly perfect as their ignorance of the institutions of the country that
they are required to serve—after duty, that is; after honor. Specifically,
my father's generation—the empire-makers—disliked Jews, regarded
blacks as low comedy relief, politicians as corrupt, Filipinos as sly . . .
still fresh in everyone's memory was the slaughter by the American
army of several hundred thousand Filipinos at the beginning of the
century: the largest experiment in genocide the world was to know until
Hitler. The West Pointers regard only one another with true reverence.

The authors of *West Point* are particularly interesting when they
discuss what goes on nowadays in the classrooms at the Academy. One
of the authors graduated in 1965 and no doubt writes from personal
experience. Since the teachers tend to be graduates, they often have no
special knowledge of the subject they teach—nor do they need to have
because each day's lesson is already prepared for them in "blocs." But
then, according to General George A. Lincoln, the Academy's academic
guru (and Nixon adviser): "West Point is an under-graduate scholarship
school without many scholars or any great motivation for learning as
far as a material proportion of each class is concerned." He seems rather
pleased by this. Galloway and Johnson are not. They believe that the
cadets are taught "the ability to think and reason without really being
able to do so."

Boys who go to West Point today do so for a variety of reasons, none
having much to do with learning. There is the romantic appeal of the
Long Gray Line. There is the cozy appeal of a life in which all important
decisions will be made by others. There is the attractive lure of retirement at an early age—not to mention translation to the upper echelons
of those corporations which do business with the Pentagon. Simply by

stepping on an escalator, the West Pointer can have the sense of duty done, of honor upheld, of country served—and self, too. It is an irresistible package. Yet an instructor at the Academy recently commented (anonymously), "The cadets at West Point are fifth rate." To which the answer must be: they are fifth-rate because that is what the system requires of them. Since they are not different from other American boys their age, their intellectual torpor is due to a system that requires loyalty and obedience above all else—two qualities that flourish most luxuriantly in the ignorant; most dangerously in the fanatic.

It is no surprise that the military elite was delighted by the anticommunist line of their civilian masters. The Truman-Acheson, Eisenhower-Dulles, Kennedy-Johnson-Rusk, Nixon-Kissinger war on commies at home and abroad was thrilling to the military. For one thing the ideals of socialism are anathema to them even though, paradoxically, the West Pointer is entirely cared for by the state from his birth in any army hospital (if he is born into a military family) to taps at government expense in a federal boneyard. Yet the West Pointer takes this coddling as his due and does not believe that a steel worker, say, ought to enjoy privileges that belong rightfully to the military elite. Retired officers are particularly articulate on this point, and their passionate letters supporting the AMA's stand against socialized medicine are often as not written from government-paid private rooms at Walter Reed.

The cold war also meant vast military appropriations for weapons. One of the few American traditions (almost as venerable as the Warner Brothers Christmas layoff) is the secretary of defense's annual warning to Congress at budget time. Since his last request for money, the diabolical Reds are once again about to pass us—or have passed us—in atomic warheads, cutlery, missiles, saddles, disposable tissues. Distraught, Congress immediately responds to this threat with as many billions of dollars as the military feel they need to defend freedom and human dignity for all men everywhere regardless of color or creed—with the small proviso that important military installations and contracts be located in those areas whose representatives enjoy seniority in Congress.

In this fashion, two thirds of the nation's federal income has been spent for more than a generation in order that the congressmen who give the generals the money they ask for will then be re-elected with money given *them* by the corporations that were awarded federal money by generals who, when they retire, will go to work for those same corporations. Beautifully, both nation and self are served because the commies are rats, aren't they? Particularly the home-grown ones.

Just before the Second War, I listened several times to Air Force generals discuss with a humor that soon turned into obsession the ease with which the White House could be seized, the Congress sent home, and the nation kept out of the war that the Jew Franklin D. Rosenfeld was trying to start against Hitler. Although Hitler was a miserable joker (and probably a crypto-Jew), he was doing our work for us by killing commies. I do not think this sort of thinking is by any means dead today. I once asked Fletcher Knebel what gave him the idea for his *Seven Days in May,* a lively and popular thriller about the possibility of a military coup in Washington. "Talking to Admiral Radford," he told me. "He scared me to death. I could just see the Joint Chiefs kicking Kennedy out."

The United States has now been a garrison state for thirty-two years. To justify all those billions of dollars spent, the military likes to have a small war going on somewhere in the world. Or as General Van Fleet (W.P. 1915) said with some satisfaction, "Korea has been a blessing. There has to be a Korea either here or some place in the world." And so these blessings continued to shower upon us until August 15. Has peace at last come to our restless empire? Well, several weeks ago the new secretary of defense warned Congress that the Soviet's iron fist is still powerful within that velvet glove. If this striking image does not get the money out of Congress, a military crisis in the Middle East, or a small war in Chile, say, ought to keep the money flowing in the right direction.

Galloway and Johnson are, I think, too hard on the individual shortcomings of the West Pointers. After all, if we didn't want them to be the way they are (militantly anti-communist, anti-politician, anti-dissenter) they would be different. A class of this sort is made not born. I have known a good many West Pointers of the imperial generation and found them to be men of considerable virtue though none had, I should say, much sense of the civilian world. But then how could they? Their education was fifth-rate; their lives remote from everyday cares; their duty and honor directed not toward the republic but toward one another.

For a half century now West Pointers have been taught that communism is America's number one enemy without ever being told what communism is. Paradoxically, fascist-minded Americans tend to admire the communist societies once they actually visit them. The Nixons and the Agnews particularly delight in the absence of dissent; not to mention the finality of all social arrangements. Certainly the world of Mao (less some of his subtler thoughts) is nothing but the civilian world as West Point would like it to be. And if Mao is not an admirer of elites—well, neither (officially) were the founders of the American republic and just look what we have created. Anomalies are the stuff of political systems.

Certainly the West Pointers would approve the puritanism of the communist societies. Galloway and Johnson give a grim picture of the sexual deprivation of the cadets which, they maintain, makes for a lifetime of uneasy relations with women—not to mention "the entire company [that] once masturbated together in the showers." Life on the Hudson was even more austere in my father's day. But there were occasional mavericks. Although G.V. never much liked Eisenhower ("a sour cuss, always on the make"), he did give Ike credit for having managed, under the most perilous conditions, to lay the wife of the post dentist. Obviously *supreme* commanders are made early.

The military-industrial-West Point complex is more than a century old. One of the first functions of the Academy was to supply engineers to the nation. West Pointers built the first railroads as well as many roads and dams. Working as engineers for the early tycoons, West Pointers were brought into close contact with the business elite of the country and the result has been a long and happy marriage.

The military was also used to protect American business interests overseas. On at least one occasion the business interests tried to get the military to overthrow a president. In 1933 the Liberty League secretly approached Major General Smedley Butler and asked him to help them remove President Roosevelt. Butler turned them down flat. He also launched the most devastating attack ever made on American capitalism. Of his thirty-three years in the Marine Corps, he declared,

I spent most of my time being a high-class muscle-man for Big Business, for Wall Street, and for the Bankers. In short, I was a racketeer, a gangster for capitalism . . . Like all members of the military profession, I never had an original thought until I left the service. . . . I helped make Mexico—and especially Tampico—safe for American oil interests in 1914. I decided to make Haiti and Cuba a decent place for the National City Bank boys to collect revenues in. . . .

He also lists among his field of operations Nicaragua, the Dominican Republic, China (where the Marines protected Standard Oil's interests in 1927). Butler summed up, "Looking back on it, I feel that I might have given Al Capone a few hints. The best he could do was operate his racket in three districts. I operated on three continents."

Our military today operates on all five continents with results that no longer please anyone except those businesses that make weapons and pay for presidential elections. The final irony is that despite all the money we pour into our military establishment it probably could not win a war against anyone—except perhaps the American people. The disaster in Vietnam showed that the services could not fight a war in a primitive country against a "highly motivated" enemy. Naturally, the West Pointers blame this defeat on the commie-weirdo-fags (and/or politicians) who forced them in the President's elegant phrase, "to fight with one arm tied behind them." Whatever that meant: after all, the military were given a half-million American troops and more than 100 billion dollars to play with. Admittedly there were a few targets they were told not to bomb, like hospitals in Hanoi—or Peking or Moscow—but secretly president and generals bombed pretty much whatever they wanted to. Perhaps the generals felt betrayed because they could not use hydrogen bombs on the jungles and dikes of North Vietnam, or attack China. Yet even the bloodthirstiest of the Pentagon hawks did not want another go 'round with Chinese ground troops after the rout we suffered in Korea.

It should be noted that the American fighting man has been pretty lousy from the beginning of the republic, and more power to him. He has no desire to kill strangers or get hurt himself. He does not like to be told what to do. For him, there is neither duty nor honor; his country is his skin. This does not make for a world conqueror. In fact, according to a 1968 study of American performance in World War II and Korea, "the US side never won unless it had a 2-to-1 superiority of forces over the other side."* Shades of George Washington, who disliked taking on the British unless he was certain to outnumber them, preferably five to one. Even then, Washington's troops were usually beaten. Like the Italians, we Americans are killers for personal profit or revenge; the large-scale stuff doesn't really grip us.

Stuart H. Loory's *Defeated: Inside America's Military Machine* is an analysis of the state of the armed forces today. If his report is true, let us hope that the Soviet military machine is in just as big a mess as ours. Lorry begins with the usual but always staggering statistics. Between 1946 and 1972 five million citizens of a free republic were drafted into the "peacetime" [*sic*] armed forces. Year in, year out, two thirds of the federal budget goes to the military. Of all military expenditures by every

*From "Ideology and Primary Group," a paper delivered by John Helmer to the annual meeting of the American Sociological Association on August 27, 1973.

nation in the world, the United States accounts for 27.6 percent. The army's PX system is America's third largest retailer. The Defense Department owns land equivalent in area to the state of Ohio. And so on.

But what are we getting in exchange for all this money spent? A fifth-rate "ticket punching" officer corps, according to Loory. Apparently no officer is allowed to stay in any job long enough to learn to do anything well. In order to be promoted, he must get his ticket punched: a brief time in the field, then to command school, to the Pentagon, etc. This moving about ("personnel turbulence" is the army's nice phrase) has resulted in what appears to be a near-total demoralization of the basic units of the army. Officers are shipped out just as they get to know the names of the men in their outfits while the problems of drugs and race occupy most of the time of the commanders, particularly in Europe. Even the nuclear forces of SAC, forever guarding the free world, are in disarray. Obviously the second law of thermodynamics is in operation, and irreversible.

Mr. Loory contrasts American troops in Germany unfavorably to the soldiers of the Bundwehr. Apparently American troops are assigned to broken-down barracks and constantly oppressed with that mindless chicken shit which so appeals to the traditional "West Point mind": if you have nothing to do, police the area. The Germans, on the other hand, have modern barracks, interesting training, a good deal of freedom, and of course a stronger currency. In a nice reversal of history, the Americans are now the Prussians—in a sloppy sort of way—while the Prussians behave as if the private soldier is actually an intelligent member of the same race as his officers.

In the wake of the defeat of the American military machine in Asia and the resulting shocks to our institutions at home, a good many questions are bound to be asked about what sort of a country we want. Fatigue and lack of resources have stopped the long march from the Atlantic to the borders of China. The West Point elite have not served us well even though they have never disguised the fact that we are number three on their list of priorities. Yet even when they try to work peacefully for the country, they are often a menace. The Army Corps of Engineers has made such an ecological mess of our rivers and lakes that Justice Douglas has termed them "public enemy number one."

Not unnaturally, the West Pointers are most successful at creating miniature West Points, particularly in Latin American (though Ethiopia and several other exotic countries have been seeded with Duty, Honor, Country academies). All around the world West Pointers are turning out military elites trained to fight not wars but those who would extend democracy at home. Galloway and Johnson have a particularly fascinating chapter on the links between West Pointers and their opposite numbers in Latin America, particularly with the dictator of Nicaragua, Tachito Somoza (W.P. 1946).

Galloway and Johnson favor placing the Academy's four regiments in four different cities, making them closer to the grass roots of, say, Harlem or of San Francisco. They feel that this would in some way acquaint the cadet corps with their third loyalty. I doubt it. I agree with Davy Crockett and Senator Wade: an aristocratic military elite is deeply contrary to the idea of this republic and its constitution. Since the next great war will be fought by computers and by highly trained technicians, we have no need of a peacetime army of two million or even of two hundred thousand. Certainly a large army controlled by the West Point elite will continue, as it has done for nearly a quarter century, to squander money and create wars.

Forgetting the morality of a republic trying to be an empire, we now lack the material resources to carry on in the old way (LBJ ran out of bombs one afternoon downstairs in his war room; later, Nixon was to run out of kerosene for his bombers). What money we have would be better used for internal improvements, in Henry Clay's phrase. After all, the two most successful nations in the world today are Japan and Germany—and neither has much of a military establishment. This simple lesson ought to be plain to America's capitalists; yet many of our magnates are as bemused by military grandeur as any plebe, misty-eyed at the thought of the Long Gray Line and by the resonant self-aggrandizing rhetoric the late Douglas MacArthur used so successfully to peddle.

Self-delusion is a constant in human affairs. Certainly without self-delusion on the grandest scale we could never have got into our present situation; and West Point has certainly made its contribution. But reality has never been West Point's bag. According to George A. Custer (W.P. 1861), "The Army is the Indian's best friend." While according to West Point's current version of what happened in Vietnam, "The War . . . ended in August of 1968 when sorely battered Communist troops were unable to engage the allied war machine." With historians like that who needs generals?

There is also mounting evidence that today's soldier will not endure much longer West Point's traditional oppression. John Helmer's thesis in "Ideology and Primary Group" makes this pretty plain. According to Helmer, the division between the West Point officer class and today's working-class soldier is now almost unbridgeable. Since middle-class men were able to stay out of the worst of the Vietnam war, the working class provided the combat troops. They quickly got the point that "in the search and destroy tactics most commonly used [the infantryman] was, strictly speaking, the bait to catch the enemy. According to the plan he was intended to be a target, a sitting duck for the other side to attack at its ultimate cost."

The same cynical use of men is at work in Europe, where working-class American troops are, if not exactly bait, political hostages to ensure a "proper" American response in case of a Soviet strike. These men don't have to be good soldiers; they don't have to be anything but on the spot. It does not take great prescience, however, to know that should a Soviet army ever occupy Paris, the United States would abandon its own troops as swiftly as it would its allies. The American empire is not about to lose a single of its cities to save all Europe—much less three hundred thousand fuck-ups (in the eyes of the West Point elite) with their drugs, their brawling, their fragging of officers whom they regard as an alien and hostile class.

Today the first order of business in the United States is the dismantling of the military machine. Obviously, we must continue to make it disagreeable for anyone who might decide to attack us (this could be done of course by not provoking other nations but that is too much to ask). Nevertheless the military budget must be cut by two thirds; and the service academies phased out.

What to do with the officer corps? That is a delicate point. West Pointers are now more and more into politics and, as always, they are on the side of reaction. Their web of connections with the military academies they have created in Latin America, Asia, and Africa makes them truly international. Also their creations may give them dangerous ideas. It is not inconceivable that a coup of the sort that General Butler refused to lead might one day prove attractive to a group of the Honor, Duty, Country boys. Let us hope that Richard Nixon never asks General Haig (W.P. 1947) to send home Congress and Supreme Court so that the sovereign might get on with the country's true business, which is the making of armaments and small wars. Finding suitable employment for our officer caste will be, as they say, a challenge.

I look guiltily at the silver cup, and think of the generals who gave it to me. On a bright day in May four years ago I stood beside my uncle, General F.L. Vidal (W.P. 1933), at the edge of an Air Force runway near

Washington, D.C. Awkwardly, my uncle held what looked to be a shoebox. "It's *heavy,*" he muttered in my ear. I shuddered. Like the contents of the box (my father's ashes), I am a lifelong thanatophobe. Behind us stood a dozen of G.V.'s classmates. Among them the solemn, pompous, haggard Leslie Groves—himself to die a few months later; and that handsome figure of the right wing, General Wedemeyer.

After the helicopter departed on its mission, the old generals of the empire commiserated with one another. The icon of their generation, the lovely athlete of a half century before, was now entirely gone, ashes settling upon the Virginia countryside. The generals looked dazed; not so much with grief as with a sense of hurt at what time does to men, and to their particular innocence. Although I have always found poignant (yes, even honorable) the loyalty of West Pointers to one another, I could not help thinking as I walked away from them for the last time that the harm they have done to this republic and to the world elsewhere far outweighs their personal excellence, their duty, their honor. But then the country that they never understood was always last in their affections and so the first of their loyalties to be betrayed.

*The New York Review of Books*
October 18, 1973

# 99

·

# THE OZ
# BOOKS

"I have just seen a number of landscapes by an American painter of some repute," wrote John Ruskin in 1856; "and the ugliness of them is Wonderful. I see that they are true studies and that the ugliness of the country must be unfathomable." This was not kind. But then the English of that day had no great liking for the citizens of the Great Republic. Twenty-four years earlier Mrs. Trollope had commented without warmth on the manners and the domestic arrangements of United Statesmen (or persons, as we must now, correctly, describe ourselves). Twelve years earlier Charles Dickens had published *Martin Chuzzlewit.* Dickens had found the American countryside raw. The cities ramshackle. The people gasping, boastful, even—yes, dishonest. This was not at all kind. But then how could these British travelers have known that in a century's time the barbarous republic beyond the western sea would not once but twice pull from the flames of war (or "conflagration" as they say in Hollywood) England's chestnuts?

In 1856 the United States was a provincial backwater. The eruption of energy that was to fuel the future empire did not begin until four years later when the Civil War broke out. By war's end the United States was a great industrial power with satanic cities every bit as ugly and infernal as Birmingham and Manchester, with a vast flat interior that was peculiarly susceptible to those drastic changes in weather (and so fortune) that make farming an exciting occupation, with a somewhat thin civilization that has not to this day quite got off the ground in the sense that Europe's nation-states were able to do in those dark confused centuries that followed on the death of Charlemagne, and Christendom.

Yet during 1856 a number of interesting things happened in the United States. Mrs. Carl Schurz opened the first kindergarten at Watertown, Wisconsin. In Chelsea, Massachusetts, the Universalist Church observed, for the first time anywhere, Children's Day. In New York City the big theatrical hit of the season was a pantomime (from London) called *Planche, or Lively Fairies.* The year's most successful book of poems was J. G. Whittier's *The Panorama and Other Poems,* a volume that included "The Barefoot Boy." People were unexpectedly interested in the care, education, and comfort of children. It is somehow both fitting and satisfying that on May 15 of the first American Children's Year Lyman Frank Baum was born.

Like most Americans my age (with access to books), I spent a good deal of my youth in Baum's Land of Oz. I have a precise, tactile memory of the first Oz book that came into my hands. It was the original 1910 edition of *The Emerald City of Oz.* I still remember the look and the feel of those dark blue covers, the evocative smell of dust and old ink. I also remember that I could not stop reading and rereading the book. But "reading" is not the right word. In some mysterious way, I was translating myself to Oz, a place which I was to inhabit for many years while, simultaneously, visiting other fictional worlds as well as maintaining my cover in that dangerous one known as "real." With *The Emerald City,* I became addicted to reading.

By the time I was fourteen, I had read Baum's fourteen Oz books as well as the nineteen Oz books written after his death in 1919 by a young Philadelphia writer named Ruth Plumly Thompson. I remember puzzling over the strange legend that appeared on the cover of each of the books that she wrote: "by Ruth Plumly Thompson founded on and continuing the famous Oz stories by L. Frank Baum." It took me years to figure out what that phrase meant.

To a child a book is a book. The writer's name is an irrelevant decoration, unlike the title, which prepares one for delight. Even so, I used, idly, to wonder who or what L. Frank Baum was. Baum looked to my eye like Barnum, as in Barnum & Bailey's circus. Was it the same person? or the circus itself? But then, who or what was Bailey? Ruth Plumly Thompson (who was always founded-on and inexorably continuing) seemed to me to be a sort of train. The plum in Plumly registered, of course. Circus. And plums. Founded on and continuing. I never thought to ask anyone about either writer. And no one thought to tell me. But then, in the 1930s very little had been written about either Baum or Thompson.

Recently I was sent an academic dissertation. Certain aspects of Baum's *The Land of Oz* had reoccurred in a book of mine. Was this conscious or not? (It was not.) But I was intrigued. I reread *The Land of Oz*. Yes, I could see Baum's influence. I then reread *The Emerald City of Oz*. I have now reread all of L. Frank Baum's Oz books. I have also read a good deal of what has been written about him in recent years. Although Baum's books were dismissed as trash by at least two generations of librarians and literary historians, the land of Oz has managed to fascinate each new generation and, lately, Baum himself has become an OK subject, if not for the literary critic, for the social historian.

Even so, it is odd that Baum has received so little acknowledgment from those who owe him the most—writers. After all, those books (films, television, too, alas) first encountered in childhood do more to shape the imagination and its style than all the later calculated readings of acknowledged masters. Scientists are often more candid in their admiration (our attempts to find life elsewhere in the universe is known as Operation Ozma). Lack of proper acknowledgment perhaps explains the extent to which Baum has been ignored by literary historians, by English departments, by. . . . As I write these words, a sense of dread. Is is possible that Baum's survival is due to the fact that he is *not* taught? That he is not, officially, Literature? If so, one must be careful not to murder Oz with exegesis.

In search of L. Frank Baum and the genesis of Oz, I have read every sort of study of him from *To Please a Child* by his son Frank Joslyn Baum and Russell P. MacFall to the meticulous introductions of Martin Gardner for the Dover reproductions of the original Oz editions (as well as Gardner's book with R. B. Nye, *(The Wizard of Oz & Who He Was)* to issues of *The Baum Bugle* (a newsletter put out by Oz enthusiasts since 1957) to the recent and charming *The Oz Scrapbook* as well as to what looks to be a Ph.D. thesis got up as a book called *Wonderful Wizard, Marvelous Land* (1974) by Raylyn Moore.

The introduction to Moore's book is written by the admirable Ray Bradbury in an uncharacteristically overwrought style. Yet prose far to one side, Bradbury makes some good points: "Let us consider two authors" (the other is Edgar Rice Burroughs) "whose works were burned in our American society during the past seventy years. Librarians and teachers did the burning very subtly by not buying. And not buying is as good as burning. Yet, the authors survived."

The hostility of librarians to the Oz books is in itself something of a phenomenon. The books are always popular with children. But many librarians will not stock them. According to the chairman of the Miami Public Library, magic is out: "Kids don't like that fanciful stuff anymore. They want books about missiles and atomic submarines." Less militaristic librarians have made the practical point that if you buy one volume of a popular series you will have to get the whole lot and there are, after all, forty Oz books.

Bradbury seems to think that the Oz books are disdained because they are considered "mediocre" by literary snobs (the same people who do not take seriously Science Fiction?). But I think that he is wrong. After all, since most American English teachers, librarians, and literary historians are not intellectuals, how would any of them know whether or not a book was well or ill written? More to the point, not many would care. Essentially, our educators are Puritans who want to uphold the Puritan work ethic. This is done by bringing up American children in such a way that they will take their place in society as diligent workers and unprotesting consumers. Any sort of literature that encourages a child to contemplate alternative worlds might incite him, later in life, to make changes in the iron Puritan order that has brought us, along with missiles and atomic submarines, the assembly line at Detroit where workers are systematically dehumanized.

It is significant that one of the most brutal attacks on the Oz books was made in 1957 by the director of the Detroit Library System, a Mr. Ralph Ulveling, who found the Oz books to "have a cowardly approach to life." They are also guilty of "negativism." Worst of all, "there is nothing uplifting or elevating about the Baum series." For the Librarian of Detroit, courage and affirmation mean punching the clock and then doing the dull work of a machine while never questioning the system. Our governors not only know what is good for us, they never let up. From monitoring the books that are read in grade school to the brass handshake and the pension (whose fund is always in jeopardy) at the end, they are forever on the job. They have to be because they know that there is no greater danger to their order than a worker whose daydreams are not of television sets and sex but of differently ordered worlds. Fortunately, the system of government that controls the school system and makes possible the consumer society does not control all of publishing; otherwise, much imaginative writing might exist only in *samizdat.*

Ray Bradbury makes his case for America's two influential imaginative writers, Baum and Edgar Rice Burroughs, creator not only of Tarzan but of John Carter in the Mars series. "John Carter grew to maturity" (in pots?) "two generations of astronomers, geologists, biochemists, and astronauts who cut their teeth on his Barsoomian beasts and Martian fighting men and decided to grow up and grow out away from earth." A decision that would never have been acceptable to our rulers if the Russians had not put Sputnik into orbit, obliging an American president of the time to announce that, all in all, it was probably a good thing for our prestige to go to the moon.

Bradbury then turns to "L. Frank Baum, that faintly old-maidish man who grew boys" (in a greenhouse?) "inward to their most delightful interiors, kept them home, and romanced them with wonders between their ears." Through Bradbury's rich style, a point is emerging: inward to delightful selves. Kept them home. Romanced them. Wonders. Yes, all that is true. And hateful to professional molders of American youth. Boys should be out of the house, competing in games, building model airplanes, beating each other up so that one day they will be obedient soldiers in the endless battle for the free world. Show us a dreaming boy (or girl) at home with a book, and we will show you a potential troublemaker.

Bradbury compares Baum to Lewis Carroll. This is a mistake. Carroll belongs, in a complex way, not only to our language's high literature but to logic. It is simple-minded and mawkish to say that "Oz is muffins and honey, summer vacations, and all the easy green time in the world" while "Wonderland is cold gruel and arithmetic at six A.M., icy showers, long" (as opposed to short?) "schools." Because of this supposed polarity, Bradbury thinks "that Wonderland is the darling of the intellectuals." On the subject of Oz, he is at his best not in this preface but in a good short story called "The Exiles" (1950).

The text of Raylyn Moore is interesting. She has read what others have written about Baum. She is perhaps too impressed by the fact that the hippies (surely they no longer exist this side of the rainbow) took up Oz in a big way. She also keeps quoting the author of *The Greening of America* as if he were some sort of authority. Fortunately, she also quotes from those who have written interestingly about Baum: Edward Wagenknecht, James Thurber (in *The New Republic,* 1934), and Henry Littlefield, who demonstrates (in *American Quarterly,* 1964) that *The Wizard of Oz* is a parable on populism "in which the Tin Woodman is seen as the eastern industrialist worker (he is discovered by Dorothy in the eastern land of the Munchkins), the Scarecrow as the farmer, and the Lion as the politician (William Jennings Bryan), who as a group approach the Wizard (McKinley) to ask for relief from their sufferings. Dorothy's magical silver shoes (the proposed silver standard) traveling along the Yellow Brick Road (gold) are lost forever in the Deadly Desert when she returns to Kansas (when Bryan lost the election)." This is certainly elaborate.

Yet Baum in his work and life (as described by those who knew him) was apolitical. He is known to have marched in a torchlight parade for Bryan in 1896, the year of McKinley's victory. He also supported Bryan in 1900. But, politically, that was it. Only once in the fairy tales have I been able to find a direct political reference. In *The Sea Fairies* there is an octopus who is deeply offended when he learns that Standard Oil is called an "octopus": " 'Oh, what a disgrace! What a deep, dire, dreadful disgrace!' " But though Baum was not political in the usual sense, he had very definite ideas about the way the world should be. I shall come to that.

L. Frank Baum was born at Chittenango in upstate New York, the son of Benjamin W. Baum, who had become rich in the Pennsylvania oil fields. The Baums came from the Palatinate and Frank Baum's grandparents were German-speaking. Grandfather Baum was a Methodist lay preacher. Frank's mother was Scots-Irish. There were eight brothers and sisters. Four died early.

Apparently the Baums enjoyed their wealth. L. Frank Baum grew up on a large estate called Rose Lawn, near Syracuse. In *Dot and Tot of Merryland* (1901) Baum describes the house's "wings and gables and broad verandas," the lawns, flowers, "winding paths covered with white gravel, which led to all parts of the grounds, looking for all the world like a map." Maps of Oz were later to be important to Baum and to his readers. Oz was . . . no, *is* an oblong country divided into four equal sections whose boundaries converge at the Emerald City, the country's capital as well as geographical center. Each of the four minor countries is a different color: Everything in the north is purple; the south red; the east blue; the west yellow. The effect, exactly, of a certain kind of old-fashioned garden where flower beds are laid out symmetrically and separated from one another by "winding paths covered with white gravel."

At twelve Baum was sent to a military academy which he hated. He escaped by developing a bad heart. Back at Rose Lawn, Baum put out a newspaper on a printing press given him by his father. Later Baum became interested in chicken breeding and acting, two activities not often linked. Happily, the indulgent father could provide Baum not only with eggs but also with a theatrical career. Because Benjamin Baum owned a string of theatres, his son was able to join a touring company at nineteen. Three years later Baum was in New York, with a leading role in Bronson Howard's highly successful play *The Banker's Daughter* (1878). According to contemporary photographs Baum was a handsome young man with gray eyes, straight nose, dark brown hair, and a period mustache that looked to be glued on; he was six feet tall, left-handed; the voice was agreeable and in later years, on the lecture circuit, he was sometimes compared, favorably, to Mark Twain.

The pieces are now falling into place. Weak heart. Dreamy childhood. Gardens of Rose Lawn. Printing press and self-edited newspaper. Chicken breeding. Theatre. At that time the theatre was as close as anyone could come to creating magic. On the rickety stages of a thousand provincial theatre houses, alternative worlds blazed like magic by limelight. In 1882 Baum wrote and played and toured in a musical "comedy" called *The Maid of Arran,* a fair success. The same year he married Maud Gage. The marriage was a true success though she was a good deal tougher than he: she spanked the children, he consoled them. Maud's mother was an active suffragette and a friend of Susan B. Anthony. Although the high-minded Puritan Gages were most unlike the easy-going Germanic Baums, relations seem to have been good between Mrs. Gage and her son-in-law, who was pretty much of a failure for the next sixteen years. Baum's theatrical career ended, literally, in flames when the sets and costumes of *The Maid of Arran* were burned in a warehouse fire. Suddenly the whole family was downwardly mobile. At twenty-nine Baum went to work as a traveling salesman for a family firm that made axle grease. He also wrote his first book, *The Book of the Hamburgs,* all about chickens.

The lives of Baum and Burroughs are remarkably similar in kind if not in detail. Each knocked about a good deal. Each failed at a number of unsatisfying jobs. Each turned late to writing. Burroughs wrote his first book at thirty-seven; he was thirty-nine when *Tarzan of the Apes* was published. Except for the chicken manual, Baum did not publish until he was forty-one; then at forty-four came *The Wonderful Wizard of Oz.* Forty appears to be the shadow-line in American lives; it must be crossed in style, or else.

Failure has never been much fun in the United States. During the last two decades of the Gilded Age and the first decade of the American Empire, failure must have been uncommonly grim. On every side, enormous fortunes were conspicuously made and spent. To be poor was either a sign of bad character or of bad genes or both. Hard-hearted predestination was in the air. *The Origin of Species* had greatly influenced United Statespersons, and throughout Baum's lifetime Darwin was constantly misread and misquoted in order to support *laissez nous faire,* the Puritan work ethic, and, of course, slavery.

In their twenties and thirties Burroughs and Baum were Darwinian rejects. Burroughs was a railroad dick; Baum operated, first, a failing store in Dakota Territory; then a failing newspaper. During the bad years, Burroughs used to tell himself stories before going to sleep (on the job, too, one would guess). Night after night he would add new episodes to his various serials. Although there is no evidence that Baum indulged in this kind of daydreaming, the best part of his day was the children's bedtime when he would improvise magical stories for them.

Powerless to affect the gray flat everyday world, Burroughs and Baum each escaped into waking dreams. The dreams of Burroughs are those of a fourteen-year-old boy who would like to be physically powerful like Tarzan or magically endowed like John Carter, who was able to defenestrate himself at will from dull earth to thrilling (pre-NASA) Mars. Sex is a powerful drive in all of Burroughs's dreams, though demurely rendered when he wrote them down. The dreams of Baum are somewhat different. They are those of a prepubescent child who likes to be frightened (but not very much) and delighted with puns and jokes in a topsy-turvy magical world where his toys are not only as large as he but able to walk and talk and keep him company. There is no conscious sex in the world of the nine-year-old. Yet there is a concomitant will to power that does express itself, sometimes in unexpected ways.

Since the quotidian did not fulfill the dreams of either Baum or Burroughs, each constructed an alternative world. Most artists do. But it is odd that each should have continued well into middle life to tell himself the sort of stories that most people cease to tell themselves in childhood or early adolescence. It is not usual to be a compulsive storyteller for an audience of one. Yet neither seemed to have had any urgent need to share his private stories with others (I count Baum's children as extensions of himself; there is no record of his inventing stories for anyone else).

Although it is hard to think of Baum as writing political allegories in support of Free Silver, his inventions do reflect the world in which he grew up. When he was a year old, in 1857, the country was swept by a Christian revival whose like we were not to see again until the Carter White House and the better federal prisons started to fill up with evangelical Christians. During Baum's prepubescence the Civil War took place. In his twelfth year Susan B. Anthony started the suffragette movement; and San Francisco fell flat on its hills. In fact, all during the last days of the century, nature was on a rampage and the weather was more than usually abnormal, as the old joke goes.

In 1893, a cyclone destroyed two Kansas towns, killing thirty-one people. I take this disaster to be the one that Baum was to describe seven years later in *The Wizard of Oz.* He himself was marginally associated with one national disaster. On December 6, 1890, Baum wrote a rather edgy "funny" column for his newspaper in Aberdeen, Dakota Territory. He turns inside out the official American line that the Sioux Indians were getting ready to massacre all the whites. Baum pretends to interview an Indian chief who tells him that the Indians are terrified of being massacred by the whites. Two weeks after this story was published, the U.S. Seventh Cavalry slaughtered three hundred Indian men, women, and children at nearby Wounded Knee. Soon afterward, Baum and his family moved to Chicago.

Since no one ever thought to investigate in any detail the sort of books Baum liked to read, we can only guess at influences. He himself mentioned Charles Reade's *The Cloister and the Hearth,* as well as Dickens and Thackeray. When Baum was still a schoolboy, American educators began to emphasize the sciences (the assembly line was on its way) and the traditional humanities gave ground to the inhumanities. Certainly Baum's lifelong interest in science and gadgetry was typical of his time and place.

The overwhelming presence in the Oz books of kings and queens, princes and princesses derives from a line of popular writing that began in 1894 with *The Prisoner of Zenda* and reached a most gorgeous peak with the publication of *Graustark* in 1901. Although Baum was plainly influenced by these books, I suspect that his love of resplendent titles and miniature countries had something to do with his own ancestry. Before Bismarck's invention of the German Empire in 1871, that particular geographical area was decorated—no, gilded—with four kingdoms (one of them, Bavaria, contained the home of Baum's ancestors), six grand-duchies, five duchies, seven principalities, and three freetowns. The adjoining Austro-Hungarian Empire was a dual monarchy containing numerous kingdoms, duchies, principalities, not to mention a constant shifting of borders that my own family (perhaps like Baum's) never satisfactorily explained to me.

According to F. J. Baum and MacFall, sixty Utopian novels were published in the United States between 1888 and 1901. The best known was Bellamy's *Looking Backward,* which Baum mildly sent up in the Aberdeen *Saturday Pioneer.* The fact that so many writers were inclined to posit an alternative society to the Gilded Age shows a certain dissatisfaction with the great republic.

Baum is sometimes regarded as a Utopian writer. But I don't think that this is accurate. Utopian writers have political ideas, and Baum seems to have had none at all. Except for a mild parody of the suffragettes, there is little to link political America with magical Oz, whose minuscule countries are governed by hereditary lords. On the other hand, Baum was a social moralist who is said to have been influenced by William Morris's *News from Nowhere,* published in 1891 (not 1892 as R. Moore states). In *The Emerald City,* nearly two decades after the publication of Morris's vision of the good society, Baum writes of Oz in somewhat similar terms: "there were no poor people . . . because there was no such thing as money, and all property of every sort belonged to the Ruler. The people were her children, and she cared for them. Each person was given freely by his neighbors whatever he required for his use, which is as much as anyone may reasonably desire." This is not the sort of society most calculated to appeal to the Librarian of Detroit.

Interestingly enough, there is no reference in the Oz books to a republic of any kind. There are no parliaments or congresses. There are no elections—a most peculiar thing for an American writer to leave out. The various rulers are all feudal except in his last book of the series *(Glinda of Oz)* where Baum introduces us, surprisingly, to a Supreme Dictator. Baum was still at work on the book in March 1919 when Mussolini founded the Fascist Party. Was he, in some way, prescient? Whether or not Baum was predicting fascism, it is significant that he associates the idea of dictatorship with democracy: " 'I'm the Supreme Dictator of all, and I'm elected once a year. This is a democracy, you know, where the people are allowed to vote for their rulers. A good many others would like to be Supreme Dictator, but as I made a law that I am always to count the votes myself, I am always elected.' " If nothing else, the years that Baum lived in Chicago had left their mark on his political thinking. Earlier in the series *(The Emerald City),* there is another elected monarch, the unhappy rabbit King of Bunnyberry. But this election was reminiscent not of Chicago but of the feudal

arrangements of the ancient Teutonic kings and their descendants, the
Holy Roman emperors.

The authors of *To Please a Child* tell us the genesis of the name Oz.
"One evening while the thunder of Admiral George Dewey's guns was
still echoing in Manila Bay, Baum was sitting in his Chicago home
telling stories to youngsters. The two events brushed each other briefly
in the course of manifest destiny and children's literature." I cannot tell
if "manifest destiny" is meant ironically. In any case, Baum says that
he was telling a story pretty much like *The Wizard of Oz* when one of
the children wanted to know where all these adventures took place.
Looking about for inspiration, Baum glanced at a copy of the *Chicago
Tribune* (dated May 7, 1898) and saw the headlines proclaiming Dewey's
victory. Then he noticed a filing cabinet with two drawers: A-N and
O-Z. The second label gave its name to Oz. True or not, there is a certain
niceness in the way that the militant phase of the American empire was
to coincide with Baum's parallel and better world.

Baum had begun to prosper in Chicago. At Mrs. Gage's insistence,
he wrote down some of the stories that he had made up for his children.
They were published as *Mother Goose in Prose* in 1897; that same year
he started a magazine called *The Show Window,* for window-dressers.
The magazine was an unlikely success. Then Baum published *Father
Goose, His Book* (1899); he was now established as a popular children's
writer. Devoting himself full-time to writing, he produced a half-dozen
books in 1899, among them *The Wizard of Oz.*

During the next nineteen years Baum wrote sixty-two books. Most of
them were for children and most of them had girl-protagonists. There
are many theories why Baum preferred girls to boys as central characters. The simplest is that he had four sons and would have liked a
daughter. The most practical is that popular American writing of that
day tended to be feminized because women bought the books. The most
predictable is the vulgar Freudian line that either Baum secretly wanted
to be a girl or, worse, that he suffered from a Dodsonian (even Humber-
tian) lust for small girls. I suspect that Baum wrote about girls not only
because he liked them but because his sort of imagination was not geared
to those things that are supposed to divert real boys (competitive games,
cowboys and Indians, cops and robbers, murder).

In the preface to *The Wizard of Oz,* L. Frank Baum says that he would
like to create *modern* fairy tales by departing from Grimm and Andersen and "all the horrible and blood-curdling incident devised" by

such authors "to point a fearsome moral." Baum then makes the disingenuous point that "Modern education includes morality; therefore the
modern child seeks only entertainment in its wondertales and gladly
dispenses with all disagreeable incident." Yet there is a certain amount
of explicit as well as implicit moralizing in the Oz books; there are also
"disagreeable incidents," and people do, somehow, die, even though
death and illness are not supposed to exist in Oz.

I have reread the Oz books in the order in which they were written.
Some things are as I remember. Others strike me as being entirely new.
I was struck by the unevenness of style not only from book to book but,
sometimes from page to page. The jaggedness can be explained by the
fact that the man who was writing fourteen Oz books was writing
forty-eight other books at the same time. Arguably, *The Wizard of Oz*
is the best of the lot. After all, the first book is the one in which Oz was
invented. Yet, as a child, I preferred *The Emerald City, Rinkitink,* and
*The Lost Princess* to *The Wizard.* Now I find that all of the books tend
to flow together in a single narrative, with occasional bad patches.

In *The Wizard of Oz* Dorothy is about six years old. In the later books
she seems to be ten or eleven. Baum locates her swiftly and efficiently
in the first sentence of the series. "Dorothy lived in the midst of the great
Kansas prairies, with Uncle Henry, who was a farmer, and Aunt Em,
who was the farmer's wife." The landscape would have confirmed John
Ruskin's dark view of American scenery (he died the year that *The
Wizard of Oz* was published).

When Dorothy stood in the doorway and looked around, she could see
nothing but the great gray prairie on every side. Not a tree nor a house broke
the broad sweep of flat country that reached the edge of the sky in all
directions.

This is the plain American style at its best. Like most of Baum's central
characters, Dorothy lacks the regulation father and mother. Some commentators have made, I think, too much of Baum's parentless children.
The author's motive seems to me to be not only obvious but sensible.
A child separated from loving parents for any length of time is going
to be distressed, even in a magic story. But aunts and uncles need not
be taken too seriously.

In the first four pages Baum demonstrates the drabness of Dorothy's
life; the next two pages are devoted to the cyclone that lifts the house
into the air and hurls it to Oz. Newspaper accounts of recent cyclones

had obviously impressed Baum. Alone in the house (except for Toto, a Cairn terrier), Dorothy is established as a sensible girl who is not going to worry unduly about events that she cannot control. The house crosses the Deadly Desert and lands on top of the Wicked Witch of the East, who promptly dries up and dies. Right off, Baum breaks his own rule that no one ever dies in Oz. I used to spend a good deal of time worrying about the numerous inconsistencies in the sacred texts. From time to time, Baum himself would try to rationalize errors, but he was far too quick and careless a writer ever to create the absolutely logical mad worlds that Lewis Carroll or E. Nesbit did.

Dorothy is acclaimed by the Munchkins as a good witch who has managed to free them from the Wicked Witch. They advise her to go to the Emerald City and try to see the famous Wizard; he alone would have the power to grant her dearest wish, which is to go home to Kansas. Why she wanted to go back was never clear to me. Or, finally, to Baum: eventually, he moves Dorothy (with aunt and uncle) to Oz.

Along the way to the Emerald City, Dorothy meets a live Scarecrow in search of brains, a Tin Woodman in search of a heart, a Cowardly Lion in search of courage. Each new character furthers the plot. Each is essentially a humor. Each, when he speaks, strikes the same simple, satisfying note.

Together they undergo adventures. In sharp contrast to gray flat Kansas, Oz seems to blaze with color. Yet the Emerald City is a bit of a fraud. Everyone is obliged to wear green glasses in order to make the city appear emerald-green.

The Wizard says that he will help them if they destroy yet another wicked witch. They do. Only to find out that the Wizard is a fake who arrived by balloon from the States, where he had been a magician in a circus. Although a fraud, the Wizard is a good psychologist. He gives the Scarecrow bran for brains, the Tin Woodman a red velvet heart, the Cowardly Lion a special courage syrup. Each has now become what he wanted to be (and was all along). The Wizard's response to their delight is glum: " 'How can I help being a humbug,' he said, 'when all these people make me do things that everybody knows can't be done? It was easy to make the Scarecrow and the Lion and the Woodman happy, because they imagined I could do anything. But it will take more than imagination to carry Dorothy back to Kansas, and I'm sure I don't know how it can be done.' " When the Wizard arranges a balloon to take Dorothy and himself back home, the balloon takes off without Dorothy. Finally, she is sent home through the intervention of magic, and the good witch Glinda.

The style of the first book is straightforward, even formal. There are almost no contractions. Dorothy speaks not at all the way a grown-up might think a child should speak but like a sensible somewhat literal person. There are occasional Germanisms (did Baum's father speak German?): " 'What is that little animal you are so tender of?' " Throughout all the books there is a fascination with jewelry and elaborate costumes. Baum never got over his love of theatre. In this he resembled his favorite author, Charles Reade, of whom *The Dictionary of National Biography* tells us: "At his best Reade was an admirable storyteller, full of resource and capacity to excite terror and pity; but his ambition to excel as a dramatist militated against his success as a novelist, and nearly all his work is disfigured by a striving after theatrical effect."

Baum's passion for the theatre and, later, the movies not only wasted his time but, worse, it had a noticeably bad effect on his prose style. Because *The Wizard of Oz* was the most successful children's book of the 1900 Christmas season (in its first two years of publication, the book sold ninety thousand copies), Baum was immediately inspired to dramatize the story. Much "improved" by other hands, the musical comedy opened in Chicago (June 16, 1902) and was a success. After a year and a half on Broadway, the show toured off and on until 1911. Over the years Baum was to spend a good deal of time trying to make plays and films based on the Oz characters. Except for the first, none was a success.

Since two popular vaudevillians had made quite a splash as the Tin Woodman and the Scarecrow in the musical version of *The Wizard,* Baum decided that a sequel was in order . . . for the stage. But rather than write directly for the theatre, he chose to write a second Oz book, without Dorothy or the Wizard. In an Author's Note to *The Marvelous Land of Oz,* Baum somewhat craftily says that he has been getting all sorts of letters from children asking him "to 'write something more' about the Scarecrow and the Tin Woodman." In 1904 the sequel was published, with a dedication to the two vaudevillians. A subsequent musical comedy called *The Woggle-Bug* was then produced; and failed. That, for the time being, was that. But the idiocies of popular theatre had begun to infect Baum's prose. *The Wizard of Oz* is chastely written. *The Land of Oz* is not. Baum riots in dull wordplay. There are endless bad puns, of the sort favored by popular comedians. There is also that true period horror: the baby-talking ingenue, a character who lasted well into our day in the menacing shapes of Fanny (Baby Snooks) Brice and the early Ginger Rogers. Dorothy, who talked plainly and to the point in *The Wizard,* talks (when she reappears in the third book) with a cuteness hard to bear. Fortunately, Baum's show-biz phase wore off and in later volumes Dorothy's speech improves.

Despite stylistic lapses, *The Land of Oz* is one of the most unusual and interesting books of the series. In fact, it is so unusual that after the Shirley Temple television adaptation of the book in 1960,* PTA circles were in a state of crisis. The problem that knitted then and, I am told, knits even today many a maternal brow is Sexual Role. Sexual Role makes the world go round. It is what makes the man go to the office or to the factory where he works hard while the wife fulfills *her* Sexual Role by homemaking and consuming and bringing up boys to be real boys and girls to be real girls, a cycle that must continue unchanged and unquestioned until the last car comes off Detroit's last assembly line and the last all-American sun vanishes behind a terminal dioxin haze.

Certainly the denouement of *The Land of Oz* is troubling for those who have heard of Freud. A boy, Tip, is held in thrall by a wicked witch named Mombi. One day she gets hold of an elixir that makes the inanimate live. Tip uses this magical powder to bring to life a homemade figure with a jack-o'-lantern head: Jack Pumpkinhead, who turns out to be a comic of the Ed Wynn–Simple Simon school. " 'Now that is a very interesting history,' said Jack, well pleased; 'and I understand it perfectly—all but the explanation.' "

Tip and Jack Pumpkinhead escape from Mombi, aboard a brought-to-life sawhorse. They then meet the stars of the show (and a show it is), the Scarecrow and the Tin Woodman. As a central character neither is very effective. In fact, each has a tendency to sententiousness; and there are nowhere near enough jokes. The Scarecrow goes on about his brains; the Tin Woodman about his heart. But then it is the limitation as well as the charm of made-up fairy-tale creatures to embody to the point of absurdity a single quality or humor.

There is one genuinely funny sketch. When the Scarecrow and Jack Pumpkinhead meet, they decide that since each comes from a different country, " 'We must,' " says the Scarecrow, " 'have an interpreter.' "

" 'What is an interpreter?' asked Jack.

" 'A person who understands both my language and your own. . . .' " And so on. Well, maybe this is *not* so funny.

The Scarecrow (who had taken the vanished Wizard's place as ruler

---

*In 1939, MGM made a film called *The Wizard of Oz* with Judy Garland. A new book, *The Making of "The Wizard of Oz"* by Aljean Harmetz, describes in altogether too great but fascinating detail the assembling of the movie, which had one and a half producers, ten writers, and four directors. Who then was the "auteur"?

of Oz) is overthrown by a "revolting" army of girls (great excuse for a leggy chorus). This long and rather heavy satire on the suffragettes was plainly more suitable for a Broadway show than for a children's story. The girl leader, Jinjur, is an unexpectedly engaging character. She belongs to the Bismarckian *Realpolitik* school. She is accused of treason for having usurped the Scarecrow's throne. " 'The throne belongs to whoever is able to take it,' answered Jinjur as she slowly ate another caramel. 'I have taken it, as you see; so just now I am the Queen, and all who oppose me are guilty of treason. . . .' " This is the old children's game I-am-the-King-of-the-castle, a.k.a. human history.

Among the new characters met in this story are the Woggle-Bug, a highly magnified insect who has escaped from a classroom exhibition and (still magnified) ranges about the countryside. A parody of an American academic, he is addicted to horrendous puns on the grounds that " 'a joke derived from a play upon words is considered among educated people to be eminently proper.' " Anna livia plurabelle.

There is a struggle between Jinjur and the legitimate forces of the Scarecrow. The Scarecrow's faction wins and the girls are sent away to be homemakers and consumers. In passing, the Scarecrow observes, " 'I am convinced that the only people worthy of consideration in this world are the unusual ones. For the common folks are like the leaves of a tree, and live and die unnoticed.' " To which the Tin Woodman replies, " 'Spoken like a philosopher!' " To which the current editor Martin Gardner responds, with true democratic wrath, "This despicable view, indeed defended by many philosophers, had earlier been countered by the Tin Woodman," etc. But the view is not at all despicable. For one thing, it would be the normal view of an odd magical creature who cannot die. For another, Baum was simply echoing those neo-Darwinians who dominated most American thinking for at least a century. It testifies to Baum's sweetness of character that unlike most writers of his day he seldom makes fun of the poor or weak or unfortunate. Also, the Scarecrow's "despicable" remarks can be interpreted as meaning that although unorthodox dreamers are despised by the ordinary, their dreams are apt to prevail in the end and become reality.

Glinda the Good Sorceress is a kindly mother figure to the various children who visit or live in Oz, and it is she who often ties up the loose ends when the story bogs down. In *The Land of Oz* Glinda has not a loose end but something on the order of a hangman's rope to knot. Apparently the rightful ruler of Oz is Princess Ozma. As a baby, Ozma was changed by Mombi into the boy Tip. Now Tip must be restored to his true identity. The PTA went, as it were, into plenary session. What effect would a book like this have on a boy's sense of himself as a future man, breadwinner and father to more of same? Would he want, awful thought, to be a Girl? Even Baum's Tip is alarmed when told who he is. " 'I!' cried Tip, in amazement. 'Why I'm no Princess Ozma—I'm not a girl!' " Glinda tells him that indeed he was—and really is. Tip is understandably grumpy. Finally, he says to Glinda, " 'I might try it for awhile,—just to see how it seems, you know. But if I don't like being a girl you must promise to change me into a boy again.' " Glinda says that this is not in the cards. Glumly, Tip agrees to the restoration. Tip becomes the beautiful Ozma, who hopes that " 'none of you will care less for me than you did before. I'm just the same Tip, you know; only—only—' "

"Only you're different!" said the Pumpkinhead; and everyone thought it was the wisest speech he had ever made.

Essentially, Baum's human protagonists are neither male nor female but children, a separate category in his view if not in that of our latter-day sexists. Baum's use of sex changes was common to the popular theatre of his day, which, in turn, derived from the Elizabethan era when boys played girls whom the plot often required to pretend to be boys. In Baum's *The Enchanted Island of Yew* a fairy (female) becomes a knight (male) in order to have adventures. In *The Emerald City* the hideous Phanfasm leader turns himself into a beautiful woman. When *John Dough and the Cherub* (1906) was published, the sex of the five-year-old cherub was never mentioned in the text; the publishers then launched a national ad campaign: "Is the cherub boy or girl? $500 for the best answers." In those innocent times Tip's metamorphosis as Ozma was nothing more than a classic *coup de théâtre* of the sort that even now requires the boy Peter Pan to be played on stage by a mature woman.

Today of course any sort of sexual metamorphosis causes distress. Although Raylyn Moore in her plot *précis* of *The Enchanted Island of Yew* (in her book *Wonderful Wizard, Marvelous Land*) does make one confusing reference to the protagonist as "he (she)," she omits entirely the Tip/Ozma transformation, which is the whole point to *The Land of Oz,* while the plot as given by the publisher Reilly & Lee says only that "the book ends with an amazing surprise, and from that moment on Ozma is princess of all Oz." But, surely, for a pre-pube there is not much difference between a boy and a girl protagonist. After all, the central fact of the pre-pube's existence is not being male or female but being a child, much the hardest of all roles to play. During and after puberty, there is a tendency to want a central character like oneself (my favorite Oz book was R. P. Thompson's *Speedy in Oz,* whose eleven- or twelve-year-old hero could have been, I thought, me). Nevertheless, what matters most even to an adolescent is not the gender of the main character who experiences adventures but the adventures themselves, and the magic, and the jokes, and the pictures.

Dorothy is a perfectly acceptable central character for a boy to read about. She asks the right questions. She is not sappy (as Ozma can sometimes be). She is straight to the point and a bit aggressive. Yet the Dorothy who returns to the series in the third book, *Ozma of Oz* (1907), is somewhat different from the original Dorothy. She is older and her conversation is full of cute contractions that must have doubled up audiences in Sioux City but were pretty hard going for at least one child forty years ago.

To get Dorothy back to Oz there is the by now obligatory natural disaster. The book opens with Dorothy and her uncle on board a ship to Australia. During a storm she is swept overboard. Marius Bewley has noted that this opening chapter "is so close to Crane's ('The Open Boat') in theme, imagery and technique that it is difficult to imagine, on comparing the two in detail, that the similarity is wholly, or even largely accidental."

Dorothy is accompanied by a yellow chicken named Bill. As they are now in magic country, the chicken talks. Since the chicken is a hen, Dorothy renames her Billina. The chicken is fussy and self-absorbed; she is also something of an overachiever: " 'How is my grammar?' asked the yellow hen anxiously." Rather better than Dorothy's, whose dialogue is marred by such Baby Snooksisms as " 'zactly," "auto'biles," " 'lieve," " 'splain."

Dorothy and Billina come ashore in Ev, a magic country on the other side of the Deadly Desert that separates Oz from the real world (what separates such magical kingdoms as Ix and Ev from our realer world is never made plain). In any case, the formula has now been established. Cyclone or storm at sea or earthquake ends not in death for child and animal companion but translation to a magic land. Then, one by one, strange new characters join the travelers. In this story the first addition is Tik-Tok, a clockwork robot (sixteen years later the word "robot" was coined). He has run down. They wind him up. Next they meet Princess Languidere. She is deeply narcissistic, a trait not much admired by

Baum (had he been traumatized by all those actresses and actors he had known on tour?). Instead of changing clothes, hair, makeup, the Princess changes heads from her collection. I found the changing of heads fascinating. And puzzling: since the brains in each head varied, would Languidere still be herself when she put on a new head or would she become someone else? Thus Baum made logicians of his readers.

The Princess is about to add Dorothy's head to her collection when the marines arrive in the form of Ozma and retinue, who have crossed the Deadly Desert on a magic carpet (cheating, I thought at the time; either a desert is impassable or it is not). Dorothy and Ozma meet, and Dorothy, "as soon as she heard the sweet voice of the girlish ruler of Oz knew that she would learn to love her dearly." That sort of thing I tended to skip.

The principal villain of the Oz canon is now encountered: the Nome King (Baum thought the "g" in front of "nome" too difficult for children . . . how did he think they spelled and pronounced "gnaw"?). Roquat of the Rock lived deep beneath the earth, presiding over his legions of hard-working nomes (first cousins to George Macdonald's goblins). I was always happy when Baum took us below ground, and showed us fantastic caverns strewn with precious stones where scurrying nomes did their best to please the bad-tempered Roquat, whose " 'laugh,' " one admirer points out, " 'is worse than another man's frown.' " Ozma and company are transformed into bric-a-brac by Roquat's magic. But Dorothy and Billina outwit Roquat (nomes fear fresh eggs). Ozma and all the other victims of the Nome King are restored to their former selves, and Dorothy is given an opportunity to ham it up:

"Royal Ozma, and you, Queen of Ev, I welcome you and your people back to the land of the living. Billina has saved you from your troubles, and now we will leave this drea'ful place, and return to Ev as soon as poss'ble."

While the child spoke they could all see that she wore the magic belt, and a great cheer went up from all her friends. . . .

Baum knew that nothing so pleases a child as a situation where, for once, the child is in the driver's seat and able to dominate adults. Dorothy's will to power is a continuing force in the series and as a type she is still with us in such popular works as *Peanuts,* where she continues her steely progress toward total dominion in the guise of the relentless Lucy.

Back in the Emerald City, Ozma shows Dorothy her magic picture in which she can see what is happening anywhere in the world. If Dorothy ever wants to visit Oz, all she has to do is make a certain signal and Ozma will transport her from Kansas to Oz. Although this simplified transportation considerably, Baum must have known even then that half the charm of the Oz stories was the scary trip of an ordinary American child from U.S.A. to Oz. As a result, in *Dorothy and the Wizard in Oz* (1908), another natural catastrophe is used to bring Dorothy back to Oz; the long missing Wizard, too. Something like the San Francisco earthquake happens. Accompanied by a dim boy called Zeb and a dull horse called Jim, Dorothy falls deep into the earth. This catastrophe really got to Dorothy and "for a few moments the little girl lost consciousness. Zeb, being a boy, did not faint, but he was badly frightened. . . ." That is Baum's one effort to give some sort of points to a boy. He promptly forgets about Zeb, and Dorothy is back in the saddle, running things. She is aided by the Wizard, who joins them in his balloon.

Deep beneath the earth are magical countries (inspired by Verne's *Journey to the Center of the Earth,* 1864? Did Verne or Baum inspire Burroughs's *Pellucidar,* 1923?). In a country that contains vegetable people, a positively Golden Bough note is sounded by the ruling Prince: " 'One of the most unpleasant things about our vegetable lives [is] that while we are in our full prime we must give way to another, and be covered up in the ground to sprout and grow and give birth to other people.' " But then according to the various biographies, Baum was interested in Hinduism, and the notion of karma.

After a number of adventures Dorothy gestures to Ozma (she certainly took her time about it, I thought) and they are all transported to the Emerald City where the usual party is given for them, carefully described in a small-town newspaper style of the Social-Notes-from-all-over variety. *The Road to Oz* (1909) is the mixture as before. In Kansas, Dorothy meets the Shaggy Man; he is a tramp of the sort that haunted the American countryside after the Civil War when unemployed veterans and men ruined by the depressions of the 1870s took to the road, where they lived and died, no doubt, brutishly. The Shaggy Man asks her for directions. Exasperated by the tramp's slowness to figure out her instructions, she says: " 'You're so stupid. Wait a minute till I run in the house and get my sunbonnet.' " Dorothy is easily "provoked." " 'My, but you're clumsy!' said the little girl." She gives him a "severe look." Then " 'Come on,' she commanded." She then leads him to the wrong, i.e., the magical, road to Oz.

With *The Emerald City of Oz* (1910) Baum is back in form. He has had to face up to the fact that Dorothy's trips from the U.S.A. to Oz are getting not only contrived, but pointless. If she likes Oz so much, why doesn't she settle there? But if she does, what will happen to her uncle and aunt? Fortunately, a banker is about to foreclose the mortgage on Uncle Henry's farm. Dorothy will have to go to work, says Aunt Em, stricken. " 'You might do housework for someone, dear, you are so handy; or perhaps you could be a nursemaid to little children.' " Dorothy is having none of this. "Dorothy smiled. 'Wouldn't it be funny,' she said, 'for me to do housework in Kansas, when I'm a Princess in the Land of Oz?' " The old people buy this one with surprisingly little fuss. It is decided that Dorothy will signal Ozma, and depart for the Emerald City.

Although Baum's powers of invention seldom flagged, he had no great skill at plot-making. Solutions to problems are arrived at either through improbable coincidence or by bringing in, literally, some god (usually Glinda) from the machine to set things right. Since the narratives are swift and the conversations sprightly and the invented characters are both homely and amusing (animated paper dolls, jigsaw puzzles, pastry, cutlery, china, etc.), the stories never lack momentum. Yet there was always a certain danger that the narrative would flatten out into a series of predictable turns.

In *The Emerald City,* Baum sets in motion two simultaneous plots. The Nome King Roquat decides to conquer Oz. Counterpoint to his shenanigans are Dorothy's travels through Oz with her uncle and aunt (Ozma has given them asylum). Once again, the child's situation *vis-à-vis* the adult is reversed.

"Don't be afraid," she said to them. "You are now in the Land of Oz, where you are to live always, and be comfer'ble an' happy. You'll never have to worry over anything again, 'cause there won't be anything to worry about. And you owe it all to the kindness of my friend Princess Ozma."

And never forget it, one hears her mutter to herself.

But while the innocents are abroad in Oz, dark clouds are gathering. Roquat is on the march. I must say that the Nome King has never been more (to me) attractive as a character than in this book. For one thing, the bad temper is almost permanently out of control. It is even beginning to worry the king himself: " 'To be angry once in a while is really good fun, because it makes others so miserable. But to be angry morning, noon and night, as I am, grows monotonous and prevents my gaining any other pleasure in life.' " Rejecting the offer of the usual anodyne, a "glass of melted silver," Roquat decides to put together an alliance of all the wicked magic figures in order to conquer Oz. He looks among his nomes for an ideal general. He finds him: " 'I hate good people. . . . That is why I am so fond of your Majesty.' " Later the General enlists new allies with the straightforward pitch: " 'Permit me to call your attention to the exquisite joy of making the happy unhappy,' said he at last. 'Consider the pleasure of destroying innocent and harmless people.' " This argument proves irresistible.

The nomes and their allies make a tunnel beneath the Deadly Desert (but surely its Deadliness must go deeper than they could burrow?). Ozma watches all of them on her magic picture. She is moderately alarmed. " 'But I do not wish to fight,' declared Ozma, firmly." She takes an extremely high and moral American line; one that Woodrow Wilson echoed a few years later when he declared that the United States "is too proud to fight" powerful Germany (as opposed to weak Mexico where Wilson had swallowed his pride just long enough for us to launch an invasion). " 'Because the Nome King intends to do evil is no excuse for my doing the same.' " Ozma has deep thoughts on the nature of evil: " 'I must not blame King Roquat too severely, for he is a Nome and his nature is not so gentle as my own.' " Luckily, Ozite cunning carries the day.

Baum's nicest conceit in *The Emerald City* is Rigamarole Town. Or, as a local boy puts it,

"if you have traveled very much you will have noticed that every town differs from every other town in one way or another and so by observing the methods of the people and the way they live as well as the style of their dwelling places,"

etc. Dorothy and her party are duly impressed by the boy's endless commentary. He is matched almost immediately by a woman who tells them, apropos nothing:

"It is the easiest thing in the world for a person to say 'yes' or 'no' when a question that is asked for the purpose of gaining information or satisfying the curiosity of the one who has given expression to the inquiry has attracted the attention of an individual who may be competent either from personal experience or the experience of others," etc. A member of Dorothy's party remarks that if those people wrote books " 'it would take a whole library to say the cow jumped over the moon.' " So it would. And so it does. The Shaggy Man decides that there is a lot to be said for the way that the people of Oz encourage these people to live together in one town "while Uncle Sam lets [them] roam around wild and free, to torture innocent people.' "

Many enthusiasts of the Oz books (among them Ray Bradbury and Russell B. Nye) point with democratic pride to the fact that there is a total absence, according to Mr. Nye, of any "whisper of class consciousness in Oz (as there is in Alice's Wonderland)." Yet Martin Gardner has already noted one example of Baum's "despicable" elitism. Later *(Emerald City),* Baum appears to back away from the view that some people are better or more special than others. "It seems unfortunate that strong people are usually so disagreeable and overbearing that no one cares for them. In fact, to be different from your fellow creatures is always a misfortune." But I don't think that Baum believed a word of this. If he did, he would have been not L. Frank Baum, creator of the special and magical world of Oz, but Horatio Alger, celebrator of pluck and luck, thrift and drift, money. The dreamy boy with the bad heart at a hated military school was as conscious as any Hermann Hesse youth that he was splendidly different from others, and in *The Lost Princess of Oz* Baum reasserts the Scarecrow's position: " 'To be individual, my friends' " (the Cowardly Lion is holding forth), " 'to be different from others, is the only way to become distinguished from the common herd.' "

Inevitably, Baum moved from Chicago to California. Inevitably, he settled in the village of Hollywood in 1909. Inevitably, he made silent films, based on the Oz books. Not so inevitably, he failed for a number of reasons that he could not have foretold. Nevertheless, he put together a half-dozen films that (as far as special effects went) were said to be ahead of their time. By 1913 he had returned, somewhat grimly, to writing Oz books, putting Dorothy firmly on ice until the last book of the series.

The final Oz books are among the most interesting. After a gall bladder operation, Baum took to his bed where the last work was done. Yet Baum's imagination seems to have been more than usually inspired despite physical pain, and the darkness at hand. *The Lost Princess of Oz* (1917) is one of the best of the series. The beginning is splendidly straightforward. "There could be no doubt of the fact: Princess Ozma, the lovely girl ruler of the Fairyland of Oz, was lost. She had completely disappeared." Glinda's magical paraphernalia had also vanished. The search for Ozma involves most of the Oz principals, including Dorothy. The villain Ugu (who had kidnapped and transformed Ozma) is a most satisfactory character. "A curious thing about Ugu the Shoemaker was that he didn't suspect, in the least, that he was wicked. He wanted to be powerful and great and he hoped to make himself master of all the Land of Oz, that he might compel everyone in that fairy country to obey him. His ambition blinded him to the rights of others and he imagined anyone else would act just as he did if anyone else happened to be as clever as himself." That just about says it all.

In *The Tin Woodman of Oz* (1918) a boy named Woot is curious to know what happened to the girl that the Tin Woodman had intended to marry when he was flesh and blood. (Enchanted by a witch, he kept hacking off his own limbs; replacements in tin were provided by a magical smith. Eventually, he was all tin, and so no longer a suitable husband for a flesh-and-blood girl; he moved away.) Woot, the Tin Woodman, and the Scarecrow (the last two are rather like an old married couple, chatting in a desultory way about the past) set out to find the girl. To their astonishment, they meet another tin man. He, too, had courted the girl. He, too, had been enchanted by the witch; had chopped himself to bits; had been reconstituted by the same magical smith. The two tin men wonder what has happened to the girl. They also wonder what happened to their original imperishable pieces.

In due course, the Tin Woodman is confronted by his original head. I have never forgotten how amazed I was not only by Baum's startling invention but by the drawing of the Tin Woodman staring into the cupboard where sits his old head. The Tin Woodman is amazed, too. But the original head is simply bored, and snippy. When asked " 'What relation *are* we?' " the head replies, " 'Don't ask me. . . . For my part, I'm not anxious to claim relationship with any common, manufactured article, like you. You may be all right in your class, but your class isn't my class.' " When the Tin Woodman asks the head what it thinks about inside the cupboard, he is told,

"Nothing. . . . A little reflection will convince you that I have had nothing to think about, except the boards on the inside of the cupboard door, and it didn't take me long to think everything about those boards that could be thought of. Then, of course, I quit thinking."

"And are you happy?"

"Happy? What's that?"

There is a further surprise when the Tin Woodman discovers that his old girlfriend has married a creature made up of various human parts assembled from him and from the other man of tin. The result is a most divided and unsatisfactory man, and for the child reader a fascinating problem in the nature of identity.

In Baum's last Oz book, *Glinda of Oz* (posthumously published in 1920), magic is pretty much replaced by complex machinery. There is a domed island that can sink beneath the waters of a lake at the mention of a secret word, but though the word is magic, the details of how the island rises and sinks are straight out of *Popular Mechanics.*

Ozma and Dorothy are trapped beneath the water of the lake by yet another narcissistic princess, Coo-eeh-oh. By the time Glinda comes to the rescue, Coo-eeh-oh has been turned into a proud and vapid swan. This book is very much a last roundup (Baum may not have written all of it). Certainly there are some uncharacteristic sermons in favor of the Protestant work ethic: "Dorothy wished in her kindly, innocent heart, that all men and women could be fairies with silver wands, and satisfy all their needs without so much work and worry. . . ." Ozma fields that one as briskly as the Librarian of Detroit could want:

"No, no, Dorothy, that wouldn't do at all. Instead of happiness your plan would bring weariness. . . . There would be no eager striving to obtain the difficult. . . . There would be nothing to do, you see, and no interest in life and in our fellow creatures."

But Dorothy is not so easily convinced. She notes that Ozma is a magical creature, and *she* is happy. But only, says Ozma, with grinding sweetness, " 'because I can use my fairy powers to make others happy.' " Then Ozma makes the sensible point that although she has magical powers, others like Glinda have even greater powers than she and so " 'there still are things in both nature and in wit for me to marvel at.' "

In Dorothy's last appearance as heroine, she saves the day. She guesses, correctly, that the magic word is the wicked Coo-eeh-oh's name. Incidentally, as far as I know, not a single Oz commentator has noted that Coo-eeh-oh is the traditional cry of the hog-caller. The book ends with a stern admonishment, " 'it is always wise to do one's duty, however unpleasant that duty may seem to be.' "

Although it is unlikely that Baum would have found Ruskin's aesthetics of much interest, he might well have liked his political writings, particularly *Munera Pulveris* and *Fors.* Ruskin's protégé William Morris would have approved of Oz, where

Everyone worked half the time and played half the time, and the people enjoyed the work as much as they did the play. . . . There were no cruel overseers set to watch them, and no one to rebuke them and find fault with them. So each one was proud to do all he could for his friends and neighbors, and was glad when they would accept the things he produced.

Anticipating the wrath of the Librarian of Detroit, who in 1957 found the Oz books to have a "cowardly approach to life," Baum adds, slyly, "I do not suppose such an arrangement would be practical with us. . . ." Yet Baum has done no more than to revive in his own terms the original Arcadian dream of America. Or, as Marius Bewley noted, "the tension between technology and pastoralism is one of the things that the Oz books are about, whether Baum was aware of it or not." I think that Baum was very much aware of this tension. In Oz he presents the pastoral dream of Jefferson (the slaves have been replaced by magic and good will); and into this Eden he introduces forbidden knowledge in the form of black magic (the machine) which good magic (the values of the pastoral society) must overwhelm.

It is Bewley's view that because "The Ozites are much aware of the scientific nature of magic," Ozma wisely limited the practice of magic. As a result, controlled magic enhances the society just as controlled industrialization could enhance (and perhaps even salvage) a society like ours. Unfortunately, the Nome King has governed the United States for more than a century; and he shows no sign of wanting to abdicate. Meanwhile, the life of the many is definitely nome-ish and the environment has been, perhaps, irreparably damaged. To the extent that Baum makes his readers aware that our country's "practical" arrangements are inferior to those of Oz, he is a truly subversive writer and it is no wonder that the Librarian of Detroit finds him cowardly and negative, because, of course, he is brave and affirmative. But then the United States has always been a Rigamarole land where adjectives tend to mean their opposite, when they mean at all.

Despite the Librarian of Detroit's efforts to suppress magical alternative worlds, the Oz books continue to exert their spell. "You do not educate a man by telling him what he knew not," wrote John Ruskin, "but by making him what he was not." In Ruskin's high sense, Baum was a true educator, and those who read his Oz books are often made what they were not—imaginative, tolerant, alert to wonders, life.

*The New York Review of Books*
September 29 and October 13, 1977

# 100
—— • ——

# E. NESBIT'S
MAGIC

After Lewis Carroll, E. Nesbit is the best of the English fabulists who
wrote about children (neither wrote *for* children), and like Carroll she
was able to create a world of magic and inverted logic that was entirely
her own. Yet Nesbit's books are relatively unknown in the United
States. Publishers attribute her failure in these parts to a witty and
intelligent prose style (something of a demerit in the land of the dull and
the home of the literal) and to the fact that a good many of her books
deal with magic, a taboo subject nowadays. Apparently, the librarians
who dominate the "juvenile market" tend to the brisk tweedy ladies
whose interests are mechanical rather than imaginative. Never so happy
as when changing a fan belt, they quite naturally want to communicate
their joy in practical matters to the young. The result has been a depressing literature of how-to-do things while works of invention are sternly
rejected as not "practical" or "useful." Even the Oz books which had
such a powerful influence on three generations of Americans are put to
one side in certain libraries, and children are discouraged from reading
them because none of the things described in those books could ever
have happened. Even so, despite such odds, attempts are being made by
gallant publishers to penetrate the tweed curtain, and a number of
Nesbit's books are currently available in the United States, while in
England she continues to be widely read.

Born in 1858, Edith Nesbit was the daughter of the head of a British agricultural college. In 1880 she married Hubert Bland, a journalist. But though they had a good deal in common—both were socialists, active in the Fabian Society—the marriage was unhappy. Bland was a philanderer; worse, he had no gift for making a living. As a result, simply to support her five children, Nesbit began to write books about children. In a recent biography, *Magic and the Magician,* Noel Streatfeild remarks that E. Nesbit did not particularly like children, which may explain why those she created in her books are so entirely human. They are intelligent, vain, aggressive, humorous, witty, cruel, compassionate . . . in fact, they are like adults, except for one difference. In a well-ordered and stable society (England in the time of the gross Edward), children are as clearly defined a minority group as Jews or Blacks in other times and places. Physically small and weak, economically dependent upon others, they cannot control their environment. As a result, they are forced to develop a sense of communality; and though it does not necessarily make them any nicer to one another, at least it helps them to see each other with perfect clarity. Nesbit's genius is to see them as clearly and unsentimentally as they see themselves, thus making for that sense of life upon the page without which no literature.

Nesbit's usual device is to take a family of children ranging in age from a baby to a child of ten or eleven and then involve them in adventures, either magical or realistic (never both at the same time). *The Story of the Treasure Seekers, The Wouldbegoods,* and *The New Treasure Seekers* are realistic books about the Bastable children. They are told by Oswald Bastable, whose style owes a great deal to that of Julius Caesar. Like the conqueror, Oswald is able through a cunning use of the third person to establish his marked superiority to others. Wondering if his younger brother H. O. is mentally retarded, he writes, "H. O. is eight years old, but he cannot tell the clock yet. Oswald could tell the clock when he was six." Oswald is a delightful narrator and the stories he tells are among Nesbit's best. For the most part they deal with scrapes the children get into while searching for treasure in familiar surroundings, and the strategies they employ in coping as sensibly as possible with the contrary world of grown-ups. In a Nesbit book there is always some sort of domestic trouble. One parent is usually missing, and there is never enough money—although to the twentieth-century reader, her "impoverished" middle-class households, each with its three servants and large house, suggest an entirely golden aristocratic age. Yet many of the children's adventures have to do with attempts to improve the family's finances.

To my mind, it is in the "magic books" that Nesbit is at her best, particularly the trilogy which involves the Five Children. In the first volume, *Five Children and It,* they encounter the Psammead, a small bad-tempered, odd-looking creature from pre-history. The Psammead is able to grant wishes by first filling itself with air and then exhaling. ("If only you knew how I hate to blow myself out with other people's wishes, and how frightened I am always that I shall strain a muscle or something. And then to wake up every morning and know that you've got to do it. . . .")

But the children use the Psammead relentlessly for their wishes, and something almost always goes wrong. They wish "to be more beautiful than the day," and find that people detest them, thinking they look like Gypsies or worse. Without moralizing, Nesbit demonstrates, literally, the folly of human wishes, and amuses at the same time. In *The Phoenix and the Carpet,* they become involved with the millennial phoenix, a bird of awesome vanity ("I've often been told that mine is a valuable life"). With the use of a magic carpet, the phoenix and the children make a number of expeditions about the world. Yet even with such an ordinary device as a magic carpet, Nesbit's powers of invention are never settled easily. The carpet has been repaired, and the rewoven section is not magic; whoever sits on that part travels neither here nor there. Since most intelligent children are passionate logicians, the sense of logic is a necessary gift in a writer of fantasy. Though a child will gladly accept a fantastic premise, he will insist that the working out of it be entirely consistent with the premise. Careless invention is immediately noticed; contradiction and inconsistencies irritate, and illusion is destroyed. Happily, Nesbit is seldom careless and she anticipates most questions which might occur to a child. Not that she can always answer him satisfactorily. A condition of the Psammead's wishes is that they last only for a day. Yet the effects of certain wishes in the distant past did linger. Why was this? asked one of the children. *"Autres temps,"* replied the Psammead coolly, *"autres moeurs."*

In *The Story of the Amulet,* Nesbit's powers of invention are at their best. It is a time-machine story, only the device is not a machine but an Egyptian amulet whose other half is lost in the past. By saying certain powerful words, the amulet becomes a gate through which the children are able to visit the past or future. Pharaonic Egypt, Babylon (whose dotty queen comes back to London with them and tries to get her personal possessions out of the British Museum), Caesar's Britain—they visit them all in search of the missing part of the amulet. Nesbit's history is good. And there is even a look at a Utopian future, which turns out to be everything a good Fabian might have hoped for. Ultimately, the amulet's other half is found, and a story of considerable beauty is concluded in a most unexpected way.

There are those who consider *The Enchanted Castle* Nesbit's best book. J. B. Priestley has made a good case for it, and there *is* something strange about the book that sets it off from the bright world of the early stories. Four children encounter magic in the gardens of a great deserted house. The mood is midnight. Statues of dinosaurs come alive in the moonlight, the gods of Olympus hold a revel, Pan's song is heard. Then things go inexplicably wrong. The children decide to give a play. Wanting an audience, they create a number of creatures out of old clothes, pillows, brooms, umbrellas. To their horror, as the curtain falls, there is a ghastly applause. The creatures have come alive, and they prove to be most disagreeable. They want to find hotels to stay at. Thwarted, they turn ugly. Finally, they are locked in a back room, but not without a scuffle. It is the sort of nightmare that might have occurred to a high-strung child, perhaps to Nesbit herself. And one must remember that a nightmare was a serious matter for a child who had no electric light to switch on when a bad dream awakened him; he was forced to continue in darkness, the menacing shadows undispelled.

My own favorites among Nesbit's work are *The House of Arden* and *Harding's Luck,* two books that comprise a diptych, one telling much the same story as the second, yet from a different point of view. The mood is somewhere between that of *The Enchanted Castle* and of the *Five Children,* not midnight yet hardly morning. Richard Harding, a crippled boy, accompanies an old tramp about England. The Dickensian note is struck but without the master's sentimentality. Through magic, Harding is able to go into the past where he is Sir Richard Harding in the age of Henry VIII, and not lame. But loyalty to the tramp makes him return to the present. Finally he elects to remain in the past. Meanwhile in *The House of Arden* a contemporary boy, Eldred, must be tested before he can become Lord Arden and restore the family fortunes. He meets the Mouldiwarp (a mole who appears on the family coat of arms). This magic creature can be summoned only by poetry, freshly composed in its honor—a considerable strain on Edred and his sister Elfrida, who have not the gift. There are adventures in the past and the present, and the story of Richard Harding crosses their own. The magic comes and goes in a most interesting way.

As a woman, E. Nesbit was not to everyone's taste. H. G. Wells described her and Hubert Bland as "fundamentally intricate," adding that whenever the Blands attended meetings of the Fabian Society "anonymous letters flitted about like bats at twilight" (the Nesbit mood if not style is contagious). Yet there is no doubt that she was extraordinary. A failed serious poet, she became of necessity a writer of children's books. But though she disdained her true gift, she was peculiarly suited by nature to be what in fact she was. As an adult writing of her own childhood, she noted, "When I was a little child I used to pray fervently, fearfully, that when I should be grown up I might never forget what I thought and felt and suffered then." With extraordinary perceptiveness, she realized that each grown-up must kill the child he was before he himself can live. Nesbit's vow to survive somehow in the enemy's consciousness became, finally, her art—when this you see remember me— and the child continued to the end of the adult's life.

E. Nesbit's failure in the United States is not entirely mysterious. We have always preferred how-to-do to let's-imagine-that. As a result, in the last fifty years we have contributed relatively little in the way of new ideas of any sort. From radar to rocketry, we have had to rely on other societies for theory and invention. Our great contribution has been, characteristically, the assembly line.

I do not think it is putting the case too strongly to say that much of the poverty of our society's intellectual life is directly due to the sort of books children are encouraged to read. Practical books with facts in them may be necessary, but they are not everything. They do not serve the imagination in the same way that high invention does when it allows the mind to investigate *every* possibility, to set itself free from the ordinary, to enter a world where paradox reigns and nothing is what it seems. Properly engaged, the intelligent child begins to question all presuppositions, and thinks on his own. In fact, the moment he says, "Wouldn't it be interesting if . . . ?" he is on his way and his own imagination has begun to work at a level considerably more interesting than the usual speculation on what it will be like to own a car and make money. As it is, the absence of imagination is cruelly noticeable at every level of the American society, and though a reading of E. Nesbit is hardly going to change the pattern of a nation, there is some evidence that the child who reads her will never be quite the same again, and that is probably a good thing.

*The New York Review of Books*
December 3, 1964.

There are so many things that people who take polls never get around to asking. Fascinated as we all are to know what our countrymen think of great issues (approving, disapproving, don't-knowing, with that native shrewdness which made a primeval wilderness bloom with Howard Johnson signs), the pollsters never get around to asking the sort of interesting personal questions our new Romans might be able to answer knowledgeably. For instance, how many adults have an adventure serial running in their heads? How many consciously daydream, turning on a story in which the dreamer ceases to be an employee of IBM and becomes a handsome demigod moving through splendid palaces, saving maidens from monsters (or monsters from maidens: this is a jaded time). Most children tell themselves stories in which they figure as powerful figures, enjoying the pleasures not only of the adult world as they conceive it but of a world of wonders unlike dull reality. Although this sort of Mittyesque daydreaming is supposed to cease in maturity, I suggest that more adults than we suspect are dazedly wandering about with a full Technicolor extravaganza going on in their heads. Clad in tights, rapier in hand, the daydreamers drive their Jaguars at fantastic speeds through a glittering world of adoring love objects, mingling anachronistic historic worlds with science fiction. "Captain, the time-warp's been closed! We are now trapped in a parallel world, inhabited entirely by women with three breasts!" Though from what we can gather about these imaginary worlds, they tend to be more Adlerian than Freudian: the motor drive is the desire not for sex (other briefer fantasies take care of that) but for power, for the ability to dominate one's environment through physical strength, best demonstrated in the works of Edgar Rice Burroughs, whose books are enjoying a huge revival.

When I was growing up, I read all twenty-three Tarzan books, as well as the ten Mars books. My own inner story-telling mechanism was vivid. At any one time, I had at least three serials going as well as a number of tried and true reruns. I mined Burroughs largely for source material. When he went to the center of the earth à la Jules Verne (much too fancy a writer for one's taste), I immediately worked up a thirteen-part series, with myself as lead and various friends as guest stars. Sometimes I used the master's material, but more often I adapted it freely to suit myself. One's daydreams tended to be Tarzanish pre-puberty (physical strength and freedom) and Martian post-puberty (exotic worlds and subtle *combinazione* to be worked out). After adolescence, if one's life is sufficiently interesting, the desire to tell oneself stories diminishes. My last serial ran into sponsor trouble when I was in the Second World War, and it was never renewed.

Until recently I assumed that most people were like myself: day-dreaming ceases when the real world becomes interesting and reasonably manageable. Now I am not so certain. The life and success of Burroughs lead one to believe that a good many people find their lives so unsatisfactory that they go right on year after year telling themselves stories in which they are able to dominate their environment in a way that is not possible in the overorganized society.

According to Edgar Rice Burroughs, "Most of the stories I wrote were the stories I told myself just before I went to sleep." He is a fascinating figure to contemplate, an archetypal American dreamer. Born in 1875 in Chicago, he was a drifter until he was thirty-six. He served briefly in the U.S. Cavalry; then he was a gold miner in Oregon, a cowboy in Idaho, a railroad policeman in Salt Lake City; he attempted several businesses that failed. He was perfectly in the old-American grain: the man who could take on almost any job, who liked to keep moving, who tried to get rich quick but could never pull it off. And while he was drifting through the unsatisfactory real world, he consoled himself with an inner world where he was strong and handsome, adored by beautiful women and worshiped by exotic races. His principal source of fantasy was Rider Haggard. But even that rich field was limited, and so, searching for new veins to tap, he took to reading the pulp magazines, only to find that none of the stories could compare for excitement with his own imaginings. Since the magazine writers could not please him, he had no choice but to please himself, and the public. He composed a serial about Mars and sold it to *Munsey's.* The rest was easy, for his fellow daydreamers recognized at once a master dreamer.

In 1914 Burroughs published *Tarzan of the Apes* (Rousseau's noble savage reborn in Africa), and history was made. To date the Tarzan books have sold over twenty-five million copies in fifty-six languages. There is hardly an American male of my generation who has not at one time or another tried to master the victory cry of the great ape as it issued from the voluptuous chest of Johnny Weissmuller, to the accompaniment of thousands of arms and legs snapping during attempts to swing from tree to tree in the backyards of the Republic. Between 1914 and his death in 1950, the squire of Tarzana, California (a prophet more than honored in his own land), produced over sixty books, while enjoying the unique status of being the first American writer to be a corporation. Burroughs is said to have been a pleasant, unpretentious man who liked to ride and play golf. Not one to compromise a vivid unconscious with dim reality, he never set foot in Africa.

With a sense of recapturing childhood, I have just reread several Tarzan books. It is fascinating to see how much one recalls after a quarter century. At times the sense of *déjà vu* is overpowering. It is equally interesting to discover that one's memories of Tarzan of the Apes are mostly action scenes. The plot had slipped one's mind . . . and a lot of plot there is. The beginning is worthy of Conrad. "I had this story from one who had no business to tell it to me, or to any other. I may credit the seductive influence of an old vintage upon the narrator for the beginning of it, and my own skeptical incredulity during the days that followed for the balance of the strange tale." It is 1888. The young Lord and Lady Greystoke are involved in a ship mutiny ("there was in the whole atmosphere of the craft that undefinable something which presages disaster"). The peer and peeress are put ashore on the west coast of Africa, where they promptly build a tree house. Here Burroughs is at his best. He tells you the size of the logs, the way to hang a door when you have no hinges, the problems of roofing. One of the best things about his books is the descriptions of making things. The Greystokes have a child, and conveniently die. The "man-child" is discovered by Kala, a Great Ape, who brings him up as a member of her tribe. As anthropologist, Burroughs is pleasantly vague. His apes are carnivorous, and they are able, he darkly suspects, to mate with human beings.

Tarzan grows up as an ape, kills his first lion (with a full nelson), teaches himself to read and write English by studying some books found in the cabin. The method he used, sad to say, is the currently fashionable "look-say." Though he can read and write, he cannot speak any language except that of the apes. He also gets on well with other members of the animal kingdom, with Tantor the elephant, Ska the vulture, Numa the lion (Kipling was also grist for the Burroughs dream mill). Then white folks arrive: Professor Archimedes Q. Porter and his daughter Jane. Also, a Frenchman named D'Arnot who teaches Tarzan to speak French, which is confusing. By an extraordinary coincidence, Jane's suitor is the current Lord Greystoke, who thinks the Greystoke baby is dead. Tarzan saves Jane from an ape. Then he puts on clothes and goes to Paris, where he drinks absinthe. Next stop, America. In Wisconsin, he saves Jane Porter from a forest fire: only to give her up nobly to Lord Greystoke, not revealing the fact that *he* is the real Lord Greystoke. Fortunately in the next volume, *The Return of Tarzan,* he marries Jane and they live happily ever after in Africa, raising a son John, who in turn grows up and has a son. Yet even as a grandfather, Tarzan continues to have adventures with people a foot high, with descendants of Atlantis, with the heirs of a Roman legion who think that Rome is still a success. All through these stories one gets the sense that one is daydreaming, too. Episode follows episode with no particular urgency. Tarzan is always knocked on the head and taken captive; he always escapes; there is always a beautiful princess or high priestess who loves him and assists him; there is always a loyal friend who fights beside him, very much in that Queequeg tradition which, Professor Leslie Fiedler assures us, is the urning in the fuel supply of the American psyche. But no matter how difficult the adventure, Tarzan, clad only in a loincloth with no weapon save a knife (the style is comforting to imitate), wins against all odds and returns to his shadowy wife.

Stylistically, Burroughs is—how shall I put it?—uneven. He has moments of ornate pomp, when the darkness is "Cimmerian"; of redundancy, "she was hideous and ugly"; of extraordinary dialogue: "Name of a name," shrieked Rokoff. "Pig, but you shall die for this!" Or Lady Greystoke to Lord G.: "Duty is duty, my husband, and no amount of sophistries may change it. I would be a poor wife for an English lord were I to be responsible for his shirking a plain duty." Or the grandchild: "Muvver," he cried, "Dackie doe? Dackie doe?" "Let him come along," urged Tarzan. "Dare!" exclaimed the boy, turning triumphantly upon the governess, "Dackie do doe yalk!" Burroughs's use of coincidence is shameless even for a pulp writer. In one book he has three sets of characters shipwrecked at exactly the same point on the shore of Africa. Even Burroughs finds this a bit much. "Could it be possible [muses Tarzan] that fate had thrown him up at the very threshold of his own beloved jungle?" It was possible since anything can happen in a day-dream.

Though Burroughs is innocent of literature and cannot reproduce human speech, he does have a gift very few writers of any kind possess: he can describe action vividly. I give away no trade secrets when I say that this is as difficult for a Tolstoi as it is for a Burroughs (even William). Because it is so hard, the craftier contemporary novelists usually prefer to tell their stories in the first person, which is simply writing dialogue. In character, as it were, the writer settles for an impression of what happened rather than creating the sense of the thing happening. In action Tarzan is excellent.

There is something basic in the appeal of the 1914 Tarzan which makes me think that he can still hold his own as a daydream figure, despite the sophisticated challenge of his two young competitors, James Bond and Mike Hammer. For most adults, Tarzan (and John Carter of Mars) can hardly compete with the conspicuous consumer consumption of James Bond or the sickly violence of Mike Hammer, but for children and adolescents the old appeal continues. All of us need the idea of a world alternative to this one. From Plato's Republic to Opar to Bondland, at every level, the human imagination has tried to imagine something better for itself than the existing society. Man left Eden when he got up off all fours, endowing his descendants with nostalgia as well as chronic backache. In its naïve way, the Tarzan legend returns us to that Eden where, free of clothes and the inhibitions of an oppressive society, a man is able, as William Faulkner put it in his high Confederate style, to prevail as well as endure. The current fascination with LSD and drugs—not to mention alcohol—is all a result of a general sense of boredom. Since the individual's desire to dominate his environment is not a desirable trait in a society that every day grows more and more confining, the average man must take to daydreaming. James Bond, Mike Hammer, and Tarzan are all dream selves, and the aim of each is to establish personal primacy in a world that, more and more, diminishes the individual. Among adults, the current popularity of these lively fictions strikes me as a most significant and unbearably sad phenomenon.

*Esquire*
December 1963

# SOME MEMORIES
# OF THE GLORIOUS BIRD
# AND AN EARLIER SELF

"I particularly like New York on hot summer nights when all the
. . . uh, superfluous people are off the streets." Those were, I think, the
first words Tennessee addressed to me; then the foggy blue eyes blinked,
and a nervous chuckle filled the moment's silence before I said whatever
I said.

Curtain rising. The place: an apartment at the American Academy in
Rome. Occasion: a party for some newly arrived Americans, among
them Frederic Prokosch, Samuel Barber. The month: March 1948. The
day: glittering. What else could a March day be in the golden age?

I am pleased that I can remember so clearly my first meeting with the
Glorious Bird, as I almost immediately called him for reasons long since
forgotten (premonition, perhaps, of the eventual take-off and flight of
youth's sweet bird?). Usually, I forget first meetings, excepting always
those solemn audiences granted by the old and famous when I was
young and green. I recall vividly every detail of André Gide's conversation and appearance, including the dark velvet beret he wore in his study
at 1-bis rue Vaneau. I recall even more vividly my visits to George
Santayana in his cell at the Convent of the Blue Nuns. All these audiences, meetings, introductions took place in that *anno mirabilis* 1948, a
year that proved to be the exact midpoint between the end of the Second

World War and the beginning of what looks to be a permanent cold war. At the time, of course, none of us knew where history had placed us.

At that first meeting I thought Tennessee every bit as ancient as Gide and Santayana. After all, I was twenty-two. He was thirty-seven; but claimed to be thirty-three on the sensible ground that the four years he had spent working for a shoe company did not count. Now he was the most celebrated American playwright. *A Streetcar Named Desire* was still running in New York when we met that evening in a flat overlooking what was, in those days, a quiet city where hardly anyone was superfluous unless it was us, the first group of American writers and artists to arrive in Rome after the war.

In 1946 and 1947 Europe was still out-of-bounds for foreigners. But by 1948 the Italians had begun to pull themselves together, demonstrating once more their astonishing ability to cope with disaster which is so perfectly balanced by their absolute inability to deal with success.

Rome was strange to all of us. For one thing, Italy had been sealed off not only by war but by Fascism. Since the early thirties few English or American artists knew Italy well. Those who did included mad Ezra, gentle Max, spurious B.B. and, of course, the Anglo-American historian Harold (now Sir Harold) Acton, in stately residence at Florence. By 1948 Acton had written supremely well about both the Bourbons of Naples and the later Medici of Florence; unfortunately, he was—is— prone to the writing of memoirs. And so, wanting no doubt to flesh out yet another chapter in the ongoing story of a long and marvelously uninteresting life, Acton came down to Rome to look at the new invaders. What he believed he saw and heard, he subsequently published in a little volume called *More Memoirs of an Aesthete,* a work to be cherished for its quite remarkable number of unaesthetic misprints and mispellings.

"After the First World War American writers and artists had emigrated to Paris; now they pitched upon Rome." So Acton begins. "According to Stendhal, the climate was enough to gladden anybody, but this was not the reason: one of them explained to me that it was the facility of finding taxis, and very little of Rome can be seen from a taxi. Classical and Romantic Rome was no more to them than a picturesque background. Tennessee Williams, Victor [he means Frederic] Prokosch and Gore Vidal created a bohemian annexe to the American Academy. . . ." Liking Rome for its many taxis is splendid stuff and I wish I had said it. Certainly whoever did was putting Acton on, since the charm of Rome—1948— was the lack of automobiles of any kind. But Acton is just getting into stride. More to come.

Toward the end of March Tennessee gave a party to inaugurate his new flat in the Via Aurora (in the golden age even the street names were apt). Somehow or other, Acton got himself invited to the party. I remember him floating like some large pale fish through the crowded room; from time to time, he would make a sudden lunge at this or that promising bit of bait while Tennessee, he tells us, "wandered as a lost soul among the guests he assembled in an apartment which might have been in New York. . . . Neither he nor any of the group I met with him spoke Italian, yet he had a typically Neapolitan protégé who could speak no English."

At this time Tennessee and I had been in Rome for only a few weeks and French, not Italian, was the second language of the reasonably well-educated American of that era. On the other hand, Prokosch knew Italian, German, and French; he also bore with becoming grace the heavy weight of a Yale doctorate in Middle English. But to Acton the author of *The Asiatics,* the translator of Hölderlin and Louise Labé was just another barbarian whose works "fell short of his perfervid imagination, [he] had the dark good looks of an advertiser of razor blades. . . ." Happily, "Gore Vidal, the youngest in age, aggressively handsome in a clean-limbed sophomore style, had success written all over him. . . . His candour was engaging but he was slightly on the defensive, as if he anticipated an attack on his writings or his virtue." Well, the young G.V. wasn't so dumb: seeing the old one-two plainly in the middle distance, he kept sensibly out of reach.

"A pudgy, taciturn, moustached little man without any obvious distinction." Thus Acton describes Tennessee. He then zeroes in on the "protégé" from Naples, a young man whom Acton calls "Pierino." Acton tells us that Pierino had many complaints about Tennessee and his friends, mostly due to the language barrier. The boy was also eager to go to America. Acton tried to discourage him. Even so, Pierino was enthralled. " 'You are the first *galantuomo* who has spoken to me this evening.' " After making a date to see the *galantuomo* later on that evening, Pierino split. Acton then told Tennessee, "as tactfully as I could, that his young protégé felt neglected. . . . [Tennessee] rubbed his chin thoughtfully and said nothing, a little perplexed. There was something innocently childish about his expression." It does not occur to the memoirist that Tennessee might have been alarmed at his strange guest's bad manners. "Evidently he was not aware that Pierino wanted to be taken to America and I have wondered since whether he took him there, for that was my last meeting with Tennessee Williams." It must be said that Acton managed to extract quite a lot of copy out of a single meeting.

To put his mind at rest, Tennessee did take Pierino to America and Pierino is now a married man and doing, as they say, well.

"This trifling episode illustrated the casual yet condescending attitude of certain foreigners towards the young Italians they cultivated on account of their Latin charm without any interest in their character, aspirations or desires." This sentiment or sentimentality could be put just as well the other way around and with far more accuracy. Italian trade has never had much interest in the character, aspirations or desires of those to whom they rent their ass. When Acton meditates upon The Italian Boy, a sweet and sickly hypocrisy clouds his usually sharp prose and we are in E. M. Forsterland where the lower orders (male) are worshiped, and entirely misunderstood. But magnum of sour grapes to one side, Acton is by no means inaccurate. Certainly he got right Tennessee's indifference to place, art, history. The Bird seldom reads a book and the only history he knows is his own; he depends, finally, on a romantic genius to get him through life. Above all, he is a survivor, never more so than now in what he calls his "crocodile years."

I picked up Tennessee's *Memoirs* with a certain apprehension. I looked myself up in the Index; read the entries and found some errors, none grave. I started to read; was startled by the technique he had chosen. Some years ago, Tennessee told me that he had been reading (that is to say, looking at) my "memoir in the form of a novel" *Two Sisters*. In this book I alternated sections describing certain events in 1948 with my everyday life while writing the book. Memory sections I called *Then*. The day-by-day descriptions I called *Now*. At the time Tennessee found *Two Sisters* interesting because he figured in it. He must also have found it technically interesting because he has serenely appropriated my form and has now no doubt forgotten just how the idea first came to him to describe the day-to-day life of a famous beleaguered playwright acting in an off-Broadway production of the failing play *Small Craft Warnings* while, in alternating sections, he recalls the early days not only of Tennessee Williams but of one Thomas Lanier Williams, who bears only a faint familial resemblance to the playwright we all know from a thousand and one altogether too candid interviews.

There is a foreword and, like all forewords, it is meant to disarm. Unfortunately, it armed me to the teeth. During the 1973 tryout of a play in New Haven, Tennessee was asked to address some Yale drama students. Incidentally, the style of the foreword is unusually seductive, the old master at his most beguiling: self-pity and self-serving kept in exquisite balance by the finest comic style since S. L. Clemens.

"I found myself entering (through a door marked EXIT) an auditorium considerably smaller than the Shubert but containing a more than proportionately small audience. I would say roughly about two-score and ten, not including a large black dog which was resting in the lap of a male student in the front row. . . . The young faces before me were uniformly inexpressive of any kind of emotional reaction to my entrance. . . ." I am surprised that Tennessee was surprised. The arrogance and self-satisfaction of drama students throughout Academe are among the few constants in a changing world. Any student who has read Sophocles in translation is, demonstrably, superior to Tennessee Williams in the untidy flesh. These dummies reflect of course the proud mediocrity of their teachers, who range, magisterially, through something called "world drama" where evolution works only backward. Teachers and taught are to be avoided.

"I am not much good at disguising my feelings, and after a few moments I abandoned all pretense of feeling less dejection than I felt." The jokes did not work. So "I heard myself describing an encounter, then quite recent, with a fellow playwright in the Oak Room Bar at Manhattan's Plaza Hotel." It was with "my old friend Gore Vidal. I had embraced him warmly. However, Mr. Vidal is not a gentleman to be disarmed by a cordial embrace, and when, in response to his perfunctory inquiries about the progress of rehearsals . . . I told him . . . all seemed a dream come true after many precedent nightmares, he smiled at me with a sort of rueful benevolence and said 'Well, Bird, it won't do much good, I'm afraid, you've had too much bad personal exposure for anything to help you much anymore.'

"Well, then, for the first time, I could see a flicker of interest in the young faces before me. It may have been the magic word Vidal or it may have been his prophecy of my professional doom." Asked if the prognosis was accurate, Tennessee looked at the black dog and said, "Ask the dog."

An unsettling anecdote. I have no memory of the Plaza meeting. I am also prone, when dining late, to suffer from what Dorothy Parker used grimly to refer to as "the frankies," or straight talk for the other person's good like frankly-that-child-would-not-have-been-born-mongoloid-if-you-hadn't. . . . An eyewitness, however, assures me that I did not say what Tennessee attributes to me. Yet his paranoia always has some basis in reality. I have an uncomfortable feeling that I was probably thinking what I did not say and what he later thought I did say. When it comes to something unspoken, the Bird has a sharp ear.

It is hard now to realize what a bad time of it Tennessee used to have from the American press. During the forties and fifties the anti-fag battalions were everywhere on the march. From the high lands of *Partisan Review* to the middle ground of *Time* magazine, envenomed attacks on real or suspected fags never let up. A *Time* cover story on Auden was killed when the managing editor of the day was told that Auden was a fag. From 1945 to 1961 *Time* attacked with unusual ferocity everything produced or published by Tennessee Williams. "Fetid swamp" was the phrase most used to describe his work. But, in *Time,* as well as in time, all things will come to pass. The Bird is now a beloved institution.

Today, at sixty-four, Tennessee has the same voracious appetite for work and for applause that he had at twenty-four. More so, I would suspect, since glory is a drug more addictive than any other as heroes have known from Achilles on (Donald Windham's *roman à clef* about Tennessee bore the apt title *The Hero Continues*). But fashions in the theater change. The superstar of the forties and fifties fell on bad times, and that is the burden of these memoirs. In sharp detail we are told how the hero came into being. Less sharply, Tennessee describes the bad days when the booze and the pills caused him to hallucinate; to slip out of a world quite bad enough as it is into nightmare land. "I said to my friend Gore, 'I slept through the sixties,' and he said, 'You didn't miss a thing.' " Tennessee often quotes this exchange. But he leaves out the accompanying caveat: "If you missed the sixties, Bird, God knows what you are going to do with the seventies."

But of course life is not divided into good and bad decades; it is simply living. For a writer, life is, again simply, writing and in these memoirs the old magician can still create a world. But since it is hardly news to the Bird that we are for the night, the world he shows us is no longer the Romantic's lost Eden but Prospero's island where, at sunset, magicians often enjoy revealing the sources of their rude magic, the tricks of a trade.

Not that a magician is honor-bound to tell the whole truth. For instance: "I want to admit to you that I undertook this memoir for mercenary reasons. It is actually the first piece of work, in the line of writing, that I have undertaken for material profit." The sniffy tone is very much that of St. Theresa scrubbing floors. Actually, Tennessee is one of the richest of living writers. After all, a successful play will earn its author a million or more dollars and Tennessee has written quite a few successful plays. Also, thirteen of his works have been made into films.

Why the poor-mouthing? Because it has always been the Bird's tactic to appear in public flapping what looks to be a pathetically broken wing. By arousing universal pity, he hopes to escape predators. In the old days before a play opened on Broadway, the author would be asked to write a piece for the Sunday *New York Times* drama section. Tennessee's pieces were always thrilling; sometimes horrendous. He would reveal how that very morning he had coughed up blood with his sputum. But, valiantly, he had gone on writing, knowing the new play would be his last work, ever . . . By the time the Bird had finished working us over, only Louis Kronenberger at *Time* had the heart to attack him.

But now that Tennessee's physical and mental health are good (he would deny this instantly; "I have had, in recent days, a series of palpitations of the variety known as terminal"), only the cry of poverty will, he thinks, act as lightning conductor and insure him a good press for the *Memoirs.* Certainly he did not write this book for the $50,000 advance. As always, fame is the spur. Incidentally, he has forgotten that in the past he *did* write for money when he was under contract to MGM and worked on a film called *Marriage Is a Private Affair,* starring Lana Turner and James Craig (unless of course Tennessee now sees in this movie that awesome moral grandeur first detected by the film critic Myra Breckinridge).

The *Memoirs* start briskly. Tennessee is a guest at a country house in Wiltshire near Stonehenge. On the grounds of the estate is a "stone which didn't quite make it to Henge." He looks himself up in *Who's Who.* Broods on his past; shifts back and forth in time. *Now* and *Then.* The early days are fascinating to read about even though the Williams family is already known to every playgoer not only from *The Glass Menagerie* but also from the many other plays and stories in which appear, inexorably, Rose the Sister, Edwina the Mother, Dakin the Brother, Cornelius the Father, Reverend Dakin the Grandfather, as well as various other relatives now identified for the first time. He also tells us how he was hooked by the theater when some St. Louis amateurs put on a play he had written. "I knew that writing was my life, and its failure would be my death. . . ."

I have never known any writer with the exception of the artistically gifted and humanly appalling Carson McCullers who cared so much about the opinion of those condemned to write for newspapers. Uneasily confronting a truly remarkable hunger for absolute praise and total notice, Tennessee admits that, when being interviewed, he instinctively "hams it up in order to provide 'good copy.' The reason? I guess a need to convince the world that I do indeed still exist and to make this fact a matter of public interest and amusement." Fair enough, Bird. But leave your old friends out.

"This book is a sort of catharsis of puritanical guilt feelings, I suppose. 'All good art is an indiscretion.' Well, I can't assure you that this book will be art, but it is bound to be an indiscretion, since it deals with my adult life. . . .

"Of course I could devote this whole book to a discussion of the art of drama, but wouldn't that be a bore?

"It would bore me to extinction, I'm afraid, and it would be a very, very short book, about three sentences to the page with extremely wide margins. The plays speak for themselves."

A wise choice: the plays do speak for themselves and Tennessee's mind is not, to say the least, at home with theory. Most beautifully, the plays speak for themselves. Not only does Tennessee have a marvelous comedic sense but his gloriously outrageous dramatic effects can be enormously satisfying. He makes poetic (without quotes) the speech of those half-educated would-be genteel folk who still maintain their babble in his head. Only on those rare occasions when he tries to depict educated or upper-class people does he falter. Somewhat reproachfully, he told me that he had been forced several times to use a dictionary while reading *Two Sisters*.

What, I asked, was one of the words you had to look up? "Solipsistic," he said. Tennessee's vocabulary has never been large (I note that he still thinks "eclectic" means "esoteric"). But then he is not the sort of writer who sees words on the page; rather he hears them in his head and when he is plugged into the right character, the wrong word never sounds.

"Life that winter in Rome: a golden dream, and I don't just mean Raffaello [Acton's 'Pierino'] and the mimosa and total freedom of life. Stop there: What I do mean is the total freedom of life and Raffaello and the mimosa. . . ." That season we were, all of us, symbolically, out of jail. Free of poverty and hack work, Tennessee had metamorphosed into the Glorious Bird while I had left behind me three years in the wartime army and a near-fatal bout with hepatitis. So it was, at the beginning of that golden dream, we met.

Tennessee's version: "[Gore] had just published a best-seller, called *The City and the Pillar*, which was one of the first homosexual novels of consequence. I had not read it but I knew that it had made the best-seller lists and that it dealt with a 'forbidden subject.'" Later, Tennessee actually read the book (the only novel of mine he has ever been able to get through) and said, "You know you spoiled it with that ending. You didn't know what a good book you had." Fair comment.

"Gore was a handsome kid, about twenty-four [*sic*], and I was quite taken by his wit as well as his appearance." Incidentally, I am mesmerized by the tributes to my beauty that keep cropping up in the memoirs of the period. At the time nobody reliable thought to tell me. In fact, it was my impression that I was not making out as well as most people because, with characteristic malice, Nature had allowed Guy Madison and not me to look like Guy Madison.

"We found that we had interests in common and we spent a lot of time together. Please don't imagine that I am suggesting that there was a romance." I don't remember whether or not I ever told Tennessee that I had actually seen but not met him the previous year. He was following me up Fifth Avenue while I, in turn, was stalking yet another quarry. I recognized him: he wore a blue bow tie with white polka dots. In no mood for literary encounters, I gave him a scowl and he abandoned the chase just north of Rockefeller Center. I don't recall how my own pursuit ended. We walked a lot in the golden age.

"I believe we also went to Florence that season and were entertained by that marvelous old aesthete Berenson." No, that was someone else. "And then one afternoon Gore took me to the Convent of the Blue Nuns to meet the great philosopher and essayist, by then an octogenarian and semi-invalid, Santayana." I had to drag Tennessee to meet Santayana. Neither had heard of the other. But Tennessee did stare at the old man with great interest. Afterward, the Bird remarked, "Did you notice how he said 'in the days when I had secretaries, *young men?*' "

In the *Memoirs* Tennessee tells us a great deal about his sex life, which is one way of saying nothing about oneself. Details of this body and that body tend to blur on the page as they do in life. Tennessee did not get around to his first homosexual affair until he was well into his twenties, by which time he had achieved several mature as well as sexually meaningful and life-enhancing heterosexual relationships. Except he wasn't really all that enhanced by these "mature" relationships. Lust for the male set his nerves to jangling. Why was he such a late-developer? Well, this was close to half a century ago, and Tennessee was the product of that Southern puritan environment where all sex was sin and unnatural sex was peculiarly horrible.

I think that the marked difference between my attitude toward sex and that of Tennessee made each of us somewhat startling to the other. I never had the slightest guilt or anxiety about what I always took to be a normal human appetite. He was—and is—guilt-ridden, and although he tells us that he believes in no afterlife, he is still too much the puritan not to believe in sin. At some deep level Tennessee truly believes that the homosexualist is wrong and that the heterosexualist is right. Given this all-pervading sense of guilt, he is drawn in both life and work to the idea of expiation, of death.

Tennessee tells of his affair with a dancer named Kip. But Kip left him; got married; died young. Then Tennessee was drawn to a pseudonymous lover in New Orleans; that affair ended in drink and violence. For a number of years Tennessee lived with an Italo-American, Frank Merlo. Eventually they fell out. They were reunited when Frank was dying of cancer. Frank's last days were sufficiently horrifying to satisfy any puritan's uneasy conscience while, simultaneously, justifying the romantic's extreme vision of the world: "I shall but love thee better after death."

The other line running through Tennessee's emotional life is what I call the Monster Women. Surrogate mothers one might say if Tennessee's own mother, Miss Edwina, were not so implacably in this world, even as I write these lines. Currently convinced that the blacks signal to one another during the long St. Louis nights by clanging the lids of the trash cans, Miss Edwina is every inch the Amanda of *The Glass Menagerie*. In fact, so powerful is Tennessee's creation that in the presence of Miss Edwina one does not listen to her but only to what he has made of her.

"I had forty gentlemen callers that day," she says complacently. We are having dinner in the restaurant of the Robert Clay Hotel in Miami. Delicately she holds a fork with a shrimp on it. Fork and shrimp proceed slowly to her mouth while Tennessee and I stare, hypnotized not only by the constant flow of conversation but by the never-eaten shrimp for just as she is about to take the first bite, yet another anecdote wells up from deep inside her . . . ah, *solipsistic* brain and the fork returns to the plate, the shrimp untouched. "Tom, remember when that little dog took the hat with the plume and ran all 'round the yard . . . ?" This is also from *The Glass Menagerie*. Tennessee nervously clears his throat. Again the shrimp slowly rises to the wide straight mouth which resembles nothing so much as the opening to a miniature letter box—one designed for engraved invitations only. But once again the shrimp does not arrive. "Tom, do you remember . . . ?"

Tennessee clears his throat again. *"Mother, eat your shrimp."*

"Why," counters Miss Edwina, "do you keep making that funny sound in your throat?"

"Because, Mother, when you destroy someone's life you must expect certain nervous disabilities."

Yet Tennessee went on adding even more grotesque ladies than Miss Edwina to his life. I could never take any of them from Carson McCullers to Jane Bowles to Anna Magnani. Yes, yes, yes, they were superb talents all. Part of the artistic heritage of the twentieth century. I concede their talent, their glory, their charm—for Tennessee but not for me. Carson spoke only of her work. Of its greatness. The lugubrious Southern singsong voice never stopped: "Did ya see muh lovely play? Did ya lahk muh lovely play? Am Ah gonna win the Pew-litzuh prahzz?" Jane ("the finest writer of fiction we have in the States") Bowles was more original. She thought and talked a good deal about food and made powerful scenes in restaurants. The best that one could say of Magnani was that she liked dogs. When Marlon Brando agreed to act with her in the film of Tennessee's *Orpheus Descending,* he warned, "When I do a scene with her, I'm going to carry a rock in each hand."

I don't know what Tennessee gets from the Monster Women, but if they give him solace nothing else matters. Certainly he has a huge appetite for the grotesque not only in art but in life. In fact, he is dogged by the grotesque. Once, in the airport at Miami, we were stopped by a plump middle-aged man who had known Tennessee whom he called Tom from the old days in St. Louis. The man seemed perfectly ordinary. He talked to Tennessee about friends they had in common. Then I noticed that the man was carrying a large string bag containing two roast turkeys and a half dozen loaves of bread. "What," I asked, "is that?" The man gave us a knowing wink. "Well, I got me two roast turkeys in there. And also these loaves of bread *because you know about the food in Miami.* " Then he was gone. It would seem that the true artist need never search for a subject; the subject always knows where to find him.

It is curious how friends actually regard one another—or think they do—when memoir-time rolls around, and the boneyard beckons. A figure of some consequence in our far-off golden age was the composer-novelist Paul Bowles. From time to time over the years, Tennessee has bestowed a number of Walter Winchellish Orchids on Paul as well as on Jane (I fear that a lifetime on Broadway has somewhat corrupted the Bird's everyday speech and prose although nothing, happily, can affect the authenticity of those voices in his head). Certainly Bowles was an early hero of Tennessee's.

But now let us see what Bowles makes of Tennessee in *his* memoir *Without Stopping.* "One morning when we were getting ready to leave for the beach" (this was Acapulco, 1940), "someone arrived at the door and asked to see me. It was a round-faced, sun-burned young man in a big floppy sombrero and a striped sailor sweater, who said his name was Tennessee Williams, that he was a playwright, and that Lawrence Langner of the Theatre Guild had told him to look me up. I asked him to come in and installed him in a hammock, explaining that we had to hurry to the beach with friends. I brought him books and magazines and rum and coke, and told him to ask the servants for sandwiches if he got hungry. Then we left. Seven hours later we got back to the house and found our visitor lying contentedly in the hammock, reading. We saw him again each day until he left."

Paul Bowles used to quote Virgil Thomson's advice to a young music critic: Never intrude your personal opinions when you write music criticism. "The words that you use to describe what you've heard will be the criticism." Bowles on Tennessee demonstrates a mastery of the unsaid. Needless to say, Tennessee read what Bowles had written about him. Now watch the Bird as he strikes . . .

"It was there in Acapulco that summer that I first met Jane and Paul Bowles. They were staying at a pension in town and Paul was, as ever, upset about the diet and his stomach. The one evening that we spent together that summer was given over almost entirely to the question of what he could eat in Acapulco that he could digest, and poor little Janie kept saying, 'Oh, Bubbles, if you'd just stick to cornflakes and fresh fruit!' and so on and so on. None of her suggestions relieved his dyspeptic humor.

"I thought them a very odd and charming couple." I think I give Tennessee that round, on points. But Bowles's prose still remains the perfect model for judgment by indirection even though, like Tennessee, he occasionally gets the facts wrong. Bowles writes: "Gore had just played a practical joke on Tennessee and Truman Capote which he recounted to me in dialect, as it were. He had called Tennessee on the telephone and, being a stupendous mimic, had made himself into Truman for the occasion. Then, complete with a snigger, he induced Tennessee to make uncomplimentary remarks about Gore's writing."

This is a curious variation on the actual story. A number of times I would ring Tennessee, using Capote's voice. The game was to see how long it would take him to figure out that it was not Capote. One day I rang and spoke to what I thought was Tennessee. But it was Frank Merlo, newly installed in the flat. I had not got beyond my imitable whine, "This is *Tru*man," when Frank began to attack Tennessee. I broke the connection. Frank never knew whether or not I had repeated his complaints to Tennessee. I did not. But years later I did tell Bowles the story.

Back to 1948: "In those days Truman was about the best companion you could want," writes Tennessee. "He had not turned bitchy. Well, he had not turned *maliciously* bitchy. But he was full of fantasies and mischief." That summer Capote arrived in Paris where Tennessee and I were staying at the Hôtel de l'Université ("A raffish hotel but it suited Gore and me perfectly as there was no objection to young callers"), and Capote would keep us entranced with mischievous fantasies about the great. Apparently, the very sight of him was enough to cause lifelong heterosexual men to tumble out of unsuspected closets. When Capote refused to surrender his virtue to the drunken Errol Flynn, "Errol threw *all* my suitcases out of the window of the Beverly Wilshire Hotel!" I should note here that the young Capote was no less attractive in his person then than he is today.

When Tennessee and I would exchange glances during these stories, Capote would redouble his efforts. Did we know that Albert Camus was in love with him? Yes, Camus! Madly in love. Recently Capote's biographer told me that the Capote-Camus connection might well prove to be a key chapter. No doubt it will also provide a startling footnote to the life story of Camus, a man known until now as a womanizer. Then Capote showed us a gold and amethyst ring. "From André Gide," he sighed. Happily, I was able to check that one out. A few days later I called on Gide in the company of my English publisher. "How," I asked in my best Phillips Exeter French, "did you find Truman Capote?" "Who?" Gide asked. I suspect that it was then, in the fabulous summer of '48, that the nonfiction novel was born.

To return again to 1948, I have a bit more to report on that season.

"Frankie and I had been out late one evening and when we returned to the apartment the transom on the front door was open and from within came the voice of Truman Capote, shrill with agitation. . . . In the apartment were Truman, Gore Vidal, and a female policeman. . . . It seemed that Truman and Gore, still on friendly terms at this point, had got a bit drunk together and had climbed in through the transom of the apartment to wait for me and Frankie."

Before this story petrifies into literary history, let me amend the record. Tennessee, an actress, and I came back to Tennessee's flat to find Capote and a friend in the clutches of the law. They had indeed been caught entering the flat. But by the time we arrived, Capote had matters well under control. Plainclotheswoman and plainclothesman were listening bug-eyed to Capote, who was telling them *every*thing about the private lives of Mr. and Mrs. Charles Chaplin.

Tennessee's asides on the various personages who have come his way are often amusing, sometimes revelatory. He describes a hilarious dinner with the Russian performer Yevtushenko, who saw fit to lecture Tennessee on commercialism, sexual perversion, and the responsibilities of art while swilling expensive wine. Tennessee admired Dylan Thomas until he actually met him and received "this put-down: 'How does it feel to make all that Hollywood money?' " There was also the snub from Sartre. Tennessee gave a party at the Hôtel de l'Université, hoping that Sartre would come. Instead the Master sat a few blocks away at a café, and for several hours he made a point of *not* coming to the party despite the pleas of various emissaries.

Tennessee omits to mention a splendid lunch given us at the Grand Véfour by Jean Cocteau, who wanted the French rights to *A Streetcar Named Desire* for Jean Marais to act in. I came along as translator. Marais looked beautiful but sleepy. Cocteau was characteristically brilliant. He spoke no English but since he could manage an occasional "the" sound as well as the final "g," he often gave the impression that he was speaking English. Tennessee knew no French. He also had no clear idea just who Cocteau was, while Cocteau knew nothing about Tennessee except that he had written a popular American play with a splendid part in it for his lover Marais. Between Tennessee's solemn analyses of the play and Cocteau's rhetoric about theater (the long arms flailed like semaphores denoting some dangerous last junction), no one made any sense at all except Marais who broke his long silence to ask, apropos the character Stanley Kowalski, "Will I have to use a Polish accent?"

Although Marais and Cocteau broke up soon afterward, Cocteau did the play without Marais. Cocteau's adaptation was, apparently, a gorgeous mess. Naked black youths writhed through beaded curtains while Arletty, miscast as Blanche, struck attitudes among peacock feathers.

The situation of a practicing playwright in the United States is not a happy one, to understate the matter. Broadway is more and more an abandoned parcel of real estate. Except for a native farce or two and a handful of "serious" plays imported from the British Isles, Broadway is noted chiefly for large and usually bad musicals. During the theater season of 1947–48 there were 43 straight plays running on Broadway. In 1974–75 there were 18, mostly imported. Adventurous plays are now done off-Broadway and sometimes off-off . . . where our memoirist ended up as a performer in *Small Craft Warnings.*

Unique among writers, the American playwright must depend upon the praise of journalists who seldom know very much about anything save the prejudices of their employers. With the collapse of a half dozen newspapers in the last third of a century, the success of a play now depends almost entirely upon the good will of the critic for *The New York Times.* The current reviewer is an amiable and enthusiastic Englishman who knows a good deal about ballet but not so much about the social and political nuances of his adopted land. Yet at sixty-four Tennessee Williams is still trying to curry favor with the press. Of *Small Craft Warnings,* "Clive Barnes" (in *The New York Times*) "was cautiously respectful. With the exception of Leonard Harris, I disregard TV reviews. I suppose they were generally negative."

Then Tennessee has second thoughts. And a new paragraph: "To say that I disregard TV reviews is hardly the total truth. How could I disregard any review which determines the life or death of a production?" How indeed? Yet after thirty years of meaningless praise and equally meaningless abuse, it is no wonder that Tennessee is a bit batty. On those rare occasions when Tennessee's literary peers have got around to looking at his work, the result has been depressing: witness, Mary McCarthy's piece "A Streetcar Named Success."

There have been complaints that these *Memoirs* tell us too much about Tennessee's sex life and too little about his art. Personally, I find the candor about his sex life interesting if not illuminating. At the worst, it will feed that homophobia which is too much a part of the national psyche. Yet perhaps it is better to write this sort of thing oneself rather than leave it to others to invent.

Recently that venerable vendor of book-chat Alfred Kazin wrote, "Vidal gets more literary mileage out of his sex life than anyone since Oscar Wilde and Jean Cocteau." This struck me as breathtakingly wrong. First, neither Wilde nor Cocteau ever exploited his sex life for "mileage." Each was reticent in public. Eventually the law revealed the private life of the first, while friends (and an ambiguous sort of unsigned memoir) revealed the life of the second. The book-chat writer does mention the admittedly too many interviews I've lately given to magazines like *Playboy* where sex is always a Solemn and Sacred subject and where I, too, am Solemn but never personal. As evidence of my seeking mileage he quotes the rather lame " 'In youth I never missed a trick . . . I tried everything . . . I could no more go to bed with somebody whose work I admired than I could . . . well, make love to a mirror. Fame in others switches off desire.' " Not, I would say, the most prurient of giveaway lines. Except in *Two Sisters,* a memoir done with mirrors, I have not used myself as a subject for private analysis on the ground that since we live in a time where the personality of the writer is everything and what he writes is nothing, only a fool would aid the enemy by helping to trivialize life, work.

A columnist reports that Tennessee was obliged to cut his *Memoirs* in half because of the "filth." I hope that we are given that other half one day; and I doubt that there will be much "filth," only indiscretions which ought to be interesting. After all, Tennessee has known or come across a great many of our time's movers and shakers. I say "come across" because for a long period he was . . . well, inattentive. Sometimes the stupefying combination of Nembutal and vodka (now abandoned) addled him. I was present when Edna Ferber (yes, Edna Ferber) came over to our table at a restaurant and introduced herself. With considerable charm, she told Tennessee how much she admired him. He listened to her with eyes that had narrowed to what Miss Ferber would have described as "mere slits." As she walked away, the Bird hissed, "Why is that woman attacking me?"

Tennessee is the sort of writer who does not develop; he simply continues. By the time he was an adolescent he had his themes. Constantly he plays and replays the same small but brilliant set of cards. I am not aware that any new information (or feeling?) has got through to him in the twenty-eight years since our Roman spring. In consequence, we have drifted apart. "Gore no longer receives me," said the Bird to one of his innumerable interviewers; and he put this down to my allegedly glamorous social life. But the reason for the drifting apart is nothing more than difference of temperament. I am a compulsive learner of new things while the Bird's occasional and sporadic responses to the world outside the proscenium arch have not been fortunate. "Castro was, after all, a gentleman," he announced after an amiable meeting with the dictator. Tell that to the proscribed fags of Cuba.

Tennessee's much publicized conversion to Roman Catholicism took place during the time of his great confusion. Shortly after the Bird was received into the arms of Mother Church, a Jesuit priest rang him up and asked if he would like an audience with the Pope? a meeting with the head of the Jesuit order? Oh yes. Yes! Tennessee was delighted. The next morning the priest arrived to take Tennessee to the Vatican where, presumably, the Pope was waiting on tenderhooks to examine the

Church's latest haul. Unfortunately, Tennessee had forgotten all about the audience. He would have to beg off, he said; he was just not up to the Pope that day. The priest was stunned. The Pope's reaction has not been recorded.

The Jesuits, however, are made of tougher material. The secretary of the Black Pope rang to say that since a cocktail party had been arranged, Mr. Williams was going to be there, or else. The Bird was present. Almost immediately, he began to ham it up about God. Now if there is anything a Jesuit likes less than chat of God, it is having to listen to the religious enthusiasm of a layman. Trying to deflect Tennessee from what was fast turning into a Billy Graham exhortation about God and goodness, one of the Jesuits asked, "How do you start to write a play, Mr. Williams?" The Bird barely paused in his glorious ascent. "I start," he said sharply, "with a sentence." He then told the assembled members of the Society of Jesus that ever since becoming a Roman Catholic, he had felt a divine presence constantly with him. The Jesuits shifted uneasily at this. Like the old trouper he is, the Bird then paused abruptly in midflight in order to see just what effect he was having. After a moment of embarrassed silence, one of the Jesuits asked, timidly, "Is this presence a *warm* presence?"

"There is," said the Bird firmly, "no temperature."

But despite the "conversion," Tennessee now writes, "I am unable to believe that there is anything but permanent oblivion after death. . . . For me, what is there but to feel beneath me the steadily rising current of mortality and to summon from my blood whatever courage is native to it, and once there was a great deal." As he ends the *Memoirs,* he thinks back upon Hart Crane, whose legend has always haunted him. But though a romantic, Tennessee is no Crane. For one thing, it is too late to choose an abrupt death at sea. For another, art is too beguiling and difficult: "life is made up of moment-to-moment occurrences in the nerves and the perceptions, and try as you may, you can't commit them to the actualities of your own history."

But Tennessee continues to try. Now he has invited the world to take a close look at him, more or less as he is (the lighting of course has been carefully arranged, and he is not one to confuse an Entrance with an Exit). The result should be gratifying. The Glorious Bird is not only recognized but applauded in the streets. When he came to sign copies of the *Memoirs* in a large Manhattan bookstore, nearly a thousand copies were sold and the store had to be shut because of overcrowding. The resemblance to the latter days of Judy Garland would be disquieting were it not for the happy fact that since Tennessee cannot now die young he will probably not die at all (his grandfather lived for almost a century). In any case, artists who continue to find exhilarating the puzzles art proposes never grow bored and so have no need of death.

As for life? Well, that is a hard matter. But it was always a hard matter for those of us born with a sense of the transiency of these borrowed atoms that make up our corporeal being.

"I need," Tennessee writes with sudden poignancy, "somebody to laugh with." Well, don't we all, Bird? Anyway, be happy that your art has proved to be one of those stones that really did make it to Henge, enabling future magicians to gauge from its crafty placement not only the dour winter solstice of our last days but the summer solstice, too— the golden dream, the mimosa, the total freedom, and all that lovely time unspent now spent.

*The New York Review of Books*
February 5, 1976

# *THE FOURTH DIARY*
# *OF ANAÏS NIN*

Last year, Anaïs Nin cabled me in Rome: Volume Four of her diaries (1944–47) was to be published. She needed my permission to print what she had written about me. Into the time machine, I thought, as I entered the bar of the Pont Royal in Paris—to find Anaïs, at sixty-seven, as beautiful as ever. "I've been on television all day. West German television, with Jeanne Moreau. In the park." She gave me a hard look. (I had been told that she thought the character of Marietta Donegal in *Two Sisters* was based on her).

"I've marked the pages where you appear. It's very systematic. Edmund Wilson was wonderful about his portrait." Fifteen-love, Vidal's serve. "Now, anything you want cut, I'll take out. But if there is too much to cut, then the whole thing comes out." I was torn. I believe nothing should be suppressed; yet I knew all about Anaïs's "portraits." Once she had copied out in a red notebook everything she had written about me over the years. I kept the notebook for some months, unopened (I had read parts of the diary before); not pleased, she took it back.

Now, drinking tea, I read dutifully the pages that she showed me (not, incidentally, the entire portrait—several fine warts were withheld for the current exhibition). I suggested that she cut a line or two involving a third person. She agreed, obviously relieved that I, too, was intent on being wonderful. Then I was reproached for *Two Sisters*.

"I didn't read it, of course—I don't read that sort of book—but I was told it was a hideous caricature." I explained that neither the character of Marietta Donegal (a racketing, boisterous American lady of letters) nor the Relationship (with Anaïs one feels that the word "relationship" deserves a capital "R"—at least to start with) between her and me in the novel-memoir was at all like ours in life; in fact, rather the reverse. But I did admit that Marietta's "philosophy" ("We must flow deeply from the core of our inner being") was very much like hers and I thought that in an age when mind was under fire and feeling worshiped, a playful travesty was in order. She took that well enough. She was aware that we no longer felt the same way about things. "Anyway, you said—I was told—that I wrote well."

Who then is Anaïs Nin? Born in 1903; daughter of a Spanish composer-pianist; brought up in France; unhappily transplanted to New York as a child, where she began to keep a diary in order to win her absent father's love—a tall order and, consequently, a vast diary running now to many millions of words.

In the early thirties Anaïs returned to France, married a wealthy businessman (not mentioned in her earlier volumes), played at being a poor artist ("Never understood until now—1945—why I had to make myself poor enough in Paris to go to the pawnshop. It was because all my friends went there, and I wanted to reach the same level of poverty and denial"), met and helped to launch Henry Miller. She also began to write poetic monologues like *House of Incest* and *Winter of Artifice*.

At the start of the war, she came back to New York, with a second wealthy husband who makes—at his request—no appearance in the diaries. Together they created a romantic Bohemian atmosphere in a five-floor walk-up apartment in the Village. Again she played at poverty (I was shocked when she told me one day that I should let her husband pay for dinner because he was not a poor artist, as they had pretended, but a banker). Failing to get her books published commercially, she printed them herself.

One of the books was a volume of short stories, *Under a Glass Bell.* Edmund Wilson praised it in *The New Yorker.* She was overnight a celebrity, and the present diary begins.

Right off, we meet her life-force companion of earlier days, Gonzalo. He is working at the press she has financed, and helped him, physically, to set up. "Gonzalo has assumed leadership. He is proud of his place, his machine, his independence. I am very tired, but content. I am proud of my human creation." She is not unlike the Feiffer heroine who wants "a strong man that I can mould." Her persistent fantasy is that she is Joan of Arc forever putting Dauphins on the throne. Unfortunately, whenever Dauphin becomes King, she becomes regicide—that is, when she does not try to seize the throne herself—a normal human power drive, as Women's Lib has taught us, but for a Latin woman of her generation, a source of shame and guilt.

As the months pass, Gonzalo does not keep his word, is destructive, must be sent to Peru—and she worries about how much of herself she gives to others: "Did my faith in Henry [Miller] make him strong enough to go on without me? Does one really create strength in others, or does one merely become that strength?" Each Relationship begins on a high note, and ends with recriminations.

Meanwhile, Edmund Wilson has fallen in love with Anaïs but she prefers the companionship of several young men ("the transparent children") who shield her from the grossness of the harsh, competitive New York world. Incidentally, although she resolutely invades the privacy of others, her own is respected. We never know whom she goes to bed with. But certain emotional patterns do keep recurring and one can work out, up to a point, her Relationships.

It is fun to watch Anaïs as she becomes a figure in the High Bohemia of New York, the world of surrealist emigrés like Breton, of such native ground figures as James Agee, Richard Wright, Maya Deren (another relationship—small "r"—which starts magically and ends with recriminations: Maya made Anaïs look old in her film "Ritual and Ordeal"). Then, 1945, we meet the twenty-year-old author of the novel *Williwaw,* Warrant Officer (still in uniform) Gore Vidal, recently returned from the Aleutians, more recently hired as an editor by E. P. Dutton—where I lasted six months in order to get them to publish Anaïs's *Ladders to Fire* and *Children of the Albatross.* Incidentally, the photograph of me in the book is labeled "Gore Vidal at seventeen." It is actually Gore Vidal at twenty-one, looking glum as a result of a dose of clap picked up the week before in Guatemala City.

Volume Four is most interesting when it deals with Anaïs's career and the way she went about promoting it. She is forever conferring with book publishers, with editors of *Harper's Bazaar* and *Town and Country,* posing for photographs, meeting helpful people, lecturing. At Harvard "I wore a black dress and a shocking pink scarf. I won many people, even some who were openly prejudiced. . . ." She frets about bad reviews, presides eventually over the dissolution of her court of young men. Like everyone else, the children fail her, too.

She strikes a "death blow" at me, ending Phase One of a long, long Relationship. Then, with a friend, she drives across America. This is much the pleasantest part of the journal, for she responds with an uncharacteristic directness and delight to landscape. In Big Sur she meets Miller again, and his new wife. Next she moves on to Aca-pulco—a fishing village in those days, and there the diary ends.

Over the years defenders of Anaïs Nin—myself included—have main-tained that whatever the shortcomings of her books, the diaries, their primal source, would one day establish her as a great sensibility. Now here they are, and I am not so certain. Admittedly, she has left out a great deal. Of the two analysts she was going to (1944–47), only one is mentioned. And at least two Meaningful Relationships are entirely omitted. What she has done is shrewdly excerpt those pages which deal with people well known to readers today. The result is not the whole truth but an interesting *tour d'horizon* of her works and days, loves and hates among the celebrated of lost time, and for me reading her is like a feast of madeleines awash with tea.

The commonest complaint about Anaïs's work is its (her) narcissism. Since I cannot think of any modern writer who is not a narcissist (if you cannot love yourself, you cannot love anyone), it seems to me unfair to accuse her of a fault common to our monkey race. Yet her self-absorp-tion does put people off and I think it has to do with what Wilson calls her "solemn, hieratic style." Not only does she write an inflated, oracu-lar prose, but she is never able to get outside her characters. This would be tolerable if she were able to illuminate their interiors; something she seldom does, and for an odd reason.

There are two kinds of narcissist: objective and subjective. The objec-tive looks into the mirror and sees the lines, sees death upon the brow, and records it. The subjective stares with rapture into the mirror, sees a vision no one else can see and, if he lacks great art, fails entirely to communicate it. At her best, Anaïs Nin can write very beautifully indeed. Suddenly a phrase gleams upon the page: she does notice things, one decides, looking forward to the next line but then the dread flow of adjectives begins and one realizes that she is not seeing but writing. Since she is not a fool, she is aware of her limitations, yet, like the rest of us, she rather treasures them. "What had happened is that I have touched off such a deep level of unconscious life that the women" (in *Ladders to Fire*) "lose their separate and instinctive traits and flow into one another. As if I were writing about the night life of woman and it all became one." Not able to deal with other women, she can only write of herself apostrophized. People exist for her only as pairs of eyes in which to catch her own reflection. No wonder their owners so often disappoint her. They want mirrors, too.

The diaries present a real problem. Anaïs is dealing with actual people. Yet I would not recognize any of them (including myself) had she not carefully labeled each specimen. She is particularly devastating in her portrait of Edmund Wilson. She disliked him almost from the beginning. But since he was the most important critic of the day, she saw a good deal of him, and played at loving friendship. At lunch, "I felt his distress, received his confession. He tells me about his sufferings with Mary McCarthy."

Later Anaïs writes to a young friend, Leonard, assuring him that she prefers his company to that of Wilson "who asserts his opinions, beliefs, and knowledge as the ultimate verity." Then she gives us a fine description of an evening at Wilson's empty house ("Mary took away all the furniture"). But "when he talked about my work, he had more to say about the flaws of 'Winter of Artifice' and little about the achievements." The evening ends with Wilson in the street, crying after her, "Don't desert me! Don't leave me alone!" Like Georges Sand, Anaïs Nin is no gentleman. She meditates on going to bed with him, but decides "if he ever tastes of me, [he] will be eating a substance not good for him, some phosphorescent matter which illuminates the soul and does not answer to lust." The Relationship ends when he offers to teach her how to write, and presents her with a complete set of Jane Austen, the perfect insult. She responds seriously, "I am not an imitator of past styles." This is splendid comedy of the Meredithean sort; made all the finer by the fact that at no point is she aware of having been in the presence of America's best mind. But then Wilson represents all that she hates, history, politics, literature. To her, mind and feeling must be forever at war. Thus has she systematically unbalanced both art and life.

If there is one theme to Volume Four, it is Anaïs's formidable will to power. Yet she is able to write, apropos my own, "For the first time I saw a contrast in our aims. [Gore's] interest is like Miller's, to meet everybody, to win the world." She is even able to record with a straight pen, "Writing in a diary developed several habits: a habit of honesty (because no one imagines the diary will ever be read)." This was written in June 1946, when, at her insistence, I was trying to get Dutton to publish the childhood diary. The diary was always meant to be read, for it was her vindication, her victory over the unloving father.

Anaïs Nin has been, literally, avant-garde. In her contempt for intellect, her mystical belief in Love (the record of human disaster in the journals is not the whole story), in her wholehearted acceptance of psychoanalysis and astrology, she was a precursor of that generation which now grooves along emotional lines she helped engineer. For them, too, there is no history, no literature, no mind. Feeling is everything and astrology, like man, is heavy. But then mind has never had more than a fragile foothold in the United States, a society where intelligence is always on sufferance, as D. H. Lawrence observed, and subject to the majority's will.

Warning to literary historians. Deal warily with Anaïs's "facts." Small example: at our first meeting, she says, I introduced myself as Lieutenant Vidal. First, I would never have used a military title; second, I was plainly a Warrant Officer, in uniform. When I pointed this out to her in the bar of the Pont Royal, she laughed gaily. "You know, I never get those things right." Nor does she correct them. Best of the lines I was not shown (and the one most apt to give pleasure to the employees at *Time*), "Gore has a prejudice against Negroes." Oh, dear. Well, I was brought up by my grandfather, a Mississippi-born senator. I have since matured. I now have a prejudice against whites.

Finally, I do not really recognize Anaïs—or myself—in these bitter pages. Yet when I think of her and the splendid times we had so many years ago, I find myself smiling, recalling with pleasure her soft voice, her French accent, and the way she always said "yatch" instead of "yacht." That makes up for a lot.

*The Los Angeles Times Book Review*
September 26, 1971

# 104

# WRITING PLAYS
# FOR TELEVISION

Until I began to write plays for television, I entertained an amiable contempt for my stagestruck playwright friends who so meekly (masochistically, I thought) submitted their talents to the irrelevant strictures of directors and stars, of newspapermen in Wilmington and of sudden, brief acquaintances in hotel rooms. I had taken to heart the failure of the prose writer in the theater. From Smollett's irritable attempts to get his tragedy produced to Henry James as he was jeered from the stage on his first night, the novelist has cut a ponderous, sad figure beneath the proscenium arch. As a novelist, I was wary, preferring to suffer my reverses and petty triumphs on the familiar ground of prose and *not* in the theater, strewn already with the corpses of illustrious confrères.

The reason for our party's failure in what should have been a natural arena is caught in Flaubert's phrase: "The theater is not an art but a secret." And the secret is deceptively simple: dialogue is not prose. It is another language, and a talent for the novel does not necessarily mean a talent for the theater. The novel is the more private and (to me) the more satisfying art. A novel is all one's own, a world fashioned by a single intelligence, its reality in no way dependent upon the collective excellence of others. Also the mountebankery, the plain showmanship which is necessary to playwriting, strikes the novelist as disagreeably broad. One must show *every* collision on the stage, while in the novel it is often a virtue to avoid the obvious scene, to come at the great moments obliquely. Even dialogue is not the same in a novel as it is on the stage. Seldom can dialogue be taken from a book and played by actors. The reason is one of pace rather than of verisimilitude. Certainly, in our country, most novelists have an accurate ear for speech; it is a gift liberally bestowed upon the good and the bad alike, the gray badge of naturalism. Yet in the novel, *duration* differs from the stage. The novelist's arrangement of dialogue is seldom as concentrated as the playwright's, whose line must finally be achieved by people talking, unassisted by an author's stage management.

Aware of the essential difference between the novel and the play, I kept happily to my own country until the black winter of 1953, when I realized in a moment of revelation that the novel as a popular art form had come to a full halt. There were many reasons. Television had stunned it. The new critics had laid it out all neat in a blue suit, a flower in its waxy hands (HERE LIES THE NOVEL, EXPLICATED), and their funeral orations were already under way in the literary quarterlies. The newspaper reviewers, lagging in their serene way some twenty years behind the fact, wanted more Kipling and less art, while the public, its attention distracted by television and the movies, firmly refused to pay five dollars for anyone's novel, aware that if a book contained enough healthy American sadism they could eventually buy it in a cheap paperback edition. By 1953, unpopular novelists like myself were living precariously on the bounty of reprint publishers; a bounty which ended when those jolly opportunists flooded the newsstands, sinking many, both good and bad. Needless to say, none of this happened quickly. Disaster approached with stealthy tread, and not until my revelation did I awaken to the harshness of the situation: that I was on the verge of providing future thesis writers with a poignant page or two of metropolitan suffering, before I went off to Africa to run rifles.

But happily, when faced with ruin, all one's cunning and resourcefulness rush to the surface, and if one's career is conducted beneath a beneficent star, crisis is healthy. I looked about me. I had been a novelist for a decade. I had been hailed as the peer of Voltaire, Henry James, Jack London, Ronald Firbank and James T. Farrell. My early, least satisfactory works had been best-sellers. Though not yet thirty years old, I was referred to in the past tense, as one of those novelists of the 1940s from whom so much had been expected.

I turned to my peers to see what they were doing. I discovered that the most colorful was writing unsuccessful musical comedies and the most talented had virtuously contrived to die. The others had dropped from view, most of them finding dim employment either in anonymous journalism or in the academy. The cleverest ones had married rich wives and traveled a lot. The prospect was not flooded with light.

But one must live, as they say, and since I do not write popular short stories or journalism, or teach, and since I was spoiled by ten years of receiving money for work that I would have done whether I had been paid or not (the happiest of lives and the luckiest), it looked very much as if I should have to turn to the fantasy world of business and get a job. At that crucial moment, I discovered television.

I had not watched television until the winter I decided to write for it. At the time, its great advantage for me was proximity. I live on the bank of the Hudson, and there to the south, in New York City, was this fine source of revenue. I was intrigued. I was soon enthralled. Right off, there is the immediacy of playwriting. There they are, one's own creations, fleshed out by living people, the symbolic detail isolated by the camera as millions of strangers in their homes watch one's private vision made public. The day after my debut in February of 1954, I was committed seriously to writing for the camera. I discovered that although the restrictions imposed by a popular medium are not always agreeable, they do at least make creative demands upon one's ingenuity. More often than not, the tension between what one is not allowed to say and what one must say creates ingenious effects which, given total freedom, might never have been forced from the imagination. The only analogy I can think of is the nineteenth-century novel. Nearly all the productions of that extraordinary age were published first in magazines edited for gentlewomen and supervised by Mrs. Grundy, her fist full of asterisks. There was so much the harried novelist could *not* say that he was impelled to freight heavily what he *could* say with other meanings, accomplishing the great things by indirection, through association and logical echo.

The same is true now in television. With patience and ingenuity there is nothing that the imaginative writer cannot say to the innocent millions. Of course the naturalistic writer has a more difficult time. He is used to making his point directly and bluntly: *You are a slut.* And he is morose when he cannot bluntly hammer out the obvious, the way he could on the stage or in the lower novel. But for my kind of second-story work, television is less confining. Also, the dramatic art is particularly satisfying for any writer with a polemical bent; and I am at heart a propagandist, a tremendous hater, a tiresome nag, complacently positive that there is no human problem which could not be solved if people would simply do as I advise. This sort of intensity, no matter how idiotic, works well in the drama if only because there is nothing more effective than having something to say.

As for the world of television, the notable characteristics are youth and enthusiasm. The dramatists, directors and producers are all young men, and their deep pleasure in this new toy is communicable and heartening. There is none of the bored cynicism one often finds in Hollywood studios, nor any of the rapacity and bad temper endemic to the theater in New York. Most television plays are bad, but considering that television uses up hundreds of new plays a year and that there have not been a hundred fine plays written in the last two thousand years, they can be excused their failures if their intentions are honorable. And at the moment, the very real sense of honor the better television writers possess lends excitement to their work.

Another novelty for me has been working with people. I had never before worked with anyone, and the thought of belonging to a group was unnerving. But to my surprise I enjoyed it. Working on a play is not unlike being stranded on an island with a group of strangers from a foundered ship's company. For ten days, actors, director, author, technicians work together, getting to know one another almost morbidly well. Then, when the play is over, sadly, sweetly, the players and the management separate, never to meet again—until the next play together.

A play on television of the sort I write is not filmed. It is seen on the air at the exact moment it is performed. The actors build their performances as they would on the stage. The only difference is that they are being photographed by three cameras and we, the audience, are watching a play as though it were a movie.

In the last two years I have written nearly twenty plays. All but seven were either half-hour plays or adaptations. Incidentally, adapting is neither easier nor more difficult than writing an original play. There is, I think, only one basic trick to it: simply knowing how to read precisely and critically. One must get the point of the work. I make this obvious comment because just as literary men are seldom playwrights, playwrights are almost never literary men, and they are usually baffled and bored by the slower, denser order of the novel. In fact, excepting the poet-dramatists, there is a good case that the drama is not literature at all but an entirely separate art requiring collective means to achieve its moments, sharing with prose nothing beyond the general human preoccupation. A gift for playwriting is only a form of cleverness, like being adept at charades or Double-Crostics, while novel writing goes, at its best, beyond cleverness to that point where one's whole mind and experience and vision *are* the novel and the effort to translate this wholeness into prose *is* the life: a circle of creation.

Of course it can be argued that a Shaw or a Chekhov achieves a comparable wholeness in the theater, but the very exceptionalness of any play which is better than viable suggests the narrow boundaries of a literary form whose effectiveness depends as much on interpretation as on the line written, the idea proposed, the light cast. We have all been moved by plays whose productions led us to believe that truth had rent the air about us, only to find later, upon reading the script, that we were tricked, or rather *served* beautifully, in the theater by a number of talents of which the writer's was but one, and perhaps the least.

There are a number of mechanical limitations in television which time may eliminate. For instance, a play done "live" is seen only once, and that is the end. So many fine performances, so many good plays written on air, with nothing to show for all the work done but a kinescope (a filmed record of the play) that because of labor-union and technical considerations may not be shown again on television. It is a waste of many talents. Someday, perhaps on the new magnetic tape, a play which is broadcast live will be accurately recorded and reshown.

One would also like to see a repertory system in television, not only for the actors of course (television *is* a kind of repertory for actors, providing the talented with work and experience) but for the redoing of plays whose value has been established; and there are now a number of interesting plays to choose from. Finally, waiting in the wings, is something called subscription television. Certain productions will be available only to those viewers who pay to see them, a miraculous state of affairs for the writer, who will then have an audience which in a sense is *his* and not accidental. Also, he will be free of those nervous men the advertisers, who now largely control television.

All things considered, I suspect that the Golden Age for the dramatist is at hand. There is so much air to be illustrated, so many eyes watching, so much money to be spent, so many fine technicians and interpreters at one's command, that the playwright cannot but thrive.

# 105

# VISIT TO A SMALL PLANET

I am not at heart a playwright. I am a novelist turned temporary adventurer; and I chose to write television, movies, and plays for much the same reason that Henry Morgan selected the Spanish Main for his peculiar—and not dissimilar—sphere of operations. The reasons for my conversion to piracy are to me poignant, and to students of our society perhaps significant.

If I may recall in nostalgic terms the near past, I began writing novels at the end of the Second World War. Those were the happy years when a new era in our letters was everywhere proclaimed. We would have, it was thought, a literature to celebrate the new American empire. Our writers in reflecting our glory would complement the beautiful hardness of our currency. But something went wrong. The new era did not materialize and the work of my generation was dismissed—for the present at least—as a false dawn. It is a fact that the novel as a popular art form retrogressed gravely in our reign. Not clever enough to interest the better critics or simple enough to divert the public, we lost the critics to pure criticism and the public to impure television. By the 1950s I and my once golden peers were plunged into that dim cellar of literature characterized as "serious," where, like the priests of some occluded god, we were left to tend our prose privately: so many exiles, growing mush-rooms in the dark.

The passage of time has only confirmed the new order. Less and less often is that widening division between the commercially possible and the seriously meaningful bridged by the rare creator who is both. Most of the large publishing events of recent years have been the crudely recollected experiences of nonwriters. Lost is the old conception of the man of letters creating a life's work to be enjoyed by the common reader in continuity. True, that nineteenth-century phenomenon never quite took root in this country; for lovely though New England's Indian summer was, winter when it came was killing. Nowadays, our better literary men seek refuge in the universities, leaving what is left of the public novel to transient primitives and to sturdy hacks. Nor, let me say, are the serious writers themselves responsible for their unpopularity, as our more chauvinistic editorial writers would have it. The good work of the age is being done, as always. Rather it is the public which has changed. Television, movies, the ease of travel . . . so many new diversions have claimed the attention of that public which once read that I think it doubtful if the novel will ever again have the enormous prestige, the universal audience it enjoyed that fine morning when an idler on a Mississippi wharf shouted to the pilot of a passing steamer: "Is Little Nell dead?" And, alas, Mistah Kurtz, he dead, too; solemnly embalmed by the Academy.

Today, the large audience holds communion in a new, more compelling establishment. I doubt if many Americans could identify a single character in a work of modern fiction, but there are few who could not describe in exact detail the latest comedian's joke on television. Yet it is vain to deplore a cultural change. If after two pre-eminent centuries the novel no longer is useful to the public, only novelists need mourn, for it is a fact of civilization that each society creates the games it wants to play and rejects those it regards as irrelevant.

The main audience has turned back to the play (in all its various forms, both "live" and filmed). Nevertheless, it is a stoic consolation for those of us whose first allegiance is to the novel to know that there will always be some serious interest in one's work and that the keys to the kingdom of prose will continue to be passed on from hand to hand. And though I rather suspect that in a century's time the novel will be as rare and private an art form as poetry today or that delicate and laborious process by which dedicated men fire glass with color, it will always be worth the doing.

Over the years I attempted three stage plays. When I was nineteen I wrote a quasi-poetical work about, Heaven alone knows why, a man who became a werewolf in Manhattan. I destroyed all copies of this early effort only to learn recently that a collector has somehow got hold of a copy, a ghastly prospect for some as yet unborn English major.

The next play I wrote was on an equally obscure subject, written in a frenzy in the spring of 1948 at Shepheard's Hotel in Cairo. Later that summer, I gave it to Tennessee Williams to read. He pronounced it the worst play he'd read in some time, and I solemnly abandoned playwriting for good, after first pointing out to him that a literary form which depended on the combined excellence of others for its execution could hardly be worth the attention of a serious writer, adding with deliberate cruelty that I did not envy him being stagestruck and his life taken up with such frivolous people as actors and directors. He agreed that I should not expose myself just yet to this sort of tedium.

Six years later, driven by necessity, I took the plunge into television, the very heart of darkness, and to my surprise found that I liked it. But despite television's raw youth there is a tradition already firmly established that comedies seldom work on the small screen and that satire never does. Like most traditions, this one is founded on a part truth. For one thing, the comedy timing of stage-trained actors is inevitably affected by the absence of human response during a performance, and for another several people sitting at home glumly staring at a television set are not apt to find anything very amusing unless it is heavily underscored by laughter from a studio audience. And plays on television are performed without audiences.

Satire presents a further difficulty for the mass audience. If satire is to be effective, the audience must be aware of the thing satirized. If they are not, the joke falls flat. Unfortunately for our native satirists, the American mass audience possesses very little general information on any subject. Each individual knows his own immediate world, but, as various research polls continually inform us, he holds little knowledge in common with others. Even political jokes, if they were allowed on television, would not have much relevance. Recently one national poll disclosed that almost half of those queried could not identify the Secretary of State. The size of the population has much to do with this collective ignorance. When Aristophanes made a satiric point, he could be confident that his audience would appreciate his slyest nuance because in a small community each citizen was bound to share with his fellows a certain amount of general information—literary, religious, and political. National units today are too large and, in America at least, education too bland to hope for much change. As a result, satire, unless done very broadly puzzles and irritates rather than amuses.

I have often thought that the domination of naturalism in our letters is directly attributable to the breakdown of the old homogeneous American society of the nineteenth century, caused by the influx of immigration, the discovery of exciting new machinery, the ease of travel. Before this burst of population and invention, an educated man, writing allusively, could assume that his readers would respond knowledgeably to a fairly large number of references both literary and social. Since 1900 this has been less and less possible, and it is no coincidence that naturalism should be to this day the preferred manner in the novel, if only because the naturalistic writer, by definition, takes nothing for granted. He assumes that the reader knows no more than he chooses to tell. He constructs a literal world of concrete detail. His narrative is easily followed. He records the surface of life with a photographer's care, leaving the interpretation, the truth of his record, to the reader's imagination. The result is that our time's most successful *popular* writing is journalism, another dagger at the novel's heart.

The idea for *Visit to a Small Planet* (from outer space arrives a charming hobbyist named Kreton whose blithe intent it is to start a war: "I mean it's the one thing you people down here do *really* well!") was rejected by three television sponsors before Philco-Goodyear Playhouse bought it. I was told that the advertisers found the premise alarming, which was certainly disingenuous of them. Had I not spun my fragile satire about the one glittering constant in human affairs, the single pastime that never palls: war? In fact, one might say that *Visit* is the happiest of pro-war plays.

But only Philco saw the charm of this conceit, and on the night of May 8, 1955, it was telecast. With some anxiety we waited for the roof to fall in. To my surprise it did not, and most people were pleased with the result. I was then informed that a producer would like me to do a stage version for Broadway. And so it came to pass. Expansion was not difficult. As a novelist, I was accustomed to using a hundred thousand words to net my meaning. My problem theatrically has always been one of compression.

After the script was ready there were the usual trials, delays, problems of temperament; each participant convinced that the others had gone into secret league to contrive his professional ruin (and on occasion cabals did flourish, for the theater is a child's world).

On January 16, 1957, the play opened in New Haven. From that moment until the New York opening on February 7, I was more dentist than writer, extracting the sharper (and not always carious) teeth. The heart of the play's argument was a scene in the second act between Kreton and the Secretary-General of the United Nations. At each performance the audience, charmed by the fooling that had gone before, grew deathly cold as the debate began. This was not what they had anticipated (a fault, I own, of the dramaturgy), and their confidence in the play was never entirely regained. A few days before we left Boston, I replaced the scene with a lighter one, involving the principals and giving the curtain to our subtlest player, the cat. The substitute was engaging; the play moved amiably; no one was shocked. (Earlier, some observers in New Haven had declared the entire conception unwholesomely menacing. If only they had seen the first draft of the play, in which I blew up the whole world at the end, the perfect curtain.) So by deliberate dulling of the edge of the satire, the farce flourished.

A number of reviewers described the play as a vaudeville, a very apt description and one in which I concur, recalling a letter from Bernard Shaw to Granville-Barker: "I have given you a series of first-rate music hall entertainments thinly disguised as plays, but really offering the public a unique string of turns by comics and serio-comics of every popular type." That of course is only half the truth, but it is the amiable half. In the case of *Visit,* the comedic approach to the theme tended to dictate the form. Having no real commitment to the theater, no profound convictions about the well-made or the ill-made play, I tend to write as an audience, an easily bored audience. I wrote the sort of piece I should like to go to a theater to see, one in which people say and do things that make me laugh. And though monsters lurk beneath the surface, their presence is sensed rather than dramatically revealed. My view of reality is not sanguine, and the play for all its blitheness turns resolutely toward a cold night. Fortunately for the play's success, the incisors were extracted out of town and the venture was a hit. But in that word "hit" lies the problem.

I was obliged to protect an eighty-thousand-dollar investment, and I confess freely that I obscured meanings, softened blows, and humbly turned wrath aside, emerging with a successful play which represented me only a little. It is not that what was fashioned was bad or corrupt; I rather fancy the farce we ended up with, and I think it has a good deal of wear in it. But the play that might have been, though hardly earth-shaking, was far more interesting and true. Like too many others I played the game stolidly according to rules I abhorred, realizing that the theater and its writers are seriously, perhaps fatally, hampered by economic pressure. Because it costs too much to put on a play, one works in a state of hysteria. Everything is geared to success. Yet art is mostly failure. It is only from a succession of daring, flawed works that the occasional masterwork comes. But in the Broadway theater to fail is death, and in an atmosphere so feverish it is difficult to work with much objectivity. Only the honest hacks have a good time of it. Cannily, they run up a banner: It's just us again, kids, trying to make a buck. And they are let off with genial contempt. It is the crankier, more difficult writers who must work at a disadvantage, and efforts to divert them into familiar safe channels are usually disastrous. Is there a solution? I see none; unless it be the decentralization of the theater to the smaller cities and to the universities, where the means of production will be less than good but the freedom greater, particularly the luxurious freedom to fail.

*The Reporter*
July 11, 1957

# 106

##### ◆

# WHO MAKES
# THE MOVIES?

Forty-nine years ago last October Al Jolson not only filled with hideous song the sound track of a film called *The Jazz Singer,* he also spoke. With the words "You ain't heard nothin' yet" (surely the most menacing line in the history of world drama), the age of the screen director came to an end and the age of the screenwriter began.

Until 1927, the director was king, turning out by the mile his "molds of light" (André Bazin's nice phrase). But once the movies talked, the director as creator became secondary to the writer. Even now, except for an occasional director-writer like Ingmar Bergman,* the director tends to be the one interchangeable (if not entirely expendable) element in the making of a film. After all, there are thousands of movie technicians who can do what a director is supposed to do because, in fact, collectively (and sometimes individually) they actually do do his work behind the camera and in the cutter's room. On the other hand, there is no film without a written script.

*Questions I am advised to anticipate: What about such true auteurs du cinéma as Truffaut? Well, *Jules et Jim* was a novel by Henri-Pierre Roché. Did Truffaut adapt the screenplay by himself? No, he worked with Jean Gruault. Did Buñuel create *The Exterminating Angel*? No, it was "suggested" by an unpublished play by José Bergamin. Did Buñuel take it from there? No, he had as co-author Luis Alcorisa. So it goes.

In the Fifties when I came to MGM as a contract writer and took my place at the Writers' Table in the commissary, the Wise Hack used to tell us newcomers, "The director is the brother-in-law." Apparently the ambitious man became a producer (that's where the power was). The talented man became a writer (that's where the creation was). The pretty man became a star.

Even before Jolson spoke, the director had begun to give way to the producer. Director Lewis Milestone saw the writing on the screen as early as 1923 when "baby producer" Irving Thalberg fired the legendary director Erich von Stroheim from his film *Merry Go Round.* "That," wrote Milestone somberly in *New Theater and Film* (March 1937), "was the beginning of the storm and the end of the reign of the director. . . ." Even as late as 1950 the star Dick Powell assured the film cutter Robert Parrish that "anybody can direct a movie, even I could do it. I'd rather not because it would take too much time. I can make more money acting, selling real estate and playing the market." That was pretty much the way the director was viewed in the Thirties and Forties, the so-called classic age of the talking movie.

Although the essential creator of the classic Hollywood film was the writer, the actual master of the film was the producer, as Scott Fitzgerald recognized when he took as protagonist for his last novel Irving Thalberg. Although Thalberg himself was a lousy movie-maker, he was the head of production at MGM; and in those days MGM was a kind of Vatican where the chief of production was Pope, holding in his fists the golden keys of Schenck. The staff producers were the College of Cardinals. The movie stars were holy and valuable objects to be bought, borrowed, stolen. Like icons, they were moved from sound stage to sound stage, studio to studio, film to film, bringing in their wake good fortune and gold.

With certain exceptions (Alfred Hitchcock, for one), the directors were, at worst, brothers-in-law; at best, bright technicians. All in all, they were a cheery, unpretentious lot, and if anyone had told them that they were *auteurs du cinéma,* few could have coped with the concept, much less the French. They were technicians; proud commercialities, happy to serve what was optimistically known as The Industry.

This state of affairs lasted until television replaced the movies as America's principal dispenser of mass entertainment. Overnight the producers lost control of what was left of The Industry and, unexpectedly, the icons took charge. Apparently, during all those years when we thought the icons nothing more than beautiful painted images of all our dreams and lusts, they had been not only alive but secretly greedy for power and gold.

"The lunatics are running the asylum," moaned the Wise Hack at the Writers' Table, but soldiered on. Meanwhile, the icons started to produce, direct, even write. For a time, they were able to ignore the fact that with television on the rise, no movie star could outdraw *The $64,000 Question.* During this transitional decade, the director was still the brother-in-law. But instead of marrying himself off to a producer, he shacked up, as it were, with an icon. For a time each icon had his or her favorite director and The Industry was soon on the rocks.

Then out of France came the dreadful news: all those brothers-in-law of the classic era were really autonomous and original artists. Apparently each had his own style that impressed itself on every frame of any film he worked on. Proof? Since the director was the same person from film to film, each image of his *oeuvre* must then be stamped with his authorship. The argument was circular but no less overwhelming in its implications. Much quoted was Giraudoux's solemn inanity: "There are no works, there are only *auteurs.*"

The often wise André Bazin eventually ridiculed this notion in *La Politique des Auteurs,* but the damage was done in the pages of the magazine he founded, *Cahiers du cinéma.* The fact that, regardless of director, every Warner Brothers film during the classic age had a dark look owing to the Brothers' passion for saving money in electricity and set-dressing cut no ice with ambitious critics on the prowl for high art in a field once thought entirely low.

In 1948, Bazin's disciple Alexandre Astruc wrote the challenging *"La Caméra-stylo."* This manifesto advanced the notion that the director is—or should be—the true and solitary creator of a movie, "penning" his film on celluloid. Astruc thought that *caméra-stylo* could

tackle any subject, any genre. . . . I will even go so far as to say that contemporary ideas and philosophies of life are such that only the cinema can do justice to them. Maurice Nadeau wrote in an article in the newspaper *Combat:* "If Descartes lived today, he would write novels." With all due respect to Nadeau, a Descartes of today would already have shut himself up in his bedroom with a 16mm camera and some film, and would be writing his philosophy on film: for his *Discours de la Méthode* would today be of such a kind that only the cinema could express it satisfactorily.

With all due respect to Astruc, the cinema has many charming possibilities but it cannot convey complex ideas through words or even, paradoxically, dialogue in the Socratic sense. *Le Genou de Claire* is about as close as we shall ever come to dialectic in a film and though Rohmer's work has its delights, the ghost of Descartes is not very apt to abandon the marshaling of words on a page for the flickering shadows of talking heads. In any case, the Descartes of Astruc's period did not make a film; he wrote the novel *La Nausée.*

But the would-be camera-writers are not interested in philosophy or history or literature. They want only to acquire for the cinema the prestige of ancient forms without having first to crack the code. "Let's face it," writes Astruc:

between the pure cinema of the 1920s and filmed theater, there is plenty of room for a different and individual kind of film-making.

This of course implies that the scriptwriter directs his own scripts; or rather, that the scriptwriter ceases to exist, for in this kind of film-making the distinction between author and director loses all meaning. Direction is no longer a means of illustrating or presenting a scene, but a true act of writing.

It is curious that despite Astruc's fierce will to eliminate the scriptwriter (and perhaps literature itself), he is forced to use terms from the art form he would like to supersede. For him the film director uses a *pen* with which he *writes* in order to become—highest praise—an *author.*

As the French theories made their way across the Atlantic, bemused brothers-in-law found themselves being courted by odd-looking French youths with tape recorders. Details of long-forgotten Westerns were recalled and explicated. Every halting word from the *auteur*'s lips was taken down and reverently examined. The despised brothers-in-law of the Thirties were now Artists. With newfound confidence, directors started inking major pacts to meg superstar thesps whom the meggers could control as hyphenates: that is, as director-producers or even as writer-director-producers. Although the icons continued to be worshiped and overpaid, the truly big deals were now made by directors. To them, also, went the glory. For all practical purposes the producer has either vanished from the scene (the "package" is now put together by a "talent" agency) or merged with the director. Meanwhile, the screenwriter continues to be the prime creator of the talking film, and though he is generally paid very well and his name is listed right after that of the director in the movie reviews of *Time,* he is entirely in the shadow of the director just as the director was once in the shadow of the producer and the star.

What do directors actually do? What do screenwriters do? This is difficult to explain to those who have never been involved in the making of a film. It is particularly difficult when French theoreticians add to the confusion by devising false hypotheses (studio director as *auteur* in the Thirties) on which to build irrelevant and misleading theories. Actually, if Astruc and Bazin had wanted to be truly perverse (and almost accurate), they would have declared that the cameraman is the *auteur* of any film. They could then have ranked James Wong Howe with Dante, Braque, and Gandhi. Cameramen do tend to have styles in a way that the best writers do but most directors don't—style as opposed to preoccupation. Gregg Toland's camera work is a vivid fact from film to film, linking *Citizen Kane* to Wyler's *The Best Years of Our Lives* in a way that one cannot link *Citizen Kane* to, say, Welles's *Confidential Report*. Certainly the cameraman is usually more important than the director in the day-to-day making of a film as opposed to the preparation of a film. Once the film is shot the editor becomes the principal interpreter of the writer's invention.

Since there are few reliable accounts of the making of any of the classic talking movies, Pauline Kael's book on the making of *Citizen Kane* is a valuable document. In considerable detail she establishes the primacy in that enterprise of the screenwriter Herman Mankiewicz. The story of how Orson Welles saw to it that Mankiewicz became, officially, the noncreator of his own film is grimly fascinating and highly typical of the way so many director-hustlers acquire for themselves the writer's creation.* Few directors in this area possess the modesty of Kurosawa, who said, recently, "With a very good script, even a second-class director may make a first-class film. But with a bad script even a first-class director cannot make a really first-class film."

A useful if necessarily superficial look at the way movies were written in the classic era can be found in the pages of *Some Time in the Sun*. The author, Mr. Tom Dardis, examines the movie careers of five celebrated writers who took jobs as movie-writers. They are Scott Fitzgerald, Aldous Huxley, William Faulkner, Nathanael West, and James Agee.

Mr. Dardis's approach to his writers and to the movies is that of a deeply serious and highly concerned lowbrow, a type now heavily tenured in American Academe. He writes of "literate" dialogue, "mas-

---

*Peter Bogdanovich maintains that Kael's version of the making of *Citizen Kane* is not only inaccurate but highly unfair to Orson Welles, a master whom I revere.

sive" biographies. Magisterially, he misquotes Henry James on the subject of gold. More seriously, *he misquotes Joan Crawford.* She did not say to Fitzgerald, "Work hard, Mr. Fitzgerald, work hard!" when he was preparing a film for her. She said "*Write* hard. . . ." There are many small inaccuracies that set on edge the film buff's teeth. For instance, Mr. Dardis thinks that the hotel on Sunset Boulevard known, gorgeously, as The Garden of Allah is "now demolished and reduced to the status of a large parking lot. . . ." Well, it is not a parking lot. Hollywood has its own peculiar reverence for the past. The Garden of Allah was replaced by a bank that subtly suggests in glass and metal the mock-Saracen façade of the hotel that once housed Scott Fitzgerald. Mr. Dardis also thinks that the hotel was "demolished" during World War II. I stayed there in the late Fifties, right next door to fun-loving, bibulous Errol Flynn.

Errors and starry-eyed vulgarity to one side, Mr. Dardis has done a good deal of interesting research on how films were written and made in those days. For one thing, he catches the ambivalence felt by the writers who had descended (but only temporarily) from literature's Parnassus to the swampy marketplace of the movies. There was a tendency to play Lucifer. One was thought to have sold out. "Better to reign in hell than to serve in heaven," was more than once quoted—well, paraphrased—at the Writers' Table. We knew we smelled of sulphur. Needless to say, most of the time it was a lot of fun if the booze didn't get you.

For the Parnassian writer the movies were not just a means of making easy money; even under the worst conditions, movies were genuinely interesting to write. Mr. Dardis is at his best when he shows his writers taking seriously their various "assignments." The instinct to do good work is hard to eradicate.

Faulkner was the luckiest (and the most cynical) of Mr. Dardis's five. For one thing, he usually worked with Howard Hawks, a director who might actually qualify as an *auteur.* Hawks was himself a writer and he had a strong sense of how to manipulate those clichés that he could handle best. Together Faulkner and Hawks created a pair of satisfying movies, *To Have and Have Not* and *The Big Sleep.* But who did what? Apparently there is not enough remaining evidence (at least available to Mr. Dardis) to sort out authorship. Also, Faulkner's public line was pretty much: I'm just a hired hand who does what he's told.

Nunnally Johnson (as quoted by Mr. Dardis) found Hawks's professional relationship with Faulkner mysterious. "It may be that he simply

wanted his name attached to Faulkner's. Or since Hawks liked to write
it was easy to do it with Faulkner, for Bill didn't care much one way
or the other. . . . We shall probably never know just how much Bill cared
about any of the scripts he worked on with Hawks." Yet it is interesting
to note that Johnson takes it entirely for granted that the director
wants—and must get—*all* credit for a film.

Problem for the director: how to get a script without its author?
Partial solution: of all writers, the one who does not mind anonymity
is the one most apt to appeal to an ambitious director. When the studio
producer was king, he used to minimize the writer's role by assigning
a dozen writers to a script. No director today has the resources of the
old studios. But he can hire a writer who doesn't "care much one way
or the other." He can also put his name on the screen as co-author
(standard procedure in Italy and France). Even the noble Jean Renoir
played this game when he came to direct *The Southerner.* Faulkner not
only wrote the script, he liked the project. The picture's star Zachary
Scott has said that the script was entirely Faulkner's. But then, other
hands were engaged and "the whole problem," according to Mr. Dardis,
"of who did what was neatly solved by Renoir's giving himself sole
credit for the screenplay—the best way possible for an *auteur* director
to label his films."

Unlike Faulkner, Scott Fitzgerald cared deeply about movies; he
wanted to make a success of movie-writing and, all in all, if Mr. Dardis
is to be believed (and for what it may be worth, his account of Fitzgerald's time in the sun tallies with what one used to hear), he had a
far better and more healthy time of it in Hollywood than is generally
suspected.

Of a methodical nature, Fitzgerald ran a lot of films at the studio.
(Unlike Faulkner, who affected to respond only to Mickey Mouse and
Pathé News). Fitzgerald made notes. He also did what an ambitious
writer must do if he wants to write the sort of movie he himself might
want to see: he made friends with the producers. Rather censoriously,
Mr. Dardis notes Fitzgerald's "clearly stated intention to work with film
producers rather than with film directors, here downgraded to the rank
of 'collaborators.' Actually, Fitzgerald seems to have had no use whatsoever for directors as such." But neither did anyone else.

During much of this time Howard Hawks, say, was a low-budget
director known for the neatness and efficiency of his work. Not until the
French beatified him twenty years later did he appear to anyone as an
original artist instead of just another hired technician. It is true that

Hawks was allowed to work with writers, but then, he was at Warner Brothers, a frontier outpost facing upon barbarous Burbank. At MGM, the holy capital, writers and directors did not get much chance to work together. It was the producer who worked with the writer, and Scott Fitzgerald was an MGM writer. Even as late as my own years at MGM (1956–1958), the final script was the writer's creation (under the producer's supervision). The writer even pre-empted the director's most important function by describing each camera shot: Long, Medium, Close, and the director was expected faithfully to follow the writer's score.

One of the most successful directors at MGM during this period was George Cukor. In an essay on "The Director" (1938), Cukor reveals the game as it used to be played. "In most cases," he writes, "the director makes his appearance very early in the life story of a motion picture." I am sure that this was often the case with Cukor but the fact that he thinks it necessary to mention "early" participation is significant.

There are times when the whole idea for a film may come from [the director], but in a more usual case he makes his entry when he is summoned by a producer and it is suggested that he should be the director of a proposed story.

Not only was this the most usual way but, very often, the director left the producer's presence with the finished script under his arm. Cukor does describe his own experience working with writers but Cukor was something of a star at the studio. Most directors were "summoned" by the producer and told what to do. It is curious, incidentally, how entirely the idea of the working producer has vanished. He is no longer remembered except as the butt of familiar stories: fragile artist treated cruelly by insensitive cigar-smoking producer—or Fitzgerald savaged yet again by Joe Mankiewicz.

Of Mr. Dardis's five writers, James Agee is, to say the least, the lightest in literary weight. But he was a passionate film-goer and critic. He was a child of the movies just as Huxley was a child of Meredith and Peacock. Given a different temperament, luck, birth-date, Agee might have been the first American cinema *auteur:* a writer who wrote screenplays in such a way that, like the score of a symphony, they needed nothing more than a conductor's interpretation . . . an interpretation he could have provided himself and perhaps would have provided if he had lived.

Agee's screenplays were remarkably detailed. "All the shots," writes

Mr. Dardis, "were set down with extreme precision in a way that no other screenwriter had ever set things down before. . . ." This is exaggerated. Most screenwriters of the classic period wrote highly detailed scripts in order to direct the director but, certainly, the examples Mr. Dardis gives of Agee's screenplays show them to be remarkably visual. Most of us hear stories. He saw them, too. But I am not so sure that what he saw was the reflection of a living reality in his head. As with many of today's young directors, Agee's memory was crowded with memories not of life but of old films. For Agee, rain falling was not a memory of April at Exeter but a scene recalled from Eisenstein. This is particularly noticeable in the adaptation Agee made of Stephen Crane's *The Blue Hotel,* which, Mr. Dardis tells us, no "film director has yet taken on, although it has been televised twice, each time with a different director and cast and with the Agee script cut to the bone, being used only as a guidepost to the story." This is nonsense. In 1954, CBS hired me to adapt *The Blue Hotel.* I worked directly from Stephen Crane and did not know that James Agee had ever adapted it until I read *Some Time in the Sun.*

At the mention of any director's name, the Wise Hack at the Writers' Table would bark out a percentage, representing how much, in his estimate, a given director would subtract from the potential 100 percent of the script he was directing. The thought that a director might *add* something worthwhile never crossed the good gray Hack's mind. Certainly he would have found hilarious David Thomson's *A Biographical Dictionary of Film,* whose haphazard pages are studded with tributes to directors.

Mr. Thomson has his own pleasantly eccentric pantheon in which writers figure hardly at all. A column is devoted to the dim Micheline Presle but the finest of all screenwriters, Jacques Prévert, is ignored. There is a long silly tribute to Arthur Penn; yet there is no biography of Penn's contemporary at NBC television, Paddy Chayefsky, whose films in the Fifties and early Sixties were far more interesting than anything Penn has done. Possibly Chayefsky was excluded because not only did he write his own films, he would then hire a director rather the way one would employ a plumber—or a cameraman. For a time, Chayefsky was the only American *auteur,* and his pencil was the director. Certainly Chayefsky's early career in films perfectly disproves Nicholas Ray's dictum (approvingly quoted by Mr. Thomson): "If it were all in the script, why make the film?" If it is not all in the script, there is no film to make.

Twenty years ago at the Writers' Table we all agreed with the Wise
Hack that William Wyler subtracted no more than 10 percent from a
script. Some of the most attractive and sensible of Bazin's pages are
devoted to Wyler's work in the Forties. On the other hand, Mr. Thomson does not like him at all (because Wyler lacks those redundant faults
that create the illusion of a Style?). Yet whatever was in a script, Wyler
rendered faithfully: when he was given a bad script, he would make not
only a bad movie, but the script's particular kind of badness would be
revealed in a way that could altogether too easily boomerang on the too
skillful director. But when the script was good (of its kind, *of its kind!*),
*The Letter,* say, or *The Little Foxes,* there was no better interpreter.

At MGM, I worked exclusively with the producer Sam Zimbalist. He
was a remarkably good and decent man in a business where such qualities are rare. He was also a producer of the old-fashioned sort. This
meant that the script was prepared for him and with him. Once the
script was ready, the director was summoned; he would then have the
chance to say, yes, he would direct the script or, no, he wouldn't. Few
changes were made in the script after the director was assigned. But this
was not to be the case in Zimbalist's last film.

For several years MGM had been planning a remake of *Ben-Hur,* the
studio's most successful silent film. A Contract Writer wrote a script;
it was discarded. Then Zimbalist offered me the job. I said no, and went
on suspension. During the next year or two S. N. Behrman and Maxwell
Anderson, among others, added many yards of portentous dialogue to
a script which kept growing and changing. The result was not happy.
By 1958 MGM was going bust. Suddenly the remake of *Ben-Hur* seemed
like a last chance to regain the mass audience lost to television. Zimbalist
again asked me if I would take on the job. I said that if the studio
released me from the remainder of my contract, I would go to Rome
for two or three months and rewrite the script. The studio agreed.
Meanwhile, Wyler had been signed to direct.

On a chilly March day Wyler, Zimbalist, and I took an overnight
flight from New York. On the plane Wyler read for the first time the
latest of the many scripts. As we drove together into Rome from the
airport, Wyler looked gray and rather frightened. "This is awful," he
said, indicating the huge script that I had placed between us on the back
seat. "I know," I said. "What are we going to do?"

Wyler groaned: "These Romans. . . . Do you know anything about
them?" I said, yes, I had done my reading. Wyler stared at me. "Well,"
he said, "when a Roman sits down and relaxes, what does he unbuckle?"

That spring I rewrote more than half the script (and Wyler studied every "Roman" film ever made). When I was finished with a scene, I would give it to Zimbalist. We would go over it. Then the scene would be passed on to Wyler. Normally, Wyler is slow and deliberately indecisive; but first-century Jerusalem had been built at enormous expense; the first day of shooting was approaching; the studio was nervous. As a result, I did not often hear Wyler's famous cry, as he would hand you back your script, "If I knew what was wrong with it, I'd fix it myself."

The plot of *Ben-Hur* is, basically, absurd and any attempt to make sense of it would destroy the story's awful integrity. But for a film to be watchable the characters must make some kind of psychological sense. We were stuck with the following: the Jew Ben-Hur and the Roman Messala were friends in childhood. Then they were separated. Now the adult Messala returns to Jerusalem; meets Ben-Hur; asks him to help with the Romanization of Judea. Ben-Hur refuses; there is a quarrel; they part and vengeance is sworn. This one scene is the sole motor that must propel a very long story until Jesus Christ suddenly and pointlessly drifts onto the scene, automatically untying some of the cruder knots in the plot. Wyler and I agreed that a single political quarrel would not turn into a lifelong vendetta.

I thought of a solution, which I delivered into Wyler's good ear. "As boys they were lovers. Now Messala wants to continue the affair. Ben-Hur rejects him. Messala is furious. *Chagrin d'amour,* the classic motivation for murder."

Wyler looked at me as if I had gone mad. "But we can't do *that*! I mean this is Ben-Hur! My God. . . ."

"We won't really do it. We just suggest it. I'll write the scenes so that they will make sense to those who are tuned in. Those who aren't will still feel that Messala's rage is somehow emotionally logical."

I don't think Wyler particularly liked my solution but he agreed that "anything is better than what we've got. So let's try it."

I broke the original scene into two parts. Charlton Heston (Ben-Hur) and Stephen Boyd (Messala) read them for us in Zimbalist's office. Wyler knew his actors. He warned me: "Don't ever tell Chuck what it's all about, or he'll fall apart." I suspect that Heston does not know to this day what luridness we managed to contrive around him. But Boyd knew: every time he looked at Ben-Hur it was like a starving man getting a glimpse of dinner through a pane of glass. And so, among the thundering hooves and clichés of the last (to date) *Ben-Hur,* there is something odd and authentic in one unstated relationship.

As agreed, I left in early summer and Christopher Fry wrote the rest of the script. Before the picture ended, Zimbalist died of a heart attack. Later, when it came time to credit the writers of the film, Wyler proposed that Fry be given screen credit. Then Fry insisted that I be given credit with him, since I had written the first half of the picture. Wyler was in a quandary. Only Zimbalist (and Fry and myself—two interested parties) knew who had written what, and Zimbalist was dead. The matter was given to the Screenwriters Guild for arbitration and they, mysteriously, awarded the credit to the Contract Writer whose script was separated from ours by at least two other discarded scripts. The film was released in 1959 and saved MGM from financial collapse.

I have recorded in some detail this unimportant business to show the near-impossibility of determining how a movie is actually created. Had *Ben-Hur* been taken seriously by, let us say, those French critics who admire *Johnny Guitar,* then Wyler would have been credited with the unusually subtle relationship between Ben-Hur and Messala. No credit would ever have gone to me because my name was not on the screen, nor would credit have gone to the official scriptwriter because, according to the *auteuri* theory, every aspect of a film is the creation of the director.

The twenty-year interregnum when the producer was supreme is now a memory. The ascendancy of the movie stars was brief. The directors have now regained their original primacy, and Milestone's storm is only an echo. Today the marquees of movie houses feature the names of directors and journalists ("*A work of art,*" J. Crist); the other collaborators are in fine print.

This situation might be more acceptable if the film directors had become true *auteurs.* But most of them are further than ever away from art—not to mention life. The majority are simply technicians. A few have come from the theatre; many began as editors, cameramen, makers of television series, and commercials; in recent years, ominously, a majority have been graduates of film schools. In principle, there is nothing wrong with a profound understanding of the technical means by which an image is impressed upon celluloid. But movies are not just molds of light any more than a novel is just inked-over paper. A movie is a response to reality in a certain way and that way must first be found by a writer. Unfortunately, no contemporary film director can bear to be thought a mere interpreter. He must be sole creator. As a result, he is more often than not a plagiarist, telling stories that are not his.

Over the years a number of writers have become directors, but except for such rare figures as Cocteau and Bergman, the writers who have gone in for directing were generally not much better at writing than they proved to be at directing. Even in commercial terms, for every Joe Mankiewicz or Preston Sturges there are a dozen Xs and Ys, not to mention the depressing Z.

Today's films are more than ever artifacts of light. Cars chase one another mindlessly along irrelevant freeways. Violence seems rooted in a notion about what ought to happen next on the screen to help the images move rather than in any human situation anterior to those images. In fact, the human situation has been eliminated not through any intentional philosophic design but because those who have spent too much time with cameras and machines seldom have much apprehension of that living world without whose presence there is no art.

I suspect that the time has now come to take Astruc seriously . . . after first rearranging his thesis. Astruc's *caméra-stylo* requires that "the script writer ceases to exist. . . . The filmmaker/author writes with his camera as a writer writes with his pen." Good. But let us eliminate not the screenwriter but that technician-hustler—the director (a.k.a. *auteur du cinéma*). Not until he has been replaced by those who can use a pen to write from life for the screen is there going to be much of anything worth seeing. Nor does it take a genius of a writer to achieve great effects in film. Compared to the works of his nineteenth-century mentors, the writing of Ingmar Bergman is second-rate. But when he writes straight through the page and onto the screen itself his talent is transformed and the result is often first-rate.

As a poet, Jacques Prévert is not in the same literary class as Valéry, but Prévert's films *Les Enfants du Paradis* and *Lumière d'été* are extraordinary achievements. They were also disdained by the French theoreticians of the Forties who knew perfectly well that the directors Carné and Grémillon were inferior to their script-writer; but since the Theory requires that only a director can create a film, any film that is plainly a writer's work cannot be true cinema. This attitude has given rise to some highly comic critical musings. Recently a movie critic could not figure out why there had been such a dramatic change in the quality of the work of the director Joseph Losey after he moved to England. Was it a difference in the culture? the light? the water? Or could it—and the critic faltered—could it be that perhaps Losey's films changed when he . . . when he—oh, dear!—got Harold Pinter to write screenplays for him? The critic promptly dismissed the notion. Mr. Thomson prints no biography of Pinter in his *Dictionary*.

I have never much liked the films of Pier Paolo Pasolini, but I find most interesting the ease with which he turned to film after some twenty years as poet and novelist. He could not have been a film-maker in America because the costs are too high; also, the technician-hustlers are in total charge. But in Italy, during the Fifties, it was possible for an actual *auteur* to use for a pen the camera (having first composed rather than stolen the narrative to be illuminated).

Since the talking movie is closest in form to the novel ("the novel is a narrative that organizes itself in the world, while the cinema is a world that organizes itself into a narrative"—Jean Mitry), it strikes me that the rising literary generation might think of the movies as, peculiarly, their kind of novel, to be created by them in collaboration with technicians but without the interference of The Director, that hustler-plagiarist who has for twenty years dominated and exploited and (occasionally) enhanced an art form still in search of its true authors.

*The New York Review of Books*
November 25, 1976

# 107

·

# GORE VIDAL

In the *Secret Miracle,* Borges remarks of his author-protagonist, "Like every writer, he measured the virtues of other writers by their perform-ances, and asked that they measure him by what he conjectured or planned." This seems to me a sad truth. Even André Gide, when young, used to wonder why it was that strangers could not tell simply by looking into his eyes what a master he would one day be. The artist lives not only with his performances (which he tends to forget), but with his own private view of what he *thinks* he has done, and most important, what he still plans to do. To the writer of a given book, what exists in print is only a small, perhaps misleading, fraction of the great thing to be accomplished; to the critic, however, it is the thing itself entire. Consequently critic and writer are seldom on the same wavelength.

As it must to all American writers who stay the course, and do not have the luck (sometimes good) to die after a first success, I am now confronted with a volume called *Gore Vidal.* It is the work of Ray Lewis White, a young professor at the University of North Carolina. For two years he has written me probing letters (sensibly, he never proposed a meeting), examined my papers at the University of Wisconsin, and immersed himself in what is probably, in plain bulk, the largest *oeuvre* of any contemporary American writer. At all times he has had my sympathy, even awe, as he worked his way through a career that has endured for a quarter century. The result is now at hand, one hundred fifty-seven dense pages, describing and judging ten novels (stopping short of the apocalyptic *Myra Breckinridge*), four plays and seven short stories. Omitted are the politics, most of the essays, the political journalism, the television writing and performing, and the movie hack work. Omitted, too, is the personal element. There are no revelations. Unlike Mary McCarthy, the Subject (as I shall now be known for modesty's sake) does not extend confidences to biographers nor, to Mr. White's credit, were they solicited. He has addressed himself entirely to the work, only bringing in the life as a means to show when and where—if not why—something was written. From this point of view, his book is meticulous and, I would suspect, accurate. Suspect because the Subject has no memory for dates or chronology. As a result, the story of his life unfolds for him like that of a stranger. Even so, the effect is disquieting: what a lot of time the Subject mis-used or simply wasted. And of all that he wrote, how little now seems to him remotely close to what he originally planned and conjectured (but still plans and conjectures).

Mr. White's detailed plot outlines of the novels and plays will doubtless not encourage many people to read the original works. Worse, in an age of non-readers, those who like to know about writing without actually reading books will be quite satisfied to skim Mr. White's study and feel that their duty to the Subject has been more than discharged since it is well known that in any year there is only One Important Novelist worth reading (there is some evidence that the Subject's year occurred at the end of the 40s). Yet perhaps it is best to be known only in outline: part of the genius of Borges is the lovely way he evades making books by writing reviews of novels that he has not written, demonstrating not only what he might so perfectly have done but inviting our respect for then not doing it.

Mr. White divides the Subject's career as novelist into three parts. The first phase was both precocious and prolific. Between the ages of nineteen and twenty-four (1945–1949), the Subject wrote and published six novels. The first was the war novel *Williwaw,* still regarded by certain romantics as a peak he was never again to scale. Among the other five novels, only *The City and the Pillar,* and perhaps *A Search for the King,* have much interest for anyone today except as paradigms of what was then the national manner: colorless, careful prose, deliberately confined to the surface of things. Then, according to Mr. White, came the second phase and the flowering.

Between 1950 and 1953 the Subject published *The Judgment of Paris, Messiah* and the short stories in *A Thirsty Evil.* These works resembled hardly at all the books that had gone before. But unfortunately the Subject was by then so entirely out of fashion that they were ignored. Only gradually did they find an audience. For some years now the paperback edition of *Messiah* has been much read, particularly on the campuses, and now *The Judgment of Paris* ("Vidal's Peacock-like novel-as-dialogue") is being discovered. But the original failure of these books made it necessary for the Subject to earn a living and so from 1954 to 1961, he wrote plays for television, Broadway, films, as well as criticism and political journalism; concluding his head-on encounter with the world by running for Congress in 1960—all in all, an interesting and profitable decade. But looking over Mr. White's neat chronology at the beginning of the book, what a waste it now seems. Yet the Subject was having his life if not art; and Strether would have approved. Then, world exhausted, the Subject resumed an interrupted novel about the apostate emperor Julian, and so became a novelist once more, embarked upon his third (and terminal?) phase.

What does Mr. White make of all this? He is cautious, as well he might be; in many quarters his author is still regarded with profound suspicion. He is adroit at demonstrating the recurring themes from book to book. He makes, however, inadequate use of the essays, relying too heavily upon newspaper interviews—usually garbled—or on taped answers to questions in which the Subject has a tendency to sound like General Eisenhower with a hangover. He also betrays his youth when he tries to reconstruct the literary atmosphere in which the books were published. He places *In a Yellow Wood* (1949) in the company of books by Busch, Heyliger, Burnett and Mayo, who also dealt with the problems of a returned veteran. It may be that these novels were most worthy but they were quite unknown at the time. *Lucifer with a Book, That Winter, Barbary Shore* were the relevant books everyone read. But then no one has yet captured the sense of excitement of the literary scene in the 40s. Between VJ day and the beginning of the Korean war, it looked as if we were going to have a most marvelous time in all the arts; and the novel was very much alive, not yet displaced at the vulgar level by movies, at the highest by film.

These complaints registered, Mr. White has written—how for me to put it?—a most interesting book, astonishingly exact in detail and often shrewd in judgment. The series to which it belongs is aimed at a university audience and Mr. White has kept within the bounds prescribed.

Here and there one sees the beginning of something extra-academic, but he shows his tact, as one must in dealing with a living author little prone to autobiography. The inner life will come later—inevitably, since all that is apt to be remembered of any mid-20th century author is his life. Novels command neither interest nor affection but writers do, particularly the colorful ones who have made powerful legends of themselves. I suspect that eventually novels will be read only to provide clues to the author's personality; and once each of his characters has been satisfactorily identified, each of his obsessions duly noted, each key turned in its giving lock, the books may then be put aside for good, leaving us with what most concerns this artless time: the story of the author as monster most sacred, the detritus of his life enriched by our fascinated gaze, the gossip of his day our day's gospel. Of such is the declining kingdom of literature in which Mr. White has staked out with some nicety the wild marches of a border lord.

*The New York Times Book Review*
September 1, 1968

# 108
### · ###

# HOLLYWOOD!

One morning last spring (June 1982), I cast a vote for myself in the
Hollywood hills; then I descended to the flats of Beverly Hills for a
haircut at the barber shop in the Beverly Wilshire Hotel, where I found
the Wise Hack, now half as old as time; his remaining white hairs had
just been trimmed; he was being manicured, the large yellow diamond
still sparkles on that finger which he refers to as a "pinkie." The Wise
Hack's eyes have lost a bit of their sparkle but then eyes that have looked
with deep suspicion into those of F. Scott Fitzgerald *and* of Y. Frank
Freeman have earned their mica glaze.

When I greeted him, he said, accusingly, "Why do you want to be
governor of this schmatteh state?" When I said that I didn't want to be
*governor* (I was a candidate for the U.S. Senate) he nodded slyly. "That's
what *I* told people," he said, cryptic as always. Then: "It's over there.
In my briefcase. This Xerox copy. You can borrow it. Everybody's in
it. Not that I know a lot of these young hotshots they got nowadays with
their beads and long hair. Remember when there was only the one head
of the studio and he was there forever? But a lot of old-timers are in it,
too. Ray's in it. Real hatchet job like that one that—you know, what's
her name, did to Dore . . ." I supplied the name of Lillian Ross. He
nodded, "I warned Dore at the time . . ."

In due course, I read the Xerox of a book—or tome as the Wise Hack would say—called *Indecent Exposure* by a journalist named David McClintick, who has examined at great length the David Begelman scandal of five years ago. As I read the book, the Wise Hack supplied me with a running commentary. Although the Wise Hack's memory for names is going fast, he has perfect recall of what goes on—or went on—behind Hollywood's closed doors. "You see, the book is told from the point of view of this one young hotshot who, when Columbia Pictures was on its ass, was made president in New York by Ray Stark and Herbert Allen, Jr., then this hotshot Alan Hirschfield . . . You know him?" A sharp look, suddenly. I said as far as I know I have never met Mr. Hirschfield. But then like the Wise Hack I can't keep straight all the young executives who come and go, talking of Coca-Cola—Columbia's new owner.

I did know the unfortunate Begelman, who had been my agent, and I had once made a film with Ray Stark twenty years ago while . . . But as the Wise Hack always says, "First you identify your characters. Then you show us your problem. Then you bring on your hero. Then you kick him in the balls. Then you show how he takes that kick. Does he feel sorry for himself? Never. Because," and I would recite along with the Wise Hack movieland's inexorable law: "Self-pity is not box office."

In 1973 Columbia Pictures was close to bankruptcy. The studio's principal supplier of films, Ray Stark, went to his old friend Charles Allen of the investment firm Allen and Company and persuaded him to buy into the studio. Stark proceeded to interest Allen's thirty-three-year-old nephew, Herbert Allen, Jr., in Columbia's management. Together they selected an employee of Allen and Company, one Alan Hirschfield, to be the president of Columbia Pictures, headquartered in New York. Thus has Hollywood always been governed. The power and the money are in New York; the studio and the glamor are in Hollywood. According to the Wise Hack, the day after Pearl Harbor was attacked, there was not a dry eye in the commissary at MGM when L. B. Mayer exhorted each of the assembled artists and artisans "to say to himself a silent prayer—at this time of national emergency—for our great president—Nicholas M. Schenck in New York."

David Begelman was made chief of production of Columbia Pictures in Hollywood. Begelman had been a highly successful agent and packager of films. He turned, as they say, Columbia Pictures around. After four years of Begelman's management the studio was a great success.

Begelman got most of the praise, which somewhat irritated Hirschfield. Even so, everything was going very nicely for everyone until . . .

In 1976 Begelman forged the actor Cliff Robertson's name to a check for ten thousand dollars made out to Robertson by Columbia. Robertson would never have known of the check if he had not got an IRS form in the mail. It is of some psychological interest that although Robertson had once been a client of Begelman, a *froideur,* as they say in Bel Air, developed between the two men when Begelman took the side of Cinerama against his client in a dispute over money. Begelman's attempts to cover up the Robertson forgery failed, and Columbia's board of directors suspended Begelman as president of the company, notified the SEC, and ordered an audit of Begelman's affairs. The press reported that there had been "financial irregularities"; the word *forgery* was not mentioned.

A second forged check surfaced, made out to the director Marty Ritt, as well as a payment to an imaginary Frenchman whose name Begelman had appropriated from one of Hollywood's leading maîtres d'hotel— Begelman's subconscious had its witty side. After a thorough investigation, the auditors reported to the board of Columbia that Begelman had embezzled $61,008; he had also taken, in unauthorized expenses, $23,-000. The board was stunned by these amounts.

"Why so little?" asked the Wise Hack, not at all rhetorically. "A real thief in that job can steal millions. This was the petty cash. Let's face it, David's a sick man. That's all." Since the Wise Hack's estimate was pretty much that of the board of directors, Begelman was reinstated on condition that he pay back what he had taken and agree to go to the village medicine man—at this time and in that place, a shrink. Plainly, they were all nuts. Now begins the agony and the ecstasy of Mr. McClintick's tale.

In an author's note, Mr. McClintick tells us that "everything in this book is real [as opposed to true?], every episode, scene, weather reference, conversation, and name (except for that of a single confidential informant)." Since Columbia's board meetings are reported with such a wealth of "real" dialogue, it would appear that the author's Deep Throat is Mr. Hirschfield himself. Certainly, he must have an astonishing memory. If not, how else could he have supplied the author with so many detailed conversations? After all, in Mr. McClintick's own words, "The minutes are summaries and contain no actual dialogue." Perhaps Mr. Hirschfield taped himself and his fellow board members.

But this is only idle supposition—one must proceed carefully with Mr. McClintick because on the page entitled "Acknowledgments" he gives "thanks also to Robert D. Sack, the finest libel lawyer in America and, not insignificantly, an astute editorial critic." Plainly, what we are in for is hardball. Curiously enough, neither author nor libel lawyer cum editorial critic is exactly straightforward on the problem of attribution. On the next page there are two epigraphs. One is an aria by John Huston on how Hollywood is a jungle. The other is a remark by David Chasman: "The New Hollywood is very much like the Old Hollywood." To the innocent reader it looks as if both Huston and Chasman had made these statements to the author. The Huston aria is dated 1950; the Chasman 1981. I had no idea of the provenance of the Chasman quotation but surely Mr. McClintick should have given prompt credit to Lillian Ross, from whose remarkable book *Picture* he lifted Huston's speech. Instead, under "Notes," on page 524, he identifies his source.

Despite the author's note, *Indecent Exposure* belongs to a relatively new genre of writing in which real people are treated as if they are characters in a fiction. Villains "smirk"; heroes "stride"; Begelman "sidled over." Although Mr. McClintick has proudly billed his book as "A True Story of Hollywood and Wall Street," he does not hesitate to enter the minds of real people. "Caressed by Muzak, Begelman sat at his elaborate *faux marbre* desk and thought about the check and about Cliff Robertson. . . . Using Robertson's name to steal the money in the first place had been a big mistake, even though it had seemed perfectly logical at the time." Incidentally, "the finest libel lawyer in America" and "astute editorial critic" does not have much of an eye or ear for English—or even the *faux anglais* of Bel Air. Dangling participles adorn Mr. McClintick's pages like hangman's nooses. Or, later, "Sitting at home on a Sunday three months later, facing an imminent investigation, Begelman decided to proceed with his plan for concealing the Pierre Groleau embezzlement." How does our author know that Begelman was sitting rather than standing? or whether or not Muzak caressed or annoyed Begelman? And wouldn't it be more dramatic to have him on the toilet instead of at his desk when he thinks about the check? Since all of this is plainly unknowable, all of this becomes untrue.

It is Mr. McClintick's thesis that good-guy Alan Hirschfield wanted to get rid of Begelman because he was a crook but he couldn't because the real power brokers at Columbia, Herbert Allen and Ray Stark, did not share his high moral standards. Mr. McClintick's Hirschfield is a highly moral man—if somewhat indecisive, because he fears not only for his job but he suspects "blackmail" might be used against him because his wife Berte was employed by the research firm E. J. Wolf & Associates, who did work for Columbia.

Thus, Mr. McClintick sets up his hero: "Reporters, especially women, enjoyed interviewing him. He was an attractive man—a six-footer of medium build with an athletic bearing, hair that was expertly coiffed even though thinning and graying, and a countenance that revealed his droll, playful personality through twinkling eyes and the trace of a smile. Relaxed and informal, he laughed easily and often, and his speaking voice was the kind of soft, gentle adult voice that children find comforting." I looked in the back of the book for affidavits from children; there were none.

Hirschfield is also from Oklahoma, which gives him a "somewhat hometown naïveté that was a deeply ingrained part of Alan's character—the Oklahoma in him—as Berte saw it. . . ." Mr. McClintick is no doubt an eastern city bumpkin, unaware that Oklahoma's rich and marvelous corruption makes Hollywood's wheeling and dealing seem positively innocent. In the text, Hirschfield usually "strides"; occasionally he "ambles." Sometimes he is "discombobulated"; even "a man in agony"; once—only once—he "whined." He is a good family man, as all good men are, and "the company of his children—Laura, thirteen; Marc, eleven; and Scott, eight—always invigorated Alan, no matter what problems might be plaguing him."

Now let us look at the villains of the book. "Although [Herbert Allen] was trim and fit, he had slightly sunken eyes which gave him a somewhat gaunt, tired look and projected coolness, cynicism, nonchalance, and even indifference, much more often than joy or sadness." This does not sound at all like a well-coiffed person to me. The author keeps fretting about those eyes. "While Herbert's slightly sunken eyes appeared to reveal fatigue and worry . . . they were an inherited characteristic," and his Uncle Charles has them, too. Even so . . . Although Mr. Hirschfield's sexual life is not discussed (marital strain is alluded to only toward the end), Herbert Allen's girlfriends are noted by name and his suite on the Carlyle Hotel's thirty-first floor is made to sound jumping: ". . . he was a bit compulsive about the physical standards he set for his women. He would mull over fine points of physique with cronies, etc.," but then Allen was "divorced in 1971—after nine years of marriage and four children." What any of this has to do with the Begelman case is a question best asked of the ghost of Jacqueline Susann, which hovers over these often steamy pages.

. . .

On the other hand, the relationship between Allen and Hirschfield is interesting. The latter was an employee of Allen and Company, a powerful investment firm run by Herbert's uncle, Charles Allen. "Hirschfield considered himself superior in intellect and business acumen to Herbert Allen, Jr., the firm's scion . . . who was four and half years younger than Hirschfield and, unlike Hirschfield, born to great wealth." This has the ring of truth. "He, not Herbert, had saved Columbia. He, not Herbert, was one of the brightest young show-business executives in the nation." Worse, the little that Herbert knew about movies he had learned from old-fashioned oldsters like Ray Stark. Fortunately, "none of Hirschfield's feelings was stated or even hinted in Herbert's presence, however. While never best friends, Alan and Herbert always had had a close, comfortable relationship which continued in the summer of 1977." Summertime for Iago.

It is odd how widely Mr. McClintick misses the point of the relationship between Allen and Hirschfield. He writes as if they were equals. They are not. Allen is, as the author puts it, a "scion"; Hirschfield is a hired hand. From Mr. McClintick's account it would appear that in the course of the drama Hirschfield may have had occasional delusions of equality—if he did, he destroyed himself because, as every scion knows from the moment he first teethes on that silver spoon, the one with the money wins because that is the American way. Since workers in the Hollywoods often make many hundreds of thousands of dollars a year, there is a tendency to think of them as rich. They are not or, as John O'Hara once said of the best-selling writer, "He has the income of a millionaire without the million dollars." David Begelman was also a hired hand. But he had developed an expertise: He could put together successful films. That is a gift so rare—and often so temporary, fashions change rapidly in movieland—that the board of Columbia forgave him his trespasses by invoking mental illness and let him go on as before. With perfect hindsight, this was a stupid thing to do; but it was done and Hirschfield made no demur.

Mr. McClintick describes Ray Stark at considerable length. "As long as anyone in Hollywood could remember, Ray Stark had been known to friend and foe alike as 'The Rabbit.'" The Wise Hack shook his head and wheezed, "News to me. And I go back to the first rewrite on that Hong Kong thing—*The World of Herman Orient*"—he meant *The World of Susie Wong;* the Wise Hack tends to mix up movie titles but he is precise when it comes to movie deals. "Although many people assumed that the tag originated as a sexual reference," Mr. McClintick delicately sows a seed, "it was a physical description coined by Fanny Brice, who was to become Stark's mother-in-law in the 1940s. . . . Although he was far from being what Herbert Allen called him—'the most important producer in Hollywood post-1948' (he had produced little of artistic distinction, and his films had won very few Academy Awards, none as best picture)—Ray Stark had accomplished something that the entertainment industry admires more than anything else because it is so elusive—commercial consistency." He means Stark's pictures made money.

In thirty years Stark had gone from hired hand (he was a writer's agent and then a movie producer) to movie mogul. When Columbia started to come apart in 1973, Stark could deal as an equal with the Allen family. Together Stark and the scion hired both Hirschfield and Begelman. Stark himself continued to make his own pictures; sometimes at Columbia and sometimes not. Mr. McClintick discusses at length the relationship between the sixty-two-year-old Stark and the thirty-three-year-old Herbert Allen: Never at a loss for a Freudian cliché, he speculates that Stark is in need of a surrogate son, following "the death, apparently by suicide, of Ray's son, Peter."

"Cheap shot," muttered the Wise Hack. "Anyway, Ray knew Herbert before the kid died." We were seated in the study of the Wise Hack's house. "I got the letters, too," he added, with a McClintickesque tight smile. "What letters?" The Wise Hack's style is often Delphic. "Here," he handed me two badly Xeroxed letters. "These have been going around the town. Just like the book." One of the letters was from our author Mr. David McClintick to Ray Stark. The other was Stark's answer.

On September 5, 1980, Mr. McClintick wrote Stark a letter. He was, he said, disappointed that he had not been able to "break through the stiffness, awkwardness and discomfort that have always characterized our relationship if it can be called a relationship."

"When Herbert and I first discussed my book nearly two years ago, he said that he would give me full cooperation and that he would do everything he could to encourage you and David Begelman to cooperate as well." Apparently, Herbert Allen and David Begelman each gave fifteen hours of time to the author—"these sessions were painful," McClintick concedes; doubtless the principals must find the resulting use of their time even more painful. "By contrast," Mr. McClintick chides, "you have granted me precisely one hour in connection with my book. (A previous hour in your office in December 1977 concerned an article for *The Wall Street Journal.*) Not only was the time far too short, but the atmosphere was hardly conducive to a relaxed and candid conversation. Furthermore, you saw fit to bring a witness—a gesture to which frightened people sometimes resort, but which I found odd in these circumstances, and even a little rude."

Unlike Allen and Begelman and the novel's hero, Hirschfield, Stark was not about to help Mr. McClintick turn him into a fictional character. But Stark had no choice; Mr. McClintick is an auteur, a creator of true fictions or fictive truths in the great line of those *ci-devant* novelists Capote and Mailer. He can invent Ray Stark as both Mailer and Capote, separately, invented Marilyn Monroe.

Mr. McClintick mounts his high horse. "Ray, I'm sure that you feel that the one hour you gave me fulfills your commitment." The word *commitment* is the giveaway—the auteur knows that he—and he alone—is the creator of this particular universe and none of his characters is going to be autonomous. "You have told me repeatedly how you rarely give any time to journalists, implying that I should be deeply honored to receive even one hour. All I can say is that I am not just another Hollywood gossip monger. I am one of the top investigative reporters in this country (Pulitzer Prize nominee) and am writing a serious book about events in which you played a major role . . . the book will include the deepest and most detailed portrait of you that has ever been written or ever will be written until someone does your biography or you do your autobiography . . ." At this moment any semi-autonomous character in a true fiction would have taken to his heels.

Stark's response is benign: "I respect you as a Pulitzer Prize nominee and, therefore, I must respect your power of observation and presume by this time you should know that I am a very private person. I doubt whether you can find a dozen quotes or two interviews given by me in the last ten years. . . . You and I have talked congenially, I believe, several times. Once at a premiere in New York and at length, I thought, in my office in California. It may have only been for an hour according to your time, but since my interest span is short, it seemed like several hours to me." Stark notes that one of his associates joined them for lunch not "as a witness because long ago I found it very difficult to refute what a writer may interpret or write regardless of there being a witness. She was along to refresh my memory.

"That misinterpretation on your part only strengthens my reluctance to break what has been my lifelong policy against interviews and personal publicity. . . . The fact that you want to give 'the deepest and most detailed portrait of me that has ever been written' certainly motivates me *not* to talk to you." Thus one of Pirandello's characters tries to leave the stage. Stark notes that "it is difficult for me to express to you that I have nothing to hide. It is merely that I have no desire to have my privacy invaded." He ends, cheerfully, "I wish that all of your efforts are fruitful for you. At least now you are in possession of one of the longest and most revealing letters that I have ever written to a member of the press."

Mr. McClintick's revenge is outright. He accuses Stark of various crimes and then says that these accusations are either untrue or unverifiable. He quotes one of Hirschfield's tirades: "Ray is in no position to threaten or blackmail. I assure every one of you that with two phone calls—to the SEC and IRS—Ray will be busy for the rest of his life. I will not hesitate to make those calls." If that is not an accusation of corporate and personal crookedness, it is hard to know what is. But our auteur has put an asterisk beside this "quotation." At the bottom of the page, there is a footnote in the smallest type that my eye can read: "This was a threat, made in the passion of a heated meeting, which turned out to be empty. Hirschfield had no evidence of any wrongdoing by Stark that would have been of interest to the SEC or IRS." This is good to know but why quote a libel that one knows to be untrue?

Later, our auteur goes even further. Somehow, Mr. McClintick obtained a copy of a letter that the columnist Liz Smith wrote to Ray Stark. "I was trying," she writes, "to explain why I had to come down harder on the Begelman affair than you might want me to, considering your friendship. All these items on my desk saying he owes you $600,-000 and you had a deal with him to take all your worthless as well as good projects for Columbia, and on and on. All that has been kept out of my column. I consider that friendship, Ray . . ."

Now for the pussy-footnote: "Of course the 'items' about a $600,000 debt and Begelman's buying Stark's 'worthless' projects for Columbia were omitted from Smith's column not because of friendship but because she could not verify them as anything more than unfounded rumors." So our auteur prints libel based on "unfounded rumors" that Liz Smith did not see fit to print, in order to make us think that Stark and Begelman were defrauding Columbia. There is no experience quite like being caught in an American journalist's true fiction where the laws of libel—not to mention grammar—often seem not to obtain.

. . .

The Begelman *affaire* is of more interest as a study in contemporary journalistic practices than it is of skulduggery in the movie business. After Begelman's reinstatement, the press found out what happened. As the storm of publicity broke over Columbia (Mr. McClintick's style is contagious) Stark and Allen remained Begelman's allies. Hirschfield waffled. Since every bad novel must have a good-guy hero, Mr. McClintick would have us believe that, from the beginning of the scandal, Hirschfield had been morally outraged and sickened by Begelman's crimes. If he had been, then he was very much out of character—or at least out of that character which our auteur has invented for him. Apparently after Hirschfield became president of Columbia, he hired a man who had been fired "from CBS Records for misappropriation of funds and was under federal indictment for income tax evasion. . . .

" 'What if Clive goes to jail?' Herbert Allen asked Hirschfield.

" 'Then he'll run it from Danbury [a federal prison in Connecticut],' Hirschfield replied, only half in jest." Later, at another studio, Hirschfield kept in office a man caught with his hand in the till. As our auteur gorgeously puts it: "Hollywood is a town that takes delight in spitting in the face of irony."

The press did a good bit of spitting, too, and Hollywood was subjected to creative as well as investigative reporting. Characteristically, *The New York Times* took the low road. They assigned that excellent young novelist and West Point graduate Lucian K. Truscott IV to thread the Hollywood maze. He did his best—but West Point and the army are not much use when it comes to reading audits. Truscott heard all the old rumors, including the perennial one that organized crime and the movie business have often had carnal, as it were, knowledge of one another. Although there is probably a good deal of truth in this, one must first discover an authentic smoking gun. Truscott's piece, according to Mr. McClintick, "was strewn with falsehoods, large and small." Old Charles Allen was labeled "The Godfather of the New Hollywood"; a photograph of crime lord Meyer Lansky was published—and, of course, there was Begelman.

"Word on the article was beginning to circulate, the price of Columbia's stock was plummeting, and at noon Friday, the New York Stock Exchange stopped trading the stock because an influx of sell orders had made orderly trading impossible." When it comes to mischief, never underestimate the power of *The New York Times.* But, for once, the *Times* had met its match. "That afternoon, Allen & Company announced publicly that it would sue *The New York Times* for $150

million for publishing false and defamatory statements. . . . Three
months later, after elaborate negotiations between lawyers for the two
sides, *The New York Times* found it necessary to publish perhaps the
most elaborate retraction, correction, and apology in the history of
major American newspapers up to that time." There is an obscure
footnote to the effect that a Mr. Abe Rosenthal, identified as the executive editor of the paper, was away at the time that the piece was published. Social notes from all over.

In due course, Begelman left Columbia. Then Hirschfield departed after
he was caught trying secretly to get Sir James Goldsmith to buy Columbia away from the Allens—the sort of behavior that is bound to
make irritable your average sunken-eyed employer. Although Hirschfield had always denied that he wanted to leave New York for Hollywood, he indeed went to Hollywood in a big way; currently, he is head
of production at Twentieth Century–Fox. Meanwhile, Columbia, Stark,
Allen and Company continue to prosper; and so it goes . . . Hollywood
is what it is.

Traditionally, bad writers like to take fierce Moral Stands. They
depict their characters in the blackest of black, and the whitest of white.
Ostensibly, Mr. McClintick is cleaning out the Augean stables of the
Republic. He will give us the lowdown about Hollywood (all that
money, all those movie stars!), a glittering cancer that is munching away
at the very heart of what is, after all—in the immortal phrase of a writer
very much like Mr. McClintick, Spiro Agnew—the greatest nation in
the country. But, surely, the author knows that Hollywood is no more
corrupt than Detroit or Washington. This is a nation of hustlers and
although it is always salutary to blow the whistle on the crooks, it is hard
to see, in this particular case, just what all the fuss is about. Begelman's
forgeries are psychologically interesting—but hardly worth a book
when we still know so little about the man. The loyalty of the board of
directors to Begelman *could* be interpreted as just that; hence, something rather rare in Hollywood. In any case, it was the board that
notified the SEC; called in the auditors; and let Begelman, finally and
messily, go. Hirschfield's problems with Herbert Allen, Jr., belong to the
realm not of morality but of the higher hustlerdom and we know, at a
glance, what makes him run.

The implicit moral of *Indecent Exposure* (thus, irony spits back) is
not the story that the book tells but the book itself as artifact, the work
of a writer who believes that he can take real people and events and

remake them, as it were, in his own image. Worse, he is so filled with an odd animus toward most of his characters that he repeats accusations that he knows to be untrue so that he can then recant them, slyly, in footnotes to the text. If the "finest libel lawyer in America" told the writer that he could get away with this sort of hit-and-run tactic, I can only defer to what is, after all, a superior knowledge of our republic's greasy laws; but as "an astute editorial critic" he should have advised the creator to forget all about instructing us in what Mr. McClintick refers to "as the lessons of power and arrogance" (which he is in no position either to learn or to apply), and simply tell the truth as far as the truth can ever be determined. This is what used to be known as journalism, an honorable trade, as demonstrated thirty years ago by Lillian Ross in her book *Picture,* where she recorded, in deadly detail, only what she herself had seen and heard at MGM during the making of *The Red Badge of Courage.* The result was definitive; and the really "real" thing.

*The New York Review of Books*
September 23, 1982

# 109

# REMEMBERING
# ORSON WELLES

Although Orson Welles was only ten years my senior, he had been famous for most of my life. I was thirteen when he made his famous Martians-are-coming radio broadcast. Then, three years later, when Welles was twenty-six, there was, suddenly, *Citizen Kane.* I was particularly susceptible to *Citizen Kane* because I was brought up among politicians and often saw more of my own father in newsreels than in life, particularly *The March of Time,* whose deep-toned thundering narrator—the voice of history itself—Welles was to evoke in his first film, whose cunning surface is so close to that of newsreel-real life that one felt, literally, at home in a way that one never did in such works of more gorgeous cinematic art as *All This and Heaven Too.*

Five years later, at the Beverly Hills Hotel, I first beheld the relatively lean Orson Welles. ("Note," Mercury Player Joseph Cotten once told me, "how Orson either never smiles on camera, or, if he has to, how he sucks in his cheeks so as not to look like a Halloween pumpkin.") On his arm was Rita Hayworth, his wife. He has it all, I remember thinking in a state of perfect awe untouched by pity. Little did I know—did he know?—that just as I was observing him in triumph, the great career was already going off the rails while the Gilda of all our dreams was being supplanted by the even more beautiful Dolores del Rio. Well, Rita never had any luck. As for Welles . . .

For the television generation he is remembered as an enormously fat and garrulous man with a booming voice, seen most often on talk shows and in commercials where he somberly assured us that a certain wine would not be sold "before its time," whatever that meant. But Welles himself was on sale, as it were, long before *his* time in the sense that he was an astonishing prodigy, as Frank Brady records in *Citizen Welles*, a long biography which, blessedly, emphasises the films in detail rather than the set of conflicting humours that made up the man.

Born in Kenosha, Wisconsin, on May 6, 1915, Welles was much indulged by a well-to-do, somewhat arty family. He was a born actor, artist, writer, magician. At fifteen, he ended his schooling. At sixteen, he was acting, successfully, grown-up parts for Dublin's Gate Theatre. At eighteen, he co-edited and illustrated three Shakespeare plays and a commercial textbook, *Everybody's Shakespeare*. At nineteen, he appeared on Broadway as Chorus and Tybalt in *Romeo and Juliet*. At twenty-two, he founded his own acting company, The Mercury Theater, whose greatest success was a modern-dress *Julius Caesar* with Welles as Brutus. The Mercury Theater then took radio by storm, dramatising novels and stories, among them H. G. Wells's *War of the Worlds*, done in a realistic radio way, using the medium to report, moment by moment, the arrival of Martians in New Jersey. The subsequent national panic augurs ill for that inevitable day when some evil Panamanian tyrant drops his Señor Buén Muchacho mask and nukes Miami.

In due course RKO gave Welles a free hand, if a limited budget, to write, direct, and star in his first film. *Citizen Kane* began a new era in the movies. For those given to making lists, *Citizen Kane* still remains on everyone's list of the ten best films; often as the best film ever made. But for Welles himself things started to fall apart almost immediately. The Hearst newspapers declared war on him for his supposed travesty of Hearst's personal life. On Kane's deathbed, he whispers the word "Rosebud." This is thought to be the key, somehow, to his life. In the film it turns out to be a boy's sled, which Mr. Steven Spielberg recently bought for $55,000. In actual life, Rosebud was what Hearst called his friend Marion Davies's clitoris, the sort of item that producers of children's films tend not to collect. Although the next film, *The Magnificent Ambersons* (1942), might have been even better than *Citizen Kane*, there was trouble with the editing—largely because Welles was in South America, failing to make a film.

For the rest of his life Welles moved restlessly around the world, acting on stage, in movies, on television. As director-actor, he managed to make *Macbeth*, *Othello*, *Chimes at Midnight* (the world from Falstaff's point of view). He also invented, as much as anyone did, the so-called film noir with *Journey into Fear* (1943), *The Lady from Shanghai* (1948), *Touch of Evil* (1958).

Everything that Welles touched as a director has a degree of brilliance, here and there, but he was always running out of money not to mention leading ladies, who kept mysteriously changing in his films, because he was often obliged to shut down for long periods of time, and then, when he started again, actors would be unavailable. In *Othello* Desdemona, finally, is a most expressive blonde wig. Meanwhile, Welles took every acting job he could to finance his own films and pay American taxes. We got to know each other in the Sixties, a period which Mr Brady regards as "the nadir" of Welles's acting career. Well, all I can say is that there was an awful lot of nadir going around in those days. In fact, Welles acted in a nadir film that I had written called *Is Paris Burning?**

In later years we appeared on television together. "You see, I have to do the talk shows to keep my lecture price up at the universities." Orson always acted as if he were broke and, I suppose, relative to the Business, he was. He seemed to live in Spain as well as Hollywood and Las Vegas, "where I am near the airport," he would say mysteriously. "Also there are no death duties in Nevada unlike, shall we say, Haiti."

Orson's conversation was often surreal and always cryptic. Either you picked up on it or you were left out. At one point, he asked me to intervene on his behalf with Johnny Carson because there had been a "misunderstanding" between them and he was no longer asked to go on *The Tonight Show* and his lecture fees had, presumably, plummeted. I intervened. Carson was astonished. There was no problem that he knew of. I reported this to Orson in the course of one of our regular lunches at a French restaurant in Hollywood where Orson always sat in a vast chair to the right of the door. There was a smaller chair for a totally unprincipled small black poodle called Kiki.

"There is more to this than Johnny will ever tell you," he rumbled.

---

*I was astonished to read in Frank Brady's *Citizen Welles* that Orson was offered the starring role in *Caligula,* "but when he read the Gore Vidal script and found it to be a mixture of hard-core pornography and violence, he peremptorily turned it down on moral grounds." Since Brady also gets the plot to *The Big Brass Ring* wrong, I assumed that he was wrong about Caligula, a part Orson could not have played even if my script for the picture had been used as written. But now, suddenly, I recalled Kenneth Tynan telling me that Orson had been upset by my original script. "You must never forget what a Puritan he is when it comes to sex."

"Much, much more. Why," he turned to the waiter with cold eyes, "do you keep bringing me a menu when you know what I must eat? Grilled fish." The voice boomed throughout the room. "And iced tea. How I hate grilled fish! But doctor's orders. I've lost twenty pounds. No one ever believes this. But then no one ever believes I hardly eat anything." He was close to four hundred pounds at the time of our last lunch in 1982. He wore bifurcated tents to which, rather idly, lapels, pocket flaps, buttons were attached in order to suggest a conventional suit. He hated the fat jokes that he was obliged to listen to—on television at least— with a merry smile and an insouciant retort or two, carefully honed in advance. When I asked him why he didn't have the operation that vacuums the fat out of the body, he was gleeful. "Because I have seen the results of liposuction *when the operation goes wrong.* It happened to a woman I know. First, they insert the catheter in the abdomen, subcutaneously." Orson was up on every medical procedure. "The suction begins and the fat—it looks like yellow chicken fat. You must try the chicken here. But then the fat—hers not the chicken's—came out unevenly. And so where once had been a Rubenesque torso, there was now something all hideously rippled and valleyed and canyoned like the moon." He chuckled and, as always, the blood rose in his face, slowly, from lower lip to forehead until the eyes vanished in a scarlet cloud, and I wondered, as always, what I'd do were he to drop dead of a stroke.

We talked mostly of politics and literature. At our last lunch, I was running in the Democratic primary for Senate. Orson approved. "I too had political ambitions, particularly back in the FDR days. I used to help him with speeches and I like to think I was useful to him. I know he thought I should have a serious go at politics some day. Well, some day came. They wanted me to run for the Senate in my home state of Wisconsin, against Joe McCarthy. Then I let them—another 'them'— convince me that I could never win because," and the chuckle began again, "I was an actor—hence, frivolous. And divorced—hence, immoral. And now Ronnie Reagan, who is both, is president." Eyes drowned in the red sea; laughter tolled; then, out of who knows what depths of moral nullity, Kiki bit a waiter's sleeve.

When I observed that acting—particularly old-time movie acting— was the worst possible preparation for the presidency because the movie actor must be entirely passive so that he can do and say exactly what others tell him to do and say, Orson agreed that although this might be true in general (we both excluded *him* from any generality), he had known two movie actors who would have been good presidents. One was

Melvyn Douglas. The other was Gregory Peck. "Of course," he was thoughtful, "Greg isn't much as an actor, which may explain why he has so good a character.'

During the last year of our occasional meetings, Orson and I were much preoccupied with Rudy Vallee. The popular singer of yesteryear was living in the mansion "Silvertip" high atop that Hollywood hill halfway up which I sometimes live. When the maestro heard that I was his neighbour, he sent me a copy of his memoirs *Let The Chips Fall* . . . Like a pair of Talmudic scholars, Orson and I constantly studied this astonishing book. Parts of it we memorised:

Somehow I have never inspired confidence. I don't think it is due to any weakness particularly evident in my face, but there is something about me, possibly a quiet reserve or shyness, that gives most people the impression that I can't do anything very well.

Each of us had his favourite moments. Mine was the telegram (reproduced) that Rudy sent the relatively unknown radio announcer, Arthur Godfrey, in 1940, to show what a keen eye and ear Rudy had for talent (for a time Vallee ran a talent agency). Orson preferred the highly detailed indictment of Rudy's protégé, "The Ungreatfulcholy Dane," Victor Borge, complete with reproductions of inter-office memoranda, telegrams sent and received, culminating in two newspaper cuttings. One headline: VICTOR BORGE SUED FOR $750,000; the other: BORGE SUED BY THE IRS.

As professional storytellers, we were duly awed by Rudy's handling of The Grapefruit Incident, which begins, so casually, at Yale.

Ironically, the dean was the father of the boy who, nine years later, was to hurl a grapefruit at me in a Boston theater and almost kill me.

Then the story is dropped. Pages pass. Years pass. Then the grapefruit motif is reintroduced. Rudy and his band have played for the dean; afterward, when they are given ice cream, Rudy asks, "Is this all we're having . . ."

Apparently one of [the dean's] sons noticed my rather uncivil question . . . and resolved that some day he would avenge this slight. What he actually did later at a Boston theater might have put him in the electric chair and me in my grave but fortunately his aim was bad. But of that more later.

Orson thought this masterful. Appetites whetted, we read on until the now inevitable rendezvous of hero and grapefruit in a Boston theatre where, as Rudy is singing—"Oh, Give Me Something to Remember You By,"

a large yellow grapefruit came hurtling from the balcony. With a tremendous crash it struck the drummer's cymbal . . ." [but] "if it had struck the gooseneck of my sax squarely where it curves into the mouth it might have driven it back through the vertebra in the back of my neck."

Of this passage, the ecstatic Orson whispered, "Conrad"—what might have been *if* Lord Jim had remained on watch.

Finally, in a scene reminiscent of Saint-Simon's last evocation of the Duchess of Burgundy, Vallee tells us how he had got the Chairman of the Board himself to come see his house and its rooms of memorabilia. Frank Sinatra dutifully toured room after room of artefacts relating to the master. Although an offending journalist gave "the impression that most of the pictures portrayed my likeness, actually, one third of the pictures are of neutral subjects or of personalities other than myself." Even so, "as Frank Sinatra rather snidely put it as we left this particular corridor, 'You would never guess who lived here.' "*

In literary matters, Orson was encyclopaedic, with an actor's memory for poetry. I have known few American writers who have had much or, indeed, any enthusiasm for literature. Writers who teach tend to prefer literary theory to literature and tenure to all else. Writers who do not teach prefer the contemplation of Careers to art of any kind. On the other hand, those actors who do read are often most learned, even passionate, when it comes to literature. I think that this unusual taste comes from a thorough grounding in Shakespeare combined with all that time waiting around on movie-sets.

*Rudy Vallee scholars will search in vain for the adverb "snidely" in *Let the Chips Fall . . .* I have taken the liberty of using an earlier version of the Sinatra visit as recorded in *My Time Is Your Time* (1962). Even though Rudy Vallee always wrote the same book, he was given to subtle changes, particularly in his use or omission of adverbs, reminiscent, in their mastery, of the grace notes in Bach. A synoptic edition of Vallee's three memoirs is long overdue, as well as a meticulous concordance.

When we had finished with politics and literature and the broiled fish, Orson told me a hilarious story of a sexual intrigue in Yugoslavia during the shooting of Kafka's *The Trial.* How was Orson to manoeuvre a willing young woman away from her escort in a bar that was connected by a dark and creaking staircase to Orson's room, and then . . . ? Each detail of this labyrinthine tale was lovingly recounted right up until the final victory in the wrong bed or room—or something. Orson was a superb dramatizer. As an actor, he was limited by his unique physical presence and that great booming conman's voice. But when it came to storytelling, he was as exciting at a corner table, talking, as he was on the screen itself in a work all his own. But the tragedy of Welles ("How," I can hear him say, eyes theatrically narrowed to slits in that great round pudding of a face, "do you define tragedy?") is that more time was spent evoking movies at corner tables than in a studio. Yet he was always seriously at work on a number of projects that he could never get the financing for.

"This time I've written a political script. Rather your kind of thing." He puffed on a cigar. He looked like Harry Lime. "You know Paul Newman. Can you put in a word for him? Because if I don't have one of the Six Bankable Boys, there's no financing. What one has to go through." He patted his stomach as if it were his dog. He looked like Falstaff. "They always ask me, aren't you glad, *cher maître,* that the old studio system is finished, that there are no more vulgar furriers controlling your films? And I say, my God, how I miss them! Even Harry Cohn. When you make fifty-two pictures a year on an assembly-line basis there is always room for an Orson Welles film. But now there is no room anywhere." He smoothed the dog's fur as if it were his stomach. Then he chuckled. "I have made an art form of the interview. The French are the best interviewers, despite their addiction to the triad, like all Cartesians." I took this well: triad = trinity, but *versus,* I would have thought, Descartes.

Orson was now in full flow. "They also have the gift of the unexpected letdown. The ultimate Zinger. "There are only three great directors in the history of the film,' they will announce. I smile shyly." Orson smiles. Cotten was right. Though he doesn't seem to be sucking in his cheeks, the corners of his mouth are drawn not up but down. "There is D. W. Griffith. I roll my eyes toward Heaven in an ecstasy of agreement. There is Orson Welles. I lower my lids, all modesty—little me? Then," his voice drops, basso profundissimo, "there is—Nicholas Ray!" Orson erupts in laughter. We meditate on the interview as art form as well as necessity for Orson, "because I don't lecture any more."

"Then why," I asked, "did you ask me to ask Carson to get you back on *The Tonight Show* so that you could get more lecture dates when you've given up lecturing?" He looked at me in true surprise. "Surely I told you I've stopped lecturing because I can't walk from the airport terminal to the gate." "You can use a wheelchair," I said. "But that would be the end of me as an actor. Word would spread I was terminally ill. Besides there is no wheelchair large enough unless I bring my own, which would make a truly bad impression."

Orson never knew that I knew how, the previous week, Orson's driver had delivered him to the restaurant's parking lot, only to find that Orson was so tightly wedged in the front seat that the car had to be taken apart so that he could get out.

"If not Newman, there's Nicholson or Beatty. Warren has consented to give me an audience. But Nicholson would be better. The story's called *The Big Brass Ring,* about a senator who's just been defeated by Reagan for president—two years from now, of course. Really right down your alley . . ."

Three years after our last lunch, Orson died at the age of seventy. He had not been able to get one of the Bankable Boys to agree to do *The Big Brass Ring* and so it is now just one more cloudy trophy to provoke one's imagination. What would Welles's Don Quixote have been like if he had been able to finish it? But then it is pleasurable to imagine what he might have done with any theme because he was, literally, a magician, fascinated by legerdemain, tricks of eye, forgeries, labyrinths, mirrors reflecting mirrors. He was a master of finding new ways of seeing things that others saw not at all.

Happily, I now know something about *The Big Brass Ring,* which was published obscurely in 1987 as "an original screen-play by Orson Welles with Oja Kodar." Wellesian mysteries begin to swirl. Who is Oja Kodar? The dust jacket identifies her as Welles's "companion and collaborator (as actress and screenwriter, among other capacities) over the last twenty years of his life. She is a Yugoslav sculptor who has had one-woman shows in both Europe and the US. The lead actress in *F for Fake* [which I've never seen] and *The Other Side of the Wind* [unreleased], she collaborated on the scripts of both films as well as many other Welles projects" . . . all unmade.

Orson never mentioned her. But then, come to think of it, except for bizarre dreamlike adventures, he never spoke of his private life. In all the years I knew him, I never set foot in any place where he was living, or met his wife, Paola Mori, who died a year after he did. I invited Orson

several times to the house where I lived within megaphone distance of
the Rudy Vallee shrine and he always accepted, with delight. Then the
phone calls would start. "I know that it is the height of rudeness to ask
who will be there, so my rudeness is of the loftiest sort. Who will be
there?" I would tell him and he'd be pleased to see so many old friends;
finally, an hour before the party began, he'd ring. "I have an early call
tomorrow. For a commercial. Dog food, I think it is this time. No, I do
not have to eat from the can on camera but I *celebrate* the contents. Yes,
I have fallen so low."

Further mysteries: there is an afterword published to the script by
Jonathan Rosenbaum, who tells us that Welles left two estates, "one of
them controlled by his wife Paola Mori and daughter Beatrice, . . . the
other controlled by Kodar." Now the two estates appear to be in equilibrium; hence, "the publication of *The Big Brass Ring* represents a major
step forward in the clarification of the invisible Orson Welles, even
though it comprises only a piece of the iceberg (or jigsaw puzzle, if one
prefers)." I prefer jigsaw puzzle. And now, for me, an essential piece is
at hand: the screenplay, which is purest Welles. He is plainly at the top
of his glittering form, which was as deeply literary as it was visual.

What, precisely, is "purest Welles"? Although every line sounds like
Welles, we are told that he based some of the story on an autobiographical sketch by Kodar. Thus, they collaborated. But the germ of the story,
one of Welles's few "originals" (a word in this context never to be let
out of quotes), was first expressed by Welles in a conversation with the
film director Henry Jaglom. Welles said that there was a story that "he'd
been thinking about for years, about an old political adviser to Roosevelt
who was homosexual, and whose lover had gotten crippled in the Spanish Civil War fighting the fascists. Now he was in an African kingdom,
advising the murderous leader—and back in the US, a young senator
who'd been his protégé was going to run against Reagan in 1984, as the
Democratic nominee." So far so Wellesian. The fascination with politics, particularly the New Deal; with homosexuality to the extent that
it involves masks and revelation; and, finally, with the relationship
between the teacher and the taught.

The action is swift. A series of images—fading campaign posters: the
defeated presidential candidate, Pellarin, walks through a restaurant
where he is recognised and cheered: he is a combination of Texas Good-
Ole-Boy and Harvard Law School. The wife, Diana, is edgy, long-
suffering, rich. Then we are aboard a yacht. Pellarin is bored. Diana

plays backgammon with a woman friend. Pellarin goes into their bedroom and finds a girl—a manicurist—stealing his wife's emerald necklace. To his own amazement, he tells her, "Keep it." With this Gidean *acte gratuit* the story takes off. When a shipwide search for the necklace begins, Pellarin realises that it will be found on the girl; so he makes her give him the jewels; then he promises her that he will turn them over to a fence at the next port, which is Tangiers.

At Tangiers Pellarin books a flight to the African country where his old mentor, Kimball Menaker, is advising the local Idi Amin. At the airport, he is ambushed by Cela Brandini, a superb portrait of the dread Oriana Fallaci in the terminal throes of requited self-love. "I am Cela Brandini," she declares with all the authority of a bush afire. "Of course you are," he says, mildly. Brandini: "And I have never asked you for an interview." Pellarin: "Guess I'm just plain lucky." Now Welles can use his second art form, the interview with tape recorder. Brandini has just interviewed Menaker, a figure that Pellarin must never see again because . . . The plot of the emerald necklace crosses with that of the search for Menaker, to be played by Welles at his most oracular, not to mention polymathematical.

As they wait in the airport lounge, Brandini plays for him some of Menaker's dialogue on her recorder, a nice narrative device. Menaker: "A message? Do I wish to send a message to the Senator from Texas? ex-chairman of the Foreign Affairs Committee? former vedette of the Hasty Pudding Club Review, our future President, and my former friend?" Brandini has interviewed Menaker as background for a piece she wants to do on Pellarin. She is aware that Menaker is the skeleton in Pellarin's closet. Had they been lovers? What glorious scandal! Brandini: "The way he speaks of you—he seems to think he's your [father]." Pellarin is pleased. She strikes, "And yet, politically—he almost killed you off." Pellarin demurs: "He didn't quite do that, you know—He killed himself." Mysteries within mysteries. A quest. Nothing now is what it seems. Pellarin, pilgrim.

Pellarin finds Menaker in the Batunga Hilton; he is in bed with a sick monkey while two naked black women play backgammon as they keep guard over him. Although the scene is about finding a fence for the emeralds (Menaker is the author of *The Criminal Underworld Considered as a Primitive Culture—An Anthropological View:* "I'm an authority on everything," he says), the subtext concerns a woman, Pellarin's lost love, a Cambodian beauty, last seen by Menaker in Paris.

Pellarin departs with the sick monkey knotted about his neck, hiding the emeralds. He joins the yacht at Barcelona. Brandini is also there. She declaims: "I'm an anarchist." Pellarin: "I wish you were a veterinarian." Brandini: "I do not think that monkey has very long to live." Pellarin: "Neither do I." Brandini: "Interesting." Pellarin: "Death? The subject doesn't capture my imagination." Brandini: "I know something about it, Pellarin. I've seen it in Vietnam, Central America—in Greece." Pellarin: "I know. There's a lot of that stuff going around." Back on the yacht, Pellarin tries to get the monkey off his neck: it falls into the sea, the emeralds clutched in its fist. How is Pellarin to get the money he "owes" the girl?

Meanwhile, Menaker is out of Africa and again in the clutches of Brandini. A reference is made to Menaker's Harvard rival, Henry Kissinger, "chief brown-noser to the Rockefellers." Menaker is concerned about Kissinger because: "He *is* getting *shorter*—Have you noticed that? He's positively *dwindling* with thwarted ambition: Metternich as the incredible shrinking man. They ought to give poor shrinking Henry one last go at State. As a foreigner, there's no higher he can go—and who knows how much smaller he can get." They speak of Menaker's influence on Pellarin. Menaker seems to him triumphant despite their association, not to mention that of Harvard. These are only minor limitations. Brandini: "You've spoken of his limitations—What are yours?" Menaker: "I'm an old man, Miss Brandini—and a faggot. I couldn't use another limitation."

Pellarin and Menaker meet. Menaker says not to worry about the emeralds: they are false. Diana sold the originals to help get Pellarin elected to Congress. She has worn paste copies ever since. So Pellarin must cash a cheque in order to give money to the girl for the worthless jewels that she stole and Pellarin lost. This is exquisite Welles. And he brings it off with Wildean panache.

Now the story of the emeralds again crosses the story of the lost love in Paris. Apparently, she is in Madrid. She wants to see Pellarin. Menaker will take him to her. Meanwhile they meditate upon identity. Menaker: "Even the great ones must have sometimes felt uncomfortable in their own skins. Caesar must have dreamt of Alexander, and Napoleon of Caesar." Pellarin: "Shit, Professor—I couldn't make their weight." Menaker: "Then think of poor Dick Nixon—mincing about inside his fortress in the Oval Room, all bristling with bugs—hoping a playback would eventually inform him who he was . . . He told us often what he *wasn't,* but he never really got it figured out." Pellarin: "Neither have I . . . You sly old son of a bitch, so *that's* what you've been getting at." Menaker: "In a perfect world, all of us should be allowed some short vacations from our own identities. Last week you were Bulldog Drummond, gentleman jewel thief. Soon you'll be hoping to sneak down that rabbit hole again to where it's always Paris in the spring." Orson Welles, who was known to all the world as Orson Welles, could never be anyone else in life but, in art, he could saw a lady in half, pull a rabbit from a hat, arrange shadows on celluloid in such a way as to be any number of entirely other selves.

Menaker leads Pellarin to "The Old Dark House." A *feria* is in progress; fireworks. Only Pellarin goes inside the house: "The scene is strange, almost surreal . . . (The action must be given in synopsis . . . The climax of this sequence is strongly erotic: to spell out its specific details would be to risk pornography) . . . A man searching and searching—up and down, from floor to floor, from room to room of an empty house, comes to discover (in a lightning flash of fireworks breaking through a shuttered window) that all along there has been someone watching him:—naked, in a shadowed chair." This is much the same scene that Orson told me at our last lunch as having happened to him. Did it? Or was he trying out the scene on me? She is found; they speak in French; make love; then she vanishes. Although the film was to be shot in black and white, Orson intended the fireworks to be in colour; at the scene's end "The colored lights fall into darkness."

Pellarin faces Menaker in the street. Menaker never delivered the letter that Pellarin had written asking the girl to marry him. Menaker did not deliver it because he wants Pellarin to go to glory. Pellarin: "Screw Pennsylvania Avenue." Menaker: "Boysie—There's nowhere else for you to go." Later, the ubiquitous Brandini strikes. She tells Pellarin that "during his sexual fantasizing about you—Dr. Menaker would masturbate into a handkerchief . . . Then, when it was stiff with his dried semen, he mailed it to his crippled friend, as . . . I don't know what: a sentimental souvenir." I must say that even at the lively fun-court of Tiberius and of his heir, Caligula, neither Suetonius nor I ever came up with anything quite so—dare I use so punitive a word?—icky. But Orson needed an emotional trigger for a nightmare flight through the city and an encounter with a blind beggar who menaces Pellarin and whom he kills. Let it come down. The police suspect; but cover for him.

Pellarin re-enters the world. A speech must be given in Brussels. Menaker is on the train, which Brandini satisfactorily misses—"dressed as usual: semi-safari with a strong hint of battle fatigues." They sing, jointly, Menaker's "hit number from the Hasty Pudding Show of nineteen twenty-nine." Then Orson adds, with his usual flourish: "If you want a happy ending, that depends, of course, on where you stop your story."

In a statement to Henry Jaglom (May 20, 1982), Orson wrote of Pellarin.

He is a great man—like all great men he is never satisfied that he has chosen the right path in life. Even being President, he feels, may somehow not be right. He is a man who has within him the devil of self-destruction that lives in every genius . . . There is this foolish, romantic side of us all . . . That is what the *circumstances* of the film are about—the theft of the necklace, the situation with the monkey, etc. All these idiotic events that one's romantic nature leads one into.

But of course Orson is describing Menaker, not Pellarin, and, again of course, Orson is describing his own "romantic nature" which led him down so many odd roads, to our enduring delight if not always his.

I have a recurring fantasy that if one were to dial the telephone number of someone in the past, one would hear again a familiar voice, and time would instantly rewind from now to then. I still have Orson's telephone number in my book (213–851–8458). Do I dare ring him and talk to him back in 1982, where he is busy trying to convince Jack Nicholson to play Pellarin for two not four million dollars? Should I tell him that he'll not get the picture made? No. That would be too harsh. I'll pretend that I have somehow got a copy of it, and that I think it marvellous though perhaps the handkerchief was, from so prudish a master, a bit much? Even incredible.

"Incredible?" The voice booms in my ear. "How could it be incredible when I stole it from *Othello*? But now I have a real treat for you. Standing here is your neighbour . . . Rudy! Overcome 'that quiet reserve or shyness.' *Sing.*"

From out of the past, I hear "My time is your time," in that reedy highly imitable voice. The after-life's only a dial tone away. "What makes you think that this is the after-life?" Orson chuckles. "This is a recording." Stop story here.

*The New York Review of Books*
June 1, 1989

# 110

## CONTAGIOUS
## SELF-LOVE

The Seventh Earl of Longford and I appeared together on British television. As the Seventh Earl was introduced to the viewers, he swung around in his chair and looked at himself in the television monitor; it was plain that he was ravished by what he saw. And I? In those few seconds I was depraved and corrupted by the sort of blind self-love that is so communicable that one is transformed. I was—am—like Onan on a peak in Darien; the prurient theater of my mind, hopelessly dominated by the fact of the Seventh Earl who made me love him as he loves him.

In front of me now is the Seventh Earl's third volume of memoirs. On the dust jacket there is a photograph *in color* of the Seventh Earl's head. He looks mighty pleased with himself—as well he ought. Beneath the picture, the words *The Grain of Wheat, an Autobiography, Frank Longford.* That's all: a vivid contrast to the Seventh Earl's billing on the slender paperback *Humility.* The title *Humility* was hardly visible, modest mauve on black, while the author's name was in stark white *Frank Pakenham, Earl of Longford.* But no matter how Frank wants to be known, I find his ruling passion perfectly irresistible.

In the present volume Frank brings us up to date. He admits right off to being an intellectual and a quotation from A. J. Cronin early on convinced me that the contents of Frank's mind are well worth a detour.

As he says, "my special kind of brain is well above average in literature."
After all, he produced "*Peace by Ordeal,* still the standard book on the
Anglo-Irish Treaty of 1931"; as for his biography of De Valera, "Sales
were highly satisfactory . . . and the English reviews were very pleasing."
Frank tells us that his college was Christchurch, "certainly the most
aristocratic college in the world." Frank's war was not much good; he
was "invalided out with a nervous breakdown" in May 1940. But Frank
turned his misfortune to tremendous advantage:

with prisoners, ex-prisoners, outcasts generally and all those who hesitate
to show their faces abroad, I have had one unfailing and unforeseen point
of contact. I can say and mean and be believed—"I also have been humiliated." The gulf is bridged as if by magic. If my sense of compassion has been
strengthened and activated from any human experience, it is from my own
infirmities and the indignities I have myself undergone.

Like Henry James, Frank does not spell out those infirmities and
indignities. We can only guess at his anguish. But he does share his
triumphs with us: "according to the *Economist,* I was an enormously
successful amateur banker." When Leader of the House of Lords, Frank
spoke on Rhodesia and "Harold Wilson and other leaders crowded in
to listen. Next day, Harold Wilson congratulated me in front of the
Cabinet." Later, "when I resigned I was overwhelmed with letters
. . . referring in glowing terms to my leadership." And why not? On one
occasion, when Leader, *Frank spoke from the back benches*! "I can't find
that a Leader of the House had ever previously done what I did."
Frank had his downs as well as his ups in politics. He was not heeded
as often as he ought to have been. He might "have swayed the issue"
on devaluation, but didn't. Serenely he records that Harold Wilson is
supposed to have noted, "Frank Longford quite useless. Mental age of
12." Frank takes this very well (after all, any *bright* 12-year-old is perfectly able to lead the Lords). But he does hope that in future Harold
"will avoid such indiscretions." Anyway, "nothing in my membership
in the Wilson Government became me so well—it was said at the
time—as the manner of my leaving it." He left it on a Point of Principle.
He "most treasures" a letter he got from someone mysteriously called
"Bobbity Salisbury." Truly great men like Clem Attlee thought the
world of Frank who also

treasures more than one of his letters running like this: "My dear Frank,
I will look into the point you mentioned as soon as possible. Yours ever,
Clem."

Yet for all the wonderful letters and compliments from his peers "I felt, and still feel, that I was largely wasted in the Cabinet." But, Frank, that's the point isn't it? To be humiliated in order that you may be able to grow as a human being, to learn compassion so that you can help us outcasts across that awful gulf.

Frank writes a lot about sinners (loves them, hates the sin). He got to know the gangster brothers Kray: "talking to me that afternoon, I am sure that they had made a resolution: never again." He befriended Ian Brady and Myra Hindley, of the Moors murders fame: "their agony is never far from my mind." Frank admits that he is sometimes criticized for his Christian treatment of murderers: "psychologists and other men assess my motives as they wish." But Frank is, simply, good. There is no other word. Best of all, he wants us to share with him through his many testaments his many good actions. That's why he writes books and appears on television programs. By reading Frank and looking at Frank people will want to be as good as he is. Of course he can be stern. Although Frank doesn't want to put homosexualists in jail, he doesn't want people to forget that "homosexual conduct . . . remains wrongful." Pornography, on the other hand is not only wrongful but must be rooted out and the makers and dispensers of it punished.

Frank reports on his still unfinished crusade against pornography. All in all, he has been having a super time even though he is a bit miffed that the press has not so far acknowledged that "I had an experience of inquiries which no one in politics could equal." Unfortunately, "these rather striking qualifications . . . were never mentioned." But more fortunately,

I was featured in the *Evening Standard* as "British worthy No. 4, my predecessors being the Duke of Norfolk, the Archbishop of Canterbury and Mick Jagger. I was interviewed times without number and was chosen by the *Sunday Times* as the most caricatured figure of 1972 . . . My citation as "Man of the Year" referred to me as Crusader Extraordinary.

Then came The Garter, "a clear reminder that I was not without recognition." And so, gartered as well as belted, on to Copenhagen. TV cameras. Strippers. Porn. Jesus. Love. Compassion. Outrage. Filth. Human decency. Where will it end, Frank?

I think I know, because Frank let a bit of the cat's whisker out of the bag when he quoted a journalist who wrote:

Lord Longford is clearly a good man. If he is not actually a saint, he is certainly the most saintly member of the Upper Chamber, and I do not overlook the Bishops.

That's it. After the humiliation of the bad war, the failed career in politics, the eccentric attempt to regulate England's morals, now comes the halo, the nimbus, the mandala, the translation to Paradise by special arrangement with Telstar. And so at God's right hand, forever and ever stands the Seventh Earl of Longford, peering happily into an eternal television monitor. Pray for us, Saint Frank. Intercede for us, and teach us to love ourselves as you loved you.

*New Statesman*
March 8, 1974

# 111

### NASSER'S
### EGYPT

"Are you German, sir?" A small, dark youth stepped from behind a palm tree into the full light of the setting sun which turned scarlet the white shirt and albino red the black eyes. He had been watching me watch the sun set across the Nile, now blood-red and still except for sailboats tacking in a hot, slow breeze. I told him that I was American but was used to being mistaken for a German: in this year of the mid-century, Germans are everywhere, and to Arab eyes we all look alike. He showed only a moment's disappointment.

"I have many German friends," he said. "Two German friends. *West* German friends. Perhaps you know them?" He pulled a notebook out of his pocket and read off two names. Then, not waiting for an answer, all in a rush, he told me that he was a teacher of Arabic grammar, that he was going to Germany, *West* Germany (he emphasized the *West* significantly), to write a book. What sort of book? A book about West Germany. The theme? He responded with some irritation: "A Book About West Germany." That was what the book would be about. He was a poet. His name was Ahmed. "Welcome," he said, "welcome!" His crooked face broke into a smile. "Welcome to Luxor!" He invited me to his house for mint tea.

As we turned from the bank of the Nile, a long, haunting cry sounded across the water. I had heard this same exotic cry for several evenings, and I was certain that it must be of ancient origin, a hymn perhaps to Ikhnaton's falling sun. I asked Ahmed what this lovely aria meant. He listened a moment and then said, "It's this man on the other side who says: will the ferryboat please pick him up?" So much for magic.

Ahmed led the way through narrow streets to the primary school where he taught. It was a handsome modern building, much like its counterparts in Scarsdale or Darien. He took me inside. "You must see what the children make themselves. Their beautiful arts." On the entrance-hall table their beautiful arts were exhibited: clay figures, carved wood, needlework, all surrounding a foot-long enlargement in clay of the bilharzia, a parasite which is carried by snails in the irrigation ditches; once it invades the human bloodstream, lungs and liver are attacked and the victim wastes away; some ninety per cent of the fellahin suffer from bilharzia. "Beautiful?" he asked. "Beautiful," I said.

On the wall hung the exhibit's masterpiece, a larger than life-size portrait of Nasser, painted in colors recalling Lazarus on the fourth day. A somewhat more talented drawing next to it showed students marching with banners in a street. I asked Ahmed to translate the words on the banners. "Our heads for Nasser," he said with satisfaction. I asked him if Nasser was popular with the young. He looked at me as though I had questioned the next day's sunrise. Of course Nasser was loved. Had I ever been in Egypt before? Yes, during the winter of 1948, in the time of the bad fat King. Had things improved? I told him honestly that they had indeed. Cairo had changed from a nineteenth-century French provincial capital surrounded by a casbah to a glittering modern city, only partially surrounded by a casbah. He asked me what I was doing in Egypt, and I told him I was a tourist, not mentioning that I had an appointment to interview Nasser the following week for an American magazine.

Ahmed's house is a large one, four stories high; here he lives with some twenty members of his family. The parlor is a square room with a high ceiling from which hangs a single unshaded light bulb. Two broken beds serve as sofas. I sat on one of the beds while Ahmed, somewhat nervously, ordered mint tea from a sister who never emerged from the dark hall. Then I learned that his father was also a teacher, and that an uncle worked in Nasser's office; obviously a prosperous family by Luxor standards.

I was offered the ceremonial cigarette. I refused; he lit up. He was sorry his father was not there to meet me. But then again, puffing his cigarette, he was glad, for it is disrespectful to smoke in front of one's father. Only recently the father had come unexpectedly into the parlor. "I was smoking a cigarette and when he came in, oh! I bit it hard, like this, and have to swallow it down! Oh, I was sick!" We chuckled at his memory.

When the mint tea arrived (passed to us on a tray from the dark hall, only bare arms visible), Ahmed suggested we sit outside where it was cool. Moonlight blazed through a wooden trellis covered with blossoming wisteria. We sat on stiff wooden chairs. He switched on a light momentarily to show me a photograph of the girl he was to marry. She was pretty and plump and could easily have been the editor of the yearbook in any American high school. He turned off the light. "We modern now. No more arranged marriages. Love is everything. Love is why we marry. Love is all." He repeated this several times, with a sharp intake of breath after each statement. It was very contagious, and I soon found myself doing it. Then he said, "Welcome," and I said, "Thank you."

Ahmed apologized for the unseasonable heat. This was the hottest spring in years, as I had discovered that day in the Valley of the Kings where the temperature had been over a hundred and the blaze of sun on white limestone blinding. "After June, Luxor is *impossible!*" he said proudly. "We all go who can go. If I stay too long, I turn dark as a black in the sun." Interestingly enough, there is racial discrimination in Egypt. "The blacks" are second-class citizens: laborers, servants, minor government functionaries. They are the lowest level of Egyptian society in every way except one: there are no Negro beggars. That is an Arab monopoly. Almsgivers are blessed by the Koran, if not by Nasser, who has tried to discourage the vast, well-organized hordes of beggars.

"To begin with, I had naturally a very light complexion," said Ahmed, making a careful point, "like the rest of my family, but one day when I was small the nurse upset boiling milk on me and ever since that day I have been somewhat dark." I commiserated briefly. Then I tried a new tack. I asked him about his military service. Had he been called up yet? A new decree proposed universal military service, and I thought a discussion of it might get us onto politics. He said that he had not been called up because of a *very interesting story.* My heart sank, but I leaned forward with an air of sympathetic interest. Suddenly, I realized I was impersonating someone. But who? Then when he began to talk and I to respond with small nods and intakes of breath, I realized that it was E. M. Forster. I was the Forster of *A Passage to India* and this was Dr.

Aziz. Now that I had the range, my fingers imperceptibly lengthened into Forsterian claws; my eyes developed an uncharacteristic twinkle; my upper lip sprouted a ragged gray moustache, while all else turned to tweed.

"When the British attacked us at Suez, I and these boys from our school, we took guns and together we marched from Alexandria to Suez to help our country. We march for many days and nights in the desert. We have no food, no water. Then we find we are lost and we don't know where we are. Several die. Finally, half dead, we go back to Alexandria and we march in the street to the place where Nasser is. We ask to see him, to cheer him, half dead all of us. But they don't let us see him. Finally, my uncle hears I am there and he and Nasser come out and, ah, Nasser congratulates us, we are heroes! Then I collapse and am unconscious one month. That is why I have *not* to do military service." I was impressed and said so, especially at their getting lost in the desert, which contributed to my developing theory that the Arabs are disaster-prone: they *would* get lost, or else arrive days late for the wrong battle.

Ahmed told me another story of military service, involving friends. "Each year in the army they have these . . . these . . ." We searched jointly—hopelessly—for the right word until E. M. Forster came up with "maneuvers," which was correct. I could feel my eyes twinkling in the moonlight.

"So these friends of mine are in this maneuvers with guns in the desert and they have orders: *shoot to kill.* Now one of them was Ibrahim, my friend. Ibrahim goes to this outpost in the dark. They make him stop and ask him for the password and he . . ." Sharp intake of breath. "He has *forgotten* the password. So they say, 'He must be the enemy.'" I asked if this took place in wartime. "No, no, *maneuvers.* My friend Ibrahim say, 'Look, I forget. I *did* know but now I forget the password but you know me, anyway, you know it's Ibrahim.' And he's right. They do know it was Ibrahim. They recognize his voice but since he cannot say the password they shot him."

I let E. M. Forster slip to the floor. "Shot him? Dead?"

"Dead," said my host with melancholy satisfaction. "Oh, they were very sorry because they knew it was Ibrahim, but, you see, *he did not know the password,* and while he was dying in the tent they took him to, he said it was all right. They were right to kill him."

I found this story hard to interpret. Did Ahmed approve or disapprove what was done? He was inscrutable. There was silence. Then he said, "Welcome," and I said, "Thank you." And we drank more mint tea in the moonlight.

I tried again to get the subject around to politics. But beyond high praise for everything Nasser has done, he would volunteer nothing. He did point to certain tangible results of the new regime. For one thing, Luxor was now a center of education. There were many new schools. All the children were being educated. In fact he had something interesting to show me. He turned on the lamp and opened a large scrapbook conveniently at hand. It contained photographs of boys and girls, with a scholastic history for each. Money had to be raised to educate them further. It *could* be done. Each teacher was obliged to solicit funds. "Look what my West German friends have given," he said, indicating amounts and names. Thus I was had, in a good cause. I paid and walked back to the hotel.

On the way back, I took a shortcut down a residential street. I had walked no more than a few feet when an old man came rushing after me. "Bad street!" he kept repeating. I agreed politely, but continued on my way. After all, the street was well lit. There were few people abroad. A shout from an upstairs window indicated that I should halt. I looked up. The man in the window indicated I was to wait until he came downstairs. I did. He was suspicious. He was from the police. *Why* was I in that street? I said that I was taking a walk. This made no sense to him. He pointed toward my hotel, which was in a slightly different direction. That was where I was supposed to go. I said yes, but I wanted to continue in *this* street, I liked to walk. He frowned. Since arrest was imminent, I turned back. At the hotel I asked the concierge why what appeared to be a main street should be forbidden to foreigners. "Oh, 'they' might be rude," he said vaguely. "You know. . . ." I did not know.

In the diner on the train south to Aswan I had breakfast with a young government official from the Sudan. He was on his way home to Khartoum. He had a fine smile and blue-black skin. On each cheek there were three deep scars, the ritual mark of his tribe—which I recognized, for I had seen his face only the day before on the wall of the Temple of Luxor. Amenhotep III had captured one of his ancestors in Nubia; five thousand years ago the ritual scars were the same as they are now. In matters of religion Africans are profound conservatives. But otherwise he was a man of our time and world. He was dressed in the latest French fashion. He had been for two years on an economic mission in France. He spoke English, learned at the British school in Khartoum.

We breakfasted on musty-tasting dwarfish eggs as dust filtered slowly in through closed windows, covering table, plates, eggs with a film of grit. A fan stirred the dusty air. Parched, I drank three Coca-Colas—the national drink—and sweated. The heat outside was already 110 degrees, and rising. For a while we watched the depressing countryside and spoke very little. At some points the irrigated land was less than a mile wide on our side of the river: a thin ribbon of dusty green ending abruptly in a blaze of desert where nothing at all grew, a world of gray sand as far as the eye could see. Villages of dried-mud houses were built at the desert's edge so as not to use up precious land. The fellahin in their ragged clothes moved slowly about their tasks, quite unaware of the extent of their slow but continual decline. In the fifth century B.C., Herodotus was able to write: "As things are at present these people get their harvest with less labor than anyone else in the world; they have no need to work with plow or hoe, or to use any other of the ordinary methods of cultivating their land; they merely wait for the river of its own accord to flood the fields." But all that has changed. Nearly thirty million people now live in a country whose agriculture cannot support half that number.

"I used to think," said the Sudanese at last, "that Egypt was a fine place, much better than the Sudan. A big country. Rich. But now I know how lucky we are. There is no one at home poor like this." He pointed to several ragged men in a field. Two lay listlessly in the sun. The others worked slowly in the field, narcotized by the heat; the diet of the fellahin is bread and stewed tea and not much of that. I asked him what he thought of Nasser's attacks on his government (recently there had been a disagreement over Nile water rights and Nasser had attacked the Sudanese President with characteristic fury). "Oh, we just laugh at him. We just laugh at him," he repeated as though to convince himself. I asked him why Nasser was continuously on the offensive not only against the West but against the rest of the Arab world. He shrugged. "To impress his own people, I suppose. We don't like it, of course. But perhaps it makes him feel big. Makes them . . ." He pointed to a group of villagers drawing water from a canal. "Makes them forget."

Aswan is the busiest and most optimistic of Egypt's cities. On its outskirts a brand-new chemical factory employs several thousand people. There is a sense of urgency in the city's life, for it is here that all of Egypt's hopes are concentrated: the High Dam is being built. When the dam—the world's largest—is completed in 1970, vast tracts of desert will be made arable and electrical power will be supplied cheaply for the whole country. It should be recalled that the United States had originally agreed to finance a part of the dam, but in 1956 John Foster Dulles withdrew our support and the Soviet obligingly filled the vacuum. Not only are the Russians now financing the dam, but their engineers are building it.

The government had arranged that I be shown around by one of the Egyptian engineers, a cautious, amiable man who spoke not only English but Russian. "I like the Russians very much," he announced firmly as we got into his car. He would show me everything, he said. Nothing to hide.

It was sundown as we approached the barren hills where a huge channel is being cut contiguous to the Nile. Ten thousand men work three eight-hour shifts. Most of the heavy work is done in the cool of the night. Off to the left of the road I noticed a fenced-in compound containing a number of small, modern apartment houses. "The Russians," said my guide. It was a pleasant scene: women chatted in doorways while through uncurtained windows one could see modern kitchens where dinners were cooking. A large sign forbade the taking of photographs.

"How many Russians are there in Aswan?" I asked. He looked at me bewildered. "What you say?" He took refuge in pidgin English. I repeated the question very slowly and distinctly. He looked puzzled. He lost all his English until I made it impossible for him not to understand me.

"You mean how many Russians altogether? Or how many Russian *engineers*?" he countered, playing for time. "After all, there are wives and children, and sometimes visitors and . . ." I told him carefully and slowly that I would like to know, first, how many Russians altogether; then I would like to know how many of those were engineers. Of course he had thought that what I wanted to know was the actual number of technicians, and in what categories. After all, there were civil engineers, electrical engineers, and so on, but none of *that* was secret. "We have no secrets! Everything open! Anything you want to know we tell you!" He beamed expansively and parked the car in front of a small circular building. Not until I got out did I realize he had not answered the question.

We now stood on a low hill with a long view of the digging. It was a startling sight. Beneath us was the vast channel already cut from the rock. The sun was gone by now, and the channel—more like a crater—was lit by hundreds of electric lights strung on poles. A perpetual haze of dust obscured the view. Russian diesel trucks roared up and down the sides of the crater, adding to the shrill chatter of drills in stone. Behind us a whole town of new buildings had been somewhat casually assembled: machine shops, technical schools, a hospital. In the desert beyond these buildings, a thousand low black tents were pitched, each with its own campfire. Here the workers lived in stern, nomadic contrast to the modern world they were making.

We entered the circular building which contained a large detailed model of the completed dam. On the walls, diagrams, maps, photographs demonstrated the work's progress and dramatized the fertile Egypt-to-be. I met more Egyptian engineers.

We studied the models and I tried unsuccessfully to sound knowledgeable about turbines. I asked how the workers were recruited. Were they local? How quickly could people who had never used machinery be trained? I was told that the fellahin were surprisingly adaptable. They were trained in schools on the spot. Most of the workers are recruited locally. "But the main thing," said my guide, "is that they know how important all this is. And they do."

I had been told that the dam was some forty weeks behind in its current schedule. But not being an expert in these matters, I could not tell from looking at what I was shown if things were going well or badly, behind or on schedule. The most I could gather was that the engineers were genuinely enthusiastic about their work. Morale is high. And I am ready to testify that they have dug a fine big hole.

We drove to the center of the channel, a good mile from the exhibition hall and at least a hundred yards below the surface of the desert. The air in the crater is almost unbreathable: part dust, part exhaust. A constant haze dims the lights on their poles. The noise is continual and deafening. Hundreds of drills in long, chattering rows break the sandstone floor of the crater, while Russian steam shovels tear at the cliff. I noticed that all the Russian machines looked improvised. No two steam shovels were alike.

We made our way to the entrance of a tunnel cut into a sandstone hill. This was a shortcut to the place where the first turbines were to be set up. At the entrance of the tunnel we were stopped by the only Russian I was to see: a gray, middle-aged man with a tired face. After a long discussion, he gave permission for me to enter the tunnel. "With every Egyptian engineer," said my guide, "there is also a Russian engineer." It was obvious who was in charge.

The tunnel was brightly lit; the noise of drilling was stunningly amplified by stone walls. I was surprised to see occasional puddles of water on the tunnel floor. I daydreamed: The diggers had struck underground springs. That meant there was water in the desert, deep down, and if there was water deep down, all of Egypt's problems were solved. Obviously no one else had figured out the true meaning of the puddles. I turned to my guide. We shouted at one another and I learned that the puddles were caused not by springs but by seepage from the nearby Nile. The nightmare of the dam builders is that the Nile's water might begin to seep at too great a rate through the sandy walls of the crater, wrecking not only the project but possibly diverting the river's course as well.

Finally, lungs protesting, I said that I had seen enough. This time two engineers drove me back to the hotel, where we drank a ceremonial beer together and I complimented them not only on their enthusiasm but on their courage. At the earliest, the dam will be completed in 1970, which means that these men are dedicating their professional lives to a single project. "But we do this, as Nasser says, for the good of our people," said my original guide solemnly. The other engineer was equally solemn: "No, for the good of all humanity." Taking advantage of this suddenly warm mood, I asked again how many Russians were working on the dam. I got two blank looks this time. "What you say?" And I was no wiser when they left.

The next day in Aswan I was able to obtain an unofficial view of what is really going on. There is a good deal of friction between Egyptians and Russians. Much of it is due to the language barrier. The Russians speak only Russian, the Egyptians speak English or French, sometimes both, but few have learned Russian. The professional interpreters are hopeless because, though they can cope with ordinary conversation, they do not know the technical terms of either language. "We use sign language mostly," said one technician glumly. "Everything is too slow."

Another problem is machinery. It is well known that the Soviet has always had a somewhat mystical attitude toward that sine qua non of the machine age: the interchangeable part. It seems to go against the Slavic grain to standardize. Consequently, when a machine breaks down (usually in six months' time) it must be replaced entirely. Efforts to "cannibalize," as the mechanics put it, are futile since a part from one drill will not fit another drill. As a result, Swedish drills are now being imported, at considerable cost.

Humanly, the Russians are praised for their ability to survive without complaint the terrible heat. "But," said one Egyptian, "heat is bad for their babies. They turn all red and get sick so they have to send them home." The Russians keep almost entirely to themselves. One of the livelier engineers was the most critical: "They don't go out; they don't dance; they don't do nothing. Just eat and drink!" He shook his head disapprovingly, for the Egyptian with any money is a happy fellow who wants to have a good time in whatever is the going way:

alcohol has lately caught on, despite the Prophet's injunction, while the smoking of hashish and kif has gone into decline, the result of stringent new laws against their sale and use. Also the emancipation of women is progressing nicely and women are to be seen in public places. Dancing is popular. In fact, the twist was the rage of Cairo's nightclubs until Nasser banned it.

Sooner or later every Egyptian connected with the High Dam denounces John Foster Dulles. He is the principal demon in the Egyptian hell, largely because the engineers still wish the Americans would come in on the dam—speaking only as technicians, they add quickly, reminding one that they are, after all, Western-trained and used to Western machinery and procedures. Also they find Western life sympathetic. But what's done is done . . . and we would look sadly at one another . . . such is Allah's will. The Soviet is committed to the dam to the end. I suspect that they wish they were out of it: spending four hundred million dollars to build the largest dam in the world in the midst of a desert is a venture more apt than not to leave all participants exhausted and disenchanted with one another. And there, but for the grace of John Foster Dulles, go we.

At my hotel in Cairo I found a message from the President's office. My appointment was canceled, but His Excellency would see me in the next few days. I telephoned the Appointments Secretary. When? They would let me know. I was to stand by. Meanwhile, there were many people in and out of the Cabinet I could see. Name anyone. I picked Mohammed Hassanein Heikal. He is editor of Cairo's chief newspaper, *Al Ahram.* He is supposed to have written *The Philosophy of the Revolution,* Nasser's *Mein Kampf* (a rather touching work reminiscent more of Pirandello than of Hitler). Heikal is the President's alter ego. An appointment was made for late that afternoon.

I had a drink in a nearby hotel bar with an English journalist who had been some years in Egypt. He is a short, red-faced man who speaks Arabic; he demonstrates the usual love-hate for Nasser which one soon gets used to. "He's a dictator, but then they all are. They have to be. He's personally honest, which few of them are. But the main thing is he's the first man ever to try to do anything for the people here. *The first.* Ever! And it's not just demagoguery. He means it. But the problems! He's inherited the old bureaucracy, the most corrupt in the world. On top of that there aren't enough trained people to run the country, much less all the new business he confiscated last year. The foreigners who used to manage things are gone. Alexandria's a ghost town. Even so, in spite of everything, he's made these people proud to be Egyptians." I said that I thought nationalistic pride, of de Gaulle's *la gloire* sort, too luxurious an emotion in a dangerous world.

"That's not the point. This isn't manifest-destiny stuff. It's that these people really believed they were inferior to everybody else. They thought they really were scum . . . wogs. For centuries. Well, Nasser's changed all that. He's shown them they're like anybody else. We said Egyptians could never run the Suez Canal. Remember? Well, they run it a lot better than we ever did." I asked him about Arab imperialism. Nasser has proposed himself as leader of the Arab world, a new Saladin. Through his radio and through the thousands of Cairo-trained school-teachers sent out to the various Arab countries, Nasser has tried to incite the people to overthrow their "reactionary" governments and to unite with him in some vague but potent hegemony.

The Englishman laughed. "The joke of course is the Egyptians aren't Arab at all. The Arabs conquered Egypt and stayed. But so have a lot of other races. Nasser himself is only part Arab. The Copts have no Arab blood, while everyone else is a mixture. The Egyptians used to be contemptuous of the Arabs. In fact, their word for Arab means a nomad, a wild man, a . . ." "Hick?" I supplied, and he nodded. "Now everyone's trying to claim pure Arab descent."

We spoke of the more ruthless side of Nasser's reign. Egypt is a police state. Arrests are often indiscriminate. Currently, a journalist is in jail for having provided an American newspaper with the information— accurate—that Nasser is a diabetic. There is nothing resembling representative government. The middle class is in a state of panic.

I asked him about Nasser personally. What sort of a man was he? I got the familiar estimate: great personal charm, most reasonable in conversation, entirely lacking in personal vanity and ostentation . . . he still lives at Heliopolis in the house he owned as a colonel. He tends to be nervous with foreigners, especially with the British and the French. They put him on the defensive. He is a devoted family man, a puritan who was profoundly shocked during his first Cairo meeting with Indonesia's President Sukarno, who gaily asked, "Now, where are the girls?" He worries about gaining weight. He admires Tito because he "showed me how to get help from both sides—without joining either." Nasser in his passion for Egypt has also declared, "I will treat with the devil himself if I have to for my country." But he is wary of foreign commitments. He has said: "An alliance between a big and a small power is an alliance between the wolf and the sheep, and it is bound to end with the wolf devouring the sheep." His relations with the Soviet are correct but not warm. He has imprisoned every Egyptian Communist he can find. He took advantage of a Soviet offer to give technical training to Egyptian students, but when he discovered that their first six months in Moscow were devoted to learning Marxist theory, he withdrew the students and rerouted them to the West. He is thought to be genuinely religious. He is obsessed, as well he might be, by the thought of sudden death.

"He's at the Barrage right now. That's his place downriver. You may as well know you're going to have a hard time seeing him." He looked about to make sure that the ubiquitous barman—a government informer—was out of earshot. Then he whispered: "Nasser was shot at yesterday." I contained my surprise and the Englishman played this dramatic scene with admirable offhandedness. "Complete censorship, of course. It won't hit the papers. He wasn't hurt, but his bodyguard was killed. So he's holed up at the Barrage for the rest of this week." Who shot at him? The Englishman shrugged. Saudi Arabia, Yemen, Syria, Iraq, Israel—any number of governments would like Nasser dead.

I sat in the anteroom of the editor of *Al Ahram*. His secretary went on with her work. I glanced at her desk (I can read upside down if the type is sufficiently large) and noted a copy of the American magazine *Daedalus*. Seeing my interest, she gave it to me. It featured an article on birth control. Heikal himself had made many marginal notes. "A problem, isn't it?" I said. She nodded. "A problem."

I was shown into the editor's office. Heikal is a short, lean man, handsome in the way that certain actors of the 30s who played suave villains with pencil moustaches were handsome. He smokes cigars. He gives an impression of great energy. He shook my hand; then he darted back to his desk where he was correcting proofs of an editorial. Would I mind? He always liked to go over them at the last minute. He made marginal notes. He puffed cigar smoke. He is an actor, I decided, giving a performance: Malraux without genius. He has the half-challenging, half-placating manner of those men who are close to a prince.

I waited patiently for quite a few minutes. Finally, he slapped his pencil down with a flourish. He was mine. I asked him how many printer's errors he had found. "Eight," he said precisely, "but mostly I like to change at the last minute." I mentioned *Daedalus* and birth control. "A problem," he said. They were doing their best, of course, but it would take twenty years to educate the people. It was a formidable task.

I then made the error of referring to *The Philosophy of the Revolution* as his book. "My book? *My* book? It is Nasser's book." I said that I had thought it was at least a joint effort. "You've been reading Robert St. John's *The Boss,*" which indeed I had. "Well, that is not the only mistake in that book," he said drily. I remarked that it was neither shameful nor unusual for politicians to be helped in their literary work. Even President Kennedy had once been accused of having used a ghost to write an entire book. "Yes," said Heikal knowledgably, "but Sorensen works for Kennedy. I don't work for Nasser. He is my friend. My leader. But I don't work for him." He discussed American politics for a moment; he was the only Egyptian politician or editor I met who knew much about American affairs. I mentioned the recent letter Kennedy had written to Nasser, a personal letter whose contents were more or less known to everyone. Nasser had been sufficiently moved to answer Kennedy personally, not going through the usual Foreign Office machinery. This exchange had been much discussed in Cairo. It was believed that a new era had begun; that the two young Presidents would understand one another. But the crux to the renewed dialogue was unchanged: What about Israel? Was there a solution to the Arab-Israel conflict?

"None," said Heikal firmly, ending all debate. "How can there be?" Before I could stop him, he was off in full tirade. I was reminded of 1948, of the seven hundred thousand Arabs driven from their Palestinian homes, of the predatoriness of Israeli foreign policy, and how it is written on the wall of the Knesset that there would one day be a Jewish empire from the Mediterranean to the Euphrates. He spoke of Jewish ingratitude. "The Arabs are the only people *never* to persecute Jews," he said with some accuracy. "English, French, Germans, Spanish, at one time or another every country in Europe persecuted them, but never we. During the last war, we were friends to them. Then they do this! They dispossess Arabs from their homes. They move into a land which isn't theirs. The Jews," he said, with a note of triumph, "are not a race, they're a religion." There is nothing quite so chilling as to hear a familiar phrase in a new context. I relished it. "They are *Europeans,*" he said grimly, coming to the point, "setting themselves up in *our* world. No, there is no solution!" But then he became reasonable. "The real fault of course is our weakness, and their strength. Our policy now is to build up Egypt. Perhaps when we are stronger economically there will be less to fear from the Israelis." This seems to be current Egyptian policy.

We discussed Nasser's "Arab socialism." Heikal was emphatic: it was

State of Being

not doctrinaire socialism. It was improvisational. Point-to-point navigation, as it were. I said that despite some of the methods used to expropriate businesses, there was no doubt that some kind of socialism was inevitable for Egypt and that Nasser had merely done the inevitable. But Heikal would not accept this small compliment. "Methods? Methods? You make us sound like Stalin, with your 'methods'!" I said I had not meant to compare Nasser to Stalin. He cut me off. "What we do is legal. Open. It is for the people. How can you accuse us of 'methods' . . ." This time I cut *him* off. With some irritation, I told him that I had no intention of repeating the various horror stories told me by those who had been ruined by his government, their businesses seized, their livelihoods ended. Even allowing for the natural exaggeration of victims, such methods were not apt to please those who were ruined by them. Nor was it only the large corporations which had been nationalized. Innumerable small businesses had also been taken over. An owner would come to work one morning to find an army officer sitting at his desk, directing what had been his business the day before.

Heikal was scornful. "So we take their money. So they are not happy. So what? At least they are still alive! That's something!" He felt this showed great restraint on the part of the government and perhaps he was right. I was reminded of Joseph Stalin's answer to Lady Astor when she asked him, "When are you going to stop killing people?" "The undesirable classes," said the tyrant, turning upon her his coldest eye, "never liquidate themselves."

Wanting to needle Heikal—an irresistible impulse—I said I didn't think that the endlessly vituperative style of Egypt's newspapers was very apt to win them any friends. Israel is the principal victim of these attacks, but any government which does not momentarily please Nasser will get the full treatment from the Arab press and radio.

Heikal took my question personally, as well he might. His voice slipped automatically into the singsong of rhetoric and denunciation. "We write this way because we feel this way. How can we help it? How can we be asked not to say what we feel so strongly? Take the British, *I hate the British.* I can't help it. I saw them. I know them. Their contempt for us. Their treachery. And over Suez they were not . . . kind." This was an unexpected word. "You came into Suez with force." "They," I murmured. "You tried to destroy us." "They," I said somewhat more loudly. "All right," he said irritably, the tide of his rhetoric briefly stemmed. "*They* wanted to destroy us. So how can we feel anything but hate for them? Look what they did to the Arab world after

1918. They brought back the kings, the sheiks, to keep us medieval. As if we were to occupy England and restore the lords, break the country up into Saxon kingdoms. So how can we express ourselves in any way except the way we do?" Like most rhetorical questions, no answer was desired.

Actually, the fulminating style is inherent in the language (*vide* the Old Testament). Semitic languages are curiously suited to the emotional tirade, even when the speaker is not himself an emotional man. By nature Nasser is an unemotional speaker. As a rule he will bore his audiences for an hour or two, droning on sensibly about the state of the nation. Then when he is in danger of losing them entirely, he allows the language to do its natural work; he proposes that all Egypt's enemies "choke in their rage" as well as other gaudy sentiments calculated to keep his torpid audience awake. Yet to give Nasser his due he is, verbally, one of the most continent of Arab leaders.

Heikal reverted to Israel. Did I realize that thirty-eight percent of their budget went for the military as opposed to thirteen percent of Egypt's budget? Having spent several days poring over the Egyptian budget, I was surprised that anyone could have come up with any figure for any department. The only ascertainable fact is that Egypt is flat broke. But I accepted his figures. I did remark that it must be distressing for Israel—for any country—to be reminded daily that its neighbors, once they awaken from their "deep slumber," will drive them into the sea. After all, no one wants to be drowned. Heikal shook his head sadly: didn't I realize that the Israeli military expenditure was for offense, not defense? I asked him point-blank: "Do you think Israel is planning an offensive war against Egypt?" He shrugged. I then mentioned his own press's continual reminder of Israel's financial dependence on the United States. This being true, did he really think that the United States would permit Israel to embark on a military adventure? We had effectively stopped Israel, France, and England at the time of Suez. Did he honestly believe that we would now allow Israel, by itself, to launch an attack on Egypt? He edged away. No, he did not think the United States would allow a unilateral action. "But," he added quickly, "you can't blame us for being on guard." Then again he reverted to what is the government's present line: we must strengthen Egypt, concentrate on home problems, create "Arab socialism," become a model for the rest of the Arab world.

As I left, I told him that if I saw Nasser at the end of the week I was perfectly willing to present to the American public Egypt's case against

Israel, just as Egypt would like it presented. Partly out of a sense of mischief (we hear altogether too much of the other side) and partly out of a sense of justice, I thought that the Arab case *should* be given attention in the American press. As of now it has been disregarded. In fact, a few years ago the Egyptians, despairing of ever seeing their cause presented impartially in the usual "news" columns, tried to buy an advertisement in *The New York Times.* They were turned down. As a result, the Egyptians are somewhat cynical about our "free press." They are also quite aware that when Israel was being founded in 1948 and the Arabs protested to Harry Truman, he told them with characteristic bluntness: "I do not have hundreds of thousands of Arabs among my constituents." Heikal laughed when I told him that the Arab point of view might one day be given in the American national press. "Your press would never let you," he said with finality, as one journalist to another. "Don't even try."

Another week passed. More appointments were made with Nasser. Each was broken at the last minute, and I was advised to be patient. He would see me soon. But then the Syrian comedy began, disrupting Nasser's schedule. The President of Syria was removed by some army colonels in Damascus. A few days later the young captains in Aleppo tried to overthrow the older officers in Damascus who had overthrown the President. The young men in Aleppo declared that they were for Nasser; they wanted union again with Egypt. Was Nasser behind this plot? Some think yes. Some think no. I suspect no. As one of his closest advisers said, with what seemed candor: "We don't even know these boys in Aleppo. They're much younger than our group." It is protocol in the Middle East that only colonels may start revolutions. Generals are too old, captains too young. In any case, the colonels in Damascus triumphed over the captains in Aleppo and then in a marvelous gesture of frustration the colonels restored the President they had overthrown in the first place. There was no one else, apparently, available for the job. But by the time this comedy had run its course I had fled Egypt, though just as I was getting on the plane to Beirut there was yet another telephone message from the President's office: "His Excellency will definitely see you tomorrow." But I was ready to go, shamefully demonstrating the difference between the amateur and the professional journalist. The professional would have remained, as Hans Von Kaltenborn once remained six weeks, to obtain an interview with Nasser. The amateur moves on.

"The Arabs are their own worst enemies," said a foreign diplomat in

Beirut. "They can't present anything to anyone without undermining themselves. They are self-destructive. In fact, many of them actually believe that since this world is a mess, why bother to alter it when what really matters is the Paradise to come." I was reminded of the Koran, where it is written that "The life of the world is only play and idle talk and pageantry."

The Arabs' religion contributes greatly to the difficulties they are experiencing in the modern world. Americans tend to believe, in a vague, soupy way, that all religion is A Good Thing. Richard Nixon was much applauded when he said that a man's religion should never be a matter of concern in politics, *unless of course he had no religion.* Nixon shook his head gravely on that one. Yet some religions are more useful than others, and some religions are downright dangerous to the human spirit and to the building of a good society.

To understand the Arab world one must understand the Koran, a work Goethe described as "A holy book which, however often we approach it, always disgusts us anew, but then attracts, and astonishes and finally compels us to respect it." It is a remarkable work which I shall not go into here except to note that its Five Pillars are: (1) the creed; (2) the prayer; (3) the fast; (4) the pilgrimage to Mecca; (5) almsgiving. One unfortunate result of the last: the holiness which accrues to almsgivers has fostered a demoralizing tradition of beggars. Also, in requesting aid of other countries, the Arab nations are profoundly self-righteous and demanding, on the high moral ground that they are doing the giver a favor by taking his money and making him more holy. The result has been that until very recently American aid to Egypt was almost never acknowledged in the press or noted in any other way, except by complaints that the giver, if he weren't so selfish, ought to come through with ever more cash, making himself that much worthier in Allah's eyes. In any event, no quo for the quid is Arab policy, as both the Soviet and ourselves have discovered.

I found myself continually asking diplomats, journalists, and old Arab hands: Why should we give *any* aid to Egypt? What do we gain by it? What should we get from it? Answers were never very precise. Naturally, there was "the Soviet threat." If we don't help Egypt, the Russians will and the Middle East will come into "the Soviet sphere." For a number of reasons this is not likely to happen. Soviet policy in the Arab world has been even more unsuccessful than our own. In 1956, after jailing the local Communists (while accepting Soviet aid for the High Dam), Nasser said quite explicitly: "The Communists have lost faith in religion, which in their opinion is a myth. . . . Our final conclusion is that we shall never repudiate it in exchange for the Communist doctrine." The Moslem world and the Marxist world are an eternity apart. Paradise here and now on earth, as the result of hard work and self-sacrifice, is not a congenial doctrine to the Arab. Also, of some importance is the Egyptian's human response to the Russians: they find them austere, dogmatic, and rather alarming.

One is also reminded that whether Nasser chooses to be absorbed by the Soviet bloc or not, at a time of chaos the Soviets *might* move in and take the country by force. This drastic shift in the world balance of power is not easy to visualize. The Soviets, already overextended financially, are not apt to take on (any more than we are) the burden of governing a starving Egypt. But if they did, it is unlikely that they would then shut down the Suez Canal (England's old nightmare), since, after cotton, the canal is the main source of Egypt's revenue. I would suggest that the strategic value of Egypt to the West is very small, and it merely turns Nasser's head and feeds his sense of unreality for us to pretend that Egypt is of great consequence. Yet it is of *some* consequence, especially now.

The principal source of irritation between Nasser and the United States is Israel, a nation in which we have a large economic and emotional interest. But I got the impression from members of the Egyptian government that the continual tirades against Israel are largely for home consumption. Nations traditionally must have the Enemy to prod them into action. President Kennedy finds it difficult to get any large appropriation bill through our Congress unless he can first prove that it will contribute to the holy war against Communism. Once he has established that he is indeed striking a blow at the Enemy, he can get any money he needs, whether it is to explore the moon or to give assistance to the public schools. In the same way, Nasser needs the idea of Israel to goad his own people into the twentieth century.

Nasser once said to Miles Copeland, "If you want the cooperation of any Middle Eastern leader you must first understand his limitations—those limitations placed on him by the emotions and suspicions of the people he leads—and be reconciled to the fact that you can never ask him to go beyond those limitations. If you feel you *must* have him go beyond them, you must be prepared to help him lessen the limitations." A most rational statement of any politician's dilemma; and one which Dulles in his blithely righteous way ignored, causing Nasser to observe with some bitterness in 1956: "Dulles asked me to commit suicide."

National leaders are always followers of public opinion. No matter how well-intentioned they might be privately, they are limited by those they govern. Paradoxically, this is truest of dictators.

Our current policy toward Nasser is sympathetic. It is hard to say to what extent he can or will respond, but it is evident that he is trying. His value to us is much greater now that he has, temporarily, given up hope of leading the Arab world, of becoming the new Saladin. He must make Egypt work first. He is perfectly—sadly—aware that Algeria and Morocco, two Arab nations potentially richer and politically more sophisticated than Egypt, may well provide new leadership for the Moslem world. His only remaining hope is to make "Arab socialism" a success. If it is, then the kings and the sheiks will eventually fall of their own corruption and incompetence, and Nasser's way will be the Arab's way.

What is our role? Since 1952 our assistance to Egypt has totaled $705,000,000. Over half this amount was given or lent in the last three years. So far the Egyptian government has been most scrupulous in its interest payments, etc. However, since July, 1961, when Nasser seized most of the nation's industries and businesses, he has opposed all private investment. The only assistance he will accept (the weak must be firm) is government-to-government, with no political strings. Again, why should we help him?

"Because," said an American economist, "any aid ties him to us, whether he likes it or not, whether he acknowledges it or not. If we help him build the new power plant in Cairo (with Westinghouse assistance), he will have to come to us in the future for parts and technicians. That's good business for us. That keeps *our* economy expanding." This, of course, is the standard rationale for America's foreign-aid program, and up to a point it is valid. Today's empires are held not with the sword but the dollar. It is the nature of the national organism to expand and proliferate. We truly believe that we never wanted a world empire simply because we don't suffer (since Teddy Roosevelt, at least) from a desire to see Old Glory waving over the parliaments of enslaved nations. But we do want to make a buck. We do want to maintain our standard of living. For good or ill, we have no other true national purpose. There is no passion in America for military glory, at least outside of Texas and Arizona. Our materialistic ethos is made quite plain in the phrase "the American way of life."

I submit that our lack of commitment to any great mystique of national destiny is the healthiest thing about us and the reason for our current success. We are simple materialists, not bent on setting fire to the earth as a matter of holy principle, unlike the True Believers with their fierce Either-Ors, their Red or Dead absolutes, when the truth is that the world need be neither, just comfortably pink and lively. Even aid to such a disagreeable and unreliable nation as Nasser's Egypt increases our sphere of influence, expands our markets, maintains our worldly empire. And we are an empire. Americans who would not have it so had best recall Pericles' admonition to those Athenians who wished to shirk imperial responsibilities. We may have been wrong to acquire an empire, Pericles said, but now that we possess one, it is not safe for us to let it go. Nor is it safe for the United States to opt out now. Luckily, our passion for trade and moneymaking and our relatively unromantic view of ourselves has made us surprisingly attractive to the rest of the world, especially to those countries whose rulers suffer from *folie de grandeur.*

Historians often look to the Roman Empire to find analogies with the United States. They flatter us. We live not under the Pax Americana, but the Pax Frigida. I should not look to Rome for comparison but rather to the Most Serene Venetian Republic, a pedestrian state devoted to wealth, comfort, trade, and keeping the peace, especially after inheriting the wreck of the Byzantine Empire, as we have inherited the wreck of the British Empire. Venice was not inspiring but it worked. Ultimately, our danger comes not from the idea of Communism, which (as an Archbishop of Canterbury remarked) is a "Christian heresy" whose materialistic aims (as opposed to means) vary little from our own; rather, it will come from the increasing wealth and skill of other Serene Republics which, taking advantage of our increasing moral and intellectual fatness, will try to seize our markets in the world. If we are to end, it will not be with a Bomb but a bigger Buck. Fortunately, under that sanctimoniousness so characteristic of the American selling something, our governors know that we are fighting not for "the free world" but to hold onto an economic empire not safe or pleasant to let go. The Arab world—or as a salesmen would say, "territory"—is almost ours, and we must persevere in landing that account. It will be a big one some day.

*Esquire*
October 1963

# 112

## MONGOLIA!

In August, Moscow's weather is like that of Bangor, Maine; the cool wind has begun to smell of snow while the dark blue sky is marred with school-of-Tiepolo clouds. Last August the rowan trees were overloaded with clusters of red berries. "Rowanberries in August mean a hard winter," said the literary critic as he showed me the view from the Kremlin terrace. "But after the hard winter," I said, sententious as Mao, "there will come the spring." He nodded. "How true!" As we pondered the insignificance of what neither had said, a baker's dozen of ornithologists loped into view. Moscow was acting as host to a world ornithological congress. To a man, ornithologists are tall, slender, and bearded so that they can stand motionless for hours, imitating kindly trees, as they watch for birds. Since they are staying at our group's hotel, we have dubbed them the tweet-tweets.

The critic asked, "Have you read *Gorky Park*?" I said that I had not because I have made it a rule only to read novels by Nobel Prize winners. That way one will never read a bad book. I told him the plot of Pearl Buck's *This Proud Heart*. He told me the plot of *Gorky Park*. "It's a really good bad book," he said. "You know, everyone's making such heavy weather about it here. I can't think why. It's wonderfully silly. An American gunman loose in Moscow!" He chuckled. "It's so surrealist." I said that they should publish it as an example of American surrealism, with a learned commentary explaining the jokes.

As we chatted, two Russian soldiers walked by us. One was in uniform; the other wore blue jeans and a T-shirt emblazoned with the words THE UNITED STATES MILITARY ACADEMY, WEST POINT. The literary critic smiled. "Could an American soldier wear a Kremlin T-shirt?" I explained to him, patiently, I hope, the difference between the free and the unfree worlds. Abashed, he changed the subject to, where was I going next? When I said, "Ulan Bator," he laughed. When I wanted to know what was so funny, he said, "I thought you said you were going to Ulan Bator." When I told him that that was exactly where I was going, to the capital of the Mongolian People's Republic (sometimes known as Outer Mongolia), he looked very grave indeed. "It is said," he whispered so that the ubiquitous KGB would not overhear us, "that the British and French embassies have a spy at the airport and that anyone who looks promising is approached—oh, very furtively—and asked if he plays bridge. You did not hear this from me," he added.

At midnight the plane leaves Moscow for Ulan Bator, with stops at Omsk and Irkutsk (in Siberia). The trip takes ten hours; there is a five-hour time difference between Moscow and Ulan Bator (U.B. to us fans). Moscow Aeroflot planes have a tendency to be on time, but the ceilings are too low for claustrophobes, and there is a curious smell of sour cream throughout the aircraft. Contrary to legend, the stewardesses are agreeable, at least on the Siberian run.

Our party included an English-born, Nairobi-based representative of the United Nations Environment Programme—White Hunter, his name. A representative of the World Wildlife Fund International who turned out to be a closet tweet-tweet—and was so named. And the photographer, Snaps. We were accompanied by the youthful Boris Petrovich, who has taught himself American English through the study of cassettes of what appears to have been every American film ever made. We had all met at the Rossya Hotel in Moscow. According to the Russians, it is the largest hotel in the world. Whether or not this is true, the Rossya's charm is not unlike that of New York's Attica Prison. In the Soviet Union the foreigner is seldom without a low-level anxiety, which can, suddenly, develop into wall-climbing paranoia. *Where are the visas?* To which the inevitable Russian answer, "No problem," is ominous indeed.

Now our little group was being hurtled through the Siberian skies to a part of Outer Mongolia where no white—or, for that matter, black—

Westerner had ever been before, or as one of our men at the American Embassy put it: "You will be the first American ever to set foot in that part of the Gobi Desert." I asked for my instructions. After all, those of us who believe in freedom must never not be busy. When I suggested that I might destabilize the Mongolian government while I was there, one of our men was slightly rattled. "Actually," he said, "no American has ever been there because there isn't anything there." My fierce patriotism was seriously tried by this insouciance. "Then why," I asked, "am I going?" He said he hadn't a clue. Why *was* I going?

It all came back to me on the night flight to Ulan Bator. The World Wildlife Fund has taken to sending writers around the world to record places where the ecology is out of joint. My task was a bit the reverse. I was to report on the national park that the Mongolian government is creating in the Gobi in order to keep pristine the environment so that flora and fauna can proliferate in a perfect balance with the environment.

As I stared out the porthole window at my own reflection (or was it Graham Greene's? The vodka bottle seemed familiar), my mind was awhirl with the intense briefings that I had been subjected to. For instance, is the People's Republic of Mongolia part of the Soviet Union? No. It is an independent socialist nation, grateful for the "disinterested" aid that it gets from the other socialist nations. When did it come into being? Sixty years ago, when the Chinese were ejected and their puppet, the Living Buddha, was shorn of his powers and the twenty-eight-year-old Damdiny Sükh, known as Ulan Bator (Red Hero in Mongolian), took charge of the state, with disinterested Soviet aid. Meanwhile, back at the Kremlin, Vladimir Ilyich Ulyanov Lenin was not entirely thrilled. Classic Marxism requires that a state evolve from feudalism to monarchy to capitalism and then to communism. As of 1920, whatever had been going on in Mongolia for two millennia, it was not capitalism. The people were nomadic. Every now and then, in an offhand way, they'd conquer the world. Genghis Khan ruled from the Danube to the Pacific Ocean, and some twelve hundred years ago, according to one account, Mongol tribes crossed from Asia to North America via the Bering Strait, making the Western Hemisphere a sort of Mongol colony. Lenin knitted his brow and came up with the following concept: "With the aid of the proletariat of the advanced countries, backward countries can go over to the Soviet system and, through certain stages of development, to communism, without having to pass through the capitalist stage." So it came to pass. In sixty years an illiterate population has become totally literate, life expectancies have increased, industries and mining have taken the place of the old nomadic way of life, and there is a boom in population. "Sixty percent of the population," said Boris Petrovich, "is under sixteen years of age." Tweet-tweet looked grim. "So much the worse for them," he said. Boris Petrovich said, "But, gosh, they need people here. Why, they've only got one and a half million people to one and a half million square kilometers. That's not enough people to feed themselves with." As the environmental aspect was carefully explained to Boris Petrovich, his eyes lost their usual keenness. "Should I," he asked me, changing the subject, "buy Lauren Bacall's book?"

Jet lag and culture shock greeted us at the airport, where blue asters had broken through the landing strip. But no one was asked to play bridge, because we were whisked aboard an Air Mongolia plane and flown five more hours to the provincial capital of Gobi Altai, the southwestern province of Mongolia. At the foot of the Altai range of mountains is the town of Altai. Here we spent the night in a two-story hotel on the main street, whose streetlamps did not turn on. Opposite the hotel is the police station. At the end of the street is a new hospital of raw cement.

We were given dinner by the deputy chairman of the province, the Soviet director of the park, and the deputy minister of forestry (under whose jurisdiction is the near-treeless Gobi), as well as two ministerial officials assigned to the United Nations Environment Programme. Toasts were drunk as dishes of mutton came and went. Money is no longer flowing from the UN, White Hunter pointed out. The Reagan administration is cutting back. The Soviet Union is making a fair contribution to the fund, but—such is the Soviet sense of fun—the money is in unconvertible rubles. This means that the Soviet contribution can be spent only in the Soviet sphere. Hence, the Gobi park.

Although Mongolia smells of mutton fat, the Mongols smell not at all, even though the Russians go on about the great trouble they have getting them to bathe. Men and women are equally handsome: tall, narrow-waisted, with strong white teeth. Some wear the national tunic with sash and boots; others wear the international uniform of blue jeans. "Why," I asked one of our Mongolian colleagues, "are there no bald men here?" He was startled by the question. "The old men shave their heads," he said, as if this was an answer. Even so, there are no bald men to be seen anywhere. Our group came to the conclusion that over the millennia bald babies were exposed at birth.

As the evening ended, I had a sense of what the English call *déjà vu.*

I had been in this company before. But where? It came to me: in my grandfather's state of Oklahoma, on one of the Indian reservations. Physically, the Mongolians are dead ringers for the Cherokees, whose nation my grandfather represented as an attorney in an effort to get some money for the land that the American government had stolen from them. All in all, the Russians are doing rather better by their Mongols than we are doing by ours.

I proposed a toast to Kublai Khan, "China's great Mongol emperor, who opened up a peaceful discourse between East and West." The Mongols at table were amused. The Russians less so. "You know," said one of the ministerials, "we are making a number of movies about Mongolian history." I did not ask if any of these films would deal with the 250-year Mongol occupation of Russia. The Russians still complain of their suffering during the Mongol occupation. "Now," said the ministerial, "we are making a movie about American Indians." When I asked what the theme was, I got a vague answer. "Oh, the . . . connections. You'll see."

The next day there was rain in the Gobi. Something unheard of, we were told. In fact, there had been a flood a few days before, and many people were said to have been drowned. Due to bad weather, the plane would not take us to the encampment. So we set out on a gray afternoon in jeeps and Land Rovers. There is no road, only a more or less agreed-upon trail.

As we left Altai, we saw a bit of the town that Snaps and I had not been allowed to see earlier that morning, when we had set out to record the real life of the Mongols, who live in what the Russians call a *yurta* and the owners call a *ger:* a round tent, ingeniously made of felt, with a removable flap across the top to let out smoke. In winter the fire is lit in the morning for cooking; then it goes out until sundown, when it is lit again for the evening meal. Apparently the *yurta* retains warmth in winter and is cool in summer. At Altai, every hundred or so *yurtas* are surrounded by wooden fences, "to hold back the drifts of snow in winter," said a Russian, or "to keep them in their particular collective," said a cynical non-Russian. Whatever, the wooden fences have curious binary devices on them: "king's ring and queen's ring," I was told by a Mongol—and no more.

Every time Snaps and I were close to penetrating one of the enclosures, a policeman would indicate that we should go back to the hotel. Meanwhile, the children would gather around until Snaps snapped; then they would shriek *nyet* and scamper off, only to return a moment later with many giggles. The older people quite liked being photographed, particularly the men on their ponies, whose faces—the ponies'—are out of prehistory, pendulous-lipped and sly of slanted eye. In costume, women wear boots; not in costume, they wear high heels as they stride over the dusty graveled plain, simulating the camel's gait.

*The Gobi Desert* by Mildred Cable with Francesca French is an invaluable look at central Asia in the twenties and thirties by two lady missionaries who traveled the trade routes, taught the Word, practiced medicine.* "The Mongol's home is his tent, and his nomadic life is the expression of a compelling instinct. A house is intolerable to him, and even the restricting sense of an enclosing city wall is unbearable." One wonders what today's Mongols think, cooped up in their enclosures. "They hate the new housing," said one official. "They put their animals and belongings in the apartment houses, and then they stay in their *yurtas.*" Others told me that, in general, the people are content, acclimatized to this bad century. "The Mongol lives in and for the present, and looks neither backward toward his ancestors nor forward to his descendants."

"Snaps, one word is worth a thousand pictures," I said. "Which word?" he asked. "That would be telling," I told him. But now comes the time when I must come to Snaps's aid and through the living word transmit to the reader's eye the wonder that is Mongolia when the monsoons are almost done with and the heat has dropped after July's 113 degrees Fahrenheit and lizards cook in Gobi.

We are in a jeep, lurching over rough terrain. The driver is young, wears a denim jacket, grins as he crashes over boulders. Picture now a gray streaked sky. In the distance a dun-colored mountain range, smooth and rounded the way old earth is. We are not yet in the Gobi proper. There is water. Herds of yaks and camels cross the horizon. But once past this watered plain, the Gobi Desert begins—only it is not a proper desert. Sand is the exception, not the rule. Black and brown gravel is strewn across the plain. Occasional white salt slicks vary the monotony. All sorts of shy plants grow after a rain or near one of the rare springs. Actually, there is water under a lot of the Gobi, in some places only a few feet beneath the surface. For those who missed out on the journeys to the moon, the Gobi is the next best thing.

*Frederic Prokosch relied heavily on the two ladies for *The Seven Who Fled.*

"The word Gobi," authority tells us (*Géographie Universelle,* P. Vidal de la Blanche et L. Gallois), "is not the proper name of a geographical area, but a common expression used by Mongols to designate a definite order of geographical features. These are wide, shallow basins in which the smooth rocky bottom is filled with sand, pebbles, or, more often, with gravel." *L'autre* Vidal tells us that, properly speaking, the Gobi covers a distance of 3,600 miles, "from the Pamirs to the confines of Manchuria." But Outer Mongolia's Gobi, together with that part of the Gobi inside China to our south and west, is the desert's heart, once crossed by the old silk route that connected the Middle Kingdom with the West.

We arrive in darkness at Tsogt, a small town on whose edge is the fenced-in administrative center of the park. We slept in spacious *yurtas,* worthy of the great Khan. In the dining *yurta* a feast of mutton had been prepared. We were joined by several Russian specialists connected with the park. One was a zoologist, given to wearing green camouflage outfits with a most rakish hat. Another had spent a winter in New York City, where "every square meter costs one million dollars."

Next day, at second or third light, we were shown a fuzzy film of all the fauna that the park contained, from wild Bactrian camels to wild bears to the celebrated snow leopard and, of course, the ubiquitous goat. But once the Gobi is entered, there are few herds to be seen, and only the occasional tweet, usually a kite or a variety of low-flying brown-and-white jay. As befits a World Wildlife Funder, Tweet-tweet was becoming unnaturally excited. Snaps, too, was in his heaven. Bliss to be in Gobi, almost.

After the film we boarded a plane that I had last flown in in 1935, and flew south across the Gobi, which I had last seen in the pages of the old *Life* magazine, circa 1935, as portrayed by Margaret Bourke-White. Time kept warping until I noticed that Snaps was furtively vomiting into his camera case; others were also queasy. When I suggested that air be admitted to the cabin, I was greeted with 1935 stares of disbelief. So we returned to base. We were then loaded into jeeps and crossed a low mountain range to the park itself.

On a high hill with dark mountains behind, the Gobi stretches as far as anyone could wish, its flatness broken by the odd mountain, set island-like in the surrounding gravel. I got out of the jeep to commune with the silence. The driver started to pluck at small dark-green clumps of what turned out to be chives. We ate chives and looked at the view, and I proceeded to exercise the historical imagination and conjured up Genghis Khan on that famous day when he set his standard of nine yak tails high atop Gupta, and the Golden Horde began its conquest of Europe. "Hey"—I heard the Americanized voice of Boris Petrovich—"did any of you guys see *The Little Foxes* with Elizabeth Taylor?" A chorus of noes did not faze him. "Well, why not?" It was Tweet-tweet who answered him. "If you have gone to the theater seriously all your life," he said sternly, "there are plays that you know in advance that you will not be caught dead at." But Tweet-tweet had not reckoned with the Russian sense of fair play. "How can you say that when you wouldn't even go *see* her in the play? I mean, so she was crucified by the reviewers . . ." Thus, put in our place, we descended into Gobi. Thoughts of Taylor's fleshy splendor had restored Genghis to wraithdom and dispersed the Horde.

We stopped at an oasis, a bright strip of ragged green in the dark shining gravel. Water bubbles up from the earth and makes a deep narrow stream down a low hill to a fenced-in place where a Mongol grows vegetables for the camp. The water is cool and pure, and the Mongols with us stare at it for a time and smile; then they lie down on their bellies and drink deeply. We all do. In fact, it is hard to get enough water in Gobi. Is this psychological or physiological? The Mongol gardener showed me his plantation. "The melons don't grow very large," he apologized, holding up a golf ball of a melon. "It is Gobi, you see." I tried to explain to him that if he were to weed his patch, the vegetables would grow larger, but in that lunar landscape I suspect that the weeds are as much a delight to him as the melons.

As we lurched across the desert to the Yendiger Mountains, we passed an empty village where nomads used to winter. Whether or not they are still allowed in the park is a moot point. No straight answer was available. We were told that certain sections of the park are furrowed off—literally, a furrow is plowed and, except for the park rangers, no human being may cross the furrow unless he wants to be detained for poaching. Are there many poachers? A few . . .

At the deserted village, each jeep took a different route toward the dark mountains in the distance. En route, the jeep that I was traveling in broke down four times. Long after the others had arrived at camp, our group was comfortably seated on a malachite-green rock, sipping whisky from the bottle and watching the sun pull itself together for a Gobi Special sunset, never to be forgotten. Tweet-tweet said that in the Galapagos Islands Tom Stoppard had worked out a numeric scale with which to measure the tasteless horror of each successive night's overwrought sunset. But I defended our Gobi Special. For once, Mother

Nature was the soul of discreet good taste. Particularly the northern sky, where clouds like so many plumes of Navarre had been dipped in the most subtle shade of Du Barry gray, while the pale orange of the southern sky did not cloy. True, there was a *pink* afterglow in the east. But then perfection has never been Mother Nature's ideal.

The jeep functional, we drove between dark brown rocks along the bottom of what looked to be an ancient riverbed until we came to a turn in the ravine, and there was the campsite. In a row: one *yurta,* a dozen pup tents, a truck that contained a generator. "This is the first electricity ever to shine in this part of Gobi," said the Soviet director. As the Mongol lads strung electric lines from tent to tent, Snaps, with narrowed eyes and camera poised, waited. "You never know," he whispered, "when you'll get a shot of electrified Mongol. *Tremendous* market for that, actually."

We were told that close to camp there is a famous watering hole where, at sundown, the snow leopard lies down, as it were, with the wild ass. But we had missed sundown. Nevertheless, ever game, our party walked halfway to the hole before settling among rocks on the ridge to fortify ourselves with alien spirits against the black desert night that had fallen with a crash about us. As we drank, we were joined by a large friendly goat. Overhead, the stars (so much more satisfactory than the ones beneath our feet) shone dully: Rain clouds were interfering with the Gobi's usual surefire light show. I found the Dipper; it was in the wrong place. There was a sharp difference of agreement on the position of Orion's Belt. Shooting stars made me think, comfortably, of war. I showed Boris Petrovich what looked to be one of the Great Republic's newest satellites. "Keeping watch over the Soviet Union," I said. "Unless," he said, "it is one of our missiles on its way to Washington. But, seriously," he added, "don't you agree that Elizabeth Taylor was a first-rate *movie* actress? You know, like Susan Hayward."

First light seized us from our pup tents, where we had slept upon the desert floor, inhaling the dust of millennia. As I prepared for a new day of adventure, sinuses aflame, there was a terrible cry, then a sob, a gasp—silence. Our friend of the evening before, the goat, was now to be our dinner.

We checked out the watering hole, which turned out to be a muddy place in the rocks; there were no signs of beasts. Again we were on the move, this time southeasterly toward the Mount Mother system. The heat was intense. We glimpsed a wild ass, wildly running up ahead of us. Some gazelles skittered in the distance. The countryside was almost always horizontal but never pleasingly flat. To drive over such terrain is like riding a Wild West bronco. As we penetrated deeper into the preserve, vegetation ceased. What thornwood there was no longer contained greenery. Thornwood—with camel and goat dung—provides the nomads with their fuel. We were told that poachers are more apt to steal the wood in the preserve than the animals.

Suddenly, all of our jeeps converged on the same spot, close to the steep dark-red Khatan Khairkhan, an island of rock rising from a dry sea. The drivers gathered around a circle of white sand some six feet in diameter. Three spurts of icy water bubbled at the circle's center. Again, the happy smiles. Mongols stare at water rather the way northerners stare at fires. Then each of us tried the water. It tasted like Badois. Camel and wild-ass dung in the immediate vicinity testified to its excellent, even curative, mineral qualities.

Halfway up the red mountain, we made camp at the mouth of a ravine lined with huge, smooth red rocks. Glacial? Remains of a sea that had long since gone away? No geologist was at hand to tell us, but in the heights above the ravine were the Seven Cauldrons of Khatan Khairkhan, where, amongst saksaul groves and elm trees, the waters have made seven rock basins, in which Tweet-tweet and White Hunter disported themselves while Snaps recorded the splendors of nature. The author, winded halfway up, returned to camp and read Mme. de La Fayette's *La Princesse de Clèves*.

That night our friend the goat was served in the famous Mongolian hot pot. Red-hot rocks are dropped into metal pots containing whatever animal has been sacrificed to man's need. The result is baked to a T. As usual, I ate tomatoes, cucumbers, and bread. We drank to the Golden Horde, now divided in three parts: Outer Mongolia, which is autonomous, thanks to the "disinterested" Soviet Union's presence; Inner Mongolia, which is part of China and filling up with highly interested Chinese; and Siberia, which contains a large Mongolian population. Since functioning monasteries are not allowed in China or Siberia, practicing Buddhists come to Ulan Bator, where there are a large school, a lamasery, and the Living Buddha. This particular avatar is not the result of the usual search for the exact incarnation practiced in ancient times. He was simply selected to carry on.

Even rarer than a functioning lamasery in Mongolia is Przhevalski's horse. These horses exist in zoos around the world, but whether or not they are still to be found in Gobi is a subject of much discussion. Some think that there are a few in the Chinese part of the Gobi; some think that they are extinct. In any case, the Great Gobi National Park plans to reintroduce—from the zoos—Przhevalski's horse to its original habitat. We drank to the Przhevalski horse. We drank to the plane that was to pick us up the next morning when we returned to base. "Will it really be there?" I asked. "No problem."

At dawn we lurched across the desert beneath a lowering sky. At Tsogt there was no plane. "No problem." We would drive four or five hours to Altai. Along the way we saw the marks that our tires had made on the way down. "In Gobi, tracks may last fifty years," one of the Russians said.

At the Altai airport low-level anxiety went swiftly to high: The plane for Ulan Bator might not take off. Bad weather. The deputy minister of forestry made a ministerial scene, and the plane left on time. There was not a cloud on the route. We arrived at dusk. The road from the airport to the city passes beneath not one but two huge painted arches. From the second arch, Ulan Bator in its plain circled by mountains looks very large indeed. Four hundred thousand people live and have their being beneath a comforting industrial smog. As well as the usual fenced-off *yurtas,* there are high-rise apartment houses, an opera house, a movie palace, functioning streetlamps, and rather more neon than one sees in, say, Rome. Although our mood was gala as we settled in at the Ulan Bator Hotel, low-level anxiety never ceased entirely to hum. Would the visas for the Soviet Union be ready in time? Had the plane reservations for Moscow and the West been confirmed? Would we get back the passports that we had surrendered upon arrival?

The next day, our questions all answered with "No problem," we saw the sights of Ulan Bator. A museum with a room devoted to odd-shaped dinosaur eggs, not to mention the skeletons of the dinosaurs that had laid them. Every public place was crowded. A convention of Mongol experts was in town; there was also a delegation of Buddhists, paying their respects to the Living Buddha, who would be, his secretary told me, too busy with the faithful to receive us that day. Undaunted, Snaps and I made our way to the Buddhist enclosure, where we found several temples packed with aged priests and youthful acolytes with shaved heads. As the priests read aloud from strips of paper on which are printed Sanskrit and Tibetan texts, their voices blend together like so many bees in a hive while incense makes blue the air and bells tinkle at odd intervals to punctuate the still-living texts. In a golden robe, the Living Buddha sat on a dais. As the faithful circled him in an unending stream, he maintained a costive frown. Outside, aged costumed Mongols of both sexes sat about the enclosure, at a millennium's remove from cement block and Aeroflot.

The United Kingdom's man in Ulan Bator, James Paterson, received us at the British Embassy. Outside, a suspicious policeman stands guard with a walkie-talkie, keeping close watch not only on the ambassador and his visitors but on the various Mongols who paused in front of the embassy to look at the color photographs, under glass, of the wedding of the Prince and Princess of Wales. The Mongols would study the pictures carefully and then, suddenly, smile beatifically. How very like, I could practically hear them say to themselves, our own imperial family—the Khans of yesteryear!

Paterson is tall and tweedy with a charming wife (in central Asia all of us write like the late Somerset Maugham). "I am allowed to jog," he said. "But permission must be got to make trips." Since he knew that I was asking myself the one question that visitors to U.B. ask themselves whenever they meet a noncommunist ambassador (there are four, from Britain, France, Canada, and India)—What on earth did you *do* to be sent here?—he brought up the subject and laughed, I think, merrily. He was raised in China; he was fascinated by the Mongol world—unlike the French ambassador who, according to diplomats in Moscow, used to go about Ulan Bator muttering, "I am here because they fear me at the Quai d'Orsay." When I asked Paterson where the French ambassador was, I was told, "He is no longer here." Tact, like holly at Christmas, festooned the modest sitting room, where a much-fingered, month-old *Economist* rested on the coffee table.

A reception was given us by the minister of forestry. He is a heavyset man with gray hair and a face much like that of the old drawings of Kublai Khan. He hoped that we had enjoyed the visit to the park. He hoped that there would be more money from the United Nations, but if there should be no more, he quite understood. White Hunter found this a bit ominous, as he favors further UN funding of the park. Tourism was discussed: A new guest complex would be built at Tsogt. The plans look handsome. Room for only eighteen people—plainly, a serious place for visiting scientists. Elsewhere, hunters are catered for.

Tweet-tweet spoke eloquently of the Wildlife Fund's work around the world. "Under its president, Prince Philip," he intoned. The Mongol translator stopped. "Who?" Tweet-tweet repeated the name, adding, "The husband of our queen." The translator could not have been more gracious. "The husband of *whose* queen?" he asked. Tweet-tweet went on to say that if it were not for the politicians, there would be world peace and cooperation, and the environment would be saved. I noticed that the minister's highly scrutable Oriental face, so unlike our veiled Occidental ones, was registering dismay. I interrupted. "As one politician to another," I said, "even though I have just lost an election, having polled only a half-million votes"—roughly a third of the population of Mongolia, I thought, in a sudden frenzy of demophilia—"I am as peace-loving as, I am sure, His Excellency is." I got a wink from the minister, and after dinner a powerful pinch of snuff. Even in Mongolia, we pols must stick together in a world made dangerous for us by well-meaning Tweet-tweets.

The next day all was in order; there was indeed no problem. The ten-hour trip took place in daylight. As we stretched our legs in Omsk, White Hunter noticed a handsome blond girl beyond the airport railings. He turned to Boris Petrovich. "What are the girls like here?" Boris Petrovich shook his head. "Well, I was only here once, when I was on the junior basketball team. We played everywhere." White Hunter said, "You mean you didn't make out?" Boris Petrovich looked shocked. "Well, gosh, I was only sixteen." I told him that in the United States many males at sixteen have not only passed their sexual peak but are burned-out cases. Boris Petrovich's eyes glittered. "I'll bet there are some movies on that," he said. "You know, that soft-porn stuff on cassettes."

Before our party separated at the Moscow airport, we agreed that the Great Gobi National Park was a serious affair and not a front for Soviet missiles or, worse, a hunters' paradise with Gobi bears and snow leopards as the lure. Snaps was thrilled with the Buddhist pictures; less thrilled with the Gobi, "of an ugliness not to be reproduced"; pleased with the pictures of the people, though we had failed to penetrate a single *yurta*. White Hunter had hopes that the United Nations would raise enough money to keep the park going. Tweet-tweet was satisfied that wildlife was being tended to. Meanwhile, Boris Petrovich darted between the two groups—one headed for London, one for Rome.

As I was leaving the reception area, he made a small speech about the necessity of good Soviet-American relations, the importance of world peace, the necessity of cooperation on environmental matters. Then he lowered his voice. "I have a question to ask you." He looked about to see if we were being overheard. Thus, I thought to myself, Philby was recruited. Swiftly, I made my decision. If I were to sell out the free world, I must be well paid. I would want a *dacha* on the Baltic, near Riga. I would want . . . "How tall," asked Boris Petrovich, "is Paul Newman, really?"

*Vanity Fair*
March 1983

# 113

# AT HOME
# IN A
# ROMAN STREET

For twenty years I have rented a small penthouse on top of the molder-
ing seventeenth-century Origo Palace in the middle of what bureaucratic Romans call the Historic Center and everyone else calls Old
Rome. The palace is at the northwest corner of a busy square that has
all the charm of New York City's Columbus Circle, minus Huntington
Hartford's masterpiece, and plus, below street level, three classical temples, home to a colony of cats, a perennial—no, millennial—reminder
that this precinct was once sacred to the goddess Isis, and the cat was,
and is, her creature. In a nearby street there is a large marble foot on
a pedestal, all that is left of Isis' cult statue. Cats now sun themselves
on her toes.

The west façade of the palace is set in a two-thousand-year-old north-
south Roman street that starts a half-dozen blocks to the north in what
was the Field of Mars (where the Roman army used to parade and now
parliament parades), continues on to the Pantheon and then to us. We
live in what was once the vestibule to a huge complex of baths, libraries,
concert halls, theaters and, of course, the Pantheon, all built by one
Marcus Agrippa, the John D. Rockefeller of his day, who wanted to
celebrate his wealth and the emperor Augustus' glory, in about that
order.

The penthouse is a small, square, rickety, twentieth-century addition to the palace; it is built around a squalid inner court, more than compensated for by two huge terraces at right angles to one another. From the south terrace we can see a corner of the Victor Emmanuel monument, a snowy-white wedding cake in the form of an antique Remington Rand typewriter, a bit of the Campidoglio, the Aventine Hill, the Synagogue, the dome of San Carlo and, directly below us, the eighteenth-century Teatro Argentina, where *The Barber of Seville* was booed on opening night while Rossini sat next door at Bernasconi's eating pastry. The pastry is still good at Bernasconi's, and the theater still functions.

From the west terrace, Sant' Andrea della Valle (Act I, *Tosca*) fills the sky to the left. We are so close to it that we can identify the wild flowers that grow out of cracks in the dome and lantern. Next, we can see, in the distance, like a gray-ridged soccer ball, Saint Peter's; then Sant' Agnese in the Piazza Navona; and, finally, best of all, the fantastic, twisted spire of Sant' Ivo alla Sapienza, Borromini's literally off-the-sky masterpiece.

In summer, when the red sun starts to drop behind Saint Peter's, birds suddenly appear—real birds, swifts, as opposed to the pigeons that use the terraces as a convention hall. From sunset to dark, the swifts do Jonathan Livingston Seagull free falls and glides with great panache. In winter, they vanish. Although Roman winters are not severe, last January a heavy snow fell on Rome and the single lemon tree on the terrace outside my bedroom window was covered with two inches of snow, framing each gold lemon in white.

Question I most hear: Why have you spent almost a third of your life in this Roman apartment? I quote Howard Hughes. When asked why he had ended up a long-nailed recluse in a sealed hotel room, he croaked with perfect candor: "I just sort of drifted into it." That's almost always the real answer to everything. But there are, of course, a thousand other reasons. Although I have a house in the unfashionable Hollywood Hills, and my subject, as a writer, is the United States, I have never had a proper human-scale village life anywhere on earth except in this old Roman street. In Los Angeles we live in our cars, en route to houses where a pool is a pool is a pool and there are only three caterers and you shall have no other. A car trip to Chalet Gourmet on the Sunset Strip is a chore not an adventure. But a trip down our street is a trip indeed.

By and large, the shops are exactly like the shops of two thousand years ago, as preserved at Pompeii and Ostia: a single deep room with a wide door that can be shuttered and a counter at the back. Produce is displayed on benches or tables on the sidewalk or in the doorway. Fresh food in season is all-important here, and we talk a lot about food. As I write, we are sweating out the first peas. No one will eat a frozen one deliberately. Sex and politics are not obsessive; but health care is. We are all hypochondriacs. In fact, Italians buy more pills per capita than any other nationality. Luckily, they usually forget to take them. In our pharmacy with its eighteenth-century rococo boiserie, there is a comfortable chair where you sit while the pharmacist takes your blood pressure, not once but, properly, twice. I trust him more than any doctor. We all do.

I know every shopkeeper in this street, and just about every old resident. We seldom have names for one another, but everyone knows everything about everyone else, and we—the older crowd, of course—study each other closely for signs of debility. We are all diagnosticians. The vegetable man's tremor is worse, we say to one another at the butcher's. We discuss Parkinson's among the Tuscan sausages. The carpenter goes by, green of face—he has been drunk for a week. We feel sorry for the wife. *Peccato*—"a shame." But the daughter is married to the hardware-store owner and pregnant again. Will she need a second caesarean?

The herb shop has been doing business for over a century: dark wooden paneling and drawers, porcelain apothecary jars with gilt Latin inscriptions. Two old brothers—not old when I first came—preside over this two-thousand-year-old anthology of herbal remedies and pleasures. An old woman suddenly turns to me, in a state of ecstasy. "I am ninety years old," she says, "and everything in the street's changed except this place. It's the same! The same!" That, I fear, is the retrograde joy of our village life.

Even our lunatics are always the same. For decades now, the flower woman goes out each day in the bus to the cemetery to steal flowers from new graves; then she returns to the street and sits in the doorway of a deconsecrated church and makes up bouquets (as I write, daffodils, tulips, and mimosa). We are worried lately about her loss of the last set of dentures. True, they did not fit, but she now looks really awful. She has also, overambitiously, acquired more plastic bags than she can carry at one time. This is worrying.

Then there is the small man in the three-piece suit with the homburg, whose brim is always curled up like Chaplin's bowler. As he makes his daily progress down the street, he looks very worried. Suddenly he will come up to you and ask the time. "What time is it?" he murmurs urgently. You tell him. He nods three times; patters off. He has never been heard to say anything else.

Beneath us in the palace, a mother and son live. She is a charming lady, somewhat bent now from a decade of sleeping in a chair so that she can watch over her son, who was sent home from the sort of institution that Governor Reagan shut down in California. At the full moon, he howls; at the dark of the moon, he storms our door, shouting for us to release the beautiful women covered with jewels locked inside. Currently, he has a full beard and looks like Karl Marx.

Next to the palace is a hole in the wall: the most popular *fruttateria* in town. Like swifts at sundown, motorcycled adolescents park on the sidewalk and swig fruit drinks. Efforts to get them on drugs or alcohol have so far failed: This is an old city.

Literature? Two blocks to our north, back of the Pantheon, Thomas Mann lived and wrote *Buddenbrooks.* Nearby, George Eliot stayed at the Minerva Hotel. Ariosto lived in Pantheon Square; Stendhal was close to us. I myself have written at least a part of every one of my books from *Washington, D.C.,* to *Lincoln* in this flat. The last chapters of *Lincoln* were composed on the dining room table.

Italo Calvino now lives at the north of the street, and we *cher confrère* one another when we meet. Then we move on. Yes, we are all growing old. But a baby's being born to the wife of the hardware-store owner, while a half-dozen babies of a few years ago are now men and women. So—plenty more where we came from. That is the lesson of the street. Meanwhile, what time is it? Free the bejeweled ladies held captive! Daffodils, tulips, and mimosa! What time is it? The same.

*Architectural Digest*
October 1985

# 114

#### ∙

# REFLECTIONS ON
# GLORY REFLECTED
# AND OTHERWISE

## I

Although the New York family of Auchincloss is of "recent arrival" (1803), as Sitting Bull used to say, they have managed, through marriage, to become related to everyone in the United States who matters—to everyone in the United States who matters, that is. For idle hypergamy and relentless fecundity there has not been a family like them since those much less attractive Mittel-Europa realtors, the Habsburgs. Although the family has produced neither a great man nor a fortune ("each generation of Auchincloss men either made or married its own money"—Louis Auchincloss in *A Writer's Capital*), there are, aside from the excellent novelist, numerous lawyers, stockbrokers, and doctors whose Cosa Nostra is the Presbyterian (*not* Episcopalian) Hospital in New York. By the mid-twentieth century, the clan's most notorious member was Hugh D. Auchincloss, Jr. A bulky man who stammered, "Hughdie" (usually known as "Poor Hughdie") was heir to a Standard Oil fortune, thanks to his father's marriage to the daughter of a Rocke-feller partner named Jennings. This worldly, I think the adjective is, match, sharply separated Hughdie's line from those of the brownstone cousinage (fifty-seven male Auchinclosses in 1957), content with their snail-like upwardly mobile marriages to Old as well as Older New York.

Early in life, at Yale, in fact, Hughdie's originality was revealed; *he was unable to do work of any kind.* Since the American ruling class, then and now, likes to give the impression that it is always hard at work, or at least very busy, Hughdie's sloth was something of a breakthrough. The word "aristocrat" is never used by our rulers, but he acted suspiciously like one; certainly he was inert in a *foreign* way. Would he move to England? But Hughdie's originality in sloth was equally original in ultimate choice of venue. He moved not to London but to Washington, DC. Not only had no Auchincloss ever moved to Washington, DC; *no one* had ever moved there without first undergoing election or appointment. As if this was not original enough, he started a brokerage firm with a million dollar gift from his oleaginous Jennings mother, and settled into an Italian palazzo next to the Japanese embassy in Massachusetts Avenue. Since the partners did all the work at the brokerage house, he had a great deal of time to woolgather and to fret whether or not he was happy. In fact, each day would end with a careful analysis of the preceding not-so-crowded hours and whether or not others—specifically, the wife of the moment—had contributed sufficiently to his happiness, a somewhat vagrant bluebird with other errands that took precedence in the nation's capital.

As the city had no life other than the political, Hughdie became a "groupie" even though he had little interest in politics as such. He believed in the virtue of the rich and the vice of the poor and that was as far as introspection ever took him. But Hughdie very much believed in celebrity (one of his most attractive monologues was of the date that he had had in youth with the film star Kay Francis) and of all celebrities the politician most fascinated him, and of all politicians the members of the United States Senate were the most visible and glamorous.

For a long time, before and after Franklin Roosevelt, presidents tended to be nonentities kept hidden in the White House while senators were always centre-stage. They were, literally, the conscript patriciate of the nation until they were elected directly in 1913. After that, though hereditary nobles continued to sit in the chamber (today one finds a Rockefeller, a Du Pont, a Pell, a Heinz, all in place, as well as such recent hustlers as the Kennedys), outsize tribunes of the people joined them and, along with Byrds, Hales, Frelinghuysens, there were Borahs, La Follettes, and Longs.

From Lincoln's murder to FDR's first inaugural the Senate was the great stage of the republic. At our own century's quarter time there were ninety-six senators, and the whole country observed these paladins with awe if not pleasure. When a powerful senator spoke, the galleries would be full. Everyone understood exactly what Borah meant when he said that he would rather be right than president, or did *Senator* Clay say it first? For Hughdie, the Senate's Reflected Glory was sun enough for him. But few political magnificos came to his Massachusetts Avenue palace during the time of his Russian-born first wife. There was a grim divorce in which an airplane propeller surreally figured. With Hughdie's second wife, the "beauteous" (*Time* magazine's adjective) daughter of the blind Senator Gore, he hit the jackpot, and she filled Merrywood, his new house—or "home" as the press liked to say even then—across the river, with senators and the Speaker, Sam Rayburn, and the likes of Walter Lippmann and Arthur Krock: my mother had persuaded Hughdie that if one wanted true Reflected Glory, certain Jews would have to be invited to the house if only to set up the reflectors.

In due course, after two children, Nina Gore Vidal Auchincloss left Hughdie for Love, and he was promptly married for his money by one of her ladies-in-waiting, who brought him two very poor but very adorable frizzy-haired step-daughters to take my place in his ample heart. For a long time there was no RG, much less G, to illuminate the sad Merrywood until one of the adorable girls married. . . . But let Hughdie state his victories in Caesarean plainstyle, written for an Auchincloss family publication: "Hugh D. Auchincloss (golf and chess) has twice been connected with the U. S. Senate through marriage; once as the son-in-law of the late Thomas Gore, senator from Oklahoma, and now as step-father-in-law of John F. Kennedy, junior senator from Massachusetts." That was it. All of it, in fact. At the end, there was to be absolute RG.

A decade later Hughdie was acclaimed "the first gentleman of the United States" by Mr. Stephen Birmingham, a society chronicler who should know. But by then Reflected Glory had so paid off that as he and I stood face to face in the Red Room of the White House, he could ask himself rhetorically, "What am I doing here? I am a Republican and I hate publicity." I have never seen anyone so happy but then, next to limelight, RG is best. At the American empire's zenith, there was poor Hughdie, a dusty mirror at the dead center of The Sacred Way.

*Tout ça change,* as the French say, but with us, unlike the French, the specifics never remain as they were. The actors are constantly changed at our capital; plays, too. I am put in mind of my native District of Columbia and its turbulent clubhouse, the Senate, by Patricia

O'Toole's *The Five of Hearts,* by Joseph Alsop's various published reminiscences, by the two Henrys, Adams and James, neither ever very far from my thoughts. In *The Five of Hearts* O'Toole describes that eponymous coven of Henry and Clover Adams, of John and Clara Hay, of Clarence King, the five who, in 1882, came together in Washington as friends and so remained until the last died in 1918, their lives illuminated—indeed set ablaze—by Reflected Glory to which Hay, as Secretary of State, gained some of the real thing; while Adams, by constantly saying that RG hurt his eyes, achieved a degree of True Glory not to mention all sorts of Last Words.

2

In youth, one does not bother with one's own relatives much less their social and historical connections. Even so, although I was unaware at mid-century of the existence of an Annapolis-bound fifth cousin, who would one day achieve Glory as our thirty-ninth president, I was very much aware that my grandfather with whom I lived was Glory; and that my father, much newsreel-ized as the Director of Air Commerce and airlines-founder, was also Glory (most glorious, in my eyes and probably everyone else's, as an All-American football player at West Point). I was also aware that when I was transported at ten from the house of the Gores in Rock Creek Park to trans-Potomac Merrywood, I had left Glory for Reflected Glory, and though Hughdie maintained a lavish, by Washington standards, household with five *white* servants, it was very clear that Senator Gore and Gene Vidal were the people that everyone read and talked about as opposed to the army of shadowy Auchinclosses and their equally dim to me (if not to Mr. Birmingham) connections up there in dirty New York City and dull Newport, Rhode Island. Give me Rehoboth Beach, Delaware, any day.

Although I, too, was RG, I knew from the start that I was out for Glory. So, too, was Henry Adams at my age. But as grandson and great-grandson of two presidents, he was positively blinded at birth by RG; later, by settling in a house opposite the White House, he was incessantly bombarded by RG waves. Unlike Adams, I got out at seventeen, and vowed that if I was not elected to anything, I would not come back to live in the capital when there were so many other worlds and glories elsewhere. At seventeen, I enlisted in the army and, Mr. Birmingham to the contrary, I was delighted to get my own life started and be rid of all the RGs of Merrywood, whom Jack Kennedy, years later, characterized to me as "the little foxes," a phrase taken from that perennial favorite, *The Old Testament,* by Lillian Hellman.

In later years, Adams's friend and mine, President Theodore Roosevelt's daughter, Alice Longworth, congratulated me every time we saw each other: "You got out. So wise. It's a mistake to end up here, as a fixture. Like me. Like Joe," she added once, gazing with benign malice at her cousin, Joe Alsop, across the room. When I was in my early teens, Joe had been a fat, bibulous journalist in his twenties who often came to Merrywood, and several times watched me as I played tennis with a schoolmate. Years later, when Joe was involved with an Italo-American sailor, Frank Merlo (soon to enter RGdom's all-time Hall of Fame as the inamorato of Tennessee Williams), he told me, "Of course I know *all* about *The City and the Pillar.* The Who, and Where, and the . . . What?" For the great majority that has since joined us, *The City and the Pillar* was a "glorious" *roman* of the Forties, whose *clef* was much sought by interested parties.

As I read with some pleasure *The Five of Hearts* I was struck, as always, by what a small world the American one was—and is. For Henry Adams at the end of the last century, the country was "a long straggling caravan, stretching loosely toward the prairies, its few score of leaders far in advance and its millions of immigrants, negroes, and Indians far in the rear, somewhere in archaic time." Today there are more millions at the rear and a few score more leaders but the ownership of the country is as highly concentrated as ever, and at the capital of the country there are still ruling families, connected by politics and marriage and bed. Like papal Rome, each old Washington family descended from a president or senator who'd come to town and stayed. The Gores were an aberration: in the eighteenth century much of that part of Maryland which is now the District of Columbia had belonged to them before they moved west, buying up sequestered Indian lands. When Thomas Pryor Gore came to the Senate in 1907, he was actually returning to the family's original homestead; also, as a senator, he was the Hearts' toga-ed enemy.

Twenty-five years earlier, Henry Adams had published anonymously the novel *Democracy,* whose villain was a powerful, corrupt United States Senator and whose protagonist, Madeleine Lee, was attracted to Glory, rather like the Five, but, unlike them, was horrified by "democracy" up close. In many ways, this novel is still one of the best about capitoline ways. Nevertheless, it was that energetic dilettante genius,

Clarence King, who saw the flaw in Adams's rendering: "The real moral is that in a Democracy, *all* good, bad and indifferent is thrown in the circling eddy of political society and the person within the whole field of view who has the least perception, who most sadly flaunts her lack of instinct, her inability to judge of people without the labels of old society" was Adams's heroine. One rather wished that King had got round to excelling at the popular novel as easily as Hay and Adams had. Certainly he had a better grasp of the whole than either Hay or Adams. Also, the gift of phrase. Of England, King wrote: "a big hopeless hell of common people to whom all doors are shut save the grave and America."

John Hay's problems with the Senate began when he first came to town as assistant to President Lincoln's secretary; later, as Assistant Secretary of State to President Harrison and, finally, most spectacularly, as Secretary of State under William McKinley and Theodore Roosevelt, when he ceased to be entirely lunar and became solar—but a sun outshone by the national sun of that huge spotted star, TR, and bedazzled as well as tormented by the ninety competitive capitoline suns clustered at the wrong end of Pennsylvania Avenue. Unlike Henry Adams, Hay was Glory by the end; but he had had to pay for his distinction in a series of pitched battles with the Senate, specifically with the arrogant senator from Massachusetts, Henry Cabot Lodge (known as "Pinky"), a one-time protégé at Harvard of the then professor Henry Adams. Cabot, with his wife, Nannie, was practically a Heart himself; and this made the duels with Hay all the more bitter.

Hay had proved to be a marvellous manager of his wife's money while Adams had inherited a fortune from his mother. As a result, they were able to build and share a joint "Neo-Agnostic" Romanesque building in Lafayette Park; here they maintained the most civilized pair of establishments in the city until . . . I suppose Mr. Birmingham would say Merrywood, which was not as unintellectual in the Thirties and Forties as it became later when the not-so-merry house in the Virginia woods was loud with girlish shrieks, slammed doors, the thud of great feminine feet on the stairs, and poor Hughdie's sighs. But then, even at its zenith, Merrywood's Reflected Glory was never much more than old limelight; certainly nothing was ever generated on the premises. There was no intelligence at the centre, only a Meredithian heroine on temporary loan from the Senate.

The love-hate of Hearts for Senate took a powerful turn when widower Henry Adams became the lover—or "lover"—of the splendid

Elizabeth Sherman Cameron, wife of Senator Don Cameron from Pennsylvania, while John Hay became the lover (without quotation marks) of the wife of his senatorial nemesis, Henry Cabot Lodge.

As a young journalist in Washington, Adams wrote, "To be abused by a senator is my highest ambition." With *Democracy,* the anonymous author was much abused by many senators, among them the suspected model for Senator Ratcliffe, James G. Blaine. On the other hand, by his love for Lizzie, Adams probably earned not the abuse but the complaisant admiration of the hard-drinking, sad senator from Pennsylvania. Certainly the triangle was a balanced one and gave Henry James the shivers—of excitement and total interest in the oddity, the sheer *Americanness of it all.

O'Toole strikes a balance between today's mindless prurience and what really matters (which once actually mattered to our mindful Protestant founders), the public life of the republic. Sex lives of the glorious and their reflectors are no more interesting in themselves than are those of the bamboozled masses that now crowd our alabaster cities and cover over with cement our fruited plains. In a society with an hereditary monarch the comings and goings of the night are duly noted for their effect upon Grace and Favour and the conduct of public affairs. But as the American oligarchy selects, at what often looks to be absentminded random, its office-managers, the private lives of these public functionaries arouse no particular interest unless there is comedy in it.

On the other hand, the private lives of the actual rulers of the country are as out of bounds to American historians as they are to all of the other paid-for supporters of that oligarchy which controls the sources of information and instruction, that is, the "media" and Academe. What is fascinating *inter alia,* in any story of the Hearts, is that the reader, often quite unprepared, is placed at the heart of the oligarchy that he has been told all his life does not—indeed cannot—exist in a "democracy." Yet the whole point to the enchanting Five is that, by birth or design, they are central to the ruling class. As in England, promising plebes have always been absorbed into the oligarchy. Although a fortune is a necessity somewhere in a patrician family, the visible players on the national stage are either plebes for sale (McKinley, Reagan, or that hypergamous railway lawyer, Lincoln) or they are energetic members of the oligarchy who take to public life in the interests of their class: the Roosevelts, the Tafts, currently Mr. Bush, of Kennebunkport, Texas. From time to time, regional oligarchies contribute to the national establishment—members of such old clans as the Byrds and the Gores, not to mention more recent combines like the Kennedys and the Longs. But as the First Gentleman of Entropy, Henry Adams, knew, all the clans wear out, usually more soon than late.

Of the Five, only Clarence King was doomed because he was merely brilliant as a geologist and talker. There was no King fortune. When he decided to make one, almost alone among his generation, he failed. The fact that he had secretly married a black nursemaid by whom he had a number of children was no help. The fact that King could not, like Hay, marry a fortune makes one suspect that, for all his potency with dusky women of the lower class or exotic foreign primitives, he could not function sexually with women of his own class. This is a common condition too little explored in our democratic orgasm-for-all-the-folks self-help (often literally) books. It might explain Clover Adams's suicide and Henry's chaste passion for Lizzie Cameron not to mention the Virgin of Chartres.

The Five set up shop in Washington, and there they remained, except for the peripatetic King. Pleased but not satisfied with the anonymous Glory of *Democracy,* Henry Adams settled in to write a history which was really autobiography, or at least family chronicle; but as he was subtle, he did not write of the administrations of the two Adams presidents—he wrote instead of their coevals and rivals, Jefferson and Monroe. Then, perversely, when he came to write a memoir, he was more historian than memoirist. In any case, Adams's writing is full of tension. To write of the deeds of others, though an act of a sort, is not *action* in the sense that Glory requires. He was permanently soured not so much by the risible republic or its imperial spin-off in whose ruins we have our dull being, but by his own inability to set foot on the national stage as had such sub-Hearts as the awful Theodore Roosevelt or the far worse "Pinky" Lodge. Even Hay was able to turn his great gift for flattering the glorious into high office.

In 1885 Clover abruptly killed herself; grief over her father's death was the official line. But somewhere in Adams's latest—last—novel, *Esther,* there are clues. The protagonist notes how "everything seems unreal" while, in real life, Clover says to her sister in that last year, "Ellen, I'm not real . . . Oh, make me real—you are all of you real!" Clover's death killed off Henry Adams. But his ghost continued to haunt Washington, where he never ceased to worship the beauteous Lizzie, or act as sardonic chorus to the American empire, enjoying, all the while, the respectful love of those young women he liked to have about him, his "nieces," as he called them. Finally, he set himself up as a sort of marriage-broker between Virgin and Dynamo, faith and machine; but that match could not be made. Happily, there were Washington politics to delight in, and the Spanish-American War, and an unruly campaign in the Pacific, and the First World War, when so many of his worst prophecies were confirmed. Next to "I win," "I told you so" are the sweetest words.

Meanwhile, Adams and Hay had the best seats to observe the national comedy. In their letters, they were so often to the witty point about the actors that two of the mummers struck back when Hay's letters were published posthumously. Theodore Roosevelt deplored Hay's "close intimacy with Henry James and Henry Adams—charming men but exceedingly undesirable companions for any man not of strong nature— and the tone of satirical cynicism which they admired . . . impaired his usefulness as a public man." TR then took full credit for everything that Hay had accomplished, while Lodge solemnly blamed Hay's problems with the Senate on Hay's bad-mouthing of that collective body. Meanly, Lodge even denied Hay's brilliance as a conversationalist, so reluctantly attested to by TR. Apparently, O. W. Holmes and J. R. Lowell were better at mealtime autocracy than Hay.

Twenty years after the death of the last of the Adams Circle I can remember half-hearing their names spoken as if they were still contemporary in a city where office-holders are constantly changed but the oligarchy never. I thought of all this recently when I spoke on alumnus John Hay at Brown University, and saw in the audience John Hay's face, the current possession of a great-grandson who wears it almost as nicely as the original Johnny Hay, who was, according to Mark Twain, "a picture to look at, for beauty of feature, perfection of form, and grace of carriage and movement."

As I described Hay's career, I thought of my own mother's involvement with Hay's grandson, John Hay Whitney, known as Jock, while, simultaneously, my symmetrically-inclined father was involved with Jock's wife, another Liz like Cameron. In fact, it was Liz Whitney who taught me how to ride in the Virginia hills during that far too short "long summer" before the Second War when my half-sister was born to grow up to marry Jock's first cousin, while summer's end—apotheosis, too—took place in 1939 when the King and Queen of England arrived in town and all of us Reflected Glory extras took to the streets and cheered them while our parents attended the garden party on the

lawn at the British Embassy, presided over by the handsome, tactless
Sir Ronald Lindsay, whose wife was Lizzie Cameron's niece, Elizabeth
Hoyt, a small dark woman often at Merrywood that summer, where she
did her best to influence the gathered magnates to come to England's
aid in a war that most Americans wanted to stay out of. My grandfather
was an "isolationist" and so was I. In fact, I did my part so well as an
America-Firster at school that, one night at Merrywood, Alice Longworth left the dinner party to come sit on my bed, and give me ammunition to use in her war against foreign entanglements in general and
cousin Eleanor in particular.

Although the oligarchy occasionally splits on the no-turning-back
issues, taking their positions to one side or the other of the Jefferson-
Hamilton fault line that runs through our history when it is not, indeed,
our only history, war has always united the oligarchy and it is then that
their house-servants, the teachers and communicators, are set to work
redecorating the American interior, removing old furniture like the Bill
of Rights to the attic, or romanticizing England and demonizing Germany and Japan in those days, the Arab world in these. The First World
War was largely a matter of the Hamiltonian oligarchs feeling their oats
while the Jeffersonians fell glumly into line.

The Second War, a continuation of the First, hurtled us into the
nuclear age as king—a harvest king as it turns out—of the castle. But
since so simpleminded a game cannot be so bloodily played by a serious
people, our domestics have been hard at work trying to disguise what
really happened. As a result, the American people now believe that the
Second World War was fought by two teams. The bad team wanted to
kill all the Jews, for reasons unknown; the good team was anti-genocide
and pro-Zion. As a veteran of that war and of the debates that led up
to it, I can only say that the fate of the Jews had no more to do with
American policy in 1941 than the ideals of democracy had to do with the
First World War. Hitler's treatment of the Jews was not known to the
American public when it was placed at war by the oligarchy in order
to stop German expansionism in Europe and Japanese in Asia, a pointless enterprise since they have now superseded us anyway.

Henry Adams was the first to anticipate and articulate the *realpolitik*
behind the wars: Germany, he said, was too small a power "to swing
the club," and prevail. He predicted the division of the world between
the United States and Russia, and as much as he disliked the English
he never ceased to favour an "Atlantic Combine" from "the Rocky
Mountains on the West" (could he have, presciently, already surrendered the California littoral to Japan?) "to the Elbe on the East."

**3**

The short, superficial biography written to be read not taught is an agreeable English speciality. The practitioners are often ladies whose research is often adequate to their task, which to my mind is a most useful one: to tell people something about the interesting or still relevant dead. After all, no one not institutionalized is expected to read, as opposed to teach or quarry, Dumas Malone's six-volume life of Jefferson, but should anyone still at large actually read it, as I did, every page, he will know profound despair. There is no sign of intelligent life anywhere in an artifact comparable only to Gutzon Borglum's Dakota cliff. True, close readers will delight in the footnotes, the work of often inspired graduate students, but the actual dead lunar text exists not to be read but to be worshipped. So there is room for another kind of book between the charming but light *Five of Hearts* and Dumas Malone. Unfortunately, those few Americans who can make sense of history can't write while those who can write usually know nothing at all. For any sensible oligarch, this is a fine arrangement; and will never be altered as long as one American university stands, endowed.

The fact that Henry Adams was not only a gifted writer but a uniquely placed historian carries no particular weight in today's world, where a field is a field, as a book editor of yesteryear used to say, assigning for review the latest biography of Queen Elizabeth I to her last biographer, with predictable (either way) results. Honourably and gracefully, O'Toole covers her complex subject, but without much sense of what they—Adams, above all—were about. Here one must trust to a biography that is literature as well as good academic scholarship, Ernest Samuel's *Henry Adams*.

At times, one senses that O'Toole has not read with sufficient care or interest Adams's Jefferson-Madison volumes, without which the Adams literary character is not graspable; but she is Gibbonian when compared to her reviewer in the Sunday *New York Times*, an Englishwoman who is also known for writing light readable books about complex figures. The reviewer's confusion about the United States in general and the Hearts in particular would have given joy to the Five, none of whom took very seriously the English who, even then, were turning into eccentric Norwegians as their once-glorious day waned. Although it is plain that the reviewer had never read or, perhaps, heard of any of the Five before she got the book to review, she pluckily strikes the notes that she thinks an American paper like *The New York Times* would want struck. She deplores but does not demonstrate the male sexism that drove

Clover Adams to suicide and Clara Hay to fat; affects astonishment over Henry Adams's "anti-semitism," as nothing compared to that of jolly *Private Eye,* which doubtless gives her a real giggle; even uses the word *zaftig* to show she knows what's what at the *Times*—rather like her ambitious compatriot, a novelist, who recently told an American interviewer that he might have been a much better writer had he been even slightly Jewish.

Genuflections to dumb Americans completed, she mounts her Norse horse. O'Toole had compared the Hearts to Bloomsbury. This is too much for the reviewer, who writes that the Hearts "had an emotional gaucheness that has no counterpart in the England of the 19th century. . . . Bloomsbury would not have gone in for those enameled Five of Hearts pins, worn as the badge of friendship. Virginia Woolf would not have been caught dead using their heart-embossed paper on which the Five wrote their sentimental missives." None of this is true, of course. There were no pins. The note-paper with the hearts was the joke of a season. There were no sentimental missives. There was a tragedy when Clover killed herself and Adams lost his world; when Hay's son died and he shattered. Otherwise, there were splendid, ironic "missives" full of splendid jokes.

Humour is more definitive of a class than anything else. The English instinctively grade humour on class lines, and the one who fails to get the joke gets a one-way ticket back to where he came from. If nothing else, Bloomsbury knew its place: at the very top of the educated middle class. They aspired no higher, and if they had it would have done no good. (Maynard Keynes was the exception, and much resented by the Woolf-pack.) Certainly, they would never have had access to the Hearts, who were too high above them, except for the Hearts' "cousin," Henry James, who lived close by, and since he treated them sweetly, they called him "Master," and not always with the humorous quotation marks.

The point to the Five is that they were far more civilized than their American, much less English, contemporaries. They cannot be compared, finally, to Bloomsbury because, reflected or true glory, they were ruling class, while the Bloomsburyites were simply educated, powerless, middle-class folk who, like Mrs. Dalloway, came all over queer when a great one drove by, pearl-grey kid-gloved hand visible at a back-seat window. American grandees have always mystified the English with their easy manners. They treat Bloomsburyites or taxi drivers as if they were equals, but it would have to be an uncharacteristically dull Bloomsburyite to remain unguarded, if not uncovered, in such a presence.

True aristos as well as idle artists, the Hearts did not take seriously the busyness of the contemporary arts, particularly as commodities. They preferred works of the past; they trafficked with Berenson. The reviewer displays a true Norse envy, when Hay hangs a Botticelli on his wall. She has also found a target. This is a "book about things: the acquisition of the marvelous art objects with which the friends stuffed their houses," and about "dependence on possessions and buildings as a source of inspiration and shame, almost a substitute for spiritual life."

Norwegians like to talk about spiritual life which, in Bloomsbury, meant Friendship, as the Hearts perfectly exemplified. Although they could afford pictures that Virginia and Leonard and Vanessa and Quentin and poor Lytton could not, their interests were not in possessions but in each other and their common, curious nation, whose history they not only recorded but helped direct, in office like Hay; in the study, as historian, like Adams; or in the drawing-rooms of Clara and Clover.

O'Toole is perhaps wise to deal as superficially as she does with the intellectual life of her characters because it is hard to dramatize something that does not exist for today's uncommon, alas, common reader, or someone like the *Times* reviewer who thinks that the Hearts wrote "sentimental" letters to each other when their letters are mostly sharp and shrewd and engaged in the world in a way quite alien to sentimentalists. She finds a lack of spiritual life (can she be born-again?) in Henry Adams, whose last decades were spent in profound spiritual meditation upon the Virgin. But then she cannot have read *Mont Saint-Michel and Chartres* or even *The Education of Henry Adams.*

The Hearts, she tells us, "lived on a knife edge between taste and tastelessness." Proof? Poor Clara Hay tried to wear a too-tight wedding dress at her wedding anniversary. But the English mind (to the extent that one can say such a thing exists, Henry Adams mutters in my ear) needs desperately to believe that its American masters are emotionally gauche yet elitist and snobbish, buyers-up of old culture to stuff houses with. When it comes to getting things wrong, the English are born masters. In fact, I was once so impressed by their inability to sort things out that I used Madame Verdurin as a prototype for their professional book-chatterers, only to find myself defeated yet again: they hadn't heard of Madame Verdurin either.

## 4

Today literature enjoys a certain prestige in the First World, and much is made of successful writers in the press and in the schools. It is salutary to find that neither Adams nor Hay took writing, as such, very seriously. Hay was one of the most popular light-verse writers of his day, and his life of Lincoln, with John Nicolay, was—well, as monumental as a Dakota mountain. But, pseudonymously, inspired by Henry Adams, Hay wrote a novel called *The Breadwinners* which was a huge success with both general public and reactionary critics.

As so many of today's celebrities and journalists seem to be born knowing, it is a very easy thing to write a popular novel if one has an exploitable name. But even today it is hard, if not impossible, to reach a wide audience with no name at all, as anonymous John Hay and Henry Adams did. But then the ease with which these two, and Clarence King, too, wrote so very well makes one suspect that education might actually play a part in a process we are taught to think of as charismatic— *creative* writing as a silver spring that gushes miraculously from the psyche's mud. Perhaps if one has learned to speak well, one can probably think well, too, and if one can then coordinate thought and speech one might be able to write it all down in a way that is agreeable for others to read. But I am sure that this is far too simple; in any case, *high* art, even for them, was elsewhere, and they revered their honorary Heart, Henry James, who had chosen to settle in backward England for reasons which they could never appreciate, though Clover Adams thought he'd be better off running a hog ranch in Wyoming. Hog ranch is bad enough, but what Clover really meant was even worse; that is, better: "hog ranch" was period slang for a whore house.

Henry James was very conscious that he had got out and that the Hearts, particularly Clover, were not entirely approving. Yet with them, as with so many American grandees of the period, Europe was just a pleasanter extension of their usual life; and far less foreign than Wyoming. It has often been noted (and never explained) how so many American writers who could get out of the great republic did so and how even those most deeply identified with the republic and its folkways— Mark Twain, Bret Harte, Stephen Crane—all managed to put in quite a lot of time on the other side of the Atlantic. *Douceur de la vie* was one reason. Also, God was doing well, extremely well, altogether too well in the last great hope of earth, while in Europe He was giving ground, if not to reason's age, to societies more interested in cohesive social form than Final Answers to All Questions. Edith Wharton believed that everything published in the States must first be made acceptable to an imaginary Protestant divine in Mississippi—probably named Gore.

In 1882, Henry James made the mistake of confiding to Clover his feeling for their native land, an emotion which had not much love in it. He was also tactless enough to regard her as America incarnate; to which her sharp response: "Am I then vulgar, dreary and impossible to live with?" But James's eye was never so cold and penetrating as when it was turned upon those he loved, and he did coolly love the Hearts if not the Republic for which they sometimes stood. From his not-yet-Norwegian outpost in the North Sea and its still splendid world metropolis, London, he could generalize of things American—of Adamses, too. "I believe that Washington is the place in the world where money—or the absence of it, matters least," he wrote Sir John Clark. As for the Adamses, "They don't pretend to conceal (as why *should* they?) their preference of America to Europe, and they rather rub it into me, as they think it is a wholesome discipline for my demoralized spirit. One excellent reason for their liking Washington better than London is that they are, vulgarly speaking, 'someone' here, and they are nothing in your complicated kingdom." This was written in the last days of our austere, deliberately *un*precedented republic. Then, in 1898, the American empire emerged with eagle-like cries (not least a mournful chirp or two from James), and in that year John Hay was recalled as ambassador from London to take over the State Department as well as such new imperial acquisitions as the Philippines. During this time of glory, Hay was aided and abetted by the English magnates; and subsequent visits to London were state affairs for the Hays, who were, most vulgarly, "someone" in the complicated, declining kingdom; for Henry Adams, too, if he chose. But he chose not to be someone, even though the raffish Prince of Wales as well as that ultimate someone, Gladstone, had admired *Democracy*.

Adams lived long enough to attend the birth of what he had conceived as "The Atlantic Combine," the bringing together of the United States and England, with the old country as the junior partner. When England ran out of money in 1914, the wooing of America began in earnest. Before, the British had encouraged their "cousins" to acquire a Pacific empire in order to contain the Russians, the Germans, and the Japanese. The Hearts, particularly Hay, played a great part in the making of this new alliance with a series of arrangements and treaties that culminated in the Hay-Pauncefote Treaty. Ironically, an adverb which sometimes does duty in these lives for "inevitably," Hay's principal antagonist in the Senate—England's, too—was Henry Cabot Lodge. Did Lodge know that Hay had so elaborately antlered him? O'Toole thinks not. But I think that he did on the ground that totally self-absorbed men, dedicated to their own glory, notice anything and everything that impinges on them.

Henry Adams records an edgy scene between the two when Lodge told Hay that he wished that he "would not look so exceedingly tired when approached on business at the department." It was Adams's view that the worn-out Hay had been "murdered" by Lodge and his senatorial allies. Certainly, after Hay's death, there was little traffic between Adams and Lodge, much less with the great presidential noise across the park. The comedy was grim, Adams wrote Lizzie Cameron. Of himself and the bereft mistress, Nannie, he observed, "We keep up a sort of mask-play together, each knowing the other to the ground. She kept it up with Hay for years to the end." Then Nannie, too, was dead and Lizzie settled in Paris, besotted by the young American poet Trumbull Stickney (friend of Cabot Lodge's poet son, Bay), whom I dutifully read at school because my favourite teacher was writing a dissertation on his work.

## 5

Not long ago, I paid my last visit to Joe Alsop. As always, I telephoned and asked him, yet again, for his address in Georgetown. He gave me, yet again, the numbers and the street: "N Street, *N* as in Nellie," he thundered. The new house was smaller than the one of his heyday; but, as ever, he was comfortably looked after by friends. I found him rather too small for my taste. The body had begun its terminal telescoping. But the brain was functioning and the large face was a healthy puce, like the brick of a Georgetown house, and the huge clown glasses magnified eyes only slightly dulled by a lifetime's reflection more of than on Glory. Nevertheless, Joe was seriously unravelling and we knew that we were meeting, somewhat self-consciously, for the last time. With loved ones, this can be painful, or so the world likes to pretend, but with a life-long acquaintance, the *envoi* can be rather fun, particularly if you are dying at a slower rate than the other.

As always, Joe was for war anywhere any time in order to "maintain the balance of power." He had used this phrase so long that no one had any idea what—or whose—power was to be balanced. I was for the minding of our own business. He sounded like his great uncle; I sounded like my grandfather. So much for development in political attitudes or increased wisdom among the subsequent generations. As always, we played roles for each other. I was Henry James, returning to the collapsing empire from wicked, thriving Europe, and Joe was Henry Adams, weary with absolute wisdom. We gossiped: this was Washington, after all, Henry James's "city of conversation."

Joe told me how he had made up with cousin Eleanor Roosevelt, the only presidential widow ever to matter, to those who matter, that is. He had spent several decades attacking her dreadful husband and mocking her nobility of character and Sapphic tendencies; but there had been a sea-change before she died, and he spoke with affection of having seen her. I doubt if the affection had been returned. "I forgive," she once said to me, small gray eyes like hard agate, "but I *never* forget." Joe had been part of the Alice Longworth circle of TR devotees and FDR disdainers, and their wit was murderous, and Eleanor a preordained victim. But she had her own murderous quality, which Joe caught nicely in *The New York Review of Books,* when he likened her sweet nursery-school teacher manner to that of his "Auntie Bye" who "had a tongue that could take the paint off a barn, meanwhile sounding quite unusually syrupy and cooing."

Joe was writing his memoirs and so unusually reflective of the past. I was undergoing the attentions of a biographer and in a most uncharacteristically down-memory-lane mood. He remarked that my father was the handsomest man he ever saw, adding, "A colonel, wasn't he?" I took the trick with: "No, a first lieutenant when he left the army." In Washington the military have no status at all. To old Washington, a "colonel" suggests someone lodged in a boarding house in E Street, with a letter to a senator as yet unacknowledged; while generals and admirals are not invited out anywhere except when they are hypergamous, as Robert McAlmon (in *Village*) notes bitterly of my father's marriage with the wealthy daughter of a United States Congressman, giving "him enough of a start so that he would become quite a figure in the army some day." But my father's wife was not wealthy, and he became quite a figure in civil aviation. Still, he was forever a colonel to Joe, while I always referred to Joe's admiral-grandfather as, "Wasn't he something in the *regular* Navy?"

We spoke of the days of our youth and just before. He was convinced

that Franklin Roosevelt could never have had an affair with the Roman
Catholic Lucy Mercer *before* she had married someone else. Afterward,
when she was no longer virgin, she could then commit adultery with an
absolvable conscience. We discussed Henry Adams's special status in
the city, which Joe had somewhat taken over. Adams never left his card
with anyone, something unheard of in those days. He also never invited
anyone to his daily breakfasts. The right people (those who were interesting), somehow, turned up. In later life, he almost never went out to
other people's houses, including the white one across the road; *they*
came to him. I recalled Eleanor's approving comment that though he
would not come *into* her house when he took his drive, he insisted that
the children come out and get in his carriage for a roughhouse.

Joe and I stayed pretty much away from the subject of Jack Kennedy,
since amongst the chroniclers of our time, Joe was chief mourner, even
widow. I did remember the amusement that "the old thing" aroused in
Jack's vigorous breast, and I was present when someone said that Joe
was getting restive, and it was time to have him over for lunch and "hold
his head," an odd expression.

Joe shared with me a liking for the English that one could—how to
put it without awakening shrieks of "elitist snob" from both sides of the
irradiated Atlantic?—"relate to," combined with no particular liking
for the fallen big sister nation. But then as the Hay-Adams generation
marked the beginning of our national primacy in the world, our generation marked the actual mastery of the whole works, and our disdain for
those who had preceded us was unkind, to say the least. Once, at
Hyannisport, the thirty-fifth president was brooding on the why and the
what of great men; he thought, not originally, that great political figures
were more the result of the times in which they lived and not so much
of character or "genius." I mentioned Churchill as a possible exception.
Jack's response was worthy of Joe, his father: "That old drunk! How
could he lose? He always knew we were there to bail him out!"

In the fragment of memoir that Alsop has so far published, he did do
a bit of a Henry Adams number when he diffidently told us how "the
WASP ascendancy," to which he belonged, was at an end, and that he
himself spoke now as an irrelevant relic of a quaint past when Washington was, in James's phrase, "a Negro village liberally sprinkled with
whites," and one wore so very many clothes and changed them so often
in a day. But Joe was putting on an act. He knew that the WASP
ascendancy is as powerful as it ever was. How could it not be? They still

own the banks. Head for head, they may be nearly outnumbered by Roman Catholics at the polls and by Jews in show biz and the press, but they still own the country, which they now govern through such non-WASP employees as Henry Kissinger, or through insignificant members of the family, like George Bush, who are given untaxing jobs in government.

Joe did manage to take a gentle swipe at cousin Eleanor, reminding us that in the old days "Eleanor Roosevelt was not only anti-Semitic, which she later honorably overcame" (like kleptomania?), "she was also quite obstinately anti-Catholic, which she remained until the end of her days." This is disingenuous, to say the least. Like everyone else, Eleanor was many people, not one. But the most important of her personas was that of politician, and no politician is going to be anti *any* minority if he can help it; unless, of course, his constituency requires that he make war on a minority, as George Wallace, say, used to do on blacks and Ronald Reagan always did on the poor. Neither Jews nor Catholics nor blacks, *as such,* figured in Eleanor's private world, which was exclusive of just about everyone or, as she explained to her husband's political manager, Jim Farley, when he complained that he was never asked to private Roosevelt functions, "Franklin is not at ease with people not of his own class." She was the same as a private person. But as a public one, she was there for everyone; hence, her implacable war with the Roman Catholic hierarchy over federal aid to education, which came to a head when that rosy Urning, Cardinal Spellman, denounced her as an unnatural mother, and she turned him into a pillar of salt in her column.

At my last meeting with Joe Alsop, I fear that our imitations of the two Henrys were not much good. For one thing, Henry James could not bear his native land and he had, most famously, given reasons (but not the right ones) why. On his last trip to Washington to see the other Henry, he wrote: "There is NO "fascination" *whatever* in anything or anyone . . ." And he was worn out with "the perpetual effort of trying to do justice to what one doesn't like." I, of course, am fascinated by my native land and my only not-so-perpetual effort involves restraining myself from strangling at the dinner table those Washington oligarchs who have allowed the republic to become a "national security state" and then refused to hold their employees to account. "Why didn't you impeach Reagan over Iran-Contras?" I asked a very great personage, indeed, a press lord. "Oh, we couldn't! It would have been too soon. You know, after Nixon."

Joe was an absolute romantic, and differed from Henry Adams in that
he thought of himself as a participant on the battlefield as a brave
journalist, which he was, and in the high councils of state, where he liked
to bustle about backstage to the amusement of the actors. As avatars,
Joe and I were not much. But we had had a very good time, I thought,
as I left the N Street house for the last time.

Happily, for Henry Adams, and all other Hearts, the problem of
Glory did not persist after middle age, when acceptance, if not wisdom,
traditionally begins. Of himself and friends, Adams wrote: "We never
despised the world or its opinions, we only failed to find out its existence.
The world, if it exists, feels in exactly the same way toward us, and cares
not one straw whether we exist or not. Philosophy has never got beyond
this point. There are but two schools; one turns the world into me; the
other turns me into the world; and the result is the same." Finally, not
they but their great friend, Henry James, united the reflection of glory
with the thing itself in a life that was all art, and it is no accident that
he should have worked the proposition through not only in his unconscious but in the imagination, the only world there is, finally, that is
graspable, artful.

On James's death-bed, he became Napoleon Bonaparte, and in his last
coherent but out-of-self raving spoke in the first person as the emperor
who personified for the Hearts' century the ultimate wordly glory.

From James's last dictations:

. . . we hear the march of history, what is remaining to that essence of
tragedy, the limp? . . .
They pluck in their tens of handfuls of plumes from the imperial
eagle . . .
The Bonapartes have a kind of bronze distinction that extends to their
fingertips . . .
across the border
all the pieces
Individual Souls, great of . . . on which great perfections are If one
does . . .

Later:

Tell them to follow, to be faithful, to take me seriously.

The secretary, Miss Bosanquet, wrote, after the end: "Several people
who have seen the dead face are struck with the likeness to Napoleon

which is certainly great." Thus, Glory and its Reflection had at last combined—not so much in death, where all things must, but in the precedent art and its true sanity.

*The Threepenny Review*
Spring 1991

# INDEX

# ABOUT THE AUTHOR

Gore Vidal was born in 1925 at the United States Military Academy, West Point, where his father was the first aviation instructor. Vidal's maternal roots are thoroughly political. As a boy, he lived with his grandfather, the legendary blind Senator T. P. Gore, to whom Vidal read. His father, Eugene Vidal, served as director of the Bureau of Air Commerce under Franklin D. Roosevelt. After graduating from Phillips Exeter Academy, Vidal enlisted at seventeen in the United States Army. At nineteen he became a warrant officer (j.g.) and first mate of the army ship *F.S. 35,* which carried supplies and passengers from Chernowski Bay to Dutch Harbor in the Aleutian Islands. While on night watch in port, he wrote his first novel, *Williwaw,* published in 1946, the year he was mustered out.

Vidal's early works include *The City and the Pillar* (1948), the short story collection *A Thirsty Evil* (1956), and two successful Broadway plays, *Visit to a Small Planet* (1957) and the prize-winning *The Best Man* (1960). Vidal also wrote a number of plays for television's "golden age" *(The Death of Billy the Kid)* as well as Hollywood screenplays *(Suddenly Last Summer).* In the sixties, three widely acclaimed novels established Vidal's international reputation as a best-selling author: *Julian* (1964), a re-creation of the world of the apostate Roman emperor who attempted to restore paganism; *Washington, D.C.* (1967), the first in what was to become a multi-volume fictional "chronicle" of American history; and the classic *Myra Breckinridge* (1968), a comedy of sex change in a highly mythical Hollywood.

*Myron* (1974), a sequel to *Myra Breckinridge,* continued to mine the vein of fanciful, sometimes apocalyptic humor that informs *Kalki* (1978), *Duluth* (1983), and *Live from Golgotha* (1992), works described by Italo Calvino as "the hyper-novel or the novel elevated to the square or to the cube." Vidal also continued to explore the ancient world in the wide-ranging *Creation* (1981). The *Boston Globe* noted, "He is our greatest living man of letters."

Gabriel García Márquez praised "Gore Vidal's magnificent series of historical novels or novelized histories" that deal with American life as viewed by one family from the Revolution to the present: *Burr* (1973), *Lincoln* (1984), *1876* (1976), *Empire* (1987), *Hollywood* (1990), and *Washington, D.C.* Vidal's interest in politics has not been limited to commentary; he ran for Congress in New York in 1960, and in 1982 came in second in the California Democratic senatorial primary.

Vidal's essays, both political and literary, have been collected in such volumes as *Homage to Daniel Shays* (1972), *Matters of Fact and Fiction* (1977), *The Second American Revolution* (1982), and *At Home* (1988). The National Book Critics Circle citation for "best critic" (1983) read: "The American tradition of independent and curious learning is kept alive in the wit and great expressiveness of Gore Vidal's criticism."

Vidal divides his time between Los Angeles, California, and Ravello, Italy.

## ABOUT THE TYPE

This book was set in Times Roman, designed by Stanley Morison specifically for *The Times* of London. The typeface was introduced in the newspaper in 1932. Times Roman had its greatest success in the United States as a book and commercial typeface, rather than one used in newspapers.